ROUTLEDGE HANDBOOK OF HISTORICAL INTERNATIONAL RELATIONS

This handbook presents a comprehensive, concise and accessible overview of the field of Historical International Relations (HIR). It summarizes and synthesizes existing contributions to the field while presenting central themes, approaches and methodologies that have driven the development of HIR, providing the reader with a sense of the diversity and research dynamics that are at the heart of this field of study. The wide range of topics covered are grouped under the following headings:

- Traditions: Demonstrates the wide variety of approaches to HIR.
- Thinking International Relations Historically: Different ways of thinking IR historically share some common concerns and areas for further investigation.
- Actors, Processes and Institutions: Explores the processes, actors, practices, and institutions that constitute the core objects of study of many HIR scholars.
- Situating Historical International Relations: Critically reflects about the situatedness of our objects of study.
- Approaches: Examines how HIR scholars conduct and reflect about their research, often in dialogue with a variety of perspectives from cognate disciplines.

Summarizing key contributions and trends while also sketching out challenges for future inquiry, this is an invaluable resource for students, academics and researchers from a range of disciplines, particularly International Relations, global history, political science, history, sociology, anthropology, peace studies, diplomatic studies, security studies, international political thought, political geography, international law.

Benjamin de Carvalho is a Senior Research Fellow at the Norwegian Institute of International Affairs (NUPI) in Oslo.

Julia Costa Lopez is a Senior Lecturer in History and Theory of International Relations at the University of Groningen.

Halvard Leira is a Research Professor at the Norwegian Institute of International Affairs (NUPI) in Oslo.

ROUTLEDGE HANDBOOK OF HISTORICAL INTERNATIONAL RELATIONS

Edited by
Benjamin de Carvalho, Julia Costa Lopez
and Halvard Leira

LONDON AND NEW YORK

First published 2021
by Routledge
2 Park Square, Milton Park, Abingdon, Oxon OX14 4RN

and by Routledge
52 Vanderbilt Avenue, New York, NY 10017

Routledge is an imprint of the Taylor & Francis Group, an informa business

British Library Cataloguing-in-Publication Data
A catalogue record for this book is available from the British Library

Library of Congress Cataloging-in-Publication Data
Names: Carvalho, Benjamin de, editor. | Costa Lopez, Julia, 1987- editor. | Leira, Halvard, 1976- editor.
Title: Routledge handbook of Historical International Relations / edited by Benjamin de Carvalho,
Julia Costa Lopez, Halvard Leira.
Other titles: Handbook of Historical International Relations
Description: Abingdon, Oxon ; New York, N.Y. : Routledge, 2021. | Includes bibliographical references and index.
Identifiers: LCCN 2020055887 (print) | LCCN 2020055888 (ebook) | ISBN 9780815347644 (hardback) |
ISBN 9781351168960 (ebook)
Subjects: LCSH: International Relations–History. | International Relations–Research.
Classification: LCC JZ1305 .R6845 2021 (print) | LCC JZ1305 (ebook) | DDC 327.09–dc23
LC record available at https://lccn.loc.gov/2020055887
LC ebook record available at https://lccn.loc.gov/2020055888

ISBN: 9780815347644 (hbk)
ISBN: 9781351168960 (ebk)
ISBN: 9781032006697 (pbk)

Typeset in Bembo
by KnowledgeWorks Global Ltd.

CONTENTS

LIST OF CONTRIBUTORS

Editors

Benjamin de Carvalho is a Senior Research Fellow at the Norwegian Institute of International Affairs (NUPI) in Oslo. He has written extensively on early modern Historical International Relations, and been active in the Historical International Relations Section of the International Section since its inception and in a number of functions. His latest publications include *The Sea and International Relations* (Manchester University Press, co-edited with Halvard Leira) and *Status and the Rise of Brazil* (Palgrave Macmillan, co-edited with Maria Jumbert and Paulo Esteves). With Halvard Leira he has also co-edited the four-volume set on Historical International Relations (SAGE).

Julia Costa Lopez is a Senior Lecturer in History and Theory of International Relations at the University of Groningen. Her research interests focus on historical international relations and international political thought, particularly in the late-medieval and early modern periods. Her work has been published in journals such as *International Organization*, *Review of International Studies*, or *International Studies Review*.

Halvard Leira is a Research Professor at the Norwegian Institute of International Affairs (NUPI). He has published extensively in English and Norwegian on international political thought, historiography, foreign policy and diplomacy. His work has appeared in, e.g., International Studies Quarterly, Review of International Studies, Millennium, Leiden Journal of International Law, and Cooperation and Conflict. Leira is co-editor of International Diplomacy (2013), Historical International Relations (2015), and the current volume. He is former section chair and programme chair of the HIST section of the ISA and was programme chair of EISA PEC2018.

Contributors

Morten Skumsrud Andersen is a Senior Research Fellow at the Norwegian Institute of International Affairs (NUPI) in Oslo and is currently researching great power politics and topics in Historical International Relations and diplomacy.

Alexander Anievas is an Associate Professor in the Department of Political Science, University of Connecticut. He is the author of *Capital, the State, and War: Class Conflict and Geopolitics in the Thirty Years' Crisis, 1914–1945* (University of Michigan Press, 2014), for which he was awarded the Sussex International Theory Book Prize, and co-author (with Kerem Nişancıoğlu) of *How the West Came to Rule: The Geopolitical Origins of Capitalism* (Pluto, 2015), winner of the ISA's International Political Sociology Section Best Book Award and BISA's International Political Economy Working Group Book Prize. He is currently working on a manuscript exploring the role of race and the far-right in the making of US hegemony and the Cold War 'liberal' international order.

Lucian M. Ashworth is a Professor in the Department of Political Science at Memorial University. His main area of research interest is the history of international thought. He is the author of *A History of International Thought* (Routledge, 2014), and many other books and articles on disciplinary and intellectual history.

William Bain is an Associate Professor of International Relations at the National University of Singapore. His research explores questions of International Relations theory, history of international thought, and political theology. He is the author or editor of *Political Theology of International Order* (2020), *Medieval Foundations of International Relations* (2016), *The Empire of Security and the Safety of the People* (2006), and *Between Anarchy and Society: Trusteeship and the Obligations of Power* (2003).

Jens Bartelson is a Professor of Political Science at Lund University. He has written mainly about the concept of the sovereign state, the philosophy of world community, and the concept of war in international thought. He is the author of *War in International Thought* (Cambridge University Press, 2017), *Visions of World Community* (Cambridge University Press, 2009), *The Critique of the State* (Cambridge University Press, 2001), and *A Genealogy of Sovereignty* (Cambridge University Press, 1995).

Martin Bayly is an Assistant Professor in International Relations Theory at the London School of Economics and Political Science. He works on Historical International Relations, empire, and South Asia. His first book *Taming the Imperial Imagination* (Cambridge University Press, 2016) was awarded the International Studies Association's Francesco Guicciardini Prize in 2018. Following a British Academy Postdoctoral Fellowship in 2016–2019, he is currently researching the histories of twentieth-century Indian international thought.

Brett Bowden is a Professor of History and Politics at Western Sydney University, Australia. He is an Elected Fellow of the Royal Historical Society (UK) and the Royal Society of New South Wales. Key publications include *The Empire of Civilization, Civilization and War, The Strange Persistence of Universal History in Political Thought, Direct Hit: The Bombing of Darwin Post Office*, and the four-volume edited collection *Civilization: Critical Concepts*. He is the recipient of the Norbert Elias Prize, the APSA Crisp Prize, the GW Symes Award, and a Distinguished Alumni Award from Flinders University.

Jordan Branch is an Assistant Professor of Government at Claremont McKenna College. He is also a Fellow at the American Council of Learned Societies and has held positions at Brown University and the University of Southern California. His publications include *The Cartographic State: Maps, Territory, and the Origins of Sovereignty* (Cambridge, 2014) and articles in *International Organization, International Studies Quarterly*, the *European Journal of International Relations, International Theory*, and *Territory, Politics, Governance*.

Quentin Bruneau is an Assistant Professor of Politics at the New School for Social Research. He is interested in the history and theory of International Relations, international political economy, and economic history. His publications are forthcoming in *International Theory* and the *Oxford Handbook of History and International Relations*. He is currently working on a book about the transformation of sovereign lending over the last two centuries.

Charles Butcher is an Associate Professor in Political Science at the Norwegian University of Science and Technology. His research interests include the structure and dynamics of historical and non-Western state systems, the onset and dynamics of resistance movements and the use of violence against civilians by armed groups in war. His work has been published in the *Journal of Conflict Resolution, Journal of Peace Research, Comparative Political Studies, International Theory*, and *International Studies Quarterly*.

Zeynep Gülsah Çapan is a Lecturer at the chair group of International Relations at the University of Erfurt. Her research focuses on history and historiography, Eurocentrism, sociology of knowledge, and postcolonial and decolonial thought. Her research has been published in journals such as *Third World Quarterly* and *International Studies Review*.

Mauro José Caraccioli is an Assistant Professor of Political Science and Core Faculty in the Alliance for Social, Political, Ethical, and Cultural Thought (ASPECT Program) at Virginia Tech, Blacksburg, VA. His work links the history of political thought, environmental politics, and theories of scholarly reflexivity. He is the author of *Writing the New World: The Politics of Natural History in the Early Spanish Empire* (University of Florida Press, 2021).

Andrew Delatolla is a Lecturer in Middle Eastern Studies at the University of Leeds and was previously Assistant Professor in International Relations at the American University in Cairo. He is interested in the intersections of race, gender, and sexuality in colonial state formation and postcolonial statehood with a focus on Lebanon, Syria, Egypt, and Turkey and the Ottoman Empire.

Robert A. Denemark, University of Delaware, is currently Visiting Scholar at the Arrighi Center for Global Studies at Johns Hopkins. His world-systems publications appear in *Review* (Braudel Center), *Journal of World-Systems Research, International Studies Quarterly, International Studies Review,* and *Cambridge Review of International Affairs*. He edited Andre Gunder Frank's posthumously published *Reorienting the 19th Century: Global Economy in the Continuing Asian Age* (Paradigm, 2014).

Richard Devetak is an Associate Professor in International Relations at the University of Queensland. His research focuses on the history of international thought, history of the states-system, and critical theories of International Relations. His publications include *Critical International Theory: An Intellectual History* (Oxford University Press, 2018).

Filipe dos Reis is an Assistant Professor at the Department of International Relations and International Organization, University of Groningen. His current research focuses on the history and politics of international law, imperial Germany, and maps. He is co-editor of two edited volumes: *The Politics of Translation in International Relations* and *Mapping European Empires: Connectivity and Cartographic Imaginaries of Power*.

Yale H. Ferguson is Emeritus Distinguished Professor of Global and International Affairs, Rutgers University, and Professorial Fellow, Division of Global Affairs, Rutgers-Newark. He and Richard Mansbach have co-authored for some 45 years, always emphasizing the close relationship of IR and History. Their seven joint books include *The Elusive Quest*; *Polities: Authority, Identities, and Change*; *A World of Polities*; and *Remapping Global Politics*; forthcoming: *Populism and Globalization*; and *Organized Violence: Past, Present, Future*.

Melody Fonseca Santos is a Term Assistant Professor at the Department of Political Science of the University of Puerto Rico, Rio Piedras Campus, and Researcher at the Institute of Caribbean Studies. Her research and teaching interests are US politics towards the Caribbean, postcolonial theory and decolonial thinking, feminist theories, and critical security studies. She has published various academic articles and book chapters on US interventionism in Haiti, US colonial politics on Puerto Rico, and current debates on Global IR and critical approaches to the discipline. Currently, she is the editor of the journal *Caribbean Studies*.

Julian Go is a Professor of Sociology at the University of Chicago. His research explores the social logics of imperial formations and modern colonialism; postcolonial/decolonial thought and related questions of social theory, epistemology, and knowledge; and global historical sociology.

Kerry Goettlich is a Lecturer in International Security at the University of Reading. He previously completed his Ph.D. in International Relations at the London School of Economics, where he was an editor of *Millennium: Journal of International Studies*. His current project examines the historical emergence of scientific practices underlying modern territoriality, such as border surveying, as they emerged in seventeenth-century colonial North America and were globalized in the late-nineteenth century. His work has appeared in the *European Journal of International Relations* and the *Oxford Research Encyclopedia of International Studies*.

Cristian Gogu is a Ph.D. candidate at the University of Connecticut. His research interest lies in the impact of global finance on Western liberal democracies.

Maj Grasten is an Assistant Professor at the Department of Management, Politics and Philosophy, Copenhagen Business School. Her research sits at the intersection of Socio-Legal Studies and Global Governance, with particular focus on International Organizations and legal bodies, experts and knowledge production in international law, and the legal foundations of markets. Among her latest publications is the edited book *The Politics of Translation in International Relations* (Palgrave, 2020).

Daniel M. Green is an Associate Professor of Political Science and International Relations at the University of Delaware, United States. A former Chair of the English School (EngS) Section and of the Historical International Relations (HIST) Section of the International Studies Association, he is currently Convener of the Nineteenth Century Working Group of HIST. He has published in many journals and collections and most recently edited *Guide to the English School in International Studies* (with Cornelia Navari, Wiley Blackwell, 2014) and *The Two Worlds of Nineteenth Century International Relations: The Bifurcated Century* (Routledge, 2018). His current book project is entitled *Order Projects and Resistance in the Global Political System: A Framework for International Relations History*.

Ryan D. Griffiths is an Associate Professor in the Department of Political Science at Syracuse University. His research focuses on the dynamics of secession and the study of sovereignty, state systems, and international orders. He is the co-author of the International System(s) Dataset (ISD). His most recent book is *Secession and the Sovereignty Game: Strategy and Tactics for Aspiring Nations* (Cornell University Press, 2021).

Xavier Guillaume teaches at the University of Groningen, the Netherlands.

Martin Hall is an Associate Professor of Political Science at Lund University, Sweden. He is mainly interested in Historical International Relations in general and state-making in particular. He is the co-author of *Essence of Diplomacy* (Palgrave) and co-editor of *Civilizational Identity: The Production and Reproduction of 'Civilizations' in International Relations* (Palgrave) and *De-Centering State Making: Comparative and International Perspectives* (Edgar Allen). Recently, Hall has published on steppe state-making, and on Swedish-Sami relations. Hall is the co-editor of the journal *Cooperation and Conflict*.

Liane Hartnett is a Lecturer at La Trobe University with an interest in intellectual history and political theory. She is the author of 'Love as a Practice of Peace: The Political Theologies of Tolstoy, Gandhi and King', which features in Vassilios Paipais' *Theology and World Politics: Metaphysics, Genealogies, Political Theologies* (2020) and the co-author, with Cian O'Driscoll, of *Sad and Laughable and Strange: At War with Just War*, which is forthcoming in *Global Society*.

Jaakko Heiskanen is a Leverhulme Early Career Fellow at the Department of Politics and International Studies, University of Cambridge. His main research interests include International Relations theory, the history of international order, nationalism, and conceptual history. His work has been published in *International Political Sociology, Cooperation and Conflict, International Theory*, and *Journal of Political Ideologies*.

Benjamin Herborth is a Senior Lecturer at the Department of International Relations and International Organization and Director of Studies of the Research Master's programme Modern History and International Relations at the University of Groningen, the Netherlands. His research interests include social and political theories in and of International Relations, the politics of security and mobility, German foreign policy, and reconstructive methodology. Cutting across these research interests is the belief that the field of International Relations, having a strong tradition of reifying both political spaces and political subjects, provides an excellent site for theorizing both. His work has been published, *inter alia*, with *Review of International Studies, International Studies Review, International Theory*, and *Cambridge University Press*.

Andrew R. Hom is a Senior Lecturer in International Relations at the University of Edinburgh. His research interests include timing and time, international theory, security, and victory in war. He is the author of *International Relations and the Problem of Time* (Oxford University Press), the co-editor of *Moral Victories: The Ethics of Winning Wars* (Oxford University Press) and *Time, Temporality, and Global Politics* (e-IR), and an Associate Editor of the journal *International Relations*.

Victoria Tin-bor Hui is an Associate Professor in Political Science at the University of Notre Dame. She received her Ph.D. in Political Science from Columbia University and her B.SSc. in Journalism and Communication from the Chinese University of Hong Kong. She is the author of *War and State Formation in Ancient China and Early Modern Europe* (Cambridge University Press, 2005). Hui's core research examines the centrality of war in the formation and transformation of 'China' in history. As a native from Hong Kong, Hui has also published analyses of the Umbrella Movement in 2014, the anti-extradition protests in 2019 and the Beijing-imposed national security law in 2020.

Beate Jahn is a Professor of International Relations at the University of Sussex and President of the European International Studies Association (EISA). She is interested in critical and classical theory, ideology, and liberalism. Her publications include *Moral und Politik* (1993), *The Cultural Construction of International Relations* (2000), *Classical Theory in International Relations* (2006), and *Liberal Internationalism* (2013).

Oliver Kessler is a Professor for International Relations at the University of Erfurt. His research focuses on Theories of International Relations, social theory of risk and uncertainty, and the boundary of IPS and IPE.

Torbjørn L. Knutsen, Ph.D. in International Studies (University of Denver, 1985), is a Professor of International Relations in the Department of Sociology and Political Science at the Norwegian University of Science and Technology (NTNU), in Trondheim, Norway. His English-language books include *The Rise and Fall of World Orders* (1999), *A History of International Relations Theory* (3rd ed., 2016), and *Ways of Knowing*, co-written with Jonathon Moses (3rd ed., 2019). His interests include Great Power politics, diplomatic history, and international terrorism.

Jorg Kustermans is an Associate Professor of international politics at the University of Antwerp, Belgium. His research interests include the conceptual history of peace, changing practices of peacemaking, and the sources of international authority. His research has appeared in a number of scholarly journals, including *Review of International Studies* and *the Chinese Journal of International Politics*. He recently co-edited *A Requiem for Peacebuilding* (Palgrave, 2021).

Heonik Kwon is a Senior Research Fellow in Social Science and Professor of Social Anthropology at Trinity College, University of Cambridge, and is the author of several prize-winning books on the Vietnam War social history and Cold War conceptual history; his most recent work is *After the Korean War: An Intimate History* (Cambridge, 2020). He is currently completing a book on Korea's Cold War experience as manifested in the religious-cultural sphere.

Christopher David LaRoche is an Assistant Professor of International Relations at Central European University. He holds a Ph.D. from the University of Toronto, and previously held research fellowships at the China Institute, University of Alberta, and Munk School for Global Affairs, University of Toronto. His research has appeared in *International Theory, International Studies Quarterly,* and the *European Journal of International Relations*.

Deborah Welch Larson is a Professor of Political Science at the University of California, Los Angeles. Her publications include *Origins of Containment: A Psychological Explanation* and *Quest for Status: Chinese and Russian Foreign Policy* with Alexei Shevchenko.

George Lawson is a Professor of International Relations at the Australian National University. His work is oriented around the relationship between history and theory, with a particular interest in global historical sociology. He applies this interest to the study of revolutions in two books, *Anatomies of Revolution* (2019) and *Negotiated Revolutions* (2005). Lawson also applies his interest in history theory to debates around global modernity, most notably in *The Global Transformation: History, Modernity, and the Making of International Relations* (2015), co-authored with Barry Buzan, which charts the ways in which a range of important dynamics in contemporary International Relations have their roots in the nineteenth-century 'global transformation'. His work has won the Francesco Guicciardini Prize and the Joseph Fletcher Prize, both from the International Studies Association, and the Hedley Bull Prize from the European Consortium of Political Research.

Luis Lobo-Guerrero is a Professor of History and Theory of International Relations at the University of Groningen. He is the author of *Insuring Security* (2010), *Insuring War* (2012), *Insuring Life* (2016), *Imaginaries of Connectivity: The Creation of Novel Spaces of Governance,* ed. (2020), and *Mapping, Connectivity, and the Making of European Empires,* ed. (2021). He is currently working on a project that seeks to understand the invention of globality in the long sixteenth century.

Joseph MacKay is a Research Fellow in the Department of International Relations at the Australian National University. He holds a Ph.D. from the University of Toronto. He works on historical international security and hierarchies, and the history of international thought. His research has appeared in the *Review of International Studies, International Studies Quarterly, International Theory,* and other venues.

Richard W. Mansbach has served as Political Science Department Chair at Rutgers-New Brunswick and Iowa State University, where he is a Professor of Political Science. He was a Marshall Scholar and has received four Fulbright fellowships. He and Yale Ferguson have co-authored seven books, including *The Elusive Quest; Polities; A World of Polities* and *Remapping Global Politics;* forthcoming: *Populism and Globalization;* and *Organized Violence: Past,* Present, *Future.*

Jeppe Mulich is a Lecturer in modern history at the Department of International Politics at City, University of London. His work takes place in the disciplinary intersection of global history, historical sociology, and International Relations. He is the author of *In a Sea of Empires: Networks and Crossings in the Revolutionary Caribbean* (2020).

Cornelia Navari is an Honorary Senior Lecturer at the University of Birmingham, United Kingdom and Visiting Professor of International Affairs at the University of Buckingham. She is the author of *Internationalism and the State in the 20th Century* (2000) and *Public Intellectuals and International Affairs* (2012); and the editor of *Theorising International Society: English School Methods* (2009), *Ethical Reasoning in International Affairs* (2013), and *Hans Morgenthau and the American Experience* (2018). With Daniel Green, she edited the *Guide to the English School in International Studies* (Wiley Blackwell, 2014) and with Molly Cochran *Progressivism and American Foreign Policy between the World Wars* (2018).

Patrick Nitzschner is a doctoral candidate at Lund University. His dissertation project engages with the concept of democratic defence, reconstructing the political interventions of early Frankfurt School theorists in exile and upon return to Germany. He has previously worked on notions of criticality and (post-)positivism in epistemology and methodology

Andreas Aagaard Nøhr is a Lecturer at the Department of International Relations and International Organization, University of Groningen. He has a Ph.D. in International Relations from the London School of Economics and Political Science. His research interests lie at the intersection between the history of political thought, International Relations, and historical epistemology. Currently, Andreas is working on two research projects: The project, *The Politics of Truth in the Western Tradition of Thought,* interrogates the relationship between truth and politics by inquiring into the conditions of possibility for the current crisis of post-truth politics, while in the other project, *Traditions of Thought: A Global Epistemology for International Relations* endeavours to explain the multiplicity of thought and action in world politics and thus attempts to theorize non-Western and comparative political thought within the purview of a global epistemology.

Joel Quirk is a Professor of Politics at the University of the Witwatersrand, South Africa. His research focuses on slavery and abolition, human mobility, social movements, repairing historical wrongs, and the politics and history of Africa. He is the author or co-editor of seven books, including *The Anti-Slavery Project: From the Slave Trade to Human Trafficking* (Penn, 2011), *Mobility Makes States: Migration and Power in Africa* (edited with Darshan Vigneswaran, Penn, 2015), and *Contemporary Slavery: The Rhetoric of Global Human Rights Campaigns* (edited with Annie Bunting, Cornell, 2018).

Ellen J. Ravndal is an Associate Professor in Political Science at the University of Stavanger, Norway. She holds a D.Phil. in International Relations from the University of Oxford and has previously taught at Lund University and the Australian National University. Her research broadly focuses on International Organizations (IOs), including the UN Secretary-General, IO autonomy, and the history of IOs, and has appeared in journals such as *Global Governance*, the *International History Review*, and the *Review of International Studies*.

Or Rosenboim is a Senior Lecturer in Modern History and Director of the Centre for Modern History at City, University of London. She has published articles on the history of international thought, world order, and federalism. Her book, *The Emergence of Globalism: Visions of World Order in Britain and the United States, 1939–1950*, was published in 2017.

Carsten-Andreas Schulz is an Assistant Professor of International Relations at the Pontificia Universidad Católica de Chile and holds a D.Phil. from the University of Oxford. His research focuses on Latin America's relationship with and contribution to international order.

Maja Spanu is a Research Fellow in International Relations and Affiliated Lecturer at the University of Cambridge. She is the co-founder of the Cambridge IR and history working group, an international network of specialists of history and international politics. Her research interests include self-determination and state formation, nationalism and citizenship, international justice, and war crimes.

Brent J. Steele is the Francis D. Wormuth Presidential Chair, Professor, and Department Chair of Political Science at the University of Utah. His research and teaching interests include topics ontological security, IR theory, international ethics, generational analysis, critical security studies, US foreign policy, and global health.

Jelena Subotic is a Professor of Political Science at Georgia State University in Atlanta. She received her Ph.D. in Political Science from the University of Wisconsin-Madison. She is the author of two books: *Yellow Star, Red Star: Holocaust Remembrance after Communism* (Cornell University Press, 2019) and *Hijacked Justice: Dealing with the Past in the Balkans* (Cornell University Press, 2009) and numerous scholarly articles on identity politics, national identity, and the Western Balkans.

Shogo Suzuki is a Senior Lecturer at the University of Manchester. His main research areas are Chinese and Japanese foreign policy and diplomatic history, as well as International Relations theory with reference to East Asia. His research has been published in journals such as *European Journal of International Relations*, *International Affairs*, and *Millennium*.

Ted Svensson is an Associate Professor at the Department of Political Science, Lund University, Sweden. His publications include *Production of Postcolonial India and Pakistan: Meanings of*

Partition (Routledge, 2013) and articles in *Review of International Studies*, *Postcolonial Studies*, *Third World Quarterly*, *Global Society*, and *Alternatives*. He is also editor of the journal *Cooperation and Conflict*.

Ann E. Towns is a Professor in Political Science at the University of Gothenburg and a Wallenberg Academy Fellow. She heads GenDip, a research program on gender and diplomacy (https://www.gu.se/en/gender-and-diplomacy). Towns is co-editor of *Gendering Diplomacy and International Negotiation* (with Karin Aggestam, 2018, Palgrave) and author of *Women and States: Norms and Hierarchies in International Society* (2010, Cambridge University Press) and numerous journal articles on gender, states, and International Relations in history.

Claire Vergerio is an Assistant Professor of International Relations at Leiden University. Her work lies at the intersection of political thought, history, and international law. She is particularly interested in the regulation of warfare and its relationship to different visions of international order, as well as in the construction of the historical narratives that underpin the disciplines of International Law and International Relations.

Tomas Wallenius is a Leverhulme Early Career Fellow in International Relations at Nuffield College, Oxford University. He works on political ideologies and International Relations. His new project investigates contested visions of citizenship and the right of movement in the era of decolonization. Tomas is also finishing a project on foreigners' property rights and the making of global capitalism. His publications include *The Case for a History of Global Legal Practices* (*European Journal of International Relations*, 2019).

William C. Wohlforth is the Daniel Webster Professor at Dartmouth College, where he teaches in the Department of Government. His most recent books are *America Abroad: The United States' Global Role in the 21st Century* (Oxford University Press, 2018), with co-author Stephen G. Brooks, and *The Oxford Handbook of International Security* (Oxford University Press, 2018), co-edited with Alexandra Gheciu.

Joanne Yao is a Lecturer in International Relations at Queen Mary University of London. Before her appointment to QMUL, she taught at Durham University and the London School of Economics and Political Science (LSE). She has also worked in the US public sector and for international non-governmental organizations. Her research interests are in IR theory, historical sociology, global and international history, international institutions, critical geography, and environmental politics.

Ayşe Zarakol is Reader in International Relations at the University of Cambridge and a Fellow at Emmanuel College. Dr Zarakol works on the evolution of East and West relations in the international order, declining and rising powers, and politics of non-Western regional powers. She is the author of *After Defeat: How the East Learned to Live with the West* (Cambridge University Press, 2011) and the editor of *Hierarchies in World Politics* (Cambridge University Press, 2017). Her articles have appeared in many journals, such as *International Organization*, *International Theory*, *International Studies Quarterly*, *European Journal of International Relations*, *Review of International Studies*. She is currently finishing up a book manuscript titled *Before Defeat: Rethinking the Decline of the East and the Future of the West*.

PREFACE AND ACKNOWLEDGEMENTS

We used to live by variation of a quote by Mark Twain: 'I am not the editor of a [handbook] and shall always try to do right and be good so that God will not make me one' (*Galaxy Magazine*, December 1870). We had been part of too many handbooks to want to edit one ourselves. We had heard too many handbook editors complain to want to edit one. Our initial reaction when Nicola Parkin from Routledge approached us because she sensed the need for a handbook of Historical International Relations (IR) was therefore one of reticence. But we were also intrigued, and to some extent felt a certain pressure and a sense of responsibility. And although we may at times have wished that we had stuck to our initial stance on editing a handbook, it goes without saying that it is with immense gratitude to all the wonderful scholars who have made this project possible that we now fondly look back on those years of labour, and with great pride and no regrets whatsoever that we publish the proceedings of that work.

When we were approached by Routledge in 2017, Historical IR had existed for a few years as its own section within the International Studies Association. Having been involved in the section since its inception and having reaped the benefits of our newly found(ed) academic home, we realized that a handbook would make the foundations of the Historical IR endeavour even stronger, by gathering a number of central people around the topics which held our common project together. In spite of ourselves, we became handbook editors.

Truth be told, we have at times come to regret that decision (as when the process of coordinating more than 60 authors felt a bit too much like herding cats), in particular when Covid-19 and other curveballs of life made the whole process grind to a standstill (and it felt as if both herder-editors and our feline authors were stuck on flypaper). Other experiences are nevertheless the ones which will stick with us. The wealth of wonderful people helping us out throughout the process has made us understand even better the extent to which Historical IR consists of an amazing community of scholars, how the subdiscipline has become ingrained in the core of the discipline and what an exceptionally generous, kind, and interesting subfield Historical IR has become.

Allow us to dwell a bit on Historical IR, for this subfield and community are the reason why this handbook has been produced in the first place. In our minds, Historical IR is an approach of its own. Related to History in its approach, it is not part of it, borrowing heavily from Historical Sociology it is nevertheless broader, and being intrinsically part of IR it explicitly looks to the past in order to find answers to current conundrums. This handbook is therefore not an attempt at *rapprochement* between the disciplines of History and IR. Historical IR was born out of the many (historical) critiques of the neo-neo historical inertia of the Cold War and spent its infancy in homelessness, at times adopted by Historical Sociology, other times sheltered by the English School. If the foundation of a separate Historical IR section can be considered the baptism of this new subfield, we suggest that this handbook be seen as the coming-of-age of Historical IR. While substantive, the chapters do not seek to be definitive. While broad, we do not claim it to be exhaustive. Our ambition was that this handbook should reflect the current state of historical work in IR, that it summarizes the work done thus far, and that it can serve as a point of departure for future research in the field.

The work has been organized alongside the traditional 'IR Circuit', meeting at conferences, and organizing workshops alongside other IR scholars. To kick-start the process, we organized an EWIS workshop in Groningen in June 2018 where many chapters were presented in draft form. Another batch of papers was presented in draft form at the Pan-European Conference on International Relations in Prague in September 2018. Based on these two sessions, the editors met on other business at an EISA exploratory symposium in Rapallo in November 2018 and hammered out final details. The EISA thus deserves many thanks for facilitating our work. Chapters were submitted, reviewed, and resubmitted through 2019 and early 2020, some authors had to pull out and others were roped in, and then Covid-19 put a break on this, as so many other processes. With a lot of goodwill and endless online meetings, the editing was nevertheless able to proceed to the conclusion in the summer and autumn of 2020.

Beyond conferences and workshops, we have had the help of many willing reviewers and advisors within and beyond the actual handbook. Handbook-authors were eager to read and comment on other chapters, and colleagues outside of the handbook jumped at the opportunity to write what they knew would be valued input in making the handbook even better. Nowhere was the generosity of the subfield more obvious than in our interactions with colleagues reviewing chapters for us, or providing us with advice on the broader project. Their prompt replies and excellent feedback are testament to the generosity of the wider community of Historical IR. In alphabetical order, our most heartfelt gratitude is thus owed to the following:

Lucian Ashworth, Martin Bayly, Zoltan Buzas, Mauro Caraccioli, Christopher Chase-Dunn, Tim Dunne, Dan Green, Xavier Guillaume, Benjamin Herborth, John M. Hobson, Torbjørn L. Knutsen, Jorg Kustermans, George Lawson, Katharine Millar, Daniel Nexon, Patricia Owens, Vassilios Paipais, Andrew Phillips, Ellen Jenny Ravndal, Or Rosenboim, Ann Towns, Claire Vergerio, and Anders Wivel.

Axel Andreas Keber provided excellent assistance in finalizing the manuscript for submission, and has done a tremendous job with the index. For their patience, professionalism, and encouragement, we thank the people at Routledge: Nicola Parkin, Rob Sorsby, and Claire Maloney.

Finally, some funding has been provided by two research projects funded by the Research Council of Norway: EMPRISE, project number 262657 and CHOIR, project number 288639.

Benjamin de Carvalho
Julia Costa Lopez
Halvard Leira
Oslo and Groningen, November 2020

1

INTRODUCTION: HISTORICAL INTERNATIONAL RELATIONS

Benjamin de Carvalho, Julia Costa Lopez and Halvard Leira

Introduction

Disciplinary International Relations (IR) grew in part out of the discipline of History. Even so, the subfield of Historical International Relations (HIR) is a relatively new one. A mere decade ago, a handbook such as this one would have seemed unthinkable. Sure, there were books about History *and* IR (Elman and Elman, 1997) and more on the way (Bukovansky et al., forthcoming), people discussed the "problem of history" in IR (Armitage, 2004; Vaughan-Williams, 2005) and it was asked what history could be in IR (Hobson and Lawson, 2008). These takes nevertheless all supposed either the existence of a divide to be bridged or a continuum where the enterprises of History and IR were commensurable. The emergence and institutionalisation of a distinct subfield over the last decade has radically changed that landscape. Writing in 2020, it is obvious that a burgeoning subfield of HIR not only exists within the discipline, but that it has come to age and is thriving. As the ensuing chapters vividly demonstrate, so much material is being produced that a stock-taking exercise is both possible and necessary. This handbook attempts just such a stocktaking.

Taking stock implies casting the nets far and wide. What follows is thus not an overview of the subjects we have decided upon as the most important in or for HIR, it is more like an inductively generated catalogue of current and past HIR. This is also not a handbook about the history of IR, as it offers no complete or coherent historical account. Rather, it seeks to give a comprehensive overview of the historical work undertaken by IR scholars over the past three decades, initially as part of different traditions or theoretical enterprises and, later, more or less consciously as belonging to the subdiscipline of IR which we now call HIR. Over the last decade, we have spent countless hours as programme chairs for conferences, members of awards committees and as supervisors and lecturers. This forms the basis for the selection of subjects below – these are the subjects which animate scholars doing HIR at the current stage. While we hope that many see the texts as concrete inspiration, we also fully expect others to be inspired by omissions.

In this introduction, we start by presenting the overall trajectory of historical work in the IR discipline, how it was central to the founding of scholarly IR but was somewhat marginalised during the Cold War, and how it has had a gradual resurgence since the 1980s, gaining steam around the turn of the century. We follow this up with a discussion of how the literature of the last decades transcended the earlier discussions about history and/in/for IR, leading up to what we see as the distinctiveness of HIR and the justification for this handbook as an IR project rather than a multidisciplinary one. Finally, we lay out the broad contents of each of the ensuing sections of the book.

Historical International Relations

As detailed in recent IR historiography, the Anglo-American (or perhaps rather, Commonwealth-American) discipline of IR grew out of a number of different academic traditions, including colonial administration, international law, history and political science (Long and Schmidt, 2005; Bell, 2009; Ashworth, 2014; Vitalis, 2015; Rosenboim, 2017; Davis et al., 2020). It makes sense to claim that international history was one of the academic midwives in IR's long formative phase. During the first decades of disciplinary development, no particular justification for turning to history was needed. For a discipline which grew partly out of History, more or less explicitly theoretically informed historical narrative was the predominant form of scholarship. The gradual move towards behavioural social science, game theory and quantitative methods from the 1960s onwards implied a less explicit focus on historical analysis (Guilhot, 2011, 2017), but history remained as a quarry for data, a testing ground for theory and a site of investigation. Quantitative research obviously relied on the coding of historical data and involved making historiographical decisions (Fazal, 2011). Historical analysis could also be found on the margins of the American discipline, for instance in World-Systems Theory (Denemark, 2021 in this volume) and the English School (e.g. Dunne, 1998). History remained one of the unacknowledged partners of IR – unacknowledged, but still formative and a constant presence. The "scientific" approaches to international relations nevertheless implied that history could no longer serve as its own justification. Furthermore, even if scholars across the discipline were clearly engaging with historical data and history (albeit often relatively recent history), there was little explicit reflection about how and why one should engage history. As Christopher Thorne lamented, history was more often than not abused in IR (1983: 123).

The situation changed in the 1980s. Within the discipline, a gradual intellectual opening up changed the terms of discussion for historically-oriented IR. The many and broad challenges against the perceived "neo-neo" consensus involved history in two distinct ways. First, as one of many different alternative approaches, historical analysis benefited from the general opening up of the discipline. Second, and more importantly, history served as one of the central spanners in the works of mainstream theorising. This was obvious in the work of thinkers as diverse as Walker, Cox, Ruggie and Kratochwil, all engaging with history to demonstrate the shortcomings of the allegedly "scientific" approaches (Cox, 1981; Ruggie, 1986, 1998; Kratochwil, 1986; Walker, 1993; see the discussion in Leira and de Carvalho, 2016). These two different openings towards history have had slightly different implications for HIR. On the one hand, studies engaging history started emerging in all corners of the discipline, some of them with a fairly traditional view of history and concerned with getting the facts straight and using them to build, modify or test theories. On the other hand, historical arguments were being engaged more thoroughly in the parts of the discipline at the time lumped together as "critical": poststructuralism, constructivism, historical sociology and so forth. It has been a guiding principle of the editors of this volume, that both of these approaches fit within the broader project of HIR.

Looking at external factors, the turn to history seems obviously related to the relatively rapidly changing conditions of world affairs since 1989. Whereas decades of Cold War and the perceived centrality of the Euro-Atlantic area enabled relatively ahistorical conceptions of an unchanging system, the breakdown of bipolarity, the multiplication of actors and the emergence of new powers in the global south led to a return to history. Faced with an uncertain future, an increasing number of scholars have looked to the past for guidance, patterns and ideas. This tendency has been clear, despite theoretical and methodological differences. Some look to the past to find recurring patterns, others to bring forth unacknowledged legacies, and yet others to denaturalise taken-for-granted concepts and ideas or to understand how we come to find ourselves in our current predicament (Bartelson, 1995; Reus-Smit, 1999; Jahn, 2000; Inayatullah and Blaney, 2004).

By the turn of the century, enough historically-oriented scholarship was coming forward for observers to comment on a possible "historical" or "historiographical" turn in the discipline (Bell, 2001). The interest and investment in historically-oriented scholarship has continued to grow since this diagnosis was first put forward, and with the growing diversity and globalisation of the discipline, the scope of HIR was broadened significantly by scholars from outside of the traditional "core" of IR (Towns, 2009; Shilliam, 2011; Vitalis, 2015; Nişancıoğlu, 2020; Manchanda, 2020; Çapan, 2020). More and more scholars are self-consciously describing their work as historical, grounding it in HIR and engaging in ever more sophisticated theoretical and empirical historical analyses. After initial explorations and excavations in many directions, it is now possible to see some cohesion emerging and to take stock of the developments.

Writing Historical IR

Thinking of HIR of course immediately brings up debates about the relations between History and IR. As noted previously, this has always been a close relation: not only were history and historians crucial in the birth of the IR discipline, but most IR work includes an (implicit) historical dimension (Hobson and Lawson, 2008). And yet, at the same time, the relation between IR and History has been extensively and explicitly debated, and these debates have both drawn on and informed the way in which work in HIR has been carried out (Suganami, 2008; Yetiv, 2011; Leira, 2015; Kratochwil, 2016).

For many years, this engagement was based on the assumption of a stark division between IR and History: where IR scholars focused on theory and concepts, on nomothetic knowledge, historians were concerned with the particular, the contingent and the ideographic. In terms of the production of historical knowledge, this led to an (implicit) inferiority complex of IR that asked how it could learn from history. In this view, the writing of historians, based on primary sources, paying minute attention to detail and historical context, mastering ancient languages and a multitude of texts, was just superior to that of theory-minded IR scholars. To be sure, what history can learn from IR was also correspondingly asked, leading to a counter-dismissal of history as pretty much an auxiliary science for IR scholars to mobilise in their pursuit of more noble, theoretical aims (Yetiv, 2011). This division of labour, and the privileging of historical writing by historians, is epitomised in Elman and Elman's claim that "all international relations theories need historical facts against which they can be measured" (1997: 7).

And yet, most reflexive engagement about history and IR since then has sought to challenge this "eternal divide" (Lawson, 2012) and instead brings both disciplines closer together. The epistemological debates in IR provided an important context for this, for the original position implied that there is a somehow complete historical record that can best be accessed by historians and from which IR scholars can consequently draw. In challenging this position, IR scholars have pointed to the problems of assuming historical objectivity, to the presence of a variety of substantive assumptions about the nature of history, to different forms of historical consciousness already present in IR and to the status of History as a social science (Vaughan-Williams, 2005; Reus-Smit, 2008; Lawson, 2012; Glencross, 2015). Ultimately, in doing so, they have tried to overcome the perceived gulf that divided History and IR in the self-image of the discipline, seeking to put both disciplines closer together along a continuum or even negating substantive difference.

In setting up this handbook, we build on this reflexive tradition as a way of thinking about HIR. And yet, we do not seek to position ourselves in the ongoing epistemological debates about the status of historical truth or the notion of historical knowledge, particularly because doing so would not do justice to the genuinely open spirit that has so far characterised this field of study. At the same time, while we sympathise with arguments that use the reflexive tradition in order to attempt to overcome the "eternal divide", this volume makes evident that the different disciplines and activities cannot easily be collapsed unto each other. HIR scholars seek to answer different puzzles, ask different questions, about different peoples and processes: ultimately, HIR writes different histories, and these are the ones that are reflected in this volume.

This means that HIR increasingly starts from the fact that historians have no privileged epistemological position from which to write history. Certainly, there is a longer tradition, reflection and experience of what the craft of writing histories involve, reflected in more extensive methodological writings, approaches and training at graduate levels that IR scholars can definitely benefit from. Ultimately, however, the writing of history relies on the linking into a narrative of a variety of pieces of past traces – sources – on the basis of a present-asked question (Thies, 2002 gives a handy how-to guide for HIR). And as the chapters in this volume emphasise, not only is there no impediment for IR scholars to write their own histories, but doing so may seem increasingly necessary. For historians engage with historical topics, select and interpret sources, and write histories in the context of conversations that, while may at some level resonate with IR concerns, are still disciplinary-specific. As kindred spirits in another discipline, HIR scholars engage with these bodies of knowledge, but relying on them in order to solve our puzzles may leave us in a state of constant short-sightedness. This is thus neither a handbook of the history of international relations nor a handbook about all historical writing and research of relevance for IR. Rather, the chapters in this handbook take stock of the historical research that is being conducted in IR, by IR scholars, in answer to IR questions.

Organisation of the volume

Handbooks come in many different shapes and forms. Some consist of topical essays, others of what amounts to annotated bibliographies. Likewise, some come with strict editorial guidelines, with overall topics to be covered in each and every chapter, while others leave the structure of each chapter to the individual authors. We have tried to steer a middle course. In recognition of the wide variety of subjects covered, we have chosen not to enforce some overarching processes or issues for all to address. We have furthermore encouraged authors to use their own voices and explore their subjects in the ways they see most fit. The point has not been to bring forth consensus views or greatest hits, but to provide a high-quality set of curated essays on the current state of HIR. However, to ensure coherence and usefulness for our readers, we have tasked all authors with undertaking two core tasks: engaging with the current state of HIR knowledge in the specific field and pointing to openings and opportunities where the field may (or should!) go in the future. The chapters in this volume in this sense constitute both an exercise in mapping the field and one in setting (possible) agendas for HIR.

As in any exercise in mapping, it is important to reflect on the selectivities at play in the composition of "the field". When two of us edited the four-volume set on HIR (Leira and de Carvalho, 2015) five years ago, it became clear to what extent HIR, unlike the fantasy of Cormac McCarthy, has, unfortunately, largely been a country for (Western-based) old men. On the one hand, for reasons we suspect are closely related to the sociology and political economy of the IR discipline, where tenure and contracts are often related to doing policy-relevant research, HIR scholarship is predominantly produced by PhD students and tenured professors. And the latter group has traditionally been dominated by Western, old (or at least middle-aged) men. On the other hand, as some excellent recent scholarship has shown, the contributions of women and minority groups have systematically been obscured (Anievas et al., 2015; Owens, 2018). However, times are changing and we have made every effort to have the selection of contributors to this handbook reflect that change. Younger scholars are proving it possible to build careers on historical research, and groups that were traditionally under-represented in HIR scholarship – women as well as academics from outside of the Western core of the IR discipline in particular – are increasingly taking part, making their mark on and becoming central in HIR conversations. Although we have not always managed, we have attempted our utmost to have this reflected in the contributors as well as the topics covered.

Traditions

IR is a discipline which has construed itself around a number of alleged theoretical traditions and debates. As Luke Ashworth demonstrates in his chapter, this is not necessarily a precise (or useful, for that matter) way of slicing and dicing the discipline. Nevertheless, since a majority of IR scholars still see themselves as rooted in (or fighting against) such traditions, we have laid out the first section of the book according to a logic of different ways of thinking IR historically within established traditions. The different chapters in this section demonstrate the wide variety of approaches to HIR and underscore our point that HIR is now being conducted in all corners of the discipline.

Before the specific traditions are presented, we nevertheless need a more solid grounding. In the first chapter of this section (MacKay and LaRoche), we get an introduction to philosophies and theories of history, and an admonition to the subfield to engage in a more explicit and critical engagement with the underlying ideas of what drives history. Moving on from this, the section first presents traditions which have put history at the centre of their investigation: the English School (Navari and Green) with its emphasis on the expansion of international society (which has inspired and provoked scholars of many theoretical stripes), World-Systems Theory (Denemark) with its focus on macro history and global systemic patterns and Historical Sociology (Go, Lawson and de Carvalho) which has moved from an interest in the emergence of the modern state system to a broader interest in global political phenomena.

The second part of the section introduces the historical work being done within the frameworks of the more generally oriented traditions of the discipline. Here we find the usual suspects, liberalism (Jahn) bridging classical liberal ideas and the more recent liberal internationalism; realism (Larson) with its oscillation between ahistoricism and structural explanations applied to history; constructivism (Bruneau) with its insistence on the historical specificity of the current international system combined with an interest in the variation between systems; poststructuralism (Nøhr) with its genealogical method and its focus on core concepts of IR/ir and International Political Theory (Rosenboim and Hartnett) with its exploration of the intersection of thought and practice.

In sum, this first section of the book illustrates how historical work can be found in all the major traditions of IR thought and how it is conducted in a multitude of ways. Despite the wide variation, these chapters also point to a number of similar topics for further exploration. There is wide agreement on the need for research to transcend singular levels of analysis and to focus instead on the interplay between levels. Likewise, writers from different traditions agree on the need to look beyond Europe, to include non-canonical writers and topics, as well as gender and race in the analyses and to explore core concepts more diligently. A common thread uniting these concerns is the desire to explore the 19th century in more depth, as a pivotal moment where many of the above-mentioned topics were established, changed or marginalised (cf. Buzan and

Lawson, 2015). As the chapters demonstrate, there are important overlaps between traditions, and a clear tendency for writers allegedly belonging to one tradition, carrying out work which could just as well be grouped within another one. This could suggest that we might be better served by thinking about our discipline in ways not guided by "traditions". The next section presents just such a take.

Thinking International Relations historically

The preceding chapters take as their starting point the continued importance of distinct intellectual traditions in the study of IR, as a way of anchoring analysis or as a starting point for pointing out glaring omissions. In his chapter, Luke Ashworth questions if a focus on traditions is the most fruitful way of thinking about disciplinary developments. While not rejecting existing narratives outright, Ashworth recognises that the narratives we tell about ourselves as a discipline are central to opening up and closing down different lines of investigation. His re-centring of disciplinary history around a set of broad central topics can thus be read as a call for opening up HIR to concerns beyond the established traditions.

Opening up can also mean rethinking, as demonstrated by our two chapters discussing acknowledged core concerns of the discipline, war (Bartelson) and capitalism (Anievas and Gogu). These chapters demonstrate convincingly how even the traditional core of the discipline benefits from being historicised. Following that, we have a set of chapters dealing with core cross-cutting topics which for a long time have been forgotten, neglected and marginalised: gender (Towns), Eurocentrism/civilisation (Bowden) and race (Yao and Dellatolla). These topics have had a resurgence in general IR over the last decades, and these chapters vividly demonstrate how important they are to HIR as well. The call for opening up is then brought more explicitly to disciplinary developments and historical trajectories beyond the geographical core of the discipline, in Latin America and the Caribbean (Fonseca), as well as in Asia (Hui). The final two chapters bring to the table two relatively recent ways of thinking IR historically, through political theology (Bain) and the concept of time itself (Hom). Theology and time tie the end of this section back to the very beginning, to philosophies and theories of history, demonstrating the need for HIR scholars to engage more explicitly with what we believe the driving forces and key concepts of history to be.

Unsurprisingly, the different ways of thinking IR historically share some common concerns and areas for further investigation. Most of these tie in with broader trends in the discipline. First, there is a focus on relationships between different cores and peripheries, in the discipline as well as in its object of study (Tickner and Wæver, 2009; Çapan et al., 2021). Second, many of the chapters relate closely to the work on hierarchy (as opposed to anarchy) in IR in general (Zarakol, 2017). Third, across modes of thinking, there is a growing interest in the many-faceted global and interconnected ways of discussing the organisation of order and violence (Barkawi, 2017; Phillips and Sharman, 2020). Finally, several of these prisms implicitly or explicitly force us to reconsider the core concepts of IR scholarship and IR practice (Berenskoetter, 2016; Leira, 2019). Taken together, these chapters urge HIR to think traditional phenomena anew and to keep engaging forgotten, marginalised and new phenomena, spaces and places.

Actors, processes and institutions

The third section of the book is broader, and self-consciously less "coherent". In line with our overall inductive project, our aim here is to showcase the breadth of the HIR project through key themes. Thus, the chapters in this section do not share a common topical focus, rather they explore the processes, actors, practices and institutions that constitute the core objects of study of many HIR scholars. Even so, we do find that the chapters cluster around some common themes.

A first theme that emerges is the centrality within HIR – just like in the discipline more broadly – of histories of the state system. Indeed, the historical exploration of the modern international, its core actors and its practices remains an important focus of the field. This is unsurprising. For one, some of the early historically minded traditions in IR, such as the English School, started from a problematisation of, and inquiry into the rise of the modern international and a comparative focus on state systems (Wight, 1977; Watson, 1992; Buzan and Little, 2000). Furthermore, the state, however understood, is also at the centre of the IR disciplinary imaginary, and, more broadly, of the imaginary of the social sciences as such (Bartelson, 2001). Many of the chapters in this section thus deal with state practices, institutions and processes, such as sovereignty or diplomacy. From these, it emerges that a good amount of HIR research is concerned with tracing the history of the practices that constitute the state, and with it, the modern international. Thus, for example, the initial chapter by de Carvalho unpacks debates about the history and emergence of sovereignty as the articulation of the political authority of the state, followed by a chapter on state formation (de Carvalho and Leira), while the subsequent chapters by Heiskanen and Spanu are concerned with the histories of how the subjects of the state have been thought.

The contribution of HIR scholarship to the understanding of the state, however, goes beyond these. As Devetak notes in his chapter on Reason of State, there are a number of concepts that are frequently used, yet their meaning is taken for granted. Many of the chapters in this section demonstrate the crucial role of HIR scholarship in unpacking the meaning and the historicity of these concepts, from reason of state to the nation to borders and territoriality. In doing so, HIR scholars are able to provide fertile grounds for novel conceptualisation. Andersen and Wohlforth's inquiry into the histories of the balance of power, for example, reveals not its universality, but rather the fundamental politics behind the concept itself. Ultimately, thus, HIR not only makes us aware of the history of international relations, but also of the historicity of the discipline and its thinking.

Second, the chapters in this section also demonstrate the importance of HIR within the so-called Imperial turn. Indeed, a large amount of current HIR work seeks to problematise traditional state-centric analytics by bringing to the fore the history (and present) of empires. As Martin Bayly writes, this move jointly responds to broader societal reflections about the American empire after the end of the Cold War, and to the turn to history itself within the discipline. For a historical account of international relations immediately encounters the centrality of empire (Keene, 2002; Barkawi and Laffey, 2002; Ravndal, 2020). The chapters in this section, however, evidence that this turn goes beyond recovering histories of empire, or even developing conceptualisations of empire. Instead, it seeks to provide a fundamentally different narrative about the emergence of the modern international by showing the global entanglements between states, empires and dynamics such as capitalism. Thus, the turn to empire cuts across the studies of a variety of practices and actors, from international law, to international organisations to insurance. With these broader shifts, as the chapters by Svensson and Kwon demonstrate, empire also becomes central in thinking about the post–1945 Cold War world.

And yet, despite the vitality of this imperial turn, much remains to be done. As Caraccioli notes, what IR means by "empires" remains suspiciously focused on the 19th-century Anglosphere. Other empires – French, German and beyond – are much less studied, raising questions not only about the resulting historical narratives, but also about the conceptual selectivities that may come from it (for exceptions, see, e.g. dos Reis, 2021). Beyond this, an important area for further development emerges from the joint discussion of both state practices and the turn to empire: the simultaneous centrality and the absence of the state. While there were important early takes on both state formation from a historical-sociological tradition (Tilly, 1990; Spruyt, 1994; Hobson, 1998), and inquiry into the state as a category of thought (Bartelson, 2001), the last two decades seem to have a relative dearth of studies that put the history of the state itself as centre (for a certain exception, see Buzan and Lawson, 2015). HIR scholars seem to either be favouring the disaggregation of the state into various practices, a focus on alternative forms of organisation such as empire, or a broader conceptual take through notions such as polity (Ferguson and Mansbach, 1996).

Finally, a third theme that emerges from the chapters in this section concerns the analytics that HIR scholars use in their research. Indeed, as has been noted elsewhere, historically minded IR scholars have been comparatively late to take stock of historiographical developments, such as the turn to social history, and thus depart from their traditional high-politics focus (Keene, 2008; Vergerio, 2018). And yet, the chapters in this section show a progressive turn towards pluralising both the types of questions that are asked and the types of sources that are used. As Leira notes in his chapter, whereas traditional diplomatic history formed the basis for much HIR work, new diplomatic histories that open up questions of gender and social practice have now become the norm in historiography and are progressively trickling into IR. This is not an isolated occurrence, but as the chapters by Vergerio, Ravndal, Goettlich and Branch exemplify, the study of a variety of state and imperial practices and institutions has been fundamentally transformed by new sets of questions and focus on different actors.

Altogether, then, these chapters offer not only an overview of key topics making up the HIR "canon" if we may call it such but also showcase a breadth of methods, approaches and onto-logical concerns. In our mind, this has been a key feature of the HIR project since its inception, namely the opening up of spaces for thinking differently, and offering alternative accounts which sit less comfortably with the IR orthodoxy. The fact that many of these accounts could now be counted as part of the IR "mainstream" itself is a testimony to the effectiveness of the HIR pro-ject in productively challenging mainstream (ahistorical) takes on international politics.

Situating Historical IR

While the previous section focuses on a variety of processes and actors that constitute the objects of study in HIR, this section critically reflects about the situatedness of these objects of study. In so doing, it engages the ways in which this situatedness affects the histories written by IR scholars and the core conceptual categories of the discipline. The section's approach to situatedness is thus both temporal and spatial. The first chapters on Rome, Greece and the Middle Ages place the focus on the pre-modern "international", broadly understood. In doing so, they show not only the ways in which the modern IR imaginary relies on particular constructions of these spaces, but also the opportunity for novel theorisation. The latter chapters focus on spaces, Europe, Asia, Latin America, Africa the Middle East, and examine the ways in which these spaces are written into our histories, but also, as Zarakol's chapter demonstrates, what they can tell us about our concepts.

Two core important themes emerge from these engagements as necessitating further attention. First, there is an imbalance in the areas that receive attention, and thus a consequent need to plur-alise the sites – temporal and spatial – that are studied in HIR. HIR engagement with Oceania, pre-Columbian America or pre-modern Africa is still largely lacking (with some exceptions, such as Ferguson and Mansbach, 1996; Warner, 2001; or Rae, 2017). And yet, what this list already highlights is that when thinking about sites of inquiry, time and space should not be under-stood as two separate dimensions. What emerges from many of the chapters in this section is that presumably temporal locations – such as "the Middle Ages" – are entangled with particular spatialities (Costa Lopez, 2016), and conversely, that apparently spatial terms – Europe being the classic example – also entail their own specific temporalities.

Ultimately, this means that the matter of pluralising the objects of study – temporally and spatially – cannot be solved by simply adding more, but also points to a need for a fundamental rethinking of the core categories that HIR uses to define its objects. As Herborth and Nitzschner argue, even if Europe draws most of the scholarly attention, its conceptual function remains taken for granted, and it is only a rethinking of it that can allow us to move past core thinking categories like Eurocentrism. More broadly, as Lewis and Wigen (1997) have pointed out in the context of critical geography, things as apparently obvious and material as the existence of separate continents are themselves the result of long, political processes of construction. Thus, the chapters in this section undertake the first step in thinking through some of the core spatial and temporal categories of HIR, but much work still remains to be done.

Approaches

As the various disciplinary traditions, topics of study and areas show, HIR is far from being a monolithic field or approach. While all HIR shares – at least at a basic level – a common concern with historicity, this translates into a highly heterogeneous field that deploys a wide variety of perspectives and methodological sensibilities. Moreover, as HIR consolidates into a distinctive field, with its own conversations, scholars are increasingly being more reflexive, specific and innovative about their approach to knowledge production. The essays in this section showcase not only this variety, but also the increasingly sophisticated ways in which HIR scholars conduct and reflect about their research, often in dialogue with a variety of perspectives from cognate disciplines.

HIR scholars are taking up the task of writing their own narratives based on primary sources. This reflects not only a distinctive ethos towards HIR research, we think, but also the development of a thriving set of research questions that while still connected to History, are properly IR. And yet, as Jeppe Mulich's chapter notes, there are still very important selectivities at play: much research is still focused on similar sources to those in diplomatic history – governmental and diplomatic records, for example – and there have been limited openings to other types of sources, from social to literary or artistic. Still, the increasing variety of sources reflects not only aim for more comprehensiveness, but also the extent to which a number of new approaches are being integrated and developed within HIR. For, as has been noted, IR, history and a number of other social sciences have evolved closely together throughout the 20th and 21st centuries, experiencing parallel shifts and turns.

Capan, dos Reis and Grasten, for example, reflect on the turns in historiography towards global, connected and entangled histories, and the ways in which IR may both benefit from engaging with them, but also adapt them so that they are most suitable to its concerns. Similarly, Kustermans unpacks the challenges in thinking historically through the recent sociology-inspired practice turn in IR, while Wallenius looks not only at the engagement with historical approaches to the study of international thought such as the Cambridge School, but also how IR efforts to improve on these methods are increasingly drawing from a variety of other areas, such as sociology or literary studies. Finally, Subotic and Steele examine the different ways in which IR scholars have engaged with the wider field of memory studies. For, as their chapter emphasises, HIR not only reflects on the past but also opens up the study of the ways in which the past is nowadays remembered and the politics involved in it.

Following from that, the different approaches also bring up the extent to which there are fundamentally different notions of historicity at play in much of HIR writing, and the ways in which this relates to how we understand the goal of HIR work itself. As Kustermans writes, much of HIR sees itself as militating against the ahistoricism of the so-called mainstream, and thus emphasising historicity and contingency. And yet, this may have led to a lack of reflection about how to conduct the type transhistorical analysis that may transcend a sometimes naive fetishising of contingency, and yet remain historically aware (Fasolt, 2014). For Kustermans, a sociologically informed Durkheimian tradition offers one such opportunity. With a similar sentiment, if coming from a very different methodological perspective, Griffiths and Butcher's chapter on quantitative approaches also seeks to set itself apart with what is sometimes the focus on contingency of some historical works. Quantitative approaches in this view not only bring to the fore the distinct challenges of conceptualisation – of studying the past with present-day concepts – but also open the door to undertaking interesting new cross-historical comparisons, an area that is certainly in need of development.

And yet, what the essays in this section and in the previous ones taken together point to is not only different ways of doing history or the variety of topics, but rather the central role and potential of HIR to destabilise and reconstitute the core categories of IR as a discipline. The two concluding chapters of the section tackle precisely this: Kessler's engagement with conceptual history brings to the fore not only that the history of concepts rests of a variety of different assumptions about the relation between social and semantic orders but also, as a result, the need to engage with the historicity and assumptions of our own concepts. The concluding chapter by Guillaume builds on this, by looking at how we order history through particular conceptual divisions, that is, particular periods. As HIR scholarship has long demonstrated (Osiander, 2001; de Carvalho et al., 2011) IR rests on a number of problematic breaks and periodisations in the narratives it tells about itself, and one of the crucial contributions of HIR is not only to debunk these myths but also, with it, to provide the tools for novel conceptualisation. Ultimately, as Guillaume argues, it is this combination of fresh theoretical reflection with careful historical engagement that will enable HIR to become a prominent conversation partner not only within IR but also, more broadly, with other humanities and social sciences.

Concluding remarks

Brilliant scholars in our past, even in the past of HIR, have asked "What is history?". Based on the essays in this volume, we find ourselves reflecting on the somewhat less ambitious question, "What is Historical IR?". Our first reaction would be to point out the extreme variation. To start with temporal scope, in this collection, we have chapters referring to events in the 14th-century BCE as well as chapters discussing 21st-century CE politics of history. Geographically, most of the globe is covered in works of HIR, although the existing studies of the polar regions have yet to be integrated with the broader discipline. When it comes to thematic and theoretical scope, our sense is that the proof is still very much in the pudding. And this is where all of the different traditions, ways of thinking, topics, actors and places tie in with the various approaches. As long as research concerned with history, however understood, is competently and transparently conducted, with methods fitting the questions raised and with the same questions emerging from or speaking directly to the field of IR, we would be inclined to consider it as HIR; for a spirit of openness is, if anything, one of this field.

By way of conclusion, let us go back in time to the early institutionalisation of the subfield of HIR. At the time of establishment (ca. 2012), the convenors were a slightly disjointed group of scholars interested in IR past, missing both a label and an institutional home. The establishment of the Historical International Relations Section (HIST) at the International Studies Association (ISA) created a profound change in the community, allowing diverse scholars to find a common home and providing aspiring scholars with hope for the future. This institutionalisation, combined with the growth in scope and depth described earlier, made it possible for a community of scholars to grow stronger. We have sought to capture the work of this community within these pages.

Looking back at this project, what we find most striking is the sheer breadth of research undertaken within HIR, and the extent to which scholars within the subfield still speak to each other. We sincerely believe that the founding principle of the HIST section has mattered here. The section was founded on a big-tent principle, where there would be no exclusion based on method, outlook or scope. This openness has been a way for a relatively diverse group of scholars to stick together peacefully, and we believe that scholars engaged in HIR ought to work hard to avoid sectarian tendencies and doctrinal statements on methodology and substance. Looking at where we stand today, we believe that it is the broad-tent approach to approaching the past that has allowed for the formation and integration of a (rather diverse, to be honest) group of scholars under a common enterprise. Keeping this together will require more openness in the future, as new voices are bound to challenge the existing boundaries. In our view, a commitment to methodological and theoretical pluralism is the foundation of a project which has been wildly successful over the last two decades, and it should continue to guide the subfield in the future.

Editing a handbook is a fantastic learning experience. Even though we thought we knew the field of HIR fairly well, reading the wonderful chapters in this collection has demonstrated beyond any doubt that there is still a lot more to explore. We are proud to have been able to collect this work and look forward to see it inspiring new generations of HIST scholars.

References

Anievas, A., Manchanda, N., and Shilliam, R., eds. (2015). *Race and Racism in International Relations*. Abingdon: Routledge.

Armitage, D. (2004). The fifty years right: intellectual history and international relations. *Modern Intellectual History*, 1 (1), 97–109.

Ashworth, L. M. (2014). *A History of International Thought. From the Origins of the Modern State to Academic International Relations*. London: Routledge.

Barkawi, T. (2017). *Soldiers of Empire: Indian and British Armies in World War II*. Cambridge: Cambridge University Press.

Barkawi, T., and Laffey, M. (2002). Retrieving the imperial: *Empire* and international relations. *Millennium – Journal of International Studies*, 31 (1), 109–127.

Bartelson, J. (1995). *A Genealogy of Sovereignty*. Cambridge: Cambridge University Press.

Bartelson, J. (2001). *The Critique of the State*. Cambridge: Cambridge University Press.

Bell, D. (2001). International relations: the dawn of a historiographical turn? *British Journal of Politics and International Relations*, 3 (1), 115–126.

Bell, D. (2009). Writing the world: disciplinary history and beyond. *International Affairs*, 85 (1), 3–22.

Berenskoetter, F., ed. (2016). *Concepts in World Politics*. London: Sage.

Bukovansky, M., Keene, E., Reus-Smit, C., and Spanu, M., eds. (forthcoming). *The Oxford Handbook of History and International Relations*. Oxford: Oxford University Press.

Buzan, B., and Lawson, G. (2015). *The Global Transformation: History, Modernity and the Making of International Relations*. Cambridge: Cambridge University Press.

Buzan, B., and Little, R. (2000). *International Systems in World History*. Oxford: Oxford University Press.

Çapan, Z. G. (2020). Beyond visible entanglements: connected histories of the international. *International Studies Review*, 22 (2), 289–306.

Çapan, Z. G., dos Reis, F., and Grasten, M. (2021). Global Histories: Connections and Circulations in Historical International Relations. In: B. de Carvalho, J. Costa Lopez, and H. Leira, eds., *Routledge Handbook of Historical International Relations*, Abingdon: Routledge.

Costa Lopez, J. (2016). Beyond eurocentrism and orientalism: revisiting the othering of Jews and Muslims through medieval canon law. *Review of International Studies*, 42 (3), 450–470.

Cox, R. W. (1981). Social forces, states and world orders: beyond international relations theory. *Millennium – Journal of International Studies*, 10 (2), 126–155.

Davis, A., Thakur, V., and Vale, P. (2020). *The Imperial Discipline: Race and the Founding of International Relations*. London: Pluto Press.

de Carvalho, B., Leira, H., and Hobson, J. M. (2011). The big bangs of IR: the myths that your teachers still tell you about 1648 and 1919. *Millennium – Journal of International Studies*, 39 (3), 735-758.

Denemark, R. (2021). World-Systems Analysis: Past Trajectories and Future Prospects. In: B. de Carvalho, J. Costa Lopez, and H. Leira, eds., *Routledge Handbook of Historical International Relations*, Abingdon: Routledge.

dos Reis, F. (2021). Empires of Science, Science of Empires: Mapping, Centers of Calculation and the Making of Imperial Spaces in Nineteenth Century Germany. In: L. Lobo-Guerrero, L. Lo Presti, and F. dos Reis, eds., *Mapping, Connectivity and the Making of European Empires*, Lanham: Rowman and Littlefield.

Dunne, T. (1998). *Inventing International Society: A History of the English School*. New York, NY: Springer.

Elman, C., and Elman, M. F. (1997). Diplomatic history and international relations theory. Respecting difference and crossing boundaries. *International Security*, 22 (1), 5-21.

Fasolt, C. (2014). *Past Sense. Studies in Medieval and Early Modern European History*. Leiden: Brill.

Fazal, T. M. (2011). *State Death: The Politics and Geography of Conquest, Occupation, and Annexation*. Princeton, NJ: Princeton University Press.

Ferguson, Y. H., and Mansbach, R. W. (1996). *Polities: Authority, Identities, and Change*. Columbia, SC: University of South Carolina Press.

Glencross, A. (2015). From 'doing history' to thinking historically: historical consciousness across History and International Relations. *International Relations*, 29 (4), 413-433.

Guilhot, N. (2017). *After the Enlightenment: Political Realism and International Relations in the Mid-Twentieth Century*. Cambridge: Cambridge University Press.

Guilhot, N., ed. (2011). *The Invention of International Relations Theory: Realism, the Rockefeller Foundation and the 1954 Conference on Theory*. New York, NY: Columbia University Press.

Hobson, J. M. (1998). The historical sociology of the state and the state of historical sociology in international relations. *Review of International Political Economy*, 5 (2), 284-320.

Hobson, J. M., and Lawson, G. (2008). What is history in international relations? *Millennium – Journal of International Studies*, 37 (2), 415-435.

Inayatullah, N., and Blaney, D. L. (2004). *International Relations and the Problem of Difference*. New York, NY: Routledge.

Jahn, B. (2000). *The Cultural Construction of International Relations: The Invention of the State of Nature*. Basingstoke: Palgrave.

Keene, E. (2002). *Beyond the Anarchical Society: Grotius, Colonialism and Order in World Politics*. Cambridge: Cambridge University Press.

Keene, E. (2008). The English school and British historians. *Millennium – Journal of International Studies*, 37 (2), 381-393.

Kratochwil, F. (2016). History, action and identity: revisiting the 'Second' great debate and assessing its importance for social theory. *European Journal of International Relations*, 12 (1), 5-29.

Kratochwil, F. V. (1986). Of systems, boundaries, and territoriality: an inquiry into the formation of the state system. *World Politics*, 39 (1), 27-52.

Lawson, G. (2012). The eternal divide? History and International Relations. *European Journal of International Relations*, 18 (2), 203-226.

Leira, H. and de Carvalho, B., eds. (2015). *Historical International Relations. 4 vols*. London: SAGE.

Leira, H. (2015). International Relations pluralism and history—embracing amateurism to strengthen the profession. *International Studies Perspectives*, 16 (1), 23-31.

Leira, H. (2019). The emergence of foreign policy. *International Studies Quarterly*, 63 (1), 187-198.

Leira, H. and de Carvalho, B. (2016). Construction time again: history in constructivist IR scholarship. *ERIS – European Review of International Studies* 3 (3), 99-111

Lewis, M. W., and Wigen, K. E. (1997). *The Myth of Continents: A Critique of Metageography*. Berkeley, CA: University of California Press.

Long, D., and Schmidt, B. C. (2005). *Imperialism and Internationalism in the Discipline of International Relations*. Albany, NY: SUNY Press.

Manchanda, N. (2020). *Imagining Afghanistan: The History and Politics of Imperial Knowledge*. Cambridge: Cambridge University Press.

Nişancıoğlu, K. (2020). Racial sovereignty. *European Journal of International Relations*, 26 (1, supplement), 39-63.

Osiander, A. (2001). Sovereignty, international relations, and the Westphalian myth. *International Organization,* 55 (2), 251-287.

Owens, P. (2018). Women and the history of international thought. *International Studies Quarterly,* 62 (3), 467-481.

Phillips, A., and Sharman, J. C. (2020). *Outsourcing Empire: How Company-States Made the Modern World.* Princeton, NJ: Princeton University Press.

Rae, H. (2017). Patterns of Identification on the Cusp of Globalization. In: T. Dunne, and C. Reus-Smit, eds., *The Globalization of International Society,* Oxford: Oxford University Press, 63-81.

Ravndal, E. J. (2020). Colonies, semi-sovereigns, and great powers: IGO membership debates and the transition of the international system. *Review of International Studies,* 46 (2), 278-298.

Reus-Smit, C. (1999). *The Moral Purpose of the State. Culture, Social Identity, and Institutional Rationality in International Relations.* Princeton, NJ: Princeton University Press.

Reus-Smit, C. (2008). Reading history through constructivist eyes. *Millennium – Journal of International Studies,* 37 (2), 395-414.

Rosenboim, O. (2017). *The Emergence of Globalism: Visions of World Order in Britain and the United States, 1939–1950.* Princeton, NJ: Princeton University Press.

Ruggie, J. G. (1986). Continuity and Transformation in the World Polity: Towards a Realist Synthesis. In: R. O. Keohane, ed., *Neorealism and its Critics,* New York, NY: Columbia University Press, 131-158.

Ruggie, J. G. (1998). *Constructing the World Polity: Essays on International Institutionalization.* London: Routledge.

Shilliam, R., ed. (2011). *International Relations and Non-Western Thought.* London: Routledge.

Spruyt, H. (1994). *The Sovereign State and its Competitors: An Analysis of Systems Change.* Princeton, NJ: Princeton University Press.

Suganami, H. (2008). Narrative explanation and international relations: back to basics. *Millennium – Journal of International Studies,* 37 (2), 327-356.

Thies, C. G. (2002). A pragmatic guide to qualitative historical analysis in the study of international relations. *International Studies Perspectives,* 3 (4), 351-372.

Thorne, C. (1983). International relations and the promptings of history. *Review of International Studies,* 9 (2), 123-135.

Tickner, A. B., and Wæver, O. (2009). *International Relations Scholarship around the World.* Abingdon: Routledge.

Tilly, C. (1990). *Coercion, Capitals and European States 1990–1992.* Oxford: Blackwell.

Towns, A. (2009). The status of women as a standard of `Civilization'. *European Journal of International Relations,* 15 (4), 681-706.

Vaughan-Williams, N. (2005). International relations and the problem of history. *Millennium – Journal of International Studies,* 34 (1), 115-136.

Vergerio, C. (2018). Context, reception, and the study of great thinkers in international relations. *International Theory,* 11 (1), 110-137.

Vitalis, R. (2015). *White World Order, Black Power Politics: The Birth of American International Relations.* Ithaca, NY: Cornell University Press.

Walker, R. B. J. (1993). *Inside/Outside: International Relations as Political Theory.* Cambridge: Cambridge University Press.

Warner, C. M. (2001). The rise of the state system in Africa. *Review of International Studies,* 27 (5), 65-89.

Watson, A. (1992). *The Evolution of the International Society: A Comparative Historical Analysis.* London: Routledge.

Wight, M. (1977). *Systems of States.* Leicester: Leicester University Press.

Yetiv, S. (2011). History, international relations, and integrated approaches: thinking about greater interdisciplinarity. *International Studies Perspectives,* 12 (2), 94-118.

Zarakol, A., ed. (2017) *Hierarchies in World Politics.* Cambridge: Cambridge University Press.

PART I

Traditions

2

THEORIES AND PHILOSOPHIES OF HISTORY IN INTERNATIONAL RELATIONS

Joseph MacKay and Christopher David LaRoche

Introduction

How do philosophies of history shape inquiry in International Relations (IR)? How should they? This chapter surveys theoretical understandings of history and the historical long haul, as they impinge on disciplinary IR. IR focuses on some of the largest human interactions in time and space—it is thus a logical site for long-range historical theorizing. Indeed, theories of history have had a direct impact on world politics, fueling revolutionary wars, decolonization, and the twentieth century's ideological struggles for 'control of the whole world's future' (Westad, 2017: 8). But the role of philosophies of history in IR is ambiguous. In Anglo-American IR, the 1960s turn to social scientific inquiry and covering laws gradually replaced the historical analysis emphasized by earlier thinkers (Aron, 1976; Carr, 2001; Niebuhr, 2008).

In many respects, the tide is now turning back. A revival of historical IR—exemplified by this volume—has motivated new theoretical and methodological inquiry (e.g., Buzan and Lawson, 2012). New research into the intellectual history of both disciplinary IR (Osiander, 1998; Schmidt, 2012) and international theory more broadly (Boucher, 1999; Armitage, 2013) has driven renewed interest in how the history of those ideas should be written (Bell, 2002; Devetak, 2017; see also Ashworth, 2021 in this volume). In political practice, recent concerns about the stability of the 'liberal world order' and its reactionary challengers—who couch their criticisms in explicitly historical terms—have prompted new examinations of how theories of history are deployed in contemporary world politics (Drolet and Williams, 2018; MacKay and LaRoche, 2018; see also Jahn, 2021 in this volume).

This chapter explains the philosophy of history and IR's relationship to it, arguing that IR scholars should be more explicitly aware of the problem of history in their own work. It proceeds in three sections. First, we unpack the philosophical or theoretical problem of history, especially as it emerged in and through European philosophy in the modern period. Second, we turn to the role—commonly tacit but often profound—of the problem of history in IR. Third, we turn to the disciplinary future, considering the role the theoretical problem of history can play in the field going forward, and how IR scholars should locate it in their work.

The philosophical problem of history

We begin with the matter of history as an object of theoretical inquiry. Although history features in most traditions of thought, it took on distinctive importance in modern European philosophy, through the thought of, for example, Hegel, Marx, Nietzsche, Heidegger, and Foucault, and it is primarily this manifestation of the philosophy of history that has informed historically Western-centric IR theory. Its roots lay in early modern philosophers such as Bacon, Descartes, and Hobbes, who distinguished changeable humanity from more durable or cyclical natural phenomena—think of the putative emergence of human society from a 'state of nature'. Drawing on Rousseau's radical version of this distinction, Kant (2006) and his successors formulated a universal or philosophical history in which practical reason 'makes sense' of the contingencies of empirical history in two linked ways (following Yovel, 1980: 6–25). First, reason shows itself to be historical—to develop across time, culminating in the moment where reason can make sense of its own historical development (a philosophical history of philosophy). Second, history can be organized by reason—the empirical details of history can be schematized according to a rational shape or form (a philosophy of history). In varying ways, Kant, Hegel, and others formulated history as a rational process, out of which human reasoning processes could reconstruct evidence of their own past operation.

Kant's universal history, which underwrites his influential arguments in *Toward Perpetual Peace*, finds directionality in history but makes no predictive claims: rational humans can hope for future moral progress, but no more.[1] Hegel and Marx went further, arguing rationality decisively shapes human political, spiritual, intellectual, and material conditions. For Kant, reason is transhistorical and thus apart from empirical history. For Hegel, reason plots out a linear or dialectical process in which human subjectivity and objectivity (freedom and necessity, respectively) converge through concrete human action, in social, political, and cultural institutions. Reason itself thus unfolds in time—or, put differently, it only occurs and emerges through history (Yovel, 1980: 4; Pinkard, 2017). The implications, on this account, were not small. For Hegel (1988: 22), this working out of the logic of history as the actualization of human freedom was 'the *final goal of the world*'. The fundamental conditions for that freedom were announced in the French Revolution and made actual in the modern state, where, animated by the French Revolutionary spirit, human beings can live 'at home' in their world (Ritter, 1982: 47–52).

In their more famous philosophy of history, Marx and Engels (1978) radicalized (or 'inverted') Hegel, foregrounding successive historical stages of material conditions—historical and dialectical materialism—defined in terms of class structure and conflict, which propelled those stages forward. The ultimate purpose of this philosophy of history was not simply to make sense of the world, as Marx's predecessors had done, but 'to *change* it' (1978: 145). As Hannah Arendt (2006: 79) summarizes, 'If one imagines that one can "make history," one cannot escape the consequence that there will be an end to history'—that is, that grand plans and assertions inevitably imply eventual transformation and completion. By contrast, Nietzsche and his descendants—including Max Weber, Oswald Spengler, and Martin Heidegger—had mixed or negative views of progress. While they saw humanity as contingently shaped by and located in history ('historicity'), they took that contingency to rule out linear conceptions of progress. If history relativizes all cultural or political values, meaningful, long-run progress makes little sense.

These philosophical reconstructions of history have dual implications for our understanding of world politics. They generated the transformative ideologies, like Marxism, that defined political life for much of the modern period. They also informed Whig histories and ideas of progress that underwrote central principles of world ordering, such as the 'standard of civilization' that separated peoples on the basis of putative temporal advancement and authorized domination of those less advanced, such as in J.S. Mill's treatment of intervention. Ideas of temporal advancement and progress continue to inform many key concepts in the social sciences, both in early authors such as Comte, Marx, and Weber, and in more recent concepts such as modernization theory and the stages of development.

They also supply later, retrospective understandings of world history—the rational reconstructions of historical grand narrative that give history meaning or the deconstructions of history that deny its coherence. When Alexandre Kojève (1980) prefigured the 'end of history' thesis (Fukuyama, 1989), or Michel Foucault (1977) diagnosed the happenstance dispersion that typifies his brand of genealogy, they made crucial theoretical choices, either assigning a grand structure to history or abjuring one. German émigré scholars arriving in North American academia brought with them historicist ideas—among them Hannah Arendt, Leo Strauss, Hans-Georg Gadamer, and to a degree Hans Morgenthau (see Zuckert, 2011). In Britain, the 'Cambridge School' of contextualist intellectual history reshaped how political, and more recently international, thought were understood. Philosophy of history has been most notably absent from parts of the English-speaking academy: analytical philosophers having almost uniformly rejected historical theorizing and historicism (canonically Popper, 2002). Even here though, robust mid-twentieth-century debates addressed matters of historical method and interpretation.[2] American pragmatists have also long concerned themselves with matters of history and historical progress (Dewey, 1916; Rorty, 1989; James, 1996). In all these instances, philosophy of history has shaped both ideologies and analyses of world historical and international political life—and has done so internationally.

Philosophy of history and International Relations

Given the intellectual reach of nineteenth- and twentieth-century philosophies of history, it should not surprise us they surfaced in early IR. For example, early realists such as Carr (2001, 2016), Niebuhr (2008), Aron (1976), and Morgenthau (1946) grappled with these questions, casting doubt on progress linked to Enlightenment rationality, science, and institutional design (Guilhot, 2017). Instead, conflict would be endemic, and history prone to stasis and repetition. Exceptionally among them, Carr in particular echoed Hegel's (1967: 13) view that history has a governing logic, visible only in hindsight. He imagined, 'the possibility of… progress subject to no limits that we can or need envisage—toward goals which can be defined only as we advance towards them, and the validity of which can be verified only in a process of attaining them' (Carr, 2001: 113). Carr was an odd realist in his choice of historical-theoretic view, but not unusual in taking these matters seriously.

Much of postwar American IR took a studied disinterest in both historical change and history as a discipline. It was commonly silent on philosophies of history as such. Treating actors (states) as isomorphic units in a durable structure of anarchy made transhistorical comparisons possible. However, these theorists still made tacit commitments about history's long term, and how to understand it.[3] Waltz's structuralism applied across historical contexts, but thereby specified how history worked: 'The texture of international politics remains highly constant, patterns recur, and events repeat themselves endlessly' (Waltz, 1979: 66).[4] This made the long run of history cyclical, which was observable in the recurrence of history's most destructive and generative processes (war and peace). Neorealism's critics had historical-theoretic commitments, too. Neoliberal institutionalists insisted on a long, gradual historical arc toward integration, peace, and prosperity: 'Improvements (as judged by cosmopolitan moral standards) are more likely to be incremental than sudden, building on the knowledge of one another created by successful cooperation' (Keohane, 1984: 257). While both concealed their presumed logics of history—behind power-political and social-evolutionary logics, respectively—they are there nonetheless. Early critical IR claimed Waltz had misunderstood not just the logic of history, but also how we can know it. Cox (1986) and Ashley (1986) both argue, albeit differently, that one's understanding of history is shaped by one's position in it. In any case, scholars elsewhere continued to take history seriously. The English School was deeply committed to the historical long run (Butterfield and Wight, 1966; Bull, 1977). Bull (1977: 65, emphasis added) cautioned that 'there is nothing *historically inevitable* ... about the idea of a society of states'. The prospect of theorizing world history on long and large terms has thus never fully vanished from the discipline's broader theoretical frame of reference (on the English School, see Green and Navari, 2021 in this volume).

As the neo-neo schools' dominance waned, theoretical interest in history reemerged in the discipline, initially through increased interest in processes of empirical historical change. Early constructivism often focused on large-scale change in world politics (see Go et al., 2021; Bruneau 2021; both in this volume). Ruggie asserted that Waltz could not 'account for, or even describe, the most important contextual change in international politics in this *millennium*' (Ruggie, 1986: 141).[5] In his own work, he increasingly located institutional and spatial aspects of world politics in time (Ruggie, 1993). Onuf (1989) insisted on a 'world of our making', implying both large potential for transformation and a moral imperative to weigh attendant responsibilities. Kratochwil (1991) reframed the relationship between normativity and decision-making by drawing on the history of modern social thought. Accounts focused on norms unfolded unavoidably in historical time (Finnemore and Sikkink, 2001). Wendt (1999: 314) argued that 'structural change' and 'cultural change' are deeply linked—both aim not just to foreground ideas, but also to link them to long-run historical transformation. He argued that a long-run liberalizing and pacifying trend in international history ran deep and was perhaps inevitable (Wendt, 1999: ch. 7, more elaborately, Wendt, 2003). In this sense, early constructivists were sophisticated, if largely tacit, theorists of history.[6] Others became more explicitly concerned with macrohistorical stasis and change, in increasingly elaborate ways (for example, Reus-Smit, 1999; Philpott, 2001; Bukovansky, 2002; Nexon, 2009; Goddard, 2018; Allan, 2018). Such accounts proliferated ways of 'making sense' of empirical history.

Beyond constructivism strictly defined, related work ranges across the transformative processes of the nineteenth century (Buzan and Lawson, 2015), the rise of capitalism (Anievas and Nişancıoğlu, 2015; see also Anievas and Gogu, 2021 in this volume), and the 'durable diversity' of the early modern Indian Ocean (Phillips and Sharman, 2015). Such accounts, especially those tracking histories outside the West, often emphasize the multilinear or polyvalent character of the historical long run. The emerging literature on hierarchies focuses on historical settings and themes in sustained ways (Zarakol, 2017). Rosenberg (2006), drawing on Trotsky, argues for tracking the 'uneven and combined' trajectories of the modern world, whereby the category of the 'international' became thinkable precisely to tie together a world following divergent (and deeply unequal) paths. A growing literature points to a distinct historical course for East Asia— but disagrees on whether it results from distinctive cultural features (Kang, 2010), differing power-political configurations (Hui, 2005; Wang, 2011), or some combination of the above (Zhang, 2015; Lee, 2016). Disagreements on historical correspondence—can the Peloponnesian or Imjin War, or categories and concepts derived thereof, be used to understand great power competition today?—have informed a debate about the rise of China (Kang and Ma, 2018).[7] Such accounts rarely reference philosophies of history directly but are united in taking seriously multiple trajectories in the long run of modern world politics, implying a pluralist conception of history.

Two recent studies usefully exemplify how long-run theorizing about history is bound up with historical IR (see de Carvalho et al., 2021 in this volume). Allan (2018) shows how emerging conceptions and practices of world ordering in modern Europe were generated in part out of shifting conceptions of the nature of the world ('cosmologies'). The process driving change follows a loop, beginning with practical or problem-solving ideas that are gradually recoded as ends in themselves, generating new cosmological conceptions of the world, which underwrite new configurations of world politics—producing new problems in need of practical solutions.

This process itself is cyclical. However, long-term movements across cycles are not. Depending on our reading, they either track long-term progress or no particular path at all.

Elsewhere, Lee (2016) reframes late imperial (or 'early modern') East Asian world order in terms of relational links between China, Korea, and Japan. These three moved through the period on distinct trajectories, as their convergences and divergences alike were shaped by their interactions. Korea and Japan charted different courses in relations with China for reasons largely of their own—but as they did so, a range of self-reinforcing trends and perhaps unintended consequences produced varying historical courses for each. While Lee's point is to explain the region on its own terms, East Asian ordering, at a higher level of aggregation, followed a distinctive historical trajectory from that of Europe. When European empires became major powers in the region, in the nineteenth century, China and Japan responded quite differently to Eurocentric world ordering, adaptively arriving at distinct strategies and producing further variation in their trajectories (Suzuki, 2009). Their trajectories in the early-twentieth century were nonetheless very different, reminding us that historical trajectory is not a one-stop shop. There are perhaps unavoidably multiple, interacting pathways through the historical long run. Lee (2016: 186) concludes by reminding us these complex interactions likely make the region's future unpredictable.

This emphasis on positionality in historical processes points to more critically minded scholars, who focus on the proliferation of perspectives from which world politics can be seen. The postcolonial turn or 'moment' in security studies (Barkawi and Laffey, 2006), predicated on worldviews from outside the developed West, shows the through-line of modern history reads differently from below or outside its triumphalist liberal, hegemonic core. Inayatullah and Blaney (2003) focus similarly on an attendant 'problem of difference', and Chowdhry and Nair (2004) point to such triumphalist narratives and 'the ways in which historical processes are implicated in [their] production'. Elsewhere, feminist scholars similarly see the long run of history as plural not just in its directionality, but in the views it affords (Tickner, 1997; Ackerly and True, 2008; Sjoberg, 2012). Such accounts scrutinize the 'priority of research questions', and not simply answers, about the workings of world political history from feminist lenses (Wibben, 2014). Others call for 'transversal' analysis that cuts across areas of inquiry, and thus across multiple historical lines or narratives (Basaran et al., 2016). Narrative approaches track these trajectories at the level of individual, personal history, and autoethnography—located in the global (Inayatullah and Dauphinee, 2016). The common theme is that views of history and time are multiple—their wager is not just against a single course, but against a single narrative of it.

Another site of theoretical engagement with history is the emerging literature on time in world politics (see Hom, 2021). Hutchings (2008) argues shared temporalities orient shared experience. She introduces the category of 'world political time' in connection with world historical long runs. While Hutchings and others (Vij, 2012; Agathangelou and Killian, 2016) are explicitly critical in their orientation, others deal with the conventional explanatory powers and possibilities of IR as a field of study. Time, McIntosh (2015) shows, is tacitly central to IR's core theoretical traditions. For Hom (2018), timing is an action. To time something is to impose a structure, sequence, or order of priority on activities in our shared political world. In sum, this multifaceted body of work is oblique in its conception of history but does not differ from philosophy of history in offering sustained theoretical engagement with the experience of temporality—whether personal or world-historical.

Few if any of these accounts identify and delineate explicit and systematic theories of history. They nonetheless imply a multiplying range of views of how history works and how it can and should be understood. Put differently, philosophies of history are most detectable in the discipline today by their proliferation. While conceptions of history and historicity remain largely tacit in

IR, including historical IR, they now imply theories of history more diverse, but perhaps also divergent, than at any time in the field's history.

Conclusion

We argue this proliferation is welcome but requires more careful acknowledgment and analysis. IR has long taken long and large empirical history seriously, aiming to make systematic sense of patterns underlying events and explaining epochal shifts in the form and function of world politics. In so doing, IR scholars have been stalked by a second set of debates about how to make sense of history as such. Nonetheless, these engagements have often been oblique. It may be that, while many scholars imply theories of history, the state of the field is less clear on overt historical theorizing. We thus close with a few open-ended prescriptive words on how largely tacit engagements with philosophies of history can be made more productively direct and explicit.

We see (at least) three ways historical IR scholars might want to engage with philosophies of history. First, they may wish to take them up and apply them explicitly. For example, many conventional liberalisms in IR imply narratives of progress; comparatively few have the courage of their convictions in making conceptions of progress systematically explicit. Similarly, many realists tell stories of historical stasis but ground their arguments in no general account of history. We think scholars implying such theories of history would benefit from making those claims explicit and confronting one another on the resulting historical-theoretic terrain. IR's resident history specialists should take this challenge especially seriously. Second, historical IR scholars may wish to adopt a 'positionality' with reference to theories of history. For example, many critical IR scholars already concern themselves with how theories of historical progress conceal domination or injustice, whether past or ongoing (Grovogui, 1996; Bell, 2016; Getachew, 2019).[8] Inversely, realist theories of stasis can be read as denying the possibility of historical emancipation. A critical positionality with regard to these *or other* theories of history might make philosophy of history itself more theoretically visible to the field, by showing how it operates both productively and destructively in our scholarship. Third, and most obliquely, philosophies of history may help scholars to sound a warning. By giving form to history and how we experience it, as scholars and citizens alike, theories of history may allow us to confront the future in new and explicit ways. We write in a time of multiple overlapping crises, including a pandemic, a changing climate, a revival of right-wing populism, and increasingly violent extremism. These events demand not just historical contextualization, but also theorization, perhaps in ways yet to be determined, that allows us to grapple with comparatively radical patterns of often unprecedented change.

In sum, we argue for renewed and more direct focus on such questions, in whatever form, for two reasons. First, making sense of the historical long run requires thinking, in general or theoretical terms, about both the form of history and the tools we can use to understand it. There can be, as the saying goes, no theory-free inquiry. IR scholars have long implied disagreements about how history works. Where disagreements can be neither resolved nor obviated, we should make our assumptions about history clear, and we should debate them. Second, tacit or explicit conceptions of history move public life. Elites appeal to progress or to nostalgia in justifying their choices and aspirations. Publics move and are moved in line with similar concerns. An eschatological belief at the end of history, an appeal to progress into the future, a fixation on power-political cyclicality, or a faith in lost greatness are all potentially implicated in shaping world politics. Attention to how these conceptions of history work should be part of our disciplinary remit as well.

Suggestions for further reading

Arendt, H. (1998). *The Human Condition.* 2nd edition. Chicago, IL: University of Chicago Press.

Hegel, G. W. F. (1988). *Introduction to the Philosophy of History.* Indianapolis, IN: Hackett Publishing.

Kant, I. (2006). In: Allen W. Wood ed., *Toward Perpetual Peace and Other Writings on Politics, Peace, and History.* Translated by David L. Colcasure. New Haven, CT: Yale University Press.

Lawson, G. (2010). The eternal divide? History and International Relations. *European Journal of International Relations,* 18 (2), 203-226.

MacKay, J., and LaRoche, C. D. (2017). The conduct of history in International Relations: rethinking philosophy of history in IR theory. *International Theory,* 9 (2), 203-236.

Melzer, A. M., Weinberger, J., and Zinman, M. R., eds. (1995). *History and the Idea of Progress.* Ithaca, NY: Cornell University Press.

Buck-Morss, S. (2009). *Hegel, Haiti, and Universal History.* Pittsburgh, PA: University of Pittsburgh Press.

Pinkard, T. P. (2017). *Does History Make Sense? Hegel on the Historical Shapes of Justice.* Cambridge, MA: Harvard University Press.

Tucker, A., ed. (2009). *A Companion to the Philosophy of History and Historiography.* Malden, MA: Wiley-Blackwell.

Notes

1 The place of Kant's universal history in his overall philosophy is debated; see Yovel (1980), Shell (1997), and Molloy (2017).

2 See articles in Dray (1966), especially by Donagan, Dray, Hempel, Mink, Passmore, and Walsh, as well as Cohen (1978) on Marx. Recent analytical work on Hegel suggests renewed interest (e.g., Brandom, 2019).

3 We simplify somewhat. While rationalism was central to American IR from the early 1960s (e.g., Schelling, 1960, 1966), anarchy talk became systematic only with Bull (1977) and Waltz (1979). See Donnelly (2015). Isomorphically minded, ahistorical rationalism nonetheless persisted throughout this period.

4 Mearsheimer (2003: 2) and Gilpin (1983: 211) make similar claims.

5 See also Hall and Kratochwil's (1993) reframing of the crusades, against neorealist readings.

6 Leira and de Carvalho (2016) provide a useful, more detailed review of constructivism's handling of history.

7 Though see also Krishna (2017).

8 See also Turner and Nymalm (2019) on how moralizing historical narratives shape perceptions of China's rise.

References

Ackerly, B., and True, J. (2008). An intersectional analysis of International Relations: recasting the discipline. *Politics & Gender,* 4 (1), 156-173.

Agathangelou, A. M., and Killian, K. D., eds. (2016). *Time, Temporality and Violence in International Relations: (De)Fatalizing the Present, Forging Radical Alternatives.* London: Routledge.

Allan, B. B. (2018). *Scientific Cosmology and International Orders.* Cambridge: Cambridge University Press.

Anievas, A., and Gogu, C. (2021). Capitalism and 'the International': A Historical Approach. In de Carvalho, B., Costa Lopez, J., & Leira, H., eds. *Routledge Handbook of Historical International Relations.* Abingdon: Routledge.

Anievas, A., and Nişancıoğlu, K. (2015). *How the West Came to Rule: The Geopolitical Origins of Capitalism.* London: Pluto Press.

Arendt, H. (2006). *Between Past and Future: Eight Exercises in Political Thought.* Penguin classics. New York, NY: Penguin Books.

Armitage, D. (2013). *Foundations of Modern International Thought.* Cambridge: Cambridge University Press.

Aron, R. (1976). *Introduction to the Philosophy of History: An Essay on the Limits of Historical Objectivity.* Westport, CT: Greenwood Press.

Ashley, R. K. (1986). The Poverty of Neorealism. In: Keohane, R. O., ed., *Neorealism and Its Critics,* New York, NY: Columbia University Press, 255-300.

Ashworth, L. M. (2021). Disciplinary Traditions and Debates: The Subject Matters of International Thought. In de Carvalho, B., Costa Lopez, J., & Leira, H., eds. *Routledge Handbook of Historical International Relations*. Abingdon: Routledge.

Barkawi, T., and Laffey, M. (2006). The postcolonial moment in security studies. *Review of International Studies*, 32 (2), 329-352.

Basaran, T., Bigo, D., Guittet E.-P., et al., eds. (2016). *International Political Sociology: Transversal Lines*. London: Routledge.

Bell, D. (2002). Language, legitimacy, and the project of critique. *Alternatives: Global, Local, Political*, 27 (3), 327-350.

Bell, D. (2016). *Reordering the World: Essays on Liberalism and Empire*. Princeton, NJ: Princeton University Press.

Boucher, D. (1999). *Political Theories of International Relations: From Thucydides to the Present*. Oxford: Oxford University Press.

Brandom, R. B. (2019). *A Spirit of Trust: A Reading of Hegel's Phenomenology*. Cambridge, MA: Harvard University Press.

Bruneau, Q. P. (2021). Constructivism: History and Systemic Change. In de Carvalho, B., Costa Lopez, J., & Leira, H., eds. *Routledge Handbook of Historical International Relations*. Abingdon: Routledge.

Bukovansky, M. (2002). *Legitimacy and Power Politics: The American and French Revolutions in International Political Culture*. Princeton, NJ: Princeton University Press.

Bull, H. (1977). *The Anarchical Society*. 3rd edition. London: Pan Macmillan.

Butterfield, H., and Wight, M., eds. (1966). *Diplomatic Investigations: Essays in the Theory of International Politics*. Cambridge, MA: Harvard University Press.

Buzan, B., and Lawson, G. (2012). Rethinking benchmark dates in international relations. *European Journal of International Relations 20(2)*, 1-26.

Buzan, B., and Lawson, G. (2015). *The Global Transformation: History, Modernity and the Making of International Relations*. Cambridge: Cambridge University Press.

Carr, E. H. (2001). *What Is History?* London: Palgrave Macmillan.

Carr, E. H. (2016). In: M. Cox ed., *The Twenty Years' Crisis, 1919–1939*. London: Macmillan.

Chowdhry, G., and Nair, S. (2004). Introduction: Power in a Postcolonial World: Race, Gender, and Class in International Relations. In: G. Chowdhry and S. Nair, eds., *Power, Postcolonialism and International Relations: Reading Race, Gender and Class*, London: Routledge, 1-32.

Cohen, G. A. (1978). *Karl Marx's Theory of History: A Defence*. Oxford: Clarendon Press.

Cox, R. W. (1986). Social Forces, States and World Orders: Beyond International Relations Theory. In: R. O. Keohane, ed., *Neorealism and Its Critics. The Political Economy of International Change*, New York, NY: Columbia University Press, 204-254.

de Carvalho, B., Costa Lopez, J., and Leira, H. (2021). Introduction: Historical International Relations. In de Carvalho, B., Costa Lopez, J., & Leira, H., eds. *Routledge Handbook of Historical International Relations*. Abingdon: Routledge.

Devetak, R. (2017). 'The battle is all there is': philosophy and history in International Relations theory. *International Relations*, 31 (3), 261-281.

Dewey, J. (1916). Progress. *International Journal of Ethics*, 26 (3): 311-322.

Donnelly, J. (2015). The discourse of anarchy in IR. *International Theory*, 7 (3), 393-425.

Dray, W. H., ed. (1966) *Philosophical Analysis and History*. New York, NY: Harper & Row.

Drolet, J.-F., and Williams, M. C. (2018). Radical conservatism and global order: international theory and the new right. *International Theory*, 10 (3), 285-313.

Finnemore, M., and Sikkink, K. (2001). Taking stock: the constructivist research program in international relations and comparative politics. *Annual Review of Political Science*, 4 (1), 391-416.

Foucault, M. (1977). Nietzsche, Genealogy, History. In: D. F. Bouchard, ed., *Language, counter-memory, practice: Selected essays and interviews*, Ithaca, NY: Cornell University Press, 139-164.

Fukuyama, F. (1989). The end of history? *The National Interest*, 16, 3-18.

Getachew, A. (2019). *Worldmaking after Empire: The Rise and Fall of Self-Determination*. Princeton, NJ: Princeton University Press.

Gilpin, R. (1983). *War and Change in World Politics*. Cambridge: Cambridge University Press.

Go, J., Lawson, G., and de Carvalho, B. (2021). Historical Sociology in International Relations: The Challenge of the Global. In de Carvalho, B., Costa Lopez, J., & Leira, H., eds. *Routledge Handbook of Historical International Relations*. Abingdon: Routledge.

Goddard, S. E. (2018). *When Right Makes Might: Rising Powers and World Order*. Ithaca, NY: Cornell University Press.

Green, D. and Navari, C. (2021). The English School and Historical International Relations. In de Carvalho, B., Costa Lopez, J., & Leira, H., eds. *Routledge Handbook of Historical International Relations*. Abingdon: Routledge.

Grovogui, S. N. (1996). *Sovereigns, Quasi Sovereigns, and Africans: Race and Self-Determination in International Law*. Minneapolis, MN: University of Minnesota Press.

Guilhot, N. (2017). *After the Enlightenment: Political Realism and International Relations in the Mid-Twentieth Century*. Cambridge: Cambridge University Press.

Hall, R. B., and Kratochwil, F. V. (1993). Medieval tales: neorealist 'Science' and the abuse of history. *International Organization*, 47 (3), 479-491.

Hegel, G. W. F. (1967). *Philosophy of Right*. Translated by T. M. Knox. London: Oxford University Press.

Hom, A. R. (2018). Timing is everything: toward a better understanding of time and international politics. *International Studies Quarterly*, 62 (1), 69-79.

Hom, A. R. (2021). Time and History in International Relations. In de Carvalho, B., Costa Lopez, J., & Leira, H., eds. *Routledge Handbook of Historical International Relations*. Abingdon: Routledge.

Hui, V. T. (2005). *War and State Formation in Ancient China and Early Modern Europe*. Cambridge: Cambridge University Press.

Hutchings, K. (2008). *Time and World Politics: Thinking the Present*. Manchester, UK: Manchester University Press.

Inayatullah, N., and Blaney, D. L. (2003). *International Relations and the Problem of Difference*. London: Routledge.

Inayatullah, N., and Dauphinee, E., eds. (2016). *Narrative Global Politics: Theory, History and the Personal in International Relations*. London: Routledge.

Jahn, B. (2021). Liberalism between Theory and Practice. In de Carvalho, B., Costa Lopez, J., & Leira, H., eds. *Routledge Handbook of Historical International Relations*. Abingdon: Routledge.

James, W. (1996). *A Pluralistic Universe*. Lincoln, NE: University of Nebraska Press.

Kang, D. C. (2010). *East Asia Before the West: Five Centuries of Trade and Tribute*. New York, NY: Columbia University Press.

Kang, D. C., and Ma, X. (2018). Power transitions: Thucydides didn't live in East Asia. *The Washington Quarterly*, 41 (1), 137-154.

Kant, I. (2006). In: Pauline Kleingeld ed., *Toward Perpetual Peace and Other Writings on Politics, Peace, and History*. Translated by D. L. Colcasure. New Haven, CT: Yale University Press.

Keohane, R. O. (1984). *After Hegemony: Cooperation and Discord in the World Political Economy*. New Haven, CT: Princeton University Press.

Kojève, A. (1980). *Introduction to the Reading of Hegel: Lectures on the Phenomenology of Spirit*. Agora paperback editions. Ithaca, NY: Cornell University Press.

Kratochwil, F. V. (1991). *Rules, Norms, and Decisions: On the Conditions of Practical and Legal Reasoning in International Relations and Domestic Affairs*. Cambridge: Cambridge University Press.

Krishna, S. (2017). China is China, not the non-west: David Kang, eurocentrism, and global politics. *Harvard Journal of Asiatic Studies*, 77 (1), 93-109.

Lee, J.-Y. (2016). *China's Hegemony: Four Hundred Years of East Asian Domination*. New York, NY: Columbia University Press.

Leira, H., and de Carvalho, B. (2016). Construction time again: history in constructivist IR scholarship. *European Review of International Studies*, 3 (3), 99-111.

MacKay, J., and LaRoche, C. D. (2018). Why is there no reactionary international theory? *International Studies Quarterly*, 62 (2), 234-244.

Marx, K., and Engels, F. (1978). In: R. C. Tucker, ed. *The Marx-Engels Reader*. 2nd edition. New York, NY: Norton.

McIntosh, C. (2015). Theory across time: the privileging of time-less theory in International Relations. *International Theory*, 7 (3), 464-500.

Mearsheimer, J. J. (2003). *The Tragedy of Great Power Politics*. New York, NY: W. W. Norton & Company.

Molloy, S. (2017). *Kant's International Relations: The Political Theology of Perpetual Peace*. Ann Arbor, MI: University of Michigan Press.

Morgenthau, H. J. (1946). *Scientific Man vs. Power Politics*. Chicago, IL: The University of Chicago Press.

Nexon, D. H. (2009). The balance of power in the balance. *World Politics*, 61 (2), 330-359.

Niebuhr, R. (2008). *The Irony of American History*. Chicago, IL: University of Chicago Press.

Onuf, N. G. (1989). *World of Our Making: Rules and Rule in Social Theory and International Relations*. Studies in international relations. Columbia, SC: University of South Carolina Press.

Osiander, A. (1998). Rereading early twentieth-century IR theory: idealism revisited. *International Studies Quarterly*, 42 (3), 409-432.

Phillips, A., and Sharman, J. C. (2015). *International Order in Diversity: War, Trade and Rule in the Indian Ocean*. Cambridge: Cambridge University Press.

Philpott, D. (2001). *Revolutions in Sovereignty: How Ideas Shaped Modern International Relations*. Princeton, NJ: Princeton University Press.

Popper, K. (2002). *The Poverty of Historicism*. London: Psychology Press.

Reus-Smit, C. (1999). *The Moral Purpose of the State: Culture, Social Identity, and Institutional Rationality in International Relations*. Princeton, NJ: Princeton University Press.

Ritter, J. (1982). *Hegel and the French Revolution: Essays on the Philosophy of Right*. Studies in contemporary German social thought. Cambridge, MA: MIT Press.

Rorty, R. (1989). *Contingency, Irony, and Solidarity*. Cambridge: Cambridge University Press.

Rosenberg, J. (2006). Why is there no international historical sociology? *European Journal of International Relations*, 12 (3), 307-340.

Ruggie, J. G. (1986). Continuity and Transformation in the World Polity: Toward a Neorealist Synthesis. In: R. O. Keohane, ed., *Neorealism and Its Critics*, New York, NY: Columbia University Press, 131-157.

Ruggie, J. G. (1993). Territoriality and beyond: problematizing modernity in International Relations. *International Organization*, 47 (1), 139-174.

Schelling, T. C. (1960). *The Strategy of Conflict*. Cambridge, MA: Harvard University Press.

Schelling, T. C. (1966). *Arms and Influence*. New Haven, CT: Yale University Press.

Schmidt, B. C. (2012). On the History and Historiography of International Relations. In: W. Carlsnaes, T. Risse-Kappen, and B. A. Simmons, eds., *Handbook of International Relations*, London: SAGE.

Shell, S. (1997). Rousseau, Kant, and the Beginning of History. In: C. Orwin and N. Tarcov, eds., *The Legacy of Rousseau*, Chicago, IL: University of Chicago Press, 45-64.

Sjoberg, L. (2012). Gender, structure, and war: what Waltz couldn't see. *International Theory*, 4 (1), 1-38.

Suzuki, S. (2009). *Civilization and Empire: China and Japan's Encounter with European International Society*. London: Routledge.

Tickner, J. A. (1997). You just don't understand: troubled engagements between feminists and IR theorists. *International Studies Quarterly*, 41 (4), 611-632.

Turner, O., and Nymalm, N. (2019). Morality and progress: IR narratives on international revisionism and the status quo. *Cambridge Review of International Affairs*, 32 (4), 407-428.

Vij, R. (2012). Temporality, civic engagement, and alterity: Indo-Kei in contemporary Japan. *Alternatives*, 37 (1), 3-29.

Waltz, K. N. (1979). *Theory of International Politics*. New York, NY: McGraw-Hill.

Wang, Y.-K. (2011). *Harmony and War: Confucian Culture and Chinese Power Politics*. New York, NY: Columbia University Press.

Wendt, A. (1999). *Social Theory of International Politics*. Cambridge: Cambridge University Press.

Wendt, A. (2003). Why a world state is inevitable. *European Journal of International Relations*, 9 (4), 491-542.

Westad, O. A. (2017). *The Cold War: A World History*. New York, NY: Basic Books.

Wibben, A. T. R. (2014). Researching feminist security studies. *Australian Journal of Political Science*, 49 (4), 743-755.

Yovel, Y. (1980). *Kant and the Philosophy of History*. Princeton, NJ: Princeton University Press.

Zarakol, A., ed. (2017). *Hierarchies in World Politics*. Cambridge: Cambridge University Press.

Zhang, F. (2015). *Chinese Hegemony: Grand Strategy and International Institutions in East Asian History*. Stanford, CA: Stanford University Press.

Zuckert, C. H., ed. (2011). *Political Philosophy in the Twentieth Century: Authors and Arguments*. New York, NY: Cambridge University Press.

3

THE ENGLISH SCHOOL AND HISTORICAL INTERNATIONAL RELATIONS

Cornelia Navari and Daniel M. Green

From the first, the English School (ES) defended historical approaches to international studies and provided the first historical theories relevant to a discipline of International Relations (IR).[1] In 1966, in the context of the British Committee on the Theory of International Politics (BC), Hedley Bull laid out the 'classical approach' in which history appeared alongside philosophy and law as the triad that should guide the study of IR and the same year Martin Wight provided two such theories in his 'Why is There No International Theory?' (Wight, 1966). The major historical theory appeared in 1984 in *The Expansion of International Society*, also in the context of the BC, which has been called 'one of the few extended and sustained metanarratives that can be found within IR' (Dunne and Little, 2014: 98). But what kind of history was intended by the British Committee is seldom inquired after. For all their rejection of 'scientism', the BC, or at least central members of it, were striving after a theory, and their returns to history were the off-shoots of their grappling with what kind of theory.

Theory and history: three English School responses

Wight's 'Why is There No International Theory?' was no casual musing by a historian. It was a direct response to the agenda laid down for the British Committee[2] by its sponsors, the Rockefeller Foundation – to consider a *theory* of IR. Wight's lecture course on the Theory of International Relations, developed during the 1950s, provided the background.[3] In the essay, Wight outlined two sorts of theory relevant to IR: a 'theory of survival' and a 'theory of diplomatics'. The 'theory of survival' dealt with the 'extremities' (as he termed them) of the international experience – 'the right of devastation and pillage in war', the right of intervention, and the prospect of nuclear war. Its subject matter was questions of 'national existence and national extinction'; it displayed 'repetition and necessity', and the appropriate method for dealing with this subject matter was the conventional body of political science 'middle-range' theory. For the generality of statecraft and the daily progress of diplomacy – in other words, everyday IR, the appropriate form of theorizing was 'historical writing', understood as 'a coherent structure of hypotheses that will provide a common explanation of phenomena'. 'Historical writing' shared the same aim as positive theories in political science, only with 'more judiciousness and modesty' (Wight, 1966, 32–33).[4] What is more relevant in the present context is the kind of history Wight had in mind. His attack on progressivism in the essay was also an attack on the progressive history that had dominated the nineteenth century and that continued to structure much of the understanding of political relations among states (see Hall, 2019). What he is recommending is a form of technical history.

The ES's second historiographical moment came in the effort to devise a comparative history of 'states systems'. Some four years after the onset of the BC, following the seminal moment when Hedley Bull first proposed that international life was not anarchic but composed into a 'society of states',[5] the BC decided to make a prolonged study of state-systems in various parts of the globe. Wight took the directing role (Vigezzi, 2005: 199–203), focusing on the 'norms and values that animate [each] system, and the institutions in which they are expressed' (Bull, 1976: 113). The result was four essays on Hellas, Persia, and the modern state-system, demonstrating a variety of beliefs, social forms, and 'animating' tendencies, with no direction or unifying theme. Aside from a fairly substantial piece by Geoffrey Hudson on China (Hudson, 1965), other studies were nugatory, and no second volume to follow *Diplomatic Investigations* appeared. Bull published Wight's studies in a stand-alone volume (Wight, 1977) to illustrate his theory of the importance of a common culture underlying any state-system.

The historian who established a comparative standard was Herbert Butterfield, to be carried forward in the well-known work by Adam Watson. In a paper for the Committee in 1965 to initiate their discussions on historic systems, Butterfield, always doubtful about Wight's culture-alone thesis, put forward the idea that 'a states-system can only be achieved by a tremendous conscious effort of reassembly after a political hegemony has broken down' (Vigezzi, 2005: 187).[6] In other words, a state-system, or international society, arises from the collapse of a previous hegemony, the end of which 'ensures the conditions' for its subsequent development. Watson developed Butterfield's thesis into a typology of state-systems that moved from a collection of independent entities, to hegemony, suzerainty, dominion, and empire (Watson, 1992), clarifying much of the Committee's previous discussions and creating a template based on the form of rule. Developing Butterfield's main thesis, he presented the Italian city-states as emerging out of the waning of the medieval theocracy, Westphalia out of the failed Habsburg bid to re-establish hegemony, and the Concert of Europe out of the near-successful French efforts to do the same.

Watson's efforts were carried forward by Buzan and Little in their *International Systems in World History* (2000). Generalizing Bull and Watson's (1984: 1) definition of an international system as 'a group of independent communities …[in which] the behavior of each is a necessary factor in the calculation of others', they plotted the historical development of both regional and global international systems from pre-modern times to the modern era, specifically defending a historical methodology, one based in their case on comparative social forms. The argument is summarized in their 1994 article, published in the *International Political Science Review*, on 'The Idea of "International System": Theory Meets History'.

The more enduring historiographical moment, and the one that was to sweep the discipline, was *The Expansion of International Society* (1984), initiated by Hedley Bull when he took up the BC chairmanship in 1978. It was a difficult time for the Committee – Rockefeller had decided, after 20 years, not to renew the grant. The previous five years, under Watson's chairmanship, it had focused on questions of justice and ethics, where discussions, though lively enough, concealed an overall standstill and, in Vigezzi's account, a 'dispersal of effort'. Returning from Australia to take up his Oxford chair, Vigezzi points to the importance of Bull's Australian and *outremer* experience, his continued focus on Order, and the growing question in Bull's mind as to whether the emerging global order could in any sense be called an 'international society'. In the event, he wrote to Watson that there had been enough 'Ethics and Morality' for the time being and proposed that the next stage of the Committee's work be devoted to Convergence and Divergence. It was the theoretical beginnings of a historical narrative that would identify central elements of the European social order and its spread to the rest of the globe.

The theory of the Expansion Narrative

The 'Expansion Narrative' is a historical narration of how functional norms and practices of international behaviour developed in Europe, to provide a form of order there, roughly in the period from 1300 to 1800 – a European international system that then spreads to the rest of the world. The expansion took place most rapidly (and forcefully) in the nineteenth century, thanks to imperialist colonization and strong social pressures. Critical, according to Gerrit Gong, was the 'Standard of Civilization' that developed especially in the last 30 years of that century (Gong, 1984). Subtly implicit in the narrative is a stage theory, in that a relatively disconnected 'international system' – with different regional subsystems – was superseded by a next phase, marked by a more intense interaction and the development of shared understandings of appropriate behaviour, which became an 'international society'.[7]

Adam Watson summarized the narrative in his 1992 *Evolution of International Society*. It portrays a developing European international society's expansion to the world as a gradual process, done by European exploration and colonization, beginning around 1500. (He proposed the Palazzo Venezia in Rome as the first embassy, established in 1437.) Crucial norms and practices were gradually developed between the major European powers: Watson highlighted the evolution of a diplomatic system (professional diplomats, embassies, and diplomatic immunity), great conferences, and treaty-making at the end of wars, balancing power, and external recognition of sovereignty. The process was gradual: one turning point, for example, is in the eighteenth century when Russia and the United States became 'members of European society' (1992: 224).

Many key developments came in the nineteenth century. Hedley Bull (1984a, 117) finds the process of creating the 'universal international society' as completed around the mid-nineteenth century, through the penetration of the last insular regional systems and the linking up of the world into one political space. Watson (1992: 227) highlights a transition in which European states at first operated separately, in conflict and competition: 'They did not yet dominate the other systems of states in the world, and had not yet created a single global system. That was to be the achievement of the nineteenth century', essentially through a process of domination. Buzan (2014: 62) presents Expansion in three phases: emergence (in Europe), transfer (to everywhere else), and then decolonization. For Dunne and Little (2014: 101), the nineteenth century was when the 'nascent global international society' forming over regional systems was overtaken by key developments, including a portentous 'transformation' in the way Europeans conceived of international society and themselves: 'European great powers in the nineteenth century began to see themselves as members of an exclusive club to which most political entities around the world were not eligible to join' (2014: 101). *Is this why we use language like "developed", "undeveloped" or "under-developed" countries?*

The Standard of Civilization was devised around the 1880s (Gong, 1984) and used to gate-keep admission to an international society that was globalizing. Gong's overall account is of an implicit standard and an explicit one (1984: 5–7); the implicit one (a European sense of cultural superiority) appeared early in the century and was the more omnipresent (e.g. Bowden, 2009; Zarakol, 2011), while the explicit one was codified much later, in the 1890s and early 1900s in legal textbooks and international legal expectations. In accordance with this standard, polities and kingdoms previously treated as sovereign entities were denied that status. Literature on the Standard is especially focused on countries not actually formally colonized, tracking their incorporation into international society through sociocultural conformities and adaptations and

29

through invitations to meetings, conferences, and treaties. Favourite cases include the Ottoman Empire, China, Japan, and Siam (Gong, 1984). Indeed, this first rendering of the Expansion Narrative in the 1970s and 1980s adopted the metaphor of 'entry' or 'incorporation' into a pre-existing European international society, tracking admission using specific dates and treaties. This thereby sidestepped the issue of outright forceful colonization.

Finally, the ES has always been concerned with the post-1945 phase, sometimes described to include the 'Revolt Against the West' (e.g. Bull, 1984b) which achieved decolonization. By this account, 'European or Western dominance of the universal international society' peaked around 1900 (Bull, 1984b: 219). Rules before decolonization were made by the West/Europe and in their own interests (Bull, 1984b: 217), but by 1900, the non-West was beginning to shape and reform international society, with five goals in mind (Bull, 1984b: 220–222): a campaign for equal sovereignty, the anti-colonial revolution, and struggles for racial equality, international economic justice, and liberation from Western cultural domination (on non-Western Historical IR, see Fonseca Santos, 2021; Svensson, 2021; both in this volume). These early ES works drew some attention to the co-constitutive and multidirectional nature of the evolution of international society, and there is some acknowledgement that once former colonies got their independence and were admitted to international society, they would have an impact. The main concern, however, was that this impact would be negative – 'quasi-states' (Jackson, 1990) would be given independence before they were ready and would not be good, responsible actors in global politics.

More recent studies have elaborated upon the expansion process, sometimes taking it in different directions (see also Bayly, 2021 in this volume). Christian Reus-Smit (2013) seeks a causal theory of why an international society of states exists, and identifies the desire for human rights and political freedom as the key driver. Expansion is then the creation of new sovereign states and the collapse of empires, a process in which decolonization events are particularly central. He identifies five historical moments in which a state-system emerged and then 'expanded through a series of imperial implosions' (2013: 15), each producing newly independent states: the Westphalian episode around 1648, the Latin American 'second wave' between 1810 and 1825 in Latin America and the Caribbean, and the post-1945 breakdown of all empires; 1919 and 1989 are other such moments.

From the historical point of view, the Expansion Narrative established a fully developed and global 'international society' as the end point of the diplomatic activity of the previous four centuries and codified its periodization. The emphasis on treaty-making at the end of wars established the basic periodization: Westphalia, Utrecht, Vienna, Versailles, with corrections and adjustments at Berlin and Bretton Woods. This periodization has been challenged – Buzan and Lawson (2015) have put forward the 1850s as a turning point, at which the world is finally one unified political-strategic system – but it has not been overturned.[8]

The Expansion Narrative today

While large-scale historical narratives – e.g. liberal-democratic expansion and 'whiggish' progress narratives that incorporate directionality, telos and ignore historical contingency – have been the subject of persistent attack, the Expansion Narrative avoids teleology for the most part and has survived attacks on grand narratives relatively unscathed. Its critics do not question that a form of expansion occurred but rather focus on the processes involved, and the ideological implications of the theory and the process itself. Many of these criticisms have been incorporated into the narrative, correcting its detail and amplifying it in significant ways. It should also be noted that

[handwritten margin note: The U.S. Acted like the West though but it's not on here...]

large-scale narratives are essential conceptual tools, conveying summary information to the general public and to students in the classroom, and are in fact omnipresent (Suganami, 2008; White, 1973). Narratives bring order to the infinite volume of facts available, highlighting some things and ignoring others. The relevant question is the accounting – do the analytic benefits of a narrative outweigh the costs? More importantly, do the criticisms directed at elements in the Expansion Narrative undercut the essential elements in the story, or do they rather amplify it and correct it?

There have, of course, been important criticisms of the Expansion Narrative. A common charge is that the Expansion story as originally represented is Eurocentric and overly impressed with Western power (Buzan, 2004: 214–216; Buzan and Little, 2000; Dunne and Little, 2014; Kayaoglu, 2010; Keal, 2003). It is also said to have sanitized a process that was often violent, and with little genuine regard for the subjects that were being incorporated (Callahan, 2004; see also Yao and Delatolla, 2021 in this volume), describing as gradual and benign a 'process of social incorporation' that was in fact repressive and exclusionary (Keal, 2003). Those brought in are said to have appreciated the order and rationality they became a part of: 'non-European polities are portrayed as embracing the rules and practices of the expanding international society' (Reus-Smit, 2013: 31), while we know that many elements of the new rules and practices were loathed and profoundly contested. Such critiques challenge the legitimacy of international society today, as the costs of conquest for victim populations are ignored (Keal, 2003). Finally, the expansion story has been found to be 'primarily descriptive not explanatory' (Reus-Smit, 2013: 31); the original narrative was not primarily concerned with why things happened.

However, Reus-Smit's recent work highlights an important causal factor, which has served to considerably amplify the historical narrative. These are the 'political struggles for freedom and recognition' (2013: 1). These drove the expansion process in part by adapting the discourses of the imperializer for processes of resistance. Nor is this just his theory. Local historians from the Middle East, Africa, Japan, and Latin America have constructed their political histories of independence or (re Japan) modernizations in terms of the Expansion Narrative, albeit an adjusted narrative in which local forces did not merely absorb but also selected elements in the Standard of Civilization discourse to serve local purposes of adaptation and change. Amitav Acharya (2001) is perhaps most relevant in this respect, but see also Carsten-Andreas Schulz (2014).

Noting that Zhang (1991) and Stivachtis (1998) had already offered their critiques, Edward Keene (2014) ambitiously criticizes the analogy frequently assumed between 'entry' and 'expansion'. Instead, he argues for a shift 'from expansion to stratification'. By this argument, we need to rethink how the nineteenth-century system itself actually functioned and ordered things, not just the idea of incorporation itself (2014: 655) – in fact, non-Western states were hardly admitted into international society on equal terms. Carsten-Andreas Schulz (2014) makes a similar point about Latin American states in the nineteenth century and the awkward case of countries nominally Western in civilizational terms. He argues that international society was 'heterarchical', with different measures of status and belonging and varying ways of including and excluding. Latin American states might have been incorporated in formal-legal terms, but were excluded on civilizational expectations. A second purpose in these studies is to take account of the new interest in hierarchy that has become prominent in IR (e.g. Bially Mattern and Zarakol, 2016). B.A. Roberson's study of the modernization of Egyptian legal codes demonstrates how Egyptian legal and political elites deliberately adopted European legal practice to counter European rights to special legal treatment (Roberson, 2009). These are innovative process breakthroughs, though still within the classical account.

Similarly, it is now realized that changes were not so easily imposed by imperial conquest (Buzan and Little, 1994, citing Laura Benton); there was always local pushback and resistance. The regional systems that were overrun and absorbed by the European system, once ignored, are now getting attention (Buzan and Little, 1994: 62; Stivachtis, 2014; Suzuki et al., 2014). But these developments imply a correction of the narrative, not its overthrow.

Tim Dunne and Reus-Smit's (2017) edited volume, *The Globalization of International Society*, is the new major revisiting of the Expansion Narrative, with some significant advances. The authors take a truly global perspective to the story and take on the 1984 Expansion collection at every point, providing compelling critiques of the classical narrative. Major theoretical and conceptual innovations are offered (Reus-Smit and Dunne, 2017a: 28–39). Perhaps most significantly, the volume rejects the incorporation/expansion model in favour of globalization processes writ large, proposing the 'globalization' of international society, not the expansion of it. This de-privileges Europe in favour of a globally interactive process. Second, they fully embrace the idea that international systems are social and therefore not distinct in any way from 'international society', in effect backing away from the ES's somewhat stadial understanding of international history. In short, there is no notion that an international system stage preceded a societal one (Reus-Smit and Dunne, 2017a: 33). Third, they choose to foreground Hedley Bull's (1977: 278) notion of the 'world political system' – all the actors and forces in the world, not just state actors enact a constant influence on the development of international society (2017a: 33–34). International society exists within and develops from 'a broader world of political actors and relations' which they call 'the world political system', and which features 'a shifting panoply of individual and institutional actors' (2017a: 34). In effect, they counsel us to take a variety of global influences into account, always. In their terms, international society is a 'governance assemblage…in which the principal units are sovereign states' (2017a: 34).

New studies consider in some detail how the world political system has shaped the evolution of international society, as 'contestation' in the globalization of international society characterizes the modern co-constitution of the culture of international society since 1945 (and the new tone is much less Eurocentric or Euro-friendly; see Bowden, 2021 in this volume). Ian Hall (2017) discusses the contours and content of the new revolt today, noting that some of those Bull identified in 1984, such as the anti-colonial revolution, have been largely resolved or displaced, but that new disagreements have taken their place. The issue of racial inequality lingers as a problem in international society, but in different forms (Klotz, 2017). Gender and gender expectations are incorporated as part of standards of civilization (Towns, 2017), something completely missing from the ES in the past, and even today.

These topics are evidence of the cultural issues at stake in the new international society. They also offer fertile possibilities for future exploration, building on the traditional ES concern about culture (as webs of norms and values). With the new lens, all the world's civilizations can be seen in relation to their contributions to an international culture. What other approaches to IR give this question so much concerted attention? In this new form, the ES is incorporating and joining many of the arguments made by postcolonial IR and its empirical points about the intercultural cogeneration of the international.

Relatedly, the ES continues to undertake a creative introspection of the central concepts of 'international society' and 'international system', which may shake up the conceptual underpinnings of the narrative itself. One argument is that a somewhat violent, disconnected 'international system' phase or stage is actually hard to substantiate empirically, such that we should shift our thinking to consider most of world history as displaying aspects and dimensions of international society alone.

Finally, the new literature is more cautious about seeing expansion/globalization as a finished process. Instead, it presents both as ongoing, with recognition that the current age of challenges to the West, the rise of the BRICS/East, and a general 'multicultural multipolarity' are, or may be, creating a different form of international society.

Conclusion

The ES's strong historical research agenda, and its singular content, are a key source of the ES's uniqueness. The ES has always been an alternative to positivist modes of theorizing, to quantitative approaches, and to a scientific-structural realism; it has always been 'interpretive, normative, and attentive to questions of identity and culture' (Epp, 2014: 33). This is the sensibility it brings to international history. No other approach or 'research program' in IR has embarked upon a concerted effort to develop a unified narrative of IR history, in which key terms and descriptors for phases and aspects of history are debated so intensely.

Taken together, the Expansion Narrative is a grand account of the history of IR, one that builds on the 1648-Westphalia state-system narrative but adds to it considerably. Crucially, it addresses colonialism better than most approaches and the social story of how practices were developed in a 'European cultural hearth' – in intense interaction with the rest of the world – and then spread elsewhere. As ES authors have noted, it therefore anticipates, by decades even, today's more fashionable renderings, both constructivist, driven by social mechanisms and norms, and the interest in norm diffusion. Its origins lie clearly in diplomatic history, and in the experience of the British Empire. It puts to the side the more common realist-oriented themes of systemic power distributions, polarities, power transitions, predicting the incidence of war, etc. Instead, it is primarily about order and the problem of securing and managing legitimacy for a presently existing order.

The overall import of the ES's theoretical contribution to historical IR should not be underrated. The Expansion Narrative and the comparative study of state-systems that the ES has pursued alongside it (Wight, 1977; Watson, 1992) have established the temporality of our present state-system and provided the historian of international relations with a common focus – the historical development of the contours of a system of sovereign states. In the course of doing so, they also provided it with a Big Question. The Expansion Narrative supported the contention that state-systems based on mutual recognition and equality are historically rare (see Phillips and Sharman, 2015), that hierarchical systems are more the norm, and that the European historical system of equal sovereigns, or at least of equal great powers who recognized each other's right to exist, is positively freakish. It is quite possible that a China-centred international society of 2050 and beyond will be hierarchical in the more usual manner. Watson identified a continuous tendency in state-systems towards hegemony, a reminder that the conditions of our present state-system are contingent historical conditions, and that other narratives are possible. Scholars should focus our attention on the historical conditions, and historical contingencies, that maintain our 'freakish order', as well as the ones that are most likely to overcome it. This is a task for historical IR, with the ES in the vanguard, for years to come.

Suggestions for further reading

Bellamy, A. J., ed. (2006). *International Society and It Critics*. Oxford: Oxford University Press.
Hall, I. (2019). The English School's Histories and International Relations. In: B. Schmidt, and N. Guilhot, eds., *Historiographical Investigations in International Relations*, London: Palgrave Macmillan, 171–201.

Linklater, A., and Suganami, H. (2006). *The English School of International Relations: A Contemporary Reassessment*. Cambridge: Cambridge University Press.

Vigezzi, B. (2014). The British Committee and International Society: History and Theory. In: C. Navari, and D. Green, eds., *Guide to the English School in International Studies*, London: Wiley Blackwell, 37–58.

Wight, M. (1966). Why is There No International Theory? In: H. Butterfield, and M. Wight, eds., *Diplomatic Investigations*, London: George Allen & Unwin, 17–34.

Notes

1 As opposed to historical theories with implications for international relations (e.g. Fischer, 1967).

2 The British Committee on the Theory of International Politics was initiated by Kenneth Thompson of the Rockefeller Foundation in 1957 to support the work of a faltering American committee on the same subject.

3 For those unfamiliar with the lectures, Bull's characterisation has the virtue of brevity: 'Each pattern or tradition of thought embodied a description of the nature of international politics and also a set of prescriptions as to how men should conduct themselves in it' (Bull, 1976: 103).

4 Wight (1966: 32–33) is anticipating the argument that conventional historians and conventional political scientists do not in fact differ much in method or philosophy; each is doing much the same thing – empirically based case studies. The main difference is that one uses primarily sociographical material and the other historiographical material.

5 In July 1961, in the paper 'International Society and Anarchy' (Vigezzi, 2005: 392–395).

6 The unpublished paper Butterfield delivered to the Committee in January was entitled 'The Historic State-System'; Vigezzi (2005: 186–188) provides an account of the contents.

7 A third, Kantian phase, of considerable liberal norm-convergence and the erosion of states under deep human solidarity is the 'world society' phase, not something we discuss here (see Wight, 1991; Buzan, 2004).

8 From the theoretical point of view, the Expansion Narrative also narrowed the ES focus on what has come to be termed 'fundamental institutions' (see Holsti, 2004; Buzan, 2004, Knudsen and Navari, 2019).

References

Acharya, A. (2001). *Constructing a Security Community in Southeast Asia: ASEAN and the Problem of Regional Order*. New York, NY: Routledge.

Bayly, M. (2021). Imperialism: Beyond the 'Re-turn to Empire' in International Relations. In de Carvalho, B., Costa Lopez, J., & Leira, H., eds. *Routledge Handbook of Historical International Relations*. Abingdon: Routledge.

Bially Mattern, J., and Zarakol, A. (2016). Hierarchies in world politics. *International Organization*, 70 (3), 623–654.

Bowden, B. (2009). *The Empire of Civilization: The Evolution of an Imperial Idea*. Chicago, IL: Chicago University Press.

Bowden, B. (2021). Eurocentrism and Civilization. In de Carvalho, B., Costa Lopez, J., & Leira, H., eds. *Routledge Handbook of Historical International Relations*. Abingdon: Routledge.

Bull, H., and Watson, A., eds. (1984). *The Expansion of International Society*. Oxford: Oxford Clarendon Press.

Bull, H. (1976). Martin Wight and the theory of international relations. *British Journal of International Studies*, 2 (2), 101–116.

Bull, H. (1977). *The Anarchical Society*. London: Macmillan.

Bull, H. (1984a). The Emergence of a Universal International Society. In: H. Bull, and A. Watson, eds., *The Expansion of International Society*, Oxford: Clarendon Press, 117–126.

Bull, H. (1984b). The Revolt against the West. In: H. Bull, and A. Watson, eds., *The Expansion of International Society*, Oxford: Clarendon Press, 217–228.

Buzan, B. (2004). *From International Society to World Society?* Cambridge: Cambridge University Press.

Buzan, B. (2014). *An Introduction to the English School of International Relations*. Cambridge: Polity Press.

Buzan, B. (2014). The Historical Expansion of International Society. In: C. Navari, and D. M. Green, eds., *Guide to the English School in International Studies*, Chichester: John Wiley & Sons, 59–75.

Buzan, B., and Lawson, G. (2015). *The Global Transformation: History, Modernity and the Making of International Relations*. Cambridge: Cambridge University Press.

Buzan, B., and Little, R. (1994). The idea of 'international system': theory meets history. *International Political Science Review*, 15 (3), 231–255.

Buzan, B., and Little, R. (2000). *International Systems in World History: Remaking the Study of International Relations*. Oxford: Oxford University Press.

Callahan, W. A. (2004). Nationalizing international theory: race, class and the English school. *Global Society*, 18 (4), 305–323.

Dunne, T., and Reus-Smit, C., eds. (2017). *The Globalization of International Society*. Oxford: Oxford University Press.

Dunne, T., and Little, R. (2014). The International System – International Society Distinction. In: C. Navari, and D. M. Green, eds., *Guide to the English School in International Studies*, Chichester: John Wiley & Sons, 91–107.

Epp, R. (2014). The British Committee on the Theory of International Politics and Its Central Figures. In: C. Navari, and D. M. Green, eds., *Guide to the English School in International Studies*, Chichester: John Wiley & Sons, 25–36.

Fischer, F. (1967). *Germany's Aims in the First World War*. New York, NY: W. W. Norton.

Fonseca Santos, M. (2021). Disciplinary Histories of Non-Anglophone International Relations: Latin America and the Caribbean. In de Carvalho, B., Costa Lopez, J., & Leira, H., eds. *Routledge Handbook of Historical International Relations*. Abingdon: Routledge.

Gong, G. (1984). *The Standard of 'Civilization' in International Society*. Oxford: Clarendon Press.

Hall, I. (2017). The 'Revolt Against the West' Revisited. In: T. Dunne, and C. Reus-Smit, eds., *The Globalization of International Society*, Oxford: Oxford University Press, 345–361.

Holsti, K. J. (2004). *Taming the Sovereigns: Institutional Change in International Politics*. Cambridge: Cambridge University Press.

Hudson, G. F. (1965). *Europe and China: A Survey of Their Relations from the Earliest Times to 1800*. London: Edward Arnold.

Jackson, R. (1990). *Quasi-States: Sovereignty, International Relations and the Third World*. Cambridge: Cambridge University Press.

Kayaoglu, T. (2010). Westphalian Eurocentrism in international relations theory. *International Studies Review*, 12 (2), 193–217.

Keal, P. (2003). *European Conquest and the Rights of Indigenous Peoples*. Cambridge: Cambridge University Press.

Keene, E. (2014). Three Traditions of International Theory. In: C. Navari, and D. M. Green, eds., *Guide to the English School in International Studies*, Chichester: John Wiley & Sons, 171–184.

Knudsen, T. B. (2019). Fundamental Institutions and International Organization. In: T. B. Knudsen, and C. Navari, eds., *International Organization in the Anarchical Society*, Cham, Switzerland: Palgrave-Springer, 23–50.

Knudsen, T. B., and C. Navari, eds. (2019). *International Organization in the Anarchical Society: The Institutional Structure of World Order*. Cham, Switzerland: Palgrave-Springer.

Reus-Smit, C. (2013). *Individual Rights and the Making of the International System*. Cambridge: Cambridge University Press.

Reus-Smit, C., and Dunne, T. (2017a). The Globalization of International Society. In: T. Dunne, and C. Reus-Smit, eds., *The Globalization of International Society*, Oxford: Oxford University Press, 18–40.

Roberson, B. (2009). Law, Power and the Expansion of International Society. In: C. Navari, ed., *Theorising International Society: English School Methods*, Houndmills: Palgrave Macmillan, 189–208.

Schulz, C.-A. (2014). Civilization, barbarism and the making of Latin America's place in 19th-century international society. *Millennium: Journal of International Studies*, 42 (3): 837–859.

Stivachtis, Y. (1998). *The Enlargement of International Society: Culture versus Anarchy and Greece's Entry into International Society*. London: Macmillan.

Stivachtis, Y. (2014). The Regional Dimension of International Society. In: C. Navari, and D. M. Green, eds., *Guide to the English School in International Studies*, Chichester: John Wiley & Sons, 109–125.

Suganami, H. (2008). Narrative explanation and international relations: back to basics. *Millennium: Journal of International Studies*, 37 (2), 327–356.

Suzuki, S., Zhang, Y., and Quirk, J., eds. (2014). *International Orders in the Early Modern World: Before the Rise of the West*. London: Routledge.

Svensson, T. (2021). Decolonisation and the Erosion of the Imperial Idea. In de Carvalho, B., Costa Lopez, J., & Leira, H., eds. *Routledge Handbook of Historical International Relations*. Abingdon: Routledge.

Vigezzi, B. (2005). *The British Committee on the Theory of International Politics (1954-1985): The Rediscovery of History*. Milan: Edizioni Unicopli.

Watson, A. (1992). *The Evolution of International Society*. London: Routledge.

White, H. (1973). *Metahistory: The Historical Imagination in Nineteenth Century Europe*. Baltimore, MD: Johns Hopkins University Press.

Wight, M. (1991). In: G. Wight, and B. Porter, eds., *International Theory: The Three Traditions*, London: Leicester University Press.

Wight, M. (1977). In: H. Bull, eds., *Systems of States*, Leicester: Leicester University Press.

Yao, J., and Delatolla, A. (2021). Race and Historical International Relations. In de Carvalho, B., Costa Lopez, J., & Leira, H., eds. *Routledge Handbook of Historical International Relations*. Abingdon: Routledge.

Zarakol, A. (2011). *After Defeat: How the East Learned to Live with the West*. Cambridge: Cambridge University Press.

Zhang, Y. (1991). China's entry into international society: beyond the standard of 'civilization'. *Review of International Studies*, 17 (1), 3–16.

4

WORLD-SYSTEMS ANALYSIS

Past trajectories and future prospects

Robert A. Denemark

A focus on the state, and a search for general laws of social behaviour, dominated the social sciences in the United States in the 1960s and 1970s. From this perspective, history was little more than a set of case studies to be considered in pursuit of those social laws when contemporary data were insufficient. World-systems analysis (WSA) emerged in the 1970s in opposition to this ahistoricism, statist orientation, and assumptions of universality. In this essay, I will introduce the intellectual foundations of the world-systems perspective, key early insights, major elements, revisionist positions, and ongoing research.

WSA adopts a critical, long-term, large-scale, whole-systems approach to the study of human interaction. From this perspective, the properties and dynamics of the various agents included in a large social system can only be understood with reference to the system in which they are embedded. A world-system is bounded geographically by the extent of interactions that are two-way, necessary, structured, regularized, and serve social reproductive functions (Friedman and Rowlands, 1977; Chase-Dunn and Hall, 1997). The 'world' in WSA represents the extent of these interaction boundaries and not the geographical extent of the planet, though the current world-system became global in the 19th century.

WSA was pioneered in the 1960s and 1970s by Immanuel Wallerstein (1972, 1974, 1976), Samin Amin (1973, 1976), Andre Gunder Frank (1966, 1967), and Giovanni Arrighi (Arrighi and Saul, 1973). Goldfrank (2012) identifies four major intellectual influences in the founding work of Wallerstein, who was the prime mover in the development of the world-systems school. The first of these influences may be found in the German Historical School, that questioned the proposed universalisms of the dominant British/Liberal perspective on state formation, and considered economic liberalism a strategy (of the momentarily dominant) and not an inevitable phase of human development. Among the more critical insights generated from these roots is that social relations should be viewed as dynamic, and therefore historically contingent, instead of homeostatic or self-equilibrating.

A second pillar of WSA comes from the sociology of Marx and Weber, whose models featured historically malleable and conflict-ridden social totalities. Marx saw the capitalist era, identified by its drive for endless capital accumulation, as featuring specific conflicts and contradictions that define social relations. For Weber, interstate conflict is the political framework of capitalism, not an aberration. Chase-Dunn (1981) traced the specific ways in which the competitive state system and the capitalist world economy constitute a single mutually reinforcing system.

The third major influence was the Annales School, and especially the work of Fernand Braudel (1972 [1949]), with its concern for the long-term deep structures of large-scale regions. Regions with few 'external' interactions were 'worlds' wherein a single division of labour exists with multiple political and cultural formations. Eschewing the study of lead personalities or high diplomacy, Braudel sees the dynamics of a world economy shaping the nature of its parts. Such relationships rest on the base level structures of everyday life and will alter as those interactions change in a process of co-constitution.

Finally, WSA is identified as an outgrowth of dependency theory. Dependency emerged in an effort to understand the limited progress of the periphery, in contradistinction to the predictions of rapid development offered by the dominant 'modernization' school, and the somewhat similar predictions of Marxism. 'Modernization' conceived of development as a problem of moving from (original) traditional (undifferentiated) social formations to the functionally differentiated social roles and tasks of the modern state. Marxism saw peripheral states as evolving into the social forms presented by industrial societies, if with a lag and perhaps some assistance in escaping the stagnant Asiatic mode. The dependency argument characterized interaction with advanced countries as both the source of exploitation that reinforced raw materials dependence and low wages, and the social context that sustained the alleged traditionalism of the underdeveloped. Gunder Frank characterized this 'Development of Underdevelopment' (1966). Ironically, modernization theorists attacked dependency for its allegedly Marxian orientation, while Marxists attacked it for its 'neo-Smithian' rejection of the primacy of the sphere of production (Brenner 1977).

WSA emerges from these origins with a rejection of the nation-state as the unit of analysis for social, political, or economic interaction, in favour of the world-system itself. WSA is deeply historical, eschewing short-termism or teleological models. Ignoring the relevant global historical context leads to myriad errors, as, for example, the idea that underdevelopment stems from various internal, national, racial, or religious proclivities.

WSA rejects some of the divisions imposed by traditional social science (Wallerstein, 1976, 1977, 1991b, 1999). Wallerstein (1996) led a research group to review the history of the social sciences in an effort to provide a series of practical suggestions for overcoming intellectual insularity. WSA sought to introduce a form of social analysis that would focus on complexity, contingency, and emergent properties. These traits were tied to chaos theory by Prigogine (1996).

The puzzle of Eastern Europe and core/periphery differentiation

WSA sought to shed light on social processes that were difficult to understand from traditional viewpoints. A key example concerns the arguments regarding the development of capitalism and the differentiation of Western and Eastern Europe into core and periphery (Chirot, 1989). European feudalism featured a myriad of small, poor territories with overlapping sovereignties (see Costa Lopez, 2021 in this volume). Change was driven by an external source. The Islamic conquest of Iberia led to efforts at reconquest. This generated the tendency for military leaders to rise on the basis of merit and not (feudal) family lineage and broke down earlier land tenure patterns. The eventual result was a very different social order, as in Portugal, featuring meritocratic leaders of a more centralized polity. The territory was more urban, cosmopolitan, and well monetized. To enhance Portugal's working capital, the state helped facilitate advances in naval architecture, maritime insurance, and facilitated the growth of an urban workforce. The new state could sponsor fleets and organize the search for gold to secure its position. Portugal emerged with a stronger state and economy. This model was replicated elsewhere in Western Europe.

Alternatively, no external invader or terminal 'crisis of feudalism' altered conditions in Eastern Europe. Land tenure schemes featured inefficient collective cultivation by peasants who could not leave the land. Growth outstripped agricultural productivity. Feudal lords had to compete surreptitiously for (illicitly mobile) labour, or to combat the tendency of peasants to flee to unsettled areas where they were free to farm and join 'Cossack armies'. In the hope of stemming the flow, feudal lords reduced the number of days a peasant had to work on the owner's fields instead of his own small plot. Feudalism appeared ready to disintegrate.

Polish landholders were rescued by the increased demand for their grain given changing conditions in the new polities of the more urbanized west. Gold poured into Poland to pay for the grain, but was used primarily for private security forces or ostentatious consumption on low-productively estates. Lords increased peasant labour dues from one day per week, all the way to six (Stavrianos, 1981: 66). Ongoing efforts towards political centralization were sidetracked by landowners wishing to retain their autonomy. To protect their power from commercial competitors, the lords promulgated laws making grain trading illegal, but rarely enforced such rules. By this mechanism, potential political competitors among the commercial elite were neutered (Denemark and Thomas, 1988).

The consolidation of a new economic system refocused Eastern Europe towards weak states, low levels of accumulation, and repression. Both well-established practices and contingency, along with individual, family, class, and polity-level actions, large-scale and long-term processes, pushed the western edges of Europe onto the road to growth and eventual capitalist development, and Eastern Europe into peripheral disadvantage, specifically because of their interaction.

The creation of an explanation for the differentiation of the advanced western and the underdeveloped eastern portions of Europe not only shed light on a long-standing historical question but played a broader intellectual role as well. In the 1960s and 1970s, the postcolonial world was suffering with persistent poverty and the solutions offered, including adherence to western political and economic models, were proving unhelpful. The search for a better understanding of underdevelopment was a high priority in academic circles, and western governments were covertly funding for some of the most conservative perspectives (Latham, 2000; Gilman, 2003). Offering an analysis that explained the phenomena, as opposed to providing endless *ad hoc* justifications for continued poverty, would open scholarship to new and more critical perspectives. Underdevelopment is not an anomaly. Power and wealth are reinforced by the terms of interaction dictated by the dominant party (Braudel, 1992: ch. 1).

This core/periphery hierarchy is further suggested by Wallerstein to include a middle-level 'semi-periphery' made up of rising peripheral areas (mostly those finding themselves in command of key resources), or declining core states. Wallerstein argued that semi-peripheral areas are often fostered by core states for ideological purposes. At once a political buffer and a powerful but largely empty economic promise, the existence of a semi-periphery offers the hope of status mobility to poor states. Students of WSA spent considerable time theorizing and evaluating the claims regarding a tripartite global status, and support for the predicted three-part differentiation proved considerable (Arrighi and Drangel, 1986; Borgatti and Everett, 1999; Karatasli and Kumral, 2018).

World-system cycles and trends

The fundamental insights of WSA lead to a deeper historical understanding of global social relations. Along with core/periphery differentiation, world-systems scholarship illuminated three cycles and three secular trends (Hopkins and Wallerstein, 1979). Each is based on a set of interactive dynamics born from tensions or contradictions in the context of the capitalist world economy. First among the cycles is that of economic growth and decline. These cycles are usually suggested to emerge from the anarchy of production and the socially determined nature of consumption. Overinvestment in times of expansion generates eventual losses, identified as downturns. An alternative view suggests that economic cycles are driven by fundamental innovations that generate economic activity across an array of sectors, but eventually diffuse (Modelski and Thompson, 1996). Not surprisingly, the political economies of growth and decline generate very different social and cultural responses.

A second cycle is that of hegemony and rivalry. Initial advantages in agriculture may lead to industrial and financial dominance as well. One possible result of the overlap of advantageous positions may be the emergence of a single polity of such wealth and power that it is capable of making global rules. But such power tends to dissipate as the exploitation upon which it is based leads to social change and global counter-coalitions. In periods of hegemony, there tends to be international peace and stability. Counter-hegemonic movements are most often manifested as revolutions or terrorist violence (on revolutions, see Lawson, 2021 in this volume). After hegemony breaks down, we find periods of rivalry characterized by intense ideological competition and direct great power conflict. A third cycle is understood as revolving periods during which labour has the advantage over owners of capital, and where capital has the advantage over workers. All of these cycles are based on contingent, long-term social phenomena that appear to reinforce or degrade sets of coordinate social patterns. None emerges exactly the same manner over time (Arrighi, 1994).

Other global and historical processes are secular in nature. The modern world-system expands as the drive to acquire wealth, especially in the downturn, fuels a search for new resources and markets. Extensive analysis by Chase-Dunn and his colleagues sees expansion proceeding in pulses at various rates (Inoue et al., 2014). A second secular trend in the modern world-system is mechanization, fuelled by the drive to acquire wealth by substituting machine for human production. Finally, the modern world-system also features a trend towards increasing commodification, as more of the fundamental elements of life move from non-market, often familial interactions, into market processes (e.g. food preparation, elder-care, child-rearing). Both of these latter trends can be seen in the work on commodity chains, labour processes, and mining, offered by Gereffi and Korzeniewicz (1994) and Bunker and Ciccantell (2005). Each secular trend derives from the world-system structure, and the impact of subsequent actions reflects back upon that structure.

Unlike more teleological perspectives, WSA shies away from predictions about post-'modern world-system' social systems. Eventually, the secular trends will approach asymptotic limits under capitalist world-system constraints and will reduce the ability of the cycles to make rebounds. As a result, and in a manner consistent with the contingent nature of social relations, there will be scant foundation upon which to predict the nature of any system that would arise with the destruction of the modern world-system. Change is inevitable, but in the wake of the decline of the longest term, largest scale social environment, its direction cannot be predicted. This does not relieve us of the responsibility to work towards progressive ends.

Revisionist positions

WSA has generated significant internal debate and at least two sustained revisionist positions. While much of contemporary WSA is focused on understanding the modern capitalist world economy (from the 16th century onward), another important strand adopted a comparative and historical orientation. Comparison can be a powerful analytical tool. The analysis of cases that are similar in critical ways can help us to identify both the unique and the common elements at play. Chase-Dunn and Hall (1997) began the study of smaller historical world-systems in search of comparative insights. The study of historical systems is especially helpful, but there remains the problem of geographical bounding. There can be no legitimate comparison among ostensibly separate systems that are not actually independent. Considerations of the fall-off of interaction effects include insights from scholars in archaeology, anthropology, and history, as well as sociology and political science (Chase-Dunn and Inoue eds., forthcoming).

A broader challenge to traditional WSA was offered by Barry Gills and Andre Gunder Frank (Gills and Frank, 1992, 2011; Frank, 1998, 2014). After studying a variety of historical world-systems, Frank and Gills argue that there are few world-system attributes that alter in a significant manner following the development of capitalism. Indeed, of the dozen or so critical differences between capitalist and earlier world-systems identified by Wallerstein, Frank contends that only one or two stand the test of historical consideration, and that is not a sufficient foundation upon which to posit the existence of an entirely separate social system (Frank, 1991).

This argument is played out in debates among scholars in several fields. Historians contend over the 'Great Divergence' between China and the west (i.e. Pomeranz, 2000). Civilizationists like David Wilkinson (1987, 1994) track world system power polarity back into the Bronze Age, and political scientists like George Modelski and William R. Thompson (1996) focus on the rise and decline of leading/innovative economic sectors that generate wealth and propel the polities in which they are developed to global leadership. Archaeologists like Andrew and Susan Sherratt (1993, 2000) and anthropologists like Kajsa Ekholm-Friedman and Jonathan Friedman (1982) have considered what pre-capitalist world-systems might look like, especially in the context of periods of significant trade in various eras of antiquity (also see Hall et al., 2011). Historians like Philippe Beaujard (2012) outlined the history of the Indian Ocean as a world system from the seventh century to the arrival of the Portuguese. Sing Chew (2018) considers early Southeast Asia.

World(-)system(s) topics and literatures

In a short review essay, there is little chance to outline even the full list of topics considered by students of the current world-system in anthropology, archaeology, geography, history, political science, and sociology. Two dedicated journals, *Review* (now retired) and *Journal of World-Systems Research*, may be consulted. Three websites with information and sets of working papers are available: one at the Institute for the Study of World-Systems (https://irows.ucr.edu/); another focuses on geographic linkages (Globalization and World Cities 'GaWC', http://www.lboro.ac.uk/gawc/Taylor.html); and a third focuses on ancient trade (http://www.archatlas.org/atlas/atlas.php). Handbooks and review essays often focus on different facets of WSA (Sanderson, 1995; Denemark, 2007; Modelski and Denemark, 2008; Babones and Chase-Dunn, 2012; Erin and Chase-Dunn, 2018; Khutkyy and Chase-Dunn, 2018). Literatures have emerged to address ideational, ideological, and agential concerns (Wallerstein, 1991; Denemark, 2007); gender, family relations, and population movements (Dunaway, 2012; Lindio-McGovern, 2012); environmental challenges (Chew, 2001; Hornborg and Crumley, 2007; Jorgenson and Rice, 2012), and inequality (Bornschier and Suter, 2010; Suter, 2010; Karatasli and Kumral, 2018). More traditional world system topics concern the incorporation of areas into expanding world system relations (Hall, 2012), trade (Nemeth and Smith, 1985; Smith and White, 1992), urbanization and geographic networks (Flint, 2010; Timberlake and Smith, 2012), great power conflict (Cioffi-Revilla, 1996; Bornschier and Chase-Dunn, 2012; Suter and Bergesen, 2018), and the rise of anti-systemic movements (Arrighi et al., 1989; Silver, 2003; Moghadam, 2012).

World-Systems Analysis and Historical International Relations

WSA and Historical International Relations overlap in crucial ways. Three methodological issues feature prominently. Much attention has been paid to the return of the study of politics in academic considerations of international relations. This is a logical move, especially in the context of the change from a hegemonic global order to one characterized by rivalry. But after discarding liberal polemics, and with significant historical study, WSA came to reject a narrow focus on the state as the primary unit of political analysis. States are hardly irrelevant, but they do not provide the context within which they themselves act, nor are they the sole (or even the most critical) structures within which individuals, social movements, cultural trends, or economic conditions emerge. Focusing too much on the state is an error.

Second, Historical International Relations will likely face the question of 'how historical' it should become. This is inevitable – and problematic. It is not possible to determine how far back into the historical record our studies should go if an attempt to do so is made prior to considerations of the historical features one is trying to understand. WSA followed the Annales School in viewing the 'long 16th century' as the logical starting point of the 'modern' system. This has proven fruitful, but not unproblematic (see the discussion in de Carvalho, 2021 in this volume). The reification of the post–'long 16th century' capitalist world economy clarified some phenomena, but clouded our ability to perceive others. *A priori* temporal boundaries are generally a trap (see Hom, 2021; Guillaume, 2021, both in this volume).

Third, Historical International Relations should do what it can to avoid intellectual closure and uni-disciplinarity (see the discussion in de Carvalho et al., 2021 in this volume). It is far more fruitful to foster a transdisciplinary intellectual community. This is true in two ways. Scholars do not have to agree on a specific intellectual foundation, much less a single academic field, to contribute. The current trend towards ring-fencing perspectives on ontological or epistemological grounds will harm our ability to find interesting questions and explore novel processes uncovered by honest scholars with different intellectual starting points. Further, no academic field is perfectly suited to such a broad task, and working together, while learning the strengths and weaknesses that exist in each, is a strategy that is important for increasing our understanding of historical international relations.

In substantive terms, it is likely that renewed concern over great power conflict will propel Historical International Relations into questions regarding systemic violence. The dynamics of hegemony and rivalry are an important starting point for understanding the nature of violence in past periods of transition. What attention has been paid, as in the case of the work of William R. Thompson (Modelski and Thompson, 1996; Reuveny and Thompson, 2007; Rasler and Thompson, 2010; Rapkin and Thompson, 2013) and others, suggests there is much more to be done.

Finally, the return of traditional and narrowly defined state-centric 'politics' in the study of international relations raises the fear that we will ignore the economic foundations of the global system. These foundations are not well illustrated by micro-foundationally oriented neoclassical liberal economics. The persistence of a core-periphery hierarchy globally, and the likelihood that recent advances in life chances by the world's poor might be undercut with the return of the dynamics of great power rivalry, suggest that material well-being and its distribution should not be ignored in the context of renewed interest in historical international relations. This is closely related to the question of inequality within states as well, as these global and local phenomena are not independent (Murphy, 2018). World-system scholars have written widely on many issues that will be of interest to students of Historical International Relations and we welcome the chance to interact.

Suggestions for further reading

Abu Lughod, J. (1989). *Before European Hegemony: The World System A.D. 1250-1350*. Oxford: Oxford University Press.

Arrighi, G., and Silver, B. (1999). *Chaos and Governance in the Modern World System*. Minneapolis, MN: University of Minnesota Press.

Kristiansen, K. (1998). The Emergence of the European World System in the Bronze Age. In: Kristiansen, K., and Rowlands, M., eds., *Social Transformation in Archaeology: Global and Local Perspectives*, London: Routledge.

Modelski, G., Devezas, T., and Thompson, W. R., eds. (2008). *Globalization as Evolutionary Process*. London: Routledge.

Taylor, P. (2013). *Extraordinary Cities: Millennia of Moral Syndromes, World-Systems and City/State Relations*. Cheltenham: Edward Elgar.

Wallerstein, I. (2000). *The Essential Wallerstein*. New York, NY: The New Press.

Wallerstein, I. (2004). *World-Systems Analysis*. Durham, NC: Duke University Press.

References

Amin, S. (1973). *Neo-Colonialism in West Africa*. New York, NY: Monthly Review Press.

Amin, S. (1976). *Unequal Development*. New York, NY: Monthly Review Press.

Arrighi, G., and Saul, J., eds. (1973). *Essays on the Political Economy of Africa*. New York, NY: Monthly Review Press.

Arrighi, G. (1994). *The Long Twentieth Century: Money, Power, and the Origins of Our Time*. London: Verso.

Arrighi, G., and Drangel, J. (1986). Stratification of the world-economy: an explanation of the semiperipheral zone. *Review*, 10 (1), 9-74.

Arrighi, G., Hopkins, T., and Wallerstein, I. (1989). *Anti-Systemic Movements*. London: Verso.

Babones, S., and Chase-Dunn, C., eds. (2012). *Routledge Handbook of World-Systems Analysis*. London: Routledge.

Beaujard, P. (2012). *Les Mondes de l'Ocean Indien (The Worlds of the Indian Ocean)*. Paris: Armand Colin.

Borgatti, S., and Everett, M. (1999). Models of core/periphery structures. *Social Networks*, 21 (4), 375-395.

Bornschier, V., and Chase-Dunn, C., eds. (2012). *The Future of Global Conflict*. London: Sage

Bornschier, V., and Suter, C. (2010). On the Evolution of Inequality in the World System. In: Suter, C., ed., *Inequality Beyond Globalization: Economic Changes, Social Transformations and the Dynamics of Inequality*, Zürich: LIT Verlag, 33-64.

Braudel, F. (1972 [1949]). *The Mediterranean and the Mediterranean World in the Age of Philip II*. Berkeley, CA: University of California Press.

Braudel, F. (1992). *Civilization and Capitalism, 15th–18th Century. Vol. 3: The Perspective of the World*. Berkeley, CA: University of California Press.

Brenner, R. (1977). The origins of capitalist development: a critique of neo-Smithian Marxism. *New Left Review*, 104, 121-140.

Bunker, S., and Ciccantell, P. (2005). *Globalization and the Race for Resources*. Baltimore, MD: Johns Hopkins University Press.

Chase-Dunn, C. (1981). Interstate system and capitalist world-economy: one logic or two. *International Studies Quarterly*, 25 (1), 19-42.

Chase-Dunn, C., and Hall, T. (1997). *Rise and Demise: Comparing World-Systems*. Boulder, CO: Westview.

Chase-Dunn, C. and Inoue, H. eds. (forthcoming). *Systemic Boundaries: Time Mapping. Globalization since the Bronze Age*. New York, NY: Springer.

Chew, S. (2001). *World Ecological Degradation*. Walnut Creek, CA: AltaMira.

Chew, S. (2018). *The Southeast Asia Connection: Trade and Polities in the Eurasian World Economy, 500 BC–AD 500*. New York, NY: Berghahn.

Chirot, D., ed. (1989). *The Origins of Backwardness in Eastern Europe*. Berkeley, CA: University of California Press.

Cioffi-Revilla, C. (1996). Origins and evolution of war and politics. *International Studies Quarterly*, 40 (1), 1-22.

Costa Lopez, J. (2021). International Relations in/and the Middle Ages. In de Carvalho, B., Costa Lopez, J., & Leira, H., eds. *Routledge Handbook of Historical International Relations*. Abingdon: Routledge.

de Carvalho, B. (2021). Sovereignty in Historical International Relations: Trajectories, Challenges and Implications. In de Carvalho, B., Costa Lopez, J., & Leira, H., eds. *Routledge Handbook of Historical International Relations*. Abingdon: Routledge.

de Carvalho, B., Costa Lopez, J., and Leira, H. (2021). Introduction: Historical International Relations. In de Carvalho, B., Costa Lopez, J., & Leira, H., eds. *Routledge Handbook of Historical International Relations*. Abingdon: Routledge.

Denemark, R. (2007). Epistemology of World System History. In *Encyclopedia of Life Support Systems*. Oxford: EOLSS Publishers.

Denemark, R. (2010). World System History. In: Denemark, R. A., Marlin-Bennett, R., eds., *The International Studies Encyclopedia*, Oxford: Wiley/Blackwell, 2553-2572.

Denemark, R., and Thomas, K. (1988). The Brenner-Wallerstein debate. *International Studies Quarterly*, 32 (1), 47-65.

Dunaway, W. (2012). The Centrality of the Household to the Modern World-System. In: Babones, S., and Chase-Dunn, C., eds., *Routledge Handbook of World-Systems Analysis*. London: Routledge, 453-461.

Ekholm-Friedman, K., and Friedman, J. (1982). 'Capital' imperialisms and exploitation in the ancient world-systems. *Review*, 6 (1), 87-110.

Erin, S., and Chase-Dunn, C. (2018). Global Political Sociology and World-Systems. In: Janoski, T., et al, eds., *Cambridge New Handbook of Political Sociology*, Cambridge: Cambridge University Press, 953-972.

Flint, C. (2010). Geographic Perspectives on World-Systems Theory. In: Denemark, R. A., Marlin-Bennett, R., eds., *The International Studies Encyclopedia*, Oxford: Wiley/Blackwell, 2828-2845.

Frank, A. G. (1966). The development of underdevelopment. *Monthly Review*, 18 (4), 17-31.

Frank, A. G. (1967). *Capitalism and Underdevelopment in Latin America*. New York, NY: Monthly Review Press.

Frank, A. G. (1991). Transnational ideological modes: feudalism, capitalism, socialism. *Critique of Anthropology*, 11 (2), 171-188.

Frank, A. G. (1998). *ReORIENT: Global Economy in the Asian Age*. Berkeley, CA: University of California Press.

Frank, A. G. (2014). *ReORIENTING the 19th Century: Global Economy in the Continuing Asian Age*. Boulder, CO: Paradigm.

Friedman, J., and Rowlands, M. (1977). Notes Toward an Epigenetic Model of the Evolution of 'Civilizations. In: Friedman, J., and Rowlands, M., eds., *The Evolution of Social Systems*, Pittsburgh, PA: University of Pittsburgh Press, 201-278.

Gereffi, G., and Korzeniewicz, M., eds. (1994). *Commodity Chains and Global Capitalism*. New York, NY: Greenwood Press.

Gills, B. and Frank, A. G. (2011 [1994]). The Modern World System under Asian Hegemony: The Silver Standard World Economy 1450-1750. Reprinted in: Manning, P., and Gills, B., eds., *Andre Gunder Frank and Global Development: Visions, Remembrances, and Explorations*. London: Routledge.

Gills, B., and Frank, A. G. (1992). World System Cycles, Crises, and Hegemonial Shifts 1700 BC to 1700 AD. *Review*, 15 (4), 621-687.

Gilman, N. (2003). *Mandarins of the Future: Modernization Theory in Cold War America*. Baltimore, MD: The Johns Hopkins University Press.

Goldfrank, W. (2012). Wallerstein's World-System: Roots and Contributions. In Babones, S., and Chase-Dunn, C., eds., *Routledge Handbook of World-Systems Analysis*, New York, NY: Routledge, 97-103.

Guillaume, X. (2021). Historical Periods and the Act of Periodisation. In de Carvalho, B., Costa Lopez, J., & Leira, H., eds. *Routledge Handbook of Historical International Relations*. Abingdon: Routledge.

Hall, T. (2012). Incorporation into and Merger of World-Systems. In: Babones, S., and Chase-Dunn, C., eds., *Routledge Handbook of World-Systems Analysis*, New York, NY: Routledge, 47-55.

Hall, T., Kardulias. P. N., and Chase-Dunn, C. (2011). World-systems analysis and archaeology: continuing the dialogue. *Journal of Archaeological Research*, 19, 233-279.

Hom, A. R. (2021). Time and History in International Relations. In de Carvalho, B., Costa Lopez, J., & Leira, H., eds. *Routledge Handbook of Historical International Relations*. Abingdon: Routledge.

Hopkins, T., and Wallerstein, I. (1979). Cyclical rhythms and secular trends of the capitalist world-economy: some premises, hypotheses, and questions. *Review*, 2 (4), 483-500.

Hornborg, A., and Crumley, C., eds. (2007). *The World System and the Earth System: Global Socioenvironmental Change and Sustainability since the Neolithic*. Walnut Creek, CA: Left Coast Press.

Inoue, H., et al. (2014). Urban Scale Shifts since the Bronze Age: Upsweeps, Collapses, and Semiperipheral Development. *IROWS Working Papers,* viewed on 20 October 2020 <http://irows.ucr.edu/papers/irows89/irows89.htm>.

Jorgenson, A. and Rice, J. (2012). The Sociology of Ecologically Unequal Exchange in Comparative Perspective. In: Babones, S., and Chase-Dunn, C., eds., *Routledge Handbook of World-Systems Analysis*, New York, NY: Routledge, 431-439.

Karatasli, S. S., and Kumral, S. (2018). Great Convergence of Third Great Divergence? Changes in the Global Distribution of Wealth. In Korzeniewicz, P. R., ed., *The World System as a Unit of Analysis: Past Contributions and Future Advances*, New York, NY: Routledge, 36-49.

Khutkyy, D., and Chase-Dunn, C. (2018). The World-System(s). In: Outhwaite, W., and Turner, S., eds., *Sage Handbook on Political Sociology*, London: Sage, 1067-1082.

Latham, M. (2000). *Modernization as Ideology: American Social Science and 'National Building' in the Kennedy Era*. Chapel Hill, NC: University of North Carolina Press.

Lawson, G. (2021). Revolutions: Integrating the International. In de Carvalho, B., Costa Lopez, J., & Leira, H., eds. *Routledge Handbook of Historical International Relations*. Abingdon: Routledge.

Lindio-McGovern, L. (2012). The Migration of Reproductive Labor from the Periphery to the Core and Semiperiphery under Neoliberal Globalization. In: Babones, S., and Chase-Dunn, C., eds., *Routledge Handbook of World-Systems Analysis*, New York, NY: Routledge, 476-478.

Modelski, G., and Denemark, R. (2008). *World System History*. Oxford: Eolss Publishers.

Modelski, G. and Thompson, W. R. (1996). *Leading Sectors and World Powers: The Coevolution of Global Politics and Economics*. Columbia, SC: University of South Carolina Press.

Moghadam, V. (2012). Anti-Systemic Movements Compared. In: Babones, S., and Chase-Dunn, C., eds., *Routledge Handbook of World-Systems Analysis*, New York, NY: Routledge, 476-478.

Murphy, C. (2018). Solving Global Problems May Require Addressing Global Inequalities. *Paper presented at the 2018 meeting of the International Studies Association*, San Francisco, CA.

Nemeth, R., and Smith, D. A. (1985). International trade and world-system structure: a multiple network analysis. *Review*, 8 (4), 517-560.

Pomeranz, K. (2000). *The Great Divergence. China, Europe, and the Making of the Modern World Economy*. Princeton, NJ: Princeton University Press.

Prigogine, I. (1996). The laws of chaos. *Review*, 19 (1), 1-9.

Rapkin, D., and Thompson, W. R. (2013). *Transition Scenarios: China and the United States in the Twenty-First Century*. Chicago, IL: University of Chicago Press.

Rasler, K., and Thompson, W. R. (2010). Systemic Theories of Conflict. In: Denemark, R. A., Marlin-Bennett, R., eds., *The International Studies Encyclopedia*, Oxford: Wiley/Blackwell,

Sanderson, S., ed. (1995). *Civilizations and World Systems: Studying World-Historical Change*. Walnut Creek, CA: AltaMira.

Sherratt, A. (1993). What would a bronze-age world system look like? Relations between temperate Europe and the Mediterranean in later prehistory. *Journal of European Archaeology*, 1 (2), 1-57.

Sherratt, A. (2000). Envisioning Global Change: A Long-Term Perspective. In R. Denemark, et al., eds., *World System History: The Social Science of Long-Term Change*. London: Routledge, 115-132.

Silver, B. (2003). *Forces of Labor: Workers' Movements and Globalization since 1870*. Cambridge: Cambridge University Press.

Smith, D. A., and White, D. (1992). Structure and dynamic of the global economy: network analysis of international trade 1965–1980. *Social Forces*, 70 (4), 857-893.

Stavrianos, L. S. (1981). *Global Rift*. New York, NY: William Morrow.

Suter, C., and Bergesen, A., eds. (2018). *The Return of Geopolitics*. Berlin: LitVerlag.

Suter, C., ed. (2010). *Inequality Beyond Globalization: Economic Changes, Social Transformations, and the Dynamics of Inequality*. Zürich: LitVerlag.

Timberlake, M. and Smith, D. A. (2012). Global Cities and World City Networks. In: Babones, S., and Chase-Dunn, C., eds., *Routledge Handbook of World-Systems Analysis*, New York, NY: Routledge, 247-255.

Wallerstein, I., ed. (1991). *Geopolitics and Geoculture: Essays on the Changing World-System*. Cambridge: Cambridge University Press.

Wallerstein, I., ed. (1991b). *Unthinking Social Science: The Limits of 19th Century Paradigms*. Cambridge: Polity.

Wallerstein, I., et al., eds. (1996). *Open the Social Sciences*. Stanford, CA: Stanford University Press.

Wallerstein, I. (1972). Three paths of national development in sixteenth-century Europe. *Studies in Comparative International Development*, 7, 95-101.

Wallerstein, I. (1974). *The Modern World-System, Vol. 1*. New York, NY: Academic Press.

Wallerstein, I. (1976). A world-system perspective on the social sciences. *British Journal of Sociology*, 27 (3), 345-354.

Wallerstein, I. (1977). The tasks of historical social science: an editorial. *Review*, 1 (1), 3-7.

Wallerstein, I. (1999). *The End of the World as We Know It: Social Science for the Twenty-First Century*. Minneapolis, MN: University of Minnesota Press.

Wilkinson, D. (1987). Central civilization. *Comparative Civilizations Review*, 17, 31-59.

Wilkinson, D. 1994. Civilizations are world systems! *Comparative Civilizations Review*, 30, 59-71.

5

HISTORICAL SOCIOLOGY IN INTERNATIONAL RELATIONS

The challenge of the global

Julian Go, George Lawson and Benjamin de Carvalho[1]

Introduction

The importance of Historical Sociology (HS) for the development of Historical International Relations (HIR) cannot be overstated. While the discipline of IR has been intimately – albeit often implicitly and tacitly – connected to History since its inception (see Lawson, 2012; in this volume, de Carvalho, Costa Lopez, and Leira, 2021), historical work in IR has tended to rely more heavily on the methods and concepts of HS than on the craft of historians. In fact, from the 1980s onwards, much of the historically oriented contributions to IR relied heavily on classic works of HS – most notably works on state formation (see Leira and de Carvalho, 2016; de Carvalho and Leira, 2021a for discussions). As IR – at least in its American guise – had almost forgotten how to be historical by the end of the Cold War, the recovery of historical thinking within the discipline happened much through HS. Thus, distinguishing between HS and HIR today is a question less of different ontologies (especially since the turn to Global Historical Sociology advocated by two of the authors of this chapter) or epistemologies (since they are largely shared), but of definition or orientation; in short, Miles' Law, 'Where you stand depends on where you sit'.

While much of the work in HIR is sociological in character, HS covers a broad spectrum of HIR. However, recent disciplinary developments within IR, notably with the institutionalization of the Historical International Relations Section (HIST) at the International Studies Association (ISA) and its European counterpart (EISA) have aimed to see the historical project within IR as a broader one, covering for instance also international law and international legal history, developments in conceptual history and the history of ideas, and more. It is no longer the case that HS covers HIR *in toto*, although it is still a central component of HIR.

At its core, HS has been concerned with understanding the roots of our current predicament. That is, how can we make sense of modernity through understanding the origins of, and paths to, modernity? Of obvious relevance to dominant strands of IR, HS scholarship examining state formation and the impact of war have been most commonly cited in IR and 'imported' into the discipline. As these speak to the dominant realist imaginary of international politics, they became powerful tools in the toolkit of early constructivists seeking to fire their first shots at the 'neo-neo' edifice in the late 1980s (see Leira and de Carvalho, 2016). Paradoxically, in spite of its association with the constructivist agenda, as Steve Smith provocatively stated in 2001 (Smith,

2001), HS in IR was and had by and large remained stubbornly statist in its approach. While speaking directly to the making of modernity in the West through telling the story of the West, HS had offered few insights into processes of global change, largely focusing on explaining the historical trajectory of a country via dynamics *internal* to that territory, combining this with attention to the ways in which other territories lacked comparable dynamics. Until relatively recently, the underlying assumption of much HS has been that historical development arose from the endogenous characteristics of a handful of powerful (Western) polities.

These tendencies are mirrored by the broader discipline. For much of its disciplinary history, IR has studied the workings of a small part of the world (the West) through a relatively sparse analytical lens (the 'states under anarchy' problematique). Only recently has IR scholarship begun to make clear the ways in which the emergence of the discipline was intimately associated with issues of colonial management (e.g. Vitalis, 2010, 2016; in this volume Bayly, 2021), the diverse range of polities that constitute the international system (e.g. Phillips and Sharman, 2015), and the myriad of social forces, from market exchanges to cultural flows, that make up 'the international' (e.g. Hobson, Lawson, and Rosenberg, 2010; Anievas and Gogu, 2021).

A number of recent works have highlighted the problems associated with such a Western statist view (e.g. Pomeranz, 2000; Christian, 2004; Belich, 2009; Osterhammel, 2014) to the extent that providing an overview of HS today without simultaneously suggesting a way out of the statist impasse is no longer tenable. Recent scholarship has shown that the world has long been a space of 'imperial globality' in which historical trajectories have been intertwined through power relations (Burton and Ballantyne, 2012: 13). Contemporary world politics sits squarely downwind from this space of 'structural entanglements'. As such, the most productive way of providing an overview of HS is through gauging the productive tension underlying a discussion of historical sociology vs *global* historical sociology. This allows for the double aim of (1) providing an overview of HS relevant to IR, while at the same time; (2) pointing at ways to make HS more global.

Historical Sociology: the need for a Global Historical Sociology

While HS as an institutional field of inquiry is multifaceted, it shares certain underlying concerns and themes. Besides its concern with temporality, which requires close attention to processes of change, sequence, and the unfolding of action over time (see Hom, 2021), historical sociology's underlying rubric is its focus on the modern; more specifically, on the emergence and constitution of modernity – or as Adams, Clemens, and Orloff (2005: 2) put it, in 'how people and societies became modern or not'. From the classical founders of historical sociology such as Karl Marx, Max Weber, and W.E.B. DuBois to its 'first wave' represented by Richard Bendix, Barrington Moore Jr., and the early work of S.N. Eisenstadt, historical sociology has sought to illuminate the dynamics and dilemmas involved in the emergence of modernity (Adams, Clemens, and Orloff, 2005: 3–7).

As noted above, a range of scholarship has begun to demonstrate that modernity has always been a transnational and global development, occurring on scales higher (and at times lower) than the nation-state, including through imperialism (e.g. Bhambra, 2007a; Goody, 1996; Pomeranz, 2000; Hobson, 2004; Sassen, 2007). Industrialization, ideas of sovereignty, and the modern, rational state: these and other core features of modernity were formed and continue to operate at transnational and global scales (Buzan and Lawson, 2015).

However, as yet, historical sociology has not fully elaborated the concepts and theories that could be used in a systematic analysis of transnational and global processes. To be clear, the issue is not that comparative historical sociology has narrowed its lens to Europe or the United States.

As historical sociologists themselves make clear (e.g. Mahoney, 2011), non-European parts of the world are firmly on the agenda. Rather, the issue is that historical sociology has not yet systematically analysed and theorized the connections *between* or *through* societies and states (whether in the West or elsewhere). In other words, historical sociology is known best for studies of state formation, economic development, gender politics, class formation, and social movements *within* states.[2] However rich such studies are, they are limited by dint of their methodological nationalism – even as transnational and global dynamics (in the form of markets, transnational ideologies, and inter-imperial conflicts) intrude on such accounts, they are rarely given adequate attention, let alone effectively theorized. At the same time, historical sociology is home to a range of comparative accounts that examine the divergent developmental pathways taken by particular states (e.g. Slater, 2010; Mahoney, 2010). Yet these studies are hindered by their internalism – again, even as transnational and global dynamics are often central to how these studies conduct their empirical analysis, such dynamics are neither effectively theorized nor integrated into causal accounts, which remain centred around endogenous factors.

This is true, in particular, of the main work that came out of the 'second-wave' of historical sociology (Adams, Clemens, and Orloff, 2005). Indeed, one can be forgiven for noting that second-wave historical sociology has suffered from the same limitations that afflicted disciplinary history decades before its transnational turn: *state-centrism* (Go, 2014). This is the assumption that social relations are territorialized along state lines (Goettlich and Branch, 2021). Social processes, as well as cultural and political relations, are treated as 'contained' by the nation-state. What counts occurs within the nation-state. Relations between states are less important; relations, processes, and forms through or 'above' nation-states are of little interest either. In the strongest form of state-centrism, such relations are bracketed out altogether.

Second-wave historical sociology is not unusual in its state-centrism – such an orientation has dominated the social sciences since their inception, or at the very least since the Second World War (Taylor, 1996; Wallerstein, 2001). For historical sociology, a particular brand of state-centrism has been manifest in at least two ways (Go, 2013). The first is the more straightforward: the main objects of analysis have been nation-states. The historian Sven Beckert (in Bayly et al., 2006: 1455) usefully conceptualizes transnational history as premised upon 'the interconnectedness of human history as a whole'; transnational history 'acknowledges the extraordinary importance of states ... but it also pays attention to networks, processes, beliefs, and institutions that transcend these politically-defined spaces'. This does not characterize second-wave historical sociology, which was instead interested in class formation, types of political regimes, collective action and revolutions, welfare states, gender relations, or economic and political development *within* national states. This is most evident in the proliferation of research and theory on the state – the very research and theory for which second-wave historical sociology became renowned (Evans, Rueschemeyer, and Skocpol, 1985). While this work fruitfully examined state policies, welfare regimes, or other state forms, it rarely, if ever, studied the international organizations that national states confronted, the transnational networks of ideas that stage managers formed part of, or the imperial webs that states were embedded within (see Nexon, 2009). Furthermore, the states theorized in this work were always 'national states' (in Tilly's, 1990 terminology), and only rarely imperial-states or city-states, or members of regional associations and interstate organizations. Finally, the study of the state itself became dominant. Why emphasize the 'state'? Why didn't historical sociologists look at migration flows or the transatlantic slave trade, trading companies or international non-governmental organizations, and global health regimes or transnational women's movements? When 'bringing the state back in', this scholarship blocked virtually everything else out.[3]

The point here is not to deny that the state is an important unit of analysis – of course, it is. Rather, the point is that a dominant focus on the state has acted as an obstacle to effective analysis not only of other units, but also to how states interacted with these. What began as an analytical move became, over time, an ontological one: the state acted as a cage not just of social scientific enquiry but of social relations *in toto*. In other words, analysts acted as if states really were containers of ideas and practices. Yet there are a myriad of actors, forms, and processes operating at different scales that states try to manage, regulate, or discipline but which they ultimately cannot.

Some second-wave scholarship recognized this point. For example, Skocpol's (1979) seminal study of social revolutions *did* include analysis of international factors. For Skocpol (1979: 22–30), the elision of international factors in previous accounts of revolution (not least by Barrington Moore, Jr.) was something she sought explicitly to rectify. Similarly, Charles Tilly (1990: 26) referred to international factors in his analysis of European state formation: 'Other states—and eventually the entire system of states—strongly affected the path of change followed by any particular state'. For Tilly (1990: 23), competition between states in the form of war and preparation for war was the determining factor in dynamics of state formation: war made states just as states made war.

But here arises the second way in which historical sociology's nation-state-centrism made its appearance – as a 'realist' theory of the international that limits this realm to the regulation of violence. For most second-wave historical sociology, the international system was treated as a bare space of 'anarchy' largely devoid of empires, transnational networks of actors, ideas that crossed borders, cultural flows, and so on. This is a radically impoverished vision of the international. There are processes, logics, and forms in the international realm that are irreducible to the actions of states, just as state policies and militaries do not exhaust the complex reality of the international system. Yet the references by second-wave historical sociologists to international dynamics were largely limited to the coercive realm. For instance, the interstate system that Tilly historicizes in *Coercion, Capital and European States, AD 990–1992* turns out not to be little more than a collection of polities battling for position in the European theatre. It is *war* that makes and remakes states: 'War drives state-formation and transformation' (Tilly, 1990: 20–23). For Tilly, the international system is a largely passive arena – a space of conflict-strewn competition between states-as-actors (Tilly, 1990: 23).[4] Similarly, Skocpol's overarching argument is that social revolutions are primarily caused by state breakdown, which is in turn most often brought about by defeat in war (Skocpol, 1979: 60–63, 186, 95–98, 104). As in Tilly's work, Skocpol's (1979: 20) bellicist theory of the state summons a realist theory of the international: the international is merely a 'structure of competing states'.

A final example is provided by Michael Mann's (1986, 1993, 2013, 2014) four-volume *The Sources of Social Power*. Mann's very warrant for his reinterpretation of the 'history of power in human societies' is that he had 'arrived at a distinctive, general way of looking at human societies that is at odds with models of society dominant within sociology and historical writing'; that is, societies should be seen as 'constituted of multiple overlapping and intersecting sociospatial networks of power' (Mann, 1986: 1). Theoretically, this view of social relations could adduce to an analysis of global networks that seep through and across nation-states rather than being contained within them. However, in Mann's empirical analysis, this promising approach does not come to fruition. Instead, when referring to global or transnational factors that explain the rise of states, classes, and capitalism, he reverts to two different, arguably opposed theorizations of global space, with one dominating the other: 'culture' (Mann, 1993: 753) and interstate competition, especially war, where the latter is the one that dominates his analysis. Such competition and war requires 'military-fiscal extraction' which imposes heavy tax burdens on populations (Mann,

1993: 214–225). In turn, this imperative impacts domestic class conflict and state formation. In Mann's work, as in Tilly's and Skocpol's, the global is *primarily* a space of war – all three theorists hold the same bellicist *cum* realist conception of the global.[5]

Historical sociology has not erred by discussing militaries or war – both are powerfully generative of how domestic and international orders have emerged and been shaped over time. The issue is that Skocpol, Tilly, and Mann reduce the international to little more than war between competitive states in a sparse environment represented by 'anarchy'. Despite repeated gestures to the productive capacity of 'the international', their analysis contains only the thinnest conceptualization of this sphere. This means that all three theorists buy into the notion that violence is largely, at least in the modern era, something carried out by and between states. This assumption omits the multiple forms of violence that escape the nation-state frame, from the procreant role played by colonial and postcolonial forces in 'Western' wars to the impact of ostensibly 'private' actors on coercive practices (see Barkawi, 2017; de Carvalho and Leira 2021b). Wedded to state-centrism and an accompanying 'states-under-anarchy' motif, the rich insights Skocpol *et al.* furnish in terms of domestic outcomes are not matched by equivalent insights into the relations that flow between or across boundaries.

Second-wave historical sociology, therefore, derived a range of resources through which to think about international, transnational, and global processes. Mann opened up the possibility of theorizing transnational 'networks' and global norms; Tilly intimated how 'empire-states' may have constituted global order; Skocpol referred to 'world historical time'. But the promise of a fully fledged 'global imagination' was not fulfilled (Magubane, 2005). Instead, state-centric modes of analysis persisted and, in some cases, largely domesticated second-wave analysis.

More recent work within the so-called third wave of historical sociology (Adams, Clemens, and Orloff, 2005) aims to go beyond the confines of the nation-state. For instance, something of a nascent transnational or global turn can be seen in recent sociological examinations of empire and colonialism (e.g. Adams, 2005; Go, 2009, 2011; Lange, Mahoney, and Hau, 2006; Mahoney, 2010; Wimmer and Feinstein, 2010), as well as in emerging work on the transnational activities of missionaries (e.g. Stamatov, 2010), trading companies (e.g. Adams, 1996; Erikson and Bearman, 2006; Wilson, 2011), maritime violence (e.g. Norton, 2014; Leira and de Carvalho, 2011; Leira and de Carvalho, 2021b), international organizations (e.g. Chorev, 2012), revolutions (e.g. Lawson, 2019), and culturally based reinterpretations of modernity (e.g. Bhambra, 2007a; Reed and Adams, 2011). A related development can be seen in the rising interest in postcolonial studies within historical sociology and social theory (e.g. Bhambra, 2007b, 2010; Boatcâ and Costa, 2010). This work can serve as the basis for a more *global* historical sociology.

Historical Sociology in IR

So too does companion work in IR. At the risk of oversimplification, there have been two main stages in the development of historical sociology in IR. The first stage, appearing around the same time as second-wave historical sociology and much influenced by it, was oriented around three core wagers. First, emphasis was placed on the interaction between national and international scales, with particular attention to the ways in which pressures emanating from the international system reshaped national societies (e.g. Hobson, 1997). Second, historical sociologists in IR sought to transcend the materialism of mainstream IR by attending to the impact of transnational ideologies and norms – here Mann's (1986) emphasis on the potentially 'transcendent' power of ideology was a key resource (e.g. Ruggie, 1993; Reus-Smit, 1999). Finally, this scholarship emphasized the importance of discontinuity in the international realm, thereby disrupting mainstream claims as to the 'enduring sameness' of world politics (e.g. Cox, 1987; Rosenberg, 1994; Spruyt, 1994; see the discussion in Leira and de Carvalho, 2016).

More recent historical sociological work in IR is less influenced by second-wave historical sociology than its predecessor. Rather, a wide range of scholarship has opened up mainstream assumptions about how to conceive and theorize 'the international'. Contemporary historical sociology in IR covers a broad range of sensibilities (materialist and ideational, structural and agency based) and examines a similarly broad range of issue-areas (from the legacies of colonialism to the development of the human rights regime). Historical sociology in IR has sought not just to unpack the different forms that international orders have taken in the past, but also the ways in which the contemporary international order cannot be treated as a predetermined given. Proponents share an understanding of the centrality of discontinuity, contingency, and particularity in international processes alongside an interest in examining how social forms and processes shape international events. As such, historical sociology in IR offers a double punch: a focus on the rich detail of historical international relations alongside an emphasis on how configurations of social relations combine in particular contexts in order to generate discrete outcomes.

If historical sociology in IR has managed to establish a foothold in the discipline, there are two challenges that scholars working in this idiom confront. First, historical sociology in IR has become somewhat unwieldy, making its *distinctive* contribution hard to identify (Lawson, 2007). Indeed, quite often, historical sociology in IR boils down to little more than a commitment to inject historical sociological insights into IR without necessarily explaining *why* IR scholarship should take note of such research. Paradoxically, therefore, just as the work of historical sociologists in IR has proliferated, so its core rationale has become less clear and the specific challenge it offers has receded from view. The second problem is rooted in a more intellectual challenge: the failure shared by both classical social theorists and IR scholars to 'theorize the international' (Rosenberg, 2006). As a discipline, IR appears to have a semipermeable membrane that allows ideas from other disciplines in, but blocks substantive traffic out.

If such looting and pillaging raids are to be curtailed, historical sociology in IR needs to make a comparable move to that undertaken by historical sociologists working in Sociology. Indeed, the task faced by the former is the mirror image to that confronting the latter. Whereas historical sociologists in Sociology are burdened by the internalism that pervades state-centrism and methodological nationalism, historical sociologists in IR are waylaid by 'externalism': the bracketing of the international realm into a discrete sphere of analysis with its own distinct logics. The simultaneous existence of multiplicity *and* interactivity – 'interactive multiplicity' – is what constitutes the field of IR; it is also what historical sociology in IR is best placed to interrogate (Hobson, Lawson, and Rosenberg, 2010).

Globalizing Historical International Relations

Where HS has contributed to the opening the state to historical inquiry in IR, as argued above, this has nevertheless happened within the confines of a statist ontology – one that can no longer be defended in light of the recent focus on the importance of transnational and global dynamics. It has also demonstrated the extent to which IR must further globalize its concepts (Çapan et al., 2021). At first glance, these may seem like odd statements to make. After all, the relationship between history and IR has often been close (Suganami, 1999; Kratochwil, 2006; Lawson, 2012). And what social scientific discipline is more 'global' than IR? However, for much of its disciplinary history, IR has been provincially oriented towards Western interests, concepts, and concerns (Hoffman, 1987; Wæver, 1998; Buzan and Little, 2001;

Hui, 2005; Shilliam, 2011). Furthermore, despite the apparent closeness between history and IR, over the past generation much mainstream IR theory has assumed an ahistorical (not to mention asocial) character, best illustrated by Waltz's (1979) neorealism and Keohane's (1984) neoliberal institutionalism. Both of these approaches take the main actors of the international system to be sovereign states. Both see states as unitary actors with interests that are predetermined and universal across time and place. And both work with the assumption that the international realm is distinct by virtue of its anarchical nature – in other words, its lack of an overarching sovereign authority. Put simply, neorealism and neoliberal institutionalisms rely upon the same assumptions about the international sphere that many second-wave historical sociologists wittingly or unwittingly incorporated in their work. This generates certain analytic and theoretical limitations, not least regarding the historical – or rather ahistorical – canvass painted by conventional IR scholarship.

IR scholarship that defends the views associated with Waltz, Keohane, and their variants see their strength as lying in the parsimony of their assumptions. Because actors are of a single kind and because the structural context of anarchy is unchanging, it is possible to reduce the international to a small number of derivative logics: a self-help system, the requirement for states to prioritize survival, a recurring security dilemma, and the mechanism of the balance of power. If anarchy stands as a constant structural condition, the international sphere appears as a continuous, static holding pen for 'actual' international relations. This means that IR scholarship is – or should be – concerned with mapping the relentless struggle for survival (as in neorealism) or the conditions for cooperation (as in neoliberalism) that take place within a timeless and spaceless anarchical system.

From this, assumption of the 'enduring sameness' of international anarchy (Waltz, 1979) flows a particular view of history. Because in structural terms at least, international relations is a realm of 'recurrence and repetition', history becomes little more than a contextless sphere of timeless 'lessons'. This lack of concern for temporality generates a selection bias in which history becomes little more than the predetermined site for the empirical verification of theoretical claims. Although *history* as a point of data collection is often present in mainstream accounts, *historicism* – a commitment to historically locating practices and dynamics, a concern for the contingent, disruptive, constitutive impact of historical events and processes, and the study of contextualized rationalities and inter-subjectivities – is largely absent. Most mainstream approaches use history merely in order to code findings, mine data, or as a source of *post factum* explanations (Isacoff, 2002; Lawson, 2012; in this volume, MacKay and LaRoche, 2021).

By taking a static picture of the structure of world politics (the anarchical states-system), much mainstream IR occludes differences between polities (such as empires and nation-states), fails to distinguish between types of international order (such as imperial and sovereign orders), ignores *social* structural forces (such as capitalism, patriarchy, and racism), and reduces agency to the actions of state managers, financiers, and generals. In this way, historically specific *social* categories – the balance of power, sovereignty, anarchy, etc. – are seen as stable, fixed entities that can be deployed without regard for time and space specificity. Such thinking results in the swallowing of a 'continuist mystique' in which the past is ransacked in order to explain the present: the contest between Athens and Sparta is transplanted to the Cold War in order to elucidate the stand-off between the United States and the Soviet Union; all wars, whether they be guerrilla insurgencies or great power conflicts, are explicable by the basic fact – or permissive context – of anarchy; and all political units – city-states, empires, nation-states, and transnational alliances – are functionally undifferentiated. The result is a 'gigantic optical illusion' that generates an isomorphic homology of social forms (Hobson, 2002).

Against this background, historical sociology in IR has sought to inject historicist insights into IR, demonstrating the hierarchical rather than anarchical formations that international orders assume (e.g. Cox, 1987; Keene, 2002; Hobson, 2014; Bially Mattern, and Zarakol, 2016), the distinctions that can be drawn between modes of international order-making (e.g. Zhang, 2009; Buzan and Lawson, 2015; Phillips and Sharman, 2015: 202), the specious historical reading of the Peace (or 'Myth') of Westphalia upon which conventional approaches rely (Osiander, 2001; Teschke, 2003; de Carvalho et al., 2011), and more. Such insights have joined the array of historically informed approaches that have emerged, or re-emerged, in recent decades, from constructivism (e.g. Ruggie, 1993; Reus-Smit, 1999, 2013; Nexon, 2009) to neoclassical realism (e.g. Schweller, 2006), and from approaches associated with the English School (e.g. Buzan and Little, 2001; Keene, 2002; Suzuki, 2009; Zarakol, 2011) to postcolonial analysis (e.g. Grovogui, 1996; Inayatullah and Blaney, 2004; Shilliam, 2011). The result is a shared concern with historicizing and, thereby, denaturalizing the ahistorical, asocial assumptions of mainstream IR.

Conclusion: addressing the global through history

There are, therefore, striking parallels between the critiques of second-wave historical sociology and the emergence of historical sociology in IR. Second-wave historical sociology generated commanding accounts of internal development and change. And Skocpol, Mann, Tilly, and others used their awareness of the historical diversity of social orders to construct searching comparative accounts that distinguished between pathways of historical development on the basis of the presence or absence of certain endogenous factors. However, this tradition tended to reduce the international to a zone of timeless geopolitical imperatives in which the main actors were independent nation-states. As a consequence, these scholars did little to close the gap between 'inside' and 'outside', 'internal' and 'external', and 'domestic' and 'international' – to the contrary, they hardened it. The 'international' was externalized from the object domain of historical sociology even as historical sociologists in IR showed how the multifaceted effects of global and transnational dynamics – processes of capitalist accumulation, cultural flows that accelerated or redirected historical pathways, or patterns of integration that extended far beyond single polities – contained a constitutive effect on dynamics of continuity and change (Hobson, Lawson, and Rosenberg, 2010).

For second-wave historical sociologists, a particular subgrouping of these effects – political-military relations – was seen as representing the limits of the international, or at least as its principal contribution to the wider academy (Mann, 2006). For their part, historical sociologists in IR, even as they worked from a wide range of sensibilities and explored a plethora of issue-areas, did little to overcome the 'externalist' logic associated with realism. Indeed, just as was the case with second-wave historical sociologists, their enquiry often served to strengthen the boundary between 'inside' and 'outside'. To this end, a concern for the interactive multiplicity of international dynamics provides a common resource through which historical sociologists working in both Sociology and IR can transcend their disciplinary shortcomings. Going beyond the state-centrism that characterizes – and constrains – second-wave historical sociology carries the promise of a truly global historical sociology in IR, one that can make sense of units and interaction well beyond the confines of the state. To be sure, states are (still) the principal forms of political authority in the contemporary world. They are also key sites of identity and affective sentiment. But, taking the state seriously means seeing it not as a static, independent object but as an entity-in-motion that is embedded within, and formed by, wider flows, circuits, and networks (Go and Lawson, 2017).

Suggestions for further reading

Adams, J., Clemens, E. and Orloff A. S., eds. (2005). *Remaking Modernity*. Durham: Duke University Press.

Bhambra, G. (2014). *Connected Sociologies*. London: Bloomsbury.

Go, J., and Lawson, G., eds. (2017b). *Global Historical Sociology*. Cambridge: Cambridge University Press.

Hobden, S., and Hobson, J., eds. (2002). *Historical Sociology of International Relations*. Cambridge: Cambridge University Press.

Skocpol, T., ed. (1984). *Vision and Method in Historical Sociology*. New York, NY: Cambridge University Press.

Wimmer, A., and Glick Schiller, N. (2002). Methodological nationalism and beyond. *Global Networks*, 2 (4), 301-334.

Notes

1 This contribution is based on Go and Lawson (2017).

2 It would be impractical to cite all of the works on these themes, but for important overviews, see: Adams, Clemens, and Orloff (2005); Calhoun (1996); and Smith (1991).

3 See the critique in Towns (2009). One notable exception is the contribution by Peter Evans to *Bringing the State Back In* (in Evans et al. 1985).

4 So important was this debt to realism that Tilly's analysis (alongside the broader move to 'Bringing the State Back In') helped to foster a resurgence in realist inspired analysis of state formation (e.g. Brewer, 1990; Downing, 1992; Ertman, 1997; Spruyt, 1994). This was not the only link between realism and historical sociology – a further example can be found in the cross-pollination of ideas between hegemonic stability theory and world systems' analysis (e.g. Chase-Dunn and Hall, 1997; Gilpin, 1981).

5 In Volume 2 of *Social Sources*, Mann (1993: 258) explicitly refers to Morgenthau as providing the model for his thinking on international relations. For discussions of Mann's realism, see Hobden (1999), Hobson (2006), and Lawson (2006); for responses, see: Mann (2006).

References

Adams, J. (1996). Principals and agents, colonialists and company men: the decay of colonial control. *American Sociological Review*, 61 (1), 12-28.

Adams, J. (2005). *The Familial State: Ruling Families and Merchant Capitalism in Early Modern Europe*. Ithaca, NY: Cornell University Press.

Anievas, A., and Gogu, C. (2021). Capitalism and 'the International': A Historical Approach. In de Carvalho, B., Costa Lopez, J., & Leira, H., eds. *Routledge Handbook of Historical International Relations*. Abingdon: Routledge.

Barkawi, T. (2017). *Soldiers of Empire*. Cambridge: Cambridge University Press.

Bayly, M. (2021). Imperialism: Beyond the 'Re-turn to Empire' in International Relations. In de Carvalho, B., Costa Lopez, J., & Leira, H., eds. *Routledge Handbook of Historical International Relations*. Abingdon: Routledge.

Bayly, C. A., Beckert, S., Connelly, M., Hofmeyr, I., Kozol, W., and Seed, P. (2006). AHR conversation: on transnational history. *American Historical Review*, 111 (5), 1440-1464.

Belich, J. (2009). *Replenishing the Earth: The Settler Revolution and the Rise of the Anglo-World, 1783–1939*. New York, NY: Oxford University Press.

Bhambra, G. K. (2007a). *Rethinking Modernity: Postcolonialism and the Sociological Imagination*. Houndmills: Palgrave-MacMillan.

Bhambra, G. K. (2007b). Sociology and postcolonialism: another 'missing' revolution? *Sociology*, 41 (5), 871-884.

Bhambra, G. K. (2010). Historical sociology, international relations and connected histories. *Cambridge Review of International Affairs*, 23 (1), 127-143.

Bially Mattern, J., and Zarakol, A. (2016). Hierarchies in world politics. *International Organization*, 70 (4), 623-654.

Boatcâ, M., and Costa, S. (2010). Postcolonial Sociology: A Research Agenda. In: E. Gutiérrez Rodríguez, M. Boatcâ, and S. Costa, eds., *Decolonizing European Sociology: Transdisciplinary Approaches*, Burlington, Surrey: Ashgate, 13-32.

Brewer, J. (1990). *The Sinews of Power: War, Money, and the English State, 1688–1783*. Cambridge, MA: Harvard University Press.

Burton, A., and Ballantyne, T. (2012). Introduction. In: A. Burton, and T. Ballantyne, eds., *Empires and the Reach of the Global*, Cambridge, MA: The Belknap Press of Harvard University Press, 1-26.

Buzan, B., and Lawson, G. (2015). *The Global Transformation: History, Modernity, and the Making of International Relations*. Cambridge: Cambridge University Press.

Buzan, B., and Little, R. (2001). Why international relations has failed as an intellectual project and what to do about it. *Millennium*, 30 (1), 19-39.

Calhoun, C. (1996). The Rise and Domestication of Historical Sociology. In: T. McDonald, ed., *The Historic Turn in the Human Sciences*, Ann Arbor, MI: University of Michigan Press, 305-338.

Çapan, Z. G., dos Reis, F., and Grasten, M., (2021). Global Histories: Connections and Circulations in Historical International Relations. In de Carvalho, B., Costa Lopez, J., & Leira, H., eds. *Routledge Handbook of Historical International Relations*. Abingdon: Routledge.

Chase-Dunn, C., and Hall, T. (1997). *Rise and Demise: Comparing World-Systems*. Boulder, CO: Westview Press.

Chorev, N. (2012). *The World Health Organization Between North and South*. Ithaca, NY: Cornell University Press.

Christian, D. (2004). *Maps of Time*. Berkeley, CA: University of California Press.

Cox, R. (1987). *Production, Power and World Order*. New York, NY: Columbia University Press.

de Carvalho, B., Costa Lopez, J., and Leira, H. (2021). Introduction: Historical International Relations. In de Carvalho, B., Costa Lopez, J., & Leira, H., eds. *Routledge Handbook of Historical International Relations*. Abingdon: Routledge.

de Carvalho, B., and Leira, H. (2021a). State Formation and Historical International Relations. In de Carvalho, B., Costa Lopez, J., & Leira, H., eds. *Routledge Handbook of Historical International Relations*. Abingdon: Routledge.

de Carvalho, B., and Leira, H. (2021b). Protestant Privateering and Overseas Expansion, ca.1570–1620. In: B. de Carvalho, and H. Leira, eds., *The Sea and International Relations*, Manchester: Manchester University Press.

de Carvalho, B., Leira, H., and Hobson, J. (2011). The big bangs of IR: the myths that your teachers still tell you about 1648 and 1919. *Millennium*, 39 (3), 735-758.

Downing, B. (1992). *The Military Revolution and Political Change*. Princeton, NJ: Princeton University Press.

Erikson, E., and Bearman, P. (2006). Malfeasance and the foundations for global trade. *American Journal of Sociology*, 112 (1), 195-230.

Ertman, T. (1997). *Birth of the Leviathan*. Cambridge: Cambridge University Press.

Evans, P. B., Rueschemeyer, D., and Skocpol, T. (1985). *Bringing the State Back In*. Cambridge/New York: Cambridge University Press.

Gilpin, R. (1981). *War and Change in World Politics*. Cambridge: Cambridge University Press.

Go, J. (2009). The 'new' sociology of empire and colonialism. *Sociology Compass*, 3 (5), 775-788.

Go, J. (2011). *Patterns of Empire: the British and American Empires, 1688–present*. Cambridge: Cambridge University Press.

Go, J. (2013). For a postcolonial sociology. *Theory & Society*, 42 (1), 25-55.

Go, J. (2014). Occluding the global: analytic bifurcation, causal scientism, and alternatives in historical sociology. *Journal of Globalization Studies*, 5 (1), 122-136.

Goettlich, K., and Branch, J. (2021). Borders and Boundaries: Making Visible What Divides. In de Carvalho, B., Costa Lopez, J., & Leira, H., eds. *Routledge Handbook of Historical International Relations*. Abingdon: Routledge.

Go, J., and Lawson, G. (2017). Introduction: For a Global Historical Sociology. In: J. Go, and G. Lawson, eds., *Global Historical Sociology*, Cambridge: Cambridge University Press, 1-34.

Goody, J. (1996). *The East in the West*. Cambridge: Cambridge University Press.

Grovogui, S. (1996). *Sovereigns, Quasi Sovereigns, and Africans*. Minneapolis, MN: University of Minnesota Press.

Hobden, S. (1999). Theorising the international system: perspectives from historical sociology. *Review of International Studies*, 25 (2), 257-271.

Hobson, J. (1997). *The Wealth of States*. Cambridge: Cambridge University Press.

Hobson, J. M. (2002). What's at Stake in Bringing Historical Sociology Back into International Relations? In: S. Hobden, and J. Hobson, eds., *Historical Sociology of International Relations*, Cambridge: Cambridge University Press, 3-41.

Hobson, J. M. (2004). *The Eastern Origins of Western Civilization*. Cambridge: Cambridge University Press.

Hobson, J. M. (2006). Eurocentrism and neorealism in the 'Fall of Mann': will the real Mann please stand up? *Millenium – Journal of International Studies*, 34 (2), 517-527.

Hobson, J. M. (2014). The twin self-delusions of IR: why 'Hierarchy' and not 'Anarchy' is the core concept of IR. *Millennium*, 42 (3), 557-575.

Hobson, J. M., Lawson, G., and Rosenberg, J. (2010). Historical Sociology. In: R. A. Denemark, ed., *The International Studies Encyclopaedia*, Oxford: Wiley.

Hoffman, S. (1987). An American Social Science: IR. In: S. Hoffman, ed., *Janus and Minerva: Essays in International Relations*, Boulder, CO: Westview, 3-24.

Hom, A. R. (2021). Time and History in International Relations. In de Carvalho, B., Costa Lopez, J., & Leira, H., eds. *Routledge Handbook of Historical International Relations*. Abingdon: Routledge.

Hui, V. T.-B. (2005). *War and State Formation in Ancient China and Early Modern Europe*. Cambridge: Cambridge University Press.

Inayatullah, N., and Blaney, D. (2004). *International Relations and the Problem of Difference*. London: Routledge.

Isacoff, J. B. (2002). On the historical imagination of international relations. *Millennium*, 31 (3), 603-626.

Keene, E. (2002). *Beyond the Anarchical Society*. Cambridge: Cambridge University Press.

Keohane, R. O. (1984). *After Hegemony*. Princeton, NJ: Princeton University Press.

Kratochwil, F. (2006). History, action and identity. *European Journal of International Relations*, 12 (1), 5-29.

Lange, M., Mahoney, J., and von Hau, M. 2006. Colonialism and development: a comparative analysis of Spanish and British Colonies. *American Journal of Sociology*, 111 (5), 1412-1462.

Lawson, G. (2006). A conversation with Michael Mann. *Millennium*, 34 (2), 477-508.

Lawson, G. (2007). Historical sociology in international relations: open society, research programme and vocation. *International Politics*, 44 (4), 343-368.

Lawson, G. (2012). The eternal divide? History and international relations. *European Journal of International Relations*, 18 (2), 203226

Leira, H., and de Carvalho, B. (2011). Privateers of the North Sea: at world's end. In: A. Colás, and B. Mabee, eds., *Mercenaries, Pirates, Bandits and Empires. Private Violence in Historical Context*, New York, NY: Columbia University Press, 55-82.

Leira, H., and de Carvalho, B. (2016). Construction time again: history in constructivist IR scholarship. *ERIS – European Review of International Studies*, 3 (3), 99-111.

MacKay, J., and LaRoche, C. D. (2021). Theories and Philosophies of History in International Relations. In de Carvalho, B., Costa Lopez, J., & Leira, H., eds. *Routledge Handbook of Historical International Relations*. Abingdon: Routledge.

Magubane, Z. (2005). Overlapping Territories and Intertwined Histories: Historical Sociology's Global Imagination. In: J. Adams, E. S. Clemens, and A. S. Orloff, eds., *Remaking Modernity: Politics, History, Sociology*, Durham, NC: Duke University Press, 92-108.

Mahoney, J. (2010). *Colonialism and Postcolonial Development*. New York, NY: Cambridge University Press.

Mahoney, J. (2011). Is comparative sociology marginal within the section? *Trajectories: Newsletter of the Comparative-Historical Sociology Section of the ASA*, 22 (2), 36-37.

Mann, M. (1986). *The Sources of Social Power. Volume I: A History of Power from the Beginning to AD 1760*. Cambridge: Cambridge University Press.

Mann, M. (1993). *The Sources of Social Power. Volume II: The Rise of Classes and States, 1760–1914*. Cambridge: Cambridge University Press.

Mann, M. (2006). Explaining international relations, Empires and European miracles: a response. *Millenium* 34 (2), 541-550.

Mann, M. (2013). *The Sources of Social Power. Volume III: Global Empires and Revolution, 1890-1945*. Cambridge: Cambridge University Press.

Mann, M. (2014). *The Sources of Social Power Volume IV: Globalizations, 1945-2011*. Cambridge: Cambridge University Press.

Nexon, D. (2009). *The Struggle for Power in Early Modern Europe*. Princeton, NJ: Princeton University Press

Norton, M. (2014). Classification and coercion: the destruction of piracy in the English maritime system. *American Journal of Sociology*, 119 (6), 1537-1575.

Osiander, A. (2001). Sovereignty, international relations, and the Westphalian myth. *International Organization*, 55 (2), 251-287.

Osterhammel, J. (2014). *The Transformation of the World: A Global History of the Nineteenth Century*. Translated by P. Camiller. Princeton, NJ: Princeton University Press.

Phillips, A. and Sharman, J. C. (2015). *International Order in Diversity: War, Trade and Rule in the Indian Ocean.* Cambridge: Cambridge University Press.

Pomeranz, K. (2000). *The Great Divergence.* Princeton, NJ: Princeton University Press.

Reed, I., and Adams, J. (2011). Culture in the transitions to modernity. *Theory and Society*, 40 (3), 247-272.

Reus-Smit, C. (1999). *The Moral Purpose of the State.* Princeton, NJ: Princeton University Press.

Reus-Smit, C. (2013). *Individual Rights and the Making of the International System.* Cambridge: Cambridge University Press.

Rosenberg, J. (1994). *The Empire of Civil Society.* London: Verso.

Rosenberg, J. (2006). Why is there no international historical sociology. *European Journal of International Relations*, 12 (3), 307-340.

Ruggie, J. (1993). Territoriality and beyond: problematizing modernity in international relations. *International Organization*, 47 (1), 139-174.

Sassen, S. (2007). *Territory, Authority, Rights: From Medieval to Global Assemblages.* Princeton, NJ: Princeton University Press.

Schweller, R. (2006). *Unanswered Threats.* Princeton, NJ: Princeton University Press.

Shilliam, R. (2011). The Perilous but Unavoidable Terrain of the Non-West. In: R. Shilliam, ed., *International Relations and Non-Western Thought*, London: Routledge, 12-26.

Shilliam, R., ed. (2011). *International Relations and Non-Western Thought.* London: Routledge.

Skocpol, T. (1979). *States and Social Revolutions.* Cambridge: Cambridge University Press.

Slater, D. (2010). *Ordering Power: Contentious Politics and Authoritarian Leviathans in Southeast Asia.* Cambridge: Cambridge University Press.

Smith, D. (1991). *The Rise of Historical Sociology.* Philadelphia, PA: Temple University Press.

Smith, S. (2001). Historical Sociology and International Relations Theory. In: S. Hobden, and J. M. Hobson, eds., *Historical Sociology of International Relations*, Cambridge: Cambridge University Press, 223-243.

Spruyt, H. (1994). *The Sovereign State and its Competitors.* Princeton, NJ: Princeton University Press.

Stamatov, P. (2010). Activist religion, empire, and the emergence of modern long-distance advocacy networks. *American Sociological Review*, 75 (4), 607-628.

Suganami, H. (1999). Agents, structures, narratives. *European Journal of International Relations*, 5 (3), 365-386.

Suzuki, S. (2009). *Civilization and Empire.* London: Routledge.

Taylor, P. J. (1996). Embedded statism and the social sciences: opening up to new spaces. *Environment and Planning A*, 28, 1917-1995.

Teschke, B. (2003). *The Myth of 1648.* London: Verso.

Tilly, C. (1990). *Coercion, Capital and European States, AD 990–1992.* Oxford: Blackwell.

Towns, A. E. (2009). The status of women as a standard of 'civilization.' *European Journal of International Relations*, 15 (4), 681-706.

Vitalis, R. (2010). The noble American science of imperial relations and its laws of race development. *Comparative Studies in Society and History*, 52 (4), 909-938.

Vitalis, R. (2016). *White World Order, Black Power Politics.* Ithaca, NY: Cornell University Press.

Wæver, O. (1998). The sociology of a not so international discipline. *International Organization*, 52 (4), 687-727.

Wallerstein, I. (2001). *Unthinking Social Science: The Limits of Nineteenth-Century Paradigms.* Philadelphia, PA: Temple University Press.

Waltz, K. (1979). *Theory of International Politics.* Reading, MA: Addison-Wesley.

Wilson, N. H. (2011). From reflection to refraction: extractive administration in British India, circa 1770–1855. *The American Journal of Sociology*, 116 (5), 1437-1477.

Wimmer, A., and Feinstein, Y. (2010). The rise of the nation-state across the world, 1816-2001. *American Sociological Review*, 75 (5), 764-790.

Zarakol, A. (2011). *After Defeat: How the East Learned to Live with the West.* Cambridge: Cambridge University Press.

Zhang, F. (2009). Rethinking the 'Tribute System': broadening the conceptual horizon of historical East Asian politics. *The Chinese Journal of International Politics*, 2 (4), 545-574.

6

LIBERALISM BETWEEN THEORY AND PRACTICE

Beate Jahn

Liberalism is generally associated with individual freedom, the protection of private property, the rule of law and government by consent in the domestic sphere or human rights, free trade, international law and organisation as well as democracy in the international sphere. These principles play a crucial role in liberalism as a political ideology and as a theoretical approach in International Relations. But they also inform foreign policies like democracy promotion, humanitarian intervention, neoliberal economic policies, multilateralism and characterise political actors like liberal parties, liberal states and, most recently, the liberal world order.

This liberal world order, according to Francis Fukuyama, was the result of the 'unabashed victory of economic and political liberalism' over its ideological competitors at the end of the Cold War (Fukuyama, 1989: 3, 4). It ushered in the end of history with 'Western liberal democracy' as 'the final form of human government' (Fukuyama, 1989: 4). While not many commentators subscribed to Fukuyama's more flamboyant claims about the end of history, his optimism regarding the realisation of a liberal world order was widely shared (Sørensen, 2000: 287; Richardson, 2001: 2). It entailed the spread of democracy and human rights, the globalisation of capitalism and a prominent role for international law and international organisations. This 'new world order', as then president Bush called it, was expected to produce freedom, prosperity and peace for all (Richardson, 2001: 2).

Today, however, this hegemony of the liberal world order is generally regarded as over (Duncombe and Dunne, 2018: 25). Democracy is on the retreat, human rights are prominently violated, neoliberal policies have generated unprecedented levels of inequality and economic crises, international institutions from the World Trade Organization (WTO) through the International Criminal Court (ICC) and the European Union (EU) are losing support from states and populations alike, civil wars and terrorism spread insecurity and antiliberal populist forces are on the rise in all parts of the world. The promises of freedom, prosperity and peace remain unfulfilled.

In light of this disjuncture between theory and practice, this chapter will first introduce conventional conceptions of liberalism and explore their role in and for the constitution of the liberal world order. The failure of this liberal project, the second part of this chapter shows, has given rise to a range of new conceptions of liberalism. These revisions, I will show in conclusion, pave the way for a new theoretical and methodological perspective in the study of liberalism – one that conceives liberalism not only as a product *of* history or a theory *about* history but also as a driving force *in* history.

Conventional accounts of liberalism

Liberalism does not have an unequivocal founder and its origins cannot be precisely dated. But John Locke provides an early systematic account of the core dimensions of liberal thought (Gray, 1986: 11). Locke argued that all men were naturally born free. Yet in order to uphold and realise this freedom, they had to have two core rights. The first was the right to private property – that is, the right to turn common property like land into private property through labour – thus ensuring economic independence. The second was the right to consent to government which guaranteed the political independence of the individual (Locke, 1994: 269–294, 336, 351). In Locke's work, these principles are mutually constitutive: private property constitutes individual freedom and individual freedom requires government by consent whose 'chief end … is the preservation of … property' (Locke, 1994: 351) and hence the freedom of the individual.

However, the attempt to realise this political vision in practice revealed, right from the start, tensions and contradictions that gave rise to a multitude of liberal theories. The first of these tensions arose from the economic dimension of liberalism. Following Locke's argument, landowners and merchants in 17th-century Britain demanded political rights on the basis of their property and this led to the *de jure* transfer of political power into the hands of commercial and capitalistic interests (Perelman, 2000: 175; Acemoglu and Robinson, 2006: 349–50). But once in power, this liberal elite systematically pursued the privatisation of common land, thus depriving large sections of the population of their independent livelihood.

The resultant economic conflicts gave rise to a second set of political contradictions. Liberal elites could not extend political rights to those sections of the population that had no interest in the protection of private property. The establishment of liberal polities thus went hand in hand with the extension of political rights to property owners only and the denial of political rights to the vast majority of the population. Throughout much of its history, therefore, liberalism was passionately antidemocratic and only made political compromises (lowering the property threshold in the second half of the 19th century and introducing universal suffrage after the First World War) under the threat of revolution and war (Acemoglu and Robinson, 2006: 29).

A third set of tensions arose between domestic and international politics. In order to address domestic divisions, Locke systematically advocated colonialism (Tully, 1993; Arneil, 1996; Tuck, 1999). He argued that land held in common was less productive than privately owned land. Colonists therefore had a right to appropriate 'common' land abroad from indigenous populations as well as from other European colonists if they 'improved' it through their labour (Locke, 1994: 296–297). These justifications for colonialism were used well into the 19th century by settlers in America, Canada, New Zealand and Australia (Ivison, 2003: 93). Colonies relieved domestic tensions by providing the opportunity to appropriate common land abroad rather than at home; colonial administration offered employment for the middle and higher classes; the poor could emigrate and better their prospects by appropriating other peoples' land; and governments were able to 'export' their criminals, poor and orphans. In short, colonialism enabled the import of economic benefits from abroad and the export of domestic political tensions. But the pursuit of colonialism required power politics and generated colonial wars – both with indigenous populations and with European competitors. Hence, the pacification of the domestic sphere went hand in hand with power politics in the international sphere.

The establishment of liberalism was thus characterised by fundamental contradictions: policies of appropriation and expropriation, political emancipation and oppression, the rule of law at home and power politics abroad. The 18th century, hence, was characterised by constant upheavals, rebellions and the threat of revolution at home (McNally, 1988: 62, 8–9; Tilly, 2004; see also Lawson, 2021) and colonial 'world' wars abroad (Bayly, 2010: 216; Burbank and Cooper, 2010: 220).

The need to explain and address these tensions led to the development of a wide range of liberal theories – each elaborating the workings of a particular dimension of liberalism, identifying the necessary policies and attributing adverse developments to nonliberal forces (compare Anievas and Gogu, 2021). Thus, the tensions created by economic inequality provide the starting point for liberal economic theories. Recognising the abject conditions of 'the laboring poor … in every improved and civilized society', Adam Smith began to 'inquire into the nature and causes of the wealth of nations' in search of a solution to the centrifugal forces that threatened to tear society apart (Smith, 1952: 340). He identified the division of labour and the 'invisible hand' of the market – the law of supply and demand – as leading to the most efficient use of natural resources and the cheapest prices. The wealth of nations could thus be increased by letting market forces work without interference from government regulation or the protection of businesses. Under such conditions, the self-interested behaviour of individuals, Smith famously argued, had the unintended consequence of promoting the good of society (Smith, 1952: 194). And free trade would have the same effect of benefitting all nations in the international sphere (Smith, 1952: 293).

Following Smith, liberal economic theories thus tend to offer economic solutions to the material and political tensions created by liberal policies – usually advocating free markets and free trade as the core means to increase productivity and wealth which is eventually expected to trickle down to all parts of the (world) population (Gilpin, 1987). This has a pacifying effect by improving the material conditions of the domestic poor; but the tremendous increase in productivity as a result of the industrial revolution in the 19th century also led to economic interdependence between states and made, as Norman Angell argued, even (international) war irrational (Angell, 1910). These core principles of liberal economic theories were historically compromised only when confronted with a serious threat of revolution or war. Triggered by widespread revolutions in the mid-19th-century, Britain introduced factory regulation and Germany the beginnings of welfare legislation. Similarly, the great depression was widely seen as having played a crucial role in the rise of fascism, communism and the outbreak of World War II, which paved the way for Keynesianism and 'embedded liberalism' in the early Cold War period (Ruggie, 1982) – only to be replaced in the 1970s by neoliberal economic policies and their renewed focus on the privatisation of property, the deregulation of markets and the liberalisation of trade (Plattner, 2008: 68).

Yet, inasmuch as the historical record does not conform to these theoretical expectations, liberal economic theories explain the disjuncture with reference to nonliberal actors and contexts. If free trade policies were not adopted, Adam Smith noted, it was because businesses kept demanding protection, governments kept interfering in the market and individuals did not behave according to rational economic principles – hence the freedom of trade was a 'Utopia' as long as actors behaved in illiberal ways (Smith, 1952: 201). Protectionism, rent-seeking, slavery, colonialism – all part and parcel of liberalism's political rather than economic form of extraction – are rational forms of behaviour in an illiberal context lacking specialised production and effective trading networks (Moravcsik, 1997: 530).

Addressing the problem of wars towards the end of the 18th century, Immanuel Kant's brief philosophical sketch 'Perpetual Peace' develops solutions that are still influential today in political, institutional and normative liberal theories (Jahn, 2005; see also Bartelson, 2021). In the first definitive article, Kant advocates republican government as a solution to wars between absolutist states because it provides the citizens who have nothing to gain from these wars with a voice (Kant, 1957: 120). Equating Kant's republican government with democracy, liberals like Woodrow Wilson subsequently based the peace of Versailles on the principles of democracy and self-determination. The same ideas also inspired the democratic (or liberal) peace thesis that was highly influential in the run-up to the end of the Cold War. Democracies, it argued, did not fight each other because democratic regimes represented the peaceful interests of the population and offered nonviolent means of conflict resolution (Doyle, 1996: 26; Russett, 1996). Peace could thus be extended by spreading democracy.

Kant's second definitive article offers international organisation as a solution to the security dilemma and can thus serve as a precursor of liberal institutionalist theories. A federation of states based on collective security arrangements, Kant argued, would make aggressive war too costly and thus establish a zone of peace (Kant, 1957: 16–18). The potential of international organisations and institutions to enable nonviolent conflict resolution and further international cooperation has consistently played a role in liberal theories from the 19th century onwards (Long and Schmidt, 2005) – though not all of them were based on Kant and not all 'Kantians' supported international organisation (see also Rosenboim and Hartnett, 2021). While British idealists were influenced by Kant's wider work, they were opposed to international organisation (Boucher, 2010), which in turn was supported by new liberals like Hobhouse, Green and Hobson who did not draw on Kant (Richardson, 2001). Yet arguments for the pacifying effect of international organisation can be found from support for the League of Nations through David Mitrany's functionalism (Long, 1995: 322; Schmidt, 2005: 67; Fritz, 2005: 156) to Keohane and Nye's theory of complex interdependence as well as regime theory and global governance (Vitalis, 2005: 171; Gorman, 2005). International organisations – from the International Monetary Fund (IMF), the World Bank, the General Agreement on Trade and Tariffs (GATT) and the North Atlantic Treaty Organization (NATO) to the Universal Declaration of Human Rights (UDHR) and support for the EU – also played a crucial role in the establishment of the 'liberal subsystem' by the United States (US) after the Second World War (Deudney and Ikenberry, 1999). The benefits of this peaceful and prosperous liberal subsystem could thus be extended by integrating new states into these institutions (see also Ravndal, 2021).

Finally, many normative, especially cosmopolitan, liberal theories are inspired by Kant's third definitive article. The moral wrongs of the colonial wars generated by (liberal) commercial states, Kant argues, have direct implications for all parts of the world and thus call for transnational law – specifically the limitation of the rights of private actors to universal hospitality – as a solution (Kant, 1957: 20–23). Following this line of argument, normative liberal theories tend to identify the level of interdependence (or globalisation) as the material basis for the universalisation of liberal principles like economic redistribution (Beitz, 1979), cosmopolitan democracy (Held, 1996; Archibugi, 1998) or respect for human rights (Linklater, 1998). And since these principles are already embodied in liberal states and institutions like the EU, the latter are accorded with the right and obligation of intervention in less (morally) advanced societies (Buchanan and Keohane, 2004: 19).

Like the economic theories, liberal political theories systematically attribute the nonliberal behaviour of liberal actors to nonliberal principles, actors and contexts. Aggressive behaviour on the part of liberal states is blamed on the nature of authoritarian governments – irrespective of their behaviour – against which liberal states have to pre-emptively defend themselves (cf. Bowden, 2021). Similarly, the antidemocratic history of liberalism is attributed to the continuing influence of illiberal principles: liberals simply had not learned yet that extending equal rights to all citizens 'need not lead to the outright plunder of the rich and the destruction of a productive economy and a civilized society' (Plattner, 2008: 60, 68). And it was the nonliberal nature of non-European societies which were unable to govern themselves or act in accordance with international law that forced liberal colonial powers to deny them equal political rights (Mill, 1984: 118). What stands in the way of liberal cosmopolitan law is the right of sovereignty or the principle of non-intervention (Tesón, 2003: 129). In short, if no liberal state has ever behaved as liberal abroad as at home, it is because the international sphere with its lack of individuals, civil society and government provides an environment 'inhospitable to liberalism' (Hoffmann, 1987: 397, 405).

This belief that the limits of liberalism simply lay in the continued existence of nonliberal actors and spaces was directly responsible for the exultant optimism at the end of the Cold War: for the implosion of the Soviet Union undermined not only the standing of its nonliberal ideology but also the power that had hitherto propped up nonliberal actors and spaces. And with their demise, liberal principles, practices and institutions could finally unfold their full potential. The end of the Cold War, in sum, seemed to demonstrate that liberalism was indeed aligned with, and an expression of, the progressive forces of history (Ikenberry, 2006: 161, 158, 146; Plattner, 2008: 29; Jahn, 2012).

The crisis of the liberal world order

Liberal theories thus became highly influential – both in academia and in practice. For once, it seemed, empirical evidence supported liberal rather than realist conceptions of international politics. And hence liberal theories provided the guiding principles for the rise of the liberal world order – and its fall the impetus for a more fundamental reconsideration of liberal theories today. This section traces the development of liberal hegemony in broadly two (overlapping) stages. The 1990s were characterised by proactive liberal international policies, early indications of their failures, followed by some theoretical adjustments and policy reforms. In the second stage, slowly gaining momentum during the 2000s, opposition to these policies grew throughout the international system and liberal actors themselves explicitly abandoned liberal domestic and international policies.

With the implosion of the Soviet Union, the bilateral Cold War order turned into a unilateral international order in which the leading liberal power and the architect of the post-1945 liberal subsystem – the US – occupied an unchallenged hegemonic position. In the absence of (powerful) nonliberal competitors, the US and its liberal allies proactively pursued the globalisation of liberal principles, practices and institutions. This included, in line with liberal political theories, democracy promotion – through funding and the extension or withholding of economic or diplomatic privileges like conditional aid (Carothers, 2000). Moreover, based on the liberal claim that democracy provided nonviolent forms of conflict resolution, the establishment of democratic regimes became a central part of peacebuilding operations during the 1990s (Paris, 2004). And in the 2000s, the liberal assumption that authoritarian governments were by definition aggressive provided the justification for regime change as a crucial goal of the military interventions in Afghanistan and Iraq (Duffield, 2001; Smith, 2007).

Following liberal economic theories, capitalist economic principles were rolled out to Eastern European states and much of the Third World. The IMF and the World Bank made aid conditional on the adoption of neoliberal economic principles: state-owned industries and public services like health care, public transport and education were privatised, labour markets were deregulated, fiscal austerity introduced, welfare states dismantled and domestic markets opened up to foreign direct investment (Shimko, 2005). These policies were also implemented in developed liberal states. Moreover, the early 1990s witnessed the institutionalisation of these principles in a variety of organisations, from the EU single market in 1992 through the inaugural summit of Asia-Pacific Economic Cooperation (APEC) in 1993, to the North American Free Trade Agreement (NAFTA) as well as the transformation of the GATT into the WTO in 1994 (Rosenberg, 2005).

Normative liberal theories justified humanitarian interventions in Somalia and Kosovo and supported the codification of a right or obligation to humanitarian intervention (Wheeler, 2000; Linklater, 2000; Habermas, 2002). Meanwhile, existing 'liberal' institutions like the EU and NATO expanded into Central and Eastern Europe; Russia and China were integrated into the WTO, new institutions like the ICC were established and pressing issues like the environment addressed through multilateral treaties (Kyoto Protocol).

Yet, already by the mid-1990s it became clear that these policies systematically failed to achieve their goals. Democracy promotion policies most commonly led to the establishment of illiberal or authoritarian democracies (Carothers, 2002: 18); the introduction of democracy through peacebuilding operations either rekindled conflict or recreated the conditions for the original conflict (Paris, 2004: 155). Regime change through military interventions did not lead to international pacification: after 18 years of war, the US is today negotiating its withdrawal from Afghanistan with the Taliban – the very political force it set out to replace; the intervention in Iraq triggered a violent insurgency and led to the destabilisation of the entire region, the rise of ISIS and an international conflict in Syria; just as the replacement of the Ghaddafi regime destabilised not only Libya but also neighbouring countries like Mali (Kuperman, 2013). Instead of leading to general prosperity, neoliberal economic policies led to painful transitions in Eastern Europe and the Third World, to rising inequality within and between states, to economic – and eventually in 2008 – a global financial crisis (Kupchan and Trubowitz, 2007: 35–6; Deudney and Ikenberry, 2012: 17, 8, 4; Dunne and McDonald, 2013: 11, 13). Humanitarian interventions, too, were not undertaken where needed (like in Rwanda), quickly abandoned when they became too costly (as in Somalia) or conducted in ways more conducive to the national interests of the intervening powers than to the protection of human rights (like in Kosovo) (de Waal, 1994; Ignatieff, 1999; Hehir, 2010).

Analysing these disappointing developments, most observers initially employed the familiar liberal explanations: arguing that the continuing existence of nonliberal principles, practices, actors and institutions was responsible for the failure of liberal policies. Thus, the World Bank blamed the lack of 'good governance' and traditional African cultures for the failures of its policies in Africa (Williams and Young, 1994: 99). Democracy promotions failed because it turned out that target states lacked the necessary state capacity, economic structures, civil society, political parties, legal system and so on (Diamond, 1996: 33). And humanitarian interventions were not successful because the interveners had not yet fully embraced the liberal moral obligation to help others in need and instead pursued their own national interests (Linklater, 2000: 493; Tesón, 2003: 129; Wheeler, 2004: 310). In the excitement of the end of the Cold War, it was argued, liberal theorists had naively overestimated the level of (liberal) development in target societies as well as the maturity of their own liberal principles and moral commitment.

Consequently, addressing these failures called for more thorough and longer lasting interventions. Peacebuilding operations required the wholesale reconstruction of target societies – from the constitution of legitimate governments through a shift in political culture to the production of new men with new ideas – along liberal lines (Jahn, 2007). A functioning market economy required 'good governance'. The introduction of democracy had to be delayed until liberal market economies had been introduced and consolidated. Paradoxically, therefore, the successful establishment of a liberal market democracy required 'illiberal' behaviour on the part of the interveners (Paris, 2004: 209). Liberal foreign policies yet again included privatisation and expropriation, political emancipation and oppression, culminating in public debates about the possibility or necessity of a new period of liberal imperialism or American empire (Cooper, 2002; Ignatieff, 2003; Bacevich, 2003).

In the first phase after the Cold War, therefore, liberal foreign and international policies systematically failed to fulfil their promises and increasingly took the form of blatant power politics. Against this background, opposition to liberal internationalism spread. Resistance against decades of liberal interference in the Middle East led to the terror attacks of 9/11; Third World states under the leadership of the BRICS resisted further trade liberalisation; African states withdrew their support for the ICC citing racist bias; and Russia openly began to pursue illiberal policies at home and abroad.

More importantly, however, in this second phase, resistance to liberal policies gained momentum in core liberal states themselves. Already under the Bush administration, the US abandoned multilateralism for unilateralism, 'unsigned' international treaties like the Kyoto Protocol and refused cooperation with the ICC. In the context of the war on terror, the US prominently violated human rights in Guantanamo Bay, Abu Ghraib and through the rendition programme (for UK cooperation, see Blakely and Raphael, 2017). The US and the UK started an illegal war of aggression in Iraq. Liberal economic policies, compounded by austerity and the financial crisis in 2008, led to extreme levels of economic inequality and hollowed out the centre of domestic politics in favour of extreme parties on the right and on the left (Kupchan and Trubowitz, 2007). Eventually, in 2016, the Brexit referendum and the Trump election catapulted populist forces into power in core liberal states. They attacked core democratic institutions like elections and an independent judiciary at home, and they explicitly pursued the opposite of liberal foreign policies: unilateralism instead of multilateralism, protectionism instead of free trade, citizenship over human rights, cooperation with authoritarian regimes instead of liberal allies, nationalism over internationalism. Moreover, these developments are not confined to the US and the United Kingdom. Populist forces have been gaining ground on every continent – from India, Turkey and the Philippines through South Africa, Hungary, Poland and Italy to Venezuela and Brazil.

These developments posit a more fundamental challenge to conceptions of liberalism. After all, the election of President Trump or the Brexit referendum can hardly be blamed on nonliberal actors and the liberal economic, political and normative policies of the post–Cold War era failed in the context of a liberal – not an illiberal – world order. Moreover, observers widely agree that it was the failure to fulfil its promises that undermined the attraction of the liberal world order. Hence, the theoretical question has arisen: why have liberal policies pursued under highly auspicious circumstances produced such counterproductive outcomes? – and it has triggered a range of different answers.

Some previously highly influential liberal theories have, for the time being, simply been abandoned. Faced with the charge that democratic peace theory lent itself to the justification of illegal and aggressive war, for example in Iraq, and was thus complicit in the production of domestic and international conflict (Smith, 2007; Ish-Shalom, 2013), this theory has all but disappeared. Similarly, Habermasian approaches identified core principles, practices and institutions of the liberal world order – the public sphere, democracy, the rule of law, human rights, constitutions, the EU, diplomacy, negotiations, mediation (Hoffmann, 1992) – as emancipatory and thus supported dominant liberal foreign policies (Linklater, 1998: 167; Pensky, 2001: xi–xii; Habermas, 2002). But when it became clear that 'the actions of powerful liberal societies' and 'the structures which cater for their interests' constituted the main danger from which 'vulnerable societies' had to be protected (Linklater, 2005: 154) – this approach was abandoned (Deitelhoff and Müller, 2005: 177, 171, 167; Linklater, 2007).

A second response to the demise of the liberal world order lies in locating the current tensions and contradictions not in liberalism itself but in its 'illiberal' American practice. It was the success of liberalism, Deudney and Ikenberry (2012) maintain, that catapulted the US into a hegemonic position which in turn enabled high-handed policies that ultimately undermined its authority. The US overlooked that capitalism generates economic inequality and imposed a 'fundamentalist capitalism' on other states; it ignored the development of different – often even better performing – models of democracy and exported its own indiscriminately; it disregarded the interests and identities of other states, regularly intervening in their internal affairs; and it rejected international treaties (Kyoto, ICC, ABM), violated international law (Guantanamo), ignored the UN (Iraq) and thus lost authority in the eyes of friends and allies alike – even while liberalism paved the way for the development of competing powers like the BRICS. This distinction between the success of liberal principles on the one hand and the responsibility of American practice on the other provides the basis for a rather optimistic assessment of the future prospects of liberalism: it requires nothing else but a reform of American foreign policy, a new grand strategy of 'democratic internationalism' including social democratic forms of redistribution to compensate the inevitable losers of the capitalist economy; cooperation with other democracies and the readiness to learn from them in order to revitalise democratic institutions at home; as well as more international collaboration and less power politics (Deudney and Ikenberry, 2012).

A third approach, in contrast, identifies the roots of the current tensions and contradictions within liberalism itself. While nationalism and cosmopolitanism are both integral elements of liberalism, historically states rarely pursue the common good – 'unless doing so is in clear alignment with their national interests'. Similarly, the claim that liberal principles of individual freedom, private property and government by consent are universally valid was historically used to justify 'deep intrusions into the domestic affairs of others' and a hierarchical international order in the form of colonialism, imperialism, the mandate system of the League of Nations, right through to recent calls for 'graduated sovereignty' and liberal imperialism (Cooper, 2002; Buchanan and Keohane, 2004; Bell, 2016; Duncombe and Dunne, 2018: 41; Bayly, 2021). Moreover, every act of appropriation in the history of liberalism – from the enclosure of common land through colonial conquests to the privatisation of education, health care, public transport and the establishment of intellectual property rights – is simultaneously an act of expropriation contributing to economic inequality. While social democratic forms of redistribution may thus indeed be necessary to offset the negative consequences of capitalism, such compromises are historically the exception rather than the rule (Ruggie, 1982; Acemoglu and Robinson, 2006). If colonialism, imperialism and a class-based elitism are therefore constitutive elements of liberalism, it follows that liberalism functions as an ideology justifying class- and race-based domestic and international hierarchies (Parmar, 2018: 172). This type of analysis comes to much more pessimistic conclusions regarding the future of liberalism. For, inasmuch as race, class and power politics play a constitutive role in and for liberal concepts, the latter cannot simply shed these burdens (Parmar, 2018: 172).

Conclusion

Current developments, in sum, reflect the uncertain fate of liberalism today. Many of the conventional features of liberalism are still part and parcel of the current world order: capitalism, international institutions and law, widespread humanitarian commitments (Duncombe and Dunne, 2018: 42) as well as democratic principles and institutions. They are, however, under serious attack. At stake in current debates about liberalism is therefore, first, whether these institutions themselves are at risk; and second, whether they are likely to deliver on traditional liberal promises of political freedom, general prosperity, respect for human rights and peace.

By highlighting that liberalism tends to produce both political emancipation *and* oppression, prosperity *and* poverty, peace *and* war, current research challenges conventional approaches that attribute the negative consequences of liberal policies by definition to nonliberal actors and contexts – and that hence fail to grasp the dynamic relations between liberal and nonliberal principles, practices, actors and spaces. Any attempt to investigate those dynamics, and hence also to answer current questions, therefore requires a theoretical and methodological shift: away from a theoretical conceptualisation of liberalism that excludes potentially relevant historical evidence, and towards historical investigations that focus on the generative relations of liberalism with all other principles, practices, actors and spaces.

Assessing the future prospects of liberal institutions therefore does not only require tracing their current developments. In light of the fact that liberal institutions are not for the first time in history under threat, it requires the systematic study of the conditions of their rise and fall in the past. Similarly, assessing the potential of liberal principles, practices and institutions to deliver on their promises calls for the systematic investigation of the results of liberal policies in *all* times and places. These studies, moreover, open up the possibility of an entirely new perspective that does not treat liberalism only as a product of history or as a theory about history but also as a powerful historical force in its own right.

If liberal policies play a constitutive role not just for liberal actors and spaces but also for nonliberal ones, then the fact that all of liberalism's nonliberal competitors – conservatism, socialism, communism, fascism, antiimperialism and even 'religious fundamentalism' from Khomeini's Iran through Saudi Wahabism to Orban's 'old-school Christian democracy' – were constituted by, and in direct relation to, liberal rule comes into view (Jahn, 2019: 11–12). And if liberal policies establish not just liberal but also nonliberal spaces, then we can investigate the international sphere as a product of liberal power politics and its justification. These nonliberal actors and spaces then do not any longer appear as external frontiers to be conquered and liberalised. Instead, studying the production of both liberal and nonliberal spaces provides the opportunity to investigate the historical dynamics that actually drive the rise and fall of liberalism – including its current predicament.

Liberalism creates its own enemies and limitations – antiliberal actors and nonliberal spaces that challenge or confine its rule and must therefore be subdued and/or liberalised. But the successful integration of nonliberal actors and spaces into the liberal sphere deprives liberalism of a nonliberal sphere into which to project the dark side of its internal tensions. Ironically, therefore, the moment of liberalism's greatest triumph – the moment of its globalisation – simultaneously marks the beginning of its demise: for now these tensions and contradictions undermine the liberal world order from within.

This was the fate of the first liberal world order at the end of the 19th century when liberal forces had established themselves in power in most European states, and almost all non-European territories had been integrated into liberal empires and a capitalist world market was thriving (Jahn, 2019: 13). Yet, it was precisely this successful extension of liberal power across the globe that abolished the external space into which to project the growing resistance among domestic and colonial populations as well as the competition between liberal powers – and that brought this liberal world order down in the First World War. Similarly, the second liberal world order and the demise of communist actors and spaces deprived liberal forces of the need to make economic and political compromises at home and abroad, thus exacerbating economic exploitation and political marginalisation and generating domestic and international resistance as well as competition between erstwhile liberal allies (Kupchan and Trubowitz, 2007). The globalisation of liberalism abolished the separation between the domestic and the international: instead of importing economic benefits from abroad, liberal populations now experience the export of investment and jobs, and instead of exporting political tensions, liberal populations are now confronted with their import in the form of refugees, migrants and terrorists. And it is the re-erection of this domestic-international divide that populist movements pursue above all – when they 'take back control', put 'America first', build walls, leave the EU or start trade wars.

Liberalism is therefore, as recent political developments and academic studies suggest, not Fukuyama's endpoint of history but rather one of its most powerful progenitors. And future research must approach it as such.

Suggestions for further reading

Doyle, M. W. (1997). *Ways of War and Peace*. New York, NY: W. W. Norton.

Freeden, M. (2005). Liberal Languages. In *Ideological Imaginations and Twentieth Century Progressive Thought*. Princeton, NJ: Princeton University Press.

Friedman, R., Oskanian, K., and Pardo, R. P., eds., (2013). *After Liberalism? The Future of Liberalism in International Relations*. Basingstoke: Palgrave.

Hovden, E. and Keene, E., eds., (2001). *The Globalization of Liberalism*. Basingstoke: Palgrave Macmillan.

Ikenberry, G. J. (2011). Liberal Leviathan. In *The Origins, Crisis, and Transformation of the American World Order*. Princeton, NJ: Princeton University Press.

Ikenberry, G. J., Parmar, I., and Stokes, D., eds. (2018). Ordering the world? Liberal internationalism in theory and practice. *International Affairs*, 94 (1), special issue, 1–5.

Jahn, B., ed. (2012). Critiquing in a time of liberal world order. *Journal of International Relations and Development*, 15 (2), special issue, 145–157.

Jahn, B. (2013). Liberal Internationalism. In *Theory, History, Practice*. Basingstoke: Palgrave.

Mehta, U. S. (1999). Liberalism and Empire. In *A Study in Nineteenth-century British Liberal Thought*. Chicago, IL: The University of Chicago Press.

Sørensen, G. (2012). A Liberal World Order in Crisis. In *Choosing between Imposition and Restraint*. Ithaca, NY: Cornell University Press.

References

Acemoglu, D. and Robinson, J. A. (2006). *Economic Origins of Dictatorship and Democracy*. Cambridge: Cambridge University Press.

Angell, N. (1910). *The Great Illusion*. London: Heinemann.

Anievas, A., and Gogu, C. (2021). Capitalism and 'the International': A Historical Approach. In de Carvalho, B., Costa Lopez, J., & Leira, H., eds. *Routledge Handbook of Historical International Relations*. Abingdon: Routledge.

Archibugi, D. (1998). Principles of Cosmopolitan Democracy. In: D. Archibugi, D. Held, and M. Köhler, eds., *Re-Imagining Political Community: Studies in Cosmopolitan Democracy*, Cambridge: Polity, 198–228.

Arneil, B. (1996). John Locke and America. In *The Defence of English Colonialism*. Oxford: Clarendon.

Bacevich, A. J., ed. (2003). *The Imperial Tense: Prospects and Problems of American Empire*. Chicago, IL: Ivan R. Dee, 93–101.

Bartelson, J. (2021). War and the Turn to History in International Relations. In de Carvalho, B., Costa Lopez, J., & Leira, H., eds. *Routledge Handbook of Historical International Relations*. Abingdon: Routledge.

Bayly, C. A. (2010). The Age of Revolutions in Global Context: An Afterword. In: D. Armitage, and S. Subrahmanyam, eds., *The Age of Revolutions in Global Context*. Basingstoke: Palgrave, 209–217.

Bayly, M. (2021). Imperialism: Beyond the 'Re-turn to Empire' in International Relations. In de Carvalho, B., Costa Lopez, J., & Leira, H., eds. *Routledge Handbook of Historical International Relations*. Abingdon: Routledge.

Beitz, C. R. (1979). *Political Theory and International Relations*. Princeton, NJ: Princeton University Press.

Bell, D. (2016). *Reordering the World: Essays on Liberalism and Empire*. Princeton, NJ: Princeton University Press.

Blakely, R., and Raphael, S. (2017). British torture in the 'war on terror'. *European Journal of International Relations*, 23 (2), 243–266.

Boucher, D., ed. (2010). *The British Idealists*. Cambridge: Cambridge University Press.

Bowden, B. (2021). Eurocentrism and Civilization. In de Carvalho, B., Costa Lopez, J., & Leira, H., eds. *Routledge Handbook of Historical International Relations*. Abingdon: Routledge.

Buchanan, A., and Keohane, R. O. (2004). The preventive use of force: a cosmopolitan institutional proposal. *Ethics and International Affairs*, 18 (1), 1–22.

Burbank, J., and Cooper. F. (2010). *Empires in World History. Power and the Politics of Difference*. Princeton, NJ: Princeton University Press.

Carothers, T. (2000). Taking Stock of US Democracy Assistance. In: M. Cox, G. J. Ikenberry, and T. Inoguchi, eds., *American Democracy Promotion: Impulses, Strategies, and Impacts*, Oxford: Oxford University Press, 181–199.

Carothers, T. (2002). The end of the transition paradigm. *Journal of Democracy*, 13 (1), 5–21.

Cooper, R. (2002). The New Liberal Imperialism, *The Guardian*. 7 April.

De Waal, A. (1994). Dangerous Precedents? Famine Relief in Somalia, 1991-93. In: J. Macrae and A. Zwi, eds., *War and Hunger: Rethinking International Responses to Complex Emergencies*, London: Zed Books.

Deitelhoff, N., and Müller, H. (2005). Theoretical paradise – empirically lost? Arguing with Habermas. *Review of International Studies*, 31 (1), 167–179.

Deudney, D., and Ikenberry, G. J. (1999). The nature and sources of liberal international order. *Review of International Studies*, 25 (2), 179–196.

Deudney, D., and Ikenberry, G. J. (2012). Democratic Internationalism. An American Grand Strategy for a Post-exceptionalist Era. *Council on Foreign Relations*, 6 November.

Diamond, L. (1996). Is the third wave over?. *Journal of Democracy*, 7 (3), 20–37.

Doyle, M. W. (1996). Kant, Liberal Legacies, and Foreign Affairs. In: M. E. Brown, S. M. Lynn-Jones, and S. E. Miller, eds., *Debating the Democratic Peace*, Cambridge: MIT Press, 3–57.

Duffield, M. (2001). *Global Governance and the New Wars*. London: Zed Books.

Duncombe, C., and Dunne, T. (2018). After liberal world order? *International Affairs*, 94 (1), 25–42.

Dunne, T., and McDonald, M. (2013). The politics of liberal internationalism. *International Politics*, 50 (1), 11–13.

Fritz, J.-S. (2005). Internationalism and the Promise of Science. In D. Long and B. C. Schmidt, eds., *Imperialism and Internationalism in the Discipline of International Relations*, Albany, NY: State University of New York Press, 141–158.

Fukuyama, F. (1989). The End of History? *National Interest*, Summer, 3–18.

Gilpin, R. (1987). *The Political Economy of International Relations*. Princeton, NJ: Princeton University Press.

Gorman, D. (2005). Liberal internationalism, the league of Nations Union, and the mandates system. *Canadian Journal of International History*, 40 (3), 449–477.

Gray, J. (1986). *Liberalism*. Minneapolis, MN: University of Minnesota Press.

Habermas, J. (2002). Letter to America. *The Nation*, 26 November.

Hehir, A. (2010). *Humanitarian Intervention. An Introduction*. Basingstoke: Palgrave.

Held, D. (1996). *Democracy and the Global Order: From the Modern State to Cosmopolitan Governance*. Cambridge: Polity.

Hoffmann, M. (1992). Third-Party Mediation and Conflict-Resolution in the Post-Cold War World. In: J. Baylis and N. R. Rennger, eds., *Dilemmas of World Politics: International Issues in a Changing World*, Oxford: Clarendon, 261–286.

Hoffmann, S. (1987). Janus and Minerva. In *Essays in the Theory and Practice of International Politics*. Boulder, CO: Westview.

Ignatieff, M. (1999). Counting Bodies in Kosovo. *New York Times*, 21 November.

Ignatieff, M. (2003). State Failure and Nation-Building. In: J. L. Holzgrefe and R. O. Keohane, eds., *Humanitarian Intervention. Ethical, Legal, and Political Dilemmas*, Cambridge: Cambridge University Press, 299–321.

Ikenberry, G. J. (2006). *Liberal Order and Imperial Ambition*. Cambridge: Polity.

Ish-Shalom, P. (2013). *Democratic Peace: A Political Biography*. Ann Arbor, MI: University of Michigan Press.

Ivison, D. (2003). Locke, Liberalism and Empire. In: P. R. Anstey, ed., *The Philosophy of John Locke: New Perspectives*, London: Routledge, 86–105.

Jahn, B. (2005). Kant, Mill, and illiberal legacies in international affairs. *International Organization*, 59 (1), 177–207.

Jahn, B. (2007). The tragedy of liberal diplomacy: democratization, intervention, statebuilding II. *Journal of Intervention and Statebuilding*, 1 (2), 211–229.

Jahn, B. (2012). Critique in a time of liberal world order. *Journal of International Relations and Development*, 15 (2), 145–157.

Jahn, B. (2019). The sorcerer's apprentice: liberalism, ideology, and religion in world politics. *International Relations*, 33 (2), 322–337.

Kant, I. (1957). In L. W. Beck, ed., *Perpetual Peace*, London: Macmillan.

Kupchan, C. A., and Trubowitz, P. L. (2007). Dead center. The demise of liberal internationalism in the United States. *International Security*, 32 (2), 25–44.

Kuperman, A. J. (2013). A model humanitarian intervention? Reassessing NATO's Libya campaign. *International Security*, 38 (1), 105–136.

Lawson, G. (2021). Revolutions: Integrating the International. In de Carvalho, B., Costa Lopez, J., & Leira, H., eds. *Routledge Handbook of Historical International Relations*. Abingdon: Routledge.

Linklater, A. (1998). *The Transformation of Political Community*. Cambridge: Polity.

Linklater, A. (2000). The good international citizen and the crisis in Kosovo. In: A. Schnabel and R. Thakur, eds., *Kosovo and the Challenge of Humanitarian Intervention: Selective Indignation, Collective Action, and International Citizenship*, New York, NY: UN University Press, 482–495.

Linklater, A. (2005). Dialogic politics and the civilising process. *Review of International Studies* 31 (1), 141–154.

Linklater, A. (2007). Towards a sociology of global morals with an 'emancipatory intent'. *Review of International Studies*, 33 (1), 135–150.

Locke, J. (1994). In P. Laslett ed., *Two Treatises of Government*. Cambridge: Cambridge University Press.

Long, D. (1995). The Harvard School of Liberal International Theory: a case for closure. *Millennium: Journal of International Studies*, 24 (3), 489–505.

Long, D. and Schmidt, B. C., eds., (2005). *Imperialism and Internationalism in the Discipline of International Relations*. Albany, NY: State University of New York Press.

Mill, J. S. (1984). A Few Words on Non-Intervention. In: J. M. Robson, ed., *The Collected Works of John Stuart Mill*, Vol. XXI., Toronto: University of Toronto Press, 109–124.

Moravcsik, A. (1997). Taking preferences seriously: a liberal theory of international politics. *International Organization*, 51 (4), 513–553.

Paris, R. (2004). *At War's End. Building Peace after Civil Conflict*. Cambridge: Cambridge University Press.

Parmar, I. (2018). The US-led liberal order: imperialism by another name? *International Affairs*, 94 (1), 151–172.

Pensky, M. (2001). Editor's Introduction. In: J. Habermas, *The Postnational Constellation. Political Essays*. Cambridge: Polity, vii–xvii.

Perelman, M. (2000). The Invention of Capitalism. In *Classical Political Economy and the Secret History of Primitive Accumulation*. Durham: Duke University Press.

Plattner, M. F. (2008). Democracy Without Borders? In *Global Challenges to Liberal Democracy*. Lanham, MD: Rowman and Littlefield.

Ravndal, E. J. (2021). International Organizations in Historical Perspective. In de Carvalho, B., Costa Lopez, J., & Leira, H., eds. *Routledge Handbook of Historical International Relations*. Abingdon: Routledge.

Richardson, J. L. (2001). Contending Liberalisms in World Politics. In *Ideology and Power*. Boulder, CO: Lynne Rienner.

Rosenberg, J. (2005). Globalisation theory: a post mortem. *International Politics*, 42 (1), 2–74.

Rosenboim, O., and Hartnett, L. (2021). International Political Thought and Historical International Relations. In de Carvalho, B., Costa Lopez, J., & Leira, H., eds. *Routledge Handbook of Historical International Relations*. Abingdon: Routledge.

Ruggie, J. G. (1982). International regimes, transactions, and change: embedded liberalism in the postwar economic order. *International Organization*, 36 (2), 379–415.

Russett, B. (1996). Why Democratic Peace? In: M. E. Brown, S. M. Lynn-Jones, and S. E. Miller, eds., *Debating the Democratic Peace*, Cambridge: MIT Press, 58–81.

Schmidt, B. C. (2005). Paul S. Reinsch and the Study of Imperialism and Internationalism. In: D. Long and B. C. Schmidt, eds., *Imperialism and Internationalism in the Discipline of International Relations*, Albany, NY: State University of New York Press, 43–69.

Shimko, K. L. (2005). International Relations. In *Perspectives and Controversies*. Boston, MA: Houghton Mifflin.

Smith, A. (1952). *An Inquiry into the Nature and Causes of the Wealth of Nations*. Chicago, IL: William Benton.

Smith, T. (2007). *A Pact with the Devil. Washington's Bid for World Supremacy and the Betrayal of the American Promise*. New York, NY: Routledge.

Sørensen, G. (2000). The Impasse of Third World Democratization: Africa Revisited. In: M. Cox, G. J. Ikenberry, and T. Inoguchi, eds., *American Democracy Promotion. Impulses, Strategies, and Impacts*, Oxford: Oxford University Press, 287–307.

Tesón, F. R. (2003). The Liberal Case for Humanitarian Intervention. In: J. L. Holzgrefe and R. O. Keohane, eds., *Humanitarian Intervention: Ethical, Legal, and Political Dilemmas*, Cambridge: Cambridge University Press, 93–129.

Tilly, C. (2004). *Contention and Democracy in Europe, 1650-2000*. New York, NY: Cambridge University Press.

Vitalis, R. (2005). Birth of a Discipline. In: D. Long, and B. C. Schmidt, eds., *Imperialism and Internationalism in the Discipline of International Relations*, Albany, NY: State University of New York Press, 159–81.

Wheeler, N. J. (2004). The Humanitarian Responsibilities of Sovereignty. In: J. Welsh, ed., *Humanitarian Intervention in International Relations*, Oxford: Oxford University Press, 29–52.

Wheeler, N.J. (2000). Saving Strangers. In *Humanitarian Intervention in International Society*. Oxford: Oxford University Press.

Williams, D., and Young, T. (1994). Governance, the World Bank, and Liberal Theory. *Political Studies*, 42 (1), 84–100.

7

REALISM

Excavating a historical tradition

Deborah Welch Larson

Historical realism

The realist strain of Historical International Relations began with the emergence of a new school of strategist-historians in the 1980s and 1990s. Classic realist theory (Morgenthau, 1978; Waltz, 1979; Gilpin, 1981) surveyed developments in international relations such as alliance formation and recurring balances of power without providing a sustained historical analysis of a particular era. Historical examples were extracted from the period, detached from an explanation of a historical case. It was therefore difficult for the reader to determine the causal importance of an illustration or its place in a sequence of events (see the discussion in de Carvalho et al., 2021 in this volume). Similarly, strategic theorists such as Thomas Schelling (1960) and Robert Jervis (1978) used history as a source of insights and illustrations for concepts such as deterrence and the balance of power, but did not write historical works themselves. In turning to history, the strategist-historians were following the tradition of earlier European realist theorists or European immigrants to the United States, such as Winston Churchill (1948–53), Arnold Wolfers (1966), Martin Wight (1977), and Henry Kissinger (1973, 1994). These realist thinkers applied realist concepts of anarchy, the balance of power, and the national interests to history, but did not test theories or try to derive generalizations divorced from context (on disciplinary developments, see Ashworth, 2021 in this volume).

Beginning in the 1980s, strategic theorists (Snyder, 1983; Mearsheimer, 1983; Posen, 1984) did in-depth historical research, often using archival sources, to test theoretical predictions. In doing so, they showed the theoretical fertility as well as the limitations of realism when applied to foreign policy. These scholars stressed realist variables such as the distribution of power, technology, economic wealth, and geopolitics as determinants of state policy, but they also included variables from other non-realist theories such as organization theory and cognitive psychology. I will review these major works to show their influence on subsequent historical realist scholarship as well as recent emendations.

Offence/Defence Theory and World War I

Initially realist historical research focused on preemptive war and the security dilemma. Jack Snyder (1983) seeks to explain why the continental countries of World War I adopted offensive military strategies, although the defence had the advantage because machine guns, enhanced firearms and artillery, and barbed wire made the offensive ruinously costly.

Along with other realist theorists in the 1980s, Snyder came to military doctrine via analogy to the study of nuclear deterrence theory and the conditions for a stable balance between nuclear powers. According to nuclear deterrence theory, mutual deterrence could be endangered by advances in weapons technology that made it possible to prevent the other side from retaliating against a first strike. Schelling (1960) argued that first-strike advantages can cause states to pre-empt even when they are only trying to preserve the status quo through reciprocal fears of a surprise attack. If offensive nuclear strategies such as counterforce increased the risk of a pre-emptive war, then by analogy, World War I could be viewed as a war that was brought about by fear of being attacked and the belief that it was advantageous to strike first.

Whereas Jervis (1978) and Quester (1977) had stressed the role of technology and geography in contributing to beliefs about an offensive advantage, Snyder emphasizes offensive military doctrines as the main reason why the continental powers adopted pre-emptive military strategies at the outset of the war (10–11). In Snyder's view, offensive military doctrines make arms races more likely, exacerbate the security dilemma, and increase the likelihood of preventive war (214).

Beliefs about the advantage of the offence reflect cognitive and motivational biases. Cognitive biases are the product of limits on human cognitive capacities and the tendency to take shortcuts. Motivational biases relate to the human need to preserve core values and interests. Military organizations have an inherent predilection for offensive military strategies, which enhance their autonomy and increase their budgets (207–208).

Before World War I, military officials in France and Germany had well-developed ideologies favouring offensive strategies that enhanced their institutional prestige and position. Russia did not, because of the lack of hierarchical organization and upheavals due to defeat in the Russo-Japanese War.

Snyder (1983: 209) allows for the importance of individual decision makers, such as the difference between the older Field Marshal Helmuth von Moltke and his successor as chief of the Imperial German Staff (1891–1906) Alfred von Schlieffen. Moltke was much more flexible in his orientation to military strategy, more willing to consider defensive strategies, and more inclined to make pragmatic adaptations to reality than the more dogmatic Schlieffen, whose plan for a two-front war contributed to early German military disasters.

Snyder (1983: 215) stresses perceptual variables as the source of decisions for military doctrine and strategy. Whether the security dilemma operates depends on how political and military officials *perceive* the offence/defence balance, even if these perceptions are wrong (Jervis, 1976, 1978).

Snyder (1983: 210) concludes that realist theory alone cannot explain military doctrine. A state's foreign policy goals, geography, the military balance, and prevailing military technology are often insufficient to predict what kind of doctrine it will adopt. A multilevel approach, therefore, is needed, one that incorporates potential biases due to the defensive needs of allies, the dogmatism of military planners, or misconstrued lessons of history.

Scott Sagan (1986) criticizes Snyder for overemphasizing military biases in favour of the offensive and neglecting political imperatives such as alliance commitments as the reason for offensive military strategies. Objecting to Snyder's characterization of military doctrine as 'irrational,' Sagan points out that the German Schlieffen plan came very close to succeeding. More important than the offence/defence balance in determining military outcomes, in Sagan's view, are the quantity and quality of the opposing forces.

Keir Lieber (2005: 94–97, 2007) contends that recent developments in German historiography, partly due to the recovery of documents, indicate that the German military had no illusions about the defensive advantages of improvements in fire power and expected the war to be prolonged and costly. Instead of a 'cult of the offensive,' he argues, Germany's desire for continental hegemony was the most important cause of World War I. In response, Snyder (2008) contends that current German history does not undermine his arguments about a military bias for the offensive. Despite their recognition of the risks of a costly war of attrition, the German military persisted in their offensive strategic planning because they saw no other alternative.

Grand strategy and World War II

In line with Snyder, Posen's (1984) explanation of military doctrine and grand strategy before World War II considers balance of power theory, offence/defence advantages, and organizational theory. Posen defines grand strategy as a theory of how to achieve security, which identifies potential threats, establishes priorities among dangers, and indicates how to overcome those threats. A military doctrine identifies military means and specifies how they should be used to achieve the goals of grand strategy (13–14).

The importance of military doctrine extends beyond a state's military policy, affecting the conflict proneness of an international environment. Posen (1984: 16–20) argues that offensive doctrines contribute to arms racing, making war more likely and more intense when it does break out. If war does occur, both sides will compete to deliver a knock-out blow, throwing all their resources into the early stages of the conflict. In contrast, defensive doctrines alleviate uncertainty about intentions by allowing status quo–minded states to adopt force postures that are clearly distinguishable from those of potential aggressors. Defensive strategies assume a longer war, so that states can afford to wait to develop and mobilize their forces until there is a compelling justification.

Posen (1984: 47–79) deduces hypotheses about the determinants of offensive and defensive military doctrines from organization theory and balance of power theory. Similar to Snyder, he argues that military organizations have a bias towards offensive doctrines that maximize their budgets and operational freedom. According to Posen, organization theory explains why military doctrine is often not well integrated with grand strategy: military organizations are concerned with their own parochial interests in increasing their budgets and enhancing autonomy rather than the national interest, which requires establishing priorities. Military doctrine is more likely to be innovative and integrative when civilians intervene in military affairs. They are more likely to do so, Posen contends, when compelling external threats raise the prospect of defeat or disaster (59–60), consistent with balance of power theory. Balance of power theory also predicts that the military doctrines will vary with individual states, depending on their relative power position and the political goals of grand strategy, as well as geographic factors and military technology (see also Andersen and Wohlforth, 2021 in this volume).

Posen argues that France was driven to adopt a defensive strategy because of its inferiority in industrial might and population to Germany. France desperately needed allies in Eastern Europe to force Germany to fight a two-front war. France also needed Britain's industrial resources and armies to defeat Germany. Because Britain was determined to avoid war at all costs, France tried to assuage British concerns by adopting a defensive doctrine that conflicted with French commitments to its allies in Eastern Europe (109–111). Domestic political constraints also played a role in in the adoption of a defensive doctrine because French conscripts were given only one year of training, inadequate to prepare them for conducting an offensive (108–109).

Britain also adopted a defensive-deterrent doctrine because it did not have sufficient economic or military resources to defend the British Empire against a coalition of Germany, Italy, and Japan. Britain's strategy for avoiding war, however, was irrational because it allowed Germany to conquer its enemies sequentially (141–143). After Britain awakened to the threat posed by Hitler in 1939, British civilians intervened in military affairs to develop a system of air defences to prevent

Germany from using strategic bombing to deliver a 'knock-out blow,' providing additional time for Britain to mobilize its superior industrial resources for a war of attrition (165–169, 171–175). Also consistent with balance of power theory is Britain's 1937 shift to rearmament when it adopted a five-year plan that doubled defence spending.

Posen's contrast between French and British grand strategies recapitulates some of the earlier conclusions of the in-depth study by Wolfers (1966). In contrast to Wolfers, however, Posen does not discuss the reluctance of Britain and France to enlist the help of the Soviet Union, essential for France's efforts to defend its Eastern European allies—Czechoslovakia, Rumania, Yugoslavia, Poland. Since it was the Red Army that bore the major burden of defeating, Germany, failure to ally with the Soviet Union is telling and consequential (Haslam, 1984: 223, 225, 227–278).

Posen attributes Nazi Germany's selection of an offensive doctrine to Hitler's goal of conquering Europe and the world. Given Germany's political isolation, Hitler relied on displays of military power and coercion to intimidate his opponents. He emphasized speed in his strategy—the blitzkrieg—so that he could defeat his enemies sequentially instead of confronting them all at once (217).

Posen concludes that balance of power theory provides the best explanation for innovation in military doctrine, largely because Britain and France, despite having militaries with similar organizational biases, adopted different military doctrines. Similar to Snyder, Posen emphasizes the role of key officials who promoted innovation in military doctrine—Air Chief Marshal Sir Hugh Dowding in developing the British air defence system, General Heinz Guderian in formulating the German blitzkrieg strategy.

Posen leaves out domestic politics and non-rational factors in explaining political decisions related to use of force—such as Chamberlain's issuance of a guarantee to Poland in March 1939 or Hitler's decision to invade Poland, at the cost of going to war against both Britain and France in 1939. Just as Chamberlain's appeasement policy was motivated in part by the British public's aversion to war, so his decision to offer Poland a guarantee was driven by a shift in public opinion and a defiant Parliament and Cabinet, the result of Hitler's invasion of a rump Czechoslovakia in defiance of his promises at Munich. Chamberlain favoured appeasement in 1938 when the military balance was favourable to Britain and shifted to deterrence when Britain and France could not carry out the commitment (Rosecrance, 1986: 87, 173–174).

Posen does not give sufficient weight to the political goals that lead leaders to choose war. If leaders are determined to go to war, they will find a way to do so, including modifying prevailing military doctrine (Shimshoni, 1990/1991). There is also little evidence political leaders consider the offence/defence balance when deciding whether and how to go to war. In such instances, we would expect political goals and perceptions of other states' intentions to be overriding. In her historical study of the uses of intelligence, Keren Yarhi-Milo (2014) did not find that British officials used German military doctrine in estimating Hitler's intentions. Offence/defence theory has often been criticized for unclear definitions, circularity, and including too many unrelated variables in the concept (Levy, 1984; Glaser and Kaufmann, 1998; Davis et al., 1998/1999).

With their references to the security dilemma and the risks of offensive doctrines, Snyder (1983) and Posen (1984) articulate what would become central concepts of defensive realism (Snyder, 1991: 11–12), which argues that states are primarily motivated by security. Security, however, is an amorphous term that can be used to describe a variety of goals, including promoting a state's ideology, acquiring overseas markets, or maintaining an empire (Zakaria, 1998: 27). In *Myths of Empire* (1991: 19), Snyder argues that he is recapturing the classical realism of Hobbes, Thucydides, and Morgenthau by adding domestic political coalitions to explain why great powers have a tendency towards overexpansion. This would later be one of the recurring themes of neoclassical realism.

Deterrence

Mearsheimer (1983) seeks to identify the military (but not political) factors that influence the success or failure of efforts at conventional deterrence. He identifies three strategies that a potential initiator of conflict may use: attrition, blitzkrieg, and limited aims strategies. An attrition strategy seeks to wear the opponent down through repeated battles. A blitzkrieg strategy relies on mobility, speed, and manoeuvre to defeat the opponent without having to engage in bloody and costly battles. Germany in World War II and Israel made effective use of the blitzkrieg to achieve stunning victories. A limited aims strategy seeks to seize a piece of territory through a surprise attack.

His principal cases include the decision by Britain and France not to launch an offensive against Germany after it invaded Poland in 1939 and the corresponding decisions by Germany to attack Poland in 1939 and France in May 1940. His treatment of the Middle East conflicts of 1956, 1967, and 1973 is relatively abbreviated, given the paucity of archival sources about Israeli or Egyptian decision-making. In his focus on strategic decisions leading up to World War II, Mearsheimer is following in the steps of Winston Churchill (1948–53), whose magisterial series of six volumes *The Second World War* deals not only with the lead-up to the war, but also strategic and coalition decisions during the war.

To lay the basis for his analysis of British, French, and German decisions concerning the early part of World War II, Mearsheimer considers their decisions before the war. Assuming that they would have to fight a long costly war of attrition against Germany, like World War I, Britain and France preferred to stay on the defensive as long as possible to conserve resources for a prolonged struggle. Both states believed that the defence had the advantage, and that an attacker could only achieve victory through material superiority, which would require time to mobilize. France also entered into alliances with states in Eastern Europe to force Germany to fight a two-front war, but without the ability to seize the offensive, could not defend its allies when they were picked off by Germany (75–76). Britain and France were deterred from launching an offensive to help Poland because they believed it would lead to a strategy of attrition that would ultimately fail. Churchill (vol. I, 1948: 336–339) as well is critical of the British and French decision to issue a deterrent threat over Poland rather than defending Czechoslovakia in 1938 (Reynolds, 2007: 108–109).

According to Mearsheimer, Germany was deterred from launching an offensive against France until it had arrived at a military strategy that promised a quick victory. Hitler informed his generals in fall 1939 that he planned to launch an offensive in the West, but his military planners could only come up with a limited aims strategy, regarded as unacceptable by the civilian leadership. By February 1940, after the blitzkrieg strategy had emerged, Hitler won their support for an invasion of France in May, a decision that was vindicated by France's swift, humiliating defeat and departure from the war.

Mearsheimer (1983: 53, 209–211) concludes that deterrence is likely to fail when the initiator is considering use of a blitzkrieg strategy because it promises victory quickly and at low cost. This hypothesis is supported by Germany's decisions to strike France in May 1940 and to invade the Soviet Union in June 1941, and Israel's decision to go to war against Egypt in 1967. Deterrence is likely to succeed, however, if attrition is the only available strategy because it is both costly and risky. With a limited aims strategy, the military may be deterred from starting a war by the risk that the defender will resist the attempted capture of territory, which could lead to a war of attrition.

Mearsheimer concludes that both political and military considerations are important for deterrence. Political factors are likely to come into play once military officials have devised an acceptable military strategy.

Mearsheimer (1983) provides a clear, informative discussion of the blitzkrieg strategy. His analysis is contradicted by some recent historical scholarship which rebuts the argument that Germany's adoption of the blitzkrieg strategy alone was responsible for its defeat of France in 1940. Instead, it was France's practice of controlled fighting, which emphasized defensive fortifications and fire power, and its failure to emplace anti-tank defences near the Ardennes Forest, that had the most causal weight in determining the outcome (May, 2000: 448–464).

Other military historians have questioned whether the German military had formulated a coherent strategy for use of the blitzkrieg by 1940. Instead, German generals had recourse to the traditional German military strategy of envelopment of enemy forces and seeking a decisive battle. Mearsheimer's argument is also contradicted by evidence that Hitler failed to attack in 1939 because of weather conditions and the loss of German war plans to the allies due to a plane crash, not because the German military had failed to devise an alternative to the attrition strategy (Cooper, 1978; Harris and Toas, 1990; Lieber, 2005: 104, 116–121).

Regardless of historical disputes, Mearsheimer's analysis of conventional deterrence broadens the discussion by focusing on strategy, and not just the balance of forces.

Balance of power theory

Balance of power theory presumes that power is observable and calculable. William Wohlforth (1993) questions that presumption by analysing how Soviet and American elites viewed the elements of power, the balance of power, and the hierarchy of power and prestige. Stephen Walt (1987: 25–32) had earlier contended that states balance against threats rather than power, and that beliefs about intentions influence threat perception. Walt bases his argument on historical cases of Middle East alliances from 1955 to 1979.

In his study of American and Soviet perceptions of power, Wohlforth (1993: 11–12) tests the equilibrium conception of the balance of power theory associated with Waltz (1979) against the hierarchical view of the international system identified with Gilpin (1981) and Organski (1968). Whereas the equilibrium model predicts the recurring formation of balances of power, the hierarchical one posits an unequal distribution of status and influence and uneven growth in power. Rising states desire more status and influence, while declining powers are reluctant to accord the new powers authority over the rules of the system. The resulting struggle for power and prestige can lead to arms competition and war.

Wohlforth studies five crisis periods during which US and Soviet elites disagreed over the relative distribution of power: the immediate post-war period 1945–1947; intensification of the rivalry in 1949–1951; a series of intense crises from 1959 to 1962; and return to Cold War between 1979 and 1985 (for a critical view of periodizations, see Guillaume, 2021 in this volume; on the Cold War, see Kwon, 2021 in this volume). In his comparison of different power distributions during the Cold War, Wohlforth is following in the tradition of the British theorist Martin Wight (1977), who compares balance of power systems. In each crisis, the Soviet Union acquired some new capability, but failed to translate the increase in power into enhanced status and influence (Wohlforth, 1993: 102, 110, 131–132, 134–135).

The Soviet claim to equal status with the United States was based largely on its conventional military power and superiority on the Eurasian land mass. The United States was prepared to acknowledge Soviet conventional military superiority, but defined power more broadly as also including economic, cultural, and political components, where the Soviet Union lagged (211).

The disjuncture between Soviet and American views of the appropriate distribution of power and influence was glossed over during periods of cooperation and détente, but eventually re-emerged as Soviet elites received increasing indications that the US government did not view the Soviet Union as an equal power. The ambiguity of feedback about the real distribution of power and prolonged periods in which each side had a different view of the world order (213, 221–222) allowed illusions to persist, making their disconfirmation all the more disruptive of normal relations.

Wohlforth argues that the balance of power is elusive because it is only after dramatic catalysing events that perceptions of power are brought into line with realities. Each state tends to define the principal components of power to flatter its comparative advantage—the size of armies for land powers, battleships for naval powers. While relative power is ambiguous, Wohlforth concludes, the status hierarchy is clear, contributing to rising powers' dissatisfaction with the existing order (290, 303).

In effect, he takes realist balance of power theory as far as possible in his analysis of Soviet foreign policy during the Cold War, ending up with a revisionist account that helped to justify neoclassical realism (Rose, 1998). Another input into neoclassical realism is Walt's (1996) study of the foreign policy of revolutionary states, including the France, the Soviet Union, and Iran. He concludes that state behaviour is not just influenced by relative power but by domestic politics and beliefs about the other's intentions, which can be influenced by ideology (339).

Neoclassical realism

Realist-infused historical scholarship indicates that realism is better able to explain patterns and outcomes in international politics than it can explain a particular state's foreign policy. To address this deficiency, the first iteration of neoclassical realists seek to add elite perceptions of power and domestic political constraints to realist explanations of foreign policy (Lobell et al., 2009). In a subsequent development, Ripsman et al. (2016) go beyond foreign policy to explain international outcomes. They conceptualize two new independent variables—the permissiveness and the clarity of the international environment. The international system varies in the range of choice available to leaders trying to preserve their state's security. In addition, the international environment does not always provide clear signals of threats and opportunities for states. Intervening variables are divided into four categories: (1) leaders' images; (2) strategic culture; (3) state-society relations; and (4) domestic institutions. This framework has been most recently applied in Taliaferro (2019) to explain US policy towards allies trying to acquire nuclear weapons.

Conclusions

The strategist-historians of the 1980s and 1990s combine political science with history, adding to previous realist history a concern with testing theories and arriving at generalizations. Whereas Wolfers, Churchill, Wight, and Kissinger were not positivists, their successors use realist concepts of balance of power, geography, and anarchy along with behavioural science to develop historically grounded theories. Realist historians diverge from much political science in supplementing theory with narrative explanation, incorporating context and other variables where necessary to achieve a more realistic historical explanation.

In so doing, these historical realists illustrate the limits of structural realist theory (Waltz, 1979). They conclude that in addition to relative power, it is necessary to consider the role of individuals, perceptions of power, organizational biases, and domestic politics. This served as the basis for neoclassical realism. Neoclassical realism layers in variables at levels of analysis other than the international system, such as perceptions, and domestic politics, while maintaining the realist emphasis on relative power and geography.

Directions for future research include the relationship between domestic politics and national security policy, especially in an era of US retrenchment. More research also needs to be done on what determines perceptions of relative power and how these affect the status hierarchy, especially in an era of power transition with a rising China and resurging Russia. To address such questions, historical realists engage in detailed historical investigation.

Suggestions for further reading

Betts, R. (1999). Must war find a way? A review essay. *International Security*, 24 (2), 166–198.
Kissinger, H. (2011). *On China*. New York: Penguin Press.
Lynn-Jones, S. (1995). Offense-defense theory and its critics. *Security Studies*, 4 (4), 660–691.
Shifrinson, J. (2018). *Rising Titans, Falling Giants: How Great Powers Exploit Power Shifts*. Ithaca, NY: Cornell University Press.
Trachtenberg, M. (2006). *The Craft of International History: A Guide to Method*. Princeton, NJ: Princeton University Press.

References

Andersen, M. A., and Wohlforth, W. C. (2021). Balance of Power: A Key Concept in Historical Perspective. In de Carvalho, B., Costa Lopez, J., & Leira, H., eds. *Routledge Handbook of Historical International Relations*. Abingdon: Routledge.
Ashworth, L. M. (2021). Disciplinary Traditions and Debates: The Subject Matters of International Thought. In de Carvalho, B., Costa Lopez, J., & Leira, H., eds. *Routledge Handbook of Historical International Relations*. Abingdon: Routledge.
Churchill, W. S. (1948–53). *The Second World War*. Six volumes. Boston, MA: Houghton Mifflin.
Cooper, M. (1978). *The German Army, 1933–1945: Its Political and Military Failure*. New York, NY: Stein and Day.
Davis, J., Finel, B., and Goddard, S. (1998/1999). Taking offense at offense-defense theory. *International Security*, 23 (3), 197–206.
de Carvalho, B., Costa Lopez, J., and Leira, H. (2021). Introduction: Historical International Relations. In de Carvalho, B., Costa Lopez, J., & Leira, H., eds. *Routledge Handbook of Historical International Relations*. Abingdon: Routledge.
Gilpin, R. (1981). *War and Change in World Politics*. Cambridge: Cambridge University Press.
Glaser, C. L., and Kaufmann, C. (1998). What is the offense-defense balance and can we measure it? *International Security*, 22 (4), 44–82.
Guillaume, X. (2021). Historical Periods and the Act of Periodisation. In de Carvalho, B., Costa Lopez, J., & Leira, H., eds. *Routledge Handbook of Historical International Relations*. Abingdon: Routledge.
Harris, J., and Toas, F. (1990). *Armoured Warfare*. New York, NY: St. Martin's.
Haslam, J. (1984). *The Soviet Union and the Struggle for Collective Security in Europe, 1933–39*. London: Palgrave Macmillan.
Jervis, R. (1976). *Perception and Misperception in International Politics*. Princeton, NJ: Princeton University Press.
Jervis, R. (1978). Cooperation under the security dilemma. *World Politics*, 30 (2), 167–214.
Kissinger, H. (1973). *A World Restored: Metternich, Castlereagh, and the Problems of Peace, 1812–22*. Boston, MA: Houghton Mifflin.
Kissinger, H. (1994). *Diplomacy*. New York, NY: Simon & Schuster.
Kwon, H. (2021). Understanding the Postcolonial Cold War. In de Carvalho, B., Costa Lopez, J., & Leira, H., eds. *Routledge Handbook of Historical International Relations*. Abingdon: Routledge.
Levy, J. (1984). The offense/defensive balance of military technology. *International Studies Quarterly*, 28 (2), 219–238.
Lieber, K. (2005). *War and the Engineers: The Primacy of Politics over Technology*. Ithaca, NY: Cornell University Press.
Lieber, K. (2007). The new history of World War I and what it means for international relations theory. *International Security*, 32 (2), 155–191.
Lobell, S., Ripsman, N., and Taliaferro, J., eds. (2009). *Neoclassical Realism, The State, and Foreign Policy*. Cambridge: Cambridge University Press.

May, E. (2000). *Strange Victory: Hitler's Conquest of France*. New York, NY: Hill and Wang.

Mearsheimer, J. (1983). *Conventional Deterrence*. Ithaca, NY: Cornell University Press.

Morgenthau, H. (1978). *Theory of International Politics*. 5th edition. New York, NY: Knopf.

Organski, A. (1968). *World Politics*. New York, NY: Knopf.

Posen, B. (1984). *The Sources of Military Doctrine: France, Britain, and Germany between the World Wars*. Ithaca, NY: Cornell University Press.

Quester, G. (1977). *Offense and Defense in the International System*. New York, NY: Wiley.

Reynolds, D. (2007). *In Command of History: Churchill Fighting and Writing the Second World War*. New York, NY: Basic Books.

Ripsman, N., Taliaferro, J., and Lobell, S. (2016). *Neoclassical Realist Theory of International Politics*. Cambridge: Cambridge University Press.

Rose, G. (1998). Neoclassical realism and theories of foreign policy. *World Politics*, 51 (1), 144–177.

Rosecrance, R. (1986/1987). Explaining military doctrine. *International Security*, 11 (3), 167–174.

Sagan, S. (1986). 1914 Revisited: allies, offense, and instability. *International Security*, 11 (2), 151–175.

Schelling, T. (1960). *The Strategy of Conflict*. Cambridge: Harvard University Press.

Shimshoni, J. (1990/1991). Technology, military advantage, and World War I: a case for military entrepreneurship. *International Security*, 15 (3), 87–215.

Snyder, J. (1983). *The Ideology of the Offensive: Military Decision Making and the Disasters of 1914*. Ithaca, NY: Cornell University Press.

Snyder, J. (1991). *Myths of Empire: Domestic Politics and International Ambitions*. Ithaca, NY: Cornell University Press.

Snyder, J. (2008). Defensive realism and the 'new' history of World War I. *International Security*, 33 (1), 174–185.

Taliaferro, J. (2019). *Defending Frenemies: Alliance Politics and Nuclear Nonproliferation in U.S. Foreign Policy*. New York, NY: Oxford University Press.

Walt, S. M. (1987). *The Origins of Alliances*. Ithaca, NY: Cornell University Press.

Walt, S. M. (1996). *Revolution and War*. Ithaca, NY: Cornell University Press.

Waltz, K. (1979). *Theory of International Politics*. Reading, MA: Addison-Wesley.

Wight, M. (1977). *Systems of States*. Leicester: Leicester University Press.

Wohlforth, W. (1993). *The Elusive Balance: Power and Perceptions during the Cold War*. Ithaca, NY: Cornell University Press.

Wolfers, Arnold. (1966). *Britain and France between Two Wars: Conflicting Strategies of Peace from Versailles to World War II*. New York, NY: W. W. Norton.

Yarhi-Milo, K. (2014). *Knowing the Adversary: Leaders, Intelligence, and Assessment of Intentions in International Relations*. Princeton, NJ: Princeton University Press.

Zakaria, F. (1998). *From Wealth to Power: The Unusual Origins of America's World Role*. Princeton, NJ: Princeton University Press.

8

CONSTRUCTIVISM

History and systemic change

Quentin Bruneau

Introduction

In the study of historical international relations, the boundaries between constructivists, English School scholars, historically inclined liberals and post-structuralists are difficult to discern. This chapter is primarily interested in macro-historical approaches to International Relations (IR) that share constructivism's interest in the role of ideas and norms, but it excludes scholars that clearly and solely identify with the English School, historical sociology and post-structuralism, as these approaches are examined in separate chapters. Above all, this chapter is concerned with scholars who have carried out historical research themselves; it is only very tangentially interested in those who explain how it should be done but have not practically carried out any such projects.

My goal here is not to assess whether constructivists are good or bad historians, whether they make an adequate use of primary sources or take sufficient stock of existing historiography (on this topic consult Leira and de Carvalho, 2016). The aim is simply to outline how constructivists, broadly defined, have engaged in historical work on international relations. To this end, it begins by examining their first forays into the history of international relations. It then moves on to explore how this early work gave rise to two fully fledged research programmes, one on the origins of the modern international system and the other on the comparison of various international systems throughout world history. Finally, it raises two contentious points emerging from this work, one pertaining to substance and the other to method. In so doing, the chapter seeks to identify some of the debates that have stemmed from constructivism's engagement with history, and the limitations that remain within constructivist work on the history of international relations.

Two challenges

Constructivism has been historical from its inception. The main purpose of constructivists' initial use of history was to mount a challenge against neorealism and neoliberalism's disciplinary hegemony. Constructivist scholars sought to show that the assumptions at their core were, historically speaking, highly questionable. As one observer put it, 'neo-realism not only misunderstands the present, but systematically misconceives the past' (Kratochwil, 1993: 69). To develop this challenge, constructivists pursued what I identify here as two distinct research strategies.[1]

Spotting discontinuity: the modern international system

The first strategy consisted in locating the origins of the modern international system of states. Its purpose was to show that the system of states was not a transhistorical structure, but a historically specific one whose very existence scholars of IR had to explain. Thus, instead of producing theoretical critiques, historically inclined constructivists drew attention to the fact that the world had not always been made up of sovereign states, and that this state of affairs had only come about with the replacement of medieval 'heteronomy,' a feudal system of multiple overlapping authorities, somewhere in the middle of the second millennium CE, in Europe (Bartelson, 1995; Hall and Kratochwil, 1993; Kratochwil, 1986; Ruggie, 1983, 1993).[2] This radical shift meant that neorealists and neoliberal scholars of IR posited a state of affairs which ought to be explained, rather than assumed away and held as a constant throughout time. Crucially, constructivist scholars claimed that this change could not possibly be accounted for without reference to ideas and epistemes, because the discontinuity in question was really a shift in terms of how people thought about the political units that constituted their world (for a contemporaneous Marxist version of this puzzle, see Rosenberg, 1994a, 1994b).[3] Taken together, these arguments implied that IR should concern itself not only with the study of the interactions between states, as neorealists and neoliberals did, but also with the conditions and reasons for the emergence of a system of states in the first place. Their historical observation also limited the applicability of theories that were based on the existence of an anarchic system of states to the early modern period and its aftermath.

This argument was groundbreaking in the context of American IR, though slightly less so beyond it. The English School in particular had already explored the issue (Bull, 2002 [1977]; Watson, 2009 [1992]; Wight, 1977). Nonetheless, this iteration of the argument enjoyed a certain success, as can be observed from the attention it received beyond constructivist circles; even rationalist scholars came to pay lip service to the importance of this medieval-to-modern shift and to the role that ideas played in its advent (Fischer, 1992; Krasner, 1995; Spruyt, 1996). As the Cold War came to an end, the static nature of international relations became less clear, and the relevance of radical discontinuities in the international system more obvious, thus creating fertile ground for the spread of these constructivist arguments.

Comparing international systems

The second strategy that historical constructivists pursued to challenge mainstream approaches took the form of a comparative history of international systems, a line of inquiry also inherited from the English School.[4] Using a variety of historical cases, they sought to demonstrate, on the one hand, that different international systems had been constituted by different kinds of units or 'polities' (Ferguson and Mansbach, 1996), i.e. not just states, and on the other hand, that the fundamental dynamics of different international systems could not be understood without reference to common cultural and normative understandings (Reus-Smit, 1999). Thus, while some constructivists were busy making the theoretical case *that* culture and ideas mattered to the operation of the international system (Wendt, 1999), others were demonstrating *how* this mattered, using cases from a variety of historical and geographical settings. This work had a certain liberal sensibility, as it examined the norms that bound the units of international systems together and permitted cooperation, not unlike the macro-historical work of prominent IR liberals (Ikenberry, 2000). But perhaps more importantly, by examining non-European international systems, this strand of work made meaningful contributions to the project of 'Global IR,' long before it was even explicitly articulated (Acharya, 2014).

It appears, then, that constructivism was historical from its early days. The two initial research strategies pursued to mount a challenge against mainstream IR had a lasting impact on historical constructivist scholarship. Indeed, out of these initial forays into historical international relations emerged two research agendas.

Tracing the origins of the modern international system

The work of the first group of constructivists on the important discontinuity marking the birth of the modern international system led to a flurry of studies on the origins of this system. Sharpening the early strokes and correcting them in substantial ways, a new group of scholars turned to this task by breaking it down, focusing on specific features of the modern international system.

Ad Europae maiorem gloriam

A first set of scholars delved into the European origins of various features of the international system. Among this group, some scholars continued searching for the moment when sovereign states became the key units of international politics. They drew attention, in turn, to the centrality of Protestant ideas around the time of the reformation for the emergence of sovereign statehood (Philpott, 2001), and to the gradual exclusion of non-state actors from the right to wage war (Thomson, 1996). Others honed in on the shift from dynastic to popular sovereignty as the main principle of legitimacy in international political culture after the American and French revolutions, and its implications for international relations, notably for war (Bukovansky, 1999, 2001; see also Hall, 1999; see the discussion in Lawson, 2021 in this volume).

Simultaneously, a number of scholars analysed the changing norms that regulated relations between states, putting striking emphasis on the development of liberal norms. This substantive preference and the little attention paid to illiberal norms involuntarily created a 'whiggish' narrative of international relations. Examples of this type of work included studies that tracked the rise of global governance (Mitzen, 2013), as well as the more specific institutional form of multilateralism (Ruggie, 1992), scholarship examining the shifting principles that underlay the practice of intervention and its metamorphosis in time, notably the expanding definition of humanity and the rise of multilateralism (Finnemore, 2004; but see also Barnett, 2011; see also Ravndal 2021 in this volume), and research bringing to light the importance of arguments against the slave trade in legitimising and bringing about decolonisation (Crawford, 2002; see also Svensson 2021 in this volume).[5] These historical constructivists' attraction to the sway of progressive ideas in IR was reminiscent of classic liberalism, to which constructivists, rather than liberal institutionalists or neoliberal scholars, were in many ways the true heirs.

Beyond Europe

The tendency to look for the origins of the modern international system within Europe was based on a historical assumption that the English School once termed the 'expansion of international society': the idea that the modern system of states emerged in Europe, along with all its key institutions (diplomacy, international law etc.), and subsequently spread to the rest of the world (Bull and Watson, 1984).[6] Under the guidance of this diffusionist story, there was no need to look outside Europe to understand the origins of the modern international system and the development of its key features. However, the increasingly obvious fact that Europe and the extra-European world had interacted frequently from the early modern period onwards, through practices such as colonialism and imperialism, put growing strain on a Eurocentric narrative that required a pristine Europe.[7] How could these relations not be constitutive of the normative structure of the international system?

A second set of constructivist scholars therefore began looking for the origins of the modern international system outside Europe, in particular in the relations between Europeans and non-Europeans (Neumann, 2011; Wigen, 2014; Zarakol, 2010).[8] One way of doing this was to examine the direct legacies of imperial and colonial representations for contemporary international relations (Doty, 1996).[9] This was also useful, normatively speaking, for those seeking to cast doubt on the complete break of our world from this not-so-distant one. Another approach consisted in recovering the extra-European origins of crucial features of our system of states, for instance modern territoriality, the origins of which apparently lay in early modern colonial practices only imported back to Europe in the late-eighteenth century (Branch, 2012).[10] Finally, some scholars attempted to show that the modern international system was precisely the unstable result of a fusion of two normative orders, a familiar European one based on the respect of states' sovereignty and an extra-European order based on the divisibility of sovereignty and the civilisation of non-European cultures (Keene, 2002; see the discussion in de Carvalho, 2021; Bayly, 2021; both in this volume).

Before I move on to the next section, I want to dwell on one of the main theoretical payoffs of this literature. Amidst growing engagement with the history of international relations between Europe and the world, researchers returned to a key assumption of mainstream IR theory: the anarchical structure of the international system. Putting the nineteenth- and early twentieth-century interactions of non-European polities with Europe at the centre of their inquiries, constructivist scholars gradually recognised that the international system had indeed been hierarchically ordered in the recent past (Hobson and Sharman, 2005; Kang, 2010; Keene, 2007, 2014; Mattern and Zarakol, 2016; Ringmar, 2012). Several polities had effectively claimed the right to command over others. While there was no single global sovereign in the nineteenth century, a club of countries, the family of civilised nations, had made good on its claims to command over others. Such an observation allowed constructivists to speak of hierarchy, even in a restricted Waltzian sense, further entrenching their challenge of mainstream IR. This both exposed the limited scope conditions of mainstream theories which assumed anarchy as a baseline and posed the historical question of when the international system had actually become anarchical.

Comparing international systems

As we saw earlier, the main alternative strand of research that historical constructivists initially pursued to challenge mainstream IR consisted in the comparison of different international systems. The initial intention was to show that the fundamental dynamics of international systems could not be grasped without a deep understanding of their ideational and normative structure. Those taking up this research strategy in later years continued this project, but also used their comparative work to develop new theoretical insights.

From the mid-noughties onwards, the first strand of work sought to deepen our understanding of the ideational underpinnings of different international systems in two different ways. First, some developed better histories of international political thought. Early work comparing international systems had already relied heavily on international political thought to define how international systems functioned (see Reus-Smit, 1999). The goal now was to give a better account of the thought of various epochs, in a more methodologically grounded fashion, integrating the insights of Cambridge School contextualism and those of conceptual history (*Begriffsgeschichte*) (Armitage, 2012; Bartelson, 2009; Bell, 2012; Keene, 2005; Pitts, 2006, 2018; Roshchin, 2013).[11] The point was to go beyond studies that consisted either in placing the likes of Machiavelli, Hobbes and Kant in the ahistorical categories of realism and liberalism or in engaging in a relatively a-contextual exegesis of their texts to recover the 'timeless' wisdom they contained. In so far as constructivism was about the ideational underpinnings of IR, it was clear that those interested in history should begin producing historically sound accounts of international political thought. This exercise was key to help constructivists identify the ideational foundations of various international systems. The second method to deepen our understanding of these systems consisted in developing better accounts of why their internal dynamics differed so radically. Though earlier work also aimed to do this, new explanations focused with more insistence on the agency side than on ideational structures (Lebow, 2008). Such work did not spend much time analysing the units of different international systems; it was more concerned with understanding the agentic drives that could explain the dynamics of these systems.

The second research pathway was the continuation of theoretical challenges to mainstream (chiefly realist) IR, focusing on two key aspects. First, historical constructivists provided a theoretical explanation of transitions between international systems (Phillips, 2010; Reus-Smit, 2013). While they had initially demonstrated that there were indeed radically different international systems throughout history, they had not provided strong theoretical accounts of transitions between systems, though, as we saw earlier, they lambasted realists for lacking the theoretical tools to do so. This was in a sense the realisation of an early promise. Second, those comparing international systems targeted an assumption central to neorealism, as well as to historical sociology: the idea that in any international system, the units would necessarily converge on one type (e.g. the state) (see Go et al., 2021 in this volume). Scholars showed that diversity among the units of the international system could not only exist but persist over time, and that one could produce a solid theoretical account of why this might be so (Phillips and Sharman, 2015).

Thus, historical constructivists comparing international systems continued to challenge realist assumptions and to deepen our understanding of international relations. They achieved this both through substantive studies about the constitution of international systems and through theoretical work on their transformation, fulfilling promises they had made two decades earlier.

Taking stock and moving forward

From early modern discontinuities to the nineteenth century

As stated earlier, constructivists initially turned to history to challenge neorealism and mainstream IR more generally. To mount this challenge, one of their strategies was to turn to the early modern period, where they identified a radical discontinuity: the emergence of a system of territorial sovereign states. In one way, this initial challenge was creaking at the seams less than a decade after it had been raised. One scholar in particular had launched a scathing attack on one of its most popular versions, namely the claim that a system of states had emerged in 1648 with the Peace of Westphalia (Osiander, 2001; see also the later de Carvalho et al., 2011). Through a close examination of the treaties constituting the Peace of Westphalia – those of Münster and Osnabrück – and of the political debates surrounding them, this study showed that there was no reason to associate this event with the emergence of a system of sovereign states. It had in fact nothing to do with such a development; if anything, this peace treaty was about the development of ideas opposed to absolute state sovereignty. This intervention raised two major questions. First, if the modern international system did not emerge in 1648, then when did it begin? Second, if the early modern world was not about states and interstate dynamics, then what was it about?

While answers to the second question remained scarce (for an exception see Nexon, 2009), constructivists had in many ways already begun answering the first question around the time when this challenge was raised and in the following years. The vast majority of those tracing the origins of the modern international system indeed pointed to the critical role of the nineteenth century (Branch, 2014; Bukovansky, 2001; Crawford, 2002; Doty, 1996; Finnemore, 2004; Reus-Smit, 1999: 6; Ruggie, 1992; Thomson, 1996), long before more explicit calls to that effect were heard (Buzan and Lawson, 2015). Furthermore, the scholar who attacked the Westphalian myth head on, Andreas Osiander, attempted to answer the question of the origins himself, arguing that no real states-system was to be found at any point before the nineteenth century (Osiander, 2007; for a Marxist view, see Teschke, 2009). Though most IR scholars still point to 1648 as the birth date of the modern international system, constructivist literature in fact seems to agree on the centrality of the nineteenth century for the emergence of a great deal of its core features. Thus, constructivists have not contented themselves with critiques of old myths, but they have in fact produced the outline for a novel answer. Yet, the Westphalian myth keeps resurfacing in research and teaching, in large part because this answer remains fragmented and scattered, an issue to which I will return in the conclusion. This question of empirical accuracy leads me to the second and final issue I wish to raise here.

What about the people?

Due to its focus on ideas, norms, culture and the like, one main methodological problem afflicts historical constructivist work. Historical constructivists have given insufficient thought to the methodological question of where we ought to look for the ideas that constitute international systems. There has been a strong temptation on the part of researchers to turn to the clearest statements of how international systems function. This concern has, inevitably, led scholars to rely heavily on the writings of great political and legal thinkers, philosophers and politicians, where such ideas can be found in their clearest form (a good example is Reus-Smit, 1999). A number of scholars have recently criticised this way of proceeding, questioning why these writings and individuals might warrant so much attention, by comparison with less well-known albeit influential practitioners (see, e.g., Keene, 2017; Wallenius, 2019). If, as one prominent historian of international law puts it, 'international law is what international lawyers do and what they think,' then international relations are likewise, what practitioners of IR do and what they think. This may not be properly captured by works that overemphasise the historical role of great thinkers.

The problem of course is that practically oriented individuals tend to spend less time laying out their views in clear treatises than great thinkers do. Historical constructivists thus need new methods to recover these individuals' thoughts. Dealing with this seemingly arcane methodological issue could yield profoundly new insights into the question of how 'the world hangs together.' One way to do this might consist in drawing on work at the intersection of international, social and cultural history (Koskenniemi, 2004; Mösslang and Riotte, 2008; but see also Cross, 2008), as well as on the insights of the 'practice turn.' By making greater use of existing histories of international practitioners, whether they are diplomats, lawyers, economists, colonial administrators, bankers, constructivists may be able to rehabilitate the agency side of their histories and provide more historically grounded accounts of change, in which social agents are not mere coat hangers for the norms and ideas recovered from great men's thought.

Conclusion

This chapter has examined the ways in which constructivists and a few closely related scholars have approached the history of international relations. Constructivists initially mounted a challenge against mainstream approaches – chiefly realism – in two main ways. First, they sought to trace the origins of the system of sovereign states, showing that it was a historically specific form of international order, and that prior ones bore little resemblance to it. This meant that realism took for granted a state of affairs that ought to be explained – a problem it was ill-equipped to address. Second, constructivists attempted to compare different international systems, showing that their core constitutive units differed vastly and that their internal dynamics could not be understood without reference to their constitutive ideas. This strategy also served to reveal the specificities of our own world, which were entirely taken for granted by mainstream theories.

These two initial challenges to mainstream approaches came to form the core research strands of historical constructivism. The first, concerned with the origins of the modern international system, was developed so as to examine the rise of various features of modern international relations, such as intervention. While many of these genealogies initially traced 'modern' features of international relations back to Europe, later work subsequently began exploring the importance of contacts between Europeans and the extra-European world in shaping modern international relations. The second research strategy, focused on the comparison of international systems, developed along different lines. Some of the scholars engaged in this type of work deepened our understanding of the ideational and normative constitution of different international orders, through both in-depth studies of international political thought and a renewed focus on agents' logics of action. Others made novel theoretical contributions based on their comparative study of international systems, in the form of explanations of systems change, and rebuttals of realist assumptions, such as unit convergence.

Has historical constructivism fulfilled its purpose, and do we still need it today? If historical constructivism initially served to challenge mainstream theories of IR, then the fact that a majority of IR scholars do not see their work as fitting within realism, liberalism, Marxism or the English School,[12] may imply that this project is at an end. But this is somewhat of a red herring. All scholars of IR define the present in relation to some idea of what international relations were like in the past, and it is truly striking how traditional these views can be even among purportedly critical scholars. In this sense, what were long seen as realist or 'mainstream' IR assumptions still pervade a great deal of courses and publications from scholars who would never identify with these groups. Nowhere is this clearer than in the case of the debate on the origins of the system of states. Despite regular attempts to debunk the Westphalian story, the myth persists across theoretical divides. The main problem is that few fully fleshed out alternatives exist; what we have are mostly fragmented and scattered critiques. The Westphalian myth thus remains as the only clearly available shorthand version of the history of the states-system for those teaching IR. Historical constructivist work therefore still faces the admittedly Sisyphean task of cobbling together new grand narratives about the making of modern international relations.

Suggestions for further reading

Alexandrowicz, C. H. (1967). *An Introduction to the History of the Law of Nations in the East Indies (16th, 17th, and 18th Centuries).* Oxford: Clarendon Press.

Branch, J. (2014). *The Cartographic State: Maps, Territory and the Origins of Sovereignty.* Cambridge: Cambridge University Press.

Hébié, M. (2015). *Souveraineté territoriale par traité.* Paris: Presses Universitaires de France.

Keene, E. (2002). *Beyond the Anarchical Society: Grotius, Colonialism and Order in World Politics.* Cambridge: Cambridge University Press.

Lebow, R. N. (2009). *A Cultural Theory of International Relations.* Cambridge: Cambridge University Press.

Phillips, A. (2011). *War, Religion and Empire: The Transformation of International Orders.* Cambridge: Cambridge University Press.

Notes

1 I am not suggesting that these are self-consciously understood as distinct schools or traditions by the scholars pursuing them.
2 The influence of Michel Foucault's work on John Ruggie and Jens Bartelson is striking.
3 Rosenberg has in some way returned to a naturalised version of the international by adopting Trotsky's theory of uneven and combined development, in which societies have replaced states as the fundamental transhistorical constituent units of the international. For an interesting analysis of the problems, this analytic move poses, see Mann (1986).
4 See, for instance, Buzan and Little (2000); Watson (2009 [1992]); Wight (1977).
5 Again, the English School had been exploring similar topics for some time (Mayall, 1990; Vincent, 1974, 1986).
6 This is generally referred to as the 'expansion of international society' among English School scholars (Bull and Watson, 1984).
7 For what is still an outstanding account of the legal and diplomatic dimension of these relations, see Alexandrowicz (1967, 1973).
8 This theme was also present in histories of international law (Anghie, 2005), and in much more familiar places for political scientists, such as Benedict Anderson's work on nationalism (Anderson, 1983).
9 The English School produced a great deal of work on this issue, focusing on the 'entry into international society' of various countries.
10 For a different view, see Schulz (2019).
11 Though some of these authors may not identify as constructivist or even IR scholars, but as political scientists engaged in the historical study of international political thought, their work has uncontestably contributed to this strand of work.
12 See TRIPS survey results for Question 18, https://trip.wm.edu/charts/#/bargraph/38/5052.

References

Acharya, A. (2014). Global international relations (IR) and regional worlds. *International Studies Quarterly*, 58 (4), 647–659.
Alexandrowicz, C. H. (1973). *The European-African Confrontation: A Study in Treaty Making*. Leiden: Sijthoff.
Anderson, B. (1983). *Imagined Communities : Reflections on the Origin and Spread of Nationalism*. London: Verso.
Anghie, A. (2005). *Imperialism, Sovereignty and the Making of International Law*. Cambridge: Cambridge University Press.
Armitage, D. (2012). *Foundations of Modern International Thought*. Cambridge: Cambridge University Press.
Barnett, M. (2011) *Empire of Humanity: A History of Humanitarianism*. Ithaca, NY: Cornell University Press.
Bartelson, J. (1995). *A Genealogy of Sovereignty*. Cambridge: Cambridge University Press.
Bartelson, J. (2009). *Visions of World Community*. Cambridge: Cambridge University Press.
Bayly, M. (2021). Imperialism: Beyond the 'Re-turn to Empire' in International Relations. In de Carvalho, B., Costa Lopez, J., & Leira, H., eds. *Routledge Handbook of Historical International Relations*. Abingdon: Routledge.
Bell, D., ed. (2012). *Victorian Visions of Global Order: Empire and International Relations in Nineteenth-Century Political Thought*. Cambridge: Cambridge University Press.
Branch, J. (2012). 'Colonial reflection' and territoriality: the peripheral origins of sovereign statehood. *European Journal of International Relations*, 18 (2), 277–297.
Bukovansky, M. (1999). The altered state and the state of nature: the French revolution and international politics. *Review of International Studies*, 25 (2), 197–216.
Bukovansky, M. (2001). *Legitimacy and Power Politics: The American & French Revolutions in International Political Culture*. Princeton, NJ: Princeton University Press.
Bull, H. (2002). *The Anarchical Society: A Study of Order in World Politics*. New York, NY: Columbia University Press.
Bull, H. and Watson, A., eds. (1984). *The Expansion of International Society*. Oxford: Oxford University Press.
Buzan, B. and Lawson, G. (2015). *The Global Transformation: History, Modernity and the Making of International Relations*. Cambridge: Cambridge University Press.
Buzan, B. and Little, R. (2000). *International Systems in World History: Remaking the Study of International Relations*. Oxford: Oxford University Press.
Crawford, N. (2002). *Argument and Change in World Politics: Ethics, Decolonization, and Humanitarian Intervention*. Cambridge: Cambridge University Press.

Cross, M. K. D. (2008). *The European Diplomatic Corps: Diplomats and International Cooperation from Westphalia to Maastricht*. Basingstoke: Palgrave Macmillan.

de Carvalho, B. (2021). Sovereignty in Historical International Relations: Trajectories, Challenges and Implications. In de Carvalho, B., Costa Lopez, J., & Leira, H., eds. *Routledge Handbook of Historical International Relations*. Abingdon: Routledge.

de Carvalho, B., Leira, H. and Hobson, J. M. (2011). The big bangs of IR: the myths that your teachers still tell you about 1648 and 1919. *Millennium*, 39 (3), 735–758.

Doty, R. L. (1996). *Imperial Encounters: The Politics of Representation in North-South Relations*. Minneapolis, MN: University of Minnesota Press.

Ferguson, Y. H. and Mansbach, R. W. (1996). *Polities: Authority, Identities, and Change*. Columbia, SC: University of South Carolina Press.

Finnemore, M. (2004). *The Purpose of Intervention: Changing Beliefs about the Use of Force*. Ithaca, NY: Cornell University Press.

Fischer, M. (1992). Feudal Europe, 800-1300: communal discourse and conflictual practices. *International Organization*, 46 (2), 427–466.

Go, J., Lawson, G., and de Carvalho, B. (2021). Historical Sociology in International Relations: The Challenge of the Global. In de Carvalho, B., Costa Lopez, J., & Leira, H., eds. *Routledge Handbook of Historical International Relations*. Abingdon: Routledge.

Hall, R. B. (1999). *National Collective Identity: Social Constructs and International Systems*. New York, NY: Columbia University Press.

Hall, R. B. and Kratochwil, F. V. (1993). Medieval tales: neorealist "science" and the abuse of history. *International Organization*, 47 (3), 479–491.

Hobson, J. M. and Sharman, J. C. (2005). The enduring place of hierarchy in world politics: tracing the social logics of hierarchy and political change. *European Journal of International Relations*, 11 (1), 63–98.

Ikenberry, G. J. (2000). *After Victory: Institutions, Strategic Restraint, and the Rebuilding of Order After Major Wars*. Princeton University Press.

Kang, D. C. (2010). Hierarchy and legitimacy in international systems: the tribute system in early modern East Asia. *Security Studies*, 19 (4), 591–622.

Keene, E. (2005). *International Political Thought: A Historical Introduction*. Cambridge: Polity.

Keene, E. (2007). A case study of the construction of international hierarchy: British treaty-making against the slave trade in the early nineteenth century. *International Organization*, 61 (2), 311–339.

Keene, E. (2014). The standard of 'civilisation', the expansion thesis and the 19th-century international social space. *Millennium – Journal of International Studies*, 42 (3), 651–673.

Keene, E. (2017). International intellectual history and International Relations: contexts, canons and mediocrities. *International Relations*, 31 (3), 341–356.

Koskenniemi, M. (2004). *The Gentle Civilizer of Nations: The Rise and Fall of International Law 1870-1960*. Cambridge: Cambridge University Press.

Krasner, S. D. (1995). Compromising Westphalia. *International Security*, 20 (3), 115–151.

Kratochwil, F. (1986). Of systems, boundaries, and territoriality: an inquiry into the formation of the state system. *World Politics*, 39 (1), 27–52.

Kratochwil, F. (1993). The embarrassment of changes: neo-realism as the science of realpolitik without politics. *Review of International Studies*, 19 (1), 63–80.

Lawson, G. (2021). Revolutions: Integrating the International. In de Carvalho, B., Costa Lopez, J., & Leira, H., eds. *Routledge Handbook of Historical International Relations*. Abingdon: Routledge.

Lebow, R. N. (2008). *A Cultural Theory of International Relations*. Cambridge: Cambridge University Press.

Leira, H. and de Carvalho, B. (2016). Construction time again: history in constructivist IR scholarship. *European Review of International Studies*, 3 (3), 99–111.

Mann, M. (1986). *The Sources of Social Power (Vol. 1)*. Cambridge: Cambridge University Press.

Mattern, J. B. and Zarakol, A. (2016). Hierarchies in world politics. *International Organization*, 70 (3), 623–654.

Mayall, J. (1990). *Nationalism and International Society*. Cambridge: Cambridge University Press.

Mitzen, J. (2013). *Power in Concert: The Nineteenth-Century Origins of Global Governance*. Chicago, IL: University of Chicago Press.

Mösslang, M. and Riotte, T., eds. (2008). *The Diplomats' World: The Cultural History of Diplomacy, 1815–1914*. Oxford: Oxford University Press.

Neumann, I. B. (2011). Entry into international society reconceptualised: the case of Russia. *Review of International Studies*, 37 (2), 463–484.

Nexon, D. H. (2009). *The Struggle for Power in Early Modern Europe: Religious Conflict, Dynastic Empires, and International Change*. Princeton, NJ: Princeton University Press.

Osiander, A. (2001). Sovereignty, international relations, and the Westphalian myth. *International Organization*, 55 (2), 251–287.

Osiander, A. (2007). *Before the State: Systemic Political Change in the West from the Greeks to the French Revolution*. Oxford: Oxford University Press.

Phillips, A. (2010). *War, Religion and Empire: The Transformation of International Orders*. Cambridge: Cambridge University Press.

Phillips, A. and Sharman, J. C. (2015). *International Order in Diversity: War, Trade and Rule in the Indian Ocean*. Cambridge: Cambridge University Press.

Philpott, D. (2001). *Revolutions in Sovereignty: How Ideas Shaped Modern International Relations*. Princeton, NJ: Princeton University Press.

Pitts, J. (2006). *A Turn to Empire: The Rise of Imperial Liberalism in Britain and France*. Princeton, NJ: Princeton University Press.

Pitts, J. (2018). *Boundaries of the International: Law and Empire*. Cambridge, MA: Harvard University Press.

Ravndal, E. J. (2021). International Organizations in Historical Perspective. In de Carvalho, B., Costa Lopez, J., & Leira, H., eds. *Routledge Handbook of Historical International Relations*. Abingdon: Routledge.

Reus-Smit, C. (1999). *The Moral Purpose of the State: Culture, Social Identity, and Institutional Rationality in International Relations*. Princeton, NJ: Princeton University Press.

Reus-Smit, C. (2013). *Individual Rights and the Making of the International System*. Cambridge: Cambridge University Press.

Ringmar, E. (2012). Performing international systems: two East-Asian alternatives to the Westphalian order. *International Organization*, 66 (1), 1–25.

Rosenberg, J. (1994a). *Empire of Civil Society: A Critique of the Realist Theory of International Relations*. London: Verso.

Rosenberg, J. (1994b). The international imagination: IR theory and 'classic social analysis'. *Millennium*, 23 (1), 85–108.

Roshchin, E. (2013). (Un)Natural and contractual international society: a conceptual inquiry. *European Journal of International Relations*, 19 (2), 257–279.

Ruggie, J. G. (1983). Continuity and transformation in the world polity: toward a neorealist synthesis. *World Politics*, 35 (2), 261–285.

Ruggie, J. G. (1992). Multilateralism: the Anatomy of an Institution. *International Organization*, 46 (3), 561–598.

Ruggie, J. G. (1993). Territoriality and beyond: problematizing modernity in international relations. *International Organization*, 47 (1), 139–174.

Schulz, C.-A. (2019). Territorial sovereignty and the end of inter-cultural diplomacy along the "Southern frontier". *European Journal of International Relations*, 25 (3), 878–903.

Spruyt, H. (1996). *The Sovereign State and Its Competitors: An Analysis of Systems Change*. Princeton, NJ: Princeton University Press.

Svensson, T. (2021). Decolonisation and the Erosion of the Imperial Idea. In de Carvalho, B., Costa Lopez, J., & Leira, H., eds. *Routledge Handbook of Historical International Relations*. Abingdon: Routledge.

Teschke, B. (2009). *The Myth of 1648: Class, Geopolitics, and the Making of Modern International Relations*. 2nd edition. London: Verso.

Thomson, J. E. (1996). *Mercenaries, Pirates, and Sovereigns*. Princeton, NJ: Princeton University Press.

Vincent, R. J. (1974). *Nonintervention and International Order*. Princeton, NJ: Princeton University Press.

Vincent, R. J. (1986). *Human Rights and International Relations*. Cambridge: Cambridge University Press.

Wallenius, T. (2019). The case for a history of global legal practices. *European Journal of International Relations*, 25 (1), 108–130.

Watson, A. (2009). *The Evolution of International Society: A Comparative Historical Analysis*. 2nd edition. Milton Park: Routledge.

Wendt, A. (1999). *Social Theory of International Politics*. Cambridge: Cambridge University Press.

Wigen, E. (2014). Go West! Turkey's entry into international society. *International Relations*, 28 (4), 468–478.

Wight, M. (1977). *Systems of States*. London: Leicester University Press.

Zarakol, A. (2010). *After Defeat: How the East Learned to Live with the West*. Cambridge: Cambridge University Press.

9

POSTSTRUCTURALISM AND THE CHALLENGE OF HISTORY

Andreas Aagaard Nøhr

The historical challenge of neo-realism

The poststructuralist concern for history takes place on the backdrop of an impasse in the modern social sciences between a-temporal structuralist approaches and approaches that favour historical interpretation. With what R. B. J. Walker (1989: 169) ironically refers to as 'life before International Relations' – the origin story of the discipline is largely told through a set vocabulary of great battles, peace treaties, lines of ascension, with themes of progress, modernity, emancipation, and of regression, violence, and tragedy. Yet the deeper layers of the story seem to all be set against some timeless background of the balance of power, security, and order – history, as such, had largely been forgotten by the discipline of International Relations (IR) (on the balance of power, see Andersen and Wohlforth, 2021 in this volume). Whether progressive, evolutionary, teleological, or centring on some kind of idea of an eternal return, this historical fable merely justifies certain theoretical outlooks. Indeed, when it comes to one of the central objects of theorizing in the discipline, there is a complete neglect for historical sensitivity (Walker, 1989: 171): 'the historicity of states and state systems recedes into the background, and world politics begins to be portrayed as a permanent game, which can appear to have followed more or less the same rules for time immemorial'. At the end of the 1980s, history had effectively given way to structure in the discipline of IR: it had become a discipline blind to the historicity of process, practice, power, and politics *qua* its structural theorizing (Ashley, 1984: 258–260).

In response, poststructuralists thus pose a historical challenge by inverting the hierarchy between theory and history: theoretical discourse cannot be allowed to enjoy a special locale outside the constraints of history, it must be historicized, and its conditions of possibility rendered visible. The 'appropriate posture' would according to Ashley (1987: 408) amount to 'an overview of international history in the making, a view from afar, from up high'. Against the static structuralism of neo-realism, the poststructuralists are interested in how 'structural patterns are constituted through historical processes of differentiation' (Walker, 1989: 175). As such, this chapter will take up the questions of how to recognize poststructuralist Historical IR (HIR). What patterns of thought, fundamental ideas, and methodological insights does it lend itself to? I shall proceed, not by outlining a set of formal criteria that needs to be followed to the letter, nor by presenting a succession of authors that handed down shards of analytical light, but by drawing attention to certain characteristics and problems that might be associated with poststructuralist thought in relation to HIR.

History is a narrative

The main thrust of poststructuralism arises from the insight that signs do not contain inherent or positive meaning; rather, meaning is derived from the difference between signs within a system of signs. Poststructuralists exploit the arbitrary nature of the sign, the uncertainty or 'slippage' between signifier (word) and signified (concept), to argue that *meaning is necessarily arbitrary*. As language is essential to communications about the past, this highlights a central problem of history: the radical indeterminacy of historical meaning. No matter how coherent the theory or how rigorous the method, there is no way in which the gap between the interpretations and the object of study can be breached and come to a close. It is not that other historiographic approaches within IR would not acknowledge this fundamental problem of historiography, but the difference between these positions and the poststructuralist lies in the fact that the former 'impose some kind of interpretive closure on the historical record' (Vaughan-Williams, 2005: 117), while the latter embrace this radical indeterminacy.

Thus, in relation to historiography, we must acknowledge that there is a difference between the past and history (Jenkins, 1991: 8): 'the past has gone and history is what historians make of it when they go to work'. There is, as with the signifier and the signified, no necessary link between the past and these narrative structures. In this way, history must be properly understood as *Le Texte Général* – that is, a never-ending series of interpretations. Or with Ashley (1987, 408–409): 'History itself is grasped as a series of interpretations imposed upon interpretations – none primary, all arbitrary'. The work of the historian, however, consists among other things in providing the past with meaning – meaning that is made intelligible by weaving traces of the past into what Hayden White (1973) termed 'narrative structures' (see the discussion in Guillaume, 2021; Hom, 2021; both in this volume). Because history as such has no inherent meaning, no simple and obvious history of events, the historian will have to discuss how narrativization of the events or facts of history have been 'emplotted' – White's initial schematization of romance, comedy, satire, and tragedy will evoke some familiarity, but was inevitably too crude. Thus, it is only when the historian weaves such narrative structures upon a collection of disparate events that we are presented with historical meaning. Campbell (1992: 263) attempts to show how works dealing with the Bosnian War adopt certain 'narrativizing structures' in their interpretation of the events themselves, arguing that this effectively leads 'many of the major assessments of the conflict [to] have reduced [the] complexity to the banalities of ethnic essentialism in order to attribute responsibility to particular individuals or groups'.

By considering history as narrative structures, poststructuralism draws long lines back to ancient modes of writing history and to the distinction between history as *res gestae*, the totality of events that constitutes the unfolding of human civilization on the one hand, and history as the *historia rerum gestarum*, the account of these events, on the other. With modernity, history comes to 'present a rational standard that lifts man above mere conventionalism and capricious subjectivism because it allows man to judge all conventions in terms of their state of progress towards the perfectly just society in which is the rational end of history' (Gillespie, 1984: 12). All approaches to history – at least in so far as they claim that history is a *res* – thus have to answer the question of what history is. That is, they have to provide a rational ground for human actuality, at the same time such attempts are in constant danger of unchecked reification. With two world wars and a long history of colonialism, conceptions that consistently sustain human dignity seem wanting. Such failures might persuade us to forsake any hope for history altogether.

Indeed, the kind of historicism that poststructuralism typically is assumed to subscribe to reverts back to an ancient understanding of history as mere chance – a path that, because it abandons any rational grounds for discussing history while at the same time refusing all cosmological or theological sources of meaning, inevitably ends in nihilism. History is merely the last great myth. Nevertheless, such a standpoint can hardly be the topic of discussion in a chapter such as this; if not for some inarticulable rational ground, there must still be something to be said about history as past events in order to attempt to provide us with some degree of meaning. In that regard, some poststructuralists would rather view the 'meaninglessness of history' as an analytical grip; one that functions to demonstrate the extent to which the meaning offered by the present is merely coincidental, and therefore can be changed by posing questions of it.

Nevertheless, that human actuality is reduced to nothing is exactly the kind of critique that we find in modernist rebuttals of poststructuralist scholarship (for an early example, see Spegele, 1992). Such critics, however, are too quick to dismiss the possibility that it is the prac- tice of asking questions of present narratives to produce new ones that makes historiography both productive and meaningful. Indeed, it would be quite unsatisfactory if poststructuralist historiography of IR were to end here with the demonstration of all modernist histories being nothing but arbitrary narratives within the possibility of a truly external evaluation. How then, sensing the unease at which such a premature ending would entail, and a desire to go a little further, do poststructuralists typically go about narrating history? There are at least two possible routes: on the one hand, there is the possibility of a history oriented towards the *future*, guided by Derrida – that draws its strength from the problem of history by emphasizing the *différance,* or rather the difference and deferral, of historical meaning (Vaughan-Williams, 2005); on the other, a history oriented and firmly lodged in the *present*, guided by Foucault – and it is the latter, even if the core of both consist in problematization, that will be the focus of the next section.

Genealogy

Poststructuralist historiography starts from the acknowledgement of a meta-historical problem – that human beings occupy an ambiguous position as both historical beings existing *within* his- tory and yet at the same time standing *outside* it contemplating its unfolding. Modern thought has offered two responses to this problem, one being a reaction to the other, and yet both are fallacies: *finalism* – to write history of the past in terms of some imagined future – and *pres- entism* – to write history of the past in terms of the present. The problem with both, however, is that they assume some supra-historical position from which they narrate the unfolding of history. Following Nietzsche, poststructuralists argue that history as a scholarly activity is firmly lodged in the present and that we, in contrast, should abandon the quest for supra-historical position by instead aiming to write history wholly from within. In doing so, they attempt to write historiographies in terms of genealogies – that is, to write 'the history of the past in terms of the past' (Bartelson, 1995: 58).

A genealogy, then, is a *history of the present* in so far as it questions the historical limits of what is taken as natural and timeless in the present. As such, the starting point of genealogy is the nominalist assumption that anything general does not exist. The genealogist then asks: how is the phenomenon under study possible? *How did we get here*? How can we account for the emergence of the various objects, subjects, and concepts that constitute our present? Not as a speaking sub- ject relating through the use of concepts to represent an object, but as discursive practices – a system of autonomous statements that organize practice – that structure a logical space of intel- ligibility between subject, objects, and concepts (See Bartelson, 1995: 69–73 for a discussion). As for instance when Molloy (2006: 15–34) points out that our current reading of Realism rests on a misreading of the classical realists as parsimonious scientists. From here, a genealogy traces how the rationalities that underlie particular discursive practices change and shift over time; how their trajectories blend, disperse, and affect one another; and how they eventually manifest themselves as what, in our contemporary discourse, is taken as natural, essential, and general (on practices, see Kustermans, 2021 in this volume). By doing so, a genealogy historicizes that which is held to be universal and transcendental and emphasizes the ways in which the genesis of the present is chaotic, contingent, singular, and still at points interconnected and somewhat discontinuous. In other words, a genealogy is a 'history of the present' that resists fixating the present in the past while at the same time avoids writing a history of the past in terms of the present – the connection between the present and the past is lodged in the activity of the problematizing the present.

Genealogy is both *effective* and *exemplary*. Effective because it responds to a call to write history; the more pertinent a problem, the more effective genealogy becomes. Exemplary in that the genealogist sticks to the traces of the past which are documented and can be confirmed: 'Genealogy is grey [as opposed to the blue of the idealist], meticulous, and patiently documentary. It operates on a field of entangled and confused parchments, on documents that have been scratched over and recopied many times', writes Foucault (1991: 76). Not because there is something real behind the apparent, but because these instances constitute the traces of past interpretations. It is these different interpretations that battle it out to clear the logical space of knowable subject, objects, and concepts. In studying these, the genealogist writes what Nietzsche calls *wirkliche Historie* or what Machiavelli calls *verita effectuale* – here, politics are studied in terms of Realpolitik and rationality in terms of *Realrationalität*, with all its accidents, coincidences, and contradictions. For example, when in 1944 Raphaël Lemkin coined the neologism 'genocide' to describe a disparate set of violence practices that were not guided by the strict principles of sovereignty and right, he did not anticipate the way in the concept of genocide would be transformed into what Meiches (2019) terms the 'hegemonic understanding of genocide' – a crime involving relatively stable group categories, with set identities and agencies.

Yet, genealogy does not pretend to arrive at the essences or the proper origins: by being exemplary, genealogy is neither essentialist nor relativist, but contextualist and elliptic. It is the very context of discursive practices, and the problems that constitute it, that restrain possible interpretations and it is elliptic in the sense that if genealogy is to justify its interpretation of the present then it must write the history of its own vantage point at the same time. In contrast to suprahistorical perspectives that attempt to totalize history, genealogy put everything into historical motion; ideals, truths, bodies, and experiences that seem to be beyond relativity are all dissolved and emerge as episodes of logical construed spaces that determine social fields. What takes place here is not reducible to a series of meaningless serious speech acts; rather, these activities are social maneuverers that carry great consequences for those involved. Thus, what is studied is the materialization of a battle where subjects emerge and play games of truth, there and there alone; Foucault (1991: 85) writes 'in a sense, only a single drama is ever staged in this non-place, the endlessly repeated play of dominations'. At its core, genealogy is an empiricist methodology: the world is not a play that simply hides a deeper truth existing beneath its layers – it is as it appears.

Genealogy is *episodic*: not in the sense of a finale of a long drama or a non-episode from which all other episodes can be comprehended, but in the sense that it takes the present as an episode among other, soon to be displaced by a new interpretation of which the genealogical reading can be seen as problematic. As when Bartelson (1995) shows how the logical space that determines our conception of sovereignty has transmuted from the Middle Ages and the Renaissance, over the classical age, to modernity. Or when Der Derian (1987) invokes instances of mytho-diplomacy, proto-diplomacy, anti-diplomacy, neo-diplomacy, and techno-diplomacy to destabilize the concept of diplomacy as merely an international culture of reciprocity among equals and the recognition of certain immunities and norms towards strangers. The point of a genealogy is not to reconstruct the past in its totality as it actually was, but rather to recount only those episodes that were effective in forming that which was identified as problematic. It does not resemble a conventional historiography of the great events and texts that make up an age or constitute a culture, but is concerned instead with only those incidents and historical accidents that are relevant to the formation of that which was demonstrated to be problematic in the present. In fact, such events and texts have to be taken with a degree of suspicion, as their 'greatness' is merely a function of the significance they are granted by a problematic present. In response, genealogy sees these earlier interpretations of greatness as part of the problems that they themselves have sought to solve, which makes history a series of reversals in the rules of interpretation.

Genealogy as a method for studying HIR is not without its problems (Vucetic, 2011). There is, for instance, an inherent danger or problem of adhering to an 'archaeological' selection of empirics when it comes to conducting a genealogy. It was with good reason that Foucault situated his studies of discourse predominantly within the human sciences, one of them being that this made it easy to delineate the particular discursive practice that he was interested in. However, this was largely a strategy that was inherited from French historical epistemologists and once their theoretical apparatus was let loose on the social world by large, it would have to be given up (Foucault, 2002 [1969]: 192–195). Sure enough, Ashley and Walker never strayed far from the 'discipline' of IR (Ashley, 1987; Roy et al., 1988, but see also Hamilton, 2016a). However, if genealogy is to aid us in studying the multiple wills at play in the bundle of power relations that constitutes IR, we must simultaneously also move to new empirical fields. This may be a more complex endeavour than first assumed and one linked to a second, more pertinent problem highlighted by the rather monotonous tendency of genealogies to stay within the empirical field of the Western tradition of thought. The question is perhaps less 'how much relativism history of ideas can afford before dissolving into pure fiction' (Bartelson, 1995: 58), but what degree of relativism is necessary for genealogy to be of any use in studying the social forces and power relations at play when different traditions of thought meet, clash, or assimilate? It is exactly in such moments that an ontology of violence (Borg, 2018) can prove problematic.

Identity and concepts

When it comes to HIR, poststructuralists have predominantly been occupied with studying *identity* and *concepts*.

Self/other or identity/alterity can be seen as an alternative to the disciplines studying more traditional problematiques of war and peace, and cooperation and conflict (Guillaume, 2011). According to Neumann (1996), scholarly interest in the self/other nexus has many origins. There is the ethnographic path where the active part of identity formation necessarily entails delineating a number of 'out-groups' from an 'in-group' – that while it might be along ethnonationalist lines might as well be formed along any other social marker. The psychological path identifies the mechanism of self-categorization as the way in which individuals become members of a group; and yet, it only remains relevant as long as it treats the self as socially situated. The Continental philosophical path is interested in how the 'dialectic of self and other' possibly forms new synthesis in the name of reason and progress. Lastly, there is what Neumann refers to as the 'Eastern excursion', which breaks with the dialectical understanding of self and other and instead proposes a dialogical one: rather than the self/other nexus being constituted by a transcendental self that knows the other, it is the problem of knowing the other that makes the self.

In contrast to modern conceptions of identity (including Realists and Liberals that consider identity, whether cooperate or social, an intrinsic property; and Constructivists who, while acknowledging the social character of identity, still maintain that corporate identities are intrinsic), poststructuralists conceive of identity as a process involving 'social *continuants*'. That is, they see 'identity as something both stable in time (it continues through time) and changing (it is an ever ongoing event that might simply reproduce itself or might evolve in a way or another according to this "direction of change")' (Guillaume, 2011: 31). Here, poststructuralists focus on othering as the main mechanism through which collective identities are formed, maintained, and transformed. Othering is what Connolly (1991: 8) refers to as the second problem of evil: 'the evil that flows from the attempt to establish security of identity for any individual or group by defining the other that exposes sore spots in one's identity as evil or irrational'. In other words, othering works through a double move towards *each* and *all*: it imposes a division between each self and other and in addition a hierarchy that places the self above the other. As Connolly also points out, the construction of othering is a 'structural temptation' – temptation, in that it is neither a necessity nor an implication of the existence of alterity; structural in that once the logic of identity is at work, structural imperatives that usually do not register on the level of conscious reflection direct ones conceptions of the other.

There are several histories of identities in IR. Well-known examples include how perceived dangers and their representation across about 500 years of history shape American identity through practices of foreign policy (Campbell, 1992); the shaping of national identities through 'imperial encounters' between the United States and the Philippines, as well as between Great Britain and Kenya (Doty, 1996); or how American identity has been shaped by a series of interventions in the Caribbean in the 20th century that strategically displaced castration anxiety (Weber, 1999). In *Uses of The Other*, Neumann (1999) explores the evolution of the European othering of Russians showing how generating counter-representations of the self is central to the process of collective identity formation: if the Other is 'barbarian', then we must be 'civilized'; if the Other is 'infidel', then we must be 'the faithful'; or if the Other is 'backwards' and 'despotic', then we must be 'modern' and 'liberal'. Decentring these Western experiences of collective identity formation, Guillaume (2011) demonstrates through a study of Japanese responses to questions of empire and multiculturalism how such dichotomized dyads collapse, and consequently how our conception of the international is stuck within the three problematiques of war/peace, cooperation/conflict, and identity/alterity.

The poststructuralist emphasis on identity as a research object involves two dangers. The first, despite its popularity among critics, does not consist in the straw man of overplaying the fragmentation of identity to a degree where conversations about commonalities between social groups become impossible, but rather how a commitment to 'nomadic identities' leaves the political open for essentializing narratives of the self. That poststructuralists argue identities are context-bound instantiations – social *continuants* in Guillaume terms – does not change the fact that a large part of political discourse consists in essentializing representations of identity. Consequently, poststructuralists are faced with a choice between political irrelevance on the one hand, as they offer no substitute for the context-traversing identities that they critique, or supplementing their critiques by fielding their own 'as if' stories about identity on the other (Neumann, 1999: 214–216). The second problem emerges once poststructuralists insist on thinking solely through binary oppositions – here mainly by considering othering as the only mechanism of collective identity formation. They neglect the fact that Othering remains a temptation, not a necessity. While the poststructuralist break from structuralism consisted in a rejection of clarifying all permutations and rendering the social open to change, it at the same time had a tendency to conceive of such change as possible only through simple dualism: normal/pathological, civilized/

barbarian, good/evil, and so on. If analytical categories only come in Manichean oppositions, then the complexities of social worlds will elude us. Indeed, as Guillaume (2011: 27) points out, 'dichotomies do not stand by themselves and are embedded in more complex systems of representation that are not necessarily dualistic'.

Concepts – the second aspect of Historical IR that poststructuralists have been interested in, has as well been a focal point of general interest in the discipline (Berenskoetter, 2017). There are many examples of poststructuralist conceptual analysis: anarchy (Walker, 1993), sovereignty (Bartelson, 1995), diplomacy (Der Derian, 1987), and genocide (Meiches, 2019) have already been mentioned; others include the state (Bartelson, 2001), world community (Bartelson, 2009), the balance of power (Andersen, 2016), the global climate (Hamilton, 2016b), or foreign policy (Leira, 2019). Concepts such as these are interesting because they present 'concrete and tangible ways of entering social worlds analytically' (Neumann, 2019: 8). The poststructuralist approach to concepts owes much to Foucault's idea of writing a history of *mentalities*, and consequently much of the work with concepts by poststructuralists follows a genealogical methodology. Yet, as this has brought IR in contact with intellectual history, there is perhaps also a homage to be payed to the German school of conceptual history, predominantly Reinhart Koselleck. However, such an intellectual marriage is not always without its contradictions, as it places its efforts somewhere in between hermeneutics and structuralism (for a comparison, see Bartelson, 1995: 53–87).

Signs are the locale of meaning. As we have seen earlier, a sign is made up of a signifier and a signified – a word and a concept. While words may have many possible meanings, they are nonetheless clarified by their context. In contrast, concepts are overloaded with meaning to a point where they are *qualitatively different* from mere words. They are essentially contested and carry with them a plethora of historical baggage and experience. Thus, words can easily be defined with reference to a context like entries in a dictionary, but concepts on the other hand must always be interpreted in relation to the semantic field in which they are located. An additional analytical distinction that cannot be overlooked, which has been instituted by some scholars is one between *analytical* and *practical* concepts: 'usage by people who are studying, talking, and writing about a phenomenon, as distinct from, say, everyday usage' (Neumann, 2019: 5). Predominantly, the purpose of such a distinction has been to buy some leeway in terms of foreseeable historical contradiction that an analysis of transhistorical concepts may lead to.

The poststructuralist engagement with concepts is faced with at least two problems. The first problem has to do with the distinction between practical and analytical concepts. In a society permeated by scientific discourse, this distinction between analytical and practical is oddly enough unaccounted for. What comes first, analytical or practical concepts? Does analytical usage spill over into practical usage, or are analytical concepts formed on the basis of practical ones? The danger being that the analysis of particular practical concepts risks being contaminated by analytical ones, while on the other hand we can be blind to how analytical concepts are implicated in practice. These questions have so far not been of much concern to poststructuralist conceptual analysis in IR.

The second problem is one that comes directly from the complexity of subject matter in IR. If the interaction between two or more polities is not only a question of political and economic relations, but also one of interlingual relations – that is, relations *across* linguistic borders – which carries with it, certain costs of interactions (Wigen, 2015: 429), then we can no longer be satisfied with an analysis of primary concepts in a single language; even if it happens to be the hegemonic language of the present. Anyone trying to interact across linguistic boundaries is always faced with a practical problem because '[t]ranscending linguistic boundaries involves *a priori* a *semantic* transaction cost [i.e. meaning is lost in translation]' (ibid., 429). In this way, practitioners are always engaged in a 'two-level language game' where their statements are always enabled and constrained by two sets of conceptual languages. Wigen proposes to study the compatibility of two different languages, through what he terms 'conceptual entanglement' – 'the extent to which concepts take their meaning from translation equivalents in other languages and draw upon meaning across linguistic boundaries' (ibid., 436). The question is whether humankind possesses some kind of 'spiritual kinship' that allows concepts to travel through individual interpretations, or whether the origins of concepts are to be found elsewhere, say in relation to the utility that a particular concept would have to a problem that any culture might have had.

Conclusion

I'd like to conclude this chapter by saying that the project of a Historical IR, which may be taken to consist of the consciences of the discipline of the past, runs into ambiguity at the very moment it is conceived as it will have to answer the question: what is history? This is also the case for poststructuralist approaches, and in the preceding chapter, I hope to have shown how exactly how they have contended with and reflected upon some of these basic problematiques of Historical IR.

Suggestions for further reading

Campbell, D. (1992). *Writing Security: United States Foreign Policy and the Politics of Identity*. Minneapolis, MN: University of Minnesota Press.
Doty, R. L. (1996). *Imperial Encounters: The Politics of Representation in North-South Relations*. Minneapolis, MN: University of Minnesota Press.
Todorov, T. (1984). *The Conquest of America: The Question of the Other*. Translated by Richard Howard. Norman: University of Oklahoma Press.
Weber, C. (1999). *Faking It: U.S. Hegemony in a Post-Phallic Era*. Minneapolis, MN: University of Minnesota Press.

References

Andersen, M. S. (2016). *A Genealogy of the Balance of Power*. PhD Thesis, The London School of Economics and Political Science (LSE).
Andersen, M. A., and Wohlforth, W. C. (2021). Balance of Power: A Key Concept in Historical Perspective. In de Carvalho, B., Costa Lopez, J., & Leira, H., eds. *Routledge Handbook of Historical International Relations*. Abingdon: Routledge.
Ashley, R. (1984). The poverty of neorealism. *International Organization*, 38 (2), 225–286.
Ashley, R. (1987). The geopolitics of geopolitical space: towards a critical social theory of international politics. *Alternatives*, 12 (4), 403–434.
Bartelson, J. (1995). *A Genealogy of Sovereignty*. Cambridge: Cambridge University Press.
Bartelson, J. (2001). *A Critique of the State*. Cambridge: Cambridge University Press.
Bartelson, J. (2009). *Visions of World Community*. Cambridge: Cambridge University Press.
Berenskoetter, F. (2017). Approaches to concepts analysis. *Millennium: Journal of International Studies*, 45 (2), 151–173.
Borg, S. (2018). Genealogy as critique in international relations: beyond hermeneutics of baseless suspicion. *Journal of International Political Theory*, 14 (1), 41–59.
Connolly, W. E. (1991). *Identity/Difference: Democratic Negotiations of Political Paradox*. Ithaca: Cornell University Press.
Der Derian, J. (1987). *On Diplomacy: A History of Western Estrangement*. Oxford: Blackwell.
Foucault, M. (1991). Nietzsche, Genealogy, History. In: P. Rabinow, ed., *The Foucault Reader: An Introduction to Foucault's Thought*, London: Penguin Books, 76–100.
Foucault, M. (2002 [1969]). *The Archaeology of Knowledge*. Translated by A. M. Sheridan Smith. London: Routledge.
Gillespie, M. A. (1984). *Hegel, Heidegger, and the Grounds of History*. Durham, NC: Duke University Press.

Guillaume, X. (2011). *International Relations and Identity: A Dialogical Approach.* London: Routledge.

Guillaume, X. (2021). Historical Periods and the Act of Periodisation. In de Carvalho, B., Costa Lopez, J., & Leira, H., eds. *Routledge Handbook of Historical International Relations.* Abingdon: Routledge.

Hamilton, S. (2016a). Genealogy of metatheory in IR: how 'ontology' emerged from the inter-paradigm debate. *International Theory,* 9 (1), 136–170.

Hamilton, S. (2016b). The measure of all things? The Anthropocene as a global biopolitics of carbon. *European Journal of International Relations,* 24 (1), 33–57.

Hom, A. R. (2021). Time and History in International Relations. In de Carvalho, B., Costa Lopez, J., & Leira, H., eds. *Routledge Handbook of Historical International Relations.* Abingdon: Routledge.

Jenkins, K. (1991). *Re-Thinking History.* London: Routledge.

Kessler, O. (2021). Conceptual History in International Relations: From Ideology to Social Theory?. In de Carvalho, B., Costa Lopez, J., & Leira, H., eds. *Routledge Handbook of Historical International Relations.* Abingdon: Routledge.

Kustermans, J. (2021). Historical Practices: Recovering a Durkheimian Tradition. In de Carvalho, B., Costa Lopez, J., & Leira, H., eds. *Routledge Handbook of Historical International Relations.* Abingdon: Routledge.

Leira, H. (2019). The emergence of foreign policy. *International Studies Quarterly,* 63 (1), 187–198.

Meiches, B. (2019). *The Politics of Annihilation: A Genealogy of Genocide.* Minneapolis, MN: Minnesota University Press.

Molloy, S. (2006). *The Hidden History of Realism: A Genealogy of Power Politics.* London: Palgrave Macmillan.

Neumann, I. B. (1996). Self and other in international relations. *European Journal of International Relations,* 2 (2), 139–174.

Neumann, I. B. (1999). *Uses of the Other: 'The East' in European Identity Formation.* Ann Arbor, MI: University of Michigan Press.

Neumann, I. B. (2019). *Concepts for International Relations: For Students and Other Smarties.* Ann Arbor, MI, University of Michigan Press.

Roy, R., Walker, R. B. J., and Ashley, R. (1988). Dialogue: towards a critical social theory of international relations – Ramashray Roy, R. B. J. Walker, and Richard Ashley. *Alternatives,* 13 (1), 77–102.

Spegele, R. D. (1992). Richard Ashley's discourse for international relations. *Millennium: Journal of International Studies,* 21 (2), 147–182.

Vaughan-Williams, N. (2005). International Relations and the 'Problem of History' *Millennium: Journal of International Studies,* 34 (1), 115–136.

Vucetic, S. (2011). Genealogy as a research tool in international relations. *Review of International Studies,* 37 (3), 1295–1312.

Walker, R. B. J. (1989). History and structure in the theory of international relations. *Millennium: Journal of International Studies,* 18 (2), 163–183.

Walker, R. B. J. (1993). *Inside/Outside: International Relations as Political Theory.* Cambridge: Cambridge University Press.

White, H. (1973). *Metahistory: The Historical Imagination of Nineteenth-Century Europe.* Baltimore, MD: John Hopkins University Press.

Wigen E. (2015). Two-level language games: international relations as inter-lingual relations. *European Journal of International Relations,* 21 (2), 427–450.

10

INTERNATIONAL POLITICAL THOUGHT AND HISTORICAL INTERNATIONAL RELATIONS

Or Rosenboim and Liane Hartnett

Introduction

In recent years, International Relations (IR) scholarship has cultivated a growing interest in history. In a parallel movement, scholars of political thought have dedicated greater attention to the international sphere of political relations, giving rise to the field of International Political Thought (IPT) at the intersection of history and theory. These intellectual developments emphasize, we suggest, the shared awareness of the importance of ideas in shaping the international realm, both in the present day and historically: by drawing on historical sources, IPT offers a wider, more variegated temporal vista on the evolution of international concepts and structures, while Historical IR (HIR) scholarship frequently embraces the study of past ideas as a key to understanding politics beyond the state. This chapter seeks to explore some of the recent works in HIR and IPT, highlighting the common traits in the two strands of scholarship, in particular the emphasis on the importance of past ideas for understanding the international realm.

IR scholars have long found in History a useful depository of past examples and case studies. Yet, often such intellectual endeavours employed historical knowledge in a superficial or simplistic manner. Lack of direct engagement with a variety of primary and archival sources, as well as a selective use of secondary sources and historical studies have not allowed IR scholars to explore the whole range of possibilities contained within the study of the past. The rise of HIR as a distinct subfield of IR has announced a concrete aim to transform the interaction between IR scholars and History.

Captured in IR mythology as the second great debate between 'scientific' and 'historical' approaches, the stark disciplinary divide between IR and History would seem to have been cemented with the rise of professionalization in post–Second World War academia. By then, the need for distinction and separation enhanced the distance between IR and History, encouraging scholars on both ends to engage in academic activities within the recognized boundaries of their discipline. Nonetheless, turning back to the origins of the discipline of IR, one cannot but notice that many of the early propagators and scholars of IR were, in fact, historians. In England, this silent overlap was particularly prominent. E. H. Carr, Alfred Zimmern and later Martin Wight were all trained as historians. In addition, many historians such as Arnold Toynbee or Herbert Butterfield were interested in themes related to IR. Apparently, the cross-fertilization between History and IR, which has intensified over the last two decades, has, in fact, longer historical and intellectual roots.

The rapprochement between historians and IR scholars has been noted not only from the perspective of IR, but also from that of History, where the study of IPT has seen a surge of interest and publications. Over the last two decades, the growing scholarly attention to the international, global and world dimensions of history has transformed the landscape of historical research. These transformations generated new research projects in the fields of intellectual history and the history of political thought, exploring IPT in a historical perspective. Scholars have uncovered past trajectories of ideas and concepts about the international sphere, embedding them within the intellectual traditions of the history of political thought.

Thus, IPT emerged as a significant and innovative field that seeks to shift the traditional state-centric narrative of intellectual history and the history of political thought to explore international, transnational and global political ideas. In this framework, the historian David Armitage (2004) announced an 'international turn' in intellectual history, where scholars honed in on themes that transcended the boundaries of states to highlight the transnational and even global dimension of the history of ideas. He argued that historians of political thought have rendered explicit what had previously been an implicit assumption of their studies, about the tendency of ideas to migrate, travel and connect people and places around the world.

The 'international turn' in the history of political thought was accompanied, it seems, by a parallel transformation in IR, which Duncan Bell (2009) described as the 'historical turn'. As historians of political thought abandoned methodological nationalism and adopted a more international outlook, a new path for a dialogue with IR has emerged. The contemporaneity of these processes may indicate that the two subfields are ready for a fruitful and insightful conversation.

The scholarly exchanges between IPT and HIR have created a rich, intellectual space for interdisciplinary dialogue, which may prove particularly beneficial for three reasons. First, IPT scholarship may widen the theoretical horizons of IR scholars and lead to an in-depth engagement with ideas and concepts hitherto ignored. Second, IPT scholarship may help challenge conventional narratives in IR by honing in on concepts' historic origins. Third, HIR may provide a rich conceptual framework for IPT scholarship, in a dialogue attuned to both historical particularism and theoretical generalizability.

This chapter is not intended as an exhaustive or definitive account of the field, but rather an initial exploration of some of the salient aspects of a scholarly universe undergoing growth and transformation. Our argument proceeds as follows. The 'Historical IR' section posits that the work of IR is inherently historical and ideational and charts but four ways in which this endeavour is pursued. The 'International Political Thought' section offers an overview of the uses of IPT in HIR, highlighting the work of scholars who actively engaged with the study of History and who sought to outline new paths to innovation in both contents and methods. The 'Empire and international thought' section focuses on empire, a theme that has received significant scholarly attention. Finally, in the 'Conclusion' section, we discuss some of the implications of the closer interplay between HIR and IPT and outline possible paths for future research.

Historical IR

The subfield of HIR has garnered much momentum since its foundation as a distinct section in the International Studies Association. However, to whatever extent the study of IR is predicated on an engagement with the past to understand or explain the present, or indeed predict the future, it is always inescapably historical and ideational. To make this claim is not to negate the many important ways in which this work differs. To draw on the classic essay by Quentin Skinner, such work might privilege texts in the hope they contain "timeless elements' in the form of 'universal ideas', even a 'dateless wisdom' with 'universal application'", it might privilege contexts of 'religious, political, and economic factors' as the 'ultimate framework' for discerning meaning, or it might opt for something in between (1969: 3–4). Similarly, it might differ in its understanding of what constitutes the archive. In this vein, it could variously turn to a text or phenomena in its attempt at sense-making. Finally, it might be driven by distinct normative endeavours and assessments of what constitutes the abiding question or *problematique* at the heart of IR, and how, where and why one ought to engage with it. These plural methods and ends testify to the multiple ways in which the study of IR engages with ideas and their historical genealogy and recognizes the importance of the past for thinking about the international. This recognition underpins George Lawson's claim that 'everyone who studies International Relations (IR) is a historian' (2018: 75). In what follows, we chart four ways in which IR scholars deliberately and consciously engage with historical thought. We posit these four approaches tend to centre on normative, disciplinary, conceptual and sociological questions, although conceding there is more overlap between them than our schema may suggest.

Normative IR's engagements with historical thought long precede the discipline's deliberate engagement with historical methods that Duncan Bell (2009) described as the 'historical turn'. Indeed, the second great debate we earlier alluded to did not so much result in the demise of historical work as much as it sharpened the cleavage across the Atlantic, which saw historical work continue to thrive in British IR. Normative IR was a fertile field for this flourishing. Normative IR engages with history primarily through what Renée Jeffery (2005) described as the 'invention of tradition', or the evocation and mobilization of history in acts of self-definition and critique. It is to be found in Martin Wight's (1991) world carved up between realists, rationalists, and revolutionaries. Equally, it is evident in international political theory's turn to the past as a trove of ethical enlightenment, exemplified in Chris Brown et al.'s (2002) *International Relations in Political Thought: Texts from the Ancient Greeks to the First World War*, which curates the works of 50 thinkers from Thucydides to Joseph Schumpeter. The purpose of the work was to introduce students and scholars of IR to 'canonical' texts and their historical and philosophical contexts.

Recent works in normative IR continue the historical work of constructing and interrogating tradition with the aim of exposition and critique. Thus, William Bain's (2020) *Political Theology of International Order* seeks to uncover the medieval theological origins of international order to counter the narrative that the modern states-system is the product of the gradual process of secularization (see also Bain, 2021 in this volume). Similarly, in a bid to highlight the promise and perils of just war thinking, Cian O'Driscoll (2019) studies the twin thematic of victory and tragedy as implicated over time in the thought of just war scholars from Cicero to Michael Walzer.

If normative IR is explicitly engaged in the construction and interrogation of tradition, disciplinary work seeks to excavate the ideational origins of IR's endeavour. Lucian Ashworth's (2014) *A History of International Thought: From The Origins of the Modern State to Academic International Relations,* for example, sought to shed light on the multiple narratives of the international's emergence. From interrogating the big bang moments of IR to their ameliorative proclivities, other works by Benjamin de Carvalho et al. (2011) and Joseph McKay and Christopher David LaRoche (2018), for instance, seek to call into question the doxa upon which our origin stories are premised and the problems they in turn perpetuate. This disciplinary work has been further enriched by the recent exploration of the many silences and exclusions upon which IR is predicated. In foregrounding the lives and legacies of scholars associated with the Howard School, Robert Vitalis' (2015) *White World Order, Black Power Politics: The Birth of American International Relations* invites us to interrogate whether IR from its inception was not in fact about race relations. Patricia Owens and Katharina Rietzler's 2021 edited collection, *Women's International Thought: A New History*, similarly seeks to recover and identify the work of neglected academic women in a bid to rewrite disciplinary history. These histories and attempts to redress them have largely centred on Anglo-American as the locus of IR. Albeit not entirely at odds with the discipline's development, these histories occlude a more plural, and indeed a truly international conception of the discipline's formation (see Fonseca Santos, 2021; Çapan et al. 2021; both in this volume). Seeking to remedy this, Ayşe Zarakol's (2010) *After Defeat*, Ian Hall's (2015) *Radicals and Reactionaries in International Thought*, Robbie Shilliam's (2015) *The Black Pacific: Anti-Colonial Struggles and Oceanic Connections* and Martin Bayly's (2021) work on the forgotten origins of South Asian IR ask what debates would be rendered audible, what paradigms perceptible, if we were to simply look beyond the Anglo-American archive (see Zarakol, 2021 in this volume).

Conceptual historical work at its core connotes a linguistic engagement with the past. This work tends to draw chiefly, albeit not exclusively, on methodologies championed by Reinhart Koselleck and Michel Foucault. If the former is typified by a turn to *Begriffsgeschichte*, the latter entails an engagement with genealogies. If the former is characterized by an exploration of the shifts in meaning over history, the latter analyses discourses or the ways in which power constructs knowledge over time (see Kessler, 2021 in this volume). Both methods seek to denaturalize concepts and reveal their historic contingency. Although they vary in focal range, these approaches are not dissimilar to what is commonly (and problematically) referred to as the 'Cambridge School', which takes as its starting point our embeddedness in speech acts and language games.

Conceptual work in IR builds upon and expands these frames. Jens Bartelson seeks to examine 'the world war made' by focussing on the meaning of war from the early seventeenth to nineteenth century. To this end, he provides an analysis of the historical ontology of war, which attempts to chart not just conceptual shifts in the meaning of 'war' but what conceptions of war have presupposed (2017: 1). Similar assumptions about the historical roots of international concepts are contained in the postcolonial scholarship of Nivi Manchanda (2020) whose *Imagining Afghanistan: The History and Politics of Imperial Knowledge* examines representations of gender, state and tribes to re-historicize Afghanistan and problematize colonial knowledge formation.

If conceptual IR is primarily concerned with the politics of knowledge production and shifts in language and meaning, historical sociology is primarily concerned with the societal. Historical sociologists are not alone in assuming societal bonds carry great importance in explaining and analysing human action, but in the context of IR, they emphasize the co-constitutive nature of history and theory. As Tarak Barkawi and George Lawson elaborate, 'theories arise historically, formed amid encounters between theorists and events and practices they experience and take part in' (2017: 2). At its crux, it seeks to incorporate 'temporality in the analysis of social processes' (2017: 2). Lawson suggests it is best conceived as 'oriented around two main thematics: first, the *transnational* and *global* dynamics that enable the emergence, reproduction and breakdown of social orders; and second, the *historical* emergence, reproduction and breakdown of transnational and global social forms' (2018: ch. 6). To whatever extent historians of ideas privilege the ideational, historical sociologists, in their embeddedness in the social, seek to illustrate how the material and ideational are always inherently in dialogue with each other. Tarak Barkawi's (2017) *Soldiers of Empire: Indian and British Armies in World War II* offers a postcolonial perspective on the making of the soldier and what animates them to participate in combat. Characteristic of Barkawi's scholarship, he posits the imperial as the formation to best understand war as a political act and societal phenomena, and in the process illuminates the forgotten, interwoven, material histories erased by Eurocentric narratives of war (contrast to Bartelson, 2021 in this volume). Contending revolutions are 'inter-social all the way down', George Lawson's *Anatomies of Revolution* offers an account of how revolutions begin, unfold and end (2019: 9). Examining revolutions from England in the seventeenth century to Ukraine in the twenty-first, he argues for the significance of revolutions not just as normative projects, but as analytical categories of social transformation and substantive processes which have shaped the modern world.

HIR is therefore a broad church united by a common endeavour, yet divided about the methods, objectives and locus of the study. Our fourfold division, however, is ultimately artifice. Normative concerns shape how we understand the archive, which concepts matter and why, what the right relationship is between the ideational and material, and indeed why we ask any historical question in the first place. Conceptual and sociological works are inextricably linked much in the same way languages are in society. Finally, each of these engagements with historical thought serves to make and unmake the discipline. In charting these differences, we have sought to illuminate something of the omnipresence of historical thought in the study of IR, suggesting that the debates and discussions which inhere in the field are somehow at their core about how and why we engage with history and ideas.

International Political Thought

IPT lies in the interstices of IR and History, and consequently many scholars of IPT traverse both disciplines. This space is rendered possible by the parallel movement we earlier described. Indeed, if the last 20 years saw the inherently historical discipline of IR self-consciously embrace historical methods, it has also seen History embrace the 'international'. The 'international turn' in intellectual history has been defined as one of the most transformative historiographical movements of the last decades (Armitage, 2013: 18). Since the 1990s historians have become more attentive to the international, transnational and global dimensions of politics, transcending the national boundaries of history-writing (Bayly et al., 2006). It has been argued that the categories of politics are not reducible to the 'state', and that conventional narratives of national history have obfuscated rather than revealed many important themes in the history of political thought (Rothschild, 2008; Bartelson, 2009; Sluga, 2013; Rosenboim, 2017).

Historians sought to define their subject matter as 'global', 'transnational' and 'international', although the differences between these categories have not always been clear. Some developments in the field of intellectual history were parallel to the emergence of historical subfields of international, transnational and global history, reflecting growing scholarly interest in human relations beyond the state. Iriye (2013) suggests that global and transnational history looks beyond national boundaries to explore interconnections across borders, discussing issues that concern humanity as a whole. By contrast, the focus on international history could be defined as the relations among nations as sovereign entities (Iriye, 2013: 10–12). While this distinction is not clear-cut or unchanging, it provides a useful starting point for investigating the abundance of recent scholarship on IPT, often united not by common themes but by a common focus on larger, potentially world-spanning spaces.

One of the questions arising from the current literature in IPT regards canon formation. Various studies pointed to a collection of key thinkers, leading intellectuals and practitioners who shaped international thought (Guilhot, 2011; Navari, 2013b). Some seek to challenge common perceptions of foundational figures in international thought. The history of British international thought has also received great attention, centring in particular on British liberal internationalists, their theories of world order and Britain's role in it (Hall and Hill, 2010; Hall, 2012; Holthaus, 2014; Sylvest, 2014; Rosenboim, 2014). While scholars have provided engaging studies of the international aspects of major political philosophers such as Grotius, Hobbes, Gentilli and Kant, we would argue that international thought should not be extrapolated from the canon of political thought, or proceed by examining what 'great political thinkers' said about world politics and international affairs (Bain, 2016; Molloy, 2017; Costa López, 2020). Studies of IPT should outflank the question of the existence and desirability of a canon of thinkers of international thought. Instead of building a new canon or reflecting on 'canonical thinkers', future research should investigate international thought by building an eclectic and transnational collection of thinkers united by a shared concern with the international dimension of politics (Keene, 2017; Vergerio, 2019).

The interplay of individuals and organizations can also provide a profitable field for the study of 'minor' or 'mid-level' thinkers of IR (Pedersen, 2015; Vitalis, 2015; Umoren, 2018). Historians and IR scholars have recently interrogated the writings of a group of British and American intellectuals and politicians, including Alfred Zimmern, Jan Smuts and Norman Angell, who are invested with the responsibility for shaping the ideology of American international interventionism, in partnership with the British Empire, to create a peaceful internationalist world order (Mazower, 2009; Ceadel, 2009; Baji, 2016). The interaction between intellectuals, public servants and policymakers has also received the attention of historians, raising questions on the reception and impact of ideas in politics. Lawyers, civil servants and economists have signalled out as important links in connecting ideas to policies between the national and international spheres (Slobodian, 2018; Huber et al., 2019; Wertheim, 2020). Yet, as recent studies have shown, religious orders and their members were also significant contributors to developing and spreading ideas about world order (Erdmann, 2005; Moyn, 2015; Thompson, 2015).

What are the spatial boundaries of IPT? Anglo-American collaboration has been important for the development of ideas about the international sphere, as historical configurations of world politics emerged in institutional frameworks such as Chatham House–based committee on 'World Order' and 'Reconstruction' (Williams, 2007). The claim that Britain and the United States were the birthplace of the academic discipline of IR in the twentieth century has justified, for many historians, the focus on these countries as the main hubs for the development of international thought (Schmidt, 1998). One alternative account highlights the importance of the imperial dimension for the foundation of IR as a discipline and the development of international thought as a whole (Davis et al., 2020). The global perspective that such a narrative opens up challenges Anglo-American historiography and constructs new political spaces for the evolution of ideas about the international. These novel interpretations of history of IR as a discipline set an example for the potential and importance of the active exchange between IR scholars and historians of IPT.

Our vision of IPT calls for a more expansive, creative approach not just to the questions of the canon, institutions and geography, but also methodology. Despite the many merits of a contextualist approach, as Joel Isaac (2016) reminds us, IPT ought to also offer concrete philosophical arguments for debate. Even in regard to 'minor thinkers' or 'mid-level thinkers' whose ideas may be limited in philosophical depth and theoretical range, it may be useful to enhance the contextualist approach with a more abstract analysis of their arguments. At the same time, contextualism serves as an important check on theoretical abstraction that bears little relevance to history or practical philosophy. The mission of IPT need not end with discussing past international theorists in their own terms but can extend to bringing to the fore their relevance to our own problems, their value in generating new theoretical arguments.

Empire and international thought

IPT is still very much a work in progress. The ever-growing historical scholarship expanded the field of investigation to include various eras and divergent themes. In his book on the foundations of international thought, Armitage (2013) suggested that historians of international thought should explore the transition from a system of empires to the current system of states.

Recent studies in IPT have shown that space between empires and states was complex, multi-layered and sometimes incoherent. In this section, we will look at a selection of studies that provide novel interpretations of empire and imperialism in the history of international thought. These path-breaking studies, we argue, represent an important contribution not only to historical studies on empires and the international, but also to IR, by offering an inspiring example for the intellectual potential embodied in interdisciplinary exchange.

The interplay of imperial and IR, and the idea of imperial political unity in the Victorian age were identified as fundamental themes in the study of international thought (Mehta, 1999; Pitts, 2005; Bell, 2006, 2007a, 2007b; Muthu, 2008; Mantena, 2010; Armitage, 2013). Pitts (2005), Mehta (1999) and Mantena (2010) have offered long-term historical vistas on the implication of liberalism in imperial projects, drawing on the writings of leading liberal thinkers, including J.S. Mill, Adam Smith and Henry Maine. These works also emphasize the highly interdisciplinary nature of Victorian international thought, where thinkers have built on their knowledge in law, economics and philosophy to theorize empire and the international sphere. The Victorian imaginary of world order is further developed in the scholarship of Duncan Bell (2007a, 2007b), who explores the notion of 'greater Britain' as an influential political trope in imperial England and interrogates the lasting legacy of empire on liberal internationalism (2016). Together, these studies shed light on the persisting contradictions of liberalism and offer insights into the continuities between liberalism's past configurations and its interpretations in IR today.

A number of studies focussed on the interwar years, with particular emphasis on the development of liberal internationalism as a political ideology in the age of imperial decline (Bisceglia, 1982; Parmar, 2002; Laqua, 2011; Gorman, 2012; Pugh, 2012; Navari, 2013a). Drawing clear temporal boundaries has not always been an easy task in the study of the history of international thought. Casper Sylvest (2009) discussed traditions and innovation in British liberal internationalism, questioning the claims of originality often attached to interwar theories, and pointing out the continuities between Victorian and Edwardian international thought, in particular regarding moral universalism. International or universal morality continued to play part in mid-century international thought, yet the relations between morality and reason were put under scrutiny as the imperial world order fell apart. A different interpretation of international morality, highlighting the repressive and exclusive aspects of the liberal imperial mindset, is advanced in Jeanne Morefield's (2005, 2014) studies of Alfred Zimmern and Gilbert Murray, as well as in her later work on the legacy of empire. Imperial apologetic patterns of international thought permeated mid-century internationalism, but came under increasing criticism as a more pluralistic approach took centre stage. Morefield provides a compelling account of the historical foundation of American foreign policy in the early twentieth-first century, by outlining the intellectual foundations of contemporary ideas in the European experience of empire.

Another strand of international thought explores the critiques of empire as a motivation for global political form (Long, 1996; Porter, 2007). In a similar critical vein, John M. Hobson discusses the impact of empire and Eurocentrism on the evolution of IR theory. Emphasizing the close connection between the racialized and discriminating imperial worldview and the development of IR theory, Hobson (2012) levels a poignant critique at current theoretical positions that fail to take stock of their problematic political assumptions. The discriminatory heritage of IR theory is also the subject of Robert Vitalis' aforementioned study, which focuses on the foundation of the American discipline of IR. Vitalis (2015) highlights the important contribution of Black international thinkers, providing a novel history of international thought through the writings of such figures as Merze Tate and Ralph Bunche. Adom Getachew's (2019) study of IPT after empire follows a similar pattern by showing the importance of Black international thinkers for making the post-imperial world order. The historical work undertaken by these scholars goes a long way to reveal the blind spots of existing scholarship and its limits. Their call for a more inclusive, self-aware and reflexive international theory is grounded in the study of the history of international thought.

The meticulous and original studies on empire by historians of international thought have contributed to a better understanding of the theoretical complexities around the political category of empire and challenged conventional narratives about the formation of the contemporary international order. Such works represent historical scholarship with a deep theoretical foundation, conversant with IR. The conceptual and historiographical influence of such groundbreaking works on empire can be traced in recent publications that employ new perspectives on the history of international thought to challenge common knowledge in IR (Zarakol, 2010; Anievas et al., 2014; Bayly, 2018; Phillips and Sharman, 2020).

Conclusion

This chapter has sought to illustrate the rich conceptual and methodological exchange that IPT facilitates between historians and scholars of IR. As exemplified in the burgeoning work on empire, IPT promises to widen the theoretical horizons of IR scholars and challenge their conventional narratives, just as HIR serves to provide a theoretical framework cognisant of the abstract and the particular. In the process, historians and IR scholars are called to confront the constitution and representation of the international: what it is, where it comes from, where it is going, and our role as scholars in understanding and explaining it. In many ways, this interdisciplinary conversation has only just begun. As it continues, we would like to signpost three themes that merit further research in the future.

First, both IPT and HIR are characterized by a significant lack of attention to gender issues, and to women as international thinkers and activists. The current state of affairs is limited to the examination of a few 'key' women scholars, who have by now joined the canon of modern international thought, most notably Hannah Arendt. Yet, as some scholars have argued, there are many more sources on the international thought of women that need to be unearthed and explored (Owens, 2018). Thus, HIR scholars with an interest in international thought can follow in the footsteps of intellectual historians and investigate archival collections to discover the contribution of women to the development of international thought. Although this examination of women's place in the canon is slowly gaining momentum, this focus remains confined to the work in the Anglo-American and Western-European archive. In addition, issues related to gender, feminism and the household are still relegated to the margins of the history of international thought, and rarely feature in HIR. More work can be undertaken to reveal the implications of gender-based social structures on international theory and to highlight the historical trajectories of feminist critiques of IR.

The second theme that deserves further exploration is non-European histories of political thought. The rise of 'global' and 'world' intellectual history has been accompanied not only by remarkable new scholarship on international thought in Africa, Asia and Latin America, but also by a greater awareness of the spatial and conceptual limits of the existing scholarship, in both IPT and IR (Shilliam, 2010; Moyn and Sartori, 2013; Anievas et al., 2014). It seems banal, four decades after Edward Said's (1978) *Orientalism*, to note that most of the histories of international thought that we have are written from the perspective of the West. Existing literature in IPT and HIR has been predominantly focused on the United States, Britain and a small selection of European states. Although this is gradually shifting, the intellectual blind spots include not only most of Africa, Asia, the Middle East and Latin America, but also 'minor' European states, such as Italy, the Scandinavian countries, Spain and Greece.

To overcome this bias, future scholarship needs to engage directly with knowledge produced in other geopolitical spheres. Such a goal seems to also require linguistic skills that are often lacking in the Anglophone world, where many scholars base their research exclusively on English sources. Mastering more than one language is a necessary condition for grappling with the history and evolution of ideas about the international sphere. For this purpose, transnational and trans-linguistic collaborations may prove a fruitful way forward. For example, there is much scope for collaborative projects that seek to outline the evolution of international thought beyond the English-speaking intellectual spheres, or at least exploring English sources in different locations, such as South Africa (Thakur and Vale, 2020). Future research in IPT and HIR may also demand greater linguistic abilities, novel archival sources and intellectual dexterity in a range of cultural and political spheres, to investigate the material and ideational history of the international on a truly global scale. Through new research strategies, that widen the geographic and linguistic scope of research, the contribution of HIR and IPT can transcend the conversation between these two subfields and embody an innovative and ambitious path for the advancement of the disciplines of History and IR as a whole.

Finally, we would like to propose that future studies in HIR and IPT extend their gaze beyond the 'usual suspects', the major thinkers and the Great Powers, to look at figures and subjects at the margins of the international order. Minor thinkers can often be better representatives of the common knowledge and views of their era than the exceptional 'great thinker' whose writings are more frequently studied. By widening our pool of international thinkers, we may hope to have a more diverse, pluralist and accurate map of the intellectual development of ideas about the international sphere. Engaging in new sources for understanding the international sphere can mean not only expanding the search geographically, into territories and regions hitherto excluded from the 'canon' of international thought but also digging deeper into the past and investigating a longer temporal arch of international thinking. Engaging with medieval and early modern international thinkers beyond the well-known canon of 'great thinkers' may provide impetus for a fresh theoretical perspective. Similarly, there may be much to be gained by understanding 'thought' as not merely contained in political works narrowly construed, but as expressed in art, music and literature.

The interplay between HIR and IPT may seem to lead smoothly to positive and optimistic conclusions about the future of such conversations. It is evident that historians and IR scholars can both benefit from a closer dialogue, which may open up new paths for research and construct new theoretical frameworks. At the same time, scholars should not lose sight of the fundamental differences between the underlying assumptions and objectives of research in IR and in History. While contextualized studies of the history of international thought may enrich our understanding of the evolution of the foundational political categories of IR, we should not neglect drawing theoretical implications for thinking about IR today. The challenge of future research will be to reflect on the desirable and possible means to translate historical case studies in political thought into an analysis of IR relevant for our own concerns. Such a challenge might draw historians and IR scholars apart but, at the same time, may lead to the crystallization of research in HIR as an insightful and rich approach to the study of IR.

Suggestions for further reading

Ashworth, L. (2014). *A History of International Thought: From the Origins of the Modern State to Academic International Relations.* London: Routledge.

Bell, D. (2016). *Reordering the World: Essays on Liberalism and Empire.* Princeton, NJ: Princeton University Press.

Moyn, S., and Sartori, A. (2013). *Global Intellectual History.* New York, NY: Columbia University Press.

Owens, P., and Rietzler, K., eds. (2021) *Women's International Thought: A New History.* Cambridge: Cambridge University Press.

References

Anievas, A., Manchanda, N., and Shilliam, R. (2014). *Race and Racism and International Relations: Confronting the Global Colour Line*. London: Routledge.

Armitage, D. (2004). The fifty years rift: intellectual history and international relations. *Modern Intellectual History*, 1 (1): 97–109.

Armitage, D. (2013). *Foundations of Modern International Thought*. Cambridge: Cambridge University Press.

Bain, W., ed. (2016). *Medieval Foundations of International Relations*. London: Routledge.

Bain, W. (2020). *Political Theology of International Order*. Oxford: Oxford University Press.

Bain, W. (2021). Political Theology and Historical International Relations. In de Carvalho, B., Costa Lopez, J., & Leira, H., eds. *Routledge Handbook of Historical International Relations*. Abingdon: Routledge.

Baji, T. (2016). Zionist internationalism? Alfred Zimmern's post-racial commonwealth. *Modern Intellectual History*, 13 (3): 623–651.

Barkawi, T. (2017). *Soldiers of Empire*. Cambridge: Cambridge University Press.

Barkawi, T., and Lawson, G. (2017). The international origins of social and political theory. *Political Power and Social Theory*, 32.

Bartelson, J. (2009). *Visions of World Community*. Cambridge: Cambridge University Press.

Bartelson, J. (2017). *War in International Thought*. Cambridge: Cambridge University Press.

Bartelson, J. (2021). War and the Turn to History in International Relations. In de Carvalho, B., Costa Lopez, J., & Leira, H., eds. *Routledge Handbook of Historical International Relations*. Abingdon: Routledge.

Bayly, M. J. (2018). *Taming The Imperial Imagination: Colonial Knowledge, International Relations, and the Anglo-Afghan Encounter, 1808-1878*. Cambridge: Cambridge University Press.

Bayly, M. J. (2021). Lineages of Indian International Relations: The Indian Council on World Affairs, the League of Nations, and the Pedagogy of Internationalism. *International History Review*, Online First.

Bayly, C. A., Beckert, S., Connelly M., Hofmeyr, I., Kozol, W., and Seed, P. (2006). AHR conversation: on transnational history. *American Historical Review*, 111 (5): 1441–1464.

Bell, D. (2006). Empire and international relations in Victorian political thought. *The Historical Journal*, 49 (1), 281–298.

Bell, D. (2007a). *The Idea of Greater Britain: Empire and the Future of World Order, 1860-1900*. Princeton, NJ: Princeton University Press.

Bell, D., ed. (2007b). *Victorian Visions of Global Order: Empire and International Relations in Nineteenth-Century Political Thought*. Cambridge: Cambridge University Press.

Bell, D. (2009). Writing the world: disciplinary history and beyond. *International Affairs*, 85 (1): 3–22.

Bisceglia, L. (1982). *Norman Angell and Liberal Internationalism in Britain, 1931–1935*. New York, NY: Garland.

Brown, C., Nardin, T., and Rengger, N. (2002). *International Relations in Political Thought: Texts from the Ancient Greeks to the First World War*. Cambridge: Cambridge University Press.

Çapan, Z. G., dos Reis, F. and Grasten, M., (2021). Global Histories: Connections and Circulations in Historical International Relations. In de Carvalho, B., Costa Lopez, J., & Leira, H., eds. *Routledge Handbook of Historical International Relations*. Abingdon: Routledge.

Ceadel, M. (2009). *Living the Great Illusion: Sir Norman Angell, 1872–1967*. Oxford: Oxford University Press.

Costa López, J. (2020). Political authority in international relations: revisiting the medieval debate. *International Organization*, 74 (2): 222–252.

Davies, A. (2020). Making a Settler Colonial IR: Imagining the 'international' in early Australian International Relations. *Review of International Studies*, First View. (Part of a forthcoming special issue on the plural origins of International Relations).

Davis, A. E., Thakur, V., and Vale, P. (2020). *The Imperial Discipline: Race and the Founding of International Relations*. London: Pluto.

de Carvalho, B., Leira, H., and Hobson J. M. (2011). The big bangs of IR: the myths that your teachers still tell you about 1648 and 1919. *Millennium*, 39 (3), 735–758.

Erdmann, M. (2005). *Building the Kingdom of God on Earth: The Churches' Contribution to Marshall Public Support for World Order and Peace, 1999–1945*. Eugene, OR: Wipf and Stock.

Fonseca Santos, M. (2021). Disciplinary Histories of Non-Anglophone International Relations: Latin America and the Caribbean. In de Carvalho, B., Costa Lopez, J., & Leira, H., eds. *Routledge Handbook of Historical International Relations*. Abingdon: Routledge.

Getachew, A. (2019). *Worldmaking after Empire: The Rise and Fall of Self-Determination*. Princeton, NJ: Princeton University Press.

Gorman, D. (2012). *The Emergence of International Society in the 1920s*. Cambridge: Cambridge University Press.

Guilhot, N. (2011). *The Invention of International Relations Theory: Realism, the Rockefeller Foundation, and the 1954 Conference on Theory*. New York, NY: Columbia University Press.

Hall, I., and Hill, L., eds. (2010). *British International Thinkers from Hobbes to Namier*. London: Palgrave MacMillan.

Hall, I. (2012). *Dilemmas of Decline: British Intellectuals and World Politics, 1945–1975*. Berkeley, CA: University of California Press.

Hall, I. (2015). *Radicals and Reactionaries in International Thought*. London: Palgrave.

Hobson, J. M. (2012). *The Eurocentric Conception of World Politics: Western International Theory 1760–2010*. Cambridge: Cambridge University Press.

Holthaus, L. (2014). G.D.H. Cole's international thought: the dilemmas of justifying socialism in the twentieth century. *The International History Review*, 36 (5), 858–875.

Huber, V., Pietsch, T. and Rietzler, K. (2019). *Women's International Thought and the New Professions, 1990-1940 Modern Intellectual History*. Published ahead of print 24 May 2019. Viewed on 20 October 2020 <https://doi.org/10.1017/S1479244319000131>.

Iriye, A. (2013). *Global and Transnational History: The Past, Present and Future*. Basingstoke: Palgrave Macmillan.

Isaac, J. (2016). Pain, Analytical Philosophy, and American Intellectual History. In: J. Isaac, J. T. Kloppenberg, M. O'Brien, and J. Ratner-Rosenhagen, eds., *The Worlds of American Intellectual History*, Oxford: Oxford University Press.

Jeffery, R. (2005). Tradition as invention: the 'Traditions Tradition' and the history of ideas in international relations. *Millennium: Journal of International Studies*, 34 (1), 57–84.

Keene, E. (2017). International intellectual history and international relations: contexts, canons and mediocrities. *International Relations*, 31 (3), 341–356.

Kessler, O. (2021). Conceptual History in International Relations: from Ideology to Social Theory?. In de Carvalho, B., Costa Lopez, J., & Leira, H., eds. *Routledge Handbook of Historical International Relations*. Abingdon: Routledge.

Laqua, D., ed. (2011). *Internationalism Reconfigured: Transnational Ideas and Movements Between the World Wars*. London: I.B. Tauris.

Lawson, G. (2018). International Relations as a Historical Social Science. In: A. Gofas, I. Hamati-Ataya, and N. Onuf, eds., *Handbook of the History, Philosophy, and Sociology of International Relations*, London: Sage, 75–89.

Lawson, G. (2019). *Anatomies of Revolution*. Cambridge: Cambridge University Press.

Long, D. (1996). *Towards a New Liberal Internationalism: The International Theory of J.A. Hobson*. Cambridge: Cambridge University Press.

Magee, G. B., and Thompson, A. S. (2010). *Empire and Globalisation: Networks of People, Goods and Capital in the British World, c. 1850–1914*. Cambridge: Cambridge University Press.

Manchanda, N. (2020). *Imagining Afghanistan: The History of Politics of Imperial Knowledge*. Cambridge: Cambridge University Press.

Mantena, K. (2010). *Alibis of Empire: Henry Maine and the Ends of Liberal Imperialism*. Princeton, NJ: Princeton University Press.

Mazower, M. (2009). *No Enchanted Palace: The End of Empire and the Ideological Origins of the United Nations*. Princeton, NJ: Princeton University Press.

McKay, J., and LaRoche, C. D. (2018). Why is there no reactionary international theory? *International Studies Quarterly*, 62 (2): 234–244.

Mehta, U. S. (1999). *Liberalism and Empire: A Study in Nineteenth-Century British Liberal Thought*. Chicago, IL: University of Chicago Press.

Molloy, S. (2017). *Kant's International Relations: The Political Theology of Perpetual Peace*. Ann Arbor, MI: University of Michigan Press.

Morefield, J. (2005). *Covenants Without Swords: Idealist Liberalism and the Spirit of Empire*. Princeton, NJ: Princeton University Press.

Morefield, J. (2014). *Empires Without Imperialism: Anglo-American Decline and the Politics of Deflection*. Oxford: Oxford University Press.

Moyn, S. (2015). *Christian Human Rights*. Philadelphia, PA: University of Pennsylvania Press.

Muthu, S. (2008). Adam Smith's critique of international trading companies: theorizing 'Globalization' in the age of enlightenment. *Political Theory*, 36 (2): 185–212.

Navari, C. (2013a). *Internationalism and the State in the Twentieth Century*. London: Routledge.

Navari, C. (2013b). *Public Intellectuals and International Affairs: Essays on Public Thinkers and Political Projects*. Dordrecht: Republic of Letters.

O'Driscoll, C. (2019). *Victory: The Triumph and Tragedy of Just War*. Oxford: Oxford University Press.

Owens, P. (2018). Women and the history of international thought. *International Studies Quarterly*, 62 (3), 467–481.

Parmar, I. (2002). Anglo-American elites in the interwar years: idealism and power in the intellectual roots of Chatham House and the Council on Foreign Relations. *International Relations*, 16 (1): 53–75.

Pedersen, S. (2015). *The Guardians: The League of Nations and the Crisis of Empire*. Oxford: Oxford University Press.

Phillips, A., and Sharman, J. C. (2020). *Outsourcing Empire: How Company States Made the Modern World*. Princeton, NJ: Princeton University Press.

Pitts, J. (2005). *A Turn to Empire: The Rise of Imperial Liberalism in Britain and France*. Princeton, NJ: Princeton University Press.

Porter, B. (2007). *Critics of Empire*. London: I. B. Tauris.

Pugh, M. (2012). *Liberal Internationalism: The Interwar Movement for Peace in Britain*. Basingstoke: Palgrave.

Rosenboim, O. (2014). Barbara Wootton, Friedrich Hayek and the debate on democratic federalism in the 1940s. *The International History Review*, 36 (5), 894–918.

Rosenboim, O. (2017). *The Emergence of Globalism: Visions of World Order in Britain and the United States, 1939–1950*. Princeton, NJ: Princeton University Press.

Rothschild, E. (2008). The archives of universal history. *Journal of World History*, 19 (3): 375–401.

Said, E. (1978). *Orientalism*. New York, NY: Pantheon.

Schmidt, B. C. (1998). *The Political Discourse of Anarchy: A Disciplinary History of International Relations*. Albany, NY: SUNY Press.

Shilliam, R. (2015). *The Black Pacific: Anti-Colonial Struggles and Oceanic Connections*. London: Bloomsbury Academic.

Shilliam, R., ed. (2010). *International Relations and Non-Western Thought: Imperialism, Colonialism and Investigations of Global Modernity*. London: Routledge.

Skinner, Q. (1969). Meaning and understanding in the history of ideas. *History and Theory*, 8 (1), 3–53.

Slobodian, Q. (2018). *Globalists: The End of Empire and the Birth of Neoliberalism*. Cambridge: Harvard University Press.

Sluga, G. (2013). *Internationalism in the Age of Nationalism*. Philadelphia, PA: University of Pennsylvania Press.

Sylvest, C. (2009). *British Liberal Internationalism, 1880–1930: Making Progress?* Manchester: Manchester University Press.

Sylvest, C. (2014). Russell's realist radicalism. *The International History Review*, 36 (5), 876–893.

Thakur, V., and Vale, P. C. J. (2020). *South Africa, Race and the Making of International Relations*. London: Rowman & Littlefield.

Thompson, M. G. (2015). *For God and Globe: Christian Internationalism in the United States Between the Great War and the Cold War*. Ithaca, NY: Cornell University Press.

Umoren, I. D. (2018). *Race Women Internationalists: Activist-Intellectuals and Global Freedom Struggles*. Berkeley, CA: University of California Press.

Vergerio, C. (2019). Context, reception, and the study of great thinkers in international relations. *International Theory*, 11 (1), 110–137.

Vitalis, R. (2015). *White World Order, Black Power Politics: The Birth of American International Relations*. Ithaca, NY: Cornell University Press.

Wertheim, S. (2020). *Tomorrow, the World: The Birth of U.S. Global Supremacy in World War II*. Cambridge: Harvard University Press.

Wight, M. (1991). *International Theory: The Three Traditions*. London: Leicester University Press.

Williams, A. (2007). *Failed Imagination? The Anglo-American New World Order From Wilson to Bush*. 2nd edition. Manchester: Manchester University Press.

Zarakol, A. (2010). *After Defeat*. Cambridge: Cambridge University Press.

Zarakol, A. (2021). Linking up the Ottoman Empire with IR's Timeline. In de Carvalho, B., Costa Lopez, J., & Leira, H., eds. *Routledge Handbook of Historical International Relations*. Abingdon: Routledge.

PART II

Thinking International Relations historically

11

DISCIPLINARY TRADITIONS AND DEBATES

The subject matters of international thought

Lucian M. Ashworth

This chapter begins from the premise that there has been such a wealth of work on disciplinary history, the history of international thought, and on marginalized voices in International Relations (IR) that it is no longer possible to write an account of traditions and debates that build on the standard post-1980 paradigms and great debates model that is so prevalent in textbooks. This standard view saw IR as broken up into paradigms, which had debated each other in three or four great debates since the First World War. Starting in the late 1990s, new studies in disciplinary history refuted the idea of a field-defining realist-idealist great debate, arguing that the rich life of traditions in twentieth-century IR could not be reduced to a simplistic realist-idealist antimony (see the summary in de Carvalho et al., 2011: 745ff). Recently, retellings of IR's postwar story have even called into question assumptions about the second and third debates, arguing that they form part of a wider attempt to bring a sense of theoretical order to IR (Ashworth, 2019). Rather, much as the study of infectious diseases does not feel a need to build its theorizing by starting with the discredited miasma theory of infection, the field needs to develop new ways of seeing its past traditions and debates that conform to the findings of recent scholarship on IR's past, and also align with the many different subject matters that constitute IR. The old model of a few traditions going through periodic great debates does not fit the facts that we know about IR's past.

In the last few decades, there have been two popular ways of dealing with the issue of debates and traditions in the disciplinary history of IR and the history of international thought. The first, flowing off earlier 1990s discussions of the myth of the 'great debate' motif in IR, was to debunk the idea of three or four great debates and to substitute alternative fine-grained readings of the origins of IR. The second was to engage with the wider literature outside of IR on traditions in political thought and produce a new reading of how different intellectual traditions developed and interacted to create IR as we now know it. The first approach engages directly with IR's self-image of its past and common sense understandings of the discipline that date from the early 1980s. The second approach takes the criticism of the great debates narratives as read, and attempts to reconstruct a new story based upon the historical evidence of the times. I will be explaining what this second approach means in the first section of this chapter. There are many excellent iterations of the two approaches, but the first might be exemplified by Brian Schmidt's edited collection on the myth of the first great debate (Schmidt, 2012), while the second by another edited collection by Hall (2015).

While both approaches are useful, they have until recently shared a common blind-spot: although criticizing the common-sense narratives of IR's self-image, they have concentrated on Western, male, and white authors who largely write in English. This does not mean that either approach necessarily has to be restricted to this specific group, although the perceived need to write against the common sense of IR has tended (especially in the case of the first approach, but also to a lesser extent in the second) to lead to a mirroring of earlier lacunae in IR over the place of gender, empire, and race (see Towns, 2021; Bayly, 2021; and Yao and Delatolla, 2021 in this volume). That said, there are many recent exceptions to this trend, and current research in the history of international thought has seen a growing awareness of marginalized voices. Yet, IR as a discipline has been predominantly an English-speaking Western, white, and male pursuit. Having said this, the broader field of international thought (of which IR is a part) has been the home of other voices. Analysing these other works, alongside the more common analyses of white Western men, I seek to develop an alternative way to explore different traditions in IR and international thought by grouping both recent analyses and past writers around five themes. The five themes are 1. political economy, 2. political geography and geopolitics, 3. women and feminism, 4. race and empire, and 5. war and security.

These themes, to the extent that they reflect both recognizable blocks of literature in the past and trends in the history of international thought, can be interpreted as traditions that have waxed and waned over time as the research priorities of international thought and the field of IR have changed. While each one has a claim to be an origin point for the field of IR, they also each speak to current concerns about the nature of global politics. While each represents a past that can be studied, the nature of these pasts have clear contemporary relevance as they speak to on-going debates and their long histories can and do act as part of the justifications for their place at the IR table. In some cases, the perception of their histories can even be used as a means of attempted exclusion, rather than inclusion. In short, these five represent broad traditions in international thought that owe their coherence to a shared subject matter. Each of these traditions has a history consisting of a past literature, as well as a set of disciplinary historians in the present who have interpreted this history. I will return to this point at the start of the second section.

This chapter will consist of two uneven sections. The first, and shorter one, will look at the concept of traditions, and lay out why it makes more sense in IR to look at traditions in terms of common subject matters, rather than in terms of ideologies or paradigms. This section will provide the theoretical underpinning to this study. The second will adumbrate the five traditions laid out above, exploring both the forms of the historical literature and debates and the way that these traditions have been reconstructed by present disciplinary historians of IR. Obviously these five traditions are not an exhaustive list, and part of the argument of this chapter is that the subject matters that make up what we know as international thought or IR are always in flux. They do, though, represent both past iterations of international thought and current subject matters regarded as integral parts of the field of IR. These also are not self-contained traditions, and it is not uncommon for individual writers or groups of authors to float between two or more. Given the newness of this approach, and the shortness of this chapter, most of my analysis of these traditions will be of English language texts. Despite this, there is much work which needs to be done on non-English writers and traditions in international thought.

Seeing traditions in terms of subject matter, rather than in terms of ideology or school clusters, is not the most common way to approach the topic of international thought. It does, though, carry with it three advantages. First, it avoids the trap of fitting past thinkers (and even present disciplinary historians) into prefabricated paradigms (see Wallenius, 2021). Since paradigms were a later innovation in IR, this helps us avoid certain worrying anachronisms (and false equivalences or divisions). Second, it accepts that the subject matter of international thought and IR has floated over the decades, and that different traditions and literatures have tended to cross in and out of IR over time. Third, it allows us to take on board insights from the philosophy of science and the history of ideas, while adapting these to the peculiar and often idiosyncratic nature of international thought and IR. It is to this idea of tradition that we turn in the first section.

Traditions as subject matter

When the question of traditions is raised, the default setting for social scientists is to think in terms of the standard ideologies taught in political theory. That international thought is not so easily divided this way is evident by the use of different names such as realist, idealist, and constructivist. That said, even in IR discussions, there is an attempt to link apparent IR traditions with broader political theory categories. Thus, idealist gets linked to liberalism, realism to conservatism, and constructivism becomes a broad brush category that takes in radical approaches. The problem with this ideologies-as-traditions approach to international thought is that past thinkers refuse to stay in their boxes. Realists turn out to be socialists, or someone lumped into the liberal category because of their support for international organizations turns out to be a Marxist or old-fashioned conservative (see Ashworth, 2014, especially Chapters 5–7). There is a bigger problem, though. The attempt to reduce the past to paradigms familiar to us from modern IR textbooks is an anachronistic exercise that imposes categories developed in the 1980s and 1990s onto past writers who did not think in those terms.

The basic problem with using what appear to be standard IR paradigms is that these are actually of very recent vintage. The standard divisions of IR into a realist paradigm (really neorealism), a liberal paradigm (mostly non-realists), and an amorphous constructivist one (a catchall for anything more radical) have their origins in the attempts of stocktakers in IR during the early 1980s to make sense of the apparent muddle that was seen to exist in IR from the 1960s. The idea of competing paradigms, linked to three or four field-defining great debates, brought a sense of pluralist order to IR (Ashworth, 2019).

Thus, 'tradition' is more often than not employed as an anachronistic attempt to code past thought using current categories. It was this problematic use of the concept of tradition that led to it being abandoned by the Cambridge school of the history of ideas in the 1960s. A modified reformulation of traditions is not without its defenders, however, and Ian Hall has successfully employed Mark Bevir's concept of tradition to debates in British IR after 1945 (Hall, 2012). Here, though, traditions become malleable concepts that can be justified by the self-awareness of their existence by contemporary practitioners. They are bundles of ideas and intellectual practices that are passed down and constantly reworked. The crucial thing here, though, is that a tradition is a multigenerational and fluid lived experience. It becomes a combination of community and sets of ideas.

My use of tradition owes much to this approach by Bevir and Hall, but in the spirit of the fluidity of the concept, I will shift the emphasis to subject matter. My concentration on subject matter is designed to achieve a broader scale view of the constituent elements of international theorizing. It is also within subject matters that the debates of past IR have taken place. There have been furious debates in IR's past, but they have tended not to be between paradigms, but rather between those studying the same subject matter. Thus, the debates over collective security and peaceful change in the late 1930s raged between those specifically interested in war and security. It was not a debate over whether this subject mattered, but rather about how the question of the use and prevention of war should be answered. Here it is worth pointing out that, while rejecting the idea of overarching and field defining great debates fits the historical evidence, this does not mean debates in the past did not happen. The crucial thing here, though, is that these were often not struggles between hard shelled and distinct paradigms, but smaller affairs between related approaches sharing a common subject matter. This is also true for the texts and exchanges often quoted as being part of the so-called great debates. These were usually lesser affairs with more limited goals. Some of these will be dealt with below.

As well as analysing the nature of each of the traditions that built up around these subject matters, each of these traditions have also benefited from analysis by recent historians of international thought. Each can also claim, in different ways, to be founding moments for the development of IR. Here it is less a case of evaluating what the 'true' origin story of IR is, and more that IR has multiple origin stories depending on what subject matter you privilege. In this sense, my chapter is also an argument for rejecting a single origin point for IR, and instead to argue that the origin point that people pick depends on the subject matter (and the slant given to it) that they see as being their primary concern. IR has multiple origins because it has multiple subject matters. Rather than a discipline with a core, IR has always been a bundle of often eclectic subjects.

This brings me to a final note on nomenclature. I have often used IR and international thought interchangeably above (cf. Rosenboim and Hartnett, 2021). This seemingly careless use of terms is actually deliberate. In theory at least there ought to be a clear distinction between the wider history of international thought (taking in all studies of the international), and the disciplinary history of IR. The problem here is that it is not all that clear on the aggregate where exactly the field of IR begins within international thought. Basically, each disciplinary historian concentrating on different subject matters will come up with different but defendable definitions. Thus, Nicolas Guilhot, concentrating on classical realist communities in the United States that were trying to make sense of the foreign policy dilemmas around them, can firmly see IR as a product of the late 1940s and 1950s (2008). For Barry Buzan and George Lawson, concentrating on the way that industrialization influenced global order, the origin point moves to the late-nineteenth century (2015), while in my own recent work, I have argued that in its modern paradigmized form, IR really only dates from the 1980s (2019). None of these are wrong. The issue is more that your answer to the question of when IR emerged is dependent on your definition of what IR is. Since, as I will show below, there are many defining traditions based on subject matter within the broad space that is IR, the question of what IR is cannot be answered without doing unscientific violence to a pluralistic field. In this sense, the boundaries of IR – and consequently of the disciplinary history of IR – will always be blurred. It is certainly contained within international thought, but it rattles around and can never be still. Consequently, to study traditions and debates in IR and international thought, we have to treat each one as an alternative story that, in the style of the film Rashōmon, gives us a different view of what it is that we are studying.

Traditions in international thought

Historically speaking, IR is a field without a single core tradition. Rather, it has always been a bundle of subject matters investigated by diverse schools of scholars. It suffered a major narrowing around 1950 with a mass extinction event, but quickly regained its diversity from the 1960s. Up to 1950, we can discern different traditions that included political economy, political geography, colonial administration, feminism, and security, although individual writers would cross the porous borders between these. The reason it is so difficult to find an origin point for IR is that each of these traditions has a distinct-but-often-related intellectual history. In this section, I summarize the histories of these traditions, with reference to the disciplinary historians who have explored them.

While my choices of subject matters are not meant to be exhaustive, there are reasons why I have chosen these five, which represent a mediation between the present and the past. Each of these are subject matters with a strong history in international thought, even if they have gone through periods of inactivity or marginalization in IR. Each is also currently of interest to groups of scholars within IR, and have been the subject of analysis by disciplinary historians or historians of international thought over the last few decades. They combine, therefore, an important presence in the past with a significant level of interest in the present.

Political economy

Before there was IR, there was International Political Economy (IPE). This may seem a strange claim given that the field of IR is often traced to 1919 or the late 1940s, while IPE's own histories start in the late 1960s (Cohen, 2008). Yet, the origins of international thought as a stand-alone intellectual endeavour can be found in debates over political economy in the last decades of the nineteenth century. The role of political economy in international thought, especially in the English-speaking world, is a story of dominance leading to marginalization, followed by a return. Yet, that marginalization within the field of IR was so powerful that histories of IPE usually take as read that their subfield was a later interloper brought forth by the new mercantilism of the 1970s (Cohen, 2008: 1).

Arguably the key text in IPE's rediscovery of its pre-1960s past was Craig Murphy's *International Organizations and Industrial Change* (1994). Murphy demonstrated how the rise in ideas of global governance, along with the development of a web of global governance built around the expanding system of international organizations, was directly linked to rapid industrial change after 1850. This also built on an earlier Marxist tradition in political economy, going back to the late-nineteenth century. Despite this earlier work, however, it was not until 2015 that Barry Buzan and George Lawson published a book-length argument in IR for the industrial origins of our modern world order (Buzan and Lawson, 2015).

Yet, with the important exception of Murphy, little has been written on the role of political economy as a tradition in late nineteenth and early-twentieth century international thought. Part of the problem here is that past international political economists have often been read differently in IR's disciplinary history, so their political economy has been displaced by their attitudes towards war, security, and international organizations. A case in point here is Norman Angell, whose work on the new internationalized political economy showed how conceptions of profit through war between great powers were obsolete (Angell, 1911). Despite Angell's obvious reliance on a materialist political economy, he has been classified in much IR conventional wisdom as an idealist.

At least Angell has survived in the textbooks. The Marxist and anti-imperialist political economist H. N. Brailsford, a contemporary and frequent sparring partner of Angell's, is rarely discussed outside of disciplinary history circles. Equally, the work of Rosa Luxemburg is rarely discussed, despite her work speaking to ongoing debates in IPE (Worth, 2012), while Karl Polanyi (whose *Great Transformation* is partially a work of IR) has been rediscovered, but still remains little used in disciplinary history (Dale, 2016; also Ashworth, 2014: 218–221). The great erasure of this tradition came in the 1950s with the development of a specific American-led IR within the university. The return of a vibrant IPE within IR would not occur until the 1970s, when a series of scholars, including Susan Strange, revamped IPE. Yet, despite this revival, knowledge of the earlier intellectual debates specific to this tradition were largely forgotten.

Underlying these debates was the game-changing role of industrialization in the late-nineteenth century. As well as changing the rules of international order (Buzan and Lawson, 2015), it also led to the discussions around the changing nature of international anarchy under industrialization (e.g. Reinsch, 1900). In short, the emergence of the study of international affairs as a separate field is a product of the globalizing processes that created a truly global political economy. Once we refocus our attention to industrialization then a number of debates in the early-twentieth century take on a different form. Thus, the difference of opinion between Brailsford and Angell before the First World War becomes a debate over what the globalization of finance and trade means for security. Is it the opportunity for the creation of a more peaceful world, as Angell saw it, or is it the cause of new imperial conflicts over markets and the control of capital, as Brailsford interpreted it? This difference would resurface in the 'does capitalism cause war' debates of the 1930s (see Ashworth, 2014: 213–216). Equally, the political economy approach of Brailsford and Angell would battle it out with the racist view of empire found in the works of A. T. Mahan both before and after the First World War (Ashworth, 2014: 103–107, 116–119).

Political geography and geopolitics

Despite the successful revival of critical geopolitics over the last few decades, reappraisals of the role of geopolitics and political geography in the history of international thought have been few. The last decade, however, has seen the emergence of several works that have explored the role of political geographers and geopoliticians in the formation of international thought in the early and mid-twentieth century (Ashworth, 2011b, 2013; Rosenboim, 2017: ch. 3). Here, though, a distinction needs to be made between political geography and geopolitics. Political geography, as a sub-discipline of the emerging field of human geography, influenced the development of international thought and IR in the early and mid-twentieth century, especially in the United States. Geopolitics, influenced by human geographers such as Friedrich Ratzel, emerges as a popular form of political geography that inspired the international thought of several key non-geographers in IR. These two groups deserve to be explored separately.

Political geography emerged in Germany in the late-nineteenth century, and in the writings of Friedrich Ratzel, it became a way of understanding the competition between states through the application of principles of topography and human geography. In Britain, Halford Mackinder applied Ratzel's logic to the relation between the British Empire and the topography of the Earth's surface. It was, though, Ellen Churchill Semple, a student of Ratzel's who popularized political geography in the English-speaking world. Semple laid down many of the basic parameters for understanding the international from a geographical point of view, particularly through the study of borders and the influence of different environmental conditions. Despite these pre-war experiments, political geography did not fully develop as a branch of international thought until the end of the First World War, and the appearance of two key texts inspired by the Paris Peace Conference (Mackinder, 1919; Bowman, 1928). What marked these works out from pre-war political geography was the abandonment of environmental determinism. In Bowman's case, this was influenced by his exposure to French political geography, which had a less determinist reading of Ratzel than anglophone geographers. Both writers stressed the importance of ideas and interactions between environment and ideology. Both saw hope in ideological changes that would offer less violent alternative futures. In other publications, Mackinder and Bowman regarded the changes associated with the League of Nations and the new diplomacy as key to these alternatives (Mackinder, 1922: 276; Bowman, 1930).

Yet, it is with an American historical geographer that political geography took a new turn relevant to recent developments in IR. A student of Semple's, Derwent Whittlesey took Semple's concept of the relationship between society and geographic conditions to a different level by arguing that the relationship was fungible: human society's also influenced the environment, and with the development of new technologies and practices, the potential for human societies to become unsustainable and damage the environment increased (Whittlesey, 1939). Whittlesey's way of looking at the international in the context of its ecology predated current green IR and planet politics. While Whittlesey was too early for global warming, his conception of how human progress changed the environment has contemporary relevance.

Alongside political geography, geopolitics emerged as an attempt to synthesize insights of political geography with current affairs. Developed by non-geographers, geopolitics remained the main conduit through which concepts of political geography entered public discussions of foreign policy and international order. Geopolitics was particularly popular in interwar Germany (Murphy, 1997) and was an important aspect of foreign policy discussions in the United States from the 1940s. Key here were the writings of Nicholas Spykman and Robert Strausz-Hupé (see Ashworth, 2014: 203–213; Rosenboim, 2017: ch. 3). The main feature of American geopolitics was the attempt to develop foreign policy advice for both wartime strategy and the anticipated post-war settlement. Distinctly internationalist and interventionist in their politics, their ideas have been explored by Schmidt (2012).

Whittlesey and Spykman also played a role in the future direction of IR in American universities through their roles at Yale University's Institute for International Studies. Spykman taught at the Institute, while Whittlesey was involved in encouraging the Institute's commitment to including political geographers on its faculty. The composition of the Institute, an important player in the development of IR in the United States during the 1940s, included a mix between political geographers and non-geographers. Spykman's early death, and the failure to rehire a political geographer at Yale after another departure, eventually undermined the part played by political geography and geopolitics in American IR. The debates that occurred between geographers and non-geographers in 1940s US IR is a story that has yet to be told. Suffice it to say that what happened at Yale formed a part of a much larger eclipsing of political geography and geopolitics in IR. Like political economy, this erasure of a tradition would be tempered by its later revival.

Women and feminism

In an important 2018 *tour de horizon* of 60 texts in the history of international thought and international political theory, Patricia Owens showed that there were wide discrepancies in the number of historical women writers cited from IR's past. While ten texts mentioned between 5 and 15 historical women, a worryingly large number mentioned none at all (Owens, 2018). One comeback to Owen's study might be that women were just in short supply in IR's past. However, this does not account for the wide discrepancies in numbers. Two other points also emerge from Owens' analysis. First, the texts mentioning historical women provided wildly different lists, suggesting that, on aggregate, there were many women writing on international affairs throughout the twentieth century. Indeed, the term 'international thought' was first extensively used by Florence Stawell (1929). Second, Owens herself has found forgotten historical women, which suggests that the historical women we do know about are but a part of a much larger group (Owens, 2018: 476–479).

Owens' interest was women writers, rather than specifically feminist ones, and it reveals that even when women wrote on distinctly non-feminist topics, they stood to be written out of the subsequent histories. The strange – almost blanket – exclusion of these writers from many histories of international thinking is an issue of deep concern. It is also a demonstration of how the *post hoc* construction of debates often distorts our view of what IR is and has been. Interestingly, of the four genres explored by Owens, disciplinary history did the best in terms of both numbers of women discussed, and the percentage of historical women to historical men (although at an average of 4.88%, this was hardly stellar).

Yet, this exclusion of women, even when those women have not been feminist, makes an important feminist point about the way that IR has marginalized women and underplayed the importance of gender. This has also included the erasing of a distinct feminist tradition in early IR that flourished before the 1950s. Some of these feminist scholars have been the subject of recent rediscovery by historians of international thought and include key early-twentieth century writers such as Helena Swanwick (Ashworth, 2011a; Stöckmann, 2018), Virginia Woolf (Wilson, 2013), and Jane Addams (Cochran, 2017).

Much of the rediscovery of early feminist IR developed as a spin-off of work that had been rediscovering interwar thinkers and debates. As a result, many of these involved British feminists who had contributed to debates around the role of war, the League of Nations, and appeasement. These included the journalist Helena Swanwick, whose work on suffrage and peace before and during the 1914–18 war led her to be a fixture of debates about the nature of international order and foreign policy (see Ashworth, 2011a; Stöckmann, 2018). Swanwick had written extensively on international affairs from a maternalist feminist perspective, and also was familiar to historians through the role she played in the Women's International League for Peace and Freedom (WILPF). More attention is now being given to the place of both the 1915 Hague Conference and WILPF in the development of a distinct feminist international thought (True and Tickner, 2018). WILPF, in particular, played an important role in providing a forum for discussions by early IR feminists (for their importance, and the richness of their contribution to contemporary debates, see Ashworth, 2020). What is more, the role of feminist international thinkers in the interwar period is also uncovering the place that feminism in particular played in the debates over appeasement (Ashworth, 2011a).

Increasingly, the history of feminism in IR seems to mirror the history of both IPE and geopolitics: after a rich history prior to 1945, it becomes marginalized in the predominantly US university-based field of IR, only to return decades later. A decade ago, it was common for both feminist and non-feminist IR scholars to assume that feminist IR emerged in the 1980s and 1990s (see the summary in Stöckmann, 2018: 218–219). This claim can no longer stand up to scrutiny. Indeed, as I write a comprehensive volume on women in the history of international thought (that also covers many key feminists) is being edited for Cambridge University Press by Patricia Owens and Katharina Rietzler (2021). While more needs to be done on the place of both women and feminism in international thought, this is increasingly a part of disciplinary history that cannot be ignored.

Race and empire

One of the women writers mentioned in the Owens and Rietzler collection is Merze Tate. Praised by Morgenthau for her work on disarmament, Tate does not just stand out as one of the few women in the US university system after 1950 studying IR, she was also one of the few African Americans. With notable exceptions, much of the literature in IR disciplinary history over the last few decades has focused on white anglophone men writing in the imperial metropoles. This has helped mask two aspects of IR's history: the roles that have been played by both imperialism and race in international thought.

The interlinked concepts of race and empire have always played a role in international thought. Many of the figures that were involved in the development of international thought before the First World War were overt racists (Hobson, 2012). A. T. Mahan, a major influence on strategic studies, based his view of international order on the idea of an ultimate violent conflict between races. Similarly, the influential US scholar Brooks Adams interpreted the rise and fall of nations in terms of racial development, while the political geographer (and student of Ellen Churchill Semple) Ellsworth Huntington saw the health of societies in terms of what he called kith groups. In the case of the last two, race was mixed with climate (see Ashworth, 2014: 103–107).

Alongside these overtly racist forebears, IR has also not fully come to terms with the extent to which the field emerged out of studies of imperialism and colonial administration. Disciplinary history has begun to confront this, with David Long and Brian Schmidt's edited collection bringing together a selection of experts writing on the influence of imperialism on IR's origins (2005). More recently, Thakur, Davis, and Vale have explored the foundation of the Union of South Africa and the role of the Round Table group around Lionel Curtis as an imperial and racial point of origin for international thought (2017). The Round Table, as conduit between empire and IR, is not unique in this regard. Much early-twentieth century international thought mixed global order and colonial administration. It is telling, for example, that the American political scientist Paul Reinsch wrote two books on colonial administration, in addition to his better-known books on world politics and the Public International Unions (Schmidt, 1998: ch. 4; Ashworth, 2014: 107–109; Ashworth, 2019: 128). As formal empires faded, IR's link to the problem of empire continued. Ian Hall has written on the equivocal nature of the English School's engagement with the broadening of international society to include non-Western and recently independent societies (Hall, 2011).

This refocusing of international thought towards empire opens another question faced by disciplinary history. Our histories of international thought tend to be histories of Western (and colonizing) IR. What of the international thought of the non-Western world, especially of those who were subject to colonialism? Robbie Shilliam has composed a fresh analysis of the 1935–36 Italian-Ethiopian conflict that has put it in the context of wider Pan-African thinking (Shilliam, 2013). Musab Younis more recently has extended this to a study of three interwar cases (Haiti, Liberia, and Ethiopia), and has explored both Western racist interpretations and the wider Pan-African literature on these cases: uncovering both a 'White' and a 'Black' Atlantic (Younis, 2018).

Another interesting trend has been the rediscovery of pre-independence Indian IR. India's role as a League member, coupled with its predominantly anglophone university system, meant that it produced a sizeable IR community that also engaged with Western anglophone IR. Stephen Legg has explored this status with frequent references to major Indian scholars writing on the League (Legg, 2014). Concentrating specifically on IR and global order, Martin Bayly has summarized several key Indian IR figures, pointing out that they tended to synthesize Indian themes with knowledge of Western international thinkers, thereby creating a related but unique international thought (Bayly, 2017). The quality and quantity of the work coming out of India at the time means that Legg and Bayly have just scratched the surface. The detailed analysis of the League and its wider ramifications found in J. C. Coyajee's *India and the League of Nations*, for example, situates itself within a broader global literature (a product, in part, of his Cambridge education) while presenting a distinctly Indian view (Coyajee, 1932).

Yet, the issue of race extends beyond the categories of formal empire. Cecelia Lynch has recently categorized race as a moral aporia that exists at the heart of IR throughout its history (Lynch, 2019). The role of race within the history of American IR has been explored in detail by Robert Vitalis, who combines an argument for the racist and segregated nature of the origins of US IR with a rediscovery of the African American Howard School of IR (Vitalis, 2015). The seemingly anti-imperialist and racially blind discipline of IR found in American universities turns out on closer analysis to be embedded in imperial ideas, and to be as racially segregated as the society it served.

War and security under anarchy

In the 1980s, it became common to talk about realist and idealist paradigms. This, though, was a recent development owing much to the absorption of Thomas Kuhn's ideas into IR. Amongst the IR stocktakers of the 1970s (and even into the early 1980s), it was more common to lump realism and idealism together as examples of two strands of a common traditional approach that stood in stark contrast to behavioural and post-behavioural approaches. This made sense to the extent that those writers referred to as realist and idealist often shared both methods and subject matter. Rather than distinguishing between what 1980s scholars saw as distinct realist and idealist paradigms, it is probably more helpful to see a larger common tradition that, as wars became more destructive and economies more integrated, saw the problem of war as paramount (see Bartelson, 2021 in this volume).

This, of course, is the traditional subject matter of IR that most current IR scholars and students are familiar with. Consequently, there is an ample and well-known literature of both disciplinary historians and historical sources to draw on. It also links to the other traditions discussed above. The work of Angell in political economy, Bowman in political geography, Swanwick in feminism, Tate at the Howard School, and Coyajee on the League all dealt directly with questions of war and security. Underlying these discussions of the prevalence of war was the question of the role of the structure of international order (Anarchy? Society? Hierarchy?).

Different disciplinary historians have traced this problem back to different origin points. For some the discourse of war under anarchy can be traced to the late-nineteenth century (Schmidt, 1998; Sylvest, 2005; Knutsen, 2008; Cochran and Navari, 2017). For others the interwar period is the focus (Long and Wilson, 1995; Ashworth, 2007). Many regard the post-1945 period as the foundation of IR through the articulation of both US classical realism (Guilhot, 2008), and the English School (Dunne, 1998; Hall; 2012). These all share an analysis of a rich tradition that explored the nature of international order, discussed whether it was a functioning international society, and argued over if (and in what way) it should be reformed.

Debates about war and security under anarchy/hierarchy/society dominate our understandings of IR and its history. Before the First World War, much of it revolved around questions of whether war still paid under the conditions of new technologies and the new imperial and global political economy. In the wake of the First World War, attention turned to the possibilities of reordering the international anarchy in order to make wars less likely, and to redirect military might into serving a policing role in the service of preventing aggressive war. Here questions of collective security, psychological changes to behaviour, and the question of whether a new multilateral diplomacy was replacing a secret bilateral one predominated. These interwar debates would feed into Second World War debates about reconstruction, and the radical surgery conducted by the Allies during 1942–45 as they constructed new organizations to deal with potential war-causing instabilities. Trade, development, and fiscal stability were all seen as important to security, and thus the subject of international agreements. With the end of US-Soviet cooperation, and the proliferation of weapons of mass destruction, the immediate importance of maintaining a fragile peace between superpowers became the dominant concern in the United States. Questions of relative power came to dominate discussions, as did the tragic and ultimately unstable nature of the system of states. These concerns refocused the classical realist and early English School to immediate questions of power and order/society.

This concentration on classical realism and the English School has come to dominate Western anglophone interpretations of IR, but in reality, its ascendency was short lived. Classical realist notions of power and tragedy were soon being challenged by approaches that, borrowing from systems theory, replaced the fungible concept of power with ideas of structure and systems. Here war played a double system-sustaining and system-destroying role. At the same time, decolonization and new wars of national liberation or proxy conflicts between the two superpowers played havoc with English School notions of international society. Both of these played into debates that are now half-remembered in IR as part of a second field-defining 'great debate'.

I have written elsewhere on how there never were separate second and third great debates (Ashworth, 2019). Rather, conflicts between classical realists and behaviouralists merged with other new approaches to create a perceived sense of theoretical confusion and drift. This perception of confusion in IR circles during the 1960s and 1970s was brought to an end by the introduction of the idea of paradigms, and the settling on three (later more) approaches in what would become known as the inter-paradigm debate of the early 1980s. Thus, rather than two debates, we find a growing pluralization of the field from the 1960s, which is eventually subjected to new attempts to impose order in the 1980s. While war and security remained the focus, there were disagreements over the global architectures that helped or hindered conflicts. Was the international system a power political state-based one, a transnational one, or a hierarchical one based on global economic inequality? This period would see the re-emergence of IPE, and by the 1990s gender and geopolitics.

Conclusion

When we refocus IR traditions around subject matters, a different set of trends emerge. A diverse field of international thought narrows in the mid-twentieth century, only for those traditions to reappear in the 1970s, 1980s, and 1990s. In this sense, 1950 represents a point where a mass extinction takes place, with vibrant traditions in political economy, geopolitics, and feminism coming to an end. At the same time, the link to imperialism and colonial administration is lost, and the writings of women and non-white writers in international thought disappear. Developments in classical realism and the English School occur concurrently with a great erasure of diverse traditions in IR. A folk memory of this erasure survives in the bowdlerized account of the realist-idealist debate, where some of those erased, such as Norman Angell, are remembered out of context. Yet, this idea of a big two-sided debate hides the large number of smaller intellectual debates within these subject matters. Whether that be the debates over capitalism and war, between political geographers and geopoliticians, feminist responses to appeasement, or Indian engagements with British and American IR, IR before 1950 engaged in many vigorous debates.

Yet, this narrowing of IR lasts little longer than a decade. A debate, partially remembered as the second great debate, sees notions of power politics challenged by ideas of systems in the 1960s, while political economy returns in the 1970s. By the 1990s, feminism and geopolitics have also returned, and in the last decade, a new appreciation of the place of empire and race has made its mark. Even the planet politics turn has its analogue in the writings of the political geographer Derwent Whittlesey. Each of these have also witnessed a corresponding rediscovery of their subject matters in earlier pre-1950 international thought by post-1990 disciplinary historians of IR. The sections above have adumbrated these new histories of political economy, political geography, women and feminism, and race and empire within the broader history of international thought.

Taking a traditions as subject matters view of IR provides a bird's eye view of the many clusters that make up international thought, but it is not the only tool we have for understanding the richness of the field. It does not displace more detailed studies, like those of Ian Hall using Mark Bevir's concept of tradition (Hall, 2012). Each subject matter contains many different clusters of scholars, and the advancement of the history of international thought requires all these tools, working at different levels of magnification.

Equally well, my list of traditions are not exhaustive. Others could and should be added as scholarship expands our horizons. There is still much that we do not know, which is underscored by the recent and partial nature of much of the work I have summarized in this chapter. While we are well served by major histories of the study of war and security under anarchy, our knowledge of the other four still contain gaps, and lack comprehensive histories. Thus, despite the excellent example set by Craig Murphy in 1994, there is still no comprehensive history of IPE before 1950. The role of political geography in international thought is still largely restricted to journal articles, while the first attempt at a comprehensive study of women in the history of international thought is only going to press this year. Similarly, our knowledge of IR outside of the confines of the North Atlantic and the English-speaking world is still sketchy, and more work needs to be done on non-Western traditions. Despite the wealth of historical scholarship on international thought that has emerged since the mid-1990s, we are still only walking along the shore of a mighty ocean.

Suggestions for further reading

Ashworth, L. M. (2019). A Historiographer's View: Rewriting the History of International Thought. In: A. Gofas, I. Hamati-Ataya, and N. Onuf, eds., *The Sage Handbook of the History, Philosophy and Sociology of International Relations*, London: Sage, 529–541.

Ashworth, L. M. (2013). Mapping a new world: geography and the interwar study of international relations. *International Studies Quarterly*, 57 (1), 138–149.

Lynch, C. (2019). The moral aporia of race and international relations. *International Relations*, 33 (2), 267–285.

Murphy, C. N. (1994). *International Organization and Industrial Change*. New York, NY: Oxford University Press.

Owens, P., and Rietzler, K., eds. (2021). *Women's International Thought. A New History*. Cambridge: Cambridge University Press.

Younis, M. (2018). Race, the world and time: Haiti, Liberia and Ethiopia (1914-1945). *Millennium*, 46 (3), 352–370.

References

Angell, N. (1911). *The Great Illusion*. Toronto: McClelland and Goodchild.

Ashworth, L. M. (2007). *International Relations and the Labour Party*. London: IB Tauris.

Ashworth, L. M. (2011a). Feminism, war and the prospects for peace. Helena Swanwick (1864-1939) and the lost feminists of inter-war international relations. *International Feminist Journal of Politics*, 13 (1), 25–43.

Ashworth, L. M. (2011b). Realism and the spirit of 1919: Halford Mackinder, geopolitics, and the reality of the League Of Nations. *European Journal of International Relations*, 17 (2), 279–301.

Ashworth, L. M. (2014). *A History of International Thought*. London & New York: Routledge.

Ashworth, L. M. (2020). Women of the Twenty Years' Crisis: The Women's International League for Peace and Freedom and the Problem of Collective Security. In: P. Owens, and K. Rietzler, eds., *Women's International Thought. A New History*, Cambridge: Cambridge University Press.

Bartelson, J. (2021). War and the Turn to History in International Relations. In de Carvalho, B., Costa Lopez, J., & Leira, H., eds. *Routledge Handbook of Historical International Relations*. Abingdon: Routledge.

Bayly, M. (2021). Imperialism: Beyond the 'Re-turn to Empire' in International Relations. In de Carvalho, B., Costa Lopez, J., & Leira, H., eds. *Routledge Handbook of Historical International Relations*. Abingdon: Routledge.

Bayly, M. J. (2017). The Forgotten History of Indian International Relations. *ORF Issue Brief*, November, Issue no. 10.

Bowman, I. (1928). *The New World*. 4th edition. Yonkers-on-Hudson, NY: World Book Company.

Bowman, I. (1930). *International Relations*. Chicago, IL: American Library Association.

Buzan, B., and Lawson, G. (2015). *The Global Transformation: History, Modernity and the Making of International Relations*. Cambridge, Cambridge University Press.

Cochran, M. (2017). The 'Newer Ideals' of Jane Addams's Progressivism: A Realistic Utopia of Cosmopolitan Justice. In: M. Cochran, and C. Navari, eds., *Progressivism and US Foreign Policy Between the World Wars*, New York, NY: Palgrave Macmillan, 143–165.

Cochran, M., and Navari, C., eds. (2017). *Progressivism and US Foreign Policy Between the World Wars*. New York, NY: Palgrave Macmillan.

Cohen, B. (2008). *International Political Economy. An Intellectual History*. Princeton, NJ: Princeton University Press.

Coyajee, J. C. (1932). *India and the League of Nations*. Madras: Waltair.

Dale, G. (2016). In search of Polanyi's international relations theory. *Review of International Studies*, 42 (3), 401–424.

de Carvalho, B., Leira, H., and Hobson, J. M. (2011). The big bangs of IR. The myths that your teachers still tell you about 1648 and 1919. *Millennium*, 39 (3), 735–758.

Dunne, T. (1998). *Inventing International Society*. Houndmills: Macmillan.

Guilhot, N. (2008). The realist gambit: postwar American political science and the birth of IR theory. *International Political Sociology*, 2 (4), 281–304.

Hall, I., ed. (2015). *Radicals and Reactionaries in Twentieth Century International Thought*. Houndmills: Palgrave Macmillan.

Hall, I. (2011). The Revolt against the West: decolonisation and its repercussions in British International Thought, 1945–75. *International History Review*, 33 (1), 43–64.

Hall, I. (2012). *Dilemmas of Decline*. Berkeley, CA: University of California Press.

Hobson, J. M. (2012). *The Eurocentric Conception of World Politics*. Cambridge: Cambridge University Press.

Knutsen, T. (2008). A lost generation? IR scholarship before World War I. *International Politics*, 45 (6), 650–674.

Legg, S. (2014). An international anomaly? Sovereignty, The League of Nations and India's princely geographies. *Journal of Historical Geography*, 43, 96–110.

Long, D., and Schmidt, B., eds. (2005). *Imperialism and Internationalism in the Discipline of International Relations*. Albany, NY: SUNY University Press.

Long, D., and Wilson, P. (1995). *Thinkers of the Twenty Years' Crisis*. Oxford: Clarendon.

Mackinder, H. J. (1919). *Democratic Ideals and Reality*. London: Constable.

Mackinder, H. J. (1922). *The Modern British State*. 2nd edition. London: George Philip.

Murphy, D. (1997). *The Heroic Earth*. Kent, OH: Kent State University Press.

Owens, P. (2018). Women and the history of international thought. *International Studies Quarterly*, 62 (3), 467–481.

Reinsch, P. S. (1900). *World Politics at the End of the Nineteenth Century*. New York & London: Macmillan.

Rosenboim, O. (2017). *The Emergence of Globalism*. Princeton, NJ: Princeton University Press.

Rosenboim, O., and Hartnett, L. (2021). International Political Thought and Historical International Relations. In de Carvalho, B., Costa Lopez, J., & Leira, H., eds. *Routledge Handbook of Historical International Relations*. Abingdon: Routledge.

Schmidt, B. (1998). *The Political Discourse of Anarchy*. Albany, NY: State University of New York.

Schmidt, B., ed. (2012). *IR and the First Great Debate*. London: Routledge.

Shilliam, R. (2013). Intervention and colonial-modernity: decolonising the Italy/Ethiopia conflict through Psalms 68:31. *Review of International Studies*, 39 (5), 1131–1147.

Stawell, F. M. (1929). *The Growth of International Thought*. London, Butterworth.

Stöckmann, J. (2018). Women, wars, and world affairs: recovering feminist international relations, 1915–39. *Review of International Studies*, 44 (2), 215–235.

Sylvest, C. (2005). Continuity and change in British liberal internationalism, c.1900–1930. *Review of International Studies*, 31 (2), 263–283.

Towns, A. (2021). Gender in Historical International Relations. In de Carvalho, B., Costa Lopez, J., & Leira, H., eds. *Routledge Handbook of Historical International Relations*. Abingdon: Routledge.

True, J., and Tickner, J. A. (2018). A century of international relations feminism: from World War I women's peace pragmatism to the women, peace and security agenda. *International Studies Quarterly*, 62 (2), 221–233.

Vitalis, R. (2015). *White World Order. Black Power Politics*. Ithaca, NY: Cornell.

Wallenius, T. (2021). How to Do the History of International Thought?. In de Carvalho, B., Costa Lopez, J., & Leira, H., eds. *Routledge Handbook of Historical International Relations*. Abingdon: Routledge.

Whittlesey, D. (1939). *The Earth and the State*. New York, NY: Henry Holt.

Wilson, P. (2013). Attacking Hitler in England: Patriarchy, Class and War in Virginia Woolf's *Three Guineas*. In H. Bliddal, C. Sylvest, and P. Wilson, eds., *Classics of International Relations*, London & New York: Routledge, 36–47.

Worth, O. (2012). Accumulating the Critical Spirit: Rosa Luxemburg and critical IPE. *International Politics*, 49 (2), 136–153.

Yao, J., and Delatolla, A. (2021). Race and Historical International Relations. In de Carvalho, B., Costa Lopez, J., & Leira, H., eds. *Routledge Handbook of Historical International Relations*. Abingdon: Routledge.

12

WAR AND THE TURN TO HISTORY IN INTERNATIONAL RELATIONS[1]

Jens Bartelson

Introduction

What started over 20 years ago as a rebellion against what then was perceived as an overly static and state-centric world view within the study of international relations is now coming of age as a vibrant and dynamic subfield devoted to the historical study of international relations broadly conceived. But to what extent has this historical reorientation contributed to a better understanding of war in world politics, given that war long has been a main preoccupation of academic international relations?

In order to answer this question, we must first consider what was at stake in the turn to history and what its claims to novelty have entailed before going on to analyse how war has been conceptualized and understood by those scholars who self-consciously have associated themselves with this turn. Hence, I will try to answer the above question by revisiting some recent scholarship in Historical International Relations which either directly or indirectly has sought to make sense of war and violent conflict in different historical and cultural contexts during the past couple of decades. Given the task at hand, I will not engage scholarship from academic international relations more broadly conceived but confine my inquiry to the growing and increasingly cohesive body of historically oriented scholarship that has emerged during the last decades.

As I shall argue, although those who have taken a turn to history have done little to challenge modern notions of war and warfare at the conceptual level, this reorientation has nevertheless brought a shift of focus away from the traditional preoccupation with the *causes of war* within the study of international relations in favour of an increased emphasis on the *effects of war* on international and global order. Yet whatever its intellectual merits, the turn to history has not yet produced a coherent understanding of the nature of war, let alone a theory about its effects. Judging from its role in this reorientation, the concept of war seems to have provided a mediating link between the traditional concerns of international relations and those of historical scholarship, thereby leaving a range of other possible functions that war might fulfil in the history of international relations unexplored. Thus, as I will conclude, Historical International Relations is challenged to develop a more coherent understanding of the role of war in world politics.

In order to assess the extent to which the turn to history has produced new insights into the function of war in academic international relations, I will start by revisiting some of the common claims of those who have taken a turn to history and discuss its impact on the study of international relations. I will then proceed to discuss some works within this subfield that have explicitly engaged the problem of war – conceptually, theoretically and empirically – in order to assess the extent to which this reorientation have yielded fresh and important insights beyond those conveyed by mainstream international relations. I will end this chapter by briefly discussing the possibility of expanding the study of war in new directions, given a historical orientation.

The turn to history

What later was proclaimed and eventually acknowledged as a turn to history in the study of international relations initially grew out of a dissatisfaction with neorealism and its inability to account for historical transformation in the international system, especially in the light of its obvious failure to understand how and why the Cold War ended the way it did. Many scholars then called for a more historically oriented approach to the study of international relations, informed by insights on modern social theory and classical historical sociology (Rosenberg, 1994; Hobson, 1998; Spruyt, 1998). But as Halvard Leira and Benjamin de Carvalho have pointed out, this initial turn to history was quite reactive and mostly programmatic in character and did not translate into any series engagement with extant historiography. Nevertheless, it turned the tide in favour of historical processes at the expense of the neorealist obsession with structure in the study of international relations (Leira and de Carvalho, 2016; de Carvalho, Costa Lopez, and Leira, 2021).

Laments to the effect that academic international relations long had failed to properly embrace history were followed by sustained attempts to bring history and historical sociology back into the core of international relations theorizing. But these attempts merely reactivated a dormant tension between the social and the historical sciences. Whereas the former has been geared to the study of the present, the latter is by definition devoted to the study of the past. Whereas the former takes a nomothetic approach to its subject matter in order to explain *why* things happen, the latter takes an ideographic approach in order to understand *how* things happen. According to those who advocated a turn to history, scholarship in international relations had long been animated by conventional presuppositions of modern social science. To the extent that scholars had bothered to consult historical scholarship at all, this was only in order to excavate from the past examples that were used to illustrate present concerns or to corroborate their theoretical assumptions. This narrow focus on the present and the biased and often anachronistic mining of historical scholarship tended to reinforce a static view of world politics, making it difficult to come to terms not only with its past but also to chart its possible future transformations in a global context (Hobson, 2002, 2007). Such a decontextualized account of world politics not only made the emergence of the modern state and the international system difficult to explain and understand, but also removed the vast multiplicity of political associations in other times and places from the scope of inquiry. Thus, to the same extent as the study of international relations was ahistorical in outlook, it was also Eurocentric more or less by default (Hobson, 2012; Bowden, 2021).

This world view found additional support in the way in which students of international relations had approached the history of international thought, and especially those texts that had been singled out as exemplars of the disciplinary canon. In historiographical terms, this meant that authors from diverse historical contexts far apart in space and time – notably, Thucydides, Machiavelli, Hobbes and Kant – were read as if they were addressing the same problems and therefore also mobilized in order to solve present ones. Foremost among the works singled out for target practice in this regard were those by Kenneth Waltz (1959) and Robert Gilpin (1981), both of whom not only maintained that international politics had remained essentially the same across the millennia, but also that the rich legacy of international thought could be best under-stood as responses to the allegedly perennial problems of war and peace. In response to this habit-ually anachronistic reading, Duncan Bell soon proclaimed the dawn of a historiographical turn within international relations, in which the 'study of the history of political thought, as well as the intellectual history of the discipline, is now taken far more seriously, studied more carefully and explicitly, and plays a greater role in shaping the theoretical debate, than it has in the past' (Bell, 2001: 123).

Apart from the presentist tendency to regard history as a repository of examples and lessons that could be invoked to support various theoretical claims, others used the historical schol-arship to debunk the nomothetic ambitions that had been underwriting much theorizing in international relations by insisting on the historical contingency and singularity of historical events (see Vaughan-Williams, 2005). Yet according to Lawson (2012), both these forms of pres-entism merely served to reinforce rather than to overcome the divide between history and academic international relations. Instead of being considered autonomous enterprises with different subject matters and approaches to them, history and international relations should be considered a common enterprise, since '[a]s such, the choice is not one between a historical enterprise which can do with or without theory, but acceptance of the fact that history *is* a social science' (Lawson, 2012: 221). Thus, from the viewpoint of international relations, the turn to history was a matter of *assimilating* those parts of historical scholarship that deemed useful to its own research agenda, rather than reorienting the study of international relations in a more ideographic and descriptive direction.

Yet behind such claims to have inaugurated a new turn, it is obvious that the turn to history also marked a *return* to a particular way of studying history and to a set of problems that had long been crucial to the study of historical sociology. Although historical sociologists had been busy trying to explain how and why modern states had emerged, their search for causes had with few exceptions been confined to domestic societies rather than to the international system within which states simultaneously had become embedded. As a consequence, and as Hobden (1999) and Rosenberg (2006) pointed out, since traditional historical sociology lacked a *sui generis* conceptualization of the international context within which states had emerged and interacted, attempts to build an *international* historical sociology on such foundations would only issue in methodological nationalism.

Much of what has been going on since then can be understood as an attempt to make sense of the modern international system in ways that do not render its existence epiphenomenal to states, thereby providing the foundations of what can be termed a more genuinely international – and later also global – historical sociology (Go, Lawson, and de Carvalho, 2021). Thus, in what is perhaps the most comprehensive survey of the benefits expected to accrue from marrying the study of historical sociology and international relations together, Lawson argued that '[t]he rejection of universal, timeless categories and their replacement by multilinear theories of world historical development gives history the chance to breathe, and agency the chance to make a difference' (Lawson, 2006: 415). From this observation, it followed that 'by renewing the interest in temporality and, and, in turn, into the various logics within which world history takes place, the Westphalian moment, and indeed the entire modern European states-system, become just one part in a much wider canvas' (Lawson, 2006: 415). Another benefit that would hopefully ensue from this union 'lies in its capacity to debunk taken-for-granted assumptions about cen-tral concepts and myths of origin in the discipline' (Lawson, 2006: 416) that had followed from widespread tendencies to impose the disciplinary concerns of the present onto an alien past. As Hobson and Lawson (2008) were to argue, scholars of international relations took onboard theories and concepts from authors like Mann, Skocpol, Giddens and Tilly in order to explain the making of modern states and the international system along with their various transform-ations during the modern era, thereby offering a double punch: 'not just a focus on the histor-ical details of particular dimensions of international relations, but also an emphasis on causal explanations wherever these were located, specifying how patterns, configurations and sets of social relations combined in particular contexts to determine certain outcomes' (Hobson and Lawson, 2008: 433).

Given these venerable sources of inspiration, it would be reasonable to expect that the marriage of historical sociology to international relations would produce an intensified focus on war as its first offspring. Yet curiously this has rather brought an increased attention to *other* mechanisms of change in the international system, as well as to *other* effects of war than those traditionally associated with theories of state-making. This endeavour has found additional support in the ambition to subject the study of international thought to the rigours of con-textualist methodology and historiography. Although both these reorientations have yielded an avalanche of books and articles in recent years, they still represent distinct strands of scholarship and with few attempts to bridge the gap between their different starting points for the benefit of a more holistic understanding of the history of modern international relations. Loose talk of a historical turn also makes it easy to forget that the modern discipline of international relations has its very roots in a tradition of political-historical writing stretching back to early modern historiography and its focus on issues of international order and the balance of power, and that the writings of some of those who led the development of the discipline – such as Raymond Aron, Stanley Hoffman and Fred Halliday to name a few – displayed a clear and distinct histor-ical orientation several decades before anything like a turn to history was proclaimed. Hence the claim that the study of international relations has been stuck with a static view of its subject matter and a rigidly nomothetic approach to its study is itself anachronistic and indicative of the extent to which the discipline of international relations has been forgetful of its own history (see also Ashworth, 2021).

Yet before proceeding to assess the extent to which the historical turn has brought any added value to the understanding of war in world politics, it is important to note that the historical turn has been met with scepticism on grounds other than the veracity of its claim to novelty. One such line of criticism concerns the futility of trying to resolve the underlying tension between structure and history that some of those who have taken the turn to history claim to have done. For example, as Tom Lundborg (2016) has argued, while the difficulties involved in trying to combine international relations and historical sociology hark back to an underlying ontological tension between the study of structure and history in the social sciences, 'the study of history, as well as of structure, cannot be separated from certain assumptions about the nature of this ground, what it consists of and who has the legitimate authority to stand on it and claim its presence and meaning' (Lundborg, 2016: 116). But as I will suggest in the concluding section, the study of war has come to provide precisely the kind of mediating link between structure and history that has made the quest for such ground appear redundant, at least for the moment.

The turn to war

Since so much work in historical sociology has been focused on the role of war in shaping the formation of modern states and the international system, we could expect that this would spill over into the historically oriented study of international relations as well. But whereas academic international relations has long been preoccupied with the causes of war, historical sociologists have been more concerned about its role in the making of states and empires. Although the turn to history has shifted concerns in the latter direction, it has also broadened the research agenda thanks to a sustained engagement with historical scholarship *outside* the confines of historical sociology. Many historically oriented scholars have thereby added important nuance and complication to the standard bellicist assumptions of much historical sociology. Rather than trying to corroborate the worn dictum according to which war made the state and the state made war empirically, pioneering statements in this field have instead emphasized the extent to which the making of states and the emergence of the international system were conditioned by a host of ideational and institutional factors that were independent of practices of warfare (Ruggie, 1993; Spruyt, 1994; Bruneau, 2021).

Yet many of those who have taken the historical turn have tried to understand how and explain why the modern international system emerged in Europe and later spread to other continents as well. This has compelled them to reassess and sometimes debunk conventional accounts of when and why a transition from a hierarchical world of empires to an anarchical world of states took place. This tendency is most clear from the many reinterpretations of the Thirty Years War and the Peace of Westphalia in 1648 that have emerged in recent decades. Whereas textbook accounts of international relations long took the Peace of Westphalia as the starting point when an international system of territorially demarcated and mutually recognizing sovereign states first emerged, both Croxton (1999) and Osiander (2001) have pointed out that this conclusion did not find much support in the treaties of Münster and Osnabrück but was rather a product of later attempts to legitimize the international system and provide its study with a semblance of intellectual cohesion. From this kind of contention has ensued a series of reassessments to the effect that the Peace of Westphalia was nothing but a false caesura in the history of international relations, (Teschke, 2003) and that the foundations of the modern international system were laid only much later largely thanks to the wide dissemination and uptake of *Le Droit des Gens* (1758) by Emer de Vattel (Beaulac, 2004).

But none of these objections has kept historically oriented scholars from continuing to attribute decisive importance to the Thirty Years War while adding considerable nuance and complication to the received view. If the initial turn to history was more programmatic than substantial, more recent scholarship is much more attuned to the historiographical debates at hand and more inclined to make use of primary sources in more sophisticated ways (Leira and de Carvalho, 2016). Yet many of the accounts of the emergence of the modern international system have taken war to be constitutive of its emergence. For example, even if Daniel Philpott is trying to explain how the meaning of sovereignty changed as a result of 'prior revolutions in ideas about justice and political authority' (Philpott, 2001: 4), these decisive shifts could nevertheless 'arose out of a crisis, often a major war, sometimes a major upheaval in the international system' (Philpott, 2001: 44) of which the Thirty Years' War was the first and paradigmatic instance. Equally focused on the Reformation and its effects on international order, Daniel Nexon (2009) has forcefully argued that the rise of religious heterodoxy in Europe produced a crisis that upset the balance of power within as well as among the composite monarchies of the day, a crisis which had a destabilizing impact on the dynastic order and eventually issued in widespread religious warfare across the continent. But as Nexon also shows, the road leading from here to an international system of sovereign states was far from straight. Not only did many composite states survive decades of religious discord, but also '[s]hifts in the nature of warfare and economic relations ultimately contributed more to a Europe composed of sovereign-territorial and nation-states than did the introduction of new religious ideas' (Nexon, 2009: 10).

Another good example of this new emphasis on the constitutive function of war in the shaping of international orders, and of the early modern international order in particular, is provided by Andrew Phillips. Understood as 'the constellation of constitutional norms and fundamental institutions through which co-operation is cultivated and conflict contained between different political communities' (Phillips, 2010: 5), international orders are sustained 'through the applications of authorized practices of organized violence' (Phillips, 2010: 6). While such orders might undergo change whenever 'the relative distribution of power and prestige between different political units is altered' (Phillips, 2010: 6), more fundamental change is likely to occur when its constitutional values and fundamental institutions change in tandem with its principle of unit differentiation.

This tendency to conceptualize international orders in terms of an amalgamation of material and ideational elements and explore multiple causes of their rise and demise has paved the way for some fascinating comparisons across time and space. Tin-Bor Hui's (2005) very sophisticated attempt to explain why a competitive system of sovereign states emerged in early modern Europe, whereas similar structural and historical preconditions in ancient China instead produced a quest for domination and empire is a case in point. By the same token, Phillips (2010) not only tries to explain how the universalist Christian order was transformed into one composed of sovereign states, but also to compare it with largely parallel developments in the Sinosphere, arguing that both processes were driven by 'a combination of institutional decay, the collapse of prevailing social imaginaries and the accompanying emergence of anti-systemic ideologies, and increases in violence interdependence both within and between political communities' (Phillips, 2010: 7).

The renewed interest in the rise and demise of international orders has also produced a series of accounts of how the sovereign state and the international system were able to spread to other continents. Understanding how the states-system was globalized has seemed especially urgent since Keene (2002) pointed to the sharp disjunction that has long existed between an 'order promoting toleration within Europe, and an order promoting civilization beyond' (Keene, 2002: 7). Some explanations of this transition place war at the centre stage, whereas others do not. Yet all of them struggle hard to avoid the obvious Eurocentrism of earlier diffusionist accounts of Western expansion. For example, as Ayse Zarakol (2010) has shown, conclusive military defeat at the hands of Western powers prompted the Ottoman Empire, Russia and Japan to adapt and conform to Western standards of statehood and emulate many of their political and social institutions in order to survive in an expansive international system dominated by Western powers. Others have emphasized how the modern international order emerged not so much as a consequence of disruptive wars but through a global transformation during the long nineteenth century. As Barry Buzan and George Lawson have argued, being the product of the combined forces of industrialization and the emergence of rational states and ideologies of progress, this global transformation meant that '[t]hose convinced of their cultural superiority and with access to advanced weapons, industrial production, medicine and new forms of bureaucratic organization gained a pronounced advantage over those with limited access to these sources of power' (Buzan and Lawson, 2015: 9), providing not only for lasting power asymmetries between core and periphery in modern international relations, but also for the declining usefulness of war as an instrument of foreign policy among core states (Buzan and Lawson, 2015: 269).

Similarly, as Andrew Phillips and Jason Sharman (2015) have noted in their study of how war, trade and rule were interconnected in the Indian Ocean during the early modern period, diversity of political forms long constituted the default setting of international orders even inside Europe. The puzzle is why such heterogeneity persisted even as interaction between actors increased, given that we would normally expect military and economic competition among units to bring about emulation and institutional convergence. But as they argue, the endurance of diversity was made possible by the fact that Europeans and regional rulers had compatible interests and broadly congruent ideas and institutions that allowed for common strategies of localization and power sharing. That pattern was reconfigured from the mid-eighteenth century onwards, when new forms of imperial rule based on notions of indivisible sovereignty began to supersede the model of divided sovereignty upon which maritime empires had previously been built (Phillips and

Sharman, 2015: 46). But as Sharman (2019) has also argued, the European expansion into other continents was not based on military superiority, but the key to their success was instead 'local support and the cultivation of indigenous allies combined with a judicious posture of European subservience when faced by far more powerful Asian empires' (Sharman, 2019: 503).

An apt way to characterize the above contributions would be to say that they are based on the founding assumption that war made the international system, and that the international system made war. This represent a significant advance on the methodological nationalism of earlier attempts to incorporate insights from historical sociology into the study of international relations, as well as a conclusive departure from earlier tendencies to naturalize the international system. But this macro shift also comes with certain meta-historical commitments. Leaving aside for the moment the inherent ambiguities of the component terms of this equivocation, it is plain from these accounts that the wars that brought the international system into being are of a different kind from those that the anarchic structure of the same system later facilitated among its component parts. Those wars that so profoundly disrupted the pre-modern world order and helped to bring the modern world into being did not take place between sovereign and territorially demarcated actors with clearly discernible identities and interests but were instead instrumental in beating such entities into being in the most literal of senses. By contrast, the wars engendered by the modern international system were precisely wars *between* such sovereign entities, and during phases of imperial expansion, wars between them and those non-European polities that were lacking these defining characteristics of modern statehood, thereby compelling them to emulate these characteristics to gain admission into the international system and enjoy whatever legal protection it offered.

But this meta-historical characterization also raises the question of how this bifurcation of the modern world has been reproduced during the last two centuries. As Arjun Chowdhury (2018) has shown, strong and well consolidated states of the kind exemplified by Western European historical experience constitute an exception in the international system. The majority of states have always been weak, beset by inner discord and often unable to cater to the most basic needs of their populations. Although European states were formed and consolidated through costly wars against alternative political forms, that path to statehood has not been accessible to the latecomers in the international system, since '*state formation itself* throws up the possibility of alternatives to the centralized state and reduces the need to emulate that institutional form, which counters the expectation that units in world politics should emulate the strongest units in order to survive' (Chowdhury, 2018: 23). Unable to monopolize violence and to deliver the basic goods that their citizens expect, and in the absence of any viable alternatives to statehood, the majority of states outside the West are condemned to a condition of lasting weakness and dysfunction as long as the structure of the modern international system remains the same. To the extent that the turn to history has also brought a macro reorientation in its wake, many phenomena previously thought to originate within individual states – such as state weakness and failure – now appear to have systemic causes with century-long trajectories of their own.

This focus on the disruptive and constitutive effects of war has arguably detracted attention from other forms of organized violence that were important in the shaping of the international system and its global expansion. European expansion and the subsequent global spread of the international system were not brought about by major wars against non-Europeans, but by other violent practices of what at least initially looks like less magnitude and intensity. Scholars of historical international relations have only recently started to inquire into how great powers have dealt with pirates and other non-state actors that have been seen as threats to international order, and how these practices have been important in reproducing the international system and maintain the distribution of power within it (Löwenheim, 2007). Others have vividly described how the creation of colonial armies and indigenous forces not only made imperialism possible, but also warfare more generally in a context characterized by multiple connections between core and periphery and the West and the rest (Barkawi, 2017). Still others have argued that however destructive processes of colonial expansion were to those unlucky to be on the receiving end, these processes nevertheless created spaces necessary for the formation of new polities and thus also for those transformations that were integral to the formation of a genuinely global international system (Mulich, 2018).

Yet the focus on the constitutive function of war in the making of international orders easily issues in a misfortune cookie, the taste of which is bitter. Although few of the authors discussed in this chapter claim to say anything about the future trajectories of the modern international order, some of their narratives are motivated by a concern that the current international order is under challenge by a variety of forces, with potentially disruptive consequences for the international system as a whole. The desire to make sense of the genesis of the international system springs partly out of a conviction that its demise is imminent. Such worries do seem proportionate to the explanatory power attributed to war and other forms of violence. If the current international order is believed to have been constituted by wars and violent practices of the past, the more likely it seems that any future changes will come only as a consequence of cataclysmic violence.

Conclusion

War remains a central concern of Historical International Relations. Less focused on its causes and more interested in its effects, historically oriented scholars have tended to regard war as both disruptive and constitutive of international orders across a series of geographical and historical contexts: major war is frequently invoked as the primary cause of transitions between international orders. Such wars are believed to affect not only the distribution of power between polities but are also believed to condition the identities and interests of these polities, as well as the fundamental institutions and norms of the international system as a whole. By investing war with so much explanatory power, the historical study of international relations has been able to provisionally resolve the perennial tension between structure and history that runs through most of the social sciences, and which has found expression in prior attempts to supplement the traditional concerns of international theory with a diachronic account of how the structures and actors of world politics once emerged and under what conditions they are likely to change. The turn to war has offered a way of overcoming the tension between these explanatory priorities and distinctive approaches to the subject matter of international relations, telling us how we got from one international order into another without any apparent loss of theoretical coherence or unnecessary sacrifice of historical detail. Yet this has come with the cost of naturalizing war itself to the point of investing it with a productive force of its own.

Still the turn to history has yielded an incomplete understanding of the role of war in world politics and has left students of historical international relations with at least three challenges. First, while focusing on its transformative effects on international orders, scholars have been less interested in the causes of war and more so in its consequences for the structure, institutions and norms of the international system. Most likely this is less a consequence of the turn to history as such, but more a consequence of their reorientation *away* from realism, coupled with a selective uptake of relevant historical scholarship. Ironically so, since before realism emerged in its structural and nomothetic incarnation in the late 1970s, many of its core assumptions had animated historical scholarship all the way from Ranke to modern diplomatic history. Although this latter field has undergone some serious intellectual convulsions during the past decades, some of these seem to have aligned it more closely with the concerns that once prompted scholars of international relations to integrate cultural factors into their explanations of international phenomena

(Reynolds, 2006; Schweizer and Schumann, 2008). A serious re-engagement with contemporary diplomatic and international history could provide students of international relations with an opportunity to study war from within a historical framework that takes the distribution of both internal state capacity and the distribution of capabilities into consideration (see also Leira, 2021).

A second challenge to the understanding of war within historical international relations comes from the historiographical turn mentioned earlier. Although the resulting historiography has been preoccupied with international thought about almost everything else but international war, scholarship within this field indicates the extent to which war among European states as well as their expansion on other continents was accompanied, and in some instances propelled by, changing justifications of war and warfare within European legal thought from the early modern period onwards (Koskenniemi, 2001; Anghie, 2007; Armitage, 2012; Pagden, 2015; Pitts, 2018). Yet there is still a curious disconnect between the historical study of international thought and the study of historical international relations proper that at least in part stems from tensions between their different epistemological starting points, tensions that are waiting to be overcome for the benefit of both (Bartelson, 2014, Rosenboim and Hartnett, 2021).

The third and final challenge comes from the current attempts to question the extent to which concepts of social theory actually can help us make non-Eurocentric sense of political orders as if they were meaningfully experienced by other people in other times and in other places outside Europe. Although many of those who took the turn to history have struggled hard to overcome the most blatant forms of anachronism and Eurocentrism, much contemporary theorizing still remains indebted to modern social theory in the shape it evolved in the early twentieth–century Europe. This has made some scholarship within Historical International Relations vulnerable to the kind of criticism that maintains that the categories and concepts of modern historical sociology and international relations embody profound and unacknowledged forms of methodological Eurocentrism that need to be overcome through a more sustained focus on international and global interconnectedness (Bhambra, 2010; Bartelson, 2015; Go and Lawson, 2017).

Suggestion for further reading

Bartelson, J. (2017). *War in International Thought*. Cambridge: Cambridge University Press.

Joas, H., and Knöbl, W. (2013). *War in Social Thought: Hobbes to the Present*. Princeton, NJ: Princeton University Press.

Kaspersen, L. B., and Strandsbjerg, J., eds. (2017). *Does War Make States? Investigations of Charles Tilly's Historical Sociology*. Cambridge: Cambridge University Press.

Nabulsi, K. (2005). *Traditions of War: Occupation, Resistance and the Law*. Oxford: Oxford University Press.

Sharman, J. C. (2019). *Empires of the Weak: The Real Story of European Expansion and the Creation of the New World Order*. Princeton, NJ: Princeton University Press.

Note

1 I would like to thank Niklas Bremberg, Benjamin de Carvalho, Adrian Hyde-Price, Stephanie Hoffman, Halvard Leira, Chiara Ruffa and Amy Verdun for valuable comments on earlier drafts of this chapter.

References

Anghie, A. (2007). *Imperialism, Sovereignty and the Making of International Law*. Cambridge: Cambridge University Press.

Armitage, D. (2012). *Foundations of Modern International Thought*. Cambridge, Cambridge University Press.

Ashworth, L. M. (2021). Disciplinary Traditions and Debates: The Subject Matters of International Thought. In de Carvalho, B., Costa Lopez, J., & Leira, H., eds. *Routledge Handbook of Historical International Relations*. Abingdon: Routledge.

Barkawi, T. (2017). States, Armies, and Wars in Global Context. In J. Go, and G. Lawson, G., eds., *Global Historical Sociology*, Cambridge: Cambridge University Press, 58–75.

Bartelson, J. (2014). International theory meets intellectual history. *Contemporary Political Theory*, 13 (4), 392–397.

Bartelson, J. (2015). Towards a genealogy of 'society' in international relations. *Review of International Studies*, 41 (4), 675–692.

Beaulac, S. (2004). *The Power of Language in the Making of International Law: The Word Sovereignty in Bodin and Vattel and the Myth of Westphalia*. Leiden: Martinus Nijhoff Publishers.

Bell, D. S. (2001). International relations: the dawn of a historiographical turn? *The British Journal of Politics and International Relations*, 3 (1), 115–126.

Bhambra, G. K. (2010). Historical sociology, international relations and connected histories. *Cambridge Review of International Affairs*, 23 (1), 127–143.

Bowden, B. (2021). Eurocentrism and Civilization. In de Carvalho, B., Costa Lopez, J., & Leira, H., eds. *Routledge Handbook of Historical International Relations*. Abingdon: Routledge.

Bruneau, Q. P. (2021). Constructivism: History and Systemic Change. In de Carvalho, B., Costa Lopez, J., & Leira, H., eds. *Routledge Handbook of Historical International Relations*. Abingdon: Routledge.

Buzan, B., and Lawson, G. (2015). *The Global Transformation: History, Modernity and the Making of International Relations*. Cambridge: Cambridge University Press.

Chowdhury, A. (2018). *The Myth of International Order: Why Weak States Persist and Alternatives to the State Fade Away*. Oxford: Oxford University Press.

Croxton, D. (1999). The peace of Westphalia of 1648 and the origins of sovereignty. *The International History Review*, 21 (3), 569–591.

de Carvalho, B., Costa Lopez, J., and Leira, H. (2021). Introduction: Historical International Relations. In de Carvalho, B., Costa Lopez, J., & Leira, H., eds. *Routledge Handbook of Historical International Relations*. Abingdon: Routledge.

Gilpin, R. (1981). *War and Change in World Politics*. Cambridge: Cambridge University Press.

Go, J. and, Lawson, G. (2017). *Global Historical Sociology*. Cambridge: Cambridge University Press.

Go, J., Lawson, G., and de Carvalho, B. (2021). Historical Sociology in International Relations: The Challenge of the Global. In de Carvalho, B., Costa Lopez, J., & Leira, H., eds. *Routledge Handbook of Historical International Relations*. Abingdon: Routledge.

Hobden, S. (1999). Theorising the international system: perspectives from historical sociology. *Review of International Studies*, 25 (2), 257–271.

Hobson, J. M. (1998). The historical sociology of the state and the state of historical sociology in international relations. *Review of International Political Economy*, 5 (2), 284–320.

Hobson, J. M. (2002). What's at Stake in 'Bringing Historical Sociology Back into International Relations? Transcending 'Chronofetishism' and 'Tempocentrism' in International Relations. In: S. Hobden, and J. M. Hobson, eds., *Historical Sociology of International Relations*, Cambridge: Cambridge University Press, 3–41.

Hobson, J. M. (2007). Reconstructing international relations through world history: Oriental globalization and the global–dialogic conception of inter-civilizational relations. *International Politics*, 44 (4), 414–430.

Hobson, J. M. (2012). *The Eurocentric Conception of World Politics: Western International Theory, 1760–2010*. Cambridge: Cambridge University Press.

Hobson, J. M. and Lawson, G. (2008). What is history in international relations?. *Millennium*, 37 (2), 415–435.

Hui, V. T. B. (2005). *War and State Formation in Ancient China and Early Modern Europe*. Cambridge: Cambridge University Press.

Keene, E. (2002). *Beyond the Anarchical Society: Grotius, Colonialism and Order in World Politics*. Cambridge: Cambridge University Press.

Koskenniemi, M. (2001). *The Gentle Civilizer of Nations: The Rise and Fall of International Law 1870–1960*. Cambridge: Cambridge University Press.

Lawson, G. (2006). The promise of historical sociology in international relations. *International Studies Review*, 8 (3), 397–423.

Lawson, G. (2012). The eternal divide? History and international relations. *European Journal of International Relations*, 18 (2), 203–226.

Leira. H. (2021). Diplomacy: The World of States and Beyond. In de Carvalho, B., Costa Lopez, J., & Leira, H., eds. *Routledge Handbook of Historical International Relations*. Abingdon: Routledge.

Leira, H., and de Carvalho, B. (2016). Construction time again: history in constructivist IR scholarship. *ERIS – European Review of International Studies*, 3 (3), 99–111.

Löwenheim, O. (2007). Predators and Parasites. In *Persistent Agents of Transnational Harm and Great Power Authority*. Ann Arbor, MI: University of Michigan Press.

Lundborg, T. (2016). The limits of historical sociology: temporal borders and the reproduction of the 'modern' political present. *European Journal of International Relations*, 22 (1), 99–121.

Mulich, J. (2018). Transformation at the margins: imperial expansion and systemic change in world politics. *Review of International Studies*, 44 (4), 694–716.

Nexon, D. H. (2009). *The Struggle for Power in Early Modern Europe: Religious Conflict, Dynastic Empires, and International Change*. Princeton, NJ: Princeton University Press.

Osiander, A. (2001). Sovereignty, international relations, and the Westphalian myth. *International Organization*, 55 (2), 251–287.

Pagden, A. (2015). *The Burdens of Empire: 1539 to the Present*. Cambridge: Cambridge University Press.

Phillips, A. (2010). *War, Religion and Empire: The Transformation of International Orders*. Cambridge: Cambridge University Press.

Phillips, A., and Sharman, J. C. (2015). *International Order in Diversity: War, Trade and Rule in the Indian Ocean*. Cambridge: Cambridge University Press.

Philpott, D. (2001). Revolutions in Sovereignty. In *How Ideas Shaped Modern International Relations*. Princeton, NJ: Princeton University Press.

Pitts, J. P. (2018). *Boundaries of the International: Law and Empire*. Cambridge, MA: Harvard University Press.

Reynolds, D. (2006). International history, the cultural turn and the diplomatic twitch. *Cultural and Social History*, 3 (1), 75–91.

Rosenberg, J. (1994). The international imagination: IR theory and 'classic social analysis'. *Millennium*, 23(1), 85–108.

Rosenberg, J. (2006). Why is there no international historical sociology? *European Journal of International Relations*, 12 (3), 307–340.

Rosenboim, O., and Hartnett, L. (2021). International Political Thought and Historical International Relations. In de Carvalho, B., Costa Lopez, J., & Leira, H., eds. *Routledge Handbook of Historical International Relations*. Abingdon: Routledge.

Ruggie, J. G. (1993). Territoriality and beyond: problematizing modernity in international relations. *International Organization*, 47 (1), 139–174.

Schweizer, K. W., and Schumann, M. J. (2008). The revitalization of diplomatic history: renewed reflections. *Diplomacy and Statecraft*, 19 (2), 149–186.

Sharman, J. C. (2018). Myths of military revolution: European expansion and eurocentrism. *European Journal of International Relations*, 24 (3), 491–513.

Spruyt, H. (1994). *The Sovereign State and its Competitors: An Analysis of Systems Change*. Princeton, NJ: Princeton University Press.

Spruyt, H. (1998). Historical sociology and systems theory in international relations. *Review of International Political Economy*, 5 (2), 340–353.

Teschke, B. (2003). *The Myth of 1648: Class, Geopolitics, and the Making of Modern International Relations*. London: Verso.

Vaughan-Williams, N. (2005). International relations and the problem of history. *Millennium*, 34 (1), 115–136.

Waltz, K. N. (1959). *Man, the State, and War: A Theoretical Analysis*. New York, NY: Columbia University Press.

Zarakol, A. (2010). *After Defeat: How the East Learned to Live with the West*. Cambridge: Cambridge University Press.

13

CAPITALISM AND 'THE INTERNATIONAL'

A historical approach

Alexander Anievas and Cristian Gogu

Introduction

While the recent 'historical turn' in disciplinary International Relations (IR) is a much-welcomed development, it must be noted that the turn to history is much more of a *return* to the discipline's recently forgotten past. For, prior to the post-1945 period, the study of the international dynamics and spread of the world capitalist order was a hallmark of many IR works. Not only can we find large tracts of research on capitalist imperialism and colonialism not *formally* associated with the discipline's official 'cannon' that are nonetheless in many ways impeccably 'IR' works for their time (Hobson, 1902; du Bois, 1915; Bukharin, 1973; Luxemburg, 2003). But it must also be remembered that IR was primarily founded as a policy science designed to solve the 'technical' problems resulting from capitalism's international expansion; in particular, the dilemmas posed by the empire-building and colonial administration activities of the white Western capitalist powers as they forcibly expanded into and occupied various nations of the Global South (Anievas, Manchanda, and Shilliam, 2015: 2; see also Ashworth, 2021; Bayly, 2021; both in this volume).

Recent 'revisionist' historiographies have correctly highlighted the racial – and often racist – foundations of IR's birth (cf. Yao and Delatolla, 2021 in this volume). Yet questions concerning the geopolitical forms and dynamics of *capitalism* were also crucial (e.g. Reinsch, 1908; Moon, 1927). For policymakers and scholars of the time, along with the discipline they helped shape, the problems of war and interstate conflict were perceived as intimately linked to the intersecting processes of social and 'racial' disorder, anti-colonial revolts, socialist-inspired revolutions, and ruinous economic competition on the world market. As such, within the Anglo-Saxon world at least, the emergence of IR as a distinct intellectual enterprise was fundamentally oriented around historical investigations into these interwoven questions of capitalist empire, imperialism, and inter-race relations (cf. Long and Schmidt, 2005; Hobson, 2012; Vitalis, 2015; Anievas, Manchanda, and Shilliam, 2015).

Consequently, much recent Historical IR finds not-so-distant echoes in these internationally attuned historical and sociological works of the past. What is more, it has been the more overtly sociological approaches within contemporary Historical IR – what some have dubbed 'international historical sociology' (Hobson, Lawson, and Rosenberg, 2010) – that have primarily dealt with the problem(atic) of capitalism: a subject that has also seen a recent efflorescence in the academy particularly in the wake of the global economic crisis of 2007–2008. From the 'new history of capitalism' literature (e.g. Beckert, 2014) and other relatedly 'global' accounts (Yazdani and Menon, 2020) to more explicitly IR works attempting to rethink capitalism's 'multicultural' or 'geopolitical' origins (e.g. Anievas and Nişancioğlu, 2015; Hobson, 2020), the study of capitalism as a distinct historical and social thematic has returned with a vengeance.

More generally, questions regarding the precise relationship between capitalism and 'the international' have been at the forefront of a number of recent IR debates. Such discussions include neo-Gramscian analyses of capitalist modernity as a geopolitically conditioned 'passive revolution' and related treatments of understanding the rise of capitalism in the context of 'uneven and combined development', postcolonial-inspired studies of the 'Eastern' origins of the modern world, and feminist and queer IR work de-naturalizing modernity's multiple intersecting structures of power, oppression, and hierarchy (see, inter alia, Bhambra, 2007; Morton, 2007; Matin, 2013; Anievas and Nişancioğlu, 2015; Buzan and Lawson, 2015; Owens, 2015; Weber, 2016; Hesketh, 2017; Roberts, 2017).

In what follows, we provide a brief overview of some of this literature, particularly as it relates to the 'international' formation and development of capitalism in history. As such, we necessarily limit ourselves to presenting a highly stylized and partial account of a very large, rich, and still growing body of literature. In conclusion, we then outline some avenues for future research that reconnect the above-noted themes of history-writing, and 'the international' to capitalist modernity's distinctive 'regime of historicity'. But first, we must ask: what is capitalism and where did it come from?

The concept of capitalism

These two questions regarding definition and origin are, in fact, related. For to say what *is* capitalism is to also delimit our object of inquiry into its formation. In other words, a given definition of capitalism always in part determines what historical factors, relations, and processes one should look for in explaining and understanding its genesis. If, for example, capitalism is associated with market-based exchange and interdependence *à la* Adam Smith, one could reasonably point to the presence of such capitalist indicators from as early as the Classic Period (200–900 CE) in the Mesoamerican and Mayan regions (Pezzarossi, 2015: 346). Social systems defined by widespread private ownership of property and vibrant market economies, other commonly associated features of capitalism, can also be traced to such pre-modern formations as the late Roman Republic and Sung Dynasty (Runciman, 1983; Hobson, 2004).

Similarly, the existence of capital-wage labour relations and 'market-dependent' economic agents – yet two more classical markers of capitalism identified by some Marxist-influenced scholars – can be found in numerous regions of the world typically considered 'pre-modern' or 'pre-capitalist'. For instance, the 16th-century diamond mines in Kollur, India employed up to 60,000 workers, while the metallurgical and mining enterprises in Kiangsu of the Sung era (960–1279) could employ 3000 wage labourers (see Anievas and Nişancioğlu, 2015: 216). The market dependency of economic agents (including wage labourers) was also a structurally pronounced feature of numerous societies in Medieval Europe (Persson, 2014).

The point is to say there are as many different ways to approaching the question of defining capitalism as there are potential problems of locating its *historical* origins. For some scholars, this is simply not an issue since it is taken as matter of fact that capitalism – in some form or another – has more or less existed throughout human history. This is particularly the case if capitalism is defined as coextensive with markets as sustained and complex market activities and exchange relations have been detected as far back as civilizations have existed. Given the presence of 'widespread mercantile activity' and even 'manufacturing' throughout much of history, Jack Goody, therefore, asks (2006: 212): 'Can we not therefore dispense with this pejorative term [capitalism] drawn from nineteenth-century Britain and recognize the element of continuity in the market and in bourgeois activities from the Bronze Age until modern times?'. If capitalism is seen as an essential characteristic of nearly *all* societies, then the problem of explaining its origins vanishes. But so too does any conception of capitalism's *historical specificity* and the possibility of its *overcoming*.

Despite much debate, there is no agreed-upon consensus to defining capitalism. Fortunately for us, we need not 'solve' this perennial dilemma here. Instead, we simply highlight that a particular problem common to all the aforementioned approaches to defining capitalism is the tendency to be both too abstract and insufficiently historicist. For historically attuned IR scholars who have sought to escape the neorealist trap of a supra-historical anarchy, the prospect of a transhistorical conception of capitalism might appear equally unappealing.

Such approaches also demonstrate a remarkable similarity in their theoretical disregard for social relations that are not immediately reducible to 'the market' or capital relation alone. As we shall see, the contributions of feminist materialism, queer theory, and postcolonialism have all shown how such acts of discarding not only erase histories and ongoing practices of violence and oppression that sit beyond the immediate operation of capital, but also mischaracterize the nature of capitalism itself. We would therefore argue that any properly historicist understanding of capitalism – past and present – would in some way incorporate such 'externalities' into its conceptual bounds since, in many instances, it is precisely those relations that sit 'outside' of capital which fundamentally shape, determine, change, and destabilize its development (Anievas and Nişancioğlu, 2018: 191–192).

The origins of capitalism

For those scholars seeking to uncover the historical origins of capitalism, contemporary explanations have largely fallen under three distinct – albeit sometimes overlapping – schools of thought. Drawing on the classical political economy tradition represented, above all, by Adam Smith's *The Wealth of Nations* (1776), liberal or 'neo-Smithian' scholars focus on how the spread of trade and market relations tended to congeal into modern capitalist societies. This dynamic is rooted in Smith's macro-sociological theory of development based upon the abstract notion of a utility-maximizing 'homo economicus' (see also Jahn, 2021 in this volume).

For Smith, it was the existence of a 'quasi-universal' systemic drive that impelled economic agents to cut costs through specialization, continuously accumulate capital, and rationalize the production process. This created ever-greater efficiency gains. Consequently, modern economic growth was the aggregate result of a multiplicity of individual economic agents acting in their own interests which in turn functioned as an abstract mechanism generalizing capitalist laws of motion across the economy as a whole. The ensuing emergence of a 'commercial society' or *capitalism* was, then, not a result of the conscious act(s) of any individual or group of individuals. Rather, it arose through the 'natural' pressures of market competition. As Robert Brenner puts it (2007: 57), 'The particular choices individuals are inclined to make and that are selected out by the system turn out, or just happen, to bring about, in the aggregate, sustained economic growth. This coincidence is of course what Smith is capturing with his notion of the invisible hand'.

For many IR approaches following Smith, capitalism is generally conceived of as a positive societal outcome that arises from the 'free' competition of self-regarding rational actors. The spread of 'free trade' and market relations is, moreover, often directly equated with the promotion of a more cooperative and peaceful international order. As a result, economic 'globalization' can be seen as transforming world politics into a series of positive-sum games whereby states can realize absolute gains. The development of market relations is in turn identified as advancing more liberal-democratic civic cultures, identities, and norms. Political relations thereby functionally follow economic integration (cf. Keohane and Nye, 1977; Ruggie, 1998; Deudney and Ikenberry, 1999; Gartzke, 2007).

Such pristinely liberal narratives are not only accepted by 'traditional' IR theories, but also evident in many self-identified 'critical' and constructivist approaches. Alexander Wendt's (1999) account of the emergence of a Western-based 'Kantian' culture of anarchy essentially repackages, in constructivist form, long-familiar liberal themes of the putatively pacifying effects of liberal-democratic identity relations (see also Linklater, 1990). For capitalism is conceived by Wendt (1999: 361–362) as a solely domestic attribute of states, fostering trust, and peaceful relations between them.

Yet it is important to recall that Smith's 'natural system of liberties' reflected a wider set of social institutions, wherein 'the economy' depended on public guarantees for private property rights, civil law for enforcing contracts, legislation for competitive markets, and public education for developing moral sentiments. Smith was indeed well aware of the need for some state intervention to underwrite certain social and moral codes of behaviour to maintain the public good (Smith, 1812). Moreover, it should be remembered that *The Wealth of Nations* was not a simple exercise in 'value-free' analysis. It was also an explicitly political intervention: a kind of 'capitalist manifesto' addressed to Smith's fellow compatriots in half-feudal Scotland. Yet Smith's work left an unresolved tension between a *transhistorical* conception of the market and a more *historically attentive* notion of capitalist social structure – a tension that was only compounded by many of Smith's later followers (Teschke and Wenten, 2016: 5–6).

The question regarding the historical origins of this social structure drove Smith's great antagonist, Karl Marx, to directly confront the implied circularity of the capital-wage labour relation. For if each side of this relation presupposed the other, the simple accumulation of one pole was insufficient as an explanation for the emergence of the other (Marx, 1976: 873). The hoarding of capital, for example, could not in and of itself produce the social conditions for the purchase of wage labour. The possibility of using capital to purchase labour-power was instead premised on the existence of a class with nothing other than their labour-power to sell: that is, the commodification of labour-power itself. What this implied, however, was a history beyond simply hoarding wealth.

Marx thus proposed that the emergence of this historically distinctive capital-wage labour relation grew out of the process of 'so-called primitive accumulation'. This process entailed not only the separation of the direct producers from their means of production (that is expropriation). It also involved the (often forcible) coming together or encounter of the possessors of capital and those who had nothing but their labour-power to sell (Anievas and Nişancioğlu, 2015: 216–218). Workers were now compelled to exchange their labour-power for a wage lower than the value their labour added to the final product. The surplus appropriated by the owner of the final product was therefore rooted in an unequal exchange of supposedly equal values: that is to say, the relation constituted a particular form of exploitation. Hence, in contrast to liberal perspectives, explanations drawing on Marx's writings typically focus on the antagonistic and hierarchical social relations that underpin capitalism. They tend to emphasize the intrinsically exploitative nature of the capital-wage labour relationship, while regarding the ensuing inter-capitalist competition as a potential source of geopolitical conflict and war (Harvey, 2003; Callinicos, 2009).

A final approach to the origins of capitalism was offered by the great German sociologist, Max Weber (2001), who sought to explain the European 'miracle' of capitalist economic growth by examining the multiple intersecting processes of macro-sociological transformation occurring over the *longue durée*. For Weber, the first 'rational' (modern) capitalist states were the result of a series of interrelated societal changes occurring throughout the European continent. Perhaps most importantly, Weber pointed to how Martin Luther challenged the supremacy of Catholicism, spawning a new Protestant consciousness that emphasized an ethic of hard work, saving, and frugality that facilitated an expanded process of wealth acquisition in Northwestern Europe. In the political sphere, kingdoms and empires transferred their power to nation-states as new nationally conscribed militaries replaced the private armies of kings and lords, while large-scale economic activities became an appendage of sovereign companies. While Weber's 'protestant ethic' thesis is today widely refuted on empirical grounds, his emphasis on multicausality and the role of geopolitical competition in explaining the origins of capitalist modernity remains influential (see, inter alia, Skocpol, 1979; Mann, 1986; Tilly, 1992; Hobson, 2004; Bhambra, 2007; Buzan and Lawson, 2015).

Weber's emphasis on geopolitical competition as a driver of capitalist transformation drew inspiration from earlier works of mercantilist political economy. For, long before Smith and Marx, the first scholar to use the concept of political economy was a French soldier, dramatist, and economist, Antoyne de Montchrétien (c.1575–1621), whose *Traicté de l'œconomie politique* (1970) aimed to describe 'the science of wealth acquisition common to the State as well as the Family' (Hoogvelt, 2001: 1). Montchrétien advocated against Aristotle's separation of economics from politics and developed an economic policy for the state in the spirit of mercantilism. The treatise was written as a combination of science and oratory to persuade King Louis XIII and his mother Queen Marie de Medici to modernize France's system of administration according to the needs of manufacturing, commerce and navigation. The proposed policies advocated for trade expansion, defended the right of merchants to large profits, and demanded a limitation on the activity of foreign merchants moving wealth out of France (Montchrétien, 1970: XXIII; 7–8fn.1).

The mercantilist 'zero-sum game' of economic and geopolitical competition thereby dovetails with the neo-Weberian idea that interstate competition was, in early modern Europe, the fundamental factor driving processes of rational state-building activities that gave birth to the modern system of sovereign states. As Michael Mann puts it (1986: 454), '[t]he growth of the modern state, as measured by finances, is explained primarily not in domestic terms but in terms of geopolitical relations of violence'. In some accounts, these systemic pressures of contending European states are also conceived as a key determinant in the rise of capitalism itself (see Mann, 1986; Tilly, 1992). Interstate competition is conceived as driving technological and organizational innovations that spurred on the development of capitalist social relations. In turn, this afforded some European states a comparative advantage in the means of violence thus laying the foundations for their subsequent rise to global dominance.

The resolute focus on Europe as the endogenous birthplace of capitalism and the modern world also finds its direct lineages in the works of Smith, Marx, and Weber. For although all acknowledged the role of non-Western societies as conduits of capital accumulation, market expansion, and resource extraction via colonialism, the primary focus of their analyses was Europe (cf. Anievas and Nişancioğlu, 2015: 146–148). Moreover, with the partial exception of Marx,[1] the classical political economy and sociology traditions were generally hamstrung by a form of methodological internalism that elevated the European experience of capitalist modernity into a *universal* stage of development through which all societies must pass, albeit at different times and velocities. Although empirically ever-present, the *international* dimensions of social change and transformation were thus relegated to the realm of contingent 'externalities'. The false sense of universality generated by such *Eurocentric* modes of enquiry has been the bane of political economy and social theory since their inception (cf. Anievas and Nişancioğlu, 2015; see also Herborth and Nitzschner, 2021; Bowden, 2021; both in this volume).

The geopolitics of capitalism

The legacy of these three different perspectives on the political economy of capitalism has had a lasting (albeit highly uneven) influence on the contemporary field of IR/International Political Economy (IPE). Realists looked back to the mercantilist vision of economics as a zero-sum proposition, wherein one state's economic gain was another state's loss and the role of wealth accumulation was largely conceived in brute power-political terms. Liberal IR reached for Smith's understanding of the intrinsically wealth-expanding properties of the modern world market where 'absolute gains' could be reaped from increasing trade and other economic transactions.

Yet, after 1945, examinations of the relationship between *historical* capitalism and 'the international' were largely side-lined in the Anglo-Saxon IR academy, just as ahistorical neoclassical economics was becoming hegemonic within disciplinary Economics and beyond. The value of capitalism as an explanatory concept quietly faded from these disciplinary discourses. Following the national independence movements and breakdown of the Bretton Woods System, scholars working in the dominant traditions of IPE tried to explain the seeming paradox between a *multiple* state-system and an ever-global *transnational* economy. As structural realists explained the contemporary epoch of world order-building through the lens of hegemonic stability theory, neo-liberals took up such concepts as 'complex interdependency' (Keohane and Nye, 1977; Gilpin, 1981). Yet both these hegemonic perspectives lost any conception of the historical specificity of capitalist social relations.

By contrast, IR scholars working outside the discipline's dominant approaches sought to 'historicize' the modern international system by investigating the changing historical relations between capitalism, sovereignty, and the multistate system (see esp. van der Pijl, 1984; Cox, 1987; Ashley, 1987; Halliday, 1987; Linklater, 1990; Ruggie, 1993; Rosenberg, 1994). Given the Marxist tradition's emphasis on the importance of capitalism to understanding modern IR, it is worth examining their contributions in some detail.

Two 21st-century Marxist IR studies by Benno Teschke (2003) and Hannes Lacher (2006) deploy Robert Brenner's groundbreaking work on the development of agrarian capitalism to investigate the making of the modern international system. Starting from the idea that capitalism first emerged exclusively in 17th-century England, Teschke and Lacher problematize conventional interpretations of the co-evolution of the international system and capitalism shared by many Marxists and IR theorists alike. The 1648 Treaty of Westphalia ending the Thirty Years' War, commonly described in mainstream IR as inaugurating the modern international system, is thereby declared a foundational 'myth' of IR (Teschke, 2003).

A central corollary of this re-periodization of the origins of capitalism and the international states-system is that the latter preceded the former. This is because the European states-system already in place was fundamentally *pre*-modern as absolutism represented 'a *sui generis* social formation, displaying a specific mode of government and determinate pre–modern and pre–capitalist domestic and international "laws of motion"' (Teschke, 2003: 191; Lacher, 2006: 78). Absolutism is thus conceived as a distinct 'mode of exploitation' that was *inimical* to the development of capitalist property relations. Unlike capitalism, the direct producers under absolutist property relations were subject to extra-economic coercion but, unlike feudalism, the coercive authorities were centralized.

As such, the international system remained pre-modern through the 18th century because it was based on a form of absolutist sovereignty: an iteration of dynastic sovereignty more centralized than the 'parcelized' sovereignty of feudalism, but still personalized in contrast to the 'abstract' state under capitalism. Hence, rather than the 1648 Westphalian peace marking the birth of the modern states-system, Teschke and Lacher argue that the international system only *started* to become modern under the geopolitical-economic pressures exerted by capitalist Britain on its continental European rivals. From this historical analysis, Teschke and Lacher claim that the 'interstateness of capitalism' cannot be derived from the nature of the capital relation itself. Instead, it must be 'regarded as a "historical legacy" of pre-capitalist development' (Lacher, 2006: 52, 60; Teschke, 2003: 145–146). For Lacher and Teschke, then, there is neither any structural connection between capitalism and a multistate system nor anything inherent to the nature of capitalism which would necessarily perpetuate it: the relationship is conceived as entirely contingent.

Such claims regarding the non-correspondence of capitalism and a multistate system lead them to a degree of ambiguity regarding the persistence of geopolitical rivalries and war under capitalism. For example, Teschke and Lacher (2007) point to the obsolescence of 'inter-imperial rivalry' within the advanced capitalist heartland. Since capitalism does not require *territorial* expansion, Teschke argues that 'we should expect it to bring about the decline of external geo-political accumulation that defined the war-driven international conduct of the feudal and abso-lutist ages', while the post-1945 architecture of international organizations could act as 'arena of peaceful inter-capitalist conflict resolution' (Teschke, 2003: 256, 267).

The idea that the post-WWII period of capitalist development has moved beyond significant geopolitical conflicts among the 'advanced' industrial powers has been forcefully challenged by a number of scholars often grouped under the label of 'theorists of the new imperialism' (see Gowan, 1999; Callinicos, 2009; Harvey, 2003). Taking off after the US-led invasions of Afghanistan and Iraq in 2001–2003, this diverse group of scholars sought to explain the persistence of geopol-itical conflict and war as intrinsic properties of capitalism. Drawing on the classical Marxist the-ories of imperialism but loosening their alleged economic determinism, these approaches sought to define contemporary capitalist imperialism as the dialectical intersection of two distinct, but mutually irreducible, 'territorial' and 'capitalist' logics of power (Harvey, 2003; Callinicos, 2009). The basic historical argument of the new imperialism theorists was that contemporary global capitalism had yet to exit the crisis of profitability ushered in by the economic crises of the late 1960s and early 1970s, and that this had resulted in the fracturing of the capitalist heartland into competing economic blocs, which would likely give rise to geopolitical struggles among them (Callinicos, 2009).

But if the world so far has avoided any repeat of the 'Thirty Years' Crisis' of the two world wars (Anievas, 2014), most states did not escape the financialization pushed by neoliberal policies that partly transformed the nature of geopolitics into a conflict between debtors and creditors. As Silvia Federici (2014: 232) has observed, 'it was through the "debt crisis", triggered in 1979 by the Federal Reserve's rise of interest rates on the dollar, that the World Bank and the International Monetary Fund (IMF), as representatives of international capital, "structurally adjusted" and de facto recolonized much of the former colonial world, plunging entire regions into a debt that over the years has continued to grow rather than becoming extinguished'. Moreover, the privat-ization of public services (housing, healthcare, education, transportation) across developed econ-omies has been accompanied by the rise of private debt for the use of those services.

The resulting inequality and the series of financial crises of the last 40 years reignited an interest in debt/credit relations (Graeber, 2011, Piketty, 2014) and how debt – both between sovereigns and between private actors – has historically been a central feature of the (re)pro-duction of capitalism (Di Muzio and Robbins, 2016, Federici, 2014). As privatization of the 'commons' advances by violence and legal sanction, debt is 'mobilized in a more systematic and intensified manner by those in the control of credit in order to shape and reshape the terrain of social reproduction for the sake of the symbolic accumulation of power represented in money' (Di Muzio and Robbins, 2016: 11). In a genealogy of capitalist debt, Di Muzio and Robbins (2016) record several historical episodes (creation of national debts in England, the United States, and British colonies and the subsequent resistance movements) in which debt was not only used to accumulate new wealth, but also to condition the lower classes to sell their assets, to take more debt, or to accept subsistence wages for their labour.

The role of (national and individual) debt in what Marxists have termed the process of 'primitive accumulation' is a subject in need of further exploration in Historical IR; particularly as the war-making activities of states have often had detrimental yet socially 'generative' fiscal consequences for their subject populations. In late 16th– and 17th-century France, for example, the war-induced fiscal pressures that the Absolutist monarchy brought to bear on the peasantry, alongside the more general economic consequences of war, hastened the dynamic of land dispossession taking place in the countryside. Rising taxes and rents drove peasant families ever deeper into poverty and debt, forcing many to sell their properties. 'Middling' and poorer peasants were consequently uprooted from the land, resulting in widespread proletarianization, the revaluation of land as capital, and the development of distinctly capitalist social relations (Heller, 2000). In these ways, war, state taxation, and debt did to the French rural economy what the enclosures had done to contemporary England: yet another instance of the uneven and variegated historical ways by which the development of capitalism has been mediated by and rooted within fundamentally 'international' processes.

Other influential Marxist-inspired approaches focused on examining the relationship between capitalism and 'the international' have also noted the constitutive force that the global economy bears on national social forces and interstate relations. Through a rigorous historicist reading of Gramsci, Adam David Morton (2007) shows how 'modern' state structures and social identities have been continually shaped by the reciprocal interaction between national 'nodes' and the globalizing tendency of capitalism. Specifically, the concepts of passive revolution and hegemony help explain the uneven development of the states-system and its impact on individual states' transitions to capitalism, as demonstrated by Italy's modern nation-state-building process and Mexico's transition to neoliberalism. Morton thereby enunciates a 'theory of survival and reorganisation of state identity through which social relations are reproduced in new forms consonant with capitalist property relations'. In so doing, he demonstrates how both the Italian and wider European state formation processes were 'shaped by the causal conditioning of the international' in the form of an ongoing process of 'passive revolution', 'whether through developments linked to the French Revolution; social forces associated with Fascism; or the growing dominance of Anglo-Saxon capitalism' (Morton, 2007: 41). This crystallizes a conception of passive revolution as an international process of cultural, socio-economic, and political transformations, but realized with the consent and active support (hegemony) of local elites, whose continued reproduction and way of life depended on their adaptation to the capitalist mode of production.

The outcome of a passive revolution also hinged on the national struggles between newly ascendant capitalist classes (the bourgeoisie) and subaltern agents (rural, poor, indigenous people). Focusing on the Zapatista movement in Mexico, Morton shows how Gramsci's theory of passive revolution contradicts any notion of the state as an externally determined 'transmission belt' for the spread of global capital. Instead, he proposes a 'nodal' understanding of the national state vis-à-vis the international sphere (Morton, 2007: 75).

This understanding of the uneven development of state apparatuses and social forces and their reciprocal interaction for understanding the history of capitalism pushes us to reject any linear conception of its development. In a similar vein, Chris Hesketh (2017) shows how other forms of organizing production, social relations, and 'ways of life' can challenge the centrality of the capitalist state as the primary locus of political contestation and maker of modernity as further demonstrated by the experience of the Zapatistas. Beyond approaches that equate modernity with the system of sovereign states focused on capitalist growth exists a multiplicity of different 'we' united through a common struggle and a common knowledge – where theory and practice combine in what Gramsci calls 'the philosophy of praxis' (Hesketh, 2017). As Morton and Hesketh show, the modern bureaucratic state develops as a node within 'uneven' and 'combined' social realities transcending the traditional IR separation of 'the international' and 'domestic' as ontologically distinct spheres of social causality and agential action. Justin Rosenberg's work (2006) further bridges this divide by conceptualizing anarchy as an emergent property of a broader macro-historical process of uneven and combined development (UCD).

According to Rosenberg, the distinctiveness of Leon Trotsky's idea of UCD is how it incorporates a specifically international dimension of social causality as an intrinsic property of historical development itself. This then opens up 'the international' to a genuinely sociological analysis that avoids both (neo)realist reifications of the international system as an absolutely autonomous ('supra-social') sphere and the classical sociological tradition's tendency to falsely subsume its distinctive causal dynamics to a conception of the social in the ontologically singular (Rosenberg, 2006).

For instance, Trotsky's own 'classical' case of combined development in Czarist Russia indicated how the processes of militarization, bureaucratic state-making, and industrialization were pursued not by an indigenous capitalist class, but by a semi-feudal monarchy concerned with their own geopolitical survival. Trotsky's understanding of development thereby reconceptualized the spread of capitalism as 'uneven (involving a staggered sequence of national industrial revolutions) and combined (in the triple sense of geopolitically interconnected, temporally compressed and sociologically hybridized)' (Rosenberg, 2013: 198).

This theorization of capitalism not only allows for the existence of multiple types of capitalist societies but also integrates into its conceptual bounds the ostensibly 'contingent' – international – sources of historical change and transformation characterizing each society's differentiated path to capitalist modernity. It thereby reconceptualizes 'the social' as ontologically plural, interactive, and thus multivalent (Matin, 2013). But this raises the question: what exactly is 'the social'? And might not attempts to position 'the international' in a wider ontology of social structure and processes replicate the implicitly reactionary conceptions of 'the social' bequeathed by the classical tradition?

Capitalism and 'the social'

This is the challenge laid down by Patricia Owens' *Economy of Force*. In a *tour-de-force* spanning Greek, Roman, and modern European philosophy, Owens (2015) argues that the rise of the social realm in European capitalist empires and states is, in fact, a modern form of household control. As such, forms of government should be theorized through their governing of the household, for 'household rule is organised around the material life needs and processes of human beings' (Owens, 2015: 287). Owens reconstructs through different historical periods the ontological understanding of *oikonomikos* – the science of household rule. Social engineering tools were initially applied internally in the competitive struggle of European states to police their own 'domesticated' subjects for increasing their productive capacities. Then, during the modern era, the United Kingdom and the United States used international counterinsurgency strategies to 'win the hearts' of disgruntled workers in the colonies and to pacify 'dysfunctional' behaviours in Vietnam, Afghanistan, and Iraq.

On Owens' account, the anarchical becomes social and governable by a bureaucratic form of state geared towards the promotion of capitalist property relations. In short, the patriarchal authority of feudal households translated into the bureaucratic apparatuses of capitalist empires and states, which enabled gendered and racialized laws that reinforced despotic and patriarchal family governance and instituted a gendered and racialized international division of labour. As such, attempts to understand 'the international' in purely social-theoretic terms reproduces the concealed forms of domination and oppression underlying 'the social' itself. Owens' main contribution to the understanding of capitalism rests in a genealogical excavation of *oikonomia* as a science of political domination and economic exploitation, which can unpack how gender, class, racial, and imperial hierarchies structure relations of (re)production under global capitalism.

Touching on related issues, Adrienne Roberts (2017) shows how law and social welfare policies targeting women are coercive and disciplinary and have been historically used to create and reproduce gendered relations of capitalist social order. Through a historical analysis of social welfare policies, penal systems, and economic development in Canada, Britain, and the United States, Roberts painstakingly demonstrates how the regulation of private and public space – and the policing of the bodies residing therein – are constitutive of the development of modern capitalism. Perhaps it should come as no surprise then that women make up the fastest rising segment of the global prison population in neoliberal capitalism (Roberts, 2017: 3).

Roberts' approach seeks to understand the ways in which power is exerted through the state, its laws, and its institutions in ways that conceal its operation. Specifically, Roberts' feminist historical materialist approach helps uncover how the deepening forms of surveillance and control 'are constitutive of "the economy"', which, in capitalist society, is *artificially* separated from other social relations, including legal relations'. The law is not an institutional mechanism separated from the economy. It is, rather, a part of the *gendered social ontology* of capitalism – 'itself *constitutive* of historically specific relations of production *and* social reproduction' (Roberts, 2017: 11,15; cf. Federici, 2004). Drawing on the Gramscian tradition, Roberts focuses on changes in social relations determined by transformations of ideas, institutions, and material capabilities, tracing the shift from one regime of punishment to another, intimately linked with the transformations in capitalist relations.

Cynthia Weber's (2016) *Queer International Relations* is another notable recent work unearthing the variegated mechanisms of domination and oppression by which different practices and discourses of modern state-making and IR are legitimized and constructed as 'normal' by comparison with other 'perverse' figurations. Particularly interesting is how Weber reconceptualizes 'sovereign statecraft as sovereign mancraft'[2] which helps us understand how the modern notion of 'sovereignty' relies on a constructed 'sovereign man', always placed in opposition to an imagined configuration of the 'homosexual'.

Although not explicitly addressing the relationship between sexuality and sovereignty, on one hand, and capitalism, on the other, Weber nonetheless highlights the capitalist nature of the various discourses of modern statecraft. 'Modernization became a securitizing system of management and rule to be imposed by the "developed" on the "underdeveloped" and the "undevelopable" to tame or to destroy their dangerous anarchy that—if left unmonitored, unmanaged, and unmodernized—threatened Western capitalist states and Western civilizational order itself' (Weber, 2016: 52). The division of labour engendered by a presumed cultural division between the 'unwanted im/migrant' and the 'domesticated citizen' and the 'securitization' of foreign lands and peoples through discourses about the 'terrorist' complements the capitalist character of sovereign statecraft (Weber, 2016: 20). In these ways, Weber challenges the dichotomies – male/female, masculine/feminine, heterosexual/homosexual, white/black, modern/primitive, etc. – used to reproduce the 'sovereign man' and the 'political delusion of sovereignty', thereby challenging its supposed historical immutability.

Capitalism and world history

By exposing how the exclusion and punishment of 'non-sovereigns' is constitutive of the sovereign and the right to participate in the capitalist order (domestic and international), Weber's work connects with other IR studies challenging Eurocentric accounts of capitalist history. For, as many postcolonial scholars have argued, Eurocentric approaches to 'the international' are problematic insofar as 'IR's ontological exclusion of cultural heterogeneity has led to its systematic blindness toward the non-West' (Matin, 2013: 9; see also Çapan, dos Reis, and Grasten, 2021 in this volume).

Correcting this blind spot, John M. Hobson (2004) shows how from 500 to 1800 'the East' was far more developed than 'the West' in terms of agrarian, industrial, bureaucratic, military, and navigational technology, which spread into Europe through Eastern-centred globalization and once assimilated by Europeans enabled their rise to global dominance. The upshot of Hobson's analysis is to thereby 'provincialize' Europe as the sole, sovereign author of sociohistorical change, demonstrating instead how 'the West' and 'East' were interconnected and co-constitutive social entities that jointly – albeit unequally – made the modern capitalist world.

This point is further brought out in the work of Alexander Anievas and Kerem Nişancioğlu (2015) who challenge established explanations of the development of capitalism, which describe a fundamentally European process, wherein a new system of production evolved within the 'internal' bounds of European feudal societies. This Eurocentric recounting of the history of capitalism is problematic since it reasserts a form of European exceptionalism, while relegating the role of non-Western agents and societies to the periphery of the history of capitalism. By focusing on the Mongolian expansion, the Ottoman-Habsburg rivalry, the Atlantic discoveries, the development of Asian colonies, and the European bourgeois revolutions, Anievas and Nişancioğlu instead highlight the centrality of non-Western societies in explaining the emergence of capitalism in Europe and its subsequent evolution into a world system. They show how each of these historical processes captures or anticipates the central dynamics and processes behind the collapse of feudalism and the emergence of capitalism.

The historical processes and events identified by Anievas and Nişancioğlu thus demonstrate how the multiple geopolitical advantages that thrust Europe to global ascendancy were based on the prior influences from the more powerful non-European societies. Insofar as there was anything exceptional about the development of capitalism in Europe, it was rooted in the 'exceptionally cruel deployment of the means of violence' against these non-European societies, whereas the very interactions with these societies actually generated these means of violence (Anievas and Nişancioğlu, 2015: 276).

For Anievas and Nişancioğlu, the critique of Eurocentrism is not only a spatial ('extra-European') one, but also a substantive or categorical one: the need to identify and explain those practices which 'enable or delimit ways of thinking about categories (capitalism)'. For there is 'no being of capitalism independent of its becoming', 'no logic to capitalism independent of its history' and, consequently, 'no categories of capitalism that operate independent of a spatio-historical setting (or the interconnections between these settings)'. The myth that capitalism is a system categorically based on the employment of 'free' wage labour only emerged after the enslavement of other non-European peoples. Hence, a non-Eurocentric history of capitalism presupposes de-naturalizing these categories by investigating the history behind them (Anievas and Nişancioğlu, 2016: 72–73).

Conclusion: capitalism, 'the international', and history-writing

Although recent IR works have sought to problematize the typically Eurocentric framings of capitalist modernity's becoming, much less attention has been paid to the question of whether there is something about 'the international' that entails a distinctive approach to history-writing itself (Davenport, 2016). It is well known that capitalist modernity produced a historically novel political order based upon the formal differentiation of the political and economic and 'inside' and 'outside' demarcations in territorial space (Rosenberg, 1994; Anievas and Nişancıoğlu, 2015). Less noted, however, is the fact that this distinctive political order was also founded upon and legitimized through a particular *order of time*. François Hartog (2015) has termed this the 'modern regime of historicity': a historically unique conception of universal linear time representing 'both a fundamental rupture between past, present, and future – as distinct temporal planes – and their relinking along a singular line that allows for continuity' (Trouillot, 2002: 231–232; see also MacKay and LaRoche, 2021; Hom, 2021; both in this volume).

Consequently, the past was divested of its long-held authority, and the circular conception of time represented by the ancient regime of historicity was replaced by a future-orientated understanding of history. This conception of history was marshalled by Enlightenment thinkers in the service of newly aspiring sovereigns who sought to liberate themselves from the antiquated authority of pope and emperor, whilst simultaneously defining themselves against their 'backward' colonial subjects to which sovereignty was denied (Fasolt, 2004: 16). The forms of sovereignty in space these political agents sought to carve out in linearly defined territorial boundaries were thus coextensive with linearly defined conceptions of sovereignty in time. And it was this latter division of history into distinct temporal planes for which the modern sovereign laid claim. As a result, individual freedom, autonomy, and 'progress' came to be conceived as resting *within* and *necessarily limited to* the internal confines of the sovereign state (Fasolt, 2004: 7; Davenport, 2016: 257).

The idea of progress entailed in these delineations in time was thereby accompanied by its obstinate demarcation in space. Progress, so to speak, stopped at water's edge. For although 'progress' could be detected in 'national histories considered in isolation', at the level of 'the international', scholars could only find 'recurrence and repetition' in which 'political action is most regularly necessitous' (Wight, 1966: 26). Thus, emerged the analytical distinction between the 'ordered' domestic realm and the 'anarchic' international upon which contemporary realist IR was founded (cf. Davenport, 2016). So while critical and Historical IR scholars have been hitherto predominately focused around engagements *with* history, perhaps the next step is a critique *of* history. For what might a historiographical approach posited upon the fractured space of 'the international' mean for rewriting the history of capitalism?

Suggestions for further reading

Anievas, A., and Nişancıoğlu, K. (2015). *How the West Came to Rule: The Geopolitical Origins of Capitalism.* London: Pluto Press.

Ashton, T. H., and Philpin, C. H. E., eds. (1985). *The Brenner Debate: Agrarian Class Structure and Economic Development in Pre-industrial Europe.* Cambridge: Cambridge University Press.

Federici, S. (2004). *Caliban and the Witch: Women, the Body and Primitive Accumulation.* Brooklyn: Autonomedia.

Mielants, E. (2007). *The Origins of Capitalism and the 'Rise of the West'.* Philadelphia, PA: Temple University Press.

Roberts, A. (2017). *Gendered States of Punishment and Welfare: Feminist Political Economy, Primitive Accumulation and the Law.* London: Routledge.

Notes

1 As numerous scholars have shown, Marx's later writings began to move beyond such Eurocentric assumptions (Stedman Jones, 2007; Anderson, 2010).
2 Initially conceptualized by Richard Ashley, this refers to modern state attempts 'to present its sovereign foundation…as if it were the singular, preexisting, ahistorical ground that authorizes all sovereign decisions in its political community' (Weber, 2016: 193).

References

Anderson, K. (2010). *Marx at the Margins: On Nationalism, Ethnicity, and Non-Western Societies*. Chicago, IL: University of Chicago Press.
Anievas, A., Manchanda, N., and Shilliam, R., eds. (2015). *Race and Racism in International Relations: Confronting the Global Colour Line*. London: Routledge.
Anievas, A. (2014). *Capital, the State, and War: Class Conflict and Geopolitics in the Thirty Years' Crisis, 1914-1945*. Ann Arbor, MI: University of Michigan Press.
Anievas, A., and Nişancioğlu, K. (2016). Why Europe? Anti-Eurocentric theory, history, and the rise of capitalism. *Spectrum: Journal of Global Studies*, 8 (1), 70–98.
Anievas, A., and Nişancioğlu, K. (2018). Lineages of capital. *Historical Materialism*, 26 (3), 167–196.
Ashley, R. K. (1987). The geopolitics of geopolitics space. *Alternatives*, 12 (4), 403–434.
Ashworth, L. M. (2021). Disciplinary Traditions and Debates: The Subject Matters of International Thought. In de Carvalho, B., Costa Lopez, J., & Leira, H., eds. *Routledge Handbook of Historical International Relations*. Abingdon: Routledge.
Bayly, M. (2021). Imperialism: Beyond the 'Re-turn to Empire' in International Relations. In de Carvalho, B., Costa Lopez, J., & Leira, H., eds. *Routledge Handbook of Historical International Relations*. Abingdon: Routledge.
Beckert, S. (2014). *Empire of Cotton: A Global History*. London: Penguin.
Bhambra, G. K. (2007). *Rethinking Modernity: Postcolonialism and the Sociological Imagination*. Houndmills: Palgrave Macmillan.
Bowden, B. (2021). Eurocentrism and Civilization. In de Carvalho, B., Costa Lopez, J., & Leira, H., eds. *Routledge Handbook of Historical International Relations*. Abingdon: Routledge.
Brenner, R. (2007). Property and Progress: Where Adam Smith Went Wrong. In: C. Wickham, ed., *Marxist History-Writing for the Twenty First Century*, Oxford: Oxford University Press, 49–111.
Bukharin, N. I. (1973 [1915]). *Imperialism and World Economy*. New York, NY: Monthly Review Press.
Buzan, B., and Lawson, G. (2015). *The Global Transformation: History, Modernity and the Making of International Relations*. Cambridge: Cambridge University Press.
Callinicos, A. (2009). *Imperialism and Global Political Economy*. Cambridge: Polity.
Çapan, Z. G., dos Reis, F., and Grasten, M. (2021). Global Histories: Connections and Circulations in Historical International Relations. In de Carvalho, B., Costa Lopez, J., & Leira, H., eds. *Routledge Handbook of Historical International Relations*. Abingdon: Routledge.
Cox, R. W. (1987). *Production, Power, and World Order*. New York, NY: Columbia University Press.
Davenport, A. (2016). The international and the limits of history. *Review of International Studies*, 42 (2), 247–265.
Deudney, D., and Ikenberry, G. J. (1999). The nature and sources of liberal international order. *Review of International Studies*, 25 (2), 179–196.
Di Muzio, T., and Robbins, R. H. (2016). *Debt as Power*. Manchester: Manchester University Press.
Du Bois, W. E. B. (1915). African roots of war. *Atlantic Monthly*, 115 (5), 707–714.
Fasolt, C. (2004). *The Limits of History*. Chicago, IL: University of Chicago Press.
Federici, S. (2014). From commoning to debt: financialization, microcredit, and the changing architecture of capital accumulation. *The South Atlantic Quarterly*, 113 (2), 231–244.
Gartzke, E. (2007). The capitalist peace. *American Journal of Political Science*, 51 (1), 166–191.
Gilpin, R. (1981). *War and Change in World Politics*. Cambridge: Cambridge University Press.
Goody, J. (2006). *The Theft of History*. Cambridge: Cambridge University Press.
Gowan, P. (1999). *The Global Gamble: Washington's Faustian Bid for World Dominance*. London: Verso.
Graeber, D. (2011). *Debt: The First 5,000 Years*. New York, NY: Melville House.
Halliday, F. (1987). State and society in international relations: a second agenda. *Millennium*, 16 (2), 215–239.
Hartog, F. (2015). *Regimes of Historicity*. New York, NY: Columbia University Press.

Harvey, D. (2003). *The New Imperialism*. Oxford: Oxford University Press.

Heller, H. (2000). Primitive accumulation and technical innovation in the French wars of religion. *History and Technology*, 16 (3), 243–262.

Herborth, B., and Nitzschner, P. (2021). Europe in Historical International Relations. In de Carvalho, B., Costa Lopez, J., & Leira, H., eds. *Routledge Handbook of Historical International Relations*. Abingdon: Routledge.

Hesketh, C. (2017). *Spaces of Capital/Spaces of Resistance: Mexico and the Global Political Economy*. Athens: University of Georgia Press.

Hobson, J. A. (1902). *Imperialism: A Study*. London: Nisbet & Co.

Hobson, J. M. (2004). *The Eastern Origins of Western Civilisation*. Cambridge: Cambridge University Press.

Hobson, J. M. (2012). *The Eurocentric Conception of World Politics: Western International Theory, 1760–2010*. Cambridge: Cambridge University Press.

Hobson, J. M. (2020). *Multicultural Origins of the Global Economy: Beyond the Western-Centric Frontier*. Cambridge: Cambridge University Press.

Hobson, J. M., Lawson, G., and Rosenberg, J. (2010). Historical Sociology. In: R. A. Denemark, and R. Marlin-Bennett, eds., *The International Studies Encyclopedia*, London: Wiley-Blackwell.

Hom, A. R. (2021). Time and History in International Relations. In de Carvalho, B., Costa Lopez, J., & Leira, H., eds. *Routledge Handbook of Historical International Relations*. Abingdon: Routledge.

Hoogvelt, A. (2001). *Globalization and the Postcolonial World*. Basingstoke: Palgrave.

Jahn, B. (2021). Liberalism between Theory and Practice. In de Carvalho, B., Costa Lopez, J., & Leira, H., eds. *Routledge Handbook of Historical International Relations*. Abingdon: Routledge.

Keohane, R., and Nye, J. S., Jr. (1977). *Power and Interdependence*. Boston, MA: Little, Brown & Co.

Lacher, H. (2006). *Beyond Globalization: Capitalism, Territoriality, and the International Relations of Modernity*. London: Routledge.

Linklater, A. (1990). *Beyond Realism and Marxism*. Basingstoke: Palgrave.

Long, D., and Schmidt, B. C., eds. (2005). *Imperialism and Internationalism in the Discipline of International Relations*. Albany, NY: SUNY Press.

Luxemburg, R. (2003 [1913]). *The Accumulation of Capital*. London: Routledge.

MacKay, J., and LaRoche, C. D. (2021). Theories and Philosophies of History in International Relations. In de Carvalho, B., Costa Lopez, J., & Leira, H., eds. *Routledge Handbook of Historical International Relations*. Abingdon: Routledge.

Mann, M. (1986). *The Sources of Social Power Volume 1: A History of Power from the Beginning to AD 1760*. Cambridge: Cambridge University Press.

Marx, K. (1976 [1867]). *Capital: A Critique of Political Economy, Vol I*. London: Penguin.

Matin, K. (2013). *Recasting Iranian Modernity: International Relations and Social Change*. London: Routledge.

Montchrétien, A. De. (1970 [1615]). *Traicté de L'Œconomie Politique*. Geneva: Slatkine Reprints. Viewed on 20 October 2020, <https://gallica.bnf.fr/ark:/12148/bpt6k55779/>.

Moon, P. T. (1927). *Imperialism and World Politics*. London: MacMillan.

Morton, A. D. (2007). *Unravelling Gramsci: Hegemony and Passive Revolution in the Global Economy*. London: Pluto.

Owens, P. (2015). *Economy of Force*. Cambridge: Cambridge University Press.

Persson, K. G. (2014). Markets and Coercion in Medieval Europe. In: L. Neal, and J. G. Williamson, eds., *The Cambridge History of Capitalism, Volume 1*, Cambridge: Cambridge University Press, 225–266.

Pezzarossi, G. (2015). A Spectral Haunting of Society: Longue Durée Archaeologies of Capitalism and Antimarkets in Colonial Guatemala. In: M. P. Leone, and Knauf, J. E., eds., *Historical Archaeologies of Capitalism*, London: Spring.

Piketty, T. (2014). *Capital in the Twenty-First Century*. Cambridge, MA: Belknap Press.

Reinsch, P. S. (1908). *World Politics at the End of the Nineteenth Century*. London: MacMillan.

Rosenberg, J. (1994). *The Empire of Civil Society*. London: Verso.

Rosenberg, J. (2006). Why is there no international historical sociology?. *European Journal of International Relations*, 12 (3), 307–340.

Rosenberg, J. (2013). Kenneth Waltz and Leon Trotsky: anarchy in the mirror of uneven and combined development. *International Politics*, 50 (2), 183–230.

Ruggie, J. G. (1993). Territoriality and beyond: problematizing modernity in international relations. *International Organization*, 47 (1), 139–174.

Ruggie, J. G. (1998). *Constructing the World Polity*. London: Routledge.

Runciman, D. (1983). Capitalism without classes: the case of classical Rome. *British Journal of Sociology*, 34 (2), 157–181.

Skocpol, T. (1979). *States and Social Revolutions*. Cambridge: Cambridge University Press.

Smith, A. (1776). *The Wealth of Nations*. London: Strahan & Cadell.

Smith, A. (1812). *The Theory of Moral Sentiments*. London: Cadell & Davies.

Stedman Jones, G. (2007). Radicalism and the Extra-European World: The Case of Karl Marx. In: D. Bell, ed., *Victorian Visions of Global Order*, Cambridge: Cambridge University Press, 186–214.

Teschke, B. (2003). *The Myth of 1648*. London: Verso.

Teschke, B., and Lacher, H. (2007). The changing 'logics' of capitalist competition. *Cambridge Review of International Affairs*, 20 (4), 565–580.

Teschke, B., and Wenten, F. (2016). Capitalism. In: F. Berenskoetter, ed., *Concepts in World Politics*, London: SAGE Publications, 157–180.

Tilly, C. (1992). *Capital, Coercion, and European States, AD 990-1992*. London: Wiley.

Trouillot, M. R. (2002). The Otherwise Modern: Caribbean Lessons from the Savage Slot. In: B. M. Knauft, ed., *Critically Modern: Alternatives, Alterities, Anthropologies*, Bloomington, IN: Indiana University Press, 220–237.

van der Pijl, K. (1984). *The Making of an Atlantic Ruling Class*. London: Verso.

Vitalis, R. (2015). *White World Order, Black Power Politics*. Ithaca, NY: Cornell University Press.

Weber, C. (2016). *Queer International Relations*. Oxford: Oxford University Press.

Weber, M. (2001 [1905]). *The Protestant Ethic and the Spirit of Capitalism*. London: Routledge.

Wendt, A. (1999). *Social Theory of International Politics*. Cambridge: Cambridge University Press.

Wight, M. (1966). Why Is There No International Theory?. In: H. Butterfield, and M. Wight, eds., *Diplomatic Investigations*, London: Allen and Unwin, 17–34.

Yao, J., and Delatolla, A. (2021). Race and Historical International Relations. In de Carvalho, B., Costa Lopez, J., & Leira, H., eds. *Routledge Handbook of Historical International Relations*. Abingdon: Routledge.

Yazdani, K., and Menon, D. M., eds. (2020). *Capitalisms: Towards a Global History*. Oxford: Oxford University Press.

14

GENDER IN HISTORICAL INTERNATIONAL RELATIONS

Ann E. Towns

Introduction

This chapter provides an overview of feminist and gender scholarship in the International Relations (IR) subfield of Historical IR. The main claim is that much like other IR subfields, and despite the centrality of gender to historical international phenomena and developments, Historical IR has done exceptionally little to integrate gender into its analyses. Historical IR is thriving, with a surge in excellent scholarship that is capturing a lot of disciplinary attention and a relatively new Historical IR section of the International Studies Association whose membership is swelling. One is hard pressed to find any gender analyses or even mention of gender in this work, however.

At first glance, it furthermore might appear as if there is little IR feminist scholarship that is historical. As this chapter will show, there is in fact a fair amount of feminist IR work which could be sorted as 'Historical IR.' The silence on gender in Historical IR scholarship is thus a bit curious, given that there is feminist IR work to draw on. It is even more curious given how much gender scholarship there is within the discipline of history, scholarship that can readily be relied upon in IR analyses. My conclusion is that Historical IR is ripe for more gender work, both in terms of scholarship that is centred on gender and in terms of scholarship that weaves gender into other central aims. Indeed, the current inattentiveness to gender in most Historical IR scholarship is hard to defend.

Charting some of the main themes that feminist scholarship has explored in Historical IR is the main aim of this chapter. More specifically, I will discuss feminist IR work on the historical processes of state-formation, war and peace, and the disciplinary history of IR. I do so at some length, since most Historical IR seems to have overlooked this work and seems not to realize how central gender is to historical processes in international politics. Much, though not all, feminist Historical IR has been intersectional in one way or another, drawing attention to the mutual constitution and complex interconnections of the hierarchies of gender and those of, e.g., class, race or sexuality. Using imperialism and diplomacy as illustrations, the chapter concludes with a brief discussion of some fruitful directions for future research in gender and Historical IR.

Before I proceed, a few brief words are in order about some of the choices upon which the chapter rests. We all know the precariousness of making disciplinary claims and of trying to determine what should or should not count as, e.g., 'history' or 'feminist scholarship.' For present purposes, I approach 'feminist' and 'gender' scholarship interchangeably and broadly, to include any work that centres on gender, sex or the categories of (or some subset of the categories) men, women and trans or non-binary people. The empirical rather than theoretical contributions are emphasized. My discussion here will furthermore focus on studies with a primary and sustained focus on historical developments in international politics, even if a range of additional publications include brief sections on the history of gender in international politics (e.g. Enloe, 1990; Tickner, 1992; D'Amico, 1999; Hooper, 2008; Carpenter, 2013). As 'Historical IR,' I focus on scholarship that addresses international politics prior to the Cold War – that way, I avoid having to determine whether feminist work from the 1980s and early 1990s, which addressed what was then a contemporary context, should now count as 'history.' Finally, I approach 'IR scholarship' conventionally, as that which focuses on international politics – generally by scholars in political science, IR or global studies departments – and is published in international politics venues. In other words, Historical IR is distinguished from international history within, e.g., the discipline of history (see de Carvalho et al., 2021 in this volume).

Feminist IR history scholarship

Since the 1980s, a massive body of feminist scholarship has emerged within IR. With the exception of the recent interest in disciplinary histories, very little of this has been sorted as Historical IR in the sense of being labelled as such in IR publications or at IR conferences. The presence of feminists and other gender scholars in the relatively new Historical International Relations Section (HIST) of the International Studies Association has been limited. It would nonetheless be a mistake to draw the conclusion that there is no feminist scholarship on historical international developments and phenomena. As I will show below, although the body of feminist IR work that is historical is not huge, a range of historical themes have been analysed in feminist IR scholarship. I will point to some such work on state-formation, war and peace, and the disciplinary history of IR.

International politics of state-formation

States are some of the most fundamental units of international politics in the modern era. It is thus not surprising that feminist scholars have analysed gender in the historical and internationalized processes of state-formation, exploring the temporally and spatially changing sets of aims, institutions and relations that make up states (e.g. Peterson, 1988, 1992, 1997; Saco, 1997; Towns, 2009, 2010, 2017). Spike Peterson's work pioneered in unearthing the masculinist premises of early state formations for an IR audience. Drawing on feminist historians and historical anthropologists, she has outlined how patriarchal gender constructions co-emerged with the early development of European states (e.g. 1988, 1992, 1997). In broad strokes, she argues, Western state formations have since their inception entailed reorganizations that disempowered women politically, economically and ideologically. She uses the emergence of the Athenian polis and the nineteenth-century European state to exemplify these patterns. The development of the polis involved altered property relations, with women losing prior claims to property; the constitution of political authority as male only with citizens as free men; an institutionalized militarism that celebrated a new form of masculinity; strict legal regulations of women's sexuality (laws codified a distinction between 'respectable women,' who provided legitimate heirs, and 'not-respectable women,' who saw to men's pleasure); and new ideas that privileged masculinist cosmologies that denigrated anything marked as feminine. In effect, in the polis, women's bodies, labour and labour products were 'placed at the service of and under control by men, who exercised that control individually and collectively through the patriarchal state' (Peterson, 1992: 36).

Subsequent work has developed these claims, looking more closely at gender and state-formation in the nineteenth and early twentieth centuries while attempting to more explicitly examine the international dimensions of state changes. For instance, my work has drawn on historical anthropology, history and native studies to draw attention to the fundamental global changes in women's political authority that took place in the nineteenth century (Towns, 2009, 2010, 2017). Prior to the nineteenth century, the world consisted of a range of polities with sex/gender arrangements of political authority that were quite diverse. Some included female rule, whereas others were male dominated. For instance, in the seventeenth and eighteenth centuries, many polities in Western Africa as well as in the Americas deployed a gender-dual organizations of decision-making, with one female and one male title-holder for each position. Many Native American and West African societies furthermore practiced gender as something flexible and varying, often including a third gender and the option of women assuming men's roles and vice versa. This in turn meant that in addition to occupying female titles, male women could participate in the male political councils.

Political authority was much more male dominated in most of the larger polities of the nineteenth century, such as the Ottoman Empire, Qing China, the Qajar Empire of Persia and the European empires. That said, while heavily male dominated, female rulers and sovereigns were sometimes tolerated. Empress Dowager Cixi ruled China from 1861 for 47 years, for instance, and there were a number of female monarchs in Europe during the absolutist era – a time when the political authority of the state was vested in the sovereign. Here, it is useful to consider Europe in the sixteenth century, as examined in Diana Saco's fabulous 1997 article in the *European Journal of International Relations* on the reign of one female sovereign, Elizabeth I. Analysing late-medieval discourses and constructs of gender, marriage and sovereignty, Saco argues that gender and marriage were integral to the practice of international politics and to state sovereignty. Saco shows that at this time, the 'the Commonwealth' was constructed 'as that which belonged to a prince (and less often a people) in whom sovereignty was vested. In a sense, then, what we today regard as "International" Relations were, more appositely, *inter-sovereign* relations. This inelegant but more accurate phrase implies a different orientation toward cross-border relationships...16th century sovereignty was not simply emplaced in a territory but embodied in a king or queen' (Saco, 1997: 293). With a physical body functioning as the sovereign, marriages became central not only to secure heirs to the throne but also to forge alliances between states and as a means to expand state dominion and rule. However, as marriage essentially constituted the husband as lord over 'his' wife, marriage – while necessary to produce heirs and avoid wars of succession – could be a threat to the sovereignty of the commonwealth. 'England, through Elizabeth, [would have to] assume the weaker, female position in the match,' as Saco points out (Saco, 1997: 298). Precautions, such as set terms and agreements, were thus common in marriages between sovereigns.

While constructions of gender, marriage, and sovereignty made women a risk as sovereigns, women were tolerated – though never preferred – as sovereigns in a range of late medieval and absolutist European states. Elite women also took on political roles as members of royal courts. However, by the late nineteenth and early twentieth centuries, state institutions and political office in Europe and across the world became populated almost exclusively by men, as women were expressly and legally banned from political decision-making and from holding public office (Towns, 2009, 2010). How this turned into a global practice of excluding women from political power is of course a complex matter. For an IR audience, it is important to note that European colonialism and the international spread of European scientific ideas about binary sex and the proper relations between men, women and the state were crucial to the global stand-ardization of male rule (e.g. Towns, 2007, 2014). The impact on the political organization of colonized areas was severe, including a fundamental restructuring of political authority as male. The colonial administrative systems of warrant chiefs, court clerks, court messengers and so on were populated exclusively by men, displacing prior forms of institutionalized female political authority. The imperative to remove women from political rule was in turn supported by the new social sciences, which provided ample evidence that female political authority was a 'savage' practice. Nineteenth-century scholarship in the emerging fields of anthropology and geography pointed to the elevated political status of women among societies in Africa, Asia and Native America, scholarship which became used as evidence that women had no place in politics in 'civilized' states (ibid.; in this volume, see Bowden, 2021).

This standardization then set the stage for the massive transnational women's movements that characterized the twentieth century, movements involving every continent and which have successfully struggled to change the norms of international society and to bring women (back) into political power, now as 'voters,' 'public officials' and 'civil servants' of reconfigured states. In *Activists Beyond Borders* (1998), Margaret Keck and Kathryn Sikkink draw on secondary sources from the discipline of history to examine the international movement for 'woman suffrage' as a transnational advocacy network that sought to alter the institutional form of democratic states. They locate the origins of the movement in Britain and the United States in the late nineteenth century, a movement which then came to connect activists and suffrage organization across borders, primarily in Europe and North America. They claim that the transnational campaign was successful in large part because suffrage as an 'issue lent itself to framing and action that appealed to the most basic values of the liberal state – equality, liberty, and democracy' (Keck and Sikkink, 1998: 53).

In my own work, relying on primary texts (pamphlets, letters, biographies etc. in English, Spanish, French and the Scandinavian languages) as well as secondary sources, I have shown that transnational suffragism extended far beyond Europe and North America (Towns, 2010). International suffrage activism furthermore emerged in four waves: a first in the Western 'core' of international society in the first two decades of the twentieth century; a second, temporally over-lapping but spatially distinct wave among socialist organizations, parties to the east in Europe, in Russia and in China; a third in Latin America between the 1940s and 1960s; and a fourth among Afro-Asian actors struggling against colonialism from the 1950s. Rather than an international norm that was established by European suffragists and that then spread without activism to states in the rest of the world, suffrage was hard won and fought for across the globe. Partly, this was because women's suffrage had been framed as a matter of 'civilization.' European suffragists had successfully argued that granting women suffrage was appropriate for 'advanced,' 'civilized' states. The implications of this for women in allegedly 'less advanced' countries was far from clear, and opponents argued that women were ill suited to vote in 'less advanced' states. Latin American, African and Asian suffragists thus had to reinterpret the appropriateness of suffrage, claiming, e.g., that the empowerment of women was a precolonial tradition of non-European societies that was worth reviving (Towns, 2010).

War and peace

Feminist scholars have also examined gender in the history of war (e.g. Elshtain, 1987; Kinsella, 2011; Inal, 2013). Indeed, it is difficult to account for how wars have been conducted without paying attention to how intricately interwoven war and gender have been. While a political philosopher rather than an empirical scholar, Jean Elshtain's (1987) *Women and War* has become a classic go-to on gender and war. Written as a series of reflections on men, women and war, the book shows that war has historically possessed an extraordinary capacity to call forth and mobilize particular and powerful identities for men and women. More specifically, and relying on an almost perplexing assortment of sources, Elshtain explores how narratives of Man as 'Just Warrior' and Woman as 'Beautiful Soul' reproduce men's identity as warriors and women's position as nurturing non-combatants. Her analysis is historical and focused on the West, starting in philosophical texts of ancient Greece and moving back and forth through the European Middle Ages, the early modern and modern periods. Elshtain furthermore argues that these deeply entrenched narratives mask the complicated realities of what men and women have actually done in war. For instance, far from pacifist, many women have been fervent supporters of war, even if they have been prohibited from participating as combatants. Warmongering women have throughout history cheered on their husbands, brothers and sons to sacrifice themselves for their community, and they have enthusiastically engaged in war-supporting activities. Deeply insightful, *Women and War* effectively shows how representations of gender and war structure individual and collective action, perpetuating themselves across time.

In the critically acclaimed and award-winning 2011 monograph *The Image Before the Weapon: A Critical History of the Distinction Between Combatant and Civilians*, Helen Kinsella develops and complicates Elshtains claims about male combatants and female civilians. Relying on rich primary sources central to international legal doctrine from early Western thought to the twentieth century, she shows that the so-called principle of distinction has been anything but given. In attempts to pin down and bring stability to what is in practice an arbitrary distinction, discourses of gender, civilization and innocence have been invoked by philosophers of law and international lawyers ranging from Aquinas, to Grotius and Vitoria, during the US civil war and in the nineteenth-century laws of war. Kinsella skilfully demonstrates that the distinction becomes no clearer by seeking recourse in ideas about combatants as men and civilians as women.

Female bodies have historically been treated as property during war. Yet as Tuba Inal shows in *Looting and Rape in Wartime, Law and Change in International Relations* (2013), when the Hague Conventions of 1899 and 1907 prohibited wartime looting of property, this did not include the female body – rape was not treated as a war crime in international law until 1998, with the Rome Statute. Inal accounts for this puzzle through a careful examination of understandings of gender and male sexuality in the laws of war and the documents surrounding them, primarily from the mid-nineteen century to the present. Much like Elshtain and Kinsella, she makes very clear that the regulation and conduct of war has historically been intimately bound up with gender.

As much feminist scholarship has shown so well, women should not be treated as a coherent category nor assumed to be 'the peaceful sex.' That said, historically, women have been legally treated as if a coherent category, banned from serving as soldiers and by and large kept out of positions involving military strategy and decision-making. Their participation in war, while crucial, has primarily been in support functions and from the sidelines. And many women, seemingly more women than men, have engaged in international mobilizations for peace. Because of the work of feminist historians, the historical peace activism of millions of women – often organized transnationally – has been well documented.

Some attention to women's historical peace activism has also made it into the discipline of IR. The historical activities of the Women's International League for Peace and Freedom (WILPF), established in 1915 to protest World War I, has been particularly well analysed by IR scholars (e.g. Meyer, 1999; Lynch, 1999; Confortini, 2011, 2012, 2013). Confortini provides a fascinating account of what she calls the 'critical methodology' of WILPF, a methodology which allowed the organization to move beyond its predominantly Western, white and liberal internationalist roots to become a critical, radical and anti-colonial force. Feminist methodologies of 'attentive thinking,' openness to multiple points of view and 'empathetic cooperation'–enabled WILPF to reformulate its mission to become a critical voice in the liberal order. However, most scholarship on women's internationalism remains within the discipline of history. For instance, there is a great deal of work among historians on the role of individual women as well as women's movements in the League of Nations (e.g. Miller, 1992, 1994). There is furthermore an excellent body of groundbreaking scholarship on the history of black women's internationalism and resistance to white, liberal world order (e.g. Blain, 2018; Umoren, 2018).

Disciplinary history of IR and histories of international thought

It seems to be a generally accepted idea that there were few women IR scholars before the 1980s, and even fewer feminist IR scholars before that time. Such ideas are now challenged by the recent surge in interest in the gendered politics of writing IR disciplinary history. For instance, Robert Vitalis' groundbreaking work on race and the birth of the US IR discipline recovers the pioneering IR scholarship of Merze Tate, trained at Oxford and Harvard and the first African-American woman professor of political science in the United States (Vitalis, 2015). A number of studies have highlighted how women scholars and thinkers such as Tate have been written out of the histories of the early years of the discipline, resulting in a collective forgetting of early women IR thinkers. These studies generally also attempt to bring some of these early women thinkers back into view (e.g. Ashworth, 2013; Hansen, 2011; Kinsella, 2014; Vitalis, 2015; Murphy, 2017; Owens, 2018; Tickner and True, 2018). In doing so, as Ashworth (2013: 39, see also Ashworth, 2021) argues, this body of work demonstrates that not only women but also feminist women 'were at the center of the development of the discipline in its first decades.'

The most ambitious ongoing attempt to write women back into the disciplinary history of IR is carried out by an interdisciplinary research team of historians and IR scholars headed by Patricia Owens at the University of Sussex (see the Leverhulme Project on Women and the History of International Thought at http://blogs.sussex.ac.uk/whit/). The aim of the project is to start documenting how women were excluded from the disciplines of international thought in the United States and Britain in the beginning of the twentieth century, with a focus on European and black diaspora women. The project also intends to recover the intellectual contributions of these women and to write a revisionist disciplinary history of IR that includes their work. Owens recently published a survey demonstrating the magnitude of the exclusion of women thinkers from IR disciplinary histories (Owens, 2018). An edited volume – *Women and International Thought: A New History* – on the history of women's international thought is forthcoming (Owens and Rietzler, 2020), as is an anthology for classroom use (Owens et al., forthcoming).

One of the thinkers highlighted in Owen's work is Lucy Philip Mair, a Cambridge graduate, lecturer in IR at the London School of Economics in the 1930s and 1940s and central scholar of colonial administration. Crucially, and like others, Mair has been ignored despite holding a position at a prestigious university. However, in the first few decades of the twentieth century, when IR emerged as a discipline, women were largely excluded from academic positions and women like Mair were exceptionally few. In discussing the disciplinary history of IR, scholars thus often also widens the analysis to examine the international thought of women outside the disciplinary confines of IR. Owen's important work on the international thought of Hanna Arendt, including the 2007 monograph *Between War and Politics: the International Relations and the Thought of Hanna Arendt*, is a case in point (see also, e.g., Lang and Williams, 2005; Owens, 2017). A number of other IR scholars, including Lynch (1999) and Tickner and True (2018), have focused on the many women who thought and wrote about international politics in the context of peace activism. Tickner and True (2018) centre on the writings of Jane Addams, US president of the Women's

Peace Party, the International Congress of Women and WILPF and recipient of the Nobel Peace Prize in 1931. Addams was active in the context of American pragmatism, a philosophical school that emphasizes contextual and experiential knowledge. Much like contemporary feminist scholarship on women, peace and security, Tickner and True point out, Addams' writings deployed a relational ontology with analyses grounded in concrete practices of men and women in peace and war. The authors conclude that the feminist pragmatist vision of the first part of the twentieth century is enduring, a legacy which the discipline of IR needs to do much more to recognize. It is worth noting, again, that readers interested in historical women's international thought have much to learn from the discipline of history. For instance, on black women's international thought, see the recent and excellent work of, e.g., Keisha Blain and Imaobong Umoren.

Conclusions

As this chapter has shown, not only is there a fair amount of feminist IR history, but it covers a broad terrain and is generally innovative and insightful. Feminist IR scholarship has demonstrated that gender has been absolutely central to what states have been made to be and how they have developed historically, since their very emergence. Gendered international processes have furthermore shaped the ideologies and identities that have animated action, of states and other collective actors, whether in war or peace. Massive transnational social movements have laboured to change state institutions and the character of IR, including the global women's suffrage movement and the women's peace movements of the first half of the twentieth century. Given what we know about the centrality of gender to historical developments in IR, the silence on gender in much Historical IR is indefensible.

Historical scholarship is still but a tiny fragment of feminist IR work, however. How gender fits into a range of question of central concern to Historical IR still remains understudied. IR studies of imperialism are screaming for attention to gender, for instance. Questions of female agency in imperialism, of masculinity and imperial relations, of sexuality, masculinity and imperial militarism and how these change across time and space are but a few themes that could be fruitfully explored by IR scholars. Indeed, we still do not have answers to some of absolutely fundamental questions. For instance, how and why did most (all?) empires come to displace women's decision-making, to instead rely almost exclusively on men in formal positions of power? On virtually any question of interest to a Historical IR audience, there is a substantial body of gender history scholarship to draw on, scholarship which in all its richness and attention to context and detail is invaluable to IR's general concern with temporally and geographically more encompassing processes.

There is furthermore exceptionally little scholarship on gender in IR histories of diplomacy (on this point, see, e.g., Aggestam and Towns, 2017, 2019; in this volume, see Leira, 2021). Gender scholars have made excellent contributions to diplomatic history, a lively subfield within history. This research often provides close and detailed accounts of the extraordinary lives and efforts of individual women, showing that women have historically filled important diplomatic functions, as unofficial envoys, behind-the-scenes negotiators and informal mediators (e.g. Sluga and James, 2015). Some, such as Lady Anne Fanshawe, ambassadress of England at the Court of Madrid (1664–1666), even served formally as diplomats. That said, modern diplomacy has been remarkably male dominated. And yet IR scholars have asked virtually no questions about the gender of diplomacy in history. Schulz (2019) argues that women participated in the diplomacy of the Mapuche prior to the seventeenth century, but that the practice of treaty making with the Spanish turned diplomatic interactions into an all-male practice as the Spanish would not negotiate with women. More generally, when, where and how did diplomacy come to encompass

159

men only? What kind of masculinity constructions infused diplomatic practice, and how have these changed over time and across space? If we take the informal diplomatic labour of women seriously, as Enloe (1990) asks that we do, in what ways might the history of diplomacy have to be reconceptualized? These are but a few of the many intriguing IR history questions that remain to be asked about gender in the history of international politics.

Suggestions for further reading

Dean, R. (2001). *Imperial Brotherhood: Gender and the Making of Cold War Foreign Policy*. Amherst: University of Massachusetts Press.

Garner, K. (2018). *Women and Gender in International History*. London: Bloomsbury.

McCarthy, H. (2014). *Women of the World. The Rise of the Female Diplomat*. London: Bloomsbury.

McClintock, A. (1995). *Imperial Leather. Race, Gender and Sexuality in the Colonial Contest*. London: Routledge.

Midgley, C., ed. (1998). *Gender and Imperialism*. Manchester: Manchester University Press.

Towns, A. E. (2010). The Inter-American Commission of Women and Women's Suffrage, 1920–1948. *Journal of Latin American Studies*, 42 (4): 779–808.

References

Aggestam, K., and A. E. Towns (2017). Introduction. In: K. Aggestam, and A. Towns, eds., *Gendering Diplomacy and International Negotiations*, New York, NY: Palgrave MacMillan, 1–22.

Aggestam, K., and A. E. Towns. (2019). The gender turn in diplomacy: a new research agenda. *International Feminist Journal of Politics*, 21 (1), 9–28.

Ashworth, L. (2013). Feminism, war and the prospects for peace. *International Feminist Journal of Politics*, 13 (1): 25–43.

Ashworth, L. M. (2021). Disciplinary Traditions and Debates: The Subject Matters of International Thought. In de Carvalho, B., Costa Lopez, J., & Leira, H., eds. *Routledge Handbook of Historical International Relations*. Abingdon: Routledge.

Blain, K. (2018). *Setting the World on Fire. Black Nationalist Women and the Global Struggle for Freedom*. Philadelphia, PA: University of Pennsylvania Press.

Bowden, B. (2021). Eurocentrism and Civilization. In de Carvalho, B., Costa Lopez, J., & Leira, H., eds. *Routledge Handbook of Historical International Relations*. Abingdon: Routledge.

Carpenter, R. C. (2013). *'Innocent Women and Children': Gender Norms and the Protection of Civilians*. Farnham, UK: Ashgate.

Confortini, C. C. (2011). Doing feminist peace. *International Feminist Journal of Politics*, 13 (3), 349–370.

Confortini, C. C. (2012). *Intelligent Compassion. Feminist Critical Methodology in the Women's International League for Peace and Freedom*. Oxford: Oxford University Press.

Confortini, C. C. (2013). How matters: women's international league for peace and freedom's trips to the Middle East, 1931-1975. *Peace & Change*, 38 (3): 284–309.

D'Amico, F. (1999). Women Workers in the United Nations: From Margins to Mainstream. In: M. K. Meyer, and E. Prügl, eds., *Gender Politics in Global Governance*, Oxford: Rowman & Littlefield, 19–40.

de Carvalho, B., Costa Lopez, J., and Leira, H. (2021). Introduction: Historical International Relations. In de Carvalho, B., Costa Lopez, J., & Leira, H., eds. *Routledge Handbook of Historical International Relations*. Abingdon: Routledge.

Elshtain, J. (1987). *Women and War*. Chicago, IL: University of Chicago Press.

Enloe, C. (1990). *Bananas, Beaches and Bases. Making Feminist Sense of International Politics*. Berkeley, CA: University of California Press.

Hansen, L. (2011). A research agenda on feminist texts and the gendered constitution of international politics in Rebecca West's Black Lamb and Grey Falcon. *Millennium*, 40 (1): 109–28.

Hooper, C. (2008). *Manly States. Masculinities, International Relations and Gender Politics*. New York, NY: Columbia University Press.

Inal, T. (2013). *Looting and Rape in Wartime: Law and Change in International Relations*. Philadelphia, PA: University of Pennsylvania Press.

Kinsella, H. (2011) *The Image Before the Weapon: A Critical History of the Distinction Between Combatant and Civilian*. Ithaca, NY: Cornell University Press.

Kinsella, H. (2014). Simone Weil: An Introduction. In: F. Roesch, ed., *Émigré Scholars and the Genesis of American International Relations: a European Discipline in America?* London: Palgrave, 176–197.

Lang, A., and Williams, J., eds. (2005). *Hannah Arendt and International Relations*. New York, NY: Palgrave Macmillan.

Leira. H. (2021). Diplomacy: The World of States and Beyond. In de Carvalho, B., Costa Lopez, J., & Leira, H., eds. *Routledge Handbook of Historical International Relations*. Abingdon: Routledge.

Lynch, C. (1999). *Beyond Appeasement: Interpreting Interwar Peace Movements in World Politics*. Ithaca, NY: Cornell University Press.

Meyer, M. K. (1999). The Women's International League for Peace and Freedom: Organizing Women for Peace in the War System. In: M. K. Meyer, and E. Prügl, eds., *Gender Politics in Global Governance*, Oxford: Rowman & Littlefield, 58–71.

Miller, C. (1992). *Lobbying the League. Women's International Organizations and the League of Nations*. PhD Thesis, Oxford University, Faculty of Modern History.

Miller, C. (1994). 'Geneva – the key to equality': inter-war feminists and the League of Nations. *Women's History Review*, 3 (2): 219–245.

Murphy, C. N. (2017). Relocating the Point of IR in Understanding Industrial-Age Global Problems. In: S. L. Dyvik, J. Selby, and R. Wilkinson, eds., *What's the Point of International Relations*. London: Routledge, 71–82.

Owens, P., and Rietzler, K., eds. (2020) *Women and International Thought: A New History*. Cambridge: Cambridge University Press.

Owens, P., Dunstan, S., Hutchings, K., and Rietzler, K., eds. (2021). *From Canon to History: An Anthology of Women's International Thought*. Cambridge: Cambridge University Press.

Owens, P. (2017). Racism in the Theory Canon: Hannah Arendt and 'the One Great Crime in Which America Was Never Involved'. *Millennium*, 45 (3): 403–424.

Owens, P. (2018). Women and the history of international thought. *International Studies Quarterly*, 62 (3): 467–481.

Peterson, V. S. (1988). *An Archeology of Domination: Historicizing Gender and Class in Early Western State Formation*. PhD Dissertation, American University.

Peterson, V. S. (1992). Security and Sovereign States: What Is at State in Taking Feminism Seriously? In: V. Spike Peterson, ed., *Gendered States: Feminist (Re)Visions of International Relations Theory*, Boulder, CO: Lynne Rienner Publishers, 31–64.

Peterson, V. S. (1997). Whose crisis? Early and post-modern masculinism. In: S. Gill, and J. H. Mittelman, eds., *Innovation and Transformation in International Studies*, Cambridge: Cambridge University Press, 185–201.

Saco, D. (1997). Gendering sovereignty: marriage and international relations in Elizabethan times. *European Journal of International Relations*, 3 (3), 291–318.

Schulz, C-A. (2019). Territorial sovereignty and the end of inter-cultural diplomacy along the 'Southern frontier'. *European Journal of International Relations*, 25 (3), 878–903.

Sluga, G., and James, C., eds. (2015). *Women, Diplomacy and International Politics since 1500*. London: Routledge.

Tickner, A. (1992). *Gender in International Relations. Feminist Perspectives on Achieving Global Security*. New York, NY: Columbia University Press.

Tickner, A., and True, J. (2018). A century of international relations feminism: from World War I women's peace pragmatism to the women, peace and security agenda. *International Studies Quarterly*, 62 (2): 221–233.

Towns, A. E. (2007). The Status of Women and the Ordering of Human Societies Along the Stages of Civilization. In: *Civilizational Identity: The Production and Reproduction of 'Civilizations' in International Relations*, M. Hall, and P. T. Jackson, eds., New York, NY: Palgrave MacMillan, 161–179.

Towns, A. E. (2009). The status of women as a standard of 'civilization.' *European Journal of International Relations*, 15 (4), 681–706.

Towns, A. E. (2010). *Women and States: Norms and Hierarchies in International Society*. Cambridge: Cambridge University Press.

Towns, A. E. (2014). Carrying the load of civilization: the status of women and challenged hierarchies. *Millennium: Journal of International Studies*, 42 (3): 595–613.

Towns, A. E. (2017). Gender, Power and International Society. In: T. Dunne, and C. Reus-Smit, eds., *The Globalization of International Society*, Cambridge: Cambridge University Press, ch. 20.

Umoren, I. (2018). *Race Women Internationalists. Activist-Intellectuals and Global Freedom Struggles*. Berkeley, CA: University of California Press.

Vitalis, R. (2015). *White World Order, Black Power Politics. The Birth of American International Relations*. Ithaca, NY: Cornell University Press.

15

EUROCENTRISM AND CIVILIZATION

Brett Bowden

Introduction

In his study of the word *civilization*, the French linguist Émile Benveniste (1971: 289) states, 'the whole history of modern thought and the principal intellectual achievements in the western world are connected with the creation and handling of a few dozen essential words which are all the common possession of the western European languages.' *Civilization* is one of the words; in fact, he asserts that it is 'one of the most important terms of our modern lexicon.' This might sound reasonable enough; I have argued at length myself (Bowden, 2009) that civilization is a significant concept in world history and international affairs. However, when we consider that Eurocentrism entails the privileging of Europe (or the West) over other parts of the world, then this statement itself might be considered an example of Eurocentrism. How so? The idea that civilization and everything that it entails is uniquely Western suggests that those attributes do not apply to rest of the world, that the non-Western world represents something other than civilization, perhaps its antitheses – barbarism or savagery. Furthermore, it overlooks the fact that Ibn Khaldûn's (1332–1406) *Muqaddimah* of 1377, an Islamic history of the world, includes concepts very similar to civilization. As stated in the text, 'It deals with such conditions affecting the nature of civilization as, for instance, savagery and sociability, group feelings, and the different ways by which one group of human beings achieves superiority over another' (Ibn Khaldûn, 2005: 35). This sounds very much like the Western conception of civilization.

This is not the only example of the close links between Eurocentrism and civilization, particularly in international history and international relations. As will be explained, the ideas and ideals of civilization, progress, and universal history, which are closely related with similar intellectual heritage, by their very nature are deeply enmeshed in discourses that many would identify as Eurocentric. In exploring these close links further, this chapter first discusses the idea of Eurocentrism in a little more detail and then takes a closer look at the concept of civilization and the associated idea of universal history.

Eurocentrism

At the heart of Eurocentrism is a view of the world – sometimes implied, sometimes explicit – that situates European (particularly Western Europe) culture, history, and values as the universal norm (Herborth and Nitzschner, 2021 in this volume). Not only are they the norm to which other Peoples' culture, history, and values are compared and judged (and usually deemed inferior), but also they are the culture, history, and values that are assumed to be appropriate and aspirational for all Peoples. With this in mind, Eurocentrism is inherently related to the West's Orientalist tendencies in defining and depicting the 'exotic East,' as identified by Edward Said (1978), both of which are in turn related to the broader European imperial enterprise, which is in part underpinned by the ideas of civilization and universal history.

Coming to prominence as a term in the 1920s, the essence of Eurocentrism was captured by Oswald Spengler (1962: 13) just prior to the First World War:

> The Western European area is regarded as a fixed pole, a unique patch chosen on the surface of the sphere for no better reason, it seems, than because we live on it – and great histories of millennial duration and mighty faraway Cultures are made to revolve around this pole in all modesty. It is a quaintly conceived system of sun and planets! We select a single bit of ground as the natural centre of the historical system, and make it the central sun. From it all the events of history receive their real light; from it their importance is judged in *perspective.*

Spengler's observations came just as the second wave of European imperial expansion (Hobsbawm, 1989) was drawing to a close on the eve of the Great War. He went on to argue that for Europe and the West the 'existence of Athens, Florence or Paris is more important than that of Lyang or Pataliputra.' That is not the case for the rest of the world, however, so 'is it permissible to found a scheme of world-history on estimates of such a sort?' He thought not; for if 'so, then the Chinese historian is quite entitled to frame a world-history in which the Crusades, the Renaissance, Caesar and Frederick the Great are passed over in silence' (Spengler, 1962: 13).

Eurocentrism is inherently related to Western ideas of civilization, progress, and teleological or universal history and comes about, in part, because of the way in which we understand history. Eric Wolf (1982: 5) makes the point that many of us 'have been taught, inside the classroom and outside of it, that there exists an entity called the West, and that one can think of this West as a society and civilisation independent of and in opposition to other societies and civilisations.' He goes on to explain how many have grown up 'believing that this West has a genealogy, according to which ancient Greece begat Rome, Rome begat Christian Europe, Christian Europe begat the Renaissance, the Renaissance the Enlightenment, the Enlightenment political democracy and the industrial revolution.' In the most recent stage of this narrative, industry is 'crossed with democracy,' which gives us 'the United States, embodying the rights to life, liberty, and the pursuit of happiness' (Wolf, 1982: 5).

It is not too hard to understand how such thinking has become commonplace when considering that one of the major – and still most studied – thinkers of the Enlightenment, Immanuel Kant (1724–1804), essentially argued as much. Kant (1963: 24–25) wrote,

> If one follows the influence of Greek history on the construction of and misconstruction of the Roman state which swallowed up the Greek, then the Roman influence on the barbarians who in turn destroyed it, and so on down to our own times; if one adds episodes from the national histories of other peoples insofar as they are known from the history of the enlightened nations, one will discover a regular progress in the constitution of states on our continent [Europe] (which will probably give law, eventually, to all others).

Isaiah Berlin (1991: 9) is quite blunt in stating that there 'is no ladder of ascent from the ancients to the moderns.' Berlin goes on to highlight the dangers associated with the bloody-minded 'pursuit of the ideal,' while Wolf (1982: 5) similarly notes how such a narrow understanding of the genealogy of the Western tradition is misleading and potentially dangerous in the wrong hands or minds. In effect, this evolutionary schema renders history as a sort of 'moral success story,' a proverbial race through time in which successive runners pass on the torch of progress and liberty (see Roberts, 1985; Stark, 2014). History becomes a story 'about the furtherance of virtue, about how the virtuous win out over the bad guys.' Moreover, quite often it turns out that the 'winners prove that they are virtuous and good' merely by winning. If, then, history is understood as the 'working out of a moral purpose in time, then those who lay claim to that purpose are by that fact the predilect agents of history' (Wolf, 1982: 5). In short, Western Europe is conceived of as at the vanguard of civilization, a driver of progress and shaper of history, largely because it believes and says so.

Eurocentric accounts of history have long had a tendency to sideline the rest of the solar system. George Hegel (1770–1831) (1956: 87), for instance, insisted that the 'Old World [is] the scene of the World's History.' In discussing the peoples of India, he (1956: 162) argued that the only people 'capable of History' are those who 'comprehend their own existence as independent, *i.e.* possess self-consciousness.' This did not apply to the peoples of India, for instance, who are 'incapable of writing History.' Hegel (1956: 163) went on to insist that it is 'because the Hindoos have no History in the form of annals (historia) that they have no History in the form of transactions (res gestæ); that is, no growth expanding into a veritable political condition.' The question for Hegel (1958: 213, para. 331), and he is not alone here, 'is how far a nomadic people … or any people on a low level of civilization, can be regarded as a state.'

As Ranajit Guha (2002: 9) explains, for Hegel, a 'people or a nation lacked history … not because it knew no writing but because lacking as it did in statehood it had nothing to write about.' With such thinking in mind, the British took it upon themselves to compile such uneven accounts of India's history as that which was prepared by James Mill and published as *The History of British India* in 1817. Despite never having visited India, Mill's *History*, an attack on William Robertson's *Historical Disquisition* of 1791, relayed to European audiences an equally mistaken image of Indian civilization as eternally backward and undeveloped. Such thinking persisted well into the twentieth century as evidenced by Ferdinand Schiller's (1926: vii) claim, 'The peoples of India appear to care very little for history and have never troubled to compile it.'

The Eurocentric thinking underpinning such positions is highlighted by Said (1978: 31–33) in a discussion of Arthur Balfour's speech to the British House of Commons of 13 June 1910 in which he insisted, 'We know the civilization of Egypt better than we know the civilization of any other country. We know it farther back; we know it more intimately; we know more about it.' By Balfour's reckoning, as with India and elsewhere, the well-being of Egypt and its people was best entrusted to the hands of the British. He continued, 'Western nations as soon as they emerge into history show the beginnings of those capacities for self-government.' But beyond Europe,

> one may look through the whole history of the Orientals … and you never find traces of self-government … Conqueror has succeeded conqueror; one domination has followed another; but never in all the revolutions of fate and fortune have you seen one of those nations of its own motion establish what we, from a Western point of view, call self-government. That is the fact.

As outlined in the following section on civilization, the capacity for self-government, European or Western-style self-government, is widely seen as a cornerstone of civilization.

Civilization

Civilization refers to both a process and a destination. Much as Ibn Khaldûn describes, it represents the process of a social collective becoming civilized, or progressing from a state of nature, savagery, or barbarism to a state of civilization. It describes a state of human society marked by significant urbanization, social and professional stratification, the luxury of leisure time, and corresponding advancements in the arts and sciences. The capacity for reasonably complex sociopolitical organization and self-government according to prevailing standards, European or Western standards, has long been thought of as a central requirement of civilization.

This, in essence, describes the function of the standard of civilization. The standard was a means used in international law to distinguish between civilized and uncivilized peoples to determine membership in the European international society of states. The concept entered international legal texts and practice in the eighteenth and nineteenth centuries under the influence of anthropologists and ethnologists who drew hierarchical distinctions between civilized, barbarian, and savage peoples based on their respective capacities for social cooperation and organization. Operating primarily during the European colonial period, the standard of civilization set the benchmark for the ascent of non-European states to the ranks of the civilized 'Family of Nations.' A civilized state required (1) basic institutions of government and public bureaucracy, (2) the organizational capacity for self-defence, (3) a published legal code and adherence to the rule of law, (4) the capacity to honour contracts in commerce and capital exchange, and (5) recognition of international law and norms, including the laws of war (Gong, 1984; Bowden, 2004, 2009; Vergerio, 2021). The treatment and role of women in society is another important marker (Towns, 2009, 2021). If a nation could meet these requirements, it was generally deemed a legitimate sovereign state, entitled to recognition as an international personality.

The inability of many non-European societies to meet these European criteria, and the concomitant legal distinction that separated them from civilized societies, led to the unequal treaty system of capitulations. The right of extraterritoriality, as it was also known, regulated relations between sovereign civilized states and quasi-sovereign uncivilized states in regard to their respective rights over, and obligations to, the citizens of civilized states living and operating in countries where capitulations were in force. As the Italian jurist Pasquale Fiore (1918: 362) explained, in 'principle, Capitulations are derogatory to the local "common" law; they are based on the inferior state of civilization of certain states of Africa, Asia and other barbarous regions, which makes it impracticable to exercise sovereign rights mutually and reciprocally with perfect equality of legal condition.' In much of the non-European world, this system of capitulations incrementally escalated to the point that it became large-scale European civilizing missions, which in turn became colonialism.

There is widespread agreement in the Western world that civilization is a good thing, or at least that it is better than the alternatives: barbarism, savagery, or a state of nature of some sort. In theory, as time passes and the further we get away from the Big Bang and the primordial soup, the more we progress both as a species and as individual human beings; the more we progress, the more civilized we become individually and collectively; the more civilized we become, the further we are removed from the vestiges of savagery and barbarism. In fact, for many in the West, civilization, progress, and modernity are by definition good things (e.g. Stark, 2014). Samuel Huntington (1998: 40) summarized the state of debate rather succinctly: 'To be civilized was good, to be uncivilized was bad.'

As with many debates, however, rarely are things so clearly black or white; there are usually many more shades of grey. For instance, in stark contrast to the rosy picture of civilization and modernity suggested above, Zygmunt Bauman (2001: 4–6) alarmingly suggests that the

Holocaust was not so much 'a temporary suspension of the civilizational grip in which human behaviour is normally held,' but a '"paradigm" of modern civilization' and modernity. This is not necessarily to suggest that civilization is 'bad' or not worth having or being a part of; it is just to highlight that along with the upsides there are some potential downsides, even a 'dark side' (Alexander, 2013).

Returning to the specifics of what civilization means, R.G. Collingwood (1992: 502–511) has outlined three distinct aspects: economic, social, and legal. Economic civilization is marked not simply by the pursuit of riches, which might be inimical to economic civilization, but by 'the civilized pursuit of wealth.' The realm of social civilization is the forum in which humankind's sociability is satisfied by 'the idea of joint action,' or what we might call community. The final mark of civilization is 'a society governed by law,' and not so much by criminal law as by civil law, 'the law in which claims are adjusted between its members.' For Collingwood (1992: 283), 'Civilization is *something which happens to a community*. … Civilization is a *process of approximation to an ideal state*.' Of course, during the various phases of European expansion, that ideal state has been represented by the great powers of Europe. In essence, Collingwood is arguing that civilized society is guided by and operates according to the principles of the rule of law.

Not too far removed from Collingwood's concern with the elimination of physical and moral force via social civilization are accounts of civilized society concerned with the management of violence, if only by removing it from the public sphere. Such a concern is extended in Bauman's account of civilization to the more general issue of producing readily governable subjects. The 'concept of *civilization*,' he argues, 'entered learned discourse in the West as the name of a conscious proselytising crusade waged by men of knowledge and aimed at extirpating the vestiges of wild cultures' (Bauman, 1987: 93). That is, the civilizing missions conducted by Europe's expansionist powers, particularly from the sixteenth century on.

This proselytizing crusade in the name of civilization is significant here, particularly when considering Jean Starobinski's (1993: 31) assertion that, 'taken as a value, civilization constitutes a political and moral norm. It is the criterion against which barbarity, or non-civilization, is judged and condemned.' As Spengler highlighted, in the Eurocentric view of the world, Europe is synonymous with civilization and is therefore the benchmark against which the rest of the world is measured and judged. A similar sort of argument is made by Anthony Pagden (1988: 33), who states that civilization 'describes a state, social, political, cultural, aesthetic – even moral and physical – which is held to be the optimum condition for all mankind, and this involves the implicit claim that only the civilized can know what it is to be civilized.' It is out of this implicit claim and the Eurocentric judgements passed in its name that the notion of the 'burden of civilization' was born.

The claim that only the civilized know what it means to be civilized is an important one, for as Starobinski (1993: 32) notes, the 'historical moment in which the word *civilization* appears marks the advent of self-reflection, the emergence of a consciousness that thinks it understands the nature of its own activity.' More specifically, it marks 'the moment that Western civilization becomes aware of itself reflectively, it sees itself as one civilization among others. Having achieved self-consciousness, civilization immediately discovers civilizations.' But as Norbert Elias (2000: 5) highlights, it is not a case of Western civilization being just one among equals, for the very concept of civilization 'expresses the self-consciousness of the West.' Moreover, 'it sums up everything in which Western society of the last two or three centuries believes itself superior to earlier societies or "more primitive" contemporary ones.' Elias further explains that in using the term civilization, 'Western society seeks to describe what constitutes its special character and what it is proud of: the level of *its* technology, the nature of *its* manners, the development of *its* scientific knowledge or view of the world, and much more' (e.g. Hanson, 2002; Murray, 2003; Morris, 2010).

Significant here is that the West is widely seen as maintaining its lofty position at the vanguard of progress and civilization. This view of the West as largely insular, self-sufficient, and boldly forging the way ahead on the path of progress and virtue is described by, among others, Robert Nisbet (1980: 8) in his work on the idea of progress. He states, 'the history of all that is greatest in the West,' such as 'religion, science, reason, freedom, equality, justice, philosophy, the arts, and so on – is grounded deeply in the belief that what one does in one's own time is at once tribute to the greatness and indispensability of the past, and confidence in an ever more golden future.' As noted above, an issue here is not only the denial of the value and achievements of other civilizations or cultures, but also the implication that they are largely stagnant; out of which comes the further implication that if anything of value is to be retrieved, it cannot be done without the assistance of a more civilized tutor.

Universal history

Eurocentrism and civilization come together in the idea of universal history (Schiller, 1972 [1789]). Universal history is an idea that remains central to the Western tradition of studying and theorizing about history, progress, civilization, and human perfectibility (Bowden, 2017). It is an all-encompassing version of history that seeks to explain and document the history of humankind as a single coherent unit of study. It is about fitting all peoples and places into the narrative of history, which means placing them somewhere on a continuum between the poles of state of nature and civilized modernity. At the same time, it means knowing that all will ultimately arrive at the same end: civilization, or Western modernity. Despite the critics of universal history and historicism more generally, as Georg Iggers (1982: 43–44; 2012) highlights, 'central to the emerging philosophies of progress' and history from the eighteenth century 'is the conception of the unity of man's history. This involves the conception that civilization is one and universal, that in the place of a variety of separate histories, there emerges one world history.' And yet, the history of humankind as sketched by the philosophes of the Enlightenment 'seldom turns out to be universal history in a true sense.' Rather, Western Europe is seen as 'the vanguard of civilization. The history of mankind thus becomes identical with the history of Western civilization' (Iggers, 1982: 44). In this form of universal history, 'the history of the West becomes ultimately the history of the non-West, as the West extends its hegemony over the world' (Iggers, 1982: 59). In essence, theorists of universal history contend that the non-Western 'world will find the completion of its historical development not in the further development of its own heritage but, because its heritage represents an earlier phase in the progress of mankind, in total Europeanization' or Westernization (Iggers, 1982: 53). The notion that all peoples are destined to travel the same path through history and arrive at the same place is precisely what is so troubling about the idea of universal history. It is the essence of its Eurocentricity.

Trends in IR

Eurocentrism, the privileging of Europe and European perspectives over those of other parts of the world, has been identified and called out by many (e.g. Grovogui, 2006; Hobson, 2012; Martin, 2013), particularly in the postcolonial era and by postcolonial thinkers. However, Eurocentrism is not just a relic of the past; it persists, sometimes implicitly or subconsciously, sometimes explicitly and proudly. In fact, it is probably fair to suggest that the twenty-first century has seen a reinvigoration of views and biases in the Western world about the historical and contemporary significance and importance of Western civilization. In line with this trend, the past couple of decades have also seen calls for the revival of standards of civilization, including standards of human rights and democracy, and standards of economic globalization and liberalization (Franck, 1992; Donnelly, 1998; Fidler, 2000; Mozaffari, 2001). As in the past, these standards are Western standards. Moreover, despite various attempts to 'decolonize' the discipline of International Relations (Capan, 2017), some of the obstacles are said to be both the fundamental building blocks of the states-system and the system itself, such that the 'Westphalian narrative perpetuates a Eurocentric bias in international relations theory' (Kayaoglu, 2010). Thus, Eurocentrism remains a challenge for the discipline, but it can no longer be glossed over as it once was.

Conclusion

The aim of this chapter has been to discuss two concepts – Eurocentrism and civilization – and how they relate to one and other, particularly in the context of international relations from the eighteenth century on. The revival of civilizational analysis and the Eurocentrism that accompanies it has a number of causes or drivers and manifests in a range of different manners. Some of the causes are as much about perceptions as realities: the idea that Western civilization is under threat, from both internal and external forces, such as large-scale immigration and the spread of multiculturalism. Outcomes have included the rise in support of anti-immigrant, nationalist, and populist political movements and parties in many countries, and not just the West. The Brexit vote in the United Kingdom and the election of Donald Trump in the United States are not unrelated. In academe, heated debates have emerged about the teaching of Western civilization (the 'great books' and thinkers), including how or even if it should be taught.

These are all issues that have a long way to go before they are fully played out, if that is even possible given the level and intensity of disagreement. What has been demonstrated herein is that the concept of civilization, widely recognized as being synonymous with Western Europe, particularly from the eighteenth century on, and then the West more generally, is in effect an example of Eurocentrism at work in that it is used to measure and judge different Peoples and cultures by European or Western standards. In short, the concept of civilization is inherently Eurocentric.

Suggestions for further reading

Amin, S. (2009). *Eurocentrism: Modernity, Religion, and Democracy*. Translated by R. Moore, and J. Membrez. 2nd edition. New York, NY: Monthly Review Press.

Bernal, M. (1987). *Black Athena*. London: Free Association Books.

Blaut, J. (2000). *Eight Eurocentric Historians*. New York, NY: The Guilford Press.

Bowden, B. (2009). *The Empire of Civilization: The Evolution of an Imperial Idea*. Chicago and London: University of Chicago Press.

Chakrabarty, D. (2000). Provincializing Europe. In *Postcolonial Thought and Historical Difference*. Princeton, NJ: Princeton University Press.

Hobson, J. (2012). *The Eurocentric Conception of World Politics: Western International Theory, 1760–2010*. Cambridge: Cambridge University Press.

Said, E. (1978). *Orientalism*. London: Routledge & Kegan Paul.

References

Alexander, J. (2013). *The Dark Side of Modernity*. Cambridge, UK, and Malden, MA: Polity.

Bauman, Z. (1987). *Legislators and Interpreters: On Modernity, Post-Modernity and Intellectuals*. Ithaca, NY: Cornell University Press.

Bauman, Z. (2001). *Modernity and the Holocaust*. Ithaca, NY: Cornell University Press.

Benveniste, E. (1971). Civilization: A Contribution to the History of the Word. In *Problems in General Linguistics*. Translated by M. Meek. Coral Gables, FL: University of Miami Press, 289–313.

Berlin, I. (1991). *The Crooked Timber of Humanity*. London: Fontana.

Bowden, B. (2004). In the name of progress and peace: the 'standard of civilization' and the universalizing project. *Alternatives: Global, Local, Political*, 29 (1), 43–68.

Bowden, B. (2017). *The Strange Persistence of Universal History in Political Thought*. New York, NY: Palgrave Macmillan.

Capan, Z. (2017). Decolonising international relations? *Third World Quarterly*, 38 (1), 1–15.

Collingwood, R. (1992). *The New Leviathan*. Edited by D. Boucher. Oxford: Clarendon Press.

Donnelly, J. (1998). Human rights: a new standard of civilization. *International Affairs*, 74 (1), 1–24.

Elias, N. (2000). *The Civilising Process*. Revised edition. Translated by E. Jephcott. Oxford: Blackwell.

Fidler, D. (2000). A kinder, gentler system of capitulations? International law, structural adjustment policies, and the standard of liberal, globalized civilization. *Texas International Law Journal*, 35 (3), 387–413.

Fiore, P. (1918). *International Law Codified and Its Legal Sanction*. New York, NY: Baker, Voorhis and Company.

Franck, T. (1992). The emerging right to democratic governance. *American Journal of International Law*, 86 (1), 46–91.

Gong, G. (1984). *Standard of 'Civilization' in International Society*. Oxford: Clarendon Press.

Grovogui, S. (2006). *Beyond Eurocentrism and Anarchy: Memories of International Order and Institutions*. New York, NY: Palgrave Macmillan.

Guha, R. (2002). *History at the Limit of World-History*. New York, NY: Columbia University Press.

Hanson, V. (2002). *Why the West Has Won: Carnage and Culture from Salamis to Vietnam*. London: Faber and Faber.

Hegel, G. (1956). *The Philosophy of History*. Translated by J. Sibree. New York, NY: Dover Publications.

Hegel, G. (1958). *Philosophy of Right*. Translated by T. M. Knox. Oxford: Clarendon Press.

Herborth, B., and Nitzschner, P. (2021). Europe in Historical International Relations. In de Carvalho, B., Costa Lopez, J., & Leira, H., eds. *Routledge Handbook of Historical International Relations*. Abingdon: Routledge.

Hobsbawm, E. (1989). *The Age of Empire 1875—1914*. New York, NY: Vintage.

Huntington, S. (1998). *The Clash of Civilisations and the Remaking of World Order*. London: Touchstone Books.

Iggers, G. (1982). The Idea of Progress in Historiography and Social Thought Since the Enlightenment. In: G. Almond, M. Chodorow, and R. Pearce, eds., *Progress and its Discontents*, Berkeley, CA: University of California Press, 41–66.

Kant, I. (1963). Idea for a Universal History from a Cosmopolitan Point of View. In: L. Beck, ed., *On History*, Indianapolis, IN: Bobbs-Merrill, 11–26.

Kayaoglu, T. (2010). Westphalian Eurocentrism in international relations theory. *International Studies Review*, 12 (2), 193–217.

Khaldûn, I. (2005). *The Muqaddimah: An Introduction to History*. Edited by N. Dawood. Translated by F. Rosenthal. Princeton, NJ: Princeton University Press.

Martin, K. (2013). Redeeming the universal: Postcolonialism and the inner life of Eurocentrism. *European Journal of International Relations*, 19 (2), 353–377.

Morris, I. (2010). *Why the West Rules—For Now: The Patterns of History, and What They Reveal About the Future*. New York, NY: Farrar, Straus and Giroux.

Mozaffari, M. (2001). The transformationalist perspective and the rise of a global standard of civilization. *International Relations of the Asia-Pacific*, 1 (2), 247–264.

Murray, C. (2003). *Human Accomplishment: The Pursuit of Excellence in the Arts and Sciences, 800 BC to 1950*. New York, NY: Harper Collins.

Nisbet, R. (1980). *History of the Idea of Progress*, London: Heinemann.

Pagden, A. (1988). The 'defence of civilization' in eighteenth-century social theory. *History of the Human Sciences*, 1 (1), 33–45.

Roberts, J. (1985). *Triumph of the West*. London: British Broadcasting Corporation.

Schiller, F. (1926). Introduction. In: E. Goddard, and P. Gibbons, eds., *Civilisation or Civilisations: An Essay in the Spenglerian Philosophy of History*, London: Constable & Company, vii–xvi.

Schiller, F. von. (1972 [1789]). The nature and value of universal history: an inaugural lecture. *History and Theory*, 11 (3), 321–334.

Spengler, O. (1962). *The Decline of the West*. Translated by C. Atkinson. New York, NY: Alfred A. Knopf.

Stark, R. (2014). *How the West Won: The Neglected Story of the Triumph of Modernity*. Wilmington, DE: Intercollegiate Studies Institute.

Starobinski, J. (1993). *Blessings in Disguise; or The Morality of Evil.* Translated by A. Goldhammer. Cambridge, MA: Harvard University Press.

Towns, A. (2009). The status of women as a standard of 'civilization'. *European Journal of International Relations*, 15 (4), 681–706.

Towns, A. (2021). Gender in Historical International Relations. In de Carvalho, B., Costa Lopez, J., & Leira, H., eds. *Routledge Handbook of Historical International Relations.* Abingdon: Routledge.

Vergerio, C. (2021). International Law and the Laws of War. In de Carvalho, B., Costa Lopez, J., & Leira, H., eds. *Routledge Handbook of Historical International Relations.* Abingdon: Routledge.

Wolf, E. (1982). *Europe and the People Without History.* Berkeley, Los Angeles and London: University of California Press.

16

DISCIPLINARY HISTORIES OF NON-ANGLOPHONE INTERNATIONAL RELATIONS

Latin American and the Caribbean

Melody Fonseca Santos

Introduction

While different authors have focused on revisiting and problematizing the foundational myths of the International Relations (IR) discipline, its 'linearity' and 'expansion' from Europe and the United States towards the 'rest' (de Carvalho et al., 2011; Ashworth, 2019), including pointing out the imperial origins of the discipline and the centrality of colonialism and race in its development (Anievas et al., 2016; Persaud and Sajed, 2018; Schmidt, 2019; see Yao and Delatolla, 2021), non-Anglophone and non-Western scholarships remain excluded from the discipline. Rather than contingent exclusionary practices, the dynamics that have marginalized these scholarships in the discipline's history are entangled to a broader issue: the geopolitics of knowledge.

As Walter Mignolo stated, the '"history" of knowledge is marked geo-historically and has a value and a place of "origin." Knowledge is not abstract, nor de-localized' (2003: 4). The geopolitics of knowledge places subjects and knowledge in power relations, which, in turn, reflects the relationship between their states—metropolis and colonies; centre, semi-periphery, and periphery—in the global order. The Eurocentrism and Anglocentrism of the discipline's historical narrative assume that it emerges in the West and 'expands' to other territories where it is welcomed without resistance and, even today, with very few modifications (see Herborth and Nitzschner, 2021 in this volume). However, the geopolitics of knowledge has been anything but linear. It involves various issues that complicate its analysis: the epistemic violence of the North-South/Centre-Semi-Periphery-Periphery transfer of knowledge sustained by the epistemicides of modernity/coloniality, globalization, and neoliberalism's repercussions on the marginalization of various groups within the Global North that relocate them to a sort of epistemic Global South, and Anglocentrism as a double force implying the centrality of British and American scholarships and their forms of knowledge production. All of the above is accentuated by English's predominance and the impossibility of translation and intelligibility beyond it.

Likewise, the consequences of disciplinary mythologies on the recognition of IR beyond Western and Anglo-Saxon scholarship, since they constitute not only the self's narrative but also the other's in a co-constitutive relation, has lacked attention. As Duncan Bell points out regarding disciplinary mythologies: 'Engines of identity construction, they help to mark and police the boundaries of disciplines, as well as shaping the self-understandings of scholars' (2009: 5). The marking and policing of boundaries have been detrimental for recognizing non-Anglophone scholarship, mainly when it draws from interdisciplinary approaches.

In order to outline a critical history of the IR discipline in a non-Anglophone context, this chapter examines the origins and development of the discipline and its main theoretical approaches in Latin America and the Caribbean. It discusses the region's most relevant theoretical contributions, such as dependency theory, peripheral realism, and decolonial thinking. As I will argue, these theoretical approaches are examples of an entangled body of knowledge that mainly rests on interdisciplinarity. Finally, I conclude by considering the challenges that must be approached to overcome the Anglocentric geopolitics of knowledge.

Origins and development of the IR discipline in Latin America and the Caribbean

Latin America and the Caribbean in the IR discipline are marked by the region's positionality in the modern colonial world/system (see Schulz, 2021). From the centre's perspective, the region is peripheral. One of the first Latin American IR scholars, Gustavo Lagos, noticed this imaginary when he highlighted that the region was part of what the world considered underdeveloped while at the same time being the only underdeveloped region also considered Western (1980: 248). This awareness motivated developing a homegrown Latin American thought: thinking the international from 'our own perspectives' (Bernal-Meza, 2018: 76).

The delinking of Latin American and the Caribbean from the centre, together with the discipline's Eurocentrism, Anglocentrism, and English's primacy, has enabled dispute around the region's theoretical production. As Briceño Ruiz and Simonoff propose, Latin American theories are disputed—when not invisibilized or denied—by the centre sustained on two premises: they are not positivist theories that can be extrapolated and empirically demonstrable and, secondly, they do not address international issues, as have previously been defined and established by the centre (2017: 51). The Global North's academic denial of Latin American and Caribbean theoretical production also fractures the possibilities of understanding Latin American contributions from their own reality: the region thinks and produces knowledge and theory from a practical positionality (Tickner, 2008).

In his work, Lagos called for a critical revision of the dominant theories from and for Latin America (1980: 250). An example of these homegrown theories is autonomy theory (Simonoff and Lorenzini, 2019; Colacrai, 2019: 122), which emerged from the 1970s as a Latin American attempt to claim a place in the global order. Tickner (2003) understands this proper and genuine way of thinking from Latin America as a bridge between dependency theory and the dominant theories of the time: realism and interdependence. However, as a theory emerging from Latin American practice, this vision of IR has only been considered as a regional doctrine by the centre.

The post–Second World War period brought the institutionalization of IR and the creation of regional institutions such as the Economic Commission for Latin America and the Caribbean (ECLAC, former ECLA), which became a fundamental pillar in the IR discipline's origins and evolution in the region. At the centre of the ECLAC, Raúl Prebisch introduced dependency theory, demonstrating that the discipline's early developments took place at regional institutions. It is quite relevant that the two primary sources for the discipline's origins were History and International Law, mainly because the first Latin American and Caribbean IR scholars were also diplomats. This characteristic underpinned how the discipline was implemented in the region.

Mexico's experience in its development of international policy is arguably linked to its diplomatic relations with the United States. These relations have informed Mexico's institutionalization of the discipline in such a way that the first centre for international studies, founded in 1940 and formerly known as Mexico City College, was a private American centre created to train diplomats to specialize in Latin American affairs. In 1951, the National Autonomous University of Mexico (UNAM) offered the first Diplomatic Sciences career. In 1960, the Center for International Studies of the Colegio de México was founded, and in 1974, the Matías Romero Institute was created as an initiative of the Ministry of Foreign Affairs (Covarrubias, 2019: 132–133).

The discipline's development through the creation of educational centres, diplomatic careers, and regional institutions was common in the rest of the region. In Brazil, the Superior Institute of Brazilian Studies was created in 1955, with the prominent role of the leading Brazilian IR scholar, Helio Jaguaribe (Fonseca and Uziel, 2019). Similarly, in 1966, the Institute of International Studies of the University of Chile was founded, and a few years later, Gustavo Lagos occupied the first IR chair (Heine and Aguirre, 2019: 171–172). In Argentina, a similar process is observed with the diplomat Juan Carlos Puig's and the discipline's institutionalization through his chair at the Universidad Nacional del Litoral (Colacrai, 2019). Lastly, the establishment of various academic headquarters of the Latin American Faculty of Social Sciences (FLACSO), firstly in Chile, followed by Argentina, Brasil, Costa Rica, Ecuador, Guatemala, México, and Paraguay, with programmes running in Cuba and the Dominican Republic (among other countries), serving as a significant guide for the consolidation of the discipline in Latin America and the Caribbean. In the Hispanic Caribbean, it is crucial to highlight Cuba's School of Foreign Service, founded in 1960 after the Cuban Revolution, and that served as a precedent for the Instituto Superior de Relaciones Internacionales Raúl Rao García. Besides FLACSO's programmes, the Dominican Republic has different graduate programmes in collaboration with foreign institutions, while in Puerto Rico, the Center for Advanced Studies of Puerto Rico and the Caribbean created the first Master's Program in International Relations and Diplomacy in 2017.

By the end of the Cold War, IR scholars' primary concern—both for mainstream and critical authors—was the need to comprehend how the 'new' international order would be defined (see Kwon, 2021). In Latin America and the Caribbean, the bipolar system's breakdown also involved a series of changes and crises that led studies on the global, regional, and local. However, it is crucial to keep in mind that the region's histories, although converging with those of the Global North, have their own characteristics. The post–Cold War era arrived in a region transitioning in various ways towards democracy.

It is essential to mention the consequences of military dictatorships in the region's intellectual development. Critical scholars from different social sciences disciplines either turn to leftist praxis and political engagement opposing these regimes or are exiled because of intense repression. Those who returned to their countries of origin often brought a perspective of analysis merged (appropriating or debating briefly) with the centre's theories. While transitional justice, Human Rights policies, and the politics of memory became a symbol of the region's intellectual identity in the post-dictatorial era, it reinforced the idea of theorization as a practical approach due to the necessity to develop a course of action for transitions to democracy.

The second wave of neoliberalism also brought the Washington Consensus and the ascription to liberal democracy and free markets mandates expressed in the North American Free Trade Agreement and the Dominican Republic-Central America Free Trade Agreement. Parallel to this, the 1990s brought a wave of resistance marked by the symbolism of 1992 (the Fifth Centenary of arrival of Columbus), and the violence it represents in the collective imaginary of Latin America and the Caribbean. Various publications emerged from other disciplines shaping what later will be understood as decolonial thinking (see below). Alternatively, the Zapatista uprising of January 1, 1994, was the time/space to rethink what international relations imply for the region. Their demands against neoliberal globalization, racism, epistemicide, and the violence of land dispossession embodied in the First Declaration of the Selva Lacandona determined a before and after in the regions' critical theorization of the local/global.

Theoretical contributions to the discipline: dependency theory, peripheral realism, decolonial thinking

Currently, IR scholarship in Latin America and the Caribbean has been challenged by the historical, epistemic, and ontological turns, which are revisiting and re-centralizing knowledge practices and methodologies from the 'margins'—as Latin American and Caribbean *saberes: mestizos, criollos*, as well as indigenous and Afro-Latin Americans perspectives (Lao-Montes, 2004; Rivera Cusicanqui, 2015; Scauso, 2016; Quick Hall, 2019). As diverse as the region, these approaches and theories are framed within a broad theoretical gaze—that includes Westernized mainstream theory, critical theory, decolonial thinking, or even surpassing these frames and embedding themselves in epistemic and ontological experiences beyond disciplinary boundaries. In this section, I delve into three different theoretical contributions, including dependency theory as Latin America's main contribution to IR, Carlos Escudé's peripheral realism as an original contribution to understanding mainstream foreign policy perspectives in the region, and finally, the contributions of the Latin American and Caribbean modernity/coloniality/decoloniality group to the IR discipline.

Dependency theory

In 1949, the Argentinian economist Raúl Prebisch published the Spanish version of 'The economic development of Latin America and its principal problems.' Considered as a 'Manifesto' (Guillén, 2007: 124; Kay, 2009: 159), it established the basis for the structuralist approach that would dominate ECLAC's reports and policies towards the region. Prebisch, Celso Furtado, Aníbal Pinto, Osvaldo Sunkel, Juan Noyola, and Victor Urquidi, among others, were known as the Latin American Structuralist Development School.

Prebisch's structuralist approach forged two main paradigms. Firstly, centre-periphery paradigm, as Cristobal Kay suggests, '[establishes] that the world economy is composed of a small number of core industrialized countries, [...] labelled as the "center," and a large number of weaker non-industrialized countries, [...] labelled as the "periphery." While the center exported industrial commodities to the periphery, the latter exported primary commodities such as tropical agricultural products and mineral products to the former' (2009: 161). Secondly, dependency theory, which 'argues that the structure of the global political economy essentially enslaves the less developed countries of the South by making them reliant to being vulnerable to the nations of the capitalist core of the North' (Balaam and Dillman, 2019: 81). This theory's development was mainly forwarded by Latin American economists, historians, and sociologists, such as Enzo Faletto, Fernando Henrique Cardoso, Aníbal Quijano, and the German-American sociologist and economic historian, Andre Gunder Frank—all of them mainly influenced by Marxist approaches. For Arlene Tickner, 'the diverse authors grouped together under the dependency label seek to explain economic underdevelopment in the periphery as the product of the specific nature of global capitalism, as well as examining the ways in which external dependency has moulded internal processes in ways that reinforce inequality and exclusion' (2003: 327).

Dependency theory introduced within the core of IR institutionalism the idea that the international division of labour not only reproduced inequalities among states, but that its structure, promoting the extraction of resources, labour, and surplus from the periphery to the centre, will prevent any possibilities of development for those at the periphery. It empirically contested modernization theories by demonstrating the impact of unequal commodity values, inflation, and the lack of capital surplus in the periphery as significant obstacles for development. It also opened the gates for a broader critique of dependency from a historical perspective, established since the colonial era and reconfigured throughout the expansion of global, industrial, and financial capitalism. Furthermore, dependency theory facilitated the basis for South-South theorization and research to understand the *longue durée* process of colonization and its material impact in the Global South. An example of this is Walter Rodney's *How Europe Underdeveloped Africa* (1972).

Although highly popular among critical scholarship in Latin America, the Caribbean, and the United States, dependency theory also received substantial criticism. Its critiques mainly emerged from the same authors developing the theory and their different approaches to whether or not the unequal capitalist system could be reformed and thus facilitate underdeveloped nations' development. On the other hand, other authors understood dependency as deeply rooted in the capitalist order; thus, it would only be overcome if capitalist society was dismantled. Another critique was its determinism, as it did not account for the conditions that created dependency in the first instance.

In recent years, a more comprehensive analysis of the practices of extractivism and neo-extractivism in the region has reflected the influence of the dependency theory perspective. Extractivism has been studied as the leading force shaping the region's positionality within the global political and economic order throughout the modern/colonial system, and as the dispositif that strengthens the unequal exchange of commodities and values in the global market. Neo-extractivism posits the complexity of how developmental policies led by progressive governments are also entangled to the extraction of resources, displacement of communities, and strengthening dependency relations with 'new' global powers such as China. The structural problem of land possession/dispossession still determines the unequal and dependent relations between land-owners (elite families and foreign corporations), farmers, indigenous, and marginalized communities within Latin American and Caribbean societies. It also reproduces dependency on the global commodities market and foreign capital investment.

Dependency theory is probably the most globally recognized Latin American theory. Despite its detractors—particularly after the end of the Cold War and the backlash of structuralist/neo-Marxist approaches—it has regained popularity in recent years due to the material turn and decolonial approaches to International Political Economy (Kapoor, 2002; Tausch, 2010).

Peripheral realism

Although the end of the Cold War re-centralized analysis around the liberal international order's characteristics and the role of the hegemonic powers in it, peripheral states' role in this order was largely overlooked. An exception can be found in the theory of peripheral realism developed by Carlos Escudé. This theory proposes that the international order is divided between states that establish the agenda and give orders, those that follow them, and those that rebel against the orders (Escudé, 1992). Escudé considers that states at the periphery should assume their role as peripheral states and follow the hegemonic agenda because they do not have the power to dictate or rebel against the agenda as the domestic political cost of resisting against the hegemon would be too high.

Peripheral realism considers the internal conditions and the relationship between account-ability to its citizens and the state's responsibility to provide guarantees, security, and how this limits their chances of rebelling against the established order. By drawing on a comparison of Costa Rican and Argentinian foreign policies, Escudé concludes that a realistic foreign policy from a peripheral country's point of view would allow for vaster stability in its relation with the hegemonic countries, as well as the possibilities of developing much needed domestic policies (Escudé, 1995; Schenoni and Escudé, 2016).

Similarly, neoclassical realism approaches small states' foreign policy considering their neces-sities to create coalitions and pursue regional integration or similar strategies to gain international recognition while maintaining domestic stability. Both theoretical frameworks provide a realist perspective from a peripheral point of view, either by focusing on the state's positionality within the global order or by considering how small and often less well-resourced states have fewer strat-egies to negotiate their place in international relations.

Arguably, peripheral realism does not distance itself from the hegemonic realist interpret-ation of power in which zero-sum games determine state relations. It neither problematizes the consequences of US imperialism and interventionism in the region nor rigorously approaches the need to embrace regional solidarities that will inevitably challenge Washington's agenda. Nevertheless, it is crucial to consider that this is an attempt to develop a realist paradigm from the periphery's perspective; additionally, from the perspective of a periphery marked by the trauma of US interventionism, military dictatorships, and debt crisis—in the past and present—threatening their democratic stability.

Peripheral realism has been recently revisited in light of the growing relations of dependency between China, Latin America, and the Caribbean. This has helped analyse both: these states' foreign policies towards China and Chinese foreign policy in different contexts (Schenoni and Escudé, 2016; Bernal-Meza, 2018).

Decolonial thinking

The Latin American and Caribbean proposal of decolonial thinking emerged from the encounters and collaborative work of the modernity/coloniality/decoloniality group that included scholars Walter Mignolo, Aníbal Quijano, Ramón Grosfoguel, Santiago Castro-Gómez, Catherine Walsh, María Lugones, among others. Delving into different critical theories, paradigms, and discip-lines—world-system theories, postcolonial and subaltern studies, black feminism, linguistics, phil-osophy, sociology, history, and anthropology—these authors argued for historical, epistemic, and ontological turns within the production of knowledge, particularly in the Social Sciences. Their works revisited the contributions of intellectuals such as José Carlos Mariátegui, Felipe Guamán Poma de Ayala, Enrique Dussel, Fernando Coronil, Frantz Fanon, Aimé Césaire, and Sylvia Wynter. As diverse as the region itself, decolonial thinkers provide a wide range of reflections that have only recently been noticed by the IR discipline.

As Ari Jerrems and I have suggested, decolonial thinking 'attempts to go beyond intellectual understandings offered by European philosophy and, in doing so, opens itself to an intercultural democratization of knowledge and a diversification of its sources beyond Western texts' (2012a: 1). Decolonial thinking, beyond a theory, represents a paradigm that results to break from the very epistemic foundations of, in this case, IR.

Among the different theoretical concepts proposed by decolonial thinkers, the most recognized and used in IR is the coloniality of power. The coloniality of power partially detaches coloniality from formal historical colonialism and thus is more adequate to understand the complex pro-cess of continuity and change (Fonseca and Jerrems, 2012a: 4). After Aníbal Quijano coined the concept of coloniality (1992), later developed as coloniality of power (2000), different decolonial authors have proposed new interpretations. Quijano's definition is grounded in world-system theories' structuralism while adding complexity by suggesting that hierarchies of race and culture have been intrinsically intermingled with capitalism since its beginning (Fonseca and Jerrems, 2012a: 4). Quijano states that 'race and the division of labor remained structurally linked and mutually reinforcing' (2000: 533). Ramón Grosfoguel and Santiago Castro-Gómez have problematized Quijano's structuralist perspective by understanding it as a heterarchy of power (2007: 18). Castro-Gómez, delving on Foucauldian analysis of power, understands the coloniality of power as a 'transversal cut,' or '*tejido onírico*' operating in different dispositifs of power (Fonseca and Jerrems, 2012a: 6). According to Castro-Gómez, the coloniality of power is composed of multiple regimes of power that work on at least three levels: microphysical, mesophysical, and macrophysical (Fonseca and Jerrems, 2012b: 115). Microphysical processes occur at the level of bodies and represent disciplinary technologies and the production of subjects. Mesophysical processes work through the control of a population, primarily through the modern Nation-State. Macrophysical processes refer to transnational phenomena such as international security dispositifs (Castro-Gómez, 2007: 163).

Although less explored by IR scholars, other concepts developed by decolonial thinkers are the coloniality of knowledge and the coloniality of being. The coloniality of knowledge is defined as the epistemic violence perpetrated at the 'encounter' with the 'other' (Dussel, 1995), producing what Boaventura de Sousa Santos has called 'epistemicide' (2010) and reproduced throughout the modern/colonial system. The coloniality of knowledge establishes European epistemology's exclusive acknowledgment, cancelling or conditioning non-European knowledge, labelling them as backward.

The coloniality of being is related to modern and colonial subjectivities constituted through modernity/coloniality and it refers to 'the lived experience of colonization and its impact on language' (Maldonado-Torres, 2007: 242), and thus, on the narrative and representation that the colonialized subject receives of himself or herself. The coloniality of being, as suggested by Walter Mignolo, 'is not inherent to the colonial subject [but it refers to] the exercise of strategies of domination' (Mignolo, 2007: 315). It does not refer to a determined and fixed subjectivities but to contested identities and techniques in a continuous negotiation process to dominate, contain, or convert the other (Fonseca and Jerrems, 2012b).

These concepts have contributed significantly to broadening and diversifying the already existent critical currents within IR. Notably, in the past decade, there has been what could be called an encounter between critical IR approaches and decolonial views in which Latin American and Caribbean contributions have gradually informed the works proposed from other areas (Çapan, 2017). This has been noted in at least three research trends. Firstly, the interest to revisit the Haitian Revolution as a space/time of rupture with modernity/coloniality and as a counter-narrative of modern linearity (Shilliam, 2008; Bhambra, 2016). Secondly, the analytical rearticulation of settler colonialism and settler societies beyond traditional views reconceptualizes modern/colonial dispossession and its legacies as a continuous practice of this dispositif of dispossession (Taylor, 2012; Forbis, 2016). Thirdly, the common challenge of going beyond the epistemic turn and proposing an ontological turn that envisions the understanding of the world beyond the world and of the human beyond the human (Blaney and Tickner, 2017).

Conclusion

This chapter briefly introduced the origins and development of the IR discipline in Latin America and the Caribbean. It discussed how their most relevant theoretical contributions (dependency theory, peripheral realism, and decolonial thinking) mainly rest on interdisciplinarity due to the impossibility to delink the local from the global. Either by taking into account internal inequalities (dependency theory), by including domestic policies within foreign policy rationalization and based on a sociological analysis of society (peripheral realism), or by approaching the modern/colonial system of power through the constant defining and undefining of the local/global, the openness to unmark the discipline's limits reflects an attempt to provide holistic theorization of political realities.

To further develop a critical history of the discipline in the region, the consequences of the geopolitics of knowledge represent four significant challenges that must be approached: (1) Revisit other forms of knowledge production that have survived and emerged in the context of more than 500 years of epistemic violence; (2) Consider Latin American and Caribbean theoretical 'hybridity' more broadly by including homegrown theorizations that may relate or dialogue with Global North approaches as the interconnectedness of IR is manifested in that hybridization; (3) Take into account the material limitations that Global South scholars face in undertaking research and contributing 'original' theories that provide an understanding of the complexities of the region; (4) Overcome Anglocentrism in our own academic spaces by supporting projects that are distant from theoretical perspectives and dynamics that do not give an account for Latin American and Caribbean forms of knowledge production and realities—forms that involve both interdisciplinarity and political positionality. This last challenge is also relevant for non-Anglophone scholarship around the world. English's centrality has also affected relationality within the Global North as is the case with Portuguese, French, and Spanish scholarship, for instance. While language gatekeepers obstruct access of scholars, theoretical exchanges are both limited by the necessity to dialogue through mainstream Anglocentric theories and nurtured by the uses of critical nondisciplinary (or marginal) approaches—such as French poststructuralism and Latin American, Caribbean, and Portuguese decolonial thinking. As has been suggested here, interdisciplinarity enables the construction of bridges for South-South, South-North, and non-Anglophone perspectives for a global discipline of IR.

Suggestions for further reading

Bosch, J. (2009). *De Cristóbal Colón a Fidel Castro. El Caribe, frontera imperial.* México D.F.: Porrúa.

Escobar, A. (2011). *Encountering Development: The Making and Unmaking of the Third World.* Princeton, NJ: Princeton University Press.

Ghosh, B. N. (2019). *Dependency Theory Revisited.* New York, NY: Routledge.

Pope Atkins, G. (2018). *Handbook of Research on the International Relations of Latin America and the Caribbean.* London: Routledge.

Williams, E. (1984). *From Columbus to Castro. The History of the Caribbean 1492–1969.* New York, NY: Vintage Books.

References

Anievas A., et al., eds. (2016). *Race and Racism in International Relations. Confronting the Global Colour Line.* London: Routledge.

Ashworth, L. M. (2019). Los mitos que me enseñó mi profesor de Relaciones Internacionales. Reconstruyendo la historia del pensamiento internacional. In: A. Lozano Vázquez, et al., eds., *¿Cien años de relaciones internacionales?: Disciplinariedad y revisionismo,* Ciudad de México: Siglo XXI, 213–249.

Balaam, D. N., and Dillman, B. (2019). Economic Determinism and Exploitation: The Structuralist Perspective. In: *Introduction to Political Economy.* 7th edition. New York, NY: Routledge, 71–96.

Bell, D. (2009). Writing the world: disciplinary history and beyond. *International Affairs,* 85 (1), 3–22.

Bernal-Meza, R. (2018). Dos aportes teóricos latinoamericanos de relaciones internacionales y su utilización por el pensamiento chino contemporáneo: los casos de Prebisch y Escudé. *Revista de Estudios Sociales,* 64, 75–87.

Bhambra, G. (2016). Undoing the epistemic disavowal of the Haitian revolution: a contribution to global social thought. *Journal of Intercultural Studies*, 37 (1), 1–16.

Blaney, D., and Tickner, A. (2017). Worlding, Ontological Politics and the possibility of a decolonial IR. *Millennium*, 45 (3), 293–311.

Briceño Ruiz, J., and Simonoff, A. (2017). La Escuela de la Autonomía, América Latina y la teoría de las Relaciones Internacionales. *Estudios Internacionales*, 49 (186), 39–89.

Çapan, Z. G. (2017). Decolonising international relations? *Third World Quarterly*, 38 (1), 1–15.

Castro-Gómez, S. (2007). Michel Foucault y la colonialidad del poder. *Tabula Rasa*, 6, 153–172.

Colacrai, M. (2019). Perspectivas teóricas, Relaciones Internacionales y Política Exterior en Argentina. Devenir y situación actual. *Estudios Internacionales*, 51 (194), 113–130.

Covarrubias Velasco, A. (2019). Las Relaciones Internacionales en México. *Estudios Internacionales*, 51 (194), 131–144.

de Carvalho, B., Leira, H., and Hobson, J. M. (2011). The big bangs of IR: the myths that your teachers still tell you about 1648 and 1919. *Millennium*, 39 (3), 735–758.

de Sousa Santos, B. (2010). Más allá del pensamiento abismal: de las líneas globales a una ecología de saberes. In H. Cairo, and R. Grosfoguel, eds., *Descolonizar la modernidad, Descolonizar Europa: Un diálogo Europa-América Latina*, Madrid: Iepala, 101–146.

Dussel, E. (1995). *1492. El encubrimiento del otro. Hacia el origen del Mito de la Modernidad.* La Paz: Biblioteca Indígena.

Escudé, C. (1992). *Realismo periférico: fundamentos para la nueva política exterior argentina*. Buenos Aires: Planeta.

Escudé, C. (1995). *Realismo de los estados débiles: La política exterior del primer gobierno de Menem frente a la Teoría de las RR. II*. Buenos Aires: Grupo Editor Latinoamericano.

Fonseca, G. Jr., and Uziel, E. (2019). Notas sobre o campo das relações internacionais no Brasil no centésimo aniversário da disciplina. *Estudios Internacionales*, 51 (194), 145–166.

Fonseca, M., and Jerrems, A. (2012a). *Why Decolonise International Relations Theory?* Working paper presented at BISA. Viewed on 20 October 2020. <https://www.academia.edu/2140460/Why_Decolonise_International_Relations_Theory>.

Fonseca, M., and Jerrems, A. (2012b). Pensamiento decolonial: ¿una 'nueva' apuesta en las RRII? *Relaciones Internacionales*, 19, 103–121.

Forbis, M. M. (2016). After autonomy: the Zapatistas, insurgent indigeneity, and decolonization. *Settler Colonial Studies*, 6 (4), 365–384.

Grosfoguel R., and Castro-Gómez, S., eds. (2007). *El giro decolonial: reflexiones para una diversidad epistémica más allá del capitalismo global*. Bogotá: Siglo del Hombre.

Guillén, A. (2007). Raúl Prebisch, crítico temprano del modelo neoliberal. *Economía UNAM*, 4 (10), 123–130.

Herborth, B. and Nitzschner, P. (2021). Europe in Historical International Relations. In de Carvalho, B., Costa Lopez, J., and Leira, H., eds. *Routledge Handbook of Historical International Relations*. Abingdon: Routledge.

Kapoor, I. (2002). Capitalism, Culture, Agency: Dependency versus Postcolonial Theory. *Third World Quarterly*, 23 (4), 647–664.

Kay, C. (2009). Latin American Structuralist School. In: R. Kitchin, and N. Thrift, eds., *International Encyclopedia of Human Geography*, Oxford: Elsevier, 159–164.

Kwon, H. (2021). Understanding the Postcolonial Cold War. In de Carvalho, B., Costa Lopez, J., and Leira, H., eds. *Routledge Handbook of Historical International Relations*. Abingdon: Routledge.

Matus, G. L. (1980). Tendencias y perspectivas del estudio de las Relaciones Internacionales: tareas para América Latina. *Estudios Internacionales*, 13 (50), 236–251.

Lao-Montes, A. (2004). De-calibanizing Caribbean rationalities. *The CLR James Journal*, 10 (1), 154–166.

Maldonado-Torres, N. (2007). On the coloniality of being: contributions to the development of a concept. *Cultural Studies*, 21 (2–3), 240–270.

Mignolo, W. D. (2003). *Historias locales/diseños globales. Colonialidad, conocimientos subalternos y pensamiento fronterizo*. Madrid: Akal.

Mignolo, W. D. (2007). El pensamiento decolonial, desprendimiento y apertura: un manifiesto. In: R. Grosfoguel, and S. Castro-Gómez, eds., *El giro decolonial: reflexiones para una diversidad epistémica más allá del capitalismo global*, Bogotá: Siglo del Hombre.

Persaud, R., and Sajed, A., eds. (2018). *Race, Gender, and Culture in International Relations. Postcolonial Perspectives*. London: Routledge.

Quick Hall, K. M. (2019). *Naming a Transnational Black Feminist Framework Writing in Darkness*. London: Routledge.

Quijano, A. (1992). Colonialidad y modernidad/racionalidad. In: H. Bonilla, ed., *Los conquistados. 1492 y la población indígena de las Américas*, Quito: LibriMundi, Tercer Mundo.

Quijano, A. (2000). Coloniality of Power, Eurocentrism and Latin America. *Nepantla: Views from South*, 1 (3), 533–580.

Rivera Cusicanqui, S. (2015). *Sociología de la imagen. Miradas ch'ixi desde la historia andina*. Buenos Aires: Tinta Limón.

Scauso, M. S. (2016). Indianismo and Decoloniality: Voices of Resistance. In P. Smith, and S. Dreher, eds., *Religious Activism in the Global Economy: Promoting, Reforming, or Resisting Neoliberal Globalization?* London and New York: Rowman & Littlefield International.

Schenoni L., and Escudé, C. (2016). Peripheral realism revisisted. *Revista Brasileira de Política Internacional*, 59 (1), 1–18.

Schmidt, B. (2019). Revisando la Historia temprana de las Relaciones Internacionales: Imperialismo, colonialismo y raza. In: A. Lozano Vázquez, et al., eds., *¿Cien años de relaciones internacionales? Disciplinariedad y revisionismo*. Ciudad de México: Siglo XXI, 250–264.

Schulz, C. (2021). Latin America: Between Liminality and Agency in Historical International Relations. In de Carvalho, B., Costa Lopez, J., and Leira, H., eds. *Routledge Handbook of Historical International Relations*. Abingdon: Routledge.

Shilliam, R. (2008). What the Haitian Revolution Might Tell Us about Development, Security, and the Politics of Race. *Comparative Studies in Society and History*, 50 (3), 778–808.

Simonoff, A., and Lorenzini, M. E. (2019). Autonomía e Integración en las Teorías del Sur: Desentrañando el Pensamiento de Hélio Jaguaribe y Juan Carlos Puig. *Iberoamericana-Nordic Journal of Latin American and Caribbean Studies*, 48 (1), 96–106.

Tausch, A. (2010). Globalization and development: the relevance of 'classical' dependency theory for the world today. *International Social Science Journal*, 61 (2), 467–488.

Taylor, L. (2012). Decolonizing international relations: perspectives from Latin America. *International Studies Review*, 14 (3), 386–400.

Tickner, A. (2003). Hearing Latin American voices in international relations studies. *International Studies Perspectives*, 4 (4), 325–350.

Tickner, A. (2008). Latin American IR and the Primacy of lo práctico. *International Studies Review*, 10 (4), 735–748.

Yao, J., and Delatolla, A. (2021). Race and Historical International Relations. In de Carvalho, B., Costa Lopez, J., and Leira, H., eds. *Routledge Handbook of Historical International Relations*. Abingdon: Routledge.

17

PRE-MODERN ASIA AND INTERNATIONAL RELATIONS THEORY

Victoria Tin-bor Hui

Introduction

Does pre-modern interstate relations in Asia challenge International Relations (IR) theories?[1] A growing body of works fault IR theories for falsely universalizing the Western experience (Tickner and Wæver, 2009). John Hobson (2012: 344) boldly declares that 'to be or not to be Eurocentric – that is the question.' As Asia sits on the opposite end of the Eurasian continent, critical scholars have turned to 'perspectives on and beyond Asia' for counterexamples (Acharya and Buzan, 2010: book subtitle). Hobson (2012: 211) rejoices that China perfectly undermines Waltz's (1979) structural realism. David Kang (2010: 2) contends that the East Asian tribute system's hierarchy brought about centuries of stability while the Western system's formal equality contributed to incessant conflicts. This chapter assesses the extent of this challenge via a critical review of the best books on pre-modern Asian international relations.

If the foil is Eurocentrism, the first order is to specify what IR theories and what Western experiences are at stake (see also Herborth and Nitzschner, 2021). Not all IR theories are about anarchy and war. Hierarchy and peace are not alien to theories of unipolarity and hegemonic stability, or the history of international relations in pre-modern Europe. Waltz's critics should refrain from submitting to his theoretical hegemony. Nevertheless, it is not unreasonable to zoom in on Waltzian structural realism because of its centrality to the literature on historical Asian international relations. While Kang takes Waltz as the key target, Yuan-kang Wang (2011: 2, 6) contends that anarchy trumps culture and refutes the assertion that IR theory is ill-suited for the non-Western world. Feng Zhang (2015: 31–32) does not follow Waltz but takes cues from him in constructing a relational theory of grand strategy. Ji-young Lee (2017: 7–8) aspires to transcend the debate between Kang's emphasis on Confucian culture and Wang's focus on relative power with an argument based on domestic legitimation.

In juxtaposing structural realism against Asian experiences, it is important to avoid committing Waltz's main mistake: being 'unhistorical, perhaps anti-historical' (Schroeder, 1994: 148). Critical to historical honesty is attention to subalterns as well as powerful actors. Cox (1981: 128) highlights that '[t]heory is always for someone and for some purpose' and calls for attention to the less powerful. While Asia may be weaker than Europe, Asian states are weaker than China and so their perspectives should be given primacy. Kang (2010: 4) contends that IR scholars should take Asia on its own terms and not as a reflection of Europe, but his claim that East Asian states voluntarily submitted to China runs the risk of replacing Eurocentrism with Sinocentrism (Callahan, 2012; Suzuki, 2009, 2021). Fairbank (1968: 12), whose argument forms the basis for Kang's argument, acknowledges that the 'Chinese world order' was 'a unified concept' only 'at the Chinese end' and as 'an ideal pattern.' Lee (2017: 11) most clearly points out that the study of 'China's hegemony' requires an understanding of the history of East Asia, not just that of China. Her deep reading of Korean sources shows that 'savvy' Korean leaders consistently 'manipulated' to protect their political independence and autonomy against Chinese control (Lee, 2017: 2, 103). Feng Zhang (2015) likewise simultaneously examines the fluctuating normative and instrumental foreign policy strategies of both China and its neighbours.

This chapter points out that, while arguments that follow China's Sinocentric top-down worldview may seem to challenge realist premises, those that consider other Asian perspectives identify more common grounds. China was not always the most powerful; when it was, relations were not always peaceful. As Yan (2011: 213–214) suggests, while 'relations of absolute equality between states lead to violent conflict,' 'relations of absolute hierarchy lead to tyranny in which the strong oppress the weak.' When voices of the weak are given their due regard, what was chronicled as hierarchy in Chinese official histories was contested by a desire for equality by secondary states in their own records. What was documented as stable peace in Chinese histories could be violent pacification for the subordinated. What appeared to be legitimate authority in the eyes of the Chinese court could be domination for weaker neighbours and equality for stronger ones.

In the rest of this chapter, the next section problematizes Confucian peace and cultural legitimacy. The discussion is anchored with the Ming's and the Qing's relations with the supposedly Confucianized states of Korea, Vietnam and Japan. The subsequent section unpacks hierarchy in the Song dynasty's relations with equal and even more powerful neighbours. The overall analysis will demonstrate that, whether the authors in question intend to critique or support Eurocentric IR theories, core books in this genre add up to a pre-modern Asia that is characterized by a mixture of peace and conflict, of cultural legitimacy and power calculation, and of hierarchy and anarchy. The conclusion will draw implications for the related agenda to construct a Chinese IR theory.

What peace and what cultural legitimacy?

Was peace the norm in pre-Modern East Asia? There is a general (mis)perception that East Asian culture was Confucian and that Confucianism dictated peace (Hui, 2018). Max Weber (1951: 169) spoke of 'the pacifist character of Confucianism.' John K. Fairbank (1974: 7) developed 'the pacifist bias of the Chinese tradition.' Recent works have largely followed the footsteps of the early giants. Many articles and books take Confucian concepts such as 'benevolence' (*ren*), 'virtue' (*de*), 'great harmony under heaven' (*tianxia datong*), and 'kingly authority' (*wangdao*) for a pacifist foreign policy. Even Wang (2011: 3), who highlights the importance of relative power, takes for granted that Confucian culture is supposed to 'constrain Chinese use of force in the past.' Kang most strongly argues, 'shared ideas, norms, and interests' created a 'Confucian society' among China, Korea, Vietnam, and Japan in 1368–1841 (Kang, 2010: 8–9). Robert Kelly (2012: 408) agrees that East Asia experienced a 'Long Peace' rooted in war-reducing Confucian ideals.

It is noteworthy that Lee depicts the opposite picture on the very first page:

> In the early modern period, China was the sole great power in East Asia… However, consider the following episodes. In 1388, Korea… sent armed forces against the Ming. In 1592, Japan invaded Korea in an attempt to conquer the Ming and build

a 'Japanocentric world order.' A few decades later, during the Ming to Qing transition in seventeenth-century China, Korea supported Ming war efforts against the more powerful, rising Qing... Japan created a self-proclaimed tributary order centered on itself, treating Qing tributaries Korea and Ryukyu as its own. Why did these less powerful East Asian actors accept, defy, or challenge China?

(Lee, 2017: 1)

Lee (2017: 178) nevertheless contends that scepticism of China's legitimate hegemony is not warranted because defiance, challenge, coercion and war are 'integral feature[s] of how the system functioned.' But does such a mix of defiance and compliance make Asian international relations culturally distinctive?

The presumption of hierarchy and peace is closely tied to the tribute system, the 'governing principle' of which is taken to be 'benevolence' (Qin, 2010: 252). China, though powerful, had no desire to use its military and economic capabilities to seek expansion (Kang, 2010: 2). Other East Asian states admired and emulated China's Confucian civilization. They demonstrated their voluntary submission to the China-centred hierarchy by 'coming to pay tribute, receiving the Chinese title, and using the Chinese calendar' (Lee, 2017: 64, 48).

Did the tribute system reflect cultural legitimacy or relative power? To answer that question, we have to know what the system was. Lee offers a rare and helpful definition. She details how both the Ming and the Qing 'crossed the boundaries of what was accepted as legitimate within the framework of typical tribute practices' (Lee, 2017: 141). First, in the ideal world, only the Chinese emperor could be the Son of Heaven while 'barbarians' could not (Lee, 2017: 49). Yet, when the 'barbarian' Manchu Qing took over the Ming, Korea complied, however reluctantly (Lee, 2017: 135). Second, the Confucian ideal held that tributes should not involve 'economic exploitation' akin to taxes and imperialism as the Mongols did to Korea (Lee, 2017: 50). Yet, the Ming 'adopted some of the most notorious Mongol practices, including demanding human tribute as well as large amounts of goods,' blurring 'the line between imperialism and... benign hegemony' (Lee, 2017: 81–83). The Manchu Qing likewise demanded royal princes as hostages and Korean troops in support of the Qing's other wars (Lee, 2017: 141). Third, the investiture practice should have signified China's respect for the political autonomy of the receiving country (Lee, 2017: 50). Yet, the Ming considered the option of annexing Korea in 1608 and again a decade later (Lee, 2017: 141). Though the Ming court eventually ruled out annexation, it employed coercive diplomacy to extract Korean compliance (Lee, 2017: 84).

Wang (2011: 149) most explicitly points out that the tribute system was coercive rather than benevolent because those who accepted Chinese supremacy were granted tributary trade privileges while those who did not were defined as inhuman, therefore deserving extermination. He contends that Vietnam and Korea were 'forced' to accept Chinese dominance by 'relative weakness, geographic proximity, and lack of a counterbalancing ally' (Wang, 2011: 150). Although Confucian scholar-officials spoke of virtues, they advocated the use of force to punish those who did not know their place in the China-centred hierarchy. Wang (2011: 126, 130, 134, 138, 144, 169) observes how they frequently advocated aggressive policies against 'insubordination' to 'a country as great as China.' Zhang (2015: 41, 65, 110, 132, 134, 139, 160) similarly notes that neighbours' refusal to 'serve the great' was repeatedly the cause for conflict because non-subservience was seen as a violation of propriety, even a crime, that deserved 'punishment.'

Kang (2010: 23, 55, 102) concurs that the tribute system was characterized by 'a mix of legitimate acceptance and rational calculation' with 'no bright line' between the two. On the whole, however, he argues against power calculation, dismissing such a view for implying that China's neighbours were 'placating China culturally while inwardly seething with resentment'

(2010: 12). To establish that secondary states saw China and Confucianism as legitimate, he cites the voluntary adoption of Chinese and Confucian ideas and institutions; the absence of evidence that Koreans, Vietnamese, or Japanese were smirking at Chinese behind their backs; and the use of the tribute system by secondary states in their dealings with one another (Kang, 2010: 68). It is interesting that Kang provides extensive citations from historians to suggest otherwise. Quoting Womack, Kang (2010: 37, 101) acknowledges that both Vietnam and Korea adopted many Chinese practices to 'preserve autonomy and independence'; as such, 'deference to China was not the same as submission.' Referencing Alexander Woodside, Kang (2010: 35) notes that Korea engaged in 'history writing as boundary maintenance' against Chinese hegemony. Regarding Vietnam, it similarly commissioned history writing 'to establish a record of autonomy from China' and 'to affirm the equality of North and South' (Kang, 2010: 39). Citing David Marr, Kang (2010: 103) observes 'subtlety' in how Vietnamese monarchs styled themselves 'king' while addressing China's emperors but 'emperor' when speaking to their own subjects. As for Japan, Kang suggests that the embrace of Confucian learning was meant to be an equalizer to dilute China's claim to supremacy, thus Japan's insistence that status rankings should be 'based not on size but on culture' (Kang, 2010: 78). What follows is a closer examination of how Korea, Vietnam, and Japan viewed their relations with China.

Korea

Korea was the supposedly 'model tributary' (Lee, 2017: 13, 43). Lee's in-depth reading of Korean state letters, court documents, and personal essays offers the best insights into Korean perspectives in the genre of Asian Historical IR. She observes that Korea's policies towards the Ming 'vacillated markedly,' from compliance in 1370, to a failed challenge in 1388, back to compliance in 1392, and then to another attempt at challenge in 1398 (Lee, 2017: 172). Korea was 'unusually aggressive' against the Ming in 1370, 1388, and 1398 (Lee, 2017: 86, 79).

Lee's detailed analysis provides an illuminating account of overt compliance but behind-the-back defiance. When the Ming first rose to power, Korea's immediate reaction was 'the fear of possible Ming invasions' (Lee, 2017: 83). In 1370, Koryo King Kongmin agreed to become a Ming tributary but also ordered a military campaign to the Liaodong region (Chinese) or Tongnyong Administration (Korean) against the Ming's warning (Lee, 2017: 87). Lee's (2017: 88) description of Kongmin's reasoning is worth quoting:

> a new tributary relationship with the Ming was a welcome development to the extent that the Ming did not repeat the kind of imperial control that the Yuan empire had exerted over Koryo Korea.... [E]ven while accepting a Ming tributary status, Kongmin wanted to be considered an equal to the Ming empire within Korea. Kongmin performed a memorial service to Heaven, which was allowed only to the Son of Heaven (meaning an emperor as opposed to a king); when the Ming founder sent his envoy to erect a tombstone and perform a memorial service that signified Koryo Korea's status as a Ming tributary, Kongmin denied the reception of the Ming emperor's edict on the pretense of sickness. Upon the Ming envoy's departure, Kongmin had the tomb-stone pulled out and thrown away. Therefore, it is through the lens of domestic concerns that one can explain why Koryo king Kongmin's decision to become a Ming tributary came in the same year that he ordered a military campaign in a strategically important area to the Ming to regain the lost territory.

In 1388, Koryo sent another army 'in a direct challenge to Ming power' after the Ming announced plans to lay claim to the same contested territory (Lee, 2017: 89). In a dramatic manner, General

Yi Song-gye turned back the army and overthrew King U. Lee recounts that Yi was sent to the battlefield by a rival faction and he knew that Liaodong would likely be 'his tomb' (Lee, 2017: 90). Even if he could score an initial victory, Koryo Korea did not have sufficient supplies to sustain a full-scale war against the Ming (Lee, 2017: 89). In 1392, Yi established the Choson dynasty and immediately sent a tribute mission to the Ming requesting investiture. Nevertheless, Choson-Ming relations remained tense for years, with the Ming executing Choson envoys and Choson preparing for a military campaign in 1398 which was eventually abandoned (Lee, 2017: 85, 92).

Zhang (2015: 77) corroborates the tale of Choson confrontation with the Ming: King T'aejong is reported to complain that he had to 'endure' the Ming's requisitions for horses, eunuchs, and virgins and restrain his 'anger.' What of the famous '*sadae* (serving the great)' policy? Choson launched the policy upon hearing Emperor Yongle's invasion of Vietnam, drawing the lesson that '[i]f our country has a little lack of the propriety of serving the great, [he] will send a punitive expedition against us' (Zhang, 2015: 76). Thus, he urged his officials to both 'serve [the Ming emperor] with utmost integrity' and 'strengthen fortifications' in the same sentence (Zhang, 2015: 76).

Lee further reports extensive power dynamics beyond shared Confucian culture. During the Imjin War (1592–1598), the Ming came to the aid of Choson Korea not 'out of a sense of Confucian obligation toward a tributary' but because of 'the realpolitik logic' that Japan's ruler Toyotomi Hideyoshi was planning to march from Korea onward to the Ming (Lee, 2017: 133). It is remarkable that the Ming's initial reaction to Japan's lightning invasion of Korea was to 'suspect possible collusion between Japan and Korea against it' (Lee, 2017: 108). At the end of the war, King Sonjo pursued 'hyper compliance' because he had to cover up his 'failures as a king' (Lee, 2017: 130).

During the Ming-Qing transition, King Kwanghae originally adjusted his Ming policy 'in accordance with shifting power balances' between the rising Manchu Qing and the declining Ming (Lee, 2017: 150). Injo dethroned Kwanghae under the pretext that the former king had abandoned his tributary obligations to the Ming. To shore up domestic legitimacy, King Injo was bound to follow a 'hyper compliance' policy with the declining Ming even though he knew that Choson could not realistically fight the rising Qing. After Manchu invasions in 1627 and 1636, Injo 'was forced to comply' (Lee, 2017: 25, 135). Korea would continue to maintain peace with the Qing until modern times. But it is noteworthy that Koreans saw the Manchus as 'barbarians' who did not represent 'the Central Efflorescence (*zhonghua*)' (Ge, 2011: 157). As a subtle form of defiance, Korea renamed their envoys from 'Missions to the Celestial Court (choch'on),' which symbolized admiration, in Ming times to 'Missions to Yan (today's Beijing) (yonhaeng),' which signalled indifference, in Qing times (Ge, 2011: 156–158).

Vietnam

KEY

Vietnam's relation with China was more frosty. Kang claims Vietnam as another example for the absence of 'smirking at Chinese behind their backs' (Kang, 2010: 68). This point is directly taken from Liam Kelley's (2005: 93) argument that there was 'no evidence of mockery' in the poetry that Vietnamese envoys composed. But why would one look for evidence of mockery in envoy poetry? After all, Vietnamese envoys proudly showed their refined poems to Chinese officials and requested prefaces to their collections (Kelley, 2005: 87, 89, 189). We should instead look for poems written for only Vietnamese consumption.

The Ming's Emperor Yongle (r. 1402–1424) once sent an army to 'punish' 'rebellious bandits' in Vietnam (Wang, 2011: 154). Kelley (2005, 14) recounts that Ming troops were 'forced to abandon their imperial pretentions in Vietnam after suffering military defeat.' The Vietnamese commander Le Loi's guerrilla tactics made it difficult for Ming troops to move supplies from the border to the Vietnamese capital (Wang, 2011: 154). Wang observes that the ensuing emperor decided to retreat, citing 'historical precedents that Vietnam had been a liability when it was annexed in the Han dynasty' (Wang, 2011: 155). Le Loi's chief minister Nguyen Trai wrote the famous poem 'Proclamation on the Pacification of Wu [China]' in the wake of the triumph over the Ming (Vuving, 2001, 64). The poem reads:

> Now think upon this Dai Viet land of ours;
> Truly is it a cultured nation.
> As mountain and river make for various lands,
> so our Southern ways must differ from the North.
> It was the Trieu, the Dinh, the Ly and Tran,
> who in succession built this country.
> Even as the Han, the Tang, the Song and Yuan,
> each was so sovereign in its own domain.
> Sometimes strong, sometimes weak,
> Yet never lacking heroes,
> we beat the ambitious Liu Yan
> and crushed Zhao Xie with his dream of grandeur.
> There was Suo Du captured at Ham Tu Pass
> and Black Horse, the Mongol
> come to grief at Bach Dang Bay.
> (O'Harrow, 1979: 168–170)

This was a declaration that, when China dared to invade as under the Han, the Tang, the Song, the Yuan, and the Ming dynasties, they would be eventually 'crushed' by Vietnamese heroes. It was also a proclamation of political equality, as 'each was so sovereign in its own domain.' It was, furthermore, an assertion of cultural parity and difference, as Dai Viet was 'a cultured nation' with its different 'Southern ways.'

Historian Womack (2012: 38, 48–49) argues that it was 'the capacity of resistance by smaller neighbors' rather than Chinese benevolence that produced relative stability. Kang (2010: 101) acknowledges that Vietnam was 'impractical to subdue.' In the twentieth century, France and the United States would learn the same bitter lesson that superior firepower was no match for Vietnamese guerrilla resistance.

Japan

If Korea and Vietnam covertly 'smirked' at China, Japan openly challenged China. Even in Kang's analysis, Japan 'grimaced at China's centrality' as it was 'on the edge,' 'the most skeptical of and uncomfortable with China's dominance' and 'never wholly embracing the Confucian society' (Kang, 2010: 55, 69, 77). In 1382, Kanenaga wrote to the Ming that 'now the world is the world's world; it does not belong to a single ruler... How could we kneel down and acknowledge Chinese overlordship?' (Wang, 2011: 149; Zhang, 2015: 94). The Ming emperor was 'outraged' but was deterred by the memory of the Yuan dynasty's failed invasion of Japan a century earlier (Zhang, 2015: 94–95). Shogan Ashikaga Yoshimitsu pursued compliance by signing 'subject, the king of Japan' both because Japan's imperial institution had been on the other side of the civil war (Lee, 2017: 97) and because Yoshimitsu tried to restore the lucrative tribute trade (Wang, 2011: 149). But his submission to China would be denounced by generations of Japanese elite.

In launching the Imjin War, Hideyoshi 'felt confident about Japanese military superiority' (Lee, 2017: 107) and openly declared his 'lifelong goal to annex China' (Wang, 2011: 174). During the Ming-Qing transition, 'Japan contemplated balancing against the Qing but abandoned the idea' (Lee, 2017: 25). Lee insists that there was 'no external balancing' as structural realists would expect. Yet, she notes that Japan 'seriously considered a military alliance' with Korea and the Ming against the Qing before it eventually 'distanced itself from China' and acted as 'a new center of a miniature international order' (Lee, 2017: 25, 143).

Hierarchy, status rankings, and peace?

Another point of contention is the argument that 'the use of the tribute system by secondary states in their dealings with one another' contributed to system stability (Kang, 2010: 68). There is a built-in contradiction to this logic: if China did not like to be second to any other states and considered any subordination 'humiliating,' why would other states that shared the same hierarchical worldview not find it humiliating to submit to the Chinese emperor or one another? Kang (2010: 73, 71) indeed observes, 'states down the hierarchy had trouble dealing with each other and with determining their own hierarchic rankings' because they 'each looked down on the other as less advanced.' As such tension stifled potentially lucrative Japanese-Korean trade, Korean and Japanese merchants forged letters that gave the delusion that their trade missions were tribute missions from a supplicant neighbour (Kang, 2010: 75–76).

What hierarchy?

While Kang, Lee, and Zhang focus on East Asia in the Ming and Qing time, Wang's inclusion of the weaker Song dynasty demonstrates the massive payoffs of looking at earlier periods of Asian international relations. If the Ming era is a poor fit for the idealized tribute system and Confucian peace, the Song era completely subverts the presumption of China-centred hierarchy. The Song was divided into the Northern Song (960–1126) and the Southern Song (1127–1279). While the Northern Song confronted the Khitan Liao and the Tangut Xi Xia, the Southern Song successively battled the Jurchen Jin and the Mongols. As illustrated by Morris Rossabi's *China Among Equals* (1983) and Tao Jinsheng's *Two Sons of Heaven* (1988), the Song was the 'lesser empire.'

Whether or not one agrees with Wang's adoption of the Waltzian term of 'anarchy,' China in Song times was a full-fledged international system. It demonstrated the makings of stateness, diplomacy, territoriality, and nationalism characteristic of the modern world (Ge, 2011: 27, 48, 55). All the units in Song times were state actors because Song's rivals had adopted Chinese institutions, modes of government, and the Chinese political vocabulary from the previous cosmopolitan Tang era (Rawski, 2010: 71–73). In the constant struggles for power, all states followed the same set of international rules in conducting foreign policy. And all were 'opportunistic in forming alliances' (Rawski, 2010: 70), switching sides as they saw fit, and dividing and conquering the opposite camp. The Northern Song allied with Xi Xia to isolate Liao, and it then formed an alliance with Jin to defeat Liao (Wang, 2011: 60, 72). The Southern Song later joined forces with the Mongols to eliminate Jin, before it was in turn conquered by the Mongols (Wang, 2011: 96). As in other multistate systems, intense military competition gave rise to territoriality. The Song negotiated a series of boundary agreements with Liao, Jin, and the Mongols (Wang, 2011: 51, 54, 89, 96).

Kang (2010: 2) emphasizes, 'the more powerful [East Asian] states became, the more stable were their relations.' It is thus of theoretical interest to observe what happened when the Song's power waxed and waned. According to Wang, when the Song court found windows of opportunity in the enemy, it would strike to seek strategic advantages and to make territorial gains.

It was capable of mobilizing as many as 1.25 million troops when necessary (Wang, 2011: 66). But nearly constant warfare drained the Song's military and financial resources. The costs of maintaining a sizeable army consumed three quarters to over 80 per cent of annual revenues (Wang, 2011: 49, 66). In the face of budget deficits and looming peasant rebellions, the Song court concluded that peace was cheaper than war.

In Wang's analysis, relative capabilities dictated not only the Song's offensive versus defensive postures, but also its relative status in each peace agreement. The 1005 Shanyuan Treaty is generally regarded as one between equals, with Song addressing Liao as the 'Great Khitan State (*da qidan guo*)' or the 'Northern Court (*beichao*)' (Wang, 2011: 53). Unfortunately for the Song, the balance of power would become increasingly unfavourable. To make matters worse, the Khitans were so well versed in Chinese international rules that they astutely employed Chinese rhetoric to signify their superiority (Rawski, 2010: 71). In 1005, Song started a 'money for peace' policy and offered 'annual bribes (*suiluo*)' of 200,000 bolts of silk and 100,000 taels of silver (Wang, 2011: 53). By 1042, Song had to agree to annually 'submit an offering (*na*)' of 300,000 bolts of silk and 200,000 taels of silver (Wang, 2011: 62). While the term 'bribe' was neutral with regard to status, the term 'offering' symbolized Liao superiority (Wang, 2011: 62). After the Song was driven south by the Jurchen Jin, it was forced to yield to further demands of subordination in treaty terms. In 1141, the Southern Song explicitly accepted its inferior status as a vassal state by agreeing to pay an annual 'tribute (*gong*)' of 250,000 taels of silver and a similar number of bolts of silk (Wang, 2011: 89). In the treaty oath, the Song addressed the Jin as the 'Superior State (*shang guo*)' and referred to itself as the 'Insignificant Fiefdom (*bi yi*)' (Wang, 2011: 89). In the treaty of 1165, the Song enjoyed an upgrade after a respectable showing on the battlefield. Song 'annual tribute (*sui gong*)' was renamed to 'annual payment (*sui bi*)' and was reduced to 200,000 units of silver and silk (Wang, 2011: 92–93). The Song ruler was allowed to call himself 'emperor,' but he still had to descend from the elevated throne when receiving state letters from Jin envoys (Wang, 2011: 92). In light of such diplomatic rituals, we can appreciate the ingenuity of Vietnam in addressing itself the 'Southern Court' and the Ming or the Qing the 'Northern Court.'

The Song was not the only dynasty that signed peace treaties with 'barbarian' regimes. To justify the treaty of Shanyuan, the Song court cited as precedent a Tang-Tibet treaty of 783. The Han dynasty had also signed treaties with the Xiongnu involving the 'exchange of oath letters' and imperial marriages in a 'bilateral relationship of equals' between 198 and 135 BCE (Rawski, 2010: 79). This alternative tradition (Ge, 2011: 47) was suppressed by scholar-officials who saw diplomatic equality with foreign states as 'unbecoming of a great country' and damaging of 'the prestige and awesomeness of the Chinese throne' (Wang, 2011: 138, 186). It is thus of critical importance that scholars pay heed to the historical records of China's neighbours.

Conclusion and implications for Chinese IR

In all, Eurocentric IR theories should, of course, learn from Asian experiences. In doing so, IR scholars should strive to uncover historical Asian international relations instead of following only official rhetoric. Scholars should also avoid imposing Sinocentrism on Asian states. When China's neighbours are given due consideration, Asian international relations turns out to be a cross between hierarchy and anarchy, peace and war, cultural legitimacy and power calculation. Future research should explore common ground as well as cultural distinctiveness.

This analysis has implications for the related agenda of Chinese IR. If critics are correct that IR scholarship inescapably reflects the perspective of the most powerful in global politics, then it is not surprising that Chinese IR scholars lament that they have long been 'consumers' of Eurocentric theories and should become 'producers of knowledge' (Wang, 2006). There are mountains of writings on the 'possibility and inevitability' of a Chinese School of IR (Qin, 2006) or an IR theory with Chinese characteristics (Callahan and Barabantseva, 2012). The core argument is that Chinese culture 'advocates moral strength instead of military power, worships kingly rule instead of hegemonic rule, and emphasizes persuasion by virtue' (Li and Worm, 2011: 70). This leads to the implication that today's China is fundamentally peaceful because of its deep origin in Chinese philosophy and culture.

Yan's volume offers a ready reference. He champions the concept of 'humane (moral) authority' based on 'virtue, benevolence, the Way, justice, law, worthies, and sages' (2011: 39, 65, 115). Although he is explicitly sceptical of the agenda to develop a Chinese School of IR (2011: 252–259), he similarly provides philosophical support for 'China's theory of harmonious world diplomacy' (2011: 62). He (2011: 37–38) contends that the rise of China will 'make the world more civilized.' Unfortunately, the concept 'humane authority' is explicitly unhistorical, representing merely 'the political *ideal* of pre-Qin thinkers' (Yan, 2011: 'A Note on the Translation,' no page number). As Qianru Yang, one of the critics contained in the volume, puts it, Yan 'abstracts from concrete historical contexts and then chooses part of the works of the pre-Qin masters and expounds these texts' (in Yan, 2011: 155). The discrepancy between rhetoric and history has led to criticisms that Chinese IR is aimed to create an 'ideological preparation for a new hegemonic world order' (Callahan, 2008: 749). Yan (2011: 65–66) offers this useful standard to assess the acceptance of a China-led hierarchy in the future:

> Whether [or not] a state is a responsible major power is not something that the state itself can decide; it is a matter of judgment by other states. Should China increase its material power without at the same time increasing its [moral leadership], China will have difficulty being accepted by the international community.

This yardstick – judgement by other states – should be equally applied to the past as to the future. As Yan (2011: 218) also acknowledges, 'A nation that cannot face historical events correctly is one that cannot win over the hearts of other states.'

Suggestions for further reading

Ge, Z. (2018). *What Is China? Territory, Ethnicity, Culture, and History.* Translated by M. Hill. Cambridge, MA: Harvard University Press.

Hui, V. (2005). *War and State Formation in Ancient China and Early Modern Europe.* New York, NY: Cambridge University Press.

Perdue, P. (2005). *China Marches West: The Qing Conquest of Central Eurasia.* Cambridge, MA: Harvard University Press.

Reid, A., and Zheng, Y., eds. (2009). *Negotiating Asymmetry: China's Place in Asia.* Honolulu, HI: University of Hawaii Press.

Wade, G., ed. (2014). *Asian Expansions: The Historical Experiences of Polity Expansion in Asia.* London: Routledge.

Zhao, D. (2015). *The Confucian-Legalist State: A New Theory of Chinese History.* Oxford: Oxford University Press.

Note

1 This chapter is part of a larger project that has received funding from the Smith Richardson Foundation, the Earhart Foundation, the United States Institute of Peace, the Fulbright Fellowship Program, the Chiang Ching-Kuo Foundation for International Scholarly Exchange, the East Asia Institute Fellows Program on Peace, Governance, and Development in East Asia supported by the Henry Luce Foundation, the Institute for Scholarship in the Liberal Arts, the Kellogg Institute for International Studies and the Liu Institute for Asia and Asian Studies of the University of Notre Dame. The author is also grateful to Julia Costa Lopez and an anonymous reviewer for very insightful comments.

References

Acharya, A., and Buzan, B., eds. (2010). *Non-Western International Relations Theory*. New York, NY: Routledge.

Callahan, W. (2008). Chinese visions of world order: post-hegemonic or a new hegemony? *International Studies Review*, 10 (4), 749–761.

Callahan, W., and Barabantseva, E., eds. (2012). *China Orders the World: Normative Soft Power and Foreign Relations*. Baltimore, MD: The Johns Hopkins University Press.

Cox, R. (1981). Social forces, states, and world orders. *Millennium*, 10 (2), 126–155.

Fairbank, J. (1968). A Preliminary Framework. In: J. Fairbank, ed., *The Chinese World Order. Traditional China's Foreign Relations*, Cambridge, MA: Harvard University Press, 1–19.

Fairbank, J. (1974). Introduction: Varieties of the Chinese Military Experience. In: F. Kierman, and J. Fairbank, eds., *Chinese Ways in Warfare*, Cambridge, MA: Harvard University Press, 1–26.

Ge, Z. (2011). *Zhaizi zhongguo [Settling In/On China]*. Taipei: Lianjing.

Herborth, B., and Nitzschner, P. (2021). Europe in Historical International Relations. In de Carvalho, B., Costa Lopez, J., & Leira, H., eds. *Routledge Handbook of Historical International Relations*. Abingdon: Routledge.

Hobson, J. M. (2012). *The Eurocentric Conception of World Politics. Western International Theory 1760-2010*. Cambridge: Cambridge University Press.

Hui, V. (2018). Confucian Pacifism or Confucian Confusion? In: A. Gofas, I. Hamati-Ataya, and N. Onuf, eds., *The SAGE Handbook of the History, Philosophy and Sociology of International Relations*, Newbury Park, CA: Sage, 148–161.

Kang, D. (2010). *East Asia Before the West: Five Centuries of Trade and Tribute*. New York, NY: Columbia University Press.

Kelley, L. (2005). *Beyond the Bronze Pillars: Envoy Poetry and the Sino-Vietnamese Relationship*. Honolulu, HI: University of Hawaii Press.

Kelly, R. (2012). A 'Confucian Long Peace' in pre-Western East Asia? *European Journal of International Relations*, 18 (3), 407–430.

Lee, J. (2017). *China's Hegemony: Four Hundred Years of East Asian Domination*. New York, NY: Columbia University Press.

Li, X., and Worm, V. (2011). Building China's soft power for a peaceful rise. *Journal of Chinese Political Science*, 16 (1), 69–89.

O'Harrow, S. (1979). Nguyen Trai's 'Binh Ngo Dai Cao' of 1428: the development of a Vietnamese national identity. *Journal of Southeast Asian Studies*, 10 (1), 159–174.

Qin, Y. (2006). Guoji guanxi lilun zhong zhongguo xuepai shengcheng de keneng he biran [The possibility and inevitability of a Chinese school of international relations theories]. *World Economics and Politics*, 3, 7–13.

Qin, Y. (2010). Struggle for Identity: A Political Psychology of China's Rise. In: B. Womack, ed., *China's Rise in Historical Perspective*. Lanham, MD: Rowman and Littlefield, 249–270.

Rawski, E. (2010). Chinese Strategy and Security Issues in Historical Perspective. In: B. Womack, ed., *China's Rise in Historical Perspective*. Lanham, MD: Rowman and Littlefield, 63–87.

Rossabi, M., ed. (1983). *China Among Equals: The Middle Kingdom and Its Neighbors, 10th-14th Centuries*. Berkeley, CA: University of California Press.

Schroeder, P. (1994). Historical reality vs. neo-realist theory. *International Security*, 19 (1), 108–148.

Suzuki, S. (2009). Exchanging Eurocentrism for Sinocentrism: A Comment on Hierarchy and Asian International Relations. University of Manchester. Accessible via Internet Archive and viewed on 31 October 2020, <https://web.archive.org/web/20150922003355/http://www.wreac.org/chinese/events/past/exchanging-eurocentrism-for-sinocentrism>. Original link: <http://www.wreac.org/chinese/events/past/exchanging-eurocentrism-for-sinocentrism>.

Suzuki, S. (2021). International Order in East Asia. In de Carvalho, B., Costa Lopez, J., & Leira, H., eds. *Routledge Handbook of Historical International Relations*. Abingdon: Routledge.

Tao, J. (1988). *Two Sons of Heaven: Studies in Sung-Liao Relations*. Tucson, AZ: University of Arizona Press.

Tickner, A., and Wæver, O., eds. (2009). *International Relations Scholarship Around the World*. New York, NY: Routledge.

Vuving, A. (2001). The references of Vietnamese states and the mechanisms of world formation. *Asien*, 79, 62–86.

Vuving, A. (2009). Operated By World Views And Interfaced By World Orders: Traditional And Modern Sino-Vietnamese Relations. In: A. Reid, and Y. Zheng, eds., *Negotiating Asymmetry: China's Place in Asia*, Honolulu, HI: University of Hawaii Press, 73–92.

Waltz, K. (1979). *Theory of International Politics*. Reading, MA: Addison-Wesley.

Wang, Y. (2011). *Harmony and War: Confucian Culture and Chinese Power Politics*. New York, NY: Columbia University Press.

Wang, Z.Y. (2006). Chengwei zhishi de shengchanzhe [Becoming a producer of knowledge]. *Shijie jingji yu zhengji [World Economics and Politics]*, 3, 1–6.

Weber, M. (1951). *The Religion of China: Confucianism and Taoism*, trans. Hans H. Gerth. Glencoe, IL: Free Press.

Womack, B. (2012). Asymmetry and China's tributary system. *Chinese Journal of International Politics*, 5 (1), 37–54.

Yan, X. (2011). In: D. Bell, and Z. Sun, eds., *Ancient Chinese Thought, Modern Chinese Power*. Princeton, NJ: Princeton University Press.

Zhang, F. (2015). *Chinese Hegemony: Grand Strategy and International Institutions in East Asian History*. Stanford, CA: Stanford University Press.

18

RACE AND HISTORICAL INTERNATIONAL RELATIONS

Joanne Yao and Andrew Delatolla

Introduction

In August 2017, Mary Beard, Professor of Classics at the University of Cambridge, became the target of online abuse for defending a BBC educational cartoon that portrayed a Roman soldier in Britain as black. In noting that the Roman Empire was multiracial and therefore Roman Britain was similarly multiracial, Beard had directly challenged the myth that Britishness, rooted in Greco-Roman civilization, had always been white (Philo, 2017). Those engaged in abusive behaviour seemed to have found it difficult to escape the modern trappings of race and racial hierarchies, which are tied to myths of civilizational and national development. This myth-linking race and civilization is one that often begins with ancient Greece, the cradle of white, Western civilization, progressing from Europe to the periphery. As such, 'civilization was an unfolding, developing mainly from its own germ; it was not a superficial acquisition but an inward growth' (Bancroft, 1890: 10). This myth proposes a global history tied to assumptions of a white, Western superiority, and its effects can be felt in much of Western historiography. This view, embedded in histories of modernity, helped structure domestic political hierarchies in much of the world and informed the development of modern International Relations (IR).

Drawing from scholarship on the intersections between race, history, and IR, this chapter provides a foundational understanding of race in historical IR. As such, it explores the historical construction of race and its relationship with IR. It locates contemporary conceptualizations of race in the same historical processes that underpin modern international order and stress race's relationship to the development of IR as an academic discipline. The chapter then explores the importance of locating histories of race and racism in international politics to better understand persistent institutional and structural inequalities. Finally, we consider the example of indigenous populations in North America, and specifically Canada, highlighting the relationship between racist intellectual and political asymmetries developed through colonialism.

The historical construction of race

Race as a global idea has complex origins and scholars have identified multiple historical processes that shaped the concept as we understand it today. Some trace the origins of race as a marker of difference to the Renaissance and the Western discovery of an autonomous and rational self beyond the theocentric (Grovogui, 2001; Wynter, 2003; Bethencourt, 2013). Others trace the word 'race', or 'raza' in the Romance languages, to the expulsion of Jewish and Moorish communities from the Iberian Peninsula and the idea of a 'negative stain' on 'clean blood' (Tilley and Shilliam, 2018: 537; see Costa Lopez, 2021 in this volume). Most view the colonial encounter, the dispossession, and mass destruction of the indigenous peoples of the New World and the subsequent transatlantic slave trade to supplement the dwindling indigenous labour supply in the colonial economy as crucial to the development of modern notions of race and racial hierarchy (Caraccioli, 2021). However, the link between imperialism and race was not always straightforward. As Duncan Bell notes, imperialism had been ongoing for centuries before the consolidation of our modern notion of race, and many of the most vocal opponents of imperialism held deeply racist views (2019: 2; also see Hobson, 2012).

Race and racism as powerful global ideas acquired their modern meaning during the 19th century. While ethnocentrism and small-scale racism existed before, Tilden Le Melle argues that racism as 'a worldwide ideological and mythological phenomenon' that shaped the international system 'is the creation of 18th and 19th century Europeans' (2009: 78). Previously, the term race often referred to social groups of all kinds not necessarily connected to skin colour.[1] However, in the 19th century, science was used to naturalize and legitimatize racial hierarchies as insights and methods from the natural science, particularly biology, were applied to human phenotypes (Vincent, 1982; Delatolla and Yao, 2019). As Siba Grovogui contends, during this period, a number of fields 'succumbed to natural history, nationalism, and the naturalization of politics' and this trend 'consecrated the notion of race, racial superiority, and the racial privilege in analyses of international relations' (2001: 433).

The advancement of scientific racism was part of larger processes in the 19th century that spurred the globalization of European international society and the transformation of world order into a core-periphery order dominated by the West (Buzan and Lawson, 2015; Dunne and Reus-Smit, 2017). Racial hierarchies elevated white European societies as civilized, rational, and the developers of progressive institutions while non-whites were deemed barbaric and in need of Western guidance. This civilizational standard legitimated and inspired imperialism as the West took on Rudyard Kipling's famous 'White Man's Burden' to civilize backwards, non-white, peoples. These 19th-century global trends placed race, as 'an interrelated set of material, ideological and epistemological practices' (Persaud and Walker, 2001: 374), at the centre of an emerging order that continues to structure international society today.

Furthermore, these racial hierarchies shaped not only how white Western societies saw their own role as civilizers of the non-white races, but also how the colonized saw themselves and their racialized identity in global politics. As Frantz Fanon observed, 'it is the settler that has brought the native into existence' and that 'the Negro, never so much a Negro as since he has been dominated by the whites' and must defend himself in those racial terms (1967: 166). Hence, the discourse of race and racial hierarchies also constituted identities in the non-white periphery and had path-dependent consequences – both ideational and material – for global politics even as decolonization put an end to formal empires (Delatolla and Yao, 2019). It was in this context in the late-19th and early-20th centuries that the academic discipline of IR was born. The next section outlines the ways in which race and racial administration were fundamental to the origins of the discipline.

The global colour line and the discipline of International Relations

Mainstream disciplinary histories of IR traditionally begin with the aftermath of the First World War and a stylised 'First Debate' between the liberal search for an end to all wars and realist scepticism of liberalism's progressive premise. Critical scholars have recently challenged this orthodoxy, particularly in the erasure of race from these narratives of IR's origins (Vucetic, 2011; Anievas, Manchanda, and Shilliam, 2014; Vitalis, 2015). Anievas, Manchanda, and Shilliam's volume (2014) begins with the premise, borrowed from W.E.B. Du Bois, that the 'problem of the twentieth century is the problem of the colour-line – the relation of the darker to the lighter race of men in Asia and Africa, in America and the islands of the sea' (1961: 23). They highlight how IR as an academic discipline was founded by white Western empires as a 'policy science designed to solve the dilemmas posed by empire-building and colonial administration' (Anievas, Machanda, and Shilliam, 2014: 2). Others have also stressed the importance of colonial administration and management of race relations as an impetus for the establishment of IR as a social science (Long and Schmidt, 2005). These histories of IR's origins place race and concern about racial hierarchy front and centre in the discipline's foundations.

Despite its importance in shaping the origins of IR, since the mid-20th century, race has all but disappeared from mainstream IR scholarship. In Roxanne Doty's survey of five prominent IR journals (World Politics, International Studies Quarterly, International Organization, Journal of Conflict Resolution, and Review of International Studies) between 1945 and 1993, she found that only one article title that included the term 'race' (1993: 445). In his search of paper titles submitted to the International Studies Association's (ISA's) annual conference and published in its flagship journal International Studies Quarterly (ISQ) between 2000 and 2008, James Mittelman found only 0.37% of submitted ISA paper titles and 0% of published titles in ISQ mentioned 'race', 'racial', 'racialised', 'racism', or 'racist' (2009: 100). Of course, some scholars during this period continued to emphasize race and racism, particularly in discussions of Third World movements, decolonization, and apartheid (see, for example, Bull, 1979; Doty, 1993; Klotz, 1995; Le Melle, 2009; Svensson, 2021 in this volume), but these studies were the exception. Why did race disappear so completely from mainstream IR debates?

For Vitalis (2010), the erasure of race from IR's disciplinary self-narratives occurred in the mid-20th century as American IR shifted from imperial and colonial governance to its current focus on great power politics, anarchy, and interstate cooperation. This move sidelined race as well as the African-American scholars who pioneered early debates. During this period, race became relegated to a domestic concern while IR became purely the domain of interstate relations; scholars such as W.E.B. Dubois, Alain Locke, Merze Tate, and Ralph Bunche were relabelled as African-American or Africana studies scholars. Debra Thompson argues that rather than experiencing amnesia over race, IR suffers from aphasia, which she defines as a 'calculated forgetting, an obstruction of discourse, language and speech' (2013: 135). In avoiding discussions of race, IR can lull itself into imagining its practices and institutions have transcended race and racism, what Vitalis calls the 'norm against noticing' racial hierarchies in global institutions and practices (2000: 333). Consequently, the disappearance of racial hierarchies from IR scholarship coincided with the sidelining of other international hierarchies – an area of IR scholarship that has also seen a recent growth (see, for example, Zarakol, 2017). Hence, the agenda forward for scholars is to recover race as central to the origins of IR as an academic discipline as well as to unearth the ways in which race has always been 'baked into' (Crawford, 2016: 1125) the institutions, norms, and practices of international politics.

Recentring race in international politics

Much work has already been done to spotlight race in IR and in the practice of international politics despite the lack of explicit discussion in political or scholarly discourse. Recent scholarship has used critical race theory to evaluate IR theorizing (Henderson, 2013; Bell, 2019). Errol Henderson (2013) highlights how race is present in the foundations of IR. He draws from Charles Mills and Emmanuel Eze in arguing that the social contract articulated by early modern political theorists, including Hobbes and Kant, was in actuality a racial contract that adopted one set of moral assumptions for whites and another set for non-whites. IR discourses of anarchy from Realists to Constructivists draw from these embedded racial assumptions and perpetuates a world where '"civilised" whites' continue to be responsible for 'providing, maintaining, and ensuring order' as non-whites continue to be subjugated (Henderson, 2013: 88). Others have focused on the racial assumptions that inform the institutions and practices of the global economy from colonial dispossession to capitalist accumulation (Chakravartty and Da Silva, 2012; Tilley and Shilliam, 2018). Branwen Gruffydd Jones highlights how a 'racialised imaginary' informs our conceptualizations of successful economies and what constitutes 'good governance' (2013: 50). By examining the ideational and material foundations of the current global order, critical scholars have been able to uncover race and racial hierarchies in many of IR's core assumptions.

Another tool used by postcolonial scholars to reverse erasure and challenge accepted assumptions is contrapuntal analysis, a technique offered by Edward Said to recover overlooked global histories. This technique sets established 'metropolitan history' alongside 'histories against which (and together with which) the dominating discourse acts' to show the multiple, overlapping, and intertwined character of these narratives (1993: 18–51). Krishna (2001) deploys this technique to demonstrate that through processes of theoretical abstraction, IR has erased questions of race from its historical narratives of the emergence of international order. Meera Sabaratnam's work uses contrapuntal analysis as a musical metaphor that allows IR to 'hear multiple melodies…in a way which discloses both the relatedness and distinctiveness of human experiences' (2017). Her historical sociological examination of Mozambique in the First World War highlights how colonialism was built on indifference to the suffering and death of non-white bodies, and that this structure continues to inform global order as manifest in the ways in which we think about the non-white bodies crossing the Mediterranean in the European refugee crisis.

Bringing race to the foreground of IR scholarship makes several important and interrelated interventions. First, highlighting race at the centre of IR's assumptions alerts us to the continuing material and ideational legacies of colonialism on core institutions of international politics. The international institutions, norms, and practices that we believe have escaped the racial injustices of the past are still in many ways bound by race, the 'most efficient instrument of social domination invented in the last 500 years' (Quijano, 2000: 1). For example, not only was race central to pivotal moments of 20th-century world politics such as the Holocaust and the international moral and legal responses to it, considerations of colonial administration and racial hierarchies also shaped the foundations of the League of Nations and UN System (Anghie, 2002; Mazower, 2009; Ravndal, 2021). Second, focusing our analytical lens on race breaks down the stark dichotomy between domestic and international politics. Studies such as Amy Baker's (2015) on American perceptions of foreign aid show how racial relations within societies shape global hierarchies and knowledge structures. However, the converse can also be true. Robbie Shilliam's (2018) analysis of the deserving and undeserving poor maintains that the 'white working class' within Britain was constituted and reconstituted by the elite's attempt to secure the British imperial order. Indeed, as Naeem Inayatullah and David Blaney (2004) argue, the division of political authority between domestic hierarchy and international anarchy does not resolve but reinforces the problem of difference. And third and finally, by focusing on race, scholars have highlighted its continued centrality for the maintenance of the current global order as 'the racialization of history and historical processes' continues to endure in IR theory (Grovogui, 2001: 426; Persaud and Sajed, 2018). Into the 21st century, race and racial inequality still shape major global concerns from immigration (Danewid, 2017), to environmental inequality (Newell, 2005), security studies

(Buzas, 2013; Howell and Richter-Montpetit, 2020), to poverty reduction and humanitarian aid (Baker, 2015; Benton, 2016).

While myriad issues in 19th - and 20th-century international history warrant a re-examination through the analytical lens of racial hierarchies, the next short section uses the history of colonialism in North America to illustrate not only how the global colour line shaped imperialism in the past but also continues to have consequences for racialized bodies in today's international politics. In particular, the section focuses on an understudied aspect of settler colonialism in the Americas – the use of residential schools as a racialized tool of intellectual and physical displacement. We find this case especially salient in the ways it illustrates the three key interventions highlighted above – how foregrounding race shows the material and ideational legacies of colonialism, challenges the stark division between domestic and international politics, and stresses the importance of race in the continued maintenance of the current global order.

Race and colonialism: the case of residential schools in North America

The use of residential schools to re-educate indigenous populations in North America starting in the late-19th century and continuing throughout the 20th century rested on the racialized premise that indigenous knowledge systems were inferior to knowledge systems developed under European modernity. Hence to enter civilized international society, indigenous communities would have to abandon their customs and traditions in favour of 'legitimate' knowledge and practices. One way to erase indigenous lifeworlds[2] was through residential schools, which removed children from indigenous families to be re-educated (Amir, 2018). The programme's goal, as Canada's Deputy Minister of Indian Affairs noted, was to 'get rid of the Indian problem... our object is to continue until there is no Indian question' (Miller, 2004: 35). In other words, residential schools would allow state authorities to displace indigenous lifeworlds and identities and fully integrate the children into the body politic as modern and governable citizens.

Material and ideational legacies of colonialism. North American residential schools showcase the lasting legacy of colonialism (Harper and Thompson, 2017). Ideationally, the racialized civilizational logic that dismissed indigenous knowledge systems and lifeworlds as inferior to Western systems is rooted in long-standing European justifications for colonialism and still informs policy towards indigenous peoples globally. Materially, residential schools subjected children to violence, including physical, sexual, and emotional abuse, in addition to long-term family separation that resulted in lasting intergenerational trauma. Moreover, these schools sought to transform children into 'useful' members of society by focusing on manual labour and the development of technical skills (Miller, 1996, 2004). This focus not only incorporated indigenous communities into the global economy, but also locked them into lower status occupations (Deiter, 1999; Friesen and Friesen, 2002). Hence, through residential schools, the continuation of colonial racial hierarchies produced a cycle of structural inequality that continues to affect indigenous communities today.

Domestic and international politics. While residential schools may seem like a matter of domestic politics, exploring the racial hierarchies that underpin these schools allows us to go beyond the stark domestic-international divide in IR. The use of child separation and re-education as instruments of social engineering to displace uncivilized elements of society is not unique to North America but reflects global 'entangled histories' and has been implemented elsewhere from Israel-Palestine, to Australia and New Zealand, to Africa, China, and Russia. Other salient examples of racialized education policy include African-Americans in the mid-20th century and current policy towards Roma today (Buzas, 2018). While the specifics of these policies developed in response to domestic contexts, the key aim – to displace indigenous lifeworlds and supplant them with European modernity – is located in histories of the 19th century international law, global governance, and, particularly, in the logics of imperial and colonial governance that produced a global order privileging white Europeans (Buzan and Lawson, 2015; Vitalis, 2015).

Continuing importance to international order. The implementation of civilizing programmes such as re-education schools that effectively erased indigenous lifeworlds has ongoing effects on the contemporary international order. While postcolonial states of the global south have limited equality in international institutions, indigenous communities without sovereign state status are not recognized as legitimate actors in international politics and are largely excluded from participation in international forums.[3] This has reinforced 'power relations that not only make indigenous peoples subjects but also subjugates them' (Lindroth, 2011: 543). In other words, projects such as re-education schools not only transform indigenous peoples into productive state subjects, but also diminish these communities' agency outside of the state system. Without formal recognition, indigenous communities are forced to work within domestic and international institutions that prioritize states and state interests – often losing the policy battle to control land and resources in the face of large-scale construction projects such as dams and pipelines that threaten the traditional use of territories. Thus, subsuming indigenous political agency under the state not only has moral implications but also restricts our ability to envision an international order beyond the state-centric model and imagine international politics otherwise.

Conclusion: continuing controversy

In this chapter, we have outlined the wealth of recent critical scholarship that has revealed the importance of race and racial hierarchies in the origins of IR as a discipline and the continuing centrality of race in the institutions, norms, and practices of international order. We have discussed the effects of and ongoing structural and institutional engagements that subjects and subjugates racialized bodies to a world order that is embedded in history. While the study of race in Historical IR has provoked important discussions concerning global power relations, world order, and the making of contemporary politics, we can continue to question how racial asymmetries are present and can be overcome.

While this chapter examined racial logics used to justify the civilizing project and its legacies, the politics of race can be further considered in relation to other characteristics such as gender and sexuality. One can question how gender played a role in the targeting of Professor Mary Beard after she defended the premise that Roman Britain was multiracial. More precisely, however, as Professor Kimberlé Crenshaw has outlined in her work on intersectionality and critical race theory, intersectionality forces researchers to consider the way that exclusions and inequalities intersect to increase barriers (1991; Cho, Crenshaw, and McCall, 2011). Although critical race theory has provided a framework to research and understand processes of racialization in politics and society, it has also exposed the allegedly racist assumptions of other theories in IR, including realism, liberalism, Marxism, and securitization (Agathangelou and Ling, 2004; Howell and Richter-Montpetit, 2020).

Despite increased scholarly attention to race in the history of international order, more engagement is necessary. Racial inequalities that persist may not be immediately evident, but IR scholars need to continuously consider the origins of theories, concepts, methodologies, and how the discipline is subdivided. With regards to the latter, this includes questioning what knowledge is worthy of reproduction in a 'canon' and what knowledge is relegated to regional and theoretical specialisms; for example, categorical divisions between 'Eastern theory' and 'theory' that reproduce the geographic-civilizational division between (Western) theory as the essential foundation while 'othering' and exoticizing knowledge produced in 'Eastern' traditions. While scholars from the European peripheries and global south are celebrated, they are relegated to a separate canon, viewed as an optional addition to the foundational anthologies, or assigned to the category of 'critical theory' (see Fonseca Santos, 2021 in this volume). Nevertheless, some scholars have brought race back to the forefront of the discipline by engaging in critical methods and highlighting structural asymmetries. Yet, the disciplinary and intellectual displacements need to be viewed in tandem with the political realities. Another way to address these inequalities in knowledge production and politics is the classroom, actively discussing the importance of race in international political history and engaging scholarship written in – and by individuals in – the global south (Krishna, 2001; Chowdhry and Rai, 2009).

Suggestions for further reading

Anievas, A., Manchanda, N., and Shilliam, R., eds. (2014). *Race and Racism in International Relations: Confronting the Global Colour Line*. London: Routledge.

Bethencourt, F. (2013). *Racisms: From the Crusades to the Twentieth Century*. Princeton, NJ: Princeton University Press, 2013.

Grovogui, S. N. (2001). Come to Africa: a hermeneutics of race in international theory. *Alternatives*, 26 (4), 425–448.

Persaud, R., and Sajed, A., eds. (2018). *Race, Gender and Culture in International Relations*. London: Routledge.

Quijano, A. (2000). Coloniality of power, rurocentrism, and Latin America. *Nepantla: Views from South*, 1 (3), 533–580.

Tilley, L., and Shilliam, R., eds. (2018). Raced markets. Special issue. *New Political Economy*, 23 (5), 534–543.

Vitalis, R. (2015). *White World Order, Black Power Politics: The Birth of American International Relations*. Ithaca, NY: Cornell University Press.

Notes

1 For example, R.J. Vincent quotes Charles Kingsley who wrote 'there is no more beautiful race in Europe than the wives and daughters of our London shopkeepers' (1982: 659).

2 The concept of lifeworlds refers to the knowledges, practices, experiences, activities, and interactions that construct the world of a community or individual.

3 Notable exceptions include the United Nations Permanent Forum on Indigenous Issues and the Arctic Council but even in these forums, indigenous peoples are not afforded the same rights or power as states.

References

Agathangelou, A., and L. H. M. Ling. (2004). The house of IR: from family power politics to the Poisies of Worldism. *International Studies Review*, 6 (4), 21–49.

Amir, R. (2018). Cultural genocide in Canada? It did happen here. *Aboriginal Policy Studies*, 7 (1), 103–126.

Anghie, A. (2002). Colonialism and the birth of international institutions: sovereignty, economy, and the mandate system of the league of nations. *NYU Journal of International Law*, 34 (3), 513–634.

Baker, A. (2015). Race, paternalism, and foreign aid: evidence from U.S. public opinion. *American Political Science Review*, 109 (1): 93–109.

Bancroft, H. H. (1890). *The Works: Essays and Miscellany*. San Francisco, CA: The History Company Publishers.

Bell, D. (2019). *Empire, Race and Global Justice*. Cambridge: Cambridge University Press.

Benton, A. (2016). Risky business: race, nonequivalence and the humanitarian politics of life. *Visual Anthropology*, 29 (2), 187–203.

Bull, H. (1979). The state's positive role in world affairs. *Daedalus*, 108 (4), 111–123.

Buzan, B., and Lawson, G. (2015). *The Global Transformation: History, Modernity and the Making of International Relations*. Cambridge: Cambridge University Press.

Buzas, Z. (2013). The color of threat: race, threat perception, and the demise of the Anglo-Japanese Alliance (1902–1923). *Security Studies*, 22 (4), 573–606.

Buzas, Z. (2018). Is the good news about law compliance good news about norm compliance? The case of racial equality. *International Organization*, 72 (2), 351–385.

Caraccioli, M. J. (2021). Early (Modern) Empires: The Political Ideology of Conceptual Domination. In de Carvalho, B., Costa Lopez, J., & Leira, H., eds. *Routledge Handbook of Historical International Relations*. Abingdon: Routledge.

Chakravartty, P., and Da Silva, D. F. (2012). Accumulation, dispossession, and debt: the racial logic of global capitalism—an introduction. *American Quarterly*, 64 (3), 361–385.

Cho, S., Crenshaw, K., and McCall, L. (2011). Towards a field of intersectionality studies: theory, applications, and praxis. *Signs: Journal of Women in Culture and Society*, 38 (4), 785–810.

Chowdhry, G., and Rai, S. M. (2009). The geographies of exclusion and the politics of inclusion: race-based exclusions in the teaching of international relations. *International Studies Perspectives*, 10 (1), 84–91.

Costa Lopez, J. (2021). International Relations in/and the Middle Ages. In de Carvalho, B., Costa Lopez, J., & Leira, H., eds. *Routledge Handbook of Historical International Relations*. Abingdon: Routledge.

Crawford, N. (2016). A discussion of Robert Vitalis's white world order, black power politics: the birth of American international relations. *Perspectives on Politics*, 14 (4), 1123–1125.

Crenshaw, K. (1991). Mapping the margins: intersectionality, identity politics, and violence against women of colour. *Stanford Law Review*, 43 (6), 1241–1299.

Danewid, I. (2017). White innocence in the Black Mediterranean: hospitality and the erasure of history. *Third World Quarterly*, 38 (7), 1674–1689.

Deiter, C. (1999). *From our Mothers' Arms: The Intergenerational Impact of Residential Schools in Saskatchewan*. Etobicoke: United Church Publishing House.

Delatolla, A., and Yao, J. (2019). Racializing religion: constructing colonial identities in the Syrian provinces in the nineteenth century. *International Studies Review*, 21 (4), 640–661.

Doty, R. L. (1993). The bounds of 'race' in international relations. *Millennium*, 22 (3), 443–461.

Du Bois, W. E. B. (1961). *The Souls of Black Folk: Essays and Sketches*. Chicago, IL: A.C. McClurg & Co.

Dunne, T., and Reus-Smit, C. (2017). *The Globalization of International Society*. Oxford: Oxford University Press.

Fanon, F. (1967). *The Wretched of the Earth*. New York, NY: Penguin Books.

Fonseca Santos, M. (2021). Disciplinary Histories of Non-Anglophone International Relations: Latin America and the Caribbean. In de Carvalho, B., Costa Lopez, J., & Leira, H., eds. *Routledge Handbook of Historical International Relations*. Abingdon: Routledge.

Friesen, J., and Friesen, V. (2002). *Aboriginal Education in Canada: A Plea for Integration*. Calgary: Detselig.

Gruffydd Jones, B. (2013). 'Good governance' and 'state failure': genealogies of imperial discourse. *Cambridge Review of International Affairs*, 26 (1), 49–70.

Harper, A. O., and Thompson, S. (2017). Structural oppressions facing indigenous students in Canadian education. *Fourth World Journal*, 15 (2), 41–66.

Henderson, E. A. (2013). Hidden in plain sight: racism in international relations theory. *Cambridge Review of International Affairs*, 26 (1), 71–92.

Hobson, J. M. (2012). *The Eurocentric Conception of World Politics: Western International Theory, 1760–2010*. Cambridge: Cambridge University Press.

Howell, A., and Richter-Montpetit, M. (2020). Is securitization theory racist? Civilizationism, methodological whiteness, and antiblack thought in the Copenhagen School. *Security Dialogue*, 51 (1), 3–22.

Inayatullah, N., and Blaney, D. L. (2004). *International Relations and the Problem of Difference*. New York, NY: Routledge.

Klotz, A. (1995). Norms reconstituting interests: global racial equality and U.S. sanctions against South Africa. *International Organization*, 49 (3), 451–478.

Krishna, S. (2001). Race, amnesia, and the education of international relations. *Alternatives*, 26 (4), 401–424.

Le Melle, T. J. (2009). Race in international relations. *International Studies Perspectives*, 10 (1), 77–83.

Lindroth, M. (2011). Paradoxes of power: indigenous peoples in the permanent forum. *Cooperation and Conflict*, 44 (4), 543–562.

Long, D., and Schmidt, B. C. (2005). *Imperialism and Internationalism in the Discipline of International Relations*. Albany: SUNY Press.

Mazower, M. (2009). *No Enchanted Palace: The End of Empire and the Ideological Origins of the United Nations*. Princeton, NJ: Princeton University Press.

Miller, J. R. (1996). *Shingwauk's Vision: A History of Native Residential Schools*. Toronto: University of Toronto Press.

Miller, J. R. (2004). *Lethal Legacy: Current Native Controversies in Canada*. Toronto: University of Toronto Press.

Mittelman, J. H. (2009). The salience of race. *International Studies Perspectives*, 10 (1), 99–107.

Newell, P. (2005). Race, class and the global politics of environmental inequality. *Global Environmental Politics*, 5 (3), 70–94.

Persaud, R. B., and Walker, R. B. J. (2001). Apertura: race in international relations. *Alternatives*, 26 (4), 373–376.

Philo, J. M. (2017). Mary Beard is Right, Roman Britain was Multi-Ethnic – so why does this upset people so much? The Conversation, August 9. Viewed on 20 October 2020, <https://theconversation.com/mary-beard-is-right-roman-britain-was-multi-ethnic-so-why-does-this-upset-people-so-much-82269>.

Quijano, A. (2000). Coloniality of power, eurocentrism, and Latin America. *International Sociology*, 15 (2), 215–232.

Ravndal, E. J. (2021). International Organizations in Historical Perspective. In de Carvalho, B., Costa Lopez, J., & Leira, H., eds. *Routledge Handbook of Historical International Relations*. Abingdon: Routledge.

Sabaratnam, M. (2017). *Decolonising Intervention: International Statebuilding in Mozambique*. London: Rowman & Littlefield International.

Said, E. (1993). The Politics of Knowledge. In: C. McCarthy, and W. Crichlow, eds., *Race, identity and representation in education*, New York, NY: Palgrave Macmillan, 306–314.

Shilliam, R. (2018). *Race and the Undeserving Poor*. Newcastle: Agenda Publishing.

Svensson, T. (2021). Decolonisation and the Erosion of the Imperial Idea. In de Carvalho, B., Costa Lopez, J., & Leira, H., eds. *Routledge Handbook of Historical International Relations*. Abingdon: Routledge.

Thompson, D. (2013). Through, against, and beyond the racial state: the transnational stratum of race. *Cambridge Review of International Affairs*, 26 (1), 133–151.

Tilley, L., and Shilliam, R. (2018). Raced markets: an introduction. *New Political Economy*, 23 (5), 534–543.

Vincent, R. J. (1982). Race in international relations. *International Affairs*, 58 (4), 658–670.

Vitalis, R. (2010). The noble American science of imperial relations and its laws of race development. *Comparative Studies in Society and History*, 52 (4), 909–938.

Vucetic, S. (2011). *The Anglosphere: A Genealogy of a Racialized Identity in International Relations*. Stanford: Stanford University Press.

Wynter, S. (2003). Unsettling the coloniality of being/power/truth/freedom: towards the human, after man, its overrepresentation—an argument. *CR: The New Centennial Review*, 3 (3), 257–337.

Zarakol, A. (2017). *Hierarchies in World Politics*. Cambridge: Cambridge University Press.

19

POLITICAL THEOLOGY AND HISTORICAL INTERNATIONAL RELATIONS

William Bain

This chapter investigates political theology as an approach to understanding international relations. It proceeds in three parts. Part one illuminates assumptions that underpin political theology as a distinct type of inquiry. This identity is mediated by a recurring analogy between divine and human. Part two examines how this analogy informs thinking about extraordinary action that transgresses the established legal order. The language of the exception is latent in all rules-based systems; legitimising humanitarian intervention is perhaps the best example of this language in international relations. Part three reflects on the implications of political theology for studying international relations. Reclaiming a theological inheritance decentres much of what is taken for granted in the field. It challenges deeply internalised interpretations of canonical figures who stand as reference points for particular theoretical traditions, and it also offers a richer understanding of basic concepts like sovereignty and anarchy. However, much of the potential of political theology in international relations remains unfulfilled. The preponderant focus on Christian experience and its bearing on modern European politics leaves little room for engaging the ways in which other traditions—Islam, Judaism, Buddhism, or Hinduism, for example—negotiate the intersection of theology and politics.

Analogies and self-understanding

Political theology is a mode of inquiry that uses theological concepts and categories to comment on political life. These concepts and categories are used, for example, to authorisea particular constitutional arrangement or to explain the nature of sovereign power. An analogy between divine and human provides the ground of such commentary. The force of this analogy, and the authority it confers, is bound up with beliefs about God's nature and attributes, and his relation to the created world. Particular conceptions of God correspond with particular understandings of politics. Emphasising God's unfettered power lends weight to absolutist theories of rule and positivist conceptions of law, and emphasising God's reason privileges interconnectedness and limits what human beings can legitimately make and do (Oakley, 2005: 26–34). Scripture abounds with imagery that portrays God as a king who rules the universe as the supreme lawgiver and judge. This, in turn, provides a model for popes and kings. Medieval theologians explained the fullness of papal power by imagining the pope as a monarch who rules the Church as God rules the universe. Likewise, secular monarchs imitated God in making laws and dispensing justice. Royal prerogative, the special power or privilege that monarchs enjoy to the exclusion of all other persons, includes the power to contravene the established legal order to perform the equivalent of a miracle in politics (Figgis, 1922: 5; Oakley, 1999). Even Thomas Hobbes, who is often thought to have made a decisive break with medieval religiosity, makes use of the divine analogy to explain the generation of the commonwealth (Martinich, 1992: 10; Bain, 2020: ch. 6). Each of these examples illustrates the way in which political theology explains the character of political life.

Yet political theology as I have described it is not prominent in International Relations scholarship. Political theology must be understood as being domiciled somewhere else. Modern theologians detect political theologies in the writings of Augustine, Thomas Aquinas, and Martin Luther; and historians of political thought describe the immortal body politic and the character of royal power in terms of political theology (Oakley, 1968; Kantorowicz, 1981). However, the most capacious home is found in political theory. With publication of Carl Schmitt's *Political Theology* (1985), it was possible to imagine political theology as a distinct and self-conscious type of inquiry (Cavanaugh and Scott, 2019: 3). Notable examples include Giorgio Agamben's extension of the secularisation of theological concepts to the fundamentals of economic life (Agamben, 2011: 4). Michael Allen Gillespie (2008) argues that the heroic story about the rejection of religion and the triumph of science conceals the theological foundation of modernity itself. Projecting God's sovereignty onto earthly rule brings Jean Bethke Elshtain (2008: 228) to the edge of the abyss of the sovereign self. The divinisation of the human will, she warns rather darkly, is a destructive dead end because the sovereign self, untethered from any transcendent truth, will eventually succumb to the power it seeks to harness. And Paul Kahn (2011) employs political theology to understand the way in which the modern state occupies the place of the sacred. His point is that modern political practices remain embedded in forms of belief that make contact with the sacred.

The intellectual ferment in political theory overshadows the paucity of achievement in the field of International Relations (IR). Talk of God has been pushed to the margins of IR scholarship because rational investigation is assumed to be the only appropriate way to study the subject. Unverifiable belief might have historical significance, but it has no place in contemporary international theory. Today, such talk is usually confined to explaining the 'resurgence of religion' and the threat it poses to the Western culture of secular modernity (Thomas, 2000; Bull, 2000: 168–169). Consequently, political theology is largely a recent import that has yet to make a significant impact. True, notions of apostasy and sin colour the thought of Martin Wight (1948) and Herbert Butterfield (1949), and a scriptural motif frames Reinhold Niebuhr's (1944) defence of democracy against moral cynicism and the latent hubris of the West. But, more often than not, political theology is a kind of jargon that draws attention—loosely to be sure—to the religious dimension of international relations. This, it must be stressed, is something quite different from systematic inquiry into the nature of God, his relation to the created world, and what this relation implies about political life. Of course, Schmitt looms large in this enterprise, but too often the claims of political theology are founded on opportunistic recitations of one or two passages. Invoking the dictum, '[s]overeign is he who decides on the exception' (Schmitt, 1985: 5), to condemn the arbitrariness of sovereign power elides a history that filters extraordinary action through considerations of rightness and goodness. And when abstracted from this history, the exception takes on the air of uncritical slogan; it is an abridgement that is enlisted in the service of practical action.

We are left with a picture of political theology that lacks the kind of intellectual composition that is required to bring otherwise disparate elements together in a coherent representation. This does not mean that the field of IR is devoid of scholarship that is worthy of attention. Nicolas Guilhot (2010) provides an account of the translation of sovereign power, and its entanglement with theology, into the technical and disciplinary language of IR theory. This, he argues, is a decisive part of the field's post-war evolution. In this respect, the realism of Niebuhr and his fellow travellers must be understood as a political and theological critique of liberal optimism and misplaced scientific certainty. Others reinterpret the thought of canonical thinkers as political theology (see Bain, 2014b; Molloy, 2017; Bain, 2019) or engage in an agenda setting exercise to re-engage what most scholars treat as discrete domains: politics and theology (Thomas 2010: Bain 2014a; Paipais, 2020). But, evidence of progress duly acknowledged, political theology is still, in the main, something that takes place outside the disciplinary walls of IR. The literature within these walls is scattered and unsystematic. There are few reference points around which to organise self-conscious debates or sustained programmes of research. There is, at present, no equivalent to Gillespie's *The Theological Origins of Modernity* or Elshtain's *Sovereignty, God, State, and Self* to guide the theorist of IR. This leads to a critical point. Kahn argues that if political theology is going to be any more than an exercise in genealogy, it must be able to show that existing political practices remain embedded in theological concepts and categories (2011: 3). Political theology must be able to look forward as well as backward, leveraging a better understanding of the past so that we can see more clearly in the present.

To see international relations more clearly, I want to revisit Schmitt's decisionist politics of the exception. My objective is to show that political theology, understood as a dialectic of past and present, illuminates a dilemma that arises in a world where belief in God is one of several possibilities that can be called upon to fix meaning. It then becomes apparent that political theology involves a great deal more than simply recognising that political concepts are secularised theological concepts. Theological concepts reflect meanings that survive the process of translation and they are modified in ways that remnants of the past are intelligible in the present. Divine sovereignty can be translated into human sovereignty, but the meaning of sovereignty may well change when it is adapted to different circumstances or invoked to address different problems. Saying that the king is sovereign and, therefore, above the law he legislates is no simple translation of the belief that God is the supreme sovereign of the universe who is subject to no necessity whatsoever. The verbal formulation of sovereignty is the same but its meaning is different in important ways (see Condren, 1985: 111). The God–king analogy supposes that the king bears a likeness to God as he judges and legislates, but likeness does not entail identity. Crucially, the politics of the exception in contemporary international relations must be evaluated in this light. As Kahn (110–111) argues, the meaning of the exception is worked out by interrogating both sides of the analogy: divine and human. That is to say, the structure of meaning that grounds the theological original must be placed alongside the political derivative. Only then will it be possible to ascertain whether the analogy is convincing and, by extension, whether exceptional action in politics is anything more than a mask for arbitrary power.

The issue here is one of acquiring greater self-understanding. But to appreciate what this involves, it is necessary to refine our understanding of political theology and its underlying orientation. Approaching political theology from the standpoint of faith posits the authority of revelation as the ultimate ground of politics. In contrast, approaching political theology from the standpoint of history presumes that arrangements of political life have theological antecedents. I want to defend the second of these approaches in an attempt to tease out the implications of the politics of the exception in contemporary international relations. This historical orientation is present in Schmitt's oft-cited contention that '[a]ll significant concepts of the modern theory of the state are secularized theological concepts (1985: 36).' The immediate implication, as I have made clear already, is that political concepts have a history that is embedded in theology. But the value of recovering this history transcends the business of identifying antecedents and forerunners; political theology also makes contact with the concerns of the here and now.

Theological and political concepts disclose a structural resemblance that conditions the possibilities of coherent thought and action. By this, I mean concepts inherited from the past continue to exert influence in how we know and explain our world. This is of great importance insofar as the exception in politics is an inheritance from a world that relied on God to fix the meaning of reality. But what is left when a concept modelled on a particular understanding of God is part of a godless world? In answering this question, we realise the promise of political theology and advance the cause of greater self-understanding.

Translating the exception

In 1999, NATO initiated a bombing campaign aimed at pacifying the dispute between Yugoslavia and the Kosovo Liberation Army. The campaign provoked a vigorous debate about the legitimacy of the intervention. NATO could not claim to be acting in self-defence and, without authorisation from the Security Council, it could not plausibly claim to be responding to a threat to international peace and security under the auspices of Chapter VII of the United Nations Charter. One argument adduced in support of the war takes refuge in the politics of the exception, describing the use of force as 'illegal but legitimate' (IICK, 2000: 4). The Kosovo War illustrates the tension that arises when normal political life, expressed by the ordinary course of international law, collides with what is required to preserve or restore a normal state of affairs. That is to say, sometimes it is necessary to transgress the requirements of law for the sake of some other good. The model for this kind of action is the God of power and might found in the Hebraic scriptures. God so understood can act contrary to the established economy of salvation, for example, to grant salvation outside the sacrament of baptism. He can act contrary to the established order of morality by decreeing that adultery is meritorious. And he can stay the course of nature, as when Daniel's three companions, Shadrach, Meshach, and Abednego, emerged unscathed by the flames of Nebuchadnezzar's fiery furnace. Though fire normally consumes whatever it touches, upon the bodies of these men, it had no effect on account of God's intervention (Daniel, 3: 19–26). It is this mode of action, the capacity to perform opposites, which Schmitt has in mind when writes: '[t]he exception in jurisprudence is analogous to the miracle in the theology (1985: 36).'

But the translation from theology to jurisprudence is not exact. Therefore, understanding where and when these languages diverge is critical in grasping the full implications of the exception in international relations. When speculating about the nature of God's power, medieval theologians distinguished absolute power from ordinary or ordained power. The juristic interpretation of this distinction centres on a presently active power that operates within the dome of history. By his ordinary power, God works through arrangements—salvational, moral, and natural—that he freely brought into existence. Yet God can act apart from these arrangements when acting according to his absolute power, should it please him to do so. To grasp the extent to which seemingly esoteric theological speculation shapes taken-for-granted principles of modern politics, law, and ethics, it is critical to take the two powers together (Oakley, 1984: 62, 1999). Medieval theologians used the distinction to vindicate God's unfettered freedom while accounting for the regularity of order. The contrast between the two powers is meant to show that God is subject to no necessity; hence, everything can be other than it is. Immutable laws of nature do not constrain God's power; he can, if he so wishes, move the heavens in a linear rather than in a circular motion. But acknowledging God's absolute power does not condemn human beings to a life of perpetual uncertainty. God is no arbitrary tyrant. They can have confidence in the gift of salvation and the orderly course of nature because God freely binds himself, through covenant and promise, to uphold what he has established. The principle here is that the only force capable of binding God's omnipotence is the divine will itself (Oakley, 1984: 62, 84, 1999: 287).

Modern theories of contract and consent, positive law and morality, and sovereignty and constitutional government are shot through with these intellectual commitments. Canon lawyers, civilian jurists, and royal apologists followed the theologians by translating these commitments for use in the worldly affairs of ecclesiastical and secular polity (see Costa Lopez, 2021 in this volume). When the law and what the law prescribes is in the power of *any* agent, it is possible for that agent to reorder what exists at present (Duns Scotus, 2017: 95–97). As with God, so too popes and kings. The early modern discourse of sovereignty flourished with the assimilation of this principle into political thought. The king, God's lieutenant on earth, possesses the capacity and the authority to make and unmake at his pleasure (Oakley, 1984: 97). At this point, however, the limits of translation come into view. Saying that the king is like God does not free the human sovereign of all restraint. A king cannot make lying or theft meritorious. The resort to absolute power is conditional inasmuch as it must be justified by reasonable cause in the service of a good end. Consequently, the politics of the exception does not licence capricious power. When a pope acts outside established law, his aim must be consistent with the spiritual mission of the Church. Likewise, a king can make law as well as override what the law prescribes, but only in matters that fall within the jurisdiction of the commonwealth. Historically, this meant that popes and kings are above human law that they can transgress in special circumstances, but they remain at all times subject to divine and natural law (see, for example, Bodin, 1992: 13–14, 33–34; Giles of Rome, 2004: 361). It is this measure of restraint which distinguishes the politics of the exception in medieval and early modern thought from what theorists of IR associate with sovereignty and a culture of impunity.

We are left to ask what this brief exploration of medieval thought tells us about the politics of the exception in international relations. Political theology offers an answer that goes beyond a better understanding of historical antecedents. Acquiring such an understanding is likely to be of little interest to the practical-minded theorist who is interested in eradicating oppression and promoting a particular notion of the good life. But this attitude is short-sighted insofar as it ignores the productive character of assumptions, embedded in particular histories, which condition how we know and explain the world. Two observations are relevant in this regard. The first is that the exception is a conspicuous feature of international relations. I have already mentioned NATO's intervention in Kosovo and the justification of 'unlawful but legitimate'. Torture, or enhanced interrogation in the 'newspeak' of the American-led War on Terror, is another example. The prohibition of torture is a peremptory norm of international law—a norm that permits no derogation—but some argue that there are occasions when the safety of the people justifies overriding this norm. This is not a recent phenomenon that exposes a peculiar pathology of contemporary global order. The partitions of Poland in the late-eighteenth century, contrary to the principle of the balance of power, can be seen as exceptions for the sake of managing change (Gulick, 1955: 41). A related problem arises in the context of the sanctity of agreements. That promises should be kept is widely recognised as a fundamental precept of all social life; however, there are occasions when changing circumstances render the terms of an agreement inequitable or dangerous. The doctrine of *rebus sic stantibus* affords a remedy by permitting states to repudiate excessively burdensome or obsolete treaty obligations (Brierly, 1963: 335–340). The point on which these examples converge is that the exception arises in all rule-based systems that are populated by free subjects. To establish a rule of law is to extend an invitation to probe and test its limits.

This leads to the second observation. While there is a structural resemblance between medieval theology and modern international relations, there comes a point when the modern exception deviates from the theological original. Political theology makes contact with present concerns by bringing this deviation to light. To appreciate the character of this contribution, we must return to God's self-imposed promise to uphold what he has freely ordained. An omnipotent God who nonetheless binds himself to work through the order of creation satisfies the twofold need to vindicate divine freedom and to sustain the regularity of the universe. Crucially, human beings can have confidence in God's promise because God is good and perfect in every way. God does not joke or deceive when he promises; as Martin Luther (1961: 261, 282) once observed, God speaks directly and earnestly, which relieves the burden of doubt. However, the matter is quite different when it comes to human analogues. Human beings are conditionally good; they are created in God's image but, unlike God, they can and do misuse their freedom to choose something that is bad because it is bad. That is, human beings should act in conformity with God's will but they are under no necessity to do so. It should come as no surprise, then, that promises given by human sovereigns do not elicit the same confidence as those given by God. The language of absolute power serves to highlight the limits of power in this context. Here it is well to remember that in politics the adjective 'absolute' refers to the perfection of power in the human sovereign, not to an unfettered freedom to command without reason or cause. Kings are not God; they imitate God, and imitation involves a representation rather than a reproduction. Therefore, popes and kings should act according to the established order of law precisely because they are not God (Oakley, 1984: 113–114).

Uncovering this historical ground reveals the arbitrariness of the exception in contemporary international relations. William of Ockham's notion of the subordination of the will illustrates the significance of this point. Free will, as he understands it, is not completely autonomous and, in that regard, it is not to be confused with Kantian self-sovereignty. A good act for Ockham is one which is governed by the right reason, and to act according to the right reason is to love God and to love what God wants. Therefore, the human will is subject to something outside itself because loving what God wants means conforming to God's command (King, 1999: 237–238). But theorists of IR no longer call on God to furnish knowledge of things and actions that should be loved. In a world that is the product of nothing more than human thought and action, the will is subordinate to nothing beyond itself. The sovereign self, having assumed the mantle of God in ordaining the arrangements of moral and political life, is the sole judge of right and goodness. This divinised self stipulates a postulate that guides and legitimises the decisions of the will. God is not excluded as a possibility, but he is not necessarily included either; common humanity or rational autonomy is more likely to be invoked to secure ground of human conduct. Yet this ground is no more secure than before. Postulates of this kind cannot be verified as such (Collingwood, 1998: 30–32); empirical investigation cannot tell us that rational autonomy is 'true' any more than it can prove the existence of God. Rational autonomy is stipulated as an assumption that is either accepted or rejected for the purpose of making sense of the world, and the claims it supports will be intelligible only to those who accept it as a postulate. In other words, its authority is mandate of the human will, just as Ockham's omnipotent God mandates the objects that human beings should love.

The arbitrary character of the exception becomes apparent when we come to realise that there is no rational method for choosing between rival postulates. The exception is an expression of free will that is intended to preserve or restore a particular state of affairs in a time of emergency. Advocates of the Responsibility to Protect often appeal to the idea of common humanity when the fury of the present demands that 'something must be done'. Gareth Evans (2008: 296) is clear about what this means: 'at the end of the day the case for R2P rests simply on our common humanity: the impossibility of ignoring the cries of pain and distress of our fellow human beings'. This call will resonate with those who embrace common humanity as their postulate. But others, who proceed from a different postulate, might interpret the same call as an apology for power. It is then a short step to corrosive cynicism: 'whoever invokes humanity wants to cheat' (Schmitt, 1996: 54). The point here is that before the tribunal of the sovereign self, modelled on an omnipotent God, fundamental postulates and the values they express are ultimately indeterminate. A postulate can be stipulated to fix a hierarchy of values; yet what is made today can be unmade tomorrow: the sovereign self can dispense with one postulate and adopt another to legitimise a preferred policy or course of action. Political theology brings to the surface what is at stake when the original structure of meaning is abandoned. Cutting away the promise of an omnipotent but absolutely good God, leaves us to repose confidence in the promise of a sovereign self who is the sole author and judge of what is right and good. The problem, of course, is that a sovereign self, governed by no transcendent good and loosed from all restraint, might be a terror to others, because the will that stipulates rational autonomy, common humanity, or some other postulate to ground the regularity of political life, is the same will that decides the exception.

Achievements and directions

In this chapter, I have explored the history of the exception to illustrate the critical potential of political theology in IR scholarship. Political theology holds out a distinctive interpretive key that unlocks meanings that are otherwise hidden by a pervasive discourse of secularisation. In this sense, political theology provides an answer to a fundamental question: how did we come to imagine international relations as we do? One way of answering this question is to excavate the assimilation of theological ideas to the institutions and practices of international relations. No doubt, sovereignty is the most obvious example in this regard (see de Carvalho, 2021 in this volume). But in recent years, this interpretive key has been used to unlock the theological character of other concepts: anarchy, balance of power, constitutionalism, and international order (Bain, 2020; see Andersen and Wohlforth, 2021 in this volume). 'Wrestling with God', as Cecelia Lynch puts it, has shaped the course and meaning of international relations. Political theology, conceived as a type of inquiry, foregrounds tensions that colour how we think about otherness, social justice, and violence in international relations (Lynch, 2020). These engagements, among others, decentre what is attributed to canonical thinkers (see Wallenius, 2021 in this volume). Recover the theological character of Hobbes's political philosophy and we find that he is less the theorist of violent anarchy than a theorist of interstate society (Bain, 2019). They also expose the fetishisation of founding myths. Modern IR did not emerge once the learned sons of the Renaissance cast off the yoke of religion. Consequently, international relations—the state systems and many of the institutions and practices that describe it—might not be the secular arrangement that most theorists assume it to be.

Excavating the theological ground of modern international relations is particularly important in a world that is no longer defined solely by the European or the Christian thought and action. Concepts like anarchy and balance of power are not neutral categories which happen to cast useful light on questions of war and peace; they are heavily laden with normative presumptions of individual freedom. The same can be said of the voluntarism that underpins the social contract tradition and positivist theories of international law. It matters enormously in a deeply plural world that these ideas are saturated with Christian understandings of individual choice and personal responsibility (Riley, 1982: ch. 1). Acquiring a better self-understanding of how 'we' arrived 'here' provides a timely reminder that common ways of thinking and speaking about international relations are culturally specific in profound ways. It is here especially that there is more work to be done. Political theology is most closely associated with Christian thought and experience; yet it is not the exclusive preserve of Christianity and its various commentators (see Paipais, 2020: chs. 5, 7). A political theology can be constructed out of the materials furnished by other faiths. For example, the priority that the Islamic theologian and philosopher Al-Ghazali ascribes to the divine will, as against the rationalist orientation of Avicenna, predates parallels in Christian thought by nearly two centuries (Marmura, 2006). Effort would be well directed not only to elucidating political theologies in faiths other than Christianity but also to working out connections and parallels between faiths. It is the task of political theology, both past and present, to recover the theological inheritance of these cultures, and their associated structures of meaning, in a world in which God is not yet dead.

Suggestions for further reading

Bain, W. (2020). *Political Theology of International Order*. Oxford: Oxford University Press.
Elshtain, J. B. (2008). *Sovereignty, God, State, and Self*. New York, NY: Basic Books.
Gillespie, M. A. (2008). *The Theological Origins of Modernity*. Chicago, IL: University of Chicago Press.
Guilhot, N. (2010). American Katechon: when political theology became international relations theory. *Constellations*, 17 (2), 224–253.
Kahn, P. (2011). *Political Theology: Four New Chapters on the Concept of Sovereignty*. New York, NY: Columbia University Press.
Molloy, S. (2017). *Kant's International Relations: The Political Theology of Perpetual Peace*. Ann Arbor, MI: University of Michigan Press.
Paipais, V., ed. (2020). *Theology and World Politics: Metaphysics, Genealogies, Political Theologies*. Cham: Palgrave Macmillan.
Schmitt, C. (1985). *Political Theology: Four Chapters on the Concept of Sovereignty*. Translated by G. Schwab. Chicago, IL: University of Chicago Press.
Thomas, S. M. (2010). Living critically and 'living faithfully' in a global age: justice, emancipation and the political theology of international relations. *Millennium*, 39 (2), 505–524.

References

Agamben, G. (2011). *The Kingdom and the Glory: For a Theological Genealogy of Economy and Government*. Stanford, CA: Stanford University Press.
Andersen, M. A., and Wohlforth, W. C. (2021). Balance of Power: A Key Concept in Historical Perspective. In de Carvalho, B., Costa Lopez, J., & Leira, H., eds. *Routledge Handbook of Historical International Relations*. Abingdon: Routledge.
Bain, W. (2014a). Rival traditions of natural law: Martin Wight and the theory of international society. *International History Review*, 36 (5), 943–960.
Bain, W. (2014b). Thomas Hobbes as a theorist of anarchy: a theological interpretation. *History of European Ideas*, 41 (1), 13–28.
Bain, W. (2019). International anarchy and political theology: rethinking the legacy of Thomas Hobbes. *Journal of International Relations and Development*, 22 (2), 278–299.
Bain, W. (2020). Political Theology of International Order. Oxford: Oxford University Press.
Bodin, J. (1992). *On Sovereignty*. Edited and translated by J. Franklin. Cambridge: Cambridge University Press.
Brierly, J. L. (1963). *The Law of Nations: An Introduction to the International Law of Peace*. Edited by H. Waldock. 6th edition. Oxford: Oxford University Press.
Bull, H. (2000). Natural Law and International Relations (1979). In: K. Alderson and A. Hurrell, eds., *Hedley Bull on International Society*, Basingstoke: Macmillan, 157–169.
Butterfield, H. (1949). *Christianity and History*. London: Charles Scribner's Sons.
Cavanaugh, W., and Scott, P. M. (2019). Introduction to the Second Edition. In: W. Cavanaugh, and P.M. Scott, eds., *The Wiley Blackwell Companion to Political Theology*. 2nd edition, West Sussex: Blackwell Publishing, 1–12.
Collingwood, R. G. (1998). *An Essay on Metaphysics*. Revised edition. Edited by R. Martin. Oxford: Clarendon Press.
Condren, C. (1985). *The Status and Appraisal of Classic Texts: An Essay on Political Theory, Its Inheritance, and the History of Ideas*. Princeton, NJ: Princeton University Press.

Costa Lopez, J. (2021). International Relations in/and the Middle Ages. In de Carvalho, B., Costa Lopez, J., & Leira, H., eds. *Routledge Handbook of Historical International Relations*. Abingdon: Routledge.

de Carvalho, B. (2021). Sovereignty in Historical International Relations: Trajectories, Challenges and Implications. In de Carvalho, B., Costa Lopez, J., & Leira, H., eds. *Routledge Handbook of Historical International Relations*. Abingdon: Routledge.

Duns Scotus, J. (2017). *John Duns Scotus: Selected Writings on Ethics*. Edited and translated by T. Williams. Oxford: Oxford University Press.

Evans, G. (2008). The responsibility to protect: an idea whose time has come…and gone? *International Relations*, 22 (3), 283–298.

Figgis, J. N. (1922). *The Divine Right of Kings*. 2nd edition. Cambridge: Cambridge University Press.

Giles of Rome (2004). *On Ecclesiastical Power*. Edited and translated by R.W. Dyson. New York, NY: Columbia University Press.

Gulick, E.V. (1955). *Europe's Classical Balance of Power: A Case History on the Theory and Practice of One of the Great Concepts of European Statecraft*. New York, NY: W.W. Norton.

IICK (2000). *Kosovo Report: Conflict, International Response, Lessons Learned*. Oxford: Oxford University Press.

Kantorowicz, E. (1981). *The King's Two Bodies: A Study in Mediaeval Political Theology*. Princeton, NJ: Princeton University Press.

King, P. (1999). Ockham's Ethical Theory. In: P. V. Spade, ed., *The Cambridge Companion to Ockham*, Cambridge: Cambridge University Press, 227–244.

Luther, M. (1961). *Luther's Works: Lectures on Genesis, Chapters 15–20*. Volume 3. Edited by J. Pelikan. Saint Louis, MO: Concordia Publishing House.

Lynch, C. (2020). *Wrestling with God: Ethical Precarity in Christianity and International Relations*. Cambridge: Cambridge University Press.

Marmura, M. (2006). Al-Ghazali. In: P. Adamson, and R. Taylor, eds., *The Cambridge Companion to Arabic Philosophy*, Cambridge: Cambridge University Press, 137–154.

Martinich, A.P. (1992). *The Two God of Leviathan: Thomas Hobbes on Religion and Politics*. Cambridge: Cambridge University Press.

Niebuhr, R. (1944). *The Children of Light and the Children of Darkness*. New York, NY: Charles Scribner's Sons.

Oakley, F. (1968). Jacobean political theology: the absolute and ordinary powers of the king. *Journal of the History of Ideas*, 29 (3), 323–346.

Oakley, F. (1984). *Omnipotence, Covenant, and Order: An Excursion in the History of Ideas from Abelard to Leibniz*. Ithaca, NY: Cornell University Press.

Oakley, F. (1999). 'Adamantine Fetters of Destiny:' The Absolute and Ordained Power of God and King in the Sixteenth and Seventeenth Centuries. In: F. Oakley, ed., *Politics and Eternity: Studies in the History of Medieval and Early-Modern Political Thought*, Leiden: Brill, 276–332.

Oakley, F. (2005). *Natural Law, Laws of Nature, Natural Rights: Continuity and Discontinuity in the History of Ideas*. New York, NY: Continuum.

Riley, P. (1982). *Will and Political Legitimacy: A Critical Exposition of Social Contract Theory in Hobbes, Locke, Rousseau, Kant, and Hegel*. Cambridge, MA: Harvard University Press.

Schmitt, C. (1996). *The Concept of the Political*. Translated by G. Schwab. Chicago, IL: University of Chicago Press.

Thomas, S. (2000). Taking religious and cultural pluralism seriously: the global resurgence of religion and the transformation of international society. *Millennium*, 29 (3), 815–841.

Wallenius, T. (2021). How to Do the History of International Thought?. In de Carvalho, B., Costa Lopez, J., & Leira, H., eds. *Routledge Handbook of Historical International Relations*. Abingdon: Routledge.

Wight, M. (1948). The Church, Russia and the West. *The Ecumenical Review*, 1 (1), 25–45.

20

TIME AND HISTORY IN INTERNATIONAL RELATIONS

Andrew R. Hom

Introduction: the rise of time and history in IR

'International Relations, what a timeless, ahistorical discipline!' So the critical refrain went for decades, as structuralist rationalism, game theory, and large-N statistical work strip-mined international politics in search of elusive empirical laws, durable equilibria, or predictable phenomena that would provide International Relations (IR) its social scientific bona fides. It is debatable whether IR was ever as timeless or without history as it seemed, given that scholars – even those happily roving in formal models or scrubbing context from evidence to produce data – have always looked to the past for inspiration and cases, commented on present dilemmas, and wagered predictions about the future (see also de Carvalho, Costa Lopez, and Leira, 2021 in this volume). It is probably fairer to charge that IR traditionally treated time and history as rough and ready concepts rather than explicit, reflexive, terms of art. Nevertheless, for the past two decades or so, IR ceased taking time and history for granted. Critical IR's interest in interdisciplinary time studies, historical sociology, and the return of big comparative histories, the emergence of historical institutionalism, the use of thick descriptive case studies by constructivists, and new disciplinary intellectual histories all foregrounded time, contingency, and historical context.

Such developments offer a salutary opportunity to take stock of the discipline's underlying concepts and animating assumptions about time and history. Other chapters in this handbook interrogate the uses of the past and the historian's craft, offering a number of clarifications and useful ways to organize our thinking about Historical IR. This chapter does so for time and temporality with the aim of explicating IR's use of time and proposing ways to combine temporal and historical IR more productively.

IR's traditional uses of time

Prior to a recent upsurge in interest, IR sporadically evoked time in discussions of surprising events (Jervis, 1991), long-term change (Dark, 1998), foreign policy (see Beasley and Hom, 2021), international conflict (Akcinaroglu and Radziszewski, 2005), or political science methods (Beck, Katz, and Tucker, 1998). But because time played a tertiary role in such researches, IR's temporal imagination hewed mostly to two binaries popular in the wider human and natural sciences – linear/cyclical and continuity/change – that unravel upon closer inspection (see MacKay and Laroche, 2021).

Linear or cyclical?

First, IR treated 'linear' and 'cyclical' time as fundamental and dichotomous concepts (Hom 2020: 5–18). Linear time encompassed a huge range of phenomena and ideas, from *the* singular path of human history, a related sequence of 'developmental stages' common to all cultures, various progressive-normative claims about the 'march of history' towards a desirable end point, the way that grand narratives privilege hegemonic agents, positivist social science, and the basic link between cause and effect. Likewise, 'cyclical time' signified 'long waves', balances of power, historical materialist dialectics, core and peripheral world systems, and other recurring political phenomena (see Hom, 2018, 2019). Almost as often, it was conflated with 'timelessness', based on the assumption recurrence somehow stands above or beyond time.[1] In both cases, scholars framed cyclical time/timelessness and linear time as natural opposites.

This prevalent way of thinking about political times proves unsustainable in at least two ways. First, it is unclear whether the opposition refers to time or history. 'Linear time' frequently helps scholars distinguish 'modernity' from earlier epochs (see Walker, 1993). But such discussions rarely devote as much attention to time itself as they do to issues of periodization or the 'shape' of events (see Guillaume, 2021). For this reason, such claims have come under scrutiny in IR and beyond (see Inayatullah and Blaney, 2004; Fasolt, 2004). 'Linear' in these accounts primarily describes progressive historical development rather than making claims about the serial nature of time *per se* (see discussion in Herborth and Nitzschner, 2021 in this volume).

Similarly, cyclicality can describe recurring event series but struggles as an alternative to linear time or as a conceptualization of time as such. If time were to pass by doubling back on itself, we would relive our lives on perpetual and perfect repeat. This, in turn, would open up questions about the extent of our time loop and the possibility of historical memory. Tellingly, while we might use 'cyclical time' to symbolize historical trends (e.g. Jarvis, 2009: 39–40), espousals of cyclical time *per se* are hard to find.[2]

Finally, a more basic linear assumption about time underpins this opposition. The 'linear time' of historical progress resolves against a wider flow that is in some way linear enough for us to select and arrange some of its phenomena in an optimistic narrative indexed to calendrical dates constructed from the linear accumulation of celestial repetitions. Similarly, 'conceptions of timelessness emphasise the persistence of repetition and return … *between chronologically distinct historical eras*' (Jarvis, 2009: 39 emphasis added; cf. Sorabji, 2006: 184–185). But if repetitious phenomena mark both 'cyclical time' and 'timelessness' (e.g. Elman and Elman, 2008: 359), it is worth asking whether this concept can bear its own weight or support IR's dominant temporal antinomy. While these interpretations of historical arcs contain temporal content, it is hard to see how they could cohere as opposing and exhaustive descriptions of time itself. They, and the assumptions from which they spring, remain several layers of abstraction removed from the lived experience of time or speculative claims about the nature of time itself. It is probably more accurate to understand their conflation with time *per se* as a matter of metaphor or idiom – familiar symbolic terms that hide assumptions even as they quickly transfer meaning in a dialogue based on a shared hermeneutic toolkit (see Elias, 1989).

Continuity or change?

Even more commonly, IR scholars distinguish between 'continuity' and 'change' in various political processes and disciplinary subfields and treat these terms as self-evident categories of almost universal pertinence. Foreign policy analysis frequently speculates on whether state policy positions evince continuity or change over time (*inter alia* Zhang, 2016: 771; Sinha, 2017;

Kakachia, Minesashvili, and Kakhishvili, 2018). The same goes for national security and grand strategy (see Lissner, 2018). According to such habits of thought, continuity and change pose 'competing perspectives on world politics' (Hughes, 1997) or rough and ready ways of interpreting systemic change (Lawson, Armbruster, and Cox, 2010) and globalization (Rupert and Smith, 2016), among others. Critical projects to develop a 'postinternational' theory or to gender international politics also deploy this binary with ease (Rosenau, 1990; Aggestam and True, 2020). Moreover, the way that arguments about 'continuity *through* change' (Qin, 2014, emphasis added) or the two working *in tandem* (Rosenau, 1990) pitch themselves as provocations further attests to the distinction's stickiness.

Much like linear vs. cyclical, the continuity-change distinction depends heavily on historical interpretation of what actors and processes matter and how particular events relate to one another. The world and we in it are always changing in ways small and great (Grosz, 1999), yet we perceive plenty of continuity, from everyday routines that help manage anxiety to the persistence of war as an instrument of policy in the states system. Going further, *some* continuity is the condition of possibility for assessing change, and vice versa. Would we apprehend and be able to explicate change without reference to some other persistent element of experience against which difference resolves as such? Would we appreciate continuity without some flux with which to compare it? What seems to matter more is the balance and quality of continuity and change in a given situation.

For instance, language relies on *continuous but manageable change* to make meaning. We assemble different combinations from a finite array of letters to make different words, order them according to syntactical rules that lend semantic import, and try to keep our sentences brief enough that they do not exceed our audience's cognitive capacities. Language depends on change to make meaning, but change highly constrained by the demands and standards of interpretive continuity (Elias, 1989: 201). The continuity of our communication would be hindered significantly if we were to begin assigning entirely random combinations of letters to common referent objects, or even to 'backward clauses writing begin to'. Yet such examples of linguistic breakdown still fall within the brute limits of continuity and change, suggesting we need more precise formulations of both terms to their functional relationship.

Beyond language, social life would be unthinkable without various admixtures of continuity and change – such as when I raise my hand and waving 'hello' to a friend across the street, and this *change* in my behaviour reproduces our friendship in the moment, ensuring its *continuity* over time. By contrast, if I were to *continue* walking without waving, my friend might wonder about a *change* in our relationship. Even this basic interaction bedevils the glib 'continuity or change' binary, and most international phenomena exceed it in complexity, nuance, and duration. Moreover, time scholars mostly agree that we become aware of time and history not only through the experience of meaningful change but also by our ability to establish continuity amidst the 'flux of experience' (see Hoy, 2009). All of which is to suggest that IR would benefit either from more sophisticated categories of time or history than continuity and change or from more clearly disclosing the theoretical and political priors informing scholarly choices about which changes and continuities get elevated to the status of empirical trends or theoretical concepts.

The problem of time lurking behind enduring binaries

The final issue with IR's traditional treatment of time, and by extension history, is that our facile reproduction of these spurious binaries contributes to their reification and naturalization, which in turn further obscure the even more durable tradition underpinning them both. This is 'the problem of time', or time understood as a universal force or malevolent god (e.g. Chronos,

Saturn) that naturally brings disorder, chaos, and death. As I discuss at length elsewhere (Hom, 2020: 11–17), this tradition of explicating time as the cause of wreck and ruin stretches back at least to pre-classical Greece and likely further to ancient religions of the Near East, and easily predates self-conscious attempts to reckon duration through technical artistry or to elaborate concepts like 'linear' or 'cyclical time',[3] or historical change or continuity. It saturates the 'canon' of Western political thought and international theory and returns in contemporary IR whenever events catch analysts or actors by surprise or as large-scale transformations near on the horizon.

On its face, this tradition does not comport easily with lines, cycles, change, and continuity. However, historical precedent offers a resolution. 'Linear' or 'cyclical' time, just like historical 'continuity' or 'change', depends upon interpretation and configuration, and coheres primarily as speculative visions about collections of meaningful events. Combined with their much more recent provenance relative to the problem of time, this suggests that they function not as master claims about time but rather as *narrative responses* to the problem of time tradition. Their straight or curved 'shape', or their admixture of continuity and change, assures us that meaningful elements persist, even if important factors are shifting, and thus provide ways to make sense of anxiety-inducing and sometimes overwhelming experiences. They substitute a tidy interpretive arc or story plot for the often messy flow of temporal existence or the complex world of international politics, and then offer actors a mimetic resource for decision and action. Such benefits make it easy for us to reproduce linear/cyclical or continuity/change claims, and thereby to conflate these practical and particular interpretations about historical experience for qualities of time itself (Hom, 2020: 101–104). If we look closer, past the layers of reification, what we routinely find in such claims are competing glosses of huge, complex, and messy political phenomena – conceptual tools that schematize time and history, reducing complexity, boosting intelligibility, and ultimately guiding action by interpolating the past and extrapolating the future for the sake of managing and controlling present circumstances (McIntosh, 2020). Yet much as the trend line interprets the data but is not that data, a linear or cyclical narrative can interpret temporal experiences and processes but becomes synonymous with time *per se* only through conflation, abstraction, and reification of just the sort that critical and historical IR scholars resist in other discussions.

IR's temporal turn

Such was the story for many years in IR. More recently, a number of critically minded scholars took closer looks at time's relationship to politics and found it much more diverse and complex than previously thought. This 'temporal turn' in critical IR produced a number of invigorating studies and new (to IR) concepts of time, from the recovery of classical notions of *chronos* (continuity), *kairos* (a moment ripe for change), and *aion* (pure becoming) (Hutchings, 2008); to a more sophisticated sociotemporality (Stevens, 2015); the dominance of 'the present' over theory (McIntosh, 2020); 'savage' (Blaney and Inayatullah, 2010), 'subaltern', and gendered temporalities (see Agathangelou and Killian, 2016), and the 'ruptured time' of trauma (e.g. Edkins, 2013) – all flowing from theoretical developments and original empirical research that make a compelling case that global politics is indeed a 'heterotemporal' realm (Hutchings, 2008). Historical institutionalists joined them in foregrounding time more resolutely than previous scholars, albeit in very different ways that emphasized the path dependence, organization 'drift', and generally deleterious effects of time's passage on institutional efficiency (see Fioretos, 2017).

For all this new research and thinking, IR's temporal antinomies and the older problem of time tradition received little scrutiny. In fact, they underwrote much of temporal turn. Much critical IR explicitly contests the 'linear time' of the state, positivism, and hegemonic history, parroting a widespread tendency to conflate historical and methodological linearity with an 'underlying "base time", "essential temporality", or "source time"' (Chambers, 2011: 198, 210). A particularly pitched example of this is the IR discourse of 'rupture', which claims to refute all intimations of linear time yet also foregrounds ruptures as resources for 'a politics otherwise' of less violence and greater affirmation in the future (Hom, 2020: 208–231). Similarly, the historical institutionalist project seeks to explain why institutions change in time, an issue typically framed as distinct from continuity (e.g. Streeck and Thelen, 2005). This research also relies on the assumption that time naturally causes decay – an assumption that unwittingly disposes the theoretical imagination to conflate stability or continuity with transcendence and the eternal (Hom, 2020: 185–207).

Two other areas of more self-consciously historical research deserve mention here: the embrace by primarily constructivist scholars of thick description and historical transformations (see Leira and de Carvalho, 2017) and the efforts of intellectual histories to historicize or place IR's central ideas and traditions in context and recover their conceptual roots (in this volume, see Wallenius, 2021; Kessler, 2021). In the case of intellectual histories informed by critical race studies, the humanities, and feminist IR, this project uncovers a theological (Guilhot, 2010), imperial (Barder, 2017), gendered (see Geeta and Nair, 2014), and racist IR lineage (e.g. Henderson, 2013) quite at odds with any disciplinary 'big bang myths' (de Carvalho, Leira, and Hobson, 2011) or claims about a 'value-free' social science. Such works not only place international politics and IR theories more firmly 'in time', but also destabilize the discipline's aforementioned 'presentism' by recovering its messy pasts.

Conclusion: bringing temporal and historical IR together

For much of its disciplinary existence, IR treated time glibly or not at all, deploying intuitive oppositions and freely conflating history with time itself. Its temporal turn yielded a much richer appreciation of the global politics of time, if uneven conceptual development. Nor did such shifts include much dialogue with emerging work in Historical IR. This is curious, given how much common cause exists between them to complexify, temporalize, historicize, and destabilize rationalist or positivistic IR. Furthermore, it remains exceedingly difficult to talk about history without talking time, or vice versa. For example, as the Cold War ended, Robert Jervis asked, 'will the future resemble the past?' After noting that 'History usually makes a mockery of our hopes and expectations', he argued 'it is clear we are entering a new world', that would 'follow patterns familiar in outline but unpredictable in detail' (Jervis, 1991: 39). A decade later, David Campbell (2001) surveyed how 9/11 'broke time' but his primary purpose was to criticize 'the return of the past in response' to the attacks, especially several forms of 'Cold War redux' in emerging discourses about the event. For both scholars, the problem of time and the issue of history intermingled closely. So historical and temporal scholars would seem to have much to discuss, but move mostly in parallel – like passengers waving between two cars travelling in the same direction. To conclude, therefore, I would like to briefly sketch three ways to redress the disconnect between historical and temporal IR.

From time and history to narrative timing

One solution is to shift history – not under time but *within* the umbrella of *timing*. My own work proposes that we reimagine time not as a natural or metaphysical entity, nor even an objective existential factor, but rather always as the product of widespread timing efforts. Timing here refers not to coincidence or opportune moments but instead to a holistic, synthetic, and creative effort to establish or maintain change processes and dynamic relationships using some rubric or frame of reference as a *timing standard*. As social agents work *to time* in this way, and represent their efforts with symbolic language that prefers static or entity-like nouns to dynamic verbs, we build up a discursive catalogue of 'times' that index various social timing efforts, some of which come to seem real, natural, and universal *only* by virtue of their widespread adoption and diffusion (Hom, 2020: 27–81). Timing theory helps us scrutinize binaries like linear/cyclical and continuity/change and proffers a historico-theoretical explanation for the problem of time as a symbolic testament to how important and difficult timing has been to human survival and coexistence throughout history.

Understood in this way, timing intentionally covers a huge swathe of human activities, from technical innovation to intersubjective discourse.[4] One of these is *narrative timing*, or the way in which stories configure actions and agents to unfold a stylized world that not only communicates meaning but also reconfigures our experience of time as a dimension amenable to understanding and action (Hom, 2020: 82–107). On this reading, Historical IR accounts are – like other stories – narrative timing devices that make sense of a past not only to enable understanding but also to inform current actions. While historical accounts often promise to place actors and events 'in their time' or to track change 'over time', when historians select and arrange such elements, they are actively timing those entities – *emplotting* them in a dynamic, intelligible whole pointing towards one outcome rather than others, whether this be the moral of the story, the explanandum, or simply the chronological end point. So while it differs in scope and content from other IR knowledge modes, Historical IR still partakes of a loose disciplinary project to understand how global relations fit together in order to anticipate or shape how they unfold in hopes of reducing suffering, improving outcomes, or forestalling apocalypse (Hom, 2020: 232–244). In this way, international history sits alongside various global 'times', but all in service of vocational timing.

Temporalizing history

Second, we can combine the insights of narrative timing with intellectual history to explicitly *temporalize* IR's genealogy. Whether in its recent racialized and imperial academic past or its more venerable and self-styled 'canon' of political thought, key thinkers, and works inspiring IR as we know it emerged from what we might call timing-intensive periods, those moments when thorny events and shocking upheavals necessitated fundamental revisions to the symbolic frameworks we use to make sense of politics. Thinkers and periods vital to the stories IR tell itself about its intellectual past consistently coincided with novel changes. In the traditional canon, Thucydides reflected on the Peloponnesian cataclysm, Plato and Aristotle responded to the near-collapse of the *polis* system (Gunnell, 1987), Augustine to the Christianization and sack of Rome (Markus, 1970), the 'Machiavellian moment' proposed how new republics establish stable order amidst crisis (Pocock, 2016), the Reformation and civil wars informed Hobbes', Locke's, and Rousseau's work (see McQueen, 2018). More recently, inchoate IR scholarship emerged from interdisciplinary efforts to restore or insulate empire and white supremacy from epochal transformations wrought by industrialized globalization, the expansion of political rights, and what one work called 'the rising tide of color' in global race relations (see Henderson, 2013). And IR's emergence as a recognizable field with pretensions to disciplinary autonomy drew anxious inspiration from the legacy of two world wars and the development of nuclear weapons. All of these political developments undercut existing knowledge and expectations and engendered mighty theoretical efforts to restore a sense of meaning and intelligibility to international politics. We could join intellectual historians in framing this as a disciplinary set of responses to the problem of time, which several of these thinkers acknowledged explicitly. But we can also go a step further to think through how IR's direct or claimed intellectual history emerged from fraught timing efforts to restore meaning and reauthorize action in the wake of destabilizing experiences.

Historicizing time

Finally, rather than reconfiguring our theoretical imagination or reinterpreting familiar intellectual forebears, IR scholars interested in bringing time and history together could tap an almost completely undiscovered empirical vein of research to historicize time as a sociopolitical phenomenon. While the temporal turn uncovered numerous diverse times at work in contemporary international life, IR has not yet taken a close look at the history of various collective timing projects. If it did, it would find a rich collection of achievements in imagining, operationalizing, and distributing time *per se* as a resource, a rule, or a dimension to be reckoned and mastered by technique. All were political, most were international.

Inter alia, the earliest cosmological myths established sources of political order partly by casting humanity at the mercy of some malicious time god (Hom, 2020: 11). The Seleucids reinvented calendrical reckoning to progressively number the years from emperor to emperor instead of restarting with each accession (Kosmin, 2019). An international competition to devise reliable seafaring clocks and thus 'discover the longitude' drove the ascendance of Western standard time (Landes, 2000). The International Meridian Conference and the rise of national empires like the United States, Germany, and the Meiji Restoration in Japan secured its dominance, not only establishing common reckoning conventions and global time zones but also trampling 'national sovereignty' in the process (O'Malley, 1990; Hom, 2010: 1163). National efforts to reinforce these conventions depended on the deployment of a power-knowledge nexus and engendered local forms of subversion (e.g. Barak, 2013). Revolutionary projects played fast and loose with the public calendar, often pushing a bridge too far and drawing staunch resistance (e.g. Shaw, 2011).

These episodes have gone almost completely unstudied in IR despite their manifestly political dynamics. But if we combine the critical IR point that all times are political with Historical IR's interest in richer understanding of the past, then there is little reason to ignore the political history of time itself (see, e.g. Ogle 2015; Richards 1999). Indeed, the strong point broached by all these preceding discussions is that if we are to take time and history seriously together, then we should weave time *in* history into IR's imagination. The history of time is the temporal ground of international politics.

Suggestions for further reading

Hom, A. R. (2020). *International Relations and the Problem of Time*. Oxford: Oxford University Press.
Hoy, D. C. (2009). *The Time of Our Lives: A Critical History of Temporality*. Cambridge, MA: MIT Press.
Inayatullah, N., and Blaney, D. L. (2004). *International Relations and the Problem of Difference*. London: Routledge.
Ogle, V. (2015). *The Global Transformation of Time: 1870–1950*. Cambridge, MA: Harvard University Press.
Richards, E. G. (1999). *Mapping Time: The Calendar and Its History*. Oxford: Oxford University Press.
Walker, R. B. J. (1993). *Inside/Outside: International Relations as Political Theory*. Cambridge: Cambridge University Press.

Notes

1 We could just as easily designate these rhythms as 'timeful' because they repeatedly fill up extended chunks of time (Hom, 2020: 97).
2 The rare example functions primarily as a counterfactual (see Sorabji, 2006: 190).
3 A Google n-gram search for variants of 'linear time' and 'cyclical time' returns few hits prior to the 1930s, making it all the more curious that IR scholars treat these terms as transhistorical and natural categories of time.
4 It shares an interest in the effortful and often contentious production of time with recent work on global synchronization (e.g. Jordheim and Wigen, 2018).

References

Agathangelou, A. M., and Killian, K., eds. (2016). *Time and Violence in IR: (De)Fatalizing the Present, Forging Radical Alternatives.* London: Routledge.

Aggestam, K., and True, J. (2020). Gendering foreign policy: a comparative framework for analysis. *Foreign Policy Analysis*, 16 (2), 143–162.

Akcinaroglu, S., and Radziszewski, E. (2005). Expectations, rivalries, and civil war duration. *International Interactions*, 31 (4), 349–374.

Barak, O. (2013). *On Time: Technology and Temporality in Modern Egypt.* Berkeley, CA: University of California Press.

Barder, A. (2017). *Empire Within: International Hierarchy and Its Imperial Laboratories of Governance.* London: Routledge.

Beasley, R. K., and Hom, A. R. (2021). Foreign Policy in the Fourth Dimension (FP4D): Locating Time in Decision Making Processes. *Foreign Policy Analysis* 17(2).

Beck, N., Katz, J. N., and Tucker, R. (1998). Taking time seriously: time-series-cross-section analysis with a binary dependent variable. *American Journal of Political Science*, 42 (4), 1260–1288.

Blaney, D. L., and Inayatullah, N. (2010). *Savage Economics: Wealth, Poverty and the Temporal Walls of Capitalism.* London: Routledge.

Campbell, D. (2001). Time is broken: the return of the past in the response to September 11. *Theory & Event*, 5 (4), 1–11.

Chambers, S. A. (2011). Untimely politics Avant La Lettre: the temporality of social formations. *Time & Society*, 20 (2), 197–223.

Dark, K. R. (1998). *The Waves of Time: Long-Term Change and International Relations.* London/New York: Pinter.

de Carvalho, B., Leira, H., and Hobson, J. M. (2011). The big bangs of IR: the myths that your teachers still tell you about 1648 and 1919. *Millennium*, 39 (3), 735–758.

de Carvalho, B., Costa Lopez, J., and Leira, H. (2021). Introduction: Historical International Relations. In de Carvalho, B., Costa Lopez, J., & Leira, H., eds. *Routledge Handbook of Historical International Relations.* Abingdon: Routledge.

Edkins, J. (2013). Novel writing in international relations: openings for a creative practice. *Security Dialogue*, 44 (4), 281–297.

Elias, N. (1989). The symbol theory: an introduction, part one. *Theory, Culture and Society*, 6 (2), 169–217.

Elman, C., and Elman, M. F. (2008). The role of history in international relations. *Millennium: Journal of International Studies*, 37 (2), 357–364.

Fasolt, C. (2004). *The Limits of History.* Chicago, IL: University of Chicago Press.

Fioretos, O., ed. (2017). *International Politics and Institutions in Time.* Oxford: Oxford University Press.

Geeta, C., and Nair, S., eds. (2014). *Power, Postcolonialism and International Relations: Reading Race, Gender and Class.* London: Routledge.

Grosz, E. (1999). *Becomings: Explorations in Time, Memory, and Futures.* Ithaca, NY: Cornell University Press.

Guilhot, N. (2010). American Katechon: when political theology became international relations theory. *Constellations*, 17 (2), 224–253.

Guillaume, X. (2021). Historical Periods and the Act of Periodisation. In de Carvalho, B., Costa Lopez, J., & Leira, H., eds. *Routledge Handbook of Historical International Relations.* Abingdon: Routledge.

Gunnell, J. G. (1987). *Political Philosophy and Time: Plato and the Origins of Political Vision.* Chicago, IL: University of Chicago Press.

Henderson, E. A. (2013). Hidden in Plain Sight: Racism in International Relations Theory. *Cambridge Review of International Affairs*, 26 (1), 71–92.

Herborth, B. and Nitzschner, P. (2021). Europe in Historical International Relations. In de Carvalho, B., Costa Lopez, J., & Leira, H., eds. *Routledge Handbook of Historical International Relations.* Abingdon: Routledge.

Hom, A. R. (2010). Hegemonic metronome: the ascendancy of Western Standard Time. *Review of International Studies*, 36 (4), 1145–1170.

Hom, A. R. (2018). Timing is everything: toward a better understanding of time and international politics. *International Studies Quarterly*, 62 (1), 69–79.

Hom, A. R. (2019). Time and International Relations Theory. In: K. H. Goetz, ed., *The Oxford Handbook of Time and Politics*, Oxford: Oxford University Press.

Hughes, B. (1997). *Continuity and Change in World Politics: Competing Perspectives*. Upper Saddle River, NJ: Prentice Hall.

Hutchings, K. (2008). *Time and World Politics: Thinking the Present*. Manchester: Manchester University Press.

Jarvis, L. (2009). *Times of Terror: Discourse, Temporality, and the War on Terror*. London: Palgrave Macmillan.

Jervis, R. (1991). The future of world politics: will it resemble the past? *International Security*, 16 (3), 39–73.

Jordheim, H., and Wigen, E. (2018). Conceptual synchronisation: from progress to crisis. *Millennium*, 46 (3), 421–439.

Kakachia, K., Minesashvili, S., and Kakhishvili, L. (2018). Change and continuity in the Foreign policies of small states: elite perceptions and Georgia's foreign policy towards Russia. *Europe-Asia Studies*, 70 (5), 814–831.

Kessler, O. (2021). Conceptual History in International Relations: from Ideology to Social Theory?. In de Carvalho, B., Costa Lopez, J., & Leira, H., eds. *Routledge Handbook of Historical International Relations*. Abingdon: Routledge.

Kosmin, P. J. (2019). *Time and Its Adversaries in the Seleucid Empire*. Cambridge, MA: Belknap Press.

Landes, D. S. (2000). *Revolution in Time: Clocks and the Making of the Modern World*. Cambridge, MA: Belknap Press.

Lawson, G., Armbruster, C., and Cox, M. (2010). *The Global 1989: Continuity and Change in World Politics*. Cambridge: Cambridge University Press.

Leira, H., and de Carvalho, B. (2017). Construction time again: history in constructivist IR scholarship. *European Review of International Studies*, 3 (3), 99–111.

Lissner, R. F. (2018). What is grand strategy? *Sweeping a Conceptual Minefield Texas National Security Review*, 2 (1), 53–73.

MacKay, J., and LaRoche, C. D. (2021). Theories and Philosophies of History in International Relations. In de Carvalho, B., Costa Lopez, J., & Leira, H., eds. *Routledge Handbook of Historical International Relations*. Abingdon: Routledge.

Markus, R. A. (1970). *Saeculum: History and Society in the Theology of St Augustine*. Cambridge: Cambridge University Press.

McIntosh, C. (2020). Theorizing the temporal exception: the importance of the present for the study of war. *Journal of Global Security Studies*, 5 (4), 543–558.

McQueen, A. (2018). *Political Realism in Apocalyptic Times*. Cambridge: Cambridge University Press.

O'Malley, M. (1990). *Keeping Watch: A History of American Time*. Washington, DC: Smithsonian Institution Press.

Pocock, J. G. A. (2016). *The Machiavellian Moment: Florentine Political Thought and the Atlantic Republican Tradition*. Princeton, NJ: Princeton University Press.

Qin, Y. (2014). Continuity through change: background knowledge and China's international strategy. *The Chinese Journal of International Politics*, 7 (3), 285–314.

Rosenau, J. N. (1990). *Turbulence in World Politics: A Theory of Change and Continuity*. Princeton, NJ: Princeton University Press.

Rupert, M., and Smith, H. (2016). *Historical Materialism and Globalisation: Essays on Continuity and Change*. London: Routledge.

Shaw, M. (2011). *Time and the French Revolution: The Republican Calendar, 1789-Year XIV*. Woodbridge: Royal Historical Society.

Sinha, A. (2017). Understanding change and continuity in India's foreign policy. *International Affairs*, 93 (1), 189–198.

Sorabji, R. (2006). *Time, Creation, and the Continuum: Theories in Antiquity and the Early Middle Ages*. Chicago, IL: University of Chicago Press.

Stevens, T. (2015). *Cyber Security and the Politics of Time*. Cambridge: Cambridge University Press.

Streeck, W., and Thelen, K. A. (2005). *Beyond Continuity: Institutional Change in Advanced Political Economies*. Oxford: Oxford University Press.

Wallenius, T. (2021). How to Do the History of International Thought?. In de Carvalho, B., Costa Lopez, J., & Leira, H., eds. *Routledge Handbook of Historical International Relations*. Abingdon: Routledge.

Zhang, Y. (2016). Introduction: dynamism and contention: understanding Chinese foreign policy under Xi Jinping. *International Affairs*, 92 (4), 769–772.

PART III

Actors, processes, and institutions

21

SOVEREIGNTY IN HISTORICAL INTERNATIONAL RELATIONS

Trajectories, challenges, and implications

Benjamin de Carvalho

Sovereignty in International Relations (IR) is as fundamental as it is contested. And while historicizing sovereignty with a view to uncover the contingent character of the international system has been one of the major achievements of Historical IR (HIR) scholars, much of IR still takes the traditional understanding for granted. Yet, it has been one of the field's major contributions to a critique of the ahistorical rationalist understanding of international politics which until the mid-1990s was largely hegemonic within the discipline of IR. As I have argued elsewhere (Leira and de Carvalho, 2016), historicizing the emergence of the sovereign state through relying on much of the work undertaken in neighbouring disciplines such as historical sociology (see Go et al., 2021, in the present volume) and international political thought was one of the more successful wedges early constructivists were able to drive through the 'neo-neo' systemic construct (see Bruneau, 2021; Nøhr, 2021; both in this volume). As Jens Bartelson has noted with regards to sovereignty, 'Long gone are the days when its meaning was uncontested and its essential attributes could be safely taken for granted by international theorists' (2014: 251).

Until then, sovereignty had been treated as unproblematic and fixed, its definition more or less universally agreed-upon, and often with reference to an overall phrase like F. H. Hinsley's statement that 'at the beginning, at any rate, the idea of sovereignty was the idea that there is a final and absolute political authority in the political community; and everything that needs to be added to complete the definition is added if this statement is continued in the following words: "and no final authority exists elsewhere"' (1986: 25–26). From the early 1990s, such definitions became contested by historically oriented social constructivists seeking to demonstrate the contingent meaning of sovereignty through changing social constructions – relying both on contingent discursive articulations and at the same time producing changing distinctions between 'inside' and 'outside'.

Historicizing sovereignty required that the field abandon its 'creationist' creed in the birth of sovereignty as a result of the collective will of European sovereigns gathered in the Westphalian lands in 1648, for the myth of 1648 had long obscured the historical emergence of sovereignty in IR. Until the 1990s, 1648 had marked the boundaries of the historical imagination for generations of IR scholars. As the edifice of Westphalia started to crumble, so did the emergence of sovereignty appear as less straightforward, and its meanings in different historical contexts multiplied. The opening up of the Westphalian border undertaken by HIR scholars (see, for instance, Osiander, 1994, 2001; Krasner, 1999; Teschke, 2003; de Carvalho et al., 2011) went hand in hand with inquiries into the origins of sovereignty and the historicity of international politics. Jointly, they brought to the fore important questions of historical methods and methodology in IR. For, although some traditions of thought in IR have felt the Westphalian straightjacket more lightly than others – claims about the continuities in thinking from Thucydides until today being a case in point – applying the modern framework of IR to distant historical cases is far from unproblematic.

Beyond Westphalia, the first attempt at defining 'sovereignty' is generally attributed to Jean Bodin (see Knutsen, 1997: 73), who in the late 1570s defined sovereignty as 'the absolute and perpetual power of a commonwealth', or (in the Latin version) as 'supreme and absolute power over citizens and subjects' (Bodin, 1992: 1). Furthermore, he claimed, 'the main point of sovereign majesty and absolute power consists of giving the law to subjects in general without their consent' (ibid.: 23). Bodin argued in 1576 that it was necessary to define sovereignty 'because no jurist or political philosopher has defined it, even though it is the chief point, and the one that needs most to be explained, in a treatise on commonwealth' (ibid.: 1). While Bodin claimed to have written the first philosophical statement on sovereignty, Bodin was nevertheless no legal innovator. In fact, most states in Europe had by that time severed or limited their authority ties to Rome if not in theory, then in practice. Bodin's conceptual statement of sovereignty, then, albeit the first one of its kind in Europe, is best understood as an organized statement of the changes which had taken place with the transformation of medieval polities towards territorial/national states (see Costa Lopez, 2021 in this volume).

Bodin's definition is first and foremost concerned with domestic sovereignty; 'external' sovereignty in the sense of there being no authority above sovereigns is deducible from domestic absolute power. His definition has nevertheless exerted a great deal of influence on how the sovereignty of the state has been understood. We hear echoes of it in Hinsley's definition above, and as Cynthia Weber has argued, the common understanding of sovereignty in IR has long been 'taken to mean the absolute authority a state holds over a territory and people as well as independence internationally and recognition by other sovereign states as sovereign state' (Weber, 1995: 1).

The aim of the current chapter is to discuss the work done in HIR on sovereignty, with a view to provide an understanding of the significance of this research to the wider field of IR, and give a brief overview of the current state of the art, in order to identify key challenges and opportunities for future research. I start the chapter by discussing some more traditional takes and contextualize them within the broader discipline of IR, before turning to more current scholarship. On the basis of these, I offer some reflections on sovereignty within the field, and the state of IR in light of this research.

Destabilizing sovereignty

The conceptual centrality of sovereignty in IR cannot be overstated. Generally understood as the principle creating domestic authority, sovereignty is at the origin of the inside/outside divide, making it constitutive of the (modern) international. As Poggi has argued, 'the state's sovereignty and its territoriality, jointly produce a most significant consequence: the political environment in which each state exists is by necessity one which it shares with a plurality of states similar in nature to itself' (1990: 23). Thus, the concept sovereignty is generally taken to consist of three distinct features, supreme authority, (territorial) limits, and external recognition. Jointly, these are conceptually constitutive of the state. Sovereignty therefore is generally understood as the constitutive pillar of international politics, as it is the principle which renders international politics among primarily territorially sovereign entities possible. While defining the formal autonomy of the state as the basic unitary actor, the principle of sovereignty also demarcates the spatiality of the units which constitute the system. Thus, while conceptually creating the main units of international politics (the 'inside'), it also produces the international environment (the 'outside'). Moreover, John Gerard Ruggie (1993) forcefully established the norm of sovereignty as quintessentially modern, demarcating the break between the medieval non-territorial order and the modern order based on distinct functionally similar territorial units.

Before turning to more contemporary takes on sovereignty in HIR, let us run through how sovereignty has been treated by IR traditions. Classical Realists such as Morgenthau have seen sovereignty as the root and *sine qua non* of the anarchical character of the international system. To be sure, Morgenthau defined sovereignty as 'a centralized power that exercised its law-making and law-enforcing authority within a certain territory' (1995: 299). Sovereignty, as we see, is closely interlinked with the conditions of possibility of the international (state) system. In fact, it is this territorialization of political authority, according to Morgenthau, which leads to the 'decentralization, weakness and ineffectiveness' of supra-national institutions (ibid.: 300; see also Williams, 2004). But while Morgenthau assumed the continuity of the doctrine of sovereignty from the end of the sixteenth century to contemporary international politics, other Realists such as E. H. Carr have held that one should not assume the immanent character of sovereignty, as few concepts remain unchanged. Thus, Carr argued, while sovereignty had always been a contested principle which emerged at the break-up of the *respublica Christiana*, it was 'likely to become in the future even more blurred and indistinct than it is at present' (1964: 229–230). Neorealists, on the other hand, have tended to underplay the contested character of sovereignty. Assuming the congruence between territory, population, and authority into the sovereign state as the central actor in international politics, Kenneth Waltz derived his (descriptive) understanding of the sovereign state from the anarchical states system: 'To say that the state is sovereign means that it decides for itself how it will cope with its internal and external problems' (Waltz, 1979: 96). In consequence, neorealists do not provide a conclusive account of the emergence of the concept of sovereignty, nor do they acknowledge its historically contingent character (see the discussion in Biersteker and Weber, 1996: 6; see also Barkin and Cronin, 1994). Conversely, neoliberal scholars have focused little on sovereignty, turning instead to 'a description of the "erosion" of state sovereignty, often confusing it with a reduction in state capabilities for independence and autonomy' (see the discussion in Biersteker and Weber, 1996: 7).

To HIR, the most useful and pertinent studies of sovereignty were initiated by the constructivist push in the mid-1990s, most notably with the works of Jens Bartelson, J. G. Ruggie, Cynthia Weber (as noted above), and R. B. J. Walker. Taking as their point of departure the inherently constructed nature of sovereignty, these authors all took upon themselves to understand the effects of discourses on authority and sovereignty. Tracing the genealogy of sovereignty, Jens Bartelson famously made the case that the concept of sovereignty should be understood as integral to neither the internal nor the external sphere of politics. Rather, Bartelson argued, it is what makes the distinction between the two spheres of politics possible. Thus, sovereignty is best conceptualized, as Bartelson argued, as a frame or parergon which 'cannot be a member of either class. It is neither inside, nor outside, yet it is the condition of possibility of both. [T]here is a ceaseless activity of framing, but the frame itself is never present, since it is itself unframed' (Bartelson, 1995: 51). What sovereignty frames, then, is a matter of historical contingency.

Such a take resonated well with R. B. J. Walker's warning that 'the very attempt to treat sovereignty as a matter of definition and legal principle encourages a certain amnesia about its historical and culturally specific character' (1995: 166). Focusing on change not only laid bare the social construction of sovereignty, but also showed the extent to which making sense of sovereignty, then, required a historical perspective. As a case in point, Daniel Philpott's *Revolutions in Sovereignty* (2001) tied the emergent sovereign state to the process of the reformation. As Biersteker and Weber (1996: 11) argued, 'neither state nor sovereignty could be assumed or taken as given, fixed, or immutable'. Rather, they argue, the socially constructed character of sovereignty can only be grasped if we 'make an effort to separate state and sovereignty' and consider 'the constitutive relationship between state and sovereignty; the ways the meaning of sovereignty is negotiated out of interactions within intersubjectively identifiable communities; and the varieties of ways in which practices construct, reproduce, reconstruct, and deconstruct sovereignty' (ibid.: 11–12). In terms of studies of sovereignty, the late 1990s and early 2000s represented a moment of collective reckoning about sovereignty, as witnessed by the sheer volume of works published on sovereignty. Together with Stephen Krasner's (1999) and Andreas Osiander's (2001) work on rebutting the myth of the immaculate conception of sovereignty at the Peace of Westphalia in 1648, these works represented a genuine watershed in studies of sovereignty in IR. Together, they ascertained the need for seeing sovereignty not as a neutral principle for territorial demarcation between states, but a social construction which, in different contexts, affected international politics in different ways.

Sovereignty, history, and International Relations

While still remaining a central object of inquiry in HIR, there have been fewer recent studies devoted solely to the concept of sovereignty. Rather, more recent work has gone in the direction of highlighting the effects of specific constructions of sovereignty, contextualizing sovereignty alongside other (non-territorial) forms of organizing political authority, and problematizing the extent to which sovereignty as understood in the West really is all that constitutive of international politics. Broadly speaking, recent HIR contributions to sovereignty can be grouped in four categories according to their main concern: (a) empires and international hierarchies, (b) law and degrees of sovereignty, (c) territoriality and practices of sovereignty, and (d) the impact of different understandings of sovereignty on the international system and IR.

The challenge posed by empires and imperialism which coexisted alongside the newly emerging territorial sovereign norm has been one of the more fruitful areas in which scholars from HIR and related disciplines have contributed recently. The work of Lauren Benton, for instance (see especially 2009), has contributed to discredit overly Eurocentric accounts highlighting the traditional understanding of the European origins of sovereignty and the spread of the international system from Europe (see also Adelman, 2009; Fitzmaurice, 2014). In processes of establishing uneven imperial rule, Benton shows the extent to which sovereignty was not a fixed norm, but changed according to circumstances and its application to anything but universal. This work dovetails the critical work of Shogo Suzuki on the expansion of international society and the socialization of Japan into international society during the Meiji period (2005; see also Hui, 2021). Suzuki provides a crucial antidote to an all too often Eurocentric discipline. Focusing on the expansion of the state-system beyond Europe, Suzuki points out that 'the Japanese imperialist response directly contradicts the English School conception of a 'universal' socialization of states that promotes mutual respect for independence and territorial integrity' (2005: 138; contrast with Watson, 1992). In so doing, he questions the commonplace assumption about the 'arrival' of international society in other parts of the world, and the progressive role of international society by pointing out that it is misguided in assuming that 'cooperative norms were transmitted to other (non-European) states in the course of the expansion of European International Society' (ibid.: 143). The work of David Armitage could also be mentioned here, as he makes the case taking the global context of the emergence of sovereignty into account by showing the extent to which the emergence of sovereignty hinged as much upon successful declarations of independence from groups previously subjected to imperial rule as on its European prehistory (Armitage, 2012). The insistence of these scholars on the global context of the emergence of sovereignty has in turn contributed to question one of the main tenets of sovereignty, namely territoriality and its spatial dimension. As a case in point, Benton mentions the fact that Bodin gives little attention to and does not even mention territory in his tracts on sovereignty. Benton notes that this omission was no oversight on Bodin's part, but that his view instead was 'consistent with an early modern construction of sovereignty as spatially elastic. Because subjects could be located anywhere, and the tie between sovereign and subject was defined as a legal relationship, legal authority was not bound territorially' (2009: 288).

The inherent open-endedness of territory and ongoing efforts of sovereign states to territorialize their lands have long been highlighted by political geographers (see Strandsbjerg, 2010; and Elden, 2013). A few studies have taken on the exploration of how sovereign states territorialized space and what the consequences of this process were for the state. Karl Appuhn (2009), for instance, has emphasized the extent to which state's attempts at mastering space contributed to the formation of the state itself. Appuhn shows how Venice's need for lumber drove the Venetian Republic to develop new and innovative techniques for governing nature, changing in the process the relationship between the Republic and the space surrounding it. Through the development and implementation of novel techniques of governance and administration of forests, Venice became 'inextricably entwined with its mainland state' developing from an insular city state to a regional state (2009: 1–19). In showing how this change took place, Appuhn problematizes political space and the techniques to govern it, showing how these changes happened gradually and how they were the result of processes of gradual imposition and resistance. In fact, he argues that between 1471 and 1548 the gradual imposition of new techniques and modes of administration on the governance of forests and the 'imposition of laws restricting local practices' gradually gave these innovations, and Venice's rule over forests far beyond its centre, a taken-for-granted quality. Appuhn's focus on problematizing territory echoes the work of Chandra Mukerji on the Gardens of Versailles through which she has shown how processes of imposing state rule on the land – territorialization – contributed to shape and change France's practices of territorial governance. In order to 'claim and manage a vast and complex territory', she argues, 'place and power had to be allied in a new way' (Mukerji, 1997). The state initiated a vast series of campaigns aimed at increasing the knowledge about its lands (see also Carroll, 2006, for an example of this). Problematizing the taken-for-grantedness of territory – which has gone hand in hand with sovereignty – has also been the subject of a few studies, and promises to be one of the avenues along which HIR scholars focusing on sovereignty beyond European shores can contribute to the ongoing debates between political theorists and global historians. The work of Jordan Branch comes to mind here as it nicely straddles the divide between critical approaches to the European story while also providing key insights into the global dimension of these processes. On the one hand, Branch shows how European notions of political space and territory were inherently problematic and hinged upon their cartographic representations (2013), while on the other, he has demonstrated how key innovations in the European business of rule were in fact devised in colonial settings and entered European practice through imperial veins (Branch, 2012).

While sovereignty in the imperial enterprise has been, as noted above, one of the key recent contributions, it has also highlighted the extent of the contingency of the legal dimension of sovereignty. Benton, for instance, highlights the importance of what we today would call 'quasi-sovereignty' to imperial agents and governance. She shows how while full sovereignty was only used for imperial polities, units within empires were often granted degrees of sovereignty (2009). We find this questioning of the indivisibility of sovereignty also in the work of Andrew Phillips and Jason Sharman (2020) who have, for instance, sought to highlight multiple forms of political organization during the early modern period, emphasizing both the imperial character of global polities as well as the quasi-sovereign role played by trading companies. Yuan Yi Zhu has in a similar vein (2020) shown the continuous application and use of concepts such as 'semi-sovereignty' and 'suzerainty' beyond European shores – concepts hitherto reserved to if not medieval times, then at least medieval Europe (see Costa Lopez, 2020, for a discussion). Finally, relating to the legal dimension of sovereignty, Christian Reus-Smit (2013) has rethought the role of the rights of individuals (as opposed to sovereign states). A similar take can be found in Luke Glanville's *Sovereignty and the Responsibility to Protect* (2014) in which he offers a new reading of the political theory of sovereignty linking it to the rights of individuals, and making the case that the absolute character of sovereignty has been overstated (on the political theory of the state, see also Devetak, 2021 in this volume).

As these contributions all make clear, sovereignty is not only historically contingent in terms of its effects, but also much less absolute, much less indivisible, and much less territorial than what the traditional understanding of sovereignty as the modern concept *par excellence*; the concept that *ipso facto* turned the medieval suzerain order into a modern state-system. These studies go a long way to point this out, and to some extent do offer new understandings, much work remains if we are to understand the workings of this concept constitutive of the discipline.

Rethinking sovereignty; rethinking IR?

The challenge that remains, then, is not only rethinking the place of sovereignty within the discipline, but perhaps also rethinking the discipline without (absolute) sovereignty (the reflections take Costa Lopez et al., 2018 as point of departure). Kathleen Davis recently offered a new take on how concepts such as sovereignty contributed to making history and time intelligible through periodizations, insisting on the extent to which medieval concepts were not supplanted by sovereignty but in fact continued to influence our understanding of history and international relations (2017). Thinking sovereignty beyond Westphalia and thinking IR beyond sovereignty is crucial for relocating and recalibrating the scope of applicability of the discipline. But whereas sovereignty is a modern idea and IR as a consequence may suffer from an embedded modernism, it does not follow that the scope conditions of IR need to be limited to modern international relations. On the contrary, as the studies discussed above show, the interest of thinking of sovereignty and international relations beyond Westphalia and beyond the West is precisely that it forces IR to abandon its modernism and broaden its own conceptual apparatus, and broaden its spatial gaze. The centrality of sovereignty for making sense of IR means that any discussion of the term is inextricably bound with difficult questions about the discipline, its possibility, and its scope conditions (see the discussion in Bartelson, 2006). Addressing these not only challenges established for periodizations such as the mythical 300 years of Peace of Westphalia (1648–1948), which Leo Gross (1948) then saw giving birth to a new order based on the UN Charter of 1948, but also questions and extends the geographical scope of the discipline beyond the West.

The main push in terms of historicizing sovereignty was addressing the temporal myopia resulting from the strong persistence of the myth of Westphalia. The constructivist push towards historicizing sovereignty discussed above was important, as it paved the way for a series of inquiries into the historical emergence of sovereignty, all seeking to abandon the 'big bang' account of Westphalia (see de Carvalho et al., 2011 for an overview). Although the constructivist avalanche of works on sovereignty around turn of the millennium contributed quite successfully to historicize and denaturalize sovereignty, making temporal variations in sovereignty explicit by showcasing how sovereignty has had different meanings at different times, it did so within the confines of a traditional narrative of sovereignty, largely leaving the *spatiality* of these contestations untouched. In consequence, as Jens Bartelson has noted, these accounts inadvertently 'reinforce[d] some of the most persistent myths about the origin of sovereignty, and […] obscured questions about the diffusion of sovereignty outside the European context'. As such, he continues, 'while international society was premised on equality and nonintervention, non-European peoples were excluded on the grounds that they were uncivilized, or that their political institutions did not fulfil the requirements of sovereign statehood. Hence, they could be legitimately subjected to imperial rule by European powers' (2014: 251). As noted above, recent studies have taken the relay from an earlier generation of scholars who were more concerned with the meanings of sovereignty and its role in international relations than in seeking out sovereignty in new worlds.

Although intrinsically 'critical' (for lack of a better term), the constructivist works on sovereignty from the 1990s still largely reproduced the Eurocentrism of a view that saw innovations in political thought as grounded in the political practice and thinking of a European core which then spread beyond European shores. As noted above, recent approaches (see for instance, Benton, 2009; Branch, 2012) have sought to address this by highlighting the extent to which global interactions and currents of people and thought formed the context of these innovations. Such works have done much to extend the spatial scope of IR through historically sound analyses, also paving the way for understanding sovereignty, its changing meanings and effects within a broader and less Eurocentric spatiality. These studies also dovetail with works on the applicability of sovereignty beyond Europe, such as Kang (2010) who has argued that in the Early Modern period a particular instantiation of sovereignty was at play in the context of a hierarchical tributary system, or Zhang, who has sought to prove that an ancient Chinese state-system in the eighth century BC already operated with an institutionalized, if not legally formalized, notion of sovereignty (2003: 47). The research agenda ahead seems clear: to what extent is sovereignty a concept with European origins, or is it rather born out of the myriad of global interactions which came to characterize an ever expanding world?

Yet, while this does bring the agenda forward, it seems to me that more recent studies of sovereignty have also left something behind. Where it is clear that current work on sovereignty has been freed from the Westphalian straightjacket, it seems to me that they have also abandoned some of the key concerns of HIR scholars and with it lost some of the critical potential of these approaches. More specifically, current work seems less preoccupied with the changing meanings of sovereignty and their effects than with contrasting sovereignty to other forms of authority.

Heralding the chapters which follow in the present handbook (Heiskanen, 2021; Spanu, 2021), I also believe that the relative lack of attention given to the relationship between sovereignty and identity in current work should be addressed, as this tension may hold the key to many challenges that have confronted our past and current predicaments, and are bound to challenge us in the future. In a time where potentially violent forms of identity politics are making their mark across the globe, it may seem curious that this aspect does not figure more prominently in current studies of sovereignty. Excavating this dimension from the writings of the late 1990s may thus be one of the more fertile grounds for future historical inquiries into changing meanings of sovereignty and their effects. As Roxanne Doty wrote, one cannot understand the meaning allocated to sovereignty at any given time, nor the construction of the inside/outside boundary, without taking historically contingent practices into account (Doty, 1996: 121–122). Rather than conceiving sovereignty as neutrally demarcating the 'location of the foundational entity of international relations theory', sovereignty ought to be seen as a 'site of political struggle', namely 'the struggle to fix the meaning of sovereignty in such a way as to constitute a particular state – to write the state – with particular boundaries, competencies and legitimacies available to it' (Weber, 1995: 2–3).

Together, recent studies of sovereignty from a historical perspective open up a space for rethinking not only the origins of sovereignty in practice and theoretical terms, but also how more foundational questions about the nature of the polities inhabiting this world affect the type of relations they entertain between themselves. What's at stake in approaching sovereignty is no less than the scope conditions of international relations as our discipline has made sense of them. The traditional story of the emergence and spread of sovereignty has tended to obfuscate the extent to which sovereignty in fact is far from a neutral delimitator of political authority, but a powerful political tool. By focusing on the process through which sovereignty is imposed across multiple spaces and temporalities, we may finally move away from seeing sovereignty as principle and uncover sovereignty as politics.

Suggestions for further reading

Biersteker, T. J., and Weber, C., eds. (1996). *State Sovereignty as Social Construct*. Cambridge: Cambridge University Press.

Cohen, J. L. (2012). *Globalization and Sovereignty: Rethinking Legality, Legitimacy, and Constitutionalism*. Cambridge: Cambridge University Press.

Hobson, J. M. (2012). *The Eurocentric Conception of World Politics: Western International Theory, 1760-2010*. Cambridge: Cambridge University Press.

Krasner, S. D. (1993). Westphalia and All That. In: J. Goldstein, and R. O. Keohane, eds., *Ideas and Foreign Policy: Beliefs, Institutions, and Political Change*, Ithaca, NY: Cornell University Press, 235–265.

Nexon, D. (2009). *The Struggle for Power in Early Modern Europe: Religious Conflict, Dynastic Empires, and International Change*. Princeton, NJ: Princeton University Press.

References

Adelman, J. (2009). *Sovereignty and Revolution in the Iberian Atlantic*. Princeton, NJ: Princeton University Press.

Appuhn, K. (2009). *A Forest on the Sea: Environmental Expertise in Renaissance Venice*. Baltimore, MD: Johns Hopkins University Press.

Armitage, D. (2012). *Foundations of Modern International Thought*. Cambridge: Cambridge University Press.

Barkin, J. S., and Cronin, B. (1994). The state and the nation: changing norms and the rules of sovereignty in international relations. *International Organization*, 48 (1), 107–130.

Bartelson, J. (1995). *A Genealogy of Sovereignty*. Cambridge: Cambridge University Press.

Bartelson, J. (2006). The concept of sovereignty revisited. *European Journal of International Law*, 17 (2), 463–474.

Bartelson, J. (2014). From empire to sovereignty—and back? *Ethics and International Affairs*, 28 (2), 251–262.

Benton, L. (2009). *A Search for Sovereignty*. Cambridge: Cambridge University Press.

Biersteker, T. J., and Weber, C. (1996). The Social Construction of State Sovereignty. In: T. J. Biersteker, and C. Weber, eds., *State Sovereignty as Social Construct*, Cambridge: Cambridge University Press, 1–21.

Bodin, J. (1992). *On Sovereignty*. Edited by J. H. Franklin. Cambridge: Cambridge University Press.

Branch, J. (2012). 'Colonial reflection' and territoriality: the peripheral origins of sovereign statehood. *European Journal of International Relations*, 18 (2), 277–297.

Branch, J. (2013). *The Cartographic State: Maps, Territory, and the Origins of Sovereignty*. Cambridge: Cambridge University Press.

Bruneau, Q. P. (2021). Constructivism: History and Systemic Change. In de Carvalho, B., Costa Lopez, J., & Leira, H., eds. *Routledge Handbook of Historical International Relations*. Abingdon: Routledge.

Carr, E. H. (1964). *The Twenty Years Crisis, 1919-1939*. New York, NY: Harper and Row.

Carroll, P. (2006). *Science, Culture, and Modern State Formation*. Berkeley, CA: University of California Press.

Costa Lopez, J. (2020). Political authority in international relations: revisiting the medieval debate. *International Organization*, 74 (2), 222–252.

Costa Lopez, J., de Carvalho, B., Latham, A. A., Zarakol, A., Bartelson, J., Holm, M. (2018). In the beginning there was no word (for it): terms, concepts, and early sovereignty. *International Studies Review*, 20 (3), 489–519.

Costa Lopez, J. (2021). International Relations in/and the Middle Ages. In de Carvalho, B., Costa Lopez, J., & Leira, H., eds. *Routledge Handbook of Historical International Relations*. Abingdon: Routledge.

Davis, K. (2017). *Periodization and Sovereignty: How Ideas of Feudalism and Secularization Govern the Politics of Time*. Philadelphia, PA: University of Pennsylvania Press.

de Carvalho, B., Leira, H., and Hobson, J. M. (2011). The big bangs of IR: the myths that your teachers still tell you about 1648 and 1919. *Millennium – Journal of International Studies*, 39 (3), 735–758.

Devetak, R. (2021). Reason of State: An Intellectual History. In de Carvalho, B., Costa Lopez, J., & Leira, H., eds. *Routledge Handbook of Historical International Relations*. Abingdon: Routledge.

Doty, R. L. (1996). Sovereignty and the Nation: Constructing the Boundaries of National Identity. In: T. J. Biersteker, and C. Weber, eds., *State Sovereignty as Social Construct*, Cambridge: Cambridge University Press.

Elden, S. (2013). *The Birth of Territory*. Chicago, IL: University of Chicago Press.

Fitzmaurice, A. (2014). *Sovereignty, Property and Empire, 1500–2000*. Cambridge: Cambridge University Press.

Glanville, L. (2014). *Sovereignty and the Responsibility to Protect: A New History*. Chicago, IL: Chicago University Press.

Go, J., G. Lawson, B. de Carvalho. (2021). Historical Sociology in International Relations. In de Carvalho, B., Costa Lopez, J., & Leira, H., eds. *Routledge Handbook of Historical International Relations*. Abingdon: Routledge.

Gross, L. (1948). The peace of Westphalia, 1648-1948. *The American Journal of International Law*, 42 (1), 20–41.

Heiskanen, J. (2021). Nations and Nationalism in International Relations. In: B. de Carvalho, J. Costa Lopez, and H. Leira, eds., *Routledge Handbook of Historical International Relations*, Abingdon: Routledge.

Hinsley, F. H. (1986). *Sovereignty*. 2nd edition. Cambridge: Cambridge University Press.

Hui, V. (2021). Premodern Asia and International Relations Theory. In de Carvalho, B., Costa Lopez, J., & Leira, H., eds. *Routledge Handbook of Historical International Relations*. Abingdon: Routledge.

Kang, D. (2010). *East Asia before the West. Five Centuries of Trade and Tribute*. New York, NY: Columbia University Press.

Knutsen, T. (1997). *A History of International Relations Theory*. Manchester: Manchester University Press.

Krasner, S. D. (1999). *Sovereignty: Organized Hypocrisy*. Princeton, NJ: Princeton University Press.

Leira, H., and de Carvalho, B. (2016). Construction time again: history in constructivist IR scholarship. *ERIS – European Review of International Studies*, 3 (3), 99–111.

Morgenthau, H. J. (1985). *Politics among Nations: The Struggle for Power and Peace*. 6th edition. New York, NY: McGraw-Hill.

Mukerji, C. (1997). *Territorial Ambitions and the Gardens of Versailles*. New York, NY: Cambridge University Press.

Nøhr, A. A. (2021). Poststructuralism and the Challenge of History. In de Carvalho, B., Costa Lopez, J., & Leira, H., eds. *Routledge Handbook of Historical International Relations*. Abingdon: Routledge.

Osiander, A. (1994). *The States System of Europe, 1640-1990: Peacemaking and the Conditions of International Stability*. Oxford: Oxford University Press.

Osiander, A. (2001). Sovereignty, international relations, and the Westphalian myth. *International Organziation*, 55 (2), 251–287.

Phillips, A., and Sharman, J. (2020). *Outsourcing Empire: How Company-States shaped the Modern World*. Princeton, NJ: Princeton University Press.

Philpott, D. (2001). *Revolutions in Sovereignty: How Ideas Shaped Modern International Relations*. Princeton, NJ: Princeton University Press.

Poggi, G. (1990). *The State: Its Nature, Development and Prospects*. Stanford, CA: Stanford University Press.

Reus-Smit, C. (2013). *Individual Rights and the Making of the International System*. Cambridge: Cambridge University Press.

Ruggie, J. G. (1993). Territoriality and beyond: problematizing modernity in international relations. *International Organization*, 47 (1), 139–174.

Spanu, M. (2021). States, People and Self-Determination in Historical Perspective. In: B. de Carvalho, J. Costa Lopez, and H. Leira, eds., *Routledge Handbook of Historical International Relations*, Abingdon: Routledge.

Strandsbjerg, J. (2010). *Territory, Globalization and International Relations: The Cartographic Reality of Space*. Houndmills: Palgrave Macmillan.

Suzuki, S. (2005). Japan's socialization into Janus-faced European international society. *European Journal of International Relations*, 11 (1), 137–164.

Teschke, B. (2003). *The Myth of 1648: Class, Geopolitics, and the Making of Modern International Relations*. London: Verso.

Walker, R. B. J. (1995). *Inside/Outside: International Relations as Political Theory*. Cambridge: Cambridge University Press.

Waltz, K. (1979). *Theory of International Politics*. New York, NY: McGraw-Hill.

Watson, A. (1992). *The Evolution of International Society: A Comparative Historical Analysis*. London: Routledge.

Weber, C. (1995). *Simulating Sovereignty. Intervention, the State and Symbolic Exchange*. Cambridge: Cambridge University Press.

Williams, M. C. (2004). Why ideas matter in international relations: Hans Morgenthau, classical realism, and the moral construction of power politics. *International Organization*, 58 (4), 633–665.

Zhang, Y. (2003). System, empire and state in Chinese international relations. *Review of International Studies*, 27 (5), 43–63.

Zhu, Y. Y. (2020). Suzerainty, semi-sovereignty, and international legal hierarchies on China's borderlands. *Asian Journal of International Law*, (forthcoming). Online first: Viewed on 10 Nov 2020, <https://doi.org/10.1017/S204425132000020X>.

22

STATE FORMATION AND HISTORICAL INTERNATIONAL RELATIONS

Benjamin de Carvalho and Halvard Leira

Although the existence of the state was for a long time the unquestioned cornerstone of IR, historical accounts of the state and, importantly, state *formation*, still entered the discipline of IR through early constructivist efforts at critiquing the ahistorical notion of the state system championed by neorealists and neoliberals alike. Relying heavily on accounts of state formation from historical sociologists, these scholars sought to demonstrate the historically contingent character of both state and state system (see, for instance, Campbell, 1998; Kratochwil, 1986; Onuf, 1991; Ruggie, 1993; Walker, 1993;; and implicit in Bartelson, 1995; Ferguson and Mansbach, 1996). The aim of this chapter is to give an overview of these works, discuss their continued relevance to IR and offer some critical remarks in order to guide future research. That being said, state formation is also one of the main theoretical contribution of Historical IR (HIR) to the discipline of IR more broadly, namely in questioning the immanence and 'takenfor-grantedness' of both state and state system (see the discussion in Hobden and Hobson, 2002).

Why should IR dwell on state formation, the sceptical reader may interject, when most of what is done on state formation is by historical sociologists. There are two reasons for that. Firstly, while many of these efforts reside outside of the traditional boundaries of the discipline proper (for notable exceptions, see Branch, 2013; Hall, 1999; Nexon, 2009; Reus-Smit, 1999; Teschke, 2003, discussed in the second part of the chapter), they have nevertheless permeated into IR to the extent that they form an intrinsic part of the disciplinary canon. As such, these accounts merit dwelling upon, and this chapter should be read as dovetailing with the chapter on Historical Sociology in the current volume (Go, Lawson, and de Carvalho, 2021), which does not go into these accounts in greater detail. These accounts, in turn, form the basis for identifying challenges and avenues for further research. Secondly, as discussed elsewhere in the volume (de Carvalho, 2021), the types of units that make up the world and their attributes greatly contribute to shape the type of interaction between units. Furthermore, these accounts were central in helping early constructivists harness their critiques of the ahistoricism of the neo-neo understanding. In fact, from the 1980s onwards, much of the historically oriented contributions to International Relations (IR) relied heavily on classic works of Historical Sociology (HS) – most notably works on state formation (see Leira and de Carvalho, 2016, for a discussion). These were successful to the point where these accounts have become commonplace in IR, and many of the historical sociologists have become household names in IR. However, as the discipline has become more global, questions are raised about the applicability of the traditional state formation narratives outside of Europe. Finally, as broader trends such as globalization and increasingly dense networks of global governance have come to make their mark on international politics, there have been many a commentator heeding the erosion of the state or even a move to a (neo) medieval global polity (cf. the critical discussion in Costa Lopez, 2021). Gauging these the validity of such claims and the potential resilience of the state in the face of these processes requires an understanding of what states consist of, and especially how they came to be. Our current predicament, then, rests largely on our capacity to make sense of how states emerged and transformed.

Historical sociology and state formation

It has become commonplace over the last decade or so to consider historical sociology to have consisted of three waves (Adams, Clemens, and Orloff, 2005).[1] The first wave is considered to consist of the classics, however defined, and need not concern us more directly here, although the influence of Marx, Weber, Hintze and Durkheim is still felt today (see Go, Lawson, and de Carvalho, 2021 in this volume, for a more detailed discussion). The current historical socio- logical study of state formation is commonly dated from the 1960s and onwards, when a second wave of historical sociology is seen to have arrived with the publication of Reinhard Bendix' *Nation-Building and Citizenship*, Barrington Moore's *Social Origins of Dictatorship and Democracy*, the republication of Norbert Elias' *The Civilizing Process* and with Charles Tilly and Stein Rokkan among the earliest proponents. Historical sociology was growing steadily in the 1970s and 1980s, drawing many of their questions from Marx, but many of their answers from Weber, as Philip S. Gorski (2004: 7) put it. As a reaction to this second wave, an alleged third wave, more heterogeneous and less coherent, emerged in the late 1990s, incorporating more culturalist work, including feminism and postcolonialism. But let us now turn to the historical sociology of state formation.

State formation was a recurring theme in the historical sociology of the second wave. The many different approaches to the historical sociology of state formation share at least one very basic puzzle, namely how the perceived criss-crossing pattern of authority and power structures which were pervasive in Europe towards the end of the mediaeval age (see Costa Lopez, 2020, 2021 in this volume) gradually split, coalesced and transformed into the states and the system of states spanning the globe in our current era. The potential time span to be covered is thus more than a millennium, and different authors emphasize different periods, according to which phe- nomena, they hold to be the most important. Nevertheless, a clear majority of studies centre their explorations between the fifteenth and eighteenth centuries, although there is wide variation in explanatory factors even within that period.

As Thomas Ertman has argued (2003), the Western tradition of thinking about the emergence of the state, its trajectory and variations in outcome has relied, and to a large extent still relies, on Max Weber and Otto Hintze (1975).[2] Charles Tilly's work is probably the most well-known to and IR readership. Tilly's edited *The Formation of National States in Western Europe* (1975) was hugely influential and largely contributed to the renewed interest in state formation in historical sociology. Many categorizations are possible within the overall Weberian trajectory, and we find it useful to distinguish between three different categories.[3]

The first category could be called economic-materialist and contains authors who in one way or another have primarily stressed economic factors in state building. Some have focused on dynamics within the state, like class struggle, commercialization of the countryside and the development of property rights. Others have focused on the development of global capitalism. Economic-materialist perspectives have had some influence on IR, but much less than the dominant perspectives, and as they have generally been less preoccupied with the international dimension they will be less central in this chapter too.

The second category could be called managerial-institutionalist and consists of authors who have chiefly stressed domestic institution-building in the state formation process. Strayer (1970) focuses mainly on the medieval period and the growth of a specialized administration, capable of managing ever larger realms, while Berman, looking at the same period, emphasizes the development of a legal order. With a somewhat different managerial-institutionalist perspective, Spruyt (1999) emphasizes how territorial sovereignty allowed the states to both integrate domestically and interact externally, while also being the most institutionally efficient providers of military power. According to Spruyt, the organizational form of the state spread because of its competitive advantage over other organizational forms: it was the most effective way of combining the functions of coercion and extraction.

Stein Rokkan could also be made to fit the managerial-institutionalist category, with his focus on the phases of state building related to the interpenetration of state and society. Rokkan, often overlooked today, is well worth dwelling on. Towards the end of his life, Rokkan (for instance 1987 [1975]) was working on an ever more complex conceptual map of Europe, where he was explicitly concerned with the internal variety among the states, and where he attempted to tie together the external and internal aspects of state building. The core of the model nevertheless remained what must be counted as Rokkan's key contribution to the historical sociology of state formation, namely the relation between centre and periphery within each state, where peripheries need not be geographical.

The second, managerial-institutionalist, category shades into the third one, which could be called military-institutionalist. The overall picture has been of so-called fiscal-military states and an 'extraction-coercion-cycle,' and the model of state formation is often referred to as 'bellicist.' This has by and large been the most influential approach to state formation, and also the one which has influenced IR the most. It is also clearly the approach which has had most to say about foreign policy and international politics.[4] Scholars within this tradition draw on Weber's definition of a state as 'a human community that (successfully) claims the *monopoly of the legitimate use of physical force* within a given territory,' and asks how that situation has come about. While there is an obvious internal component here, in the pacification of the territory, stressed famously by Elias, the second wave theorists like Tilly, Giddens and Mann, were much more concerned with the external use of force and the financing of it. For the sake of brevity, we do not make a point of discerning the fine-grain between the different contributions. Suffice it to note about the differences, that whereas Giddens and Mann have focused on military capacity and military technology and Poggi and Ertman on internal institutions, they have all been concerned with the pressures of the international system of states on the individual states.

Importantly, all of the authors have been concerned with the pressures of the international system of states on the individual states. Charles Tilly has obviously been the most explicit in linking state building and war, famously arguing both that 'War made the state, and the state made war' (Tilly, 1975: 42) and that war-making and state-making could be understood as a form of organized crime, the 'quintessential protection racket' (Tilly, 1985: 169). Key to Tilly's approach is the stress on the contingency of state formation. The ambition of the group working with *The Formation of National States in Western Europe* was explicitly to offer alternatives to the then established view that the emergence of the state in Europe was the result of continuous processes of rationalization and broadening of political participation. Instead, Tilly and his colleagues focused on initial conditions and diverging (largely contingent) paths to the emergence of the state. Tilly's take on state formation centred on the processes of coercion and extraction: war-making forced states to consolidate their apparatuses – bureaucracies, means of governance, means of policing – and to fund these efforts which in turn forced states to extract resources from their populations through means of taxation which increasingly were made permanent. Both mechanisms, in turn, reinforced each other creating a momentum for centralizing rulers. The money gathered through different forms of taxation allowed for increased concentration of physical power, which again made it easier to extract more resources. In short, as Tilly himself put it, 'war made the state, and the state made war.' As the argument goes, surrounded by other political entities and at repeated war, rulers desired to strengthen their military resources. To achieve this, they sought to extract more taxes from their realms.

As Mann (1986: 490) puts it, 'The growth of the modern state, as measured by finances, is explained primarily not in domestic terms but in terms of geopolitical relations of violence.' Although Mann presents four sources of social power: ideological, economic, military and political, it is relatively obvious that he in the end privileges military power. Tilly (1992: 14) is even more direct, arguing that 'the state structure appeared chiefly as a by-product of rulers' efforts to acquire the means of war.' Writing against the view which conflated the state and society or which saw the state just as an arena for the aggregation of preferences of different social groups, Mann argued, 'the state is not an arena where domestic economic/ideological issues are resolved, rather it is an arena in which military force is mobilized domestically and used domestically and, above all, internationally.' The autonomy of the state, Mann argues, derives from the state's 'territorially-centralized form of organization' (Mann, 1984: 185).

Most of the military-institutionalist scholars privilege developments of the sixteenth and seventeenth centuries and material factors. If matters do not impact directly on the extraction/coercion-cycle, they simply do not show up in the account. This is true for the intellectual aspects of the military revolution as well as for nationalism. All told, many of the traditional accounts of state formation pay surprisingly little attention to society, apart from its economic aspects. Poggi, on the other hand, presents an account which does pay heed to society and the internal organization of the state and which acknowledges important developments in the eighteenth century and later. His account falls somewhere between the military-institutionalist and managerial-institutionalist categories. Drawing on continental European sources, among them Habermas and Koselleck, he argues that state building goes from feudalism via the *Ständestaat* to absolutist rule and finally the constitutional state. Although chiefly concerned with the establishment of political institutions, Poggi (1990: 42-46) also considers intellectual developments and the role of law. In the transition from absolutism to the constitutional state, he (Poggi, 1978: 79–85) emphasizes the role played by civil society and public opinion, and how it could work in unison with the absolutist rulers to move gradually towards a more constitutional system.

State formation and International Relations

As noted, the dominant military-institutional account of state building has been criticized on a number of counts. We will mention the two most important ones and add a third of particular relevance to IR. The first, and general critique, has been that the military-institutionalist accounts have been too materialist, and not concerned enough about ideas and intellectual factors, like theories of state and statecraft, law and science (apart from military technology).[5] The many different specific critiques along these lines point to a lack of sustained interest in the knowledge-dimension of state formation. At the most general level, the alleged third (or culturalist) wave of historical sociology can be seen as a response to these shortcomings (Steinmetz, 1999). More specifically, Gerhard Oestreich (1982: 36, cf. van Gelderen, 2003) lamented almost forty years ago, that the focus on army organization and taxation had led authors to ignore the many theories of practical government of the sixteenth and seventeenth centuries, and in general the intellectual foundations of state building. Over the ensuing decades, conceptual historians, in particular those associated with the Cambridge School, have vastly increased our knowledge of how people historically have thought about the state and its relations with other states.

The second critique has been directed mainly at the application of the military-institutionalist perspective to IR and concerns how insights from the historical sociology of state formation, particularly Tilly's version, have tended to reify the dichotomies of inside/outside and state/society (Leander, 2009). Although this reification is to some extent an effect of reading historical sociology through IR glasses, it should be noted that Tilly, in his work on state formation, does to a large extent treat inside and outside as discrete categories and shows little interest in society as anything other than a field for intervention from the state. The problem with this double reification is that it obscures both processes that transcend the dichotomies and the ensuing enmeshment, and the very processes whereby the distinctions were made in the first place. Rob Walker (1993) and others have demonstrated convincingly how the distinction between inside and outside was first made around 1600, and Habermas, Foucault and others have discussed the many-faceted processes of the eighteenth century, which were part of the production of the distinction between state and society. Reifying the dichotomies is thus quite simply non-historicist historical sociology.

The third critique is a further specification of the second and concerns how the military-institutionalist accounts have dealt with IR. The military-institutionalists generally incorporate an unarticulated analytical perspective of the international context, where war is considered to be a transhistorically valid concept. As Kestnbaum (2005: 249) argues, these approaches largely ignore 'whether war has an internal logic and structure that may vary in sociologically significant ways. Never asked is how warfare actually works' (see also Bartelson, 2021 in this volume). On the question of war it is worth noting the recent publication of *Does War Make States? Investigations of Charles Tilly's Historical Sociology* by Lars Bo Kaspersen and Jeppe Strandsbjerg (2017) which gathers a number of critical essays questioning the central tenet of Tilly's theory. In addition to soften and contextualize some of Tilly's claim, the book draws our attention to experiences beyond Europe, emphasizing the relative inadequacy of the framework to account for state formation outside of the early modern European context. This charge of Eurocentrism is not new, as other authors have probed the validity of the Tillyan framework on other continents before. Most notably, Miguel Angel Centeno has sought to specify additional conditions necessary in Latin America (2002), while Jeffrey Herbst has sought to apply the framework to the African context (1990).

The unspoken premise is that states or state-like entities have been pursuing relatively similar external activities across the millennia, and thus that the actions of ancient Egypt, or at least the actions of medieval polities, are understandable in our current terms. In and of itself, there is nothing wrong with an analytical concept of foreign policy, and it is hard to conceive of a social science without analytical concepts at all. However, there is an inherent danger in applying our current concepts analytically to earlier times, namely that one overestimates the similarities, seeing the past in terms of our present. If we discuss the foreign policy of ancient Egypt, it is ever so simple to imagine an Egyptian minister of foreign affairs directing an Egyptian ministry of foreign affairs, thinking along the same lines as our current ministers of foreign affairs. Hobden and Hobson's (2002) critique of IR can in fact also be applied to certain ways in which historical sociology conceptualizes the past, creating a tendency to reify, naturalize and eternalize our current age and to extrapolate it backwards into history in a reversed path dependency.

To recapitulate, there are a number of different approaches to state formation within historical sociology, and we have chosen to highlight the traditional military-institutionalist account, as well as the accounts of Rokkan and Poggi, both more influenced by a managerial-institutionalist perspective. We have also discussed three central criticisms of the dominant approach, its lack of interest in knowledge, its reification of inside/outside and state/society and its ahistorical approach to foreign policy and international politics. These critiques have been important to those within HIR seeking to highlight the international dimension of state formation.

Within IR, John Herz' early work on the state (1957) is important and often overlooked today. His contribution was a pioneering one in many ways. Firstly, within IR, it was an early move towards searching for answers to current predicaments in long-term historical developments. Furthermore, discussing the future trajectory of the sovereign territorial state, Herz did much of the theoretical groundwork which today characterizes studies of the state under conditions of globalization. As he argues, 'the change-over is not even uniform and unilinear. On the contrary, in concepts as well as in policies, we witness the juxtaposition of old and new (or several new) factors, a coexistence in theory and practice of conventional and new concepts, of traditional and new policies.' Writing in 1957, Herz argued that both the meaning and function of the state ('the basic protective unit') had become 'doubtful.' On the basis of his inquiry into the historical rise of the state, Hertz raises questions about the future trajectory and function of the state and the possibility of finding security in the nuclear age. He argues, 'the nation-state is giving way to a permeability which tends to obliterate the very meaning of unit and unity, power and power relations, sovereignty and independence.'

More recently, Rodney Bruce Hall's *National Collective Identity* (1999) and Christian Reus-Smit's *The Moral Purpose of the State* (1999) contributed to make state formation an explicit concern to IR scholars. Rodney Bruce Hall addressed what he calls the 'strongly state-centric' discipline of IR (1999: 4). By ignoring the collective identity of societal actors, Hall argued, IR theory has been largely unable to explain 'historical change in the international system' (ibid.: 5). For, Hall maintains, 'changes in the collective identity of societal actors transform the interests of relevant collective actors that constitute the system' (ibid.). State interests are thus not to be understood as immutable, as mainstream IR theory would have it. Instead, they are largely the product of collective identities which change over time. Thus, rather than the realist 'will-to-power,' Hall argues that domestic and global orders are the product of a 'will-to-manifest-identity' (ibid.: 6). The international behaviour of actors – such as balancing, alliance formation and conflicts – thus cannot be understood without reference to the framework formed by their collective identities (ibid.: 9).

Christian Reus-Smit takes a related and complementary approach, but rather than enquiring, as Hall does, into how the social identity of actors shapes interaction at the systemic level, Reus-Smit's concern is with how international institutions shape the identity and interests of state actors (1999: 22). However, Reus-Smit stresses that the standard constructivist understanding of the principle of sovereignty as the basis of the state's social identity is insufficient. Rather, he postulates, it must be recognized that 'the identity of the state is grounded in a larger complex of values than simply the organizing principle of sovereignty' (ibid.: 29–30). The social identity of states is firmly entrenched in the normative structure of international society. What Reus-Smit does is, so to speak, to turn Rodney Bruce Hall's account on its head: instead of emphasizing how the identity of polities contributes to the systemic interaction, Reus-Smit suggests that it is the normative system which provides the state with its moral purpose, which in turn forms the basis for its identity. While he recognizes that the collective identity of states has been different in different periods, change itself is nevertheless not addressed.

These works have failed to create much of a research program in IR, and their focus on identity from the late 1990s has not been fully followed up on in more recent studies. However, Daniel Nexon (2009) has addressed the problem both Hall and Reus-Smit have with addressing the drivers of change, finding this in the transnational networks of power which followed from the reformations. According to Nexon, these contributed largely to tearing down remnants of imperial structures in Europe. But again, where the international is given more explanatory power, the focus is shifted away from the formation of states to the erosion of empires. Another study worth noting here is *The Cartographic State* by Jordan Branch (2013). Branch addresses the conditions of possibility of states, the extent to which the formation of states required a change in mentalities of power, in geographical imaginaries, and the extent to which shifts in technologies of map-making and diffusion contributed to these.

State formation, the state and the state system

As seen above, the 'import' of concerns with state formation into IR has given rise to a number of 'IR proper' contributions to that literature. Interestingly, however, this has not led to a comparable surge in theorizing about the state or the state system. As the key actor in international politics, the state is central to most theories of international politics.[6] In fact, whether these make the state the cornerstone of their claims, or seek to move beyond the state, they nevertheless ground their claims in the changing reach of state power. For all the concern IR has had with the state, it has become commonplace to notice that there have been relatively few efforts to study the state in IR. Curiously, perhaps, the current wave of research on empire does not find its counterpart in studies of the state. To the extent that the state has been the object of historical scrutiny in IR, it is largely through the concept of sovereignty (see, for instance, Bartelson, 1995; de Carvalho, 2021 in this volume, provides an overview), and through studies of state formation.

In terms of how to conceptualize the state, IR scholars have for the most part been content with adopting some variation of the Weberian canonical definition of the state in terms of its particular means, the monopoly of violence: 'Ultimately, one can define the modern state sociologically only in terms of the specific means peculiar to it, as to every political association, namely the use of physical force' (Weber, 1978: 78). Thus one should comprehend the state in terms of the means peculiar to it, namely as 'a human community that (successfully) claims the monopoly of the legitimate use of physical force within a given territory [...] The state is considered the sole source of the 'right' to use violence' (ibid.).

Yet, while it may be useful to operate with Weber's ideal type for analytical purposes, however banal it may seem, it may be worthwhile noting that no state is ever alone in the world. This is important to keep in mind, as the theories of state formation outlined above all tend to focus on how states have evolved after the initial 'spark' kickstarting their 'formation' (see discussion in the conclusion). Among historical sociologists, little is said about the international system, its logic and precisely how it contributed to the formation of states. International politics, diplomacy and foreign policy are seldom mentioned in the analyses, more often than not the term is covered simply by 'war.'[7] Paradoxically, this is also where the international dimension of state formation seems to have been the most crucial (except, perhaps, for the competition between states). Michael Mann, for instance sees the role of the system of states as crucial, as it provided of the spark which ignites the process: 'The European state system was not simply the "political environment" in which the absolutist state and nation-state developed. It was the condition, and in substantial degree the very source of that development' (1986 112). Yet, precisely what role the international had in the process is seldom inquired into. Illustrating the diversity within the military-institutionalist category, it should be noted that Poggi (1978: 61), even though he points to the same mechanisms of state competition, is much more explicit about co-constitution, arguing that the overall result of power struggle could just as well stem from the individual rulers' desire for increased control as from systemic pressure. To Poggi, it seems, the international dimension seems to have been secondary to the formation of states, as he held that state, sovereignty and territoriality 'jointly produce a most significant consequence: the political environment in which each state exists is by necessity one which it shares with a plurality of states similar in nature to itself' (1990: 23).

The case for a history of the state system, then, is rather dire. There is little agreement among scholars as to when and how the system emerged; little agreement as to how (and whether) it undergoes change; and little agreement about what constitutes the system. For a discipline which has the international system as its main framework, it is surprising how little attention IR scholars have paid to the historical development of the international system and its consequences. This may be due in part to the fact that to many IR scholars, the central feature of the international system is precisely its alleged permanence and the timeless nature of its workings. Yet, in spite of a number of historical studies of the constituent parts of the state system, most notably diplomacy, warfare and great power politics, only few major works have taken on the state system as a whole.[8] As Barry Buzan and Richard Little have charged, 'despite more than a century of intensive discussion about the nature of the international system, it is difficult to deny how underdeveloped the concept continues to be. Even the more sophisticated accounts of the international system fail to address some of the most elementary questions' (2002: 204). Buzan and Little attribute this in part to the discipline's tendency towards presentism and ahistoricism.

Whatever the merits of such a critique, that situation is currently changing in IR, much as the result of work undertaken by HIR scholars. Much of the critique levied above is a critique of the lack of concern historical sociologists have had with the international (as such, it dovetails nicely with the critique in Go, Lawson, and de Carvalho, 2021 in this volume), and recent works such as *The Global Transformation* (2015) do much to address it. Furthermore, IR scholars working on the topic have included the international to a larger extent – although not always in a problematizing way (see, for instance, Hall, 1999; Reus-Smit, 1999). As highlighted elsewhere in the volume (Bartelson, 2021; Caraccioli, 2021; de Carvalho, 2021; Leira, 2021), we can also discern the emergence of a clear research program on hierarchies and empires dealing with the international or global dimension of the broad changes which took place between the fifteenth and the eighteenth centuries (see, for example, Bayly, 2021 in this volume).

Transformation against formation: a plea for muddying the water

To sum up, historical sociological theories of state formation have been hugely influential in IR, as they were crucial in propelling social constructivism as an approach from the late 1980s onwards. Furthermore, they inspired a number of historical works in HIR, works in which the international is given larger explanatory power than in the works of historical sociologists. Yet, the agenda on state formation to a large extent contributed to cover up the need for studies of the state and the state system. Critiques of this were many, most notably calls for a focus on empires. Where the traditional story of state formation is one of emerging states and vanishing empires, critics held that empires never vanished, and that states were also empires. An emerging literature among global historians, combined with a theoretical turn from anarchy to hierarchy has, in turn, has given the impetus for a broad research program on empires in HIR. The story could end here. That would, however, be less than helpful. Let us therefore expand on four aspects which we believe future research ought to be mindful of.

Firstly, as noted above, the literature on state formation has had a strong emphasis on Europe and the European experience. Now, this is not a critique we believe should necessarily be levelled against those authors. Firstly, many of these writings are aimed directly as critiques of the thereunto prevalent view that there was a path dependency to state formation, and that sequences having taken place in Europe could be made to repeat themselves beyond Europe. There is thus a critical element to these writings which we tend to oversee, given that the point about the contingency of these processes has become so well established. Furthermore, a number of these scholars also studied state formation outside of Europe, and from a different perspective, although those writings have tended to remain on the fringes of the state formation canon. The writings of Aristide Zolberg, one of Tilly's early collaborators, come to mind (see, for instance, Zolberg, 1983) as works worthy of bringing back into the canon. However, in terms of future research, it seems clear – as noted with respect to the works of Centeno (2002) and Herbst (1990) that making sense of the state cannot happen as long as we take a specific space as our point of departure and bracket out the multiplicity of encounters happening across borders and seas.

Secondly, while excavating empires and imperialism from the statist amnesia is crucial to a better understanding of the emergence and changing nature of international politics and of the international *tout court*, there may be dangers associated with such a project. The main danger may lie in that we come to simply replace one set of concepts by another set; state by empire, state formation by imperialism, anarchy by hierarchy and state system by global power networks. The problem with this is not only that neither state nor state system is given a fair trial, or that it is historically inadequate. There is a danger in that studies of empire replace the state IR misses out on the most rewarding aspect of this new agenda, namely enquiring into how empires *and* states interacted in the early modern period with a view to theorize international politics from a truly open perspective.

Our two next points relate back to the beginning of this chapter and relate to problematic path dependencies which have accompanied us since the emergence of the second wave of historical sociology and Tilly's masterful 1975 volume. Our third point, then, concerns a blind spot in the state formation literature, namely the role of culture, religion and identity in the processes of state formation. Just as there are a number of reasons why IR did not focus on these much before the 1990s, there are many reasons why they do not figure prominently in accounts of the emergence of the state. One of these is the importance of the work done in 1975 by Tilly and his colleagues in delineating a research agenda on the formation of the state. For if their effort brought the state in, it left the nation out. State and nation were thus seen as two different phenomena, and few studies undertook to understand their emergence *qua* nation-state. As Tilly noted,

> We began work intending to analyze state-making and the formation of nations interdependently. As our inquiry proceeded, we concentrated our attention increasingly on the development of states rather than the building of nations. There were several reasons for this drift. One was the greater ease with which we could arrive at some working agreement of the meaning of the word 'state.' 'Nation' remains one of the most puzzling and tendentious items in the political lexicon. Another was our early fixation of the periods in which the primacy (of) [sic.] states was still open to serious challenge [...] A third was the bias in our original set of topics toward the extractive and repressive activities of states. The bias was deliberate. The singling out of the organization of armed forces, taxation, policing, the control of food supply and the formation of technical personnel stresses activities which were difficult, costly, and often unwanted by large parts of the population.
>
> (Tilly, 1975: 6)

As alluded to in Heiskanen (2021 in this volume; see also de Carvalho, 2016), there is a need to address this bias by 'bringing back in' (sic) the collective identity and the nation into conceptualizations of state formation. Such a move may also help recover and harness some of the critical potential of first-generation constructivism which has been left untapped by second-generation constructivists (see Leira and de Carvalho, 2016, for a critique).

Finally, our last point is a cautionary one. There has been some debate among historical sociologists about the correct vocabulary to use to best describe the processes inquired into. While some have sought to highlight state *making* as an alternative with clearer agency, other alternatives to formation have also been discussed: emergence, crystallization, development. Each of them comes with their own conceptual baggage. Formation, while being fairly neutral, nevertheless implies the formation of a new type of polity which by extension supplants whatever polity was there before. And, however many qualifiers we use, the terms still leave these connotations. In an interview in 2007, recollecting the process around his first contributions to the state formation literature, Charles Tilly stated,

> I made a mistake. And that is in the title of the book and the polemical essays that form part of the introduction and conclusion [that I wrote] I deliberately adopted the term 'state formation'. Now why did I do that? Because I wanted to stress the alternative to the idea of 'political development'. I thought, and I persuaded my colleagues, that this was a neutral term. Well it was a mistake. Almost immediately people started using the term 'state formation' teleologically. So, the question is: 'Is this state formed yet?' And so you got numerous essays on 'the failure of state formation in fill in the blank' or something like that. And I thought: another mistake! […] I now talk about 'state transformation'. [Although] there is no neutral term because people have teleological agendas whenever they think about the history of states.
>
> (Tilly, 2007)

In line with Tilly, we would like end by suggesting that the focus of macro-historical processes moves away from ends and beginnings, moves away from units supplanting other units, and instead focus on how certain types of polities give rise to others, how different units interact with each other, how that interaction contributes to large-scale processes of change and how polities may gain a new guise and transform over time.

Suggestions for further reading

Centeno, M. A. (2002). *Blood and Debt: War and the Nation-State in Latin America*. University Park, PA: Penn State Press.

Kaspersen, L. B., and Strandsbjerg, J., eds. (2017). *Does War Make States? Investigations of Charles Tilly's Historical Sociology*. Cambridge: Cambridge University Press.

Strayer, J. R. (1970). *On the Medieval Origins of the Modern State*. Princeton, NJ: Princeton University Press.

Tilly, C. (1992). *Coercion, Capital and European States. AD 990-1992*. Oxford: Blackwell.

Notes

1 Before starting, a caveat must be made regarding literature we discuss here. Even though there have been important French and German traditions straddling historical sociology, much of the work under that explicit name has been carried out in the Anglosphere. Our initial focus will thus be on this tradition, while we get back to criticisms drawing on other traditions below. In Germany, a number of historians, particularly the ones concerned with social and conceptual history such as Reinhard Koselleck, have traditionally come close to historical sociology, while part of Jürgen Habermas' scholarship also clearly fits the label. In France, the work of Foucault, Bourdieu and their collaborators and students comes to mind.

2 It should be noted that some more systemic takes in IR have adopted other perspectives, such as the neo-Marxist studies of the state and the international system presented by Immanuel Wallerstein (1974) or in the work of Perry Anderson (e.g. 1996).

3 A number of academics have attempted to systematise the different approaches according to commonalities in explanatory factors. Philip S. Gorski (1999: 147) simply suggests a division between Marxist perspectives (with Anderson and Wallerstein as examples) and institutionalist (read Weberian) perspectives (represented by Tilly, Poggi and Downing). This is simply too undifferentiated to be useful. Casting a more fine-grained net, both Poggi (2004) and Rae (2002: 24–38) suggest trichotomies, and fusing the two gives us a rather fuller picture. Poggi calls the perspectives managerial (exemplified by Strayer and Berman), military (Collins, Hintze, Tilly) and economic (Moore, Anderson), while Rae calls the approaches materialist (Wallerstein), institutionalist (North/Thomas, Spruyt) and power-based (Elias, Giddens, Mann, Tilly).

4 Compare Strayer (1970: 27), 'The reasons for this concentration on internal affairs are obvious. The fragmented condition of Europe and the weakness of its political units did not permit any sustained or long-range activity in external affairs. […] In a Europe without states and without boundaries the concept of "foreign affairs" had no meaning, and so no machinery for dealing with foreign affairs was needed.'

5 For the natural sciences, see Carroll's (2006) fascinating study of Ireland.

6 This does not amount to say that they are the only actors around in world politics. Few would defend such a claim, and even Kenneth Waltz acknowledged, 'states are not and never have been the only international actors […] The importance of nonstate actors and the extent of transnational activities are obvious' (1979: 93–94).

7 A telling example of this can be found in Poggi's book on the development of the modern state, where we find the following index-entry for foreign policy: '*See also* Power struggle between states' (Poggi, 1978: 171).

8 Interestingly, this is the opposite situation from state formation, where most of the work consists of larger studies. There are, to be sure, notable exceptions to this.

References

Adams, J., Clemens, E. S., and Orloff, A. S. (2005). Introduction: Social Theory, Modernity and the Three Waves of Historical Sociology. In: J. Adams, E. S. Clemens, and A. S. Orloff, eds., *Remaking Modernity. Politics, History, and Sociology*, Durham, NC: Duke University Press, 1–72.

Anderson, Perry. (1996). *The Lineages of the Absolutist State*. New York, NY: Verso.

Bartelson, J. (1995). *A Genealogy of Sovereignty*. Cambridge: Cambridge University Press.

Bartelson, J. (2021). War and the Turn to History in International Relations. In: B. de Carvalho, J. Costa Lopez, and H. Leira, eds., *Routledge Handbook of Historical International Relations*. Abingdon: Routledge.

Bayly, M. (2021). Imperialism: Beyond the 'Re-turn to Empire' in International Relations. In: B. de Carvalho, J. Costa Lopez, and H. Leira, eds., *Routledge Handbook of Historical International Relations*. Abingdon: Routledge.

Branch, J. (2013). *The Cartographic State: Maps, Territory, and the Origins of Sovereignty*. Cambridge: Cambridge University Press.

Buzan, B., and Little, R. (2002). International Systems in world history: remaking the study of international relations. In: S. Hobden and J. M. Hobson, eds., *Historical Sociology of International Relations*. Cambridge: Cambridge University Press.

Campbell, D. (1998). *Writing Security. United States Foreign Policy and the Politics of Identity*. Minneapolis, MN: University of Minnesota Press.

Caraccioli, M. J. (2021). Early (Modern) Empires: The Political Ideology of Conceptual Domination. In: B. de Carvalho, J. Costa Lopez, and H. Leira, eds., *Routledge Handbook of Historical International Relations*. Abingdon: Routledge.

Carroll, P. (2006). *Science, Culture and Modern State Formation*. Berkeley, CA: University of California Press.

Costa Lopez, J. (2020). Political authority in international relations: revisiting the medieval debate. *International Organization*, 74 (2), 222–252.

Costa Lopez, J. (2021). International Relations in/and the Middle Ages. In: B. de Carvalho, J. Costa Lopez, and H. Leira, eds., *Routledge Handbook of Historical International Relations*. Abingdon: Routledge.

de Carvalho, B. (2016). The making of the political subject: subjects and territory in the formation of the state. *Theory and Society*, 45 (1), 57–88.

de Carvalho, B. (2021). Sovereignty in Historical International Relations: Trajectories, Challenges and Implications. In: B. de Carvalho, J. Costa Lopez, and H. Leira, eds., *Routledge Handbook of Historical International Relations*. Abingdon: Routledge.

Ertman, T. (2003). State Formation and State Building in Europe. In: T. Janoski, R. Alford, A. Hicks, and M. Schwartz, eds., *The Handbook of Political Sociology: States, Civil Societies, and Globalization*, Cambridge: Cambridge University Press, 367–383.

Ferguson, Y., and Mansbach, R. (1996). *Polities: Authority, Identities, and Change*. Columbia, SC: University of South Carolina Press.

Go, J., Lawson, G., and de Carvalho, B. (2021). Historical Sociology in International Relations: The Challenge of the Global. In: B. de Carvalho, J. Costa Lopez, and H. Leira, eds., *Routledge Handbook of Historical International Relations*. Abingdon: Routledge.

Gorski, P. S. (1999). Calvinism and State-Formation in Europe. In: G. Steinmetz, ed., *State/Culture: State Formation after the Cultural Turn*, Ithaca, NY: Cornell University Press, 147–181.

Gorski, P. S. (2004). Reply. *Comparative and Historical Sociology*, 15 (4), 7–10.

Hall, R. B. (1999). *National Collective Identity: Social Constructs and International System*. New York, NY: Columbia University Press.

Heiskanen, J. (2021). Nations and Nationalism in International Relations. In: B. de Carvalho, J. Costa Lopez, and H. Leira, eds., *Routledge Handbook of Historical International Relations*. Abingdon: Routledge.

Herbst, J. (1990). War and the State in Africa. *International Security*, 14 (4), 117–139.

Herz, J. (1957). Rise and demise of the territorial state. *World Politics*, 9 (4), 473–493.

Hintze, O. (1975). In: F. Gilbert, ed., *The Historical Essays of Otto Hintze*, New York, NY: Oxford University Press.

Hobden, S., and Hobson, J. M., eds. (2002). *Historical Sociology of International Relations*. Cambridge: Cambridge University Press.

Kestnbaum, M. (2005). Mars Revealed: The Entry of Ordinary People into War among States. In: J. Adams, E. S. Clemens, and A. S. Orloff, eds., *Remaking Modernity. Politics, History, and Sociology*, Durham, NC: Duke University Press, 249–285.

Kratochwil, F. (1986). Of systems, boundaries, and territoriality: an inquiry into the formation of the state system. *World Politics*, 39 (1), 27–51.

Leander, A. (2009). *Signposting Four Pitfalls: A Reflection on Historical Sociology and IR*. Working Paper, Copenhagen Business School. Available at and viewed on 15 November 2020, <http://openarchive.cbs.dk/cbsweb/handle/10398/7968>.

Leira. H. (2021). Diplomacy: The World of States and Beyond. In: B. de Carvalho, J. Costa Lopez, and H. Leira, eds., *Routledge Handbook of Historical International Relations*. Abingdon: Routledge.

Leira, H., and de Carvalho, B. (2016). Construction time again: history in constructivist IR scholarship. *ERIS – European Review of International Studies*, 3 (3), 99–111.

Mann, M. (1984). The autonomous power of the state: its origins, mechanisms and results. *European Journal of Sociology*, 25 (2), 185–213.

Mann, M. (1986). *The Sources of Social Power. Volume I: A History of Power from the Beginning to A. D. 1760*. Cambridge: Cambridge University Press.

Nexon, D. H. (2009). *The Struggle for Power in Early Modern Europe: Religious Conflict, Dynastic Empires, and International Change*. Princeton, NJ: Princeton University Press.

Oestreich, G. (1982). *Neostoicism and the Early Modern State*. Foreword by B. Oestreich and H. G. Koenigsberger. Cambridge: Cambridge University Press.

Onuf, N. G. (1991). Sovereignty: outline of a conceptual history. *Alternatives*, 16 (4), 425–446.

Poggi, G. (1978). *The Development of the Modern State. A Sociological Introduction*. Stanford, CA: Stanford University Press.

Poggi, G. (1990). *The State, Its Nature, Development, and Prospects*. Stanford, CA: Stanford University Press.

Poggi, G. (2004). Formation and Form: Theories of State Formation. In: K. Nash, ed., *The Blackwell Companion to Political Sociology*, Oxford: Blackwell, 95–106.

Rae, H. (2002). *State Identities and the Homogenisation of Peoples*. Cambridge: Cambridge University Press.

Reus-Smit, C. (1999). *The Moral Purpose of the State: Culture, Social Identity and Institutional Rationality in International Relations*. Princeton, NJ: Princeton University Press.

Rokkan, S. (1987 [1975]). Dimensjoner ved statsdannelse og nasjonsbygging: Et mulig paradigme for utforskning av variasjoner i Europa. In: S. Rokkan, ed., *Stat, Nasjon, Klasse*, Oslo: Universitetsforlaget, 347–380.

Ruggie, J. G. (1993). Territoriality and beyond: problematizing modernity in international relations. *International Organization*, 47 (1), 139–174.

Spruyt, H. (1999). *The Sovereign State and Its Competitors*. Princeton, NJ: Princeton University Press.

Steinmetz, G., ed. (1999). *State/Culture. State-Formation after the Cultural Turn*. Ithaca, NY: Cornell University Press.

Teschke, B. (2003). *The Myth of 1648: Class, Geopolitics, and the Making of Modern International Relations*. London: Verso.

Tilly, C., ed. (1975). *The Formation of National States in Western Europe*. Princeton, NJ: Princeton University Press.

Tilly, C. (1985). War Making and State Making as Organized Crime. In: P. Evans, D. Rueschemeyer, and T. Skocpol, eds., *Bringing the State Back In*, Cambridge: Cambridge University Press, 169–191.

Tilly, C. (2007). Charles Tilly interviewed by Daniel Little. University of Michigan, 15 December 2007. Available at and viewed on 15 Nov 2020, <https://www.youtube.com/watch?v=b51Dkbh8XCA>.

van Gelderen, M. (2003). The State and Its Rivals in Early-Modern Europe. In: Q. Skinner, and B. Stråth, eds., *States & Citizens. History, Theory, Prospects*, Cambridge: Cambridge University Press, 79–96.

Walker, R. B. J. (1993). *Inside/Outside. International Relations as Political Theory*. Cambridge: Cambridge University Press.

Wallerstein, I. (1974). *The Modern World-System: Capitalist Agriculture and the Origins of the European World-Economy in the Sixteenth Century*. Volume 1. New York, NY: Academic Press.

Waltz, K. (1979). *Theory of International Politics*. New York, NY: McGraw-Hill.

Weber, M. (1978). In: G. Roth, and C. Wittich, eds., *Economy and Society*. 2nd edition. Two volumes. Berkeley, CA: University of California Press.

Zolberg, A. (1983). The formation of new states as a refugee-generating process. *The ANNALS of the American Academy of Political and Social Science*, 467 (1), 24–38.

23

NATIONS AND NATIONALISM IN INTERNATIONAL RELATIONS

Jaakko Heiskanen

Introduction

One of the historically unique characteristics of modern international relations is that they are interactions between formally equal and equivalent nation-states; it is this 'global monoculture' of nation-states that differentiates the modern international order from its more heterogeneous predecessors (Phillips and Sharman, 2015: 1). Over the years, the discipline of IR has produced a substantial body of historical and theoretical literature on the 'state' side of the nation-state (e.g. James, 1986; Jackson, 1990; Spruyt, 1994; Bartelson, 2001; Branch, 2013; see de Carvalho and Leira, 2021 in this volume). In comparison, the 'nation' side of the nation-state been relatively neglected by IR scholars, even as it has been subjected to detailed analysis by sociologists and historians (e.g. Gellner, 1983; Hobsbawm, 1992; Anderson, 2006; Hirschi, 2012). The neglect of nations and nationalism in IR is rather surprising for a discipline that, after all, derives its name from the nation. Nations and nationalism are absolutely central to the theory and practice of modern international relations, yet their role has been systematically downplayed or ignored by IR scholars. As will be detailed below, the neglect of nations and nationalism is no mere oversight, but a constitutive disavowal that makes it possible to analyse international relations as interstate relations.

The chapter is divided into three sections. The first section provides a historical overview of the development of nationalism, highlighting the ambivalent relationship between nationalism and the state. The second section describes the conceptual frameworks through which IR scholars have grappled with the ambivalence of nationalism and how, in the process, they have transformed international relations into interstate relations. The final section explores the difficulties that plague attempts to move 'beyond' the nation-state and what such a move might entail for IR as a discipline.

Historical overview

At the core of nationalism is the concept of the nation, which derives from the Latin *natio* and originally signified a community of birth. In the medieval period, this term was used to designate groups of people sharing a common origin, such as university students hailing from geographically or linguistically related regions (Hirschi, 2012: 78–81). It was during the transition from the

244

late medieval to the early modern era that the word 'nation' started to be used with reference to the population of a country in several European languages, thus imbuing this concept with a new political dimension. Some of the earliest examples of the political use of the term can be found in England and the Netherlands in the sixteenth century. The backdrop to this semantic transformation was the Protestant Reformation and the resultant upsurge of confessional and constitutional strife, which heralded the fragmentation of medieval Christendom (Gorski, 2000). In the context of these upheavals, the formerly universal Catholic Church splintered into a multiplicity of 'national' churches and religion was subordinated to state-building endeavours. Not only did religious identities acquire a newfound significance in defining the foreign policy choices of states (de Carvalho, 2014), early modern state-building initiatives also spurred attempts at 'national' homogenisation through the conversion or expulsion of heretics from the state's domains (Rae, 2002).

The growing body of scholarship on the early modern origins of nationalism offers a vital corrective to the prevailing 'modernist' view, which has seen nationalism as the exclusive product of the eighteenth and nineteenth centuries (e.g. Gellner, 1983; Hobsbawm, 1992). Nevertheless, it would be misleading to claim that the nationalism of the early modern period was identical to that of the modern era. In contrast to the secular and territorialised guise of modern nationalism, early modern nationalism remained deeply embedded within a religious and dynastic framework. The early modern era was the era of the 'confessional state' rather than the 'national state' (de Carvalho, 2014). As Caspar Hirschi (2012: 3) notes in his important survey of the pre-modern roots of nationalism, 'there was a remarkable time lag between the creation of nationalist language and the implementation of nationalist politics. By the end of the fifteenth century, the concept of the nation was almost fully developed in scholarly literature, whereas in political practice, imperialist, dynastic and religious principles would prevail for another three centuries'. It was not until the eighteenth and nineteenth centuries that the religious principle of *cuius regio, eius religio* gave way to the nationalist principle of *cuius regio, eius natio*.

The rise of modern nationalism is largely coterminous with the rise of popular sovereignty, which wrested sovereignty away from God and placed it in the hands of the people. In the words of Bernard Yack (2001: 517), 'wherever popular sovereignty leads, nationalism seems to follow'. The reason behind the close association between the two discourses is that popular sovereignty revolves around an aporia: who are the sovereign people? Taken by itself, the principle of popular sovereignty is unable to demarcate or legitimate the boundaries of the political unit (see de Carvalho, 2021 in this volume). Modern political nationalism offers the solution to this quandary by grounding the abstract political unit in a concrete ethnocultural conception of the people as a nation that is both prepolitical and territorially delimited (Connor, 1981; Yack, 2001; Abizadeh, 2012). In the oft-quoted words of Ernest Gellner (1983: 1): 'Nationalism is primarily a political principle, which holds that the political and the national unit should be congruent'. Or, in the more succinct formulation of Eric Hobsbawm (1992: 19): 'nation = state = people'.

Theories of popular sovereignty were already circulating among medieval political philosophers, but these ideas were not yet implemented in political practice. Political legitimacy was instead derived from various other sources, including divine right, royal blood, right of conquest, right of inheritance, and/or the provision of services such as protection. What all of these pre-modern sources of legitimacy had in common was 'the negative presumption that legitimacy had nothing to do with those who were ruled. The masses were solely the object, not the source of political authority' (Connor, 1981: 207). As a basis of political practice, popular sovereignty did not acquire widespread currency until the American and French Revolutions at the end of the eighteenth century. In 1787, the political fiction of 'we, the people' was institutionalised in the constitution of the newly independent United States (Taylor, 1999: 226). Two years later, the French

Revolution reconfigured the political meaning of the nation concept. The terms *nation* and *patrie* had been a recurrent feature of French political debates for several decades, but they had no bearing on political legitimacy structures and could be invoked by supporters and critics of the royal government alike. Prior to the revolution, the concept of the nation remained 'a highly generalized rhetorical figure that was compatible with all sorts of different political or constitutional orientations'. It was only from 1789 that the nation was 'redefined […] from a diffuse sentiment to a specific program for political and constitutional action' (Sewell, 2004: 96). This shift was epitomised by the Declaration of the Rights of Man and of the Citizen, promulgated by the French National Assembly in the first year of the revolution, which proclaimed that 'the source of all sovereignty resides essentially in the nation' (quoted in Connor, 1978: 382). In addition to revolutionising domestic legitimacy structures, the French Revolution and the ensuing Napoleonic Wars also transformed the nature of external relations between European polities from a dynastic to a national model, paving the way for the emergence of modern international relations (Bukovansky, 1999).

The significance of the American and French Revolutions notwithstanding, it must be emphasised that 'nation-formation is a process, not an occurrence or event' (Connor, 1990: 99). Until the end of the nineteenth century, even in seemingly long-standing nation-states like France, national consciousness remained an elite phenomenon. The penetration of national consciousness deeper into the social fabric required a massive expansion of literacy rates and transport networks that was only achieved after the industrial revolution gathered speed in the second half of the nineteenth century (Weber, 1976). If the spread of nationalism 'vertically' to the lower rungs of society was a drawn-out and uneven process, the same is true for the 'horizontal' propagation of the nation-state globally. By 1920, following a series of anticolonial revolutions in Latin America, the national unifications of Italy and Germany, and the dissolution of the Habsburg, Romanov, and Ottoman empires, the bulk of the Western hemisphere was divided into nation-states. However, European imperialism still prevailed over a large portion of Asia and virtually the whole of Africa. This imperial arrangement was underpinned by civilisational and racial hierarchies that effectively rendered the nation-state a privileged preserve of the white West (see Bayly, 2021 in this volume). It was not until the second half of the twentieth century that this imperial order was dismantled, as anticolonial movements appropriated nationalist language and extended its application to the colonies (Manela, 2007; Getachew, 2019). Today, there is hardly any state, whether democratic or authoritarian, that does not claim to exercise political power in the name of a nation or people.

Given that nations are historical artefacts rather than natural entities, their boundaries are always open to contestation by other nations and nationalist movements. Indeed, the number of potential nations is infinitely greater than the number of states that have ever existed (Connor, 1972; Walby, 2003). This inherent contestability of nations inscribes a crucial ambivalence into the relationship between nationalism and the state. As Rogers Brubaker (1998: 300) observes, nationalism can take both 'state-framed' and 'counter-state' forms. In its state-framed variant, nationalism is the principal source of state legitimacy in the age of popular sovereignty. In its counter-state variant, by contrast, nationalism constitutes an ever-present threat to the integrity of the state by legitimating secessionist and irredentist claims. Modern nationalism thus suffers from a kind of autoimmune disease that leads it to constantly turn against its own creations: no sooner has a nation-state been established that its boundaries are subjected to nationalist contestation from within and without. Paradoxically, nationalism is both poison and cure for the legitimacy issues of the modern state. As the next section demonstrates, this ambivalent relationship between nationalism and the state also explains IR's contradictory attitude toward nations and nationalism.

Nations and nationalism in IR theory

The presumed equivalence of 'nation' and 'state' has been one of the defining features of IR theory. In spite of its name, the field of IR has traditionally taken the political concept of the state rather than the ethnocultural concept of the nation as its principal point of departure. Terms such as 'national interest', 'national security', and 'national defence' are thus habitually and unthinkingly used by IR scholars with reference to sovereign states. As Felix Berenskoetter (2014: 263) observes, there is a widespread tendency to 'collapse the nation into the state by conveniently assuming that the former is supervened by the latter'. Even those IR scholars who take the role of culture and identity in world politics seriously tend to use the terms 'national identity' and 'state identity' more or less interchangeably (e.g. Bloom, 1990; Doty, 1996; Lebow, 2016). For example, in an article intended to clarify the meaning of 'national identity' in IR, Paul Kowert (1998: 4–5) differentiates between 'internal' and 'external' dimensions of the concept. Internally, national identity is about 'the cohesion or uniformity of the nation-state's parts', while externally it refers to 'a nation-state's distinctiveness, as compared with other nation-states'. Both dimensions of national identity are thus explicitly defined in relation to the state or nation-state as a political unit, rather than the nation as an ethnocultural entity.

When the nation and the state are treated as interchangeable, nationalism can be understood as the glue that holds a sovereign state together: 'the better the state', Kenneth Waltz writes, 'the more nationalistic' it is. In this framing, nationalism is the 'centripetal force' that makes it possible to conceive of states as coherent agents (Waltz, 1959: 177–178). This understanding of nationalism as a source of the state's sovereignty is rarely explicitly theorised but instead tends to form an unthinking background assumption that allows IR scholars to focus on what they are really interested in: the interactions between pregiven nation-states. More common is the inverse argument focusing on state failure. Hence, the 'failed' or 'quasi' states of the Global South are characterised as 'nation-states only in name' (Mayall, 1990: 112) or as 'state-nations' rather than 'nation-states' (Rejai and Enloe, 1969). In his study of Third World statehood, for example, Robert Jackson (1990: 41) asserts that 'very few new states are "nations" either by long history or common ethnicity or successful constitutional integration'. What is required of the new postcolonial states, or so the argument goes, is a process of 'nation-building' to construct a solid national identity to underpin the state. State-framed nationalism is thus posited, implicitly if not explicitly, as a key criterion of successful statehood. Seen in this light, the discipline of IR represents one of the best (or worst) examples of 'methodological nationalism' – namely the assumption that 'the nation-state is the natural and necessary form of society in modernity' (Chernilo, 2006: 6). Significantly, IR's methodological nationalism is not reducible to the use of explicitly nationalistic terms such as 'nation-state' or 'nation-building'; it is also sedimented in seemingly neutral analytical concepts like 'sovereignty' (Heiskanen, 2019) and 'anarchy' (Zarakol, 2017). The basic theoretical toolkit of IR is deeply intertwined with a nationalist worldview that considers the territory of the earth to be neatly divided into congruent and self-contained nation-states.

Although the political use of the word 'nation' is widespread in IR, the older meaning of the word as an ethnocultural entity has not disappeared. In fact, the equation of nationhood with statehood has been the subject of periodic criticism precisely on the grounds that it distorts the original meaning of the word 'nation'. In a classic article published in 1978, for example, Walker Connor (1978: 383) argues that names such as 'United Nations', 'International Relations', and 'International Law' are all 'misnomers' insofar as they actually have the political concept of the state as their point of reference. Much confusion could be avoided, Connor suggests, if the discipline of 'International Relations' were renamed 'Interstate Relations'. Two decades later, the same line of argument was restated by Lowell Barrington (1997) in an article on 'the misuse of key concepts in political science'. For the likes of Connor and Barrington, the nation is first and foremost an ethnocultural community of people, and thus something very different from a state, which is a legal and political institution. A similar opposition of nation and state also characterises the IR literature on nationalist conflict. According to Stephen Van Evera (1994: 11), for instance, an important measure of the likelihood of regional war is 'the nation-to-state ratio', where a nation is understood as a community of people united by shared ethnocultural characteristics. If the nations of a given region outnumber the states, Van Evera argues, this increases the likelihood of conflict in that region. Likewise, Benjamin Miller (2007: 20) considers 'the regional state-to-nation balance' a key variable in assessing whether a region is war-prone. Instead of treating the nation and the state as complementary or interchangeable, these scholars view the nation as something very different from, or even directly opposed to, the state.

When the nation and the state are depicted as opposites, nationalism is no longer seen as a source of, but as a threat to, the state's unity and legitimacy. According to J. Samuel Barkin and Bruce Cronin, for example, nationalism entails a 'historical tension' between 'state sovereignty' and 'national sovereignty'. In different historical periods, one or the other principle has been dominant: when prevailing international norms favour state sovereignty, state borders tend to be stable, but when prevailing international norms favour national sovereignty, secessionist and irredentist movements tend to triumph. Ultimately, however, the two principles are irreconcilable: 'it is impossible to completely satisfy the statist and nationalist principles simultaneously' (Barkin and Cronin, 1994: 108). A similar conceptual dichotomy informs James Mayall's *Nationalism and International Society*, which represents one of the most thorough explorations of the role of nationalism in international relations. In Mayall's account, the modern international order emerged out of an 'ideological confrontation' between the conflicting principles of state sovereignty and national self-determination (Mayall, 1990: 35–36). In this oppositional framing, nationalism is cast as an external force that threatens the sovereignty of the state and disrupts the habitual practice of international relations qua interstate relations.

To sum up, the theorisation of nations and nationalism by IR scholars is characterised by two contradictory framings. On the one hand, the nation is deemed equivalent to the state, while nationalism is seen as the principal source of the state's legitimacy and coherence. In this framing, nations and nationalism are located at the centre of IR's subject matter. At the same time, however, this framing denies nations and nationalism a truly autonomous role in international relations by subordinating them to the sovereign state: the nation and the state are treated as congruent, while international relations become synonymous with interstate relations. On the other hand, the nation can be depicted as something that is different from, or even directly opposed to, the sovereign state, while nationalism is cast as a destabilising force that engenders irredentist and secessionist claims. Instead of being the centripetal force that holds the state together, nationalism is cast as a centrifugal force that threatens to pull states apart. If the first framing entails nationalism silently melting into the background of modern international relations, then the second framing depicts nationalism as something external to, or in excess of, international relations proper. In both cases, however, the end result is the same: international relations are transformed into interstate relations. Nations and nationalism are thereby relegated to a spectral existence, haunting the states-system in banal phrases such as 'national security' or 'national interests' and materialising only in moments of state breakdown and crisis (see Heiskanen, 2019).

Beyond the nation-state?

If nations and nationalism are historically contingent phenomena, this means that they are neither inevitable nor eternal. To take the world of nation-states as given, as IR usually does, is to succumb to methodological nationalism. Yet the attempt to move beyond the nation-state is fraught with peril. The literature criticising methodological nationalism is vast and diverse, but two main approaches may be identified. The first and more common approach is to locate nations and nationalism in the past, specifically in the modern era, thereby opening up the possibility of a postnational and postnationalist future. As the twentieth century was coming to a close, many commentators believed that the social, economic, cultural, and political developments associated with 'globalisation' were bringing about the end of the nation-state's hegemony – a 'borderless world' seemed to beckon (Ohmae, 1990). An especially powerful statement along these lines can be found in the work of Ulrich Beck. In Beck's estimation, globalisation represents a fundamental challenge to the basic categories of modern social and political science, which has taken the nation-state as its pregiven starting point. The old world of nationally organised industrial societies is being replaced by a new cosmopolitan world characterised by catastrophic global risks such as nuclear conflict and climate change. Taking a stand against the methodological nationalism of modern social and political science, Beck has advocated for a 'methodological cosmopolitanism' that seeks to move beyond the frame of the nation-state (Beck, 2000, 2007).

The main issue with the first approach is that it unwittingly ends up reproducing the very methodological nationalism that it seeks to overcome (Chernilo, 2006: 13; Closs Stephens, 2013: 29). Indeed, Beck's critique of methodological nationalism has echoes of the linear modernisation narratives that characterised the work of modern social theorists such as Karl Marx and Émile Durkheim. According to these scholars, nationalism belonged to an earlier stage of social evolution and would be superseded by new forms of supranational attachment in the future (Wimmer and Glick Schiller, 2002: 303). A similar attitude to nationalism characterises much of the discussion on globalisation, or at least the earlier and less sophisticated literature on the topic. Implicitly or explicitly, Jürgen Osterhammel (2013: 694) notes, the overriding assumption has been that 'nationalism and nation-state came first and then globalization came second'. By setting up a stark conceptual and/or historical dichotomy between the modern world of nation-states and the postmodern world of globalisation, these approaches reify the nationalistic interpretation of the modern world that they seek to escape (see Guillaume, 2021 in this volume).

The second critique of methodological nationalism is both more and less radical. It is more radical because it rejects not only the historical permanency of the nation-state, but also the view that the nation-state has been the natural organising principle of society in the modern era (Chernilo, 2006: 13-16). At the same time, it is less radical insofar as it accepts the persistence of nationalism in the present (Closs Stephens, 2013). In a nutshell, the overarching claim is that the nation-state has never possessed a monopoly on the organisation of the social world and has always coexisted with other forces. The focus of critique thus shifts away from denouncing a monolithic conception of modern nationalism and towards exploring the ambivalence and opacity of nationalism in both the past and the present. Rather than approaching 'the history of nationalism in black-and-white, before-and-after terms', the aim is to 'capture the variety and history of nationalism in its many hues of gray' (Gorski, 2000: 1461). Consequently, this line of critique also refuses to identify another master concept – such as 'globalisation' or 'cosmopolitanism' – as the privileged organising principle of contemporary social and political science. Instead, the issue of methodological nationalism becomes relativised and located alongside other potentially pathological methodological tendencies that include 'methodological imperialism', 'methodological globalism', and 'methodological cosmopolitanism' (Chernilo, 2006: 15; see also Çapan et al., 2021 in this volume).

The critique of methodological nationalism and the decentring of the nation-state have important implications for IR as a discipline. After all, as this chapter has shown, the worldview traditionally espoused by IR scholars is thoroughly parasitic on nationalism. The debates over the future of the nation-state are thus also, at least in part, debates over the future of the discipline. The decentring of the nation-state is reflected, for example, in the tentative displacement of the term 'international relations' by broader notions such as 'world politics' and 'global politics' that also encompass a multiplicity of non-state actors alongside nation-states (e.g. Mansbach and Rafferty, 2008; Baylis et al., 2014). A related trend is the cumulating critique of the concept of anarchy, which has traditionally served as the theoretical keystone of the discipline by distinguishing the 'anarchical' international realm from the 'sovereign' national society (e.g. Milner, 1991; Hobson, 2014; Bially Mattern and Zarakol, 2016). As Ayşe Zarakol (2017: 266) underscores, the concept of anarchy 'derives from and reproduces the political project of the nation-state'. The historicisation and decentring of the nation-state thus entail a historicisation and decentring of IR's theoretical toolkit more generally. Irrespective of whether or not the nation-state is in terminal decline, foregrounding the nationalistic underpinnings of IR's conceptual apparatus is an important step towards a more reflexive scholarly practice that might also allow IR theories to better 'travel' to other times and places beyond modernity (see Çapan and Zarakol, 2018).

Suggestions for further reading

Bartelson, J. (2009). *Visions of World Community*. Cambridge: Cambridge University Press.
Billig, M. (1995). *Banal Nationalism*. London: Sage.
Breuilly, J. (1993). *Nationalism and the State*. 2nd edition. Manchester: Manchester University Press.
Chatterjee, P. (1993). *The Nation and Its Fragments: Colonial and Postcolonial Histories*. Princeton, NJ: Princeton University Press.
Greenfeld, L. (1996). *Nationalism: Five Roads to Modernity*. Cambridge, MA: Harvard University Press.
Mandelbaum, M. (2020). *The Nation/State Fantasy: A Psychoanalytical Genealogy of Nationalism*. Basingstoke: Palgrave Macmillan.
Smith, A. D. (1986). *The Ethnic Origins of Nations*. Oxford: Basil Blackwell.

References

Abizadeh, A. (2012). On the demos and its kin: nationalism, democracy, and the boundary problem. *The American Political Science Review*, 106 (4), 867–882.
Anderson, B. (2006). *Imagined Communities: Reflections on the Origin and Spread of Nationalism*. Revised edition. London: Verso.
Barkin, J. S., and Cronin, B. (1994). The state and the nation: changing norms and the rules of sovereignty in international relations. *International Organization*, 48 (1), 107–130.
Barrington, L. W. (1997). 'Nation' and 'nationalism': the misuse of key concepts in political science. *PS: Political Science and Politics*, 30 (4), 712–716.
Bartelson, J. (2001). *The Critique of the State*. Cambridge: Cambridge University Press.
Baylis, J., Smith, S., and Owens, P., eds. (2014). *The Globalization of World Politics: An Introduction to International Relations*. 6th edition. Oxford: Oxford University Press.
Bayly, M. (2021). Imperialism: Beyond the 'Re-turn to Empire' in International Relations. In de Carvalho, B., Costa Lopez, J., & Leira, H., eds. *Routledge Handbook of Historical International Relations*. Abingdon: Routledge.
Beck, U. (2000). *What Is Globalization?* Cambridge: Polity.
Beck, U. (2007). The cosmopolitan condition: why methodological nationalism fails. *Theory, Culture & Society*, 24 (7/8), 286–290.
Berenskoetter, F. (2014). Parameters of a national biography. *European Journal of International Relations*, 20 (1), 262–288.
Bially Mattern, J., and Zarakol, A. (2016). Hierarchies in world politics. *International Organization*, 70 (3), 623–654.
Bloom, W. (1990). *Personal Identity, National Identity and International Relations*. Cambridge: Cambridge University Press.
Branch, J. (2013). *The Cartographic State: Maps, Territory, and the Origins of Sovereignty*. Cambridge: Cambridge University Press.

Brubaker, R. (1998). Myths and Misconceptions in the Study of Nationalism. In J. Hall, ed., *The State of the Nation: Ernest Gellner and the Theory of Nationalism*, Cambridge: Cambridge University Press, 272-306.

Bukovansky, M. (1999). The altered state and the state of nature: the French Revolution and international politics. *Review of International Studies*, 25 (2), 197-216.

Çapan, Z. G., dos Reis, F. and Grasten, M. (2021). Global Histories: Connections and Circulations in Historical International Relations. In de Carvalho, B., Costa Lopez, J., & Leira, H. eds. *Routledge Handbook of Historical International Relations*. Abingdon: Routledge.

Çapan, Z. G., and Zarakol, A. (2018). Between 'East' and 'West': Travelling Theories, Travelling Imaginations. In: A. Gofas, I. Hamati-Ataya, and N. Onuf, eds., *The Sage Handbook of the History, Philosophy and Sociology of International Relations*, London: Sage, 122-133.

Chernilo, D. (2006). Social theory's methodological nationalism: myth and reality. *European Journal of Social Theory*, 9 (1), 5-22.

Closs Stephens, A. (2013). *The Persistence of Nationalism: From Imagined Communities to Urban Encounters*. London and New York: Routledge.

Connor, W. (1972). Nation-building or nation-destroying? *World Politics*, 24 (3), 319-355.

Connor, W. (1978). A nation is a nation, is a state, is an ethnic group, is a.... *Ethnic and Racial Studies*, 1 (4), 377-400.

Connor, W. (1981). Nationalism and political illegitimacy. *Canadian Review of Studies in Nationalism*, 8 (2), 201-228.

Connor, W. (1990). When is a nation? *Ethnic and Racial Studies*, 13 (1), 92-103.

de Carvalho, B. (2014). The confessional state in international politics: Tudor England, religion, and the eclipse of dynasticism. *Diplomacy & Statecraft*, 25 (3), 407-431.

de Carvalho, B. (2021). Sovereignty in Historical International Relations: Trajectories, Challenges and Implications. In de Carvalho, B., Costa Lopez, J., & Leira, H., eds. *Routledge Handbook of Historical International Relations*. Abingdon: Routledge.

de Carvalho, B., and Leira, H. (2021). State Formation and Historical International Relations. In de Carvalho, B., Costa Lopez, J., & Leira, H., eds. *Routledge Handbook of Historical International Relations*. Abingdon: Routledge.

Doty, R. L. (1996). Sovereignty and the Nation: Constructing the Boundaries of National Identity. In: T. J. Biersteker, and C. Weber, eds., *State Sovereignty as Social Construct*, Cambridge: Cambridge University Press, 121-147.

Gellner, E. (1983). *Nations and Nationalism*. Oxford: Blackwell.

Getachew, A. (2019). *Worldmaking after Empire: The Rise and Fall of Self-Determination*. Princeton, NJ: Princeton University Press.

Gorski, P. (2000). The mosaic moment: an early modernist critique of modernist theories of nationalism. *American Journal of Sociology*, 105 (5), 1428-1468.

Guillaume, X. (2021). Historical Periods and the Act of Periodisation. In de Carvalho, B., Costa Lopez, J., & Leira, H., eds. *Routledge Handbook of Historical International Relations*. Abingdon: Routledge.

Heiskanen, J. (2019). Spectra of sovereignty: nationalism and international relations. *International Political Sociology*, 13 (3), 315-332.

Hirschi, C. (2012). *The Origins of Nationalism: An Alternative History from Ancient Rome to Early Modern Germany*. Cambridge: Cambridge University Press.

Hobsbawm, E. (1992). *Nations and Nationalism Since 1780: Programme, Myth, Reality*. Cambridge: Cambridge University Press.

Hobson, J. M. (2014). The twin self-delusions of IR: why 'hierarchy' and not 'anarchy' is the core concept of IR. *Millennium: Journal of International Studies*, 42 (3), 557-575.

Jackson, R. (1990). *Quasi-States: Sovereignty, International Relations, and the Third World*. Cambridge: Cambridge University Press.

James, A. (1986). *Sovereign Statehood: The Basis of International Society*. London: Allen & Unwin.

Kowert, P. (1998). National identity: inside and out. *Security Studies*, 8 (2/3), 1-34.

Lebow, R. N. (2016). *National Identities in International Relations*. Cambridge: Cambridge University Press.

Manela, E. (2007). *The Wilsonian Moment: Self-Determination and the International Origins of Anticolonial Nationalism*. Oxford: Oxford University Press.

Mansbach, R., and Rafferty, K. (2008). *Introduction to Global Politics*. London: Routledge.

Mayall, J. (1990). *Nationalism and International Society*. Cambridge: Cambridge University Press.

Miller, B. (2007). *States, Nations, and the Great Powers: The Sources of Regional War and Peace*. Cambridge: Cambridge University Press.

Milner, H. (1991). The assumption of anarchy in international relations: a critique. *Review of International Studies*, 17 (1), 67-85.

Ohmae, K. (1990). *The Borderless World: Power and Strategy in the Interlinked Economy*. London: HarperCollins.

Osterhammel, J. (2013). Nationalism and Globalization. In: J. Breuilly, ed., *The Oxford Handbook of the History of Nationalism*, Oxford: Oxford University Press, 694-707.

Phillips, A., and Sharman, J. C. (2015). *International Order in Diversity: War, Trade and Rule in the Indian Ocean*. Cambridge: Cambridge University Press.

Rae, H. (2002). *State Identities and the Homogenisation of Peoples*. Cambridge: Cambridge University Press.

Rejai, M., and Enloe, C. (1969). Nation-states and state-nations. *International Studies Quarterly*, 13 (2), 140-158.

Sewell, W. (2004). The French Revolution and the Emergence of the Nation Form. In M. Morrison, and M. Zook, eds., *Revolutionary Currents: Nation Building in the Transatlantic World*, Lanham: Rowman & Littlefield, 91-126.

Spruyt, H. (1994). *The Sovereign State and Its Competitors: An Analysis of Systems Change*. Princeton, NJ: Princeton University Press.

Taylor, C. (1999). Nationalism and Modernity. In: R. Biener, ed., *Theorizing Nationalism*, Albany, NY: State University of New York Press, 219-246.

Van Evera, S. (1994). Hypotheses on nationalism and war. *International Security*, 18 (4), 5-39.

Walby, S. (2003). The myth of the nation-state: theorizing society and polities in a global era. *Sociology*, 37 (3), 529-546.

Waltz, K. (1959). *Man, the State and War: A Theoretical Analysis*. New York, NY: Columbia University Press.

Weber, E. (1976). *Peasants into Frenchmen: The Modernization of Rural France, 1870–1914*. Stanford: Stanford University Press.

Wimmer, A., and Glick Schiller, N. (2002). Methodological nationalism and beyond: nation-state building, migration and the social sciences. *Global Networks*, 2 (4), 301-334.

Yack, B. (2001). Popular sovereignty and nationalism. *Political Theory*, 29 (4), 517-536.

Zarakol, A. (2017). Why Hierarchy? In: A. Zarakol, ed., *Hierarchies in World Politics*, Cambridge: Cambridge University Press, 266-274.

24

STATES, PEOPLE AND SELF-DETERMINATION IN HISTORICAL PERSPECTIVE

Maja Spanu

On the surface it seemed reasonable: let the people decide.
It was in fact ridiculous because the people cannot
decide until somebody decides who are the people.

(Jennings, 1956: 55–56)

Introduction

International Relations (IR) scholarship agrees that with the end of World War I and then later after World War II and with decolonisation, self-determination came to formally constitute a core principle of the international order along with its cognate norms: sovereign equality, non-interference, human rights. Scholarship also agrees that it was in the name of self-determination – whether understood as self-government, autonomy or the right to choose one's own destiny – that transitions from imperial systems of unequal entitlements to nation-states took place throughout the 20th century, leading to the system of states that we know today. However, whereas states are at the heart of the study of IR, for a number of different reasons that this chapter will delve into, these very same theories have largely remained silent over the constitution and functioning of the nexus between states and people. This is not to say that IR has entirely overlooked this nexus or the study of self-determination. There are numerous exceptions even across mainstream approaches that this chapter will discuss. Yet, when examined, the relationship is mostly scrutinised from a systemic perspective that either constructs the nation-state as the 'endpoint' of self-determination (thus overlooking what happens once states are formed) or that only peripherally looks at what happens domestically (as if this did not matter so much for the international). This 'domestic' relationship is mostly scrutinised and untangled in cognate bodies of literature to historically sensitive IR scholarship: political thought on the one hand, and literature on state formation, nationalism and citizenship on the other.

This chapter sets out to discuss these various bodies of literature. The second section addresses the gap in dominant IR theories, drawing attention to works that have been engaged in untangling the relation between states and people. The third section discusses scholarship that has focused specifically on self-determination, highlighting its limitations. The fourth section discusses literature in political thought on social contract theory and popular sovereignty whilst revealing risks entailed in neglecting political and social practices, and focusing instead on 'canonical' thinkers who have operated with racial, class and gender biases. The fifth section presents some of the contributions of literatures on state formation, nationalism and citizenship. This section focuses specifically on how these bodies of literature provide a more nuanced understanding of dynamics of inclusion, exclusion and identity within nation-states which could helpfully be used to inform historically sensitive IR studies on states, people and self-determination.

States and people in IR theory

Arguably, the relationship between states and people is central to any definition of sovereignty and to any explanation of the making of the system of states. However, IR theories have either taken this nexus for granted or have overlooked it. At least two explanations for this gap exist, and they are both historical and disciplinary. First, in the Cold War decades, mainstream approaches in IR participated in erecting states as the stable units of sovereign authority across time and space. Positivist in its epistemology and rationalist in its ontology, much of the very Western-centric scholarship at the time constructed states as 'monolithic' entities with a fixed presence in the international realm. With rare exceptions, processes of state formation, negotiations and changes in forms of political authority did not attract much interest at all (see also de Carvalho and Leira, 2021). Second, with the exception of neoliberalism, traditional IR approaches have viewed the relationship between states and people as 'merely' belonging to the domestic realm.

To be sure, the late 1980s and early 1990s brought important transformations to IR. For example, the implosion of the Soviet Union and the inability of any of the dominant paradigms in IR to predict the end of the Cold War showed that what happened domestically could explain structural change. The almost concurrent resurgence of nationalist claims on the international scene further stressed the importance of the domestic sphere for the study of IR (see also Heiskanen, 2021). Even those authors traditionally less interested in domestic politics such as neorealists were suddenly concerned with explaining violence and the upsurge of exclusive identity politics in former Yugoslavia, Rwanda or Somalia. Renewed attention to ethnic politics, genocide and crimes against humanity reminded that these were neither new nor simply internal matters. The early 1990s signalled the end of an international order formally characterised as in the Cold War by the principle of non-interference in states' domestic affairs. The early 1990s also marked a shift to the Cold War disciplinary blindness to, for example, mass atrocities, population transfers and mistreatments exercised within state borders.

For the past three decades, IR has increasingly considered – whether directly or indirectly – the relation between states and people. However, the extent of the engagement has varied. Before moving to the literature that directly tackles this relation, this section sketches how the main approaches within IR have engaged with nationalism, state formation and self-determination.

Realism

Classical realists such as E.H. Carr (1945), a historian, and Hans Morgenthau (1948), a legal theorist, engaged each in their way, with nationalism, perhaps also as a result of the post–World War II context they were writing in. Unlike classical realism, neorealism has been advancing structural arguments about the international system largely bracketing off the relevance of the domestic sphere (and of changes in it) for international politics. Kenneth Waltz did write about states' domestic structure, but he saw it as separate in its nature from the international sphere, and in relation to functions and roles rather than to the relationship between authorities, institutions and people (1979: 81–82). While a state's international standing will depend on domestic capabilities, internal characteristics, identities and behaviour do not matter so much.

From the 1990s, several neorealists started granting attention to the relation between states and people. In 1999, Stephen Krasner wrote on how more powerful states impose domestic standards to weaker states regarding treatment of internal populations (even if the latter often do not uphold them). Krasner noted constant violations of sovereignty over time due to power inequalities and hypocrisy (Krasner, 1999). In a different vein, a year later Jack Snyder wrote about the historical upsurge of violence in democratising states (Snyder, 2000). States in transition from authoritarian/single-party systems to democratic rule would witness higher levels of violence due to the sudden introduction of multiparty elections and the instrumentalisation of nationalist discourses. Unlike numerous other realists, for both Krasner and Snyder state identities matter. However, identities remain instrumental to political objectives of elites. This therefore remains very much of a top-down approach. The people follow what authorities tell them to do, but in this perspective, they are also deprived of much agency or free will.

Neoliberalism

Neoliberalism starts with the assumption that individual and collective interests of domestic populations shape the decisions that states take domestically and internationally. Andrew Moravcsik, for example, investigates this link historically whilst also being interested in the cognate question of why do states construct treaties that constrain domestic behaviour regulating how populations should be treated (2000: 2). Moravcsik argues that it is generally newly established democracies that push for the creation of standards of accountability related to the 'good' treatment of domestic groups simply because of domestic political self-interest. Governments seek to prevent domestic oppression and international conflict through international symbols, standards and procedures that secure domestic democracy. They are constrained by fear that domestic laws might be struck down. This is at least in part in contrast with Snyder's argument that democratisation and the extension of the right to vote actually leads to more nationalism and violence. In general, neoliberals include norms in their analyses but they argue that actors use them strategically to further their interests. The constitutive dimension of political culture, domestically, is therefore overlooked. As put by Mlada Bukovansky, for neoliberals 'culture helps us get what we want, but it does not make us who we are' (2002: 36). Put differently, the constitution of identities domestically is overlooked.

Interpretivism and constructivism

In the early 1990s, scholars influenced by what could be termed a 'delayed' linguistic turn in IR called for the need to deconstruct sovereignty and historicise processes of state formation (Walker, 1993; Bartelson, 1995; Biersteker and Weber, 1996). Less interested in the nexus between states and people, they did open up space to question domestic identities and their transformations. John Agnew famously wrote about the 'territorial trap' in which much rationalist scholarship had, in his view, fallen. The reification of states as fixed units of sovereign space meant that, 'the territorial state [*was*] viewed as existing prior to and as a container of society' (1994: 58–59). R. B. J. Walker suggested that the distinction between political theory and IR had mistakenly rested on the conception that state sovereignty constituted the timeless boundary between the domestic and international realms (Walker, 1993). This assumption, he claimed, had dominated and impoverished the study of world politics. It precluded the possibility of thinking about other historical forms of spatial-temporal authority, such as, for instance, empires, and about transitions from one form to the other. Focused on historicising territory over people, this scholarship nonetheless showed that state formation was in no way a 'natural' or obvious process.

Since then, historically sensitive interpretivist scholarship has revealed that relations of legitimation, forms of political authority and collective action and boundaries of political communities are far from being given or static. On the contrary, they have been constantly renegotiated, and this matters domestically and internationally. Constructivist research in particular showed that such 'domestic' issues influence state behaviour as well as broader transformations in international behaviour and norms (Hall, 1999; Bukovansky, 2002; Rae, 2002). For interpretivism and constructivism, at the core of the relation between state and people are identity and legitimacy. Norms, values and ideas define what the appropriate identity of a state should be and political legitimacy is inextricably related to such definition.

Working at the intersection of historical sociology and IR, Rae shows how, historically, elites have sought to homogenise population identities through mass atrocities and expulsion during processes of state formation (2002). During state-building, elites have regularly used all available means to homogenise state identity, from institutional and legal instruments to active violence. Rae also stresses, however, that the homogenisation of domestic populations is less and less tolerated internationally. This does not mean that international actors will intervene to stop mass violence, as the situation of the Rohingya in Myanmar since the 1970s proves. However, an international judgement regarding the domestic practices can be made, stressing the interconnectedness of the domestic and the international levels. International judgement influences domestic legitimacy and, vice-versa, a government whose practices are largely deemed illegitimate domestically can be stigmatised internationally. Rae's work focuses on mass atrocities and expulsion. However, the study of the establishment and, importantly, the functioning of the nexus between states and people beyond extreme situations once new states' identities are formed is more rarely the object of research in Historical IR. As we shall see in the next section, even those interpretivist authors who study self-determination tend to overlook its domestic implications, focusing instead on a systemic perspective.

Self-determination in Historical IR

Unlike legal studies and political theory, which have made regular interventions on the matter, the study of self-determination has only attracted attention from a limited number of IR scholars. In political theory, in particular during the decolonisation years, self-determination engaged scholars who sought to understand what the principle meant in light of postcolonial independences (Cobban, 1969; Emerson, 1971). With the end of Cold War and the upsurge of conflicts in the name of ethnic allegiances, the question reappeared. Ever since, discussions have turned towards what self-determination ought to mean and how it ought to be used (Coppieters and Sakwa, 2003). Rather than seeking to associate given meanings to self-determination, several international lawyers have instead been driven by the primary concern to historicise it (Hannum, 1990; Cassese, 1995; Ratner, 1996). In turn, because of reasons peculiar to the intellectual history of the discipline, in IR the study of self-determination has long been overlooked.

Who, then, is interested in self-determination in IR? From the mid-1990s, the study of empire gained momentum especially in American IR. The works of Alexander Motyl (2001) and Hendrik Spruyt (1994, 2005) are cases in point. Each in their own way, these authors have been interested in making sense of ends of empires and in comprehending their trajectories as preceding the formation of the contemporary sovereign order. However, less interested in studying transitions from one form of political authority to the other, these studies have been mostly concerned with explaining empire as a form of political authority, and with comparing different regimes. Over recent years, a considerable number of works have been released, addressing specifically transitions from imperial orders (based on unequal systems of entitlements) to the modern system of states (supposedly based, instead, on sovereign equality internationally, and equality of national citizens domestically). Because the principle of self-determination of people has been invoked and used historically during transitions from empires to nation-states, scholars concerned with the making of the contemporary sovereign order have therefore taken it into account in their studies. Scholars of the English School (with their grand narratives on the so-called expansion of international society) and constructivists (with their interpretive approach to understanding change over time) have discussed in detail the making of the modern system of states, to which self-determination is pivotal (see also Navari and Green, 2021; Bruneau, 2021).

Constructivists and English School authors agree that during the 20th century, self-determination became the accepted standard for membership and statehood in the 'international society' (Clark, 2007; Hurrell, 2007; Glanville, 2014). These authors acknowledge that self-determination has thus become the principle at the heart of both the legitimacy of states and of international society. However, in their treatment of self-determination, both bodies of scholarship are problematic in three key respects. First, with one exception – James Mayall's 1990 work – neither body of work has fully engaged with self-determination. Instead, the idea has been regularly studied in association with, and subordination to, other core principles of international order such as sovereignty (Fabry, 2010; Glanville, 2014) or human rights (Donnelly, 1998). Second, inasmuch as both literatures recognise that self-determination has been constitutive of new states, neither has engaged with the implications of the relationship between self-determination and legitimate statehood after empire. What happens once new states are formed? (How) does the domestic realisation of self-determination impact states' legitimacy? These are questions that remain largely unanswered because existing accounts tend to restrict the story of the expansion of international society to the establishment of new states, overlooking subsequent implications for international membership and order. Third, these literatures end up neglecting fundamental aspects, often dismissed from the study of IR as belonging to the domestic realm and thus not being relevant to a 'truly' international analysis. We are then left unable to adequately explain, for example, one of the central puzzles of state formation in the 20th century: how can self-determination be embedded in an emancipatory language of liberation from empires and, increasingly, of human rights, while inequalities exist in many states formed on the basis of self-determination?

Instead, what is present in the extant literature is a general appreciation that the meaning associated with self-determination has changed over time. Some emphasis has been put on the interwar period and on the post–Cold War years (Jackson Preece, 1998). Mostly, though, IR scholars have directed their attention in interesting ways to the post–World War II wave of decolonisation (Jackson, 1990; Crawford, 2002; Reus-Smit, 2013, see also Svensson, 2021), joining a similar interest in the discipline of history (Burke, 2002; Simpson, 2014). Decolonisation years (roughly from 1950 until 1970), these authors agree, represent an important moment to be studied as they set the grounds for the contemporary order. Decolonisation was indeed the moment in which self-determination was invoked to bring colonial empires to an end and to globalise the nation-state system as we know it today. It was also the moment in which self-determination was embedded in the language of human rights and further entrenched in the current body of international law (Burke, 2002; Reus-Smit, 2013).

In this literature, however, the question as to what happened both domestically and internationally historically once self-determination was proclaimed and statehood recognised after imperial demises remains unanswered. But engaging with only one side of the story bears at least one major, teleological risk. It leaves the reader with the sense that the nation-state was achieved globally, against imperial political hierarchies and discrimination. It thus seems that largely the model of the nation-state, along with its defining values of equality and, increasingly, inclusion, is constructed as the inescapable endpoint of self-determination. In other words, in much of this broadly defined interpretivist scholarship, self-determination ends where sovereignty starts. The nexus between states and people once new states are formed remains largely overlooked.

This absence seems to be directly related to the conception of the international system that interpretivists share. Constructivists, English School proponents and, more widely, interpretivists identify systemic change with a shift in organising principles of the system, such as, for instance, sovereignty. They therefore view the external reconfiguration of the system in accordance with these principles. Because these authors have a social conception of the international system, they are ultimately concerned with the emergence of a system based on externally independent states. It is therefore not an overstatement to say that they largely view the nation-state as the inevitable conclusion of self-determination of peoples. While this is important to understand dynamics of socialisation in the broader process of formation of the system of states, accounts of the making of the system of states tend to end where sovereignty starts. Once self-determination is realised and statehood is recognised, implications of these processes seem to no longer fit into accounts of interest. In other words, these authors are concerned with the formation of the international system of states to the extent that it leads to a given configuration of the international architecture. How the bond between states and people is established and functions within an existing polity is, however, less the object of interest. To further comprehend this nexus, we therefore have to turn to social contract literature in political thought. Though central to understand the making and functioning of the bond between states and people, as we will see, this literature also bears several important limitations.

States and people in political thought

The bond between states and people is at the heart of political philosophy. Philosophers have written over centuries about matters related to political communities, sovereignty and self-government. Scholars working at the intersection of the history of political thought and of IR have thus drawn much of their attention to specific thinkers presented as the 'canons' of such ideas. While one may go back to the ancient Greeks, it is social contract theory that, unsurprisingly, has most clearly addressed the nexus between states and people. Whether this has not necessarily been framed as 'the study of self-determination' (if only because the term started being regularly used in the 19th century and was generalised in the early 20th century), social contract theory is the approach in philosophy that views individuals' and groups' obligations (whether moral or political) as dependent on a 'contract' (understood primarily as a metaphorical agreement) among them. This contract allows individuals and groups to constitute the society and institutions in which they exist in the way they deem most appropriate. It therefore directly connects with the idea of self-determination because a contract presupposes taking into consideration, of course in different forms over time, the will of individuals and peoples – to choose a political arrangement, a form of political authority or a government, and also to change it.

The first scholar primarily associated with social contract theory is Thomas Hobbes. The point has been made that earlier conceptions of contract theory and popular sovereignty resided in the thought of early modern thinkers, including Jean Bodin (Lee, 2016). However, Hobbes' theory on the state of nature is largely viewed as central to the establishment of the bond between states and people (Malcolm, 2002). For Hobbes, the social contract serves to escape a state of nature that is unbearable. Because the state of nature is so 'nasty, brutish and short' (Hobbes, 2017: ch. XIII) and that individuals are faced with the constant risk of falling again in it (preface by Brooke in Hobbes, 2017), societies need an absolute authority to govern them. In Hobbes' view, any rational individual wants to escape the state of nature and for this reason will accept hierarchical authority in the form of a monarch.

For John Locke, the state of nature is something quite different. In 1690, Locke defined the natural state of man as 'perfect freedom' and 'equality'. By no 'manifest declaration of his Will' has God 'set one above the other' (Locke, 1960: II.4). As a result, for Locke, individuals contract with each other to create a society, but they are not contractually obliged to their government. In Locke's view, governors are merely trustees who can be removed if they fail their trust (Glanville, 2014: 63). So not only are governors accountable to their own people, but also, if deemed necessary, the people have the power to dissolve a government and constitute a new one. Unlike Hobbes, for Locke the idea of 'popular sovereignty', namely that the legitimacy of a government depends on the consent of the governed, is central.

As Mlada Bukovansky argues, Locke's conception of popular sovereignty was integrated later in the 1776 American Declaration of Independence (2002: 215). Equality and freedom were, in the Declaration, on the grounds of the consent of the governed. The American Declaration was later used as a basis to forge national declarations across the globe (Armitage, 2008). Swiss philosopher Jean-Jacques Rousseau also recovered Locke's conception, adding that, 'every authentic act of the general will obliges or favours all citizens equally' (Rousseau, 1950: CS, II, ix). More precisely, for Rousseau, it is the 'laws' strict impersonality or universality' that produces an 'equality between the citizens such that they all engage themselves under the same conditions and should all benefit from the same rights' (Putterman, 2010: 12).

As Glanville has stressed, for Rousseau, the rights of man are in fact in contradiction with the demands of the general will, insofar as the social contract gives the 'body politic an absolute power over all its members' (2014: 67). The 'people' expressing the general will thus become for Rousseau a unified body. He explained this tension as a shift from natural to civil liberty. In 20th-century theory and 20th-century practice, though, the notion of general will was used to justify very different visions of what the unity of the body politic meant.

Several 19th-century political thinkers on self-government remodelled their theories of consent of the governed and of popular sovereignty. In particular, Rousseau's vision of the people as a single unit of interest influenced various authors who made the association between self-government and external non-interference. In the early 19th century, Lord Castlereagh hinted at such an equation, suggesting that in the name of national equality, 'people should be allowed to determine their own internal political arrangements' (Glanville, 2014: 78). Giuseppe Mazzini and John Stuart Mill further elaborated this idea. In his writings in support of a unitary Italian nation, Mazzini alluded to the two dimensions, the will of people and non-interference, as two faces of a single concept. For Mazzini, the Italian nation would bring alien rule to an end through the exercise of self-determination. In turn, national independence in the form of the nation-state would then allow fully fledged individual liberty (Recchia and Urbinati in Mazzini, 2009). Recchia and Urbinati make the point that Mazzini's works constitute the origins of what came to be known later as the 'leading pioneer of Wilsonian internationalism' (2009: 3). Mill also developed a not dissimilar conception of 'liberal nationalism'. Mill claimed, 'a completely popular government is the only polity which can make out any claim to this character' namely, 'the claim of all to participate to sovereign power' (Mill, 2009: 57). Similarly to Mazzini, Mill stressed that this would be 'next to impossible in a country made up of different nationalities' (2009: 284).

This conception of 'liberal nationalism' was paralleled in the 19th century by the works of German and Central European romantics. *Mitteleuropean* romantics saw nations as groups defined along the concept of the *Volk* (translated from German as people and nation). A nation was constituted by a group of equal members linked by shared historical traditions if not just by ethnic ties. Equality of rights for individuals within the community was thus equated to kinship allegiances. Over the years, visions on ethnic nationality and institutional nationalism were integrated in the discourses of public intellectuals and political leaders of minority groups, which in Central and Eastern Europe fought for the establishment of their 'own' nation-states against European aristocratic Empires. The unity of these kin groups was given further political expression in 1919 at the Paris Peace Conference. Indeed, despite American President Woodrow Wilson's initial promise to recognise the principle of self-determination for all during World War I, 'peoples' entitled to self-government became after the war those ethnic groups that had mobilised national sentiment during the 19th century, under the Austro-Hungarian, German, Ottoman and Russian empires. These were the same groups that had been the object of attention of political philosophers a few decades earlier.

Both 'liberal nationalist' and ethnically restrictive conceptions of popular sovereignty presented here reveal what looks like an inextricable tension. On the one hand, notions of political equality and equality of rights have lain at the heart of political communities' formation and legitimacy; on the other, how the boundaries of political communities are formed clearly matter for who can gain access these rights and status. Equality within the community can thus be highly exclusive, depending on the criteria that define it. If a people has a right to fully express its political will and to determine itself, how is the people defined? Who is entitled to be part of the political community and thereby enjoy political equality and rights? Delineations of political communities and their membership criteria have varied importantly in the views of social contract theorists (and still do today – John Rawls, 1971, being one of them) and of 19th-century authors mentioned above. This, however, also opens up cracks in the understanding of political equality that philosophers have held.

For German and Central European intellectuals such as Ernest Renan, Johann Fichte and Friedrich Schelling, for example, equality was defined exclusively, along ethnonational kinship ties. However, the line between a so-called civic nationalism (in which supposedly principles of inclusion and equality apply irrespective of individual and group differences) and a so-called ethnic nationalism (favouring instead distinctions based on kinship ties and allegiances) was certainly not the only divide. Mazzini, for instance, equated self-government to universal male suffrage. Women were simply excluded from the right to vote. Mill, on the other hand, explicitly claimed that although representative government was ideally the best form of political organisation, 'the natural tendency of representative government as of modern civilisation *(wa)*s towards collective mediocrity' (Mill, 2009: 141). For this reason, he went on, universal suffrage ought to be allocated to 'those who can write, read and count arithmetically (...) and it would not be society to exclude him but his own laziness' (Mill, 2009: 165). Though Mill refers to the intellectual laziness of individuals who are not literate enough to be part of the body politic, it is difficult not to note the class bias that characterises his thought.

Moreover, both Mazzini and Mill expounded the then widely held view that not every people on the planet was anyway ready, or advanced enough, to be able to express their own will and certainly not for self-government. Self-government was a notion bound up with other ideas of imperial and racial stratification used to 'sort' peoples both domestically and internationally. Philosopher Charles Mills has argued that a 'racial contract' that is deeper than the 'social contract' actually characterises Western societies, institutions and thought historically (Mills, 1997). The racial contract was established at the beginnings of the colonising enterprise in the modern period both symbolically, to privilege white men, and politically, to stratify individuals and be able to control the lands and resources of those casted as inferior. The racial contract thus determines who can enter the social contract and get access to its freedom and equality premises.

Egalitarian understandings of the political community have thus been accompanied by exclusive and hierarchical arguments. Hierarchies concerned who, on the planet, was deemed ready for self-government following established 'standards of civilisation' (Gong, 1984). In the domestic domain of the states and empires where these thinkers lived, the tension revolved around the idea of political equality in the body politic, and exclusive criteria of partial or full access to it. Race, gender, class and ethnic ties were the usual markers of such hierarchical views.

At the start of the 20th century, racial, class and ethnic hierarchies were disputed in a sudden and subversive manner. In 1913, Joseph Stalin argued that national self-determination concerned all peoples on the planet, with no exceptions (1945). If invoked by oppressed populations (rather than externally granted by more powerful states), self-determination would liberate them from the domination of imperial powers and subsequently allow them to join a centralised state. The idea was reformulated and internationalised a year later in what became the Leninist doctrine (Lenin, 1951). These seminal texts fed movements for independence within empires as well as class and gender struggles for greater equality, both in the metropoles and in the colonies. Practice, however, did not often reflect such ideas. With some exceptions, decolonisation was internationally postponed to the 1960s. Domestically, in contexts characterised by political struggles for equality and recognition, things did not really turn out as expected. In the Soviet Union, for example, women were far from being equal to men as, instead, Bolshevik's ideology suggested (Chatterjee, 2002).

Before moving to the next section, I want to draw attention to two points that follow from the above discussion. First, much of the scholarship at the intersection of history of political thought and of IR has constructed 'canons' of thought that, however, are mostly Western. It thus focuses on Western white men who have written about popular sovereignty, social contract, self-government and self-determination often without even questioning their own spatial and temporal biases. As if what they wrote constituted a quasi-universal or a-temporal 'theory' on the nexus between states and people. This tendency, though, risks omitting from the history of political thought non-Western thinkers who, nonetheless, have thought about sovereignty, democracy and political community such as W. E. B. Du Bois and Marcus Garvey (on this, see Shilliam, 2006, 2010).

Second, even the 'ideal man' that philosophers from Hobbes to Rawls have used to illustrate the rational choice that individuals supposedly make to abide to the social contract is very much a Western, white and masculine construct pictured as representing a universal experience. Yet, this depiction leaves out all other experiences and individuals who fall outside of this narrow category. As feminist and race-oriented scholars have argued at length, one experience is not enough to explain political behaviour (Pateman and Mills, 2013). To be sure, entering the 'non-Western archive of thought' (Shilliam, 2010: 12) is not an easy task because of language boundaries but also because non-Western thinkers have been much influenced by Western ideas of modernity.

However, when we focus on specific thinkers that we view as foundational to the relation between states and people, we do have to remember that, first, they read history in specific ways; second, that while what we read today is their thought, social and political practices did not necessarily follow, or at least not in the way expected or described by them. Philosophers' thought is marked by normative projects and ambitions that, no matter how clear to the reader, do not necessarily reflect what happens out there. To further understand in practice the nexus between states and people, diversity of conceptions and allegiances and how these relations have evolved over time, we can then look into scholarship that uses historical experience to create analytical categories. Literature that has been dealing with this is varied, but we will see that scholarships on state formation, nationalism and citizenship have important insights to offer.

State formation, nationalism and citizenship

Max Weber saw states as the combination of territory and people united by elites' and bureaucracies' legitimate domination militarily, economically and politically (1978). For Charles Tilly, state formation occurs following external war making, internal elimination of rival forces, elimination of threats to domestic population and economic extraction (1992). Marxist sociologists such as Philip Gorski specifically stress the exploitative and dominating aspects in state formation (1993). With a top-down focus, sociological explanations have largely focused on state administrations and economic capacities disregarding the constitution of populations and their identities (de Carvalho, 2016: 61–62). The formation of identities is thus associated with the rise of nationalism, as if these did not matter before. However, once we start considering historically the constitution of the bond between states and people, the picture looks quite differently. Within states, multiple identities have been historically at work (Lebow, 2016) and so have multiple claims to self-determination as in Yugoslavia just before its 1990s' break-up. In turn, national identities can sometime go well beyond territorial borders as in the case of diasporas, exercising forms of transnational nationalism (Ragazzi, 2017). Suffice to look at the history of minority groups from the peace treaties of Westphalia (1648) and through the nineteenth and 20th century to realise that groups and their rights have been as much an object of domestic than external concern (Jackson Preece, 1998).

How populations and state identities are constituted is far from being a linear or uncontested process. The relationship between states and people has very much to do with forms of power and modes of government. How do states govern and produce certain types of identities? How do groups identify with and mobilise around given identities? Michel Foucault tells us that states govern individuals by dominating them and constituting them as subjects (1982). He also stresses that this is a complex social process by which individuals are made part of the dominating apparatus to have them further comply. Individuals internalise state logics of dominations. de Carvalho completes this picture, conceptualising what he terms 'subjectivation', that is the process of politicisation of subjecthood when individuals, from being subjects of the king become subjects of the state (2016).

Understanding the making of 'subjects' in processes of state formation speaks directly to the question of political legitimacy at the heart of the bond between states and people. In dynastic sovereignty, legitimacy comes from god via the queen or the king; in colonial empires, political legitimacy is accompanied by other justifications such as civilising discourses. In both cases, there is a vertical relation between an unquestioned authority and subjects. Popular sovereignty challenges this vertical conception, as legitimacy comes at least in theory from 'below' and is grounded on the consent of the governed and self-determination. At the same time, however, and centrally for our discussion, the way the political community is delineated matters for how rights are allocated and exercised domestically. In other words, just as we saw at the end of the previous section, not everyone is entitled to the same treatment, status and rights within a polity. Not all individuals or groups members of a political community can equally exercise their political will.

Historically, the allocation of rights to some and the denial of entitlements to others has facilitated (and often preceded) the execution of mass atrocities, genocide, crimes against humanities (Rae, 2002). In the interwar years, numerous minorities were denied political, social and cultural rights and, for instance, were thus unable to vote. Today, so-called liberal states regularly exclude and stratify through their immigration and citizenship laws as well as welfare policies individuals and groups (Morris, 2003). Examining how nationalism and citizenship have been practiced and understood through history helps questioning the egalitarian promise carried in the notion of a democratic political community based on the will of people. A glance into states' behaviour, past and present, quickly reveals that this promise is simply not met in practice. Who is included and who is excluded? What are the grounds for these inclusions and exclusions? What do these mean for how identities of states are formed and for their behaviour?

IR scholarship has largely remained silent on these questions. Nationalism is conspicuously peripheral to IR (considerable exceptions include Mayall, 1990; Hall, 1999; Rae, 2002; Lebow, 2016), while citizenship is even less studied (rare exceptions include Linklater, 2007; Ragazzi, 2017; Spanu, 2020). The fields of nationalism and citizenship studies, though, have brought key insights that call into question the conflation of states and nations in IR (see Heiskanen, 2021). I only want to mention here the three key contributions that these literatures have brought specifically to a discussion on the bond between states and people, and on self-determination. First, viewing states and nations as coinciding is historically incorrect since it obscures the possibility of having multiple identities within states (Gellner, 1983; Hobsbawm, 1990; Breuilly, 1993; Pettit, 1999). Second, as postcolonial scholars of nationalism have argued, this view neglects the social, symbolic (and imperial) origins of identities and of national sentiment then leading to self-determination claims (Chatterjee, 1993; Mamdani, 1996; Pettman, 1998: 155). Third, it omits considerations on normative and legal aspects, as allegiances translate into diverse institutional bonds between states and people (Kymlicka, 1996). Yet, in a discussion on the historical relation between states and people questions of status and of rights, their recognition and allocation are central.

Rights refer to the entitlements that state authorities grant to domestic population. They are the means by which individuals and groups come to constitute and take part to the domestic political community whilst representing at least in principle guarantees for protection against violations and mistreatments. Since after World War II, liberal literature in Political Theory has distinguished equality of rights (social, political, civic) and political equality as the defining criteria for the delineation of nation-states and of their membership (Marshall, 1949). If these criteria have become the key tenets of liberal states, history shows us that they may be more reflective of a normative liberal project than of actual state practices. Discourses about political equality of individuals and equality of rights as constitutive of the nation-state have been constructed in opposition to conceptions of unequal entitlement attached to empires. However, as much nationalism and citizenship literature show us, in practice, the allocation and exercise of rights within nation-states rarely – if at all – follow these 'ideal' lines. This then complexifies the relation between states and people, the definition of the latter and the implication that this definition has for how the will of the people and self-determination are both practiced and intellectualised.

Conclusion

Self-determination is a core principle of the international order that defines the bond between states and peoples in particular ways. However, as this chapter has shown, IR scholarship has either overlooked or not adequately scrutinised this nexus and its implications for states' behaviour and identity. The chapter has therefore drawn attention to related bodies of literature that have, in different ways, delved into it: from political thought, to literature on state formation, nationalism and citizenship. The discussion stressed the contributions of each body of scholarship, whilst revealing respective limits. For political thought, very often (though not always) limits revolved around the blindness to racial, class and gender components. Diverse treatments and unequal entitlements within nation-states are, in turn, aspects that literature on nationalism and citizenship in particular have considered when examining the formation of nations and national identities within states.

As historically oriented IR scholarship is becoming increasingly sensitive to histories of diversity, contestation and domination, when pursuing new research agendas it may be worth remembering what much of the pre-existing academic work has silenced. As the above discussion has revealed, despite the formal abolition of empire, hierarchies and orderings in population groups have been pervasive historically even in political systems that supposedly call for political equality. Why, however, we might ask, is this the case? Looking at the implications of self-determination once new states are formed, at the functioning of the bond between states and people may help us find answers that, so far, have been excluded because casted as belonging to the domestic realm. Additionally, as IR scholarship is engaging with emotions and trauma (Hutchison, 2018), future work may use this bridge to enquiry into the role of collective memory in the constitution of state and national identities. Hobsbawm reported that Renan once said: 'getting its history wrong is part of being a nation' (1990: 12).[1] Research in Historical IR can further untangle the deeply complex connections between past and present.

Suggestions for further reading

Getachew, A. (2019). *Worldmaking after Empire: The Rise and Fall of Self-Determination*. Princeton, NJ: Princeton University Press.
Knop, K. (2002). *Diversity and Self-Determination in International Law*. Cambridge: Cambridge University Press.
Koskenniemi, M. (1994). National self-determination today: problems of legal theory and practice. *The International and Comparative Law Quarterly*, 43 (2), 241–269.
Lake, M., and Reynolds, H. (2007). *Drawing the Global Colour Line: White Men's Countries and the International Challenge of Racial Equality*. Cambridge: Cambridge University Press.
Manela, E. (2007). *The Wilsonian Moment: Self-Determination and the International Origins of Anticolonial Nationalism*. Oxford: Oxford University Press.

Note

1 Ernest Renan actually wrote 'L'oubli et je dirai même l'erreur historique sont un facteur essentiel de la formation d'une nation et c'est ainsi que le progrès des études historiques est souvent pour la nationalité un danger' (in Hobsbawm, 1990: 12).

References

Agnew, J. (1994). The territorial trap: the geographical assumptions of international relations theory. *Review of International Political Economy*, 1 (1), 53–80.
Armitage, D. (2008). *The Declaration of Independence: A Global History*. Cambridge, MA: Harvard University Press.
Bartelson, J. (1995). *A Genealogy of Sovereignty*. Cambridge: Cambridge University Press.
Biersteker, T., and Weber, C., eds. (1996). *State Sovereignty as Social Construct*. Cambridge: Cambridge University Press.
Breuilly, J. (1993). *Nationalism and the State*. Chicago, IL: University of Chicago Press.
Bruneau, Q. P. (2021). Constructivism: History and Systemic Change. In de Carvalho, B., Costa Lopez, J., & Leira, H., eds. *Routledge Handbook of Historical International Relations*. Abingdon: Routledge.
Bukovansky, M. (2002). *Legitimacy and Power Politics: The American and French Revolutions in International Political Culture*. Princeton, NJ: Princeton University Press.
Burke, R. (2002). *Decolonization and the Evolution of International Human Rights*. Philadelphia, PA: University of Pennsylvania Press.
Carr, E. H. (1945). *Nationalism and After*. London: Macmillan.
Cassese, A. (1995). *Self-Determination of People*. Cambridge: Cambridge University Press.
Chatterjee, C. (2002). *Celebrating Women: Gender, Festival Culture, and Bolshevik Ideology, 1910-1939*. Pittsburgh, PA: University of Pittsburgh Press.

Chatterjee, P. (1993). *The Nation and its Fragments : Colonial and Postcolonial Histories*. Princeton, NJ: Princeton University Press.

Clark, I. (2007). *International Legitimacy and World Society*. Oxford: Oxford University Press.

Cobban, A. (1969). *The Nation State and National Self-Determination*. London: Collins.

Coppieters, B., and Sakwa, R. (2003). *Contextualizing Secession: Normative Studies in Comparative Perspective*. Oxford: Oxford University Press.

Crawford, N. (2002). *Argument and Change in World Politics Ethics, Decolonization, and Humanitarian Intervention*. Cambridge: Cambridge University Press.

de Carvalho, B. (2016). The making of the political subject: subjects and territory in the formation of the state. *Theory and Society*, 45 (1), 57–88.

de Carvalho, B., and Leira, H. (2021). State formation and historical international relations. In de Carvalho, B., Costa Lopez, J., & Leira, H., eds. *Routledge Handbook of Historical International Relations*. Abingdon: Routledge.

Donnelly, J. (1998). Human rights: a new standard of civilization? *International Affairs*, 74 (1), 1–23.

Emerson, R. (1971). Self-determination. *The American Journal of International Law*, 65 (3), 459–475.

Fabry, M. (2010). *Recognizing States: International Society and the Establishment of New States Since 1776*. Oxford: Oxford University Press.

Foucault, M. (1982). The subject and power. *Critical Inquiry*, 8 (4), 777–795.

Gellner, E. (1983). *Nations and Nationalism*. Ithaca, NY: Cornell University Press.

Glanville, L. (2014). *Sovereignty and the Responsibility to Protect: A New History*. Chicago, IL: The University of Chicago Press.

Gong, G. (1984). *The Standard of 'Civilization' in International Society*. Oxford: Clarendon Press.

Gorski, P. S. (1993). The Protestant ethic revisited: disciplinary revolution and state formation in Holland and Prussia. *American Journal of Sociology*, 99 (2), 265–316.

Hall, R. B. (1999). *National Collective Identity: Social Constructs and International Systems*. New York, NY: Columbia University Press.

Hannum, H. (1990). *Autonomy, Sovereignty, and Self-Determination: The Accommodation of Conflicting Rights*. Philadelphia, PA: Pennsylvania University Press.

Heiskanen, J. (2021). Nations and Nationalism in International Relations. In de Carvalho, B., Costa Lopez, J., & Leira, H., eds. *Routledge Handbook of Historical International Relations*. Abingdon: Routledge.

Hobbes, T. (2017). *Leviathan*. Edited and with an introduction by C. Brooke. London: Penguin UK.

Hobsbawm, E. (1990). *Nations and Nationalism Since 1780: Programme, Myth, Reality*. Cambridge: Cambridge University Press.

Hurrell, A. (2007). *On Global Order: Power, Values, and the Constitution of International Society*. Oxford: Oxford University Press.

Hutchison, E. (2018). *Affective Communities in World Politics: Collective Emotions After Trauma*. Cambridge: Cambridge University Press.

Jackson Preece, J. (1998). *National Minorities and the European Nation-States System*. Oxford: Oxford University Press.

Jackson, R. (1990). *Quasi-States: Sovereignty, International Relations, and the Third World*. Cambridge: Cambridge University Press.

Jennings, I. (1956). *The Approach to Self-Government*. Cambridge: Cambridge University Press.

Krasner, S. (1999). *Sovereignty: Organized Hypocrisy*. Princeton, NJ: Princeton University Press.

Kymlicka, W. (1996). *Multicultural Citizenship: A Liberal Theory of Minority Rights*. Oxford: Oxford University Press.

Lebow, R. N. (2016). *National Identities and International Relations*. Cambridge: Cambridge University Press.

Lee, D. (2016). *Popular Sovereignty in Early Modern Constitutional Thought*. Oxford: Oxford University Press.

Lenin, V. I. (1951). *The Right of Nations to Self-Determination*. New York, NY: International Publishers.

Linklater, A. (2007). *Critical Theory and World Politics: Citizenship, Sovereignty and Humanity*. London: Routledge.

Locke, J. (1960). *Two Treaties of Government*. Introduction and critical apparatus by P. Laslett. London: Mentor.

Malcolm, N. (2002). *Hobbes's Theory of International Relations*. Oxford: Oxford University Press.

Mamdani, M. (1996). *Citizen and Subject: Contemporary Africa and the Legacy of Late Colonialism*. Princeton, NJ: Princeton University Press.

Marshall, T. H. (1949). *Citizenship and Social Class, and Other Essays*. Cambridge: Cambridge University Press.

Mayall, J. (1990). *Nationalism and International Society*. Cambridge: Cambridge University Press.

Mazzini, G. (2009). *A Cosmopolitanism of Nations: Giuseppe Mazzini's Writings on Democracy, Nation Building, and International Relations*. Edited and with an introduction by S. Recchia and N. Urbinati. Princeton, NJ: Princeton University Press.

Mill, J. S. (2009). *Considerations on Representative Government.* Waiheke Island: Floating Press.

Mills, C. W. (1997). *The Racial Contract.* Ithaca, NY: Cornell University Press.

Moravcsik, A. (2000). The origins of human rights regimes. *International Organization,* 54 (2), 217–252.

Morgenthau, H. (1948). *Politics Among Nations: The Struggle for Power and Peace.* New York, NY: A. A. Knopf.

Morris, L. (2003). Managing contradiction: civic stratification and migrants' rights. *The International Migration Review,* 37 (1), 74–100.

Motyl, A. (2001). *Imperial Ends: The Decay, Collapse, and Revival of Empires.* New York, NY: Columbia University Press.

Navari, C., and Green, D. (2021). The English School and Historical International Relations. In de Carvalho, B., Costa Lopez, J., & Leira, H., eds. *Routledge Handbook of Historical International Relations.* Abingdon: Routledge.

Pateman, C., and Mills, C. (2013). *The Contract and Domination.* Cambridge: Polity Press.

Pettit, P. (1999). *Liberty as Non-Domination.* Oxford: Oxford University Press.

Pettman, J. J. (1998). Nationalism and after. *Review of International Studies,* 24 (5), 149–164.

Putterman, E. (2010). *Rousseau, Law and the Sovereignty of the People.* Cambridge: Cambridge University Press.

Rae, H. (2002). *State Identities and the Homogenisation of Peoples.* Cambridge: Cambridge University Press.

Ragazzi, F. (2017). *Governing Diasporas in International Relations: The Transnational Politics of Croatia and Former Yugoslavia.* London: Routledge.

Ratner, S. (1996). Drawing a better line: UTI possidetis and the borders of new states. *The American Journal of International Law,* 90 (4), 590–624.

Rawls, J. (1971). *A Theory of Justice.* Cambridge, MA: Harvard University Press.

Reus-Smit, C. (2013). *Individual Rights and the Making of the International System.* Cambridge: Cambridge University Press.

Rousseau, J.-J. (1950). *The Social Contract and Discourses.* Translated and with an introduction by G. D. H. Cole. New York, NY: E. P. Dutton and Company.

Shilliam, R. (2006). What about Marcus Garvey? Race and the transformation of sovereignty debate. *Review of International Studies,* 32 (3), 379–400.

Shilliam, R. (2010). *Non-Western Thought and International Relations.* London: Routledge.

Simpson, B. (2014). The Biafran secession and the limits of self-determination. *Journal of Genocide Research,* 16 (2–3), 337–354.

Snyder, J. (2000). *From Voting to Violence: Democratization and Nationalist Conflict.* New York, NY: Norton.

Spanu, M. (2020). The hierarchical society: the politics of self-determination and the constitution of new states after 1919. *European Journal of International Relations,* 26 (2), 372–396.

Spruyt, H. (1994). *The Sovereign State and its Competitors: An Analysis of Systems Change.* Princeton, NJ: Princeton University Press.

Spruyt, H. (2005. *Ending Empire: Contested Sovereignty and Territorial Partition.* Ithaca, NY: Cornell University Press.

Stalin, J. (1945). *Marxism and the National Question.* Moscow: Foreign Languages Pub. House.

Svensson, T. (2021). Decolonisation and the Erosion of the Imperial Idea. In de Carvalho, B., Costa Lopez, J., & Leira, H., eds. *Routledge Handbook of Historical International Relations.* Abingdon: Routledge.

Tilly, C. (1992). *Coercion, Capital, and European States, AD 990-1992.* Oxford: Blackwell.

Walker, R. B. J. (1993). *Inside Outside : International Relations as Political Theory.* Cambridge: Cambridge University Press.

Waltz, K. (1979). *Theory of International Politics.* Reading, MA: Addison-Wesley.

25

BORDERS AND BOUNDARIES

Making visible what divides

Kerry Goettlich and Jordan Branch

The concepts of 'borders' and 'boundaries' are in some sense inherently central to International Relations (IR). According to one IR textbook, for example, if there is anything that defines the discipline's object of analysis, it might be summed up in the phrase 'cross-border transactions' (Brown and Ainley, 2009: 7). Studying IR, then, at some level, presupposes an understanding of borders. Within IR, many different perspectives have been developed towards this end, from the neoliberal view of borders as a potential institution for reducing transaction costs (Simmons, 2005) to constructivist analyses of the norm of territorial integrity (Zacher, 2001) to studies by scholars associated with post-structuralism on how borders are 'infused through bodies and diffused across society and everyday life' (Vaughan-Williams, 2009).

The terms 'border' and 'boundary', as well as related concepts such as 'frontier' and 'territory', are difficult to define and have shifted in meaning over time and space. Indeed, among geographers, the meanings of such terms in different languages and traditions have been subject to debate (Kristof, 1959; Juricek, 1966; Amilhat Szary, 2015). When scholars have made explicit distinctions, these often have to do with, for example, the difference between formal and informal institutions, or the distinction between wide 'borderland' areas and precisely demarcated borderlines. Most IR scholarship reviewed in this chapter, however, does not make a clear distinction between 'border' and 'boundary'. We follow this usage, treating them here as interchangeable terms referring to the spatial limits of polities. Similarly, scholars have adopted differing approaches to 'territory' and 'territoriality'. A range of IR scholars adopt Robert Sack's (1986) analytical notion of territoriality as an attempt to define and control an area, while Stuart Elden's (2013) genealogical and conceptual-historical approach to the emergence of the term 'territory' itself has also been influential.

Historical IR is an area of the discipline where comparatively little work has been done which takes as its primary goal the analysis of 'borders' or 'boundaries' *per se*, either in terms of what those concepts have meant in the past, or in terms of what has happened on borderlines or in the spaces between polities. That said, there is plenty of IR scholarship which, in one way or another, engages with the history of borders and boundaries, as well as scholarship in other disciplines on the history of borders which IR has made use of. This chapter provides a brief overview of this work, approaching the topic from two different angles. First, we review Historical IR scholarship which has been concerned with changes over long periods of time in the international system, which engages in one way or another with the character and role of borders and boundaries.

Second, we explore a number of themes in IR research on territory and borders more generally in which scholars either draw on historical work or could fruitfully do so. In the final section, we point out some challenges in working with the topic which we suggest Historical IR should consider, as well as opportunities for future research.

Modernity and borders

While the scope of IR as a discipline is difficult to define in its early decades, interest in the history of borders emerged in geopolitical writings somewhere around the turn of the twentieth century. This occurred within a global context where a large number of boundaries, particularly across the colonized world, were being rapidly drawn, or redrawn in new ways. A major part of what concerned scholars at that time was the relationship between more and less 'civilized' societies, a distinction many of them thought could explain the disappearance of vague frontier zones and the appearance of linear borders. Friedrich Ratzel argued that 'civilized' societies had replaced wide frontiers and 'no man's lands' with thinner and more fixed borders because they had learned to use their land more efficiently and thus valued it more highly (see Febvre, 1973). This thesis, along with much of Ratzel's work, was brought to English-speaking scholarship by American geographer Ellen Semple (1907) and had a significant impact on the way borders have been seen in historical perspective. In a similar vein, former Viceroy of India Lord Curzon's (1907) lecture on *Frontiers* continues to be influential. In the lecture, Curzon applauded what he considered progress in Western empires' political and technical practices of delimiting and demarcating borders, arguing that recent advances held out promise for a more peaceful world.

For the most part, such discussions were not of central concern to IR as it became a more distinct discipline later in the twentieth century. For example, an article by Leo Gross (1948), which played an important role in defining the 1648 Peace of Westphalia as a central historical benchmark for IR, says nothing explicitly about 'borders' or 'boundaries' between states. More important for Gross was the establishment of sovereign states recognizing no superior authority, with the geographical nature of polities, territorial or otherwise, taking on background significance at most. One exception to this was John Herz (1957), who argued that the development of nuclear weapons would result in a growing permeability of 'the political atom, the nation-state'. This prediction rested on the basis that the territorial state originated in Europe's gunpowder revolution, in which castles could no longer provide sufficient protection for political communities and had to be replaced by large systems of fortifications surrounding a territory. The later invention of airpower, and then the atomic bomb, however, mitigated and would eventually make irrelevant the 'hard shell' that could be provided by fortification, and therefore potentially the territorial state itself.

Herz later retracted the prediction, but the basic idea remained of looking to the geographical organization of international politics, as it has historically changed in form over the *longue durée*, in order to understand seismic shifts occurring in the contemporary world. After 1979, when Kenneth Waltz's *Theory of International Politics* (Waltz, 1979) was published, this became increasingly important for many scholars criticizing neorealism for its inability to explain systemic change, which became an even more central concern with the end of the Cold War and increasing interest in globalization. This way of coming at the history of borders in international relations is best exemplified by John Ruggie's (1993) article, 'Territoriality and Beyond'. For Ruggie, one of the main problems with neorealism was that it denied that differentiation among units was important for international relations. On the contrary, Ruggie argued for an 'epochal study of rule', for which 'modes of differentiation are nothing less than the focus'. In this long-term historical perspective, 'the distinctive feature of the modern system of rule is that it has differentiated its subject collectivity into territorially defined, fixed, and mutually exclusive enclaves of legitimate dominion' (Ruggie, 1993: 151–152). In this way, Ruggie hoped to develop a vocabulary for understanding contemporary changes associated with globalization.

In making this argument, Ruggie put exclusive territoriality, and by extension, certain kinds of borders, at the centre of what defined modernity for international politics, setting a lasting agenda for Historical IR scholars. The article offered no 'theory' of this transformation but outlined a number of European historical dynamics that worked in its favour, perhaps the most distinctive of which is called change in 'social epistemes'. By this was meant certain new ways of understanding the world, particularly the single-point perspective in European art, which made possible 'a view of society as a collection of atomistic and autonomous bodies-in-motion in a field of forces energized solely by scarcity and ambition' (Ruggie, 1993: 157–158). This metaphysical shift led on the one hand to the territorialization of political authority and on the other, paradoxically, to its 'unravelling', by necessitating an extraterritorial institution of diplomacy and, eventually, multilateralism. In order to conceptualize the impact of social epistemes on sovereignty, Ruggie relied on the image of 'disjoint', or completely interlocking territorial spaces, implying at least an idea of linear borders and the absence of zonal frontiers.

Beginning in the 1990s, then, a body of IR literature developed which was inspired by the kinds of questions Ruggie had been asking, within which the history of borders played a role in various ways (see Nøhr, 2021 in this volume). Its coherence around any single question should not be overstated, but the basic concern was the way in which international systems, almost exclusively European, have changed over the course of centuries. For Hendrik Spruyt (1994), the question was how the sovereign state in Europe eliminated competing types of polities which had also grown out of increased commercial activity after 1000. In contrast to accounts from historical sociology such as that of Charles Tilly (1992), which stressed the war-making ability of the sovereign state, Spruyt drew attention to its organizational capacity, which he argued was better suited to take advantage of growing trade. Alternately, from a Marxist perspective, Benno Teschke (2003) argued for a focus on a shift from feudal to capitalist property relations in understanding modern sovereignty (see Costa Lopez, 2021 in this volume).

Changing social epistemes, or political ideas, also provided a basis for scholarship on systemic change, as part of the turn to constructivism which IR was undergoing more broadly (Hall, 1999; Philpott, 2001; Bruneau, 2021). Reus-Smit (1999), in particular, while ultimately interested in the roots of multilateralism more than territorial sovereignty, took seriously Ruggie's identification of territorial borders as an important part of the modern system of sovereign states. Contrary to many other accounts, Reus-Smit argued that the geographical extension of sovereignty was not specified until the 1713 Peace of Utrecht, which eliminated any possible dynastic union between the crowns of France and Spain.

Furthermore, some have taken seriously the problems Ruggie raised for understanding borders across history without completely adopting his methodological perspective (e.g., Larkins, 2010; Strandsbjerg, 2010). For example, some scholars interested in the origins of modern territoriality have drawn on a genealogical approach, in which concepts such as sovereignty and territory have no stable, final meaning, which can be 'bundled' and 'unbundled', as Ruggie had put it. Jens Bartelson (1995) conducts a genealogy of sovereignty, not without implications for the spatial boundaries of the concept, in which political authority was gradually associated with territorial space within legal contestations between the Holy Roman Empire, the Roman Church, and the various principalities of Christendom. The trend is exemplified in a 1313 Papal Bull, which gave legitimacy to the phrase '*rex in regno suo est imperator* [the king is emperor in his kingdom], where *regno* now had acquired an unequivocal territorial signification' (Bartelson, 1995: 99). Yet the border itself becomes more important in the 'Classical Age' after the Renaissance, when it comes to be imagined as a physical separation between states, reflecting an emerging distinction between domestic and foreign policy. Stuart Elden's (2013) genealogical study *The Birth of Territory* is also relevant here, as there is significant overlap in substance, although it is not primarily written for an IR audience. Elden sees a recognizable concept of territory in the term *territorium*, as it was adapted from Roman law in the fourteenth century, and, like Bartelson, gives great importance to the formulation of the idea of *rex in regno suo est imperator*. Also similarly to Bartelson, Elden sees a separate important shift occurring in the seventeenth century, but this time through the work of Gottfried Leibniz, which explicitly tied sovereignty and territory together.

The work in IR that has been done on the history of territorial sovereignty and the state system has important implications for the study of borders in Historical IR (see de Carvalho, 2021; de Carvalho and Leira, 2021; both in this volume). Jordan Branch's study of the role of cartography in the origins of territorial sovereignty in Europe has foregrounded the question of how political authority has been defined, and of when and how a territorial definition became predominant and excluded other possibilities (Branch, 2014). Even in the Peace of Utrecht, authority in Europe continued to be specified in treaties by lists of places, jurisdictions, and objects, rather than by describing the course of a borderline, while at the same time European empires in the Americas had long been using linear borders.

Many questions yet remain to be answered arising from Historical IR's longstanding interest in the way in which international politics came to be dominated by the fragmentation of political space into interlocking, or, as Ruggie put it, 'disjoint' territories. While many different explanations exist for the emergence of territorial sovereignty in Europe, there is much room for new interpretations of the apparent universalization of linear borders worldwide. It may be tempting to explain the latter in terms of the 'expansion' of Europe or of an already existing international society to the rest of the world through imperialism (e.g., Bull and Watson, 1984; see Navari and Green, 2021 in this volume). Western imperialism is undoubtedly a part of the answer, but this explanation is rarely supported with careful empirical study. The fact that until the late-nineteenth century European empires throughout the Eastern Hemisphere used a variety of different terms in negotiating over space with non-Western polities, rather than purely linear borders, suggests the process was not so simple. As Kerry Goettlich (2019) has argued, the history of linear borders is related to, but distinct from the history of territorial sovereignty, with linear borders only becoming consistently applied in practice globally starting in the late-nineteenth century. The long-term sociological process of rationalization, or the privileging of certain forms of quantifiable, secular, and 'scientific' knowledge, offers one potential explanation for the linearization of borders which may avoid some of the difficulties of existing theories.

Related discussions in IR

Beyond these (relatively few) explicitly historical interrogations of borders and boundaries, IR scholarship across a number of related issues could be brought into productive conversation with historical work.

For example, there is an extensive literature on territorial conflict in IR. This has relied on a variety of methodological approaches and empirical strategies, but it has largely focused on contemporary conflicts or recent history—the nineteenth and twentieth centuries. (See Toft, 2014 for a useful review.) For example, quantitative cross-national studies have posited a number of causal drivers and mechanisms to account for why some disputed territories result in violent conflict (e.g., Huth, 1996) or why some conflicts have led to changes in the location of state borders (e.g., Goertz and Diehl, 1992). Although some more qualitative studies have problematized the historical nature of boundaries (e.g., Lustick, 1993), most studies of territorial conflict have taken the linear and territorial character of state boundaries as unproblematic and have instead focused on how the location of those boundaries results from or leads to conflict. In other words, they have largely ignored Ruggie's point about the importance of change in the mode of differentiation. Given the historical period that much of this literature works on, the approach taken may be analytically useful and unproblematic. As noted above, even those studies that put the emergence of state territoriality (and linear boundaries) at a late date tend to mark the early-nineteenth century as an important point of consolidation. Yet it could still be useful for this discussion of territorial conflict to note the historical emergence of boundaries, especially for discussions of the possibility change in the dynamics of territorial conflict in the face of changing borders today. Some studies have begun down this path, focusing on issues around the role of historical boundaries in conflict (e.g., Carter and Goemans, 2011; Abramson and Carter, 2016).

Studies of other border-related issues could see similar benefits, such as the debate around the usefulness of territorial partition for ameliorating ethnic conflict (e.g., Kaufmann, 1996; Sambanis, 2000; Chapman and Roeder, 2007; among others). Again, this literature largely takes the type of division between polities as given and then asks about drawing new borders as a way to solve conflict—rather than how new or contested borders can lead to conflict. This also has been a productive discussion when applied to the contemporary international system, defined fundamentally by territorial borders, but might also be usefully expanded to think through diverse *forms* of partition rather than merely its presence. There are definitely opportunities for further theory development and historical empirical work here. A similar point applies to the literature on territorial indivisibility—the way in which certain spaces appear to be impossible to divide with a traditional boundary and how that makes them persistent sources of conflict (e.g., Toft, 2003; Hassner, 2009; Goddard, 2010). The category of indivisibility itself is constituted by the hegemony of linear division in today's international system.

Finally, research on twentieth-century transformations in what borders mean and how likely they are to be altered has demonstrated change over time *within* the framework of linear boundaries. Research has been done in this vein in IR at least since the collapse of Western colonialism in the late-twentieth century raised questions of what would and should become of borders left behind by the imperial powers, and what the consequences of maintaining or altering them would be. Many anti-colonial politicians at the time, such as Kwame Nkrumah (1963: 7), criticized existing borders as relics of the Berlin Conference of 1884–1885 which had to be rejected. The historical logic often taken from this by IR was that African borders, unlike European borders, 'are not the walls and moats of history…whose traces mark the military conflicts and diplomatic compromises of the nation's past', but instead dangerously cut across 'tribal geography', due to the geographically ill-informed nature of the 'colonial accident' (Zartman, 1965). At the same time, some scholars contested these generalizations, such as Saadia Touval (1966), who argued that Africans' 'relationships with Europeans played a role in the process' of dividing up the continent (see Quirk, 2021).

Different understandings of the history of colonial borders are of great importance for wider debates on sovereignty and statehood in the Global South. Because decolonization had essentially been a legal formality without socioeconomic substance, the colonial borders left intact gave little basis on which to build stable national communities (Jackson and Rosberg, 1982). This explained, as Jackson (1990) later put it, the problem of 'quasi-states', or states maintained externally by an international society that treated them as sovereign despite being overrun internally with civil war and corruption. Jeffrey Herbst (1989), while mainly agreeing on the characterization of the problem, argues that the discarding of any requirement of effective control in deciding boundaries had already occurred long ago in the colonial period, through the concept of the protectorate. It was this legal fiction, which bears some similarity to Jackson's concept of the 'quasi-state', that had enabled the colonial powers to avoid war. The impossibility of drawing any 'natural' borders in Africa is what led the colonial powers to that system, just as it encouraged African leaders to maintain the same borders after decolonization. Siba Grovogui (1996), however, entirely rejects Jackson's view that the misfortunes of African states are mostly due to the fact that 'Western powers have been unduly charitable to quasi states and their leaders by granting full sovereign immunity', drawing attention instead to the role of continued Western interventions of many kinds, including their efforts in favour of maintaining colonial boundaries (see Svensson, 2021).

Building on existing work on the persistence of colonial borders, IR scholars' interest in the border-drawing principle of *uti possidetis*, from international law, increased after the breakup of the USSR and Yugoslavia. While, in Roman law, the principle originally referred to favouring the actual possessor of an item in a property dispute, literally meaning 'as you possess', in modern international law, it has come to mean adopting former administrative borders as new international borders in cases of decolonization or state collapse. Because, as some argued, it had been applied historically in the decolonization of Latin America and Africa, it should also be applied in the collapse of communist states. Some scholars of international law disputed this in terms of its consequences of potentially encouraging separatism or preventing alternative boundaries from being considered which might be better suited to local conditions (Ratner, 1996). Others noted that it rested on a questionable interpretation of the history of postcolonial border drawing, pointing out that *uti possidetis* was not actually historically applied as often or considered as binding as proponents hold (Lalonde, 2002).

For many IR scholars, however, the increasingly common practice of respecting inherited boundaries pointed towards changes in international norms on the possession of territory. Zacher (2001) noted that changes to the boundaries of states have become less frequent, especially after the middle of the twentieth century. He explains this by referring to an increasingly predominant 'territorial integrity norm' which holds that border changes through force are no longer legitimate. In addition to analysing the legal principle of *uti possidetis* as a norm, this argument also drew on scholarship detailing the historical abolition, since the First World War, of a previously existing principle in international law entitling states to sovereignty over any territory successfully captured in war (Korman, 1996). Other authors have taken this discussion one step further, noting the consequences of operating in a world where borders are so rarely changed for issues ranging from state strength (Atzili, 2012) to the conquest and 'death' of states (Fazal, 2007). These debates can help foreground the ways in which linear borders can be transformed in function and meaning even as they persist in their fundamental definition.

All of these show the promise of fruitful research, if we can bring Historical IR work on territory, boundaries, and their emergence into conversation with literature on territorial conflict, boundary disputes, and secessionism today. Of course, even within Historical IR, there are numerous questions about the emergence of linear borders which remain to be asked, and challenges and opportunities for future research, explored next.

Challenges and opportunities

One of the main challenges existing in scholarship on the history of borders and boundaries is Eurocentrism. This is especially evident in the fact that many of the most cited pieces of work on the origins and history of the state system deal exclusively with Europe (Herborth and Nitzschner, 2021). Others do engage with other regions, but primarily insofar as they received ideas, practices, and institutions already developed in Europe, which could also be considered problematic (Chakrabarty, 2000). Eurocentrism is not just a normative problem in that it involves treating the history of some people and places as *a priori* more important than others, but it is also a problem for a discipline such as IR which claims to have global significance and is not meant to be European area studies.

There has been work in IR, and particularly in Historical IR, which looks beyond the West for important features of international politics, sees the West and the non-West as co-constitutive, and questions and decentres the use of theories developed with Europe in mind as universal theories. Yet there remains very little work challenging the idea that the kind of borders taken for granted as universal today originated in the particular experience of Europe, with a few exceptions. IR scholars, in particular, who have looked at the role of abstract space in cartography and modes of representation have pointed to the 1494 Treaty of Tordesillas and other examples of European empires using linear borders to divide up colonial territories centuries before this was a common practice within Europe (Larkins, 2010: 169–194; Strandsbjerg, 2010: 92–110; Branch, 2014: 100–119). Aside from cartography, different property regimes set up by imperial powers and settler colonists also played a role in encouraging the surveying and demarcation of these borders on the ground (Goettlich, 2018). Questions remain, however, surrounding the potential role of colonized people in the process of linearizing borders, as well as the ways in which border ideas and practices travel between imperial peripheries and centres.

A different way to approach a non-Eurocentric history of borders and boundaries is suggested by historian Peter Perdue's (1998) observation that during the seventeenth century, 'as the result of mutual contacts, the major Eurasian states negotiated fixed, linear borders'. In particular, this refers to the 1639 Ottoman-Persian Treaty of Zuhab, the 1689 Chinese-Russian Treaty of Nerchinsk, and the 1699 Habsburg-Ottoman Treaty of Karlowitz. Perdue raises many questions for scholars of Historical IR interested in borders and boundaries: to what extent were the logics of these distant but roughly similarly timed border treaties linked to each other? To what extent were state authorities aware of far-away changes in boundary policies? To what extent might these treaties, which predated most comparable institutions within Western Europe, have affected the latter?

The issue of language differences, however, means that Eurocentrism is no easy problem to solve. Differences among 'Western' languages and traditions create enough confusion on their own even when they have long been debated by scholars. Consider, for example, the multiple and contradictory understandings of the term 'frontier' and its Romance-language cognates, which can mean either a more or less well-defined boundary or specifically the opposite of that, a wide borderland area (Juricek, 1966). But there is much work ahead, especially where translation issues have not been sufficiently addressed. As Amanda Cheney (2017) has pointed out, for example, the use of the ambiguous term 'suzerainty' to express in English the status of Tibet before the twentieth century has hindered scholarly attempts to understand how Tibet became a part of the Chinese state. Future research, then, might focus in a similar way on how terms such as 'boundary' and 'frontier' have been used or misused to translate historical institutions and practices.

A second challenge is suggested by the ambiguous relationship between the concepts of borders and boundaries, the aspects of borders and boundaries which exceed the simple cartographic appearance of lines, and the kinds of geographical extremities of historical polities which stretch the definitions of 'border' and 'boundary'. Most polities in human history have not specified their boundaries in the linear way which is routine among states today, and such frontiers should not be ignored in Historical IR. Even when maps of historical polities, made contemporaneously or more recently, portray evenly controlled territory and fixed boundaries, political and legal geographies were often more complex, layered, and fluid, a point which historians such as Lauren Benton (2010) stress. Because linear borders are often seen as a product of European history, this challenge is intimately related to Eurocentrism. IR scholars should avoid reading history only to find phenomena that are familiar to a Eurocentric perspective. Doing so could result in missed opportunities; studying spatial ideas, practices, and institutions in historical contexts where linear borders were less commonplace could be useful for understanding the role of borders more generally in geopolitics. For example, Burak Kadercan (2017) looks at the ways in which the Ottoman Empire used different kinds of more or less 'hard' or 'soft' borders for different ends and with different results.

A further opportunity for future study is in the lack of a coherent literature or conversation around the history of borders and boundaries, particularly in IR. As suggested above, while there is plenty of literature on borders and boundaries generally in IR, this has been less the case in specifically historically oriented IR, and the topic has generally tended to be treated via one or another related areas, such as sovereignty or the state system. One way to meet this challenge would be to treat it as a matter of taking stock of the large amount of work that historians have done on borders and boundaries, and synthesizing or bringing them to bear on one another. Particularly useful in-depth historical studies include Thongchai Winichakul's (1994) work on the evolving territoriality of Siam within its imperial encounter with Britain and France, as well as Peter Sahlins' (1989) study of the French-Spanish border, focusing on dynamics among inhabitants of the frontier and their relations with state officials. Part of this work of making sense of the bigger picture has been done by historians themselves (Benton, 2010; Maier, 2017). But IR, we think, has much potential to contribute to the historical study of borders and boundaries, as an area of inquiry explicitly focused on the international.

Suggestions for further reading

Benton, L. (2010). *A Search for Sovereignty: Law and Geography in European Empires, 1400–1900*. Cambridge: Cambridge University Press.

Elden, S. (2013). *The Birth of Territory*. Chicago, IL: University of Chicago Press.

Febvre, L. (1973). Frontière: The Word and the Concept. In: P. Burke, ed., *A New Kind of History: From the Writings of Febvre*. Translated by K. Folca, London: Routledge, 208-218.

Maier C. (2017). *Once Within Borders: Territories of Power, Wealth, and Belonging since 1500*. Cambridge, MA: Harvard University Press.

Ruggie, J. G. (1993). Territoriality and beyond: problematizing modernity in international relations. *International Organization*, 47 (1), 139-174.

Sahlins, P. (1989). *Boundaries: The Making of France and Spain in the Pyrenees*. Berkeley, CA: University of California Press.

References

Abramson, S., and Carter, D. (2016). The historical origins of territorial disputes. *American Political Science Review*, 110 (4), 675-698.

Amilhat Szary, A. (2015). Boundaries and Borders. In: J. Agnew, V. Mamadouh, A. Secor, and J. Sharp, eds., *The Wiley Blackwell Companion to Political Geography*, Malden, MA: John Wiley & Sons.

Atzili, B. (2012). *Good Fences, Bad Neighbors: Border Fixity and International Conflict*. Chicago, IL: University of Chicago Press.

Bartelson, J. (1995). *A Genealogy of Sovereignty*. Cambridge: Cambridge University Press.

Branch, J. (2014). *The Cartographic State: Maps, Territory, and the Origins of Sovereignty*. Cambridge: Cambridge University Press.

Brown, C., and Ainley, K. (2009). *Understanding International Relations*. 4th edition. Basingstoke: Palgrave Macmillan.

Bruneau, Q. P. (2021). Constructivism: History and Systemic Change. In de Carvalho, B., Costa Lopez, J., & Leira, H., eds. *Routledge Handbook of Historical International Relations*. Abingdon: Routledge.

Bull, H., and Watson, A., eds. (1984). *The Expansion of International Society*. Oxford: Oxford University Press.

Carter, D. B., and H. E. Goemans. (2011). The making of the territorial order: new borders and the emergence of interstate conflict. *International Organization*, 65 (2), 275-309.

Chakrabarty D. (2000). *Provincializing Europe: Postcolonial Thought and Historical Difference*. Princeton, NJ: Princeton University Press.

Chapman, T., and Roeder, P. (2007). Partition as a solution to wars of nationalism: the importance of institutions. *American Political Science Review*, 101 (4), 677-691.

Cheney, A. (2017). Tibet lost in translation: sovereignty, suzerainty and international order transformation, 1904–1906. *Journal of Contemporary Asia Studies*, 26 (107), 769-783.

Costa Lopez, J. (2021). International Relations in/and the Middle Ages. In de Carvalho, B., Costa Lopez, J., & Leira, H., eds. *Routledge Handbook of Historical International Relations*. Abingdon: Routledge.

Curzon, G. (1907). *Frontiers*. Oxford: Clarendon Press.

de Carvalho, B. (2021). Sovereignty in Historical International Relations: Trajectories, Challenges and Implications. In de Carvalho, B., Costa Lopez, J., & Leira, H., eds. *Routledge Handbook of Historical International Relations*. Abingdon: Routledge.

de Carvalho, B., and Leira, H. (2021). State Formation and Historical International Relations. In de Carvalho, B., Costa Lopez, J., & Leira, H., eds. *Routledge Handbook of Historical International Relations*. Abingdon: Routledge.

Fazal, T. (2007). *State Death: The Politics and Geography of Conquest, Occupation, and Annexation*. Princeton, NJ: Princeton University Press.

Goddard, S. (2010). *Indivisible Territory and the Politics of Legitimacy: Jerusalem and Northern Ireland*. Cambridge: Cambridge University Press.

Goertz, G., and Diehl, P. (1992). *Territorial Changes and International Conflict*. London: Routledge.

Goettlich, K. (2019). The rise of linear borders in world politics. *European Journal of International Relations*, 25 (1), 203-228.

Goettlich, K. (2018). Enclosure and Survey Rationality: The Private Origins of Territorial Borders. Paper presented at the International Studies Association, San Francisco, 7 April.

Gross L. (1948). The Peace of Westphalia, 1648–1948. *The American Journal of International Law*, 42 (1), 20-41.

Grovogui, S. (1996). *Sovereigns, Quasi Sovereigns, and Africans: Race and Self-Determination in International Law*. Minneapolis, MN: University of Minnesota Press.

Hall, R. (1999). *National Collective Identity: Social Constructs and International Systems*. New York, NY: Columbia University Press.

Hassner, R. (2009). *War on Sacred Grounds*. Ithaca, NY: Cornell University Press.

Herborth, B. and Nitzschner, P. (2021). Europe in Historical International Relations. In de Carvalho, B., Costa Lopez, J., & Leira, H., eds. *Routledge Handbook of Historical International Relations*. Abingdon: Routledge.

Herbst, J. (1989). The creation and maintenance of national boundaries in Africa. *International Organization*, 43 (4), 673-692.

Herz, J. (1957). Rise and demise of the territorial state. *World Politics*, 9 (4), 473-493.

Huth, P. (1996). *Standing Your Ground: Territorial Disputes and International Conflict*. Ann Arbor, MI: University of Michigan Press.

Jackson, R. (1990). *Quasi-States: Sovereignty, International Relations, and the Third World*. Cambridge: Cambridge University Press.

Jackson, R., and Rosberg, C. (1982). Why Africa's weak states persist: the empirical and the juridical in statehood. *World Politics*, 35 (1), 1-24.

Juricek, J. (1966). American usage of the word 'frontier' from colonial times to Frederick Jackson Turner. *Proceedings of the American Philosophical Society*, 110 (1): 10-34.

Kadercan, B. (2017). Territorial design and grand strategy in the Ottoman Empire. *Territory, Politics, Governance*, 5 (2), 158-176.

Kaufmann, C. (1996). Possible and impossible solutions to ethnic civil wars. *International Security*, 20 (4), 136-175.

Korman, S. (1996). *The Right of Conquest: The Forcible Acquisition of Territory in International Law and Practice*. Oxford: Clarendon Press.

Kristof, L. (1959). The nature of frontiers and boundaries. *Annals of the Association of American Geographers*, 49 (3): 269-282.

Lalonde, S. (2002). *Determining Boundaries in a Conflicted World: The Role of Uti Possidetis*. Montreal: McGill-Queen's University Press.

Larkins J. (2010). *From Hierarchy to Anarchy: Territory and Politics before Westphalia*. New York, NY: Palgrave Macmillan.

Lustick, I. (1993). *Unsettled States, Disputed Lands: Britain and Ireland, France and Algeria, Israel and the West Bank-Gaza*. Ithaca, NY: Cornell University Press.

Navari, C., and Green, D. (2021). The English School and Historical International Relations. In de Carvalho, B., Costa Lopez, J., & Leira, H., eds. *Routledge Handbook of Historical International Relations*. Abingdon: Routledge.

Nkrumah, K. (1963). *Africa Must Unite*. New York, NY: Frederick A. Praeger.

Nøhr, A. A. (2021). Poststructuralism and the Challenge of History. In de Carvalho, B., Costa Lopez, J., & Leira, H., eds. *Routledge Handbook of Historical International Relations*. Abingdon: Routledge.

Perdue, P. (1998). Boundaries, maps, and movement: Chinese, Russian, and Mongolian empires in early modern central Eurasia. *The International History Review*, 20 (2), 263-286.

Philpott D. (2001). *Revolutions in Sovereignty: How Ideas Shaped Modern International Relations*. Princeton, NJ: Princeton University Press.

Quirk, J. (2021). Africa and International History. In de Carvalho, B., Costa Lopez, J., & Leira, H., eds. *Routledge Handbook of Historical International Relations*. Abingdon: Routledge.

Ratner, S. (1996). Drawing a Better Line: *UTI Possidetis* and the Borders of New States. *American Journal of International Law*, 90 (4), 590-624.

Reus-Smit, C. (1999). *The Moral Purpose of the State: Culture, Social Identity, and Institutional Rationality in International Relations*. Princeton, NJ: Princeton University Press.

Sack, R. (1986). *Human Territoriality: Its Theory and History*. Cambridge: Cambridge University Press.

Sambanis, N. (2000). Partition as a solution to ethnic war: an empirical critique of the theoretical literature. *World Politics*, 52 (4), 437-483.

Semple, E. (1907). Geographical Boundaries—I. *Bulletin of the American Geographical Society*, 39 (7), 385-397.

Simmons, B. (2005). Rules over real estate: trade, territorial conflict, and international borders as institution. *Journal of Conflict Resolution*, 49 (6), 823-848.

Spruyt, H. (1994). *The Sovereign State and its Competitors*. Princeton, NJ: Princeton University Press.

Strandsbjerg, J. (2010). *Territory, Globalization and International Relations: The Cartographic Reality of Space*. Basingstoke: Palgrave Macmillan.

Svensson, T. (2021). Decolonisation and the Erosion of the Imperial Idea. In de Carvalho, B., Costa Lopez, J., & Leira, H., eds. *Routledge Handbook of Historical International Relations*. Abingdon: Routledge.

Thongchai Winichakul (1994). Siam Mapped: A History of the Geo-Body of a Nation. Honolulu, HI: University of Hawai'i Press.

Teschke, B. (2003). *The Myth of 1648: Class, Geopolitics, and the Making of Modern International Relations*. London: Verso.

Tilly, C. (1992). *Coercion, Capital, and European States, AD 990–1992*. London: Blackwell.

Toft, M. (2003). *The Geography of Ethnic Violence: Identity, Interests, and the Indivisibility of Territory*. Princeton, NJ: Princeton University Press.

Toft, M. (2014). Territory and war. *Journal of Peace Research*, 51 (2), 185-198.

Touval, S. (1966). Treaties, borders, and the partition of Africa. *The Journal of African History*, 7 (2), 279-293.

Vaughan-Williams, N. (2009). The generalised bio-political border? Re-conceptualising the limits of sovereign power. *Review of International Studies*, 35 (4), 729-749.

Waltz, K. (1979). *Theory of International Politics*. Boston, MA: McGraw-Hill.

Zacher, M. W. (2001). The territorial integrity norm: international boundaries and the use of force. *International Organization*, 55 (2), 215-250.

Zartman, I. (1965). The politics of boundaries in North and West Africa. *The Journal of Modern African Studies*, 3 (2), 155-173.

26

REASON OF STATE

An intellectual history

Richard Devetak

Introduction

There are few concepts that have shaped the modern system of states as much as reason of state. It goes to the heart of the political rationalities that have dominated modern international relations and tied the state to a cluster of core concepts such as sovereignty and security as well as prudence, policy, interest, and balance of power. The state possesses a rationality or logic of its own that cannot be reduced to the imperatives or precepts of law, morality, or even democratic will-formation, but is fundamentally casuistic. This is what makes reason of state so central to modern politics even if it is often overlooked, misunderstood, or decried. For good or ill, as idea, doctrine, or practice, it has left an indelible mark on the world of politics.

Reason of state is a term of political art that emerged in the sixteenth century. There is an agreement among historians that the phrase seems to have circulated quite widely and been in common use by the middle of the sixteenth century (Tuck, 1993: 39; Höpfl, 2004: 84; Malcolm, 2007: 92–93). The first recorded use of the phrase 'reason of state', however, seems to be in the writings of Francesco Guicciardini, the Italian statesman and historian and friend of Machiavelli. He introduced the phrase '*ragion di stato*' in *Dialogo del Reggimento di Firenze* (1521–1525) to point out the limitations of thinking about politics from the perspective of Ciceronian civil philosophy. Not long after that, Giovanni della Casa used the phrase '*ragione degli stati*' (reason of states) in an oration to Emperor Charles V around 1547 (Burke, 1991: 479). So the term clearly circulated as a term of political discourse on the Italian peninsula during the sixteenth century even if it was not until the turn of the seventeenth century that it became a popular term of political discourse across Europe and was rendered into vernacular languages as *raison d'état*, *razón de estado*, and *Staatsräson*. This chapter presents the concept of reason of state in historical perspective, showing its emergence and reception as a distinctive form of political reasoning or morality across different local contexts from early modernity to the twentieth century. One notable fact about reason of state is its neglect as an object of investigation in the academic discipline of International Relations (IR).

Receptions of reason of state

Since the late sixteenth century when the concept became a popular term of political discourse, it has been viewed as a blight on political life and a by-word for a depraved, morally bereft, Machiavellian power politics in which the ends justify the means. As Campanella remarked in his *Aforismi Politici* (1601), reason of state was an 'invention of tyrants' used to justify violations of moral and legal codes (quoted in Viroli, 1992: 267). A century and a half later, the enlightened founders of the American republic would take an equally damning view of reason of state (Vagts, 1970). Like the balance of power and absolutist monarchy, it was thought to represent the worst of European politics: the *arcana imperii* or 'secrets of state' that entangled states in morally bereft alliances and foreign policies and were inimical to good government (see also Andersen and Wohlforth, 2021).

In what remains the most important modern account of reason of state, Friedrich Meinecke tried to rescue reason of state from ignominy. '*Raison d'ètat*', he stated (Meinecke, 1957: 1), is simply the 'fundamental principle of national conduct, the State's first Law of Motion. It tells the statesman what he must do to preserve the health and strength of the State'. For Meinecke, reason of state speaks to the practical issues of statecraft that are most fundamental to the state's existence. This inevitably raises ethical issues about statecraft, which Meinecke frames as a tension or trade-off between *Kratos* ('behaviour prompted by the power-impulse') and *Ethos* ('behaviour prompted by moral responsibility') (Meinecke, 1957: 5). This has remained a central characteristic of twentieth century treatments of reason of state. Whether used by proponents or critics of the concept, reason of state has come to represent the gap between politics and morals (Bobbio, 2000: 80).

In the study of international relations today, reason of state retains the intellectual baggage of a morally dubious politics and is associated with legitimizing unjust wars, human rights violations, and various forms of illiberalism. Given the strong reaction to reason of state, it is curious that it is rarely analysed at length. More often than not, it is merely mentioned in passing, emptied of its rich history and conceptual nuance, and reduced to an instrumental and immoral form of political reason used by states to defend indefensible actions and policies. In particular, the notion 'reason of state' has generally been subsumed by the tradition of realism. The tendency has been to situate reason of state on a historical continuum with *Realpolitik* and power politics (Vincent, 1982: 73–74). Indeed, given the realist emphases on power and national interests, it is unsurprising that their histories tend to focus more on *Realpolitik* as a 'foreign policy based on calculations of power and the national interest', as Henry Kissinger (1994: 137) put it (see also Larson, 2021).

Another approach within the realist tradition, according to Terry Nardin (1992: 16), accepts that necessity permits states to derogate from morality altogether. If statesmen and public officials are to 'protect the community, … [they] must often act in ways that not only seem, but really are, immoral. Prudence simply overrides morality'. This is an argument from expediency. However, as Nardin (1992: 15) explained, rather than representing a completely amoral outlook, realists generally consider reason of state to be the 'ethical outlook' peculiar to states. Realists may be moral sceptics, but for the most part they do not deny a 'morality of states' (Vincent, 1986: 1) that permits conduct in 'extraordinary situations' that would be considered immoral in 'ordinary situations'. In Duncan Bell's (2010: 99) words, realism 'challenges *moralism*, not *morality*'; it argues that 'the reasons for overriding the constraints of ordinary morality in emergency situations are themselves moral' (Nardin, 1992: 15). J. D. B. Miller (1979: 43) puts this realist view in stark but clear terms: 'There is no higher morality than reason of state'.

Recent intellectual histories of international thought have sought to contextualize the emergence of reason of state. Rather than treating it as an object of normative opprobrium or theoretical disrepute, international intellectual historians such as Lucian Ashworth (2014: ch. 2) and Edward Keene (2005: ch. 4) have explained how it arose as part of new humanist and natural law responses to the turbulence caused by confessional and dynastic conflict in the late sixteenth and early seventeenth centuries. Reason of state, they argue, was inextricable from efforts theoretically and rhetorically to legitimize or defend forms of government, religious and imperial allegiance, and balances of power in Europe. In other words, they have shown reason of state to be a formative concept in the emergence of the modern system of states. The following sections expand upon the ground prepared by intellectual historians in IR and political theory to give a more detailed and historically contextualized exposition of the concept of reason of state.

Machiavelli, the art of state, and reason of princes

It is Niccolò Machiavelli whose name is most closely associated with reason of state. Indeed, the term 'Machiavellian' was universally used as a pejorative, 'a synonym for political duplicity, scheming, and the pursuit of power and glory, regardless of religious, moral, and legal constraints and considerations' (Höpfl, 2004: 85). In the early years of what we now call the Thirty Years' War, a series of propaganda pieces on either side of the confessional conflict accused each other of Machiavellianism (Malcolm, 2007: 41–42). Machiavelli's name, it was found, could be used in a range of different contexts to denounce an adversary or enemy for unscrupulous, unethical conduct, whether or not the conduct was consistent with the actual thinking of the Florentine secretary.

Writing in the 'mirror for princes' genre, Machiavelli offered his advice to the recently returned Medici ruler, Lorenzo, Duke of Urbino. In *The Prince*, Machiavelli advised the new prince how to maintain his rule. What was most shocking about his advice was its open and explicit willingness to depart completely from Christian morality by operationalizing an approach to princely rule that possessed a political legitimacy detached from conventional moralities and rationalities. Machiavelli did not deny the existence of morality or that it could play a part in politics. Nor did he consign politics to irrationality. But he did reject the submission of politics to conventional forms of moral and political reasoning. It is for this reason that Croce (1946: 45) and others have argued that he articulated the autonomy of politics.

In *The Prince*, Machiavelli presented an argument for treating the requirements of princely rule as distinct from other duties, relieving the prince of constraints usually applied to the private citizen or Christian subject. Indeed, much of *The Prince* relates to the prince's interest in maintaining his rule; not just protecting the principality from external threats, but also against internal threats to his position as ruler. It might be more accurate to describe Machiavelli's advice in *The Prince* as an expression of 'reason of princes'. This was a form of reason that responded to necessity, that considered results ('*si guarda al fine*'), and that did not refrain from dissimulation, mendacity, the use of force, and other ruthless and sometimes violent practices that would be considered wicked or evil from the perspective of conventional moralities (Machiavelli, 2005: chs. 15–19). But its object was the prince and securing the prince's rule.

The point here is that politics permits not only a different form of morality, but also demands a different form of reasoning that is unique to itself. The exercise of political rule could not and should not be restrained by conventional forms of morality or reasoning. This is captured in a saying attributed to Cosimo de Medici, that Machiavelli reported in *Florentine Histories*, that 'states were not held with paternosters in hand' (Machiavelli, 1988: 283). Paternosters or rosary beads were instruments the church put in the hands of believers to maintain the discipline and piety of Christians. But rulers should not feel constrained by religious doctrine in the conduct of government; instead, they should employ a distinctly *political* rationality which was not bound by Christian morality. As Machiavelli put it in chapter xviii of *The Prince*,

> a prince, and especially a new prince, cannot observe all those things by which men are considered good, for in order to maintain the state he is often obliged to act against his promise, against charity, against humanity, and against religion
>
> (Machiavelli, 2005: 62)

Machiavelli (2005: 61) did not advocate evil, but he did argue that a prince 'should know how to enter into evil [*male*] when forced by necessity'. While it was preferable for government to be conducted within the bounds of conventional morality, Machiavelli knew that politics could not be so constrained, that circumstances would compel decisions and actions that would violate conventional morality but would be morally justifiable according to the demands of political necessity.

Unsurprisingly, given the deeply religious character of European politics at the time, Machiavelli's advice became notorious almost immediately for its apparently ignoble legitimation of political wickedness. In 1539, Cardinal Reginald Pole referred to *The Prince* as a book '*scriptum ab hoste humani generis ... Satanae digito scriptum*' [written by the enemy of the human race ... written with the devil's hand] (quoted in Petrina, 2016: 15).

But the more specific context in which Machiavelli wrote *The Prince* was one less influenced by religion than by the Italian peninsula's geopolitical restructuring in which principalities and kingdoms began to overrun and replace republics (Skinner, 1978: 113). This is not the place for an extended treatment of Machiavelli's conception of politics, but it is worth outlining the broader geopolitical changes to which *The Prince* responded. As Maurizio Viroli documented in his richly detailed study of reason of state's emergence, Machiavelli and Guicciardini were crucial in shaping the conceptualization of politics as an art of government. The traditional Ciceronian conception of politics as the art of preserving a *respublica* was challenged, and in many cases displaced, by politics as the 'art of the state' (Viroli, 1992: 2–3). If the former was concerned to foster and protect the republic's institutions of law and justice, the latter was concerned with the state's interests and security as defined by a prudence detached from justice and law.

In the context of geopolitical and constitutional change in the Italian peninsula, the art of good government was unmoored from its Ciceronian or republican framework and attached to a new style of politics captured in the expression 'the art of the state'. According to Viroli, the shift also represented a clash between competing conceptions of reason: On the one hand, Ciceronian reason (*recta ratio*) which is concerned with 'universal principles of equity that must govern our decisions in legislating, counselling, ruling and administering justice' (Viroli, 1992: 3); and on the other, reason of state which is concerned with reason in 'an instrumental sense, meaning the capacity to calculate the appropriate means of preserving the state' (Viroli, 1992: 4).

As we have seen, however, Machiavelli's 'art of the state', at least as articulated in *The Prince*, was more like a 'reason of princes'. Machiavelli's advice was geared towards the prince maintaining his grip on the state; Michel Foucault (2007: 243) puts it more precisely: 'What Machiavelli sought to save, to safeguard, is not the state but the relationship of the Prince to that over which he exercises his dominion'. But the Florentine secretary was nonetheless an important 'precursor of the *raison d'état* writers' (Tuck, 1993: xii). Over the next century, reason of princes would evolve into a fully developed reason of state, where rulers were advised to adopt new knowledges and rationalities specifically for preserving the state itself, rather than the prince and his rule.

Beyond Machiavelli: responding to religious war

An important development of Machiavelli's reason of princes was the emergence late in the sixteenth century of a new form of humanism, according to Tuck (1993: ch. 3). Inspired more by Tacitus and Seneca than Cicero, and reviving Stoicism and scepticism, thinkers such as Montaigne and Justus Lipsius justified the Machiavellian art of state on the basis of political order. The sixteenth century witnessed the outbreak of bloody confessional conflict across Europe during the Reformation, especially in France, England, the Low Countries, and the Holy Roman Empire (Greengrass, 2014). Luther's intentions may not have been political, but the unintended consequences of his challenge to the Church certainly were (Stollberg-Rilinger, 2018: 61), inflaming conflict between confessionalizing states (Schilling, 2008; de Carvalho, 2014).

In France, religious violence reached a peak with the St. Bartholomew's Day massacre of 1572 which targeted French Calvinists (known as Huguenots) and was said by Protestants to have been orchestrated by Catherine de Medici, mother to the ruling French king, Charles IX. Incidentally, Catherine was daughter of Lorenzo de Medici, Duke of Urbino, to whom Machiavelli dedicated *The Prince*. While there is no surviving evidence that the King or his mother orchestrated the massacre (Holt, 1995: 90), the accusation gained traction because Catherine's surname and nationality had become synonymous with Machiavellian deception and ruthlessness (Jensen, 1978; Sutherland, 1978).

In the context of religious and civil war, the new humanist thinking of Montaigne, Lipsius, and others allowed for rulers to depart from conventional morality and law in the quest for public peace. Montaigne, for example, argued that it was legitimate for a prince to 'break his word and faith under conditions of necessity', invoking a distinction between the morality of ordinary duty and that of 'state matters', which is a 'reason more publike, and more powerfull' (quoted in Tuck, 1993: 56). Similarly, Lipsius legitimized the derogation from conventional laws and morality when political circumstances made it necessary, allowing for the prince to '*play the fox*, especially if the good and publike profit' require it (quoted in Tuck, 1993: 57). These new humanists 'imbibed and refined Machiavelli's ideas' by drawing upon their wide-ranging erudition in counselling prudence and casuistry in matters of state (Jones, 2015: 229–230; Leira, 2008).

Botero: Counter-Reformation and anti-Machiavellianism

The most significant attempt to systematically elaborate reason of state was written by the Piedmontese ex-Jesuit, Giovanni Botero (1544–1617). After leaving the Society of Jesus in 1580, Botero served as secretary to notable personages, Carlo Borromeo, the archbishop of Milan, and Duke Carlo Emanuele of Savoy, who sent him to Paris as a diplomatic envoy, where he witnessed the French religious wars at first hand. Later, he relocated to the papal court in Rome in the service of Cardinal Federico Borromeo (cousin of Carlo), where the Roman Renaissance continued to flower under the urban development program of Sixtus V. Not unlike Machiavelli, Botero thus enjoyed a proximity to the stuff of politics and international affairs. It was during his time in Rome that Botero enjoyed a period of prolific intellectual output, including a book that would launch the conceptual career of reason of state.

Though not considered to be a political thinker of the first rank, he was, like Machiavelli, something of a pioneer. His book, *Della ragion di Stato* (*The Reason of State*), first published in Venice in 1589, was a major publishing success, passing through multiple editions in several European languages over the following century (Bireley, 2017: xvi). Most significantly, it popularized the phrase 'reason of state' by introducing further modification to the 'mirror for princes' genre of which it was an outgrowth. An even greater publishing success was Botero's *Relazioni Universali* (*Universal Relations*), which appeared in four parts between 1591 and 1596 (Bireley, 2017: xviii). This 'compendium of contemporary knowledge about the known world', as Bireley (2017: xix) puts it, was written at the instigation of Cardinal Federico Borromeo who called for better information about the state of the world, both Christian Europe and beyond. '*Relazioni*' in this context refers to situation reports or overviews of other countries, a mix of geography, demography, and political analysis. The English translation of the full title gives a good idea of the book's content: *Relations of the Most Famous Kingdomes and Common-wealths thorowout the World: Discoursing of their Situations, Religions, Languages, Manners, Customes, Strengths, Greatnesse and Policies* (1630). What this suggests is that Botero recognized how vital it was to collect and to update knowledge of the surrounding political landscape for those engaged in politics. Situations change, and states had to keep up with these changes if their policies were to be successful. This recognition was already present in his *The Reason of State* which advised rulers on the kinds of knowledge needed to govern effectively.

Before elaborating Botero's argument in *The Reason of State,* it is important to outline the political and intellectual contexts to which it forms a response. Europe had experienced convulsive political change. Foremost were the effects of the Reformation that reverberated across Europe, challenging the authority of the papacy and the Catholic Church and triggering murderous confessional conflict and political upheaval. Relatedly, the dynamics of state-building, led by ambitious and glory-seeking rulers, began transforming the political structures and improving the administrative capacities of European states (see also de Carvalho, 2021). Third, global expansion not only brought Europe into connection with the non-European worlds across the oceans, Europe's imperial powers acquired vast territories and generated access to new resources and wealth, thus enabling state-building efforts (see also Caraccioli, 2021). Intellectual changes occurred alongside these political ones. Towards the end of the sixteenth century, the Renaissance gave rise to the aforementioned 'new humanism' (Tuck, 1993: chs. 2, 3), exemplified by the publication of Lipsius's *On Constancy* (1584) and *Six Books of Politics* (1589), and Montaigne's *Essays* (1580–1588). The changed intellectual and geopolitical context compelled states to reform the arts of government and statecraft and to rethink the form of political reason that served them.

Acknowledging the need for reform, Botero's intention with *The Reason of State* was to demonstrate that effective and good government could adhere to Catholic doctrine despite the apparent prevalence of Machiavellian statecraft across Europe. Like Machiavelli, he adapted the 'mirror for princes' genre to his purposes; but his declared intention was to reject the political reasoning associated with Machiavelli. Indeed, in the 'Dedication' to his *The Reason of State*, Botero named Machiavelli, Tacitus, and Tiberius Caesar as proponents of an intolerable mode of political reasoning. Machiavelli's reason of state, he said, had 'little respect for conscience', while Tiberius 'cloaked his tyranny and cruelty in a most barbarous law of majesty' (Botero, 2017: 1). He shuddered at the 'wicked, tyrannical means' which were being lauded as 'the norm and pattern of the way that states ought to be administered and governed' (Botero, 2017: 2); and he lamented the counsel of 'impious' and 'foolish' men who tell princes 'that heresies have nothing to do with politics' (Botero, 2017: 213). This 'barbarous style of government', he said, 'is so shamelessly opposed to the law of God to the point of saying that some things are licit by reason of state and others by conscience' (Botero, 2017: 2). Botero's aim was to redeem reason of state for a Christian ruler and polity; to bring statecraft under Catholic doctrine by revising the language of politics and political analysis and expanding the knowledge on which government depends (Braun, 2017: 272).

Botero defines what he means by reason of state in the very first sentence of his book. 'The Reason of state', he says (Botero, 2017: 4), 'is knowledge [*notizia*] of the means suitable to found, conserve, and expand dominion'. It should be noted that by expansion Botero does not mean only external enlargement of the state's territory through conquest; he also means the internal 'augmentation' of a state's powers and resources (*forze*), including the 'amplification' of dominion through industry and trade (Keller, 2015: 38), and by 'defending the public good' (Botero, 2017: 213). In the 1596 edition, Botero (2017: 4 fn. 2) added that reason of state 'cannot be reduced to ordinary and common reason'. In other words, it is the reason specific to statecraft, whether the founding, conserving, or expanding of states. After grading powers according to their size (large, small, and, most optimal, middle-sized), Botero (2017: chs. 9–11) discusses a conventional topic of 'mirror for princes' literature: the requisite virtues of a prince. Steering clear of Machiavelli's flipping of conventional moral virtues by prizing justice, liberality, and other virtues aimed at the benefit of others, Botero (2017: 17–18) nonetheless agrees with the Florentine that a prince must also possess two essential virtues of the military and political arts: prudence and valour.

Regarding prudence, Botero insists that it is crucial that a ruler acquires the kind of knowledge that moral philosophers and those schooled in the art of politics (the '*politici*') are concerned with. 'Moral philosophy', he says, 'communicates knowledge of the common passions', while politics ('*la politica*') teaches how to temper or support those passions in pursuit of good government (Botero, 2017: 34). Ideally, the prince will also be knowledgeable about the arts of peace and war, but if not, he should take counsel from those who are (Botero, 2017: 34–35). Indeed, Botero (2017: 36) advises that the ruler should retain the services of experts in a range of professions, including mathematics, philosophy, the military, and rhetoric. These experts provide knowledge and counsel that 'sharpens' a ruler's prudence in decision-making. In addition to the expert counsel of these professionals, Botero (2017: 36) asserts the importance of experience, acquired directly or indirectly by reading histories and by considering the reports of ambassadors, soldiers, spies, merchants, and others experienced in affairs of state and commerce.

One of Botero's key insights that would spawn a related form of political analysis was the term 'interest'. In his discussion of prudence, Botero compiled a list of maxims in the style of Guicciardini's *Ricordi* (1965), beginning with the statement, which he believed should be taken as given, 'that in the deliberation of princes interest overcomes every other consideration' (Botero, 2017: 41). In a ruler's consideration of alliances and treaties, commitments should only be 'based on interest', Botero (2017: 41) pronounced. In a later addition, Botero equated interest with reason of state: 'reason of state is little else than reason of interest' (quoted in Malcolm, 2007: 94). By the middle of the seventeenth century, the concept of interest had achieved wide currency in European political thought. It provided an influential idiom with which counsellors, whether public officials or aspiring members of the public, could analyse the present domestic or international situation and offer policy advice to governments (Gunn, 1968; Walter, 2015). Duc de Rohan's *Treatise of the Interest of the Princes and States of Christendome* (1641: 1), which opened with the pithy statement that 'Princes command the people, and interest commands the prince', was a major intervention in advancing what Ryan Walter calls 'interest analysis'. With the proliferation of interest analysis, the crucial point was to distinguish between 'true' and 'false' interest, or as Samuel Pufendorf (2013: 7–8) put it in his contribution to the genre, between 'real' and 'imaginary' and between 'perpetual' and 'temporary' interests. While self-preservation was the fundamental ground of a state's interest, the counsellor to government must calculate how the growth in another state's power and wealth or how shifts in the balance of power impact on a state's foreign policy (Devetak, 2013: 127–131). This required extensive analysis of the present state of the European states-system.

Botero's analysis of reason of state marked an important modification to the 'mirror for princes' literature by arguing that statecraft required good counsel based on an extensive range of knowledges. His emphasis on prudence and interest influenced a raft of new humanist writings that, in different ways, legitimated the state-building enterprises of both small territorial city-republics and large kingdoms and empires, both Protestant and Catholic states. The ends or purposes of government could therefore be delinked from the private faith or interests of the ruler and ascribed to the state as an impersonal entity possessing its own needs and interests and its own forms of reason and morality (Skinner, 1989).

While Botero still tied reason of state to Catholic doctrine, for others writing in the seventeenth century such as Thomas Hobbes and Samuel Pufendorf, reason of state became the *modus vivendi* of a sovereign state accountable to itself only, acting in the interests of its self-preservation and security, and mobilizing the 'forces' of a state's strength in pursuit of the public good. As Ian Hunter (1993/1994: 89) puts it, 'the survival and security of the state itself emerged as the prime directive of political thought and action'. It was in this context that Hobbes and Pufendorf wrote two of the most powerful and influential treatises in defence of the sovereign state in the seventeenth century.

Sovereignty and reason of state: from Hobbes and Pufendorf to the democratic present

Hobbes's *Leviathan* and Pufendorf's (1934) *Law of Nature and Nations* both operated at high levels of abstraction compared to Machiavelli, Guicciardini, and Botero. Despite their differences, all three Italian writers were primarily concerned with the mundane political art of government (Foucault, 1991) and were uninterested in philosophically grounding political power and authority in law. By contrast, Hobbes and Pufendorf set about theorizing the state within their elaborate philosophical architectures of civil science and natural law, respectively. Though several decades separated the Italian Catholic from the English and German Protestants, the violence of civil and religious war persisted, and formed the context to which their legitimations of state sovereignty must be seen as improvised responses. Overcoming the confessional conflicts and civil wars required the establishment of a morally and religiously neutral sovereign authority, they argued. To achieve peace, the sovereign had to deprive conflicting parties of appeals to any authority beyond the state (Koselleck, 1988; see also Bain, 2021). The 'reconstruction of government as a strictly "worldly" management of the state', to use Hunter's (1993/1994) words, necessitated the kind of governmental rationality outlined by Botero, albeit without the Italian's commitment to Counter-Reformation Catholic politics.

To govern effectively and to meet the challenges of statecraft, the sovereign would need to develop reason of state. In a passage worth quoting at length in *Leviathan*'s chapter 'Of Counsell', Hobbes (1968: 307–308) says:

> For seeing the business of a commonwealth is this, to preserve the people in peace at home, and defend them against foreign invasion, we shall find, it requires great knowledge of the disposition of mankind, of the rights of government, and of the nature of equity, law, justice, and honour, not to be attained without study; and of the strength, commodities, places, both of their own country, and their neighbours; as also of the inclinations, and designs of all nations that may any way annoy them.

The forms of knowledge required to rule effectively, says Hobbes, includes not only the kind derived from natural law ('the disposition of Man-kind', 'the Rights of Government', and 'the nature of Equity, Law, Justice, and Honour'), but also from interest analysis (of the 'strength' and 'designs' of one's own and other states). Hobbes (1968: 308) goes on to say that in respect of a state's relations with other states, '*It is necessary to be acquainted with the Intelligences, and Letters* that come from thence, *and with all the records or Treaties, and other transactions of State* between them' (emphasis in original). Hobbes is here alluding to the importance of diplomatic knowledge acquired through the correspondence of ambassadors, envoys, spies, and merchants for reason of state. Hobbes is pointing out here that a good understanding of the international environment and up-to-date information of politics and events abroad are vital to reason of state.

While Pufendorf is best known for his abstract treatises on natural law, he also made major contributions to more concrete historical studies of the European states-system in his *The Present State of Germany* (1667/2007) and *Introduction to the History of the Principal Kingdoms and States of Europe* (1682). Botero's *Universal Relations* pioneered a genre that was taken up by Pufendorf and many other writers such as Rohan and Slingsby Bethel (Devetak, 2015). The purpose of these writings was to provide a usable account of the present state of Europe or the world; a compendium of knowledge and information based on situation reports of individuals states that could assist governments in policymaking. When governments achieved an accurate understanding of the geopolitical context and analysed the interests of rival and neighbouring states, they would be better positioned to determine their own interests and craft more effective policies. In other words, reason of state demanded of sovereigns that they absorb information and intelligence offered by wise and experienced counsellors with expertise in a range of different knowledge areas.

This is a view that has continued into the twentieth and twenty-first centuries with thinkers from Max Weber to Henry Kissinger. But it is a view that leaves the tension between reason of state and universal principles such as justice or democracy unresolved. For liberal and social democratic states in which democratic will-formation is taken to be the vital source of modern political legitimacy, reason of state may be perceived as undemocratic and unconcerned with justice. Whilst there is no doubt that reason of state is not in itself a democratic or just ground, it has historically grounded the security and sovereignty of liberal and social democratic states and their pursuit of justice. Given the global prominence of democracy and justice, how reason of state can be reconciled with justice and democracy in different national and international contexts is a topic requiring further historical and empirical research from both political theorists and international intellectual historians. But at present IR scholars seem reluctant even to examine reason of state.

Conclusion

Early in the seventeenth century, the political advisor and writer, Ludovico Zuccolo (1930: 25) could complain that 'not only the counsellors in the courts and doctors in the schools, but barbers and other base artisans in the shops and meeting-places discuss and debate reason of state and believe they know which things are done for reasons of state and which are not'. By the late seventeenth century in England, authors could quip that 'from the Lord to the fiddler, all are grown states-men' (Anonymous, 1680: 1). In other words, the seventeenth century gave rise to the assumption that everyone could reason like a statesman. Reason of state was no longer a secret or mystery confined to the corridors of state power; it was a concept which the public, as much as statesmen and public officials, could use to discuss matters of politics. But, as Botero made clear, reason of state could not be reduced to common forms of reason or morality. It is unique to the political sphere.

In the twentieth century, Max Weber (1948) would reiterate this point, albeit in a more secular register, affirming that politics creates its own forms of reason and morality distinct from other life spheres (Hunter, 1993/1994). Meinecke (1957: 6) too treated reason of state as a distinct sphere of ethical life in which the statesman's 'moral accomplishment' is to make 'an altruistic self-sacrifice in the service of a higher task'. In other words, recalling Weber's differentiated life spheres, he sees the state as an end in itself and possessing its own legitimate form of political morality, namely, reason of state. Beyond demanding 'a high degree of rationality and expediency', Meinecke (1957: 6) recognized that reason of state also required of the public official or statesman that they cultivate a specific ethical comportment. The 'statesman', he says, 'should educate and form himself culturally'. Consistent with the Stoic thinking of Lipsius, this involves 'suppress[ing] his emotions and his personal inclinations' as so as 'to ascertain the practical interests of the State' (Meinecke, 1957: 6).

Like any important term of political discourse, reason of state has always been vigorously contested. It remains the object of moral opprobrium to those committed to universal moral truths and principles and a single unified moral world. But to those who accept the world's division into historically instituted life spheres, it is important to acknowledge ethical plurality. From the latter perspective, reason of state is not a degenerate form of political thinking in which the ends justify the ends. It is the form of reason and attendant morality that has grown out of the modern states-system. With the advent of reason of state, the state became an end in itself and the object of specialized forms of knowledge. An important ethical consequence was that the state could be said to possess its own legitimacy and its own forms of reason and morality, neither of which required the non-political validation of philosophy or religion. As one historian reflected, 'In the long run the emancipation of political action from moral restraint can be considered of at least equal importance with the struggle of liberty against authority' (Mosse, 1968: 4).

Suggestions for further reading

Borrelli, G. (2017). *Machiavelli, Ragion di Stato, Polizia Cristiana: Genealogie 1.* Napoli: Edizione Cronopio.

Condren, C. (2011). Reason of state and sovereignty in early modern England: a question of ideology? *Parergon*, 28 (2), 5–27.

Church, W. (1972). *Richelieu and Reason of State.* Princeton, NJ: Princeton University Press.

Curtis, C. (2011). Advising monarchs and their counsellors: Juan Luis Vives on the emotions, civil life, and international relations. *Parergon*, 28 (2), 29–53.

Donaldson, P. (1988). *Machiavelli and Mystery of State.* Cambridge: Cambridge University Press.

Dreitzel, H. (2002). Reason of state and the crisis of political aristotelianism: an essay on the development of seventeenth-century political philosophy. *History of European Ideas*, 28 (3), 163–187.

Keller, V. (2012). Mining Tacitus: secrets of empire, nature and art in the reason of state. *British Society for the History of Science*, 45 (2), 189–212.

von Friedeburg, R. (2016). *Luther's Legacy: The Thirty Years War and the Modern Notion of 'State' in the Empire, 1530s to 1790s,* Oxford: Oxford University Press.

Zarka, Y. C., ed. (1994). *Raison et Déraison d'Etat: Théoreticiens et théories de la raison d'Etat aux XVIᵉ et XVIIᵉ Siécles.* Paris: Presses Universitaires de France.

References

Andersen, M. A., and Wohlforth, W. C. (2021). Balance of power: a key concept in historical perspective. In de Carvalho, B., Costa Lopez, J., & Leira, H., eds. *Routledge Handbook of Historical International Relations.* Abingdon: Routledge.

Anonymous. (1680). Crackfart and Tony; or The Knave and the Fool: in a Dialogue over a Dish of Coffee. London: s.n.

Ashworth, L. (2014). *A History of International Thought: From the Origins of the Modern State to Academic International Relations.* London: Routledge.

Bain, W. (2021). Political Theology and Historical International Relations. In de Carvalho, B., Costa Lopez, J., & Leira, H., eds. *Routledge Handbook of Historical International Relations.* Abingdon: Routledge.

Bell, D. (2010). Political Realism and the Limits of Ethics. In: D. Bell, ed., *Ethics and World Politics.* Oxford: Oxford University Press, 93–110.

Bireley, R. (2017). Introduction. In: Botero, ed., *The Reason of State.* Translated and edited by R. Bireley, Cambridge: Cambridge University Press.

Bobbio, N. (2000). *In Praise of Meekness: Essays on Ethics and Politics.* Translated by T. Chataway. Cambridge: Polity Press.

Botero, G. (2017). *The Reason of State.* Translated and edited by R. Bireley. Cambridge: Cambridge University Press.

Braun, H. (2017). Knowledge and counsel in Giovanni Botero's ragion di stato. *Journal of Jesuit Studies*, 4 (2), 270–289.

Burke, P. (1991). Tacitism, scepticism, and reason of state. In: J. H. Burns, and M. Goldie, eds., *The Cambridge History of Political Thought, 1450-1700,* Cambridge: Cambridge University Press, 479–498.

Caraccioli, M. J. (2021). Early (Modern) Empires: The Political Ideology of Conceptual Domination. In de Carvalho, B., Costa Lopez, J., & Leira, H., eds. *Routledge Handbook of Historical International Relations.* Abingdon: Routledge.

Croce, B. (1946). *Politics and Morals.* Translated by S. J. Castiglione. London: George Allen and Unwin.

de Carvalho, B. (2014). The confessional state in international politics: Tudor England, religion, and the eclipse of dynasticism. *Diplomacy and Statecraft*, 25 (3), 407–431.

de Carvalho, B. (2021). Sovereignty, the State and the International System. In de Carvalho, B., Costa Lopez, J., & Leira, H., eds. *Routledge Handbook of Historical International Relations.* Abingdon: Routledge.

Devetak, R. (2013). 'The Fear of Universal Monarchy': Balance of Power as an Ordering Practice of Liberty. In: T. Dunne, and T. Flockhart, eds., *Liberal World Orders*, Oxford: Oxford University Press.

Devetak, R. (2015). Historiographical foundations of modern international thought: histories of the European states-system from Florence to Göttingen. *History of European Ideas*, 41 (1), 62–77.

Foucault, M. (1991). Governmentality. Translated by R. Braidotti. Revised by C. Gordon. In: G. Burchell, C. Gordon, and P. Miller, eds., *The Foucault Effect: Studies in Governmentality*, London: Harvester Wheatsheaf, 87–104.

Foucault, M. (2007). *Security, Territory, Population: Lectures at the Collège de France, 1977-1978.* Edited by M. Senellart. Translated by G. Burchell. Houndmills: Palgrave Macmillan.

Greengrass, M. (2014). *Christendom Destroyed: Europe 1517-1648.* London: Penguin.

Guicciardini, F. (1965). *Maxims and Reflections of a Renaissance Statesman (Ricordi).* Edited by N. Rubinstein. Translated by M. Domandi. New York, NY: Harper and Row.

Gunn, J. A. W. (1968). 'Interest will not lie': a seventeenth century political Maxim. *Journal of the History of Ideas*, 29 (4), 551–564.

Hobbes, T. (1968). *Leviathan.* Edited by C. B. MacPherson. Harmondsworth: Penguin.

Holt, M. P. (1995). *The French Wars of Religion, 1562-1629.* Cambridge: Cambridge University Press.

Höpfl, H. (2004). *Jesuit Political Thought: The Society of Jesus and the State, c. 1540-1630.* Cambridge: Cambridge University Press.

Hunter, I. (1993/1994). Bureaucra, critic, citizen: on some styles of ethical life. *Arena Journal*, 2 (1), 77–101.

Jensen, D. L. (1978). Catherine de Medici and her Florentine friends. *Sixteenth Century Journal*, 9 (2), 57–74.

Jones, D. M. (2015). Reason, statecraft and the art of war: a politique reassessment. *Global Discourse*, 5 (2), 225–235.

Keene, E. (2005). *International Political Thought: A Historical Introduction.* Cambridge: Polity.

Keller, V. (2015). *Knowledge and the Public Interest, 1575-1725.* Cambridge: Cambridge University Press.

Kissinger, H. (1994). *Diplomacy.* New York, NY: Touchstone.

Koselleck, R. (1988). *Critique and Crisis: Enlightenment and the Pathogenesis of Modern Society.* Cambridge, MA: MIT Press.

Larson, D (2021). Realism: Excavating a Historical Tradition. In de Carvalho, B., Costa Lopez, J., & Leira, H., eds. *Routledge Handbook of Historical International Relations.* Abingdon: Routledge.

Leira, H. (2008). Justus Lipsius, political humanism and the disciplining of 17th century statecraft. *Review of International Studies*, 34 (4), 669–692.

Machiavelli, N. (1988). *Florentine Histories.* Translated by L. F. Banfield, and H. C. Mansfield, Jr., Princeton, NJ: Princeton University Press.

Machiavelli, N. (2005). *The Prince.* Translated and edited by P. Bondanella. Oxford: Oxford University Press.

Malcolm, N. (2007). *Reason of State, Propaganda, and the Thirty Years' War: An Unknown Translation by Thomas Hobbes.* Oxford: Clarendon Press.

Meinecke, F. (1957). *Machiavellism: The Doctrine of Raison d'ètat and Its Place in Modern History.* Translated by D. Scott. London: Routledge and Kegan Paul.

Miller, J. D. B. (1979). Morality, Interests and Rationalisation. In: R. Pettman, ed., *Moral Claims in World Affairs*, Canberra: ANU Press, 36–51.

Mosse, G. L. (1968). *The Holy Pretence: A Study in Christianity and Reason of State from William Perkins to John Winthrop.* New York, NY: Howard Fertig.

Nardin, T. (1992). Ethical Traditions in International Affairs. In: T. Nardin, ed., *Traditions of International Ethics*, Cambridge: Cambridge University Press, 1–18.

Petrina, A. (2016). *Machiavelli in the British Isles: Two Early Modern Translations of The Prince.* London: Routledge.

Pufendorf, S. (1934). *Of the Law of Nature and Nations.* Translated by C. H. Oldfather, and W. A. Oldfather. Oxford: Clarendon Press.

Pufendorf, S. (1667/2007). *Present State of Germany.* Translated by E. Bohun. Edited by M. J. Seidler. Indianapolis, IN: Liberty Books.

Pufendorf, S. (2013). *An Introduction to the History of the Principal Kingdoms and States of Europe.* Translated by J. Crull. Edited by M. J. Seidler. Indianapolis, IN: Liberty Books.

Schilling, H. (2008). *Early Modern European Civilization and its Political and Cultural Dynamism.* Lebanon, NH: University Press of New England.

Skinner, Q. (1978). *The Foundations of Modern Political Thought. Volume One: The Renaissance*. Cambridge: Cambridge University Press.

Skinner, Q. (1989). The State. In: T. Ball, J. Farr, and R. Hanson, eds., *Political Innovation and Conceptual Change*, Cambridge: Cambridge University Press, 90–131.

Stollberg-Rilinger, B. (2018). *A Short History of the Holy Roman Empire*. Translated by Y. Mintzker. Princeton, NJ: Princeton University Press.

Sutherland, N. M. (1978). Catherine de Medici: the legend of the Wicked Italian Queen. *Sixteenth Century Journal*, 9 (2), 45–56.

Tuck, R. (1993). *Philosophy and Government, 1572-1651*. Cambridge: Cambridge University Press.

Vagts, A. (1970). 'Reason of state' in America. *Jahrbuch für Amerikastudien*, 15, 237–244.

Vincent, R. J. (1982). Realpolitik. In: J. Mayall, ed., *The Community of States: A Study in International Political Theory*, London: Routledge, 73–84.

Vincent, R. J. (1986). *Human Rights and International Relations*. Cambridge: Cambridge University Press.

Viroli, M. (1992). *From Politics to Reason of State: The Acquisition and Transformation of the Language of Politics, 1250-1600*. Cambridge: Cambridge University Press.

Walter, R. (2015). Slingsby Bethel's analysis of state interests. *History of European Ideas*, 41 (4), 489–506.

Weber, M. (1948). Politics as a Vocation. In: *From Max Weber: Essays in Sociology*. Translated and edited by H. H. Gerth, and C. Wright Mills, London: Routledge, 77–128.

Zuccolo, L. (1930). Della Ragione di Stato (1621). In: B. Croce, and S. Caramella, eds., *Politici e Moralisti del Seicento*, Bari: Laterza e Figli, 25–41.

27

BALANCE OF POWER

A key concept in historical perspective

Morten Skumsrud Andersen and William C. Wohlforth

The balance of power is arguably the best known theoretical concept in the study and practice of international politics. Michael Sheehan labels it 'one of the most important concepts in history' (1996: 1). 21st century leaders like Vladimir Putin and Xi Jinping are almost as prone to describe their countries' policies in balance-of-power terms as were their 18th or 19th century predecessors. Analysts and journalists, too, are as reliant on the concept as ever. And the idea is still central in academic theory and research. 'No other single proposition about international politics', Brooks and Wohlforth write, 'has attracted more scholarly effort than the balance of power. It is perhaps as central in today's thinking as it has been at any time since the Enlightenment' (2008: 7; see also Larson, 2021). As Stephen Walt (2017) quipped, 'If you took an introduction to international relations course in college and the instructor never mentioned the "balance of power," please contact your alma mater for a refund'.

But precious few who deploy the balance of power idea know much of its historical development or are aware of the extraordinary variation in its use by both political actors and intellectuals. Scholars and analysts routinely invoke the idea's pedigree as a certification of its universality and undisputable importance, but few interrogate that history to see what lessons it really holds for the balance of power.

In this chapter, we rectify this oversight and explore the implications of doing so for International Relations (IR) scholarship. We present compact accounts of the concept's history and its role in IR theory that will benefit any student of international politics who wants to get up to speed on the historical idea and practice of the balance of power. We then review the results of scholars' efforts to evaluate the essential balance-of-power proposition against historical evidence. This periodic search for historical evidence of the workings of the balance of power represented a key area of overlap between history and IR. And although this engagement between IR and history was contentious at times (e.g. Schroeder, 1994; Elman et al., 1995), it nonetheless yielded important insights—though not the ones aficionados of the concept were hoping to find.

We contend that the balance of power is not a universal empirical law, that it does not merit explanatory precedence, and we criticize the common practice of framing research questions around the failure of international systems to conform to the expected norms of balancing. It follows that neither the way the concept itself has been *used* throughout history nor the effectiveness of the concept in *explaining* historical events and developments can justify the way the balance of power has been applied in IR. That raises a question that we tackle next: why do analysts continue to use the balance of power despite its shortcomings? We argue that it has survived because it has been extremely *useful* for a range of different purposes beyond its core propositions—it has consistently and successfully been linked to other political issues across time and place. In short, the balance of power has never been only about the 'balance of power'.

The implication is that there are several historical and theoretical issues that are not currently a part of the debates about the balance of power but should be. We conclude by arguing that scholars should not abandon balance-of-power theory, but expand it by rethinking some realist assumptions, incorporating other theoretical traditions and methodologies, and investigating more thoroughly how the balance of power is used in practical politics.

The balance of power through time

The balance of power's appeal owes much to its pedigree. For at least the past four centuries, politicians, diplomats, and writers have deployed the concept to argue, debate, and formulate foreign policy and diplomatic doctrines. Many thinkers detect balance of power logic in sources long predating the European states system itself, from the Athenian historian Thucydides' account of the Peloponnesian War from 431 BCE to the Hindu statesman and philosopher Kauṭilya's classic treatise on the art of politics, *Arthashastra*, in roughly 300 BCE. Many more see it as central to Machiavelli's account of the relations of strength between the Italian city-states in the 1400s, and in Guicciardini's *History of Italy* (see also Devetak, 2021). In 1742, David Hume argued that the principle of the balance of power 'is founded so much on common sense and obvious reasoning, that it is impossible it could altogether have escaped antiquity' (Hume, 1987 (1742): 337).

This gives rise to the sense that the balance of power idea captures essential, timeless features of any political system comprising relatively autonomous territorially based polities. The historian Leopold von Ranke proposed that the balance of power is 'the principle in modern history which weaves otherwise unintelligibly divergent strands into an understandable whole'—'the principle which gives unity to the political plot of European history' (quoted in Haas, 1953: 442–443). Later, Hans Morgenthau argued that it was the 'repetitive character of international politics, that is, the configurations of the balance of power, that lends itself to theoretical systematization' (2000 (1970): 45). Further, the history of the IR discipline shows that much of the inspiration for developing balance of power theory came from the doctrines of political leaders and diplomats in the past. Present-day balance of power theory therefore has an intimate connection to both history and political practice. Realism has been the main exponent of balance of power thinking, and a core feature of realist thought is precisely that some fundamental mechanisms of international politics remain valid across centuries. Because the balance of power is assumed to be universalistic, and because it has been deployed by political actors for centuries, scholars often summon historical examples where the balance of power has worked to avoid hegemony to illustrate the explanatory force of the concept.

Though the idea of balancing may have been around for a long time, it was not until the latter half of the 17th century—as the European states system was consolidating—that it was established as a frequently used political concept. This was also the period when the mediaeval and Christian idea of a 'universal monarchy' ruling all the world—or at least the polities of Europe—was losing its positive connotations (Pagden, 1995). As organizing communities increasingly came to be considered a human and not heavenly task, state expansion and European hegemony came to be feared. Here, the balance of power concept was fighting on the frontlines; if one could establish or maintain balance, a universal monarchy could be prevented. This would mean peace for Europe, and peace within individual states. The balance of power thus came to be considered one of the institutions of the European states system.

The balance of power was considered a conscious strategy to organize political communities and their relations. This was due to the emerging concept of *interest*. We find one of the first consistent uses of the term 'interest' in one of the early, important publications on the balance of power in Europe. Henri duc de Rohan (1638) there argues that instead of following irrational passions and the advice of unreliable councillors, parties should pursue their goals as defined by the objective requirements of interest and the maintenance of the European balance of power. Consequently, the common view, and demand, was that the interest of rulers should not be private, but express the interest of the people—later of the nation. A working balance of power, then, relied on discovering and following the true interest of the various states.

The 18th and 19th century balance of power logics were also linked to arguments concerning the standards of civilization. Reason and civilization were often considered a requirement for a properly functioning balance, where a state's interests were discovered and acted upon, whilst at the same time taking other states' interests into account. This would also require a certain restraint by the actors involved in the balancing effort, a restraint possible only in states led by reason, not passions, ambition, and private interests. The states of India, for instance, were judged to be incapable of any balance of power because of their lack of reason and their savage dispositions: a balance of power was not 'compatible with the character, principles and constitutions' of the Indian states (Parliament of Great Britain, 1833: 245), where 'war, rapine and conquest' were considered legitimate pursuits, 'prosecuted…with a savage disregard of every obligation of humanity and public faith' (ibid.: 370). India lacked the 'just and moderate principles' of the 'Christian states that constitute the Commonwealth of Europe' (ibid.: 320).

The balance of power was about hierarchy also as far as it relied on the 'great powers' of Europe. A corollary was that there existed regional sub-balances in Europe in addition to the overall balance of power. For instance, in the 18th century European states system, Britain, Spain, or France were centrally important powers 'in the very midst of this system' (Bolingbroke, 1932 (1735): 56), whilst Austria or Sweden were less central players. These states were placed in a hierarchy according to their importance for European politics and balance of power dynamics, later formalized during the Congress system of 1815–1822 when the great powers were holding the reins of the European, hierarchical system. Furthermore, states on the fringes of Europe, like Turkey, the Balkans, or other 'oriental' states, whilst occasionally considered relevant, were not included into the European balance of power. In sum, the balance of power concept was used to distinguish between and stratify the different polities that made up the European order, and was also used to distinguish between the inside and outside of Europe itself.

For most part of the 18th century, it was Britain that invoked the balance-of-power concept the most in its diplomacy. Britain considered itself an indispensable 'balancer' in the European states system. To maintain balance, one should aid the weak against the strong, and Britain conceived of itself as the country that could tip the scales in any one direction, as it saw fit. The role of the balancer, it was argued both in Britain and abroad, gave Britain unprecedented power—not only as a Great Power in Europe, but also as the decisive weight in the scale. It was Britain's duty to assure that no one could become a 'universal monarch', ruling the entire continent. Britain protected Europe and thereby protected itself, by means of the balance of power.

However, opposition to—and scepticism concerning—the balance of power concept also has a long pedigree. Increasingly in the 18th century, German lawyers started criticizing the balance of power for being merely propaganda and a politically convenient pretext for partisan actions. Loathing historical generalizations and universalistic concepts, these authors, and increasingly many with them, returned to the concept of particular state interests instead of the abstract and systemic concerns with the balance.

One of the most vocal critics of the balance of power was the German scholar Gottlob von Justi. No power has ever acted on the balance-of-power principle, he argued, as 'they have only used this theoretical system to gain allies, and to hide their particular interest and their passions that lead them to war'. The balance of power has camouflaged self-interests and the 'real motives' of states and diplomats (von Justi, 1758: 116). The balance of power has been driven by envy and fear, Justi argued, not by altruism or a concern for the common interest of Europe. It has been a cause of war, not the remedy. Following in Justi's footsteps, a later liberal critic, Richard Cobden, criticized the balance of power for being the treacherous dealings of princes and governments. In the 1830s, attacking the British foreign secretary Lord Palmerston's traditional ideas of Britain as a 'holder of the balance', he termed the balance of power 'not a fallacy, a mistake, an imposture—it is an undescribed, indescribable, incomprehensible nothing' (Cobden, 1867 (1836): 257–258).

The balance of power was not discarded because of these attacks, but increasingly became associated with protecting the independence of states: the common interest of Europe became less important than the role of the balance of power in protecting state interests and national positions. This prepared the ground for a new round of criticism: the balance of power came to be associated with a world of deceitful and secret diplomacy amongst state elites. Liberals considered the lack of transparency a leading cause of war—decisions were taken behind closed doors, and there was no accountability for the diplomats and politicians only following their own interests.

Richard Cobden considered the United States an ideal in this respect: 'America, with infinite wisdom, refuses to be a party to the "balance of power"' (Cobden, 1867 (1836): 280). Indeed, a century later, after US president James Monroe had proclaimed his 'Monroe Doctrine' in 1823, claiming the American continent as the exclusive domain of US foreign policy and urging US withdrawal from European affairs, the country defined its moral purpose in opposition to the balance of power. President Woodrow Wilson disputed the moral value and practical viability of the balance of power, associating it with the destructive power politics of the 'old world'. Wilson argued that the balance of power must be replaced by a 'community of power'—a league of nations.

After two World Wars, and as the Cold War set on, some held that the balance had become irrelevant because of nuclear weapons. Others defended the old lessons from European diplomacy, and the concept of the balance of power, which now once again became more widely accepted, also in the United States. Hans Morgenthau argued that nuclear policy was not a foreign policy tool, but a means of ensuring that the national interest can be supported by traditional means. Nuclear policy is a background condition that must be managed through cooperation, where peace and stability are the goal. The balance of power is not obsolete, he maintained: it operates, day to day, in the shadow of nuclear policy—which is a different matter entirely (Morgenthau, 1969: 207–209).

The balance of power as academic theory

In the Cold War, the balance-of-power principle, as developed by generations of diplomats in Europe, was introduced to the United States in the context of a search for a comprehensive theory of international politics. US academics took the practices of European diplomats as their cue to develop the theory we now know as Realism in IR—the argument initially being that the real-world practice of diplomats should be the ultimate reality test for any theory (Guzzini, 2004: 546). Traditional diplomatic practices had to be systematized and made readily available for some sort of theoretical and scientific generalization, and the balance-of-power principle was seen as ideal for that purpose (see also Leira, 2021).

This spurred an array of writings on the implications of the concept, debating such issues as whether it promotes peace or war, whether it is European or also extra-European, whether there is only one balance or many sub-balances, the connexions between balancing and deterrence, the balance of power as a mechanical-structural system or as intentional foreign policy prescription, whether it guarantees the independence of all states or only of the 'great powers', to mention only some. Although primarily associated with realism in IR, the concept is discussed in other approaches as well. For instance, Richard Little (2007) investigates the balance of power as 'metaphor, myth and model' from an English School perspective, whilst Stacie Goddard (2009) connects the balance-of-power concept to a constructivist theory of legitimation and rhetorical coercion. Also, international historians of various leanings have discussed the concept.

Others have lamented the state of balance-of-power theory. One problem often stressed is that the concept 'has too many meanings' (Sheehan, 1996: 2) and is 'vague' (Claude, 1989). The early writings on the balance of power had 'considerable defects', since they failed to distinguish between the different meanings of the concept. There was little 'logical coherence' or 'analytical acuteness' (Anderson, 1993: 150); 'very often it was no more than a phrase used to inhibit thought. Frequently appealed to, it was seldom analysed in real depth or formulated with genuine rigour' (Anderson in Black, 1983: 55). Paul Schroeder laments 'the ambiguous nature of the concept and the numerous ways it has been defined, the various distinct and partly contradictory meanings given to it in practice and the divergent purposes it serves [...] and the apparent failure of attempts to define balance of power as a system and specify its operating rules' (1989: 135).

As we argue below, this ambiguity and diversity of meanings are not necessarily a defect, but is inherent to any widely deployed and disseminated concept. For now, the key point is that, despite all the vagueness and heterogeneity of the concept, the typical analytical move in the literature is to acknowledge the various meanings and uses, while trying to find a 'core meaning', or a 'central proposition' of the concept.

One such core set of assumptions of balance of power theory is that power-maximizing, territorial states interact rationally in a system of anarchy. The prime goal of any such state is the survival of the political unit. The main threat to the state's survival would be hegemony—a concentration of power large enough for one actor to influence, coerce, invade, or extinguish other states at will. Such a degree of domination could even do away with the very system of independent states, as the other states in the system combined would not be able to balance the power of the hegemon. Given this existential threat, a central prediction of balance of power theory is that the higher the probability of hegemony, the larger the inclination of states (or at least great powers) to balance (Wohlforth, 2004: 215). Therefore, it predicts that hegemonies do not arise in multistate systems, as balancing coalitions will emerge to prevent it: the balance of power is taken to be a mechanism that makes states redouble their internal efforts to generate power and join the weaker part against the strong, to balance the distribution of power amongst states in the international system. The balance of power is constantly assessed to find out whether realignments might be necessary because of emerging or shifting threats and new developments within or between states in the system.

From this vantage point, balancing would be the dominant strategy for any rationally led state when hegemony is in the offing. Most often, however, such connotations to rational calculation and intention in balancing, are not at the core of balance of power theory. Rather, as in the workings of an 'invisible hand', the rational actions of states within a system, perpetually threatened by the possibility of hegemony, when added up result in a balance—be it intentional or not. The system of states, then, is an unintended consequence of states acting to defend their own interests under the constraints of anarchy (Levy, 2004: 32).

Contemporary debates over the balance of power as a concept often involve attempts at improving or amending the concept by introducing notions of 'soft balancing', or associated explanations like 'bandwagoning', 'buckpassing', or 'hegemonic transition' (Organski, 1968; Wright, 1983 (1942); Walt, 1987; Christensen and Snyder, 1990), particularly as concerns rising powers and the failure of states to gang up against US hegemony. This concept is therefore used by scholars to analyse the implications of shifting distributions of power across the state system— it is one of our *theories* of international politics.

Systemic balance-of-power theory and historical evidence

The oft-cited connection between balance of power theory and the political practice of state leaders and diplomats confronts a paradox, however: whilst much academic balance of power theory is inspired by and premised upon the historical practices of diplomats and politicians, these actors would often be the first to question the universality of the balance of power. For instance, as against reading the balance of power as a timeless principle of international politics, British Prime Minister Canning, a centrally placed actor indeed, asked:

> is the balance of power a fixed and unalterable standard? Or is it not a standard perpetually varying, as civilization advances, and as new nations spring up, and take their place among established political communities? [...] To look to the policy of Europe, in the times of William and Anne, for the purpose of regulating the balance of power in Europe at the present day, is to disregard the progress of events, and to confuse dates and facts which throw a reciprocal light upon each other (Walsh, 1835: 466).

Does Canning's scepticism about a universal balance of power practice apply to efforts to translate the idea into a universal social science theory of states systems? For decades, scholars vigorously rejected any such scepticism; yet that is indeed the main implication of most recent research. The only way to render the theory generalizable across time is to distil it to its core as a systemic defence against hegemony or the rule by the strong. The balance of power, then, should involve actions affecting the systemic distribution of capabilities that would not have been taken if not for the presence or potential of a hegemonic threat (Wohlforth, 2004: 218). Over the past quarter century, extensive research efforts have yielded three main challenges to such systemic balance of power theory: first, empirical tests of the theory's core propositions fail. Second, the behaviour, priorities, and intentions of states do not match the theory's general assumptions. Third, the most successful recent empirical tests are of more conditional versions of the theory that add on crucial scope conditions. Success for these tests are important, but they essentially add up to refutations of the more universal theory.

Balance of power theory was accepted as a staple of international relations statecraft long before it was ever subjected to careful empirical evaluation. For the wave of empirical studies that eventually appeared, to an important degree, scholars have John Vasquez (1997) to thank. His critical evaluation of realist theory, with the signature claim that it was a 'degenerating research program', sparked a series of debates that helped focus scholars on the challenge of testing the theory (Elman and Elman, 2003). One important implication of that outpouring of empirical research was that the only reliable way to test the systemic version of balance of power theory was over very long spans of history (Wohlforth in Elman and Elman, 2003). Jack Levy's rigorous review of the relevant literature yielded arguably the best formulation of the core proposition of systemic balance-of-power theory: 'hegemonies do not form in multistate systems because perceived threats of hegemony over the system generate balancing behavior by other leading states in the system' (Levy, 2004: 37). This proposition contains two elements: that hegemonies do not form, and that the main reason they do not form is because of the causal mechanisms identified in the theory, namely balancing behaviour by major powers. Neither of these propositions holds up to empirical scrutiny (Kaufman et al., 2007; Wohlforth et al., 2007).

To be sure, in the European international system familiar to so many scholars, hegemony—a condition under which one major power amasses enough capabilities to coerce or otherwise dominate the other major powers—is generally regarded not to have occurred. But in many other interstate systems that meet all the formal requirements of balance of power theory spanning centuries of history, hegemonies routinely formed. There are numerous reasons for this finding, not least of which is the fact that other crucial social science theories such as the theory of collective goods and institutional theory point in directions different than balance of power theory. Over time, balance of power theory's balancing mechanisms only managed to trump those identified in other theories under very specific circumstances, perhaps including those that obtained through key periods of European history, but do not reliably obtain elsewhere. Close inspection, moreover, reveals that in many cases where hegemonies do not form, the reasons do not lie within balance of power theory. Often—and as even Canning alluded to in the quote above—the key factor that prevents systems from falling under the sway of one dominant power is the expansion of the system into new areas and the emergence of new actors previously external to the system. Many other factors played a role in different international systems. The key point is that even to explain cases where hegemony does not occur, it is necessary for scholars to go beyond the core set of assumptions that define systemic balance of power theory.

A second and related challenge is the finding that, overall, the systemic imperative of countering hegemony just does not loom as large in the strategies of great powers as most readings of balance of power theory (and lore) would lead us to expect (see Wohlforth, 2004). Because so many factors besides balancing conspire against hegemony and because states have so many preferences and goals that have nothing to do with the issues of hegemony, the desiderata associated with balance of power theory are often of low salience. In conducting foreign policy, many policymakers act on other long-term threats, such as underdevelopment and poverty, marginalization, or more limited national and regional security threats. Importantly, they do so even when invoking the balance of power in their rhetoric. Even if some countries would certainly prefer a more even distribution of power, they do not seem to be willing to pay the costs of balancing. And concerning 'internal balancing'—the generation of power internally by a state for the purpose of checking hegemony—there are many reasons why states would want economic development, and a more efficient administration and exploitation of their resources other than for checking a potential hegemonic threat. In other words, state agendas are extremely varied, and not universally characterized by a primary focus on the problem of hegemony (Wohlforth, 2004: 233).

The third challenge to systemic balance of power theory comes from comparatively successful empirical tests of more limited theories. By showing that balancing sometimes does indeed figure in explaining the absence of hegemony in some interstate settings, these studies help explain the failure of more universal versions. Jack Levy and William Thompson, for example, report evidence that 'core propositions about balancing strategies and the absence of sustained hegemonies apply to the European system and perhaps to some other autonomous continental systems but not to the global maritime system' (2010: 7). By successfully identifying the conditions under which the core balance-of-power proposition may well work, this research by implication helps to identify all the situations in which it is unlikely to work: namely any system containing non-contiguous great powers, especially those separated by oceans or other barriers to territorial conquest. Given the crucial roles played by such offshore great powers as England/Britain, Japan, and the United States, the consequent limitations on the implications of balance of power theory are profound.

An important implication is the need to clarify what the balance of power is *not*. If balance of power theory is divorced from the concern with hegemony, it becomes a surrogate for security policies writ large. If any defensive move by any state is shoehorned into balance of power terms, the concept simply becomes a synonym for security policy. If the concept is defined too broadly, then all security policy and diplomacy is balancing, and the concept lacks analytical purpose; a theory that seems to apply everywhere, always, is likely of little utility (Wohlforth, 2004: 234). At the same time, analysts need to be careful not to translate all politics having to do with the international system's leading state into balance of power terms. The most powerful state in the system may well elicit a lot of responses from other actors, but not all those actions are truly caused by the concentration of capabilities in the system.

Why the balance of power is so popular

Despite such fundamental challenges to both logic and utility, the balance of power has been and is still a core concept of international politics. Why is this so? One reason is that the theory and practice of the balance of power have never really been only about 'the balance of power' as we know it, but an array of different issues and concerns. In all its manifestations, balance of power theory is indeed general and has a broad scope. That the balance of power is a blurry concept, and difficult to pin down, is repeated in many introductions to the theory. However, the *consequences* of this is not only that hypotheses concerning the balance are difficult to test, that a clear definition is necessary, or that one should identify the core propositions of the theory—it is also that the concept has been extraordinarily *useful* (cf. Kessler, 2021).

It is a useful concept not necessarily in the sense of it being useful for the concept's proclaimed theoretical purposes, but for a range of other purposes as well: it can be connected and linked to many policies and issues in legitimate ways, precisely because it is so multifaceted and common. Indeed, the historical record shows how the balance of power concept has been central to how practitioners have made sense of their surroundings and have promoted their political projects for more than 350 years (Andersen, 2016). In controversies and policy debates, the balance-of-power concept has emerged, been deployed, and changed through contingently linking it to other concerns. In IR, in some ways, the practical success of the balance of power concept has become its own explanation.

As noted, the core proposition of balance of power theory is qualified by aggregating auxiliary hypotheses and assumptions. At times, this seems to correspond to developments in real-world events during and after the Cold War. 'Soft balancing', for instance, became relevant with the increasing supremacy of the United States, and the lack of balancing against it. However, these are not only recent attempts at rescuing a fundamental concept from empirical challenges in a radically changing security environment: the point here is that aggregating assumptions has *always been the case*. There was never a 'pure' version of the balance of power, and there was never a consensus on what the balance of power was and was not. A widely used concept can be linked to many different issues precisely because it is so common and vague—the concept has always been part of something else, precisely because of its widespread use and many different meanings.

Treating the concept as a self-contained theoretical tool only overlooks important aspects of it. Taking its historical and contemporary usefulness seriously is an alternative to considering the balance of power a universalistic theory. It has been around for a long time, not because of its unchanging, timeless insights, but because of the versatility of its use. As noted above, through the years, the concept has proved useful to those arguing for the idea of the national interest, about monarchies and succession, Protestantism, civilization, and European community. To clarify this claim, let us look at three different examples of usefulness: as a foil for academic research, and as an argument for restraint and prudence in foreign policy by both policy makers and academics.

The first example concerns the attempt to develop the concept into a modern social science theory, which reached its apex in Kenneth Waltz. His seminal *Theory of International Politics* extracted from classical realism the standard balance of power explanation for failed hegemony (e.g. Gulick, 1955; Dehio, 1959) and clarified it dramatically by transforming it into a rigorously stated general theory. His simple proposition—that anarchy (e.g. any system of territorial sovereign polities interacting with each other) plus the assumption of state survival as a minimum goal would yield both balancing behaviour and recurring balances, or at least the absence of hegemony, over the long-term—proved strikingly attractive to scholars as an idea but not at first as a practical research enterprise. The normative appeal of the balance of power idea to many scholars (see below) meant that this basic proposition went unquestioned for decades. In fact, in much of the most prominent work on the balance of power by early realists, there is very little detailed discussion of what the balance of power as theoretical concept really entails and means, except for references to historical cases as 'prototypes', and highly general formulations. Scholars rather focused on other aspects of Waltz's theory, notably claims about differing patterns of behaviour between bipolar and multipolar systems, or especially the challenges to interstate cooperation.

Thus, an ostensible balance of power theory appeared to have major influence over IR in North America and increasingly in the United Kingdom and Europe without scholars actually focusing on its core balancing proposition. Indeed, part of what made the theory so popular was its convenient role as a foil. In the 1980s, case study researchers inaccurately pulled from Waltz's writings quasi-deterministic predictions about foreign policy and reported the finding that balancing imperatives could not actually account for state behaviour in very specific contexts as disconfirming results. In the 1990s, formal theorists translated the core balancing theory into abstract axioms whose patent falsity could be ascertained by the most cursory glance at international history; and quantitative researchers translated those axioms into large-N tests that again disconfirmed them (Niou et al., 1989; Bueno de Mesquita and Lalman, 1992). These were useful evaluations of propositions inspired by Waltz's writings, but they did not constitute actual tests of the core balance of power proposition. The result was a situation in which balance of power theory seemed to loom large, though its core arguments remained unexamined. As noted above, when scholars finally got around to actually *testing* that core proposition of balance of power theory, they found that the tendency towards balance is hardly universal, though it appears to apply, if weakly, in some interstate systems.

The second example concerns the official use of the concept to legitimate foreign policy. During the congress of Vienna, the balance of power was not much invoked. Rather, a European *equilibrium* was the order of the day (Schroeder, 1989). Seemingly a semantic point only, this had consequences: equilibrium addressed social forces attacking the European system itself, rather than skirmishes *within* the system (see Forsyth, 1980: 525). Furthermore, the five great powers heading the Congress were increasingly opposed, and considered a new, collective 'universal monarchy'. The congress powers were seen to be sacrificing smaller, independent European states on the altar of the European equilibrium (Jarrett, 2014: 136). Debating the Congress in 1815, in an instructive comment, James Mackintosh argued, 'the independence of nations is the end: the balance of power is only the means. To destroy independent nations in order to strengthen the balance of power, is the most extravagant sacrifice of the end to the means' (Hansard, 1815: col. 909). One counterreaction to the Congress system, then, in part led by Britain after the Congress of Verona, was a reintroduction of the balance of power concept in new garbs, i.e. with new links and associations. Now, rather than emphasizing the integrity of the European system as the concept had previously done (and as the Congress now did), the balance of power was deployed to protect state independence and promote anti-interventionism. This, it was argued, was what prudent balance of power politics really had been and was about—a balance of power, Mackintosh argued, that had 'been lost sight of' and 'seemed entirely forgotten'. In short, politicians effectively linked the balance of power to other concepts: independence, anti-interventionism, restraint, prudence, and—eventually—nationalism. Britain eventually abandoned the Congress system. The balance of power concept started out as a positive promise for the common interest of the European states system, where the balance of power was regularly used to *justify* interventions. In a twist of plot, the concept was then used to condemn the Congress of Vienna. When the Congress failed, actors rhetorically mobilized the balance of power in its classical sense to argue *against* interventions.

The third case concerns scholars' policy advocacy during and after the Cold War. The balance of power became equated with Realist theory, and Realist theory began to be associated with the normative preference for *restraint* in US foreign policy, and in foreign policy in general. Here, the balance of power is tailor-made to stand as the putatively objective scholarly argument for restraint. This began early in the post-war period but again, Waltz is a superb example. He argued that bipolarity and nuclear deterrence had transformed the requisites of balance such that internal efforts were sufficient. It followed that there was no need for anything other than a minimal deterrent, and there was absolutely no need for any competition in the so-called Third World whatsoever. This transformed his theory from an explanation of the Cold War to a critique of US foreign policy in the Cold War. Most of what we know as the Cold War then became a huge puzzle for his theory, notably the fundamental thrust of much US and Soviet foreign policy from about 1960 onwards (see also Kwon, 2021). Both superpowers built gigantic nuclear arsenals that went well beyond any conception of minimal deterrence, and they expended massive effort in regional competition in Asia, Africa, and Latin America. Most realists viewed this as dangerously misguided and they invoked balance-of-power terms and phraseology in making that case.

In much realist scholarship, then, the balance of power is best understood not as an academic theory but as a basic conservative prudential assumption about the world, which holds that if you push the world, it pushes back. Pushed to extreme, it becomes an academic version of Murphy's Law: for great powers, whatever can go wrong will go wrong when trying to expand. The modern variant really ends up centring on *identity and nationalism* as fundamental drivers of big outcomes in world politics. At the end of the day, scholars like Mearsheimer, Posen, Layne, Walt, Schweller, and many others have moved closer to classical early 20th century and early Cold War liberal and progressive scepticism about *interventionism* of all sorts, with its antecedents lodged in the Congress system.

Reinventing the Balance of Power (again)

Is the balance of power concept obsolete, and should we abandon the concept? When scholars discuss balancing behaviour today, as with Russia and China, it is indistinguishable from mere defence, or standard security rivalry. In today's discussion of emerging great power rivalries, there is not a lot of explicit reference to the balance of power as a theory at all. Now, people do not seem to need it when discussing this new phenomenon. There are of course those who cite this as evidence that unipolarity has ended and we are now in a multipolar world. Conversely, if we indeed *are* witnessing the rise of great power balancing today, it is rarely noted that this is the precise opposite of the original theoretical proposition, for what people call balancing today is increasing as US power *declines*.

Abandoning the concept altogether, however, is not ideal. The balance of power concept is a central part of Historical IR—including the history of the discipline. Ignoring the balance of power would mean ignoring the historical empirics on the emergence, development, use, and impact of the concept.

We have argued that the linking of the balance to *other concerns* is key. If this makes sense, then there would be a number of overlooked historical and theoretical issues that should become a part of the debates about the balance of power. This is also a means to make us rethink the balance of power in IR and encourage new approaches to using and studying it. Recent literature suggests that alternative approaches to the balance of power is indeed possible, and should be further explored.

First, one should take historical context and contingency seriously. Steven E. Lobell (2018) argues that policymakers rarely balance against overall state power, but rather *disaggregate* power and capabilities to identify threatening states. In turn, they balance against separate elements of the other state's military and material portfolio, whilst regularly ignoring their aggregate capability. Historical episodes normally coded as underbalancing or nonbalancing might therefore be instances of appropriate, *targeted* balancing. Contrary to conventional wisdom, Lobell argues that Britain did balance against the Axis powers before and during the Second World War, whilst during the Napoleonic wars, Britain and Russia target-balanced against specific elements of French power. Lobell thus introduces context and intervening variables—like geography, technology, domestic politics, and the conceptions of political leaders—to balance of power theory, whilst retaining the core theoretical proposition.

Second, it is crucial to clearly define what one is talking about when addressing the balance of power. Dan Nexon (2009), for instance, argues that we must expand what *balancing* entails—it is not only about balance of power theory as we know it in IR. Balancing behaviour, Nexon argues, 'should involve a range of possible practices designed to rectify a security deficit rather than to maximize power for its own sake'. This is in need of theorization; balancing strategies go beyond military power and should be studied as a phenomenon in its own right, not necessarily linked to a realist theoretical apparatus.

Third, we should expand the universe of cases pertaining to all facets of the balance of power or balancing. Wohlforth et al. (2007) and Victoria Hui (2021) have already made important contributions to this. They show how the balance of power has not impeded the formation of hegemonies. Victoria Hui, for instance, argues that the principles of ancient China were comparable to the modern states system and yet, hegemonies prevailed. Any balance or equilibrium there might be can often be traced to factors such as external pressures or internal policy failure. We should use an expanded sense of balance of power and balancing, including contingent links to other policy issues, to study underexplored cases in world history and to revisit episodes of balancing, underbalancing, or nonbalancing with new tools.

Fourth, there should be more detailed, historical, and hermeneutical analyses of the balance of power idea, and how it has been deployed. Andersen (2016) has argued that the concept of balance of power is a strategic resource that has been at the heart of political contestation over the past few centuries, and that contemporary usage of the concept has covered up these tracks. He traces the history of how the balance of power started off as a way of preserving a supposed European commonwealth, for then to become a notion that makes possible the denial of the existence of any such thing as 'international society' in favour of a state-centric approach to international relations, and how that confusing 'origin' and subsequent history defines the parameters of contemporary debates about 'the balance of power'. There should be more studies on how analogous concepts have been deployed in other social and semantic contexts—how did historical actors in polities and empires across Asia and the Middle East, for instance, talk about stability and desired collective outcomes across polities?

Such new avenues for research have in common taking historical context seriously—not only as related to the core proposals of balance of power theory or as a source of residual explanations—but as fundamentally affecting international collective action and the system level (Nexon, 2009). Rather than sticking with a balance of power theory frozen in time, this would entail precisely how contingent links have been forged or broken between the balance of power, security policies, and other issues. Whilst concepts may remain the same, the historical context change, and so do the conceptual links the balance of power maintains with other concepts and issues.

Suggestions for further reading

Anderson, M. S. (1970). Eighteenth-Century Theories of the Balance of Power. In: R. Hatton, and M. S. Anderson, eds., *Studies in Diplomatic History*, London: Longman, 183-198.
Bull, H. (1977). *The Anarchical Society*. New York, NY: Columbia University Press.
Butterfield, H., and Wight, M., eds. (1966). *Diplomatic Investigations*. London: George Allen and Unwin.
Mearsheimer, J. (2001). *The Tragedy of Great Power Politics*. New York, NY: Norton.
Morgenthau, H. (1948). *Politics among Nations: The Struggle for Power and Peace*. New York, NY: Alfred A. Knopf.
Paul, T. V., Fortman, M., and Wirtz, J. J. (2004). *Balance of Power: Theory and Practice in the 21st Century*. Stanford, CA: Stanford University Press.
Schweller, R. L. (2008). *Unanswered Threats*. Princeton, NJ: Princeton University Press.
Walt, S. M. (1987). *The Origins of Alliances*. Ithaca, NY: Cornell University Press.
Wright, M., ed. (1975). *Theory and Practice of the Balance of Power, 1486–1914: Selected European Writings*. London: Dent.

References

Andersen, M. S. (2016). *A Genealogy of the Balance of Power*. PhD Thesis, London School of Economics and Political Science.
Anderson, M. S. (1993). *The Rise of Modern Diplomacy, 1450–1919*. London: Longman.
Black, J. (1983). The theory of the balance of power in the first half of the eighteenth century: a note on sources. *Review of International Studies*, 9 (1), 55-61.
Bolingbroke, H. St. J. (1932 (1735)). *Defence of the Treaty of Utrecht*. Cambridge: Cambridge University Press.
Brooks, S. G., and Wohlforth, W. C. (2008). *World Out of Balance*. Princeton, NJ: Princeton University Press.
Christensen, T. J., and Snyder, J. (1990). Chain gangs and passed bucks: predicting alliance patterns in multipolarity. *International Organization*, 44 (2), 137-168.
Claude, I. L. (1989). The balance of power revisited. *Review of International Studies*, 15 (2), 77-85.
Cobden, R. (1867 (1836)). Russia. In: R. Cobden, ed., *The Political Writings of Richard Cobden. Volume I*, London: William Ridgway, 155-354.
de Mesquita, B. B., and Lalman, D. (1992). *War and Reason*. New Haven, CT: Yale University Press.
Dehio, L. (1959). *The Precarious Balance*. New York, NY: Alfred A. Knopf.
Devetak, R. (2021). Reason of State: An Intellectual History. In de Carvalho, B., Costa Lopez, J., & Leira, H., eds. *Routledge Handbook of Historical International Relations*. Abingdon: Routledge.
duc de Rohan, H. (1638). *A Treatise of the Interest of the Princes and States of Christendome*. London: Henry Hunt.
Elman, C., and Elman, M. F., eds. (2003). *Progress in International Relations Theory: Appraising the Field*. Cambridge, MA: MIT Press.
Elman, C., Elman, M. F., and Schroeder, P. W. (1995). History vs. neo-realism: a second look. *International Security*, 20 (1), 182-195.
Forsyth, M. (1980). The old European states-system: Gentz versus Hauterive. *The Historical Journal*, 23 (3), 521-538.

Goddard, S. E. (2009). When right makes might: how Prussia overturned the European balance of power. *International Security*, 33 (3), 110-142.

Gulick, E. V. (1955). *Europe's Classical Balance of Power*. New York, NY: W.W. Norton.

Guzzini, S. (2004). The enduring dilemmas of realism in international relations. *European Journal of International Relations*, 10 (4), 533-568.

Haas, E. B. (1953). The balance of power: prescription, concept, or propaganda. *World Politics*, 5 (4), 442-477.

Hansard, T. C. (1815). *The Parliamentary Debates from the Year 1803 to the Present Time*. Volume XXX. London: Longman.

Hui, V. (2021). Premodern Asia and International Relations Theory. In de Carvalho, B., Costa Lopez, J., & Leira, H., eds. *Routledge Handbook of Historical International Relations*. Abingdon: Routledge.

Hume, D. (1987 (1742)). Of the Balance of Power. In: D. Hume, ed., *Essays Moral Political and Literary*, Indianapolis, IN: Liberty Fund, 332-341.

Jarrett, M. (2014). *The Congress of Vienna and Its Legacy*. London: I.B. Tauris.

Kaufman, S. J., Little, R., and Wohlforth, W. C., eds. (2007). *The Balance of Power in World History*. New York, NY: Palgrave Macmillan.

Kessler, O. (2021). Conceptual History in International Relations: From Ideology to Social Theory?. In de Carvalho, B., Costa Lopez, J., & Leira, H., eds. *Routledge Handbook of Historical International Relations*. Abingdon: Routledge.

Kwon, H. (2021). Understanding the Postcolonial Cold War. In de Carvalho, B., Costa Lopez, J., & Leira, H., eds. *Routledge Handbook of Historical International Relations*. Abingdon: Routledge.

Larson, D. (2021). Realism: Excavating a Historical Tradition. In de Carvalho, B., Costa Lopez, J., & Leira, H., eds. *Routledge Handbook of Historical International Relations*. Abingdon: Routledge.

Leira, H. (2021). Diplomacy: The World of States and Beyond. In de Carvalho, B., Costa Lopez, J., & Leira, H., eds. *Routledge Handbook of Historical International Relations*. Abingdon: Routledge.

Levy, J. S. (2004). What Do Great Powers Balance Against and When?. In: T. V. Paul, J. J. Wirtz, and M. Fortmann, eds., *Balance of Power. Theory and Practice in the 21st Century*, Stanford, CA: Stanford University Press, 29-51.

Levy, J. S., and Thompson, W. R. (2010). Balancing on land and at sea: do states ally against the leading global power?. *International Security*, 35 (1), 7-43.

Little, R. (2007). *The Balance of Power in International Relations*. Cambridge: Cambridge University Press.

Lobell, S. E. (2018). A granular theory of balancing. *International Studies Quarterly*, 62 (3), 593-605.

Morgenthau, H. (2000 (1970)). The Intellectual and Political Functions of Theory. In: A. Linklater, ed., *International Relations. Critical Concepts in Political Science*, London: Routledge, 43-54.

Morgenthau, H. J. (1969). *A New Foreign Policy for the United States*. New York, NY: Frederick A. Praeger.

Nexon, D. H. (2009). The balance of power in the balance. *World Politics*, 61 (2), 330-359.

Niou, E. M., Ordeshook, P. C., and Rose, G. F. (1989). *The Balance of Power: Stability in International Systems*. Cambridge: Cambridge University Press.

Organski, A. F. K. (1968). *World Politics*. New York, NY: Knopf.

Pagden, A. (1995). *Lords of All the World*. New Haven, CT: Yale University Press.

Parliament of Great Britain. (1833). *Appendix to the Report from the Selected Committee of the House of Commons on the Affairs of the East-India Company*. London: J.L. Cox & Son.

Schroeder, P. W. (1989). The nineteenth century system: balance of power or political equilibrium?. *Review of International Studies*, 15 (2), 135-153.

Schroeder, P. W. (1994). Historical reality vs. neo-realist theory. *International Security*, 19 (1), 108-148.

Sheehan, M. J. (1996). *The Balance of Power: History and Theory*. London: Routledge.

Vasquez, J. A. (1997). The realist paradigm and degenerative versus progressive research programs. *American Political Science Review*, 91 (4), 899-912.

von Justi, J. H. G. (1758). *Die Chimäre des Gleichgewichts von Europa*. Altona: David Iversen.

Walsh, R. (1835). *Select Speeches of the Right Honourable George Canning*. Philadelphia, PA: Key and Biddle.

Walt, S. M. (2017). Who's afraid of the balance of power? Foreign policy. Viewed on 31 October 2020, <https://foreignpolicy.com/2017/12/08/whos-afraid-of-a-balance-of-power/>.

Wohlforth, W. C. (2004). Revisiting Balance of Power Theory in Central Eurasia. In: T. V. Paul, J. J. Wirtz, and M. Fortmann, eds., *Balance of Power. Theory and Practice in the 21st Century*, Stanford, CA: Stanford University Press, 214-238.

Wohlforth, W. C., Little, R., Kaufman, S. J., et al. (2007). Testing balance-of-power theory in world history. *European Journal of International Relations*, 13 (2), 155-185.

Wright, Q. (1983 (1942)). *A Study of War*. Chicago, IL: University of Chicago Press.

28

DIPLOMACY

The world of states and beyond

Halvard Leira

Introduction

Diplomatic history was one of the building blocks of early International Relations (IR) scholarship and has remained an implicit backbone of much state-centred theorising. But the institution and function of diplomacy long remained understudied in the discipline, and its history was largely taken for granted. Diplomatic History itself long remained impervious to the many changes in disciplinary History, retaining a view of states and their actions closely aligned with realist notions of international relations. Over the last three decades, significant changes have taken place in both disciplines, creating possibilities for a much more broad-ranging engagement with diplomacy for Historical IR, and for a significant reconceptualisation of diplomacy both past and present. Scholars have, as of yet, only started to explore these possibilities.

The chapter is intended to give a broad overview and for that reason includes references to Diplomatic History as well as the study of diplomacy within IR. Diplomatic History, understood as the historical study of political relations between polities, is relevant to all kinds of Historical IR dealing with politics. It has been, and continues to be, a key empirical resource for IR. In this chapter, diplomacy is also understood more broadly as a historical phenomenon. This broader understanding necessitates some specifications. First, the topic of this chapter is (primarily) diplomacy analytically understood. Conceptual explorations have established that 'diplomacy' only emerged as a practical concept in Europe at the tail end of the 18th century. Nevertheless, scholars typically explore phenomena at earlier times and other places under the heading of diplomacy. Acknowledging the risks of anachronism, this chapter follows convention. Furthermore, the broader understanding moves beyond states. Both within Diplomatic History (particularly in the so-called New Diplomatic History) and within IR, increased emphasis has been put on understanding and exploring diplomacy in its own right, not simply as a vehicle for state policies. In IR, drawing on the English School, there has been a focus on the *institution of diplomacy*, while Diplomatic History has focused more on *diplomatic functions* (Navari and Green, 2021). The first has privileged regularised, rules-based patterns of interaction and explored its emergence, development and spread. The second has paid more attention to actors engaged in inter-polity activities of different sorts. Both approaches are based on an analytical understanding of diplomacy, and in practice there has been a lot of overlap in how scholars have approached the empirical phenomena. Implicit in these analytical takes is the (perhaps irresolvable) tension between continuity and novelty, between seeing diplomacy as a phenomenon with some sort of essence across time and space and using diplomacy simply as a label for different phenomena with some abstract similarities.

In this chapter, the aim is threefold. First, I establish the baseline, the traditional approach to diplomacy within Historical IR (and IR as such). This is followed by a more detailed discussion of some of the most important trends in recent scholarship on diplomacy. This review is by necessity multidisciplinary. Finally, I point out possible avenues for further research and some possible implications for the overall study of IR.

Traditional diplomacy traditionally understood

The study of diplomatic history was a central pillar of the discipline of History as it was professionalised in the 19th century. When IR gradually emerged in the first decades of the 20th century, even though the actual academics were not necessarily historians, diplomatic history was one of the empirical bases of the discipline. However, within IR, diplomatic history would be put to very specific disciplinary uses, particularly in the United States after the Second World War. Diplomatic history would become a repository of proofs, of the origin-stories of the discipline and of a better way of organising international politics than what the current situation offered. Briefly told, diplomatic history would help legitimise the distinctiveness of international politics, and the dominance of realist thought within the discipline. With the later developments of the English School of IR, diplomacy as such started receiving more specific attention, but still within a broadly realist framework.

The origin-stories of the IR discipline typically latched on to the treaties of Westphalia and 1648 as the empirical starting point for international relations as an object of study (de Carvalho et al., 2011). Even so, in the effort to establish continuity and legitimise a realist worldview, political thinkers and diplomatic practices of earlier ages were invoked. The go-to reference on the emergence of modern diplomacy would become diplomatic historian Garrett Mattingly's *Renaissance Diplomacy* (1955), but of even more direct importance for the discipline would be the work of Felix Gilbert, in branding Machiavelli and Guicciardini as forerunners of realism, and in reading early American diplomacy in the light of this realism (Gilbert, 1961, 1965; cf. Guilhot's (2017) recent analysis on the connections between Gilbert and IR realism). Both Mattingly and Gilbert present a view of diplomacy as a stable phenomenon in an anarchical world system, underpinning the world of states. The same logic, presuming that systemic pressures would yield similar processes across time and space, can be found in later analyses of Ancient Greece (Adcock and Mosley, 1975; see also Knutsen, 2021) and the 14th century BCE Egyptian Amarna system (Cohen and Westbrook, 2000), among diplomatic historians and IR-scholars alike. While some IR-scholars did dabble in diplomatic history of this kind, studying the emergence, development and spread of diplomacy, it is telling that most of the second volume of collected texts in *Diplomacy* (Jönsson and Langhorne, 2004), dealing with the history of diplomacy, is filled with historians. Here we get the standard story of diplomacy, from Greece and Rome (and a detour through ancient China), via Byzantium to Early Modern Europe and the developments of the last five centuries (see Knutsen and Hall, 2021).

Even more than the origins of diplomacy, realist thinkers were concerned with the diplomatic history of the 17th, 18th and 19th centuries. The concert of Europe was considered by classical realists to be the epitome of international stability, and this stability was in no small part attributed to the workings of the so-called classical diplomacy. For Hans Morgenthau, IR was supposed to recreate the wisdom of this diplomacy, which had been embodied in what he referred to as the 'aristocratic international' (Morgenthau, 1948: 184–187, see also Guzzini's (2004) reading of this).

Focusing more on the 'great men' conducting diplomacy, but also with reference to the concert of Europe, Henry Kissinger (1957) presented a view of the statesman as a mediator between the inside of the state and its surroundings.

Common to much of this traditional approach to diplomacy and its history was an implicit realism; state-centric and with emphasis on power politics. The Eurocentrism of most of the literature is also obvious. This fundamental realist approach to international politics fit well with the dominant trends in Diplomatic History, which remained little moved by the many theoretical and methodical developments in History more generally. Thus, in the late 1990s, it made sense to try to tease out the possible interrelationships between (realist) IR and Diplomatic History (Elman and Elman, 2001).

There were, however, openings in other directions inherent in the realist reading of diplomatic history. Implicit in Morgenthau's account, and to some extent also in Kissinger's, was an understanding of diplomacy as something more than just the interaction between diplomats. This would be explored more fully by the English School, famously conceiving of diplomacy as one of the key institutions of international society (Bull, 1977). The entire argument about diplomacy as a regularised and ordered phenomenon in its own right was historically grounded, but writers associated with or inspired by the English School writers have also made more detailed studies of diplomacy in history (for an overview of the first generations, see Neumann 2003). A lot of the more or less historical work conducted in diplomatic studies in IR over the last three decades is traceable back to the English School.

Diplomacy reconsidered

There was a certain owl of Minerva quality to the late 1990s flirtation between realist IR and Diplomatic History. Two decades later, it is safe to say that neither the disciplines nor the dialogues look the same. What used to be taken for granted has been challenged, and entirely new questions have emerged. Scholars have examined for instance what diplomacy is, how it emerged (and where), in what forms it emerged, which actors were central to its emergence and development, what diplomacy can tell us about international relations more broadly and how specific forms of diplomacy have emerged historically. Briefly told, recent scholarship in IR and Diplomatic History has challenged what diplomacy is, how and where it emerged, what its key players have been and how specific subtopics have made their way onto the diplomatic agenda. That is not to say that traditional diplomatic history has been left behind, the journals *Diplomacy and Statecraft* and *Diplomatic History* still publish primarily work focusing on state actions and interactions.

The changes came earlier to IR than to Diplomatic History. In what still reads as a post-structural reinterpretation of the English School take on diplomacy, James Der Derian (1987) in the mid-1980s challenged the taken-for-granted understanding of diplomacy and suggested that its emergence and development had to be fundamentally rethought. He famously argued that diplomatic culture should be understood as 'the mediation of estrangement by symbolic power and social constraints' (Der Derian, 1987: 42) and challenged the notion of a stable, continuous diplomacy. Drawing on conceptual history, these insights were pursued in even more detail over the next decades (Constantinou, 1996; Leira 2016). Current scholarship makes it clear that a practice-concept of diplomacy only emerged with the French Revolution, and that the concept has undergone significant change since that. While this does not invalidate an analytical use of 'diplomacy', as noted in the introduction, it cautions scholars to consider the scope and generality when making claims about diplomacy before the 19th century.

Accepting that this something we call diplomacy is a relatively recent phenomenon, scholars still have explored how its predecessors emerged, and how alternative forms of regularised interaction among polities emerged and developed in other parts of the world. Through an opening up to social, intellectual and cultural history, Diplomatic History underwent its own changes from around 2000, leading to the development of what is often referred to as New Diplomatic History. The premise for this development was a gradual uptake in particular of social and cultural history, a broadening of the view of what counted as 'diplomatic' activity and an opening up towards the social sciences. Historians in this new burgeoning field have explored freely what can be understood as diplomacy and diplomats, focusing on all that which surrounds the negotiations etc., chronicled by earlier generations of historians, and drawing in a variety of new sources. They have for instance explored diplomatic practice, individual ambassadors, diplomatic families and rituals. This emerging research programme now dwarfs the historical study of diplomacy within IR, but there is sustained self-conscious work being done to reduce the differences between the disciplines. Diplomatic historians have increasingly looked to the social sciences for theoretical and methodological inspiration, and IR-scholars have brought insights from New Diplomatic History to bear on questions of particular relevance to their own discipline.

Most periods of diplomatic history have been influenced by these changes. As of yet, there has been little renewed work on ancient diplomacy coming forward, but Jones' (1999) take on ancient diplomacy as kinship diplomacy foreshadowed much of the later revisionist Diplomatic History. On Byzantine diplomacy, Nicholas Droucourt (2012) has provided new insights on the relations across religious borders, while Iver B. Neumann (2006) has read Byzantine diplomacy as an exercise in sublimating the barbarians (see also Costa Lopez, 2021). More systematic attention has been paid to early modern diplomacy, and it could well be argued that the initial push for a New Diplomatic History emerged among historians working on this period, such as Daniela Frigo (2000, 2008). A key milestone was the publication of a special issue of *Journal of Medieval and Early Modern Studies* in 2008, with the title 'Toward a new diplomatic history' (Watkins, 2008). A number of monographies and collections have followed. Of particular interest to IR-scholars should be Sowerby and Hennings (2017), which covers a wide range of different topics and sketches changes in diplomacy over 400 years. A very valuable stocktaking of scholarly developments can be found in Sowerby (2016).

Taken together, the already existing studies suggest that the traditional understanding of the emergence and early development of modern diplomacy must be substantially revised on a number of accounts. At the outset, the very notion of a sharp break happening with the Italian Renaissance must at least be modified. This has become obvious by the reading of diplomacy in a wider cultural context. Viewed from the vantage point of the mid-20th century, early modern diplomacy could be read as a specific and novel phenomenon. But as soon as scholars started to study diplomatic practices in more detail (see e.g. Bombi, 2012), as well as the context in which they operated, diplomacy appeared as a lot less distinctive and novel (Fletcher and De Silva, 2010). There were important continuities in practice from the middle ages, and significant learning from other systems and activities. Early modern diplomacy had multiple roots and uneven trajectories. Much like in the contemporary networks of trade (on which diplomacy drew), diplomatic interaction relied on kinship (Williams, 2010). Diplomatic representatives thus typically also were interwoven in complex and multiple loyalties, looking out for themselves, their families and their past, current and possible future benefactors (Spangler, 2011). The notion of a strict principal-agent relationship between prince and ambassador can thus not be maintained.

The relationship between principals and agents is problematised even more obviously when attention is turned to the historical development of one of the often unacknowledged and unrecognised parts of modern foreign services – the consuls (Leira and Neumann, 2012). Often derided as the poor cousins of diplomas, consuls could and did engage creatively in creating space for themselves and their sending-state and ensure that the proper duty of care was invoked towards their fellow countrymen. The consular institution emerged centuries before the acknowledged start of permanent diplomacy and developed partly separately from diplomacy well into the 19th century.

Of even more striking importance, recent scholarship has stressed how the self-evident gendered nature of the classical diplomacy is not applicable to earlier periods (see Towns, 2021). A systematic turn to letters as source material has made a rereading of the emergence and development of early modern diplomacy possible (Daybell, 2001). Letters, typically seen as 'private', and thus irrelevant source material, have turned out to provide new insights about diplomacy and the role of women's conduct (Daybell, 2011). Added to this new source material has been a rekindling of interest in kinship in history and historical anthropology, with a focus on individual royal women as mothers, daughters and sisters and as nodes in the royal and aristocratic networks of Early Modern Europe, with a main focus on marriages and marriage strategies (Hohkamp, 2011). Further studies have brought in further women; ambassadresses and ladies in waiting. An amazing collection of work on these topics was collected in *Women, Diplomacy and International Politics since 1500* (Sluga and James, 2016). Predominantly, these women were conducting what we recognise as diplomacy, by virtue of being women. By being women, they were able to carry out specific functions, not available to the same extent to the men they were working alongside. Women carried out tasks later reserved for men, and male diplomats were supposed to be able to handle the whole of the diplomatic household. Diplomacy in this period thus emerges as much less masculinised than what is commonly recognised.

While the traditional perceived core features of early modern diplomacy have been challenged head on, scholars have also looked to the margins and fringes of the acknowledged European tradition, as well as completely beyond it, to see how interactions between European and other entities might have changed diplomacy and to explore if there were alternative avenues to diplomacy. These kinds of studies draw on the tradition going back to Said (1978) and Todorov (1984), questioning how Europe has forced the European diplomatic system on everyone else, how indigenous traditions have been ignored and how alternative forms of diplomacy have been systematically excluded from the academic study of diplomacy.

Recent explorations of traditional European diplomacy, have, as noted above, stressed how it implied less of a break with the past and less exclusivity than previously acknowledged. Studies of the immediate neighbourhood suggest that European diplomacy was also more shaped by interaction with alternative ways of conducting relations between polities. Although their main focus is on state-formation, Iver B. Neumann and Einar Wigen (2018), drawing on detailed diplomatic and other history, also pinpoint how interactions with the steppe, in important ways, nudged how European polities dealt with external others. Interactions with Muslim others were even more important. Key features of the consular system grew out of interactions between Christian traders and Muslim rulers (Leira and Neumann, 2011), and the interaction-zones would prove to be fertile ground for diplomatic innovation and improvisation (Windler, 2001).

Looking even further, scholars have explored diplomatic interactions which developed independently of the European system. In North America, the Iroquois system of tribes around the Great Lakes developed a sophisticated system for interaction, based on *wampum*. Earlier research had detailed how this system should be seen as a diplomatic system in its own right, and Morten S. Andersen and Iver B. Neumann (2012) utilised these insights to make more general points about diplomatic practice. Based on a much higher number of polities, and lasting for much longer, the Asian diplomatic system has been studied in significant detail, by historians as well as IR-scholars (Kang, 2010; Kelly, 2012; Sverdrup-Thygeson, 2012).

As all of these contributions have highlighted, diplomacy remains Eurocentric. While acknowledging this, Iver B. Neumann (2012) argued that we could hardly expect it to be otherwise, since Europe has forced itself on the world for five centuries. Even so, most would agree that our study of diplomacy should include these other pathways, not only to demonstrate historical diversity but also to suggest that tomorrow might look very different than today. The charge of Eurocentrism has directed attention at unequal relations. Such relations were obvious for centuries in consular cases but came to the full fore with European colonialism. While the late 18th century allowed for creative diplomatic interaction between European sovereigns and North African principalities (Windler, 2001), by the early decades of the 19th century relations between Europe and the rest were typically imperially and hierarchically structured with Europeans on top and everyone else below (Keene, 2007).

Moving chronologically fast forward, it should also be noted that the perhaps most burgeoning field of New Diplomatic History, is the one dealing with the history of the last century. It is impossible to do justice to the developments here in a short chapter, but extremely summarily, all of the above challenges, approaches and widening of scope apply to this diplomatic history of the recent past. Scholars are exploring a broader range of actors, a broader range of practices and more diverse forms of diplomacy, using a much more varied set of analytical tools. One telling example could be the analysis of the League of Nations secretariat drawing on the theory of Bourdieu (Gram-Skjoldager and Ikonomou, 2019). Recent explorations have also concerned specific forms of diplomacy, comparing and contrasting across time. Public diplomacy, for instance, which has become a hot topic over the last 15 years, is widely acknowledged to have a prehistory during the Cold War. Recent research has underscored how this public diplomacy was not only state-centric (Scott-Smith and Snyder, 2013) and, as Helmer Helmers (2016) argues, it can also make sense to understand the practices of news dissemination in Early Modern Europe in light of public diplomacy. Likewise, while there is an emerging field of sports diplomacy, drawing mainly on recent and Cold War examples (Rofe and Tomlinson, 2020), there are also explorations of sports diplomacy from the first decades of the 20th century (Kidambi, 2013; Liston and Maguire, 2016). Much the same goes for studies of previously overlooked practises and the materiality of diplomacy. What has often been dismissed as mere ritual and paraphernalia has been reconsidered as core parts of what makes diplomacy and the diplomat. Gift-giving has for instance been studied across both time and space, from antiquity to the current age (Biedermann et al., 2017; Leira and Neumann, 2016; for a consideration of transhistorical practices see Kustermans, 2021), while diplomacy as such has been interrogated in light of the performing arts (Welch, 2017). Many of these examples also relate closely to the questions of hierarchy and diplomacy mentioned above. While some of this work is published in journals like *The International History Review* and *The Hague Journal of Diplomacy*, the recently established *Diplomatica* is emerging as the flagship journal of New Diplomatic History.

The New Diplomatic History has produced a wealth of new knowledge about the Early Modern period, as well as the 20th century. Much like in IR, the long 19th century remains somewhat underexplored. Some examples do exist. In an important early collection, Mösslang and Riotte (2008) placed diplomacy and diplomats between 1815 and 1914 squarely in the wider world they inhabited. Questions of gender and diplomacy have also been pursued into the 19th and early 20th centuries, detailing how women were forced out of diplomacy (Mori, 2015), and very slowly fought their way back into it (Towns, 2010; McCarthy, 2014). Some explorations have also been made of the diplomatic household and the importance of kinship.

Conclusion

While studies of diplomacy within IR were much quicker than Diplomatic History to challenge the orthodoxy, Diplomatic History has caught up and surpassed IR in a few short years. For

Historical IR, the recent developments present not only an enormous opportunity, but also a few challenges. The opportunity is clear in that new research opens up new ways of historicising diplomacy and thinking IR historically. The challenges are not new. First, with rapid developments in Diplomatic History, it becomes imperative for IR-scholars dealing with diplomacy to keep at least informed about recent developments. For several decades, IR-scholars could for instance content themselves with referring to Mattingly when writing about the emergences of modern diplomacy. This simply won't do anymore. Second, while historians have always asked somewhat different questions than IR-scholars, the New Diplomatic History accentuates some of these differences. The move towards individual actors and specific practices implies even more granular and detailed studies than what was traditionally the case. For the IR-scholar, the challenge becomes to make these detailed readings relevant for the kinds of questions asked in our discipline. To the extent that the changes in Diplomatic History mirror changes in the other social sciences, this challenge should be manageable, even if synthetic accounts become more difficult.

As the above paragraphs have demonstrated, the challenges to Diplomatic History have followed general patterns well known to the IR-scholar. This is also reflected in the macrotrends in the field. The growing interest in hierarchical relations is obvious. This finds expression not only in a growing number of studies of imperial diplomacy, but also, when coupled with an interest in overlooked actors and processes, in postcolonial approaches and in studies of gender and gender roles. The attention paid to previously overlooked phenomena is also clear in the explorations of the diplomatic work in international organisations, e.g. the League of Nations, and the new attention paid to diplomatic rituals. Historical IR and the New Diplomatic History should be able to find many fruitful avenues for cooperation on topics such as these. Temporally, both disciplines could also gain from turning their analytical gaze more squarely on the period of 'classical diplomacy' and the upheavals which came before and after this period, to the long 19th century.

Suggestions for further reading

Constantinou, C. (1996). *On the Way to Diplomacy*. Minneapolis, MN: University of Minnesota Press.

Leira, H. (2016). A Conceptual History of Diplomacy. In: C. M. Constantinou, P. Sharp, and P. Kerr, eds., *The SAGE Handbook of Diplomacy*, London: Sage, 28–38.

Sluga, G., and James, C., eds. (2016). *Women, Diplomacy and International Politics since 1500*. Milton Park: Routledge.

Sowerby, T. A. (2016). Early modern diplomatic history. *History Compass*, 14 (9), 441–456.

Sowerby, T. A., and Hennings, J., eds. (2017). *Practices of Diplomacy in the Early Modern World c. 1410–1800*. Milton Park: Routledge.

Watkins, J., ed. (2008). Toward a new diplomatic history. *Special issue of Journal of Medieval and Early Modern Studies*, 38 (1).

References

Adcock, F., and Mosley, D. J. (1975). *Diplomacy in Ancient Greece*. London: Thames and Hudson.

Andersen, M. S., and Neumann, I. B. (2012). Practices as models: a methodology with an illustration concerning wampum diplomacy. *Millennium*, 40 (3), 457–481.

Biedermann, Z., Gerritsen, A., and Riello, G. (2017). Global Gifts In *The Material Culture of Diplomacy in Early Modern Eurasia*. Cambridge: Cambridge University Press.

Bombi, B. (2012). The Roman rolls of Edward II as source of administrative and diplomatic practice in the early fourteenth century. *Historical Research*, 85 (230): 597–616.

Bull, H. (1977). *The Anarchical Society: A Study of Order in World Politics*. Houndmills: Macmillan.

Cohen, R., and Westbrook, R., eds. (2000). *Amarna Diplomacy: The Beginnings of International Relations*. Baltimore, MD: Johns Hopkins University Press.

Costa Lopez, J. (2021). International Relations in/and the Middle Ages. In de Carvalho, B., Costa Lopez, J., & Leira, H., eds. *Routledge Handbook of Historical International Relations*. Abingdon: Routledge.

Daybell, J. (2011). Gender, Politics and Diplomacy: Women, News and Intelligence Networks in Elizabethan England. In: R. Adams, and R. Cox, eds., *Diplomacy and Early Modern Culture*, Houndmills: Palgrave, 101-119.

Daybell, J., ed. (2001). *Early Modern Women's Letter Writing, 1450-1700*. Houndmills: Palgrave.

de Carvalho, B., Leira, H., and Hobson, J. M. (2011). The big bangs of IR: the myths that your teachers still tell you about 1648 and 1919. *Millennium*, 39 (3), 735-758.

Der Derian, J. (1987). *On Diplomacy: A Genealogy of Western Estrangement*. Oxford: Blackwell.

Droucort, N. (2012). Passing on political information between major powers: the key role of ambassadors between Byzantium and some of its neighbours. *Al-Masāq*, 24 (1), 91-112.

Elman, C., and Elman, M. F., eds. (2001). *Bridges and Boundaries. Historians, Political Scientist, and the Study of International Relations*. Cambridge, MA: BCSIA.

Fletcher, C., and DeSilva, J. M. (2010). Italian ambassadorial networks in early modern Europe – an introduction. *Journal of Early Modern History*, 14 (6), 505-512.

Frigo, D. (2008). Prudence and experience: ambassadors and political culture in early modern Italy. *Journal of Medieval and Early Modern Europe*, 38 (1): 15-34.

Frigo, D., ed. (2000). *Politics and Diplomacy in Early Modern Italy. The Structure of Diplomatic Practice, 1450–1800*. Cambridge: Cambridge University Press.

Gilbert, F. (1961). *To the Farewell Address: Ideas of Early American Foreign Policy*. Princeton, NJ: Princeton University Press.

Gilbert, F. (1965). *Machiavelli and Guicciardini: Politics and History in Sixteenth-Century Florence*. Princeton, NJ: Princeton University Press.

Gram-Skjoldager, K., and Ikonomou, H. A. (2019). The construction of the league of nations secretariat. Formative practices of autonomy and legitimacy in international organizations. *The International History Review*, 41 (2), 257-279.

Guilhot, N. (2017). *After the Enlightenment. Political Realism and International Relations in the Mid-Twentieth Century*. Cambridge: Cambridge University Press.

Guzzini, S. (2004). The enduring dilemmas of realism in international relations. *European Journal of International Relations*, 10 (4), 533-568.

Helmers, H. (2016). Public diplomacy in early modern Europe. Towards a new history of news. *Media History*, 22 (3-4), 401-420.

Hohkamp, M. (2011). Do Sisters have Brothers? Or the Search for the 'rechte Schwester': Brothers and Sisters in Aristocratic Society at the Turn of the Sixteenth Century. In: C. H. Johnson, and D. W. Sabean, eds., *Sibling Relations And The Transformations Of European Kinship, 1300-1900*, New York, NY: Berghahn Books, 65-83.

Jones, C. P. (1999). *Kinship Diplomacy in the Ancient World*. Cambridge, MA: Harvard University Press.

Jönsson, C., and Langhorne, R., eds. (2004). *Diplomacy: Volume I-III*. London: Sage Publications.

Kang, D. C. (2010). *East Asia Before the West: Five Centuries of Trade and Tribute*. New York, NY: Columbia University Press.

Keene, E. (2007). A case study of the construction of international hierarchy: British treaty-making against the slave trade in the early nineteenth century. *International Organization*, 61 (2), 311-339.

Kelly, R. E. (2012). A 'Confucian Long Peace' in pre-Western East Asia? *European Journal of International Relations*, 18 (3), 407-430.

Kidambi, P. (2013). Sport and the Imperial bond: the 1911 'All-India' cricket tour of Great Britain. *The Hague Journal of Diplomacy*, 8 (3-4): 261-285.

Kissinger, H. (1957). *A World Restored. Metternich, Castlereagh and the Problems of Peace 1812–22*. Cambridge: Riverside Press.

Knutsen, T. L. (2021). Ancient Greece: War, Peace and Diplomacy in Antiquity. In de Carvalho, B., Costa Lopez, J., & Leira, H., eds. *Routledge Handbook of Historical International Relations*. Abingdon: Routledge.

Knutsen, T. L. and Hall, M. (2021). Rome: Republic, Monarchy and Empire. In de Carvalho, B., Costa Lopez, J., & Leira, H., eds. *Routledge Handbook of Historical International Relations*. Abingdon: Routledge.

Kustermans, J. (2021). Historical Practices: Recovering a Durkheimian Tradition. In de Carvalho, B., Costa Lopez, J., & Leira, H., eds. *Routledge Handbook of Historical International Relations*. Abingdon: Routledge.

Leira, H., and Neumann, I. B. (2011). The Many Past Lives of the Consul. In: J. Melissen, and A. M. Fernandez, eds., *Consular Affairs and Diplomacy*, Leiden: Martinus Nijhoff Publishers, 225-246.

Leira, H., and Neumann, I. B. (2012). Consular Diplomacy. In: P. Kerr, and G. Wiseman, eds., *Diplomacy in a Globalizing World*, Oxford: Oxford University Press, 160-174.

Leira, H., and Neumann, I. B. (2016). Beastly diplomacy. *The Hague Journal of Diplomacy*, 12 (4), 337-359.

Liston, K., and Maguire, J. (2016). Sport, empire, and diplomacy: 'Ireland' at the 1930 British Empire Games. *Diplomacy & Statecraft*, 27 (2), 314-339.

Mattingly, G. (1955). *Renaissance Diplomacy*. Boston, MA: Houghton Mifflin.

McCarthy, H. (2014). *Women of the World: The Rise of the Female Diplomat*. London: Bloomsbury.

Morgenthau, H. J. (1948). *Politics Among Nations; The Struggle for Power and Peace*. New York, NY: Alfred A. Knopf.

Mori, J. (2015). How women make diplomacy: the British Embassy in Paris, 1815–1841. *Journal of Women's History*, 27 (4), 137-159.

Mösslang, M., and Riotte, T., eds. (2008). *The Diplomats' World: A Cultural History of Diplomacy, 1815–1914*. Oxford: Oxford University Press.

Navari, C., and Green, D. (2021). The English School and Historical International Relations. In de Carvalho, B., Costa Lopez, J., & Leira, H., eds. *Routledge Handbook of Historical International Relations*. Abingdon: Routledge.

Neumann, I. B. (2003). The English School on diplomacy: scholarly promise unfulfilled. *International Relations*, 17 (3), 341-369.

Neumann, I. B. (2006). Sublime diplomacy: byzantine, early modern, contemporary. *Millennium*, 34 (3), 865-888.

Neumann, I. B. (2012). Euro-centric diplomacy: challenging but manageable. *European Journal of International Relations*, 18 (2), 299-321.

Neumann, I. B., and Wigen, E. (2018). *The Steppe Tradition in International Relations*. Cambridge: Cambridge University Press.

Rofe, J. S., and Tomlinson, A. (2020). The untold story of FIFA's diplomacy and the 1966 World Cup: North Korea, Africa and Sir Stanley Rous. *International History Review*, 42 (3), 505-525.

Said, E. (1978) *Orientalism*. New York, NY: Pantheon.

Scott-Smith, G., and Snyder, D. J. (2013). 'A Test of Sentiments': civil aviation, alliance politics, and the KLM challenge in Dutch-American relations. *Diplomatic History*, 37 (5), 917-945.

Spangler, J. (2011). Those in Between. Princely Families on the Margins of the Great Powers – The Franco-German Frontier, 1477–1830. In: C. H. Johnson, D. W. Sabean, S. Tauscher, and F. Trivellato, eds. *Transregional and Transnational Families in Europe and Beyond. Experiences Since the Middle Ages*, New York, NY: Berghahn Books, 131-154.

Sverdrup-Thygeson, B. (2012). A neighbourless empire? The forgotten diplomatic tradition of Imperial China. *The Hague Journal of Diplomacy*, 7 (3), 245-267.

Todorov, T. (1984). *The Conquest of America: The Question of the Other*. New York, NY: Harper & Row.

Towns, A. (2010). *Women and States: Norms and Hierarchies in International Society*. Cambridge: Cambridge University Press.

Towns, A. (2021). Gender in Historical International Relations. In de Carvalho, B., Costa Lopez, J., & Leira, H., eds. *Routledge Handbook of Historical International Relations*. Abingdon: Routledge.

Welch, E. R. (2017). *A Theater of Diplomacy International Relations and the Performing Arts in Early Modern France*. Philadelphia, PA: University of Pennsylvania Press.

Williams, M. K. (2010). 'Dui Fratelli… Con Dui Principi': family and fidelity on a failed diplomatic mission. *Journal of Early Modern History*, 14 (6), 579-611.

Windler, C. (2001). Diplomatic history as a field for cultural analysis: Muslim-Christian relations in Tunis, 1700-1840. *The Historical Journal*, 44 (1), 79-106.

29

INSURANCE, TRADE, AND WAR[1]

Luis Lobo-Guerrero

De futuris contingentibus non es determinate veritas.[2]

However important trade has been to the development of international relations, the topic has received relatively little coverage in Historical IR. Among historians, trade has on the other hand been much studied. One example of such work has its roots in the *Annales* school – most notably associated with the work of Fernand Braudel – on trade around the Mediterranean, as well as the Indian Sea (see, for instance, Chaudhuri, 1985). Another example can be found in the institutional economic history of Douglass North and others. These traditions have had an impact on the discipline of history as a whole which is not the case in International Relations (IR). In IR, most work on trade has been on contemporary trade, and only recently have IR scholars turned their attention to the historical importance of trade, most notably in relation to war (see, for instance, Phillips and Sharman, 2015) and consular diplomacy (Leira and Neumann, 2008). Yet trade has been a key driver of expansion and innovation. In the present chapter, I propose to examine the importance of trade through the lens of insurance. In so doing, I seek to make the case for treating trade not as a stand-alone phenomenon, but in relation to its effects on other domains. Examining the trade/insurance nexus helps us shed new light on forms of governance and rethink many of the categories we often take for granted in our analyses, such as sovereignty.

I do so by examining how sovereignty, which is central to the understanding of contemporary liberal governance, creatively combines traditional technologies of security such as defence and diplomacy with forms of actuarial thinking and practice. What I call 'insurantial sovereignty', then, relates to the promotion and protection of political community and the portrayal of economic expressions of life in the way of political economies. Insurantial sovereignty constitutes a vast phenomenon with multiple manifestations in different historico-political experiences. The site for the production of insurantial sovereignty, which I will deal with in this chapter, is that of insurance and war. It constitutes a space from which to study the ways in which forms of insurance, and moreover, imaginaries of insurance (Ewald, 1991), have been complicit in making possible expressions of sovereignty such as the waging of war.

Although relationships between insurance and war have attracted relatively little academic attention (with the exception of Kingsley, 1911; Royce, 1914; Clark, 2004a,b), evidence of them in the modern period is abound. For example, insurance has been used in modern warfare as an intelligence instrument and also as a source for the funding of war efforts. A prominent case in point is that of Germany during the Nazi period. Gerald Feldman's historical study of the collaboration of the insurance company Allianz with the Third Reich between 1933 and 1945 demonstrated how life insurance records were used to expropriate the capital invested in the lives the regime had decided to destroy (2003: 236–277). Feldman narrates how actuarial records were used to locate and expropriate assets of 'the enemies of the people and the State' such as Jews and communists at home and in the conquered territories (2001: 391–395). The history of Allianz during that period closely illustrates the ways in which the insurance industry was employed as a means to further the interests of the regime.

The relationship between insurance and war for the Third Reich was even more complex and has the potential to contribute to a different political understanding of the war effort, as recently declassified documents in the United States National Archives seem to indicate (US National Archives, 2011). According to Fritz, German companies at the beginning of the war controlled close to forty-five per cent of the worldwide reinsurance industry, an element which provided the regime with a valuable source of information on the lives and property of many enemy, as well as friendly countries (2001b). Although a private business, the influence of the Nazi regime transformed the informational resources of the industry into intelligence material with which to dominate the economic spheres of the conquered territories.

Insurance practices also proved useful in the Allies' counter-intelligence efforts. For example, the American X2, part of the Office of Strategic Services (OSS) created to coordinate espionage activities behind enemy lines, established in 1943 a small Insurance Intelligence Section which proved its value in acquiring the blueprints of several industrial facilities, some even within concentration camps, for which reinsurance was being sought in the market (Fritz, 2001b). Based on neutral countries, intelligence agents with an insurance background sought to underwrite enemy assets as a way of identifying targets of strategic relevance to the enemy (see Naftali, 1993; Fritz, 2001a: Page A1, Section National/Foreign). The use of insurance for intelligence purposes was not restricted to Germany and to the Allies. Through declassified documents in the United States, it is now known, for example, that in 1941 'the San Francisco office of a British insurer resold coverage of the Panama Canal… to two Japanese firms'. A report of the OSS mentions that '[i]n connection with this insurance, there was forwarded to Tokyo a detailed description of the locks, all machinery in connection therewith, exact location, etc.' (as cited by Fritz, 2001a: Page: A1, Section National/Foreign).

These experiences in employing insurance as an instrument of war are but an example of an intimate relationship developed in the modern period between practices of statehood and the use of actuarial resources as instruments for government (see also Anievas and Gogu, 2021). Those relationships, as will be shown later, have their origins in late seventeenth and early eighteenth–century efforts to encompass developments derived from the Probabilistic Revolution into strategies aimed at balancing moral economic orders with the political economies of states. In the process, the primordial governmental concern of achieving security within and outside the state gave rise to the wider phenomena detailed here as insurantial sovereignty. Rather than seeking to analyse this form of sovereignty in the abstract and the general, the example here (based on the book cited in note 1) concentrates on exploring insurance and war relations in the specificities of the British experience of employing maritime insurance as an instrument of war beginning with the Napoleonic Wars and ending with the twenty-first century.

Maritime insurance and its use in time of war in Britain goes back to the long eighteenth century and results from interactions between financial actors at the City of London and political actors represented at Westminster. Through such interaction an alliance of power developed which materialised in the creation of a commercial empire lasting until the first half of the twentieth century (see, e.g., O'Brien, 1998, 2000). Central to the political economy of empire that emerged out of these power relations was the relationship between the resources and strategies needed for the projection of naval and military power and those required for international trade. Such interaction is evident in a notable feature of the late mercantile era which has attracted the attention of numerous economic and political historians. It is the fact that while Britain sustained protracted war efforts abroad at a high cost to the public purse, a system of domestic liberties and parliamentary control of the state developed (Stone, 1994: 6–7; see also Jahn, 2021). Presented in the literature as the 'Brewer Paradox', the balance between public and private power that characterised the system was mediated to an important extent, by insurance imaginaries, practices, and products –an issue which remains vastly under-researched. While insurers, as merchants, acquired significant amounts of government debt, mainly in the form of Navy bonds, they became increasingly active in affecting the security strategies, tactics, and environments of an international sphere on which international trade depended. By interacting with government entities and officials they slowly developed an active partnership with the state which under today's terms could be understood as a partnership in risk management. Its effects were felt at strategic, tactical, and operational levels through which the Committee of Lloyd's of London and its members portrayed their commercial interests. Their activity involved issues as diverse as intelligence gathering and sharing, investment in government debt, the provision of a basic form of social welfare, and the recognition of acts of gallantry by naval and merchant officers. The details of this partnership which materialised a form of insurantial sovereignty in the late-eighteenth century are made explicit through the interaction between Lloyd's of London and the Board of Admiralty during the Napoleonic Wars detailed at the end of the chapter and evidenced through correspondence sustained between these two bodies. However, in order to understand the significance of that partnership in the politics of empire, it is important to begin by analysing the significance of insurance practices and relationships as a moral economic issue. To do so, the chapter starts by offering a genealogy of the moral economy of insurance starting in the early-seventeenth century.

The Probabilistic Revolution, rational prognosis, and a globalising order

Insurantial sovereignty is a political effect of the Probabilistic Revolution. Much has been written within IR about the Peace of Westphalia as the founding myth of European sovereignty upon which a structural condition of anarchy in the international system derived (e.g. Teschke, 2003). Much has been written as well about how the *Jus Publicum Europeum* became a foundation of war amongst equals within a 'comprehensive spatial order' which fell into crisis with the advent of the First World War (e.g. Schmitt, 2003: 140–210, 227–237; Rasch, 2005; Odysseos and Petito, 2006, 2007; Hooker, 2009). From then onwards attempts to theorise the new 'nomos of the earth', in the form of the disciplined study of IR, evolved, from the efforts of the interwar period into the analysis of bipolarity of the Cold War heavily influenced by realist, neorealist, and liberal perspectives, into the 1980s. Towards the end of that period and beyond the trauma the Cold War meant for IR (e.g. Gaddis, 1993), the discipline began to move beyond its state-centrism incorporating many so-called post-structuralist aspects of power (see also Nøhr, 2021), a trend that consolidated way beyond 9/11. Within these writings, however, compendiums of which can be found in most comprehensive textbooks on IR theory, the political effects of the Probabilistic Revolution, a central constitutive aspect of the modern period, has been surprisingly absent.

The Probabilistic Revolution was part of a wider intellectual transformation in late-seventeenth and early-eighteenth century Europe which involved, in the words of the Bielefeld collective[3], 'a new pragmatic rationality that abandoned traditional ideals of certainty; and a sustained and remarkably fruitful attempt to apply mathematics to new domains of experience' (Gigerenzer et al., 1989: 1). These transformations materialised in the unfolding of a form of mathematics with which the probability of occurrence of future events could be measured (see, e.g., Krüger et al., 1987a,b; Daston, 1988; Gigerenzer et al., 1989; Hald, 2003; Hacking, 2006). The *need* to know the likelihood of something occurring in a future also revealed a form of reasoning for which *expectation* was a central element. This idea of a present, understood as contingent (see, e.g., Dillon, 2007), relied on the reasonable capacity to formulate future events and prepare for them. *Evental* thinking, as the rationality that informed an actionable present, became the mode for governing a future that ceased to be eschatological in design and became the opportunity for a new order of governance focused on the generation of profit and wealth (see also Bain, 2021; Guillaume, 2021).

Evental thinking and the contingent life it supported was not a phenomenon restricted to what we know today as scientific knowledge. It encompassed a modern imaginary evident in everyday life activities such as gambling and insurance, to more technical ones such as jurisprudence, data analysis, and inductive inference (Gigerenzer et al., 1989: xiii).

It also had, as key historians on this topic have noted, an effect on matters of government from its early inception. For example, after the efforts of the second Anglo-Dutch war of 1665–1667 which diminished the economic and naval capacities of the Dutch state to defend itself, Holland faced the threat of a French invasion for which it was necessary to build an army. The then Grand Pensioner of Holland (prime minister) Johan de Witt, proposed to raise funds by selling life annuities and demonstrated how to do so in a report to the States General in 1671 (Geddes and De Witt, 1879; Hald, 2003: 123). De Witt was the author of a series of letters originally written to the Estates-General of the United Provinces of Holland and West Friesland in 1671 which are recognised as one of the earliest attempts to incorporate the new mathematics of probabilities to aleatory contracts, such as annuities (Daston, 1988: 27). Although de Witt resigned in 1672 and was murdered by a mob when France invaded the Republic later that year, his attempt to raise funds for war by pricing the value of the lives of citizens through life annuities was an early indication of how government and insurance, particularly in the realm of defence, were to be related in subsequent centuries.

De Witt, as a seventeenth-century mathematician and statesman, exemplified a tradition of rule that was to be felt in various parts of Europe after the mid-seventeenth century under the rubric of 'political arithmetic'. This logic, known originally by the contributions made by William Petty to the problem of governing Ireland, then under English rule (Petty, 1690), employed statistics and statistical thinking as a means to identify populations objects of government and control (Petty, 1690; Buck, 1977: 102–111; Buck, 1982; Hoppit, 1996; Hacking, 2006). The very fact, however, that political arithmetic *emerged* denotes another epistemological feature of the order of government developing in seventeenth-century Europe which has not deserved enough attention in the study of Political Science and IR.

Political arithmetic is the application, in the modern period, of evental thinking as a pragmatic rationality that abandons traditional ideas of certainty and engages instead with employing ways of knowing, such as statistics (see, e.g., Desrosieres, 1993), to achieve '*reasonable* certainty'. The practices involved in such endeavour imply a voracious appetite on behalf of the state to 'foreknow' what is likely to happen, or to employ reasonable calculus to anticipate the likelihood and implications of an event 'taking place'. This shift in rationality relates to what Reinhart Koselleck analysed in the form of 'rational prognosis' as characterising the temporality of the state that emerged in the late-seventeenth and early-eighteenth centuries.

At the same time, and paradoxically, prognosis implies that events and scenarios construed as possible and potential are to be acted upon. The basis for modern Western governance is the capacity to formulate issues in terms of possible and potential events in a structured way such that it constitutes a political agenda. When the traditional ideas of certainty of the Christian onto-political imaginary are abandoned, uncertainty must be embraced by employing reasonable calculation to decide on what is to happen and how can those likelihoods be enhanced or diminished as a way of promoting and protecting the values upon which specific livelihoods and lifestyles rely.

Something else is required in the process of including those possible and potential issues into an agenda of government and rule. It is something that takes place at the intersection between the feral uncertainty of unthought events and scenarios, and the assessment of their likelihood and effects. It is a uniquely Western modern moment, and although evidence of its originating ideas date back to the medieval Renaissance (see Lobo-Guerrero, 2011: ch. 1), it unfolds with and during the Probabilistic Revolution. It is what we know, after the second half of the seventeenth century, as *Risk*. The following reflection by Ian Hacking expresses the uniquely Western modern dimension of this idea.

> Why did the European travellers find no sense of risk among the 'savages'? Because risk is the calculating concept that modulates the relations between fear and harm. The primitive did not calculate. Calculation began to dominate instinct, tradition and collective wisdom, in a measured way, only in seventeenth-century Europe.
>
> (Hacking, 2003: 26–27)

The transformation of feral – or untamed – uncertainty into something that can be acted upon in the form of events or scenarios constitutes what I like to refer to as 'the magical moment of risk'. Its magic relies on the obscureness of the process since the use of probabilities as a reasonable calculus of the uncertain takes place once uncertainty has been domesticated in the form of 'desirable' and 'undesirable' events.

While formulating events and scenarios, a contingent present is instantiated and acquires the recognisable form of practices intended to promote and protect particular ways of being in the world. These security practices, which of course overflow the realm of the military and traditional security sites such as the police and civil defence, determine political agendas and are used to mobilise the fear of uncertainty around which populations are governed (see, e.g., Massumi, 2007; Amoore and De Goede, 2008; Closs-Stephens and Vaughan-Williams, 2008). This idea goes to the core of the problem of political community, not in terms of the Hobbesian state of nature explained by Wolin as the condition of political nothingness (2004: 218), but as a matter of regulating, and specifically of *authorising*, the formulation of events and scenarios around which a present is to be governed. The replacement of the monopoly of prophecy by one of rational prognosis becomes evident in the ways in which uncertainty is rendered manageable in the form of risk.

The remarkable feature of rational prognosis in the Western modern art of government is therefore, not only the formulation, imagination (De Goede, 2008), and authorisation of the events and scenarios upon which it proceeds, but also the very possibility of rendering an uncertain into something that can be *traded* under the name of risk. This is where the metaphor of the magical moment becomes the site of the technological rationality of risk. The magical refers to the alchemic function of transforming uncertainty into something fungible; that is, amenable to trade and exchange as risk.

The alchemic transformation of uncertainty into risk, which relates to the emergence and operation of the late-seventeenth century rationality of government mentioned before, acquired a central role in British governance and security. Traces of this can be found as early as the Napoleonic Wars but quite concretely in the insurance and war schemes of the two world wars of the twentieth century. It is a rationality that employs knowledge and imaginaries of actuarial science and practice as an instrument with which to create sites of government characteristic of a liberal political economy.

The origins of this rationality remain vastly under-researched, although there is plenty of evidence that demonstrates that its emergence was premised on the concept of *interest* and the political economy that developed around its articulation. Interest, it has been argued, became a principle of behaviour with which to govern individuals as 'interested subjects'.

This idea of interests becoming the intersection of the private and the public and constituting a polity finds resonance with the depiction of insurantial sovereignty resulting from maritime insurance and war relations. The understanding of the intersection, however, requires an engagement with the technologies that support an 'interests-based rationality of risk'. This is not a claim for a technological ontology of instruments such as insurance. It is instead a way to investigate how a rationality of risk developed as a result of complex interactions, evidenced in the form of relationships (as will be explained later), through which technologies like insurance have operated throughout the modern period. The analysis matters greatly to the understanding of liberal governance since the outcome of those relations comes in the form of security effects. For example, the insurantial form of sovereignty has contributed to the shaping of an international sphere characterised not by anarchy, as traditional IR theory has understood it, but by an active engagement with an 'order-ing' of the world in terms of risk and the management of uncertainty in which the state has been an effect of power rather than simply an actor.

Insurantial sovereignty and Historical International Relations

In light of the considerations mentioned previously, insurantial sovereignty and the moral economies from which it results cannot be summed up into a general theory of power. What can be identified are specific forms of insurantial sovereignty that relate to what Foucault referred to as the microphysics of power. As read by Deleuze, these refer not to the 'miniaturisation of visible and articulable forms; instead, it signifies another domain, a new type of relations, a dimension of thought that is irreducible to knowledge' (Deleuze, 2006: 62).

For a start, forms of insurantial sovereignty challenge the distinction between threat and risk-based approaches to security (see, e.g., Rasmussen, 2001; Aradau et al., 2008; Lobo-Guerrero, 2010). Traditional threat-based approaches to security have focused on the ways danger is produced, managed, controlled, and destroyed in relation to specific referent objects, mainly states (e.g. Buzan, 1991; Wheeler and Booth, 2007; for a critique, see: Debrix and Lacy, 2009). They rely primarily on intelligence as a source of knowledge to inform defence and security policies. Risk-based approaches to security, in contrast, have emphasised entities or populations at risk (e.g. Ewald, 1986, 1991; O'Malley, 2004; Ericson et al., 2004; Aradau and Van Munster, 2007; Amoore and De Goede, 2008). They are based on stochastic models and forms of speculation to construct, interpret, and manage contingency which is usually expressed in the form of probabilities of potential loss and/or gain and its likely impact (e.g. Amoore and De Goede, 2008; Müller, 2009; Lobo-Guerrero, 2011). The study of the ways in which insurance has been employed, in one form or another as an instrument of government, collapses those distinctions and moves forward the research agenda of security studies into an area which involves problems traditionally studied by political economy and political theory. Approaching insurance/war relationships as security phenomena does not deny the existence, operation, and value of the state system. It does not deny either the importance of territoriality and authority when analysing security problems. What it does is that it reclaims these traditional categories into the realm of the political and rather than approaching them as ontological objects of protection, it observes them as effects of a productive relationality.

Transcending the threat/risk divide relates also to moving beyond the now traditional Schmittian understanding of politics as based on the friend/enemy distinction (Schmitt, 2007). Underlying the cases of insurantial sovereignty is a parallel understanding of the political, which can be understood as 'the concerted art of managing uncertainty'. Such an understanding does not require thinking security in terms of existential threats to an object of protection, as for example the 'Copenhagen School' has argued (e.g. Buzan et al., 1998; Buzan and Wæver, 2003; Balzacq, 2011). It does not require either to phrase the security problem in terms of emancipation and oppression (e.g. Booth, 1991). Instead, security becomes a matter of the relationship obtained between the order of governance that results from transforming uncertainty into an instrument of government in the form of risk, and the lifestyles and livelihoods referent of protection. Risk management, as the practice of security, becomes then a continuous problematisation of the order of being in the world, a problematisation that makes the political a contingent matter. In contrast with a Schmittian perspective to the political, it does not produce a confrontational problematisation. Risk management is not the result of a zero-sum game. Neither is it the result of Hegelian dialectics since it is continuously exposed to the singularity of the surprise. If artfully performed, it will result in profit and gain for the parties involved.

There is of course a utopian aspect to such an understanding of security, and utopias of this kind have been articulated in projects for a peaceful 'international'. In 1911, for example, Darwin Kingsley, president of the New York Life Insurance Company, published a collection of addresses promoting the idea that life insurance, if marketed aggressively around the world, would promote peace and reduce the likelihood of wars amongst states.

A second utopia on the use of insurance and insurantial logic to promote international peace was the address by Josiah Royce, a professor at Harvard University, to the Philosophical Union of the University of California at Berkeley in 1914 (Royce, 1914). Royce proposed the application of the principle of insurance to international affairs to 'quiet fears and encourage faithfulness' among an organisation of member states for the mutual insurance against risks (Royce, 1914: x). The risks he had in mind were those of war, but also, earthquakes, volcanic eruptions, pestilence, hurricanes, recurrent famine, and maritime disasters. Many of them have already been explored in the international arena, albeit, under a different economic rationality – financial securitisation supported by financial derivatives in the form of catastrophic bonds – for instance. In the case of international security, states party to an insurance scheme would not be interested in attacking another member since a share of the damages inflicted on the enemy would be paid for at home (note the parallel with the case of insuring enemy property in time of war).

What these utopian formulations failed to observe, however, is that the so-called principle of insurance cannot be taken for granted and should not be accepted as a universal norm. The principle of insurance as a formula, which assumes a way of understanding and managing 'un-certainties' in the world and in life, is not innocent in any way. If taken as a principle, insurance translates an order of the real into an imaginary in which uncertainties can be managed as risk and can employ actuarial technologies and knowledge to that end. If the so-called principle of insurance is assumed instead as a site from which to interrogate the complex power relations that make it possible, it becomes then a window from which observe its political dimension and to realise that insurantial utopias such as those of Kingsley and Royce are but the logical conclusion of their faith in a technology of insurance. This is to say that the possibility of understanding an international community as an outcome of an insurance principle is very different from the kind of analysis offered in this book. What the forms of insurantial sovereignty studied in subsequent chapters reveal are rationalities of government and it is those rationalities, when observed in their details, that challenge the threat/risk divide in the study of security within IR.

Insurantial sovereignty, as partnerships in risk, makes a contribution to the understanding of sovereignty as produced in social and political interaction (e.g. Bartelson, 1995; Weber, 1995; Edkins, 1999; Edkins et al., 2004). It moves the debate beyond an understanding of sovereignty as synonymous with 'sovereign statehood' (Edkins et al., 2004: 3) and provides an alternative grammar to understand how sovereignty is continuously constituted in liberal environments in which the state is but an expression of power. As noted by Edkins et al. and by the contributors to that volume, 'power is not something that is centralised and possessed, but rather something that is present in and formative of social relations, and does not exist in advance of the entities to which it gives rise' (Edkins et al., 2004: 2). What matters ultimately in the tradition of political analysis exposed in this book is the intimate relationality out of which moral economies of security result.

Insurantial sovereignty, as analysed here, also contributes to transcend the problem identified by Bartelson as the difficulty of imagining political order beyond the state (Bartelson, 2001). By re-problematising sovereignty in light of the Probabilistic Revolution which rendered the uncertain a political matter, it is possible to reimagine an international beyond the norms, legitimacy, and authority of the state-system. The orders underlying forms of insurantial sovereignty relate, not to state-based political community but also to the surprise of the event as the ground on which the contingent dimension of the political takes place.

Suggestions for further reading

Borscheid, P., and Haueter, N. V. (2012). *World Insurance: The Evolution of a Global Risk Network*. Oxford: Oxford University Press.

Desrosieres, A. (1993). *The Politics of Large Numbers: A History of Statistical Reasoning*. Cambridge, MA: Harvard University Press.

Lobo-Guerrero, L. (2012). *Insuring War: Sovereignty, Security and Risk*. London: Routledge.

Notes

1 This chapter is an edited and abridged version of Lobo-Guerrero (2012: 1–20).

2 'For future events, the truth is indeterminate'. Classical quotation from Aristotle, quoted by Koselleck, R. (2004: 18) as used by Guicciardini (Koselleck's reference is given as '*Ricordi* (Bari, 1935) II:58 ff.'), in *Futures Past* (Koselleck, 2004), note 13, 278.

3 The Bielefeld collective was a group of historians of ideas that convened in Bielefeld in the late 1980s to produce three collectively publications on the Probabilistic Revolution.

References

Amoore, L., and De Goede, M., eds. (2008). *Risk and the War on Terror*. London: Routledge.

Anievas, A., and Gogu, C. (2021). Capitalism and 'The International': A Historical Approach. In de Carvalho, B., Costa Lopez, J., & Leira, H., eds. *Routledge Handbook of Historical International Relations*. Abingdon: Routledge.

Aradau, C., Lobo-Guerrero, L., and van Munster, R. (2008). Security, technologies of risk, and the political: guest editors' introduction. *Security Dialogue*, 39 (2–3), 147–154.

Aradau, C., and van Munster, R. (2007). Governing terrorism through risk: taking precautions, (un)knowing the future. *European Journal of International Relations*, 13 (1), 89–115.

Bain, W. (2021). Political Theology and Historical International Relations. In de Carvalho, B., Costa Lopez, J., & Leira, H., eds. *Routledge Handbook of Historical International Relations*. Abingdon: Routledge.

Balzacq, T., ed. (2011) *Securitization Theory: How Security Problems Emerge and Disolve*. London: Routledge.

Bartelson, J. (1995). *A Genealogy of Sovereignty*. Cambridge: Cambridge University Press.

Bartelson, J. (2001). *The Critique of the State*. Cambridge: Cambridge University Press.

Booth, K. (1991). Security and emancipation. *Review of International Studies*, 17 (4), 313–327.

Buck, P. (1977). Seventeenth-century political arithmetic: civil strife and vital statistics. *Isis*, 68, 67–84.

Buck, P. (1982). People who counted: political arithmetic in the eighteenth century. *Isis*, 73, 28–45.

Buzan, B. (1991). *People, States and Fears: An Agenda for International Security Studies in the Post-Cold War Era.* New York, NY: Harvester Wheatsheaf.

Buzan, B., and Wæver, O. (2003). *Regions and Powers: A Guide to the Global Security Order.* Cambridge: Cambridge University Press.

Buzan, B., Wæver, O., and de Wilde, J. (1998). *Security: A New Framework for Analysis.* London: Lynne Rienner Publishers.

Chaudhuri, K. N. (1985). *Trade and Civilisation in the Indian Ocean.* Cambridge: Cambridge University Press.

Clark, G. (2004a). Insurance as an instrument of war in the 18th century. *The Geneva Papers on Risk and Insurance*, 29 (2), 247–257.

Clark, G. (2004b). Waging War with Insurance in Eighteenth-Century Britain. In: C. Thomann, and J.-M. Graf von der Schulerburg, eds., *War, Terrorism and Insurance in Europe after September 11, 2001*, Karlsruhe: Verlag Versicherungswirtschaft, 7–32.

Closs-Stephens, A., and Vaughan-Williams, N., eds. (2008). *Terrorism and the Politics of Response: London in a Time of Terror.* London: Routledge.

Daston, L. (1988). *Classic Probability in the Enlightenment.* Princeton, NJ: Princeton University Press.

De Goede, M. (2008). Beyond risk: premediation and the post-9/11 security imagination. *Security Dialogue*, 39 (2), 155–176.

Debrix, F., and Lacy, M. (2009). *The Geopolitics of American Insecurity: Terror, Power and Foreign policy.* London: Routledge.

Deleuze, G. (2006). *Foucault.* London: Continuum.

Dillon, M. (2007). Governing through contingency: the security of biopolitical governance. *Political Geography*, 26 (1), 41–47.

Edkins, J. (1999). *Sovereignty and Subjectivity.* Boulder, CO: Lynne Rienner.

Edkins, J., Shapiro, M., and Pin-Fat, V., eds. (2004). *Sovereign Lives: Power in Global Politics.* London: Routledge.

Ericson, R., Doyle, A., and Barry, D. (2004). *Insurance as Governance.* Toronto: University of Toronto Press.

Ewald, F. (1986). *L'Etat providence François Ewald.* Paris: Grasset.

Ewald, F. (1991). Insurance and Risk. In: G. Burchell, C. Gordon, and P. Miller, eds., *The Foucault Effect: Studies in Governmentality, with Two Lectures and an Interview with Michel Foucault*, Chicago, IL: The University of Chicago Press, 197–210.

Feldman, G. (2001). *Allianz and the German Insurance Business 1933-1945.* Cambridge: Cambridge University Press.

Feldman, G. (2003). Civil commotion and riot insurance in fascist Europe. *Financial History Review*, 10, 165–184.

Fritz, M. (2001a). Cloaked Business. *The Boston Globe.* November 19.

Fritz, M. (2001b). The Secret (Insurance) Agent Men. *Los Angeles Times.* September 22.

Gaddis, J. L. (1993). International relations theory and the end of the cold war. *International Security*, 17 (1), 5–58.

Geddes, J., and de Witt, J. (1879). *History of the Administration of John de Witt, Grand Pensionary of Holland.* New York, NY: C.K. Paul & Co.

Gigerenzer, G., Swijtink, Z., Porter, T., Daston, L., Beatty, J., and Krüger, L., eds. (1989). *The Empire of Chance: How Probability Changed Science and Everyday Life.* Cambridge: Cambridge University Press.

Guillaume, X. (2021). Historical Periods and the Act of Periodisation. In de Carvalho, B., Costa Lopez, J., & Leira, H., eds. *Routledge Handbook of Historical International Relations.* Abingdon: Routledge.

Hacking, I. (2003). Risk and Dirt. In: R. Ericson, and A. Doyle, eds., *Risk and Morality*, Toronto: University of Toronto Press, 22–47.

Hacking, I. (2006). *The Emergence of Probability: A Philosophical Study of Early Ideas About Probability Induction and Statistical Inference.* 2nd edition. Cambridge: Cambridge University Press.

Hald, A. (2003). *History of Probability and Statistics and their Applications Before 1750.* Hoboken, NJ: John Wiley & Sons.

Hooker, W. (2009). *Carl Schmitt's International Thought: Order and Orientation.* Cambridge: Cambridge University Press.

Hoppit, J. (1996). Political arithmetic in eighteenth-century England. *Economic History Review*, 49 (3), 516–540.

Jahn, B. (2021). Liberalism between Theory and Practice. In de Carvalho, B., Costa Lopez, J., & Leira, H., eds. *Routledge Handbook of Historical International Relations.* Abingdon: Routledge.

Kingsley, D. P. (1911). *Militant Life Insurance and Other Addresses.* New York, NY: New-York Life Insurance Company.

Koselleck, R. (2004). *Futures Past: On the Semantics of Historical Time.* New York, NY: Columbia University Press.

Krüger, L., Daston, L., Heidelberger, M., Gigerenzer, G., and Morgan, M. S., eds. (1987a). *The Probabilistic Revolution: Ideas in History,* Volume 1, Boston, MA: MIT Press.

Krüger, L., Gigerenzer, G., and Morgan, M. S., eds. (1987b). *The Probabilistic Revolution: Ideas in History,* Volume 2. Boston, MA: MIT Press.

Leira, H., and Neumann, I. B. (2008). Consular representation in an emerging state: the case of Norway. *The Hague Journal of Diplomacy,* 3 (1), 1–19.

Lobo-Guerrero, L. (2010). The International Political Sociology of Risk. In: *International Studies Online, – International Studies Encyclopaedia, International Studies Association Compendium Project,* Volume 7, 4418–4436. Oxford: Oxford University Press

Lobo-Guerrero, L. (2011). *Insuring Security: Biopolitics, Security and Risk.* London: Routledge.

Massumi, B. (2007). Potential politics and the primacy of preemption. *Theory and Event,* 10 (2). 10.1353/tae.2007.0066

Müller, B. (2009). *Security, Risk and the Biometric State: Governing Borders and Bodies.* London: Routledge.

Naftali, T. (1993). *X2 and the Apprenticeship of American Counterespionage, 1942-1944.* Ph.D. Dissertation, Harvard University.

Nøhr, A. A. (2021). Poststructuralism and the Challenge of History. In de Carvalho, B., Costa Lopez, J., & Leira, H., eds. *Routledge Handbook of Historical International Relations.* Abingdon: Routledge.

O'Brien, P. K. (1998). Inseparable Connections: Trade, Economy, Fiscal State, and the Expansion of Empire, 1688-1815. In: P. J. Marshall, ed., *The Oxford History of the British Empire, Volume II: The Eighteenth Century.* Oxford: Oxford University Press, 53–77.

O'Brien, P. K. (2000). Merchants and Bankers as Patriots or Speculators? Foreign Commerce and Monetary Policy in Wartime, 1793-1815. In: J. J. McCusker, and K. Morgan, eds., *The Early Modern Atlantic Economy,* Cambridge: Cambridge University Press, 250–277.

O'Malley, P. (2004). *Risk, Uncertainty and Government.* London: Glasshouse Press.

Odysseos, L., and Petito, F. (2006). Introducing the international theory of Carl Schmitt: international law, international relations, and the present global predicament(s). *Leiden Journal of International Law,* 19 (1), 1–7.

Odysseos, L., and Petito, F., eds. (2007). *The International Political Thought of Carl Schmitt: Terror, Liberal War and the Crisis of Global Order.* London: Routledge.

Petty, W. (1690). *Political Arithmetick.* London: Printed for Robert Clavel at the Peacock, and Hen. Mortlock at the Phoenix in St. Paul's Church-yard.

Phillips, A., and Sharman, J. (2015). *International Order in Diversity: War, Trade and Rule in the Indian Ocean.* Cambridge: Cambridge University Press.

Rasch, W. (2005). Special issue: world orders: confronting Carl Schmitt's the nomos of the Earth. *South Atlantic Quarterly,* 104 (2), whole issue.

Rasmussen, M. V. (2001). Reflexive security: NATO and international risk society. *Millennium – Journal of International Studies,* 30 (2), 285–309.

Royce, J. (1914). *War and Insurance; an Address Delivered before the Philosophical Union of the University of California at its Twenty-Fifth Anniversary at Berkeley, California, August 27, 1914.* Berkeley, CA: University of California Press.

Schmitt, C. (2003). *The Nomos of the Earth in the International Law of the Jus Publicum Europeaum.* New York, NY: Telos Press Publishing.

Schmitt, C. (2007). *The Concept of the Political: Expanded Edition.* Chicago, IL: University of Chicago Press.

Stone, L., ed. (1994). *An Imperial State at War.* London: Routledge.

Teschke, B. (2003). *The Myth of 1648: Class, Geopolitics, and the Making of Modern International Relations.* London; New York: Verso.

US National Archives. (2011). Records of the Office of Strategic Services (Record Group 226) 1940-1947. Entry 210. Boxes 1-538. Location: 250 64/21/1. CIA Accession: 79-00332A. Viewed on 30 October 2020, <http://www.archives.gov/iwg/declassified-records/rg-226-oss/>.

Weber, C. (1995). *Simulating Sovereignty: Intervention, the State and Symbols Exchange.* Cambridge: Cambridge University Press.

Wheeler, N. J., and Booth, K. (2007). *The Security Dilemma: Fear, Cooperation, and Trust in World Politics.* Houndsmills, Basingstoke: Palgrave Macmilan.

Wolin, S. S. (2004). *Politics and Vision: Continuity and Innovation in Western Political Thought, Expanded Edition.* Princeton and Oxford: Princeton University Press.

30

INTERNATIONAL LAW AND THE LAWS OF WAR

Claire Vergerio

Introduction

International law is commonly defined as the law that operates between states, and International Relations (IR) scholars have long considered its history to be fundamentally intertwined with the development of the international system. This is perhaps most clearly exemplified by the emphasis in the discipline on peace treaties, with Westphalia (1648), Vienna (1815), and Versailles (1919) constituting classic historiographical landmarks. The overlap is hardly surprising, as some of the most influential founders of the discipline—most famously Hans Morgenthau—were originally scholars of international law (Koskenniemi, 2001: 413–509).

Standard accounts of the history of international law track the development of its different branches, from the law of embassies and the determination of international legal subjecthood, to the law of the sea and the laws of war. These different branches of international law are generally considered to have contributed to the development of the international system in different ways and to varying degrees. Often highlighted as particularly essential by IR scholars are the law of embassies, as the foundation of modern diplomacy, and the laws of war, as the mechanism enabling the regulation of conflict amongst independent sovereignty entities (see notably Bull, 2002).

The laws of war (also referred to as the law of war, or in more contemporary parlance, the law of armed conflict or international humanitarian law) are generally considered to be a subset of international law. They are the rules that regulate the use of force, whether in terms of what suffices as an appropriate cause for war (*jus ad bellum*), what may be inflicted on the opponent (*jus in bello*), and more peripherally, what should guide the process of making peace (*jus post bellum*). These laws are considered to have emerged from a long tradition of seeking to regulate conduct in war, with a first important turning point in the early modern period, and a second in the late-nineteenth century.

In the early modern period, Alberico Gentili (1552–1608) and Hugo Grotius (1583–1645) are celebrated as the first jurists to have pulled together the various rules of conduct that existed for warfare and compiled them into standalone legal treatises separated from questions of military strategy. In the late-nineteenth century, the laws of war were actually codified through a famous series of initiatives, beginning with the Lieber Code of 1863 and culminating in The Hague Conference of 1899 and 1907. This codification eventually provided the basis for the 1949 Geneva Conventions, which continue to be the main legal framework regulating both international and (though to a much lesser extent) domestic conflicts to this day. While these laws have generally been understood primarily as an attempt to limit the horrors of war (Brownlie, 1963; Best, 1980; Howard et al., 1994), more critical scholars have also suggested that they may in fact ultimately legitimize violence rather than restrict it (Jochnick and Normand, 1994; Nabulsi, 1999; Kennedy, 2009).

If the laws of war are only one specific component of contemporary international law, then why write a chapter on international law *and* the laws of war? First, IR scholars have long sought to analyze international conflicts, and in their foray into the history of international law, the laws of war have attracted much more attention than, for instance, the law of territorial settlement (see Bartelson, 2021). Second, and more importantly, while the laws of war only form a small part of general international law today, they are considered to have been central to the historic development of international law as a broader field, both in its early modern phase and, perhaps even more explicitly, through its emergence from the 1870s onward as the modern, professional discipline that we know.

Taking stock of this link, the chapter unfolds in three parts. First, I outline the overarching narrative found in classic accounts of the history of international law and highlight its three main tenets. Second, I briefly summarize the two main alternative approaches to the history of international law that have emerged since the 1990s and underline the specific challenges they have raised to the classic narrative. Finally, I turn to the recent attempts to take these alternatives further, notably by acknowledging the limitations that come with intertwining the history of international law so closely with that of the laws of war.

Historicizing international law: classic accounts

Classic accounts of the history of international law have traced the steady development of international law over centuries, with a heavy emphasis on the leaps made during the early modern period. These works focused predominantly on the thought of great jurists, often enumerating the main contributions of Vitoria, Grotius, Pufendorf, Vattel, and the like. Hugo Grotius, the seventeenth-century Dutch prodigy long considered the founder of international law, has occupied a particularly prominent place in these accounts, with his 1625 treatise on *The Laws of War and Peace* deemed the cornerstone of early modern international law. Three broad features of these types of accounts are particularly noteworthy: the framing of the development of international law as an attempt to regulate relations between independent sovereign states, the sense of continuity between early modern developments and contemporary international law, and the emphasis on the importance within this broad endeavor of the development of the laws of war.

This account of the history of international law has been especially popular within the discipline of IR, and in many respects, it remains solidly anchored in the collective imagination of IR scholars. Its manifestations are visible across theoretical approaches, from classical realism to constructivism. The most commonly encountered trope is perhaps the idea that Grotius was the first to put forward the ideas of state sovereignty and/or of international society and that these would then become concretely expressed with the Peace of Westphalia (Philpott, 2001: 3; Morgenthau, 2005: 254). After all, IR's surprisingly resilient love affair with the myth of 1648 dovetails perfectly with this account of a handful of late sixteenth and early seventeenth–century thinkers providing us with the fully fledged intellectual underpinnings of the modern states-system. It is thus no surprise that this specific account of the history of international law has found a particularly resilient home within the discipline of IR.

It must also be noted that part of the continued popularity of this account in the discipline has to do specifically with the work of scholars identified with the English School (see Navari and Green, 2021 in this volume). More than any other group of IR scholars, they shared a keen interest in the history of the development of international law and saw it as deeply intertwined with the development of international society. According to the most prominent figure of the school, Hedley Bull, international law is one of the core institutions of international society and provides the basic rules of conduct in an anarchical world of independent sovereign states who would agree to bind themselves to these laws in order to avoid a complete state of nature (Bull, 2002). The idea that international law had developed out of the need to regulate relations between independent sovereign states, including the vexing issue of warfare, and that its most important roots were in the early modern period, notably during the decades around the peace of Westphalia, echoed many of the English School's most important claims about the development of the modern states-system. As perhaps the single most historically-oriented approach in IR prior to the historiographical turn of the early 2000s, the English School has left a legacy in terms of its engagement with the history of international law that continues to run deep within broader histories of IR.

Rethinking the history of international law

However, amongst certain IR scholars, and more systematically within the expanding field of the history of international law, this conventional account has come under increasing scrutiny. The 1990s saw a turning point in the historiography of international law with the growing impact of two related intellectual *courants*: Third World Approaches to International Law (TWAIL) and the broader New Approaches to International Law (NAIL). Scholars within these research agendas have challenged the two first central tenets of the conventional account of the history of international law, painting a strikingly different picture of its development over time.

'Third World Approaches to International Law'

To begin with, TWAIL scholars have consistently undermined the idea that international law emerged primarily as an attempt to regulate relations between independent sovereign states. Instead, they point to the symbiotic relationship between the development of international law and the rise of European empires. International law did not develop as an attempt to regulate relations within what IR scholars would term an 'anarchical' system or society, but in order to cement the various forms of hierarchical domination Europeans gradually imposed over Latin America, Asia, and Africa (the seminal work remains Anghie, 2005, see also Caraccioli, 2021 in this volume).

More specifically the claim is that international law and international jurists and publicists played an essential role in European territorial expansion. For instance, these jurists elaborated, recovered, and expanded legal concepts—from *terra nullius*, to the 'standard of civilization,' and the classic concept of sovereignty—in order to legitimize European control over new lands and peoples. Even more explicitly, they were actively involved in the practice of empire-building. Grotius, for instance, was defending the rights of navigation of the Dutch East India Company, arguably the most important agent of seventeenth-century European expansionism, while many of the more important late nineteenth–century international lawyers were involved in the Berlin Conference of 1884–1885, where European powers met to further buttress their expansionary activities on the African continent.

TWAIL scholars have had a significant impact within the history international law, and their core arguments have now been made by numerous scholars who do not necessarily identify with that particular approach (Sylvest, 2008; Fitzmaurice, 2012; Koskenniemi et al., 2017; Pitts, 2018). Interestingly, these arguments were also developed in a virtually parallel fashion within IR scholarship, notably via critiques of the English School's earlier work (Keene, 2002; an earlier though more specific foray in this area is Gong, 1984). As such, the idea that imperial considerations underpinned the development of the core doctrines and concepts of international law is now relatively well-established, both within the specific field of the history of international law and increasingly within the broader discipline of IR.

'New Approaches to International Law'

For their part, scholars working within the broader NAIL approach have notably undermined the conventional account's emphasis on the continuity between the early modern history of international law and its contemporary instantiation. Their own version highlights the nineteenth century as constituting a significant disjuncture in the history of international law rather than a mere additional step within its longer development (Koskenniemi, 2001; Nuzzo and Vec, 2012). Directly critiquing the teleological character of early histories of international law, the starkest versions of this scholarship argue that the history of international law in the early modern period merely constitutes the 'prehistory of international law' (Koskenniemi, 2010), a phase during which international law was so qualitatively different from what it would develop into in the nineteenth century that is has to be understood in entirely different terms.[1] At the heart of this alternative account is a story about the emergence of international law as a self-styled 'scientific discipline' in the late-nineteenth century.

Much of the debate about continuity and discontinuity hinges on the way one understands the emergence of positivism. Positivism, in a nutshell, encompasses the attempt to systematize international law and render it more scientific. It is considered to have emerged in opposition to the natural law approach and to have sought to ground international law pragmatically in the consent of states rather than in nobler religious or secular visions of morality. In some accounts, seventeenth-century jurists such as Richard Zouche (1590–1661) and Cornelius van Bynkershoek (1673–1743) can already be identified as positivists in a certain sense (Lesaffer, 2011), while eighteenth-century Vattel 'represents an important bridge between the naturalism of the absolutist era and the positivism of the modern' (Reus-Smit, 1999: 132–133). By contrast, proponents of the nineteenth-century discontinuity thesis tend to criticize these labels as wishful back-projections owing more to typological fantasies than to historical realities. The positivist turn in international law, they tell us, has to be understood within the broader nineteenth-century rise of scientific and legal positivism; they identify the late eighteenth–century lawyer Georg von Martens as the founder of the modern positivist tradition of the discipline, emphasizing that his approach would only start taking off from the 1830s (Nuzzo and Vec, 2012).

A new picture of the history of international law

These alternative accounts of the history of international law have gathered increasing support over recent years, and while their somewhat fragmented nature has prevented them from entirely replacing the conventional account, they have displaced it irreversibly. Nowadays, it has become unsound to speak of the historical development of international law without mentioning either the role of empire or the emergence of the discipline in the late-nineteenth century. While certain aspects of these alternative accounts remain debated, their broad claims have become widely accepted, and the old conventional account of the history of international law is increasingly veering toward becoming a mere historiographical curiosity.

Remarkably, though, despite their radical departures from the conventional account both in terms of focus and chronology, these alternative accounts leave relatively intact the idea that the development of the laws of war was essentially the fulcrum upon which modern international law emerged. In what remains perhaps the most famous contribution of TWAIL scholarship to the history international law, Antony Anghie explores the imperial underpinnings of international law through a novel interpretation of Francisco de Vitoria's 1532 reflections on the legality of Spain's wars against the 'Indians newly discovered' (Anghie, 2005). Similarly, Martti Koskenniemi's groundbreaking account of the development of the discipline of international law in the late-nineteenth century emphasizes the central role of a group of individuals who sought to codify international law and particularly the laws of war (Koskenniemi, 2001). In both cases, the law of war thus remains at the center of the narrative of the development of international law, whether one places the beginning of the story in the early modern period or in the nineteenth century.

New directions

A more recent wave of work has sought to broaden the scope of what constitutes the history of international law, and in doing so, it has indirectly undermined this third aspect of the conventional narrative as well. The conventional account of the history of international law placed significant emphasis on the development of the laws of war in large part because it was so heavily focused on the writings of 'great thinkers' who often couched their writings in terms of 'the laws of war and peace.' New works have highlighted not only the limitations of this conventional approach, but also of the alternative accounts (NAIL and TWAIL) that continue to take these elements for granted, and they are now opening up radically new avenues for further research.

Two main trends stand out (though this is by no means an exhaustive list of new research in the field). First, historians of international law and IR scholars have emphasized the problems that stem from telling the history of international law through collections of great thinkers and the need to explore and systematize alternative approaches. Second, these scholars have pointed to the tendency to anachronistically project the contemporary division between public and private international law back into the early modern period. In doing so, they suggest, we have drastically underestimated the importance of 'private' international legal developments for the broader history of international law, most notably the crucial role played by economic considerations and the shifts in the architecture of property rights. In both cases, these scholars have opened research avenues that give little importance to the law of war in the development of international law and that call for new foci entirely. I discuss them in turn.

Beyond 'great thinkers'

A first set of scholars have taken issue with the persistent tendency to tell the history of international law by outlining the ideas of a few famous individuals, from Vitoria, Grotius, and Vattel to Georg von Martens, Travers Twiss, and Hersch Lauterpacht. The main points made within this new area of scholarship can be divided into two distinct sets of insights.

The first set pertains to the idea that if we focus on a few 'great thinkers' in establishing the history of international law, we essentially miss the forest for the tree (see Wallenius, 2021 in this volume). Part of the issue here stems from the relatively commonsensical yet rarely acknowledged fact that individuals singled out as great thinkers are rarely representative of their own time (Keene, 2017). The more pressing problem, though, is about identifying what exactly constitutes 'international law,' particularly when we look for it during the period prior to its codification from the late-nineteenth century onward. While the conventional practice has been to focus on the writings of famous jurists and publicists, recent years have witnessed a turn toward the study of treaties signed amongst states and other political entities (Lesaffer, 2004; Keene, 2007; Hébié, 2015). This has sparked a more systematic turn toward the study of the history of international law as a complex and hardly ever linear practice, rather than merely as an almost teleological collection of famous texts (Benton and Ford, 2016; Wallenius, 2019).

The second set of insights owes much to critical disciplinary history and emphasizes the importance of analyzing how we ended up with this canon of 'great thinkers' to begin with. It is now becoming clear that the aforementioned conventional history of international law was constructed in the late nineteenth and early-twentieth century (Craven, 2012; Koskenniemi, 2012; Smeltzer, 2018; Amorosa, 2019). This went hand in hand with the establishment of international law as a scientific discipline, and crucially, it fundamentally reshaped the way international law was conceptualized (Craven, 2012: 22). In fact, it is perhaps precisely because of this late nineteenth–century retroactive construction of the history of international law through the thought of famous individuals that the actual practice of international law over centuries long remained a blind spot. The point, then, is to trace this nineteenth-century shift, and crucially, to account for the purposes that nineteenth-century lawyers sought to serve with their new historical narratives.

Beyond the public/private divide

A second group of scholars have historicized the division between public and private international law and emphasized both the contingency and the relative novelty of the split. In doing so, they have underlined the significant gaps that have been left in accounts of the history of international law that focus predominantly on matters that fall into the contemporary category of public international law: sovereignty, war, freedom of the seas, and the like. Instead, they point to the need to more effectively incorporate what would today be considered private international law (or even domestic private law) matters into the broader history of international law, especially matters pertaining to economic interests and social property relations (Koskenniemi, 2016).

The case for the importance of these 'private law' matters for the development of early modern international law is a compelling one. For example, if one considers the importance of Europe's ruling families for early modern international relations and the numerous wars of succession that rocked the continent throughout the period, it is not hard to believe that family law played a central role in Europe's high politics (Teschke, 2002). Even more importantly, though, one of the boldest claims made by this new stream of research is that the so-called prehistory of international, i.e. its history prior to the nineteenth century, was deeply intertwined with the development of the discipline of economics (Koskenniemi, 2010: 339). Beyond strengthening the idea of a disjuncture between early modern and nineteenth-century international law, this attempt to entirely reappraise the nature of early modern international law is likely to generate much debate over the coming years.

More broadly, this interest in the role of 'private' international law in the broader development of international law since the early modern period is a thriving new area of research, and it has resonated particularly well with scholars affiliated with historical sociology (see Go et al., 2021). New works are emerging notably on the links between the development of international law, empires, and the history of capitalism (Pal, 2020), the role of chartered companies in the 'prehistory of private international law' (Cavanagh, 2017), the centrality of foreigners' property rights in the construction of the nineteenth-century liberal international order (Wallenius, 2018), and the way in which the international lawyers who populated the US State Department in the early twentieth–century advanced American imperialism through their representation of US corporations with business overseas (Coates, 2016). Thus, while overarching works on the history of international law continue to focus quite heavily (if not almost exclusively) on areas within public international law (for a recent example, which also follows the 'great thinkers' approach, see Kadelbach et al., 2017), the coming years might ultimately witness a fairly significant change of emphasis.

Wither the laws of war?

These new developments do not seem to bode well for the laws of war, which, despite some continued interest in their broadly defined history (e.g. Simms and Trim, 2011; Glanville, 2014), appear to be irremediably losing their centrality in accounts of the development of international law. Yet, in light of the continued importance of the laws of war in the contemporary world, there is arguably much to gain from reappraising their history based on the recent progress of the field. Both the move away from great thinkers and the much more critical engagement with the public/private distinction could be applied to our current histories of the laws of war, with potentially highly fruitful results (for an example of the former, though focused on twentieth-century developments, see Alexander, 2015). This is yet another area for further research, one that might significantly alter our understanding of the relationship between the laws of war, international law at large, and the development of the modern states-system.

Conclusion

This chapter has provided a brief overview of what international law and the laws of war substantively entail, why they are often considered to be intertwined historically, and what the historical literature on the subject has highlighted, both in IR and beyond. With the emergence of an actual subfield focused on the history of international law in the late 1990s (populated predominantly by lawyers and historians), many of the old tropes of the classic account of the history of international law still central to much IR scholarship have been discarded. Following the critiques of TWAIL and NAIL scholars, as well as a handful of parallel developments in Historical IR, it has become incongruous to speak of international law as an institution that was established primarily in order to regulate relations between sovereign states, or to imagine the development of international law as a continuous and relatively linear process from the early modern period to the twentieth century. The imperial underpinnings of the development of international law are now well-established, as is the disjuncture constituted by the development of international law as a scientific discipline in the late-nineteenth century. IR accounts of the relationship between international law and international relations that ignore these insights may well be in need of substantive revisions.

Ironically, however, the recent developments within the historiography of international law have brought this field closer to the concerns of Historical IR scholars. Indeed, the most promising areas in the history of international law currently involve moving beyond the exegesis of a canon of famous figures and investigating the development of international law as a practice. The tools for doing so are very much those at the heart of the Historical IR agenda: accounting for crucial socioeconomic contexts, investigating the doings of various communities of practice, shedding light of on the construction of disciplinary tropes—to name a but a few. As such, there has perhaps never been a better time for scholars of Historical IR to engage more actively with international law and its contested history.

Suggestions for further reading

Alexandrowicz, C. (2017). *The Law of Nations in Global History*, Oxford: Oxford University Press.

Benton, L. (2009). *A Search for Sovereignty: Law and Geography in European Empires, 1400–1900*. Cambridge: Cambridge University Press.

Grewe, W. (2000). *The Epochs of International Law*. Berlin: Walter de Gruyter.

Koskenniemi, M. (2002). The Epochs of International Law. *International and Comparative Law Quarterly*, 51 (3), 746-751.

Neff, S. (2005). *War and the Law of Nations: A General History*. Cambridge, MA: Cambridge University Press.

Neff, S. (2014). *Justice among Nations: A History of International Law*. Cambridge, MA: Harvard University Press.

Note

1 Though of course, some elements of continuities are hardly contested, such as the persistent (if perhaps underappreciated) reliance on Roman law (Lesaffer, 2016).

References

Alexander, A. (2015). A Short History of International Humanitarian Law. *European Journal of International Law*, 26 (1), 109-138.

Amorosa, P. (2019). *Rewriting the History of the Law of Nations: How James Brown Scott Made Francisco de Vitoria the Founder of International Law*. Oxford: Oxford University Press.

Anghie, A. (2005). *Imperialism, Sovereignty and the Making of International Law*. Cambridge: Cambridge University Press.

Bartelson, J. (2021). War and the Turn to History in International Relations. In de Carvalho, B., Costa Lopez, J., & Leira, H., eds. *Routledge Handbook of Historical International Relations*. Abingdon: Routledge.

Benton, L., and Ford, L. (2016). *Rage for Order: The British Empire and the Origins of International Law 1800–1850*. Cambridge, MA: Harvard University Press.

Best, G. (1980). *Humanity in Warfare: The Modern History of the International Law of Armed Conflicts*. London: Weidenfeld & Nicolson.

Brownlie, I. (1963). *International Law and the Use of Force by States*. Oxford: Clarendon Press.

Bull, H. (2002). *The Anarchical Society: A Study of Order in World Politics*. Basingstoke: Palgrave.

Caraccioli, M. J. (2021). Early (Modern) Empires: The Political Ideology of Conceptual Domination. In de Carvalho, B., Costa Lopez, J., & Leira, H., eds. *Routledge Handbook of Historical International Relations*. Abingdon: Routledge.

Cavanagh, E. (2017). The Atlantic Prehistory of Private International Law: Trading Companies of the New World and the Pursuit of Restitution in England and France, 1613–43. *Itinerario*, 41 (3), 452-483.

Coates, B. (2016). *Legalist Empire: International Law and American Foreign Relations in the Early Twentieth Century*. Oxford: Oxford University Press.

Craven, M. (2012). The Invention of a Tradition: Westlake, The Berlin Conference and the Historicisation of International Law. In: L. Nuzzo, and M. Vec, eds., *Constructing International Law: The Birth of a Discipline*, Frankfurt am Main: Vittorio Klostermann.

Fitzmaurice, A. (2012). Liberalism and Empire in Nineteenth Century International Law. *The American Historical Review*, 117 (1), 122-140.

Glanville, L. (2014). *Sovereignty and the Responsibility to Protect: A New History*. Chicago, IL: University of Chicago Press.

Go, J., Lawson, G., and de Carvalho, B. (2021). Historical Sociology in International Relations: The Challenge of the Global. In de Carvalho, B., Costa Lopez, J., & Leira, H., eds. *Routledge Handbook of Historical International Relations*. Abingdon: Routledge.

Gong, G. (1984). *The Standard of Civilization in International Society*. Oxford: Clarendon Press.

Hébié, M. (2015). *Souveraineté territoriale par traité*. Paris: Presses Universitaires de France.

Howard, M., Andreopoulos, G., and Shulman, M., eds. (1994). *The Laws of War: Constraints on Warfare in the Western World*. London: Yale University Press.

Jochnick, C., and Normand, R. (1994). The Legitimation of Violence: A Critical History of the Laws of War. *Harvard International Law Journal*, 35 (1): 49-95.

Kadelbach, S., Kleinlein, T., and Roth-Isigkeit, D. (2017). *System, Order, and International Law: The Early History of International Legal Thought from Machiavelli to Hegel*. Oxford: Oxford University Press.

Keene, E. (2002). *Beyond the Anarchical Society: Grotius, Colonialism and Order in World Politics*. Cambridge: Cambridge University Press.

Keene, E. (2007). A Case Study of the Construction of International Hierarchy: British Treaty-Making Against the Slave Trade in the Early Nineteenth Century. *International Organization*, 61 (2), 311-339.

Keene, E. (2017). International Intellectual History and International Relations: Contexts, Canons and Mediocrities. *International Relations*, 31 (3), 341-356.

Kennedy, D. (2009). *Of War and Law*. Princeton, NJ: Princeton University Press.

Koskenniemi, M., Rech, W., and Jimenez Fonseca, M., eds. (2017). *International Law and Empire: Historical Explorations*. Oxford: Oxford University Press.

Koskenniemi, M. (2001). *The Gentle Civilizer of Nations: The Rise and Fall of International Law 1870–1960*. Cambridge: Cambridge University Press.

Koskenniemi, M. (2010). International Law and Raison d'État: Rethinking the Prehistory of International Law. In: B. Kingsbury, and B. Straumann, eds., *The Roman Foundations of the Law of Nations*, Oxford: Oxford University Press, 297-339.

Koskenniemi, M. (2012). A History of International Law Histories. In: B. Fassbender, A. Peters, S. Peter, and D. Högger, eds., *The Oxford Handbook of the History of International Law*, Oxford: Oxford University Press, 943-971.

Koskenniemi, M. (2016). Expanding Histories of International Law. *American Journal of Legal History*, 56 (1), 104-112.

Lesaffer, R. (2004). *Peace Treaties and International Law in European History: From the Late Middle Ages to World War One*. Cambridge: Cambridge University Press.

Lesaffer, R. (2011). The Classical Law of Nations (1500–1800). In: A. Orakhelashvili, ed., *Research Handbook on the Theory and History of International Law*, Cheltenham: Edward Elgar, 408-440.

Lesaffer, R. (2016). Roman Law and the Intellectual History of International Law. In: A. Orford, F. Hoffmann, and M. Clark, eds., *The Oxford Handbook of the Theory of International Law*, Oxford: Oxford University Press, 38-58.

Morgenthau, H. (2005). *Politics Among Nations*. Boston, MA: McGraw-Hill.

Nabulsi, K. (1999). *Traditions of War: Occupation, Resistance, and the Law*. Oxford: Oxford University Press.

Navari, C., and Green, D. (2021). The English School and Historical International Relations. In de Carvalho, B., Costa Lopez, J., & Leira, H., eds. *Routledge Handbook of Historical International Relations*. Abingdon: Routledge.

Nuzzo, L., and Vec, M., eds. (2012). *Constructing International Law: The Birth of a Discipline*. Frankfurt am Main: Vittorio Klostermann.

Pal, M. (2020). *Jurisdictional Accumulation: An Early Modern History of Law, Empires, and Capital*. Cambridge: Cambridge University Press.

Philpott, D. (2001). *Revolutions in Sovereignty: How Ideas Shaped Modern International Relations*. Princeton, NJ: Princeton University Press.

Pitts, J. (2018). *Boundaries of the International: Law and Empire*. Cambridge, MA: Harvard University Press.

Reus-Smit, C. (1999). *The Moral Purpose of the State: Culture, Social Identity, and Institutional Rationality in International Relations*. Princeton, NJ: Princeton University Press.

Simms, B., and Trim, D. (2011). *Humanitarian Intervention: A History*. Cambridge: Cambridge University Press.

Smeltzer, J. (2018). On the Use and Abuse of Francisco de Vitoria: James Brown Scott and Carl Schmitt. *Journal of the History of International Law*, 20 (3), 345-372.

Sylvest, C. (2008). 'Our Passion for Legality': International Law and Imperialism in Late Nineteenth-Century Britain. *Review of International Studies*, 34 (3), 403-423.

Teschke, B. (2002). Theorizing the Westphalian System of States: International Relations from Absolutism to Capitalism. *European Journal of International Relations*, 8 (1), 5-48.

Wallenius, T. (2018). *The Liberal Myth: Foreigners' Property Rights and the Making of Modern World Politics*. Doctoral Thesis, University of Oxford.

Wallenius, T. (2019). The Case for a History of Global Legal Practices. *European Journal of International Relations*, 25 (1), 108-130.

Wallenius, T. (2021). How to Do the History of International Thought?. In de Carvalho, B., Costa Lopez, J., & Leira, H., eds. *Routledge Handbook of Historical International Relations*. Abingdon: Routledge.

31

INTERNATIONAL ORGANISATIONS IN HISTORICAL PERSPECTIVE

Ellen J. Ravndal

Introduction

Since international organisations (IOs) first emerged in the 19th century, they have become a central feature of contemporary international relations. Intergovernmental organisations (IGOs) are official sites of interaction between states. IGOs like the United Nations, the World Trade Organisation (WTO), or the World Health Organisation (WHO) are important forums where states meet to discuss responses to the latest security crisis, agree on trade policies, or decide appropriate measures against COVID-19, malaria, and other diseases. IGOs as forums of states serve as focal points for international norms and decision-making. However, IOs are not merely forums where other actors meet, but also important actors in their own right. IGO secretariats prepare agendas, write reports, and implement policies, and as such exert considerable influence in international relations. International non-governmental organisations (NGOs) such as Amnesty International, Doctors Without Borders/Médecins Sans Frontières, or Greenpeace can also make a difference through their advocacy work and operations on the ground. IOs – both IGOs and NGOs – have played central roles in international affairs since their emergence, and an examination of their histories can therefore shed light not merely on the development of the IOs themselves (interesting as this is!), but also on broader trends of international relations.

This chapter provides a brief overview of the history of IOs, both IGOs and NGOs, and an assessment of current scholarship on their emergence and development in Historical IR and related disciplines. The chapter identifies five major areas of current scholarship related to (i) the genesis of IOs; (ii) internationalism, world government, and transnational society; (iii) IOs as actors and the development of an independent International Civil Service (ICS); (iv) neglected actors and sources of agency; and (v) IOs and imperialism. At time of writing, the scholarship by historians is the most extensive, with scholars in IR, international law, sociology, anthropology, and geography also entering the debate. This chapter discusses relevant books and articles regardless of the disciplinary home of the author because they all form part of the same debate. The conclusion, however, highlights the ways in which disciplinary IR scholars are making novel contributions and argues that IR scholars are well poised to examine how IOs are connected to broader international trends and what role they play in the constitution of international order. IOs are forums for interaction of other actors, as well as actors in their own right. They both reflect and in turn shape international norms. IR scholars can make a unique contribution to our understanding of IOs as integrated parts of bigger patterns by asking 'IR questions' of the history of IOs.

A brief history of international organisations

IOs, both IGOs and NGOs, first emerged in the 19th century. Depending on your choice of definition, there are several candidates for the first IGO. The Rhine River Commission established by the Congress of Vienna in 1815 was the first international commission setup to deal with the common problem of navigation on a river shared between several states (Lyons, 1963: 13; Iriye, 2002: 10–11; Reinalda, 2009: 29), yet its membership was restricted to European riparian states. The European Commission for the Control of the Danube, established in 1856, on the other hand, did extend membership to non-riparian states, making it another candidate for the label of first '*international*' organisation (Yao, 2019). The Superior Council of Health founded in 1838 included delegates from the Ottoman Empire, and was thus the first to include non-European states (Iriye, 2002: 11). A strong case for the label of the first '*modern*' IGO can be made for the International Telegraph Union (ITU) of 1865, the first of the so-called international public unions. This was the first organisation with truly open membership policies and aspirations to universal global membership. It was the first to set up a permanent secretariat (1868), and the first to operate on the later standard model of recurring conferences of state representatives as the highest decision-making organ, while day-to-day operations and implementation were in the hands of a secretariat. The ITU became a model for later IGOs established to deal with postal services, railroads, intellectual property, standardisation, and other new technologies and government services (Murphy, 1994; Reinalda, 2009; Fari et al., 2015).

From the 1860s onwards, new IGOs were formed with increasing speed. By one count, there were seven IGOs in existence in 1870, rising to 24 by 1900 and 50 in 1913 (Reinalda, 2009: 92–93). A more conservative measure, excluding regional organisations like the river commissions, gives a list of 33 IGOs founded before 1914 (Murphy, 1994: 47–48). Although the number of new IGOs created in this period was far from insignificant, it was dwarfed by the growth of NGOs in the same time period. By 1914, one source claims, fully 466 international NGOs had been established (Speeckaert, 1957; Lyons, 1963: 14). To this day, the number of NGOs remains much larger than the number of IGOs. According to the authoritative source of the *Yearbook of International Organisation*, in 2015, there were 273 IGOs and 8976 international NGOs, of conventional type, in existence (Union of International Associations, 2015: table 2.1). If we include a wider range of actors, the total number of international NGOs today surpasses 20,000 (Davies, 2013: 1; see also Union of International Associations, 2015: table 2.1).

Not only are there a greater number of international NGOs than IGOs, but they also have a much longer history. The first transnational civil society organisations were various religious orders, charities, and missionary societies. The Sovereign Constantinian Order claims to have been established as early as the 4th century. By the end of the 16th century, at least 90 Roman Catholic international NGOs were in existence, alongside organisation of other Christian denominations and Islamic organisations such as the Sufi Naqshbandiyyah (Davies, 2013: 20–21). Outside of religious societies, the opportunities for transnational contacts remained limited, and most studies argue that modern international NGOs emerged in the 19th century in parallel to the development of IGOs at that time (Iriye, 2002; Reinalda, 2009; Davies, 2013). The development of both IGOs and NGOs were connected to broader trends of globalisation, industrialisation, and the professionalisation of government administration. New technologies such as the telegraph and the railway brought people into closer contact. Governments sought to regulate and coordinate these new technologies through IGOs (Murphy, 1994; Hanrieder and Zangl, 2015). Simultaneously, closer cross-border contacts also gave rise to a 'global consciousness,' or internationalism, and offered civil society the means to organise into NGOs (Iriye, 2002: 11; see also Davies, 2013).

The League of Nations, established after the First World War, represents further important innovations in the development of IGOs. The League of Nations was the first universal IGO with a general mandate. Earlier universal IGOs like the ITU or the Universal Postal Union (UPU) had each focused on a specific issue area. The International Union of American Republics (later called the Pan-American Union, today the Organization of American States), established in 1890, was the first IGO with a general mandate spanning issues of arbitration and international law, trade, communication technologies, health, and more, but its membership was limited regionally (and politically) to republican states in the Americas (Reinalda, 2009: 131–133; MacKenzie, 2010: 6). A second important innovative feature of the League of Nations was the creation of the ICS. Although some precedents existed in earlier permanent secretariats, the League of Nations secretariat established by its first Secretary-General, Sir Eric Drummond, was the first secretariat with an international staff theoretically loyal only to the organisation and independent from national influence (Newman, 2007: 435; Newman and Ravndal, 2019). Even those who have described the League as a failure overall have acknowledged the importance of the foundation of the ICS in Geneva. Walters argued, 'the creation of a secretariat international alike in its structure, its spirit, and its personnel, was without doubt one of the most important events in the history of international politics' (Walters, 1952: 76). Pedersen's recent study of the League agrees: 'Nothing the League produced was more quietly revolutionary than the international Secretariat. There was no real precedent' (Pedersen, 2015: 46).

Although the 1930s are widely seen as a period of decline and failure of IGOs and the broader peaceful and cooperative aspirations of the international community, IOs continued to operate throughout the period. Looking beyond interstate crisis and war, recent research highlights, for example, the continuing contributions of the League of Nations in areas of minority rights, economic policy, or the administration of mandate territories (e.g. Clavin, 2013; Pedersen, 2015). During the Second World War, the numbers of international conferences and congresses may have decreased, but IGO secretariats continued to work throughout the war years, and most member states kept up their payment of membership fees (Herren, 2016).

The discredited League of Nations was replaced by the United Nations (UN) in 1945, and with it came a large number of new IGOs in different areas of international affairs. Older IGOs like the ITU or the UPU became specialised agencies in the UN system, alongside new organisations such as the WHO and the organisations of the Bretton Woods system. Outside the UN system, new regional organisations were established, such as the Arab League (1945), NATO (1949), and the Organisation of African Unity (1963, now the African Union). The next decades saw further growth in the numbers of IGOs and international NGOs. In 1951, the *Yearbook* records 123 IGOs and 832 international NGOs in existence. By 1970, this had increased to 242 IGOs and 1993 international NGOs (Union of International Associations, 2015: table 2.9). During the Cold War, the Soviet Union sought to establish its own organisations, for example the Cominform (1947), to compete with those it considered to be Western creations, but its efforts in this regard were not entirely successful, and throughout the period, it remained a member of the UN and joined various specialised agencies (Mazower, 2012: 247–248). Nonetheless, the number of IGOs reached a peak at 378 in 1985, before declining to around 230–240 in the early 2000s (Union of International Associations, 2015: table 2.9).

The number of international NGOs has continued to grow throughout the Cold War and the decades since, with the 1960s–1980s being a particularly important period in their development.

Conflict and fragmentation at the time seems to have actually stimulated, rather than hampered, the formation of new NGOs during this period (Davies, 2013:141). New NGOs emerged focused on human rights (e.g. Amnesty International, 1961; Human Rights Watch, 1978), nuclear disarmament (e.g. Pugwash Conference, 1957), and the environment (e.g. WWF, 1961; Greenpeace, 1971). The end of the Cold War brought a new period of optimism for the potential of NGOs to influence international affairs as a force for good. NGOs and transnational civil society were given credit for contributing to the end of Communism in Eastern Europe, and transnational coalitions such as the International Campaign to Ban Landmines became more common (Davies, 2013: 154–155). Like the spread of new communication technologies in the latter half of the 19th century which allowed the creation of modern NGOs, the Internet and social media seems to have offered new opportunities for transnational civil society to organise and mobilise in the 21st century. Yet this has not been a unidirectional success story. Authoritarian governments, too, have been able to employ the new tools of social media to spread their visions of the world, and in many states, NGOs are facing increasingly difficult working conditions. Many IGOs, too, face growing demands in the 21st century, not unrelated to the growth of civil society. Traditional IGOs are frequently criticised for their lack of accountability, transparency, and legitimacy (e.g. Koppell, 2010; Keohane, 2011; Bexell, 2014).

Research on the history of international organisations

The traditional narrative of the history of IOs broadly conforms to a liberal internationalist approach and portrays the growth of IOs as part of a continuing progress towards a more peaceful world (in this volume see Jahn, 2021). These ideas are visible in books published in the middle of the 20th century (Mangone, 1954; Claude, 1956; Lyons, 1963), but also in more recent accounts (e.g. Ikenberry, 2001; Iriye, 2002; Schlesinger, 2003; Kennedy, 2006). Although there is a clear connection between internationalism and the growth of IOs, most recent scholarship on the history of IOs are more critical of their subject matter and follow from the view that 'institutions are not, as some liberals would have us believe, neutral arenas for the solution of common problems but rather sites of power, even of dominance' (Hurrell, 2005: 56; see also Chimni, 2016). In a recent survey of the history of IOs since 1945, Bhupinder Chimni identifies three strands of critical history: Marxist, feminist, and Third World histories of IOs (Chimni, 2016). Although Chimni seems unaware of the extensive literature on IOs by historians, his observation holds true if we also include this scholarship. As this chapter shows, with the exception of some scholarship on the genesis of IOs, the majority of recent publications on the history of IOs apply a critical approach to their subject matter.

This section reviews contemporary literature on this history of IOs, by IR scholars, historians, and others, in relation to five areas: (i) the genesis of IOs; (ii) internationalism, world government, and transnational civil society; (iii) IOs as actors and the development of an independent ICS; (iv) neglected actors and sources of agency in the story of IOs; and (v) how imperial structures were present in the creation of IOs and how IOs in turn reproduced imperial structures and helped to legitimate empires.

The genesis of IOs

One key question IR scholars keep returning to is the question of why states have established IGOs and why they join them. By joining an IGO, or any international agreement, states limit their future options and thereby compromise their sovereignty. This puzzle requires explaining. Liberal institutionalist studies employing a rational choice approach argue that states will join an IGO if the benefits of doing so outweigh the costs to their sovereignty (Abbott and Snidal, 1998). Studies of human rights treaties, for example, have found that democratising states will seek to join 'democratic' IGOs, such as human rights treaties, precisely because of their sovereignty costs. Bearing such costs can send a signal to other states, and domestic constituencies, that the regime is committed to democracy (e.g. Hafner-Burton et al., 2015). This is a functional and state-centric account of IGO creation and IGO history – states establish them to serve a function and join them when it suits their purpose – but what have historically been those purposes and reasoning for establishing IGOs?

The literature has put forward competing and complementary explanations as to why states first turned to IGOs in the 19th century. Some argue that IGOs are essentially established by hegemons to consolidate their influence and their vision of international order at the end of major conflict (e.g. Ikenberry, 2001). Thus, for example, the UN and the Bretton Woods system represent attempts by the United States to order the world to their liking after the Second World War. A broad strokes history of IGOs seem to provide support for this view. The first attempt by states to set up international institutions to manage international order was the Concert of Europe established by the great powers at the Congress of Vienna (1814–15). Under the Concert system, the great powers would convene conferences to deal with diplomatic crises, and once states acquired the habit of meeting for diplomatic purposes, the conference practice soon expanded to other areas such as health (Huber, 2006), new communication technologies, statistics (Randeraad, 2011), and arbitration and international law. From this, it was a short step to establish permanent structures and permanent secretariats to service these conferences, and with that step the modern IGO was born, set up in response to a need of states for coordination and continuity (Reinalda, 2009).

Another version of a functionalist argument focuses not on the actions of great powers or hegemons, but on the needs of the capitalist system and states' responses to industrialisation (see Anievas and Gogu, 2021). Murphy (1994) describes the history of IGOs in three waves linked to the development of key technologies: the telegraph (ITU), radio (the International Radiotelegraph Union), and satellites (Intelsat). In response to industrialisation and the development of new technologies, IGOs were established to serve two primary functions: to foster industry and commerce and to manage potential conflicts with social groups which might oppose or suffer from an expansion of industry (Murphy, 1994: 34).

Finally, recent literature also identifies a further motivation for states to establish and join IGOs in their quest for status. States may seek to set up new IGOs, to join existing ones, to host their headquarters, and to place their nationals in prominent positions within them because these acts can confirm or confer status. In the late 19th and early 20th century, non-European states sought membership of IGOs to confirm their status as 'sovereign' and 'modern' states (Ravndal, 2018). Japan, for example, sought to use membership of the UPU to strengthen its position in negotiations with Britain (Howland, 2014). In the post-1945 era, newly independent states tried to leverage IGO membership and to reform existing IGOs to protect and strengthen their postcolonial independence (Getachew, 2019). Small- and medium-sized states, such as Canada and Norway, have also historically taken advantage of the opportunities offered by IGOs to strengthen their status (e.g. de Carvalho and Neumann, 2015).

Internationalism, world government, and transnational civil society

IGOs are official sites of interaction between states, and as such it is no wonder that many histories of IOs or explanations of the genesis of IOs tend to focus on states. But IGOs are not merely forums for state interaction, they also sit at the intersection of broader trends of international, and transnational, society. They are 'a channel for the relations between states, as well as between a myriad of nongovernmental and voluntary organizations, networks, political movements, and individuals' (Amrith and Sluga, 2008: 252). Historians turned to the study of IGOs and NGOs as part of a broader 'transnational turn.' Focusing on IOs – and using their archival collections – promised a means of overcoming the national bias of traditional diplomatic history, and a fruitful avenue for examining the circulation of ideas and practices across and between local, regional, national, and global levels (Kott, 2011).

A focus on internationalism is not new. Indeed, early studies of IOs frequently linked these new organisational forms to the growth of an international consciousness or spirit (e.g. Reinsch, 1911; Hobson, 1915; Sayre, 1919). The traditional narrative, as we have seen, broadly falls within the liberal internationalist tradition and tells the story of IOs as one of progress to a gradually more connected and peaceful world. Liberal internationalism and utopian ideals have played a role in the history of IOs, and as such should form part of the research on the history of IOs. But as Mark Mazower cautions, 'when historians confuse the utopianism of their subject with their own it is easy to be led astray' (Mazower, 2009: 6). The resulting accounts often give a one-sided view of IO history and may fuel unrealistic expectations about what IOs can and should be doing today.

Many recent accounts offer a more nuanced view of the connections between internationalism and IOs, which also take into account competing forms of internationalism such as imperial, socialist, or fascist internationalism (e.g. Sluga and Clavin, 2017). Scholars have also discussed ways in which IGOs and internationalism have been used to protect national independence and strengthen state sovereignty, contrary to the liberal internationalist story (e.g. Mazower, 2012; Sluga, 2013).

Related to discussions of internationalism and international thought, we also find histories which examine ideas such as world government. Throughout the history of IOs, they have been linked to an eventual establishment of a world government (for an overview, see Yunker, 2011). The problem of how to organise, order, and govern the world has occupied scholars and politicians at various times in the 19th and 20th centuries. Some recent scholarship into this intellectual history and how it connects to the growth of IOs include Mazower's (2012) overview of internationalism and the growth of global governance during the 19th and 20th centuries, Rosenboim's (2017) examination of American and British global thought in the mid-20th century, Slobodian's (2018) study of neoliberal thought and its influence on and through IGOs from the League of Nations to the WTO, and Getachew's (2019) analysis of visions of a post-imperial world order by anticolonial intellectuals and politicians.

Finally, NGOs, which outnumber IGOs nearly 100-to-1, also form an integral part of the story. Scholars have examined the histories of NGOs as a separate phenomenon (Davies, 2013) and connected to the growth of an international society or culture (Boli and Thomas, 1999; Iriye, 2002). Others have looked at the histories of individual NGOs or of particular time periods, such as the International Red Cross (Forsythe, 2005), Amnesty International (Hopgood, 2006), or Save the Children (Droux, 2014). All of these studies have contributed to our understanding of the connections between IOs and transnational civil society.

IOs as actors and the establishment of international administration

The first wave of historical studies of IOs tended to focus on IOs as forums, and therefore as a lens to examine broader trends of international and transnational history. The role of IOs as actors has been somewhat neglected, although this is starting to change.

In broader IR scholarship, studies of IOs as actors mostly apply a liberal institutionalist or constructivist approach and examine to what extent IGOs and their representatives can act autonomously from the member states, or what tools states have at their disposal to control IGO staff (for two foundational texts, see Barnett and Finnemore, 2004; Hawkins et al., 2006). The majority of this large and growing literature give an ahistorical impression. Although scholars may examine historical cases, or discuss the evolution of IOs, their main concern is to explain contemporary theoretical questions.

Recently, however, some historians have also turned their attention to the development of IO autonomy and the institutional histories of IOs. Such institutional histories have mostly focused on the League of Nations secretariat and the transition from the League to the UN (e.g. Auberer, 2016; Jackson and O'Malley, 2018). Scholars have examined the establishment of the ICS and discussed the process by which secretariats and the representatives of IOs gain autonomy (Dykmann, 2015; Ravndal, 2017; Gram-Skjoldager and Ikonomou, 2019). Although fewer in numbers, some publications also examine the establishment of the earliest IGOs such as the ITU and its secretariat (Fari et al., 2015).

Neglected actors and sources of agency

The majority of recent historical work on IOs seeks to question and reassess taken-for-granted assumptions about the genesis and development of IGOs and NGOs in line with the goals and aspirations of critical scholarship. One way to do so is to identify hitherto neglected actors and sources of agency.

The conclusion from this literature is that the creation and development of IOs was not solely the purview of Western great powers and their representatives. Latin American states, for example, played important roles in the formation of IOs, both global and regional, and the development of international law from the late 19th century onwards (Fawcett, 2012; Finnemore and Jurkovich, 2014; Sikkink, 2014; Schulz, 2021). Japan was able to take advantage of its membership in IOs to improve its position vis-à-vis the Western great powers (Howland, 2014; Howland, 2015), as did other peripheral states (Ravndal, 2018). In the UN General Assembly, 'Southern' actors found a venue where they could use their numerical majority to change the agenda (Irwin, 2012; O'Malley, 2018). 'Southern' actors also made crucial but largely overlooked contributions to the establishment of the Bretton Woods system in general and the discourse of development aid in particular (Helleiner, 2014). Through its focus on neglected actors and forgotten agency, the scholarship on histories of IOs shares similarities with the so-called Third World Approach to International Law (TWAIL) and Global IR (Chimni, 2006; Acharya and Buzan, 2019; see also in this volume Vergerio, 2021).

IGOs and imperialism

Another strand of critical research on the history of IOs investigates how imperialism left its lingering influence in these new institutions. Susan Pedersen (2015) details how European practices of colonialism continued in the League of Nations mandate system and the Permanent Mandates Commission. Mark Mazower (2009) has likewise shown how the imperial powers sought to establish the UN as a way to safeguard their empires. Going beyond the League and the UN, a recent edited collection gathers analysis of the interconnections of imperialism and internationalism to and through various IGOs and NGOs (Jerónimo and Monteiro, 2018).

The 'standard of civilization' was a principle of international law used by the European states during the era of imperialism to safeguard their empires and adjudicate the boundaries of which states were recognised as members of the 'club.' It is now widely accepted that the 'standard of civilization' and imperial hierarchies formed part of international law in the 19th century, and thus that their influence has continued into modern international system today (Koskenniemi, 2001; Keene, 2002; see also Bowden, 2021 in this volume). Recent scholarship on the history of IOs has demonstrated that this principle also influenced the formation of early IGOs, such as the Danube River Commission (Yao, 2019).

By reproducing the principle of 'the standard of civilisation' or providing a venue for imperial powers to protect their interests, IGOs served to (re)create political hierarchies in the world. As a recent study by Viola (2020) argues, IGOs simultaneously produced equality and hierarchies in the international system, and IGOs thus contribute to the stratification of the international system. Recent historical scholarship on IOs provides additional support for this argument. Membership policies of IGOs in the 19th century allowed colonies to become full members alongside sovereign states. This reflects the fact that the international system at that time was still one of empires and served to legitimate the colonial holdings of European empires and to boost the voting power of European imperial powers (Ravndal, 2020). But once allowed membership in IGOs, colonial territories could sometimes take advantage of this situation to consolidate its government and improve its case for full independence. India, for example, could use its League of Nations membership to prepare the ground for independence (Legg, 2014). Other scholars have demonstrated that experts from colonial states could influence the formation of global norms, for example in relation to health issues (Akami, 2017). Thus, the relationship between IGOs and imperialism is complex. IGOs have served to protect and legitimate empires, while simultaneously providing a venue for non-Western states and anticolonial movements to further their cause.

Conclusion

The history of IOs, both IGOs and NGOs, are an emerging and dynamic field of study in international history and Historical IR. IOs sit at the intersection of broader trends of international relations and bring together a number of other actors, both state and non-state. IOs are central platforms and mechanisms for the constitution of international order. The history of IOs may be a fascinating topic of study in and of themselves, but they are also an apt lens through which to study broader developments of international norms and practices. The majority of current scholarship on the history of IOs classify as 'critical' scholarship that seeks to question taken-for-granted assumptions and highlight the continuing influence of power and unequal power structures through and in IOs. Current scholarship has problematised and provided more nuance to the relationship between IOs and internationalism, highlighted the crucial influence of non-state and non-Western actors, and explored the 'dark' sides of IOs in their connections to imperialism and the 'standard of civilization.'

These trends of scholarship do not as yet provide a single unified narrative to replace the liberal narrative of progress by traditional IO history. But to do so would in many ways conflict with the new scholarship's guiding principles. The trends identified are often conflicting and contradictory. IGOs served to legitimise empire and reproduce structures of imperialism and European racialised hierarchies yet could also offer a platform and voice for non-European states and peoples to influence international politics. It is precisely in highlighting the complex, nuanced, and interconnected histories of IOs that IR scholars and historians of IOs are making a contribution to diversify and reassess the discipline of IR.

Suggestions for further reading

Davies, T. (2013). *NGOs: A New History of Transnational Civil Society*. London: Hurst & Company.

MacKenzie, D. (2010). *A World Beyond Borders: An Introduction to the History of International Organizations*. Toronto: University of Toronto Press.

Mazower, M. (2012). *Governing the World: The History of an Idea*. New York, NY: The Penguin Press.

Mitzen, J. (2013). *Power in Concert: The Nineteenth-Century Origins of Global Governance*. Chicago and London: The University of Chicago Press.

Reinalda, B. (2009). *Routledge History of International Organizations: From 1815 to the present day*. London and New York: Routledge.

Sayward, A. L. (2017). *The United Nations in International History*. London: Bloomsbury Academic.

Sluga, G., and Clavin, P., eds. (2017). *Internationalisms: A Twentieth-Century History*. Cambridge: Cambridge University Press.

Yunker, J. A. (2011). *The Idea of World Government: From Ancient Times to the Twenty-First Century*. London and New York: Routledge.

References

Abbott, K. W., and Snidal, D. (1998). Why states act through formal international organizations. *The Journal of Conflict Resolution*, 42 (1), 3–32.

Acharya, A., and Buzan, B. (2019). *The Making of Global International Relations: Origins and Evolution of IR at its Centenary*. Cambridge: Cambridge University Press.

Akami, T. (2017). Imperial polities, intercolonialism, and the shaping of global governing norms: public health expert networks in Asia and the League of Nations Health Organization, 1908–37. *Journal of Global History*, 12 (1), 4–25.

Amrith, S., and Sluga, G. (2008). New histories of the United Nations. *Journal of World History*, 19 (3), 251–274.

Anievas. A., and Gogu, C. (2021). Capitalism and 'The International': A Historical Approach. In de Carvalho, B., Costa Lopez, J., & Leira, H., eds. *Routledge Handbook of Historical International Relations*. Abingdon: Routledge.

Auberer, B. (2016). Digesting the League of Nations: planning the international secretariat of the future, 1941–1944. *New Global Studies*, 10 (3), 393–426.

Barnett, M. N., and Finnemore, M. (2004). *Rules for the World: International Organizations in Global Politics*. Ithaca, NY, and London: Cornell University Press.

Bexell, M. (2014). Global governance, legitimacy and (de)legitimation. *Globalizations*, 11 (3), 289–299.

Boli, J., and Thomas, G. M. (1999). *Constructing World Culture: International Nongovernmental Organizations since 1875*. Stanford, CA: Stanford University Press.

Bowden, B. (2021). Eurocentrism and Civilization. In de Carvalho, B., Costa Lopez, J., & Leira, H., eds. *Routledge Handbook of Historical International Relations*. Abingdon: Routledge.

Chimni, B. S. (2006). Third world approaches to international law: a manifesto. *International Community Law Review*, 8, 3–27.

Chimni, B.S. (2016). International Organizations, 1945-Present. In Cogan, J. K., Hurd, I., & Johnstone, I., eds. *The Oxford Handbook of International Organizations*. Oxford: Oxford University Press, 113–130.

Claude, I. L. (1956). *Swords into Plowshares: The Problems and Progress of International Organization*. New York, NY: Random House.

Clavin, P. (2013). *Securing the World Economy: The Reinvention of the League of Nations, 1920-1946*. Oxford: Oxford University Press.

de Carvalho, B., and Neumann, I. B. (2015). *Small State Status Seeking: Norway's Quest for International Standing*. Abingdon: Routledge.

Droux, J. (2014). From child rescue to child welfare: the Save the Children International Union facing world warfare (1939–1947). *Journal of Modern European History*, 12 (3), 377–397.

Dykmann, K. (2015). How international was the secretariat of the League of Nations. *The International History Review*, 37 (4), 721–744.

Fari, S., Balbi, G., and Richeri, G. (2015). *The Formative Years of the Telegraph Union*. Newcastle upon Tyne: Cambridge Scholars Publishing.

Fawcett, L. (2012). Between West and non-West: Latin American contributions to international thought. *The International History Review*, 34 (4), 679–704.

Finnemore, M., and Jurkovich, M. (2014). Getting a seat at the table: the origins of universal participation and modern multilateral conferences. *Global Governance*, 20 (3), 361–373.

Forsythe, D. P. (2005). *The Humanitarians: The International Committee of the Red Cross.* Cambridge: Cambridge University Press.

Getachew, A. (2019). *Worldmaking after Empire: The Rise and Fall of Self-Determination.* Princeton, NJ: Princeton University Press.

Gram-Skjoldager, K., and Ikonomou, H. A. (2019). The construction of the League of Nations secretariat. Formative practices of autonomy and legitimacy in international organizations. *The International History Review*, 41 (2), 257–279.

Hafner-Burton, E. M., Mansfield, E. D., and Pevehouse, J. C. W. (2015). Human rights institutions, sovereignty costs and democratization. *British Journal of Political Science*, 45 (1), 1–27.

Hanrieder, T., and Zangl, B. (2015). The Embedded State: The New Division of Labor in the Provision of Governance Functions. In Liebfried, S., Huber, E., Lange, M., et al., eds. *The Oxford Handbook of Transformations of the State*. Oxford and New York: Oxford University Press, 253–268.

Hawkins, D. G., Lake, D. A., Nielson, D. L., et al. (2006). *Delegation and Agency in International Organizations.* Cambridge: Cambridge University Press.

Helleiner, E. (2014). Southern pioneers of international development. *Global Governance*, 20 (3), 375–388.

Herren, M. (2016). International Organizations, 1865-1945. In Cogan, J. K., Hurd, I., & Johnstone, I., eds. *The Oxford Handbook of International Organizations*. Oxford: Oxford University Press, 91–112.

Hobson, J. A. (1915). *Towards International Government.* New York, NY: The Macmillan Company.

Hopgood, S. (2006). *Keepers of the Flame: Understanding Amnesty International.* Ithaca, NY: Cornell University Press.

Howland, D. (2014). Japan and the Universal Postal Union: an alternative internationalism in the 19th century. *Social Science Japan Journal*, 17 (1), 23–39.

Howland, D. (2015). An alternative mode of international order: the international administrative union in the nineteenth century. *Review of International Studies*, 41 (1), 161–183.

Huber, V. (2006). The unification of the globe by disease? The international sanitary conferences on cholera, 1851-1894. *The Historical Journal*, 49 (2), 453–476.

Hurrell, A. (2005). Power, Institutions, and the Production of Inequality. In Barnett, M., & Duvall, R., eds. *Power in Global Governance*. Cambridge: Cambridge University Press, 33–58.

Ikenberry, G. J. (2001). *After Victory: Institutions, Strategic Restraint, and the Rebuilding of Order after Major Wars.* Princeton and Oxford: Princeton University Press.

Iriye, A. (2002). *Global Community: The Role of International Organizations in the Making of the Contemporary World.* Berkeley, CA: University of California Press.

Irwin, R. M. (2012). *Gordian Knot: Apartheid and the Unmaking of the Liberal World Order.* Oxford: Oxford University Press.

Jackson, S., & O'Malley, A. (2018). *The Institution of International Order: From the League of Nations to the United Nations.* London and New York: Routledge.

Jahn, B. (2021). Liberalism between Theory and Practice. In de Carvalho, B., Costa Lopez, J., & Leira, H., eds. *Routledge Handbook of Historical International Relations*. Abingdon: Routledge.

Jerónimo, M. B., and Monteiro, J. P. (2018). *Internationalism, Imperialism and the Formation of the Contemporary World: The Pasts of the Present.* Basingstoke: Palgrave Macmillan.

Keene, E. (2002). *Beyond the Anarchical Society: Grotius, Colonialism and Order in World Politics.* Cambridge: Cambridge University Press.

Kennedy, P. (2006). *The Parliament of Man: The United Nations and the Quest for World Government.* London: Penguin Books.

Keohane, R. O. (2011). Global governance and legitimacy. *Review of International Political Economy*, 18 (1), 99–109.

Koppell, J. G. S. (2010). *World Rule: Accountability, Legitimacy, and the Design of Global Governance.* Chicago and London: University of Chicago Press.

Koskenniemi, M. (2001). *The Gentle Civilizer of Nations: The Rise and Fall of International Law 1870-1960.* Cambridge: Cambridge University Press.

Kott, S. (2011). Les organisations internationales, terrains d'étude de la globalisation: Jalons pour une approche socio-historique. *Critique internationale*, 52 (3), 9–16.

Legg, S. (2014). An international anomaly? Sovereignty, the League of Nations and India's princely geographies. *Journal of Historical Geography*, 43, 96–110.

Lyons, F. S. L. (1963). *Internationalism in Europe, 1815-1914.* Leyden: A. W. Sythoff.

Mangone, G. J. (1954). *A Short History of International Organization*. New York, NY: McGraw-Hill Book Company.

Mazower, M. (2009). *No Enchanted Palace: The End of Empire and the Ideological Origins of the United Nations*. Princeton and Oxford: Princeton University Press.

Murphy, C. N. (1994). *International Organization and Industrial Change: Global Governance since 1850*. Oxford: Oxford University Press.

Newman, E. (2007). The international civil service: still a viable concept? *Global Society*, 21 (3), 429–447.

Newman, E., and Ravndal, E. J. (2019). The International Civil Service. In Stone, D., & Moloney, K., eds. *The Oxford Handbook of Global Policy and Transnational Administration*. Oxford: Oxford University Press, 165–181.

O'Malley, A. (2018). *The Diplomacy of Decolonisation: America, Britain and the United Nations during the Congo crisis 1960-1964*. Manchester: Manchester University Press.

Pedersen, S. (2015). *The Guardians: The League of Nations and the Crisis of Empire*. Oxford: Oxford University Press.

Randeraad, N. (2011). The international statistical congress (1853–1876): knowledge transfers and their limits. *European History Quarterly*, 41 (1), 50–65.

Ravndal, E. J. (2017). 'A force for peace': expanding the role of the UN secretary-general under Trygve Lie, 1946-1953. *Global Governance*, 23 (3), 443–459.

Ravndal, E. J. (2018). Acting like a state: non-European membership of international organisations in the nineteenth century. In Bartelson, J., Hall, M., & Teorell, J., eds. *De-Centering State Making: Comparative and International Perspectives*. Cheltenham: Edward Elgar, 175–196.

Ravndal, E. J. (2020). Colonies, semi-sovereigns, and great powers: IGO membership debates and the transition of the international system. *Review of International Studies*, 46 (2), 278–298.

Reinsch, P. S. (1911). *Public International Unions: Their Work and Organization*. Boston and London: Ginn & Company.

Rosenboim, O. (2017). *The Emergence of Globalism: Visions of World Order in Britain and the United States, 1939-1950*. Princeton, NJ: Princeton University Press.

Sayre, F. B. (1919). *Experiments in International Administration*. New York and London: Harper & Brothers Publishers.

Schlesinger, S. C. (2003). *Act of Creation, The Founding of the United Nations: A Story of Superpowers, Secret Agents, Wartime Allies and Enemies, and Their Quest for a Peaceful World*. Boulder, CO: Westview Press.

Schulz, C. (2021). Latin America: Between Liminality and Agency in Historical International Relations. In de Carvalho, B., Costa Lopez, J., & Leira, H., eds. *Routledge Handbook of Historical International Relations*. Abingdon: Routledge.

Sikkink, K. (2014). Latin American countries as norm protagonists of the idea of international human rights. *Global Governance*, 20 (3), 389–404.

Slobodian, Q. (2018). *Globalists: The End of Empire and the Birth of Neoliberalism*. Cambridge, MA: Harvard University Press.

Sluga, G. (2013). *Internationalism in the Age of Nationalism*. Philadelphia, PA: University of Pennsylvania Press.

Speeckaert, G. P. (1957). *Les 1.978 organisations internationales fondées depuis le Congrès de Vienne* Brussels: Union des Associations Internationales.

Union of International Associations. (2015). *Yearbook of International Organizations*.

Vergerio, C. (2021). International Law and the Laws of War. In de Carvalho, B., Costa Lopez, J., & Leira, H., eds. *Routledge Handbook of Historical International Relations*. Abingdon: Routledge.

Viola, L. A. (2020). *The Closure of the International System: How Institutions Create Political Equalities and Hierarchies*. Cambridge: Cambridge University Press.

Walters, F. P. (1952). *A History of the League of Nations*. Oxford: Oxford University Press.

Yao, J. (2019). 'Conquest from barbarism': the Danube Commission, international order and the control of nature as a standard of civilization. *European Journal of International Relations*, 25 (2), 335–359.

32

REVOLUTIONS

Integrating the international

George Lawson

The new age of revolution

Revolutions have had a major impact on the development of modern international order. Writing in the late 1970s, Martin Wight (1978: 92) wrote that over half of the preceding 500 years had featured some kind of conflict between revolutionary and counter-revolutionary states. The period since the publication of Wight's book may well be the most revolutionary in history – we are living in a 'new age of revolution' (Goldstone, 2016: ii). In the contemporary world, revolutions are everywhere: on the streets of Kobane, Minsk, and Hong Kong; in the rhetoric of groups like Extinction Rebellion and Black Lives Matter; and in the potential of technologies to reshape people's lives. Rarely do weeks go by without a revolution of one kind or another being proclaimed.

If this is right, it matters a great deal for world politics. Although no revolution has ever delivered in full on its promises, revolutions have bought dramatic changes in their wake. The French Revolution introduced the notions of nationalism and popular sovereignty, concepts of political 'left' and 'right', the metric system, and a conflict between absolutism and republicanism that dominated European politics during the 19th century. The Russian Revolution pioneered a model of state-led industrialization that was a powerful draw for many states around the world during the 20th century. The Chinese, Vietnamese, and Cuban revolutions exemplified variants of southern revolution that resonated around the insurgent 'Third World' during the Cold War (see also Kwon, 2021; Svensson, 2021). The Egyptian Revolution of 1952 established a form of military-led social transformation that inspired revolutionary movements in the region during the 1950s and 1960s, just as comparable uprisings in Tunisia and Egypt inspired unrest in North Africa and the Middle East in 2011. The 'people power' uprisings in Eastern and Central Europe in 1989 have served as the lodestone for a range of 'unarmed' revolutions in the contemporary world. Whatever form revolutions have taken, they stand as a challenge to status quo authority, both at home and abroad, by virtue of the example they set in overcoming seemingly overwhelming forces and in their capacity to generate substantial changes both to the texture of their home societies and to international orders. Revolutions and the *avoidance* of revolutions, whether through autocratic modernization, reform programmes, or counter-revolution, are not occasional punctuation marks, but the very grammar of modern world history.

Given the ways in which revolutionaries have often presented their challenge as *international* projects, it is curious that revolutions have not received more attention from scholars of International Relations (IR) (Lawson, 2011, 2015; Rao, 2016). IR scholarship has usually treated revolutions as problems to be solved rather than as constitutive of international order (for exceptions, see: Walt, 1996; Halliday, 1999; Bukovansky, 2002; Panah, 2002; Anievas, 2015; Rao, 2016; Allinson, 2019; Lawson, 2019). This residual disciplinary location may be part of broader silences in IR regarding the ways in which unruly politics have shaped the development of modern international order. But even so, IR's neglect of revolution is striking. This chapter examines why this neglect matters and offers a fuller appreciation of the relationship between revolutions and IR. Before this, though, it establishes what revolutions are.

What are revolutions?

In recent years, figures as varied as Abu Bakr al-Baghdadi, Emmanuel Macron, Tarana Burke, Xi Jinping, Tawakkol Karman, and Elon Musk have been labelled as revolutionaries, while the hugely popular musical Hamilton and the even more popular Star Wars series have eulogized revolutionary struggle. This broadening of the concept of revolution goes beyond its take-up by the mass media and in popular culture – revolution is a gaming company (revolution.co.uk), a venture capitalist firm (www.revolution.com), and even a protection treatment for cats and dogs (https://www.revolution.com.au/). But is revolution really just a marketing trope, investment strategy, or pet service? And can it be street mobilization, social movement, and technological breakthrough at the same time? If revolution is everywhere, perhaps it is nowhere.

This issue is complicated by an equally common, but apparently contradictory, belief – that revolutions are irrelevant to a world in which the big issues of governance and economic development have been settled. In the contemporary world, revolutions 'offer little promise and pose little threat' (Mayer, 2001: 3). With the passing of state socialism in the Soviet Union, it is supposed, revolutions appear more as minor disturbances than as projects of deep confrontation and systemic transformation. What is left, for good or for bad, are pale imitations: anaemic (small 'r') revolutions rather than 'real', 'proper', and 'authentic' (big 'R') Revolution.

Both of these positions are untenable. While the former makes revolution so all-encompassing that it becomes an empty term without substantive content, the latter fails to see the enduring appeal of attempts to overturn existing conditions and generate alternative social orders. But why have we become so confused about revolutions? In part, it is because revolutions are not static objects of analysis, but processes that change in form across time and place. Revolutions have been conducted by nationalists in Algeria and Angola, slaves in Haiti, constitutionalists in America and France, communists in Russia, China, Nicaragua, and Afghanistan, radical military groups in Libya and Ethiopia, peasants in Mexico, Cuba, and Vietnam, a curious coalition of leftists, students, merchants, and clergy in Iran, and an even curiouser mix of Islamists, youth, labour organizations, and 'ultra' football fans in Egypt. At the same time, the concept of revolution exists in every major language group in the world. A study of its etymology would need to take in the Greek concepts of *epanastasis* (revolution), the Arabic terms thawra (rebellion) and *inqilab* (revolution), the notions of *mered* (rebellion), *hitkomemut* (uprising), *meri* (revolt), and *kesher* (plot) in classical Hebrew, the Chinese word *geming* (change of life, fate, or destiny), and the Latin verb *revolvere* (to return).

Probing deeper into the European meaning of the term reveals further diversity. In Ancient Greece, the idea of revolution was linked to the movement contained within Aristotle's trinity of democracy, oligarchy, and tyranny. In the Middle Ages, the concept was used to denote something circular, the turning of wheels rather than fundamental rupture, as in the elliptical movement of planets surveyed by Copernicus in his *De revolutionibus orbium coelestium* ('On the Revolutions of Celestial Spheres'). During the early modern period, the term began to be associated with sudden, dramatic political changes (Harris, 2015: 27, 34). By the early part of the 19th century, the constitutional revolutions of America and France had become seen as archetypal – the latter in particular crystalized the notion of revolution as a deliberate act, signified by the emergence of a distinct category of *révolutionnaire* (revolutionary) (Baker, 2015: 95, 102). From this point on, revolution was a future-oriented act – an ongoing project of potentially unlimited duration. During the 20th century, revolutions became primarily associated with violent ruptures from one type of social order (capitalist and/or colonial) to another (socialist and/or post-colonial). After the collapse of the Soviet Union, many commentators argued that revolution had taken another turn, becoming variously 'unarmed' (Ritter, 2015), 'negotiated' (Lawson, 2004), conjoined with reform programmes to generate a new category of 'refolution' (Garton Ash, 1989), or reconnected with older notions of return, as captured in Jürgen Habermas's (1990) notion of 'rectifying revolutions'. In the present day, as noted earlier, revolution is increasingly caught between two extremes: denigration on the one hand and catch-all term on the other.

A second source of confusion lies in the close relationship between revolutions and other processes of social change – revolutions are part of a broader family associated with social transformation. First, a number of revolutions in the modern era were preceded or succeeded by civil wars, including those in France, Russia, China, Cuba, Nicaragua, Afghanistan, and Angola. Thomas Paine and Edmund Burke, hardly natural bedfellows, shared the view that England's Glorious Revolution in 1688 was both a revolution and a civil war (Armitage, 2015: 67). Second, the effects of coup d'états can on occasion be revolutionary. The coup by Augusto Pinochet in Chile in 1973, the putsch against the monarchy led by Muammar Qaddafi in Libya, and the Francoist *golpe militar* in Spain set in motion radical economic and political programmes that significantly recast their societies. Third, rebellions (here used synonymously with revolts) are also closely associated with revolutions. Often, disenfranchised groups from slaves to peasants have been in a state of virtually continuous rebellion, taking part in processes that have induced revolutions from Haiti to Nicaragua, and from Algeria to Mexico. Fourth, transitions from authoritarian to democratic orders often overlap with revolutionary dynamics, most obviously in the negotiated settlement that ended apartheid in South Africa. Finally, although reform movements are usually seen as distinct from, or as barriers to, revolutions, there are several occasions when reforms by governments have hastened rather than prevented revolution. In 18th century France, for example, the programme of limited reform instigated by Louis XVI emboldened the provincial *parlements* (appeal courts), the newly empowered bourgeoisie, and peasants taking part in rural uprisings. The weakness of the monarchy was revealed by its reforms, allowing the middling classes of burghers and merchants to press for more radical changes. Defeat in the Seven Years' War with England, the example of a successful revolution in America, and the growth of new ideas like nationalism coupled with elite fracture in turning reform into revolution.

Revolution, therefore, appears in relation to, rather than opposition from, other forms of social change. Civil wars, coup d'états, rebellions, transitions, reform programmes, and revolutions are intimately connected, overlapping and running into each other at a number of junctures (Lawson, 2006). However, although revolutions bleed – sometimes literally – into other processes of social change, they also retain a relative autonomy from them. In their most basic sense, revolutions can be understood as the reorganization of everyday life – they seek permanent shifts rather than temporary changes to the texture of social relations. In this way, revolutions consist of several dimensions simultaneously: a symbolic revolution that seeks to destroy pre-revolutionary tropes and reforge new forms of symbolic order; a political revolution that aims to overthrow the old regime and reconstruct systems of governance; and an economic revolution that intends to recast relations of production, value, and exchange. In short, a revolution is a *collective mobilization that attempts to quickly and forcibly overthrow an existing regime in order to transform political, economic, and symbolic relations.*

Each aspect of this definition is important: 'collective mobilization' contrasts with processes of elite-driven change, many of which can be radical – China since its 1978 'opening up' and some contemporary Gulf monarchies serve as cases in point; 'quickly' distinguishes revolutions from longer-running processes of evolutionary change, such as the two centuries or more of British parliamentary reform; 'forcibly' illustrates the importance of conflict, compulsion, and transgression to revolutions – contained forms of contention ranging from civil rights legislation, extending the suffrage, or introducing shock therapy programmes may have dramatic consequences, but this does not equate to the forceful opening of previously restricted orders conjured by revolutions; 'overthrow' exemplifies the extra-constitutional component of revolutions, while also distinguishing them from more partial processes such as democratic transitions; both 'transform' and the inclusion of political, economic, *and* symbolic orders illustrate the systemic quality of revolutionary change; 'attempt' signifies that there are many more unsuccessful than successful revolutions and a large number of revolutionary situations that do not lead to revolutionary outcomes. If we only included successful cases of revolution that fulfilled each aspect of this definition, discussion would be limited to a handful of cases.[1] In this sense, the point is not to see this definition in a static sense, as a template to which revolutions must comply. Such a move would not only elide the variety of forms that revolution takes, but it would also struggle to make sense of unsuccessful revolutions and the many revolutionary situations that do not lead to revolutionary outcomes. There are many revolutionary movements, but far fewer successful revolutions.

Revolutions and the international

If this serves as a working definition of revolutions, how might we capture their international components? And how, as a result, might IR contribute more productively to the study of revolutions? There are three starting points for this analysis. First is the notion held by revolutionaries that the international system – whether understood as imperialist, capitalist, racist, or a combination of all three – operates as a structure of oppression. Second, there is the sense that revolutionary states pose a challenge to this system, one that is overtly emancipatory. And third, there is the internationalism of revolutionary states: that their struggle is not contained by the limits of state borders or power politics, but one that transcends existing boundaries (Halliday, 2008). Marx and Engels (1967 [1848]: 46–47), for example, thought that communism could not exist 'as a local event. The proletariat can only exist on the world-historical plane, just as communism, its activity, can only have a world historical existence'. Lenin made this point starkly: 'global class, global party, global revolution'. In 1968, protestors in European capitals chanted: 'Paris, London, Rome, Berlin, we shall fight and we shall win'; many of the principal intellectual currents of the '68-ers' were drawn from the work of 'Third World' figures such as Mao and Ho Chi Minh. Che Guevara (2002 [1968]: 62) globalized these sentiments into a battle cry of anti-imperialism in his 'Message to the People of the World':

> How close and bright would the future appear if two, three, many Vietnams flowered on the face of the globe ... what difference do the dangers to a human being or people matter when what is at stake is the destiny of humanity. Our every action is a battle cry against imperialism and a call for the unity of the peoples.

Revolutionary movements, therefore, run counter to many of the ground rules of international order (sovereignty, the sanctity of international law, and diplomacy), proclaiming ideals of universal society and global insurrection. Revolutions challenge international order in a number of ways ranging from disrupting existing patterns of trade and interstate alliances to questioning whole systems of rule. To take one example, the challenges of the Bolshevik Revolution were short-term, prompting the withdrawal of Russian forces from World War One; medium-term, in the provision of support for like-minded movements – the Soviet Union invaded Poland in 1920, provided aid for German revolutionaries in 1923, supported the Republicans during the Spanish Civil War from 1936 to 1939, and helped to install socialist regimes in Europe and Asia during the late 1940s; and long-term, in the establishment of a systemic alternative to democratic capitalism. As with other revolutions, the outcomes of the Bolshevik revolution included new alliances that, in turn, induced a conflict between the revolutionary state and a counter-revolutionary coalition that sought to contain it.

The Bolshevik revolution, like many other revolutions, challenged the credibility of the existing international system and, with it, the credibility of the system's great powers. This, naturally, prompted a response: in order to justify their position at the apex of the international system, great powers must act decisively in the face of a revolutionary challenge (Bisley, 2004: 56). Occasionally, this action takes place in support of the revolutionary movement, as with the 1989 revolutions in Central and Eastern Europe. More frequently, great powers act to suppress such revolutions, seeing them as threats to international order, as was the case in Haiti, France, Russia, Algeria, Vietnam, and elsewhere. Edmund Burke's notion that the French Revolution was likely to 'infect' its neighbours stands as an exemplary illustration of this tendency. As he told the House of Commons in 1791, when it came to containing the Jacobin virus, 'Holland might justly be considered as necessary a part of this country as Kent' (in Simms, 2011: 109). In terms of its vision and character, counter-revolution is just as internationalist as revolution.

Counter-revolution is aimed at containing the triple challenge – normative, ideological, and strategic – that revolutionary states represent. Intervention by counter-revolutionary states is both informal, covering covert practices and cultural ties, and formal, taking in propaganda, training, aid, and the provision of arms. Nick Bisley (2004: 52–53) distils these forms of aid into five sets of activities: first, direct military intervention, as in US intervention alongside white armies during the Russian Civil War; second, financial aid and clandestine support for counter-revolutionary forces, as with US support for Nicaraguan Contras or Mujahedeen groups in Afghanistan and Pakistan during the 1980s; third, low scale harassment, such as propaganda campaigns, public diplomacy, and the jamming of radio signals common to Western strategies in Eastern and Central Europe during the Cold War; fourth, deprivation, such as sanctions, of the kind that the United States has sustained against the Iranian and Cuban revolutionary regimes; and fifth, disruption, through the non-recognition of revolutionary states and associated practices, such as the expulsion of Cuba from the Organization of American States (OAS) in 1962. Counter-revolutionary policies frequently combine two or more of these activities. US involvement in the Russian Civil War included a financial package ($450 million for the post-Tsarist government and almost $200 million for use against the Bolsheviks after the October Revolution), armed intervention (9,000 American troops were sent to Siberia and nearly 5,000 to North Russia), plus assistance in the form of food relief, medical aid, and the like (Tardelli, 2013).

On occasion, counter-revolutionary forces succeed in rolling back revolutions – examples include much of continental Europe in 1848–49, the Dominican Republic in 1965, Grenada in 1983, and Syria in 2011. More frequently, these campaigns lead to protracted struggles between the revolutionary regime and counter-revolutionary forces. Although counter-revolutionary forces often enjoy a military superiority over revolutionary movements, the latter contain a political advantage, particularly in terms of legitimacy. For example, although the 1968 Tet Offensive by the North Vietnamese was a military success for the United States and its allies, it marked a political defeat for counter-revolutionary forces, so much so that military requests for funding were thereafter refused by Congress and President Johnson decided not to stand for re-election (Mack, 1975; Willbanks, 2007: chs. 6–7). A similar assessment can be made of the French military victory over the *Front de Libération Nationale* (FLN) in Algeria, which was eroded by both the illegitimacy of its methods, particularly the widespread use of torture, and the FLN's concerted, and highly successful, public information campaign (Connelly, 2003; Byrne, 2016). Regardless of outcome, the crucial point is that revolution and counter-revolution are less two entities than one, joined in a shared, if mutually destructive, relationship.

Revolution and war are also tightly meshed (see also Bartelson, 2021). On the one hand, revolutionary states are far more likely than other states to enter into violent civil war: over one million people died in the Mexican revolution and the country's subsequent civil unrest between 1910 and 1917, around three million Russians died in the civil war between 1917 and 1921, and close to five million Chinese were killed in the first five years of Mao's post-1949 revolutionary regime (Westad, 2007: 322; Beissinger, 2014: 6). On the other hand, revolutionary states are both twice as likely as non-revolutionary states to induce interstate war and much more likely to win these wars (Maoz, 1989: 204; also see Colgan, 2013). This is, in part, because revolutionary states devote far greater resources to their militaries than non-revolutionary states – major social revolutions have been followed by an average 264% increase in defence budgets (Carter et al., 2012: 452).

As Stephen Walt (1996) notes, revolutions intensify the prospects of war in three ways. First, revolutions provide a window of opportunity for states to improve their position vis-à-vis other states – because revolutionary regimes are beset by civil strife and elite fracture, other states may seize the chance to attack the revolutionary regime. Second, this window of opportunity generates 'spirals of suspicion' as the uncertainty produced by the revolution heightens levels of insecurity that, in turn, raise threat perceptions (Walt, 1996: 33). Finally, revolutionary states seek to export their revolution both as a way of shoring up their fragile position at home and because of their ideological commitment to an alternative international order. Concomitantly, counter-revolutionary states assume that the revolution will spread unless it is 'strangled in its crib' and that revolution will be relatively easy to reverse (Walt, 1996: 43). This 'perverse combination' of insecurity and overconfidence heightens the prospects of interstate conflict (Walt, 1996: 40). By increasing uncertainty and fear, by altering capabilities, and by raising threat perceptions, revolutionary states begin a process that, quite often, engenders interstate conflict. A mutual lack of understanding on both sides of the revolutionary confrontation, augmented by ideological polarization, produces an unstable international environment. War between revolutionary and counter-revolutionary forces emerges from an 'over-reaction to over-perceived revolutionary dangers' (Mayer, 1977: 202).

Revolutions, therefore, are always international events. At times, the international effects of revolution are symbolic – for example, revolutionary Haiti was the first independent state to recognize the legitimacy of the Greek revolution in 1820. At other times, it is material – the Cuban revolutionary regime has provided armed support to a range of liberation movements, as well as humanitarian assistance to states throughout the global south. Yet there is a paradox at the heart of the relationship between revolutionary states and the international system – revolutionary states must establish relations with other states and coexist with the system's rules, laws, and institutions, even while professing to reject these practices. Although the Declaration of the Rights of Man claimed that 'the sovereignty of peoples is not bound by the treaties of tyrants', the French revolutionary regime signed a resolution on non-intervention in 1793, stating that 'the invasion of one state by another state tends to threaten the liberty and security of all'

(Armstrong, 1993: 217–218, 227). Even when they did annex territory, revolutionaries appealed more to old regime treaty law than to revolutionary principles (see also Vergerio, 2021). For their part, the Soviet revolutionary regime enjoyed a selective approach to international law, arguing through the principle of 'socialist legality' that promises must be kept (*pacta sunt servanda*) and that new circumstances invalidated previous treaties (*rebus sic stantibus*). In this way, foreign loans were annulled, but rules on the treatment of prisoners of war upheld. Following the normalization of Chinese-US relations during the period of détente in the early 1970s, China ended its support for black radical groups and switched its allegiance in Angola from the Soviet-backed MPLA (*Movimento Popular de Libertação de Angola*) to UNITA (*União Nacional para a Independência Total de Angola*), a group supported by both the United States and apartheid South Africa (Frazier, 2015: 206–207).

Pressures to conform, therefore, act as a counterweight to claims of global insurrection. Despite challenging existing forms of international order, revolutionary states play their part in reproducing regimes governing trade, alliances, and security. On the one hand, revolutionary states exhibit a particular form of *revolutionary sovereignty* – a claim that simultaneously legitimizes international intervention and domestic autarchy. On the other hand, in order to function as states, revolutionary states are forced to give up some of their revolutionary aims.

Revolutionary theory and the international

The previous section laid out some of the substantive connections between revolutions and international relations. This section deepens these connections by anchoring them more systematically within existing approaches to the study of revolutions.

Revolutionary theorists often claim to have sufficiently incorporated the international aspects of revolutions into their analyses. Theda Skocpol (1979: 14), for example, argued that 'social revolutions cannot be explained without systematic reference to *inter*national structures and world historical development' (emphasis in original). Skocpol (1973: 30–31, 1979: 19–24) highlighted the formative role played by two international factors in the onset of revolutions: the uneven spread of capitalism and interstate (particularly military) competition. Both of these factors were embedded within 'world historical time', by which Skocpol (1979: 23) meant the overarching context within which interstate competition and capitalist development took place. Charles Tilly (1990: 186) also highlighted the importance of interstate competition, arguing that, 'All of Europe's great revolutions, and many of its lesser ones, began with the strains imposed by war'. Jack Goldstone (1991: 24–25, 459–460) widened this focus by noting the ways in which rising populations across a range of territories served to foster state fiscal crises (by increasing prices and decreasing tax revenues), heighten elite fracture (as competition between patronage networks was sharpened), and prompt popular uprisings (as wages declined in real terms). Mark Katz (1997: 13, 29) noted the ways in which 'central revolutions', such as France in 1789, fostered waves of 'affiliated revolutions' (also see Markoff, 1996; Sohrabi, 2002; Beck, 2011).

This 'retrieval' of the international by revolutionary theorists has been extended by a number of more recent works. Jack Goldstone (2014: 19, 21–22) highlights a variety of ways through which 'favorable international relations' serve as the conditions for societal instability, plus lists a range of factors, from demographic changes (such as rising populations) to shifting interstate relations (such as the withdrawal of external support for a client), by which international processes help to cause revolutions. Of John Foran's (2005), five 'indispensable conditions' that are said to have enabled revolutions in the 'Third World' to take place, two – dependent development and world-systemic opening – are overtly international. Charles Kurzman (2008) has noted the ways in which a wave of constitutional revolutions in the early part of the 20th century spread over widely dispersed territories, from Mexico to China. Kurzman (2008: 8) argues that this wave acted as a 'dress rehearsal' for later events, most notably the 1989 revolutions in Central and Eastern Europe. Colin Beck (2011: 193) sees such waves as likely to increase 'as the level of world culture more rapidly expands', an argument that finds support in Mark Beissinger's (2014: 16–17) database of revolutionary episodes, which shows a marked increase in both the depth and breadth of revolutionary waves over the past century. Daniel Ritter (2015: 5) emphasizes the ways in which an international context characterized by the 'iron cage of liberalism' traps authoritarian states into accepting at least the rudiments of democratic practices. If authoritarian regimes are to maintain the benefits of ties with Western states, from arms to aid, they must open up a space for non-violent opposition to emerge – the structural context of *international* liberalism provides an opening within which *domestic* non-violent opposition can mobilize.

Given this proliferation of interest in the international components of revolutions, it could be argued that contemporary revolutionary scholarship has solved the 'problem' of the international. It is certainly the case that these accounts have gone a long way to opening up a productive exchange between revolutions and IR. However, there remains considerable work to be done – the international has not yet been theorized 'all the way down'. Three motivations lie behind this claim. First, despite increasing attention to the multiple connections between revolutions and the international, this relationship remains unevenly examined, being highly visible in some work (e.g. Foran, 2005; Kurzman, 2008; Goldstone, 2014; Beck, 2014; Ritter, 2015), yet all but invisible in others (e.g. Thompson, 1995; Parsa, 2000; Goodwin, 2001; Slater, 2010). Clearly there is much still to do in terms of mainstreaming international factors into the analysis of revolutions. Second, use of the international is often reduced to a handful of factors. In Skocpol's analysis, for example, interstate competition is a surrogate for military interactions, particularly defeat in war. Hence, 'wars … are the midwives of revolutionary crises' (Skocpol, 1979: 286). Such a view neglects the ways in which a cornucopia of international processes, from transnational cultural repertoires to interstate alliance structures, affect the onset of revolutions. Third, much revolutionary scholarship has incorporated international factors via a strategy of 'add and stir', grafting international factors *onto* existing theoretical scaffolding rather than integrating such factors *within* a single framework. This point is worth examining in more depth.

As noted previously, John Foran (2005: 18–23) sees revolutions in the 'Third World' as emerging from the interaction of five 'indispensable conditions': dependent development, which exacerbates social tensions; exclusionary, personalistic regimes, which polarize opposition; political cultures of opposition, which legitimize revolutionary movements; economic downturns, which radicalize these movements; and a world-systemic opening, which denotes a 'let-up' of external constraints. Two of Foran's five causal conditions are overtly international: dependent development and world-systemic opening. Yet these factors contain little by way of causal force. The first, dependent development, is a virtually universal condition of core-periphery relations –what 'peripheral' society lacks widespread dependence of one sort or another on a metropole? Even given Foran's (2005: 19) rendering of dependent development as a specific process of accumulation ('growth within limits'), the concept is wide enough to be applicable to every 'Third World' state. This is something borne out by Foran's (2005: 255) own analysis, in which dependent development appears as a near constant of both successful and unsuccessful revolutions. In other words, the causal weight attributed to dependent development is nil; it serves as the background condition within which revolutions may or may not take place. And in this sense, to posit relations between polities as dependent is less to assert a causal relationship than it is to describe the condition of every peripheral state around the world. Without further specificity as to the quality and quantity of dependent development, the term becomes little more than an inert backdrop.

At first glance, Foran's (2005: 23) second international category – world-systemic opening – by which he means a 'let-up' of existing international conditions through interstate wars, depressions, and other such crises – appears to be more promising. Yet, here too, the causal agency of the international is significantly curtailed as world-systemic opening is seen merely as the final moment through which the 'revolutionary window opens and closes' (Foran, 2005: 252). In other words, the structural preconditions that lie behind revolutions lie elsewhere – in *domestic* regime type, cultures of opposition, and socio-economic conditions. World-systemic opening is the final curtain call on a play that has largely taken place elsewhere.

In this way, both of the international components of Foran's analysis are limited to walk-on roles: dependent development is the background from which revolutions may or may not occur; world-systemic opening is the final spark of a crisis that has been kindled elsewhere. The sequence through which Foran's analysis works is highly significant: international (dependent development), domestic (exclusionary, repressive regimes), domestic (cultures of opposition), domestic (economic downturns), and international (world-systemic opening). The fact that Foran's sequence differentiates international and domestic in this way reproduces the analytic bifurcation that his analysis hoped to overcome. Such a bifurcation occludes the myriad ways in which Foran's ostensibly domestic factors are deeply permeated by the international: exclusionary regimes are part of broader clusters of ideologically affiliated states, alliance structures, and client-patron relations; cultures of opposition are local-transnational hybrids; socio-economic conditions are heavily dependent on market forces that transcend state borders. Rather than integrating the international throughout his casual sequence, Foran maintains an empirical and theoretical bifurcation between domestic and international. And he loads the causal dice in favour of the former.

Foran's deployment of the international is emblematic of much recent revolutionary scholarship. For instance, Jack Goldstone (2001: 146), although clear that international factors contribute in multifaceted ways to both the causes and outcomes of revolutions, is equally clear about the division of labour that exists between these two registers:

> Although the international environment can affect the risks of revolution in manifold ways, the precise impact of these effects, as well as the overall likelihood of revolution, is determined *primarily* by the internal relationships among state authorities, various elites, and various popular groups (emphasis added).

In similar vein, Goldstone's (2014) more recent work makes much of the ways in which international factors serve as important conditions for, and causes of, revolutions. Yet, with the exception of noting the propensity of revolutions to stoke interstate war, international factors largely drop out of Goldstone's account of revolutionary processes and outcomes. In this way, even fourth-generation scholarship that claims to fully incorporate international factors into its analysis can be seen as containing two shortcomings: first, the maintenance of an analytical bifurcation between international and domestic; and second, retaining a residual role for the international. How might an approach that sought to more thoroughly integrate the international into the study of revolutions proceed?

An inter-social approach

This section answers this question by outlining an 'inter-social' approach to revolutions (also see Lawson, 2019). The term inter-social is preferred to alternatives such as intersocietal, international, and interstate in that it does not presume that the objects of analysis are societies, nations, or states, respectively. Rather, it examines the relationship between 'external' and 'internal' dynamics wherever these are found: in ideas that cross borders, amongst networks of revolutionary actors, in asymmetrical market interactions, and more. An inter-social approach is concerned with the ways in which differentially located, but interactively engaged, social sites affect the development of revolutions without containing a prior presumption of what these social sites are.

An inter-social approach to revolutions starts from a simple premise: events that take place in one location are both affected by and affect events elsewhere (see also Çapan et al., 2021). A number of transnational histories have pointed to the ways in which revolutionary events contain an international dimension that supersedes the national-state frame (e.g. Stone, 2002; Adelman, 2008; Hunt, 2010). To take one example, the onset of the French Revolution cannot be understood without attention to the expansionist policies of the French state during the 17th and 18th centuries – between 1650 and 1780, France was at war in two out of every three years. This bellicosity, a product of pressures caused by developments in rival states as well as domestic factors, brought increased demands for taxation that, over time, both engendered factionalism in the *ancién regime* and led to chronic state debt (Stone, 2002: 259–260; Hazan, 2014: 38). The interactive dimensions of international relations also affected events during the revolutionary period. For example, in 1792, as the Jacobins were losing influence to the Girondins, leading Girondins pressed the state into international conflict.[2] As France's foreign campaigns went increasingly badly, the Committee of Public Safety, a leading site of Jacobin authority, blamed the Girondins for betraying the revolution and committed France to a process of domestic rad-icalization: the Terror (see Hazan, 2014: 299–303 for a critique of the use of this term). In this way, domestic political friction induced international conflict that, in turn, opened up space for heightened domestic polarization. The Jacobins identified the Girondins as unrevolutionary traitors, speculators, and hoarders, while identifying themselves as the guardians of the revolution, a process that prompted a wave of popular militancy, most notably the *levée en masse* (Stone, 2002: 194–208; also see Crépin, 2013).

Inter-social relations also played a fundamental role in the outcomes of the revolution. First, the revolutionary regime annexed Rhineland and Belgium and helped to ferment republican revolution in several neighbouring countries, including Holland, Switzerland, and Italy. Second, the revolution prompted unrest throughout Europe, including Ireland, where a rebellion against English rule led to a violent conflict and, in 1800, the Acts of Union between the United Kingdom of Great Britain and Ireland. Third, the threat from France was met by extensive counter-revolution abroad. In England, for example, *habeas corpus* was suspended in 1794, while legislation ranging from the Seditious Meetings Act to the Combination Acts was introduced in order to contain the spread of republicanism. Although the French did not generate an international revolutionary party, many states acted as if they had done just this, instituting domestic crackdowns in order to guard against the claim made by Jacques-Pierre Brissot that, 'we [the French revolutionary regime) cannot be at peace until all Europe is in flames' (cited in Palmer, 1954: 11).

An inter-social approach builds from this understanding of the generative role of transboundary entanglements. Empirically, an inter-social approach charts the ways in which relations between people, networks, and states drive revolutionary dynamics. Highlighting these empir-ical connections, whether direct or indirect, realizes the *descriptive* advantages of an inter-social approach. To date, the development of such a descriptive inter-social approach has been most evident in transnational, global, and economic history (e.g. Armitage and Subrahmanyan., 2010). However, the richness of this scholarship has not been matched by work that adequately explores the *analytical* advantages of an inter-social approach. Analytically, an inter-social approach is concerned with the ways in which the logics of differentially located, but interactively engaged, social sites affect the causal pathways of revolutions. Such interrelations take many forms: the withdrawal of support to a client state from a patron, the pressures that emerge from the fusion of 'advanced' technologies in 'backward' sectors of the economy, the transmission of revolutionary ideas, the desire to emulate both revolution and counter-revolution, and so on. In both descriptive and analytical forms, inter-social interactions are less the product of revolutions than their drivers.

The promise of an inter-social approach rests on its capacity to theorize what otherwise appears as historical surplus: the logics contained within the inter-social dynamics that constitute revolutionary processes. Inter-social relations form an interactive crucible for each and every case of revolution. The external whip of international pressures, added to the uneven histories within which social orders develop, produce an inter-social logic that has not, as yet, been effectively theorized in the study of revolutions. It is the task of an inter-social approach to identify these dynamics and demonstrate their generative role in the formation of revolutionary processes. Although it can be difficult both analytically and descriptively to avoid using nation-state frames, there is no scholarly rationale for maintaining the bifurcation between international and domestic. Revolutions are amalgams of transnational and local fields of action. Revolutions are inter-social all the way down. This insight is the basis for a fuller engagement between IR and revolutionary studies (also see Lawson, 2015, 2019).

Conclusion

Revolutions matter in three ways: as *substantive* processes that have played a central role in shaping the modern world; as *analytical* categories that overlap with, but do not fully merge into, other processes of social transformation; and as *normative* projects for and against which people have fought and died. This much is clear. What is less clear is how to draw together the study of revolutions with disciplinary IR. Despite the closeness of the relationship between actual existing international relations and revolutions, IR has contributed relatively little to their study. In the contemporary world, revolutions are more likely to be studied by sociologists, historians, and comparativists than IR scholars. This is both a shame and a mistake. It is a shame because it is a missed opportunity for IR to contribute to an issue-area on which it has much to say. It is a mistake because, without a contribution from IR, the international components of revolutions are somewhere between absent and neglected. This chapter has sought to show how the study of revolutions and IR can be better integrated. The task ahead is to generate scholarship that can fill in the space opened up by this move.

Suggestions for further reading

Arendt, H. (1963). *On Revolution*. London: Penguin.

Beck, C. (2015). *Radicals, Revolutionaries and Terrorists*. Cambridge: Polity.

Chenoweth, E., and Stephan, M. J. (2011). *Why Civil Resistance Works*. New York, NY: Columbia University Press.

Foran, J., Lane. D., and Zivkovic, A., eds. (2008). *Revolution in the Making of the Modern World*. London: Routledge.

Lawson, G. (2019). *Anatomies of Revolution*. Cambridge: Cambridge University Press.

McAdam, D., Tarrow, S., and Tilly, C. (2001). *Dynamics of Contention*. Cambridge: Cambridge University Press.

Nepstad, S. E. (2011). *Nonviolent Revolution*. Oxford: Oxford University Press.

Rowbotham, S. (2014). *Women, Resistance and Revolution*. London: Verso.

Selbin, E. (2010). *Revolution, Rebellion, Resistance*. London: Zed.

Notes

1 Colin Beck (2018) finds that research on revolution is, in general, skewed towards a few landmark cases: Nicaragua, France, Russia, Cuba, Iran, Vietnam, and China. Overall, Beck finds three main biases in the social science of revolutions: first, towards 'great revolutions'; second, towards 20th century revolutions; and third, towards revolutions seen to be 'progressive'. According to Beck, 75% of historical-comparative books on revolution focus on 'leftist' or 'democratic' revolutions, while only 15% survey religious or 'reactionary' cases, almost all of which examine the 1979 Iranian Revolution. This is a big problem. It means that conservative revolutionary movements are omitted, from fascism to militant Islamism. It also means that, if revolutions are successful by definition, most studies are selecting on the dependent variable. This, in turn, means that there is not enough study of *why* so many revolutionary movements are unsuccessful, not least because of successful counter-revolutionary projects.
2 At the heart of the generalized, Girondin-Jacobin conflict was a personal clash between Brissot and Robespierre. As Brissot called (successfully) for war with Austria, arguing that French troops would be greeted as liberators, Robespierre responded with an apposite prognosis: '*personne n'aime les missionnaires armés*' ('no one likes armed missionaries'). This is a lesson that subsequent revolutionaries have been slow to learn.

References

Adelman, J. (2008). An age of imperial revolutions. *American Historical Review*, 113 (2), 319–340.

Allinson, J. (2019). Counter-revolution as international phenomenon: the case of Egypt. *Review of International Studies*, 45 (2), 320–344.

Anievas, A. (2015). Revolutions and international relations: rediscovering the classical bourgeois Revolutions. *European Journal of International Relations*, 21 (4), 841–866.

Armitage, D. (2015). Every Great Revolution is Also a Civil War. In: K. M. Baker, and D. Edelstein, eds., *Scripting Revolution*. Palo Alto, CA: Stanford University Press, 57–68.

Armitage, D., and Subrahmanyan, S., eds. (2010). *The Age of Revolution in Global Context*. Basingstoke: Palgrave.

Armstrong, D. (1993). *Revolution and World Order*. Oxford: Oxford University Press.

Baker, K. M. (2015). *Revolutionising Revolution*. In: K. M. Baker, and D. Edelstein, eds., *Scripting Revolution*. Palo Alto, CA: Stanford University Press, 71–102.

Bartelson, J. (2021). War and the Turn to History in International Relations. In de Carvalho, B., Costa Lopez, J., & Leira, H., eds. *Routledge Handbook of Historical International Relations*. Abingdon: Routledge.

Beck, C. (2011). The world-cultural origins of revolutionary waves. *Social Science History*, 35 (2), 167–207.

Beck, C. (2014). Reflections on the revolutionary wave in 2011. *Theory and Society*, 43 (2), 197–223.

Beck, C. (2018). The structure of comparison in the study of revolution. *Sociological Theory*, 36 (2), 134–161.

Beissinger, M. (2014). *The Changing Face of Revolution as a Mode of Regime Change, 1900-2012*. Paper Presented at the Comparative Workshop on Mass Protests, LSE, 13–14th June.

Bisley, N. (2004). Revolution, order and international politics. *Review of International Studies*, 30 (1), 49–69.

Bukovansky, M. (2002). *Legitimacy and Power Politics*. Princeton, NJ: Princeton University Press.

Byrne, J. (2016). *Mecca of Revolution*. New York, NY: Oxford University Press.

Çapan, Z. G., dos Reis, F., and Grasten, M. (2021). Global Histories: Connections and Circulations in Historical International Relations. In de Carvalho, B., Costa Lopez, J., & Leira, H., eds. *Routledge Handbook of Historical International Relations*. Abingdon: Routledge.

Carter, J., Bernhard M., and Palmer, G. (2012). Social revolution, the state, and war: how revolutions affect war-making capacity and interstate war outcomes. *Journal of Conflict Resolution*, 56 (3), 439–466.

Colgan, J. (2013). Domestic revolutionary leaders and international conflict. *World Politics*, 65 (4), 656–690.

Connelly, M. (2003). *A Diplomatic Revolution: Algeria's Fight for Independence and the Origins of the Post-Cold War Era*. Oxford: Oxford University Press.

Crépin, A. (2013). The Army of the Republic: New Warfare and a New Army. In: P. Serna et al., eds., *Republics at War, 1776-1840: Revolutions, Conflicts, and Geopolitics in Europe and the Atlantic World*. New York, NY: Palgrave, 131–148.

Foran, J. (2005). *Taking Power: On the Origins of Third World Revolutions*. Cambridge: Cambridge University Press.

Frazier, R. T. (2015). *The East is Black*. Durham, NC: Duke University Press.

Garton Ash, T. (1989). *The Uses of Adversity: Essays on the Fate of Central Europe*. London: Penguin.

Goldstone, J. (1991). *Revolution and Rebellion in the Early Modern World*. Berkeley, CA: University of California Press.

Goldstone, J. (2001). Towards a fourth generation of revolutionary theory. *Annual Review of Political Science*, 4, 139–187.

Goldstone, J. (2014). *Revolution: A Very Short Introduction*. Oxford: Oxford University Press.

Goldstone, J. (2016). *Revolution and Rebellion in the Early Modern World*. 2nd edition. London: Routledge.

Goodwin, J. (2001). *No Other Way Out*. Cambridge: Cambridge University Press.

Guevara, C. (2002 [1968]). Create Two, Three, Many Vietnams. In: M. del Carmen Ariet García, ed., *Global Justice*. New York, NY: Ocean.

Habermas, J. (1990). What does socialism mean today? The rectifying revolution and the needs for new thinking on the left. *New Left Review*, 183, 3–21.

Halliday, F. (1999). *Revolution and World Politics*. London: Palgrave.

Halliday, F. (2008). Revolutionary Internationalism and its Perils. In: J. Foran, D. Lane, and A. Zivkovic, eds., *Revolution in the Making of the Modern World*. London: Routledge, 65–80.

Harris, T. (2015). Did the English Have a Script for Revolution? In: K. M. Baker, and D. Edelstein, eds., *Scripting Revolution*. Palo Alto, CA: Stanford University Press, 25–40.

Hazan, E. (2014). *A People's History of the French Revolution*. London: Verso.

Hunt, L. (2010). The French Revolution in Global Context. In: D. Armitage, and S. Subrahmanyan, eds., *The Age of Revolution in Global Context*. Basingstoke: Palgrave, 20–36.

Katz, M. (1997). *Revolutions and Revolutionary Waves*. New York, NY: St Martin's.

Kurzman, C. (2008). *Democracy Denied, 1905-1915*. Cambridge, MA: Harvard University Press.

Kwon, H. (2021). Understanding the Postcolonial Cold War. In de Carvalho, B., Costa Lopez, J., & Leira, H., eds. *Routledge Handbook of Historical International Relations*. Abingdon: Routledge.

Lawson, G. (2004). *Negotiated Revolutions*. London: Ashgate.

Lawson, G. (2006). Reform, Rebellion, Civil War, Coup d'État and Revolution. In: J. DeFronzo, ed., *Revolutionary Movements in World History*. Santa Barbara, CA: ABC-CLIO.

Lawson, G. (2011). Halliday's revenge: revolutions and international relations. *International Affairs*, 87 (5), 1067–1085.

Lawson, G. (2015). Revolutions and the international. *Theory and Society*, 44 (4), 299–319.

Mack, A. (1975). Why big nations win small wars. *World Politics*, 27 (2), 175–200.

Maoz, Z. (1989). Joining the club of nations: political development and international conflict. *International Studies Quarterly*, 33 (2), 199–231.

Markoff, J. (1996). *Waves of Democracy*. Thousand Oaks, CA: Pine Forge.

Marx, K., and Engels, F. (1967 [1848]). *The Manifesto of the Communist Party*. London: Penguin.

Mayer, A. (1977). Internal Crisis and War Since 1870. In: C. C. Bertrand, ed., *Revolutionary Situations in Europe, 1917-22*. Montreal: University of Quebec Press, 201–233.

Mayer, A. (2001). *The Furies: Violence and Terror in the French and Russian Revolutions*. Princeton, NJ: Princeton University Press.

Palmer, R. R. (1954). The world revolution of the west. *Political Science Quarterly*, 69 (1), 1–14.

Panah, M. (2002). Social revolutions: the elusive emergence of an agenda in international relations. *Review of International Studies*, 28 (2), 271–292.

Parsa, M. (2000). *States, Ideologies and Revolutions*. Cambridge: Cambridge University Press.

Rao, R. (2016). Revolution. In: F. Berenskoetter, ed., *Concepts in World Politics*. London: Sage, 253–270.

Ritter, D. (2015). *The Iron Cage of Liberalism*. Oxford: Oxford University Press.

Simms, B. (2011). A False Principle in the Law of Nations: Burke, State Sovereignty, (German) Liberty, and Intervention in the Age of Westphalia. In: B. Simms, and D. Trim, eds., *Humanitarian Intervention: A History*. Cambridge: Cambridge University Press, 89–110.

Skocpol, T. (1973). A critical review of Barrington Moore's 'Social origins of dictatorship and development'. *Politics and Sociology*, 4 (1), 1–34.

Skocpol, T. (1979). *States and Social Revolutions: A Comparative Analysis of France, Russia and China*. Cambridge: Cambridge University Press.

Slater, D. (2010). *Ordering Power: Contentious Politics and Authoritarian Leviathans in Southeast Asia*. Cambridge: Cambridge University Press.

Sohrabi, N. (2002). Global waves, local actors: what the young Turks knew about other revolutions and why it mattered. *Comparative Studies in Society and History*, 44 (1), 45–79.

Stone, B. (2002). *Reinterpreting the French Revolution: A Global Historical Perspective*. Cambridge: Cambridge University Press.

Svensson, T. (2021). Decolonisation and the Erosion of the Imperial Idea. In de Carvalho, B., Costa Lopez, J., & Leira, H., eds. *Routledge Handbook of Historical International Relations*. Abingdon: Routledge.

Tardelli, L. (2013). *Fighting for Others*. PhD Thesis, London School of Economics.

Thompson, M. (1995). *The Anti-Marcos Struggle: Personalistic Rule and Democratic Transition in the Philippines*. New Haven, CT: Yale University Press.

Tilly, C. (1990). *Capital, Coercion, And European States, AD 990-1992*. Oxford: Blackwell.

Vergerio, C. (2021). International Law and the Laws of War. In de Carvalho, B., Costa Lopez, J., & Leira, H., eds. *Routledge Handbook of Historical International Relations*. Abingdon: Routledge.

Walt, S. (1996). *Revolutions and War*. Ithaca, NY: Cornell University Press.

Westad, A. (2007). *The Global Cold War*. Cambridge: Cambridge University Press.

Wight, M. (1978 [1946]). *Power Politics*. Leicester: Leicester University Press.

Willbanks, J. H. (2007). *The Tet Offensive: A Concise History*. New York, NY: Columbia University Press.

33

IMPERIALISM

Beyond the 're-turn to empire' in International Relations

Martin J. Bayly

The aide said that guys like me were 'in what we call the reality-based community,' which he defined as people who 'believe that solutions emerge from your judicious study of discernible reality.' I nodded and murmured something about enlightenment principles and empiricism. He cut me off. 'That's not the way the world really works anymore,' he continued. 'We're an empire now, and when we act, we create our own reality. And while you're studying that reality – judiciously, as you will – we'll act again, creating other new realities, which you can study too, and that's how things will sort out. We're history's actors … and you, all of you, will be left to just study what we do'.

(Suskind, 2004)

When Ron Suskind of the New York Times found himself on the receiving end of this frank assessment of American power, offered by an aide in White House of the George W. Bush administration, he was observing a sea-change in America's view of itself. The designation of 'American Empire' was nothing new, but the 9/11 attacks ushered in over two decades of United Stares–led intervention largely into parts of the world previously under the sway of European imperial powers. It wasn't simply the projection of power, but the language and style of that projection that marked a rupture moment. Policies of regime change, the deployment in Iraq and Afghanistan of counterinsurgency doctrines crafted during colonial wars of decolonization, the discourse of 'rogue states', a global campaign of counterterrorism fought through the suspension of legal rights, and the Manichean division of the world into enemies and friends; all marked a more strident era of American dominance. The military, economic, and cultural dimensions of the US foreign policy agenda from 2001 appeared to indicate that the 'unipolar moment' was in fact an imperial moment.

America's imperial turn was reflected in the social sciences too. In a reminder of the ongoing and intimate connection between contemporary world politics and the substantive and theoretical concerns of International Relations (IR), the discipline witnessed its own 'turn' to empire. But empire and imperialism had never really gone away. In fact, an appreciation for the impacts and legacies of European imperialism in particular is essential in comprehending the ways in which world politics appears today. The material and normative dominance of the 'west' (despite numerous and growing challenges to this); the delineation of borders across the continent of

Africa, the Middle East, South Asia, and beyond; the presence of large-scale South Asian diaspora throughout the Indian Ocean region and beyond; the discourse of 'civilized' and 'uncivilized' states, or in more contemporary parlance, 'failed states', 'ungoverned spaces', and 'rogue states'; and the presence of the P5 on the UN Security Council, all of these features of world politics can be traced back to empire and imperialism in the seventeenth, eighteenth, and nineteenth centuries; patterns of empire that in turn were parasitic upon other imperial polities and their legacies elsewhere.

What is surprising is not so much that we live in a world beset by the ongoing consequences of imperialism, but that until relatively recently the IR discipline was so proficient in what Robert Vitalis has termed the 'willful forgetting' of empire (2005: Loc. 2415; Bell, 2009). A cursory study of the IR canon bears this out. Kenneth Waltz's *Theory of International Politics* (1979) contains no index references to 'empire', and 'imperialism' features in his text largely as a critique of the economic theories of Hobson and Lenin. Amongst the index entries for Mearsheimer's *The Tragedy of Great Power Politics* (2001), Alexander Wendt's *Social Theory of International Politics* (1999), and Keohane and Nye's *Power and Interdependence* (1977), the terms 'empire' or 'imperialism' do not appear once. This is despite the fact that many of the case studies presented within those texts derived not from a world of nation-states, but of empires too. This isn't just about leaving empire out, but overlooking those subject to imperial rule. As Tarak Barkawi (2010) suggests, the failure of social science and IR to deal with questions of empire and imperialism left the discipline inadequate 'to the experiences and histories of most of the peoples and places on the planet'. The move, in recent years, towards what has been termed 'global IR' (Acharya, 2014; see also Çapan et al., 2021 in this volume), has made this observation more urgent. Above all, given the theme of this volume, as history clearly shows, nation-states are a relatively new invention. World politics, including for much of the twentieth century, has been primarily the story of empires not states.

For all these critiques, the 'imperial turn' has made its mark. In recent years, the study of empire and imperialism has been rejuvenated within IR. This has pulled in multiple dimensions. Some, partly motivated by the renaissance of American empire, have explored the political form of empire and its impact on systems of world order (Nexon and Wright, 2007; Phillips, 2010). Elsewhere, taking inspiration from intellectual history and the 'historiographical turn' within international political thought, imperialism and its intersection with internationalism have featured once more within the disciplinary purview (Long and Schmidt, 2005; Bell, 2001, 2007). In addition, and linked to this, the imperial turn has prompted disciplinary self-reflection as IR has considered its own imperial roots (Schmidt, 1998; Muppidi, 2012; Vitalis, 2015). In what follows I shall explore each of these developments in turn, including their payoffs for the IR discipline, before considering those areas of imperial history that IR has still yet to explore.

Bringing empire back in: the political form of empire

Empire may not always have been a 'hot topic' within IR, but Michael Doyle's (1986) volume *Empires* provides a prominent exception. Better known for his work on democratic peace theory, Doyle's earlier work sought to comprehend the political form taken by imperial rule, in the process offering a definition that provided a way marker for later scholars. For Doyle, empire was constituted by 'effective control, whether formal or informal, of a subordinated society by an imperial society', where effective control means control over sovereignty. 'Imperialism', was therefore 'the process of establishing and maintaining' this basic political relationship (Doyle, 1986: 19).

Significant in Doyle's work was the manner in which he sought to incorporate existing explanations for imperialism, drawing upon both history and IR. Outlining the spatial form of empire, he delineated 'metrocentric' approaches where imperialism resulted from a metropolitan urge, as with Lenin and Hobson's stress on the acquisitive nature of capitalism for instance. Meanwhile, 'pericentric' approaches brought in the doyennes of the 'Cambridge School' of imperial history, Gallagher and Robinson (1953), who stressed the peripheral motivations for imperial expansion, emphasizing the importance of 'informal empire' in comprehending imperialism overall. Here, empire was not so much about the whims of Emperors and their cabinets, but rather about the inevitable expansion into what Doyle termed 'imperializable peripheries' – spaces with no, or at best highly divided government; undifferentiated economies; and with absent or highly divided loyalties (Doyle, 1986: 19). Finally, 'systemic' approaches allowed for the incorporation of mainstream IR theories, notably Waltz's structural realism, which identified the system as the key variable shaping the political form of empire.

Empires reflected then a particular attitude towards the purpose of disciplinary IR. Key here was the elaboration of essential attributes of empire as primarily a political relationship. This was an attempt to pin down the mechanics of imperialism as a means of cross-case comparison. However, as Daniel Nexon and Thomas Wright (2007) argued two decades later in their own contribution to the debate, few IR scholars took up the discussion that Doyle reignited. Whereas Doyle laid the emphasis on the essential attributes of imperial units, Nexon and Wright's contribution entered the debate at the level of order. Doyle's extraction of 'empire' from 'imperialism' carried with it the implicit distinction between an empire as a form of polity, and the international order within which it was located. This entailed an assumption that has tended to bedevil the treatment of empire within IR as whole: The idea that empire was essentially the state writ large. For Nexon and Wright, what was missing was not so much a theorizing of empire as a unitary polity, but rather a theorizing of imperial orders as a set of relations. Empire had evaded treatment within IR because imperial orders tended to be treated as some form of hegemonic order, or pattern of preponderance, when in fact, imperial orders historically were frequently nested within other forms of order, including anarchic, bipolar, and multipolar orders.

Nexon and Wright's approach therefore offered a jailbreak from the tendency to socialize empire into a state-centric order within IR. Imperial power was instead theorized as a relational form of power, deriving from the positional relationship between metropoles and periphery actors. Imperial orders were thus based on hierarchical 'heterogeneous contracting' with a diversity of periphery actors. Local intermediaries were invested with power precisely because of their relationship with the central authority, but were kept in check by the possibility that their status may be revoked and passed to another if they fail to keep to the contract. Imperial metropolitan actors thereby exerted control through their capacity to 'divide and rule' – to play local intermediaries off one another.

Although largely unacknowledged this heterogeneous contracting and indirect rule model of empire resonated with some of the moves within imperial history at the time. Notable here is Tony Ballantyne's notion of empire as consisting of a series of webs rather than the more traditional 'empire from above' narrative (Ballantyne, 2014). In many ways, this continued the genealogy of indirect or informal empire models begun by Gallagher and Robinson, adapted in different ways through the likes of Chris Bayly and Thomas Metcalf (Bayly, 1996; Metcalf, 2008). Nexon and Wright's model also had the benefit of explaining how the United States could be described as an empire without exhibiting many of the characteristics traditionally associated with imperialism (at least not in the post–Cold War era), notably direct rule and permanent territorial conquest. Meanwhile, a shift away from describing essentialist qualities of empire as a political form, towards relational patterns of intersocietal encounter, hints at the works of postcolonial scholars and those who have sought to bring 'metropole' and 'periphery' in a more complex relational whole (Barkawi and Laffey, 2002; Ballantyne and Burton, 2012; Steinmetz, 2016).

But metropole-periphery models, as Nexon and Wright pointed out, remained essentially ideal-typical understandings of imperialism, raising the question of historical veracity. Direct imperial conquest didn't die out in the nineteenth century, indeed the third imperialist wave of the twentieth century, which included imperial expansions by countries such as Germany, Italy, and Japan, in many ways reflected the old-fashioned model of imperialism. These forms of imperialism coexisted with more informal and indirect patterns as with the British Empire in South Asia, whose independence movements were mobilized precisely in opposition to an apparently reinvigorated imperialist threat from both East and West in the early decades of the twentieth century. Meanwhile, the pattern of French empire had always resembled a more metrocentric form of direct rule where French colonies were perceived as *départments* of the French state. These differing structures not only challenged the ideal-typical models laid out by Doyle, Nexon, and Wright, and others, but also shaped the ways in which those empires operated, their longevity, and the patterns of resistance that they faced.

Indeed, the agency of 'periphery' actors – those subject to imperialism and colonialism – is itself worthy of greater analysis and study, including the impacts these agents had on imperial and world politics (Viksand, 2020). It is true, for instance, that the 1857 mutiny in India only saw limited impact on other colonial spaces at least beyond the immediate South Asian region, despite colonial and para-colonial ties between these spaces (Bose, 2006). But later patterns of resistance against empire clearly profited from the ability of periphery segments to collaborate and share across so-called imperial firewalls (Nexon and Wright, 2007). The League Against Imperialism set up in the 1927 Brussels Conference provides one prominent example, an organization that thrived precisely because of shared outlooks among diverse so-called periphery segments, and their corralling under wider banners of socialist and Marxist internationalisms (Raza, Roy, and Zachariah, 2015; Louro, 2018).

More broadly to suggest that peripheries didn't engage in some form of collaboration or intellectual political social or cultural contact only works as an assumption if we ignore subaltern histories, the history of ideas, and indigenous knowledge orders (Bayly, 1996). Anti-imperialism had a political, intellectual, and social life too – one which refutes the all-pervasive hegemony of imperial order (Getachew, 2019). The recent turn towards a narrative of imperial 'anxieties' has also shown just how fearful imperial power was; a fear that regularly manifested in displays of performative violence and collective punishment (Condos, 2017; Wagner, 2017). The danger here is that IR's insistence on abstraction forces it to incorporate a largely top-down – maybe even conservative – form of imperial history, in this instance unwittingly writing out the voices of those subject to imperial rule. This is just one example of how IR once more privileges the voice of the powerful, and opens up the critique from critical, postcolonial, and decolonial scholars on the essentially imperialist character of IR, and the coloniality of its knowledge (more on this later).

So we reach an impasse. Once again, history fights back against the concepts that social science demands as the cost of doing business. A theory that tries to capture everything is no theory at all, but questions remain as to the level of conceptual abstraction we are comfortable with. At what point do we end up doing damage to the history that we seek to bring into the discipline? These are surely questions that cut across the entire enterprise of Historical IR.

An empire state of mind: the historiography of imperial thought

One of the difficulties then of dealing with empire within IR relates to the ontological stability of the term. The same may also be said of 'state', 'territoriality', 'sovereignty', and a host of other concepts that are central to the discipline. But empire is perhaps unique in its apparent capacity not only to encompass these other concepts, but also in its variability across time and space. The semantic range of imperialism is broad enough to incorporate territorial and non-territorial forms (for example epistemic imperialism, capitalist accumulation, neo-imperialism). It can be said to express multiple forms of sovereignty (divided, direct, indirect). Frequently, the category of 'state' is nested within the imperial form, and indeed in many cases, states can be seen as constituted by empire. This is apparent in the fact that in the political thought of empire, 'state' was a term often used interchangeably with terms such as 'nation', 'commonwealth', 'government', 'body politic', 'political union', and 'sovereign' (Bell, 2007: 98–99). Attention to the political thought of imperialism, part of what has been termed the 'historiographical turn' (Bell, 2001), presents a second front in the study of empire within Historical IR. If empire has the capacity to create its own reality, then one of the most obvious manifestations of this was in the universe of ideas that constituted imperial thought – or what Jay-Z and Alicia Keys might call, an 'empire state of mind'.

Rather than attempting to fix the conceptual content of empire, studies of imperial thought have instead explored its multivalent intellectual worlds. Duncan Bell's wide-ranging exploration of European ideologies of empire challenges the notion of a monolithic form of imperial rule both in theory and in practice (Bell, 2006, 2007, 2016). Empire was justified and critiqued on the basis of legal, ethical, moral, cultural, and commercial imperatives, as well as its political and strategic rationales. Key here was the relationship between empire and Liberal ideologies with respect to the pursuit of free trade, the pacific benefits of commerce, and more embodied ideas of civilizational development (Pitts, 2005; see also Jahn, 2021).

A central binary distinction that these ideologies opened up was that between so-called civilized and uncivilized states, a distinction that corresponded as much with perceptions of political organization, as with judgements over the moral status of subject populations (Gong, 1984; see also Bowden, 2021). According to this logic, empire was justified on the grounds of its benevolent cultivation of more civilized practices. This was a legal and normative distinction that reached 'all the way down'. At the macro-level, 'uncivilized' powers were located in a separate normative universe justifying a general derogation from the established practices of interstate conduct, including in relation to the laws of war. But at a micro-level too, the representation of subject populations by colonial administrators, political officers, and orientalist scholars alike frequently revolved around stadial tropes of barbarism, savagery, and capacities for commercial or even intellectual intercourse. Colonial knowledge thereby justified and sustained the practices of colonial governmentality, whilst also feeding upwards into wider patterns of ordering the world that found a location in legal discourses and international organizations (Simpson, 2004; Bayly, 2016; Bayly, 2019).

The implications for IR of attention to the intellectual worlds of empire are profound. First, we perceive more clearly the co-implication of imperial thought, imperial practice, and international political theory, including canonical texts within IR theory (Buck-Morss, 2000; Pitts, 2005; Lowe, 2015). As Edward Keene (2002) has shown through his reappraisal of Grotius' work, imperialism carried with it the presumption that beyond the European system of states, sovereign-territoriality was not assumed. The sovereign prerogatives of public authorities were seen as divisible 'such that it would be possible for sovereignty to be divided between several institutions within a single political community, or ... for a state to acquire some of the sovereign prerogatives that had originally belonged to another and exercise them on its behalf' (2002: 3). Furthermore, Grotius' understanding of the law of nations allowed for the private appropriation of unoccupied lands and in the absence of established political authority the right to wage 'private war' in their defence. Significant here is not just the legal provision for what would be commonly understood as colonialism, but the fact that this goes against one of the central organizing principles of international society (in the English School sense), namely the principle of indivisible sovereign-territoriality.

Second, attention to the legal dimensions of imperial thought in particular has also challenged the mythology of the essentially egalitarian nature of international law (see Vergerio, 2021 in this volume). Key here was the nineteenth-century shift from naturalist conceptions of international to a more positivist reading, in other words, a shift from a transcendental set of practices to a more 'scientific' reading, based on the dictates of a professional legal class, and the product of sovereign will, [i.e. the 'civilized' (European) powers of the family of nations] (Pitts, 2007; Sylvest, 2007). In this sense, Antony Anghie (1999) points to the complicity between positivism and colonialism, where a body of international law was constructed around the practical requirement of ruling over 'peripheral' societies. Taking this further, and again with reference to the misconceptions of the English School, Gerry Simpson (2004) has explored the tradition of 'anti-pluralism' within the international legal system, as evidenced in the category of 'outlaw states' in international society. Contemporary discourses of 'rogue', 'failed', or 'backlash' states, familiar to International Criminal Court proceedings and Security Council resolutions, can accordingly trace a genealogy back to the 1815 Vienna Congress, and arguably, in terms of the 'barbarian' distinction, back to the 'Pax Romana' of the Roman empire. Such arguments have also helped to sustain the move from anarchy to hierarchy in the theorizing of international order (Hobson and Sharman, 2005; Zarakol, 2017; Barnett, 2017; Spanu, 2020).

Third, although this has perhaps been underappreciated within Historical IR, are the spatial dimensions of empire (see Goettlich and Branch, 2021). In theory and in practice, empire rarely covered space in a uniform fashion. Striking here is the intersection of legal provisions, colonial knowledge, and the spatial regimes of imperial and colonial authority. Lauren Benton's groundbreaking work (2009) exploring the confluence of sovereignty, law, and geography has disturbed the 'logical and perhaps even comforting ... narrative of European empires as generating a slow but steady rationalization of space', one that was encouraged by the refining of cartographic practice at the time, and cemented most emblematically in the pink shading of British imperial maps. As Benton's work demonstrates, empire, as a political, legal, and geographical order 'did not cover space evenly but composed a fabric that was full of holes, stitched together out of pieces ... politically fragmented; legally differentiated; and encased in irregular, porous, and sometimes undefined borders' (Benton, 2009: 2). Overlapping with this, and arguably overlooked within IR, has been Ann Laura Stoler's description of 'imperial formations': 'macropolities whose technologies of rule thrive on the production of exceptions and their uneven and changing proliferation. ... harboring and building on territorial ambiguity, redefining legal categories of belonging and quasi-membership, and shifting the geographic and demographic zones of partially suspended rights' (Stoler, 2006: 128). As this suggests, imperial geographies, and their politics of legality were productive not only of certain types of space, but of certain categories of people: Imperial spatializations had (and arguably continue to have) social effects, productive of 'shadow populations', 'zones of exclusion', and zones of 'privileged exemption'. The point here is that these sites should be seen as anomalous but rather at the very core of imperial practice in producing spaces of scaled sovereignty and differentiated subjecthood. The capacity for imperial formations to capture spaces as diverse as the Federally Administered Tribal Areas of Pakistan, the Mediterranean, and the US-Mexican border should prompt IR to take notice.

Both Benton and Stoler's works offer escape routes from what John Agnew described as IR's 'territorial trap' (1994). In particular, and as David Strang (1996) has shown, here we can bring in the voluminous travel and exploration literature that was generated by the imperial encounter, a literature that was productive of a host of geographical imaginations, often peddled by the 'scientific' learned societies of imperial metropoles (Bayly, 2016). Bell's study of the idea of 'Greater Britain' (2007) demonstrates how these imperial geographies could operate on a global scale. Spatializations produced by the British Empire sought to tie together the English-speaking settler colonies, and even the United States, under an imperial 'federation', an idea that found avatars in for instance the 'Closer Union' project that sought to reorganize East African colonies. Federative ideas also migrated into the post-imperial visions of anti-colonial thinkers (Getachew, 2019; Fezjula, 2020). As an attempt at imperial reform 'Greater Britain' ultimately failed, but the idea lives on in the notion of the 'Anglosphere' upon which pro-'Brexit' campaigners in the United Kingdom have pinned such high hopes (Bell, 2017).

Fourth, imperial ideologies had productive effects in a more practical sense, with consequences for world order and practices of IR. What Buzan and Lawson (2015) have termed 'ideologies of progress' (including liberalism itself) manifested in new forms of governmental management by which 'rational states' sought to comprehend and manage their subject populations. The advent of the 'colonial state' served to systematize knowledge and inculcate a new cadre of professional bureaucrats – a shift that was reflected back into metropolitan spaces. At the frontiers of colonial and imperial spaces, new methods of cartography offered a 'scientific' and fixed delimitation of space for Europeans unfamiliar with the reach of these newly acquired territories (Branch, 2013; Goettlich, 2018). It was in this drive towards mapping which was then imported back to Europe, and not the Peace of Westphalia, that Jordan Branch (2013) locates the origins of the territorial sovereign state and the possibility of IR as such.

Finally, the scientification of government had implications for foreign policy and the conduct of military operations too as forms of knowledge shaping the official mind became more generic and sterile. This signalled a move towards 'utile forms' (Ansorge and Barkawi, 2014) away from the more embodied and fluid colonial knowledge of early scholar-practitioners. For Patricia Owens (2015), it was in the colonial 'small wars' and counterinsurgency campaigns of imperial states, and particularly the wars of decolonization, that the advent of a particular rendering of the 'social' was operationalized – one which harkened back to the doctrines of 'household management' first elaborated by Ancient Greek philosophy. Combined with the differentiation of subject populations along scales of savagery and barbarianism, these ideologies of progress also demonstrated a 'dark side' (Buzan and Lawson, 2015). The use of colonies as 'imperial laboratories' (Barder, 2015; Go, 2020) offered sites for new experiments in government. Often these were reflected back to imperial metropoles. Prison camps, policing, the surveillance state, and neoliberal economics all originated in 'periphery' spaces as projects of formal and informal imperial experimentation.

An imperial social science: International Relations

To return to Vitalis (2005) and the 'wilful forgetting' of empire within IR, we ought to remind ourselves that 'forgetting' is the key word here. Whilst the contemporary IR discipline spent much of the twentieth century focussing on states, Vitalis' work shows us that at its origins, IR was a profoundly imperial discipline concerned not with relations between states, but with colonial administration, imperial relations, and 'race management' (2015; Davis, Thakur, and Vale, 2020; see also Yao and Delatolla, 2021). The 'turn' to empire then is partly conceived as a 're-turn' to the foundational purposes of political science and IR as a source of 'useful knowledge' for imperial powers. This undermines one of the central creation myths of the IR discipline, that it was developed for the purposes of understanding and preventing the horrors of the First World War with the establishing of the Woodrow Wilson Chair at the University of Aberystwyth (Wilson, 1998). Rather than a debate between idealism and realism, a more accurate framing is accordingly one between internationalism and imperialism (Long and Schmidt, 2005). The legacies of this were faintly visible even with the rise of the heroic age of theory. As the English School theorist, Martin Wight, put it: 'the question of relations with barbarians was a political problem forming a bridge between international relations and colonial administrations' (cited in Schmidt, 2005: 44). Hans J Morgenthau's observation in Politics Among Nations that the disappearance of 'politically empty spaces' on colonial frontiers demanded a reformed theoretical vision shows how 'internationalism', and its 'scientific' treatment could be seen as emergent from imperialism (1967: 52). Following Tarak Barkawi (2010): 'Repeatedly, it would seem, IR was founded amidst empire, but discovered instead only a world of sovereign states and their collective action problems'.

IR is not alone in its complicity with imperialism and colonial administration. Sociology, Anthropology, and Geopolitics can all trace their roots in colonial modernity and the need for 'useful knowledge' as means of instructing colonial administration (Asad, 1973; Steinmetz 2013; Kearns, 2009). But the discipline does stand out in its unwillingness to confront these origins – a reflection perhaps of a general apathy towards disciplinary history within the field (Long and Schmidt, 2005; Bell, 2009). There are, however, more urgent imperatives here too not only in addressing the Eurocentrism of disciplinary knowledge at its origins but also in bringing in those aspects that have been lost along the way – notably race and violence. Whilst early twentieth-century scholars of international politics may have disagreed on the best ways to organize colonies, or prevent war, they did agree on the central problematic of race management in international affairs. The popular prediction of 'race war' attests to this. By justifying imperial rule as the continuation of white dominance over subject peoples, Vitalis (2015) exposes the racist, white supremacist, discourses central to American IR at birth. Key here are the 'counter-networks' that resisted these arguments, networks that connected together spaces as diverse as Sugar Hill in Harlem, New York; Port of Spain, Trinidad; Camden in London, United Kingdom; and Ghana's capital, Accra.

Difference, or the management of difference, therefore lay at the core of IR's disciplinary project at its inception (Inayatullah and Blaney, 2004) and in this sense, as postcolonial and critical scholarship has also shown, we can point to the deep coloniality of disciplinary knowledge (see Caraccioli, 2021). Himadeep Muppidi (2012) has shown how IR's 'narrative protocols' serve to perpetuate the representation of non-westerners through 'zooalogical modalities' and a 'numerative gaze'. In this sense, the origins of IR in colonial knowledge are all too apparent. Accordingly, instead of a discipline that is alive to the constant presence of violence and death, IR is complicit in the explaining away of mass violence through implicitly dehumanizing 'others' and rationalizing-by-numerating the exercise of military force. It is in parallel with this that decolonial scholars have pushed for an epistemic flight from IR's foundations in European modernity and its intimate connections with imperialism (Agathangelou and Ling, 2004; Shani, 2008; Bilgin, 2008; Sabaratnam, 2017).

Terrae incognitae: where next for empire and Historical IR?

Where does this all leave us? At a conceptual level, one of the principle payoffs from this body of work has been the challenge that has been mounted towards the analytical bifurcation of empires vs. states. A teleological vision of the unproblematic shift from an imperial system, to a system of states, sometime after the Second World War is no longer viable. Empire has not emerged from this literature as simply a unit in itself to be placed alongside state units. Instead, the multivalent nature of European empires in particular is revealed. Empires have been shown to consist of actors and ideas that transcend public and private realms. The growth of mercantile imperialism, the role of private companies, and their sometimes ambivalent relationship with 'state' power complicate the ontology of states vs. empires, showing how polities in the international system were frequently nested within each other. Long-standing concepts of 'informal' vs. 'formal' empire – well-established within imperial history – have been brought more systematically into IR. Above all, through greater historical consciousness, the historical ontology of these concepts has also been revealed. Empire meant different things in different spaces, at different times. As a result, perhaps unsurprisingly a significant part of the imperial turn has been dominated by approaches deriving from historical sociology and 'global' historical sociology (Buzan and Lawson, 2015; see also Go, Lawson and de Carvalho, 2021).

Yet for all the recovery of imperialism within IR in recent years, the story of non-western imperialism has been far less apparent. Such studies offer new insights into the structural variety of international systems, as shown in Manjeet Pardesi's (2017) studies of Mughal and Islamicate Asia, or through Andrew Phillips and Jason Sharman's work on the hybrid forms of sovereignty that emerged through the East India Company's expansion into the Indian Ocean region (Phillips and Sharman, 2015; Phillips, 2016). Equally important are studies of the movements that opposed European empires. The collapse of the Ottoman Empire in the early twentieth century and its afterlives in the Pan-Islamist movement, which resonated across colonized spaces from Afghanistan to South East Asia, has been well covered by international historians (Aydin, 2007). Yet curiously these movements have made limited impact in IR – despite their echoes with recent events in the Middle East, and the somewhat eclectic political ideologies of the so-called Islamic State (Devji, 2015). Alongside this, the political life of Pan-Asianism, which grew out of a modernist critique of European imperialism, and paradoxically also a modernist pursuit of colonies for imperial Japan, also offers an as yet underexplored example of global inter-imperial dynamics. These entanglements of European and non-European imperialism, including the ways in which they were navigated and even exploited by anti-colonial groups, offer one potential avenue for new research.

Attention to non-European imperial thought, and anti-imperial political thought also, offers a deeper research programme on empire as a global phenomenon – including theorizations from 'non-western' perspectives. Here an analytical bifurcation of the imperial west and the non-imperial non-west will not do. Anti-colonial liberation movements galvanized around ideas of anti-imperialism with profound implications for world politics, that is clear, but broader traditions of thought are also apparent that complicate a simple binary logic. In the South Asian context, for instance, internationalist visions, ideas of hierarchy, and imperialism were extracted from the sacred texts of the Hindu Vedas and scholarly texts, including those produced in the context of expanding and contracting imperial polities, such as Kautilya's *Arthashastra*. The recovery of these histories and archaic tracts of statecraft by South Asian scholars served a purpose for nationalist thinkers who sought to showcase the intellectual vitality of South Asia against the degenerative orientalist representations of certain European scholars. Here, the response to imperialism, its intellectual worlds, and its international effects are shown to be just as important as the study of empire itself. In a sense, whilst IR had its imperial origins, it had its anti-imperial origins too. Understanding the entanglements between these worlds offers a 'global IR' that is worthy of the name.

Aside from these macro-level topics of order, scale, and intellectual history, the study of empire in Historical IR might also turn its attention to more micro-level studies of imperial practice. The generation and diffusion of practices of trade, commerce, law, land management, population management, policing, intelligence, or military activity for instance, across and between imperial spaces, offers new understandings of the ordering effects of imperial governance, its spatial reach, as well as its legacies. One notable absence here are studies of the practices of imperial violence, the frequent silencing of which offers a host of ethical as well as methodological challenges. The recent lawsuit brought against the UK Foreign and Commonwealth Office by Kenyan victims of torture perpetrated by the British government during the emergency era of the 1950s provides a case in point.

Finally, on a methodological point, it is striking that for all of the talk of a 're-turn' to empire in IR and the co-presence of a more historically informed programme of research, the use of primary source materials remains relatively uncommon (see Mulich, 2021). As the historiographical turn has shown 'the archive' is a term that encapsulates a variety of sources and one area that has seen growth has been the recovery of overlooked historical works of political thought, and even travel accounts. But the exploration of national, organizational, and local archives still seems to be viewed by many IR scholars as something that historians do. It might be said that in its quest to deal with empire more comprehensively, for IR to avoid regurgitating outdated debates in imperial history, it should engage with primary sources with the same vigour that it engages with secondary sources. For all of the problems with the construction of the archive, its silences, and its occlusions, a reliance upon only secondary sources is the equivalent of attempting to learn about the past by only visiting museums – these are curated collections.

If this can be achieved, IR offers a suite of theoretical approaches, and scales of analysis that are not always in the forefront of the historian's mind. Historical IR has ameliorated IR's traditional instrumentalization and distortion of history through slavish adherence to concepts and theory. But opportunities may also be explored to speak back to the instrumentalization and distortion of theory that the discipline of history is sometimes guilty of. One avenue here is to engage with the 'multi-axial' frameworks for analysis that global historians have developed off the back of the achievements of imperial history (Ballantyne and Burton, 2012). Given IR's competence with theorizing and operating across multiple analytical levels, there is an opportunity for IR to bring a different range of questions to the debate on the historical and ongoing presence of empire in world politics and to sharpen its disciplinary contribution.

World politics continues to echo its imperial pasts. The reverberations of racism and imperial nostalgia that have been visited upon European and North American politics can find equivalents in the hyper-nationalist projects of Xi Xinping, Narendra Modi, and Vladmir Putin. The spatial imaginaries of 'Tianxia', the BJP's attempted recovery of 'Greater India', or conceptions of Eurasia located in the writings of Russian Conservative thinkers such as Alexander Dugin, all provide reminders of the ongoing presence of imperial imaginaries. Assessing the implications of these for IR is only achievable if IR begins to confidently craft its own histories.

Suggestions for further reading

Ballantyne, T. and Burton, A. (2012). Empires and the Reach of the Global. In: E. S. Rosenberg, ed., *A World Connecting (1870–1945)*, Cambridge MA: The Belknap Press of Harvard University Press.

Biccum, A. R. (2018). What is an empire? Assessing the postcolonial contribution to the American Empire Debate. *Interventions*, 20 (5), 697-716.

Doty, R. L. (1996). *Imperial Encounters: The Politics of Representation in North-South Relations*. Minneapolis, MN: University of Minnesota Press.

Go, J. (2011). *Patterns of Empire: The British and American Empires, 1688 to the Present*. Cambridge: Cambridge University Press.

Mulich, J. (2018). Transformation at the margins: imperial expansion and systemic change in world politics. *Review of International Studies*, 44 (4), 694-716.

References

Acharya, A. (2014). Global international relations (IR) and regional worlds: a new agenda for international studies. *International Studies Quarterly*, 58 (4), 647-659.

Agathangelou, A. M. and Ling, L. H. M. (2004). The house of IR: from family power politics to the poises of worldism. *International Studies Review*, 6 (4), 21-49.

Anghie A. (1999). Finding the peripheries: sovereignty and colonialism in nineteenth-century international law. *Harvard International Law Journal*, 40 (1), 1-71.

Ansorge, J. T. and Barkawi, T. (2014). Utile forms: power and knowledge in small war. *Review of International Studies*, 40 (1), 3-24.

Asad, T., ed., (1973). *Anthropology and the Colonial Encounter*. London: Ithaca Press.

Aydin, C. (2007). *The Politics of Anti-Westernism in Asia*. New York, NY: Columbia University Press.

Ballantyne, T. (2014). *Webs of Empire: Locating New Zealand's Colonial Past*. Vancouver: UBC Press.

Barder, A. (2015). *Empire Within: International Hierarchy and its Imperial Laboratories of Governance*. Abingdon, UK: Routledge.

Barkawi, T. (2010). Empire and Order in International Relations and Security Studies. In: R. A. Denemark, ed., *The International Studies Encyclopaedia, Vol. III*. Chichester: Wiley-Blackwell, 1360-1379.

Barkawi, T. and Laffey, M. (2002). Retrieving the imperial: empire and international relations. *Millennium: Journal of International Studies*, 31 (1), 109-127.

Barnett, M. (2017). Hierarchy and Paternalism. In: A. Zarakol, ed., *Hierarchies in World Politics*. Cambridge: Cambridge University Press, 66-94.

Bayly, C. A. (1996). *Empire and Information: Intelligence Gathering and Social Communication in India, 1780-1870*. Cambridge: Cambridge University Press.

Bayly, M. J. (2016). *Taming the Imperial Imagination: Colonial Knowledge, International Relations, and the Anglo-Afghan Encounter*. Cambridge: Cambridge University Press.

Bayly, M. J. (2019). Mountstuart Elphinstone, Colonial Knowledge, and 'Frontier Governmentality' in Northwest India, 1849-1878. In S. M. Hanifi, ed., *Mountstuart Elphinstone in South Asia: Pioneer of British Colonial Rule*. London: Hurst and Co, 249-393.

Bell, D. (2001). International relations: the dawn of a historiographical turn? *British Journal of Politics and International Relations*, 3 (1), 115-126.

Bell, D. (2006). Empire and international relations in Victorian political thought. *Historical Journal*, 49 (1), 281-298.

Bell, D. (2007). *The Idea of Greater Britain*. Princeton, NJ: Princeton University Press.

Bell, D. (2009). Writing the world: disciplinary history and beyond. *International Affairs*, 85 (1), 3-22.

Bell, D. (2016). *Reordering the World: Essays on Liberalism and Empire*. Princeton, NJ: Princeton University Press.

Bell, D. (2017). The Anglosphere: new enthusiasm for an old dream. *Prospect Magazine*. February 2017. Viewed 15 October 2020, <https://www.prospectmagazine.co.uk/magazine/anglosphere-old-dream-brexit-role-in-the-world>.

Benton, L. (2009). *A Search for Sovereignty: Law and Geography in European Empires, 1400-1900*. Cambridge: Cambridge University Press.

Bilgin, P. (2008). 'Thinking past 'Western' IR'. *Third World Quarterly*, 29 (1), 5-23.

Bose, S. (2006). *A Hundred Horizons: The Indian Ocean in the Age of Global Empire*. Cambridge, MA: Harvard University Press.

Bowden, B. (2021). Eurocentrism and Civilization. In de Carvalho, B., Costa Lopez, J., & Leira, H., eds. *Routledge Handbook of Historical International Relations*. Abingdon: Routledge.

Branch, J. (2013). *The Cartographic State: Maps, Territory, and the Origins of Sovereignty*. Cambridge: Cambridge University Press.

Buck-Morss, S. (2000). Hegel and Haiti. *Critical Inquiry*, 26 (4), 821-865.

Buzan, B. and Lawson, G. (2015). *The Global Transformation: History, Modernity and the Making of International Relations*. Cambridge: Cambridge University Press.

Çapan, Z. G., dos Reis, F. and Grasten, M., (2021). Global Histories: Connections and Circulations in Historical International Relations. In de Carvalho, B., Costa Lopez, J., & Leira, H., eds. *Routledge Handbook of Historical International Relations*. Abingdon: Routledge.

Caraccioli, M. J. (2021). Early (Modern) Empires: The Political Ideology of Conceptual Domination. In de Carvalho, B., Costa Lopez, J., & Leira, H., eds. *Routledge Handbook of Historical International Relations*. Abingdon: Routledge.

Condos, M. (2017). *The Insecurity State: Punjab and the Making of Colonial Power in British India*. Cambridge: Cambridge University Press.

Davis, A., Thakur, V. and Vale, P. (2020). *The Imperial Discipline: Race and the Founding of International Relations*. London: Pluto Press.

Devji, F. (2015). ISIS: Haunted by sovereignty. *Spiked Review*. December 2015. Online. Viewed 15 October 2020, <https://www.spiked-online.com/2015/12/18/isis-haunted-by-sovereignty/>.

Doyle, M. (1986). *Empires*. Ithaca, NY: Cornell University Press.

Fezjula, M. (2021). The Cosmopolitan Historiography of Twentieth-Century Federalism. *The Historical Journal*, 64 (2), 477-500.

Gallagher, J. and Robinson, R. (1953). The imperialism of free trade. *The Economic History Review*, 6 (1), 1-15

Getachew, A. (2019). *Worldmaking After Empire: The Rise and Fall of Self-Determination*. Princeton, NJ: Princeton University Press.

Go, J. (2020). The imperial origins of American policing: militarization and imperial feedback in the early 20th century. *American Journal of Sociology*, 125 (5), 1193-1254.

Goettlich, K. (2018). The rise of linear borders in world politics. *European Journal of International Relations*, 25 (1), 203-228.

Goettlich, K., and Branch, J. (2021). Borders and Boundaries: Making Visible What Divides. In de Carvalho, B., Costa Lopez, J., & Leira, H., eds. *Routledge Handbook of Historical International Relations*. Abingdon: Routledge.

Go, J., Lawson, G., and de Carvalho, B. (2021). Historical Sociology in International Relations: The Challenge of the Global. In de Carvalho, B., Costa Lopez, J., & Leira, H., eds. *Routledge Handbook of Historical International Relations*. Abingdon: Routledge.

Gong, G. (1984). *The Standard of 'Civilization' in International Society*. Oxford: Oxford University Press.

Hobson, J. M. and Sharman, J. C. (2005). The enduring place of hierarchy in world politics: tracing the social logics of hierarchy and political change. *European Journal of International Relations*, 11 (1), 63-98.

Inayatullah, N. and Blaney, D. L. (2004). *International Relations and the Problem of Difference*. New York, NY: Routledge.

Jahn, B. (2021). Liberalism between Theory and Practice. In de Carvalho, B., Costa Lopez, J., & Leira, H., eds. *Routledge Handbook of Historical International Relations*. Abingdon: Routledge.

Kearns, G. (2009). *Geopolitics and Empire: The Legacy of Halford Mackinder*. Oxford: Oxford University Press.

Keene, E. (2002). *Beyond the Anarchical Society: Grotius, Colonialism and Order in World Politics*. Cambridge: Cambridge University Press.

Long, D. and Schmidt, B., eds., (2005). *Imperialism and Internationalism in the Discipline of International Relations*. Albany, NY: State University of New York Press.

Louro, M. (2018). *Comrades Against Imperialism: Nehru, India, and Interwar Internationalism*. Cambridge: Cambridge University Press.

Lowe, L. (2015). *The Intimacies of Four Continents*. Durham, NC: Duke University Press.

Metcalf, T. (2008). *Imperial Connections: India in the Indian Ocean Arena, 1860–1920*. Vancouver: UBC Press.

Morgenthau, H. J. (1967). *Politics Among Nations*. 4th edition. New York, NY: Knopf.

Mulich, J. (2021). International Relations in the Archive: Uses of Sources and Historiography. In de Carvalho, B., Costa Lopez, J., & Leira, H., eds. *Routledge Handbook of Historical International Relations*. Abingdon: Routledge.

Muppidi, H. (2012). *The Colonial Signs of International Relations*. London: Hurst.

Nexon, D. H. and Wright, T. (2007). What's at stake in the American Empire debate. *American Political Science Review*, 101 (2), 253-271.

Owens, P. (2015). *Economy of Force: Counterinsurgency and the Historical Rise of the Social*. Cambridge: Cambridge University Press.

Pardesi, M. (2017). Region, system, and order: the Mughal Empire in Islamicate Asia. *Security Studies*, 26 (2), 249-278.

Phillips, A. (2010). *War, Religion, and Empires: The Transformation of International Orders*. Cambridge: Cambridge University Press.

Phillips, A. (2016). Global IR meets global history: sovereignty, modernity, and the international system's expansion in the Indian Ocean Region. *International Studies Review*, 18 (1), 62-77.

Phillips, A. and Sharman, J. (2015). *International Order in Diversity: War, Trade, and Rule in the Indian Ocean*. Cambridge: Cambridge University Press.

Pitts, J. (2005). *A Turn to Empire: The Rise of Imperial Liberalism in Britain and France*. Princeton, NJ: Princeton University Press.

Pitts, J. (2007). Boundaries of Victorian International Law. In: D. Bell, ed., *Victorian Visions of Global Order: Empire and International Relations in Nineteenth-Century Political Thought*. Cambridge: Cambridge University Press, 67-88.

Raza, A., Roy, F., and Zachariah, B, eds. (2015). *The Internationalist Moment: South Asia, Worlds, and World Views, 1917–39*. Delhi: Sage.

Sabaratnam, M. (2017). *Decolonizing Intervention: International Statebuilding in Mozambique*. London: Bowman and Littlefield.

Schmidt, B. (1998). *The Political Discourse of Anarchy: A Disciplinary History*. Albany, NY: State University of New York Press.

Schmidt, B. (2005). Paul S. Reinsch and the study of imperialism and internationalism. In: D. Long and B. Schmidt, eds., *Imperialism and Internationalism in the Discipline of International Relations*. Albany, NY: State University of New York Press, 43-70.

Shani, G. (2008). Toward a post-Western IR: the *Umma, Khalsa Panth*, and critical international relations theory. *International Studies Review*, 10 (4), 722-734.

Simpson, G. (2004). *Great Powers and Outlaw States*. Cambridge: Cambridge University Press.

Spanu, M. (2020). The hierarchical society: the politics of self-determination and the constitution of new states after 1919. *European Journal of International Relations*, 26 (2), 372-396.

Steinmetz, G. (2016). Social fields, subfields and social spaces at the scale of empires: explaining the colonial state and colonial sociology. *The Sociological Review Monographs*, 64 (2), 98-123.

Steinmetz, G., ed., (2013). *Sociology and Empire: The Imperial Entanglements of a Discipline*. Durham and London: Duke University Press.

Stoler, A. L. (2006). On degrees of imperial sovereignty. *Public Culture*, 18 (1), 125-146.

Strang, D. (1996). Contested Sovereignty: The Social Construction of Colonial Imperialism. In: T. J. Biersteker and C. Weber, eds., *State Sovereignty as Social Construct*. Cambridge: Cambridge University Press, 22-49.

Suskind, R. (2004). Faith, Certainty, and the Presidency of George W. Bush. *New York Times Magazine*. October 17. Viewed 15 October 2020, <https://www.nytimes.com/2004/10/17/magazine/faith-certainty-and-the-presidency-of-george-w-bush.html>.

Sylvest, C. (2007). The Foundations of Victorian International Law. In: D. Bell, ed., *Victorian Visions of Global Order: Empire and International Relations in Nineteenth-Century Political Thought*. Cambridge: Cambridge University Press, 47-66.

Vergerio, C. (2021). International Law and the Laws of War. In de Carvalho, B., Costa Lopez, J., & Leira, H., eds. *Routledge Handbook of Historical International Relations*. Abingdon: Routledge.

Viksand, S. G. (2020). Contentious Colonies: The Positional Power of Imperial Peripheries. *Review of International Studies*. First View, doi:10.1017/S0260210520000170.

Vitalis, R. (2005). Birth of A Discipline. In: D. Long and B. Schmidt, eds., *Imperialism and Internationalism in the Discipline of International Relations*. Kindle Edition. Albany, NY: State University of New York Press.

Vitalis, R. (2015). *White World Order, Black Power Politics: The Birth of American International Relations*. Kindle Edition. Ithaca: Cornell University Press.

Wagner, K. (2017). *The Skull of Alum Beg: The Life and Death of a Rebel of 1857*. London: Hurst.

Wilson, P. (1998). The Myth of the First Great Debate. *Review of International Studies*, 24 (5), 1-15.

Yao, J., and Delatolla, A. (2021). Race and Historical International Relations. In de Carvalho, B., Costa Lopez, J., & Leira, H., eds. *Routledge Handbook of Historical International Relations*. Abingdon: Routledge.

Zarakol, A. (2017). *Hierarchies in World Politics*. Cambridge: Cambridge University Press.

34

DECOLONISATION AND THE EROSION OF THE IMPERIAL IDEA

Ted Svensson

Introduction

Decolonisation matters. It matters for our understanding of past and current international relations as well as for the lived, everyday experiences of those, in particular, who are citizens of former empires and colonies. Even though 20th-century decolonisation failed to end actual imperial practices, it did bring about an outright refutation of empire as a legitimate form of rule. Decolonisation after the Second World War, in other words, differed markedly from imperial demise and colonial secession belonging to earlier periods. Calls for a perpetual end to empire were forcefully and compellingly put forward on the basis of notions of self-determination, nationhood, and indivisible sovereignty.

The successful attainment of independence for many colonies between the 1940s and 1970s held immense implications for the arrangement of the international system, as it, firstly, induced a reconsideration of what sovereign agency and equality denoted. The crucial role played by nationalist and anti-imperial movements in effectuating wide-ranging decolonisation, secondly, exposed the limitations of attributing too much weight to the transference of imperial conceptions of 'good government' and 'popular participation', as this held no real promise of a more inclusive international order. Decolonisation after the Second World War happened despite, not foremost due to, the activities and efforts of European empires. That is, the impetus for and the particular content of decolonisation were foremost shaped by 'distinctive political trajectories' formed 'in the colonies', rather than through the extension or outgrowth of strictly 'European phenomena' (see Getachew, 2016: 839*f*). Finally, notwithstanding the revisionary impact of 20th-century decolonisation, the process of decolonising in an all-encompassing sense is yet to be fully achieved: dependencies remain, imperial aspirations persist, and there is a continuous and pressing need to attend to the important task of 'decolonising' International Relations (IR) as an academic discipline.

Temporalising decolonisation

There are numerous possible time periods to study as containing instances of decolonisation. However, what makes earlier episodes of 'resistance to imperial dominion over a given territory and people, resulting in the achievement of some alternative form of rule' distinct from the undoing of European imperialism in the 20th century is that the former did not engender a delegitimising of empire as such (Collins, 2016: 1; see also Clapton, 2017: 361). By taking this insight as its starting point, the chapter places emphasis on decolonisation as it occurred after the Second World War. It, hence, sides with accounts that accentuate the distinctiveness of decolonisation from the Second World War and onwards, as this equals a period during which empire as an admissible and justifiable form of rule, not only specific empires, was rendered hollow and largely invalidated (Collins, 2016: 3; see also Hopkins, 2017: 742). What was invalidated was the idea of empire, not empire as practice, it should be stressed (see Caraccioli, 2021).

Not everyone will agree to the chosen delimitation. For example, in his 'Global Patterns of Decolonization, 1500–1987', David Strang (1991)—as the title conveys—adopts a different periodisation. Rather than making the redundancy of the idea of empire the principal condition for delimiting how to study decolonisation, Strang identifies 'the transmission of the nation-state model from Western powers to their dependencies' as being of overriding importance, since it informed, structured, and set the limits for 'possible and appropriate action' (ibid.: 432; see also 1990: 847). According to this view, we need a temporally expansive approach to decolonisation, in order to fully come to terms with the impact that 'the emergence and diffusion of Western models of popular sovereignty' had on subsequent developments (see Strang, 1992: 368). In Strang's reading, it was '[t]he ideology of popular sovereignty' that undermined and vitiated imperial rule both at its core and edges as well as facilitated 'the reconstruction of the colony as a sovereign nation-state'; as a consequence, efforts to make imperial undertakings consistent 'with theories of popular sovereignty typically hasten[ed] decolonization' (ibid.). These points are clearly derived from and applicable to periods before 20th-century decolonisation. Yet, as this chapter elucidates, the decolonisation that took place after the Second World War exhibits qualitative novelties as regards its impact on international order and its positing of a permanent end to empire through the notions of self-determination and indivisible sovereignty.

Insisting on the uniqueness of 20th-century decolonisation is not the same, however, as disregarding the significance of prior events. In addition to the previously mentioned transference and emulation of the nation-state model, the parallel diffusion of decolonisation itself has to be acknowledged. That is, acts of successful independence from imperial sceptre propelled further, ensuing cases of decolonisation. Anti-imperial movements aspiring to turn colonies into nation states found inspiration in and legitimised their efforts by gesturing towards preceding enactments of 'national liberation' (Strang, 1990: 847f). At a certain point, this gave rise to 'a sense of the inevitability of decolonization and routinized its achievement' (ibid.: 848). Emphasising decolonisation after the Second World War is certainly congruent with portraying the growth of anti-colonial nationalism as an important enabling backdrop. Without earlier experiences of contesting and negating imperial paramountcy on the basis of calls for popular sovereignty, and the presence of vigorous anti-imperial movements that could be installed as legitimate agents of independence and postcolonial statehood, the wholesale dismantling of imperialism in the 20th century would not have been conceivable.

Akin to Strang, A. G. Hopkins holds a more comprehensive view of what decolonisation denotes while discerning 'two great waves of decolonisation': one which commenced at the end of the 18th century 'with revolutions in the New World that resulted in the creation of independent states in the Americas', whereas the second was initiated through the cessation of the Second World War and led to the establishment of a significant number of new states in Asia and Africa (2017: 729f). Hopkins, however, also intimates the possibility to go one step further when maintaining that '[m]ost of the continental European states that joined the rush into "new" imperialism at the close of the [19th] century were, in one way or another, former French colonies' and that the creation of new nation states in Europe during the 19th century might, consequently, be regarded as instances of decolonisation (ibid.: 733). He, moreover, insists that there needs to be a recognition of dominions ('the old colonies of white settlement') as undergoing decolonisation in the post-war period, and that the partial disintegration of the United States' 'own insular empire' as well as 'China's long struggle to free itself from foreign control' ought to be included in '[t]he story of post-war decolonisation'—even though China was 'never formally colonised' (ibid.: 734, 737f). Such inclusion of China brings attention to the important question of whether to speak of decolonisation only in relation to formally controlled colonies or to other territories and polities as well. Although the focus in the present chapter is on the decolonisation of formally colonised parts of the world, events in the 20th century undoubtedly have relevance beyond individual states in Asia, Africa, and elsewhere, as the momentous changes to international order attest to.

Stressing its wider import and consequence is necessary in order to rectify what remains a comparative silence on decolonisation in IR scholarship. Nicolas Guilhot accurately contends that 'the student of international relations looking for clues about decolonisation in the core canon of IR theory is bound to be disappointed' and notes that 'the end of empire was not so much analysed as "decolonisation" as it was seen as a process of worldwide diffusion of "nationalism"' (Guilhot, 2014: 701f; see also Vitalis, 2015: 120). In Guilhot's appraisal, part of the reason for this longstanding inattention to and downplaying of decolonisation lies in realism's refusal to regard 'the colonial problem' as anything else than 'a series of claims to political, legal, and economic equality which the realists easily dismissed as wishful attempts to gloss over the political, economic, and racial differences that constituted "reality"' (Guilhot, 2014: 715).[1] We, hence, need to bring into the next section the dual awareness that decolonisation should neither be reduced to the mere spread of nationalism nor to the view that 'the colonial problem' and opposition to it rested on a unifying singularity, beneath and beyond concrete anti-imperial struggles and aspirations.

The demise of empire and the inception of postcolonial nation-building

The scale of decolonisation after the Second World War is remarkable. In 1945, as Neta C. Crawford estimates, '[n]early 600 million people lived in colonies, mandates, or protectorates' and Britain alone 'had over 60 overseas colonies, mandates, or protectorates including over 450 million people' (2002: 292). Similarly, Strang has observed that '130 colonial dependencies of Western states became recognized independent states or were fully incorporated as parts of sovereign states during the twentieth century' (1990: 846). This pattern is highly significant since '[a] world-system composed of sovereign states may be quite unlike one made up of empires' (ibid.), to which we should affix *is* unlike. Even though the actual end of imperial ambitions is a wholly different matter—as exemplified by the continued control of overseas territories by former empires, by 'imperial wars' being fought in the present century, the imperial ambitions of China, and of nation states functioning as empires towards some of their constituent regions—20th-century decolonisation must be seen as fundamentally changing the composition of the international system and conceptions of what constitutes a state proper. If 19th-century empire-making consisted of conceptualising, through international law and political theory, why non-European polities did not meet the standards of complete and recognisable statehood, 20th-century decolonisation marks a mounting inability to draw up such distinctions and exclusions (see Bayly, 2021).

Two key facets of 20th-century decolonisation are the abrupt termination of empire that occurred in many former colonies and the concomitant transitioning from imperial subjugation to postcolonial statehood. In relation to the first, Martin Shipway germanely remarks that 'in the main it took only about twenty years for most of the formal structures and institutions of colonialism (though not nearly so comprehensively of their associated mentalities) to be swept away' (2008: 1), and Dipesh Chakrabarty notes that it was 'a time when both the category "empire" and actual, historical European empires truly seemed to have seen the sun set over them' (2005: 4813; see also Reus-Smit, 2011: 222*f*). In hindsight, these developments might seem given, as part of an expected teleology—i.e. as an inevitable extension of the diffusion of the nation-state model as well as of acts eroding imperial authority (see Heiskanen, 2021). However, it is notable that it occurred despite that '[e]xplicit policies of imperial retreat were the exception rather than the rule in the immediate post-war period' (Shipway, 2008: 236). Odd Arne Westad confirms this while portraying decolonisation in most cases as 'no easy walk to freedom—[since] the colonial powers often attempted to come back from the grave to reassert themselves in the immediate postwar era' (2005: 89).

Westad's own example is France, which on the day of 'its own liberation from Germany', violently suppressed 'an independence rally in the town of Setif in Algeria, killing hundreds of civilians', and he, furthermore, brings to our attention how '[b]y the time the last French soldiers withdrew from North Africa, in 1962, more than half a million people had been killed, almost all on the Algerian side' (ibid.). On the one hand, these points alert us to the openness and indeterminacy of the future of empire in the wake of the Second World War. On the other hand, it reveals an evident tension between attempts to construe decolonisation as due to 'a long-term process of globalization: [namely,] the diffusion and dissemination of European norms and practices' (see Collins, 2016: 13) and the divergent perception that it happened not because of, but in opposition to, these norms and practices.

A more promising attempt to depict decolonisation as corresponding to 'a globalising process'—i.e. one that accounts for the agency of those who primarily prompted and were affected by it—suggests that 'anti-colonial insurgences and wars' had transformative effects that were not already 'precipitated by other, more Eurocentric factors' (Thomas and Thompson, 2013: 144). This claim is based on the observation that 'the methods and practices involved had [...] lasting resonance insofar as they increasingly defined new normative standards of anti-state violence by non-state actors and groups' (ibid.). In this sense, decolonisation was 'global and globalising' rather than foremost 'national', as 'colonial conflicts were inter-related, characterised by the transmission of ideas and practices from one region to another' (ibid.: 154). Such an approach rightly puts emphasis on acts and experiences of anti-imperialism rather than on the global dissemination and emulation of European norms and practices.

We find yet another reason for not accepting a view of decolonisation as mainly the consequence a dispersed and universalised Europe in Samuel Moyn's statement that 'it was the promise of self-determination rather than any supervening concept of international rights that resounded around the world' (2012: 85). As Moyn makes clear, the 'principle that decolonization universalized [...] was that of collective liberation, not human rights' (ibid.: 86). Any account of 20th-century decolonisation is, in other words, incomplete if it fails to recognise, on the one hand, the agency of those opposing the imposition of imperial rule and, on the other hand, the deficiency of ascribing too much sway and benign intention to European ideas and standards as spread through imperial commitments.

Core traits of 20th-century decolonisation

There are two main tendencies in the extant literature on decolonisation (Shipway, 2008: 8). The first equates it 'with the End of Empire, and the end of the British Empire in particular', whereas the second depicts it—in line with what was accentuated above—as taking place 'from below', i.e. as an expression of a multitude of anti-colonial struggles (ibid.). Nonetheless, irrespective of the opted-for emphasis, viz. the entropic demise of empire or the successful opposition to empire, a key characteristic of decolonisation after the Second World War was the argument that 'colonized peoples ought to be able to "self-define" how they are governed, and [that] "nation" was the proper unit into which people should be organized' (Collins, 2016: 3; see also in this volume Spanu, 2021). Put differently, with 20th-century decolonisation, 'the abstract idea of nationhood [...] became [...] a near universal value' Collins, 2016: 3. We might expand on this by noting that, although the emergence of the territorial state as a blueprint for statehood is often associated with 19th-century state-making, it was through 20th-century decolonisation that its full relevance and potential found realisation. Or, to be more precise, 'one of the more radical developments of the twentieth century was the spread and legal acknowledgment of notions such as self-determination and sovereign equality' (Zarakol, 2018: 849). Even though these developments hardly effectuated a state of affairs where 'modern' states successfully afford either 'sovereignty *for*' or '*over*' their citizenry (ibid.: 851), they were still tied to conceptions of statehood as based on territoriality and indivisible sovereignty (de Carvalho, 2021). Decolonisation, consequently, ended not only imperial paramountcy, but also indirect rule as a mode of governing 'quasi-sovereign' polities.

If we, in light of the previous discussion, are to isolate the most crucial aspects of 20th-century decolonisation, the most evident candidates are, first, the redundancy of empire as a way to justify authority claims and to order the international and, second, the globalised acceptance of the nation as a principal and legitimate ground for political community and statehood (see Heiskanen, 2021). The two evidently emerged in a coeval and reciprocal sense, i.e. '[e]ven if "nation" was hard to define, its political potency as the antidote to "empire" was growing' during the first half of the 20th century (Collins, 2016: 3; see also Manela, 2007: 5). It is imperative that the idea and imagery of the nation state 'provided a ready receptacle into which all anti-colonial grievances and aspirations could be channelled, and just as crucially a political exit route for colonial powers themselves' (Collins, 2016: 7). As such, it became a nodal point for the confluence of rising claims to national liberation and the coeval decline of European empires. '[T]he universalization of the nation-state', thus, ought to be seen as that which 'stands as the pivot between the causes of decolonization and its consequences, legacies, and continuities' (ibid.: 9).

A third crucial feature of decolonisation after the Second World War, and of its reshaping of international order and its constituent parts, is its effects on imaginaries and realities of distributive justice. Moyn has described it as 'easily the most startling event with the widest-ranging implications in the history of distributive justice' since it led to the making of 'whole zones of entitlement and demand that had simply been off the grid and left out of account for too long' (2018: 98). Hence, 20th-century decolonisation represents genuine novelty if considered from the angle of the possibility of enunciating claims to justice and parity. It opened up novel opportunities to demand and exercise ownership and self-government and to be of equal sovereign standing. Decolonisation, in sum, denoted and harboured rupture and change proper, or phrased differently, 'by the mid-twentieth century the behavioral norm and prescriptive normative beliefs' were fundamentally altered—'colonial empire, as an accepted system of political organization' was superseded by a drive to enable colonies to become independent (Crawford, 2002: 132). While the nullifying of colonialism as a system remains one of the main affordances of 20th-century decolonisation, we should be careful to not overstate the general acceptance of the idea 'that states should not keep colonies because it is wrong to deny nations and individuals political self-determination' (see ibid.: 132, 138). As we know, extensive external influence is still imposed on certain states and much contemporary state behaviour fits the designation internal colonialism.

New international realities

More than three decades ago, Robert H. Jackson conveyed the view that we need to attend to the international level while considering the significance of 20th-century decolonisation. In his analysis of the 'transferring [of] sovereign statehood' as part of post-1945 decolonisation, he saw how it 'fashioned if not a new, then at least a substantially revised, set of international arrangements which differ dramatically from those imperial ones that previously obstructed the globalization of equal sovereignty' (1987: 520). In Jackson's assessment, decolonisation amounts to 'the sort of basic historical change which we have perhaps come to take for granted but which signals a fundamental alteration in the constitutive principles of sovereignty' (ibid.: 524). Again, we see how what is really 'an international regime change of the first importance' (see ibid.: 526) in retrospect might seem given and inexorable, even part of a neatly linear chain of events. On the contrary, the consequences of the change were cataclysmic to the extent that today 'the key if not the sole criterion of statehood is legal independence, based on the ground of self-determination, which is of course a juridical and not an empirical condition' (ibid.: 532). Elaborating on the latter, Jackson claims that the achieved independence of many past colonies was 'based primarily on an external universal right rather than an internal particular reality' (ibid.; see also Barnett, 1995: 85). A limitation of his argument is that the same critique can be levelled at any state construct—states are always objects of 'misrecognition' and attributed a provisional wholeness exactly through the failure of harmonising ideal conceptions of sovereignty with an 'internal particular reality' (see Epstein, 2018; see also Vieira, 2019: 158).

An additional way of nuancing Jackson's depiction of the internal particular reality of former colonies is to allow for decolonisation from the 1940s and onwards to not be exclusively associated with a dual desire for territorial statehood and for nationhood defined in clearly demarcated and communitarian terms. After all, it was not only the nation state that was the assumed and projected vessel of anticolonial endeavours, as 'subaltern internationalisms like pan-Arabism and pan-Africanism' decisively testify to (Moyn, 2012: 90), and which the initial overriding aspiration of 'French West African political leaders' after the Second World War to realise 'a federation of African states with each other and with France', rather than distinct and 'independent nation-states', further corroborates (Cooper, 2014: 2). Both of these examples counter the conventional assumption that the sole available trajectory was one of nation-building that, in a wanting fashion, sought to mimic European antecedents (see ibid.: 9*f*). Instead, we discern how, '[r]ather than a seamless and inevitable transition from empire to nation, anticolonial nationalists refigured decolonization as a radical rupture—one that required a wholesale transformation of the colonized and a reconstitution of the international order' (Getachew, 2019: 17).

One site where such transformation was attempted and, to some extent, achieved was within the framework of the United Nations (UN) (Barnett, 1995: 84*ff*). Between 1945 and 1965, the number of UN members rose from 51 to 117, mainly as an effect of decolonisation. Considering the swiftly growing membership, it is germane to point out that '[i]n the hierarchy of priorities of the new nations no issue exceed[ed] in importance their commitment to securing a speedy and complete end of Western colonialism' (Kay, 1967: 787). It is, hence, interesting to note that, when *The Declaration on the Granting of Independence to Colonial Countries and Peoples* was adopted in 1960, the nine abstentions came from Australia, Belgium, the Dominican Republic, France, Portugal, Spain, the Union of South Africa, the United Kingdom, and the United States (ibid.: 793; see also Reus-Smit, 2011: 234*ff*). These abstentions by most of the main agents of imperialism were indicative of 'a form of victory', as 'the draft in question [...] proclaimed "the necessity of bringing to a speedy and unconditional end colonialism in all its forms and manifestations"' (Kay, 1967: 794). The declaration, in other words, turned the elimination and rejection of imperialism into a formal expectation (Strang, 1990: 854) and it made self-determination a right of 'all people' and enshrined the need to categorically end 'the practice of colonialism' (Turner, 2013: 1195). It might, accordingly, be argued that the 'successful forging between 1960 and 1966 of an international moral consensus against the continuation of Western colonialism', primarily through the work of newly admitted members, should be seen as 'an outstanding achievement' (Kay, 1967: 808). The new members successfully put focus on the discontinuance of colonialism as an imperative issue to be addressed by the UN.

Postcolonial statehood as genuine rupture

A core question to attend to while considering the establishment of postcolonial states in the 20th century is that of whether to conceive of their transitioning from colonies to independent states as foremost representing rupture or continuity. Although previous parts of the chapter have insisted on the novelty that decolonisation stands for, an influential and divergent view on this matter has been Partha Chatterjee's suggestion that decolonisation—in the particular case of India yet by implication also elsewhere in the postcolonial world—merely resulted in instances of 'passive revolution' (see 1986: 49; cf. Chakrabarti and Cullenberg, 2003: 145*ff*). Barry Buzan and George Lawson capture the gist of the notion while describing it as the scenario 'when a revolutionary crisis yielded not radical rupture, but a form of "revolution-restoration" in which dominant classes and state elites combined to deploy crisis for their own ends' (2015: 143). Although it might be tempting to frame the long-term failure to achieve equivalence and parity between the former imperial metropoles and peripheries in terms of passive revolution, as a general point it is untenable (see Lawson, 2021 in this volume). On the one hand, it fails to properly affirm the 'world-making' aspirations of anticolonial nationalism (see Getachew, 2019) and, on the other hand, even in the specific case of India, it does not capture what the constituent moment most crucially represented, i.e. a radical departure and detachment from the previous imperial order—one marked not only by authoritarianism and a denial of citizenship rights but which also exercised authority by varyingly employing direct and indirect rule.

A related and equally problematic view is 'the Whiggish story' regarding the transferring, as part of imperial commitments, of liberal and democratic institutions that eventually facilitated and spawned 'the creation of a Commonwealth of free and equal nations' (see Hall, 2011: 56). However, while it is evident that 'the sovereign state form' has been adopted globally, it is a development that should be attributed to 'decolonization rather than imperialism' (Hobson and Sharman, 2005: 65). It might even be argued that imperialism, instead of facilitating a widespread distribution of sovereignty, chiefly allowed for 'non-sovereign political formations' to viably exist 'well into the 20th century' (ibid.: 72). The setting up of democratic institutions and the realisation of the territorial state were achievements by anti-imperial elites—not gifts by liberal-minded imperialists. It is important to keep in mind that 'the collective imperial polities [of the long 19th century] cannot be merely referred to as states that conformed to the practice of Westphalian sovereignty, notwithstanding the sovereign status of the metropole' (ibid.: 74). What this refers to is how the European empires of the long 19th-century, by being grounded in an acceptance of sovereignty as divisible, consisted of an amalgam of polities that were attributed more or less external sovereignty, more or less international status and agency (Keene, 2002: 93; Benton, 2010). Nevertheless, the change that decolonisation actuated should not be exaggerated. It is clear that decolonisation did not universalise 'pure Westphalian sovereignty'; rather, the international is still made up of 'the coexistence of multiple hierarchical arrangements alongside anarchy' (Hobson and Sharman, 2005: 80).

Another reason for depicting 20th-century decolonisation in terms of rupture is found in how the Second World War became a testament to the many horrors that Western states had committed towards each other—which, in turn, came to undermine existing narratives about the righteousness of 'rule by "superior" over "inferior" on grounds of the "standard of civilisation"' (Buzan, 2014: 584). It was the war and how it laid bare the hollowness of such a projected standard that, to a large degree, catalysed decolonisation on a grander scale, by allowing for references to be made to 'a transcendental right of self-determination', while disqualifying 'all arguments about unreadiness for self-government in the modern world' (ibid.).[2] Again, to argue that decolonisation made certain imageries and modes of structuring the international outmoded is not the same as completely disregarding the continuation of actual practices. As Buzan perceptibly remarks, even though '[d]ecolonisation [...] put an end to the "standard of civilisation" as a term of polite public discourse', there are 'various contemporary practices of conditionality and discrimination that constitute the new "standard of civilisation" in modern form', including human rights, democracy, and development (ibid.: 585*f*; see also Keene, 2002: 139). In other words, the exclusionary practices and hierarchies of the colonial era, which were grounded in a professed ability to distinguish between a civilized inside and its outside, are nowadays re-enacted and perpetuated within a distended and inclusive international society (see Buzan, 2014: 592). Nevertheless, even though exclusions and demotions endured, they did so within an order based on 'formal sovereign equality' instead of 'formal structures of inequality' (Buzan and Lawson, 2015: 204).

While many have been inclined to equate this new order with a 'Western-global' international society—produced through the transmutation of 'Western international society' into an actuality with 'planetary' reach and by the world being populated by 'states that [are] homogeneous, if only in the sense of being sovereign equals' (see ibid.: 176*f*)—there are good reasons for complicating this picture, beyond agreeing to descriptions of Western norms and institutions as having totalising qualities. First, in the wake of 20th-century decolonisation, 'foreign intervention was largely understood as infringement on sovereignty and exception from the right of non-intervention [requires] careful moral and legal justification to be regarded as legitimate by members of the international community' (Bartelson, 2018: 188). *All* members, that is. The broad expectation after 1945, even in cases of initial territorial partition, has been that 'empires should be broken up, but the successor nation-states should be preserved intact, irrespective of the national complexity they might contain' (Österud, 1997: 179). There are now, to creatively employ and subvert Jackson's terminology (see previously), a multiplicity of 'internal particular realities' that are recognised as worthy of preservation and perpetuation.

Second, it should also be stressed that decolonisation does not embody 'the universalization of a pre-existing pluralist ethic but rather its initial application' (Clapton, 2017: 358). It would be misleading to deploy imageries of a universal expansion of an existing order when the reality is that prior to 20th-century decolonisation what we find is 'a single, anti-pluralist and hierarchical society' composed of European and non-Europeans polities alike (ibid.: 359), i.e. a world of 'structural interconnections' that requires us to see how 'the development of [...] international order' had European as well as colonial origins (Seth, 2011: 168, 172*f*).

Decolonisation as an unfinished project

Michael Collins raises an important point, which summarises the overall position adopted in the present chapter, when writing that '[f]lag independence in Asia and Africa was not the end of decolonization as a practical or intellectual problem[;] [i]t was, however, the manifestation of a profound reshaping of the international system and its normative architecture after 1945' (2016: 3). At the same time as it allowed for fundamental changes to take place, much work remains before we are able to speak of decolonisation proper. The deliberate focus in this chapter has been on the period in which many former colonies formally transitioned into becoming independent postcolonial states, but the lasting consequences of both this very process and the colonialism and imperialism that preceded it deserve IR's sustained and full attention (in the vein of, for example, Bhambra, 2014; Gruffydd Jones, 2006; Shilliam, 2010). A lot more also needs to be done in order to bring about a truly global IR when it comes to grasping the varied meanings of self-determination, sovereignty, territory, etc. that went into anti-imperial political theory and praxis (Çapan et al., 2021). These things should be done not only to allow empirical richness and nuance and to make it less viable to always and immanently detect Europe and its traces in our objects of study but also in order to lay bare the systematic omissions of IR—such as race, caste, and the provincial qualities of Europe itself.

The chapter has clearly not carried out any of these urgent tasks. What it has aspired to do, however, is to firmly depart from reaffirming the idea of a past Europe as the origin and foundation on which the current international order is built and modelled. It is, finally, still much needed to ask for 'real *positive decolonization*' echoing Adebayo Adedeji, i.e. a form of decolonisation that is more than the mere granting of 'freedom from being owned by others', and which will only be achieved once former colonised populations 'are effective participants in the world economy and have commensurate share in global power' (Adedeji cited in Crawford, 2002: 137). Such a positive decolonisation is, as we know, yet to come.

Suggestions for further reading

Hager Jr., R. P. and Lake, D. A. (2000). Balancing empires: competitive decolonization in international politics. *Security Studies*, 9 (3), 108-148.

Hansen, P. and Jonsson, S. (2015). *Eurafrica: The Untold History of European Integration and Colonialism*. London: Bloomsbury Publishing.

Jansen, J. C. and Osterhammel, J. (2017). *Decolonization: A Short History*. Princeton, NJ: Princeton University Press.

Pham, Q. N. and Shilliam, R., eds. (2016). *Meanings of Bandung: Postcolonial Orders and Decolonial Visions*. London: Rowman & Littlefield International.

Spruyt, H. (2005). *Ending Empire: Contested Sovereignty and Territorial Partition*. Ithaca, NY: Cornell University Press.

Svensson, T. (2013). *Production of Postcolonial India and Pakistan: Meanings of Partition*. London: Routledge.

Notes

1 Guilhot insists that '[d]ecolonisation, with its ideologies of progress, its eschatological resonances, its revolutionary rhetoric, its universalistic claims, its moral language, and above all with its explicit goal of erasing differences between post-colonial countries and their former imperial masters, was at odds with realism' (2014: 700; see also Hall, 2011: 48*f*).

2 Additional factors related to the war impacted on decolonisation. Beyond making the 'barbarism' of the imperial metropoles obvious, it opened up the possibility of non-cooperation and it forced the British to unwillingly accept tenets of 'wartime Wilsonianism' that afforded 'subordinate states additional weapons to wield against their imperial masters' (Yellen, 2019: 1291, 1310). Recruitment of soldiers as a part of imperial war efforts also helped undermine and alter existing categorisations and differentiations (Barkawi, 2017). With specific reference to Indians serving in the British army, Tarak Barkawi concludes that '[i]n unsettling the Raj's reifications, war served as a great denaturalizing force for Indians and British alike' (see ibid.: 8*f*).

References

Barkawi, T. (2017). *Soldiers of Empire: Indian and British Armies in World War II*. Cambridge: Cambridge University Press.

Barnett, M. (1995). The new United Nations politics of peace: from juridical sovereignty to empirical sovereignty. *Global Governance*, 1 (1), 77-97.

Bartelson, J. (2018). *War in International Thought*. Cambridge: Cambridge University Press.

Bayly, M. (2021). Imperialism: Beyond the 'Re-turn to Empire' in International Relations. In de Carvalho, B., Costa Lopez, J., & Leira, H., eds. *Routledge Handbook of Historical International Relations*. Abingdon: Routledge.

Benton, L. (2010). *A Search for Sovereignty: Law and Geography in European Empires, 1400–1900*. Cambridge: Cambridge University Press.

Bhambra, G. K. (2014). *Connected Sociologies*. London: Bloomsbury.

Buzan, B. (2014). The 'standard of civilisation' as an English School concept. *Millennium: Journal of International Studies*, 42 (3), 576-594.

Buzan, B. and Lawson, G. (2015). *The Global Transformation: History, Modernity and the Making of International Relations*. Cambridge: Cambridge University Press.

Çapan, Z. G., dos Reis, F. and Grasten, M., (2021). Global Histories: Connections and Circulations in Historical International Relations. In de Carvalho, B., Costa Lopez, J., & Leira, H., eds. *Routledge Handbook of Historical International Relations*. Abingdon: Routledge.

Caraccioli, M. J. (2021). Early (Modern) Empires: The Political Ideology of Conceptual Domination. In de Carvalho, B., Costa Lopez, J., & Leira, H., eds. *Routledge Handbook of Historical International Relations*. Abingdon: Routledge.

Chakrabarti, A. and Cullenberg, S. (2003). *Transition and Development in India*. New York, NY: Routledge.

Chakrabarty, D. (2005). Legacies of Bandung: decolonisation and the politics of culture. *Economic and Political Weekly*, 40 (46), 4812-4818.

Chatterjee, P. (1986). *Nationalist Thought and the Colonial World: A Derivative Discourse*. Minneapolis, MN: University of Minnesota Press.

Clapton, W. (2017). Pluralism, decolonization and international society. *The Cambridge Review of International Affairs*, 30 (4), 350-367.

Collins, M. (2016). Decolonization. In: Mackenzie, J. M., ed., *The Encyclopedia of Empire*, Hoboken, NJ: John Wiley & Sons.

Cooper, F. (2014). *Citizenship between Empire and Nation: Remaking France and French Africa, 1945–1960*. Princeton, NJ: Princeton University Press.

Crawford, N. C. (2002). *Argument and Change in World Politics: Ethics, Decolonization, and Humanitarian Intervention*. Cambridge: Cambridge University Press.

de Carvalho, B. (2021). Sovereignty in Historical International Relations: Trajectories, Challenges and Implications. In de Carvalho, B., Costa Lopez, J., & Leira, H., eds. *Routledge Handbook of Historical International Relations*. Abingdon: Routledge.

Epstein, C. (2018). The productive force of the negative and the desire for recognition: lessons from Hegel and Lacan. *Review of International Studies*, 44 (5), 805-828.

Getachew, A. (2016). Universalism after the post-colonial turn: interpreting the Haitian Revolution. *Political Theory*, 44 (6), 821-845.

Getachew, A. (2019). *Worldmaking after Empire: The Rise and Fall of Self-Determination*. Princeton, NJ: Princeton University Press.

Gruffydd Jones, B., ed. (2006). *Decolonizing International Relations*. Lanham, MD: Rowman & Littlefield.

Guilhot, N. (2014). Imperial realism: post-war IR theory and decolonisation. *The International History Review*, 36 (4), 698-720.

Hall, I. (2011). The revolt against the West: decolonisation and its repercussions in British international thought, 1945–75. *The International History Review*, 33 (1), 43-64.

Heiskanen, J. (2021). Nations and Nationalism in International Relations. In de Carvalho, B., Costa Lopez, J., & Leira, H., eds. *Routledge Handbook of Historical International Relations*. Abingdon: Routledge.

Hobson, J. M. and Sharman, J. C. (2005). The enduring place of hierarchy in world politics: tracing the social logics of hierarchy and political change. *European Journal of International Relations*, 11 (1), 63-98.

Hopkins, A. G. (2017). Globalisation and decolonisation. *The Journal of Imperial and Commonwealth History*, 45 (5), 729-745.

Jackson, R. H. (1987). Quasi-states, dual regimes, and neoclassical theory: international jurisprudence and the Third World. *International Organization*, 41 (4), 519-549.

Kay, D. A. (1967). The politics of decolonization: the new nations and the United Nations political process. *International Organization*, 21 (4), 786-811.

Keene, E. (2002). *Beyond the Anarchical Society: Grotius, Colonialism and Order in World Politics*. Cambridge: Cambridge University Press.

Lawson, G. (2021). Revolutions: Integrating the International. In de Carvalho, B., Costa Lopez, J., & Leira, H., eds. *Routledge Handbook of Historical International Relations*. Abingdon: Routledge.

Manela, E. (2007). *The Wilsonian Moment: Self-Determination and the International Origins of Anticolonial Nationalism*. Oxford: Oxford University Press.

Moyn, S. (2012). *The Last Utopia: Human Rights in History*. Cambridge, MA: Harvard University Press.

Moyn, S. (2018). *Not Enough: Human Rights in an Unequal World*. Cambridge, MA: Harvard University Press.

Østerud, Ö. (1997). The narrow gate: entry to the club of sovereign states. *Review of International Studies*, 23 (2), 167-184.

Reus-Smit, C. (2011). Struggles for individual rights and the expansion of the international system. *International Organization*, 65 (2), 207-242.

Seth, S. (2011). Postcolonial theory and the critique of International Relations. *Millennium: Journal of International Studies*, 40 (1), 167-183.

Shilliam, R., ed. (2010). *International Relations and Non-Western Thought*. London: Routledge.

Shipway, M. (2008). *Decolonization and its Impact: A Comparative Approach to the End of the Colonial Empires*. Oxford: Blackwell Publishing.

Spanu, M. (2021). States, People and Self-determination in Historical Perspective. In de Carvalho, B., Costa Lopez, J., & Leira, H., eds. *Routledge Handbook of Historical International Relations*. Abingdon: Routledge.

Strang, D. (1990). From dependency to sovereignty: an event history analysis of decolonization 1870–1987. *American Sociological Review*, 55 (6), 846-860.

Strang, D. (1991). Global patterns of decolonization, 1500–1987. *International Studies Quarterly*, 35 (4), 429-454.

Strang, D. (1992). The inner incompatibility of empire and nation: popular sovereignty and decolonization. *Sociological Perspectives*, 35 (2), 367-384.

Thomas, M. and Thompson, A. (2013). Empire and globalisation: from 'high imperialism' to decolonisation. *The International History Review*, 36 (1), 142-170.

Turner, O. (2013). 'Finishing the job': the UN Special Committee on Decolonization and the politics of self-governance. *Third World Quarterly*, 34 (7), 1193-1208.

Vieira, M. (2019). The decolonial subject and the problem of non-Western authenticity. *Postcolonial Studies*, 22 (2), 150-167.

Vitalis, R. (2015). *White World Order, Black Power Politics: The Birth of American International Relations*. Ithaca, NY: Cornell University Press.

Westad, O. A. (2005). *The Global Cold War: Third World Interventions and the Making of Our Times*. Cambridge: Cambridge University Press.

Yellen, J. A. (2019). Wartime Wilsonianism and the crisis of empire, 1941–43. *Modern Asian Studies*, 53 (4), 1278-1311.

Zarakol, A. (2018). Sovereign equality as misrecognition. *Review of International Studies*, 44 (5), 848-862.

35

UNDERSTANDING THE POSTCOLONIAL COLD WAR

Heonik Kwon

The second half of the twentieth century is sometimes depicted as an exceptionally peaceful era in modern history, in contrast to the century's first half, which witnessed two wars of great magnitude. In this pacific view of the Cold War, which is not uncommon in the scholarship of modern European and transatlantic history, the Cold War was an unconventional conflict: it was fought mainly according to political, economic, ideological and polemical means; the powerful nations that waged this war kept building arsenals of weapons of mass destruction in the hope that they would never have to use them, and the threats of mutually assured destruction came to assure one of the longest times of international peace among industrialised nations. These strange features of the Cold War as being neither real war nor genuine peace, which Mary Kaldor succinctly explains with the idiom of an 'imaginary war', makes it difficult to come to terms with its history according to the conventional antinomy of war and peace (Kaldor, 1990). George Orwell sums up this oddity of the Cold War in his *Nineteen Eight-Four* with the emphatic statement, 'War is Peace' (on war and Historical International Relations [IR], see Bartelson, 2021 in this volume).

Turning our attention to the historical horizons outside Europe and the transatlantic, however, the pacific view of Cold War history runs into obstacles. The term 'Cold War' refers to the prevailing condition of the world in the second half of the twentieth century, divided into two separate paths of political modernity and economic development. In a narrower sense, it means the contest of power and will between the two dominant states, the United States and the Soviet Union, which, according to Orwell, set out to rule the world between them under an undeclared state of war, being unable to conquer one another (cited from Westad, 2005: 2). In a broader definition, however, the Cold War also entails the unequal relations of power among the political communities that pursued or were driven to pursue a specific path of progress within the binary structure of the global order. The 'contest-of-power' dimension of the Cold War has been an explicit and central element in Cold War historiography; in contrast, the 'relation-of-domination' aspect has been a relatively marginal and implicit element. Highlighting these two contrary aspects of the global conflict, Walter LaFeber states that the questions of *which* Cold War and *whose* Cold War are central to any effort to understand Cold War history in a global perspective (LaFeber, 1992: 13). In a similar light, Geir Lundestad and Odd Arne Westad emphasise the importance of political and revolutionary struggles for decolonisation in the making of the Cold War global order (Lundestad, 1991; Westad, 2005). Their view is that the experience of the Third World is pivotal to Cold War global politics and, therefore, the history of decolonisation is integral to the history of the bipolarisation of world politics.

It is important to note that the Cold War took violent forms especially in the regions that underwent the advent of political bipolarity as part of the political process of decolonisation. In this light, this chapter deals with three interrelated issues concerning the interface between Cold War history and the history of decolonisation. First, it asks why the Cold War becomes a legitimate subject of the history of violence once we broaden our interest to include postcolonial historical milieus. Second, it considers the related issue that the violence of the Cold War can be conceptualised broadly in terms of two forms: on the one hand, an imaginary violence – most notably, the threat and fear of thermonuclear destruction – and, on the other, a non-imaginary, real violence that tore apart the physical and moral integrity of numerous human communities. It explores the duplex character of the Cold War's violence, adopting what may be called a historical anthropological approach that is attentive to questions of plurality and unity in human historical experience. The destruction of the Cold War first became apparent in Northeast and Southeast Asia. Drawing briefly upon the violent postcolonial Cold War experience in Korea and Vietnam, finally, the chapter will explore how the duplex character of Cold War violence, imaginary and non-imaginary, can be discussed as an issue of the Cold War in Asia.

Two faces of the Cold War

In December 1955, the US Gallup Poll conducted a survey on the meaning of the Cold War. Their question to Americans was: 'Will you tell me what the term 'COLD WAR' means to you?' The responses to this survey question were diverse and revealing. The pollsters classified the following as correct answers: 'war through talking, not down and out fighting; not a hot war; a subtle war, without arms – a diplomatic war, state of enmity between countries but will not become a total, all-out war; war without actual fighting; political war, battle of words among powers to gain prestige among their nations; like a bloodless war'. The correct answers included: 'doing what you want to do and disregarding the other country's opinion; war of nerves; peaceful enemies; propaganda to agitate the reds against democracy; nations can't agree among themselves – bickering back and forth; uncertainty between foreign countries and this country; battle of wits'. The Gallop pollsters classified other responses as incorrect: 'cold war just like a hot war – as in Korea just as many boys being killed – that was supposed to be a cold war; fighting slow – no one knows what they are doing; war where no war is declared; fighting for nothing; real war all over the world; where everybody was at war; like a civil war'.

The distance between 'a bloodless diplomatic war' and 'real war all over the world like a [global] civil war' is huge, and we can infer from the above episode that these radically different understandings of the Cold War coexisted at the initial stage of the global confrontation. It is interesting to discover that these contrary conceptions of the Cold War were expressed in the context of the post–Korean War American society. The Korean War, for Americans, was part of their nation's police action in the world at the time of the Cold War. About 30,000 American lives were lost in this conflict, not to mention 2 million Korean lives. Their nation fought in both European and Asian spaces during World War II (WWII). It continued to be involved militarily in Asia after WWII, whereas in Europe, the country's post-war involvement took different means that were primarily political, diplomatic and economic. These bifurcating understandings of the early Cold War, between America's relation to post-war Europe, on the one hand, and its actions in the post-war Asia-Pacific on the other, is squarely present in the result of the 1955 polls. What is interesting about the episode is also the fact that one stream of interpretation was assigned to a categorical mistake. The pollsters classified the Cold War as a bloodless or political war as correct answers, relegating the opposite view of the Cold War world as a world civil war to an uninformed, mistaken understanding of the concept of Cold War.

These two radically different images of the Cold War, and related unresolved issues relating to the place of violence in Cold War history, persist even now, many years after the end of the Cold War. In the south-eastern region of the Korean peninsula, for instance, there is a village once known in the environs as a *moskoba* (Moscow) – the wartime reference for a communist stronghold. Each year, people originally from this village return to their homeland in order to join the ceremony held on behalf of their family and village ancestors, mainly to visit their graves scattered on the hills around the village. On these occasions, the relatives from distant places are pleased to meet each other and exchange news – but not always so. When a man cautiously suggested to his lineage elders recently that the family might consider repairing a neglected ancestral tomb, the harmony of the family meal held after the tomb visit was disrupted. One elder left the room in a fury, and others remained silent throughout the ceremonial meal. The man who proposed the idea was the adopted son of the person buried in the neglected tomb, having been selected for this role by the family elders for a ritual purpose. The elder whom he offended happened to be a close relative of the deceased. The ancestor had been a prominent anti-colonial communist youth activist before he died at a young age in a colonial prison without a descendent. The elder's siblings were among the several dozen village youths who left the village together with the retreating communist army during the chaos of the Korean War (1950–1953). Such phenomena were widespread in the early months of the war when local communities were exposed to the pre-emptive and retributive violence against the so-called collaborators committed liberally by both sides of the war as the frontier of war moved. The elder believes that this catastrophe in village history and family continuity could have been avoided if the ancestor buried in the neglected tomb had not brought the seeds of 'red ideology' to the village in the first place. Beautifying the ancestral tomb was unacceptable to this elder, who believed that some of his close kinsmen had lost, because of the ancestor, the social basis on which they could be properly remembered as family ancestors (Kwon, 2020: 65–68).

The morality of ancestral remembrance is as strong in the Vietnamese cultural tradition as it is in the Korean. These two countries also share the common historical experience of being important sites and symbols in Asia for the American leadership in the global struggle against international communism. In recent years, since the Vietnamese political leadership initiated a general economic reform and regulated political liberalisation in the country in the late 1980s, there has been a strong revival of ancestral rituals across Vietnamese villages. Such rituals were previously discouraged by the state hierarchy who regarded them as being incompatible with the modern secular, revolutionary society. In the communities of the southern and central regions (what was South Vietnam during the Vietnam War), a notable aspect of this social development has been the introduction to the ancestral ritual realm of the identities previously excluded from public memory. The memorabilia of the hitherto socially stigmatised historical identities, such as those of former South Vietnamese soldiers, have become increasingly visible in the domestic and communal ritual space (Kwon, 2006: 161–164).

In a village south of Danang, a commercial and administrative centre of Vietnam's central region, a family has a compelling history in this regard. The family's grandfather was a former labourer soldier of the French colonial army. In 1937–1938, the French colonial authority in Indochina conscripted a large number of labourers from the central region of Vietnam and shipped them to the great Mediterranean city of Marseilles. There, in the city's *poudrerie*, 2000 Vietnamese conscripts manufactured gunpowder for the French army and, under the Vichy regime, for the German army under French management. Some of these Vietnamese labourer soldiers objected to their situation and joined the French resistance, whereas others continued to endure the appalling working conditions in the factory. After sharing the humiliating experience of German occupation with the French citizens, these foreign conscripts found themselves in a highly precarious situation following their return home in 1948: the leaders in the Vietnamese revolutionary movement distrusted them, indeed looked upon them as collaborators with the colonial regime; and the French took no interest in their past service to their national economy or their contribution to the resistance movement against the German occupiers. Many of these returnees perished in the ensuing chaos of war – the First Indochina War (or what the Vietnamese call the War Against France) – and many of their children joined the revolutionary resistance movement in the following era during the Second Indochina War (which the Vietnamese call the War Against America).

The family's grandfather is one of the few returnees who survived the carnage and has an extraordinary story of survival to tell: how he rescued his family in 1953 from the imminent threat of summary execution by pleading to French soldiers in their language. He accomplished this again in 1967 thanks to the presence of an American officer in a pacification team who understood a few words of French as a result of having fought in Europe during WWII. The man's youngest brother died unmarried and without a descendent, so the man's eldest son now performs periodic death-remembrance rites on behalf of the fallen. His brother was killed in action during the Vietnam War as a soldier of the South Vietnamese army, and his eldest son is a decorated former partisan fighter belonging to the National Liberation Front.

The precarious condition of life that confronted this family and many other people in this region for many years is often referred to as *xoi dau* by the locals. Xoi dau refers to a ceremonial Vietnamese delicacy made of white rice flour and black beans. Used also as a metaphor, the term conveys how people of these regions experienced the Vietnam War. As a metaphor, xoi dau refers to the turbulent conditions of communal life during the war, when the rural inhabitants were confronted with successive occupations by conflicting political and military forces. At night, the village was under the control of the revolutionary forces; during the daytime, the opposing forces took control. Life in these villages oscillated between two different political worlds governed by two mutually hostile military forces. The people had to cope with their separate, yet equally absolute, demands for loyalty and with the world changing politically so frequently that sometimes this anomaly almost appeared normal. Xoi dau conveys the simple truth that, when you eat this food, you must swallow both the white and black parts. This is how xoi dau is supposed to be eaten, and this is what it was like living a tumultuous life seized by the brutally dynamic reality of Vietnam's civil and international war.

The meaning of xoi dau, of course, is not the same as the meaning of the Cold War as we usually understand it; yet, the extreme conditions of human life that this Vietnamese idiom refers to are very much part of Cold War history as the latter was experienced by people in central Vietnam and many other communities in the decolonising world (on decolonisation, see Svensson, 2021 in this volume). Moreover, the experience of xoi dau is hardly a thing of the past and is very much part of contemporary history, involving vigorous communal efforts to come to terms with the ruins of the past destruction existing in communal life. The same is true with the village in South Korea mentioned earlier.

Decolonisation and the Cold War

The violence of the Cold War, such as that which inflicted enduring wounds and crises on these families, was typically intertwined with the process of decolonisation. In this sense, we may start thinking about the Cold War's globally encompassing, yet regionally and locally variant histories, in terms of two broad realities: the imaginary war in Europe and North America on the one hand and, on the other, the postcolonial experience of bipolar politics in which the very concept of the Cold War becomes problematic and contradictory (on global histories, see Çapan et al., 2021 in this volume). Yale historian John Lewis Gaddis calls the second half of the twentieth century a 'long peace', an exceptional period of international peace in contrast to what came before, the first half of the century characterised by two gigantic wars among nations and empires (Gaddis, 1987). A late historian of modern Europe, Tony Judt, objected to Gaddis' characterisation of the Cold War as a long peace, however. He writes, 'This way of narrating cold war history reflects the same provincialism. John Lewis Gaddis has written a history of America's cold war. As a result, this is a book whose silences are especially suggestive. The 'third world' in particular comes up short' (Judt, 2008: 371).

Indeed, as LaFeber notes, the era of the Cold War was far from a peaceful time when seen in a broad perspective; it witnessed over 40 million human casualties across territories (LaFeber, 1992: 13). The experience of bipolar politics certainly varied in intensity and in temporality across regions. The most violent manifestation of the global Cold War took its earliest tolls in Southeast and Northeast Asia, represented by the outbreak of the First Indochina War (1945–1954) and the Korean War. In the following decades, while a new total war was being waged in Vietnam and its neighbouring counties, the Cold War's political violence became much more transnational and generalised, engulfing many nations and communities in Africa, the Middle East and Latin America during what the historian of the Middle East, Fred Halliday, calls the Second Cold War (Halliday, 1983). It is against this historical background that the celebrated Colombian writer Gabriel Garcia Marquez once said that nations in Central and South America did not have a moment's rest from the threat and reality of mass violence during the so-called cold war (cited from Grandin, 2004: 170). The reality of mass violence endured in Latin America may have been different in intensity and in character from that suffered by the Koreans in the 1950s and by the Vietnamese in the 1960s, which incorporated a totalising war as well as systematic state political violence. Moreover, not all postcolonial states and communities experienced the Cold War in terms of armed conflicts or in other exceptional forms of political violence. South Asia is a notable example. Despite these exceptions, however, it is reasonable to conclude that, for a great majority of decolonising nations, the Cold War was hardly a period of long peace.

The claim that the Cold War was a global conflict should not mean, therefore, that the conflict was experienced in the same terms all over the world. Cold War politics permeated developed and underdeveloped societies, Western and non-Western states and colonial powers and colonised nations alike; in this sense, it was a truly global reality. However, the historical experience and the collective memory of the Cold War contain aspects of radical divergence between the West and the postcolonial world (Westad, 2005: 73–109; Kwon, 2010). The recognition that a Cold War with mass human casualties and a Cold War without them are different entities, however, should not be taken to mean that these two histories are not comparable or commensurable. Dissecting the whole of the global Cold War into different constituent parts is for the purpose of creating a new image of the whole rather than dismantling the image of the whole. Even within the history of mass death, there are elements of diversity. The US experience of the Cold War does not collapse to the paradigm of the imaginary war or the long peace as easily as does the dominant European experience. The United States has a memory of mass sacrifice of American lives from the era of the Cold War, not least in relation to the Korean and Vietnam conflicts. This collective memory of mass sacrifice, however, is not the same as the memory of mass death kept in Vietnam or in Korea. Consisting principally of the heroic death of armed soldiers, the American memory distinguishes the United States from the rest of the West, whose dominant memory of the Cold War encompasses a painful but largely deathless confrontation between political groupings, but it is also distinct from the collective memories of death in the wider world during the Cold War, chiefly the tragic mass death of ordinary civilians. In the sphere of the history of violence and related realm of death commemoration, therefore, we cannot easily say that Europe and America constitute a single community of shared collective memory called the West. But nor can we easily reconcile America's memory of heroic death and sacrifice in the struggle against communism with the memories of mass tragic death associated with the same struggle in the rest of the world.

Although the recent development in Cold War studies has made a notable contribution to diversifying Cold War narratives, an equally important question remains critically unexplored. The plurality of the Cold War experience is not merely an issue of comparative history between Asia and Europe; instead, it may be discussed as part of a specific regional history.

Witnessed in the relatively narrow sphere of East Asia, the early Cold War was manifested differently among the societies that constitute this regional entity. For instance, Japan experienced the early Cold War in a manner that is closely akin to how nations in Western Europe underwent the era: with the imperative post-WWII socio-economic reconstruction, a growing economic prosperity and an unprecedented era of international peace. In the late 1960s, Japanese society underwent forceful social protests and generational upheaval, which Immanuel Wallerstein dubbed a 'revolution in the world-system' (Wallerstein and Zukin, 1989: 441–449). Provoked by the tragedy of the Vietnam War and the West's role and complicity in it, the multi-sited, simultaneous civil protest in 1967–1969 transformed the social fabric of Japan as well as that of the United States and several Western European nations. However, the so-called world revolution hardly had any ramifications elsewhere in Asia or Japan's neighbouring societies.

We can apply the same idea of Cold War historical plurality to other political societies in Asia. The fate of Korea in the 1950s, which involved a destructive civil war, is not that remote from the experience of political societies in the Middle East and Africa in the 1970s and the 1980s, during which many of these societies were swept into a civil war or a similar crisis. The behaviour of some of the East Asian states (such as China and North Korea) in the 1970s comes close to that of some of the Western states during the general crisis of the early Cold War in the 1950s: maintaining the peace of an imaginary war at home while playing a role in the escalation of a total war crisis elsewhere in the postcolonial world. It is a known historical fact (although one that is not yet satisfactorily researched) that North Korea and China were deeply implicated in the crisis of the Second Cold War across the African continent, from Sudan and Uganda to Angola and Zimbabwe. By then, these state entities were both in and out of the Cold War, having assimilated an ideology of non-alignment in thought, yet, in practice, engaging vigorously in the international postcolonial sphere with a self-conscious and sometimes self-centred revolutionary zeal. Meanwhile, South Korea, together with Taiwan and some other political entities in Southeast Asia, joined, with considerable success, what some Cold War historians call 'the right kind of revolution' – economic development as a Cold War power struggle – while maintaining within its domestic political sphere a military-led authoritarian political order and radical politics of containment with regard to civil society, which is fairly akin to how societies in Latin America underwent the Cold War era (Latham, 2010: 10–35; see also Schulz, 2021 in this volume).

Conclusion

If we approach the plurality of Cold War experiences in this way, we may say that Cold War history has a fractal formation. A fractal theory of social structure and political system is very much a part of the development of modern social anthropology. It posits that the whole and each of the parts that together constitute the whole have an identical structural form – as in the study of the segmentary kinship and political system of traditional Africa (Fortes and Evans-Pritchard, 1940).

Concerning the subject matter at hand, this idea conveys that a new way of conceptualising Asia's place in modern global history may be possible. Asia's Cold War experience is in many ways distinct and even contrary to how Europe underwent the era of political bipolarity. The Cold War in Asia was far from an imaginary war, and we are not sure whether it is over and done with today. Parallel to these differences in form and in temporality, however, Asia's Cold War has elements within it, an attention to which can render the region's experience of bipolar modernity in a similar image of the global Cold War. Considered this way, Asia's Cold War was other than an imaginary war and, at once and in part, very much an imaginary war. We can see in it not only the long peace of Europe but also the turbulent fates of Africa, the Middle East and Latin America. In the end, it appears that Asia's Cold War is not an Asian history but rather a global history in the guise of an Asian history.

If the Cold War was both an imaginary war and at the same time a generalised experience of political terror and mass death, we need to tell its history accordingly, inclusive of the seismic death events experienced by communities, rather than considering the latter only perfunctory marginal episodes in an otherwise peaceful, balanced contest for power. In regard to the Cold War's duplicity in terms of the presence and absence of mass violence, Mary Kaldor argues that the Cold War 'kept alive the idea of war, while avoiding its reality. [No conventional warfare] broke out on European soil. At the same time, many wars took place all over the world, including Europe, in which more people died than in the Second World War. But because these wars did not fit our conception of war, they were discounted' (Kaldor, 2001: 29–30). Kaldor believes that these 'irregular, informal wars of the second half of the twentieth century' took place 'as a peripheral part of the central conflict', and she argues that these 'informal wars' are becoming the source of new post–Cold War bellicosity. If we follow Kaldor, it appears that Cold War history has a concentric conceptual organisation consisting of a 'formal' history of relative peace in the centre and 'informal' violence on the periphery. The Cold War was both an idea of war in the exemplary centre and a reality of revolutionary war and chaotic violence in the peripheral terrains. At the centre, the end of the Cold War was a largely peaceful event and opened a constructive development of transnational integration, whereas in the periphery, the same 'end' gave birth to a new age of aggression. In this view of the Cold War and what comes after it, the Cold War was not only an ambiguous phenomenon, being neither real war nor genuine peace, but also a highly contradictory phenomenon, experienced as an idea of war for some and as a reality of prolific organised violence for others.

The above comment from an eminent observer of modern Europe demonstrates that our understanding of the Cold War is still grounded in a concentric spatial hierarchy. This chapter proposes that confronting the centre/periphery hierarchy in the conception of the Cold War is critical to a grounded understanding of the political history of the bipolar era. The effort involves an attention to the violence of the Cold War and its variant forms, real or imaginary. It also involves the recognition that the violence of the Cold War was experienced varyingly within a region as well as between different regional entities. Communities in Asia did not experience the Cold War in an identical way, just as bipolar politics was manifested differently between post-WWII Europe and postcolonial Asia. Orwell's 'War is Peace' continues to be meaningful for understanding the nature of the Cold War, yet for reasons that depart from what he had in mind when he coined the expression. How to reconcile the radically different historical experiences and related divergent historical memories of the global conflict goes beyond an issue of academic research in significance. Rather, it constitutes a vital, unresolved issue of public policy in the international sphere, relevant to efforts to build up transnational solidarity in the face of common contemporary threats to human security.

Suggestions for further reading

Gaddis, J. L. (1989). *The Long Peace: Inquiries into the History of the Cold War*. New York, NY: Oxford University Press.

Kaldor, M. (1990). *The Imaginary War: Understanding the East–West Conflict*. Cambridge, MA: Blackwell.

Kwon, H. (2010). *The Other Cold War*. New York, NY: Columbia University Press.

LaFeber, W. (1992). An End to Which Cold War? In: M. J. Hogan, ed., *The End of the Cold War: Its Meanings and Implications*, New York, NY: Cambridge University Press, 14–17.

Masuda, H. (2015). *Cold War Crucible: The Korean Conflict and the Post-War World*. Cambridge, MA: Harvard University Press.

Westad, O. A. (2005). *The Global Cold War: Third World Interventions and the Making of Our Times*. Cambridge: Cambridge University Press.

References

Bartelson, J. (2021). War and the Turn to History in International Relations. In de Carvalho, B., Costa Lopez, J., & Leira, H., eds. *Routledge Handbook of Historical International Relations*. Abingdon: Routledge.

Çapan, Z. G., dos Reis, F., and Grasten, M. (2021). Global Histories: Connections and Circulations in Historical International Relations. In de Carvalho, B., Costa Lopez, J., & Leira, H., eds. *Routledge Handbook of Historical International Relations*. Abingdon: Routledge.

Fortes, M., and Evans-Pritchard, E. E., eds. (1940). *African Political Systems*. Oxford: Oxford University Press.

Gaddis, J. L. (1987). *The Long Peace: Inquiries into the History of the Cold War*. New York, NY: Oxford University Press.

Grandin, G. (2004). *The Last Colonial Massacre: Latin America in the Cold War*. Chicago, IL: University of Chicago Press.

Halliday, F. (1983). *The Making of the Second Cold War*. London: Verso.

Judt, T. (2008). *Reappraisals: Reflections on the Forgotten Twentieth Century*. New York, NY: Penguin.

Kaldor, M. (1990). *The Imaginary War: Interpretations of East–West Conflict in Europe*. Oxford: Blackwell.

Kaldor, M. (2001). *New and Old Wars: Organized Violence in a Global Age*. Stanford, CA: Stanford University Press.

Kwon, H. (2006). *After the Massacre: Commemoration and Consolation in Ha My and My Lai*. Berkeley, CA: University of California Press.

Kwon, H. (2020). *After the Korean War: An Intimate History*. Cambridge: Cambridge University Press.

Latham, M. E. (2010). *The Right Kind of Revolution: Modernization, Development, and U.S. Foreign Policy from the Cold War to the Present*. Ithaca, NY: Cornell University Press.

Lundestad, G., ed. (1991). *East, West, North, South: Major Developments in International Politics, 1945–1990*. Oslo: Norwegian University Press.

Schulz, C. (2021). Latin America: Between Liminality and Agency in Historical International Relations. In de Carvalho, B., Costa Lopez, J., & Leira, H., eds. *Routledge Handbook of Historical International Relations*. Abingdon: Routledge.

Svensson, T. (2021). Decolonisation and the Erosion of the Imperial Idea. In de Carvalho, B., Costa Lopez, J., & Leira, H., eds. *Routledge Handbook of Historical International Relations*. Abingdon: Routledge.

Wallerstein, I., and Zukin, S. (1989). 1968, Revolution in the world-system: theses and queries. *Theory and Society*, 18 (4), 431–449.

PART IV

Situating Historical IR

36

ANCIENT GREECE

War, peace and diplomacy in antiquity

Torbjørn L. Knutsen

'Ancient Greece' was a littoral civilization located around the Aegean Sea during the 5th and 4th centuries BC.[1] The geographic context conditioned the economic and political activities of the region. The dry and cragged land made political centralization difficult. There were no vast and fertile pastures to sustain a wealthy and powerful landowning aristocracy in ancient Greece. Under these conditions, there emerged a great number of self-governed states. There may have been about a thousand of them. The majority were located along the Aegean coastline and marked by a common, maritime civilization. Most of the states were small; the island of Keos had four *poleis*, each of them counting about 1000 inhabitants. Sparta, Corinth and Thebes were large. Athens was the largest of them all; it had close to 150,000 inhabitants at its peak around 430 BC.

Did these city states constitute an international system? International Relations (IR) scholars tend to assume that they did. Some authors even argue that we can profitably study their interaction and infer lasting lessons about international behaviour. Different authors such as Donald Kagan (2004), Victor Davis Hanson (2006), Ned Lebow (2007), Joseph Nye (2016) and Graham Allison (2017) argue that we have much to learn from the ancient Greeks; that by carefully studying them, we can gain a better understanding of our own 21st-century world. But can we?

To answer such questions it is necessary to carefully assess the sources on which IR authors have drawn for their knowledge about ancient Greece. Especially the great Greek historians like Herodotus (2009) and Thucydides (1996), on whom IR scholars have tended to rely heavily, wrote mainly about war. Herodotus traced the long conflict between the Greeks and the Persians around 490–480 BC. Thucydides chronicled the Peloponnesian War between two great alliances – the Delian League and the Peloponnesian League – between 431 and 404 BC. Why have IR scholars been so preoccupied with Herodotus and, especially, Thucydides? Why have they tended to read his *Peloponnesian War* as a case of simple, bipolar rivalry?

The short and simple answer is that IR scholars discovered ancient Greece during the Cold-War years and that have read the story of the Peloponnesian War as a historical parallel to the superpower rivalry of their own time. There is a longer answer as well. But it needs to be prefaced by an overview of the academic field of IR.

The exaggerated bipolarity

When IR emerged as a scholarly field, in the wake of World War I, references to ancient Greece, to Thucydides and to the Peloponnesian War were non-existent. IR authors of the 1920s were not as interested in ancient wars as in contemporary peace and in the promise of a stable future order based on international law.

This changed around 1930, when Great-Power conflicts resumed. The authority of the League of Nations was shaken – as was the optimism of the IR scholars. They turned their attention away from discussions concerning the legal framework of an international order and towards the limits of international law and to the capabilities and interests of sovereign states. They discussed the failure of Versailles and argued that goodwill and pure intentions alone did not guarantee stable peace. Some of them wondered why the sensible actions of well-meaning leaders could produce unintended conflict and strife (Niebuhr, 1932) and were puzzled by why the interaction of well-meaning, moral and peaceful men could produce immoral and belligerent consequences. Reinhold Niebuhr (1941) claimed that this was one of the ironic or 'tragic' aspects of international politics.

After World War II, the Cold War and the nuclear rivalry of the superpowers highlighted these aspects of irony, made the possibility of tragedy more acute and accentuated the question of unintended consequences of well-meaning, moral acts (see Kwon, 2021 in this volume). The tragic aspects of international politics directed the attention of some scholars towards ancient Greece (Marshall, 1947; Morgenthau, 1978) – to tragic plays in which human beings are inescapably trapped by forces beyond individual will and reason (Gewen, 2020). In the early 1950s, this sentiment was addressed by IR scholars through the concept of the 'security dilemma' – i.e. the idea that a nation which seeks to increase its security, may instil fear in other nations, who then seek to increase *their* security, and so on in an escalation of fear and insecurity. This dynamic might well draw nations into an arms race and even lead to a war that no one really wants (Herz, 1951; see also Larson, 2021 in this volume). The early references to Thucydides appeared in this context. First, when IR authors explored international events in the light of their new concept of 'polarity'. They noted that the Cold War and the ancient Peloponnesian War were both bipolar constellations and waxed eloquently on their similarities (Waltz, 1959: 157f, 198f, 210; Gilpin, 1981; Aron, 1984 (1962): 145ff).

Some scholars were dubious of this superficial application of ancient authors to international politics in the nuclear age. British scholars were particularly sceptical. Martin Wight (1977) set out his reservations in *De systematibus civitatum*, a small classic in comparative macropolitics. Adam Watson (1992) probed the interrelations of ancient Greek city states with an attitude of distance and scepticism. American authors, however, were eager to draw on Thucydides. His *Peloponnesian War* was invoked to boost the scientific study of war in US war colleges in the 1970s (Stradis, 2014). The quantitative investigations of Choucri and North (1975) found in Thucydides the universal phenomenon of a balance-of-power mechanism. Organski and Kugler (1980) portrayed both classical Greece and the Cold-War world as bipolar systems where, when one nation expands and is about to overtake another, power transitions may cause misunderstandings and frictions, which in turn may lead to war.

This argument was refined and cultivated by Kenneth Waltz (1979: 127, 186f). And, even more so by Robert Gilpin (1981), who leaned heavily on Thucydides when he explored systemic causes of war. Graham Allison (2017) took the power transition argument a step further. He identified 16 historical cases of bipolar rivalry and claimed that more than a dozen of them had ended in war. Allison then allowed what he called the 'Thucydides trap' to shine an explanatory light on his analysis of a looming rivalry among the United States and China.

'The dynamic Thucydides identified will intensify in the years ahead', Allison (2017: ix) wrote. He implored US and Chinese statesmen to show wisdom and restraint lest an increasing rivalry plunge them into conflict, crisis and war.

Allison is right, of course. It is always useful to study the past in order to draw lessons for the present. But it is a dangerous sport (May, 1975). And there are many things that ought to arise suspicion: the late entry of ancient authors into IR, the selective use of them and the search for universal regularities across space, time and deep gaps of technological differences are only some of them. This should prompt us to ask whether there is more to learn from these differences about the infinite variety of human experience than to emphasize superficial similarities in an effort to infer regularities and universal laws.

Diplomacy in the classical age

The Greek world was a littoral civilization unified and marked by the Aegean. It was a seafaring civilization that evolved exchange, trade, a certain division of labour and a modest degree of economic interdependence. However, its most significant unifier was the Ionian language. It was spoken (and written) over all over the Aegean from the earliest times. This common language carried a rich literary tradition, a communal religion and sets of common religious and social practices. The Greek world was unified by a set of self-consciously held norms and values. The people who shared them referred to themselves as '*Hellenes*'. The language was the primary marker of a common identity. All Greeks viewed their linguistically unified civilization as superior to all others. They drew a clear distinction between themselves and people who did not speak Greek – whom they referred to as 'barbarians' (Keene, 2005: 22ff).

The Greeks did evolve rudimentary norms or rules of protocol. 'Rudimentary', because these norms varied from one *polis* to the next. Thucydides (2,97), for example, suggests that gift-giving was common. Yet, he writes about it as if this practice was not firm. He notes that when dealing with the Thracians, it was 'quite impossible to get anything done without a present'. So, although mechanisms of communication and coordination existed, they were neither particularly codified nor standardized. These relations were ad hoc and at best a form of proto-diplomacy (Der Derian, 1991).

Centuries before the classical period, the Greeks arranged festivals of religions and sports – such as the four-yearly Olympics and the Panathenaic festival. In the *Iliad*, Homer tells a story of how 'Neleus had sent a four-horse chariot to Elis to run in their games and compete for a tripod' (Homer, 2011: XI.699f). This early mention of games is an important indicator of diplomatic activity, because it required messengers to distribute invitations. Also, since war was suspended as long as the games lasted, truces, ceasefires and armistices had to be negotiated. The Olympic Games took place every four years, so that such negotiations obeyed a quadrennial regularity. And as the number of athletic festivals increased during the classical period, these kinds of interrelations became more frequent and more complex.

The Greek city states interacted frequently and regularly. Yet, they did not produce a diplomatic system of permanent missions. Rather, theirs was an ad hoc practice of dispatching and receiving envoys. It included guarantees of safe passage – a minimum requirement for any diplomatic system, since rulers cannot reliably communicate and exchange views without it. Herodotus and Thucydides note the regular use of *diplomas* – folded and sealed documents which gave the bearer privileges, such as protection while travelling. These *diplomas* – which in turn gave rise to the term 'diplomacy' – were unlikely to have provided fully reliable protection. Thucydides notes that envoys were accompanied by bodyguards.

Herodotus writes about *presbeis* – or 'elders' – who served as envoys on special missions and delivered their messages orally. He also discusses the *keryx*, who were heralds with special rights of protection. Thucydides adds that the *keryx* tended to travel alone and preceded the envoys to assess the safety of the route. Envoys would then follow in groups of several *presbeis*.

Members of these groups were appointed by the popular assembly to represent the *polis*. Distinct constituencies proposing their own *presbys* instructed him to represent them. As a result, the delegation as a whole would reflect the various points of view of the assembly at home. After a delegation arrived at a host *polis*, it would usually present its errand before the host assembly. Here the delegates would not speak with one voice but mirror the diversity of their own *polis*. This was hardly conducive to effective diplomacy, as the diversity of the delegation could easily be exploited by the hosts (Nicolson, 1954: 11).

The Greek world did not have a system of permanent legations/embassies (more broadly on diplomacy, see Leira 2021 in this volume). It did, however, have *proxeni* – men who were citizens of one *polis* (e.g. Athens) but who lived in another (e.g. Corinth) and there served as 'friend' or 'representative' of his native *polis* (Walbank, 2008). The *proxenos* communicated messages between the *poleis* but did not negotiate. Negotiations were made by envoys.

Anarchy and order in Ancient Greece

Classical Greece displayed a remarkable cultural efflorescence. It included astonishing artistic and literary achievements as well as seminal contributions to Western political philosophy, engineering, education and other spheres of life – and it would have a striking influence on the later development of Western civilization. Yet, these extraordinary achievements did not take place in an age of order, stability and peace. Rather, they occurred during a period of incessant war.

This constant warfare is apparent in Herodotus. It is confirmed by famous philosophers – when they, once in a blue moon, touch upon interstate relations. Plato, for example, lets Clinias the Cretan observe that city states are engaged in ceaseless wars against each other. He notes that 'the peace of which most men talk … is no more than a name; in real fact, the normal attitude of a city to all other cities is one of undeclared warfare' (Plato, 1941: 1227 (I.626); also, Barker, 1959: 187, 429). Aristotle (1981) agrees. This impression of undeclared warfare as a normal condition among states is supported by Thucydides, whose *Peloponnesian War* is dominated by military preparations, campaigns and battles.

Modern IR scholars have found in these authors support for a Realist approach to interstate relations – i.e. the view that the main actors of IR are states; that no state wants to give up its independent status voluntarily; and that this makes it difficult, if not impossible, to establish common laws to guide interstate behaviour. In the 18th century, moral philosophers added the claim that such a lawless system (which the Greeks referred to as an *anarkhia*) was rendered orderly by a balance-of-power principle (Hume, 1985 (1741)). IR Realists often argue that Thucydides invokes a balance-of-power logic and that he should be counted as the first practitioner of their discipline.

A Greek balance-of-power system?

When IR scholars read Herodotus, they tend to observe balance-of-power principles in his description of how the Greek city states coordinated their military efforts around 490 BC to contain the advance of Persia. When they read Thucydides, they see balance-of-power principles at work among the *poleis* in the wake of the Persian retreat. Furthermore, they observe balance-of-power mechanisms in Thucydides' narrative of how the Athenians (in the 480s) converted the anti-Persian alliance into a league and placed its headquarter on the island of Delos. Some (Gilpin, 1981) see balance of power at work in Sparta's reaction to Athenian expansion through the 460s.

It is easy to attribute tit-for-tat dynamics, game-theoretical constellations (Nye, 2016) and strategic dilemmas (Allison, 2017) to the relations among the Greek *poleis*. And it is easy to interpret this as the operations of a balance-of-power mechanism. It is, however, unwarranted to conclude that this mechanism was the ordering principle of an ancient 'interstate system'. An interstate system is usually defined in terms of its boundaries, its duration and its two components: first, its constituent units, which in the classical Greek case would be the self-governing *poleis*; second, the relations among the units, which is far more difficult to ascertain. The *poleis* of classical Greece related to each other commercially and politically. But were they regular and strong enough to constitute a system? The economic relations developed a certain division of labour, but hardly amounted to a system of interdependence. The political relations amounted to a proto-diplomacy, at best.

Since IR scholars draw on Herodotus and Thucydides and emphasize warfare, it may be argued that ancient Greece constituted a warfare system. But did it last long enough to qualify as such? The incessant warfare among the *poleis* carried such a high cost that the system quickly exhausted itself. In the long run, their interaction was unsustainable.

An early observer testifies to this. When Persian king Xerxes the Great planned his invasion of Greece in 485 BC, one of his generals, Mardonios, commented that the Hellenes were fighting each other to death for no particular reason. Pressed for an explanation, he charged the Greeks for being 'obstinate and stupid'.

> For whenever [the Hellenes] declare war on one another, they seek out the finest and most level land and go there to fight, so that the victors depart from the field only after great damage has been done, and I won't say anything at all about the defeated, for they are completely destroyed. What they ought to do, since they speak the same language and use heralds and messengers, is to thus put an end to their differences and employ any means other than battle to become reconciled (Herodotus, 7.9b).

Mardonios' account describes a dysfunctional system, caught in a spiral of wanton violence. He was at loss to explain this. Mardonios may have been incorrect in thinking that the Greeks were too stupid to know their own good – after all, when Xerxes launched his attack, the Greeks coordinated their forces and outsmarted him. However, his puzzlement is valuable.

Realist shortcuts

Some IR realists draw lessons from classical Greece and apply them to modern world affairs (Allison, 2017). This involves a disregard for several differences between ancient and modern states – both concepts and structures that the moderns have but the ancients lack (such as sovereignty and law, and systems of administration and coordination). There are, in other words, limits as to how far the parallels between the states of the ancient and the contemporary world can be pushed (see de Carvalho, 2021 in this volume).

With the end of the Cold War, it must be expected that its concepts of bipolar competition will fade from IR discussions of ancient Greece and be replaced by other terms and preoccupations. New readings of Thucydides may, for example, note that the largest *poleis* of the classical world were not so much akin to modern states as they were to empires. After their victory over Persia (in the 480s), the Greeks united in the Delian League. Its purpose was to block and contain Persian power. The League members all pitched in to build a navy for that purpose. After a while, however, some League members observed that the Athenians invested League funds into their own naval power. The Athenians built up maritime dominance, and other members of the Delian League suspected them of exploiting the League for their own political ends. This suspicion was boosted around 470, when the island of Naxos attempted to break out of the Delian League. Athens reacted by promptly besieging the island with its powerful fleet and forcing Naxos back into the fold. In 431, the tensions between the Delian League and the Peloponnesian League erupted into war. Its outbreak is neatly summarized in Thucydides' (1:23) famous quote, 'it was the rise of Athens and the fear that this instilled in Sparta that made the [Peloponnesian] war inevitable'.

When Athens is perceived as a growing empire rather than a territorial state, it puts a slightly different cast on it. First, the rise of Athens involved maritime control over networks of trade and transportation. In the 480s BC, the Athenians exploited Greek fear of the Persians to consolidate the Delian League; then they exploited the League to gain dominance over a ready-made system of production and maritime distribution of goods and natural resources. Athens, in other words, showed all the signs of an expanding empire. It was 'unlike any state which had existed in Europe up to this point' (Price and Thonemann, 2011: 123; see also de Romilly, 2008).

Second, the Peloponnesian War was not a neat bipolar contest. Thucydides describes a confusing mêlée of rapidly shifting alliances. The Greek *poleis* fought incessantly among themselves – much like Mardonios had observed a few decades before. The bipolar nature of the war can at best be seen as an abstract, historical tendency.

Third, a bipolar tendency is apparent only as long as analytic attention is directed exclusively towards the Hellene *poleis*. Mardonios is a Persian general and offers an outside perspective that expands the boundaries of the 'system'. For him, Greece is an element of a larger region in which the powerful Persian Empire is the major actor. From this wider perspective, the westward expansion of Persia (around 490 BC) was a significant reason for why the Greek *poleis* organized the Delian League in the first place. Also, when the Peloponnesian War broke out 60 years later (in 431 BC), the Persian king sat on the sidelines at first. Later, he practiced a skilful policy of balancing. He tried to profit from the Peloponnesian War by prolonging it – by letting Athens and Sparta 'wear each other out, at a small expense and with little risk to himself' (Thucydides, 8:46). The Persian king decided to support Sparta and the enemies of Athens in order to, 'after reducing the Athenian power as much as he could, forthwith to rid the country of the [Spartans]' (idem; see also Cawkwell, 1997: 119; Rung, 2008).

Thucydides notes that the Persian king supported Sparta in the war against Athens, and that the support was conditioned on the promise that Sparta would allow Persia to repossess the Greek cities in Ionia, which had long been under Athenian hegemony, as soon as Athens was defeated (Thucydides, 8.58). But at this point, *The Peloponnesian War* abruptly ends. Thucydides noted the Persian influence but did not live to complete the story. He died before he could write about how Athens was conquered, how Sparta became the dominant power of the region and how it placed Athens under a draconian administration. He did not write about how Sparta broke its agreement with Persia and, instead of returning the Greek cities in Asia Minor to Persian control, took on a role as liberators of all the Greeks. He did not tell the story of how Sparta launched a great campaign against 'the barbarians' on behalf of the Ionian cities in Asia Minor and how, during the 390s BC, the Persian barbarians crushed Sparta. Greece, exhausted after 30 years of war, mustered little resistance to the expanding Macedonian empire, which then easily conquered it.

Conclusions

Modern IR authors commonly see classical Greece as a system of city states. Also, they observe balance-of-power mechanisms at work in it. As long as they use the balance-of-power term carefully and in a restricted sense, there is nothing wrong with that. When one state becomes stronger than others, it will threaten weaker neighbours and provide an incentive for them to unite in a defensive coalition. This is the balance-of-power principle expressed in the simplest possible terms. And there is little doubt that relations among Greek city states operated along such lines (on the balance of power, see Andersen and Wohlforth, 2021 in this volume).

However, this balance-of-power mechanism was hardly a stabilizing force. It produced no lasting order and no stable peace. In fact, constant quarrels and wars among the Greek *poleis* exhausted them in less than a century. The stories of ancient authors like Thucydides leave little doubt about the destructive nature of that war. Numbers of modern scholars suggest that Attica lost half of its population during the course of the Peloponnesian War (Hansen, 1988).

The Persian general, Mardonios, observed this self-destructive tendency of the Greeks early on. He puzzled over it. And he noted that the city states of ancient *Hellás* held norms and values in common – they 'spoke the same language and [used] heralds and messengers' in their steady interaction. In other words, they had that 'common framework of their endeavors', which Morgenthau (1978: 226) identified as a necessary precondition for the balance-of-power mechanism to work. The various *poleis* ought therefore to have been able to agree on the basic rules of the interstate game and 'put an end to their differences and employ any means other than battle to become reconciled' (Herodotus, 7.9b). So, why didn't they?

How can we explain that the city states of ancient Greece constituted a balance-of-power system but that it produced no lasting order – that it was, to put it bluntly, an unsustainable system? Mardonios put it down to Greek obstinacy and stupidity. This chapter presents a simple, alternative explanation, viz., that the Greeks preferred war. They cultivated competition, contest and war more than they cherished cooperation, harmony and peace.

Ancient Greek authors emphasized ideals like equality and *thymos*. Equality – equal worth of free men – provided the basis for public activity, political participation and democratic decision-making. In Athens, every free citizen had a right (and a duty) to serve in the army, join the popular assembly, participate in the meetings at the *pnyx* and partake in the decision-making of government. Athenian democracy had no bureaucratic elite – and consequently no professional diplomats. In fact, many city states had no professional politicians or administrators of any kind. The *poleis* were in fact governed by amateurs.

Several *poleis* were democracies, but their interaction produced no democratic peace. Their democracy was not based on cooperative values but on competitive ideals. The free citizens served in the hoplite army where they received military training. Their ideal was that of the independent citizen-soldier (Pritchard, 2019). To capture these ideals, it is necessary to include Herodotus and Thucydides in a wider fan of primary sources – which includes epigraphic and archaeological evidence, the epic poems of Hesiod and Homer, the authors of tragedies and comedies and the great philosophers.

Plato associated the Greek ideal with *thymos*, by which he meant a desire for respect and recognition (Fukuyama, 1992), with pride, honour and with noble virtues like courage, selflessness, self-sacrifice and self-sufficiency. These were masculine ideals. They drove citizen ambitions towards excellence – and help us explain the remarkable cultural efflorescence as demonstrated by the achievements in arts, literature and athletics. But they also throw some explanatory light on the drive for competition and battle. And this drive affected not only the behaviour of Greek males within the individual *polis*, but it also affected the interaction among the *poleis*.

These masculine virtues produced costs so high that they rendered the system unsustainable. They were toxic virtues because they had dysfunctional effects for the relations among the *poleis*.

And here lies another lesson of classic Greek IR: common values may be a necessary precondition for a stable balance-of-power system. But this is not in and of itself sufficient to sustain such a system. To have a stable and sustainable international system, the common values must also be of the right kind. They must include virtues like cooperation and common cause.

Suggestions for further reading

Adcock, F. E., and Mosley, D. J. (1975). *Diplomacy in Ancient Greece*. London: Thames and Hudson.
Hall, E. (2014). *Introducing the Ancient Greeks*. New York, NY: W. W. Norton.
Lee, C., and Morley, N., eds. (2012). *A Handbook to the Reception of Thucydides*. New York, NY: Wiley.
Low, P. (2009). *Interstate Relations in Classical Greece*. Cambridge: Cambridge University Press.
Price, S., and Thonemann, P. (2011). *The Birth of Classical Europe*. London: Penguin.
Robinson, C. E. (1955). *Hellas: A Short History of Ancient Greece*. Boston, MA: Beacon Press.
Wilson, N. (2005). *Encyclopedia of Ancient Greece*. London: Routledge

Note

1 A useful vantage point is the arrangement, common among historians, of the long historical lines of the eastern Mediterranean in five simple periods: the bronze age, the 'dark age' (1100–800 BC), the archaic period (800–490 BC), the classical period (490–323 BC), and the Hellenistic period (323–31/30 BC, the emergence of the Roman Empire).

References

Allison, G. (2017). *Destined for War?* Cambridge, MA: Harvard University Press.
Andersen, M. A., and Wohlforth, W. C. (2021). Balance of Power: A Key Concept in Historical Perspective. In de Carvalho, B., Costa Lopez, J., & Leira, H., eds. *Routledge Handbook of Historical International Relations*. Abingdon: Routledge.
Aristotle. (1981). *Politics*. Harmondsworth: Penguin.
Aron, R. (1984 (1962)). *Paix et guerre entre les nations*. Paris: Calman-Lévy.
Barker, E. (1959). *The Political Thought of Plato and Aristotle*. New York, NY: Dover.
Cawkwell, G. L. (1997). The peace between Athens and Persia. *Phoenix*, 51 (2), 115–130.
Choucri, N., and R. C. North. (1975) *Nations in Conflict*. San Francisco, CA: W. H. Freeman & Co.
de Carvalho, B. (2021). Sovereignty in Historical International Relations: Trajectories, Challenges and Implications. In de Carvalho, B., Costa Lopez, J., & Leira, H., eds. *Routledge Handbook of Historical International Relations*. Abingdon: Routledge.
de Romilly, J. (2008). Thucydides and the Cities of the Athenian Empire. In: P. Low, ed., *The Athenian Empire*, Edinburgh: Edinburgh University Press, 277–293.
Der Derian, J. (1991). *On Diplomacy*. Oxford: Blackwell.
Fukuyama, F. (1992). *The End of History and the Last Man*. New York, NY: Free Press.
Gewen, B. (2020). *The Inevitability of Tragedy. Henry Kissinger and his World*. New York, NY: W. W. Norton.
Gilpin, R. (1981). *War and Change in World Politics*. Cambridge: Cambridge University Press.
Hansen, M. H. (1988). *Three Studies in Athenian Democracy*. Copenhagen: Kongelige Danske Videnskabernes Selskab.
Hanson, V. D. (2006). *A War Like No Other: How the Athenians and Spartans Fought the Peloponnesian War*. New York, NY: Random House.
Herodotus. (2009). In Strassler, R., ed. *The Histories*. New York, NY: Random House.
Herz, J. (1951). *Political Realism and Political Idealism*. Chicago, IL: Chicago University Press.
Homer. (2011). *The Iliad and the Odyssey*. San Diego, CA: Canterbury Classics.
Hume, D. (1985 (1741)). Of the Balance of Power. In: D. Hume, *Essays. Moral, political and literary*, Indianapolis, IN: Liberty Classics, 332–342.
Kagan, D. (2004). *The Peloponnesian War*. London: Penguin.

Keene, E. (2005). *International Political Thought: A Historical Introduction*. Cambridge: Polity.

Krentz, P. (1982). *The Thirty at Athens*. Ithaca, NY: Cornell University Press.

Kwon, H. (2021). Understanding the Postcolonial Cold War. In de Carvalho, B., Costa Lopez, J., & Leira, H., eds. *Routledge Handbook of Historical International Relations*. Abingdon: Routledge.

Larson, D (2021). Realism: Excavating a Historical Tradition. In de Carvalho, B., Costa Lopez, J., & Leira, H., eds. *Routledge Handbook of Historical International Relations*. Abingdon: Routledge.

Lebow, N. (2007). Thucydides and deterrence. *Security Studies*, 16 (2), 163–188.

Leira. H. (2021). Diplomacy: The World of States and Beyond. In de Carvalho, B., Costa Lopez, J., & Leira, H., eds. *Routledge Handbook of Historical International Relations*. Abingdon: Routledge.

Lorimer, J. (1877). Le problème final de droit international. *Revue de droit international et de législation comparée*, 9 (2), 161–206.

Marshall, G. C. (1947). Speech at Princeton University, 22 February 1947. *Department of State Bulletin*, 16, 390–392.

May, E. R. (1975). *'Lessons' from the Past: The Use and Abuse of History in American Foreign Policy*. Oxford: Oxford University Press.

Morgenthau, H. (1978). *Politics among Nations*. New York, NY: Alfred A. Knopf.

Nicolson, H. (1954). *The Evolution of the Diplomatic Method*. London: Constable.

Niebuhr, R. (1932). *Moral Man, Immoral Society*. New York, NY: Charles Scribner's Sons.

Niebuhr, R. (1941). *The Nature and Destiny of Man*. New York, NY: Charles Scribner's Sons.

Nye, J. (2016) *Understanding International Conflicts*. London: Longman.

Organski, A. F. K., and Kugler, J. (1980). *The War Ledger*. Chicago, IL: University of Chicago Press.

Plato. (1941). The Laws. In: H. Cairns, and E. Hamilton, eds., *Plato. The Collected Dialogues*, Princeton, NJ: Princeton University Press, 1225–1514.

Price, S., and Thonemann, P. (2011). *The Birth of Classical Europe*. London: Penguin.

Pritchard, D. M. (2019). *Athenian Democracy at War*. Cambridge: Cambridge University Press.

Stradis, A. (2014). Thucydides in the Staff College. In: C. Lee, and N. Morley, eds., *A Handbook to the Reception of Thucydides*, New York, NY: Wiley, 425–445.

Thucydides. (1996). In Strassler, R., ed. *The Peloponnesian War*. New York, NY: Simon & Schuster.

Walbank, M. (2008). Proxeny and Proxenos in Fight-Century Athens. In: P. Low, ed., *The Athenian Empire*. Edinburgh: Edinburgh University Press, 132–139.

Waltz, K. N. (1959). *Man, State and War*. New York, NY: Columbia University Press.

Waltz, K. N. (1979). *Theory of International Relations*. Reading, MA: Addison-Wesley.

Watson, A. (1992). *The Evolution of International Society: A Comparative Historical Analysis*. London: Routledge.

Wight, M. (1977). *Systems of States*. Leicester: Leicester University Press.

37

ROME

Republic, monarchy and empire

Torbjørn L. Knutsen and Martin Hall

Students of International Relations (IR) have paid too little attention to the Roman Empire. They have too long thought of Rome as ancient history and of empires as scarcely relevant for interstate relations; yet, symbols of Roman power are visible in all the major capitals of the West. Republican ideals are praised, whereas imperial practices are regularly condemned; however, as Roman history readily demonstrates, the distinction between Republic and Empire is not nearly as neat as often assumed.

'Republic' refers to a mixed form of government that involves some element of popular participation. 'Empire' refers to an expansive, usually heterogeneous, territory under single domination or control. Roman history shows that expansion took place under the Republic. And that once the Empire was formally declared, expansion slowed significantly down. It more or less ground to a halt after the death of Emperor Trajan in AD 117.

Rome, in other words, was (almost) always an empire, but not always a republic. The Roman Republic and the Roman Empire have both shaped international relations. The Great Powers of the West evolved their systems of administration and governance in the shadow of Rome's example – as the colonnades, triumphal arches and imperial eagles in Berlin, London, Paris and Washington indicate. Less visible, but even more important, the systems of Roman law and administration undergird many of the world's powerful states.

IR and Rome

Traditional IR concentrated on the interaction of contemporary states. Until the end of the Cold War, few IR scholars ventured beyond the world of the sovereign, territorial state. Realist nestors in the field – E.H. Carr, Hans Morgenthau and Kenneth Waltz among them – paid little or no attention to empires. The reason for this neglect is easy to divine: IR scholars built their field of study around a sharp distinction between empires (hierarchy) and states systems (anarchy). They focused on states – sovereign states – and the system that their interaction constitutes. They pushed empires outside of their purview. When traditional IR scholars ventured beyond Westphalia, they looked for anarchical systems, such as Ancient Greece, China during the period of the Warring States and Renaissance Europe.

There are exceptions. Michael Doyle (1986: 83) argued that Rome deserved the attention of IR scholars for three qualities: 'its size, its successful integration of diverse peoples, and its duration'. Discussions of ancient Rome are found among authors who approach IR through the concept of an international society (as opposed to that of an interstate system). Thus, discussions of Rome can be found among members of the English-school (Watson, 1992; Buzan and Little, 2000) and among some authors who were raised in the French tradition (Bozeman, 1960; Aron, 1984). These scholars tend to view Rome as an international society, held together by one broad government allowing a wide variety in local government and religious, cultural and moral traditions (Bozeman, 1960: 175).

During the Cold War, when IR was dominated by the bipolar rivalry between the two nuclear superpowers, echoes of Rome existed in the more or less quiet assumption that the United States was a Republic, whereas the USSR was an Empire. The distinction, which enhanced the positive connotations of the label 'republic' and the negative ones of 'empire', blazed through scholarship and popular culture alike.[1] Luttwak (1976) attracted much attention when he claimed that American foreign-policymakers could learn valuable strategic lessons from the Roman Empire. When the Soviet Union collapsed in 1991 and the United States was seen as the sole superpower and the commander of a new, unipolar international system, discussions of empire flared up in a spate of articles and books that suddenly likened the United States to Rome and its empire – such as, Weltmacht Amerika: *Das neue Rom, Colossus, Are We Rome?* (Münkler, 2001; Bender, 2003; Fergusson, 2004; Murphy, 2007).

The Roman Republic

Rome originated as a village and evolved into a city-state under Etruscan kings. At around 500 BC, the whole of the Italian peninsula was covered by city-states of various ethnic origins – Latin, Greek, Etruscan and Samnite to mention a few. Rome was one of many city-states. Rome's conquest of its Etruscan neighbour, Veii, in 390 BC marks the beginning of Roman ascendency. Rome built a protective city wall at this time and began to form defence alliances, whose members slipped in under Roman hegemony during the course of the mid-fourth century BC. One reason for this drift was associated with the nature of Rome's social order. Another was the strength and efficiency of its army.

Origins, order and law

After abolishing the rule of the Etruscan monarchs, the Romans appointed 'a body of legislators' (Livy, 1998: III.31.7). They drew on Hellene sources and established a republic along the lines of the Greek *politeia*: a mixed constitution which sought to combine the best elements of monarchic, aristocratic and democratic rule (Polybius, 1962: ch. 6; on ancient Greece, see Knutsen, 2021 in this volume).

Rome was deeply affected by Greek ideas in its early years. However, whereas ancient Greece remained a system of competing city-states, Rome created a large, unified society. One force behind this unification was the integrative mechanism of good laws. Another was the strength and efficiency of its army.

The early Romans separated law from religious command; they took the power to legislate human interaction away from the priests. Then they gave it to a class of jurists who recognized that human interaction involved an infinite variety of circumstances and realized that they could not regulate all of them; so they sought to provide broad, simple principles of obligation, which all young Romans had to learn by heart (Livy, 1998: V.43.6). Over time these obligations were converted into principles of law and left to lawyers, whose professional reasoning was cultivated into a science. Rome's legal scholars would, for example, distinguish between public law and civil law. The first (*ius publicum*) would protect the Roman community and the interests of the State; the second (*ius privatum*) was designed to protect the rights of individuals. The lawyers would elaborate on the concept of obligation – distinguish between types of obligation and rank them by importance.[2] The political power of Rome tended to concentrate around those officials who made, interpreted and executed the law. The smooth workings of a tripartite system of actors – the makers, the interpreters and the executioners of law (Polybius, 1962: book 6).

The expanding Republic

Why did Rome's expand so fast? Polybius (1962) argued that the answer lay in Rome's pragmatic and flexible constitution conditioned by the balance between the three constitutional elements of consuls, senate and popular assemblies (roughly corresponding to de Montesquieu's (1989: 170ff) principles of executive, legislative and judicial power).

The literature that addresses Roman expansion is enormous. It is useful to depict it as strung along a continuum with inductive approaches on the one hand and deductive on the other. Towards the inductive end are the historians who rely on painstaking studies of textual and archaeological sources (on the use of sources more generally, see Mulich, 2021 in this volume). They often begin their discussion by demonstrating Rome's superior militarily power (Delbrück, 1975). Towards the deductive end are IR scholars who tend to view Rome through social, anthropological or economic theories (de Ste. Croix, 1981). In-between are authors like Rostovzeff (1957), Harris (2016) and others who note that although Rome was militarily superior, complex interplays existed between armed forces, political leaders, economic interests and the public. Harris, for example, argues that free citizens supported war because victory brought them booty and loot. The Roman elite supported war because victories gave military glory, and glory was needed to pursue a political career in Rome. However, war was popular only as long as the Roman military was powerful, effective and successful.

The 'Harris thesis' is essentially a unit-level, culturalist explanation for Rome's expansion and success. Martial ideals, fierce intra-senatorial competition for scarce public offices and the expediency of providing land and largesse for the lower classes drove the Roman Empire. This thesis should primary be understood as a corrective of the 'defensive imperialism' view that has long dominated Roman studies (Frank, 1914). But the thesis has in turn been criticized by Eckstein (2006), Burton (2019) and others who lean more towards the deductive end of the continuum. They tend to agree that Roman culture was bellicose, but note that since *all* Mediterranean cultures at the time were also bellicose, this alone cannot explain the exceptional Roman expansion and success. Indeed, Eckstein rejects unit-level explanations and turns to systemic-level explanations instead, and explicitly to IR Realism, using power-transition theory and security dilemma logics to explain Rome's expansionist drive. Eckstein concedes one explanatory unit attribute: the Roman unique capacity for assimilating non-Romans. Burton (2011, 2019) accepts several of Eckstein's IR-Realist points, but adds a constructivist layer of explanation in suggesting that unit-level, internal culture mediated systemic pressures and shaped the responses. Mattingly (2013) adds perspectives from postcolonial studies and identity theory to portray Roman society as composed of diverse populations whose experience of empire varied greatly.

In either case, where did original Roman power and efficiency come from? One answer is related to size. Recruitment was required by law, and the number of citizens who met the requirements was high – about 10% of all free men by the estimation of Delbrück (1975: 259ff). As a result, the Republic could draft more soldiers than its neighbours. Another source of Roman power was its military organization. The Republic organized its men into smaller units of 120–160, whose discipline was superior to the looser formations of Rome's opponents. For reasons of size and organization, the armies of the Republic tended to win wars. And Rome tended to expand with each new victory (Eckstein, 2006).

The Punic turning point

Third-century Rome was still a relatively small power in a wider Mediterranean context. To the east of Rome were the leagues of Greek city-states and the post-Alexandrian monarchies in Egypt, Macedon and Asia Minor. To the west was the North-African city-state of Carthage, whose settlements and dependencies in Spain, Sicily and Sardinia commanded the Mediterranean. It controlled most of it by the fourth century BC.

When Carthage pressured the Greek city-state of Messana (on Sicily) in 264 BC, the Sicilians asked Rome to intervene. The result was the Punic Wars. They were enormously costly, both in capital and in manpower. During the first Punic War (264–241), Rome built a huge navy to complement its formidable land power. The Second Punic War (218–201) involved battles on sea as well as on land – in Italy, Spain and Greece. Rome won, and its victory was consolidated by the short and decisive third Punic War, which utterly destroyed Carthage in 146 BC.

The victory altered Rome's foreign-policy behaviour. It removed Rome's external rival. Also, it altered Rome's internal dynamics: it increased the size and changed the composition of the army and altered the political economy of the Republic. We are tempted to call the resulting compound 'the military-agricultural complex'. In the short run, it intensified the expansion of the Republic. In the longer run, it undermined the Republic and created, in effect if not in name, a monarchy.

With Carthage gone, no one could contain the expanding Republic. Its stunningly efficient fighting forces won victories on virtually all fronts. But the Romans developed another skill as well: they developed a diplomatic ability to convert military victory into political order. Once a war was over, the victorious generals would invite the defeated commanders to negotiations about the terms of surrender. The Romans, who had displayed a ruthless show of force in battle, would now show respect. Instead of negotiating out of vindictiveness, they would show lenience and good will. They would conduct a conciliatory diplomacy. In some cases, they might even throw Roman citizenship and rights into the bargain (Aron, 1984: 224).

Over time, the Roman Republic would include an increasing number of satellites to its expanding system of metropolitan dominance. The system grew in complexity because the terms upon which each new province was included depended upon local negotiations whose outcome would vary from one case to the next. Each new province would submit to Roman rule on different terms. The accumulated result would be a cosmopolitan society of great variation. It was, in effect, an empire in all but name.

The military-agricultural complex

During the third century BC, wars were fought in distant territories. Also, wars became prolonged and military service extended. As a result, it became impossible for many legionaries to maintain their farms. At the same time, victory and conquest occasionally led to sizeable inflows of capital and slaves into the Roman economy. The new wealth would be unequally distributed, making some aristocrats very rich. They would buy up land and work it with slaves.

The outcome was a vicious cycle. As land concentrated on steadily fewer hands, the number of landowners declined. This reduced the pool of citizens that could be drafted into the legions.

Concentration of wealth would increase social inequality as well as the size of the urbanized proletariat. Over the next 200 years or so, the Senate passed various measures to rectify the situation. But the solution invariably involved the conquest of new lands to dole out as colonies to proletarized veterans. Military victories thus reinforced the vicious cycle, leading to ever more hunger for land, which in turn necessitated conquest and the establishment of colonies. This military-agricultural complex also led to an ever-increasing concentration of wealth to the aristocracy, as wealth was strongly connected to land (Hall, 1999).

The East-West split

Spurred by the military-agricultural complex, the Romans expanded fast. In the west, they encountered 'barbarians'. Julius Caesar (1951: 28ff) found them quarrelsome and poor (cf. Tacitus, 1970: no. 33) and imposed order upon them by draconian means. The Romans established garrisons, founded cities, incorporated new territories as provinces under Rome and ruled directly through Roman officials (backed by Roman legions).

In the east, the Romans faced 'civilized' societies. These were often large and differentiated with big cities, sophisticated economies and a centralized political system ruled by kings or emperors. Here, the Romans co-opted the ruling class, agreed to respect local laws and ruled under the guise of alliances (de Montesquieu, 1965: 69f). The conquests in the east produced different institutions from those in the west. And as the institutions evolved, the differences would, in due time, divide the empire. The eastern half would be stable and long-lasting. The western half would be contentious and marked by cleavages and tensions.

Civil wars and the fall of the Republic

Rome's military leaders found westward expansion lucrative. Wealth – silver and slaves – flowed into Rome where it would exacerbate the problems of the late Republic. Wealthy generals and aristocrats would buy up more land and create an impoverished stock of farmers/citizens/legionaries that would swell the urban proletariat and fuel sociopolitical crises in the metropolis.

The central government lost control. Civil wars broke out among powerful and ambitious generals – first between Marius and Sulla, then between Pompey and Caesar. Each expanded the empire in order to enrich themselves and maintain the loyalty of their legions. The vast imperial expansion of the first century BC was not the policy of the Roman Senate; rather it was a consequence of competition among powerful generals and their semiprivate armies. The final contest between Marcus Antonius and Caesar's adoptive son Caesar Octavian ended with victory for Octavian (Augustus) in 31 BC. This ended the power of the generals and the civil wars. It also put an end to imperial expansion.

The Roman Empire

Augustus revolutionized Roman rule. He instituted reforms that ended the chaos and instability of the late Republic (Doyle, 1986: 93–97). Most importantly, he consolidated Rome's military power. He centralized the Roman army and placed it under his own, personal command. Augustus alone assumed the right to command Rome's military forces – a right denoted by the term *imperare*, which allowed him to call himself emperor and to refer to his realm as the Empire (on other empires, see Caraccioli, 2021; Bayly, 2021; both in this volume).

The imperial structure

Augustus maintained the discourse and trappings of the Republic, but he in effect turned the Republic into a monarchy. He streamlined a structure that had been formed by a century-long evolution – a historical process that had produced a complex web of 'places over which Rome exercised power' (Caesar, 1951:130). While maintaining the discourse and trappings of the Republic, Augustus in effect turned the Republic into a monarchy. A rough outline of the result may be indicated by three concentric circles:

1. The inner circle was the Roman metropolis.
2. The intermediate circle represented the provinces that were tied most intimately to Rome. This circle tended to expand westwards, where Roman law was enforced and where the inhabitants were often granted Roman citizenship.
3. The outer circle indicated the areas where Rome stationed its legions and upheld order by a constant presence, but where the institutions of order were traditional and local. This circle tended to expand eastwards, where it would include border regions, beyond which existed territories that were outside the purview of Roman control.

This is a very rough approximation. But it makes the important point that the Roman Empire did not describe a hub-and-spoke structure (Nexon and Wright, 2007: 253). Augustus' streamlining left ample room local autonomy (especially in the east). More importantly, inter-province trade was huge. And while Rome taxed this trade, it did not manage its provinces as colonies (in the modern sense), retaining them 'in a division of labor controlled by the metropolitan regions' (Bang, 2009: 116). Indeed, Ando (2018: 180) suggests that the Roman themselves did not see their empire as a unified entity, 'but as an international space constructed through myriad, purely bilateral instruments'. Bang (2013: 428) goes further and suggests that the empire 'may perhaps best be likened to an international society where the Roman monarch claimed preeminence among subject peoples as well as rival kings and states'.

Many roads lead from Rome: legacies of empire

The Roman Empire was flexible and durable; bending before the winds of time, adapting to changes of History. Augustus' reform was a major adaptation. Others followed. Two centuries later, for example, Constantin converted to Christianity and replaced pagan officials with fellow Christians. Also, he established a separate administrative structure in the eastern part of the empire, with Constantinople as its capital.

Institutions of diffusion

Constantine's division expressed an old civilizational fault-line that divided Europe into two political cultures. It also formalized and deepened it. Institutions east of this fault-line survived for another millennium. The western half, however, collapsed under the impact of the fourth-century crisis. It took several hundred years before a new order evolved from the ruins of the western empire – first a feudal order; then an order based on territorial command wielded by merchants and kings and legitimized by theologians (Spruyt, 1994); finally, an order based on sovereign states (Knutsen, 2016: ch. 2).

Even though the Empire collapsed and its political structure unravelled, its civilization continued to have a formative influence on the evolution of Europe, the West and the world. Its greatest influence was carried by institutions of faith, education and law.

Faith and the church

The Christian Church was a veritable international organization, a wide network led by the pope, who emerged as a strong wielder of political power. The Christian religion was a powerful source of norms and values, which sustained and shaped political thought and behaviour all over the West. In the wake of Rome's collapse, the Church was the main source of order in Europe. As secular rulers emerged during the High Middle Ages, the pope was a significant rival of monarchs and emperors who accepted and bowed to his authority. His power is still reflected in many spectacular cathedrals.

Education

The Church had a monopoly of higher education. Cathedral schools were centres of scholarship and learning. For hundreds of years, they inculcated Christian norms and Roman values in steadily new generations of Europeans. The content of higher education was built around the late-Roman notion of 'liberal arts' (*idem*). Its language was Latin – the command of which unified a Western elite of intellectuals that spoke thousands of local languages. To learn Latin, it was necessary to study texts by Cicero, Caesar, Sallust and other Roman writers. This educational system had a formative impact on the West that can hardly be exaggerated. For example, it encouraged individualism and disseminated norms and notions of individual rights.

Law

The influence of Rome received an additional boost during the early renaissance with the rediscovery of the classical cultures of Greece and Rome. This happened at a time when the contours of the modern state emerged along the North-Atlantic rim. Particularly important was the 12th-century discovery of the Justinian codex. This digest of Roman laws furnished the juridical basis for the state formations that emerged during the early modern history of Europe. The legal concepts of Rome have remained basic to both civil and common laws in Europe ever since and were – through the practices of European colonialism – exported to other parts of the world.

Political theory

The values and ideals of Rome have been kept alive up to the present day. There have been changes along the way. One of the major changes occurred during the 18th century, when the ancient ideals of Rome – republican as well as imperial – encountered the new ideas of the Enlightenment.

Enlightenment thinkers developed new concepts of 'the self' and 'self-determination' – both in terms of individual rights as well as of collective identity. Such new ideas fused with ancient ideas of Roman governance. Baron de Montesquieu, for example, developed an influential theory of the checks and balances of state powers by reading Polybius (1962) and studying the politics of the Roman Republic.

Ideals of the Roman Empire are evident in the way that the rulers of modern Europe adopted ancient symbols of greatness. The Russian title of 'tsar' is derived from 'Caesar' and the tsarist court was awash with Roman symbols – as reflected in eagles, banners, officers' uniforms – and entertained a self-image of Moscow as 'the new Rome'. The Austro-Hungarian emperor perceived himself as a successor to the Holy Roman Empire. So did the German Kaiser after the creation of the German Empire in 1871. These rulers carried the symbols of Rome, their meanings sustained by the Latin schools, which were the stepping stones to good jobs and higher office and a socializing mechanism for the elites. With the rise of Napoleon, the self-image of France shifted from a Carolingian origin to one that drew on the history of Rome. By the end of the late 19th century, the Great Powers of the west were not mere nation states, they were all empires.

Rome and the United States

The Great Power that was most directly influenced by the Roman ideals was the United States. After the War of Independence, the 13 former British colonies first emerged as independent states and then as an entirely new political entity; a federation of states. This new entity was constructed along Roman ideals. These were sustained by the American Latin schools, where new generations studied Sallust, Caesar and Cicero with such intensity that they were more familiar with the people and events of ancient Rome than they were with the contemporary affairs of Europe (Richard, 1994).

During the 1780s, when American activists debated the nature of their new nation, they referred to themselves by Roman names. The name of 'Publius' was used to sign a series of articles in 1787/1788, written by the three influential activists James Madison et al. (1987). The American Founding Fathers modelled their New Nation explicitly on Rome – not on the Empire, but on the Republic which preceded it.

They had a deep admiration for the Roman Republic and were deeply concerned about the transition from Republic to Empire. This transition, and the associated fear of imperial corruption, has informed American politics to this day. Whenever the United States has engaged in foreign adventures and sent troops abroad, critics have tended to warn about imperial tendencies – formulated in a discourse that echoes classic accounts of how the Roman Republic deteriorated into Empire (Salter, 1899). This habit is equally present on the right side of America's political spectrum (Buchanan, 2002) as on the left (Chomsky, 2005; Petras, 2014).

Conclusions

Interstate anarchy is a simple and seductive model of IR. It was developed in the West, in a pre-democratic age of strong monarchies. It is not an optimal model for the 21st century, in which the day-to-day behaviour of states are constrained by international institutions and by a world-economy marked by interdependence and globalization. Rome, seen as an international society composed of many different actors but obeying common principles of law, may be a better model.

Of course, the important differences between the Roman Empire and the current world should not be neglected: there was no democracy either in Rome or the empire-cum-society; state capacity was low; and there was no concept of any form of supranational authority or institution. And yet, the thickness of vertical as well as horizontal integration, the emphasis on law, the *structural* acceptance of a preeminent power within this society, all suggest that IR neglect the dynamics of the Roman Empire to its detriment.

Suggestions for further reading

Champion, C. B. (2004). *Roman Imperialism: Readings and Sources*. Oxford: Blackwell.

Le Glay, M., Voisin, J.-L., Le Bohec, Y., Cherry, D., Kyle, D. G., and Manolaraki, E. (2009). *A History of Rome*. New York, NY: Wiley-Blackwell.

Grant, M. (1978). *History of Rome*. New York, NY: Scribner's.

Harper, K. (2017). *The Fate of Rome: Climate, Disease, and the End of an Empire*. Princeton, NJ: Princeton University Press.

Hildinger, E. (2002). *Swords against the Senate: the Rise of the Roman Army and the Fall of the Republic*. Cambridge, MA: Da Capo Press.

Schiedel, W. (2019). *Escape from Rome: The Failure of Empire and the Road to Prosperity*. Princeton, NJ: Princeton University Press.

Notes

1 Cf. the bipolar constellation in the Star Wars movies, in which the multi-species freedom fighters of the Republic are pitted against the robotic forces of the (evil) Empire.

2 It is often noted that the political philosophy of Rome was poor compared to that of the Greeks; but it must be added that the Romans inferred broad principles from Greek philosophy and founded a legal science on them. The Greeks were concerned with law (cf. Plato, 1970) but they did not refine it into a science. In fact, no institutional framework of contractual security was evolved by any other people in the ancient world that could match that of Roman law (Bozeman, 1960).

References

Ando, C. (2018). Empire as State: The Roman Case. In: J. L. Brooke, J. C. Strauss, and G. Anderson, eds., *State Formations: Global Histories and Cultures of Statehood*, Cambridge: Cambridge University Press, 175–189.

Aron, R. (1984 (1962)). *Paix et guerre*. Paris: Calmann-Lévy.

Bang, P. F. (2009). Commanding and Consuming the World: Empire, Tribute, and Trade in Roman and Chinese History. In: W. Scheidel, ed., *Rome and China: Comparative Perspectives on Ancient World Empires*, Oxford: Oxford University Press, 100–120.

Bang, P. F. (2013). The Roman Empire II: The Monarchy. In: P. F. Bang, and W. Scheidel, eds., *The Oxford Handbook of the State in the Ancient Near East and Mediterranean*, Oxford: Oxford University Press, 412–470.

Bayly, M. (2021). Imperialism: Beyond the 'Re-turn to Empire' in International Relations. In de Carvalho, B., Costa Lopez, J., & Leira, H., eds. *Routledge Handbook of Historical International Relations*. Abingdon: Routledge.

Bender, P. (2003). *Weltmacht Amerika: Das Neue Rom*. Stuttgart: Klett-Cotta.

Bozeman, A. B. (1960). *Politics and Culture in International History: from the Ancient Near East to the Opening of the Modern Age*. New Brunswick, NJ: Transaction Publishers.

Buchanan, P. (2002). *A Republic, Not An Empire: Reclaiming America's Destiny*. New York, NY: Regnery Publishing.

Burton, P. J. (2011). *Friendship and Empire: Roman Diplomacy and Imperialism in the Middle Republic (353–146 BC)*. Cambridge: Cambridge University Press.

Burton, P. J. (2019). *Roman Imperialism*. Leiden: Brill.

Buzan, B., and Little, R. (2000). *International Systems in World History*. Oxford: Oxford University Press.

Caesar, J. G. (1951). *The Conquest of Gaul*. Harmondsworth: Penguin.

Caraccioli, M. J. (2021). Early (Modern) Empires: The Political Ideology of Conceptual Domination. In de Carvalho, B., Costa Lopez, J., & Leira, H., eds. *Routledge Handbook of Historical International Relations*. Abingdon: Routledge.

Chomsky, N. (2005). *Imperial Ambitions*. New York, NY: Metropolitan Books.

de Montesquieu, C.-L. de S. (1965). *Considerations on the Causes of the Greatness of the Romans and their Decline*. New York, NY: Free Press.

de Montesquieu, C.-L. de S. (1989). *The Spirit of the Laws*. Cambridge: Cambridge University Press.

de Ste. Croix, G. E. M. (1981). *The Class Struggle of the Ancient Greek World*. New York, NY: Cornell University Press.

Delbrück, H. (1975). *Warfare in Antiquity*. Lincoln: University of Nebraska Press.

Doyle, M. W. (1986). *Empires*. Ithaca, NY: Cornell University Press.

Eckstein, A. M. (2006). *Mediterranean Anarchy, Interstate War and the Rise of Rome*. Berkeley, CA: University of California Press.

Fergusson, N. (2004). *Colossus: The Rise and Fall of the American Empire*. New York, NY: Penguin.

Frank, T. (1914). *Roman Imperialism*. New York, NY: Macmillan.

Hall, M. (1999). *Constructing Historical Realism*. PhD dissertation. Lund: Lund Political Studies.

Harris, W. V. (2016). *Roman Power: A Thousand Years of Empire*. Cambridge: Cambridge University Press.

Knutsen, T. L. (2016). *A History of International Relations Theory*. Manchester: Manchester University Press.

Knutsen, T. L. (2021). Ancient Greece: War, Peace and Diplomacy in Antiquity. In de Carvalho, B., Costa Lopez, J., & Leira, H., eds. *Routledge Handbook of Historical International Relations*. Abingdon: Routledge.

Livy. (1998). *The Rise of Rome, Books 1–5*. Oxford: Oxford University Press.

Luttwak, E. (1976). *The Grand Strategy of the Roman Empire from the First Century AD to the Third*. Baltimore, MD: Johns Hopkins University Press.

Madison, J., Hamilton, A., and Jay, J. (1987). *The Federalist Papers*. London: Penguin.

Mattingly, D. J. (2013). *Imperialism, Power and Identity: Experiencing the Roman Empire*. Princeton, NJ: Princeton University Press.

Mulich, J. (2021). International Relations in the Archive: Uses of Sources and Historiography. In de Carvalho, B., Costa Lopez, J., & Leira, H., eds. *Routledge Handbook of Historical International Relations*. Abingdon: Routledge.

Münkler, H. (2001). *Empires: The Logic of World Domination from Ancient Rome to the United States*. Oxford: Polity.

Murphy, C. (2007). *Are We Rome?* New York, NY: Houghton Mifflin Harcourt.

Nexon, D., and Wright, T. (2007). What's at Stake in the American Empire Debate. *American Political Science Review*, 101 (2), 253–271.

Petras, J. (2014). *The Politics of Empire*. Atlanta, GA: Clarity Press.

Plato. (1970). *The Laws*. Harmondsworth: Penguin Classics.

Polybius. (1962). *The Histories*. London: Macmillan.

Richard, C. L. (1994). *The Founders and the Classics*. Cambridge, MA: Harvard University Press.

Salter, W. M. (1899). *Imperialism*. Chicago: Alfred C. Clark & Co.

Spruyt, H. (1994). *The Sovereign State and Its Competitors*. Princeton: Princeton University Pres

Tacitus. (1970). *Histories*. Cambridge: Cambridge University Press.

Watson, A. (1992). *The Evolution of International Society*. London: Routledge.

38

INTERNATIONAL RELATIONS IN/AND THE MIDDLE AGES

Julia Costa Lopez

The Middle Ages in International Relations

At first sight, looking at Historical International Relations literature on the Middle Ages would seem a rather simple endeavour. Although casual mentions to 'the medieval' are relatively common when compared to other topics or periods, the amount of literature is visibly smaller. Most International Relations (IR) scholarship that engages with the medieval does so in order to assess specific theoretical points, for the period is seen as a 'hard case' against which IR theories can be tested. Thus, for example, Markus Fischer focused on central medieval lords in order to test the neorealist idea that anarchy forces similar constraints on all political units, regardless of time period or cultural constraints (Fischer, 1992). From a Marxist perspective, Benno Teschke sought to understand the period through the evolution of social property relations, showing how these constituted different political units and created opposing strategies of reproduction for lords and peasants (Teschke, 2003). Most famously, Ruggie used the Middle Ages and the medieval-to-modern transition as a way of illustrating the historicity of political structures and thus of international dynamics against the timelessness of neorealism (Ruggie, 1993). While all these authors do indeed highlight a variety of dynamics about medieval international relations, the mode of historical engagement has been somewhat problematic (Hall and Kratochwil, 1993). Against this, a growing body of constructivist-inspired scholarship has sought to recover more historicised understandings of the period, pointing to the existence of distinctive patterns of order (Osiander, 2007; Phillips, 2010; Latham, 2012; see also Bruneau, 2021) and seeking to unpack distinctively medieval ideas and their lasting influence (Holland, 2010; Bain, 2017).

However, the importance of the medieval for IR is not limited to these historical engagements. On the contrary, the Middle Ages are arguably an ever-present, silent counterpart to much IR theorising, as they constitute a fundamental stepping stone in both the core historical narratives and the conceptual apparatus of the discipline. On the one hand, the oft-cited story about the emergence of International Relations across different IR traditions – from the English School, to constructivism, to standard textbook accounts that focus on the Peace of Westphalia – starts with the Middle Ages (de Carvalho et al., 2011; Bull, 2012). A heteronomous system, controlled by the competing universalisms of Papacy and Empire, gave way to the modern international system of sovereign states. Thus, the importance of the medieval in this view is not what it can tell us itself, but rather that 'it is the precursor to the Westphalian order that arose in Europe and was imposed from there onto the rest of the world' (Buzan and Albert, 2010: 332).

This derivative significance, however, is symptomatic of something important: the role of the medieval goes beyond its place in the self-narrative of IR, and extends to its foundational role in core concepts of the discipline (see also Kessler, 2021). As Kathleen Davis has pointed out, the historical formation of a concept as central for the IR imaginary as that of sovereignty, historically relied on the creation of a feudal and religious medieval past. First, in the sixteenth century, the battles over the notion of sovereignty and the location of authority led to the creation of the idea of 'feudalism' (see also Reynolds, 1994). Second, in the context of the colonial encounter, feudalism, slavery, and the medieval were 'grouped together and identified as a characteristic of Europe's past and of a non-European present' (in IR see Jahn, 2000; Davis, 2008: 8; also Herborth and Nitzschner, 2021). Thus, 'the "Middle Ages" as we know it today is a… reification of categories that emerged as a means of legitimising sovereignty and [colonial] conquest' and as such they are the 'narrative and conceptual basis of "modern politics"' (Davis, 2008: 9, 26).

If this is correct, the foundational conceptual apparatus of IR – be it sovereignty or colonialism, depending on the tradition – relies on, and is legitimated by, a particular (fictional) category of 'the medieval', and IR will therefore be conceptually limited as long as it does not undertake efforts to address this 'medieval' past. In this chapter, I focus on three ways of reimagining the Middle Ages that may potentially be fruitful in disentangling the medieval from its fixed connotations. First, I consider how to break with the notion of the singular, unified medieval by looking at alternative periodisations and breaks within what is conventionally considered to be the Middle Ages. Second, I challenge the isolation and locality of the period by looking into global connections and circuits at the time. Finally, I tackle the role of the medieval in reproducing a specific metageography of Europe by looking at how it can point to alternative spaces and spatial imaginaries.

Ruptures and continuities

A first starting point in order to challenge the imaginary of the medieval in IR is to problematise its unity. While a number of IR scholars have highlighted the important changes throughout the period (Teschke, 1998; but also Latham, 2012), the IR imaginary continues to be anchored in a notion of *the* medieval as singular. This is evident, for example, in the literature on neomedievalism, which, thinking that the imaginary of the sovereign state system is no longer helpful to understand our contemporary world, seeks to find a 'therapeutic redescription' (Deibert, 1997) or 'heuristic device' (Friedrichs, 2001) in *the* medieval system. This is problematic, for lumping together ten centuries of European history under a common label and under a homogenous imaginary is the core move that constitutes the medieval as the Other of modern politics (Davis, 2008). And yet, transcending this singular imaginary and unpacking different periods, ruptures, and continuities within the Middle Ages is not an easy task (see also Guillaume, 2021). However, it is one that not only can help us gain a better historical understanding, but also provide fertile ground to reimagine core concepts in IR. In this section, I point to this by critically examining debates over two interlinked ruptures: the medieval-to-modern break itself, and the so-called twelfth-century renaissance.

A core current in historiography problematises the mere existence of a big rupture between medieval and modern forms of politics in the sixteenth or seventeenth centuries, as is commonly assumed in IR (for a discussion in IR see Costa Lopez et al., 2018). Rather, one is to find a continuity between late-medieval and early modern political structures to the point that they would form a single period in terms of political language and practice. Indeed, insofar as there were changes, these were incremental (see, for example, Pennington, 1993; Bellomo, 1995; Bagge, 1997). Underpinning this challenge to the divide, as Cary Nederman notes, is the view that 'the changes separating medieval from modern patterns of political thought were largely cosmetic and unworthy of sustained analysis' (Nederman, 2009: xvii). This tradition, thus, seeks to bridge the abysmal divide by which the modern founds itself anew through an association with antiquity, and unpack the fundamental role of the medieval in the constitution of modernity (Bain, 2017).

In pointing to medieval/modern continuities, this narrative ultimately proposes different moments of break. Specifically, it draws attention to what has historiographically been seen as a moment of fundamental transformation, but that has nevertheless received very little attention in IR: the twelfth century renaissance (Benson et al., 1987). The term refers to a series of fundamental transformations in the social and political organisation of Latin Christendom starting in the mid-eleventh century and continuing well into the thirteenth. Socio-economically, Europe underwent what some scholars have termed an 'economic boom' (Wickham, 2016: 121): a demographic explosion saw the population triple between 950 and 1300, urban centres increased in size and number, monetised exchange became more common, and trade – both local and long-distance – acquired progressively more importance. In conjunction with these changes, there were also wide cultural and political changes. The period saw not only the appearance of universities, but also an intellectual transformation, with the development of new understandings of reason, nature, community, the development of new scholarly and teaching techniques in scholasticism, an expansion of interest in reading and books beyond monastic centres, and a new relation to the classics (Maxwell, 1993; Southern, 1995; Le Goff, 2018).

Crucially for IR scholars, political authority also fundamentally transformed. On the one hand, closely entangled with the changes above, the Church underwent a process of reform in the late eleventh century. The so-called Gregorian reform involved not only the establishment of some fundamental principles – such as clerical celibacy – but also an attempt to gain independence from secular structures. The Investiture Controversy (in IR see Hall, 1997; Osiander, 2007; Grzymala-Busse, 2019) saw a conflict between Pope Gregory VII and future Holy Roman Emperor Henry IV for the control of bishop and abbot appointments, beginning what historians have called a crisis of Church and State (Tierney, 1964). Secular authorities – not only the empire and kings, but also a variety of other office holders – resisted this process, and in doing so rearticulated their basis for legitimacy and attempted to progressively assert more control. A case in point, this period saw the appearance of increasingly sophisticated bureaucracies and taxation systems that made use of the wealth and increasing monetisation to provide revenue for rulers, secular, and ecclesiastic alike, leading to an overall trend towards centralisation of rule (Watts, 2009).

The need to rearticulate the grounds for authority meant that this conflict was closely intertwined with the intellectual developments mentioned above, leading ultimately to a transformation in the vocabulary and imaginary that governed political dynamics. Within this centralising and urban society, for example, university-trained Roman and canon lawyers acquired a more prominent role (Bellomo, 1995; Brundage, 2008), with the *ius commune* becoming a crucial political language to articulate, manage, and also dispute political authority (Costa Lopez, 2020). The take-off of the intellectual environment, in a context where conflicts with Muslim polities in the Eastern Mediterranean and, especially, in the Iberian peninsula had led to an increase in intellectual exchange and connections, also brought about the reacquaintance, translation, and elaboration with classical authors such as Aristotle, heavily mediated by the interpretations of Muslim and Jewish scholars. This in itself introduced an additional political language – Aristotelianism – with distinctive understandings of politics, authority, and legitimacy that lasted well into the early modern period if not beyond (Black, 1992; Nederman, 1996; Kempshall, 1999).

The implications of this double reorientation – both challenging the medieval/modern separation, and the focus on the twelfth century renaissance – for Historical IR narratives are crucial, and yet far from clear. Indeed, although this literature has not yet gained much traction in IR, it is worth noting that the two core attempts deploy it in entirely opposing ways. On the one hand, Osiander looks at late-medieval and early modern politics in order to show that 'the medieval-to-modern shift was… really much less of a "shift", than use usually implied, to the point that it was never even completed during the *ancien régime*' (Osiander, 2001a: 121). Linked to extensive work that also problematises Westphalia as a moment of rupture (Osiander, 2001b; de Carvalho et al., 2011), this perspective understands that the late-medieval and early modern world were characterised by the non-identification of society and rulers. Indeed, this system included both the articulation of a joint Christian society and its government by a multiplicity of rulers who, in material terms, struggled to project power. It is thus not until the nineteenth century that we would be able to see an international system of corporately-understood states. The second strand in IR, exemplified by Andrew Latham, takes an opposing understanding, while also situating the end-break of the period sometime in the nineteenth century. In this view, however, it is the beginning of the period that deserves our attention. Starting in the end of the thirteenth century, and certainly by the beginning of the fourteenth, the shift in political ideas (and disputably in political practice) led to an articulation of supreme political authority that would enable us to speak of sovereignty at least two centuries before we usually think. Paired with this, the development of specific, corporate notions of political community allows us to meaningfully talk about the beginnings of statehood, and thus a true (medieval) system of states (Latham, 2012).

Towards a global Middle Ages?

A second component of the IR medieval imaginary is its local character. At one level, when compared to later periods, and particularly to an IR imagination that takes the post-nineteenth century world as its starting point (Buzan and Lawson, 2015), there is a core of truth to the idea that communication, transportation, and power projection were significantly more challenging, and thus to the idea that by-and-large politics took place on a more local scale (Osiander, 2001a). At the same time, however, this works historiographically to reinforce an image of medieval Europe as a unit evolving somewhat in isolation and – at most – relating to other parts of the world only through war (Costa Lopez, 2016). Indeed, most IR works on the period only focus on intra-European dynamics, with the idea that IR-relevant contacts beyond this not only begin after 1492, but are distinctively what constitutes the advent of modernity (Buzan and Lawson, 2014). Alternatively, a number of works do mention interactions beyond Latin Christendom, but in that case, these are patently limited to war. For Teschke, for example, the internal dynamics of reproduction of the feudal system created a need for more land, which led to outward movements in the form of external conquest (Teschke, 1998: 332). More commonly, the violence of the external relations of medieval Europe is reinforced by the emphasis on the crusades.

The crusades is the generic term for a series of military campaigns that started in the eleventh century and were legitimised, and in some cases also coordinated, by the Church through ideas of defence and expansion of the Roman Christian faith.[1] Although the common idea for a crusade portrays it as a holy war against Muslim polities, crusades were also called against a variety of other groups. The Albigensian crusade (1209–1229), for example, was declared against the Catharist heresy, which had its strongholds in the Languedoc region in modern France (Sumption, 2011). Interestingly, and rather underexplored in IR, the crusades in the Eastern Mediterranean led to the establishment of distinct, new polities – the so-called Latin Crusader states (Barber, 2012). In IR, the crusades have been seen as expressive of the fundamentally religious and intolerant nature of the period, which pitted Latin Christendom against most of its others (Alkopher, 2005; Latham, 2011). An important literature relativises this overarching view. For starters, thinking that religious devotion and structural antagonism constitutes the basis of the crusades exhibits a form of religious reductionism that portrays the Middle Ages as an era of religious fanaticism (Davis, 2008). Rulers could undertake take part in a crusade for a variety of reasons, only some of which religious. Crusades not only allowed for special taxation, but, as some IR scholars have started to point out (Blaydes and Paik, 2016), crusading could be an effective tool for rulers to legitimise themselves and assert control within their territories.

Beyond highlighting the multiple motives and dimensions of the crusades, however, an even wider body of work brings to the fore the fact that war was by no means the only mode of interaction (Costa Lopez, 2016). For starters, even within a war context such as the late-medieval Iberian Peninsula, alliances between Christian and Muslim polities were not only possible, but also frequent, as were members of different faiths fighting together (Catlos, 2014). But not only this, relations within and across the borders of Latin Christendom were much more varied, including collaboration, exchange, conflict, and strategic interaction. The point is not to counter the dramatic image of interfaith violence that usually characterises the crusades with an equally idealised notion of enlightened cooperation – *convivencia* in the traditional historiography of medieval Iberia (Soifer, 2009). Rather, border areas and exchanges offer a complex picture of coexistence and living together of different religious communities, characterised more by pragmatism and convenience: trade, collaboration, friendship occurred daily, as did conflict, and on occasion, violence. This violence moreover, cannot be reduced merely to the dimension of religion: economic conditions, political anxieties, and communal relations all played a part (Catlos, 2014). In a discipline like IR with an increasing interest in understanding communal violence (Balcells, 2017), exploring and recovering these varied lineages beyond reductionist notions of medieval religious violence is imperative.

And yet, the problem with the portrayal of the medieval as externally war-like in IR is not only solved by pointing to the multiple modes of interaction even in a crusading context. On the contrary, it is important to start by recognising that this notion of the medieval is imbricated in the construction of a common macro-historical narrative of IR: that of a progressively globalised world. The standard version of the narrative is well captured by Buzan and Lawson. In their well-known article, they set 1500 as the first primary benchmark date of IR, as it 'marked the expansion of the international system to planetary scale' and 'paved the way for the huge intensification of the global economy… during later periods' (Buzan and Lawson, 2014: 453). The point here is not to deny the significance of the opening of trans-Atlantic and Indian Ocean routes, nor is it to deny later intensifications of interaction. Rather, it is to interrogate – and challenge – how this leads to a particular understanding of the medieval in IR: a view of medieval Europe as isolated.

This narrative is increasingly being countered by a wealth of literature that, under the banner of the Global Middle Ages, highlights the crucial importance of cross-regional connections and influences in the period (Bentley, 1993; Holmes and Standen, 2018). With little reception in IR, this literature points to two important arguments: first, Latin Christendom was not isolated, but rather maintained a number of important and constant connections with various other parts of the world. From long-distance trading routes such as the medieval Silk Roads (Beckwith, 2011; Hansen, 2012) to contacts with African polities (Weber, 2015), to the broad circulation of travel narratives (Muldoon, 2010), medieval Europe neither was nor thought of itself as existing in isolation. Second, and of crucial relevance for IR, not only did these connections exist, but they were crucial for political, social, and economic evolution to the point that we cannot understand medieval Europe without unpacking its global embedding (Hobson, 2004).

The Black Death provides a case in point (see Anievas and Nişancıoğlu, 2015). We mentioned above the twelfth-century renaissance and the important socio-economic changes and demographic expansion that accompanied it. And yet, in conventional periodisations, this flourishing is said to stop in the fourteenth century, not only due to the Hundred Years' War, but also due to the devastating effect of the Black Death. An epidemic of bubonic plague between 1347 and 1353, it killed over a third of Europe's population, which did not recover until the early sixteenth century. The spread of the plague points to the fundamentally connected nature of the Medieval world. The plague originated in Mongolia, where the largest outbreaks took place. The Mongol empire was a large polity that in the thirteenth and fourteenth century controlled large portions of the Eurasian steppe (Neumann and Wigen, 2018). Contacts between Medieval Europe and the Mongols started in the thirteenth century (Jackson, 2005), both violent and diplomatic, so by the time the plague emerged, there were established trade routes and regular contacts that facilitated the transmission and spread of the epidemic. Indeed, the plague started with arrival in Venice of a fleet of merchant ships returning from trading with Mongol-connected ports in the Black Sea. This is just a brief illustrative example, but it points to the fact that the continued reproduction in IR of the locality, isolation, and war-proneness of the Middle Ages is not only historiographically untenable, but also conceptually problematic for Historical IR.

Where was the Middle Ages?

The consideration of the Global Middle Ages above highlights how the Middle Ages is not just a temporal category but also a spatial one. In what constitutes one of the clearest exercises in Eurocentrism, when we refer to the Middle Ages, we usually mean 'medieval Europe'.[2] This highlights the extent to which 'the medieval' is imbricated in the reproduction of what Lewis and Wigen call metageography: 'a set of spatial structures through which people order their knowledge of the world' (1997: ix). The problem here is not (only) the elision of Europe as the underlying unmarked category, but rather the extent to which this works to reproduce and naturalise Europe itself as an entity throughout history, both spatially and politically (see also Herborth and Nitzschner, 2021). And yet, precisely because metageographies are historical devices, historical study of past times is something that can help us challenge these underlying spatial assumptions. In what follows, I illustrate this point through two potential areas for IR to explore: the international relations of Byzantium and of the Mediterranean.

Byzantine International Relations

Byzantium constitutes an interesting case in the IR imaginary. While above we focused on debates about the end of the Middle Ages, Byzantium provides an interesting perspective on IR disciplinary narratives about the end of antiquity and the beginning of the medieval period. Indeed, as has been noted, IR texts that adopt a long-historical view most commonly start with Greece and Rome, and then jump directly to the Renaissance and the beginning of modernity. The fall of the Roman Empire is what marks the start of the Middle Ages. And yet, it is worth noting that what fell is the Western Roman Empire, for the Eastern Roman Empire, with capital in Constantinople, remained as a polity until the fifteenth century. For the first few centuries, until the rhetoric of Empire was recovered in the Latin West through the coronation of Charlemagne, the Eastern 'Greek' Roman Empire was the only part rhetorically associating itself to the classical empire. And not only this, but at least until the ninth century, when relations between Latins and Greeks equalised, there was a clear hierarchy in relations between Byzantium and the Kingdoms of the West. And yet, despite this relevance, IR has for the most part failed to take Byzantium into account.

A brief example can help illustrate the importance of Byzantium for Historical IR. A crucial argument within some constructivist approaches to the Middle Ages is the so-called Roman

Law thesis. According to it, we owe the development of the modern notion of sovereignty to the rediscovery of Roman Law, for this would have provided a notion of either private property (Kratochwil, 1995) or representation (Holland, 2010) upon which sovereignty could be based. In doing so, once again, a direct link is established between modern politics and classical Antiquity that presents the Middle Ages as parenthetical period. A brief look at what is meant by Roman Law, however, reveals the ways in which this is founded upon a specific imagination of Europe: for 'Roman Law' in this narrative is nothing but a set of legal compilations ordered in the sixth century by Emperor Justinian I, who ruled the Byzantine empire from 527 to 565 A.D. The *Corpus Iuris Civilis* as used in the late Middle Ages[3] included three compilations commissioned by Justinian which put together the teachings of classical-age jurists (Digest), compiled the fundamental laws of the Empire (Codex) and summarised the Digest as a textbook (Institutes). The fourth book (Novellae) was compiled later, but also during Justinian's reign, in order to update the Codex. By eliding this history, not only does IR instantiate a specific spatial imaginary whereby only Western Europe counts in the evolution of international relations, but the fundamental role of Byzantine thought and political practice is elided: for these compilations both mediated the transmission of the thought of classical jurists – by selecting which excerpts were included – but they also contained a large amount of distinctly byzantine law, and thus political thought.

Realising this is important because it draws attention to the fact that by eliding these histories not only is IR creating a historically problematic narrative about its evolution, nor is it only reproducing a specific spatial imaginary, but is also missing the opportunity to explore an entirely different tradition of international thought and practice. Indeed, spanning over a millennium, the Byzantine empire was an entire, evolving political system, with a complex system of relations with a variety of polities (see Shepard, 2019) towards both East and West. Byzantium had a very developed diplomatic system, including distinct practices and a specific diplomatic corps, which is usually overlooked by standard accounts of the emergence of diplomacy (Mattingly, 1988; Shepard and Franklin, 1992). And as the example of Justinian's compilations shows, it had developed traditions of political thought that, while also drawing on the Roman imperial experience, constituted an independent tradition (Nicol, 1988). Historical IR would thus do well to explore this polity in its search for alternative historical imaginaries.

The Medieval Mediterranean

And yet, as Holmes and Standen note, 'the risk here is the acceptance of [other] regions into the Middle Ages only if they are demonstrably different from Europe, a position which paradoxically maintains the normative character of the European Middle Ages as the ones that really count' (2018: 18). Indeed, challenging the Eurocentrism in the notion of the medieval is not only about focusing on hitherto ignored locations, but also thinking spatially differently. There is indeed a long tradition in medieval history of thinking alternative geographies that has until now received little attention in IR. Starting with Braudel's *La Mediterranée et le Monde*, the history of the medieval Mediterranean is a burgeoning area of study.[4]

First, placing the Mediterranean centre-stage leads to an analytics of connections that can help us transcend substantivist approaches in Historical IR that have tended to focus on polities (Jackson and Nexon, 1999). Venetian and north-African traders and their networks and enclaves, missionary movements, or privateers are but a few of the groups that come to the fore if we analyse patterns of connection and exchange in the sea (Abulafia, 2011; Goldberg, 2012). From a cultural perspective, the Mediterranean constitutes an area of strong interaction, leading some to place the emphasis on patterns of 'mutual intelligibility' (Catlos and Kinoshita, 2017). Indeed, the frequent exchange led for example to the emergence of the *lingua franca*, a simplified version of Italian with Arabic and Spanish influences that enabled communication and trade (Mallette, 2014). Finally, a distinctive strand takes the notion of environmental history seriously[5] and thinks the Mediterranean as a distinctive ecological system, where topographical features interact in historically-specific ways with human activity (Horden and Purcell, 2000). Doing so is interesting not only because it affords a completely different spatiality based on ecological features, but also because it serves to destabilise periodisations by adopting a wider, transhistorical view.

The medieval Mediterranean thus points to the potential for IR not only to discover new historical modes of relations, but also to further new analytics that through focus on different spatial imaginations, such as water basins, can help develop new conceptual possibilities and challenge the conceptual essentialisms that underpin the discipline (Phillips and Sharman, 2015; Guillaume and Costa Lopez, 2021).

Conclusion

This chapter started by pointing to the infrequent yet fundamental role of the Middle Ages in both the historical narratives of origin of IR and in underpinning the conceptual apparatus of the discipline. The 'medieval' functions as the constant, unified Other for modern international relations unto which a variety of images of what we are *not* can be projected. The fact that this goes beyond historical narratives and encompasses the core conceptual apparatus of IR makes this problem extremely difficult to tackle, for if Kathleen Davies is correct, and the core concepts of sovereignty and colonialism contain in themselves the exclusion of the medieval, how can the discipline even begin to tackle the period with its conceptual apparatus? It would seem that we should just conclude that attempting to unpack medieval international relations is an anachronism in itself, which historically minded people should stay clear of (Herborth, 2021). And yet, it is precisely because its role is at once so fundamental and difficult to tackle, that the historical and conceptual pay-off of the medieval for historical IR is so high.

Suggestions for further reading

Bain, W. (2017). *Medieval Foundations of International Relations*. London, Routledge.
Canning, J. (2011). *Ideas of Power in the Late Middle Ages, 1296–1417*. Cambridge: Cambridge University Press.
Holmes, C., and Standen, N., eds. (2018). The Global Middle Ages. *Past & Present*, Supplement 13.
Valérian, D. (2014). The Medieval Mediterranean. In: P. Horden, and S. Kinoshita, eds., *A Companion to Mediterranean History*, Oxford, Blackwell: 77–90.
Watts, J. (2009). *The Making of Polities: Europe, 1300–1500*. Cambridge: Cambridge University Press.

Notes

1 The literature on the crusades is vast. A good classical entry point is Riley-Smith (2005).
2 There are of course literatures concerning other places that also use the notion of the Middle Ages, most notably a Marxist-inspired sociological literature on Tokugawa society in Japan (Ikegami, 1995). Although this is usually done in an effort to decentre Europe (Guillaume, 2014: 4), it still reproduces the connection between the Middle Ages, Europe, and feudalism.
3 One would need to start by making the precision that, although IR has situated this process in the Early Modern period, Roman Law was 'rediscovered' in the Latin West in the twelfth century, in the context of the cultural changes mentioned above.
4 Approaches within Mediterranean History are extremely varied (for a critical review see Horden, 2017).
5 The theoretical sophistication of this strand of literature serves as a good corrective to any stereotyped notion of historians as merely doing ideographic work.

References

Abulafia, D. (2011). *The Great Sea: a Human History of the Mediterranean*. Oxford: Oxford University Press.

Alkopher, T. D. (2005). The social (and religious) meanings that constitute war: the Crusades as Realpolitik vs. Socialpolitik. *International Studies Quarterly*, 49 (4), 715–737.

Anievas, A., and Nişancıoğlu, K. (2015). *How the West Came to Rule. The Geopolitical Origins of Capitalism*. London: Pluto Press.

Bagge, S. (1997). Medieval and renaissance historiography: break or continuity? *The European Legacy* 2 (8), 1336–1371.

Balcells, L. (2017). *Rivalry and Revenge: the Politics of Violence During Civil War*. Cambridge: Cambridge University Press.

Barber, M. (2012). *The Crusader States*. New Haven, CT: Yale University Press.

Beckwith, C. I. (2011). *Empires of the Silk Road: A History of Central Eurasia from the Bronze Age to the Present*. Princeton, NJ: Princeton University Press.

Bellomo, M. (1995). *The Common Legal Past of Europe. 1000–1800*. Washington, DC: The Catholic University of America Press.

Benson, R. L., Constable, G., and Lanham, C. D. (1987). *Renaissance and Renewal in the Twelfth Century*. Cambridge, MA: Harvard University Press.

Bentley, J. H. (1993). *Old World Encounters: Cross-Cultural Contacts and Exchanges in Pre-Modern Times*. New York, NY: Oxford University Press.

Black, A. (1992). *Political Thought in Europe 1250–1450*. Cambridge: Cambridge University Press.

Blaydes, L., and Paik, C. (2016). The impact of holy land crusades on state formation: war mobilization, trade integration, and political development in Medieval Europe. *International Organization*, 70 (3), 551–586.

Brundage, J. A. (2008). *The Medieval Origins of the Legal Profession. Canonists, Civilians, and Courts*. Chicago, IL: Chicago University Press.

Bruneau, Q. P. (2021). Constructivism: History and Systemic Change. In de Carvalho, B., Costa Lopez, J., & Leira, H., eds. *Routledge Handbook of Historical International Relations*. Abingdon: Routledge.

Bull, H. (2012). *The Anarchical Society. A Study of Order in World Politics*. New York, NY: Palgrave Macmillan.

Buzan, B., and Albert, M. (2010). Differentiation: a sociological approach to international relations theory. *European Journal of International Relations*, 16 (3), 315–337.

Buzan, B., and Lawson, G. (2014). Rethinking benchmark dates in international relations. *European Journal of International Relations*, 20 (2), 437–462.

Buzan, B., and Lawson, G. (2015). *The Global Transformation: History, Modernity and the Making of International Relations*. Cambridge: Cambridge University Press.

Catlos, B. (2014). *Infidel Kings and Unholy Warriors. Faith, Power, and Violence in the Age of Crusade and Jihad*. New York, NY: Farrar, Straus and Giroux.

Catlos, B. A. (2014). *Muslims of Medieval Latin Christendom, c. 1050–1614*. Cambridge: Cambridge University Press.

Catlos, B. A., and Kinoshita, S. (2017). *Can We Talk Mediterranean? Conversations on an Emerging Field in Medieval and Early Modern Studies*. Cham, Switzerland: Palgrave Macmillan.

Costa Lopez, J. (2016). Beyond eurocentrism and orientalism: revisiting the othering of Jews and Muslims through medieval canon law. *Review of International Studies*, 42 (3), 450–470.

Costa Lopez, J. (2020). Political authority in international relations: revisiting the medieval debate. *International Organization*, 74 (2), 222–252.

Costa Lopez, J., de Carvalho, B., Latham, A. A., Zarakol, A., Bartelson, J., and Holm, M. (2018). Forum: in the beginning there was no word (for it): terms, concepts, and early sovereignty. *International Studies Review*, 20 (3), 489–519.

Davis, K. (2008). *Periodization and Sovereignty: How Ideas of Feudalism and Secularization Govern the Politics of Time*. Philadelphia, PA: University of Pennsylvania Press.

de Carvalho, B., Leira, H., and Hobson, J. M. (2011). The Big Bangs of IR: the myths that your teachers still tell you about 1648 and 1919. *Millennium – Journal of International Studies*, 39 (3), 735–758.

Deibert, R. J. (1997). 'Exorcismus Theoriae': pragmatism, metaphors and the return of the medieval in IR theory. *European Journal of International Relations*, 3 (2), 167–192.

Fischer, M. (1992). Feudal Europe, 800–1300: communal discourse and conflictual practices. *International Organization*, 46 (2), 427–466.

Friedrichs, J. (2001). The meaning of new Medievalism. *European Journal of International Relations*, 7 (4), 475–501.

Goldberg, J. (2012). *Trade and Institutions in the Medieval Mediterranean: The Geniza Merchants and Their Business World*. Cambridge: Cambridge University Press.

Grzymala-Busse, A. (2019). Beyond war and contracts: the medieval and religious roots of the European state. *Annual Review of Political Science*, 23 (1), 19–36.

Guillaume, X. (2014). *International Relations and Identity: A Dialogical Approach*. Abingdon: Routledge.

Guillaume, X. (2021). Historical Periods and the Act of Periodisation. In de Carvalho, B., Costa Lopez, J., & Leira, H., eds. *Routledge Handbook of Historical International Relations*. Abingdon: Routledge.

Guillaume, X., and Costa Lopez, J. (2021). International Terraqueous Relations. In: B. de Carvalho, and H. Leira, eds., *The Sea in International Relations*, Manchester: Manchester University Press.

Hall, R. B. (1997). Moral authority as a power resource. *International Organization*, 51 (4), 591–622.

Hall, R. B., and Kratochwil, F. V. (1993). Medieval tales: neorealist 'science' and the abuse of history. *International Organization*, 47 (3), 479–491.

Hansen, V. (2012). *The Silk Road: A New History*. Oxford: Oxford University Press.

Herborth, B. (2021). Denying the international. *Cambridge Review of International Affairs*. Forthcoming.

Herborth, B. and Nitzschner, P. (2021). Europe In Historial International Relations. In de Carvalho, B., Costa Lopez, J., & Leira, H., eds. *Routledge Handbook of Historical International Relations*. Abingdon: Routledge.

Hobson, J. M. (2004). *The Eastern Origins of Western Civilisation*. Cambridge: Cambridge University Press.

Holland, B. (2010). Sovereignty as *Dominium*? Reconstructing the constructivist Roman law thesis. *International Studies Quarterly*, 54 (2), 449–480.

Holmes, C. and Standen, N. (2018). Introduction: towards a global Middle Ages. *Past & Present*, 238 (Supplement 13), 1–44.

Horden, P. (2017). The Maritime, the Ecological, the Cultural—and the Fig Leaf: Prospects for Medieval Mediterranean Studies. In: B. A. Catlos and S. Kinoshita, eds., *Can We Talk Mediterranean? Conversations on an Emerging Field in Medieval and Early Modern Studies*, Cham: Springer, 65–79.

Horden, P., and Purcell, N. (2000). *The corrupting sea: a study of Mediterranean history*. Oxford: Blackwell.

Ikegami, E. (1995). *The Taming of the Samurai: Honorific Individualism and the Making of Modern Japan*. Cambridge, MA: Harvard University Press.

Jackson, P. (2005). *The Mongols and the West, 1221–1410*. Harlow: Pearson/Longman.

Jackson, P. T., and Nexon, D. H. (1999). Relations before states: substance, process and the study of world politics. *European Journal of International Relations*, 5 (3), 291–332.

Jahn, B. (2000). *The Cultural Construction of International Relations: the Invention of the State of Nature*. Basingstoke: Palgrave.

Kempshall, M. S. (1999). *The Common Good in Late Medieval Political Thought*. Oxford: Clarendon Press.

Kessler, O. (2021). Conceptual History in International Relations: From Ideology to Social Theory?. In de Carvalho, B., Costa Lopez, J., & Leira, H., eds. *Routledge Handbook of Historical International Relations*. Abingdon: Routledge.

Kratochwil, F. V. (1995). Sovereignty as *Dominium*: Is There a Right of Humanitarian Intervention? In: G. M. Lyons, and M. Mastanduno, eds., *Beyond Westphalia? State sovereignty and international intervention*, Baltimore, MD: Johns Hopkins University Press, 21–42.

Latham, A. A. (2011). Theorizing the Crusades: identity, institutions, and religious war in Medieval Latin Christendom. *International Studies Quarterly*, 55 (1), 223–243.

Latham, A. A. (2012). *Theorizing Medieval Geopolitics. War and World Order in the Age of the Crusades*. New York, NY: Routledge.

Le Goff, J. (2018). What did the Twelfth-Century Renaissance *Mean*? In: P. Linehan, J. L. Nelson, and N. Costambeis, eds., *The Medieval World*, London: Routledge, 734–745.

Lewis, M. W., and Wigen, K. E. (1997). *The Myth of Continents. A Critique of Metageography*. Berkeley: University of California Press.

Mallette, K. (2014). Lingua Franca. In: P. Horden, and S. Kinoshita, eds., *A Companion to Mediterranean History*, Oxford: Blackwell, 330–344.

Mattingly, G. (1988). *Renaissance Diplomacy*. New York, NY: Dover Publications.

Maxwell, K. (1993). The Atlantic in the eighteenth century: a southern perspective on the need to return to the 'Big Picture'. *Transactions of the Royal Historical Society*, 3, 209–236.

Muldoon, J. (2010). *Travellers, Intellectuals, and the World Beyond Medieval Europe*. Farnham: Ashgate Publishing Limited.

Nederman, C. J. (1996). The meaning of "Aristotelianism" in medieval moral and political thought. *Journal of the History of Ideas*, 57 (4), 563–585.

Nederman, C. J. (2009). *Lineages of European Political Thought: Explorations Along the Medieval/Modern Divide from John of Salisbury to Hegel.* Washington, DC: Catholic University of America Press.

Neumann, I. B., and Wigen, E. (2018). *The Steppe Tradition in International Relations: Russians, Turks and European State Building 4000 BCE–2017 CE.* Cambridge: Cambridge University Press.

Nicol, D. M. (1988). Byzantine Political Thought. In: J. H. Burns, ed., *The Cambridge History of Medieval Political Thought c.350–c.1450*, Cambridge: Cambridge University Press, 49–80.

Osiander, A. (2001a). Before sovereignty: society and politics in Ancien Regime Europe. *Review of International Studies*, 27 (5), 119–145.

Osiander, A. (2001b). Sovereignty, international relations, and the Westphalian myth. *International Organization*, 55 (2), 251–287.

Osiander, A. (2007). *Before the State. Systemic Political Change in the West from the Greeks to the French Revolution.* Oxford: Oxford University Press.

Pennington, K. (1993). *The Prince and the Law, 1200–1600. Sovereignty and Rights in the Western Legal Tradition.* Berkeley: University of California Press.

Phillips, A. (2010). *War, Religion and Empire: The Transformation of International Orders.* Cambridge: Cambridge University Press.

Phillips, A., and Sharman, J. C. (2015). *International Order in Diversity: War, Trade and Rule in the Indian Ocean.* Cambridge: Cambridge University Press.

Reynolds, S. (1994). *Fiefs and Vassals. The Medieval Evidence Reinterpreted.* Oxford: Oxford University Press.

Riley-Smith, J. (2005). *The Crusades: A History.* London: Continuum.

Ruggie, J. G. (1993). Territoriality and beyond: problematizing modernity in international relations. *International Organization*, 47 (1), 139–174.

Shepard, J. (2019). Approaching Byzantium. In: J. Shepard, ed., *The Cambridge History of the Byzantine Empire c.500–1492.* Cambridge: Cambridge University Press, 2–20.

Shepard, J., and Franklin, S. (1992). *Byzantine Diplomacy: Papers from the Twenty-fourth Spring Symposium of Byzantine Studies, Cambridge, March 1990.* Ashgate: Variorum.

Soifer, M. (2009). Beyond convivencia: critical reflections on the historiography of interfaith relations in Christian Spain. *Journal of Medieval Iberian Studies*, 1 (1), 19–35.

Southern, R. W. (1995). *Scholastic Humanism and the Unification of Europe. Vol. I: Foundations.* Oxford: Blackwell.

Sumption, J. (2011). *The Albigensian Crusade.* London: Faber & Faber.

Teschke, B. (1998). Geopolitical relations in the European Middle Ages: history and theory. *International Organization*, 52 (2), 325–358.

Teschke, B. (2003). *The Myth of 1648: Class, Geopolitics, and The Making of Modern International relations.* London: Verso.

Tierney, B. (1964). *The Crisis of Church and State, 1050–1300.* Englewood Cliffs, NJ: Prentice-Hall.

Weber, B. (2015). An incomplete integration into the Orbis Christianus. Relations and Misunderstandings between the Papacy and Ethiopia (1237–1456). *Medieval Encounters*, 21 (2–3), 232–249.

Wickham, C. (2016). *Medieval Europe.* New Haven, CT: Yale University Press.

39

EARLY (MODERN) EMPIRES

The political ideology of conceptual domination

Mauro J. Caraccioli

Much has been written about theories of empire in the last two decades.[1] Indeed, the prodigious outbreak of scholarly turns, moments, and calls to arms have made the word as difficult to define as *culture, nature,* or, in recent times, *globalization* (Burbank and Cooper, 2011; Ghosh, 2012; Immerwahr, 2019). Yet despite the proliferation of contemporary works attending to history's multiple imperial moments, providing a definition for empire doesn't seem to be the problem, but rather how to use it as a concept. Asking scholars to think *contextually* about empire seems ironically less helpful in this regard. The requisite periodization of the term's meanings often leads to debates concerning the risks of anachronism, instead of tracing the continuities and ruptures between imperialism's many constitutive parts. Empire, as presumed, has brought together many viewpoints under its shadow, but to very little unity (see the discussion in Guillaume 2021 in this volume).[2]

To study the so-called early empires presents an added difficulty for historians of ideas. For one, it is impossible to write the history of an empire without considering how its emergence made particular models of historical inquiry possible (Cañizares-Esguerra, 2006b; Ince, 2018; Wigen, 2018). Second, and more problematic, is how the moniker 'early' applies to the so-called ancient past (see Knutsen, 2021 in this volume) as much as to the 'early modern' empires of the sixteenth century. That ambiguity, I will contend, was itself exploited by writers of the early modern world, as they sought to fashion a set of New World empires in the idealized form of imperial antiquity, but with the contents of an entirely novel set of tools and practices.

In this chapter, I look to the study of early empires as one such type of conceptual narrative, in particular the ways that modern empires have justified their logics of conceptual domination. As imperial missions became more ambitious in territorial scope, scholars in sixteenth-century and seventeenth-century empires engaged the historical craft in order to paint their own endeavours as continuations (more so than revivals) of past imperial conquests (Pocock, 2001–2015; Cañizares-Esguerra, 2001; MacCormack, 2007; Morefield, 2014). Although practical demands on imperial governance dramatically differ across empires and scholarly intentions, the ideological ethos remains curiously consistent: *the modern is used as a means to revive the past, but the past buttresses the modern in unexpected ways.* While many have argued that such dynamics form part of the illocutionary force of all political acts, my aims go further than rhetorical reconstruction. As part of the Cambridge School approach to intellectual history – only recently engaged by International Relations (IR) scholars – contextualist inquiry traditionally focuses on the polemical circumstances under which terms like sovereignty, civilization, and even empire are strategically used for various (often contradictory) purposes (Kalmo and Skinner, 2011). To establish an empire is to tell the story of how people have been conquered. More than this, however, imperial dominance is crystallized by having those same subjects tell the story of their conquest in new and adaptive ways (Owensby, 2008; Rabasa, 2011; Premo, 2017). Writing about empire therefore entails focusing on dimensions of language that go beyond examining primary sources, to also conveying how key concepts in a story are linked and delinked over time.

Recent scholarship in Imperial Studies and Political Theory has shown that imperialism is more than a territorial and ideological project; it is a conceptual one as well (Bell, 2016; Daggett, 2018; Getachew, 2019; see also Bayly 2021 in this volume). As Historical IR evolves more consciously into an interdisciplinary field, it is useful to place previously told stories about empire and IR in conversation with those found in cognate disciplines (see Go et al., 2021 in this volume). I begin by mapping, reviewing, and categorizing some of the foundational texts and debates over the proper definition of empire within contemporary IR. I then go on to illustrate the ways in which scholars of Historical IR can draw on transdisciplinary encounters with areas such as the history of science to think of early modern empires in a more co-constitutive light. Lastly, I draw on recent advances in the study of Colonial Spanish America as a concrete illustration of how early (modern) empires act as projects of conceptual domination. Specifically, I showcase how the natural history of the New World served an indispensable role in forming the allegedly timeless imaginary of the early Spanish Empire. As others have maintained, the idea of an Old World transforming the New has given way to an Atlantic paradigm that looks at the colonization of the Americas as a transformative experience for Europe's intellectual and ideological horizons of possibility (Seed, 1995: 69–99; Cañizares-Esguerra, 2001: 63–102; Simon, 2017: 3–14). That adaptation, I conclude, serves as a reminder that imperial memories reveal not just the motivation for new societies but also new theories.

How to write the history of IR and empire

To begin, a brief clarification on what I mean by 'early' empires. My central intellectual wager is that imperial power takes on a distinctive character in the sixteenth and seventeenth centuries, most notably in the Americas and their transformation of European norms of historical inquiry (Caraccioli, 2021). The reasons have as much to do with distinct Spanish, British, and French attempts to rhetorically claim a Greco-Roman inheritance, as they do with the realities of governance in unknown, far-off lands. Writing any history of empire thus entails the reconstruction of the assumed possibilities and boundaries of imperialism – both are exercises in imagination. To be more precise, however, there's something methodologically counterintuitive (but I would say rewarding) about going back into the past to reflect on the hegemonic projects of empire-building and, indeed, empire-writing. Through a kind of reflexive historiography, we can understand not just the relationship between empires' past and present but also, as I will show, the beginnings of a global political theory of empire that is attentive to the future.

Despite the recent growth of IR scholarship on imperialism, proliferation has not brought about greater clarity on the normative logics of empire. Various examples focus on what empire means in the context of American hegemony, as well as how to engage in meta-analyses of empires' past and present. However, these are views located strictly *within the borders* of an empire (Nexon and Wright, 2007; Andersen, 2016) or *comparatively* across regions (Shirk, 2017; Mulich, 2020). To be fair, this is a monumental task given the range of available sources, approaches, and phases one can observe. Yet while IR as a scholarly field was born out of the concerns of colonial administrators and different forms of imperial rule (Vitalis, 2015), much of its academic production has turned a blind eye to questions of normativity. As Brian Schmidt notes, a way to remedy this oversight is by studying various discourses about imperialism and colonialism generated by IR scholars, as these '[provide] an opening to investigate the way in which identities are constructed in the field of international relations and how particular subjects are either included or excluded from its purview' (Schmidt, 1998: 235).

For contemporary IR scholars, much of the interest in empire has a twofold, divergent trajectory: the intellectual historiography first generated by E.H. Carr's *The Twenty Years' Crisis* (1964) and the multiple immersions into international history produced by scholars like Isaac Deutscher (1985); see also: Rosenberg 1996), Stanley Hoffmann (1977), and Michael Doyle (1986). The early Realist hagiography of figures as seemingly disparate as Thucydides, Machiavelli, and Hobbes produced a variant of scholarship focused on the timeless qualities of Greco-Roman grandeur and its potential as a mirror for the present imperial moment. The concern with 'might over right' was not just a materialist insight, but also one interested in the relation between powerful forces and powerful ideas. As one recent volume puts it, 'Just as the end of the Cold War, in which Thucydides had been read as the key text for understanding a bipolar world, led not to the abandonment of the [*History of the Peloponnesian War*] but to its reinterpretation as a crucial text for understanding a multi-polar, anarchic world, so the failure of a foreign policy sanctioned by Thucydides has led not to the abandonment of the text but to its re-appropriation and redeployment in new contexts for new purposes' (Lee and Morley, 2015: 2; see also: Murray, 1997: 33–46). Over time, however, empire became a kind of shadow of itself, a 'second image' facet of broader international structures defined by anarchy (Waltz, 1977: 20–27). Kenneth Waltz (among others) relegated existing theories of imperialism to 'reductionist' readings of global politics, insufficiently scientific to account for the systemic character of IR, where '[the] whole is understood by studying its elements in their relative simplicity and by observing the relations between them' (Waltz, 1977: 39). Against the parsimony of Waltz, scholars like Doyle understood the relation between empire and the study of IR as a disorienting endeavour: 'empire turns on their heads the central insights of international relations theorists. Imperialism's foundation, is not anarchy, but order, albeit an *order* imposed and strained' (Doyle, 1986: 11). In that ideology of imposition, Doyle recognized that the constituent features of empire are ungeneralizable, making it 'impossible to address the question of how empires were established and maintained, and how they fell, without resort to historical narration' (Doyle, 1986: 13). To that end, Doyle's observations left the matter of empire's significance for global politics up for rhetorical debate, rather than engaging in any sustained meditation on what the narration of empires affords historians of imperialism.

Missing in early foundational accounts of empire therefore was a reflection on why this type of historical exercise was particularly appealing to our scholarly community? For Waltz, it was about science; for Doyle, it was about scholarly humility. Neither acknowledges the imperial moment they were writing in, with IR scholars increasingly compelled to offer policy relevance to a US government poised to take full advantage of Soviet decline. This is what Hoffmann (among others) tried to first draw attention to when he described America as 'the one-eyed leading the cripples'. Political scientists, he warned, were guilty of translating an emergent international system as a way of making power tangible, 'either because they want it…or because they fear it and want to understand the monster […] And in the postwar years, what part of power was more interesting than the imperial bit?' (Hoffmann, 1977: 47). Being 'too close to the fire', Hoffmann reasoned, should bring the fragmented discipline of IR, 'if not together, at least in perspective' (Hoffmann, 1977: 59). What the paradoxes of the world (and the field) unequivocally illustrated was the desperate need for greater historical reflection.

None of this is new for scholars of Historical IR. Yet returning to Hoffmann's warnings of imperial presentism can nevertheless help those of us studying imperial histories today by recognizing that the conceptual baggage of empire is too heavy to engage on our own (Morefield, 2014; Dahl, 2018). Rather than thinking about empire as a source of hierarchical wisdom or our disciplinary pathologies, we should think about past theories of empire and imperialism as reflexive vocabularies to understand evolving ideologies of conquest. In the next section, I examine how IR scholars have attempted that investigation through the inversion of the imperial narrative of civilization and greater attention to empire's contexts of production.

Dissident historiography and the early modern past

Between the late 1980s and early 2000s, dissident IR scholarship (broadly labelled 'Critical IR' today) brought back the reality of American Empire to journals and texts across the Anglosphere. Very few of its advocates, however, delved into the historiography of earlier empires, not least the early modern ones. Two exceptions bookending this period are David Campbell's *Writing Security: United States Foreign Policy and the Politics of Identity* (1992) and Beate Jahn's *The Cultural Construction of International Relations: The Invention of the State of Nature* (2000). Both texts engaged the great Debate at Valladolid (1550–1551) between the Dominican friar Bartolomé de Las Casas (1484–1566) and the notorious jurist Ginés de Sepulveda (1494–1573) over the conduct of Spanish conquest in the sixteenth century. The debate is deemed as the first modern altercation between advocates for 'Just War' against the New World's indigenous peoples (Sepulveda) and defenders of imperial tutelage for indigenous peoples as extension of European Christendom (Las Casas). It also served IR scholars as a conceptual vehicle to make sense of questions of cultural incommensurability.

Campbell saw the European and New World encounter as a foundational moment in the birth of a narrative of identity and difference, calling it 'an imaginary on the horizons of European thought that prepared the grounds for later encounters' (Campbell, 1992: 106; Alker, 1992). His analysis painted modern forms of empire as continuations of Civilization's battle against Barbarism. Going beyond Campbell, however, Jahn raised the bar for IR scholars to think empirically about the past, urging us to locate deeply held beliefs and misconceptions of modern political thought, including the identity/difference dichotomy, as 'based directly or indirectly on a variety of interpretations of the state of nature identified with and to be empirically studied among Amerindian peoples' (Jahn, 2000: xiv).

The Conquest of the New World was thus not just a conceptual crucible for international theory, but an empirical one as well in need of demystification. Jahn's thesis would require, in her words, disrupting 'two commonly held beliefs [...] the common representation of modern political and social thought, domestic and international, as an endogenously European cultural development', on the one hand, and on the other, 'that the distinction between political and international theory is based on [...] a basic difference between the "nature" of international politics and the "nature" of domestic politics' (Jahn, 2000: xiv–xv). While one of Imperial Spain's most long-standing contributions to the canon of Western political thought is the concept of a state of nature, contemporary accounts of its origins largely circumvent the evangelizing, anthropological, and naturalist work that informs it. A broader understanding of that empirical foundation would help clarify the concept's political implications and its divergent trajectories.

Neither Spain's imperial objectives nor the pagan practices of Amerindians represented enough reason to have the legal debates over the humanity of indigenous peoples. Indeed, Jahn argues, it was the very challenge of New World environments to 'the cultural meaning of the world – established through European historical experiences and interpreted through the prism of the Christian faith' that justified having the argument (Jahn, 2000: 35). Yet while Jahn's text captures a formative moment in the break with the medieval world and the construction of a conceptual state of nature, it is perhaps also an illustrative example of the types of readings that Historical IR must be careful to engage with and unpack. Jahn's account, for example, cuts itself off from its historical referent at the moment where perhaps the culture-nature dynamic it deploys is at its most tense and profound – at the cusp of what historians of Colonial Spanish America call the Spiritual Conquest (Jahn, 2000: 113–131). Rather than asking how knowledge about the New World was produced and used to buttress a future empire, Jahn instead focuses on how this process of knowledge formation helps establish the IR's epistemic core.

Much of IR's relation to imperial knowledge is characterized by similarly ambitious, though ambivalent conclusions. As contemporary critics have shown, IR's replacement of empire with the concept of anarchy was an expression of the juridical inequality that shaped relations between 'civilized' and 'barbaric' territories (Zarakol, 2011; see also Bayly, 2021 in this volume). Yet between Campbell and Jahn's work, there were also several important historiographical efforts to document that fascination with hierarchies of inequality. David Boucher's *Political Theories of International Relations* (1998), for example, traces the intellectual development of IR thought across 2,000 years of the Western intellectual canon. Boucher himself does not broadly reflect on the imperial question, however, except to note the missed opportunities it offered for IR scholars and political theorists to join forces and become 'acutely aware of the issues to which a system or community of sovereign states gave rise' (Boucher, 1998: 6). Instead of cultivating this dialogue, he concludes, theorists of international politics, unlike political theorists in the classical sense, 'developed their own vocabulary and concepts, indifferent to the overtures from some of the most significant political philosophers of the twentieth century' (Boucher, 1998: 6).

Much of that indifference changed at the turn of the millennium. Several changes in the sociology of the discipline led to the popularization of more interpretivist approaches to histories of imperialism. The *Borderlines* series published by the University of Minnesota Press accelerated the so-called Cultural Turn in IR, highlighting the richness of postcolonial and continental theorizing in global politics and shifting historical theorizing away from the Anglophone world (Rojas, 2001; Anand, 2007; Da Silva, 2007). Additionally, the publication of Michael Hardt and Antonio Negri's *Empire* (2000) moved the analytic lens of imperialism towards new and rich horizons, sparking a resurgence in the intellectual origins of empire as, 'the political subject that effectively regulates…global exchanges, the sovereign power that governs the world' (Hardt and Negri, 2000: xi). Key foundational myths of IR's imperial past – such as the Peace of Westphalia in 1648 (Teschke, 2003), as well as the so-called secularization ethos of the territorial state (Nexon, 2009) – were increasingly challenged. Indeed, greater analysis of IR's assumptions and misconceptions concerning the early modern past brought greater attention to the methodologies of imperial writing and its overlap with intellectual history. As David Armitage has noted, the long-awaited return of history into the study of international relations highlighted 'the maturity of the history of international thought as a subfield of intellectual history' and in the process has opened 'new conversations between historians, political theorists, International Relations scholars and international lawyers which would be continuous with those before the modern contest of the faculties drove them so forcefully, though not irreversibly, apart' (Armitage, 2004: 109). Today's scholarly landscape clearly reflects this opening of conversations, with greater work in Historical IR looking beyond questions of sovereignty, anarchy, and institutionalism to include legal pluralism, religious identity, and settler colonialism, among other themes broadly part of an eclectic, contextualist revival (Barder, 2015; Agmon, 2017; Bishara, 2017; McLarren and Stahl, 2020).

Armitage's hopefulness aside, however, Historical IR's theoretical and transdisciplinary richness has only started to tackle the question of how scholars of the past wrote the histories of their imperial projects or for that matter the *histories written by imperial subjects* (Fuerst, 2018). It has barely scratched the surface of how scholars today reproduce tenacious tropes and grand narratives of the past that buttress (if not vindicate) the current state of the world and the field (de Carvalho et al., 2011). Across recent IR work on empire is the ambition to engage the richness of history from the vantage point of constituent elements, events, and discourses, more so than the prefigured writings and refinements of intellectuals of statecraft (Guillaume, 2011). Yet for all its attention to multiple analytic registers, the emphasis on 'interdependent' contexts nevertheless remains at the level of established histories that reflect the concerns of the present rather than the innovations of the past. This type of analytic confidence over terms such as 'global', 'modernity', and even 'world history' allows scholars to make such claims as, 'Global modernity pulled the world into a single system, within which the consequences of the changes in the mode and distribution of power were widely and deeply felt…Not until the nineteenth century did the world become a global system in which core states could quickly and decisively project the new mode of power around the world' (Buzan and Lawson, 2015: 2). What does that type of contextualism offer beyond a focus on 'great thinkers' or 'great ideas' in service of IR's perpetually reimagined aspirations as a science – social or otherwise? Instead, what would it look like to do a history of empire for IR scholars that begins with the agents and ordinary subjects of empire rather than our contemporary predilections?

Faith, science, history: early empires as conceptual domination

To better illustrate this dilemma between the writers and thinkers of imperial history, I turn here to the Spanish Conquest of the New World. Much like Tzvetan Todorov (1999) did with his monumental book, *The Conquest of America: The Question of the Other* (first published in 1982), my goal here is not to focus on the macro-narratives that shaped the contexts of the encounter. Instead, I want to offer a micro-political portrait (Subotic, 2020) of a group of imperial missionaries tasked with making sense of the New World's seemingly boundless possibilities. Part of a broader series of debates, exchanges, and disputes over the proper means of documenting the New World's peoples and natural environments, Spanish Catholic missionaries engaged in a distinctly empirical transformation of historical writing. In the process, they attempted to craft a new narrative for empire that blended past and present.

By melding faith, empiricism, and empire, these same missionaries would transform how Europeans would imagine the Americas, but also how both British and Spanish American thinkers would theorize New World politics (Brading, 1993; Cañizares-Esguerra, 2006a). I should say at the outset that the sixteenth-century revival of Greco-Roman ideals, practices, and methods such as astronomy, botany, zoology, pharmacology, and particularly natural history was an emergent process with a peculiar cultural and uneven development across Southern Europe. In this regard, Imperial Spain was both at the cusp of so-called Renaissance ideals, but also slow to adapt its unique religious and territorial dynamics (Pagden, 1988). Natural history in particular was an especially exemplary field of narrative inquiry, with various writings by chroniclers, explorers, and, most notably, missionaries laying out a distinct set of empirical foundations for modern political thinking, especially as these studies developed through the New World's colonization. To that end, I want to propose reading natural history as a distinct genre of early modern political thinking, with a global trajectory born out of the various cultures of study and translation emerging in the sixteenth century (Marroquín Arredondo and Bauer, 2019).

At its height, Imperial Spain claimed possession over the largest known territorial expanse of its time. Yet the culture of state secrecy that shaped its scientific endeavours remains an obstacle for historical interpretation (Goodman, 2002; Portuondo, 2009: 103–108). Although knowledge-accumulation was encouraged, *knowledge-dissemination* proved far more politically risky. Yet there are broader institutional dynamics to account for as well. As John H. Elliot has documented, one of the most influential myths of our age of sovereign states is to overplay the extent to which territorial unity is the *de jure* governing principle of modernity. Instead, Elliot points to the history of 'composite states' across the fifteenth and sixteenth centuries as an alternative (and at the time desirable) path of political aggrandizement. In this composite model, units with a strong administrative core, '[coexisted] with a myriad smaller territorial and jurisdictional units jealously guarding their independent status' (Elliot, 2009: 6). Hence the model of national histories is not only inadequate to study the cultures informing scientific exploration in the Americas, but also it can be downright misleading.

Given the composite status of the Spanish empire – which included not only the imperial metropolis and viceroyalties in the New World, but also multi-ethnic territories across the Netherlands and Germany, alongside a wide array of corporate entities from missionary orders to commercial clearing houses – the links between its symbolic power and influence over its agents are far from straightforward (Phelan, 1960). That diffusion of power is what allowed, on the one hand, for jurists and philosophers to actively debate imperial policy towards indigenous peoples in Spain, but also generated, on the other hand, the culture of bureaucratic rivalry that pits colonial municipalities, merchants, and missionary orders against each other for jurisdiction over indigenous labour and well-being. While some Spanish thinkers wrote treatises in urban capitals, others braved the elements to tell of the unknown and build altogether new analytic vocabularies. In sum, the 'Empire' was shaped by groups and individuals on the so-called geographical margins just as much as by the learned men in the courts (Hamilton, 1963; Pagden, 1982: 60–61; Braun, 2007: 21–25; Bentancor, 2017; Fuerst, 2018).

Moreover, as historians of science have increasingly documented, the Spanish encounter with the lands, peoples, and creatures of the New World played a decisive role in the emergence of a modern, scientific world view across Europe (Gerbi, 1985; Pratt, 1992; Barrera-Osorio, 2006: 81–100; Cañizares-Esguerra, 2006b: 7–13). The distinct environments of the Americas fuelled a vital concern with perennial questions regarding the state, the boundaries of legality, national identity, civilization, in addition to inquiries into the ecological origins of its landscapes. If nature was the catalyst, the study of natural history was the means to arrive at a whole set of new questions. As Shawn Miller notes in his *An Environmental History of Latin America* (2007), one such set of new concerns was rethinking what writing history was all about:

> History without nature is not only self-serving, it is inaccurate, shortsighted, and potentially perilous to the human story line. For the drama to be complete, we must cast both nature and culture in the roles of protagonist, for each have dealt the other health and sickness, aid and harm, and life and death…All of our histories need not be environmental, but in some of our histories, nature and culture deserve equal billing.
>
> (Miller, 2007: 2)

Beyond the potential material benefits of seemingly boundless natural resources, the spirit of conquest was thus paralleled by a spirit of inquiry. Just as Charles V had sought to rebrand the Spanish nation under the Romanesque mantra of *Plus Ultra*, so too did natural historians aspire to become a 'Pliny' of the New World (Pagden, 1995: 11–28; Cañizares-Esguerra, 2006b: 14–45).

In order to tell a story of conquest that accounted for the ecological and human diversity of the New World, natural historians aimed their writing at its very landscapes. Many of them initially employed the classical frameworks of Aristotle and Pliny to explain the nature of the New World (Acosta, 2002). The sheer novelty of these spaces made the stretching and challenging of ancient sources pragmatically necessary, yet also controversial.

Like the writers of epic romances before him, for example, the historian Gonzalo Fernández de Oviedo (1478–1557) wrote of an exotic, liminal land populated by eroticized pineapples and delicious iguanas (de la Rosa, 2002; Paden, 2007). His attempt to collect and classify as much as possible of the New World's environments led Oviedo to posit American nature as an inviting space, where, in Kathleen Ann Myers words, 'the reader can praise the wonders of God's creation' (Myers, 2007: 80). Yet when writing of the arduous tasks, he endured to produce his *General and Natural History of the Indies*, Oviedo nevertheless finds great uncertainty in the experience of New World nature, hoping that his readers will, 'be satisfied with what I have seen and lived with many dangers…enjoy it and suffer none of them, and may he [sic] be able to read it in his own country without undergoing such hunger and thirst, heat and cold, or innumerable other travails, without venturing into storms at sea, nor the misfortunes one suffers in those lands' (Myers, 2007: 150).

Las Casas, as well, saw in the Americas a lost Edenic paradise (de Las Casas, 2003). In his mind, seemingly untouched lands and peoples were proof that God had once ruled over this allegedly new space and that Spanish conquest threatened its pristine order. As he reports on the kingdoms of Naco and Honduras, for instance, before the arrival of conquering Spaniards they had 'seemed a true paradise of delights and were more populous than the most frequented and populous land on earth. And now we have passed there and come that way, and we saw them in such devastation and so wanting in inhabitants that any person, however hard he might be, his heart would break in grief to see it' (de Las Casas, 2003: 38). Both men therefore view the environments of the New World as spaces of great beauty, but also great uncertainty and instability. Though the sources of that volatility vary – for Oviedo they emerge from the native peoples, for Las Casas from the Spaniards – key in their rhetorical strategies is to place upon Imperial Spain a kind of providential charge.

These two examples form part of a broader tapestry of sixteenth-century writings that sought to dominate the mysteries of the New World with the power of wonder and the written word. Indeed, subsequent generations of natural historians would find themselves repeating some of the tropes first articulated by Oviedo and Las Casas. They would also, however, overcome the narrative limits of earlier natural historians, in the process building a new set of rhetorical motifs and strategies. As with most of IR's analytic vocabulary, the shadow of the twentieth century makes it difficult to find the invisible voices of empire in a world so thoroughly shaped by states and theories of great statesmen. Even with the exemplary work by Campbell, Jahn, Teschke, and Nexon, among many others, IR's investigations into the early histories of the modern world struggle to shake off the disciplinary glasses in search of a state-centric foothold (Costa Lopez et al., 2018). Yet one need not go far to find literature that looks at the global history of early empire in analytically sophisticated and holistic ways. As recent studies on the writing of imperial laws demonstrate, there is already a rich engagement with how the imperial past intertwines with the present (Benton, 2002; Burbank and Cooper, 2013; Ross, 2015). The challenge is to articulate the lost links between empires now gone and the ones still in our midst.

Conclusion: stories of empires lost

While no field of scholarly inquiry – from anthropology to informatics, world literature to development studies – remains untouched by the influence of imperial grandeur and aspiration, very little of Anglophone IR has reflected on the languages and geopolitical realities that make its inquiries possible. That omission should not be presumed accidental. As Edward Said noted almost 30 years ago in *Culture and Imperialism* (1993), 'the power to narrate, or to block other narratives from forming and emerging, is very important to culture and imperialism, and constitutes one of the main connections between them' (Said, 1993: xiii). Thus, despite the lack of attention to the ways in which contemporary imperial rhetorics shape scholarly output on the past, present, and future of empires, the links between the rhetorics of empire and the exercise of control is an especially opportune point of departure to engage the state of the field. Even such as it is, much can be learned about empire by simply asking how the term is put to work.

Going back to the Spanish Conquest of the New World, the written text was an important symbol of the experience of discovery, particularly as an expression of eye-witness authority. Writing, Todorov maintains, ultimately marks the 'triumph' of Europeans over the Amerindians (Todorov, 1999: 251–252). Walter Mignolo singles out this attitude as part of the 'remarkable tendency [in the West] to link history with rhetoric instead of philosophy', interpreting the absence of written language as a sign of a people's barbarism (Mignolo, 1995: 136). According to this perspective, it was from a particular standpoint on the writing of history that 'Spanish men of letters appointed themselves to write the history that Amerindians could not properly write because of their lack of letters' (Mignolo, 1995: 129). While Todorov and Mignolo's work aimed to clarify how textual referents are indicative of the larger dynamics of modernity, contemporary scholars have extended this logic to the experiences of commercial, administrative, and scholarly classes in fundamentally alien landscapes. The Americas were perceived as a laboratory for empirical learning, as much as they were considered a space of salvation, or, a site of imperial management. Alongside conquistadors, priests, alchemists, collectors, astrologers, painters, and curious men of letters, Oviedo and Las Casas were amongst the first chroniclers of the Americas that brought with them old assumptions about natural hierarchies, yet developed a new vocabulary for experiential knowledge.

As the scholarly literature in Historical IR increasingly teaches us, it takes more than being a military victor to tell a history of conquest. Indeed, there is a rich intellectual repertoire of strategies enacted once peace has been forged and the project of consciousness-building begins. As I have shown above, what differentiates more recent interventions into the colonial past from foundational works is the attention to changing meanings of the global exchanges and transformations that all empires are a part of. The above therefore highlights several important areas of research for scholars of Historical IR to consider in any investigation of the subject of 'early' empires. From this account, there are three lessons this chapter has aimed to establish: one sociological, the other conceptual, and the last methodological.

First, the history of IR as a field shows how recurring attempts and missed opportunities to tackle the subject of empire have generated important critiques of past and contemporary forms of imperialism, yet have neglected to dive deep into the broader historiography of the term. Some of this may be conviction, or academic pragmatism, but some of it may also be a product of IR's own predisposition for advising, if not serving, the great halls of power. Living in a time of empire is no unique feat for a scholar of history; rather, it is what we do with the knowledge about empire available to us that can make a difference.

Second, the transdisciplinary encounters that IR scholars have embarked on over the last 20 years are illustrative of important methodological changes that enrich conceptions of empire beyond the vernaculars of national histories towards thinking of the world as a product of global history. Local contexts of production are far from dismissed in this literature, but rather repositioned to take a much stronger place alongside the grand narratives that are typically deployed to explain change and continuity in international contexts. For the purposes of studying imperialism, for example, the history of science teaches us that religion (among other systems of belief) plays an important part in the shaping of empire and its histories.

Lastly, despite having spent a good deal of space thinking about empire's past, I have said very little about how we ought to write about empire in the future. One glaring area in need of interrogation, for example, is IR's long-standing Anglophonic bias (Cheney, 2017; Wigen, 2018: 34–36; Caraccioli et al., 2020). As British and American imperialisms have taken turns as sources of intellectual and academic knowledge over the rest of the world in the last 200 years, there has been no need to re-establish a new *lingua franca* for empire as seen in previous centuries. The monolingual links between the two empires left the fabrication of a distinct kind of imperial knowledge uninterrupted, particularly as the United States took up its title as what David Slater calls the 'post-colonial imperial power' of the twentieth century (Slater, 2004: 13; see also: Manchanda, 2020). Yet despite the 'special relationship' that emerged from linguistic and ideological proximity, the same reciprocity has not happened in developing new theories of empire.[3] Whether it be literal or symbolic, translation is about making an alien world familiar to new and ever-changing audiences. When it comes to the story of empire, what makes its narratives persistent is not simply the tensions between the exotic and familiar, but rather the extent to which the narration of its history is rendered foundational or meant to be forgotten. May we all never forget what it is about empires that makes our writing on them possible.

Suggestions for further reading

Cañizares-Esguerra, J. (2001). *How to Write the History of the New World: Histories, Epistemologies, and Identities in the Eighteenth-Century Atlantic World.* Stanford, CA: Stanford University Press.

Restall, M. (2002). *Seven Myths of the Spanish Conquest.* New York, NY: Oxford University Press.

Morefield, J. (2014). *Empires Without Imperialism: Anglo-American Decline and the Politics of Deflection.* New York, NY: Oxford University Press.

Wigen, E. (2018). *State of Translation: Turkey in Interlingual Relations.* Ann Arbor, MI: University of Michigan Press.

Notes

1 According to Jennifer Pitts, the field of Political Theory especially, 'has come slowly and late to the study of empire, relative to other disciplines'. Much of the 'recent sustained attention to questions of empire and imperialism', she goes on, 'has at least two distinct sources: the turning, finally, of attention to a field of study that had occupied other scholars for more than two decades; and the sense, shared by a broad global public, that contemporary global structural inequalities, and especially American unilateralism and militarism after 2001, demanded a reinterrogation of the idea of empire' (Pitts, 2010: 211).

2 As Anthony Pagden notes, 'Because of their size and sheer diversity, most empires have in time become universal, cosmopolitan societies. In order to rule vast and widely separated domains, imperial governments have generally found themselves compelled to be broadly tolerant of diversity of culture and sometimes even belief, so long as these posed no threat to their authority…But if they have generally tolerated diversity, empires have also inevitably transformed the peoples whom they have brought together' (Pagden, 2003: xxiii).

3 As Ron Suskind famously reported an aide of the George W. Bush's administration (2000–2008) say, 'We're an empire now, and when we act, we create our own reality. And while you're studying that reality – judiciously, as you will – we'll act again, creating other new realities, which you can study too, and that's how things will sort out. We're history's actors…and you, all of you, will be left to just study what we do' (Suskind, 2004).

References

Acosta, J. (2002). *Natural and Moral History of the Indies.* Translated by F. López-Morillas. Durham, NC: Duke University Press.

Agmon, D. (2017). *A Colonial Affair: Commerce, Conversion, and Scandal in French India.* Ithaca, NY: Cornell University Press.

Alker, Jr., H. (1992). The humanistic moment in international studies: reflections on Machiavelli and Las Casas. *International Studies Quarterly*, 36 (4), 347–371.

Anand, D. (2007). *Geopolitical Exotica: Tibet in Western Imagination*. Minneapolis, MN: University of Minnesota Press.

Andersen, M. (2016). Semi-cores in imperial relations: the cases of Scotland and Norway. *Review of International Studies*, 42 (1), 178–203.

Armitage, D. (2004). The fifty years' rift: intellectual history and international relations. *Modern Intellectual History*, 1 (1), 97–109.

Barder, A. (2015). *Empire Within: Hierarchy and Its Imperial Laboratories of Governance*. New York, NY: Routledge.

Barrera-Osorio, A. (2006). *Experiencing Nature: The Spanish American Empire and the Early Scientific Revolution*. Austin, TX: University of Texas Press.

Bayly, M. (2021). Imperialism: Beyond the 'Re-turn to Empire' in International Relations. In de Carvalho, B., Costa Lopez, J., & Leira, H., eds. *Routledge Handbook of Historical International Relations*. Abingdon: Routledge.

Bell, D. (2016). *Reordering the World: Essays on Liberalism and Empire*. Princeton, NJ: Princeton University Press.

Bentancor, O. (2017). *The Matter of Empire: Metaphysics and Mining in Colonial Peru*. Pittsburgh, PA: University of Pittsburgh Press.

Benton, L. (2002). *Law and Colonial Cultures: Legal Regimes in World History, 1400-1900*. New York, NY: Cambridge University Press.

Bishara, F. (2017). *A Sea of Debt: Law and Economic Life in the Western Indian Ocean, 1780-1950*. New York, NY: Cambridge University Press.

Boucher, D. (1998). *Political Theories of International Relations*. New York, NY: Oxford University Press.

Brading, D. (1993). *The First America: The Spanish Monarchy, Creole Patriots, and the Liberal State, 1492-1867*. New York, NY: Cambridge University Press.

Braun, H. (2007). *Juan de Mariana and Early Modern Spanish Political Thought*. Burlington, VT: Ashgate.

Burbank, J., and Cooper, F. (2011). *Empires in World History: Power and the Politics of Difference*. Princeton, NJ: Princeton University Press.

Burbank, J., and Cooper, F. (2013). Rule of Law, Politics of Empire. In: L. Benton, and M. Ross, eds., *Legal Pluralism and Empires, 1500-1850*, New York, NY: New York University Press, 279–293.

Buzan, B., and Lawson, G. (2015). *The Global Transformation: History, Modernity and the Making of International Relations*. New York, NY: Cambridge University Press.

Campbell, D. (1992). *Writing Security: United States Foreign Policy and the Politics of Identity*. Minneapolis, MN: University of Minnesota Press.

Cañizares-Esguerra, J. (2006a). *Puritan Conquistadors: Iberianizing the Atlantic, 1550-1700*. Stanford, CA: Stanford University Press.

Cañizares-Esguerra, J. (2006b). *Nature, Empire, and Nation: Explorations of the History of Science in the Iberian World*. Stanford, CA: Stanford University Press.

Caraccioli, M. J. (2021). *Writing the New World: The Politics of Natural History in the Early Spanish Empire*. Gainesville, FL: University of Florida Press.

Caraccioli, M. J., Wigen, E., Costa Lopez, J., Cheney, A., and Subotic, J. (2020). Interlingual Relations: Approaches, Conflicts, and Lessons in the Translation of Global Politics. *International Studies Review*, 1–31. Online first: Viewed on 30 October 2020, <https://doi.org/10.1093/isr/viaa019>.

Carr, E. H. (1964). *The Twenty Years' Crisis, 1919-1939: An Introduction to the Study of International Relations*. New York, NY: Harper Collins Publishers.

Cheney, A. (2017). Tibet lost in translation: sovereignty, suzerainty and international order transformation, 1904-1906. *Journal of Contemporary China*, 26 (107), 769–783.

de la Rosa, A. C. (2002). Representing the New World's nature: wonder and exoticism in Gonzalo Fernández de Oviedo y Valdes. *Historical Reflections/Réflexions Historiques*, 28 (1), 73–92.

Costa Lopez, J., De Carvalho, B., Latham, A., Zarakol, A., Bartelson, J., and Holm, M. (2018). Forum: in the beginning there was no word (for it): terms, concepts, and early sovereignty. *International Studies Review*, 20 (3), 489–519.

Da Silva, D. (2007). *Toward a Global Idea of Race*. Minneapolis, MN: University of Minnesota Press.

Daggett, C. (2018). *The Birth of Energy: Fossil Fuels, Thermodynamics, and the Politics of Work*. Durham, NC: Duke University Press.

Dahl, A. (2018). *Empire of the People: Settler Colonialism and the Foundations of Modern Democratic Thought*. Lawrence, KS: University Press of Kansas.

De Carvalho, B., Leira, H., and Hobson, J. (2011). The big bangs of IR: the myths that your teachers still tell you about 1648 and 1919. *Millennium: Journal of International Studies*, 39 (3), 735–758.

de Las Casas, B. (2003). *An Account, Much Abbreviated, of the Destruction of the Indies*. Edited by F. W. Knight. Translated by A. Hurley. Indianapolis, IN: Hackett Publishing Co.

Deutscher, I. (1985). *Marxism, Wars & Revolutions: Essays from Four Decades*. New York, NY: Verso.

Doyle, M. (1986). *Empires*. Ithaca, NY: Cornell University Press.

Elliot, J. H. (2009). *Spain, Europe, and the Wider World, 1500-1800*. New Haven, CT: Yale University Press.

Fuerst, J. (2018). *New World Postcolonial: The Political Thought of Inca Garcilaso de la Vega*. Pittsburgh, PA: University of Pittsburgh Press.

Gerbi, A. (1985). *Nature in the New World: From Christopher Columbus to Gonzalo Fernandez de Oviedo*. Pittsburgh, PA: University of Pittsburgh Press.

Getachew, A. (2019). *Worldmaking After Empire: The Rise and Fall of Self-Determination*. Princeton, NJ: Princeton University Press.

Ghosh, D. (2012). Another set of imperial turns? *The American Historical Review*, 117 (3), 772–793.

Go, J., Lawson, G., and de Carvalho, B. (2021). Historical Sociology in International Relations: The Challenge of the Global. In de Carvalho, B., Costa Lopez, J., & Leira, H., eds. *Routledge Handbook of Historical International Relations*. Abingdon: Routledge.

Goodman, D. (2002). *Power and Penury: Government, Technology and Science in Philip II's Spain*. New York, NY: Cambridge University Press.

Guillaume, X. (2011). *International Relations and Identity: A Dialogical Approach*. New York, NY: Routledge.

Guillaume, X. (2021). Historical Periods and the Act of Periodisation. In de Carvalho, B., Costa Lopez, J., & Leira, H., eds. *Routledge Handbook of Historical International Relations*. Abingdon: Routledge.

Hamilton, B. (1963). *Political Thought in Sixteenth-Century Spain*. Oxford, UK: Clarendon Press.

Hardt, M., and Negri, A. (2000). *Empire*. Cambridge, MA: Harvard University Press.

Hoffmann, S. (1977). An American social science: international relations. *Daedalus*, 106 (3), 41–60.

Immerwahr, D. (2019). *How To Hide an Empire: A History of the Greater United States*. New York, NY: Farrar, Strauss and Giroux.

Ince, O. (2018). *Colonial Capitalism and the Dilemmas of Liberalism*. New York, NY: Oxford University Press.

Jahn, B. (2000). *The Cultural Construction of International Relations: The Invention of the State of Nature*. Chippenham, UK: Palgrave.

Kalmo, H., and Skinner, Q., eds. (2011). *Sovereignty in Fragments: The Past, Present and Future of a Contested Concept*. New York, NY: Cambridge University Press.

Knutsen, T. L. (2021). Ancient Greece: War, Peace and Diplomacy in Antiquity. In de Carvalho, B., Costa Lopez, J., & Leira, H., eds. *Routledge Handbook of Historical International Relations*. Abingdon: Routledge.

Lee, C., and Morley, N., eds. (2015). *A Handbook to the Reception of Thucydides*. Malden, MA: Wiley-Blackwell.

MacCormack, S. (2007). *On the Wings of Time: Rome, the Incas, Spain, and Peru*. Princeton, NJ: Princeton University Press.

Manchanda, N. (2020). *Imagining Afghanistan: The History and Politics of Imperial Knowledge*. New York, NY: Cambridge University Press.

Marroquín Arredondo, J., and Bauer, R., eds. (2019). *Translating Nature: Cross-Cultural Histories of Early Modern Science*. Philadelphia, PA: University of Pennsylvania Press.

McLarren, K., and Stahl, B. (2020). The Holy See as Hybrid Actor: Religion in International, Transnational, and World Society. In: M. Barbato, ed., *The Pope, the Public, and International Relations: Postsecular Transformations*, New York, NY: Palgrave, 189–201.

Mignolo, W. (1995). *The Darker Side of the Renaissance: Literacy, Territoriality, and Colonization*. Ann Arbor, MI: University of Michigan Press.

Miller, S. (2007). *An Environmental History of Latin America*. New York, NY: Cambridge University Press.

Mulich, J. (2020). *In a Sea of Empires: Networks and Crossings in the Revolutionary Caribbean*. New York, NY: Cambridge University Press.

Murray, A. (1997). *Reconstructing Realism: Between Power Politics and Cosmopolitan Ethics*. Staffordshire, UK: Keele University Press.

Myers, K. (2007). *Fernández de Oviedo's Chronicle of America: A New History for a New World*. Translations by N. M. Scott. Austin, TX: University of Texas Press.

Nexon, D. (2009). *The Struggle for Power in Early Modern Europe: Religious Conflict, Dynastic Empires, and International Change*. Princeton, NJ: Princeton University Press.

Nexon, D., and Wright, T. (2007). What's at stake in the American empire debate. *American Political Science Review*, 101 (3), 253–271.

Owensby, B. (2008). *Empire of Law and Indian Justice in Colonial Mexico*. Stanford, CA: Stanford University Press.

Paden, J. (2007). The iguana and the barrel of mud: memory, natural history, and hermeneutics in Oviedo's Sumario de la natural historia de las Indias. *Colonial Latin American Review*, 16 (2), 203–226.

Pagden, A. (1982). *The Fall of Natural Man: The American Indian and the Origins of Comparative Ethnology*. New York, NY: Cambridge University Press.

Pagden, A. (1988). The reception of the 'new philosophy' in eighteenth-century Spain. *Journal of the Warburg and Courtauld Institutes*, 51, 126–140.

Pagden, A. (1995). *Lords of All the World: Ideologies of Empire in Spain, Britain and France c.1500-c.1800*. New Haven, CT: Yale University Press.

Pagden, A. (2003). *Peoples and Empires: A Short History of European Migration, Exploration, and Conquest, from Greece to the Present*. London, UK: Modern Library Chronicles.

Phelan, J. L. (1960). Authority and flexibility in the Spanish imperial bureaucracy. *Administrative Science Quarterly*, 5 (1), 47–65.

Pitts, J. (2010). Political theory of empire and imperialism. *Annual Review of Political Science*, 13, 211–235.

Pocock, J. G. A. (2001–2015). *Barbarism and Religion*. 6 Volumes. New York, NY: Cambridge University Press.

Portuondo, M. (2009). *Secret Science: Spanish Cosmography and the New World*. Chicago, IL: University of Chicago Press.

Pratt, M. (1992). *Imperial Eyes: Travel Writing and Transculturation*. New York, NY: Routledge.

Premo, B. (2017). *The Enlightenment on Trial: Ordinary Litigants and Colonialism in the Spanish Empire*. New York, NY: Oxford University Press.

Rabasa, J. (2011). *Tell Me The Story of How I Conquered You: Elsewheres and Ethnosuicide in the Colonial Mesoamerican World*. Austin, TX: University of Texas Press.

Rojas, C. (2001). *Civilization and Violence: Regimes of Representation in Nineteenth-Century Colombia*. Minneapolis, MN: University of Minnesota Press.

Rosenberg, J. (1996). Isaac Deutscher and the lost history of international relations. *New Left Review*, 215 (1), 1–15.

Ross, R. (2015). Binding in conscience: early modern English Protestants and Spanish Thomists on law and the fate of the soul. *Law and History Review*, 33 (4), 803–837.

Said, E. (1993). *Culture and Imperialism*. New York, NY: Vintage Books.

Schmidt, B. (1998). *The Political Discourse of Anarchy: A Disciplinary History of International Relations*. Albany, NY: SUNY Press.

Seed, P. (1995). *Ceremonies of Possession in Europe's Conquest of the New World, 1492-1640*. New York, NY: Cambridge University Press.

Shirk, M. (2017). 'Bringing the state back in' to the empire turn: piracy and the layered sovereignty of the eighteenth century Atlantic. *International Studies Review*, 19 (2), 143–165.

Simon, J. (2017). *The Ideology of Creole Revolution: Imperialism and Independence in American and Latin American Political Thought*. New York, NY: Cambridge University Press.

Slater, D. (2004). *Geopolitics and the Post-Colonial: Re-Thinking North-South Relations*. Malden, MA: Blackwell Publishing.

Subotic, J. (2020). Ethics of Archival Research on Political Violence. *Journal of Peace Research*, 1–13. Online first: Viewed on 30 October 2020, <https://journals.sagepub.com/doi/abs/10.1177/0022343319898735>.

Suskind, R. (2004). Faith, Certainty and the Presidency of George W. Bush. *The New York Times Magazine*. October 17. Online. Viewed on 30 October 2020, <https://www.nytimes.com/2004/10/17/magazine/faith-certainty-and-the-presidency-of-george-w-bush.html>.

Teschke, B. (2003). *The Myth of 1648: Class, Geopolitics, and the Making of Modern International Relations*. New York, NY: Verso.

Todorov, T. (1999). *The Conquest of America: The Question of the Other*. Norman, OK: University of Oklahoma Press.

Vitalis, R. (2015). *White World Order, Black Power Politics: The Birth of American International Relations*. Ithaca, NY: Cornell University Press.

Waltz, K. (1977). *Theory of International Politics*. Reading, MA: Addison-Wesley Publishing Co.

Zarakol A. (2011). *After Defeat: How the East Learned to Live with the West*. New York, NY: Cambridge University Press.

40

EUROPE IN HISTORICAL INTERNATIONAL RELATIONS

Benjamin Herborth and Patrick Nitzschner

Introduction

At first glance, almost all of the historical work done in International Relations (IR) appears to be about Europe. Historical IR would thus seem to exacerbate a similar trend in history and historiography. Europe is taken for granted as self-evident centre and starting point both geographically and intellectually (Chakrabarty, 2000; Hobson, 2012; Çapan, 2016; Çapan et al. 2021 in this volume). In order to corroborate such an observation, historically oriented introductions to IR, though themselves an exception rather than the rule, are a case in point. In *Force and Statecraft*, for example, Paul Lauren et al. (2020) treat the emergence of great powers in Europe as the paradigmatic case to introduce international politics with a historical bent at large. In *Understanding Global Conflict: An Introduction to History and Theory*, Joseph Nye and David Welch (2017) expound a widely shared narrative starting with the Peace of Westphalia and gradually zooming in on contemporary international politics via the Concert of Europe and two World Wars. If it features at all in such conventional accounts, the non-European world appears as a target of imperial expansion and colonial violence and/or settlement (see Bayly, 2021; Caraccioli, 2021; both in this volume).

It is precisely because Europe is by and large taken for granted as the centre of geographical and intellectual attention, however, that it remains conceptually underexplored. The presumption of Europe goes without saying. Paying conceptual attention to Europe from the point of view of Historical IR thus not only sheds light on something previously neglected. It also allows us to explore what has been at stake in upholding Europe as a blind spot hidden in plain sight in much of the historically oriented work in IR. In order to do so, we will focus on what Europe does rather than on what Europe is.[1] This is to say that rather than mapping out more or less comprehensively who said what about Europe, we seek to reconstruct how Europe figures as an element of what Edward Said (2003 (1979): 71) termed 'imaginative geography'.

In a nutshell, we suggest that Europe has not been conceptualized and has not been theorized in historical terms, because Europe itself represents an implicit theory of history, which organizes historical accounts that appear immediately plausible and relevant to the field of Historical IR conventionally understood (in this volume see also MacKay and LaRoche, 2021; and Hom, 2021). Unpacking this implicit theory, we suggest, not only allows us to get a clearer sense of what 'Europe' does in terms of conceptual work. It also opens up a wider range of historical and political imagination in thinking about Europe in the past, present, and future. The argument proceeds as follows: in the following section, we discuss how 'Europe' is conceptually nested in the political semantics of modern politics and international relations. Specifically, we engage with key texts from both the English School tradition and Historical Sociology in order to demonstrate how Europe is used to invoke a linear, teleological view of history (on these, see also Go et al., 2021; Navari and Green, 2021, both in this volume). The third section follows up on such teleological uses of Europe by zooming in on debates on European integration as a vanguard project to overcome the perils of anarchy in international politics. In conclusion, we point to the potential of non-teleological readings of Europe.

Europe as the project of modernity

IR imagines itself as quintessentially modern (Ruggie, 1993; Inayatullah and Blaney, 2004; Shilliam, 2010; Buzan and Lawson, 2015). A historical imagination cast in terms of modernity derives its rhetorical thrust from a simple yet powerful distinction. The modern sets itself apart from what had come before. It does so not only in the sense of marking a difference, but also in terms of evoking a sense of progressive development. The simple scheme before/after is thus imbued with historical meaning and, to the extent that such meaning is organized around binary oppositions with an inbuilt moral compass (e.g. modern/pre-modern, civilized/barbarian, reason/superstition), implicit normative judgement. We have previously suggested that 'Europe' is not only the empirical site where such a type of historical imagination is both thought up and put to test. Rather, 'Europe' is woven deeply into the fabric of IR's historical imagination in such a way that the conceptual work done by what appears to be merely a geographical denomination is easily overlooked. As part of a powerful 'imaginative geography', Europe conjures up a series of implicit connotations which practically amount to a substantive theory of history featuring fixed ideas of centre and periphery as well as progress and development. To the extent that Europe stands on the progressive, advanced, and morally cherished side of the distinctions organizing its imaginative geography, Europe figures as both vanguard and *telos* of history.

Having long served as a safe haven for historical work in a summarily ahistorical discipline, the English School is a fruitful resource for the articulation of historical common sense. *The Expansion of International Society*, a classic collection of essays from an English School perspective (Bull and Watson, 1984a), states with exemplary clarity: 'The purpose of this book is to explore the expansion of the international society of European states across the rest of the globe, and its transformation from a society fashioned in Europe and dominated by Europeans into the global international society of today' (Bull and Watson, 1984b: 1). Bull and Watson proceed to distinguish the key concept of international society from the less ambitious notion of an international system. An international system accounts for a thin layer of strategically coordinated behaviour simply by virtue of the fact that a multiplicity of sovereign states exists in a context of interaction which forces them to take each other into account. International society, by contrast, adds a thickening layer of normative integration by means of 'rules and institutions'. Notably, the normative upshot of the normatively 'underdeveloped' notion of the international system had been that actors could only encounter one another on a simple plane of strategic interaction, i.e. as moral equals. Normative integration in international society, by contrast, is expressive of a moral progress which is originally pioneered in Europe and then spreads across the world.

More recent works within the English School context have been quick to acknowledge that this is 'a story of non-Europeans being integrated into an essentially Western order, socialized to accept European international norms and practices'. As an antidote, Tim Dunne and Christian Reus-Smit seek to foreground how 'international society was, from the outset, profoundly influenced by encounters, engagements, and interactions between Europeans and non-European peoples, producing a global international order that is culturally and politically far more complex than the conventional narrative allows' (Dunne and Reus-Smit, 2017a: viii). The dual move here is to give voice and agency to non-European actors and, consequently, to add complexity to the ensuing account of global order. Embracing the 'ubiquity of cultural diversity', however, Dunne and Reus-Smit (2017b: 37–39) already presuppose cultural diversity. Compare this with the sense of puzzlement expressed in Dipesh Chakrabarty's *Provincializing Europe*. Chakrabarty, too, starts from the observation that Western and European thinkers have devised universal accounts of world history in complete ignorance of its overwhelming majority. This is not what puzzles him. The 'everyday paradox of third-world social science' is, on the contrary, that third-world social scientists themselves find such ignorant accounts surprisingly helpful in making sense of third-world societies. 'What allowed the modern European sages to develop such clairvoyance with regard to societies of which they were empirically ignorant? Why cannot we, once again, return the gaze?' Chakrabarty's answer to the puzzle speaks immediately to the semantic work that Europe is doing in our political and historical imagination:

> Only 'Europe', the argument would appear to be, is *theoretically* (that is, at the level of the fundamental categories that shape historical thinking) knowable; all other histories are matters of empirical research that fleshes out a theoretical skeleton that is substantially 'Europe'
>
> (Chakrabarty, 2000: 29; see also Grovogui, 2016)

The more detailed discussion of the narrative of an 'expansion' of international society provides us with an almost ideal typical template of the semantic labour performed by 'Europe'. Articulated initially as a taken-for-granted vanguard site of world history, 'Europe' comes under critical scrutiny as the one-sidedness of the conventional narrative appears both analytically wanting and normatively problematic. In response, a Eurocentric bias is rightfully diagnosed, non-European voices are brought into the conversation, and entangled and connected histories appear as a plausible way forward (Bhambra, 2010; Bilgin, 2016). Next to these important problem shifts, however, questions as to how the political semantics of 'Europe' has shaped our political imagination in ways that cut across such connections remain open. The somewhat stylized template holds, too, for an overview of uses of Europe at the intersection of IR and Historical Sociology. Here, too, an initial wave of scholarship posits Europe as the vanguard site of world-historical change.

Daniel Philpott (2001), for instance, recounts the conventional narrative of 'Westphalia' instituting a multiplicity of sovereign states in opposition to 'medieval European unity', the return of which he traces in the European Union (EU) suggesting that 'for the first time since the demise of the Holy Roman Empire, a significant political authority other than the state, one with formal sovereign prerogatives, became legitimate within the boundaries of the Westphalia system' (Philpott, 2001: 40). Historiographical doubts regarding these watersheds aside, Europe is posited as the site where world-historical benchmarks occur (see also de Carvalho and Leira, 2021 in this volume).[2] The rest of the world appears only 'in relation to Europe'. Similarly, Rodney Bruce Hall (1999), though committed to a stronger constructivist vision of history in terms of 'hopeful nondeterminism', discusses the development of national collective identity in relation to international systems through a series of exclusively European examples. In Benno Teschke's iconoclastic effort to debunk *The Myth of 1648* (2003), structural transformations are explained in terms of changes in European property regimes.

To the extent that identity is conceived relationally, i.e. in relation to an 'other', the constitutive role of non-European voices has been brought to the fore. Iver Neumann (1999), for instance, has focused on the way in which Russia and 'the East' figured in European identity formation, John

Hobson (2004) has highlighted the *Eastern Origins of Western Civilization*, and Ayse Zarakol (2010) has traced non-Western histories of coming to terms with being relegated to secondary status (see also Rae, 2017; Bilgin, 2017). More recently, Jason Sharman (2019) has debunked the myth of European expansion being the quasi-natural consequence of European military superiority as a historiographically dubious effort to project 19th-century common sense onto the early modern era and consequently ignore Europe's comparative weakness. Taking issue with narrating the history of capitalism as a predominantly European affair, Alexander Anievas and Kerem Nişancıoğlu (2015) have highlighted the role of global processes and non-European societies. Works such as these provide rich and nuanced accounts by placing European history in a broader global context. The historical imagination of Europe in IR is enriched rather than undermined by critiques of Eurocentrism. However, important as historical attention to non-European voices may be, the project of provincializing Europe is not an empirical one. Chakrabarty's eponymous account indeed starts from the observation that Europe as a region 'has already been provincialized by history itself' (Chakrabarty, 2000: 3). Europe as an implicit theory of history, however, remains a historical force and a political problem to be reckoned with.[3]

European integration in history and theory

Much of the critical literature on predominant uses of Europe as an implicit theory of history has prompted research to focus on something other than just Europe. The prevalence of Europe, being used in such a manner, as an implicit theory of history, becomes particularly obvious, though, in the burgeoning literature on European integration. This, it would seem, is not least the case because European Integration Theory (EIT) constitutes a quite distinct realm of inquiry within the related fields of Political Science and IR which decidedly deals with Europe, conceived as the European Union. However, it is a common misperception that this exceptionality can be traced back to the EU as an object of study *sui generis*. Quite the contrary, integration theorists aimed for generalizability beyond their empirical and theoretical vantage point from the very beginning. This ambition is rooted in the *Zeitgeist* of EIT's foundational period, the 1950s. In the aftermath of the Second World War, émigré scholars persecuted by National Socialist Germany sought to theoretically come to terms with their experiences of fascism. In political theory, Hannah Arendt examined *The Origins of Totalitarianism*. In IR, her close 'thinking partner' Hans J. Morgenthau attempted to open up theoretical trajectories for overcoming the 'tragedy of the nation state' (Kostagiannis, 2014). EIT followed in the same vein, with Ernst B. Haas theorizing 'the conditions under which the state as we understand it disappears, disintegrates, weakens, changes' in order to 'get rid of' totalitarian states (Haas and Kreisler, 2000). While it would seem only natural that the EU served as nothing more than a starting point for greater goals like these, Haas' neofunctionalism set itself apart from coeval theorizations. Unlike his fiercely anti-behaviouralist contemporaries like Morgenthau who was steeped in the intellectual traditions of old Europe (Rösch, 2015), Haas' goal was to find a generalizable, positive explanation for regional integration in Europe and beyond. He was not merely interested in a theory of European integration but rather sought to explain integration in varied contexts, studying the EU as a 'laboratory', as a starting point for developing hypotheses and committing to rigorous empirical testing of their explanatory value (Haas 1960; see also Rosamond 2005). A broader debate on 'regional integration' would thus presume Europe as template and telos (Haas, 1970; Schmitter, 1970; Mattli, 1999).

Haas' theoretical propositions, of course, have become widely contested. Not least Stanley Hoffmann's (1966) intergovernmentalism emerged as a fierce contender of supranationalist readings of the integration process, emphasizing state bargains over neofunctionalism's institutional incrementalism and thereby questioning the very possibility of thorough integration in the realm of 'high politics'. However, Hoffmann's reliance on the question of the Westphalian nation state and its sovereign interest, European constructs par excellence, did not break the path towards conceptual-historical attention to Europe. What would have posed a greater challenge to the project of EIT at large were Hoffmann's (1977: 57) reservations, comparable to those of Morgenthau, against the behaviouralist logic of science that still underpins progressive stories of integration. Yet, these reservations never gained much traction in integration theory. Haas' model of doing science set the tone for integration theories to come. Andrew Moravcsik's liberal intergovernmentalism is a case in point. While sticking to Hoffmann's emphasis on state interests and restating them as economically defined, Moravcsik is closer to Haas in setting EIT's standard of validity: only 'distinctive hypotheses and objective methods' tested 'against the best alternative theories' would qualify theoretical interlocutors who, according to Moravcsik, need to offer no less than 'empirical confirmation' (Checkel and Moravcsik, 2001: 266). This mode of inquiry determines the mode of contestation in the field: much of EIT develops theory-guided explanations of integration processes and operationalizes them for hypothesis testing, at times with the aim to make future predictions. In combination with modelled assumptions of rational behaviour and methodological individualism, it unites EITs such as liberal intergovernmentalism, institutionalisms, and multilevel governance theory. What keeps these integration theories distinguishable is their key variable: the question whether state bargains, individual decision-making under institutional constraints, or layered and intertwined, multilevel decision-making processes best approximate integration outcomes. The most crucial commonality, however, is that they are all committed to a reading of history that is grounded in the experience of the EU. While supranationalist readings rely on a quasilinear, progressive story of integration, their intergovernmentalist contenders espouse a circular reading of history that foregrounds the state's sovereign interest as a natural limitation of integration. Neither seems to think of history politically as an open-ended process.

The reliance of integration theories on either a teleological narrative of progressive integration or on a stalling of integration that would cement the status quo has occasionally provoked the accusation that EIT would have largely been occupied with 'celebrating through analysis the institutional bargains of the past' (Gilbert, 2008: 643). Indeed, EIT has been consistently occupied with its namesake 'integration'. Even with the introduction of constructivist bedrock concepts to EIT, authors remained occupied with developing 'testable constructivist hypotheses on European integration' (Checkel and Moravcsik, 2001: 219), with making constructivist concepts 'empirically applicable to international relations' (Risse, 2000: 7) and EIT.[4] This focus on integration may be the reason why the Brexit referendum was met with puzzlement in much of the field. Integration theorists were first alerted to the possibility of disintegration in the mid-2010s, with challengers to the idea of progressive integration anticipating a stalling, but not a rollback. Several subsequent theorizations of disintegration seem to be in accordance with their precursors, calling for a 'consistent and coherent set of testable statements' regarding 'the crucial factors and mechanisms that influence phenomena such as European disintegration' (Vollaard, 2014: 2). For this endeavour, existing integration theories remain the basis: additional concepts, especially of constructivist origin, are added to reinstate a progressive narrative of integration theory (e.g. Börzel and Risse, 2018). But strikingly, and despite the largely austere, scientific tone of respective contributions, normatively charged positions on (dis-)integration are resurfacing. For some, disintegration is a potentially contagious, even lethal risk (Schnapper, 2017), 'an existential dilemma for the European project as such' (van Meurs et al., 2018: 263), a question of survival (Webber, 2017). To rephrase Frederic Jameson's (2005: 199) *bon mot*, it seems to be easier for integration theory to imagine an end to Europe than an end to integration traditionally conceived. What remains strikingly absent is an attempt to rethink the historical, normative, and epistemological commitments of integration theory when encountering perceived crises.

In the philosophy of science, it seems, the crisis of integration theory has been foreseen. For the late Edmund Husserl (1970 (1936)), a misguided scientific rationalism lies at the heart of another 'European crisis', characterized not by a lack of integration but by a lack of reflexive, normative, and not least, historical thinking.[5] It is particularly striking that integration theory, which initially set out to become a scientific lesson from history, today reminds us of such an absence of historical and conceptual reflection. This seems to be the case because EIT has become overly focused on *integration*, much less on what is *European* about it. Of course, the idea of an integrated Europe that served as the initial normative impetus for EIT remains very present, if implicit. But EIT has progressively rendered integration an unproblematic means and simultaneously seems to have lost sight of its European end. Resources for questioning the orthodox story of integration and its 'Europe' are readily available, but much of EIT displays a lack of engagement with these 'dissident voices' (Manners and Whitman, 2016). A historical perspective on EIT could do more than just bring these voices (back) in: it would be imperative to reflect upon the mechanisms that enable the hegemony of an integrationist telos of Europe in the first place. Not least if we were to salvage Haas' idea of Europe as a lesson from history, we would need to scrutinize EIT's very own 'geographies of knowledge of world politics' (Agnew, 2007) and their historical production.

Conclusion

The gist of our argument has been to tease out the curious ways in which Europe and Historical International Relations have become coterminous to such an extent that any attempt to single out parts of the literature on Historical IR as dealing specifically with Europe would be futile. Instead, we have sought to trace uses of Europe in the semantics of modern politics and international relations. Specifically, we have argued that it is through these very uses of Europe that an implicit theory of history is articulated which posits Europe simultaneously as vanguard and telos of world history.

Taking issue with such an implicit teleology is not only a matter of a historiographical critique. It also speaks to the way in which uses of Europe condition and curtail our political imagination – of Europe and beyond. It effects what Barry Hindess has aptly called the 'temporalization of difference' (Helliwell and Hindess, 2005; Hindess, 2007). By inscribing particular political concerns into a developmentalist narrative, the terrain of political engagement is effectively reorganized. Instead of an open-ended encounter between position and opposition, we are left with the temporalized hierarchies of the advanced and the mature vis-à-vis a difference that may still be growing up. Chakrabarty's metaphor of a 'waiting room' of history brilliantly captures the way in which a teleological account of Europe effects a spatial and temporal reordering of our political imagination (Chakrabarty, 2000: 8). The waiting room is separated in space and suspended in time, as its occupants are waiting for admission rather than arrival.

This may serve as a reminder of how difficult it is to think beyond Europe when core categories of our political thought as well as our everyday political language (think, e.g. of development aid) are shaped by a particular articulation of Europe. Bringing non-European voices into the conversation will continue to be indispensable. But to the extent that cultural difference is equated with non-European voices, i.e. to the extent that cultural difference is different in relation to a fixed idea of Europe, the underlying image of Europe itself may remain by and large unchallenged. At the same time, in terms of avenues for future research, it follows that, for those substantively interested in Europe, defensive reactions against critiques of Eurocentrism are fundamentally unwarranted. It is precisely by not taking Europe for granted that a wider range of historical and political engagements with Europe becomes possible.

Suggestions for further reading

Anderson, P. (2009). *The New Old World*. London: Verso.

Chakrabarty, D. (2000). *Provincializing Europe: Postcolonial Thought and Historical Difference*. Princeton, NJ: Princeton University Press.

Gowan, P., and Anderson, P., eds. (1997). *The Question of Europe*. London: Verso.

Le Goff, J. (2009). *The Birth of Europe*. Hoboken, NJ: John Wiley & Sons.

Tilly, C. (2004). *Contention and Democracy in Europe, 1650-2000*. Cambridge: Cambridge University Press.

Wilson, K., and van der Dussen, J., eds. (2005). *The History of the Idea of Europe*. London: Routledge.

Notes

1 For a more systematic outline and exploration of such an approach in relation to the concept of 'the West', see Hellmann and Herborth (2017) and Herborth and Hellmann (2017).

2 For a critical discussion of historiographical myths, see de Carvalho et al., (2011). On Westphalia, specifically, see Osiander (1994, 2001), Teschke (2003), and Stark Urrestarazu (2019). For a critique of the mobilization of the Middle Ages as the constitutive other of European modernity, see Costa Lopez 2020, 2021.

3 The political upshot of a view of Europe which takes its history to be contentious and open-ended rather than teleological becomes particularly clear in Charles Tilly's (2004: 257–259) contention that proposals to transfer models of social and political organization from Europe to the rest of the world fatally ignores how such models are abstracting from the century-long social and political struggle which gave rise to them.

4 It should be clarified that operationalizing the idea of social construction for hypothesis-testing takes away from its potential to explore the historical construction of the concept of Europe as such. In order to construct hypotheses, a given concept of Europe inevitably needs to be presupposed.

5 Ironically, thus, Husserl who himself set out to restore his own version of the European telos can be held against the contemporary teleology of EIT and its positivist thrust.

References

Agnew, J. (2007). Know-where: geographies of knowledge of world politics. *International Political Sociology*, 1 (2), 138–148.

Anievas, A., and Nişancıoğlu, K. (2015). *How the West Came to Rule: The Geopolitical Origins of Capitalism*. London: Pluto Press.

Bayly, M. (2021). Imperialism: Beyond the 'Re-turn to Empire' in International Relations. In de Carvalho, B., Costa Lopez, J., & Leira, H., eds. *Routledge Handbook of Historical International Relations*. Abingdon: Routledge.

Bhambra, G. K. (2010). Historical sociology, international relations and connected histories. *Cambridge Review of International Affairs*, 23 (1), 127–143.

Bilgin, P. (2016). 'Contrapuntal reading' as a method, an ethos, and a metaphor for global IR. *International Studies Review*, 18 (1), 134–146.

Bilgin, P. (2017). *The International in Security, Security in the International*. Abingdon: Routledge.

Börzel, T., and Risse, T. (2018). From the euro to the Schengen crises: European integration theories, politicization, and identity politics. *Journal of European Public Policy*, 25 (1), 83–108.

Bull, H., and Watson, A., eds. (1984a). *The Expansion of International Society*. Oxford: Clarendon Press.

Bull, H., and Watson, A. (1984b). Introduction. In: H. Bull, and A. Watson, eds., *The Expansion of International Society*, Oxford: Clarendon Press, 1–9.

Buzan, B., and Lawson, G. (2015). *The Global Transformation: History, Modernity and the Making of International Relations*. Cambridge: Cambridge University Press.

Çapan, Z. G. (2016). *Re-writing International Relations: History and Theory Beyond Eurocentrism in Turkey*. London: Rowman & Littlefield.

Çapan, Z. G., dos Reis, F. and Grasten, M. (2021). Global Histories: Connections and Circulations in Historical International Relations. In de Carvalho, B., Costa Lopez, J., & Leira, H., eds. *Routledge Handbook of Historical International Relations*. Abingdon: Routledge.

Caraccioli, M. J. (2021). Early (Modern) Empires: The Political Ideology of Conceptual Domination. In de Carvalho, B., Costa Lopez, J., & Leira, H., eds. *Routledge Handbook of Historical International Relations*. Abingdon: Routledge.

Chakrabarty, D. (2000). *Provincializing Europe: Postcolonial Thought and Historical Difference*. Princeton, NJ: Princeton University Press.

Checkel, J., and Moravcsik, A. (2001). A constructivist research program in EU studies?. *European Union Politics*, 2 (2), 219–249.

Costa Lopez, J. (2020). Political authority in international relations: revisiting the medieval debate. *International Organization*, 74 (2), 222–252.

Costa Lopez, J. (2021). International Relations in/and the Middle Ages. In de Carvalho, B., Costa Lopez, J., & Leira, H., eds. *Routledge Handbook of Historical International Relations*. Abingdon: Routledge.

de Carvalho, B., and Leira, H. (2021). State Formation and Historical International Relations. In de Carvalho, B., Costa Lopez, J., & Leira, H., eds. *Routledge Handbook of Historical International Relations*. Abingdon: Routledge.

de Carvalho, B., Leira, H., and Hobson, J. M. (2011). The big bangs of IR: the myths that your teachers still tell you about 1648 and 1919. *Millennium*, 39 (3), 735–758.

Dunne, T., and Reus-Smit, C., eds. (2017a). *The Globalization of International Society*. Oxford: Oxford University Press.

Dunne, T., and Reus-Smit, C. (2017b). The Globalization of International Society. In: T. Dunne, and C. Reus-Smit, eds., *The Globalization of International Society*, Oxford: Oxford University Press, 18–40.

Gilbert, M. (2008). Narrating the process: questioning the progressive story of European integration. *JCMS: Journal of Common Market Studies*, 46 (3), 641–662.

Go, J., Lawson, G., and de Carvalho, B. (2021). Historical Sociology in International Relations: The Challenge of the Global. In de Carvalho, B., Costa Lopez, J., & Leira, H., eds. *Routledge Handbook of Historical International Relations*. Abingdon: Routledge.

Grovogui, S. (2016). *Beyond Eurocentrism and Anarchy: Memories of International Order and Institutions*. Basingstoke: Palgrave.

Haas, E. (1960). *Consensus Formation in The Council of Europe*. Berkeley, CA: University of California Press.

Haas, E. (1970). The study of regional integration: reflections on the joy and anguish of pretheorizing. *International Organization*, 24 (4), 607–646.

Haas, E., and Kreisler, H. (2000). Ernst Haas Interview. Conversations with History. Institute of International Studies, UC Berkeley. Viewed on 31 October 2020, <http://globetrotter.berkeley.edu/people/Haas/haas-con3.html>.

Hall, R. B. (1999). *National Collective Identity: Social Constructs and International Systems*. New York, NY: Columbia University Press.

Helliwell, C., and Hindess, B. (2005). The temporalizing of difference. *Ethnicities*, 5 (3), 414–418.

Hellmann, G., and Herborth, B., eds. (2017). *Uses of the West: Security and the Politics of Order*. Cambridge: Cambridge University Press.

Herborth, B., and Hellmann, G. (2017). Introduction: Uses of the West. In: G. Hellmann, and B. Herborth, eds., *Uses of the West: Security and the Politics of Order*, Cambridge: Cambridge University Press, 1–10.

Hindess, B. (2007). The past is another culture. *International Political Sociology*, 1 (4), 325–338.

Hobson, J. M. (2004). *The Eastern Origins of Western Civilisation*. Cambridge: Cambridge University Press.

Hobson, J. M. (2012). *The Eurocentric Conception of World Politics: Western International Theory, 1760-2010*. Cambridge: Cambridge University Press.

Hoffmann, S. (1966). Obstinate or obsolete? The fate of the nation-state and the case of Western Europe. *Daedalus*, 95 (3), 862–915.

Hoffmann, S. (1977). An American social science, international relations. *Daedalus*, 106 (3), 41–60.

Hom, A. R. (2021). Time and History in International Relations. In de Carvalho, B., Costa Lopez, J., & Leira, H., eds. *Routledge Handbook of Historical International Relations*. Abingdon: Routledge.

Husserl, E. (1970 (1936)). *The Crisis of European Sciences and Transcendental Phenomenology: An Introduction to Phenomenological Philosophy*. Evanston, IL: Northwestern University Press.

Inayatullah, N., and Blaney, D. L. (2004). *International Relations and the Problem of Difference*. Abingdon: Routledge.

Jameson, F. (2005). *Archaeologies of the Future: The Desire Called Utopia and other Science Fictions*. London and New York: Verso.

Kostagiannis, K. (2014). Hans Morgenthau and the tragedy of the nation-state. *The International History Review*, 36 (3), 513–529.

Lauren, P. G., Craig, G. A., and George, A. L. (2020). *Force and Statecraft: Diplomatic Challenges of Our Time*. Oxford: Oxford University Press.

MacKay, J., and LaRoche, C. D. (2021). Theories and Philosophies of History in International Relations. In de Carvalho, B., Costa Lopez, J., & Leira, H., eds. *Routledge Handbook of Historical International Relations*. Abingdon: Routledge.

Manners, I., and Whitman, R. (2016). Another theory is possible: dissident voices in theorising Europe. *JCMS: Journal of Common Market Studies*, 54 (1), 3–18.

Mattli, W. (1999). *The Logic of Regional Integration: Europe and Beyond*. Cambridge: Cambridge University Press.

Navari, C., and Green, D. (2021). The English School and Historical International Relations. In de Carvalho, B., Costa Lopez, J., & Leira, H., eds. *Routledge Handbook of Historical International Relations*. Abingdon: Routledge.

Neumann, I. B. (1999). *Uses of the Other: 'The East' in European Identity Formation*. Minneapolis, MN: University of Minnesota Press.

Nye, J. S., and Welch, D. A. (2017). *Understanding Global Conflict & Cooperation: Introduction to Theory & History*. London: Pearson Education.

Osiander, A. (1994). *The States System of Europe, 1640-1990: Peacemaking and the Conditions of International Stability*. Oxford: Clarendon Press.

Osiander, A. (2001). Sovereignty, international relations, and the Westphalian myth. *International Organization*, 55 (2), 251–287.

Philpott, D. (2001). *Revolutions in Sovereignty: How Ideas Shaped Modern International Relations*. Princeton, NJ: Princeton University Press.

Rae, H. (2017). Patterns of Identification on the Cusp of Globalization. In: T. Dunne, and C. Reus-Smit, eds., *The Globalization of International Society*, Oxford: Oxford University Press, 63–81.

Risse, T. (2000). Let's argue. Communicative action in world politics. *International Organization*, 54 (1), 1–39.

Rosamond, B. (2005). The uniting of Europe and the foundation of EU studies: revisiting the neofunctionalism of Ernst B. Haas. *Journal of European Public Policy*, 12 (2), 237–254.

Rösch, F. (2015). *Power, Knowledge, and Dissent in Morgenthau's Worldview*. Basingstoke and New York: Palgrave Macmillan.

Ruggie, J. G. (1993). Territoriality and beyond: problematizing modernity in international relations. *International Organization*, 47 (1), 139–174.

Said, E. W. (2003 (1979)). *Orientalism*. London: Penguin Books.

Schmitter, P. C. (1970). A revised theory of regional integration. *International Organization*, 24 (4), 836–868.

Schnapper, P. (2017). Brexit and the Risk of European Disintegration. In: N. Da Costa Cabral, J. Gonçalves, and N. Cunha Rodrigues, eds., *After Brexit*, Cham: Palgrave Macmillan, 83–99.

Sharman, J. (2019). *Empires of the Weak. The Real Story of European Expansion and the Creation of the New World Order*. Princeton, NJ: Princeton University Press.

Shilliam, R., ed. (2010). *International Relations and Non-Western Thought: Imperialism, Colonialism and Investigations of Global Modernity*. London: Routledge.

Stark Urrestarazu, U. (2019). *Theatrum Europaeum: Identitätspraxis und Internationale Ordnung auf Friedenskongressen*. Wiesbaden: Springer VS.

Teschke, B. (2003). *The Myth of 1648: Class, Geopolitics, and the Making of Modern International Relations*. London: Verso.

Tilly, C. (2004). *Contention and Democracy in Europe, 1650-2000*. Cambridge: Cambridge University Press.

Van Meurs, W., De Bruin, R., Van de Grift, L., Hoetink, C., Van Leeuwen, K., and Reijnen, C. (2018). *The Unfinished History of European Integration*. Amsterdam: Amsterdam University Press.

Vollaard, H. (2014). Explaining European disintegration. *JCMS: Journal of Common Market Studies*, 52 (5), 1–18.

Webber, D. (2017). Can the EU Survive? In: D. Dinan, N. Nugent, and W. E. Peterson, eds., *The European Union in Crisis*, London: Palgrave, 336–359.

Wilson, K., and van der Dussen, J., eds. (2005). *The History of the Idea of Europe*. London: Routledge.

Zarakol, A. (2010). *After Defeat: How the East Learned to Live with the West*. Cambridge: Cambridge University Press.

41

AFRICA AND INTERNATIONAL HISTORY

Joel Quirk

Writing about Africa and Africans should not be an easy or straight-forward task. This is chiefly because of the enduring effects of European imperialism and colonialism, which ensure that efforts to grapple with the history and politics of the continent and its peoples continue to be weighed down by all kinds of ideological and political dynamics. As Achille Mbembe (2017: 7) has observed, '[t]he fierce colonial desire to divide and classify, to create hierarchies and produce difference, leaves behind wounds and scars'. These wounds are particularly deep. Europeans have consistently juxtaposed negative images regarding Africa and Africans with favourable images of themselves and have appealed to these binaries to justify many forms of historical exploitation and subjugation, including the transatlantic slave trade and colonial conquest. These and other related issues make it difficult to disentangle the history of Africa from the history of knowledge production about Africa.

This chapter approaches the relationship between African history and International Relations (IR) scholarship from three main angles. In the first section, I focus upon the politics of knowledge production, with a specific focus upon the dimensions and effects of Eurocentric classifications. In the second section, I focus upon the historical relationships between peoples in Africa and other parts of the globe. This means considering important regional variations, with particular reference to exchanges spanning the Atlantic, Indian Ocean and Sahara. In the final section, I consider efforts to theorise and understand the history of political authority. Due to the relative paucity of literature which engages with African history from an IR perspective, the chapter draws upon insights from related disciplines.

The politics of knowledge production

Peoples in Africa are frequently reduced to clichés, stereotypes and crude generalisations by outsiders from other parts of the world. This has been famously satirised by Binyavanga Wainaina: 'treat Africa as if it were one country. It is hot and dusty with rolling grasslands and huge herds of animals and tall, thin people who are starving. Or it is hot and steamy with very short people who eat primates. Don't get bogged down with precise descriptions' (Wainaina, 2005). While stereotypes are by no means uncommon, on this occasion they are directly implicated in larger political and historical processes, since there is a long history of crude generalisations about Africa being invoked to justify and legitimate external interventions.

It is here that the politics of knowledge production take centre stage. Much of what is 'known' about the history and politics of Africa has been written by Europeans, in European languages, for European audiences and, in many cases, to advance European interests (Allman, 2019; Mbembe, 2021). Of particular importance here is the relationship between knowledge and power, which was especially pronounced under colonial rule. European impressions of the different peoples whom they encountered in Africa were frequently superficial and misleading, yet these impressions nonetheless had a profound impact upon colonial laws and policies, which in turn had further effects upon their 'native' subjects. These effects were strongest in relation to identity, where fluid and overlapping conceptions of identity tended to 'harden' under colonial regimes based upon essentialised models of tribe, race and gender (Lynch, 2018). As Archie Mafeje (1971: 253) famously demonstrated, colonial anthropology did not so much describe as create: 'if tribalism is thought of as peculiarly African, then the ideology itself is particularly European in origin'.

Several different markers of difference can be identified here. As Mahmood Mamdani (2012: 74) has argued, 'the colonial state was based on a double discrimination, racial and tribal … Race was said to be about a hierarchy of civilization, whereas tribe was said to reflect cultural (ethnic) diversity within a race'. Until (at least) the mid-twentieth century, tribe was the main reference point for theorising differences amongst Africans, while race was the main reference point for differences between Africans and Europeans. The history of racial classification is long and complex (see, e.g., McGrane, 1989; Kendi, 2016; Yao and Delatolla, 2021). For the purposes of this chapter, I am primarily concerned with pseudo-scientific version of race which became dominant over the nineteenth century, which understood race in terms of innate and insurmountable differences between 'superior' and 'inferior' groupings. It should come as no surprise that Europeans positioned themselves in the former category, paving the way for racially coded hierarchies which saw the 'superiority' of European civilisation measured in roads, clothes, morals and machines (e.g., Hobson, 2012: 33–130).

European states and peoples ritually compared themselves to their non-Europeans counterparts, which meant that Africans would be chiefly defined in terms of stylised qualities which they were said to *lack* in comparison to Europeans. This overall approach was most infamously expressed through a series of binary oppositions: enlightenment/darkness, civilised/savage, Christian/pagan, white/black, modern/primitive and advanced/backwards (Mudimbe, 1988; Grovogui, 1996: 11–110). These binaries not only provided an ideological foundation for European 'superiority', they also played a major role in helping to legitimate the global expansion of European power and authority. Within IR circles, these dynamic is prominently associated with the European 'standard of civilisation', which was invoked to compel non-European rulers to transform their institutions and practices to more closely align to European expectations (e.g. Bowden, 2021). Most of the literature associated with this standard focus upon non-European states such as Thailand, Japan or Turkey who escaped direct European colonisation. However, these cases need to be recognised as the exception not the rule. No corner of Africa entirely escaped colonialism, although its duration could be measured in either centuries (Angola) or years (Ethiopia).

European colonial rule in Africa was chiefly justified using appeals to paternalism. As the word itself implies, paternalism is modelled upon the hierarchical relationship between father and child. European authority was said to be both necessary and desirable because the 'inferiority' of Africans and other non-Europeans limited their capacity for independent agency, rendering them akin to children in need of parental oversight. At the infamous Congress of Berlin in 1885 (Berlin Conference, 1885: article 6) Europeans justified the 'partition' of Africa in terms of a self-proclaimed obligation to 'watch over the preservation of the native tribes, and to care for the improvement of the conditions of their moral and material well-being … bringing home to them the blessings of civilization'. Throughout history, paternalism has played a key ideological role in justifying systems of exploitation and domination. Enslaved Africans labouring on plantations in the Americas were said to be sustained by the benevolence of their enslavers. European conquerors in Africa maintained that their 'native' subjects benefitted from colonial rule. Appeals to paternalism served a similar ideological function in both cases: cloaking elite interests in the language of altruism and benevolence (Quirk, 2021).

Paternalism has been a recurring feature of the politics of knowledge production about Africa. One of the main issues here is a recurring disconnect between what Europeans said they were doing and what they were actually doing, which creates an additional layer which must be negotiated when it comes to writing about African politics and history today (Grovogui, 2013). Consequentially, IR scholars do 'not come to Africa innocently but through recourse to an already existing archive – the colonial library – whose knowledge capital structures and almost always insinuates itself in, and contaminates, discourses on and about Africa' (Wai, 2018: 9–10). The concept of a colonial library is drawn from V.Y. Mudimbe, whose seminal work has grappled with the enduring effects of colonial knowledge practices and related efforts to reinterpret and challenge these practices from an African standpoint.

One of Mudimbe's (1991: 4) primary arguments is that colonial knowledge practices can be analysed in terms of:

> three principal arenas of conversion: the colonial commissioner's transmutation of 'savage spaces' into 'civilized settings'; the anthropologist's codifying of humans, institutions, and beliefs by their particularity vis-à-vis a functional model; and the Christian missionary's self-sacrifice amongst 'primitives' in the struggle between 'true light' and local tradition.

Taken together, these knowledge practices comprise a library of texts, symbols and systems of thought which define both Africa and Africans in terms of difference and deviance. As scholars such as Oyèrónké Oyéwùmí (1997: 152) have demonstrated, further ideological and political effects can also be found when it comes to the imposition of European models of gender, resulting in a dynamic where 'the process of inferiorizing the native, which was the essence of colonization, was bound up with the process of enthroning male hegemony' (see also Tamale, 2020). Much of Oyèwùmí's analysis is devoted to interactions between the history of the Yoruba in (what became) Nigeria and the much larger history of colonialism, racism and allied knowledge practices. The need for this broader canvas can be primarily traced the homogenisation of Africa and Africans into a singular and reductive category by Europeans. The Yoruba did not think of themselves as 'Africans' prior to contact with Europeans, but the category of African emerged as a central referent thanks to the effects of both the transatlantic slave trade and colonisation. Shared experiences of racism, enslavement and/or colonialism paved the way for new forms of identity and belonging which connected otherwise distinct peoples from many parts of the continent, and between Africa and peoples of African descent in Europe and the Americas (e.g., Gilroy, 1993; Falola and Agbo, 2019).

Political opposition to systems of European domination also played a central role in consolidating a shared sense of African identity and consciousness. Divisions between Europeans and Africans could not be dissolved, since they were hardwired into ideology and experience, so most energies were instead directed towards building a different foundation for the African side of the binary, which was tainted by European racism. Some influential examples of this larger theme include Aimé Césaire and Léopold Senghor's concept of Négritude, and W.E.B. Du Bois and Cheikh Anta Diop's historical focus on African cultural unity (e.g., Diop, 1978;

Du Bois, 2001; Wilder, 2015). These Pan-African approaches were especially influential in the mid-twentieth century, when colonial rule was eroding and there was hope for a new and different order.

It has subsequently become clearer, however, that the legacies of European colonialism cannot be easily transcended. One counterpoint comes from Kwame Appiah (1993: 60), who cautions against 'nativism' as a form of reverse discourse: 'while Western criteria of evaluation are challenged, the way in which the contest is framed is not … The Western emperor has ordered the natives to exchange their robes for trousers: their act of defiance is to insist on tailoring them from homespun material'. These sentiments comprise part of the rationale behind the now familiar distinction between the postcolonial and decolonial. While the former points to the continuation of colonial systems and mentalities, the latter 'calls for recognition of alternative knowledges and alternative ways of knowing, as part of re-opening vistas of liberation from global imperial designs and colonial matrices of power' (Ndlovu-Gatsheni, 2013). Despite growing efforts to decolonise knowledge practices, there is little doubt that the colonial library remains hegemonic and that efforts to write about Africa therefore take place in its shadow.

Regional histories and networks of cross-cultural exchange

Histories of Africa frequently begin with two recurring motifs. The first is Africa as the cradle of humankind, the original home of our species from which all humanity is descended. The second is the rich diversity of the continent. This is partly expressed in terms of physical geography, which ranges from the desserts of the Sahara to the jungle of the Congo Basin, and partly expressed in terms of differences amongst the numerous peoples who call Africa home, which include many different faiths, languages, cultures and political configurations. This diversity is worth emphasising here, because it provides an important corrective to the temptation to project the homogenising imperatives of the colonial period backwards in time. Most accounts of African history are structured in terms of the precolonial, the colonial and the postcolonial. These last two themes have a degree of internal coherence (although colonialism started much earlier than the late-nineteenth century in Luanda and Cape Town and also lasted beyond the mid-twentieth century, especially in Southern Africa). However, the precolonial tends to function as a catch all which runs together anything which happened prior to colonial conquest (see Guillaume, 2021). The language of pre- also tends to be associated with a broader tendency to view everything prior to colonisation as prelude, which gets briefly mentioned in passing before getting to the main concern: European colonialism and its effects.

There is not really a shared and singular 'precolonial' history of Africa. There are instead many different regional and local histories and networks of cross-cultural exchange. The familiar dividing line between North Africa and Sub-Saharan (or 'Black') Africa is not particularly helpful either. There were constant exchanges which saw people, goods and ideas move across the Sahara (e.g., Lecocq, 2015). One well-known example is the 1591 battle of Tondibi, where Moroccan invaders defeated the forces of a declining Songhay empire in what is now Mali (the modern name being derived from the empire which proceeded Songhay), bringing about a regional realignment which saw one of the largest states in African history collapse, resulting in a fragmented landscape where successor states struggled for dominance (Thornton, 1999: xii, 21–25). The complications associated with drawing a clear line between North and Sub-Saharan Africa are exacerbated by the fact that Sub-Saharan Africa is not a single region either. Take, for example, the trading cities of Mombasa, Mogadishu and Zanzibar in Eastern Africa, which were integrated into the Indian Ocean World (IOW) from the eighth century onwards, building upon a distinctive Swahili culture (e.g., Vernet, 2015). Prior to the nineteenth century, the political history of the Swahili coast was largely separate from that of the Sahel. Much the same can be said of most Khoisan speaking peoples in Southern Africa. Since space is limited, I've decided to briefly consider three key spheres of cross-cultural exchange which connected parts of the continent to other corners of the globe: the Sahara, Indian Ocean and Atlantic Ocean.

The history of trans-Saharan trade is strongly associated with the Islamic faith, which primarily came to Western Africa via trade, rather than conquest, and has been key referent for collective identity for over a thousand years. It was also central to how the rest of the world was imagined. Mecca was venerated as holy site, and pilgrimage emerged as a tool of statecraft, such as the famous journey of thousands of kilometres by the fabulously wealthy Mansā Mūsā, ruler of the Mali Empire, in the 1320s. As Ghislaine Lydon (2009: 3; see also Kane, 2016) observes:

> … Islam structured both the organization of long-distance caravan trade and the operation of trade networks. Muslim merchants and traders used their Arabic literacy and access to writing paper to draw contractual agreements and dispatch commercial correspondence, while depending on their mutual trust in God.

Written sources in Arabic constitute a key source of information on Western Africa, which ensures that that there is frequently greater information available on this historical region than in many parts of the continent (although both archaeology and oral histories can help to close the gap). Extensive trade routes helped to move both goods and people backwards and forward from north to south (i.e. spanning states bordering the Mediterranean to states bordering the Atlantic, and most regions in between) and from west to east (i.e. spanning Senegambia to Egypt and the Middle East via northern Nigeria and Lake Chad) (Austen, 2010: 28–29). The most prominent trade goods from Western Africa were gold and slaves. It has been estimated that around four million people were forced across the Sahara between 800 and 1900. Enslaved Africans were also traded in East Africa, with another two million slaves coming 'to Egypt by way of the Nile Valley from Ethiopia and the Southern Sudan', and perhaps an additional four million reaching 'the Middle East and India via the Red Sea and the Indian Ocean' (Austen, 2010: 32).

Enslavement was also a key component of the political and social order of Western Africa. This was especially true of the empires of Mali and Songhay: 'as Islam and empire became tightly intertwined, slavery became increasingly insinuated within both' (Gomez, 2018: 17). This longstanding nexus between enslavement and Islam also had a profound influence upon regional patterns of warfare, which escalated over the course of the eighteenth and nineteenth centuries. The most famous example of this larger dynamic is the Sokoto Caliphate (centred in what became northern Nigeria), which was founded in 1804 and rapidly acquired a major empire through a series of wars fought under the banner of Jihad. One recent influential interpretation of Jihad in West Africa comes from Paul Lovejoy (2016), who argues that Sokoto should be approached as a revolutionary state whose ideology and agenda can be best understood within the context of the more familiar 'Age of Revolutions'. Like many other states in the region, Sokoto was connected to both the Sahara and the Atlantic.

Islam also played an important role in parts of Eastern Africa. As Edward Alpers (2013: 41) observes 'Arabic, the language of Islam, became the lingua franca of western Indian Ocean trade, while Islamic law provided a legal framework for regulating trade'. Over many centuries, traders and rulers from parts of Arabia and Africa joined their counterparts in the Indian subcontinent, South East Asia and East Asia to develop extensive networks which have come to be analysed in terms of the IOW. One of the defining features of the IOW was its cultural and political diversity. No single power was able to establish their dominance (although both Portugal and Oman emerged as key maritime powers in East Africa at different points), which meant that circuits of exchange required collaboration across cultural divides (e.g., Chaudhuri, 1985; Sheriff, 2010). Europeans could be significant without necessarily being dominant. This is captured by Alessandro Stanziani (2014: 2), who points to three main phases:

> ... a long period stretching from antiquity to the rise of Islam (eighth to tenth centuries); then from the global IOW of Islamic, Mughal, and Ming-Qing powers to the coexistence of these polities with Western empires (eleventh to eighteenth centuries); and finally, the dominance of the West.

Similar sentiments have been expressed by Andrew Phillips and Jason Sharman (2015: 18), writing from an IR perspective, who point to 'a durably diverse international system'.

Both goods and people would enter and leave Eastern Africa via the IOW, with trading networks sometimes reaching considerable distances into the interior of the continent. One notable route saw gold mined in the inland state of Mutapa (present day Zimbabwe), transported to the coast at Sofala (now in Mozambique) and then taken to Kilwa (now in Tanzania) to be 'exchanged for cloth and other manufactures from India and the Middle East' (Pearson, 2008: 323). Another key example comes from Zanzibar, which came to dominate the global market in cloves during the nineteenth century (Cooper, 1977). We also have numerous examples of Africans being transported to other regions, and of chattel labour being imported from other parts of the IOW to Africa, including Cape Town. Some of these circuits persisted in the nineteenth century via indentured labour.

The history of cross-culture exchange across both the Sahara and Indian Ocean does not begin with European contact. There were long periods were European were peripheral to the story, and when they did intrude they were not necessarily dominant. IR theorists tend to begin their histories at the point where Europeans first came onto the scene, and/or to regard everything prior to European ascendance as prehistory (Suzuki et al., 2014). One of the most significant problems here is a widespread tendency to take evaluative criteria drawn from European history, most notably sovereign statehood and shared collective identity, and to then ritually catalogue all of the ways in which other parts of the globe deviate from these Eurocentric ideal types (see Zarakol, 2021; Herborth and Nitzschner, 2021). One key problem with this approach is that cultural diversity and political pluralism is the historical norm, not the exception, so it should not be surprising that arrangements elsewhere look different to those in Europe. Pluralism only appears as a 'deviation' if you use Eurocentric criteria.

Europeans played a much more central role in the history of Atlantic Africa than the other two regions considered to date (at least prior to the nineteenth century). Deep-water vessels did not play a major role prior to European incursions, so the arrival of ships capable of navigating the Atlantic Ocean marked the beginning of a major transformation. Portuguese vessels were the first to make contact, and they were the most successful European state when it came establishing permanent territorial control (e.g. Cape Verde, Elmina, São Tomé). From the 1570s, this included a colony in Angola which became the most significant colonial conquest in Atlantic Africa prior to the nineteenth century, and which in turn played a major role in the emergence of significant numbers of Euro-Africans, or 'Atlantic creoles' (see Heywood and Thornton, 2007). In addition, the Portuguese both sent and received a large number of diplomatic envoys, and also deployed their military forces to build alliances and secure economic opportunities (Northrup, 2002: 5). They were subsequently joined by the French, Dutch, Spanish and British, amongst others. It is a mistake to view the history of this period through a lens which exclusively focuses upon relations between Europeans and Africans, since political interactions within Africa did not necessarily feature Europeans, but the frequency and intensity of these cross-cultural exchanges were nonetheless sufficient to point to the emergence of a regional system (Pella, 2014: 148).

The history of Atlantic Africa is entwined with the history of the colonial Americas. This connection primarily arises through the transatlantic slave trade, which saw an estimated 12.5 million enslaved Africans forced onto ships which took them to the Americas, where their forced labour made an indispensable contribution to building the 'New World' (slavevoyages.org). Far more enslaved Africans went to the Americas than Europeans prior to the nineteenth century: '[b]y 1820' nearly '8.7 million slaves had departed from Africa to the New World, as opposed to only 2.6 million whites ... and from 1760 to 1820 this emigrating flow included 5.6 African slaves for every European' (Davis, 2006: 80). While Europeans also traded for gold and ivory, these ventures were largely overshadowed by enslavement by the seventeenth century.

With the notable exception of Angola, Europeans rarely penetrated into the African interior but were instead usually confined to the coast, where their presence was more often negotiated than imposed (Green, 2019: 365). At some ports, small permanent settlements with European and Euro-African resident populations emerged, such as Cape Coast, Anomabu and Ouidah. This can be contrasted with sites such as Bonny, Old Calabar, Loango, Cabinda and Malemba, where trade mostly depended on ship-to-shore interaction, though temporary storehouses were sometimes erected. These arrangements were not a discretionary choice where Europeans had the capacity to invade at any time yet refrained from doing so for centuries. It has instead been traced to a lack of capacity to project power inland. As David Eltis (2000: 147) argues, 'what happened in the Americas was what Europeans wanted to do in Africa but could not bring about'.

The Atlantic trade in enslaved Africans began prior to 1492 and persisted until the 1860s. Over the centuries, complex systems were developed to regularise the terms of exchange. These included the provision of credit via pawnship, mechanisms for resolving contract disputes, the emergence of brokers and trading communities and the standardisation of cross-cultural units of exchange, such as the 'bar' (Gambia, the Windward Coast and Bonny), 'trade ounces' (Gold Coast and Ouidah), 'coppers' (Old Calabar) and 'pieces' or 'cloths' (Loango and Angola). Many of these systems involved the adaptation of pre-existing models, communities and preferences which predated European contact (Quirk and Richardson, 2014).

Growing European demand for enslaved Africans had catastrophic effects upon the interior of Atlantic Africa, producing a political economy of violence that bound together coastal sites with evolving hinterlands where countless wars and raids were driven by the economic and political incentives of this external demand. Crucially, this carnage was primarily directed towards, but not always solely confined to, peoples who were regarded as enemies or outsiders. The capacity of slave suppliers within Africa to externalise – sometimes only partially or temporarily – the social and political costs of enslavement was fundamental to this political economy, which persisted throughout the second half of the nineteenth century, when the staggered end of the transatlantic slave trade resulted in the redirection of enslaved Africans into regional economic networks, contributing to the emergence of a 'slave mode of production' within some parts of Western Africa (e.g., Law, 1995; Coquery-Vidrovitch, 2009: 185–205).

States, political authority and 'rights-in-persons'

Within IR circles, the state in Africa has most frequently been defined using a logic of subtraction, which involves taking the 'modern/Western' state as benchmark, and then focusing upon the ways in which political authorities within Africa fall short of this ideal (e.g., Grovogui, 2001; Quirk and Vigneswaran, 2015). This logic is most prominently associated with the twin concepts of 'quasi-states' and 'failed' states, which have strongly informed efforts to theorise postcolonial

African politics (see also Svensson, 2021). However, it also been applied to political authority in Africa prior to colonisation, where many scholars refrain from using the category of 'state', and instead prefer to talk in terms of polities, or political communities. This approach is exemplified by Hedley Bull, whose chapter on Africa for *The Expansion of International Society* (1984: 102) clearly distinguishes between 'European states and African political communities', and also makes reference to 'polities comparable in size to modern African nation-states' (1984: 113). This can be contrasted with the approach of Jeffrey Herbst (2014: 37), who maintains that the widespread assumption 'that states and systems of states did not exist in Africa simply because the European model was not followed demonstrates, at the minimum, a lack of imagination and, more importantly, a rather narrow conception of how power can be organized'. Even the 'European model' can be best understood as stylised ideal type, given the variegated nature of European history.

Herbst contends that states and state systems can be found in Africa prior to European colonisation, but that political authority also displayed a number of distinctive features. These features are partly traced to the effects of low population densities, at least in comparison to most of China or Europe, which meant that land was frequently abundant while labour remained scarce (yet there are also some key exceptions here, such as Ethiopia) (Herbst, 2014: 16; see also Austin, 2008). In addition, agricultural production was relatively flexible, so communities faced with threats were not always obliged to defend valuable fixed infrastructure or major urban centres, and could therefore migrate and rebuild their lives at manageable cost. Herbst goes on to link this to a series of hurdles associated with 'broadcasting power'. These are said to have created systems of governance defined by differences 'between what control of the political center meant and what the partial exercise of power amounted to in the hinterland', with authority taking the form of 'concentric circles' radiating outwards, including tributary relations (Herbst, 2014: 41, 45; see also Bayart, 1993: 21).

Rather than focusing on conquering fixed territories, political elites frequently concentrated their efforts upon both controlling and acquiring people (Herbst, 2014: 37–41). This dynamic is frequently framed in terms of rights-in-persons (or wealth in people), which refers to networks of dependency, hierarchy and patronage, with junior members within a community providing services, support and material goods for their superiors, while their superiors in turn offered their qualified patronage and protection to their subordinates. These rights were not held by individuals, but through 'kin groups acting as corporate bodies' (Miers and Kopytoff, 1977: 9). One key example here is the payment of bridewealth, which typically connects different lineages in complex ways which go far beyond a union between two individuals (Goody, 1973). As many scholars have demonstrated, marriage frequently played a foundational role when it came to building and consolidating political and personal power in many corners of Africa. This is captured by Emily Osborn (2011:4), whose history of Upper Guinea prior to colonisation focuses upon mutually reinforcing dynamics between 'household-making and state-making'. Osborn points to a form of statehood that is 'highly flexible and knitted together by patron-client, marital, and kinship ties', but which 'nonetheless exists as an autonomous, identifiable political institution that stands apart from, or independent of, any one person, officeholder, clan, or kin group' (2011: 5).

Enslavement and slave trading are also integral to the 'rights-in-persons' approach. Since political power was predicated upon control over people, rather than control over land, both slave raiding and trading regularly played a key role in state-building. It is important to distinguish here between trading slaves to outsiders and incorporating enslaved outsiders into an already established political and social order. While African states typically pursued both of these strategies simultaneously, the transatlantic slave trade often tipped the balance in favour of the former, which had further effects upon state-building. This dynamic has frequently been linked to the 'predatory states thesis', which emphasises the relationship between state-building and wars of enslavement and conquest. This thesis has been linked to prominent states such Oyo, Asante, Futa Jallon and Segu (Klein, 2001: 49; Osborn, 2011: 6). However, these states need to be understood as the exception not the rule: 'perhaps 30 percent of Atlantic Africa's area was occupied by states with surface areas larger than 50,000 square kilometers', while the rest 'was occupied by small, even tiny, states' (Thornton, 1998: 14). There are a number of cases where the category of state is not especially useful, leading to the analysis of decentralised 'stateless societies'. Importantly, these societies were not necessarily defenceless against their neighbours (Hawthorne, 2013).

The extent to which rulers within Atlantic Africa were able to exercise independent agency remains hotly contested. Many Marxist inspired historians, such as Walter Rodney and Samir Amin, have concentrated their analysis upon the position of Atlantic Africa (and Africa more broadly) within a European dominated global economy. Two key strands of this approach can be briefly highlighted here. First, there is a strong insistence that 'the process by which captives were obtained on African soil was not trade at all. It was through warfare, trickery, banditry, and kidnaping', and should therefore be approached as 'social violence rather than trade in any normal sense of the word' (Rodney, 2018: 121). Second, there is an emphasis on economic dependency, demographic decline, political fragmentation and underdevelopment, whose effects are said to linger to the present day. Europeans initiated the transatlantic trade and were its overwhelming beneficiaries, and whatever short term gains might have accrued to African middlemen proved to be ephemeral and counterproductive: '[r]educed to the function of supplying slave labour for the plantations of America, Africa lost its autonomy' (Amin, 1972: 511).

Agency needs to be understood as both an historical and moral issue. Limited scope for agency (or autonomy) means a limited degree of responsibility, while greater scope for independent agency opens the door to a greater share of responsibility for atrocity. Neither of these approaches are especially satisfying, since the former goes against the grain of decades of effort to restore subaltern agency, while the later runs the risk of portraying centuries of dependency as 'the outcome of African initiative' (Mamdani, 1996: 10). The broad terms of this dynamic will be familiar to IR theorists of structure and agency, but it does not necessarily follow that these differences can be resolved by moving towards a 'mutually constitutive' position, since it is the nature of the underlying structure which is ultimately at issue. It is also clear, moreover, that the equation tends to look quite different once the focus shifts from immediate calculations to longer term cumulative effects. The overall picture of the transatlantic slave trade is clearly not a positive one, since it resulted in catastrophic levels of violence, death and insecurity which were not conducive to long-term economic and political development. There is also no question that Europeans were the main beneficiaries and perpetrators, and that things would have been very different absent external demand for forced labour. There are still arguments to be had about the dimensions and effects of the trade, especially at a micro level, but it would be a mistake to try and minimise or obscure these two larger points.

Concluding remarks

IR scholars have remarkably little to say about the history and politics of Africa prior to the European colonial conquests of the nineteenth century. The dominant impulse has been to start with the colonial state and to then focus on how and why it has changed with the passage of time. Two influential examples of this broader trend come from Robert Jackson and Christopher Clapham, whose books have both played a major role in informing analysis of the state in Africa. The history of Africa prior to colonial rule is almost entirely absent in both cases. Jackson begins his narrative with an imaginary dialogue with a British civil servant from 1936, who is said to find the notion of decolonisation as a general principle 'inconceivable' (Jackson, 1991: 14).

Similarly, Clapham begins his narrative (1996: 30) by focusing upon the ways in which European colonialism 'transformed the map of Africa' and then moves on to focus upon the characteristics of the colonial state and the later effects of decolonisation. The colonial state enters the narrative as a pre-established fact, leaving little space to consider how and why political authority had been configured previously. This has the effect of consolidating, rather than challenging, the dominant position of the European sovereign state. It also results in a lack of meaningful engagement with the numerous acts of violence which were used to establish colonial states in the first place (e.g., Falola, 2009; Walter, 2017). Many IR scholars have far more to say about the end of colonisation than the beginning, which risks doing an injustice to the endemic wars and systems of subjugation which were fundamental to colonial conquest.

The main aim of this chapter has been to make the case for considering the history of Africa prior to colonisation on its own terms, rather than as a preamble to the main event. As we have seen, this has meant grappling with important regional variations and patterns of cross-cultural exchange associated with the Sahara, Indian and Atlantic Oceans, which quickly reveal the limitations of a still widespread tendency to conceptualise Africa in singular terms. In addition, I have also attempted to highlight some of the problems and limitations associated with the application of Eurocentric evaluative standards to the politics and history of Africa. Many IR histories begin at the point where Europeans arrive on the scene and/or secure a dominant position, which can result in a failure to engage with scenarios where Europeans are either entirely absent or relevant but not dominant. As we have seen, similar kinds of complications also tend to arise when African states and peoples are exclusively benchmarked against stylised images of European states and peoples, which too often results in a focus upon what they are perceived to lack, rather than how they are actually organised. Efforts to write about Africa and Africans invariably take place under the shadow of the colonial archive. Its ideological effects cannot be escaped, but they can be interrogated.

Suggestions for further reading

Alpers, E. (2013). *The Indian Ocean in World History*. Oxford: Oxford University Press.
de Heredia, M. I., and Wai, Z., eds. (2018). *Recentering Africa in International Relations: Beyond Lack, Peripherality, and Failure*. London: Palgrave.
Gomez, M. (2018). *African Dominion: A New History of Empire in Early and Medieval West Africa*. Princeton, NJ: Princeton University Press.
Green, T. (2019). *A Fistful of Shells: West Africa from the Rise of the Slave Trade to the Age of Revolution*. London: Penguin.
Mudimbe, V.Y. (1988). *The Invention of Africa: Gnosis, Philosophy, and the Order of Knowledge*. Bloomington, IN: Indiana University Press.
Oyèwùmí, O. (1997). *The Invention of Women: Making an African Sense of Western Gender Discourses*. Minneapolis, MN: University of Minnesota Press.

References

Allman, J. (2019). #HerskovitsMustFall? A Meditation on whiteness, African studies, and the unfinished business of 1968. *African Studies Review*, 62 (3), 6–39.
Alpers, E. (2013). *The Indian Ocean in World History*. Oxford: Oxford University Press.
Amin, S. (1972). Underdevelopment and dependence in black Africa: origins and contemporary forms. *The Journal of Modern African Studies*, 10 (4), 503–524.
Appiah, K.A. (1993). *In My Father's House: Africa in the Philosophy of Culture*. Oxford: Oxford University Press.
Austen, R. (2010). *Trans-Saharan Africa in World History*. Oxford: Oxford University Press.
Austin, G. (2008). Resources, techniques, and strategies south of the Sahara: revising the factor endowments perspective on African economic development, 1500–2001. *Economic History Review*, 61 (3), 587–624.
Bayart, J.-F. (1993). *The State in Africa: The Politics of the Belly*. London: Longman.

Bowden, B. (2021). Eurocentrism and Civilization. In de Carvalho, B., Costa Lopez, J., & Leira, H., eds. *Routledge Handbook of Historical International Relations*. Abingdon: Routledge.

Bull, H. (1984). European states and African political communities. In: H. Bull, and A. Watson, eds., *The Expansion of International Society*, Oxford: Clarendon Press.

Chaudhuri, K. N. (1985). *Trade and Civilisation in the Indian Ocean: An Economic History from the Rise of Islam to 1750*. Cambridge: Cambridge University Press.

Clapham, C. (1996). *Africa and the International System*. Cambridge: Cambridge University Press.

Cooper, F. (1977). *Plantation Slavery on the East Coast of Africa*. New Haven, CT: Yale University Press.

Coquery-Vidrovitch, C. (2009). *Africa and the Africans in the Nineteenth Century: A Turbulent History*. London: M. E. Sharpe.

Davis, D. (2006) *Inhuman Bondage: The Rise and Fall of Slavery in the New World*. Oxford: Oxford University Press.

Diop, C. A. (1978). *The Cultural Unity of Black Africa: The Domains of Matriarchy & of Patriarchy in Classical Antiquity*. Chicago, IL: Third World Press.

Du Bois, W. E. B. (2001). *The Negro*. Philadelphia, PA: University of Pennsylvania Press.

Eltis, D. (2000). *The Rise of African Slavery in the Americas*. Cambridge: Cambridge University Press.

Falola, T. (2009). *Colonialism and Violence in Nigeria*. Bloomington, IN: Indiana University Press.

Falola, T., and Agbo, C. (2019). The Prospects and Challenges of Pan-Africanism. *Oxford Research Encyclopedia of Politics*, Oxford: Oxford University Press, DOI: 10.1093/acrefore/9780190228637.013.718.

General Act of the Berlin Conference on West Africa, 26th February 1885, Article Six. Available online. Viewed on 31 October 2020, <https://loveman.sdsu.edu/docs/1885GeneralActBerlinConference.pdf>.

Gilroy, P. (1993). *The Black Atlantic: Modernity and Double-Consciousness*. Cambridge, MA: Harvard University Press.

Goody, J. (1973). Bridewealth and Dowry in Africa and Euroasia. In: J. Goody, and S. Tambiah, eds., *Bridewealth and Dowry*. Cambridge: Cambridge University Press, 1–58.

Gomez, M. (2018). *African Dominion: A New History of Empire in Early and Medieval West Africa*. Princeton, NJ: Princeton University Press.

Green, T. (2019). *A Fistful of Shells: West Africa from the Rise of the Slave Trade to the Age of Revolution*. London: Penguin.

Grovogui, S. N. (1996). *Sovereigns, Quasi Sovereigns, and Africans: Race and Self-Determination in International Law*. Minneapolis, MN: University of Minnesota Press.

Grovogui, S. N. (2001). Sovereignty in Africa: Quasi-Statehood and Other Myths in International Theory. In: K. Dunn, and T. Shaw, eds., *Africa's Challenge To International Relations Theory*, London: Palgrave, 29–45.

Grovogui, S. N. (2013). Deferring Difference: A Postcolonial Critique of the 'Race Problem' in Moral Thought. In: S. Seth, ed., *Postcolonial Theory and International Relations: A Critical Introduction*, New York, NY: Routledge, 106–123.

Guillaume, X. (2021). Historical Periods and the Act of Periodisation. In de Carvalho, B., Costa Lopez, J., & Leira, H., eds. *Routledge Handbook of Historical International Relations*. Abingdon: Routledge.

Hawthorne, W. (2013). States and Statelessness. In: J. Parker, and R. Reid, eds., *The Oxford Handbook of Modern African History*, Oxford: Oxford University Press, DOI: 10.1093/oxfordhb/9780199572472.013.0004.

Herborth, B., and Nitzschner, P. (2021). Europe in Historical International Relations. In de Carvalho, B., Costa Lopez, J., & Leira, H., eds. *Routledge Handbook of Historical International Relations*. Abingdon: Routledge.

Herbst, J. (2014). *States and Power in Africa: Comparative Lessons in Authority and Control*. 2nd. ed. Princeton, NJ: Princeton University Press.

Heywood, L., and Thornton, J. (2007) *Central Africans, Atlantic Creoles, and the Foundation of the Americas, 1585-1660*. Cambridge: Cambridge University Press.

Hobson, J. (2012). *The Eurocentric Conception of World Politics: Western International Theory, 1760-2010*. Cambridge: Cambridge University Press.

Jackson, R. (1991). *Quasi-States, Sovereignty, International Relations and the Third World*. Cambridge: Cambridge University Press.

Kane, O. O. (2016). *Beyond Timbuktu: An Intellectual History of Muslim West Africa*. Cambridge, MA: Harvard University Press.

Kendi, I. X. (2016). *Stamped from the Beginning: The Definitive History of Racist Ideas in America*. New York, NY: Nation Books.

Klein, M. (2001). The slave trade and decentralized societies. *The Journal of African History*, 42 (1), 49–65.

Law, R., ed. (1995). *From Slave Trade to 'Legitimate' Commerce: The Commercial Transition in Nineteenth-Century West Africa.* Cambridge: Cambridge University Press.

Lecocq, B. (2015). Distant shores: a historiographic view on trans-Saharan space. *The Journal of African History,* 56 (1), 23–36.

Lovejoy, P. (2016). *Jihaād in West Africa during the Age of Revolutions.* Athens, OH: Ohio University Press.

Lydon, G. (2009). *On Trans-Saharan Trails: Islamic Law, Trade Networks, and Cross-Cultural Exchange in Nineteenth-Century Western Africa.* Cambridge: Cambridge University Press.

Lynch, G. (2018). Ethnicity in Africa. In *Oxford Research Encyclopedia of African History.* Oxford: Oxford University Press, DOI: 10.1093/acrefore/9780190277734.013.32.

Mafeje, A. (1971). The ideology of 'tribalism'. *The Journal of Modern African Studies,* 9 (2), 253–261.

Mamdani, M. (1996). *Citizen and Subject: Contemporary Africa and the Legacy of Late Colonialism.* Princeton, NJ: Princeton University Press.

Mamdani, M. (2012). *Define and Rule: Native as Political Identity.* Cambridge, MA: Harvard University Press.

Mbembe, A. (2017). *Critique of Black Reason.* Durham, NC: Duke University Press.

Mbembe, A. (2021). *Out of the Dark Night: Essays on Decolonization.* New York, NY: Columbia University Press.

McGrane, B. (1989). *Beyond Anthropology: Society and the Other.* New York, NY: Columbia University Press.

Miers, S., and Kopytoff, I. (1977). African 'Slavery' as an Institution of Marginality. In: S. Miers, and I. Kopytoff, eds., *Slavery in Africa: Historical and Anthropological Perspectives,* Madison, WI: University of Wisconsin Press, 3–81.

Mudimbe, V.Y. (1988). *The Invention of Africa: Gnosis, Philosophy, and the Order of Knowledge.* Bloomington, IN: Indiana University Press.

Mudimbe, V.Y. (1991). *Parables and Fables: Exegesis, Textuality, and Politics in Central Africa.* Madison: University of Wisconsin Press.

Ndlovu-Gatsheni, S. (2013). *Empire, Global Coloniality and African Subjectivity.* New York, NY: Berghahn Books.

Northrup, D. (2002). *African's Discovery of Europe, 1440-1850.* Oxford: Oxford University Press.

Osborn, E. L. (2011). *Our New Husbands are Here: Households, Gender, and Politics in a West African State from the Slave Trade to Colonial Rule.* Athens, OH: Ohio University Press.

Oyèwùmí, O. (1997). *The Invention of Women: Making an African Sense of Western Gender Discourses.* Minneapolis, MN: University of Minnesota Press.

Pearson, M. (2008). Islamic Trade, Shipping, Port States and Merchant Communities in the Indian Ocean, Seventh to Sixteenth Centuries. In: D. Morgan, and A. Reid, eds., *The New Cambridge History of Islam. Volume 3: The Eastern Islamic World, Eleventh to Eighteenth Centuries,* Cambridge: Cambridge University Press, 317–365.

Pella, J. A. (2014). *Africa and the Expansion of International Society: Surrendering the Savannah.* London: Routledge.

Phillips, A., and Sharman, J. (2015). *International Order in Diversity: War, Trade and Rule in the Indian Ocean.* Cambridge: Cambridge University Press.

Quirk, J. (2021). Political Cultures. In: H. Altink, ed., *A Cultural History of Slavery and Human Trafficking in the Age of Global Conflict,* London: Bloomsbury.

Quirk, J., and Richardson, D. (2014). Europeans, Africans and the Atlantic world, 1450–1850. In: S. Suzuki, Y. Zhang, and J. Quirk, eds., *International Orders in the Early Modern World: Before the Rise of the West,* London: Routledge, 158–178.

Quirk, J., and Vigneswaran, D. (2015). Mobility Makes States. In: D. Vigneswaran, and J. Quirk, eds., *Mobility Makes States: Migration and Power in Africa,* Philadelphia, PA: University of Pennsylvania Press, 1–35.

Rodney, W. (2018). *How Europe Underdeveloped Africa.* London: Verso.

Sheriff, A. (2010). *Dhow Cultures of the Indian Ocean: Cosmopolitanism, Commerce and Islam.* London: Hurst.

Slave Voyages. Emory Center for Digital Scholarship. Viewed on 31 October 2020, <https://www.slavevoyages.org>.

Stanziani, A. (2014). *Sailors, Slaves, and Immigrants: Bondage in the Indian Ocean World, 1750–1914.* New York, NY: Palgrave.

Suzuki, S., Zhang, Y., and Quirk, J., eds. (2014). *International Orders in the Early Modern World: Before the Rise of the West.* London: Routledge.

Svensson, T. (2021). Decolonisation and the Erosion of the Imperial Idea. In de Carvalho, B., Costa Lopez, J., & Leira, H., eds. *Routledge Handbook of Historical International Relations.* Abingdon: Routledge.

Tamale, S. (2020). *Decolonization and Afro-Feminism.* Ottawa: Daraja Press.

Thornton, J. (1998). *Africa and Africans in the Making of the Atlantic World, 1400-1800*. Cambridge: Cambridge University Press.

Thornton, J. (1999). *Warfare in Atlantic Africa, 1500-1800*. London: Routledge.

Vernet, T. (2015). East African Travelers and Traders in the Indian Ocean: Swahili Ships, Swahili Mobilities ca.1500–1800. In: M. Pearson, ed., *Trade, Circulation, and Flow in the Indian Ocean World*, New York, NY: Palgrave, 167–202.

Wai, Z. (2018). Africa in/and International Relations: An Introduction. In: M. Iñiguez de Heredia, and Z. Wai, eds., *Recentering Africa in International Relations: Beyond Lack, Peripherality, and Failure*, London: Palgrave, 1–30.

Wainaina, B. (2005). How to Write About Africa. *Granta*, 92. Also online. Viewed on 31 October 2020, <https://granta.com/how-to-write-about-africa/>.

Walter, D. (2017). *Colonial Violence: European empires and the use of force*. London: Hurst.

Wilder, G. (2015). *Freedom Time: Negritude, Decolonization, and the Future of the World*. Durham, NC: Duke University Press.

Yao, J., and Delatolla, A. (2021). Race and Historical International Relations. In de Carvalho, B., Costa Lopez, J., & Leira, H., eds. *Routledge Handbook of Historical International Relations*. Abingdon: Routledge.

Zarakol, A. (2021). Linking up the Ottoman Empire with IR's Timeline. In de Carvalho, B., Costa Lopez, J., & Leira, H., eds. *Routledge Handbook of Historical International Relations*. Abingdon: Routledge.

42

INTERNATIONAL ORDER IN EAST ASIA

Shogo Suzuki

Introduction

The global spread of the Westphalian international order has become such an entrenched part of our lives that it is almost impossible to think of alternative ways of ordering international politics today. We frequently talk of the sovereign state, the 'nation', and the nation state as if they had existed since time immemorial; bar territorial disputes, existing borders between sovereign states have taken on an almost ahistorical quality and are treated as if they have always 'been there'. Governments fall into the trap of ahistoricism, too: the Chinese government, which is currently embroiled in a number of territorial disputes, has a penchant for claiming that certain territories are 'sacred' and 'inalienable' parts of the sovereign territory of the People's Republic of China, even though the concept of the sovereign state did not exist in East Asia until the late nineteenth century.

The historical reality, however, is much more complex. What is often referred to as the 'Westphalian' international order, characterised by sovereign equality and sovereign state, only spread to the non-Western world in the late nineteenth century to the early twentieth century (Bull and Watson, 1984; Gong, 1984; Suzuki, 2009, see also Navari and Green, 2021).[1] Prior to this, the world consisted of multiple 'international orders', each with their own norms that stipulated how interstate interactions (or more accurately, interactions between the regional polities) should be conducted. The discipline of International Relations (IR), which often begins 'international history' from the peace treaties of Westphalia (1648),[2] has tended to look at the past from a position of European primacy. It therefore ignores this empirical reality, as well as the fact that prior to the rise of Europe, the non-Western world was able to dictate to the Western rulers the terms of diplomatic interaction and trade (and given their relative weakness vis-à-vis the non-European polities, they had little choice in this matter). Western actors, often attracted to the 'Orient' and its products and markets, were active, but relatively unimportant participants in many of these regional international orders (Suzuki et al., 2013).

The region we now call 'East Asia' was no exception to this. Prior to the expansion of the Europe-centred international order to the region in the late-nineteenth century, East Asia had its own international order, with a set of norms that dictated the institutional form of interstate relations. More importantly, this order proved to be remarkably durable. An examination of the lost world of the East Asian international order merits closer examination because of its importance in world history. Furthermore, in the context of the discipline of IR, greater focus on this international order helps us relativise and historicise the often assumed centrality of the 'Westphalian' international order. It serves as an important corrective to the Eurocentric focus the discipline has often been criticised for (see also Hui, 2021).

The East Asian international order

The East Asian international order has usually been discussed in IR in the context of an initial clash of international orders in the late-eighteenth and early-nineteenth centuries, when the British sent the Macartney and Amherst Missions (1793 and 1816) to the Chinese empire to seek trading opportunities. The missions are famous because of the diplomatic disputes between the two parties. The Chinese side insisted that Lord Macartney perform the kowtow to the Chinese emperor, as the latter was the Son of God and ruler of the country that sat on the apex of civilisation. Lord Macartney, who was versed in the Westphalian norms of sovereign equality, refused to do this, considering the kowtow as demeaning to both Britain and his king. Eventually, the Chinese compromised. Lord Macartney was allowed an audience with the Qianlong Emperor, only to have his requests for increased trade to be rebuffed. Lord Amherst was not as lucky—his refusal to perform the kowtow was not viewed kindly by the Jiaqing Emperor, who refused the former's request for an audience.

While the Chinese case is often cited as the most famous case of the clash between the Europe-based and East Asian international (partly because the latter is conflated with the 'Chinese world order', as noted below), these encounters were by no means limited to the Chinese empire. For instance, during the Togugawa shogunate (1603–1867), Dutch traders had to present themselves to the *shōgun* in Edo (present-day Tokyo), where they were required to participate in ceremonial rituals that served to highlight the superiority of the Japanese ruler. As one observer put it, 'kneeling, he [the Dutch trade representative] bow'd his forehead quite down to the ground, and so crawl'd backwards like a crab, without uttering one single word. So mean and short a thing is the audience we have of this mighty Monarch' (Toby, 1991: 193). This sign of subservience obviously clashes with the notion of sovereign equality, but the Western actors were in no position to challenge these potentially humiliating requirements, and neither were the Asian rulers always disposed to granting them special favours and waiving the requirement to observe local diplomatic etiquette. These incidents also highlight the encounter of two very different international orders. If the European international order was—at least in theory—based on the fundamental norm of sovereign equality, the East Asian international order operated on the basis of sovereign hierarchy. How, then, did this very different international order come about?

Historical origins of the East Asian international order

The East Asian international order is often—misleadingly—known as the 'Chinese world order' (Fairbank, 1968). This is because the intellectual roots of its normative framework can be traced back to Confucianism, and also because it was the Chinese empire that was the first polity to institutionalise these norms in their diplomatic relations by implementing the so-called tribute system (*chaogong tixi*). It is extremely difficult to pinpoint when the East Asian international order emerged, as this was a gradual and evolutionary process. Zhang (2001: 52; also see He, 1998: 32) states that the tribute system (which is the most visible institutional expression of the East Asian international order), 'as special trading arrangements can be traced back to at least the Han Dynasty' (206 B.C.–220 A.D.) in China, and gradually spread beyond the Chinese empire.

The tribute system, and along with it, the East Asian international order, reached its institutional apex during the Ming (1368–1644) and Qing (1644–1911) dynasties, and this is the 'ideal type' that is discussed here. It is important that we should pay 'adequate attention to [the tribute system's] historical evolution' to avoid giving a 'misleading impression that it was somehow static and unchanging throughout history' (Zhang, 2009: 553). Nevertheless, it is worth keeping in mind that the constitutional norms of the East Asian international order— namely the hierarchical ordering of interstate relations, and diplomacy conducted on the basis of rituals designed to shore up the social hierarchy—endured in some form or other until the late-nineteenth century, when the Meiji leadership of Japan annexed the Ryūkyū Kingdom and gradually pushed the Choson dynasty in Korea to end its tributary relations with the Qing dynasty in China (Suzuki, 2009).

The East Asian international order, characterised by the hierarchical and ritualistic diplomatic system known as the 'tribute system', did not apply to all of China's external relations. As Zhang (2009: 553) reminds us with regard to historical Chinese international politics, the tribute system was 'only one—though perhaps the most prominent—among several institutions in the historical East Asian system' and 'cannot alone capture the whole sphere of China's foreign relations because they were only partly expressed in the institutional practices of the tribute system'. As Onuma (2000: 13) notes,

> Various bodies politic or independent human groups did not always share the norms based on…Sinocentrism. Especially for nomads in Central Asia, who were regarded by China as northern or Western barbarians, China was just one of many foreign powers which they would obey when it was powerful, and exploit when it was weak.

In face of the nomads' military strength, the Chinese emperor was at times forced to acknowledge equality with the nomadic rulers (Rossabi, 1983). It is also questionable as to whether or not the nomads internalised the norms of the East Asian international order and adopted them in their interstate relations with polities other than the Chinese empire.

Nevertheless, this does not mean that the tribute system, and the East Asian international order, should be seen as an idiosyncratic institution that China applied only to a handful of its neighbours. While norms that underpinned the East Asian international order did indeed originate from China, these norms spread beyond the borders of China and were internalised by a significant number of states who can be considered core members of the East Asian international order. Fairbank's Sinocentric bias is blind to the fact that Korea, the Ryūkyū Kingdom (present-day Okinawa), Vietnam, and Japan internalised (albeit at different times) the norms of the East Asian international order and reproduced these norms in their diplomatic relations beyond those with the Chinese empire. The degree to which a shared culture necessary for the emergence of some kind of international order to emerge remains a hotly contested subject (Wight, 1977: 46; O'Hagan, 1995, 2002: 108–131; Buzan and Little, 2000: 199–215; Huntington, 2002), and it remains beyond the scope of this chapter to address fully this question. Nonetheless, it does seem significant that all these states were, to varying degrees, heavily influenced by Chinese culture. The political elite used Chinese characters, and were influenced by Confucianism. All states had experimented with a Chinese-style centralised bureaucratic government at some point in their history. It seems highly possible that this shared culture played a crucial role in helping the diffusion and internalisation of the norms that governed interstate relations within the East Asian international order.

Interstate relations in the East Asian international order

Confucianism stipulated that social harmony would be best maintained through the observation and maintenance of appropriate social hierarchies (such as father and son, husband and wife, teacher and student, ruler and subjects, etc.), and this belief was extended to the Chinese empire's external relations as well. The 'moral purpose' of the state in the East Asian international order was to reproduce these 'proper' social orderings of the world (Reus-Smit, 1999; Zhang, 2001) and achieve cosmic harmony. This influenced the institutional form of the East Asian international order, which was characterised first and foremost by its hierarchical ordering of polities, rather than sovereign equality. The Chinese emperor was (at least within the empire) believed to be the Son of Heaven, and the sole individual capable of mediating between Heaven and Earth. He was therefore placed at the apex of the international social hierarchy. Other polities were expected to acknowledge this by showing their submission to the Chinese emperor through the presentation of tribute (often in the form of valuable local produce) and the observation of social rituals—which included the famous kowtow—that confirmed the Chinese emperor's superior position. In return, the Chinese emperor provided the foreign rulers with a seal of investiture confirming the latter's legitimacy to rule their lands, a calendar (something which symbolically confirmed the emperor's divine right to mediate between heaven and earth), and gifts that were often of greater value than those presented by the foreign rulers. The foreign emissaries were also allowed to stay in the capital for a limited period and engage in trade tax-free. All of this was designed to demonstrate the generosity and benevolence a legitimate ruler was to show towards his subordinates.

Much attention has been focused on the degree to which the East Asian international order's norms of interstate relations, epitomised by the tribute system, applied to the Chinese empire's foreign policy. Numerous studies have highlighted the limits of China's ability to enforce the norms of the East Asian international order to other polities, particularly with regard to its claims to be the most civilised polity under heaven (Fairbank, 1968; Rossabi, 1983; Zhang, 2001, 2009). This was partly intended as a corrective to the inherent Sinocentrism that was visible in the works pioneered by Fairbank (Zhang, 2009: 555–557), and highlights the geographical limits of the East Asian international order, as well as the importance of moving beyond the 'ideal type' of the tribute system of the Ming and Qing era and appreciating better the East Asian international order's historical evolution.

These works have made valuable contributions to our understanding of the East Asian international order, but they are nevertheless limited in their ability to explain the longevity of this particular international order (and of course, this is not their focus). This is not to deny that resistance to Chinese hegemony or claims to civilisational superiority occurred. The important point, however, is that these contestations took place firmly within the normative structures of the East Asian international order. While reminding us of the importance of avoiding Sinocentrism, many of these works seem to inadvertently fall into this very same trap, as they seem to portray acceptance of the norms of the East Asian international order in almost zero-sum terms: this order is deemed to exist only when Chinese hegemony is accepted, and if not, it is treated as if it ceases to exist.

These works are thus blind to the fact that much of the normative structures of the East Asian international order continued to inform how China's neighbours interacted with one another (Sakayori, 1993; Hamashita, 1999), even if they refused to accept the normative supremacy of the Chinese empire. These polities constructed their own tribute systems separate from the Chinese tribute system, and often claimed civilisational superiority within them. For example, R. P. Toby's (1991) important study of Japanese diplomacy during the Tokugawa shogunate (1603–1867) shows that Japan, despite rejecting tributary relations with the Qing dynasty in China, was also structuring its interstate relations modelled on the tribute system. In similar fashion to the Chinese practice of providing calendars to 'inferior' polities, the shogunate issued Chinese merchants with a trade pass that used the Japanese calendar to symbolise their superior hierarchical position. As Toby (1991: 199) states,

> The Chinese were barbarians: the credentials were dated in the Japanese calendar; they called China 'T'ang,' the formal name usually used in diplomatic discourse…. If the Chinese merchants accepted the use of the Japanese calendar, were they not also signalling Chinese acknowledgement of Japan's central role in the world yielding the center to Japan?

While Tokugawa Japan's relations with the Choson dynasty in Korea were formally conducted on the basis of equality, the Korean emissaries' processions to the shogun's castle were effectively treated as tributary missions, and seen to symbolise foreign recognition of the Tokugawa shogunate's legitimacy to rule. The Ryūkyū Kingdom was also expected to provide tributary missions to the Tokugawa shogunate, and was treated as an inferior.

Similarly, the Vietnamese rulers conducted their foreign relations with their neighbours along the lines of the tribute system, demanding tribute from their regional neighbours. The Lê dynasty of 1472, for instance, claimed equality with China because it was a 'learned country', and demonstrates 'Vietnamese confidence in its equal status with China, as well as a Vietnamese form of "Sinocentrism" which sees its neighbouring peoples as "barbarians"' (Sakayori, 1993: 52–53).

The East Asian international order and International Relations theory

The East Asian international order and its institutional expression, the tribute system, has been the subject of much interest. China's rise and perceptions of Western 'decline', combined with a more general discomfort with the Eurocentric focus of IR, have produced a number of works that seek to move beyond the confines of the 'Westphalian straitjacket' (Hobson, 2007: 93). David C. Kang (2003, 2007, 2012) has enthusiastically embraced the tribute system as a means of moving beyond Eurocentric IR's obsession with the concept of anarchy. He has argued that a better understanding of Asian international politics requires greater sensitivity to 'hierarchy' which (unlike Europe) was the norm in the region. East Asia saw greater stability compared to Europe because the Chinese empire's superiority was accepted as legitimate. This, Kang (2012: 2) argues, made the region more stable than Europe, which was marked by 'incessant interstate conflict'. It is therefore not particularly surprising for Kang that we did not witness—at least until the early 2000s—concerted efforts to balance against China in Asia. Chinese hegemony was actually the historical norm, and the rise of China was simply just a return to this well-established reality (Kang, 2007).

Chinese authors have also enthusiastically embraced this order as a potential alternative to the current Western-dominated international order. Much is made of the Chinese empire's alleged lack of interest in military or political intervention in its neighbours as long as proper diplomatic rituals of the tribute system were observed. It is often argued that Chinese visions of international order, which are contrasted to a highly conflictual European international order, provide a potential ethical alternative to the current Westphalian sovereign state system. Tingyang Zhao (2006: 36), for instance, states,

> …taking into account the successes of the All-under-Heaven pattern in Chinese history to have bring [sic] long periods of peace and stable society.., in contrast with the inability of the United Nations pattern to deal with international conflicts…we might be encouraged to find in the All-under-Heaven pattern the theoretical potential to resolve international and inter-cultural problems.

Yaqing Qin (2007: 330) echoes this theme when he argues that the 'holistic' and inclusive (but hierarchical) nature of the Chinese international order stands in contrast to 'the Western dualistic view of the two opposites, where an inevitable conflict is implied', and could bring about an 'ideal world of harmony and order based upon morality and selflessness' because it 'takes care of the whole world, believing in and aiming at a harmonious whole'. However, it is worth noting that these Chinese debates on the Tribute System and its positive aspects were informed by then-president Hu Jintao's concept of 'harmonious world' (Callahan, 2008: 758). Given the difficulty of maintaining complete independence from the Chinese Communist Party in public life in the People's Republic of China, it is perhaps unsurprising that Chinese scholars have forwarded these somewhat laudatory 'Chinese' theories of IR—after all, '[t]heory is always for someone and for some purpose' (Cox, 1996: 87).

Beyond the political agenda of theorising and justifying 'China's peaceful rise', these laudatory depictions of the East Asian international order have been criticised on a number of grounds. First, there are questions about whether or not the legacy of hierarchy in the East Asian international order still matters. Nationalism, which entered the region in the late-nineteenth and early-twentieth centuries, has been hugely influential, and was the crucial unifying ideology that resulted in the decolonisation of Asia. What grounds are there to assume that nationalism will suddenly cease to matter, and Asian states will readily accept Chinese regional hegemony once more (Acharya 2003/2004; see also Heiskanen, 2021)?

Second, whether or not the East Asian international order was inherently peaceful compared to Europe is contestable. As Johnston (1995) has shown, China was not always benevolent towards its neighbours, and advocated a very hard, realist military strategy towards the Mongols. There are other factors to consider, such as geographical proximity and technological limitations, as well as methodological issues of how we define and count 'military conflict' in East Asia when we compare this to Europe. Furthermore, some of these arguments are soaked with a political agenda. As Callahan (2008: 755) points out, the narrative of a benevolent hegemon is often 'used…to explain why China is not a threat to world order in the twenty-first century', particularly among scholars based in the People's Republic of China. It is argued that because of these desirable qualities of stability in the Sinocentric hierarchical system, a new hierarchical system based on the ancient Pax Sinica could be a positive development for the international community.

Finally, there are questions as to whether or not the latest wave of theorising on the East Asian international order really does succeed in their agenda of moving beyond the Eurocentrism that has dogged IR for such a long time. The geographical focus is different, for sure—but as noted above, many authors gloss over the various contestations among members of the East Asian international order over their position in the hierarchical order, and too often ignore the existence of non-Chinese tribute systems that operated alongside the Chinese one. This rather ironically results in nationalistic and Sinocentric IR theory, which merely replaces the 'West' with China. Kang (2007: 43) seems to fall in this trap when he notes that 'traditional international order in East Asia encompassed a regionally shared set of norms and expectations that guided relations and yielded substantial stability'. He depicts Vietnam as holding a genuine sense of reverence towards China (Kang, 2005: 62; Kang, 2007: 43), ignoring the fact that the Vietnamese kings used the title of 'emperor', which was theoretically reserved for the Chinese emperor only. Even Japan, which refused to send any tribute missions to Qing China, is depicted as accepting Chinese material and moral supremacy (Kang, 2005: 64). The non-Chinese members of the East Asian international order seem almost stripped of their agency.

Future research on the East Asian international order

So what research can be done on the East Asian international order? There are potentially many pathways, but to this day, the longevity of the East Asian international order remains 'an enduring puzzle' (Zhang, 2001: 52). Existing works frequently fall back on a variation of hegemonic stability theory (Gilpin, 1982) and argue that China's neighbours entered into tributary relations with the Chinese empire in order to ensure their security. Tribute states could thus expect some form of Chinese protection when they faced invasion from other polities. Their display of allegiance to the Chinese empire also prevented incurring the wrath of the regional hegemon (Ogura, 2001; Kang, 2007, 2012).

David Kang's work (2007, 2012) is a typical example of this genre. While cognisant of normative factors, Kang nevertheless argues that the 'benefits' associated with acquiescence to Chinese dominance are assumed to have played a crucial role in sustaining the longevity of Pax Sinica, which ultimately resulted in a remarkably stable system in which interstate war was absent in comparison to the 'anarchic' European international system (Kang, 2007: 37). Not surprisingly, material gains were of crucial importance in non-Chinese states' acceptance of Chinese domination and their lowly social status in the Asian international system. '[T]rade with China was a key element of international relations', Kang asserts, 'because China was a lucrative and advanced market' (Kang, 2005: 61; 2007: 41–43; cf. Ogura, 2001). Accepting a subordinate position in the Asian international system also meant entering a form of alliance. In addition to acquiring the Chinese emperor's legitimation of their rule in their domains, the non-Chinese rulers could—at least in theory—count on China extending its protection from attack by others, as it was the emperor's paternal duty to look after his subjects in times of need.

These explanations, however, cannot explain adequately why the tribute system remained in place for over two millennia despite the waxing and waning of Chinese power. If interests of survival were the only concern for entering into tribute relations with China, we would expect the tributary states to disregard totally the norms of the East Asian international order whenever Chinese power was perceived to be on the wane. Yet, the norms of the East Asian international order continued to govern the interstate relations between its members right up until the end of the nineteenth century. Furthermore, there were some cases where recognition of social status and legitimacy bestowed by the Chinese emperor via tributary relations became important to certain rulers (Suzuki, 2009: 42–43; cf. Onuma, 2000: 10, 13–14), thus suggesting that the norms of the East Asian international order had been internalised to a large degree.

Given the limitation of purely materialist explanations, perhaps one big question is the role of a shared culture in sustaining international order. While we should be cautious about overemphasising non-Chinese states' acceptance of Chinese norms, particularly Sinocentrism, it is undoubtedly true that states like Korea, Japan, Vietnam, and the Ryūkyū Kingdom did have a 'shared a common image of the world' derived from Sinocentrism (Onuma, 2000: 11), and incorporated certain elements of Chinese culture or systems of governance, notably central bureaucratic rule and writing systems (Kang, 2005: 57–58; Nishijima, 1994: 164).

Today, the rise of militant Islamic fundamentalism has shaken the optimistic belief in the 'rationality' of humankind to overcome cultural difference and establish some sort of social order with each other. Despite the intensive criticism it has received, Huntington's 'clash of civilisations' thesis is being seen in a more favourable light by some quarters. Was a shared culture really the crucial 'glue' that provided the longevity of the East Asian international order? Or did the East Asian international order prevail until the late-nineteenth century simply because its members were under some sort of 'Gramscian hegemony', and alternative visions of international order were simply 'unthinkable' until the European powers, and the 'Westphalian' international order, reached the shores of Asia?

These questions also bring us to the eternal political science question of power. If we are to accept that Chinese philosophy spread throughout the East Asian international order and achieved some kind of 'Gramscian hegemony', how was this achieved? This framework certainly provides us with some answers to why resistance to Chinese hegemonic norms took place within the East Asian international order, rather than outside of it (that would have to wait until the late-nineteenth century), but the process by which this was constructed should provide us with a fascinating case study of how Chinese power, and power in general, operated.

Answering these questions, however, has formidable challenges. While the problem of Sinocentrism has been noted multiple times, it seems that many scholars regularly fall into this trap again. To an extent this is understandable, as a comprehensive understanding of the East Asian international order requires an extensive knowledge of classical Chinese (whose forms differ according to the period under scrutiny), as well as classical Vietnamese, Korean, and Japanese. For the most part, this area of study has (unsurprisingly) been the territory of historians, who possess these skills. Future research would require greater cooperation between IR and historiography, and this should be encouraged. IR has often been criticised for its 'cherry-picking' of historical 'facts', and better collaboration with historians would help the discipline in enriching and strengthening its engagement with history. Furthermore, this approach would presumably help us incorporate the voices and experiences of other non-Chinese states, and rid us of the Sinocentrism that has come to replace Eurocentrism.

The longevity of the East Asian international order means that to understand East Asian international politics, and indeed modern Asia, 'is an effort to trace how each country and area within Asia attempted to cope with the transformation of the tribute system' (Hamashita, 2009: 16). A deeper exploration of the East Asian international order is long overdue. Only when we address this lacuna will we 'Get Asia right'.

Suggestions for further reading

Arano, Y. (1988). *Kinsei nippon to ajia*. Tokyo: Tōkyō daigaku shuppankai.

Fairbank, J. K., ed. (1968). *The Chinese World Order*. Cambridge, MA: Harvard University Press.

Hamashita, T. (1997). *Chōkō shisutemu to kindai ajia*. Tokyo: Iwanami shoten.

Hevia, J. L. (1995). *Cherishing Men from Afar: Qing Guest Ritual and the Macartney Embassy of 1793*. Durham, NC: Duke University Press.

Kim, K. H. (1980). *The Last Phase of the East Asian World Order: Korea, Japan, and the Chinese Empire, 1860–1910*. Berkeley, CA: University of California Press.

Tashiro, K. (1982). Foreign relations during the Edo period: Sakoku Reexamined. *Journal of Japanese Studies*, 8 (2), 283–306.

Yamamoto, T. (1975). *Betonamu chūgoku kankeishi: kyoku shi no taitō kara shinfutsu sensō made*. Tokyo: Yamakawa shuppansha.

Notes

1 Here, the 'West' is used as shorthand for Europe and North America.

2 Of course, it should be acknowledged that this is not always the case, as Realists have at times examined ancient Greece or the Warring States period of China. However, this is done highly selectively in the context of 'proving' Realism's decidedly ahistorical claims of Realists that the international system has always been anarchical, and that the insights of realist theory apply universally, regardless of the historical or geographical context.

References

Acharya, A. (2003/2004). Will Asia's past be its future? *International Security*, 28 (3), 149-164.

Bull, H., and Watson, A., eds. (1984). *The Expansion of International Society*. Oxford: Oxford University Press.

Buzan, B., and Little, R. (2000). *International Systems in World History: Remaking the Study of International Relations*. Oxford: Oxford University Press.

Callahan, W. A. (2008). Chinese visions of world order: post-hegemonic or a new hegemony? *International Studies Review*, 10 (4), 749-761.

Cox, R. (1996). *Approaches to World Order*. Cambridge: Cambridge University Press.

Fairbank, J. K., ed. (1968). *The Chinese World Order*. Cambridge, MA: Harvard University Press.

Gilpin, R. (1982). *War and Change in World Politics*. Cambridge: Cambridge University Press.

Gong, G. W. (1984). *The Standard of 'Civilization' in International Society*. Oxford: Clarendon Press.

Hamashita, T. (1997). *Chōkō shisutemu to kindai ajia*. Tokyo: Iwanami shoten.

Hamashita, T. (1999). Higashi ajiashi ni miru kai chitsujo. In: T. Hamashita, ed., *Higashi ajia sekai no chiiki nettowaaku*, Tokyo: Yamakawa shuppansha.

Hamashita, T. (2009). Change and Continuity in East Asian 1800-2000: Dynamism and Transformation of Geo-Political China Region. Paper presented at the Conference on 'Improving the Human Destiny', Institute of Humanities and Social Sciences, Lingnan University, 11–12 June.

He, F. (1998). Huayi zhixu lun. *Beijing daxue xuebao (philosophy and social science edition)*, 35 (6), 30-45.

Heiskanen, J. (2021). Nations and Nationalism in International Relations. In de Carvalho, B., Costa Lopez, J., & Leira, H., eds. *Routledge Handbook of Historical International Relations*. Abingdon: Routledge.

Hobson, J. M. (2007). Is critical theory always for the white West and for Western imperialism? Beyond Westphalian towards a post-racist critical IR. *Review of International Studies*, 33, 91-116.

Hui, V. (2021). Premodern Asia and International Relations Theory. In de Carvalho, B., Costa Lopez, J., & Leira, H., eds. *Routledge Handbook of Historical International Relations*. Abingdon: Routledge.

Huntington, S. P. (2002). *The Clash of Civilizations and the Remaking of World Order*. New York, NY: The Free Press.

Johnston, A. I. (1995). *Cultural Realism: Strategic Culture and Grand Strategy in Chinese History*. Princeton, NJ: Princeton University Press.

Kang, D. C. (2003). Getting Asia wrong: the need for new analytical frameworks. *International Security*, 27 (4), 57-85.

Kang, D. C. (2005). Hierarchy in Asian international relations: 1300-1900. *Asian Security*, 1 (1), 53-79.

Kang, D. C. (2007). *China Rising: Peace, Power, and Order in East Asia*. New York, NY: Columbia University Press.

Kang, D. C. (2012). *East Asia Before the West: Five Centuries of Trade and Tribute*. New York, NY: Columbia University Press.

Kim, K. H. (1980). *The Last Phase of the East Asian World Order: Korea, Japan, and the Chinese Empire, 1860–1910*. Berkeley, CA: University of California Press.

Navari, C., and Green, D. (2021). The English School and Historical International Relations. In de Carvalho, B., Costa Lopez, J., & Leira, H., eds. *Routledge Handbook of Historical International Relations*. Abingdon: Routledge.

Nishijima, S. (1994). *Yamataikoku to higashi ajia: kodai nippon to higashi ajia*, Tokyo: Yoshikawa kōbunkan.

O'Hagan, J. (1995). Civilisational conflict? Looking for cultural enemies. *Third World Quarterly*, 16 (1), 19-38.

O'Hagan, J. (2002). *Conceptualizing the West in International Relations Thought: From Spengler to Said*. Basingstoke: Palgrave.

Ogura, K. (2001). *Chūgoku no ishin nippon no kyōji*. Tokyo: Chūō kōron shinsha.

Onuma, Y. (2000). When was the law of international society born – an inquiry of the history of international law from an intercivilizational perspective. *Journal of the History of International Law*, 2 (1), 1-66.

Qin, Y. (2007). Why is there no Chinese international relations theory? *International Relations of the Asia-Pacific*, 7 (3), 313-340.

Reus-Smit, C. (1999). *The Moral Purpose of the State: Culture, Social Identity, and Institutional Rationality in International Relations*. Princeton, NJ: Princeton University Press.

Rossabi, M., ed. (1983). *China Among Equals: The Middle Kingdom and Its Neighbors, 10th-14th Centuries*. Berkeley, CA: University of California Press.

Sakayori, M. (1993). Kai shisō no shosō. In: Y. Arano, M. Ishii, and S. Murai, eds., *Ajia no naka no nihonshi (vol. 5): jiishiki to sōgo rikai*, Tokyo: Tōkyō daigaku shuppankai.

Suzuki, S. (2009). *Civilization and Empire: China and Japan's Encounter with European International Society.* London: Routledge.

Suzuki, S., Zhang, Y., and Quirk, J., eds. (2013). *International Orders in the Early Modern World: Before the Rise of the West.* Abingdon: Routledge.

Tashiro, K. (1982). Foreign relations during the Edo period: Sakoku Reexamined. *Journal of Japanese Studies,* 8 (2), 283–306.

Toby, R. P. (1991). *State and Diplomacy in Early Modern Japan: Asia in the Development of the Tokugawa Bakufu.* Stanford, CA: Stanford University Press.

Wight, M. (1977). *Systems of States.* Leicester: Leicester University Press.

Yamamoto, T. (1975). *Betonamu chūgoku kankeishi: kyoku shi no taitō kara shinfutsu sensō made.* Tokyo: Yamakawa shuppansha.

Zhang, F. (2009). Rethinking the 'Tribute System': broadening the conceptual horizon of historical East Asian politics. *Chinese Journal of International Politics,* 2 (4), 545–574.

Zhang, Y. (2001). System, empire and state in Chinese international relations. *Review of International Studies,* 27 (5), 43–63.

Zhao, T. (2006). Rethinking empire from a Chinese concept 'All-under-Heaven'. *Social Identities,* 12 (1), 29–41.

43

LINKING UP THE OTTOMAN EMPIRE WITH IR'S TIMELINE

Ayşe Zarakol

Introduction

This chapter explores state-building efforts of the (early modern) Ottomans[1] by drawing from the revisionist historical scholarship on this empire[2] that emerged in the last few decades. The goal is to show, through this example, that treating Europe as a self-contained unit across time and ignoring non-European historical developments has resulted in problematic theorising in IR. This chapter demonstrates that extending the gaze of inquiry beyond Europe to a case such as the Ottoman Empire raises troubling questions about the causal mechanisms posited in the IR literature about the emergence of the modern state and the states system, the modern understanding of sovereignty, as well as the supposed lifespan of its material and social hierarchies.

Sovereignty is one of the foundational assumptions of IR, because most of our theories see sovereign states as the primary – if not the only – building blocks of the system (Lawson and Shilliam, 2009: 658; see also Krasner, 1995–1996: 121; see also de Carvalho and Leira, 2021 in this volume). Perhaps surprisingly for a social science concept, there is also a considerable degree of consensus in the field as to what sovereignty entails at a minimum: most IR definitions of sovereignty can be reduced to the components of 'supreme authority' and 'territory' (Bartelson, 2018; see also Philpott, 1995). When we think about modern sovereignty, we look for the presence of two factors: (1) *the centralisation of political authority*, i.e. the elimination of rival authority claims, external and internal, (2) *territoriality*, i.e. the expectation that political authority is claimed over a unified and bounded territory (as opposed to people or specific symbolic sites etc.). We could add that discussions of modern sovereignty usually assume external recognition, i.e. that these facts, on the ground, are acknowledged by the representatives of other similarly formed entities (see de Carvalho, 2021 in this volume).

Because the presence of sovereign states thus defined determines the scope conditions of IR theories, even in its most ahistorical moments, IR has been obliquely interested in at least *when* modern sovereignty emerged (as well as how).[3] In the traditional narrative, the Peace of Westphalia (1648) is said to have transformed the world from one dominated by religious divisions to one of territorial sovereign states. For the last few decades, however, the Westphalian narrative and the accompanied dating of modern sovereignty back to the seventeenth century have come under criticism. The majority of attacks have come from scholars who disagree that anything resembling the modern state emerged from the Treaty of Westphalia. The overwhelming majority of these scholars date the emergence of modern state to a much later period (see, e.g., Reus-Smit, 1999; Croxton, 1999; Beaulac, 2000; Osiander, 2001; Krasner, 2001; Kayaoglu, 2010; Buzan and Lawson, 2015; Branch, 2011; Bartelson, 2018. See also Benton, 2009; Elden, 2013), arguing that territoriality in the modern sense did not exist before the nineteenth century; nor did the principle of external recognition (see Goettlich and Branch, 2021 in this volume). A related line of criticism sees the Westphalian discourse as a project of nineteenth-century international jurists (see, e.g., Osiander, 2001), which has been repurposed for yet other political ends in the twentieth century (see, e.g., Kayaoglu, 2010; Schmidt, 2011).

There are also criticisms which deal explicitly with the various Eurocentric assumptions of the Westphalian narrative. The criticisms in this camp are best summed up by what John Hobson calls 'the *Eurocentric big bang theory* of world politics' (2012a: 32; see also Hobson, 2009, 2012b; de Carvalho et al. 2011). Hobson characterises most explanations of sovereignty in IR as assuming that 'the big bang of modernity explodes within Europe in 1648, having previously unfolded through an evolutionary process that is entirely endogenous to Europe, before the sovereign state is exported to the East through imperialism and proto-globalization' (2012a: 33). The big bang theory also demarcates the East from the West, relegating it 'to a backward ghetto that endures only regressive and barbaric institutions,' condemned to follow in the West's shadow, while the West is inscribed with all the progressive properties (2012a: 33). Some scholars in this camp have in fact linked the aforementioned criticisms around the dating of the modern system explicitly with the criticisms around Eurocentrism, arguing that one of the sources of the normative stratification of the international system is the projection of nineteenth-century developments back into history (Kayaoğlu, 2010). Broadly speaking, two types of remedies have been offered for the problem of Eurocentrism in the literature. A number of scholars have been challenging the notion that Europe's progress was self-propelling by offering accounts in which they show that developments in Europe were not endogenously driven but rather very much influenced by developments in what is now called the East (see Anievas and Nişancıoğlu, 2013, 2015; Nişancıoğlu, 2014; Hobson, 2004, 2009, 2012a; see in this volume Suzuki, 2021). Yet others have been challenging the dissemination narrative and the notion that sovereignty was imported unproblematically to the rest of the world (see Suzuki, 2009; Zarakol, 2011, 2014; also Anghie, 2002: 520; Shilliam, 2006). This type of argument usually focuses on the developments of the post-nineteenth-century period, with a critical lens.

In this chapter, I develop the Ottoman Empire as a site of comparative inquiry in its own right. Conceiving of (what is now labelled) the non-Western world either as the source or the victim of Western developments may inadvertently reproduce the idea that modern sovereignty could emerge *only* in Western Europe. This chapter explores the extent to which the Ottoman polity manifested claims and practices of exclusive supreme authority (as well as other trends towards political centralisation).[4] The overarching argument is that for the majority of its existence, the Ottoman Empire was not lagging behind the developments in Europe in terms of state-building. In some aspects, it was ahead of Europe and others it experienced in parallel. The gap that is thought to exist is mostly a product of nineteenth-century thinking and dynamics of recognition particular to that century (as detailed in Zarakol, 2011, 2014, 2018b, 2020). This should also usher in the realisation that institutions that are considered to be foreign imports in this part of the world also have local roots or parallels.

Supreme political authority in a 'non-European' context

The question here is whether the IR literature *actually* supposes polities outside of Europe never to have developed notions of absolute political authority. Because the IR literature says little about what was happening outside of the European context that is being studied, but abounds with claims of novelty and revolution[5]; however, the casual reader could easily that philosophical justifications of supreme political authority and/or political centralisation in Western Europe were without parallel in human history. Could the silence of the IR literature in this regard be taken as evidence of a belief that absolute claims to sovereignty by political authority did not exist outside of Europe? In the European political thought tradition (upon which IR cursorily draws), there is a long-standing notion of 'Oriental Despotism,' a label attributing non-European monarchs all sorts of tyrannical powers (see, e.g., Çırakman, 2001; Hobson and Sharman, 2005: 88).[6] Stripped of its stigma (Zarakol, 2011, 2014), 'Oriental Despotism' sounds very much like absolute monarchy (see also Çırakman, 2001: 56–57), so it seems unlikely that anyone is entirely unaware that absolute notions of sovereignty existed outside of Europe. The claim of novelty for European state-building, then, must rest on something else. One possibility is that claims of absolute sovereignty in non-European polities are not seen as 'innovative' because of the (erroneous) beliefs that such polities have been static over time (see, e.g., Hobson and Sharman, 2005: 88), and that they have exhibited practices that are believed to be evidence of their irrationality, such as deifying rulers, whereas in the European context, the rise of absolutism is believed to be linked with secularisation and rationalisation. Another possibility – albeit one that is at odds with the negative judgement of the supposed tyranny of Eastern rulers – is that such claims of absolute sovereignty are assumed merely to be claims, without any corresponding manifestations towards centralisation of authority on the ground.[7] This may be another reason why they are not taken seriously by the literature.

I entertain each possibility in the next two sections. First, I explore whether the Ottomans (as a stand-in for other polities similarly ignored by the IR literature) ever had notions of absolute sovereignty for their political rulers and demonstrate that the Ottomans, far from being static in this regard, developed such notions against a more traditional backdrop of divided sovereignty, very much like their European counterparts, and around the same time, if not earlier. In the second, subsection, I explore to what extent notions of absolutism translated to practices and institutions of centralisation on the ground and demonstrate significant trends in this direction until the seventeenth century.

The Ottoman 'Innovation' of absolutism

The origins of the Ottoman Empire date back to the thirteenth century, when the Ottomans were a small frontier band in Western hinterland of Anatolia, competing for territory with other small *beylik* (principality) formed in the wake of the collapse of the Seljuk sultanate of Rum in Asia Minor, which had gradually withered away under the onslaughts of the Crusades from the West and Mongols from the East. There are a lot of foundational myths about the early Ottomans, many of which date back to fifteenth-century revisionism by the Ottomans themselves. These myths, coupled with dearth of evidence about what the Ottomans were up to before their arrival on the world-historical stage, make this period a controversial one for modern historians. We can nevertheless posit that the thirteenth- and fourteenth-century Anatolian context they were operating in had a particular conceptualisation of sovereignty, which was an amalgamation of the Near Eastern imperial tradition (Persian, Byzantine etc.) and the Islamic one. Neither tradition pointed towards absolutism, support for which developed fifteenth century onwards.

As the Ottoman tribe had been nomadic until their arrival on the historical stage, we can assume that they did not have their own settled administrative traditions to draw upon. Without necessarily declaring that the Ottomans owed all of their approaches to state-building to the Byzantine and Seljuks,[8] we can nevertheless note that they did borrow quite liberally especially in the early years from the 'Byzantino-Seljuk' civilisation that characterised thirteenth-century Anatolia (Darling, 2000: 134, 2011: 26). The Ottomans were neighbours with the Byzantine empire, and there was intermarriage between the ruling families. The early Ottoman armies were very heterogeneous, 'mixing Christians with Muslims and often directed against coreligionists, [with a] focus on booty and territorial expansion rather than conversion' (Darling, 2000: 135). Byzantine warriors were given land as well as administrative positions (Kafadar, 1995; Darling, 2011).

From the Byzantines, the Ottomans can be said to have borrowed a type of 'multiculturalism' and a taste for imperial titles. For example, the fourth Ottoman sultan, Bayezid I (1389–1402), was married to a Serbian woman and had Christians among his advisors as well as vassals: 'Bayezid… intended the Ottoman Empire to be a hybrid, multi-religious and multi-cultural state, despite fulminations of clerics on both sides' (Darling, 2011: 41–42). His legacy was tarnished quite a bit after he was defeated and captured by Timur's Mongolian armies at the Battle of Ankara (1402). Nevertheless, the multicultural traditions of the polity persisted, and in these traditions, we can find echoes of other Near Eastern empires. After the conquest of Constantinople, Mehmed II (1451–1481) invoked Byzantine symbols to legitimise his rule: 'He built himself one palace in the Byzantine style and one in the Timurid style, issued a law code in imitation of Justinian's, and employed Byzantine and Anatolian writers as well as artists working in the Italian, Greek, Persian and Turkish traditions' (Darling, 2011: 48).[9] The conquest of Constantinople solidified the Ottoman takeover of various Byzantine institutions and practices: 'in the eyes of many, and perhaps especially of his recent converted or still Christian subjects, [Mehmed II] had thereby tacitly inherited the status of the Roman emperor' (Black, 2011: 204). Indeed, the legacies of the imperial conceptions were most evident in the titles that the Ottoman rulers used: 'The Ottomans were quick to take up the Persian titles "emperor (hüdavendigar)" and "the universal ruler who protects the world (padisah-i alempanah)" foreign rulers frequently addressed the Ottoman Sultan as "emperor"…Thus Islamic and non-Islamic concepts were strung together' (Black, 2011: 207).

Yet, these imperial titles are not by themselves enough to suggest the development of notions of absolute sovereignty, because in Near Eastern imperial polities, such claims were undercut in principle by competing claims of religious authority and in practice by limited centralisation. It would take a more radical reconceptualisation of sovereignty to move the Ottomans in an absolutist direction. In order to understand the significance of this development, however, we must first understand the role of religious authority in this geography up to the fourteenth century. Islam influenced initial Ottoman attitudes to sovereignty in two ways: through the lens of *ghaza* (holy conquest) and through the aforementioned example of the Seljuk legacy,[10] a precursor 'Muslim' empire. Neither tradition pointed to the absolute sovereignty of the Ottoman ruler. Let's start with *ghaza*.

Osman I (r. 1299–1323) is the quasi-mythical founder of the Ottoman polity. He was most likely in vassalage relationship with the Mongol ruler of the Il-khanate (Tezcan, 2009: 84). Osman's son, Orhan (r. 1323–1362), was the first Ottoman ruler to use the title *ghazi*, invoking a more pronounced Islamic identity (while recruiting Christians as foot soldiers and being married to a Byzantine princess).[11] Despite the heterodoxy of the warriors mentioned above, the *ghazi* identity became more pronounced as an ideology of conquest after the second half of the fourteenth century, when the Ottoman rulers stopped being able to lead all of the raids and started having to delegate at least some authority to other frontier *beys* (warlords), 'some of whom were not of Ottoman origin and did not identify strongly as Ottomans' (Darling, 2011: 36). It could thus be argued that the Ottomans developed a stronger religious ethos as they acquired vassals of their own, thus needing a legitimating ideology.

Whatever the source, we can note that Islam interpreted through the lens of *ghaza* points to a comparatively weak role for the Ottoman ruler, as sort of *primus inter pares* among other *ghazi* warriors (or as a feudal lord among his vassals) (Tezcan, 2009: 84). In fact, the Islamic angle initially did the Ottomans little favour in their quest for authority, for several reasons. To begin with, the 'Ottoman' family had no special pedigree – e.g. prophetic lineage – that gave them any higher religious authority than any other *ghazi*. Furthermore, in traditional Islamic (Sunni) understanding, even pedigreed political rulers had very limited legitimacy in terms of domestic governance. They had no lawmaking authority; it was up to the *ulama* to interpret (and thus make) laws according to *sharia*. A proper *ulama* class emerged in the Ottoman Empire only after the fifteenth century, but even before that, the Sufi dervish lodges were critical to recognising and legitimising the *ghaza* of the Ottomans.

But what is the conception of sovereignty that so limited political authority in Islam? Simplifying a bit, we can note that Islam emerged in the sixth century with a fusion of political power and religious authority in the person of the Prophet Mohammad, a 'hyper-sovereign' who was simultaneously a military leader, political ruler and religious lawgiver (Zarakol, 2017). The Islamic polity that Mohammad created was not sustainable as he created it, however. Mohammad's hyper-sovereign status depended on his unique role as 'the last Messenger of Allah,' a role which could not be replicated by the Caliphs.[12] The Umayyad dynasty (of Caliphs) [661–750] did not help matters by abusing their position and thereby a cementing a conviction among the growing *ulama* (jurist) caste (of Sunnis)[13] that the Caliph should not exercise any lawmaking power. The Caliphs' authority thus waned, whereas the *ulama* grew strong. Trying to cling to power, the subsequent Abbasid dynasty (of Caliphs) [850–1258] increasingly came to rely on (manumitted and converted) slave soldiers recruited from non-Arabic populations, creating the *mamluk* institution which would play a role in subsequent Islamic polities (Crone, 2003). Once introduced, this practice spread throughout the area under Muslim influence, and slaves came to replace free, native soldiers. They later became increasingly influential and autonomous political actors on their own right. This is how the institution of Caliph lost its military power as well.

By the time, the Seljuk Empire had formed in the eleventh century, the Caliph had thus been reduced to but a person in Baghdad, with some symbolic religious authority but no real political *or* military power. The Seljuk sultan (or any Muslim monarch), meanwhile, had the power of the sword to enforce order and execute wars, but no lawmaking authority: 'In theory the ruler was a shepherd…for all his services to Islam even so great a warrior as Saladin held only profane power' (Crone, 2003: 88). Legislative authority rested with the *ulama*, who did not answer to any centralised authority: 'avoidance of the state remained the norm' (Crone, 2003: 88). In this tradition, political rule was 'something which sat on top of society, not something which was rooted in it…' (Crone and Hinds, 2003: 109). The Seljuk Empire was a clear manifestation of this pattern: 'A religio-political pattern emerged under which Islamic justice was administered by the ulama as Judges, while military power became the basis of social order and legitimate political authority' (Black, 2011: 99). This was the legacy of divided sovereignty[14] that the Ottomans inherited as they consolidated their rule over what used to be Seljuk lands. During their first century, the Ottomans were thus operating in an ideational context that did not support political rulers in their quest for absolute sovereignty. There was one other influence, however, that pointed in the opposite direction: the Turco-Mongolian legacy.

The Mongolians had a very specific notion of world sovereignty for their rulers that, unlike most other societies of this time, was not subservient to (or time-sharing with) religious authority: the 'Chinggisid universalist notion of sovereignty rested on the view that divine dispensation to rule the world was given to Chinggis Khan and his descendants. Fittingly, Chinggis Khan was considered a divine legislator' (Burak, 2013b: 595). Furthermore, they introduced the notion of *yasa* to areas they conquered, which was not 'a fixed written legal code,' but rather 'an evolving body of individual decrees, regulations, and practices that had been instituted or sanctioned by Chinngis Khan… a kind of unwritten "constitution"' (Burak, 2013b: 595). It is hard to know the extent to which the Ottomans of the thirteenth century were exposed to such Mongolian notions as a result of their vassalage. It is also possible that as a Turkic tribe, the Ottomans already carried the notion of world sovereignty with them on their journey from Central Asia to Western Anatolia.[15] Some of the uncertainty about this earlier period stems from the fact that Ottomans themselves engaged in quite a bit of historical revisionism in the fifteenth century, after Bayezid I was humiliated by the Timurid invasions, erasing any positive referents to Mongolians.

Recently, there has been speculation by historians that Timurid invasions were particularly influential on the Muslim empires of Western Asia. By the sixteenth century, all major Islamic polities, including the Ottomans, introduced dynastic laws (*kanun* in the Ottoman case), contravening long-established Islamic practice. The Ottoman sultans of the sixteenth century started to circumvent tradition by first actively adapting a particular school of jurisprudence (*Hanafi*) and second by developing an 'imperial learned hierarchy with fairly standardized career and training tracks' (Burak, 2013b: 584). In 1556, Süleyman I (The Magnificent; The Lawgiver) took the unprecedented step of specifying which text the students of the imperial education system were to study: 'By specifying an imperial jurisprudential canon, the Ottoman sultans, and more generally the dynasty, sought to point to specific texts and opinions within the Hanafi school that members of imperial hierarchy were to consult and teach' (Burak, 2013b: 586). The dynastic law allowed for the creation of charitable cash endowments, for example, which *shari'a* (Islamic/jurists' law) forbid due to the involvement of interest. There also emerged in this period a political thought literature that occupied itself with justifying the efforts by the Sultans to centralise their authority and bring the *ulama* under their control. Also in the second half of the sixteenth century, the Ottomans toyed with the practice of producing official dynastic history accounts with similar goals of justifying their centralised rule.[16]

Practices of centralisation in the Ottoman Empire and their discontents

The previous section argued that in the fifteenth and sixteenth centuries, the Ottomans too developed notions akin to absolutism against a more traditional backdrop of divided sovereignty (this pattern can also be generalised to other post-Mongolian Islamicate empires). This section will demonstrate that this development was not just notional but also manifested in a number of institutional changes which can be seen as evidence of strong centralising trends.

Centralisation efforts were underway well before the Battle of Ankara, and once the polity was reconstituted in 1413 they continued at full speed well into the sixteenth century. A significant development was the creation of a centralised bureaucracy. *Ghazi* vassals came to be replaced with governors, giving way from a feudal arrangement to a patrimonial one. Mehmed II recreated the traditional Islamic practice of the *mamluk* (slave soldiers) in a rather 'innovative' manner (Tezcan, 2009: 90): he 'developed a new army and *bureaucracy*, based on recruitment of non-Muslim youths as loyal servants of the Sultan without social connections… These provided the Sultan's personal troops…Janissaries; and they staffed the central bureaucracy' (italics added) (Black, 2011: 200). This development of a slave bureaucracy 'could not have happened in the absence of strong monetary economy that financed it' (Tezcan, 2009: 91), which was made possible by the development of 'the *akçe* zone between the Danube and the Euphrates, an area in which many different currencies had been in place' (Tezcan, 2009: 89), another accomplishment of Mehmed II, and with interesting implications for territoriality. The slave-servants of the sultan became the new "nobility" of the land, but without the ability to produce heirs, thereby making it impossible to build strong bases of opposition to royal authority. By the time of Süleyman I [the Magnificent], the bureaucratic system seemed to have reached such a level of perfection that everything functioned like clockwork, with considerable centralised control.

A significant development was the emergence of an 'absolutist court' towards the end of the sixteenth century (Tezcan, 2009: 92). Murad III (r. 1574–1595) elevated or created a new court offices as counterbalances to existing networks of patronage, offices such as the chief white eunuch (*kapu agasu*), the superintendent of the harem (also a eunuch), the chief gardener. Furthermore, 'this rise of the court as a center of administrative power was also reflected in the role that royal women were playing in politics' (Tezcan, 2009: 92), who, like other personalities of the courts, frequently interfered with judicial and other bureaucratic appointments. Murad III also interfered in financial management of the empire, farming out various lucrative sources of taxation to people close to the court.

Another radical development was that the *ulama* were brought, at least for a while, under the Sultan's authority. The previous section explained why this was a revolutionary development within the (Sunni) Islamic context. It was achieved after Selim I (r. 1512–1520) conquered Mecca and Medina and with it earned additional support for the Ottoman claim to the Caliphate.[17] As discussed in the previous section, traditionally, the Caliph had considerable symbolic power but no practical authority over the *ulama* who remained autonomous in their decisions. With his new title, however, Selim was emboldened to challenge the by then long-standing Islamic tradition of political rulers leaving the *ulama* alone: when, for instance, the Şeyhülislam (the head of ulama) 'protested against the decision by Selim to have 150 treasury officials executed, the Sultan replied that this was "a violation of the Sultan's authority…No-one [has] the right or competence to question what the Sultan commands or forbids". The men were executed' (Black, 2011: 204, citing İnalcık, 1973: 94). 'Selim's son Süleyman I [The Magnificent] (r. 1520–1546) further extended the Sultan's law-making authority; hence his Turkish title as *Kanuni*; literally, lawgiver. For the very first time, *kanun* (dynastic or profane) law held priority over *sharia* (jurists or Islamic law)' (Burak, 2013a, 2013b).

The Ottoman sultans of the fifteenth and sixteenth centuries thus enjoyed a degree of centralised sovereignty unknown to both previous Islamic rulers and even to their European counterparts of the time. The Ottoman Sultans of the period, like their European counterparts, also ruled over numerous subordinate political communities but enjoyed much greater control over such communities, and instead of relying on bargains and contracts with local notables for their indirect rule, they managed the empire through the adapted Islamic institution of *mamluk*, a bureaucratic cadre of converts (*devsirme*) with no ties to any local community and with loyalty to no one but the Sultan. Also of great importance in this period is the emergence of twin rivalries with the Habsburg to the West and Safavids to the Southeast, with transformational effects for all involved. In fact, developments within these three polities (and perhaps the Mughals also) mirror each other considerably, with implications for the IR literature on the evolution of the international system which has thus far focused only on the Habsburg and ignored the Ottomans, Safavids and Mughals almost entirely.[18] Partly due to this imperial competition, there were serious efforts underway to homogenise the Muslim population of the empire, such as the promulgation of a new criminal law code that policed the boundaries of orthodoxy and public morality, the promotion of mosque worship through the imposition of new fines for irregular attendance and the construction of an unprecedented number of mosques in order to stabilise mosque congregations and monitor them easily.

By the end of the sixteenth century, however, these centralisation efforts had created and/or empowered a number of actors who could check the power of the throne, sometimes in alliance with the other discontented groups: the bureaucrat-administrators represented by the *viziers* (top-ranking administrator, later the equivalent of prime ministary), the *janissaries* (soldiers) and the *ulama* (jurists). From the seventeenth century onwards until the nineteenth century, these groups, together or interchangeably, successfully limited Ottoman absolutism and contributed to the decentralisation of the empire. First, the transformation of the *mamluk* system into a patrimonial bureaucracy inevitably empowered the viziers at the top of the pyramid vis-a-vis the Sultan (Tezcan, 2009: 96). Not all of the viziers challenged the Sultan's power, but as they gained some autonomy, they did not always do the bidding of Sultan either, sometimes conspiring with groups to depose the Sultan, especially from the seventeenth century onwards (Tezcan, 2009: 100). Administrator bureaucrats fought with the absolutist court over especially over tax farming privileges.

The second group who refused to recognise the supreme authority of the absolutist court were ironically the *janissaries*, given that they were originally conceived as loyal appendages of the Sultan. The *janissary* army had come to replace the *gazi* warrior model within the first century of the Ottoman Empire. Until the seventeenth century, the *janissaries* were made up of originally non-Muslim children raised through the *devsirme* system, whose ties to family was thus severed and were not allowed to marry themselves (until 1556). By the seventeenth century, however, Muslim born youth could join the corps, and the number of *devsirme* declined. As their numbers swelled, the Ottoman army transformed from a military institution to a financial one, as membership in the army came with tax collection privileges and other lucrative appointments such as guild stewardships (Tezcan, 2009: 189). Most *janissaries* had come to be involved in other professions: 'These one-time professional soldiers had become a group who first of all were artisans and guildsmen and only incidentally were on the military payroll' (Tezcan, 2009: 202). *Viziers*, threatened by the growth of the absolutist court, deliberately expanded the Ottoman army throughout this period as a counter-pressure group (Tezcan, 2009, 184). By the seventeenth century, the *janissaries* had thus become a serious check on the power of the Ottoman absolutist court.

The seventeenth century thus opened with the Ottoman court facing troubles in all corners: war with the Habsburgs in the West and the *Jalali* rebellions in Anatolia. *Jalali* rebellions were essentially revolts by Anatolian administrators, preachers and soldiers demanding autonomy from the throne over tax collection privileges. The similarities between the *Jalali* rebellions and the English Revolution of 1640 have been noticed by Jack Goldstone, who links these and other rebellions in this period to common structural changes, such as 'population growth, accompanied by increasing urbanization and velocity of monetary circulation, press[ing] on limited food supplies and [leading] to steadily rising prices' which 'undermined government finances' and 'precipitated popular uprisings' (Goldstone, 1998: 109–110). Within the Ottoman Empire, this situation strengthened anti-court sentiments (Tezcan, 2009: 65). During the seventeenth century, the *janissaries* would frequently demand the execution of various court officials believed to be corrupt, as well as requiring (and sometimes succeeding in) the dethronement of the Sultan. In 1622, the *janissaries* took the unprecedented step of regicide. The victim was Osman II [The Young] (r. 1618–1622), who had been enthroned at a very young age, and was supported by advisors who favoured absolutist policies,[19] which he had pursued with eagerness against the *janissaries* and the *ulama*.

This brings us to the third group acting as a check on Ottoman practices of absolute sovereignty: the *ulama*, who were involved in the aforementioned rebellion as well as many others. Just like the viziers and the *janissaries*, the *ulama* had initially been mostly a beneficiary of the centralising tendencies of the Ottoman polity. Some of the *ulama* had served as administrators in the early empire. Though weakened as a result of sixteenth-century centralisation efforts, the *ulama* nevertheless regained some of their power in the second half of the century. In the seventeenth century, neither the absolutists nor their opponents could make any moves without appealing for support from the *ulama*, which made them a very powerful group. The *ulama* thus started intervening even on decisions about who should be enthroned.

The regicide of Osman II in 1622 was a fundamental rupture in the organisation of sovereignty within the Ottoman Empire, ushering in the period Tezcan calls the Second Empire (1622–1826)[20], 'best…symbolized by a spider web with the monarch at the center but not on top of anyone else' (Tezcan, 2009: 193). The seventeenth century thus was a period when absolutism and its centralising tendencies were almost fatally defeated in the Ottoman Empire by various resistance groups: 'Of the ten reigns by the nine sultans who occupied the Ottoman throne between 1603 and 1703, six ended with dethronements' (Tezcan, 2009: 1). This period is remembered in modern Turkey as the 'decline' period of the empire. If we adopt a comparative lens, however, a different reading is possible: 'The movement in England from late-Tudor absolutism to an increasingly limited monarchy under the Stuarts is well defined and widely accepted. In the Ottoman Empire, there appears to be a parallel to the English case in the double enthronement (1618 and 1622) of the mentally incompetent Mustafa I sandwiched around the deposition and regicide of (Genç [The Young] Osman II)' (Andrews and Kalpaklı, 2005: 322, as cited in Tezcan, 2009: 5). Tezcan asks, 'How have we been led to believe that the English Civil War, which led to the execution of Charles I in 1649, and the "Glorious" Revolution of 1688, which dethroned Charles I's son James II, were advances in the history of limited government, whereas the regicide of the Ottoman Sultan Ibrahim in 1648 and the deposition of Ibrahim's son Mehmed IV in 1687, for instance, were simply signs of decline?' (Tezcan, 2009: 5). It is possible to see such depositions also as an evolution in Ottoman understanding about the limits of sovereign power, very much in parallel with Europe, if different in manifestation (see also Tezcan, 2009; Zarakol, 2011, 2020).

Conclusion: implications for IR

There have been well-placed calls in recent IR literature to visit how non-European regions may have contributed to what are considered European achievements. What is still missing, however, is the scrutiny of non-European polities not just as contributors to European development, but as sites with their own organic political trajectory. The moment we extend our gaze beyond Europe, it becomes irrefutably clear that many processes considered to have caused a number of European 'achievements' from the emergence of modern sovereignty to the 'rise of the West' were in fact not unique to Europe. The implications of these observations for IR are significant.

The divergent fates of the Ottoman Empire (and similarly situated polities) and Europe in the nineteenth century will have to be re-explained given these broad parallels, focusing on factors that were actually present in Europe but absent in the Ottoman Empire, and vice versa. Differences in the arrangement of the economy, especially the absence of capitalist development (if true), make a good starting place (see, e.g., Düzgün, 2018b). The absence of overseas domains is another (with possible implications on spatial and legal reasoning), with the caveat, however, that recent research shows that the Ottomans, too, had their age of exploration in the Indian Ocean in the sixteenth century and were not behind Europe in terms cartography (see, e.g., Casale, 2010). Another factor that was present in Europe but not in the Ottoman Empire is the nobility (or a hereditary landowning class). Ultimately, this is where the origin for parliamentary politics lies in Western Europe, whereas in the Ottoman Empire, it was the *ulama* that fulfilled the same function of checks on absolutism, but obviously the parliamentary mechanism was absent and was only introduced in the nineteenth century. Yet that is more of an explanation for lack of democratic development rather than state-building. Finally, what the Ottoman Empire had but Western Europe did not,[21] especially after the Inquisition, was heterogeneous demographics. Until the nineteenth century, the Ottoman rulers left their non-Muslim subjects relatively undisturbed, even in periods where heterodox Muslim sects were ruthlessly targeted (Zarakol, 2020). That they did so obscures the extent Ottoman communities were partaking in many the same homogenising (or 'civilising') dynamics that are considered to have given rise to nation-states in Europe. Given the parallel precursors discussed above, it is not that hard to imagine the Ottoman Empire happening on a version of what we understand as 'modern sovereignty' with only a few tweaks to the timeline, with a Sultan here and there making a slightly different decision. To the extent that the Ottomans 'lagged behind' Europe in terms of state-building, they did so only by decades, if that, not by centuries, and they started doing so relatively late in world-historical terms, in the eighteenth or nineteenth century, once again demonstrating the pivotal role that period has played in IR.

Suggestions for further reading

Düzgün, E. (2018a). Capitalism, Jacobinism and international relations: re-interpreting the Ottoman path to modernity. *Review of International Studies*, 44 (2): 252–278.

Düzgün, E. (2018b). Property, geopolitics, and eurocentrism: the 'great divergence' and the Ottoman Empire. *Review of Radical Political Economy*, 50 (1), 24–43.

Kadercan, B. (2017). Territorial design and grand strategy in the Ottoman Empire. *Territory, Politics and Governance*, 5 (2), 158–176.

Neumann, I. B., and Welsh, J. M. (1991). The Other in European self-definition: an addendum to the literature on international society. *Review of International Studies*, 17 (4), 327–348.

Tansel, C. B. (2016). Geopolitics, social forces, and the international: revisiting the 'Eastern Question'. *Review of International Studies*, 42 (3), 492–512.

Yurdusev, N. (2004). *Ottoman Diplomacy: Conventional or Unconventional?* London: Palgrave Macmillan.

Wigen, E. (2014). Go West! Turkey's entry into international society. *International Relations*, 28 (4), 468–478.

Notes

1 The Ottomans have attracted some attention in the International Relations (IR) literature, primarily as a foil to the formation of the European society of states. In recent years, however, the literature has gone well beyond this English school understanding to using the Ottomans in studies of comparative state formation, economic development and territoriality. Much of this literature focuses on the later period, however. See further readings section at the end.

2 Empire is a bit of a misnomer; the Ottomans did not conceive themselves as such – see Wigen (2013). But for intelligibility purposes, I retain this label throughout.

3 See Hobson (2009) and de Carvalho et al. (2011) for an overview of how the sovereignty literature in IR has evolved. As Lawson and Shilliam put it (2009: 660), the IR literature is not short of theories about how 'sovereignty appeared: in the *cuius regio, eius religio* (whose the region, his the religion) clauses instituted at the Treaties of Augsburg (1555) and Westphalia (1648) (Wight, 1992); in the interstate wars and geopolitical struggles ushered in by the European military revolution of the sixteenth and seventeenth centuries (Gilpin, 1981; Mann, 1988; Tilly, 1990); in normative shifts associated with shifting understandings of territoriality (Ruggie, 1983), religious belief (Philpott, 2001; Nexon, 2009) and statehood (Reus-Smit, 1999); via fundamental shake-ups to the constitution of modern subjectivity (Walker, 1993; Bartelson, 1995; Weber, 1995); or in the development of private property rights and other processes associated with the emergence of industrial capitalism (Rosenberg, 1994; Teschke, 2003).'

4 For space reasons and also because this component assumed by most to have developed late in Europe as well. I have dealt with the territorialisation angle elsewhere – see Zarakol (2018a,b).

5 Philpott's book, for instance, is called *Revolutions in Sovereignty*.

6 Çırakman (2001) argues that initially the real targets of European writers charging the Ottomans with despotism were their own absolutist states. She also suggests that the negative judgement of the Ottomans emerged in the eighteenth century. Previously, both negative and positive images existed in the European literature.

7 Of course, it is also debatable whether European rulers' claims of absolute sovereignty were more than claims. See, e.g., Krasner (2001): 20.

8 This thesis was later challenged by Paul Wittek, who advanced the *ghazi* thesis instead, which is also challenged by even more recent historiography.

9 Some historians, e.g. Baki Tezcan, dispute the existence of this law code, arguing that this was a sixteenth-century attribution to Mehmed.

10 The Seljuk influence on the Ottomans came primarily by way of the neighbouring beylik (principality) that the Ottomans absorbed into their rule during the fourteenth century. These beyliks had come into existence in the wake of the Seljuk collapse, and many were directly connected to the Seljuk administrative heritage. Some of the early Ottoman administrators had previously served in other Turkish beylik and brought that experience with them.

11 There is an extensive debate in the literature as to whether the early Ottomans were genuine zealots and if so, how that could be reconciled with the heterodox constitution of their warrior bands. See Darling (2011, 2000), Wittek (1938), Kafadar (1991, 1995).

12 Caliph means deputy.

13 Space does not allow for a discussion of sectarian differences. For the Ottomans, the Sunni lineage is more determinative.

14 For a comparison with Europe, see Zarakol (2017).

15 Another possibility is that the founder-king-blessed by-dreams narrative already existed in the region (no matter whence it originated) and the Ottomans may have absorbed it from the local population. (Darling, 2011: 27).

16 It should go without saying that such efforts also had plenty of discontents. See, e.g., Darling (2011). Nevertheless, even such resistance itself is evidence that the Ottomans were developing notions of absolute sovereignty (and practices of centralisation) throughout the fifteenth and sixteenth centuries.

17 The Abbasid dynasty had ended in 1295 – after that point, the claim to caliphate was contested by several parties, including the Mamluks in Egypt. When they lost control of the holy lands to the Ottomans, they also lost the whatever legitimacy they had to this claim. Ottomans first had laid claim to this title in early part of the fourteenth century.

18 The few exceptions to this rule include Anievas and Nisancıoğlu (2015), Phillips and Sharman (2015), Pardesi (2017), Neumann and Wigen (2018). For more, see my forthcoming book, *Before Defeat* (Zarakol, under contract).

19 The *Treasury of Justice* (author anonymous) tract from his reign argues that the sultan was the Caliph of God, i.e. equal to a prophet in terms of lawmaking power.

20 The dating is Tezcan's. It is possible to argue that Murad IV (r. 1623–1640) belongs in the previous period, given his absolutist tendencies.

21 Or put another way, Western European polities faced heterogeneous demographics mostly in their overseas colonies.

References

Anderson, P. (1974). *Lineages of the Absolutist State*. London: Verso.

Andrews, W., and Kalpaklı, M. (2005). *The Age of Beloveds: Love and the Beloved in Early Modern Ottoman and European Culture and Society*. Durham: Duke University Press.

Anghie, A. (2002). Colonialism and the birth of international institutions: sovereignty, economy and the mandate system of the League of Nations. *NYU Journal of International Law and Politics*, 34 (3), 513–633.

Anievas, A., and Nişancıoğlu, K. (2013). What's at stake in the transition debate? Rethinking the origins of capitalism and the 'rise of the west'. *Millennium*, 42 (1), 78–102.

Anievas, A., and Nişancıoğlu, K. (2015). *How the West Came to Rule*. Chicago, IL: Pluto Press/The University of Chicago Press.

Bartelson, J. (1995). *A Genealogy of Sovereignty*. Cambridge: Cambridge University Press.

Bartelson, J. (2018). Dating sovereignty. In: Forum: In the beginning there was no word (for it): terms, concepts, and early sovereignty. *International Studies Review*, 20 (3), 489–519.

Beaulac, Stephane. (2000). The Westphalian Legal Orthodoxy - Myth or Reality? *Journal of the History of International Law*, 2, 148–77.

Benton, L. (2009). *A Search for Sovereignty*. Cambridge: Cambridge University Press.

Black, A. (2011). *The History of Islamic Political Thought*. 2nd edition. Edinburgh: Edinburgh University Press.

Branch, J. (2011). Mapping the Sovereign State: Technology, Authority, and Systemic Change. *International Organization*, 65 (1), 1–36.

Burak, G. (2013a). Faith, law and empire in the Ottoman 'age of confessionalization' (fifteenth–seventeenth centuries): the case of 'renewal of faith'. *Mediterranean Historical Review*, 28 (1), 1–23.

Burak, G. (2013b). The second formation of Islamic law: the post-Mongol context of the Ottoman adoption of a school of law. *Comparative Studies in Society and History*, 55 (3), 579–602.

Buzan, B., and Lawson, G. (2015). *The Global Transformation*. Cambridge: Cambridge University Press.

Casale, G. (2010). *The Ottoman Age of Exploration*. Oxford: Oxford University Press.

Çırakman, A. (2001). From tyranny to despotism: the enlightenment's unenlightened image of the Turks. *International Journal of Middle East Studies*, 33 (1), 49–68.

Collins, R. (1997). An Asian route to capitalism: religious economy and the origins of self-transforming growth in Japan. *American Sociological Review*, 62 (6), 843–865.

Crone, P. (2003). *Slaves on Horses*. Cambridge: Cambridge University Press.

Crone, P., and Hinds, M. (2003). *God's Caliph*. Cambridge: Cambridge University Press.

Croxton, D. (1999). The peace of Westphalia of 1648 and the origins of sovereignty. *The International History Review*, 21 (3), 569–591.

Darling, L. (2000). Contested territory: Ottoman holy war in comparative context. *Studia Islamica*, 9 (91), 133–163.

Darling, L. (2008). Political change and political discourse in the early modern Mediterranean world. *Journal of Interdisciplinary History*, 38 (4), 505–531.

Darling, L. (2011). Reformulating the *Gazi* narrative: when was the Ottoman state a *Gazi* state? *Turcica*, 43: 13–53.

de Carvalho, B. (2021). Sovereignty in Historical International Relations: Trajectories, Challenges and Implications. In de Carvalho, B., Costa Lopez, J., & Leira, H., eds. *Routledge Handbook of Historical International Relations*. Abingdon: Routledge.

de Carvalho, B., and Leira, H. (2021). State Formation and Historical International Relations. In de Carvalho, B., Costa Lopez, J., & Leira, H., eds. *Routledge Handbook of Historical International Relations*. Abingdon: Routledge.

de Carvalho, B., Leira, H., and Hobson, J. M. (2011). The big bangs of IR: the myths that your teachers still tell you about 1648 and 1919. *Millennium*, 39 (3), 735–758.

Düzgün, E. (2018b). Property, geopolitics, and eurocentrism: the 'great divergence' and the Ottoman Empire. *Review of Radical Political Economics*, 50 (1), 24–43.

Elden, S. (2013). *The Birth of Territory*. Chicago, IL: The University of Chicago Press.

Elias, N. (2000 (1939)). *The Civilising Process*. New York, NY: Blackwell.

Gilpin, R. (1981). *War and Change in World Politics*. Cambridge: Cambridge University Press.

Goettlich, K., and Branch, J. (2021). Borders and Boundaries: Making Visible What Divides. In de Carvalho, B., Costa Lopez, J., & Leira, H., eds. *Routledge Handbook of Historical International Relations*. Abingdon: Routledge.

Goldstone, J. (1998). The problem of the 'early modern' world. *Journal of the Economic and Social History of the Orient*, 41 (3), 249–284.

Held, D. (1995). *Democracy and Global Order*. Cambridge: Polity Press.

Hobson, J. M. (2004). *The Eastern Origins of Western Civilization*. Cambridge: Cambridge University Press.

Hobson, J. M. (2009). Provincializing Westphalia: the Eastern origins of sovereignty. *International Politics*, 46 (6), 671–690.

Hobson, J. M. (2012a). The other side of the Westphalian frontier. In: S. Seth, ed., *Postcolonial Theory and International Relations*, Milton Park: Taylor & Francis, 32–48.

Hobson, J. M. (2012b). *The Eurocentric Conception of World Politics*. Cambridge: Cambridge University Press.

Hobson JM, Sharman JC. (2005). The Enduring Place of Hierarchy in World Politics: Tracing the Social Logics of Hierarchy and Political Change. *European Journal of International Relations*, 11(1), 63–98.

İnalcık, H. (1973). *History of the Ottoman Empire Classical Age / 1300–1600*. London: Weidenfeld and Nicholson.

Kafadar, C. (1991). On the purity and corruption of the Janissaries. *Turkish Studies Association Bulletin*, 15 (2), 273–280.

Kafadar, C. (1995). *Between Two Worlds: the Construction of the Ottoman State*. Berkeley, CA: University of California Press.

Kayaoğlu, T. (2010). Westphalian eurocentrism in international relations theory. *International Studies Review*, 12 (2), 193–217.

Krasner, S. D. (1995–1996). Compromising Westphalia. *International Security*, 20 (3), 115–151.

Krasner, S. D. (2001). Rethinking the sovereign state model. *Review of International Studies*, 27 (5), 17–42.

Lawson, G., and Shilliam, R. (2009). Beyond hypocrisy? Debating the 'fact' and 'value' of sovereignty in contemporary world politics. *International Politics*, 46 (6), 657–670.

Mann, M. (1988). *States, War and Capitalism*. Oxford: Blackwell.

Neumann, I. B., and Wigen, E. (2018). *The Steppe Tradition in International Relations*. Cambridge: Cambridge University Press.

Nexon, D. (2009). *The Struggle for Power in Early Modern Europe*. Princeton, NJ: Princeton University Press.

Nişancıoğlu, K. (2014). The Ottoman origins of capitalism: uneven and combined development and Eurocentrism. *Review of International Studies*, 40 (2): 325–347.

Osiander, A. (2001). Sovereignty, international relations and the Westphalian myth. *International Organization*, 55 (2), 251–287.

Pardesi, M. S. (2017). Region, system, and order: the Mughal Empire in Islamicate Asia. *Security Studies*, 26 (2), 249–278.

Phillips, A., and Sharman, J. C. (2015). *International Order in Diversity: War, Trade and Rule in the Indian Ocean*. Cambridge: Cambridge University Press.

Philpott, D. (1995). Sovereignty: an introduction and brief history. *Journal of International Affairs*, 48 (2), 353–368.

Philpott, D. (2001). *Revolutions in Sovereignty*. Princeton, NJ: Princeton University Press.

Reus-Smit, C. (1999). *The Moral Purpose of the State*. Princeton, NJ: Princeton University Press.

Rosenberg, J. (1994). *The Empire of Civil Society: A Critique of the Realist Theory of International Relations*. London: Verso.

Ruggie, J. G. (1983). Continuity and Transformation in the World Polity: Towards a Neorealist Synthesis. In: R. O. Keohane, ed., *Neorealism and its Critics*, New York, NY: Columbia University Press, 131–157.

Ruggie, J. G. (1995). Territoriality and beyond: problematizing modernity in international relations. *International Organization*, 47 (1), 139–173.

Schmidt, S. (2011). To order the minds of scholars: the discourse of the peace of Westphalia in international relations literature. *International Studies Quarterly*, 55 (3), 601–623.

Shilliam, R. (2006). What about Marcus Garvey? Race and the transformation of sovereignty debate. *Review of International Studies*, 32 (3), 379–400.

Suzuki, S. (2009). *Civilization and Empire: China and Japan's Encounter with European International Society*. London: Routledge

Suzuki, S. (2021). International Order in East Asia. In de Carvalho, B., Costa Lopez, J., & Leira, H., eds. *Routledge Handbook of Historical International Relations*. Abingdon: Routledge.

Teschke, B. (2003). *The Myth of 1648*. London: Verso.

Tezcan, B. (2009). Lost in historiography: an essay on the reasons for the absence of a history of limited government in the early modern Ottoman Empire. *Middle Eastern Studies*, 45 (3), 477–505.

Tilly, C. (1990). *Coercion, Capital and European States AD 990–1990*. Oxford: Blackwell.

Walker, R. B. J. (1993). *Inside/Outside*. Cambridge: Cambridge University Press.

Weber, C. (1995). *Simulating Sovereignty*. Cambridge: Cambridge University Press.

Wigen, E. (2013). Ottoman concepts of empire. *Contributions to the History of Concepts*, 8 (1), 44–66.

Wittek, Paul. 1938. *The Rise of the Ottoman Empire*. London: Royal Asiatic Society.

Wight, M. (1992). *International Theory: The Three Traditions*. Leicester: Leicester University Press.

Zarakol, A. (2011). *After Defeat: How the East Learned to Live with the West*. Cambridge University Press.

Zarakol, A. (2014). What made the modern world hang together: socialisation or stigmatisation? *International Theory* 6 (2), 311–32.

Zarakol, A. (2017). States and ontological insecurity: a historical rethinking. *Cooperation & Conflict*, 52 (1), 48–68.

Zarakol, A. (2018a). A Non-Eurocentric Approach to Sovereignty. In: J. Costa Lopez, B. de Carvalho, A. Latham, A. Zarakol, J. Bartelson, and M. Holm, Forum: In the beginning there was no word (for it): Terms, Concepts, and Early Sovereignty. *International Studies Review*, 20 (3), 489–519.

Zarakol, A. (2018b). Sovereign equality as misrecognition. *Review of International Studies*, 44 (5): 848–862.

Zarakol, A. (2020). Ottomans and Diversity. In: A. Phillips, and C. Reus-Smit, eds., *Cultural Diversity and International Order*, Cambridge: Cambridge University Press.

Zarakol, A. (under contract). *Before Defeat: Rethinking the Decline of the East and the Future of the West*. Cambridge: Cambridge University Press.

44

LATIN AMERICA

Between liminality and agency in Historical International Relations

Carsten-Andreas Schulz

Introduction

Recent Historical International Relations (HIR) and Global History both share a commitment to moving beyond the Eurocentric narrative of the 'rise of the West.' Yet both struggle to come into terms with Latin America, the large and heterogeneous region that encompasses the former Iberian colonies in the Americas. The region is neither the site of great power conflict that has traditionally been the focus of IR research—especially in the English-speaking world—nor does Latin America neatly fit into the West/non-West frame that informs subaltern and postcolonial perspectives (Brown, 2015: 369; Long, 2018: 1372–1373).

The term 'Latin America' is itself inherently Eurocentric. Nineteenth-century French intellectuals coined the notion of a 'Latin race' that had come under pressure from the Anglo-Saxon peoples. Spanish Americans then appropriated the notion in the aftermath of the Mexican-American War (1846–1848) in response to US support for filibustering expedition in Central America (Ardao, 1980; Gobat, 2013: 1346). The embrace of the region's *latinidad* reflected a shared identity, especially among Spanish America's creole elite—the descendants of Europeans born in the Americas—who gradually began to refer to the region as Latin America.[1] The term reflected a strong sense of belonging to the Western world, to the region's Christian heritage, European languages, and the belief in the universality of Enlightenment thought. However, 'Latin America' always implied a certain sense of liminality.[2] As Fawcett (2012) points out, Latin America is neither fully Western nor clearly outside the West. It is deeply influenced by European colonialism, but not an 'outsider' of the Western world.

This chapter argues that Latin America's ambiguous 'in-betweenness' has hindered understanding the region's historical place in global politics. The chapter first reviews how conventional accounts have (mis)construed this place. It then discusses scholarship that engages with Latin America's ambiguity in both historical and theoretical terms, rather than treating the region merely as an appendix of Europe and the West. The chapter concludes by identifying future directions for research, highlighting the need to consider the nature and scope of Latin Americans' agency in HIR.

Lingering Eurocentrism

Eurocentric narratives of the 'rise of the West' have fallen out of favour. More recent debates focus on global (uneven) connections across time and world regions (see also Çapan et al., 2021). However, this scholarship wrestles to make sense of Latin America's place in the making of the 'modern' world. It recognizes the global transformative impact of the conquest and the 'Columbian exchange,' but it largely understands these events through a European lens. As a result, historians and International Relations (IR) scholars tend to treat the region's societies as extensions of Europe and the West, ignoring the contradictions that arose from Latin America's liminality.

The Columbian exchange

Columbus' arrival in the Caribbean in 1492 set in motion an unprecedented exchange of food, livestock, and diseases. What Crosby (1972) termed the 'Columbian exchange' had devastating effects on the New Worlds' native inhabitants. Infectious diseases and unfettered exploitation wiped out the Caribbean's native population in the first years of the conquest. The rapid spread of diseases destabilized indigenous polities. Local allies and smallpox aided Hernán Cortés in the Siege of Tenochtitlan (today's Mexico City), paving the way for the defeat of the Aztec Empire in 1521. Smallpox and measles spread rapidly throughout the American continents, sometimes even outpacing the European colonizers. In South America, the Incan Emperor Huayna Capac—under whose rule the Tawantinsuyu reached its peak—likely died of smallpox before Francisco Pizarro's arrival in 1524. After the death of his eldest son and heir apparent, the empire descended into civil war. The Spanish *conquistadores* exploited the raging internecine conflict to their advantage. Pizarro captured and executed the last emperor in 1532. The impact of pathogens and shifting local alliances are easily forgotten in accounts that traditionally emphasize Europeans' superior military technology and strategy (Sharman, 2019). Despite the growing interest in non-European empires, the dearth of HIR scholarship about pre-Columbian polities is striking (for exceptions, see Ferguson and Mansbach, 1996; Jones, 2007).

In the Old World, the high-yielding crops introduced from the Americas—potatoes in Europe and sweet potatoes and cassava in Africa and Asia—allowed for sustained population growth; quinine, made from the bark of the cinchona tree native to South America's Andes, offered protection against malaria, facilitating later European exploration and colonization of tropical regions. The introduction of Old World crops to the Americas made coffee and sugar widely available to consumers, especially in Europe where they fuelled early industrialization (de Vries, 2008). Producing sugar, however, required heavy manual labour. Given the high demand and facing a rapidly dwindling local population, Europeans enslaved and transported over 12 million Africans to the Western Hemisphere between the sixteenth and nineteenth centuries. Brazil, the principal market for slaves in the Americas, only abolished slavery in 1888.

New World silver lay at the heart of the emerging global trade network. The discovery of silver at Potosí (today's Bolivia) and Zacatecas (Mexico) in the 1540s led to a mining boom. Spanish America became the world's principal supplier of silver from the sixteenth to late-eighteenth century. Silver catalysed the colonization of the American mainland and stimulated commerce across Eurasia (Braudel's 'circulatory system'). The establishment of Manila in 1571 provided Spain with an *entrepôt* to direct trade with Asia. The colonization of the New World shifted the centre of global trade towards the Atlantic, placing Europe increasingly at the centre.

Spain's silver mines in the New World, and the ensuing Atlantic trade more generally, played an important part in causing the 'great divergence' that set Western Europe apart from the rest of the world. Economic historians and political scientists disagree on the effects of Iberian colonialism (Acemoglu et al., 2005; Mahoney, 2010). However, both underscore the importance of the resources from the New World to explain Western economic growth and industrialization. Yet despite the centrality that these accounts place on the American continents, their inhabitants are largely absent or passive subjects. In debates on the 'great divergence,' Latin America is treated as an extension of Europe and thus overlooked.

The same can be said about the ideational impact of the conquest. Columbus' 'discovery' had a profound impact on Europeans' self-perception and world views (O'Gorman, 1961; Todorov, 1984). A prime example is the so-called Valladolid debate (1550–1551) between Juan Ginés de Sepúlveda and Bartolomé de las Casas concerning the rights of the native inhabitants of the Americas. Legal historians and IR scholars have long argued that the dispute laid the foundation of what would become international humanitarian and human rights law (see also Vergerio, 2021). Mirroring debates about the economic and political 'rise of the West,' Latin America features prominently, but without playing an active role; it is Europe's reaction to and reflection on the New World that seems to matter. However, as more recent accounts show, much can be gained from considering Latin American political and legal history on its own terms (see Benton, 2002; Becker Lorca, 2014).

The difficulty of dealing with liminality

There is a long tradition in the humanities and social sciences of treating Latin American societies as laggard copies of Europe (see Centeno and López-Alves, 2001). In the eighteenth century, European writers popularized the 'degeneration thesis,' a common trope that goes back to the early conquest. In this view, the flora and fauna of the New World were inherently inferior to those of the Old World (Gerbi, 2010 [1973]; Pagden, 1990). The deleterious effects of the New World environment were thought to extend to the native inhabitants as well, adding further justification to European domination. Europeans also portrayed the non-indigenous population as degenerated and effeminate. Elites in the Americas responded accordingly. Thomas Jefferson's *Notes on the State of Virginia* (1785) documented the rich natural environment and the quality of the new state's political institutions in defence of 'the race of the whites, transplanted from Europe' (cited in Elliott, 2006: 328). After their expulsion from the Spanish Empire in 1767, exiled Jesuits penned the Spanish American response, exalting the splendour and cultural achievements of Americas' indigenous civilizations (for example, Clavijero's *Historia antigua de México*).

The end of colonial rule in Latin America came in the wake of the Napoleonic Wars. Frances' occupation of the Iberian Peninsula in 1808 triggered a legitimacy crisis throughout the Spanish realm. The creole-controlled *cabildos* (town councils) initially declared for the disposed king. However, once restored to the throne, Ferdinand VII attempted to re-establish the status quo ante, provoking declarations of independence throughout Spanish America. In Portugal, Napoleon's invasion led to the evacuation of the court to Rio de Janeiro under British protection. Later attempts to reduce Brazil to its former colonial status provoked elites to push for greater autonomy, leading Pedro I to declare independence in 1822. Whereas the continuation of Braganza rule provided some legitimacy to the new regime, Spanish America became embroiled in long and destructive civil wars.

Despite their purportedly European heritage, the nascent states were increasingly seen as unstable and their inhabitants inherently unruly. The turn of the nineteenth century saw the emergence of the political distinction between North and South America. Cultural and racial prejudice informed European and, increasingly, US perceptions of the region. In 1823, President James Monroe famously declared that the Western Hemisphere would be closed to European (re)colonization. What became known as the Monroe Doctrine has long exhibited a tension between the 'Western Hemisphere' idea—the belief that the republics of the Americas stand in a special relationship to one another (Whitaker, 1954)—and the 'hegemonic presumption' of the United States (Lowenthal, 1976).

Schoultz (1998), for example, highlights how anti-Catholicism and contempt for widespread racial miscegenation in Latin American influenced early US foreign policy. This was combined with a much older anti-Spanish prejudice dating back to the Protestant propaganda of the sixteenth-century Dutch Revolt. The principle of 'manifest destiny' exploited these prejudices in justifying westward expansionism (Pike, 1992). Although these pejorative views are well documented in the US case (as is their gendered character), they were more widespread. Despite recognizing the new states diplomatically, European powers hesitated to treat them as fully fledged members of the international order (Schulz, 2014).

Historical IR accounts wrestle with Latin America's liminality. Consider the English School narrative of the evolution of modern international society as the result of the fragmentation of Latin Christendom and the global expansion of an originally European order. Because the descendants of Europeans built the new states in the Americas, the English School long regarded the 'admission' of Latin America' as unproblematic (Watson, 1984; for a critique, see Schulz, 2014; Lubbock, 2020). Although recent revisionist accounts have focused on the exclusion of the ancient polities in Asia, Latin America has received little attention.

Similarly, constructivists that focus on the liberal and republican discourses of creole elites often miss the inherent contradiction within these arguments (Reus-Smit, 2013; but see Simon, 2017). Latin American elites felt the tension between their 'insider' and 'outsider' status keenly. 'Completing civilization' became an important driver for state-led modernization (Obregón, 2006). In the late nineteenth century, it also became a battle cry in Argentina's and Chile's military campaigns to crush indigenous resistance against state consolidation.

Rather than treating Latin American states as 'backwards' copies of European models, understanding the region's political history and debates requires engagement with its ambiguous international position, and the way in which elites internalized and contested this discourse.

The difference that liminality can make

While the previous section focused on the ongoing struggle to overcome the Eurocentric tendency to view Latin America as a laggard copy of European societies, this section explores historically oriented IR debates that take Latin America on its own terms.

Global (historical) IR from Latin America

In contrast to English-speaking mainstream IR, which only recently rediscovered hierarchy, Latin American accounts have long highlighted the uneven and unequal development of international order (see also Fonseca Santos, 2021).

Latin Americans' critique of commodity export dependency is well known and goes back, at the least, to the Bourbon Reforms of the late colonial period. In the wake of WWI, this sensibility consolidated into a particular type of historicist international political economy that emphasizes the distinction between 'core' and 'periphery' (see Deciancio, 2016). In the 1960s and 1970s, dependency theory emerged out of this intellectual tradition as a response to modernization theory and the view that Latin America 'fell behind' (the West). For the proponents of 'Latin American structuralism,' underdevelopment resulted from the region's integration into a capitalist world economy and the internal contradictions this entailed (Furtado, 1970; Cardoso and Faletto, 1979 [1969]). Importantly, in contrast to dependency theory's reception in the Global North, Latin American variants emphasize historical processes and contingencies in this development.

In Latin America, the divide between (diplomatic) history and IR has been less stark than in the United States, whose theories and approaches dominate the field. For example, in Brazil, the so-called Brasília School stands for an explicitly historical mode of IR centred on Latin America's 'insertion' into an hierarchical international order (Bernal-Meza, 2005; Cervo, 2008; Chagas-Bastos, 2018). In the Southern Cone, historically informed accounts focus on the strategies that have allowed countries to maintain or increase their autonomy despite overbearing structural constraints (see Tickner, 2003). Much of this scholarship takes the sovereign nation state for granted. However, the same influences from historicist political economy are also evident in critical and postcolonial theories (Quijano, 2000).

In more recent years, debates about Global IR have opened a venue for dialogue between these approaches. The historical orientation of Latin American scholarship has much to offer, given the recent 'historical turn' in English-speaking IR.

Leveraging liminality

The engagement with Latin America's ambiguous position can help to revise existing theories derived from European history, as well as offering new conceptual and theoretical tools.

For example, Latin America raises important questions about the relationship between state-building and war. Centeno (2002), for example, shows how Tilly's bellicist theory—according to which large-scale interstate war leads to state consolidation, which in turn makes the state more capable of waging large-scale war—offers little insight into Latin America. Because of the timing of independence and the availability of international capital, Latin American states were not obliged to turn inward to fund their military conflicts. As a result, interstate war leads to indebtedness rather than the creation of consolidated state bureaucracies. Other authors have elaborated on this point, emphasizing the need to consider internal conflict and interstate rivalry that falls below the level of war (Mares, 2001; Thies, 2005; Martín, 2006).

Others have responded to the Latin American 'anomaly' by focusing on the region's diplomatic and legal culture. For authors in the English School tradition, Latin America represents a historically evolved regional international society that rejects the use of force as a legitimate tool of statecraft (Hurrell, 1998; Kacowicz, 2005; Merke, 2015; see also Navari and Green, 2021). Early nineteenth–century Latin Americans promoted diplomacy and international law as a means of avoiding open war. The stabilizing of interstate relations was deemed necessary to forestall costly and destructive conflicts that threatened to undo their state-building projects and might leave the region vulnerable to reconquest or foreign intervention. Spanish American creoles—typically trained in law—agreed on the principle of *uti possidetis juris*, by which the boundaries of the new states should correspond with those of the colonial administrations they inherited. While this agreed-upon norm did not prevent territorial annexation, it did provide an external criterion that informed negotiations. Even today, boundary disputes generally arise in areas that were not clearly demarcated during the colonial period (the Amazon, the Atacama Desert, or Patagonia). This originally Latin American norm was later adopted in other postcolonial regions, notably Africa, and also informed the creation of new states after the Cold War (see also Svensson, 2021).

Latin American agency

HIR scholarship in and about Latin America long concentrated on US-Latin America relations. Because of the vast power asymmetries in the Western Hemisphere and given that long list of US (or US-sponsored) interventions, studies discounted the agency of Latin Americans in their dealings with the United States. Whereas diplomatic history written in the United States focused on US actions and interests, Latin American historiography predominantly dealt with states' resistance to US domination. This tendency has been particularly pronounced in the literature on the Cold War. However, recent scholarship has fundamentally challenged the view that sees Latin Americans as mere subjects of great power politics. Drawing on multi-archival research, numerous accounts demonstrate that Latin American governments were able to pursue their own agendas and even manipulated Washington under the constraints of the Cold War (Spektor, 2009; for example, Harmer, 2011; Brands, 2012; Keller, 2015; Long, 2015). This has also led to a more general reconsideration of US-Latin American relations.

Another growing literature examines Latin American contributions to international norms and institutions (see Long, 2018). In the nineteenth century, Latin American jurists and diplomats spearheaded institutional innovations. Regional conferences provided a platform for developing multilateralism and (regional) international law. In the late-nineteenth century, US attempts to promote regional cooperation through Pan-American conferences drew heavily on Latin American precedent (Grandin, 2006). The Pan-American movement anticipated many of the global initiatives that took shape after WWI under US leadership. For Latin Americans, regional cooperation and international law provided both a means to constrain the United States (Friedman and Long, 2015; Scarfi, 2016) and to pursue their own policy agendas (Petersen and Schulz, 2018). Because of the long history of regionalism that involved Latin American states, this is a fruitful area for further historically oriented research.

Legalism also informed Latin Americans' relationship with Europe and the wider world. Finnemore, for example, maintains that Latin America's participation at the Second Hague Conference (1907) was instrumental in shaping norms about sovereignty and non-intervention (2003: 24–51), and in creating expectations about universal participation at international conferences (Finnemore and Jurkovich, 2014; but see Schulz, 2017). Recent scholarship has also re-examined Latin America's relationship with the League of Nations. Whereas the conventional view regarded Latin America's role as largely passive due to the organizations' focus on European affairs, scholarship emphasizes Latin Americans' interest in creating a counterweight to Washington in Geneva (Vargas Garcia, 2000; Fischer, 2012; McPherson and Wehrli, 2015, see also Ravndal, 2021). Regarding the second half of the twentieth century, scholarship further shows that Latin Americans shaped the 'social purpose' of the Bretton Woods institutions towards promoting state-led development (Helleiner 2014); that Latin American interventions had transformative effects on the nature of sovereign territory through the negotiation of the Law of the Sea (García-Amador, 1974); and that Latin Americans played an important role in creating and strengthening the international human rights regime (Sikkink, 2014; Kelly, 2018).

Conclusion

HIR is increasingly moving away from Eurocentrism. However, because of Latin America's ambiguous position, these accounts tend to emphasize the centrality of Latin America in global transformations while simultaneously denying its active role. As this chapter has argued, future research should engage more directly with the region's liminality.

Latin America offers ample opportunity to revisit existing concepts and theories about large-scale historical processes, as evident in the discussion about the relationship between state formation and war. Recent historiography that explicitly engages with the 'entanglements' of the region with the United States and the wider 'Atlantic world' has also led to a reconsideration of Latin American agency.

Furthermore, there is an increasing recognition of Latin American contributions to international norms and institutions, especially concerning sovereignty. What this literature has in common is an appreciation of the role that Latin American's liminality—as neither 'insiders' nor clear 'outsiders'—had in facilitating these innovations. The status of Latin American states as sovereign and independent provided Latin American actors with access to diplomatic and legal circles. At the same time, however, their experience differed significantly enough from their European and US counterparts to give them a distinct perspective.

Latin America's place in global politics tends to be viewed through a Eurocentric prism. This is particularly evident in the lack of interest in the politics of pre-Columbian societies. Despite growing literatures on non-European polities across time and space, the rich and diverse history of political communities before the arrival of the Europeans remains almost completely unexplored by HIR.

Suggestions for further reading

Adelman, J. (2006). *Sovereignty and Revolution in the Iberian Atlantic*. Princeton, NJ: Princeton University Press.

Davis, H., Finan, J., and Peck, F. (1977). *Latin American Diplomatic History: An Introduction*. Baton Rouge, LA: Louisiana State University Press.

Elliott, J. (2006). *Empires of the Atlantic World: Britain and Spain in America, 1492–1830*. New Haven, CT: Yale University Press.

Gobat, M. (2018). *Empire by Invitation: William Walker and Manifest Destiny in Central America*. Cambridge: Harvard University Press.

Muldoon, J. (1994). *The Americas in the Spanish World Order: The Justification for Conquest in the Seventeenth Century*. Philadelphia, PA: University of Pennsylvania Press.

Tenorio-Trillo, M. (2017). *Latin America: The Allure and Power of an Idea*. Chicago, IL: University of Chicago Press.

Topik, S., Marichal, C., and Frank, Z. (2006). *From Silver to Cocaine: Latin American Commodity Chains and the Building of the World Economy, 1500–2000*. Durham: Duke University Press.

Notes

1 South America or *América meridional* remained the preferred term for most of the nineteenth century. Contemporaries did not consider Haiti as a part of Latin America, and Brazilians have been lukewarm about their Latin American identity ever since.
2 For a conceptual discussion, see Mälksoo (2012).

References

Adelman, J. (2006). *Sovereignty and Revolution in the Iberian Atlantic*. Princeton, NJ: Princeton University Press.

Acemoglu, D., Johnson, S., and Robinson, J. (2005). The Rise of Europe: Atlantic Trade, Institutional Change, and Economic Growth. *American Economic Review*, 95 (3), 546–579.

Ardao, A. (1980). *Génesis de la idea y el nombre de América Latina*. Caracas: Centro de Estudios Latinoamericanos Rómulo Gallegos.

Becker Lorca, A. (2014). *Mestizo International Law: A Global Intellectual History 1842–1933*. Cambridge: Cambridge University Press.

Benton, L. (2002). *Law and Colonial Cultures: Legal Regimes in World History, 1400–1900*. Cambridge: Cambridge University Press.

Bernal-Meza, R. (2005). *América Latina en el mundo: el pensamiento latinoamericano y la teoría de relaciones internacionales*. Buenos Aires: Nuevohacer, Grupo Editor Latinoamericano.

Brands, H. (2012). *Latin America's Cold War*. Cambridge: Harvard University Press.

Brown, M. (2015). The Global History of Latin America. *Journal of Global History*, 10 (3), 365–386.

Çapan, Z. G., dos Reis, F. and Grasten, M., (2021). Global Histories: Connections and Circulations in Historical International Relations. In de Carvalho, B., Costa Lopez, J., & Leira, H., eds. *Routledge Handbook of Historical International Relations.* Abingdon: Routledge.

Cardoso, F., and Faletto, E. (1979 [1969]). *Dependency and Development in Latin America.* Translated by M. Urquidi. Berkeley, CA: University of California Press.

Centeno, M. (2002). *Blood and Debt: War and the Nation-State in Latin America.* University Park, PA: Pennsylvania State University Press.

Centeno, M., and López-Alves, F. (2001). *The Other Mirror: Grand Theory through the Lens of Latin America.* Princeton, NJ: Princeton University Press.

Cervo, A. (2008). *Inserção internacional: formação dos conceitos brasileiros.* São Paulo: Saraiva.

Chagas-Bastos, F. (2018). La invención de la inserción internacional: fundaciones intelectuales y evolución histórica del concepto. *Análisis Político*, 31 (94), 10–30.

Crosby, A. (1972). *The Columbian Exchange: Biological and Cultural Consequences of 1492.* Westport: Greenwood Press.

de Vries, J. (2008). *The Industrious Revolution: Consumer Behavior and the Household Economy, 1650 to the Present.* Cambridge: Cambridge University Press.

Davis, H., Finan, J., and Peck, F. (1977). *Latin American Diplomatic History: An Introduction.* Baton Rouge, LA: Louisiana State University Press.

Deciancio, M. (2016). International Relations from the South: A Regional Research Agenda for Global IR. *International Studies Review*, 18 (1), 106–119.

Elliott, J. (2006). *Empires of the Atlantic World: Britain and Spain in America, 1492–1830.* New Haven, CT: Yale University Press.

Fawcett, L. (2012). Between West and non-West: Latin American Contributions to International Thought. *The International History Review*, 34 (4), 679–704.

Ferguson, Y. H., and Mansbach, R. W. (1996). *Polities: Authority, Identities, and Change.* Columbia: University of South Carolina Press.

Finnemore, M. (2003). *The Purpose of Intervention: Changing Beliefs about the Use of Force.* Ithaca, NY: Cornell University Press.

Finnemore, M., and Jurkovich, M. (2014). Getting a Seat at the Table: The Origins of Universal Participation and Modern Multilateral Conferences. *Global Governance: A Review of Multilateralism and International Organizations*, 20 (3), 361–373.

Fischer, T. (2012). *Die Souveränität der Schwachen: Lateinamerika und der Völkerbund, 1920–1936.* Stuttgart: Franz Steiner.

Fonseca Santos, M. (2021). Disciplinary Histories of Non-Anglophone International Relations: Latin America and the Caribbean. In de Carvalho, B., Costa Lopez, J., & Leira, H., eds. *Routledge Handbook of Historical International Relations.* Abingdon: Routledge.

Friedman, M. P., and Long, T. (2015). Soft Balancing in the Americas: Latin American Opposition to U.S. Intervention, 1898–1936. *International Security*, 40 (1), 120–156.

Furtado, C. (1970). *Economic Development of Latin America: A Survey from Colonial Times to the Cuban Revolution.* Cambridge: Cambridge University Press.

García-Amador, F. V. (1974). The Latin American Contribution to the Development of the Law of the Sea. *American Journal of International Law*, 68 (1), 33–50.

Gerbi, A. (2010 [1973]). *The Dispute of the New World: The History of a Polemic, 1750–1900.* Translated by J. Moyle. Pittsburgh, PA: University of Pittsburgh Press.

Gobat, M. (2013). The Invention of Latin America: A Transnational History of Anti-Imperialism, Democracy, and Race. *The American Historical Review*, 118 (5), 1345–1375.

Gobat, M. (2018). *Empire by Invitation: William Walker and Manifest Destiny in Central America.* Cambridge: Harvard University Press.

Grandin, G. (2006). Your Americanism and Mine: Americanism and Anti-Americanism in the Americas. *The American Historical Review*, 111 (4), 1042–1066.

Harmer, T. (2011). *Allende's Chile and the Inter-American Cold War.* Chapel Hill, NC: University of North Carolina Press.

Helleiner, E. (2014). *Forgotten Foundations of Bretton Woods: International Development and the Making of the Postwar Order.* Ithaca, NY: Cornell University Press.

Hurrell, A. (1998). An Emerging Security Community in South America? In: E. Adler, and M. N. Barnett, eds., *Security Communities*, Cambridge: Cambridge University Press, 228–264.

Jones, C. (2007). Hierarchy and Resistance in American State-Systems 1400–1800 CE. In: S. Kaufman, R. Little, and W. Wohlforth, eds., *The Balance of Power in World History*, Basingstoke: Palgrave Macmillan, 176–198.

Kacowicz, A. (2005). *The Impact of Norms in International Society: The Latin American Experience, 1881-2001.* Notre Dame: Notre Dame Press.

Keller, R. (2015). *Mexico's Cold War: Cuba, the United States, and the Legacy of the Mexican Revolution.* New York, NY: Cambridge University Press.

Kelly, W. (2018). *Sovereign Emergencies: Latin America and the Making of Global Human Rights Politics.* Cambridge: Cambridge University Press.

Long, T. (2015). *Latin America Confronts the United States: Asymmetry and Influence.* New York, NY: Cambridge University Press.

Long, T. (2018). Latin America and the Liberal International Order: An Agenda for Research. *International Affairs*, 94 (6), 1371–1390.

Lowenthal, A. F. (1976). United States and Latin America: Ending the Hegemonic Presumption. *Foreign Affairs*, 55 (1), 199–213.

Lubbock, R. (2020). Rights, Recognition and Norms in the Making of Latin American International Society: An Historical Materialist Interpretation. *Journal of International Relations and Development*, 23 (2), 237–261.

Mahoney, J. (2010). *Colonialism and Development: Spanish America in Comparative Perspective.* Cambridge: Cambridge University Press.

Mälksoo, M. (2012). The Challenge of Liminality for International Relations Today. *Review of International Studies*, 38 (2), 481–494.

Mares, D. R. (2001). *Violent Peace: Militarized Interstate Bargaining in Latin America.* New York, NY: Columbia University Press.

Martín, F. E. (2006). *Militarist Peace in South America: Conditions for War and Peace.* New York, NY: Palgrave McMillan.

McPherson, A., and Wehrli, Y. (2015). *Beyond Geopolitics: New Histories of Latin America at the League of Nations.* Albuquerque, NM: University of New Mexico Press.

Merke, F. (2015). Neither Balance nor Bandwagon: South American International Society Meets Brazil's Rising Power. *International Politics*, 52, 178–192.

Muldoon, J. (1994). *The Americas in the Spanish World Order: The Justification for Conquest in the Seventeenth Century.* Philadelphia, PA: University of Pennsylvania Press.

Navari, C., and Green, D. (2021). The English School and Historical International Relations. In de Carvalho, B., Costa Lopez, J., & Leira, H., eds. *Routledge Handbook of Historical International Relations.* Abingdon: Routledge.

O'Gorman, E. (1961). *The Invention of America: An Inquiry into the Historical Nature of the New World and the Meaning of Its History.* Bloomington, IN: Indiana University Press.

Obregón, L. (2006). Completing Civilization: Creole Consciousness and International Law in Nineteenth-Century Latin America. In: A. Orford, ed., *International Law and Its Others*, Cambridge: Cambridge University Press, 247–264.

Pagden, A. (1990). *Spanish Imperialism and the Political Imagination: Studies in European and Spanish-American Social and Political Theory, 1513–1830.* New Haven, CT: Yale University Press.

Petersen, M. and C.-A. Schulz. (2018). Setting the Regional Agenda: A Critique of Post-Hegemonic Regionalism. *Latin American Politics and Society*, 60 (1), 102–127.

Pike, F. B. (1992). *The United States and Latin America: Myths and Stereotypes of Civilization and Nature.* Austin, TX: University of Texas Press.

Quijano, A. (2000). Coloniality of Power and Eurocentrism in Latin America. *International Sociology*, 15 (2), 215–232.

Reus-Smit, C. (2013). *Individual Rights and the Making of the International System.* Cambridge: Cambridge University Press.

Scarfi, J. P. (2016). In the Name of the Americas: The Pan-American Redefinition of the Monroe Doctrine and the Emerging Language of American International Law in the Western Hemisphere. *Diplomatic History*, 40 (2), 189–218.

Schoultz, L. (1998). *Beneath the United States: A History of U.S. Policy toward Latin America.* Cambridge: Harvard University Press.

Schulz, C.-A. (2014). Civilisation, Barbarism and the Making of Latin America's Place in 19th-Century International Society. *Millennium: Journal of International Studies*, 42 (3), 837–859.

Schulz, C.-A. (2017). Accidental Activists: Latin American Status-Seeking at the Hague. *International Studies Quarterly*, 61 (3), 612–622.

Sharman, J. C. (2019). *Empires of the Weak: The Real Story of European Expansion and the Creation of the New World Order*. Princeton, NJ: Princeton University Press.

Sikkink, K. (2014). Latin American Countries as Norm Protagonists of the Idea of International Human Rights. *Global Governance*, 20 (3), 389–404.

Simon, J. (2017). *The Ideology of Creole Revolution: Imperialism and Independence in American and Latin American Political Thought*. Cambridge: Cambridge University Press.

Spektor, M. (2009). *Kissinger e o Brasil*. Rio de Janeiro: Zahar.

Svensson, T. (2021). Decolonisation and the Erosion of the Imperial Idea. In de Carvalho, B., Costa Lopez, J., & Leira, H., eds. *Routledge Handbook of Historical International Relations*. Abingdon: Routledge.

Tenorio-Trillo, M. (2017). *Latin America: The Allure and Power of an Idea*. Chicago, IL: University of Chicago Press.

Thies, C. (2005). War, Rivalry, and State Building in Latin America. *American Journal of Political Science*, 49 (3), 451–465.

Tickner, A. (2003). Hearing Latin American Voices in International Relations Studies. *International Studies Perspectives*, 4 (4), 325–350.

Todorov, T. (1984). *The Conquest of America: The Question of the Other*. 1st edition. New York, NY: Harper & Row.

Topik, S., Marichal, C., and Frank, Z. (2006). *From Silver to Cocaine: Latin American Commodity Chains and the Building of the World Economy, 1500–2000*. Durham: Duke University Press.

Vargas Garcia, E. (2000). *O Brasil e a Liga das Nações (1919–1926): Vencer ou não perder*. Porto Alegre/Brasília: Editora da Universidade UFRGS/FUNAG.

Vergerio, C. (2021). International Law and the Laws of War. In de Carvalho, B., Costa Lopez, J., & Leira, H., eds. *Routledge Handbook of Historical International Relations*. Abingdon: Routledge.

Watson, A. (1984). New States in the Americas. In: H. Bull, and Watson, A., eds., *The Expansion of International Society*, Oxford: Clarendon Press, 127–141.

Whitaker, A. (1954). *The Western Hemisphere Idea: Its Rise and Decline*. Ithaca, NY: Cornell University Press.

PART V

Approaches

45

INTERNATIONAL RELATIONS IN THE ARCHIVE

Uses of sources and historiography

Jeppe Mulich

Introduction

The discipline of International Relations (IR) has gone through something of a historicist revival over the last two decades. A growing interest in history is changing the discipline, with more and more scholars engaging critically with history as a process, rather than as a passive repository of case studies and data sets. Curiously this emerging body of Historical IR scholarship has had relatively little to say about how to do this type of work. With a few notable exceptions (e.g. Suganami, 2008; Leira, 2015; Cello, 2017), the historical turn has largely left debates over methods and methodology to others, preferring instead to focus on theorizing world politics, analysing historical patterns of interaction, and recharting the history of the discipline itself. The present chapter is in some ways an attempt to start a debate over these neglected topics by considering the ways in which historical IR scholarship has been approaching historical source material, primary as well as secondary, and suggesting some useful lessons from the methodological debates in disciplinary history.

The chapter begins with a brief overview of the ways in which recent IR scholarship has approached the use of history in general and the use of historical sources more specifically. It then delves into a deeper discussion of the two main types of historical sources – secondary sources, or historiography, and primary sources, especially archival ones. This is followed by a conclusion that outlines some of the possible trends in the field and potential challenges associated with conducting this type of historical research in IR.

Historical IR is composed of a very large body of diverse work, often only unified by a shared interest in the human past, and as such it is exceedingly hard to make generalizable statements about the scholarship in the field. It is therefore worth saying at the outset that the following sections will often make sweeping generalizations and paint crude typologies that do not do justice to the diversity of approaches and perspectives within the field. These typologies are only meant to be useful in thinking through common trends and challenges, not to paint a comprehensive or accurate picture of all the work being done in the field.

Approaches to historical research in IR scholarship

IR scholarship can be said to display three different broad approaches to historical research – history as case study, history as data set, and history as change over time. These perspectives are of course not mutually exclusive, and many works draw on more than one approach, but distinguishing between them goes some way towards illuminating the patterns of research in the field (see also MacKay and LaRoche, 2021).

Most work that engages in theory testing or illustration through case studies necessarily relies on history as the main body of examples to draw on. This is true not just for IR but also for any social science that makes heavy use of the case study as a research model. Anything that has happened, whether in the recent or distant past, is part of history and as such requires a certain sensitivity to historical context. This poses a certain challenge to theory testing via case study in IR, as much of the theory that has traditionally been put to the test is explicitly ahistorical or claims to be universally applicable irrespective of period.[1] In fact, many of the long-standing theoretical paradigms in IR have no inherent concept of historical time. Despite this conceptual problem, many case studies in practice show a great deal of sensitivity to the historical context of their cases, even when the theory they are testing seems to dismiss time as a relevant factor (e.g. Schweller, 2006). Indeed, a major argument in the field has been whether or not case studies taken from different times and places prove or disprove the viability of universal, seemingly ahistorical theories like the balance-of-power (Hui, 2005; Wohlforth et al., 2007). In this and other ways, there has been considerable movement towards a more historically informed use of case studies in IR, especially when they are specifically employed to critique, subvert, or nuance the universalizing claims of existing theories (Nexon, 2009; Phillips and Sharman, 2015).

The second major approach is to see history as a repository of quantifiable data. Almost all quantitative work in IR starts with what is in one way or another historical material, in the sense of being aggregates of past events, but the extent to which this data is treated as *history* varies greatly (see also Butcher and Griffiths, 2021). As with case studies, there is a spectrum of approaches from a more ahistorical mode of organizing and charting data drawn from an undifferentiated or generalized past to a much more granularly historical mode of inquiry that retains some degree of context. On the one end of the spectrum, we find large-scale data sets like the Correlates of War project which seek to provide the tools to identify generalizable and, ideally, universal rules based on observable patterns in the aggregate. History as a source of Big Data, if you will. On the other, more granular ends are studies like Edward Keene's work on nineteenth-century imperial treaties (2014) or Ryan Griffiths' study of twentieth-century secessions (2014), both of which aggregate and quantify events across fairly broad swaths of time but do so with an explicit awareness of their historical context and while emphasizing the importance of seeing them as embedded within longer trajectories, rather than as abstracted data points.

The third approach is arguably the one closest to disciplinary history – namely to see history first and foremost as a process of change over time. This encompasses a broad set of works that ask actual historical questions or in other words seek to explain why and how certain aspects of international politics have emerged, changed, or disappeared over the course of history (Hobson, 2004; Zarakol, 2011; Leira, 2011; Reus-Smit, 2013; Buzan and Lawson, 2015; Halperin and Palan, 2015). It also covers research that has focused on charting and explaining variation over time, whether in state forms, international systems, or specific practices (Spruyt, 1994; Ferguson and Mansbach, 1996; Buzan and Little, 2000).

The English School in particular has a long-standing tradition of taking this approach to historical work (Bull and Watson, 1984; Watson, 1992; Keene, 2002, see also Navari and Green, 2021) and the same is true for constructivist studies of norm development (Thomson, 1994; Bartelson, 1995), but other schools of thought have tended to think less about history as a process of change and more as a relatively static series of events. This has arguably changed with the reinvigorated interest in Historical IR in the last few years, and currently, time and change are emerging as topics of fruitful discussion in their own right (e.g. Hom, 2018, 2021; Younis, 2018). These trends have gone some way towards moving the discipline beyond a narrow fixation on points of origin towards other ways of thinking through change over time (de Carvalho et al., 2011; Buzan and Lawson, 2014), exemplified by recent works that fuse together historical and IR perspectives in novel and conceptually productive ways (e.g. Anievas, 2014; McCourt 2014; Bayly, 2016).

As mentioned above, these three broad approaches are not mutually exclusive but can be combined in various ways. Work that explicitly theorizes change over time usually incorporates analysis based on data sets or case studies, and the move towards mixed methods in the field means that big-picture quantitative analyses are often supplemented by more in-depth qualitative case studies, and vice versa.

Uses of sources

All of the approaches outlined above can be based on primary or secondary sources or, as is increasingly the case, a mix of the two. While synthetic historiographical work was long the standard in IR, more scholarship is now being produced on the basis of primary source historical research. This work often relies on specific genres of sources, the choice of which tends to correspond to certain historical subfields with their own internal debates and developments. Thus, changing methods in international history have been reflected in the way in which IR scholars have used official diplomatic correspondence and similar archival materials (see also Leira, 2021), and the fields of legal history and international law and organizations have developed in frequent conversation with one another. Meanwhile, other methodological trends and innovations in disciplinary history have been much slower to filter into historical IR work, for both good and bad reasons.

The most frequently used primary sources remain official government documents of various kinds, including diplomatic dispatches, policy white papers, parliamentary debates, and similar texts typically found in national and state archives. This body of material roughly equates to what international or diplomatic historians have been basing their work on since the birth of history as an academic discipline in the nineteenth century, and state archives remain the preferred repositories for a great deal of historians. As international history went through its own internal crises in the 1980s and 1990s, confronted by mounting criticisms of parochialism and insularity posed by transnational historians, the solution was by and large to move towards a more global and multi-archival research program, rather than one rejecting the fundamental centrality of government archives (Iriye, 1989; Westad, 2000). IR scholars have found similar use for these types of official sources, which document the myriad ways in which states interact through diplomacy, military conflict, treaty negotiations, or aid programs. The reading of such officially produced texts has also been fruitfully combined with the personal papers of actors involved in the events being studied, whether they are diplomats, politicians, or other on-the-ground actors, in order to flesh out accounts that might otherwise appear as overly top-down narratives (Helleiner, 2014; Barkawi, 2017).

In a somewhat similar vein, IPE scholars make frequent use of historical sources in the form of statistics, trade data, and demographic information recorded by governmental and non-governmental bodies. This type of information, the bread and butter of economic historians, might not always appear to researchers as an example of historical source material, but it is none the less subject to many of the same issues and challenges as other non-numerical sources are. Even when statistical yearbooks and similar reports are mined as input for aggregate data sets, as described above, good research practice is to submit them to a critical reading that pays attention to their historical context and potential distortions or limitations (Cipolla, 1991). This is especially important since the creation of such sources was often quite a self-aware act of mapping out societies and economies, with the explicit aim of shaping their future trajectories (Tooze, 2001).

A different body of IR scholarship, more broadly tied to the historical subfield of intellectual history, has relied on another type of sources – published theoretical, scholarly, or polemical texts. The intersection of political theory and intellectual history has long been a thriving area of study, and many IR scholars interested in subjects like war, peace, and sovereignty have at various times engaged with debates in this interdisciplinary field (Bartelson, 1995; Teschke, 2003). Such interactions have increased substantially in the last decade, as intellectual historians have engaged in a more sustained fashion with the global and international dimensions of their subjects (Moyn and Sartori, 2013; Armitage, 2013) and IR scholars for their part have re-examined the historical dimensions and trajectories of key theoretical concepts (e.g. Rosenboim, 2017; Costa Lopez et al., 2018). Because of the inheritance from both intellectual history and political theory, IR work of this type operates with what is arguably the most fully articulated methodological foundation in the field, even if it is largely characterized by a single approach – that of the contextualist Cambridge School (Skinner, 1969; see also Wallenius, 2021). Perhaps because of its precarious relationship to neighbouring academic fields, IR as a discipline has always seemed unusually obsessed with its own foundations and genealogy. In recent years, this long-standing meta-disciplinary work has been enriched greatly by a growing literature on the intellectual history of IR, presenting close readings of momentous debates and uncovering marginalized bodies of work in the discipline's past (i.e. Ashworth, 1999, 2012; Vitalis, 2015). This more inward-looking historical work is somewhat distinct from the work on international political thought that traces the discursive genealogy of concepts and ideas, but it employs some of the same methodologies borrowed from intellectual history, often paired with theories taken from sociology and history of science.

Another set of sources frequently used by IR scholars are those of court cases and legal records, which not surprisingly implies a kinship with legal history. Scholars of international law and organizations have made use of a variety of legal sources to illuminate questions of norm development, institutional arrangements, and the transition from imperial to post-imperial international systems (Keene, 2007; Kinsella, 2011; Mantilla, 2018; Yao, 2019). These materials include treaty texts, charters, conventions and accords, and other sources of international law, alongside court transcripts and trial records, especially from international judicial bodies like the ICC and the ICJ. Legal sources that fall outside this body of well-established modern international law are still relatively underused in IR work, but there are some examples of emerging scholarship engaging with everything from medieval canon law to revolutionary constitutions and transnational legal debates (Becker Lorca, 2014; Costa Lopez, 2016; Mulich, 2017). The broader field of international law has recently witnessed an interesting internal debate over the use of historical materials. Scholars like Anne Orford have argued that the use of historical methods in international law has by and large been for the purpose of 'policing anachronism' with a narrowing and 'conservative effect on international law scholarship' (2017: 301). This critique has been countered by legal historians, most prominently Lauren Benton, who argues that it is 'based on a limited understanding of the historical approach it criticizes' and ignores what has in fact been a flourishing of different historical approaches and methodologies in recent years, most of which are not just interested in contextualizing particular moments and texts but seek to add significantly to contemporary understandings of law and legal politics (2019: 2–3). This debate is illuminating because it points towards an issue in international studies more broadly, namely a tendency among some scholars to collapse differences and see history as a single perspective, more concerned with myth-busting or providing contextual correctives than with generating theoretical contributions of its own.[2] Such accusations of needless historicism risk stymying the growth of a subfield that is in some ways still germinating, blocking much-needed methodological debates rather than participating in them in productive ways.

Despite the flourishing of historical scholarship in the field, there are still many types of sources that have been put to comparatively little use. This is especially true for the broad swath of unconventional historical materials that have permeated disciplinary history since the cultural turn of the early 1980s, including visual sources, literary texts, and various examples of material culture. In part, the explanation for the lack of engagement with this body of sources lies in the type of research questions IR scholars are traditionally interested in asking, including those associated with state power, inter-polity interactions, and large-scale organized violence. Nonetheless, as the cultural turn has shown, even the most traditional political questions can be illuminated from non-traditional angles and sources that seem to belong in one domain often have a lot to say about other aspects of the world (e.g. Winter, 1995; Cregan, 2007; Eustace, 2012). Indeed, some of these themes have begun to filter into IR scholarship, through recent engagements with cartographic sources and the spatial turn in history (Branch, 2014; Goettlich, 2019) or with the history of science (Caraccioli, 2017), as well as via rereadings of well-known events through unexpected sources, including spiritual and religious texts (Shilliam, 2013).

Finally, another welcome recent trend has been the gradual shift in chronological attention backwards in time. For a long time, the majority of historical IR work using primary sources focused on modern or contemporary history, seemingly satisfied with covering those periods that left easily identifiable ministerial and departmental archives behind, preferably of the sort containing mostly type-written pages. The reasons for this narrowed focus are manifold and arguably have as much to do with practical accessibility as they do with intellectual justification, but a growing body of literature shows that engaging with the world before the twentieth century, and beyond Western states, can be immensely productive. This scholarship has covered topics ranging from the medieval origins of inter-polity systems to the political practices of early modern East Asia, but a common thread running through the work is that temporal or spatial broadenings of our research can lead to radical reimagining of what exactly constitutes international relations, and how the international itself came to be in the first place (for recent overviews, see Bain, 2017; Brook et al., 2018).

Engaging the historiography

The alternative to doing archival research is, essentially, to rely on the archival research of others. Using secondary sources as the main basis of historical analysis is not inherently problematic. Indeed, it can often be desirable or even necessary, either due to the scope of the project or because of linguistic or other barriers to work in primary sources. But doing this type of synthetic, historiographical work does present challenges different from those associated with archival research.

Perhaps the greatest challenge is to engage the historiography as a living body of work, rather than as a source of static information. History as a discipline is characterized just as much by debate, contestation, and revision as IR is, but too often historical works are approached with the presumption that they present largely agreed-upon narratives or uncontentious analyses (Lawson, 2010). This is just as problematic as if one were to read a defensive neorealist account of nuclear disarmament, with the assumption that it represented the settled academic consensus in IR. The problem is only exacerbated when the historical works drawn upon are of an older date, representing perspectives that are not just parts of a multisided debate but also lag behind later revisions and discoveries.

In this sense, then, historiography is a moving target. Drawing on secondary sources requires a certain understanding of the ongoing debates of the field and relaying these contentions in some way is an important aspect of writing synthetic historical IR. Historical interpretations cannot and should not be treated as settled fact in the majority of cases. What is more, the debates in history might mirror some of the debates in IR, but others are wholly distinct and work under different logics and with different stakes. This makes the problem even harder and demands more of the IR researcher in terms of reading broadly in the historical literature (MacDonald, 2009).

The work on China's historical role in world politics provides an illuminating example of this challenge (see also Hui, 2021; Suzuki, 2021). The long history of regional politics in East Asia has garnered renewed interest because of China's rise in the post–Cold War world, and a slew of work has been published on the topic within IR. The Qing Empire has been a particular focus of study, given its importance as an expansionist power in both East and Central Asia during its reign from the mid-seventeenth century to the Xinhai Revolution in 1911. However, much of this work has relied heavily on the so-called Harvard School of China scholarship primarily associated with the late John K. Fairbank and his many doctoral students. This work was especially influential in the United States from the 1950s to the 1970s, but it has continued to frame certain themes in Chinese historiography. These themes include the centrality of the Opium Wars as the origin point of 'modern' Chinese history; the contrast between the pre-modern Qing Empire and the modern colonial empires of nineteenth-century Europe and America; and the sinicization or integration of the Manchu ruling elite into the dominant Han Chinese culture, most closely associated with historian Ping-ti Ho (1967).

Around the same time that IR scholars began turning their eyes to China as a rising power, in the 1990s, a renewed interest in the Qing Empire reverberated through Chinese history. What became known as the New Qing History provided a strongly revisionist interpretation of the Manchu Dynasty, in large part because of a new focus on Manchu language sources, rather than the previous reliance on sources produced in Chinese (Waley-Cohen, 2004). This shift in sources and methods led to a range of major revisions, including a move from the older sinicization thesis to one emphasizing the longevity and importance of Manchu identity; a reinterpretation of the nineteenth century as a moment of crisis and reform, rather than forceful modernization wrought by outside forces; and a global or comparativist turn, casting the Qing Empire as another example of a multicultural, expansionist colonial empire, alongside rather than contrasted with contemporary empires like the Ottomans or the British (Elliott, 2001; Hostetler, 2001; Perdue, 2005). Unfortunately, these historiographical developments have taken a very long time to filter into the predominant IR narratives, which too often continue to rely on outdated and overly simplistic visions of China's historical role in East Asia (for recent critiques, see Chong, 2014; Phillips, 2018).[3]

At times, the problem is less about overly complicated historiographies and more about underdeveloped ones. This was arguably the case when IR scholars rediscovered the history of mercenaries, as modern private military companies (PMCs) became a major topic of conversation at the turn of the twenty-first century. A slew of works were published, which in different ways interrogated the history of mercenary companies, public/private violence, and emerging state regulation of force, primarily in order to make statements about contemporary challenges posed by PMCs. But most of this work relied on secondary sources for their historical analyses, and these sources were in many cases really only one account – the work of Anthony Mockler (1969). As Sarah Percy has convincingly shown, this reliance on a single secondary source led to the reproduction of what was essentially a flawed narrative about the history of mercenaries, with serious implications for the analytical and policy-oriented conclusions drawn (Percy, 2007).

Relying on a single source is always problematic, especially when that source is rather spectacularly out of date.

Thinking through the archive

Perhaps the greatest limitation of relying solely on secondary sources is that it prevents us from answering questions we did not know to ask. Working with secondary sources sets up certain historiographical parameters, and despite our best attempts at reading the literature in creative ways, we are still limited by the original research of others. The only solution, then, is sometimes to venture into the archives ourselves, not just to find answers that do not appear in other works but also to discover new questions. Historical hypotheses and research questions have to evolve in a hermeneutic way during the process of archival research. In this sense, the archive is not just a space for *answering* questions or testing hypotheses but also one for *generating* those very questions. The historical immersion associated with sustained archival work is, perhaps, the best antidote to presentism and ahistorical tendencies. But the archive is, of course, not without problems.

Archives can be understood in a narrow and a broad sense. The first, and perhaps the most common in the Anglo-American academy, is as organized collections of documents pertaining to the past. These are often created by government bodies, but can also be non-governmental collections associated with companies, universities, or other public or private organizations. In the broader sense, archives can be seen as repositories of information about the past. This is not limited to textual sources, official or otherwise, but can include everything from images, sounds, sculptures, and landscapes – natural as well as man-made (Boyer, 1994; Hayden, 1995; Stoler, 2013). Even the bodies of historical subjects, living or dead, can be seen as archives in their own right, presenting physical maps of lived experiences (Newman, 2003).

Archives composed primarily of textual sources remain the most commonly used ones, in history as well as in IR, and official state archives are chief among them. The move towards digitization means that more and more of these collections are now available remotely, at least selections of them, and along with published source collections and online databases of other primary sources, like The Avalon Project (at Yale Law School), the David Rumsey Historical Map Collection, or Early European Books Online, the twenty-first-century scholar can do a great deal of international historical research from the comfort of a university office or a library work station.

Even if one uses online and digitized archival holdings, a certain level of immersion should still be the goal. This need not be a comprehensive commitment in the Skinnerian sense (Skinner, 1969), a feat which is not just Herculean in scope but also runs the risk of missing the tree for the forest, but it does require a critical and creative engagement with the archive and its materials. While it might be strategically useful, simply dipping into archives in order to pull out choice quotes and illustrative snippets does not provide much in terms of new discoveries, making it particularly hard to uncover things that you did not know to seek out in the first place. It also prevents one from engaging in a deeper reflection on the nature of the information stored in the archive, an exercise that requires more than just a brief visit or a keyword search, but which is crucial to fully comprehend the implications of the knowledge generated through archival research.

Archives are not uncontested or neutral spaces. Rather, they are sites of social and political authority and continued negotiation – manifestations of historical power and of narratives that stretch across time, often well into the present (Cook and Schwartz, 2002). Knowledge is produced and stored in an archive through processes of selection and silencing, infused at every step with the power to narrate the past. This might seem like a commonsensical notion in a post-Foucauldian world, but the long shadow cast by Ranke and other empiricist, nineteenth-century historians means that too many scholars still think of the archive as a site of unfiltered truth, or at the least as a sort of neutral knowledge bank (Steedman, 2001).

Awareness of the production of knowledge requires the ability to identify and read historical silences. According to Michel-Rolph Trouillot, 'any historical narrative is a particular bundle of silences, the result of a unique process, and the operation to deconstruct these silences will vary accordingly' (1995: 27). Archives have their own histories and silences are introduced throughout the process of archiving the past – both in the initial creation of files, in the subsequent selection of materials to preserve, and in later processes of revision, curation, and censoring. Not all sources survive, sometimes because of historical coincidences, when an archival site is struck by natural disaster, when a careless curator or guest misplaces a file, or when a fire ravages a government building, and sometimes because of political or strategic choice. Such choices are often made in a deliberate effort to obfuscate and rewrite the past, making the work of historians difficult. This was certainly the case during the period of decolonization in the British Empire, from the 1950s to the 1970s, as the Colonial Office engaged in Operation Legacy – a massive effort to destroy or conceal any and all documents that might embarrass the imperial administration (Sato, 2017). The British Empire was hardly alone in such efforts, making it challenging to get a full picture of a host of events even after purported declassification dates.

Imperial and colonial archives are perhaps the best example of the relationship between knowledge, power, and the selective preservation of the past. As Frederick Cooper and Ann Stoler have pointed out:

> … it is clear that the colonial archives on which we are so dependent are themselves cultural artefacts, built on institutional structures that erased certain kinds of knowledge, secreted some and valorised others … We cannot just do colonial history on our given sources; what constitutes the archive itself, what is excluded from it, what nomenclatures signal at certain times are themselves internal to, and the very substance of, colonialism's cultural politics.
>
> (1997: 17–18)

Colonialism thus created its own archive, leaving behind vast amounts of information that are extremely hard to disentangle from their imperial origins and yet remain the most comprehensive source of information about those very structures we have available. Archives are not only examples of colonial and state power, but also of the sexual and gender relations embedded into this power (Burton, 2007).[4] The erasure of non-male subjects in so many archival records is but one example of an even broader gendering of archival materials that led nineteenth-century pioneers of disciplinary history to characterize the practice of archival research as among the most masculine of academic activities (Smith, 1998: 116–129). In the words of Leopold von Ranke, the task of the professional (male) historian was to seek out the sources locked away in the archive like 'so many princesses, possibly beautiful, all under a curse and needing to be saved' (quoted in Smith, 1995: 1165).

While power relations thus infuse the archive at multiple levels, this should not prevent us from making creative use of the sources contained within it. Reading primary sources against the grain has long been a tradition in historical work, and it is often a necessary part of the process of archival research. Deconstructing the silences in the archive is, as Trouillot indicated above, one part of this task. But there are other ways to recover information that the archive was never meant to provide. Documents produced by courts, governments, and intelligence agencies can provide intimate windows into the lives of individuals swept up in the processes of governance and surveillance, whether in revolutionary Paris (Darnton, 1984; Farge, 2013) or in DDR-era Berlin (Ash, 1997). Entire colonial archives can be read not as storehouses of facts but as ethnographic sites, revealing social epistemologies of force and governance from the past and present. Proclamations, trials, and decrees can be used to uncover legal, social, and political practices, when participants are no longer around to be observed or interviewed in person (Burbank, 2004; Brown, 2008). All of these approaches naturally require care, so as not to delve too far into speculation or unfounded conjecture, but they are none the less extremely useful when moving beyond the bare claims to historical truth presented in the archive itself.

All of this to say, then, that archival materials are extremely useful for those interested in historical IR, but they require careful reflection; close and sometimes unorthodox reading; and an appreciation of what is stored and said as well as what is silenced or left out.

Conclusion

The advice given in the preceding sections can be summed up as follows: see historiography as a living body of work, continually developing through ongoing debates and contestations; and think of the archive as a partially charted territory, requiring maps as well as a willingness to seek out still-unexplored corners with an open mind. As with most other methodological guidelines, this is of course easier said than done and conducting historical work within IR adds its own challenges.

There are major practical challenges associated with conducting immersive archival research. The very act of reading primary sources can demand particular skills, as many older documents require training in palaeography or specialized language studies to be decipherable. Language itself is often a barrier to entry, especially when it comes to the type of multinational work that IR scholars typically engage in. Some of these linguistic barriers can be offset with translated sources, but that adds another layer of interpretation and selection between the researcher and the materials. Finally, there are the logistical challenges associated with spending weeks in archives across the world, something that is both costly and time-consuming – and which has led many a historian to focus on rather narrow questions, which can be comfortably answered from the convenient and air-conditioned reading rooms of the US National Archives in College Park or the British Library in London. Yet the rewards of doing granular, multi-sited work are well worth the effort it takes to access these repositories, as long as one is conscious of their limitations. What is more, both linguistic and logistical challenges can be overcome to some extent by transnational collaboration between researchers, something historians have traditionally been rather hesitant to do, but to which IR is more accommodating.

A different obstacle to archival work in IR is the limit of space. IR is still predominantly a journal discipline, and work that makes extensive use of archival sources requires a significant amount of space.[5] This is arguably one of the main reasons why history is still one of the few disciplines overwhelmingly focused around the academic monograph. The limitations of journal word counts thus make it hard to produce the kind of work that draws extensively on original archival research and moves beyond a single case study, but recent trends might point towards some partial solutions. First and foremost is the Annotation for Transparent Inquiry (ATI) initiative, which for all its potential issues does provide ways of adding further materials and deeper historiographical materials as appendices, annotations, and expanded discursive notes. For an interesting and promising example of this type of work in practice, see the online appendix to Paul Musgrave and Daniel Nexon's article in *International Organization* (Musgrave and Nexon, 2018). Such additions to articles are still only partial solutions, however, and the fact remains that

storical work still benefits tremendously from the expanded scope of monographs, a
y endangered genre within IR scholarship.

....allenge for those engaging in historiographical work is keeping up with parallel but not
always overlapping or even mutually engaged literatures. Seeing historiography as a moving
target requires a type of sustained engagement with the literature that is hard enough to keep
up with within one's own subfield, let alone in other fields. But it is a challenge worth taking up
and perhaps an indication of a broader need for increased interdisciplinary engagement on issues
and questions of common interest. This is not just a task that falls to the historically inclined IR
scholar, however, as historians would do equally well to engage with the thriving field of historical IR despite the perceived barriers to entry.

As IR has once again become interested in serious historical work, the discipline of history
has done disappointingly little to engage IR scholarship. While the dying breeds of diplomatic
historians have always been relatively happy to engage in conversations with IR scholars (e.g.
Haber et al., 1997; Gaddis, 1997), newer currents of global and transnational history have been less
involved in those types of cross-disciplinary engagements. This is a shame as the recent interest in
historical work within IR provides a unique opportunity to foster dialogue between the fields, a
dialogue that would no doubt be beneficial to both sides. While IR scholars have much to learn
from historians at the methodological level, as has hopefully been made clear throughout this
chapter, historians – and particularly global historians – have plenty to learn from IR as well. Even
as global historians have done much to showcase how no historical processes or actors can be
fully isolated from the transnational processes of the last two centuries, they have done relatively
little to theorize these entanglements, leading to conceptual gaps in what are otherwise fascinating accounts of the history of globalization. In a similar vein, global historians can learn from IR
scholars when it comes to thinking through the connections between the various levels of analysis
they employ. Conceptualizing how micro- and macro-historical analyses of global and regional
processes fit together is a question that historical IR is uniquely well-situated to answer, and which
global historians have avoided tackling for too long.[6] There is, in other words, plenty of room for
further cooperation and mutual learning in the disciplinary space between history and IR.

Suggestions for further reading

Arnold, J. H., Hilton, M., and Ruger, J., eds. (2017). *History after Hobsbawm: Writing the Past for the Twenty-First
Century*. Oxford: Oxford University Press.
Burton, A., ed. (2005). *Archive Stories: Facts, Fictions, and the Writing of History*. Durham, NC: Duke University
Press.
Farge, A. (2013). *The Allure of the Archive*. New Haven, CT: Yale University Press.
Lawson, G., and Hobson, J. (2008). What is history in international relations? *Millennium*, 37 (2), 415–435.
Sewell, W. (2005). *Logics of History: Social Theory and Social Transformation*. Chicago, IL: University of Chicago
Press.
Stoler, A. (2009). *Along the Archival Grain: Epistemic Anxieties and Colonial Common Sense*. Princeton, NJ:
Princeton University Press.
Tilly, C. (2006). Why and How History Matters. In: R. Goodin and C. Tilly, eds., *The Oxford Handbook of
Contextual Political Analysis*, Oxford: Oxford University Press, 417–437.

Notes

1 As IR scholarship has increasingly moved towards middle-range theory, these universal theories have
   somewhat fallen to the wayside (Jackson and Nexon, 2013). That has not solved the issue of historical
   time; however, as middle-range theory often operates in ways that ignore issues of change over time in
   favour of situated specificity.

2 This distinction between IR as a theory-generating field and history as a space to craft narratives and provide context is present even in work that sets out to lessen the divide between the two, including several of the contributions to the pioneering volume *Bridges and Boundaries*. See Elman and Elman (2001) and, for a critique, Lawson (2010).

3 The story is further complicated by the response to the New Qing History within the People's Republic of China. Many modern-day Chinese historians thus reject the revisionist take on the Manchu Dynasty, but from a very different standpoint than the older US historiography. Namely, the notion of seeing China as a colonizer rather than a colonized power flies in the face of the official CCP narrative, as does the emphasis on expansionism and contestation rather than peaceful coexistence within Asia (Wu, 2016).

4 On the broader relationship between colonial power, knowledge, and gender, see in particular the work of Anne McClintock (1995). For more recent historiography, see the edited volume by Stephan Miescher et al. (2015).

5 It is telling that many IR journals still do not have established ways of referencing archival materials in their style guides, leaving it up to individual authors and editors to handle something that ought to be determined by more universal standards.

6 For a full discussion of these and other potential points of engagement, see Lawson and Mulich (forthcoming).

References

Anievas, A. (2014). *Capital the State and War.* Ann Arbor, MI: University of Michigan Press.

Armitage, D. (2013). *Foundations of Modern International Thought*. Cambridge: Cambridge University Press.

Arnold, J. H., Hilton, M., and Ruger, J., eds. (2017). *History after Hobsbawm: Writing the Past for the Twenty-First Century*. Oxford: Oxford University Press.

Ash, T. (1997). *The File: A Personal History*. London: HarperCollins.

Ashworth, L. (1999). *Creating International Studies*. London: Routledge.

Ashworth, L. (2012). The poverty of paradigms: subcultures, trading zones and the case of liberal socialism in interwar international relations. *International Relations*, 26 (1), 35–59.

Bain, W., ed. (2017). *Medieval Foundations of International Relations*. New York, NY: Routledge.

Barkawi, T. (2017). *Soldiers of Empire*. Cambridge: Cambridge University Press.

Bartelson, J. (1995). *A Genealogy of Sovereignty*. Cambridge: Cambridge University Press.

Bayly, M. (2016) *Taming the Imperial Imagination*. Cambridge: Cambridge University Press.

Becker Lorca, A. (2014). *Mestizo International Law*. Cambridge: Cambridge University Press.

Benton, L. (2019). Beyond anachronism: histories of international law and global legal politics. *Journal of the History of International Law*, 21, 1–34.

Boyer, M. (1994). *The City of Collective Memory*. Cambridge, MA: MIT Press.

Branch, J. (2014). *The Cartographic State*. Cambridge: Cambridge University Press.

Brook, T., van Walt van Praag, M., and Boltjes, M., eds. (2018). *Sacred Mandates*. Chicago, IL: University of Chicago Press.

Brown, V. (2008). *The Reaper's Garden*. Cambridge, MA: Harvard University Press

Bull, H., and Watson, A., eds. (1984). *The Expansion of International Society*. Oxford: Clarendon Press.

Burbank, J. (2004). *Russian Peasants Go to Court*. Bloomington, IN: Indiana University Press.

Burton, A., ed. (2005). *Archive Stories: Facts, Fictions, and the Writing of History*. Durham, NC: Duke University Press.

Burton, A. (2007). Archive Stories: Gender in the Making of Imperial and Colonial Histories. In: P. Levine, ed., *Gender and Empire*, Oxford: Oxford University Press, 281–294.

Butcher, C., and Griffiths, R. D. (2021). Quantitative Approaches: Towards Comparative and Trans-Regional Approaches in Historical International Relations. In de Carvalho, B., Costa Lopez, J., & Leira, H., eds. *Routledge Handbook of Historical International Relations*. Abingdon: Routledge.

Buzan, B., and Lawson, G. (2014). Rethinking benchmark dates in international relations. *European Journal of International Relations*, 20 (2), 437–462.

Buzan, B., and Lawson, G. (2015). *The Global Transformation*. Cambridge: Cambridge University Press.

Buzan, B., and Little, R. (2000). *International Systems in World History*. Oxford: Oxford University Press.

Caraccioli, M. (2017). The learned man of good judgment: nature, narrative and wonder in José de Acosta's natural philosophy. *History of Political Thought*, 38 (1), 44–63.

Carvalho, B. de, Leira, H., and Hobson, J. (2011). The big bangs of IR: the myths that your teachers still tell you about 1648 and 1919. *Millennium*, 39 (3), 735–758.

Cello, L. (2017). Taking history seriously in IR: towards a historicist approach. *Review of International Studies*, 44 (2), 236–251.

Chong, J. I. (2014). Popular narratives versus Chinese history: implications for understanding an emergent China. *European Journal of International Relations*, 20 (4), 939–964.

Cipolla, C. (1991). *Between History and Economics*. Walden, MA: Wiley Blackwell.

Cook, T., and Schwartz, J. (2002). Archives, records, and power: the making of modern memory. *Archival Science*, 2 (1), 1–19.

Cooper, F., and Stoler, A., eds. (1997). *Tensions of Empire*. Berkeley and Los Angeles: University of California Press.

Costa Lopez, J. (2016). Beyond eurocentrism and orientalism: revisiting the othering of Jews and Muslims through Medieval Canon Law. *Review of International Studies*, 42 (3), 450–470.

Costa Lopez, J., et al. (2018). Forum: In the beginning there was no word (for it): terms, concepts, and early sovereignty. *International Studies Review*, 20 (3), 489–519.

Cregan, K. (2007). Early modern anatomy and the Queen's body natural: the sovereign subject. *Body & Society*, 13 (2), 47–66.

Darnton, R. (1984). *The Great Cat Massacre and Other Episodes in French Cultural History*. New York, NY: Basic Books.

Elliott, M. (2001). *The Manchu Way*. Stanford, CA: Stanford University Press.

Elman, C. and Elman, M. eds. (2001). *Bridges and Boundaries*. Cambridge, MA: MIT Press.

Eustace, N. (2012). *1812: War and the Passions of Patriotism*. Philadelphia, PA: University of Pennsylvania Press.

Farge, A. (2013). *The Allure of the Archives*. New Haven, CT: Yale University Press.

Ferguson, Y., and Mansbach, R. (1996). *Polities: Authority, Identities, and Change*. Columbia, SC: University of South Carolina Press.

Gaddis, J. (1997). History, theory, and common ground. *International Security*, 22 (1), 75–85.

Goettlich, K. (2019). The rise of linear borders in world politics. *European Journal of International Relations*, 25 (1), 203–228.

Griffiths, R. (2014). Secession and the invisible hand of the international system. *Review of International Studies*, 40 (3), 559–581.

Haber, S., Kennedy, D., and Krasner, S. (1997). Brothers under the skin: diplomatic history and international relations. *International Security*, 22 (1), 34–43.

Halperin, S., and Palan, R., eds. (2015). *Legacies of Empire*. Cambridge: Cambridge University Press.

Hayden, D. (1995). *The Power of Place*. Cambridge, MA: MIT Press.

Helleiner, E. (2014). *Forgotten Foundations of Bretton Woods*. Ithaca, NY: Cornell University Press.

Ho, P. (1967). The significance of the Ch'ing period in Chinese history. *The Journal of Asian Studies*, 26 (2), 189–195.

Hobson, J. (2004). *The Eastern Origins of Western Civilization*. Cambridge: Cambridge University Press.

Hom, A. (2018). Silent order: the temporal turn in critical international relations. *Millennium*, 46 (3), 303–330.

Hom, A. R. (2021). Time and History in International Relations. In de Carvalho, B., Costa Lopez, J., & Leira, H., eds. *Routledge Handbook of Historical International Relations*. Abingdon: Routledge.

Hostetler, L. (2001). *Qing Colonial Enterprise*. Chicago, IL: Chicago University Press.

Hui, V. (2005). *War and State-formation in Ancient China and Early Modern Europe*. Cambridge: Cambridge University Press, 2005.

Hui, V. (2021). Premodern Asia and International Relations Theory. In de Carvalho, B., Costa Lopez, J., & Leira, H., eds. *Routledge Handbook of Historical International Relations*. Abingdon: Routledge.

Iriye, A. (1989). The internationalization of history. *American Historical Review*, 94 (1), 1–10.

Jackson, P., and Nexon, D. (2013). International Theory in a Post-Paradigmatic Era. *European Journal of International Relations*, 19 (3), 543–565.

Keene, E. (2002). *Beyond the Anarchical Society*. Cambridge: Cambridge University Press.

Keene, E. (2007). A case study of the construction of international hierarchy: British treaty-making against the slave trade in the early nineteenth century. *International Organization*, 61 (2), 311–339.

Keene, E. (2014). The standard of 'civilisation', the expansion thesis and the 19th century international social space. *Millennium*, 42 (3), 651–673.

Kinsella, H. (2011). *The Image before the Weapon*. Ithaca, NY: Cornell University Press.

Lawson, G., and Hobson, J. (2008). What is history in international relations? *Millennium*, 37 (2), 415–435.

Lawson, G. (2010). The eternal divide? History and international relations. *European Journal of International Relations*, 18 (2), 203–226.

Lawson, G., and Mulich, J. (forthcoming). Global History and International Relations. In: M. Bukovansky, et al., eds., *The Oxford Handbook of History and International Relations*. Oxford: Oxford University Press.

Leira, H. (2011). *The Emergence of Foreign Policy: Knowledge, Discourse, History*. PhD dissertation, University of Oslo.

Leira, H. (2015). International relations pluralism and history – embracing amateurism to strengthen the profession. *International Studies Perspectives*, 16 (1), 23–31.

Leira. H. (2021). Diplomacy: The World of States and Beyond. In de Carvalho, B., Costa Lopez, J., & Leira, H., eds. *Routledge Handbook of Historical International Relations*. Abingdon: Routledge.

MacDonald, P. (2009). Those who forget historiography are doomed to republish it: empire, imperialism and contemporary debates about American power. *Review of International Studies*, 35 (1), 45–67.

MacKay, J., and LaRoche, C. D. (2021). Theories and Philosophies of History in International Relations. In de Carvalho, B., Costa Lopez, J., & Leira, H., eds. *Routledge Handbook of Historical International Relations*. Abingdon: Routledge.

Mantilla, G. (2018). Forum isolation: social opprobrium and the origins of the international law of internal conflict. *International Organization*, 72 (2), 317–349.

McClintock, A. (1995). *Imperial Leather*. New York, NY: Routledge.

McCourt, D. (2014). *Britain and World Power since 1945*. Ann Arbor, MI: University of Michigan Press.

Miescher, S., Mitchell, M., and Shibusawa, N., eds. (2015). *Gender, Imperialism and Global Exchanges*. Malden, MA: Wiley Blackwell.

Mockler, A. (1969). *The Mercenaries*. New York, NY: Macmillan.

Moyn, S., and Sartori, A., eds. (2013). *Global Intellectual History*. New York, NY: NYU Press.

Mulich, J. (2017). Empire and violence: continuity in the age of revolution. *Political Power and Social Theory*, 32, 181–204.

Musgrave, P., and Nexon, D. (2018). Defending hierarchy from the moon to the Indian Ocean: symbolic capital and political dominance in early modern China and the Cold War. *International Organization*, 72 (3), 591–626.

Navari, C., and Green, D. (2021). The English School and Historical International Relations. In de Carvalho, B., Costa Lopez, J., & Leira, H., eds. *Routledge Handbook of Historical International Relations*. Abingdon: Routledge.

Newman, S. (2003). *Embodied History*. Philadelphia, PA: University of Pennsylvania Press.

Nexon, D. (2009). *The Struggle for Power in Early Modern Europe*. Princeton, NJ: Princeton University Press.

Orford, A. (2017). 'International Law and the Limits of History.' In: W. Wouter, M. de Hoon, and A. Galán, eds., *The Law of International Lawyers: Reading Martti Koskenniemi*, Cambridge: Cambridge University Press, 297–320.

Percy, S. (2007). *Mercenaries*. Oxford: Oxford University Press.

Perdue, P. (2005). *China Marches West*. Cambridge, MA: Harvard University Press.

Phillips, A. (2018). Contesting the Confucian peace: civilization, barbarism and international hierarchy in East Asia. *European Journal of International Relations*, 24 (4), 740–764.

Phillips, A., and Sharman, J. (2015). *War, Trade and Rule in the Indian Ocean*. Cambridge: Cambridge University Press.

Reus-Smit, C. (2013). *Individual Rights and the Making of the International System*. Cambridge: Cambridge University Press.

Rosenboim, O. (2017). *The Emergence of Globalism*. Cambridge: Cambridge University Press.

Sato, S. (2017). 'Operation Legacy': Britain's destruction and concealment of colonial records worldwide. *Journal of Imperial and Commonwealth History*, 45 (4), 697–719.

Sewell, W. (2005). *Logics of History: Social Theory and Social Transformation*. Chicago, IL: University of Chicago Press.

Schweller, R. (2006). *Unanswered Threats*. Princeton, NJ: Princeton University Press.

Shilliam, R. (2013). Intervention and colonial-modernity: decolonising the Italy/Ethiopia conflict through Psalms 68:31. *Review of International Studies*, 39 (5), 1131–1147.

Skinner, Q. (1969). Meaning and understanding in the history of ideas. *History and Theory*, 8 (1), 3–53.

Smith, B. (1995). Gender and the practices of scientific history: the seminar and archival research in the nineteenth century. *American Historical Review*, 100 (4), 1150–1176.

Smith, B. (1998). *The Gender of History*. Cambridge, MA: Harvard University Press.

Spruyt, H. (1994). *The Sovereign State and Its Competitors*. Princeton, NJ: Princeton University Press.

Steedman, C. (2001). *Dust*. Manchester: Manchester University Press.

Stoler, A. (2009). *Along the Archival Grain: Epistemic Anxieties and Colonial Common Sense*. Princeton, NJ: Princeton University Press.

Stoler, A. L., ed. (2013). *Imperial Debris*. Durham, NC: Duke University Press.

Suganami, H. (2008). Narrative explanation and international relations: back to basics. *Millennium*, 37 (2), 327–356.

Suzuki, S. (2021). International Order in East Asia. In de Carvalho, B., Costa Lopez, J., & Leira, H., eds. *Routledge Handbook of Historical International Relations*. Abingdon: Routledge.

Teschke, B. (2003). *The Myth of 1648*. London: Verso.

Thomson, J. (1994). *Mercenaries, Pirates, and Sovereigns*. Princeton, NJ: Princeton University Press.

Tooze, A. (2001). *Statistics and the German State, 1900-1945*. Cambridge: Cambridge University Press.

Trouillot, M. (1995). *Silencing the Past*. Boston, MA: Beacon Press.

Vitalis, R. (2015). *White World Order, Black Power Politics*. Ithaca, NY: Cornell University Press.

Waley-Cohen, J. (2004). The new Qing history. *Radical History Review*, 88: 193–206.

Wallenius, T. (2021). How to Do the History of International Thought?. In de Carvalho, B., Costa Lopez, J., & Leira, H., eds. *Routledge Handbook of Historical International Relations*. Abingdon: Routledge.

Watson, A. (1992). *The Evolution of International Society*. London: Routledge.

Westad, O. A. (2000). The new international history of the Cold War: three possible paradigms. *Diplomatic History*, 24 (4), 551–556.

Winter, J. (1995). *Sites of Memory, Sites of Mourning*. Cambridge: Cambridge University Press.

Wohlforth, W. C., Little, R., and Kaufman, S. J. (2007). Testing balance-of-power theory in world history. *European Journal of International Relations*, 13 (2), 155–185.

Wu, G. (2016). New Qing history: dispute, dialog, and influence. *The Chinese Historical Review*, 23 (1), 47–69.

Yao, J. (2019). 'Conquest from Barbarism': the Danube commission, international order and the control of nature as a standard of civilization. *European Journal of International Relations*, 25 (2), 335–359.

Younis, M. (2018). Race, the world and time: Haiti, Liberia and Ethiopia (1914–1945). *Millennium*, 46 (3): 352–370.

Zarakol, A. (2011). *After Defeat*. Cambridge: Cambridge University Press.

46

HISTORY AND MEMORY

Narratives, micropolitics, and crises

Jelena Subotic and Brent Steele

How do we remember history? How do we learn it in the first place? And what are the implications of such a link between history and memory for international politics, not only of the past, but of the present and future?

The relationship between history and memory is a fraught one. For Pierre Nora, history is what is no longer, what is past. Memory, however, is alive, it is what is now: 'memory is a bond tying us to the eternal present; history is a representation of the past' (Nora, 1989: 8). Another way of conceptualising the history/memory relationship is by understanding history as delineating a 'separation of past and present,' and providing a narration of events that constitute 'the past' (Cubitt, 2013: 28). Memory, on the other hand, blurs this separation and provides a continuation between the past and the present (Cubitt, 2013: 30).

The discipline of History has engaged in this debate for quite some time (e.g. Lowenthal, 1985; Butler, 1989; Hutton, 1993). Increasingly, however, there is an acute awareness that the 'past' can never be precisely separated from the 'present' in which it is being analysed but is always interpreted with the present sensibilities, awareness, norms, and values. Further, the past – specifically, our memory of the past – informs and makes sense of our present, is a foundational block of individual and then national identity, and is always in the service of political projects in the present. This chapter, then, understands history and memory as mutually constitutive and applies this framework to the analysis of the role of historical memory (memory of history) in International Relations (IR). We first briefly outline how historical memory gets constructed. We then discuss sites and sources of research on historical memory in IR, as well as major theoretical approaches in this field. We conclude by assessing this research agenda and recommending paths ahead.

Construction of historical memory

How does historical memory get constructed and by whom? Maurice Halbwachs suggested that memory develops by collectives rather than purely by a sum of individuals (Halbwachs, 1980). There are as many memories as there are collectives. But memory does not just form out of thin air; it is conditioned by 'external stimuli' that help with the collection and recollection of history. History itself can be and often is fragmented, and we often recollect history not only by what it is, but *where* we first experience it. We need the space, and place, and people where we confront the transmission of historical fragments to formulate them into a meaningful narrative.

Paul Ricoeur summarises this process, 'to remember we need others ... not only is the type of memory we possess not derivable in any fashion from experience in the first person singular, in fact the order of derivation is the other way around' (Ricoeur, 2004: 120). We may feel as if we own our memories, and indeed the ability to hold a memory varies across individuals – some have 'amazing' memories, others do not. Yet even those who can recall a memory with seemingly perfect clarity require a social setting, a context for recollection and *of* recollection. Put another way, to the extent that memories are shared, they are 'activated' by a particular surrounding (conversation, space, or other sensory stimuli). The recollection of a particular memory occurs within a setting, a space that we travel back in time to recall the particular event or feeling of that time. Ricoeur writes, 'childhood memories are an excellent reference in this regard. They take place in socially marked places: the garden, the house, the basement, and so on ...' (2004: 120).

History and memory are thus tied together through three types of processes. First, history and memory are socially conditioned and reinforced. Individually, we may *gain* historical insights and accounts through texts, but we *retain* those in the form of a story or account – a narrative – often told by and with others to us. Second, history and memory are connected spatially. The most readily apparent space where memory gets transferred would seem, for most readers of this essay, the school or college classroom. Here both the first and second processes are connected, with the classroom being an important space for understanding history, calling and recalling it. Yet it is a space with people, the teacher or professor a key but not necessarily the sole authority figure.

Yet, classrooms are only one site, space, or place where history and memory are linked. Others include our more mundane social settings like coffee shops or pubs, school and family reunions, churches, places of employment, and museums. These are all held together by the importance of the people we engage with during such (re)calling. And, furthermore, every one of these spaces includes asymmetric forms of authority that further shape how we remember histories: for instance, in the aforementioned classroom, a professor or teacher; in a church, the priest, pastor, or an important parishioner; and in a museum, a docent who answers questions and provides a script regarding important details that other historical accounts fail to mention.

Combined with the social and spatial is a third link between history and memory – the sensory. The most important sense is of course sight, in remembering we use our eyes to read, to see, to envision. But smell (like that of an old book) and touch (the way the book felt in our hands, or how we feel standing in front of a statue) can also be powerful forms of recall. Put another way, to recall a particular historical fact and to place it in a narrative, requires a sense triggered to a time, space, and place where we first experienced that fact and where someone, or something, made it make sense.

Politics is of course involved in the process of memory construction every step of the way. Narratives – stories that help us make sense of history – are fundamentally political. They involve choices by the narrator of what to include, exclude, and how to sequentially fit information, such as events and characters, together. If these choices resonate with us, they become *our* choices and our narratives. Told to and with a number of audiences, issued as a marker that makes us part of a community who also retells it, and reinforced in a number of spaces, narratives become part of our daily routines in grappling with our past and placing our Selves within the flow of it up through our present. Individuals become invested not only intellectually but *emotionally* in the narrative itself. As such, narratives about history implicate ourselves, our political communities, and our individual and group identities. In some cases, state identity is defined specifically by the incorporation of past trauma into contemporary sense of self (Wang, 2008; Mälksoo, 2009; Subotic, 2018). In others, a sense of shared trauma can create a feeling of a transnational community of memory that crosses state boundaries (Hutchison, 2010).

Sites and sources

Scholars of historical memory and IR have engaged multiple different types of materials, sites, and sources in their studies. Significant amount of this scholarship has analysed monuments, memorials, as well as commemorative practices such as national days of remembrance to tease out the ways in which historical memorialisation shapes contemporary state identity or policy.

Work on memorialisation practices, for example, has established how a certain memory of the past becomes nationally institutionalised through cultural routinisation – through museum exhibits, or unveiling of monuments and memorials (Williams, 2007). Public commemoration, then, can be understood as a form of both domestic political governance (as political leaders organise narratives about the past into a hegemonic system of meaning that gives them continuing legitimacy) but also of international governance (as it systematises, classifies, and organises diverse practices into a fairly uniform set of rules) (Lischer, 2019).

Scholars have also looked at very specific types of memorialisation events such as, for example, centenary celebrations (Steele, 2017). Centenary commemorations provide opportunities for reevaluation of past events and reaffirmation of national and state identities. They nurture nationalism (see also Heiskanen, 2021). Critically, though, they serve to construct historical memory through specific political programs, by creating connections with historical figures and pivotal events across time and space, making national time and history appear constant, linear, and inevitable (Quinault, 1998; Gonzales, 2007). History, then, becomes shared destiny for all members of the national community (Zerubavel, 1995).

Another line of analysis in IR work on historical memory has focused on ways in which physical sites of traumatic memory serve as locations of foreign policy creation (see also Goettlich and Branch, 2021; Mulich, 2021). In addition to the foundational work at this nexus (e.g. Edkins, 2003; Bell, 2006; Zehfuss, 2007; Langenbacher and Shain, 2010; Fierke, 2014), more recent research has analysed how physical sites of commemoration (such as locations of concentration camps, killing sites, or memorials) serve to construct foreign policy through the enduring meaning they have as material reminders of collective trauma. Through regularised and routinised commemorative practices – museum exhibitions, mourners' gatherings, political speeches, performative candle lighting, flowers, or objects placement – these sites contribute to the construction of state identity both domestically and internationally (Auchter, 2014; Subotic, 2020).

Specifically, physical sites of memory serve a critical role in foreign policymaking – as material, visual, repositories of narrative claims of past violence that are easily invoked for contemporary foreign policy objectives. They are material summaries of violence or injustice that serve as shortcuts for larger foreign policy claims. They work as analogies – they are visual prompts of violence that happened in the past and serve as a warning for the future. They also exist in real time and space and are thus much more readily available for the articulation of historical claims and narratives in the present.

These physical sites of memory often become nationalised and then anchored to represent collective memory and national identity (Savage, 1994). Official memorial sites further perform a collective memory building function by inviting visitors to be a part of the collective narrative and themselves contribute to the construction of a particular national past (Yanık and Hisarlıoğlu, 2019). Physical sites of traumatic memory, then, continuously remind the national community both of its past, but also of its responsibility to prevent the collective trauma from repeating in the future.

Approaches to historical memory in International Relations

A number of approaches in IR have explored these links between history and memory with each touching on the themes of identity and politics introduced above. Here we focus on three – ontological security studies (OSS), security history, and generational analysis.

A concept first developed by psychologist R.D. Laing (1962), and articulated within Giddens's (1984, 1991) broader structurationist social theory, ontological security refers to the practices and processes of agents aiming to secure their identity through time and space. In OSS, two devices or concepts demonstrate the important links between memory and history: (1) (auto)biographical narratives and (2) 'historicity' (the use of history to make history). OSS in IR has explored the narrative aspect of ontological security from both conventional (taking the narrative as an analytical given) and critical (treating it as politically problematic) angles (Kinnvall, 2004; Mitzen, 2006; Zarakol, 2010; Berenskoetter, 2014; Subotic, 2016).

Less acknowledged is the concept of historicity (Steele, 2008: 88) – the use of the past to make sense of the present (Kinnvall, 2004; Innes, 2010; Browning and Joenniemi, 2013; Bayly, 2015). The process of narrating history is an expression of social agency across all 'levels of analysis' important in IR, from the individual, to the group, to the nation-state and beyond. This feature of ontological security binds the individual with their social group, as participating in the narration of a collective history marks individuals with group status and socialisation (Steele, 2008). Further work on ontological security has foregrounded the importance of the material environment that enables a telling of particular historical narratives (Ejdus, 2017), an issue we return to below. Once a part of that 'telling,' individuals and groups may – like the routines that are a part of their daily lives – be resistant to challenges of established historical interpretations. This is because these challenges are as much challenges to their own identities, their own views of themselves, and their place in their group's histories.

The emotional and affective components of the ontological security process are, therefore, also important for the politics of historical memory. OSS have brought forth the importance of embarrassment, guilt, and shame (Zarakol, 2010; Subotic and Zarakol, 2013; Browning and Joenniemi, 2017) as features of ontological *in*security, experienced when a critical situation challenges the routines that uphold an individual's, or group's, identity. Traumas are the most notable events that disrupt the ontological security of individuals and groups, challenging the narratives of an individual and group self (Kinnvall, 2004; Innes and Steele, 2014). Most immediately, 'traumatic experiences disrupt the ability to channel certain events into a coherent narrative' (Steele, 2008: 56). Yet traumas at the group level are also opportunities for a retelling of a past story. They provide ways in which the past can be reinterpreted to help fasten the present. Traumas are occasions when ontological insecurity is confronted by the securitisation of history. This is important both for what is collectively remembered and, more pressingly, what is forgotten.

A more recent trend in OSS's investigations of history, memory, and emotions has been the study of nostalgia. Nostalgia for individuals helps in the ontological security process as a 'mechanism to address loss of self-esteem' and to 're-establish symbolic relations with significant others' (Lupovici, 2016: 69). Nostalgia can be a 'healthy' way to acknowledge a past that is gone, something that is embedded in routines that help an actor go on with their place in the present. Yet it also serves a political function in its 'pathological' expressions when actors become attached to a fantasy of the past, one that is presumed to be politically urgent in a contemporary present as well (Sucharov, 2013: 544). While nostalgia had been overlooked as a device by ontological security scholars for some time (Lupovici, 2016: 69), the increasingly central role history plays in memory and identity has put nostalgia in the background and foreground of very recent OSS, especially its role in Brexit (Browning, 2018), and the contemporary rise in populist and nationalist politics.

A recently introduced concept of 'mnemonical security' (Mälksoo, 2015), which describes state disciplining of historical memory in pursuit of its security needs, has established an even more direct relationship between historical memory and ontological security. Specifically, Mälksoo defines mnemonical security as 'the idea that distinct understandings of the past should be fixed in public remembrance and consciousness in order to buttress an actor's stable sense of self as the basis of its political agency' (Mälksoo, 2015: 222). Through the process of mnemonical securitisation – or securitisation of historical memory – states have attempted to criminalise 'undesirable' memory through legal means (such as, for example, new laws criminalising denial of communist crimes in some Eastern European states modelled after laws criminalising Holocaust denial in Germany or France). Mälksoo demonstrates how these attempts can lead to depoliticisation of historical remembrance and foreclosing of any discussion about the 'good' and the 'bad' past (Mälksoo, 2014). What they do instead is secure a particular historical memory for the political needs of the present.

These themes overlap with a second emerging research field that directly deals with history and memory in IR: the security history literature on the role of success, victory, or 'winning' in war. Some of this scholarship focuses on how the experience of 'victory' (O'Driscoll, 2015; Hom et al., 2017) or the ill-defined goal of 'winning' a war based on a historically constructed past precedent can serve to perpetuate rather than restrict the length of a war. Combining this theme with the previously discussed scholarship on ontological security, Subotic and Steele (2018) argue that the United States' 'routine' of 'winning' past wars was called into question by the more ambiguous endings to the Iraq and Afghanistan theatres of the so-called war on terror. This ontological insecurity has been a pervasive condition of US politics with marked results – both domestic and international – since 2001.

As the opposite of winning, a war can be a traumatic experience for political communities, such trauma enables a number of reinscriptions and reinterpretations of the past in order to fortify a present and near-future. In fact, political communities can take past defeats and reconfigure them in present-day politics as heroic efforts that serve to mobilise publics for particular contemporary foreign policy actions. Matt McDonald's (2010) analysis of the Howard administration in Australia, for example, demonstrated how the disastrous Battle of Gallipoli in 1915 was turned into a positive resource almost one century later in order to justify Australian participation in the Iraq War. This was a socially important set of practices that depended on the 'image' of the Australian 'digger' as the embodiment of Australian identity and its themes of 'mateness' and 'reckless valor.' We return to this possibility below in the context of the 'Lost Cause' revisionist account of the US Civil War by the white South.

A third research field that explores the link between history and memory (and identity) is generational analysis. This research agenda developed throughout the 20th century in several waves or series (Steele and Acuff, 2012). Building in part on Roskin (1974) and Kuhn (1962), several developments in IR theory in the 1990s through today – most directly the increasing prominence of 'constructivist' social theory in IR – paved the way for a third wave of generational analysis which brought the struggle of generational conflict more sharply into focus (McCourt, 2012; Steele and Acuff, 2012; Youde, 2012).

A constitutive moment in the generational analysis story is the *formative experience* that shapes a generational cohort. Often times this formative experience is related to the failings of a previous generation's policies. In US foreign policy history, these are often wars or other national moments of disaster (such as Pearl Harbor, Vietnam, or, more recently, the 2000s War on Terror). Yet they can often include broader issues, such as political economic events (depressions, recessions panics, etc.), which are experienced as opportunities (via 'crises' or 'exogenous shocks'), to move away from previous policies and ways of approaching the global political economy (Seabrooke, 2007; Widmaier et al., 2007).

Generational analysis takes a view of history and memory that both overlaps *and* contrasts with that which Halbwachs asserted regarding the social, spatial, and sensory-conditioned factors for collective memory construction. Formative experiences are both individual but also collective and social. An individual may 'experience' such an event only indirectly, but as Halbwachs would expect, these formative periods shape a generation through their circulations in social institutions of a generation. The engagement and causal interpretation of the formative experience (who or what produced it, how to enable or avoid a similar event in the future) are reinforced by, and help further define, a generational cohort.

Yet this generational conflict, on the other hand, exposes a distinction with Halbwachs' and his followers' assumptions regarding historical memory. For generational analysis, over time there is an increasing amount of information that is transfixed solely through that generation's existing images and theories, and an increasing distance that generation finds itself from the *social* and *societal* realities of the day. The formative experience of the past is used to reinterpret the present, and as such a generational cohort continues to 'live in the past,' but in the present.

Conclusion

While we cannot provide in-depth illustrations that precisely trace the *stakes* of collective memory, we can see those stakes playing out in a number of contexts. For instance, in the United States, the so-called Lost Cause revisionist account of the South's purposes in the US Civil War (1861–1865), which denies slavery as the central cause of the war, remains salient even though it has been largely discredited by most historians (Domby, 2020).

And yet the links between the Lost Cause myth and especially white American memories of the US Civil War persist. Some of this resilience is due to its embeddedness in various institutions, including the role of universities throughout the South, the historians they employed, and the classes they offered. One other notable development that proceeded apace during this time was the construction and placement of monuments and memorials to Confederate soldiers throughout the South. Most of these were placed in a number of public sites, including courthouses, parks, schools, and cemeteries. Much like the 'little Romes' which enabled the 'symbolic universe' of Imperial Rome to be enacted in the Empire's provincial capitals for centuries (Acuff, 2012), Confederate statues demonstrate the importance of the social and material spaces, which enable a type of collective, historical memory. Far from being monuments of their time, most of these statues were instead erected much later, as defiant, and even triumphant, markers of a South 'liberated' from federal soldiers post-reconstruction, and especially in the 1890s and 1900s (Gunter et al., 2016).

The fact that sharp, and often violent debates about statues and memorials have shaped contemporary politics – not just in the United States but everywhere – is further evidence of the importance of sites as sources of research on history and memory. This chapter has therefore one important implication for the *politics* of historical memory. It suggests that efforts to contest historical memory, as found in the Lost Cause narratives and monuments in the US South, must

and have to proceed through the well-argued and meticulously researched historical acco
that scholars have produced over the previous decades. Moves towards counter-memory
re-establish more inclusive and comprehensive histories will need to continue to find ways to
channel the emotive, routinised, and sensory features of memory we described in this chapter.

Suggestions for further reading

Bentley, T. (2015). *Empires of Remorse: Narrative, Postcolonialism and Apologies for Colonial Atrocity*. London: Routledge.

Budryte, D. (2020). *Memory and World Politics*. In: P. James, ed., Oxford Bibliographies.

Dixon, J. M. (2018). *Dark Pasts: Changing the State's Story in Turkey and Japan*. Ithaca, NY: Cornell University Press.

He, Y. (2009). *The Search for Reconciliation: Sino-Japanese and German-Polish Relations since World War II*. Cambridge: Cambridge University Press.

Lind, J. (2008). *Sorry States: Apologies in International Politics*. Ithaca, NY: Cornell University Press.

Resende, E. S. A., and Budryte, D. (2014). *Memory and Trauma in International Relations: Theories, Cases, and Debates*. London: Routledge.

Wang, Z. (2014). *Never Forget National Humiliation: Historical Memory in Chinese Politics and Foreign Relations*. New York, NY: Columbia University Press.

References

Acuff, J. M. (2012). Spectacle and space in the creation of premodern and modern polities: toward a mixed ontology of collective identity. *International Political Sociology*, 6 (2), 132–148.

Auchter, J. (2014). *The Politics of Haunting and Memory in International Relations*. New York, NY: Routledge.

Bayly, M. J. (2015). Imperial ontological (in)security: 'buffer states', international relations and the case of Anglo-Afghan relations, 1808–1878. *European Journal of International Relations*, 21 (4), 816–840.

Bell, D. (2006). *Memory, Trauma and World Politics: Reflections on the Relationship between Past and Present*. Basingstoke: Palgrave Macmillan.

Berenskoetter, F. (2014). Parameters of a national biography. *European Journal of International Relations*, 20 (1), 262–288.

Browning, C. S. (2018). Brexit, existential anxiety and ontological (in)security. *European Security*, 27 (3), 336–355.

Browning, C. S., and Joenniemi, P. (2013). From fratricide to security community: re-theorising difference in the constitution of Nordic peace. *Journal of International Relations and Development*, 16 (4), 483–513.

Browning, C. S., and Joenniemi, P. (2017). Ontological security, self-articulation and the securitization of identity. *Cooperation and Conflict*, 52 (1), 31–47.

Butler, T. (1989). *Memory: History, Culture, and the Mind*. Oxford: B. Blackwell.

Cubitt, G. (2013). *History and Memory*. Manchester: Manchester University Press.

Domby, A. H. (2020). *The False Cause: Fraud, Fabrication, and White Supremacy in Confederate Memory*. Charlottesville, VA: University of Virginia Press.

Edkins, J. (2003). *Trauma and the Memory of Politics*. Cambridge: Cambridge University Press.

Ejdus, F. (2017). 'Not a heap of stones': material environments and ontological security in international relations. *Cambridge Review of International Affairs*, 30 (1), 23–43.

Fierke, K. M. (2014). Who is my neighbour? Memories of the Holocaust/al Nakba and a global ethic of care. *European Journal of International Relations*, 20 (3), 787–809.

Giddens, A. (1984). *The Constitution of Society: Outline of the Theory of Structuration*. Berkeley, CA: University of California Press.

Giddens, A. (1991). *Modernity and Self-identity: Self and Society in the Late Modern Age*. Stanford, CA: Stanford University Press.

Goettlich, K., and Branch, J. (2021). Borders and Boundaries: Making Visible What Divides. In de Carvalho, B., Costa Lopez, J., & Leira, H., eds. *Routledge Handbook of Historical International Relations*. Abingdon: Routledge.

Gonzales, M. J. (2007). Imagining Mexico in 1910: visions of the patria in the centennial celebration in Mexico City. *Journal of Latin American Studies*, 39 (3), 495–533.

Gunter, B., Kizzire, J., and Kent, C. (2016). *Whose Heritage?: Public Symbols of the Confederacy*. Montgomery, AL: Southern Poverty Law Center, 21 April.

Halbwachs, M. (1980). *The Collective Memory*. New York, NY: Harper & Row.

Heiskanen, J. (2021). Nations and Nationalism in International Relations. In de Carvalho, B., Costa Lopez, J., & Leira, H., eds. *Routledge Handbook of Historical International Relations*. Abingdon: Routledge.

Hom, A. R., O'Driscoll, C., and Mills K., eds. (2017). *Moral Victories: The Ethics of Winning Wars*. Oxford: Oxford University Press.

Hutchison, E. (2010). Trauma and the politics of emotions: constituting identity, security and community after the Bali bombing. *International Relations*, 24 (1), 65–86.

Hutton, P. H. (1993). *History as an Art of Memory*. Hanover: University Press of New England.

Innes, A. J. (2010). When the threatened become the threat: the construction of asylum seekers in British media narratives. *International Relations*, 24 (4), 456–477.

Innes, A. J., and Steele, B. J. (2014). Memory, Trauma and Ontological Security. In: E. Resende, and D. Budryte, eds., *Memory and Trauma in International Relations: Theories, Cases, and Debates*, London: Routledge.

Kinnvall, C. (2004). Globalization and religious nationalism: self, identity, and the search for ontological security. *Political Psychology*, 25 (5), 741–767.

Kuhn, T. S. (1962). *The Structure of Scientific Revolutions*. Chicago, IL: University of Chicago Press.

Laing, R. D. (1962). Ontological Insecurity. In *Psychoanalysis and Existential Philosophy*. 41–69.

Langenbacher, E., and Shain, Y. (2010). *Power and the Past: Collective Memory and International Relations*. Washington, DC: Georgetown University Press.

Lischer, S. K. (2019). Narrating atrocity: genocide memorials, dark tourism, and the politics of memory. *Review of International Studies*, 45, 805–827.

Lowenthal, D. (1985). *The Past is a Foreign Country*. Cambridge: Cambridge University Press.

Lupovici, A. (2016). *The Power of Deterrence: Emotions, Identity and American and Israeli Wars of Resolve*. Cambridge: Cambridge University Press.

Mälksoo, M. (2009). The memory politics of becoming European: the East European subalterns and the collective memory of Europe. *European Journal of International Relations*, 15 (4), 653–680.

Mälksoo, M. (2014). Criminalizing communism: transnational mnemopolitics in Europe. *International Political Sociology*, 8 (1), 82–99.

Mälksoo, M. (2015). 'Memory must be defended': beyond the politics of mnemonical security. *Security Dialogue*, 46 (3), 221–237.

McCourt, D. M. (2012). The 'Problem of Generations' Revisited: Karl Mannheim and the Sociology of Knowledge in International Relations. In: B. J. Steele, and J. M. Acuff, eds., *Theory and Application of the 'Generation' in International Relations and Politics*, New York, NY: Springer, 47–70.

McDonald, M. (2010). 'Lest we forget': the politics of memory and Australian military intervention. *International Political Sociology*, 4 (3), 287–302.

Mitzen, J. (2006). Ontological security in world politics: state identity and the security dilemma. *European Journal of International Relations*, 12 (3), 341–370.

Mulich, J. (2021). International Relations in the Archive: Uses of Sources and Historiography. In de Carvalho, B., Costa Lopez, J., & Leira, H., eds. *Routledge Handbook of Historical International Relations*. Abingdon: Routledge.

Nora, P. (1989). Between Memory and History: Les lieux de mémoire. *Representations*, 26, 7–24.

O'Driscoll, C. (2015). At all costs and in spite of all terror? The victory of just war. *Review of International Studies*, 41 (4), 799–811.

Quinault, R. (1998). The cult of the centenary, c. 1784–1914. *Historical Research*, 71 (176), 303–323.

Ricoeur, P. (2004). *Memory, History, Forgetting*. Chicago, IL: University of Chicago Press.

Roskin, M. (1974). From Pearl Harbor to Vietnam: shifting generational paradigms and foreign policy. *Political Science Quarterly*, 89 (3), 563–588.

Savage, K. (1994). Politics of Memory: Black Emancipation and the Civil War Monument. In: J. R. Gillis, ed., *Commemorations*, Princeton, NJ: Princeton University Press.

Seabrooke, L. (2007). The everyday social sources of economic crises: from 'great frustrations' to 'great revelations' in interwar Britain. *International Studies Quarterly*, 51 (4), 795–810.

Steele, B. J. (2008). *Ontological Security in International Relations: Self-Identity and the IR State*. London: Routledge.

Steele, B. J. (2017). Centenary (inter)national, 1914–1924: the politics of commemoration and historical memory in international relations. *Australian Journal of Politics & History*, 63 (3), 339–344.

Steele, B. J., and Acuff, J. M., eds. (2012). *Theory and Application of the 'Generation' in International Relations and Politics*. New York, NY: Springer.

Subotic, J. (2016). Narrative, ontological security, and foreign policy change. *Foreign Policy Analysis*, 12 (4), 610–627.

Subotic, J. (2018). Political memory, ontological security, and holocaust remembrance in post-communist Europe. *European Security*, 27 (3), 296–313.

Subotic, J. (2020). Foreign policy and physical sites of memory: competing foreign policies at the Jasenovac memorial site. *International Politics*, 57, 1012–1029.

Subotic, J., and Steele, B. J. (2018). Moral injury in international relations. *Journal of Global Security Studies*, 3 (4), 387–401.

Subotic, J., and Zarakol, A. (2013). Cultural intimacy in international relations. *European Journal of International Relations*, 19 (4), 915–938.

Sucharov, M. (2013). Imagining ourselves then and now: nostalgia and Canadian multiculturalism. *Journal of International Relations and Development*, 16 (4), 539–565.

Wang, Z. (2008). National humiliation, history education, and the politics of historical memory: patriotic education campaign in China. *International Studies Quarterly*, 52 (4), 783–806.

Widmaier, W. W., Blyth, M., and Seabrooke, L. (2007). Exogenous shocks or endogenous constructions? The meanings of wars and crises. *International Studies Quarterly*, 51 (4), 747–759.

Williams, P. (2007). *Memorial Museums: The Global Rush to Commemorate Atrocities*. Oxford: Berg Publisher.

Yanık, L. K., and Hisarlıoğlu, F. (2019). 'Writing History with One's Own Body': Necrogeopolitics, Necropolitical Spaces and the Everyday Spatial Politics of Death in Turkey. In: B. Bargu, ed., *Turkey's Necropolitical Laboratory: Democracy, Violence, and Resistance*, Edinburgh: Edinburgh University Press.

Youde, J. (2012). The Generational Shift in South African Foreign Policy. In: B. J. Steele, and J. M. Acuff, eds., *Theory and Application of the 'Generation' in International Relations and Politics*, New York, NY: Springer.

Zarakol, A. (2010). Ontological (in)security and state denial of historical crimes: Turkey and Japan. *International Relations*, 24 (1), 3–23.

Zehfuss, M. (2007). *Wounds of Memory: The Politics of War in Germany*. Cambridge: Cambridge University Press.

Zerubavel, Y. (1995). *Recovered Roots: Collective Memory and the Making of Israeli National Tradition*. Chicago, IL: University of Chicago Press.

47

HOW TO DO THE HISTORY OF INTERNATIONAL THOUGHT?

Tomas Wallenius

Before considering 'how to do the history of international thought?', we need to briefly discuss 'what is international thought?' to paraphrase Martin Wight's term. Wight contrasted political theory, which concerns itself with the organisation of domestic relations within a state, with international theory whose subject matter consists of speculation on how relations between states are ordered (Wight, 1966; see also the discussion in Navari and Green, 2021 in this volume). It is useful to note that this includes both analysis of actually existing relations between states as well as notions of how international relations ought to be organised. The idea of international relations as, at least primarily, interstate relations is of course the conventional viewpoint among International Relations (IR) scholars (Bull, 1977; Wendt, 1999).

There exist at least two possible alternative visions to the usual state-centric viewpoint. One emphasises the centrality, as well as the relative novelty, of ideas concerning the ordering of 'the global' (Hurrell, 2007). Though humans have of course imagined geographically limited spheres of experience and knowledge as their world for a very long time – Greek and Roman notions of the oikoumene/orbis terrarum provide a Eurocentric illustration of this point – there is an important shift after 1500 when voyages of discovery made it possible for, at first Europeans, to begin speculating about the global on the basis of increasing and relatively accurate knowledge about our world as a whole that included the Americas. It has been argued that further turning points in conceptualising 'the global' followed around 1860 and 1970 due to technological shifts (Bell, 2013).

A second viewpoint seeks to explicitly question the state-centric take by highlighting the novelty and specificity of a world divided into sovereign states (see de Carvalho, 2021 in this volume). If the subject matter of IR is limited to the study of interstate relations then that leaves out most of history as empires and other hierarchical structures have played a predominant role in ordering relations between different human communities. This viewpoint thus seeks to broaden the subject matter of international thought to ideas relating to ordering relations between different political communities of which the modern sovereign state is just one recent and specific type (Keene, 2005). Thinking about the changing ways in which humans have imagined the nature and limits of a political community allows us to question the usual fairly rigid distinction between doing political or international thought (Brett, 2011; Linklater, 1998).

I will follow this second viewpoint on what international thought is for the purposes of the chapter, as this broader definition allows me to illustrate key questions in how to do intellectual history through a focus on the evolution of that most reified of notions, the modern sovereign state. I will also subscribe to the semantic shift from 'theory' to 'thought' among students of political ideas. The point of this move is to emphasise that most political theorising is a mundane and practical activity. It is not exclusively practiced in the ivory tower and is also not necessarily particularly explicit or sophisticated (Freeden, 2004). All societies, including the 'international' one, have contested ideas on how they are ordered.

A timeless discussion

An influential strand of the early 20th–century practice of intellectual history was somewhat ironically distinguished by its relative ahistoricism. These writers, for whom the term textualists may serve as a useful label, primarily approached intellectual history as a timeless discussion organised around enduring questions that human beings had talked about for over two millenia. This approach is nowadays most famously associated with the American philosopher Arthur Lovejoy, who founded the *Journal of the History of Ideas* in 1940 (Burrow, 2007; Skinner, 1969). For textualists, the main focus lies in close readings of the works of pre-eminent past thinkers whose thought is perceived as relevant for our contemporary world as they were in effect discussing the same timeless issues that we confront today. This was a history from peak to peak. There is no point in studying the obscure forgotten writings of second-rate intellectuals when one can learn from canonical masters such as Plato and Aquinas. In terms of political ideas, the textualist vision entailed imagining a relatively coherent and self-conscious European tradition of political theory that centred on the problematic of the political community and stretched from the ancient Greek city-state to the nation state in contemporary Europe and its North American offshoot. This type of history of political thought was centred in the United States and usually practiced in political science (or philosophy) departments rather than history faculties. Before concluding this short sketch, it is useful to note that works by writers such as Lovejoy do at times include not inconsiderable attention to the historical milieu of political ideas (Grafton, 2006; McMahon, 2014). Thus, though the notion of textualism does not do complete justice to early 20th–century scholars, it arguably captures an important dimension of their preoccupations and serves as a useful ideal type of how to do intellectual history (on international political thought, see Rosenboim and Hartnett, 2021 in this volume).

The textualist vision of political theory as an ageless lunchtime discussion at a celestial gentlemen's club frequented by European great thinkers is relevant for IR scholars as it bears considerable similarities to the conventional approach to intellectual history as practiced within the discipline. As the problematic of the international has been conceptualised as more or less timeless, it follows that one can reconstruct an equally ageless and relevant tradition of thinking about the international. If the international is indeed a 'realm of recurrence and repetition', in Wight's words (1966, 26), this then makes say Thucydides immediately relevant for contemporary (or Cold War era) concerns. There is however a significant contrast with political theory in that IR scholars have tended to more explicitly subdivide international theory into timeless alternative visions of the international, which are then contrasted and studied comparatively (Bartelson, 1996; Schmidt, 2002). This has been done most explicitly in the context of the classical English school, on which I will focus due to its role as an important precursor to the historical turn in IR.

For Wight international theory could be organised into three analytical traditions: realism, rationalism and revolutionarism (Wight, 1991). These were to a large extent reproduced by Hedley Bull's trichotomy of the Hobbesian, Grotian and Kantian traditions (Bull, 1977). Wight viewed these ideal types as useful abstractions that allowed scholars to make sense of a multitude of bygone international thought through noting similarities as well as shifts in arguments made across wide temporal distances. Thus, Wight can in his famous essay outlining the three traditions for example bring to the reader's attention the resemblances between radical arguments made by various religious fanatics in early modern Europe, French Jacobins as well as latter-day Bolsheviks. It is useful to emphasise that these analytical traditions primarily served the role of ideal types of thinking about the international. Wight for example notes in the context of revolutionary thought that it is not always clear that the traditions are continuous and self-conscious historical ones. He also shows awareness of the analytical limitations of the toolkit. The rationalist tradition is described as the broad middle road of European thought that at times seems so heterogeneous as to potentially lose its usefulness as a concept. It is also noted that particular thinkers are also often complex and not easily pigeon holed into a particular strand of thought, as with the possible intellectual fog surrounding Hegel's viewpoints. Despite of these caveats, it is clear that the notion of the existence of relatively unchanging transtemporal patterns of thought has played an important role in how IR scholars have traditionally viewed the exercise of intellectual history. It is thus worthwhile to now consider an influential critique of the conventional viewpoint on intellectual history.

A contextual turn

Quentin Skinner wrote perhaps the most famous essay on method in intellectual history in 1969. The basic point was that in order to understand a text such as *Leviathan* or *The Prince*, one needs to reconstruct why its author wrote it. In order to do this, the scholar needs to uncover the less meticulously analysed contemporary political debates in which Thomas Hobbes or Niccolo Machiavelli were engaged (on reason of state, see Devetak, 2021 in this volume). This requires going beyond a close reading of the text itself in order to situate it in a particular historical context. For Skinner, thinkers are primarily concerned with political questions that were relatively specific to their time rather than participants in a self-conscious transtemporal discussion concerning a limited number of ageless theoretical issues. Skinner explicitly positioned the essay as an alternative viewpoint to the then influential textualist approach to intellectual history, most notably identified with Lovejoy's writings (Bevir, 2011; Skinner, 1969).

Though Skinner explicitly builds on the then prominent linguistic turn in philosophy in making his two-step argument that in order to truly understand the meaning of a text one needs to discover its author's intention and that this is only possible through uncovering the text's discursive context (for a critique Bevir, 1992), perhaps the key point in understanding Skinner's take is in recognising that it is a historian's historicist critique of intellectual history as it had been practiced by philosophers and political scientists. It was perhaps the specific historical context of the textualist ascendency in the study of political ideas that made Skinner's explicit historicism resonate. Though it is important to note that there are notable differences in emphasis among the scholars educated as historians in Cambridge conceptualised as an eponymous school – as an illustration John Pocock has been more interested in wholesale sketching of past languages of politics rather than uncovering particular authorial intentions – they all share a broad historicist inclination that comes across clearly and polemically in their most prominent member's early essay (Bevir, 2011; Burrow, 2007).

It may be worth to briefly illustrate the contextualist turn with reference to Skinner's empirical work. This has been mainly concerned with the study of the shift from a medieval to a modern conception of (European) political theory. According to Skinner one of the key, if not the key, dimension of this transformation was the invention of the modern concept of the state as an impersonal entity that held sovereignty and was separate from the person of its prince (on state formation, see de Carvalho and Leira, 2021 in this volume). Skinner argues that authors such as Machiavelli and Hobbes play pivotal roles in this transformation. In order to approximate why they are making these innovative ideological moves, it is necessary to painstakingly recreate their ideological milieu (e.g. Skinner, 2002, ch. 14). As Skinner's project spans for centuries from the renaissance to the aftermath of the reformation, this is a massively ambitious and in practice somewhat longue durée undertaking. It is on these grounds that Skinner has at times been accused of going around his own rigorous early methodological standards that conceived the main task of the historian as the construction of a primarily contemporary context rather than a diachronic grand narrative. A sympathetic critic may also point out that this methodologically historicist story is in terms of its primary focus not completely different from that of the earlier textualists. The object of inquiry is still the Western tradition of political ideas, and Skinner's primary rationale for studying political context is to 'enable us to return to the classic texts ... with a clearer prospect of understanding them' (1978, xiii; also Wallenius, 2018). Despite these substantive continuities, the contextual approach remains useful as a contrasting ideal type of how to do intellectual history. More practically, it has established itself as the mainstream approach in the history of political thought and also more recently become a very influential framework for the study of international thought.

In disciplinary terms, there are two dimensions to the contextualist shift. Firstly, IR scholars have grown explicitly critical of the earlier mainstream notion of how to study international theory that I have illustrated with reference to the classical English school. On the other hand, historians of political thought have increasingly come to realise that theories of politics within communities constitute only half of the story. As an illustration of the consequences of this shift, let us consider the traditional notion of separate Hobbesian, Grotian and Kantian patterns of international thought. Recent work has to a considerable extent challenged the usefulness of these abstractions in understanding the evolution of European international thought. It has instead been argued that these three writers should be contextualised as contributors to the influential early modern natural rights tradition (Bartelson, 1996; Tuck, 1999). This work, which draws on insights by Voltaire and Jean-Jacques Rousseau, substituting a largely ahistorical analytical conception of a tradition of thought with a historical and contextual one results in a considerably different understanding of intellectual history.

The influential conventional notion of a liberal tradition (Doyle, 1997) has also been questioned by work challenging the idea that liberalism necessarily entails an anti-imperialist viewpoint. It has been pointed out that seeing a straight line from Immanuel Kant's relatively cosmopolitan position to contemporary liberal thought misses how the construction of immense European colonial empires during the 19th century was to a considerable extent rationalised through liberal arguments, including by canonical thinkers such as John Stuart Mill and Alexis de Tocqueville (Jahn, 2005; Pitts, 2005). This work is part of a broader trend towards a more global perspective in the study of European political thought, which has also highlighted how the works of Francisco de Vitoria and Hugo Grotius, conventionally seen as fathers of international law, cannot be understood without acknowledging the great emphasis they place on the analysis of relations between European and non-European communities (Anghie, 2005; Keene, 2002; see Bayly, 2021; Caraccioli, 2021; both in this volume). Though not all of this scholarship draws explicit methodological inspiration from Skinner's contextualism, its historicist sensibility is broadly speaking compatible with Skinner's agenda. The fact that the contextualist approach has become the mainstream viewpoint on the history of international thought among historically minded IR scholars – if not perhaps the discipline as a whole – can in addition be gauged from the method sections of recent textbooks (Brown, Nardin, and Rengger, 2002; Keene, 2005). Having now outlined the new orthodoxy, I will next turn to consider potential lines of criticism as well as the question of possible alternatives.

Contextualism contested?

The question of whose thinking is worth studying is a good starting point to what is possibly the most interesting critique of the contextual approach to intellectual history. The basic argument would be that though Skinner and his epigoni do a great job in recontextualising the likes of Hobbes, Kant and Grotius, a primary focus on the linguistic moves of exceptional thinkers offers at best a partial and perhaps more urgently an unrepresentative viewpoint on the history of political ideas. This point of course builds on a paradox readily acknowledged by Skinner: the exceptional nature of a great theorist such as Hobbes, who is seen to tower above his contemporaries, makes him a very bad guide for understanding broader currents of political thought in 17th-century Europe. In a similar vein, contextualising John Rawls is probably not going to help us a lot in understanding the ideological currents that characterised world politics in the era that followed 1945. It may be that a plausible case can be made for shifting the spotlight even more so from great thinkers to thinking done in other parts of the stage, which consists of their broader ideological context.

The notion of studying the role of ideas and culture in broader political practice – rather than in the ivory tower – is of course not a novel one. And there exist a number of literatures that can serve as points of reference for a turn to practice in the study of international thought. The most obvious one is perhaps the self-conscious constructivist tradition, which consolidated the viewpoint that culture is worth some attention among mainstream IR scholars (Wendt, 1999). Historical studies, often tracing the evolution of notions of political legitimacy (Bukovansky, 2002; Reus-Smit, 1999), have played an important role in this cultural turn, which can be at least partly contextualised as a reaction against the increasingly narrowly rationalist assumptions of mainstream North American IR. Constructivism has in recent years been complemented by work applying a practice viewpoint to the study of world politics. This work focuses on the study of practices, such as diplomacy or international law, as key sites of world politics (Brunnée and Toope, 2011; Costa Lopez, 2016; Wallenius, 2019). In terms of theory, some authors also conceptualise a habitual and implicit logic of practicality that plays a separate if complementary role to the more well-known constructivist idea of a logic of appropriateness focused on normative reasoning (Adler and Pouliot, 2011).

In order to not to completely reinvent the wheel, it is useful to note that the study of international thought in practice has important earlier exponents, including the classical English school. Wight was explicit about the need to trawl bygone international thought from forgotten literatures not included in the narrow canon of political theory (Holzgrefe, 1989; Keene, 2017; Wight, 1966) and more broadly speaking the historical study of practices, such as diplomacy and international law, constituted the second dimension of the group's research agenda. This study of the evolution of the institutions of international society, to employ the school's own jargon, included an important ideational dimension (Bull, 1977; Gong, 1984; Keens-Soper, 1978; Wight, 1977).

We are also importantly not restricted to political science in terms of alternative templates for the study of international thought. The role of ideas and culture in human society is studied across the humanities and social sciences. As an illustration historiographical approaches with which political scientists are less familiar may offer intriguing viewpoints for the study of international thought. It has been argued that the focus on uncovering authorial intention in Skinner's contextualism implicitly ignores the issue of a text's reception (Vergerio, 2019). Literary historians have in contrast emphasised the importance of the study of contested receptions in order to understand a text's historical importance since at least Hans-Robert Jauss' essay from 1967. For Jauss reception does not remain constant and uncontested. The 'understanding of the first reader will be sustained and enriched in a chain of receptions from generation to generation; in this way the historical significance of a work will be decided' (1982, 20). More broadly speaking the study of bygone ideas is central to the practice of cultural history. These historians have criticised the Olympian preoccupations of conventional intellectual history and sought to excavate more mundane patterns of thought. This sensibility, which can be understood as doing anthropology across time, argues that the thought of the forgotten many, and not only the canonical few, is worth studying and can be innovative (Darnton, 1971; also Wallenius, 2018). This naturally includes excavating the often excluded thought of marginalised groups, such as women and non-Europeans in the context of an international society dominated by European men (Owens, 2018; Shilliam, 2010; also ch. by Ashworth). Cultural historians have also importantly paid extensive attention to how new ideas become diffused, through technologies such as printing or sites such as coffee houses, within the public sphere, which ties in with literary scholars' emphasis on the study of receptions that is somewhat downplayed by contextualism (Blanning, 2002; Darnton, 1995).

As an illustration of how the turn towards the study of political ideas in practice has had important results, let us briefly consider the origins of the modern sovereign state. In contrast to Skinner whose primary focus is on treatises, scholars have turned their attention to practices such as treaty making, which allows for a novel viewpoint for process tracing broader shifts in political ideology in which theorists such as Hobbes do not perhaps play such a central role. The rise of the sovereign state can be tracked in the changing language of treaties. These become binding not only to the signatory prince but also his successors. The prince is also slowly replaced by the sovereign state as a member of international society and becomes merely its ruler (Roshchin, 2006). The origins of the novel though nowadays default notion of an international order consisting of territorially bounded states that exercise exclusive sovereignty can in equal vein be analysed through treaty making (Branch, 2012). This work on the external dimension of sovereignty naturally builds on earlier work that was for a time overshadowed by Skinner's primary focus on the domestic theory of the sovereign state (Hinsley, 1966). Practice orientated work has equally highlighted the importance of relations between Europeans and non-Europeans, both in hierarchical and more equal contexts, for the evolution of the modern concept of sovereignty (Alexandrowicz, 1967; Anghie, 2005; Branch, 2012; Gong, 1984; Keene, 2002; Koskenniemi, 2001). In empirical terms, non-European international thought remains a key underexplored site for further work in a research field that has conventionally been marked by its Eurocentrism (Liu, 2004; Shilliam, 2010; Zarakol, 2018).

After having outlined some potential lines of criticism of the contextual approach, it may be worth briefly considering the counter argument. If one looks at Skinner's later empirical works rather than his early essay on method, it is clear that he does in practice engage with the changing reception of political ideas across time, the role of largely forgotten ideologists such as Marsilius of Padua, as well as literary genres that offer us insight into the ideas that co-constituted the broader practice of politics (e.g. 1978, 2002). The key take away from contextualism is not the study of the authorial intentions of prominent theorists but rather that political ideas can only be understood as interventions in specific historical debates. Yet the challenge in simply equating the contextualist approach with a broader historicist sensibility may lie in the fact that the latter has been around for a long time. Even if we do not want to go to Herodotus, the call for a contextual understanding of human societies and an awareness of the possibility of great change across time has been prominent since at least the 19th century (Burrow, 2007).

A case for closure?

I will conclude by briefly considering whether there is any point in doing the history of international thought. Are we doomed to be self-indulgent antiquarians whose reconstruction of the political ideas of lost worlds offers no clues for addressing our present predicament? Or alternatively gravediggers who seek to apply bygone thinkers' ideas to contemporary political problems, in the process modifying and mixing them with our ones by applying them outside of their historical context? Would we be better off by being honest about the need to do our own thinking?

Perhaps the most prominent optimistic answer argues that excavating forgotten political worlds can help us step outside of the box of our own unquestioned background assumptions. Skinner argues that realising how different our contemporary political thought is from our predecessors highlights the fact that ideologies have and still can change radically. Despite there being no transhistorical off the shelf solutions to be discovered in classic texts, bygone thought is interesting precisely because it sought answers to very different rather than timeless questions (Skinner, 1969). It must though be noted as a potential qualification that the very act of doing the history of political ideas, for example analysing the shift from medieval to modern European political theory, presupposes the existence of at least a relatively constant concept of 'the political' as a dimension of human societies that can be recognised across time. A critical historicist sensibility that highlights the contingency and specificity of the origins of the contemporary social world is of course not necessarily restricted to a conventional fairly narrow understanding of intellectual history but can also include other historiographical sensibilities including the study of political ideas in practice as well as more materialist preoccupations such as those of the Marxist tradition (Tully, 2002).

A second possible defence for intellectual history is that without it we are more likely to reinvent the wheel on a more regular basis. Many recent debates within IR mirror older now forgotten discussions (Schmidt, 2002). Even though we must, to paraphrase Skinner, do our own thinking in terms of the specific problems facing us, intellectual historians are struck by not only the strangeness but at times the somewhat analogous nature of past patterns of thought. As an illustration, let us consider the fact that the problematic of fostering cooperation between narrowly social self-interested actors, which still orients most IR scholars, hails not from 20th-century social theory but to a significant extent mirrors the early modern natural rights thought of Grotius and Hobbes.

My final tentative point is that the history of political ideas is a worthy endeavour because there exists popular demand for historicist, and at times critical, analysis of the making of our contemporary social world as evidenced by bookstore offerings and newspaper op-eds of varying quality. To paraphrase Allen Lane on Penguin's business model, scholars of the history of international thought should keep in mind the possibility of the existence of a considerable and global intelligent reading public, with a potential interest in learning more about the deeply contested and vastly different ways in which the political ordering of our world has been imagined.

Suggestions for further reading

Bartelson, J. (1996). Short circuits: society and tradition in international relations theory. *Review of International Studies*, 22 (4), 339–360.

Bell, D. (2013). Making and Taking Worlds. In: S. Moyn, and A. Sartori, eds., *Global Intellectual History*, New York, NY: Columbia University Press, 254–279.

Darnton, R. (1971). In search of the enlightenment: recent attempts to create a social history of ideas. *The Journal of Modern History*, 43 (1), 113–132.

Gordon, P. (2012). What is Intellectual History? A Frankly Partisan Introduction to a Frequently Misunderstood Field. Viewed 20 October 2020, <http://projects.iq.harvard.edu/files/history/files/what_is_intell_history_pgordon_mar2012.pdf>.

Jauss, H. R. (1982). Literary History as a Challenge to Literary Theory (1967). In: H. R. Jauss, ed., *Toward an Aesthetic of Reception*, Translated by T. Bahti, Brighton: Harvester Press, 3–45.

Keene, E. (2017). International intellectual history and international relations: contexts, canons and mediocrities. *International Relations*, 31 (3), 341–356.

Shilliam, R. (2010). *International Relations and Non-Western Thought. Imperialism, Colonialism and Investigations of Global Modernity*. London: Routledge. (Chapter 1).

Skinner, Q. (1969). Meaning and understanding in the history of ideas. *History and Theory*, 8 (1), 3–53.

Vergerio, C. (2019). Context, reception, and the study of great thinkers in international relations. *International Theory*, 11 (1), 110–137.

Wight, M. (1966). Why is There No International Theory? In: M. Wight, and H. Butterfield, eds., *Diplomatic Investigations. Essays in the Theory of International Politics*, London: George Allen.

References

Adler, E., and Pouliot, V. (2011). International Practices: Introduction and Framework. In: E. Adler, and V. Pouliot, eds., *International Practices*, Cambridge: Cambridge University Press, 3–35.

Alexandrowicz, C. H. (1967). *An Introduction to the History of the Law of Nations in the East Indies: (16th, 17th and 18th Centuries)*. Oxford: Clarendon Press.

Anghie, A. (2005). *Imperialism, Sovereignty and the Making of International Law*. Cambridge: Cambridge University Press.

Bayly, M. (2021). Imperialism: Beyond the 'Re-turn to Empire' in International Relations. In de Carvalho, B., Costa Lopez, J., & Leira, H., eds. *Routledge Handbook of Historical International Relations*. Abingdon: Routledge.

Bevir, M. (1992). The errors of linguistic contextualism. *History and Theory*, 31 (3), 276–298.

Bevir, M. (2011). The Contextual Approach. In: G. Klosko, ed., *Oxford Handbook of the History of Political Philosophy*, Oxford: Oxford University Press.

Blanning, T. C. W. (2002). *The Culture of Power and the Power of Culture. Old Regime Europe, 1660-1789*. Oxford: Oxford University Press.

Branch, J. (2012). 'Colonial reflection' and territoriality: the peripheral origins of sovereign statehood. *European Journal of International Relations*, 18 (2), 277–297.

Brett, A. (2011). Changes of State. In *Nature and the Limits of the City in Early Modern Natural Law*. Princeton, NJ: Princeton University Press.

Brown, C., Nardin, T., and Rengger, N. J. (2002). *International Relations in Political Thought: Texts from the Ancient Greeks to the First World War*. Cambridge: Cambridge University Press.

Brunnée, J., and Toope, S. J. (2011). Interactional International Law and the Practice of Legality. In: E. Adler, and V. Pouliot, eds., *International Practices*, Cambridge: Cambridge University Press, 108–136.

Bukovansky, M. (2002). *Legitimacy and Power Politics. The American and French Revolutions in International Political Culture*. Princeton, NJ: Princeton University Press.

Bull, H. (1977). *The Anarchical Society. A Study of Order in World Politics*. 3rd edition. Basingstoke: Palgrave.

Burrow, J. W. (2007). *A History of Histories: Epics, Chronicles, Romances and Inquiries from Herodotus and Thucydides to the Twentieth Century*. London: Allen Lane.

Caraccioli, M. J. (2021). Early (Modern) Empires: The Political Ideology of Conceptual Domination. In de Carvalho, B., Costa Lopez, J., & Leira, H., eds. *Routledge Handbook of Historical International Relations*. Abingdon: Routledge.

Costa Lopez, J. (2016). *The Legal Ordering of the Medieval International*. Oxford: University of Oxford.

Darnton, R. (1995). *The Forbidden Best-Sellers of Pre-Revolutionary France*. New York, NY: W. W. Norton.

de Carvalho, B. (2021). Sovereignty in Historical International Relations: Trajectories, Challenges and Implications. In de Carvalho, B., Costa Lopez, J., & Leira, H., eds. *Routledge Handbook of Historical International Relations*. Abingdon: Routledge.

de Carvalho, B., and Leira, H. (2021). State Formation and Historical International Relations. In de Carvalho, B., Costa Lopez, J., & Leira, H., eds. *Routledge Handbook of Historical International Relations*. Abingdon: Routledge.

Devetak, R. (2021). Reason of State: An Intellectual History. In de Carvalho, B., Costa Lopez, J., & Leira, H., eds. *Routledge Handbook of Historical International Relations*. Abingdon: Routledge.

Doyle, M. W. (1997). *Ways of War and Peace*. New York, NY: W. W. Norton.

Freeden, M. (2004). Ideology, Political Theory and Political Philosophy. In: G. Gaus, and C. Kukathas, eds., *Handbook of Political Theory*. London: Sage.

Gong, G. W. (1984). *The Standard of "Civilization" in International Society*. Oxford: Clarendon Press.

Grafton, A. (2006). The history of ideas: precept and practice, 1950-2000 and beyond. *Journal of the History of Ideas*, 67 (1), 1–32.

Hinsley, F. H. (1966). *Sovereignty*. London: Watts.

Holzgrefe, J. L. (1989). The origins of modern international relations theory. *Review of International Studies*, 15 (1), 11–26.

Hurrell, A. (2007). *On Global Order. Power, Values, and the Constitution of International Society*. Oxford: Oxford University Press.

Jahn, B. (2005). Kant, Mill, and illiberal legacies in international affairs. *International Organization*, 59 (1), 177–207.

Keene, E. (2002). *Beyond the Anarchical Society. Grotius, Colonialism and Order in World Politics*. Cambridge: Cambridge University Press.

Keene, E. (2005). *International Political Thought: An Historical Introduction*. Cambridge: Polity.

Keens-Soper, M. (1978). The Practice of a States-System. In: M. Donelan, ed., *The Reason of States. A Study in International Political Theory*. London: Allen & Unwin.

Koskenniemi, M. (2001). *The Gentle Civilizer of Nations. The Rise and Fall of International Law 1870-1960*. Cambridge: Cambridge University Press.

Linklater, A. (1998). *Transformation of Political Community: Ethical Foundations of the Post-Westphalian Era*. Cambridge: Polity.

Liu, L. H. (2004). *The Clash of Empires: The Invention of China in Modern World Making*. Cambridge, MA: Harvard University Press.

McMahon, D. M. (2014). The Return of the History of Ideas. In: D. M. McMahon, and S. Moyn, eds., *Rethinking Modern European Intellectual History*, Oxford: Oxford University Press.

Navari, C., and Green, D. (2021). The English School and Historical International Relations. In de Carvalho, B., Costa Lopez, J., & Leira, H., eds. *Routledge Handbook of Historical International Relations*. Abingdon: Routledge.

Owens, P. (2018). Women and the history of international thought. *International Studies Quarterly*, 62 (3), 467–481.

Pitts, J. (2005). *A Turn to Empire. The Rise of Imperial Liberalism in Britain and France*. Princeton, NJ: Princeton University Press.

Reus-Smit, C. (1999). The Moral Purpose of the State. In *Culture, Social Identity, and Institutional Rationality in International Relations*. Princeton, NJ: Princeton University Press.

Rosenboim, O., and Hartnett, L. (2021). International Political Thought and Historical International Relations. In de Carvalho, B., Costa Lopez, J., & Leira, H., eds. *Routledge Handbook of Historical International Relations*. Abingdon: Routledge.

Roshchin, E. (2006). The concept of friendship: from princes to states. *European Journal of International Relations*, 12 (4), 599–624.

Schmidt, B. (2002). On the History and Historiography of International Relations. In: W. Carlsnaes, B. Simmons, and T. Risse, eds., *Handbook of International Relations*, London: Sage, 3–22.

Skinner, Q. (1978). Foundations of Modern Political Thought: Volume One. In *The Renaissance*. Cambridge: Cambridge University Press.

Skinner, Q. (2002). *Visions of Politics: Volume 2. Renaissance Virtues*. Cambridge: Cambridge University Press.

Tuck, R. (1999). *The Rights of War and Peace. Political Thought and the International Order From Grotius to Kant*. Oxford: Oxford University Press.

Tully, J. (2002). Political Philosophy as a Critical Activity. *Political Theory*, 30 (4), 533–555.

Wallenius, T. (2018). *Beyond the Canon. Rethinking the History of International Political Thought*. Unpublished manuscript.

Wallenius, T. (2019). The case for a history of global legal practices. *European Journal of International Relations*, 25 (1), 108–130.

Wendt, A. (1999). *Social Theory of International Politics*. Cambridge: Cambridge University Press.

Wight, M. (1977). *Systems of States*. Leicester: Leicester University Press.

Wight, M. (1991). In: G. Wight, and B. Porter, eds., *International Theory. The Three Traditions*, Leicester: Leicester University Press for the Royal Institute of International Affairs.

Zarakol, A. (2018). A non-Eurocentric approach to sovereignty. In: Costa Lopez, J., de Carvalho, B., Latham, A. A., Zarakol, A., Bartelson, J., and Holm, M. (2018). Forum: in the beginning there was no word (for it): terms, concepts, and early sovereignty. *International Studies Review*, 20 (3), 489–519.

48

GLOBAL HISTORIES

Connections and Circulations in Historical International Relations

Zeynep Gülsah Çapan, Filipe dos Reis and Maj Grasten

Introduction

This chapter provides an overview of Global History as a field within history and identifies its relevance for International Relations (IR). Global History has figured in debates within the discipline of history to the extent that observers note a 'boom' (Fillafer, 2017: 3), 'trend' (Sachsenmaier, 2011: 2) and 'turn' (Moyn and Sartori, 2013: 3). It has even been suggested that Global History is the 'fastest-growing field within the discipline' (Conrad, 2016: 1). Certainly, global historical literature has proliferated. Several global histories have recently been published. These include a global history of power (Duindam, 2016), the United States' Declaration of Independence (Armitage, 2008), the Napoleonic Wars (Mikaberidze, 2020), modern historiography (Iggers et al., 2008) and even history as discipline (Woolf, 2011). This development is located within a more general '"global" revolution in the social sciences' and humanities (Go and Lawson, 2017: 1). There are now a vast number of introductions to the field, compendia and bridging exercises to other research areas – running through labels such as 'global intellectual history' (Moyn and Sartori, 2013) or 'global historical sociology' (Go and Lawson, 2017).

Global History has been presented as a remedy to cure the discipline of history of its 'two birth defects', methodological nationalism and Eurocentrism (Conrad, 2016: 3). Traditionally, history was mostly treated as *national* history by historians, with the treatment of the nation-state as the main unit of investigation and national histories as isolated from one another (ibid.). Thereby, '[k] nowledge of the world was…discursively and institutionally prestructured in such a way as to obscure the role of exchange relationships' in a historical perspective (ibid.). Eurocentrism implies that 'Europe' is treated as the driving force of all developments and world history (see the discussion in Herborth and Nitzschner, 2021 in this volume). Trajectories are then explained through particular binary characteristics attributed to 'Europe', such as developed, modern and rational (in contrast to Europe's Other which is underdeveloped, traditional and mystical) (Çapan, 2017a). 'Europe' is constructed as a discrete, isolated and separate spatial unit in which all developments originate and expand in a self-generative way. There is also a temporal element in play with all developments occurring first in Europe and the rest catching up. These characteristics are inscribed into and are conditioned by a spatio-temporal hierarchy that has been continuously rearticulated through history writing.

There has recently been increased interest in Global History among IR scholars, following 'the turn to history' and the development of a subfield, denominated as Historical IR (see Buzan and Lawson, 2015; Phillips and Sharman, 2015; Phillips, 2016; Barkawi, 2017). In this contribution to the *Handbook*, we argue for the relevance of Global History to the 'historical turn' in IR and sketch out what specifically should be imported into IR from the burgeoning literature on Global History. To this end, the chapter identifies three main, and yet distinct approaches to Global History. We reconstruct scholarship conceptualising Global History as (1) a hermeneutic device for extending the analytical scale of history through space; (2) as history of globalisation understood as an integrative process over time; and (3) an approach that prioritises entanglements, connections, circulations and exchange as units of investigation from a historical perspective. This later approach stands in stark contrast to the traditional territorial logics that have underpinned the methodological biases of history writing as outlined above. We argue that if we decouple global history from globalisation and, in doing so, move beyond an understanding that reduces global history to the 'history of globalization', and analytical units to spatially confined containers, Global History holds great promise for IR scholars. A broader conception of Global History, which subsumes a sensibility to entanglements, connections and co-constitution, offers a way out of reproducing the two birth defects in history writing – methodological nationalism and Eurocentrism – in historical research in international studies (cf. Çapan, 2017b). It is the third approach to Global History that we outline in this chapter and refer to as *Global History as entanglements*.

The intention in this chapter is not to pin down what Global History is, or should be, and provide a clear-cut definition. This is nearly impossible because of the term's proliferation and its proximity to (and often overlap with) closely related, yet separate, approaches such as 'International', 'World', 'Transnational' or 'Big History' (see next section; cf. Sachsenmaier, 2011: 2, 70–78).[1] Different approaches to Global History do not only operate with diverging notions of the 'global' but also with different ideas of what history is and should be. In addressing three approaches (i.e. space, process and entanglements) in the following two sections of this contribution, we identify what should be brought into IR (and what should best be left out) from a history discipline marked by methodological nationalism. In the final section, we identify how three prominent works in Historical IR have deployed Global History in an analytical move towards recognising global connections and circulations in writing histories of international relations.

From World History to the History of Global Integration

We identify a first approach to Global History that can be described as an extension of history in *space*. Thinking beyond the borders of one's own polity has a long trajectory and has been instrumental in various disciplinary traditions of history writing concerned with the 'global'. For instance, early attempts of writing *Ecumenical Histories* can be identified in ancient Greek, Arabic and Chinese chronicles, often dating back several thousand years. These histories placed the historiographer's own polity at the centre and constructed the known world around it (for further discussion, see Benjamin, 2014). During the European Enlightenment, *Universal Histories* went a step further in aspiring to cover the entire planet. It was common, however, to narrate the history of mankind as a sequence of various civilising stages with the European Enlightenment project as the final stage. The problems of centrism and hierarchisation persisted. *World Histories* are often universal in scope, but attempt to abandon teleological narratives of progress (early attempts can be found in the writings of Leopold von Ranke, Oswald Spengler and Arnold Toynbee). Here, the main impetus is to escape the constraints of national history by broadening the scope of historical inquiry by comparing different 'civilisations'.

A more recent wave of World-Historical scholarship was initiated by William McNeill's (1963) acclaimed *The Rise of the West*. For McNeill, world history meant the *rise* of Western civilisation vis-à-vis cultural influences from other civilisations. Civilisations were *not* conceptualised as bounded self-contained objects (see also McNeill, 2005: 68). However, McNeill remained substantively Eurocentric in arguing that the making of the modern world ultimately resulted from the expansion of Western civilisation.[2] A second wave of World History emerged from the 1990s onwards as an (often failed) attempt to overcome this Eurocentric bias by including other non-Western civilisations, and assigning them equal agency as Western civilisation in the development of world history.[3] However, these attempts at extending history in space by thinking beyond the borders of one's own polity have resulted in world history being written as a history of monads, meaning that the objects of study (e.g. empires, civilisations or regions) remain static, impenetrable and ahistorical entities. As these objects are plotted into an already extended space of the global, connections through which the 'global' is constructed are left out of historical inquiry.[4]

This blind spot is to some extent addressed in a second approach to Global History which focuses on the history of globalisation as an integrative *process*, underlining its temporal dimension. It incorporates events, ideas and subjects into a linear historical process of globalisation by which the world became more connected, (unequally or equally) interdependent and integrated (cf. Held et al., 1999; Osterhammel, 2014). This was not an historiographic topic before the 1990s as '[h]istorians were slow to take up globalization as a source of interest' (Hunt, 2014: 70). This approach to Global History was aimed at redressing '[t]he idea of Western history as universal (global) history [which] emerged in the 19th century' (Hobson, 2006: 408) and history's 'symbiotic relationship with nationalism' (ibid.: 3).

However, understanding globalisation as an incremental and integrative process often implies a quasi-teleological understanding of history itself. In other words, a history of globalisation takes 'existing processes, encapsulated in the "factors of globalization" and traces them as far back in the past as seems necessary and useful' (Mazlish, 1998: 389). Such an approach 'streamlines history and formats it to the single criterion of connectedness' creating a 'myth of continuity', where the 'quest for the origins of globalization' – as there has to be a 'definite starting point' – teeters on obsession (Conrad, 2016: 99–100). Hunt (2014), for instance, points to the co-constitutive role of the 'non-West' and the role played by intermediaries. The 'West did not globalize the world on its own; adventurous and enterprising people across the world brought various locales into greater interconnection and interdependence with each other. Since globalisation is not therefore a uniquely Western creation, the globalization paradigm must be modified to take account of these multiple origins and processes' (Hunt, 2014: 27). Hobson (2004) traces in *The Eastern Origins of Western Civilization* the rise and scope of what he refers to as 'Oriental globalization' in the East 'which was more advanced than the West between 500 and 1800' (ibid.: 2) and caused the rise of the West. Indeed, 'Oriental globalisation was the midwife, if not the mother, of the medieval and modern West' (ibid.: 36). The West, in turn, was 'the unconscious heir of the industrial revolution of Sung China' (ibid.: 192). Quijano (2000) pleas for an alternative geopolitical vantage point in offering an alternative non-Eurocentric history of globalisation and its origins: 'America [the Americas] was the first modern and global geocultural identity. Europe was the second and was constituted as a consequence of America, not the inverse' (ibid.: 552).

However, the linear progressive narrative of globalisation which underpins the *process* approach to Global History is not fully redressed by these interventions. Despite incorporating more diverse sources of historical development in its explanatory apparatus, additions are still plotted into a progressive, linear and universalising story of globalisation. These interventions also reinforce the persistence of bounded and mutually exclusive geographical categories in history writing. Process approaches do carry a set of (local) particularities with them that potentially work towards decentring history. However, we caution against over-determining the distinction between the West and the non-West in writing the history of globalisation. As argued by Bilgin (2008: 5–6), 'there may be elements of "non-Western" experiences and ideas built in to those ostensibly "Western" approaches to the study of world politics. The reverse may also be true. What we think of as "non-Western" approaches to world politics may be suffused with "Western" concepts and theories'. Bio- and geopolitical binaries are unwittingly reinvented in attempts at overcoming them in writing histories of globalisation. A viable way out of the trap of 'sterilis[ing] the history of the "West" by leaving out "non-Western" challenges, interventions and contributions' (ibid.: 6) is to identify and trace entanglements, connections, circulations and exchange as vehicles for the production of historical contingencies.

Global History as Entanglements

A third approach to Global History focuses on *entanglements*. This approach does not conceive the 'global' as a single unit of analysis, nor treat events, ideas and subjects as factors to be incorporated into a larger globalising historical process. It serves to overcome the methodological nationalism that defines most historical writing and, consequently, confronts Eurocentrism. This confrontation proceeds by approaching events, ideas and subjects as inextricably entwined, rather than occurring within bounded entities (such as the nation-state or self-contained civilisations). Whereas the two approaches outlined above trace historical events and developments back to specific starting points, focusing on entanglements does not conceive of time and space as static totalities, but as mutable in historical processes of globe-making and in various situated practices of projecting particular meanings into the notion of 'global'.

Global History as entanglements traces links, interconnections and circulations of ideas, peoples, institutions or technologies. In this sense, it has affinities with *Comparative History* and *Transnational History*. Comparative History focuses on comparing and contrasting units in the search for differences and similarities. However, despite its stated purpose of overcoming the limitations of single case studies, Comparative History continues to take units of analysis as bounded entities that efface internal differences (Conrad, 2016: 40). Challenging the nation-state as the main unit of analysis in global history writing, Transnational History 'focuses on either phenomena (for example, processes of cultural transfer) or entities (for example, transnational organisation) that *transcend* national states' (Olstein, 2015: 16, emphasis added). Yet, according to C.A. Bayly, 'transnational' can be 'a restrictive term' since before 1850 'large parts of the globe were not dominated by nations so much as by empires, city-states, diasporas, etc.' (quoted in Bayly et al., 2006: 1442; see also Bayly, 2021 in this volume).

Now, a number of scholars within Global History have moved away from comparisons between what appears as bounded entities, towards identifying and tracing connections and circulations, that is, entanglements. Nation-states and civilisations do not exist in isolation, nor are they fixed historical entities (see de Carvalho and Leira, 2021; Spanu 2021; Heiskanen, 2021; all in this volume). A focus on entanglements means that points of origin and spatial schemes can neither be taken as given nor employed as fixed points of reference for tracking a linear historical process. They are constructed through entanglements. It is the entanglement of events, ideas and subjects that create particular and passing temporal and spatial hierarchies which constitute the 'global'. In line with this, IR scholars (though not identifying themselves directly as 'Global Historians') have increasingly underlined connections, entanglements and co-constitution as mechanisms through which the 'international' is developed (Bader, 2015; Bilgin, 2016a,b; Owens, 2016; Çapan et al. 2021).

Finally, there are different modes of studying entanglements. We turn to two important contributions to Global History as entanglements that deploy a micro-level and a macro-level approach, respectively. A micro-level approach concerns the tracing of life histories and biographies of single individuals or groups of actors. This reveals the juxtaposition, entanglement and exchanges between different social worlds. A macro-level approach addresses how larger structural changes are entangled and thus co-constitutive. 'Global' historical inquiries are not necessarily a matter of the 'right' scale; both approaches concern how ideas and practices travel and connect through specific instances of interaction and exchange. Natalie Zemon Davis's (2007) study of Joannes Leo Africanus, born al-Wazzan, in *Trickster Travels: A Sixteenth-Century Muslim Between Worlds* illustrates the first approach. Davis reconstructs the life of Leo Africanus (1494–1554), an Arab author, diplomat and traveller. Born in Muslim Granada, raised in Morocco, captured by Spanish pirates, and subsequently employed by Pope Leo X, Davis explores 'how a man moved between different polities, made use of different cultural and social resources, and entangled or separated them so as to survive, discover, write, make relationships, and think about society and himself' (Davis, 2007: 30). The life history of Leo Africanus provides an account of how intercultural connections and encounters unfold within different power hierarchies and condition the circulation, mutual influence and constitution of ideas and knowledge.

Andrew Zimmerman's (2010) monograph *Alabama in Africa: Booker T. Washington, the German Empire, and the Globalization of the New South* illustrates the second way in which we suggest entanglements can be studied. It is an illustrative account of how ideas and practices, here in relation to the changing cotton industry in the context of a new industrial era in 19th century, developed not within one bounded space but in an entangled manner through histories of empire that brought the American South, the German Empire and Togoland, at that time a German colony, together. Zimmerman traces how the abolition of slavery and serfdom along with the development of new technologies within the cotton economy resulted in novel approaches to employ 'free' labour in production. These entwined developments constructed a new socio-economic classification in the American South: 'Negro' free labour. The American South became a model for European colonial rule in Africa, beginning with an expedition by some of its agricultural experts to Togo in 1901 under agreement with the German government. Experiences from this expedition would inform discussions on agricultural labour and modernisation in the Prussian East, especially with regard to Polish migrant workers. To summarise, it was in *points of interaction* between American, European and African histories that social orders were constituted and sedimented and ideational schemes took shape, rather than in bounded and distinct spaces of origin.[5]

Global History in Historical International Relations

In this section, we turn to three prominent interventions in Historical IR that each approach *Global History as entanglements* to counter methodological nationalism and Eurocentrism (see also Bartelson, 1995; Bell, 2001; Barkawi and Laffey, 2002; Hobson, 2002; Teschke, 2003; Buzan and Little, 2010; de Carvalho et al., 2011; Lawson, 2012; Buzan and Lawson, 2015; Bayly, 2016; Barkawi, 2017). We suggest that these three monographs, all published in 2015, serve as illustrations for how Global History can be deployed in IR. However, we want to restate our caution here against tracing historical events and evolutions back to specific starting points and conceiving of time and space as static totalities when analytically identifying and assigning agency to non-Western actors and communities in the context of (re)writing histories of international relations. *Global History as entanglements*, in our view, necessitates a consistent analytical engagement with entanglements, connections, circulations and exchange as units of investigation from a historical perspective. This contrasts with traditional territorial and temporal logics which should be treated as mutable in historical processes of globe-making.

Challenging the conventional story of how capitalism emerged, Anievas and Nisancioglu's (2015) *How the West Came to Rule* traces 'extra-European agency' to overcome the Eurocentric bias inherent in the history of capitalism. As suggested in the introduction to this chapter, historical developmental trajectories are too often explained through particular binary characteristics attributed to 'Europe', which are inscribed into a spatio-temporal hierarchy that has been continuously rearticulated in history writing. Events that are understood to be progressive (e.g. the rise of capitalism) are depicted as originating in Western Europe. Anievas and Nisancioglu (2015: 5) challenge the enactment of the 'historical distinction between tradition and modernity through a spatial separation of "West" and "East"', which works as a vehicle for excluding the 'East' from the history of capitalism's emergence. As a remedy, the authors widen 'the spatial optic of capitalism's emergence' to 'offer a fundamental rethinking of the origins of capitalism and the emergence of Western domination that puts non-Western sources at the forefront of analysis' (ibid.: 6). The book points to the 'contributions' of the Mongolian and Ottoman Empires, American 'discoveries' and the colonisation of Asia, to the development of capitalism.

Barry Buzan and George Lawson's (2015) *The Global Transformation* focuses on the transformation of the 19th century and its importance for understanding international relations. This transformation involved 'a complex configuration of industrialization, rational state-building and ideologies of progress' which changed 'the distribution of power' causing 'a shift from a "polycentric world with no dominant centre" to a "core-periphery" order in which the centre of gravity resided in the West' (Buzan and Lawson, 2015: 1). The authors point to the importance of 'inter-societal interactions' and 'entangled histories' as a vehicle for this global transformation. Modernity did not only emerge in Europe. Modernity was a global process that 'happened first in Britain'; yet '[i]nter-societal processes on a global scale were constitutive of the British experience', including the global cotton economy (ibid.: 25). Three dynamics underpin inter-societal interactions: imperialism and the extraction of raw materials in colonies by European powers; the dominant control by European powers over trade; and how innovative advances made by Europeans were conditioned by 'the emulation and fusion of non-European ideas and technologies' (ibid.: 31; on trade, see Lobo-Guerrero, 2021 in this volume).

In *International Order in Diversity* (2015), Andrew Phillips and J.C. Sharman critically address the persisting idea in mainstream IR scholarship that enduring interaction between different political units results over time in their mutual resemblance (i.e. in functionally equivalent sovereign states). They suggest that, historically, 'international systems have consisted of a bewildering diversity of political units, ranging from city-leagues through to feudal monarchies, confederacies and sprawling imperial realms' (Phillips and Sharman, 2015: 1), the interaction between which reinforced political and institutional heterogeneity. '[C]halleng[ing] a Eurocentric view of Global History' prevalent among IR scholars, the authors defy the mainstream IR narrative that late medieval Latin Christendom in Europe was more politically fragmented than 'other civilizational centres'. This narrative conceives this process to result in the early emergence of the modern sovereign state as a particularly Western innovation 'that supposedly did not exist in other Old World societies'. The consequence is a European prerogative to 'coercively remake the world's polities along Western lines through imperialism and then decolonization' (ibid.: 7; on decolonisation, see Svensson, 2021 in this volume). *International Order in Diversity* demonstrates how various organising principles (e.g. heteronomy and suzerainty) of non-Western powers allowed unlike political units, including sovereign states, chartered company sovereigns and empires, to coexist and maintain order over time within the Indian Ocean international system from 1500 to 1750. This 'International Relations has almost totally neglected' (ibid.: 6). It was *interaction*, not European institutional exceptionalism, that allowed European powers to expand into the Indian Ocean region. This approach, according to the authors, radically departs from 'the traditional triumphalist "rise of the West" historiography' in IR (ibid.: 8).

While these studies of global history have made important contributions to the discussion on how to counter Eurocentrism and methodological nationalism in IR, biases persist. The historical turn in IR was premised on the belief that historicising events, concepts and the field of IR in general constituted an important tool in decentring and decolonising the discipline. However, as this contribution has argued, Eurocentrism and methodological nationalism were already present within the discipline of history. When findings, trends and topics from history are brought into IR, Eurocentrism and methodological nationalism might be imported as well. For this reason, it is important to not only problematise Eurocentrism and methodological nationalism in IR but also identify their sources and treatment in the discipline of history itself (see Walker, 1989; Campbell, 1998; Finney, 2001; Vaughan-Williams, 2005; Çapan, 2016).

Conclusion

Histories of the 'international' and the development of concepts such as security, capital, sovereignty and civilisation have been predominantly concerned with three interlinked stories: the story of the rise of the West, the story of the development of capitalism and the story of the development of modernity. Recently, critical perspectives have increasingly questioned these macronarratives and their constitutive chronologies, teleologies and spatial imaginaries, interrupting the linear, progressive and parochial stories upon which the idea(s) of the 'international' is built. This contribution argues for the relevance of the burgeoning field of Global History for IR. In particular, *Global History as entanglements* offers a means for IR to engage Global History in a way that can problematise and transcend Eurocentric assumptions underpinning historical research in the discipline. What *Global History as entanglements* recognises is not only that there is no fixed unit of analysis but also there is no fixed and isolated space where events unfold, and ideas originate.

Suggestions for further reading

Conrad, S., and Sachsenmaier, D. (2007). *Competing Visions of World Order: Global Moments and Movements, 1880s-1930s*. Houndmills: Palgrave Macmillan.
Frank, A. G. (1998). *ReOrient: The Global Economy in the Asian Age*. Berkeley: University of California Press.
Ogle, V. (2015). *The Global Transformation of Time: 1870-1950*. Cambridge, MA: Harvard University Press.
Sachsenmaier, D. (2018). *Global Entanglements of a Man Who Never Travelled: A Seventeenth-Century Chinese Christian and His Conflicted Worlds*. New York, NY: Columbia University Press.

Notes

1 On these terms, see also Mazlish (2005). Global History is strongly influenced, but also distinct from, for example, world-systems theory, the Annales school, connected history, postcolonial history/studies and the study of multiple modernities (for further discussion see Conrad, 2016: ch. 3).

2 McNeill admitted in 1990 that his earlier work came 'in the form of intellectual imperialism' as it took the 'world as a whole, and [tried] to understand global history on the basis of cultural diffusion' of the West (McNeill, 1990: 2, see also McNeill, 2005).

3 For an attempt to introduce this understanding of World History to IR, see Linklater (2007).

4 For a discussion of the link between Global History and the spatial turn in the humanities and social sciences, see Middell and Naumann (2010). Moreover, the recent trend of Big History works on a logic of extending the temporal dimension of Global History.

5 In the words of Zimmerman (2010: 238), the 'question of whether the southern United States pursued a Prussian path, or, for that matter, whether Prussia and West Africa pursued a southern path, depends upon separating categories of knowledge from the transnational histories in which they emerged. The Prussian path, like the American path or the West African path, resulted from transnational networks of capital, social science, racial ideologies, and empire'.

References

Anievas, A., and Nisancioglu, K. (2015). *How the West Came to Rule: The Geopolitical Origins of Capitalism*. London: Pluto.

Armitage, D. (2008). *The Declaration of Independence: A Global History*. Cambridge: Harvard University Press.

Bader, A. D. (2015). *Empire Within: International Hierarchy and Its Imperial Laboratories of Governance*. Abingdon: Routledge.

Barkawi, T. (2017). *Soldiers of Empire*. Cambridge: Cambridge University Press.

Barkawi, T., and Laffey, M. (2002). Retrieving the imperial: empire and international relations. *Millennium*, 31 (1), 109–127.

Bartelson, J. (1995). *A Genealogy of Sovereignty*. Cambridge: Cambridge University Press.

Bayly, M. (2021). Imperialism: Beyond the 'Re-turn to Empire' in International Relations. In de Carvalho, B., Costa Lopez, J., & Leira, H., eds. *Routledge Handbook of Historical International Relations*. Abingdon: Routledge.

Bayly, M. J. (2016). *Taming the Imperial Imagination: Colonial Knowledge, International Relations, and the Anglo-Afghan Encounter, 1808-1878*. Cambridge: Cambridge University Press.

Bayly, C. A., Beckert, S., Connelly, M., Hofmeyr, I., Kozol, W., and Seed, P. (2006). Conversation: on transnational history. *American Historical Review*, 111 (5), 1441–1464.

Bell, D. (2001). International relations: the dawn of a historiographic turn? *British Journal of Politics and International Relations*, 3 (1), 115–126.

Benjamin, C. (2014). 'But from this time forth history becomes a connected whole': state expansion and the origins of universal history. *Journal of Global History*, 9 (3), 357–378.

Bilgin, P. (2008). Thinking Past 'Western' IR? *Third World Quarterly*, 29 (1), 5–23.

Bilgin, P. (2016a). 'Contrapuntal reading' as a method, an ethos, and a metaphor for global IR. *International Studies Review*, 18 (1), 134–146.

Bilgin, P. (2016b). How to remedy Eurocentrism in IR? A complement and a challenge for *The Global Transformation*. *International Theory*, 8 (3), 492–501.

Buzan, B., and Lawson, G. (2015). *The Global Transformation: History, Modernity and The Making of International Relations*. Cambridge: Cambridge University Press.

Buzan, B., and Little, R. (2010). World history and the development of non-Western international relations theory. In: A. Acharya, and B. Buzan, eds., *Non-Western International Relations Theory: Perspectives on and beyond Asia*, London: Routledge, 197–220.

Campbell, D. (1998). MetaBosnia: narratives of the Bosnian War. *Review of International Studies*, 24 (2), 261–281.

Çapan, Z. G. (2016). *Re-Writing International Relations: History and Theory Beyond Eurocentrism in Turkey*. London: Rowman & Littlefield.

Çapan, Z. G. (2017a). Writing international relations from the invisible side of the abyssal line. *Review of International Studies*, 43 (4), 602–611.

Çapan, Z. G. (2017b). Decolonising international relations? *Third World Quarterly*, 38 (1), 1–15.

Çapan, Z. G., dos Reis, F., and Grasten, M., eds., (2021). *The Politics of Translation in International Relations*. Houndmills: Palgrave.

Conrad, S. (2016). *What is Global History?* Princeton, NJ: Princeton University Press.

Davis, N. Z. (2007). *Trickster Travels: A Sixteenth-Century Muslim Between Worlds*. London: Hill and Wang.

de Carvalho, B., and Leira, H. (2021). State Formation and Historical International Relations. In de Carvalho, B., Costa Lopez, J., & Leira, H., eds. *Routledge Handbook of Historical International Relations*. Abingdon: Routledge.

de Carvalho, B., Leira, H., and Hobson, J. M. (2011). The big bangs of IR: the myths that your teachers still tell you about 1648 and 1919. *Millennium*, 39 (3), 735–758.

Duindam, J. (2016). *Dynasties: A Global History of Power, 1300-1800*. Cambridge: Cambridge University Press.

Fillafer, F. L. (2017). A world connecting? From the unity of history to global history. *History and Theory*, 56 (1), 3–37.

Finney, P. (2001). Still 'marking time'? Text, discourse and truth in international history. *Review of International Studies*, 27 (3), 291–308.

Go, J., and Lawson, G. (2017). Introduction: For a Global Historical Sociology. In: J. Go, and G. Lawson, eds., *Global Historical Sociology*, Cambridge: Cambridge University Press, 1–34.

Heiskanen, J. (2021). Nations and Nationalism in International Relations. In de Carvalho, B., Costa Lopez, J., & Leira, H., eds. *Routledge Handbook of Historical International Relations*. Abingdon: Routledge.

Held, D., McGrew, A., Goldblatt, D., and Perraton, J., eds. (1999). *Global Transformations: Politics, Economics and Culture*. Cambridge: Polity Press.

Herborth, B., and Nitzschner, P. (2021). Europe in Historical International Relations. In de Carvalho, B., Costa Lopez, J., & Leira, H., eds. *Routledge Handbook of Historical International Relations*. Abingdon: Routledge.

Hobson, J. (2006). East and west in global history. *Theory, Culture & Society*, 23 (2–3), 408–410.

Hobson, J. M. (2002). What's at Stake in 'Bringing Historical Sociology back into International Relations?' In: S. Hobdon, and J. M. Hobson, eds., *Historical Sociology of International Relations*, Cambridge: Cambridge University Press, 3–41.

Hobson, J. M. (2004). *The Eastern Origins of Western Civilization*. Cambridge: Cambridge University Press.

Hunt, L. (2014). *Writing History in the Global Era*. New York, NY: W. W. Norton.

Iggers, G. G., Wang, Q. E., and Mukherjee, S. (2008). *A Global History of Modern Historiography*. London: Routledge.

Lawson, G. (2012). The eternal divide? History and international relations. *European Journal of International Relations*, 18 (2), 203–226.

Linklater, A. (2007). World history and international relations. *International Relations*, 21 (3), 355–359.

Lobo-Guerrero, L. (2021). Insurance, Trade and War. In de Carvalho, B., Costa Lopez, J., & Leira, H., eds. *Routledge Handbook of Historical International Relations*. Abingdon: Routledge.

Mazlish, B. (1998). Comparing global history to world history. *The Journal of Interdisciplinary History*, 28 (3), 385–395.

Mazlish, B. (2005). Terms. In: M. Hughes-Warrington, ed., *Palgrave Advances in World History*, Houndmills: Palgrave Macmillan, 18–43.

McNeill, W. H. (1963). *The Rise of the West*. Chicago, IL: The University of Chicago Press.

McNeill, W. H. (1990). 'The rise of the west' after twenty-five years. *Journal of World History*, 1 (1), 1–21.

McNeill, W. H. (2005). *The Pursuit of Truth: A Historian's Memoir*. Lexington, KY: University Press of Kentucky.

Middell, M., and Naumann, K. (2010). Global history and the spatial turn: from the impact of area studies to the study of critical junctures of globalization. *Journal of Global History*, 5(1), 149–170.

Mikaberidze, A. (2020). *The Napoleonic Wars: A Global History*. Oxford: Oxford University Press.

Moyn, S., and Sartori, A. (2013). Approaches to Global Intellectual History. In: S. Moyn, and A. Sartori, eds., *Global Intellectual History*, New York, NY: Columbia University Press, 3–30.

Olstein, D. (2015). *Thinking History Globally*. London: Palgrave Macmillan.

Osterhammel, J. (2014). *The Transformation of the World: A Global History of the Nineteenth Century*. Princeton, NJ: Princeton University Press.

Owens, P. (2016). International historical what? *International Theory*, 8 (3), 448–457.

Phillips, A. (2016). Global IR Meets Global History: Sovereignty, Modernity, and the International System's Expansion in the Indian Ocean Region. *International Studies Review*, 18 (1), 62–77.

Phillips, A., and Sharman, J. C. (2015). *International Order in Diversity: War, Trade and Rule in the Indian Ocean*. Cambridge: Cambridge University Press.

Quijano, A. (2000). Coloniality of power, Eurocentrism, and Latin America. *Nepantla*, 1 (3), 533–580.

Sachsenmaier, D. (2011). *Global Perspectives on Global History: Theories and Approaches in a Connected World*. Cambridge: Cambridge University Press.

Spanu, M. (2021). States, People and Self-determination in Historical Perspective. In de Carvalho, B., Costa Lopez, J., & Leira, H., eds. *Routledge Handbook of Historical International Relations*. Abingdon: Routledge.

Svensson, T. (2021). Decolonisation and the Erosion of the Imperial Idea. In de Carvalho, B., Costa Lopez, J., & Leira, H., eds. *Routledge Handbook of Historical International Relations*. Abingdon: Routledge.

Teschke, B. (2003). *The Myth of 1648: Class, Geopolitics, and the Making of Modern International Relations*. London: Verso.

Vaughan-Williams, N. (2005). International relations and the 'problem of history'. *Millennium*, 34 (1), 115–136.

Walker, R. B. J. (1989). History and structure in the theory of international relations. *Millennium*, 18 (2), 163–183.

Woolf, D. (2011). *A Global History of History*. Cambridge: Cambridge University Press.

Zimmerman, A. (2010). *Alabama in Africa: Booker T. Washington, the German Empire, and the Globalization of the New South*. Princeton, NJ: Princeton University Press.

49

HISTORICAL PRACTICES

Recovering a Durkheimian tradition

Jorg Kustermans

Introduction

The idea of this chapter is to present the examination of 'historical practices' as a distinct approach to the study of Historical International Relations (HIR). Such endeavour immediately runs into a problem, because the concept around which the approach is supposed to centre has no conventional meaning. What does it mean to speak of 'historical practices'? Assuming that practices refer to the 'things that we do,' what does the adjective add to the noun? What makes a practice into a historical practice?

Three answers spring to mind.

First: a historical practice is a practice of the past. *Its antonym: a present-day practice.*

Historical practices, on this view, are the things that people used to do, but that we do not do anymore. To centre the study of *HIR* on historical practices in this first sense is to insist on the peculiarity of the past, on the past being a foreign country where people did all sorts of strange, antiquated things.

Second: a historical practice is a practice laden with the past. *Its antonym: a revolutionary practice.*

Historical practices, on this view, are those things that we do, still today, in which we recognize significant traces from the past. To centre the study of *HIR* on historical practices in this second sense is to insist on path-dependency, on the ways in which old habits work on even the most innovative undertakings.

Third: a historical practice is a practice that withstands the test of time. *Its antonym: a fleeting practice.*

Historical practices, on this view, are the things that people have been doing *at all times* – past, present, and supposedly future. To centre the study of *HIR* on historical practices in this third sense is to draw attention to functional equivalencies between societal institutions of historically diverse societies, to the elemental dimension in the most progressive ways-of-doing-things, to humanity finding expression in even the strangest custom.

It should be noted at the outset that centring the study of *HIR* on the examination of historical practices, in either sense of the notion, is not common. Obviously, in many historical narratives about international relations, reference will be made to this or that practice. Nobody denies that practices exist. But neither does anybody – almost anybody – make much theoretical ado about them in *HIR*. In marked contrast, IR theory and International Political Sociology have experienced a 'practice turn' for some time now (Neumann, 2002; Adler and Pouliot, 2011; Adler-Nissen, 2014), which argues that social life unfolds 'in and through practice.' That basic intuition can be developed in a number of ways, two of which have been especially prominent (Kustermans, 2016). A first strand emphasizes the causal importance of the myriad of everyday interactions and thus warns against overestimating the causal importance of holistically conceived social structures. A second strand stresses the 'practical' nature of action and counsels against overly stylized accounts of human activity. It explains that people always act within concrete, oftentimes messy, situations and on the basis of largely inarticulate, embodied knowledge.

It should be noted that, much as the concept of practice(s) plays a limited part in *HIR*, so does the idea of 'history' – let alone 'historical practices' – play a minor part in IR's practice turn. As a result, when I present, in later sections of this chapter, the examination of 'historical practices' as a worthwhile approach to the study of *HIR*, I will not be reconstructing an existing approach but will be introducing a possible alternative one.

'Practices' in Historical International Relations

From one point of view, 'practices' are ubiquitous in *HIR*. It is impossible to give an account of any historical period or of the development of any historical phenomenon without making reference to the importance of this or that social practice. However, rarely does the notion achieve theoretical significance.

Consider just three examples from recent books in HIR, each of undisputed scholarly merit. In *War in International Thought*, Jens Bartelson (2017: 34, emphasis added; see also Bartelson, 2021 in this volume) contends that the 'double bind between war and the state' did not emerge as an idea with Charles Tilly, but that it 'was forged historically and [that] it informed and legitimized *practices* of state formation' (see de Carvalho and Leira, 2021 in this volume). In a similar vein, in *International Order in Diversity*, Andrew Phillips and Jason Sharman (2015: 6; emphasis added) explain that 'the Mughals and the Dutch and English company sovereigns' could accept […] that two rulers would hold different sovereign prerogatives over the same territory [and that both] engaged in *practices* of localization to legitimize and stabilize the resulting accommodations.' The final example comes from Julian Go and George Lawson's (2017) programmatic introduction to their *Global Historical Sociology*. Thus, Go and Lawson (2017: 3, emphasis added) warn against 'the danger in naturalizing in our analyses what is constructed in *practice*' and also explain that 'international orders themselves change as norms, rules, and *practices* are contested' (ibid.: 29; emphasis added).

These examples could be multiplied. What they show is that it is common to make reference to 'practices' in historical narratives about world politics, but equally that such references typically lack theoretical significance. One could supplant Bartelson's 'practices of state-formation' with 'processes of state formation' and no meaning would be lost. The same holds for Philips and Sharman's 'practices of localization.' In both cases, the notion of 'practices' does no theoretical work. In Bartelson's account, 'concepts' do the theoretical work: concepts legitimize practices/ processes (on concepts and conceptual history, see Kessler, 2021 in this volume). In Philips and Sharman's argument, 'localization' does the theoretical work: localization legitimizes political arrangements. The lack of theoretical significance shows in Go and Lawson's remarks too. To stipulate that social facts are the products of social construction says as much, if not more, than to say that they are 'constructed in practice.' Where else, after all, would they be constructed, except 'in practice'? Similarly, when international orders change because their constitutive norms, rules, and practices are being contested, then those orders change because of acts of contestation, not because 'practices' are being contested in addition to norms and rules. It appears that everybody agrees that social actors engage in 'practices,' but that nobody finds it necessary to attribute particular methodological or theoretical significance to that observation.

This state of affairs contrasts sharply with the popularity of practice-theoretical approaches in many other subfields of the discipline of IR (Adler and Pouliot, 2011; Bueger and Gadinger, 2018) and in the broader social and human sciences (Schatzki et al., 2001), including the occasional – necessarily occasional, as we will explain – reflection in the field of History (Spiegel, 2005). Things look somewhat different when one examines the work of a number of younger scholars in HIR, some of whom find inspiration in the 'practice turn' in IR (e.g. Mulich, 2018; Wallenius, 2019;). As yet, however, this remains a minor movement, which has not inspired much methodological reflection yet on the particularity (or particular merit) of examining 'historical practices' in HIR.

Two plausible explanations come to mind. The first boils down to a lack of need. It is not that scholars in HIR dismiss 'practice theory' expressly. It is rather that they feel (or at least felt) no need or desire to have their scholarship centre on the notion. It is as though they are happy to concede the basic intuitions of the 'practice turn' – that social life evolves constantly 'in and through practice' – but that they simultaneously understand, not without reason, that such basic ontological truisms do not get us far in terms of explaining concrete outcomes or engaging more substantive questions.

The second possible explanation for the peripheral theoretical status of practices in HIR concerns the prehistory of this burgeoning sub-discipline. Early manifestations of what is today evolving into HIR typically went by the name of International Historical Sociology and took the form of introducing 'historical sociology' into 'international relations.' As a result, the endeavour focused, by and large, on some of the topics that had long been central to historical sociology – to wit, the (trans)formation of states (now situated within a transforming system of states) and the emergence and development of capitalism. In line with this substantive focus, classical sociological inspiration was drawn, in the main, from Weberian and Marxist scholarship (Smith, 2002) and, as a result, did not devote much explicit theoretical or methodological attention to 'practices,' and certainly not to 'historical practices.'

The English School, it should be noted, stands as a partial exception to this assessment of a lack of practice-theoretical sensibility in the prehistory of HIR (Navari, 2011). There is a distinct sense in which the primary institutions of international society – war, diplomacy, greatpowerhood, international law, balance of power – are theorized as practices: as the tangible things that diplomats and other state agents find themselves actually doing (cf. Keene, 2014); and it is certainly also the case that scholars of the English School have always sought to come to terms with the historicity of those key international practices: their particular historical provenance and their fate as they travelled in historical time (see Navari and Green, 2021 in this volume). There is the beginning of an engagement with the idea of 'historical practices' here – but only a beginning.

'History' in contemporary practice theory

I have noted that most *HIR* recognizes a number of core claims of contemporary 'practice theory' because those principles coincide with some core propositions of modern, secular, and post-Darwinian history-writing. I would summarize those shared intuitions with the statement that 'life is process.' To which one might add the further intuition that process lacks purpose. To the extent that they are social-scientific projects, both *HIR* and contemporary practice theory nonetheless seek to account for 'patterns' (of behaviour and development) and their structuring effects on the course of life. They seek to describe how life evolves and why it evolves as it does. However, whereas most *HIR* at this point takes recourse to concepts other than 'practices,' practice theory persists and seeks to elucidate the evolution of social life with reference to the very characteristics of 'practice' itself. In different articulations, contemporary practice theory appears to want to claim that *history is practice and practice is history*. This is, in large part, theoretical grandstanding, although the claim can, at the cost of losing some of its grandeur, be cashed out fruitfully in empirical terms too.

One articulation of the argument holds that seemingly 'marginal' practices actually form the locus of social change (Mulich, 2018). The argument achieves its purchase most clearly in comparison with alternative theories of social change, such as those positing that the clear-sighted introduction of new ideas and concepts reroutes patterns of historical development. Such accounts of the sources of social change are misplaced, it is the argument, because new concepts will die a quick death if they do not reflect an earlier change in practice, which, in turn, is taken to result from practitioners' creative engagement with the 'practical' exigencies of concrete, localized situations. Thus, a recent analysis of the standard of civilization argues convincingly that 'the origins of this [nineteenth-century legal] norm lie in legal practice instead of the doctrinal writings of great thinkers such as Vattel or Wheaton' (Wallenius, 2019: 119). It was diplomats and parliamentarians who cooked up the idea, which was introduced into Wheaton's and Vattel's legal doctrine posthumously by way of 'practices' of editorial intervention. Practice makes history in this and similar stories, but it makes history by means of necessarily situational practical action, and not, I must stress here, by means of the performance of 'historical practices' in any of the senses specified in the introduction to this chapter.

Compare Bourdieu's notion of the *habitus*, which has been a key concept in contemporary practice theory, including in IR's practice turn. The *habitus* is always the *habitus* of an individual person, although people in similar (though never quite identical) social structural positions will develop a similar *habitus*. The *habitus* describes an embodied 'matrix of perceptions, appreciations, and actions' (Bourdieu, 1972: 261), which finds its source in history. As a matter of fact, the *habitus* is history, it is all of (experienced) history soaked into a person. It is 'individual and group history sedimented in the body, social structure turned mental structure and sensorimotor engine' (Wacquant, 2016: 66).

Bourdieu is a nuanced thinker, though. He understood that 'the world' can evolve at different (faster) paces and in different directions than individual *habituses* do. The theoretical function of the concept was never to fetishize or hypostatize 'the past.' Bourdieu rather intended to draw attention to the recurring experience of discrepancy between (slowly evolving and steadily accumulating) *habitus* and (inevitably changing) social world, as well as the kinds of adjustments, some of which ill-adapted, that such discrepancy gives occasion to. *Habitus* implies 'lag' and practices being laden with the past, it does not imply inevitable, stubborn continuity. *Habitus* explains, for instance, why its memory of great-powerhood motivates Russia to engage in 'quixotic practices' that are ill-attuned, because of changes in the mores of international society, to its quest for recognition as a great power (Neumann and Pouliot, 2011). *Habitus*, that is, thematises historical practices in the second sense (practices laden with the past), but note that it mobilizes these mainly in the sociological analysis of the present, and with an eye to the future, but not primarily in the analysis of 'history' or 'historical development.'

Other versions of contemporary practice theory do take that route. Thus, Theodore Schatzki (2010: 221) has sought to reconceptualise the nature of history from a practice-theoretical perspective, coming to the conclusion that 'human history, the realm and course of the past, embraces myriad configurations of activities and material events that occur to and within bundles of persisting and metamorphosing practices and arrangements.' 'Persisting and metamorphosing practices' are what I have dubbed 'historical practices' in the second sense of that term. All social practices are historical practices, on this view, and historical practices, because of their crucial role in inspiring and guiding the doings of human beings, are seen to have a decisive influence on the course of history. On this view, if *HIR* wants to come to grips with evolutions and events in international relations, it will have to centre its analyses on how myriad historical practices shape those evolutions and mediate our experience and the impact of these events. I do wonder, though, if this does not bring us back to square one. I fear that Schatzki's philosophical conclusions will have historians and practice theorists agree that social life is process but that they will have historians proceeding much as they did before, trying to describe that process to the best of their ability.

Historical practices in Durkheimian social science

In the introduction to this chapter, I identified three possible meanings of the notion 'histor-ical practices': practices of the past, practices laden with the past, and practices that withstand time. Thus far, none of these notions forms the theoretical centre of a distinct approach to HIR. Practices are ubiquitous in HIR, but the notion itself has little theoretical or methodological significance. In contemporary practice theory, the situation is obviously different. 'Practices' are front and centre there, and, what is more, many scholars in contemporary practice theory under-stand practices to (almost) always be laden with the past. All practices are historical practices (in the second sense). It is my assessment, however, that HIR will not take to this argument much, or least not to its claims of paradigmatic significance. Historical practices (in the second sense) capture historiographical common sense. From the historians' point of view, the theoretical cele-bration of 'practices laden with the past' must represent much ado about nothing, or at least about nothing especially noteworthy within the confines of their own profession. They will be glad to assist sociologists of the present but do not reap much benefit from it themselves.

This leaves us with 'practices of the past' and with 'practices that withstand time.' In an important sense, these notions embody contrasting attitudes to the past and contrasting motiv-ations to study it. They have scholars who observe a different Gestalt when they gaze at the past (and try to grasp 'history'). When scholars scout for 'practices of the past,' they are struck by the particularity – and often peculiarity – of past ways of doing things. When they watch out for 'practices that withstand time,' however, they will be enamoured, and occasionally horrified, by the seeming universality of human conduct. One gets a bit of the fascination with 'practices of the past' in some *HIR*, as when we are summoned to appreciate the distinctiveness of ancient and early-modern Chinese diplomacy, with its tribute-bearing and its *kowtow* (Ringmar, 2012) or when people insist that medieval conceptions of 'world' order were fundamentally different from modern conceptions of 'international' order (Hall and Kratochwil, 1993). In contrast, one finds relatively little in *HIR* of the desire to identify sociologically meaningful universals, or to identify a shared 'animating principle' in those practices that many agree recur across historically diverse international societies.

One major exception is Laust Schouenborg's (2017) *Institutions in World History*, which identi-fies four 'functions' which all (international) societies perform: legitimacy and membership, con-flict regulation, trade, and governance through the institutionalization of culturally variable yet functionally equivalent practices. A second exception that comes to mind is James Der Derian's (1987) *On Diplomacy*, which sketches a history of diplomacy animated by the idea that dip-lomacy characteristically concerns the 'mediation of estrangement.' The book shows diplomacy *withstanding time*: notwithstanding far-reaching cultural and technological changes in the envir-onment of diplomacy, and notwithstanding its historically variable forms (which often find their cause in the changing environment), the practice of diplomacy thus far persists and retains its basic function of mediating estrangement. From Der Derian's account, it has all the appearance that diplomacy is a 'general phenomenon' and that it should be approached as such (Leira, 2017: 5).

Der Derian's type of analysis comes closer to what a sociology of historical practices would amount to than Schouenborg's. The reason is that it does not take its departure in the concept of society and does not scout for practices in light of the supposed functional needs of any such society, but rather theorizes the function of a historically recurrent practice (*in casu*: diplomacy) from the bottom up, grounded in the careful reconstruction of that practice.

In order to clarify the approach, I want to bring in the Durkheimian tradition in social science, represented foremost by Emile Durkheim himself and his close collaborator Marcel Mauss. Due to the dominance of Weberian and Marxist scholars in historical sociology, it is little-known that Durkheim and his circle always insisted on the need to historicize social facts and that many of their more concrete research projects consisted in the historical reconstruction (and sociological interpretation) of human practices that they believed to be *withstanding time*. Durkheim studied such institutions as 'corporations' (1969 [1893]) and 'religion' (2015 [1912]), whereas Mauss, for his part, focused on more circumspect phenomena such as 'personhood' (1938), 'prayer' (2003 [1909]), and 'gift-giving' (2012 [1925]). But in each of these cases, both Durkheim and Mauss would insist that they are social *practices* ('things being *done,*' 'organized *activities*') and also that that they were persisting across historical periods, that they were 'historical practices' (in the third sense) indeed. What is more, they thought and wrote systematically about what it implied to situate basic human practices at the centre of an historical social science. Four characteristics mark the Durkheimian analysis of 'historical practices.'

First, the primary purpose of a Durkheimian social science of historical practices is to lay bare the constitutive elements and basic function of said practices. This approach does not study history for the sake of knowing or recollecting the particularity of the past (cf. Durkheim, 2015: 37: 'pour le seul plaisir d'en raconteur les bizarreries et les singularités'), but neither does it necessarily study history for the sake of accounting for the present situation. Rather, the purpose, apart from understanding the operation of the practice better, is to discover that which is 'human' about the practice, and thus 'to reveal an essential aspect of humanity' (Durkheim, 2015: 38). Thus, Durkheim's sociology of religion does not primarily examine whether (or why) modern society is secularizing, but it wishes to find out what 'religion' is (Durkheim's answer: the separation of the sacred from the profane and the creation of a church) and how 'religion' – as manifested in beliefs and rites – expresses essential aspects of the human condition (Durkheim's interpretation: human beings' dependence on their groups for 'moral' sustenance).

Second, Durkheim and Mauss show a fascination with origins. Durkheim describes the aboriginal religion of the peoples of Australia, which sits at the centre of his *Formes élémentaires* as a 'very archaic religion' and insists on the necessity of studying 'the most primitive' religion (2015: 37). In his historical account of 'corporations,' he similarly stresses the importance of the 'corporation' having 'ancient origins' (1969). Likewise, Marcel Mauss (2012) focused his interpretation of gift-giving on an examination of 'forms and reasons of exchange in archaic societies.' It is important to be clear about the nature of this fascination. It was not naive. Durkheim (2012: 45) knew very well that 'much as any human institution, religion begins nowhere.' Historical practices have no ultimate origin. If Durkheimians nonetheless insist on studying 'historical practices' in their primitive manifestation, it is because their constitutive elements would be more easily perceptible there. Further historical evolution complicates social practices. What is more, without a proper interpretation of the practice as it originally manifested itself, it becomes very difficult to interpret later developments correctly. This is the reason that Durkheim (2015: 141–154) insists that 'totemism' (and not 'animism' or 'naturism') constitutes the 'primitive' form of religion. We will misunderstand the nature of present-day religions if we misinterpret the nature of primitive religions.

Third, nothing in their approach suggests that they consider social practices to be immutable. The precise *form* that social practices assume, as well as the precise articulation of the 'representations' that circulate within them, change significantly through time. Durkheim (2015: 566–569) recognizes about contemporary religions that they have 'individualized' and 'universalized' and he is very clear that (the details of) religious beliefs vary dramatically between historical religions. Durkheim is concerned about the reasons for these shifts and mentions both broader cultural evolutions, as well as more 'coincidental' factors, such as invasions. Mauss explains changes in the forms of gift-giving practices in a similar way and both show an awareness that the 'primitive practices' that they focus their attention on – as reported by travellers and early ethnographers – have been influenced (or sullied) by the encounter with the European colonizer. However, notwithstanding their appreciation of endless change, their main concern remains to perceive, underneath surface changes of form, the continuity of function and thus the continuity of the practice in question.

Fourth, Durkheimian social science reveals a remarkable interest in the future. It studies the primitive articulation of practices, as well as their subsequent permutations and present forms, with at least one eye set firmly on the future of the practice. It often reveals a worry about the strains that 'historical practices' are put under in modern society. 'Corporations' have been outlawed. 'Religion' is being rivalled by science. Rulers appear to have forgotten the art of gift-giving. At the same time, however, there is typically the belief that the practice will persist or, if it has disappeared, that it will stage a comeback. As long as the need to which practices correspond exists, as long as the structural conditions that call forth particular practices pertain, practices will be performed *in one form or another*. Thus, Durkheim (1995: 430) concludes *The Elementary Forms* by stating that:

> There are no immortal gospels, and there is no reason to believe that humanity is incapable of conceiving new ones in the future. As to knowing what the symbols will be in which the new faith will come to express itself, whether they will resemble those of the past, whether they will better suit the reality to be expressed – that is a question that exceeds human faculties of prediction and that, moreover, is beside the point.

Its very persistence is what makes a historical practice into an historical practice indeed. But for a practice to persist, it should not be clung to stubbornly. For a practice to persist, it needs to be attuned to the environment. One notes that the notion of 'historical practices' achieves a strong moral connotation: they appear as depositories of wisdom, as guides into the future.

Is it possible to study historical practices?

Let us assume that 'historical practices' (*that withstand time*) exist and that it would be worthwhile to make them the object of study in *HIR*. The assumption will create concerns about methodology, about how best to gain knowledge of such practices. Doubts have been raised about the very possibility of studying 'historical practices' (of any kind) at all. Thus, Tomas Wallenius (2019: 105) observes that '[the] usual methods for studying social practices are not directly applicable to the historical study of [...] practices as the practitioners of the world of yesterday are dead.' Supposedly, and not implausibly, one studies practices by observing their performance, so that ethnography – direct, prolonged observation in a natural setting – is the methodology of choice for research on practices. Given that it is quite simply impossible to do ethnographic research in the past (because one cannot travel to the past), one cannot meaningfully study 'practices of the past' either.[1] I find this a strange argument, because it would seem to invalidate a lot of historical scholarship. If the trustworthy reconstruction of activity (be that activity e~~r~~ within 'practices' or more free-running activity) demands the direct observation of sai~~d~~ how could historians write any history at all? 'Events,' on many accounts, are the b~~read~~ ~~and~~ butter of history-writing. But past 'events' (and probably present events) cannot be observed. No present-day scholar can be present at a past event. It is impossible, and yet it does not seem to be considered impossible for the skilled historian to reconstruct past events and to interpret their significance. Typically what they do is to draw – critically – on contemporary accounts of said events. In a similar way, and with the same critical attitude, the scholar of 'historical practices' can and should draw on contemporary accounts of these practices. Durkheimian social scientists, for their part, will often draw on existing historiography, but they too will be well-advised to take account of contemporary accounts of historical practices, and to regularly re-examine such primary sources first-hand (see Mulich, 2021 in this volume).

It is *not* impossible to study 'historical practices,' as long as one has access – if necessary mediated by historians' scholarship – to contemporary, quasi-ethnographic accounts of the practice in question. Because the Durkheimian social scientist will often want to reconstruct the historical evolution of those practices *that withstand time*, it will indeed often be necessary, for practical reasons, to draw on existing historiography. There is simply too much ground to cover. Mind you, though, that teamwork could dampen that situation of dependency (Détienne, 2008: 24). Specialists of different historical periods and peoples, each familiar with the relevant primary sources, could collaborate to reconstruct the diverse manifestations of the (supposedly) selfsame practice. A possible implication hereof is that the stringently orchestrated, multi-authored monograph – and thus not the research article – may well prove the most adequate method of publication for research on 'historical practices.'

Should we study historical practices?

It is possible, then, to centre the study of historical international relations on the examination of 'historical practices.' *But is it desirable too?* The question does not concern a possible colonization of HIR by the Durkheimian project, but concerns rather the approach eking out a corner of its own within HIR, for it to flourish and from which to engage other scholarship in HIR (and in IR more generally). Although I once wrote a rather critical analysis of 'the practice turn in IR' (Kustermans, 2016), I am inclined to answer the question in the affirmative. The main reason is that it will introduce a concern with 'history proper' into HIR, without identifying history with contingency. The Durkheimian project was a project of anthropological generalization, which worked on the assumption of a 'shared humanity' – shared between the people and societies of different epochs and different civilizations. What 'humanity' shares is a number of fundamental practices. Re-introducing such notion of a shared humanity – in full cognizance of the evolutionist legacy which lurks in the shadow of such re-introduction – should make for a worthy, normative contribution to the overall project of Historical International Relations.

Suggestions for further reading

Bellah, R. (1959). Durkheim and history. *American Sociological Review*, 24 (4), 447–461.
Karsenti, B. (1997). *L'homme total. Sociologie, anthropologie et philosophie chez Marcel Mauss*. Paris: PUF.
Kratochwil, F. (2018). *Praxis: On Acting and Knowing*. Cambridge: Cambridge University Press.
Lechner, S., and Frost, M. (2018). *Practice Theory and International Relations*. Cambridge: Cambridge University Press.
Schatzki, T. (1996). *Social Practices: A Wittgensteinian Approach to Human Activity and the Social*. Cambridge: Cambridge University Press.

Note

1 Durkheim and Mauss drew a lot on ethnographic reports for their research on archaic practices. To the extent that 'archaic' signals temporal precedence, the choice of words does not make much sense. Archaic societies and modern societies were co-present.

References

Adler, E., and Pouliot, V., eds. (2011). *International Practices*. Cambridge: Cambridge University Press.

Adler-Nissen, R. (2014). *Opting Out of the European Union: Diplomacy, Sovereignty, and European Integration*. Cambridge: Cambridge University Press.

Bartelson, J. (2017). *War in International Thought*. Cambridge: Cambridge University Press.

Bartelson, J. (2021). War and the Turn to History in International Relations. In de Carvalho, B., Costa Lopez, J., & Leira, H., eds. *Routledge Handbook of Historical International Relations*. Abingdon: Routledge.

Bourdieu, P. (1972). *Esquisse d'une théorie de la pratique*. Paris: Seuil.

Bueger, C. and F. Gadinger. (2018). *International Practice Theory: Second Edition*. Basingstoke: Palgrave Macmillan.

de Carvalho, B., and Leira, H. (2021). State Formation and Historical International Relations. In de Carvalho, B., Costa Lopez, J., & Leira, H., eds. *Routledge Handbook of Historical International Relations*. Abingdon: Routledge.

Der Derian, J. (1987). *On Diplomacy: A Genealogy of Western Estrangement*. Oxford: Basil Blackwell.

Détienne, M. (2008). *Comparing the Incomparable*. Stanford, CA: Stanford University Press.

Durkheim, E. (1969). *The Division of Labor in Society*. Translated by G. Simpson. New York, NY: The Free Press.

Durkheim, E. (1995). *The Elementary Forms of Religious Life*. Translated by K. Fields. New York, NY: The Free Press.

Durkheim, E. (2015). In: M. Achimastos, ed., *Œuvres, Tome 1: Les formes élémentaires de la vie religieuse*, Paris: Classiques Garnier.

Go, J., and Lawson G. (2017). Introduction: For a Global Historical Sociology. In: J. Go, and G. Lawson, eds., *Global Historical Sociology*, Cambridge: Cambridge University Press, 1–34.

Hall, R. B., and Kratochwil, F. (1993). Medieval tales, neorealist science, and the abuse of history. *International Organization*, 47 (3), 479–491.

Keene, E. (2014). Where should we look for modern international thought? *Contemporary Political Thought*, 13 (4), 397–402.

Kessler, O. (2021). Conceptual History in International Relations: from Ideology to Social Theory? In de Carvalho, B., Costa Lopez, J., & Leira, H., eds. *Routledge Handbook of Historical International Relations*. Abingdon: Routledge.

Kustermans, J. (2016). Parsing the practice turn: practice, practical knowledge, practices. *Millennium: Journal of International Studies*, 44 (2), 175–196.

Leira, Halvard. (2017). The Making of a Classic: On Diplomacy 30 Years On. *New Perspectives*, 25 (3), 67–73

Mauss, M. (1938). Une Catégorie de l'Esprit Humain: La Notion de Personne, Celle de «Moi». *The Journal of the Royal Anthropological Institute of Great Britain and Ireland*, 68 (2), 263–281.

Mauss, M. (2012). *Essai sur le don: Forme et raison de l'échange dans les sociétés archaïques*. Paris: Presses Universitaires de France.

Mulich, J. (2018). Transformation at the margins: imperial expansion and systemic change in world politics. *Review of International Studies*, 44 (4), 694–716.

Mulich, J. (2021). International Relations in the Archive: Uses of Sources and Historiography. In de Carvalho, B., Costa Lopez, J., & Leira, H., eds. *Routledge Handbook of Historical International Relations*. Abingdon: Routledge.

Navari, C. (2011). The concept of practice in the English school. *European Journal of International Relations*, 17 (4), 611–630.

Navari, C., and Green, D. (2021). The English School and Historical International Relations. In de Carvalho, B., Costa Lopez, J., & Leira, H., eds. *Routledge Handbook of Historical International Relations*. Abingdon: Routledge.

Neumann, I. (2002). Returning practice to the linguistic turn: the case of diplomacy. *Millennium: Journal of International Studies*, 31 (3), 627–651.

Neumann, I., and Pouliot, V. (2011). Untimely Russia: hysteresis in Russian-Western relations over the past millennium. *Security Studies*, 20 (1), 105–137.

Phillips, A., and Sharman, J. (2015). *International Order in Diversity: War, Trade and Rule in the Indian Ocean.* Cambridge: Cambridge University Press.

Ringmar, E. (2012). Performing international systems: two East-Asian alternatives to the Westphalian order. *International Organization*, 66 (2), 1–25.

Schatzki, T. (2010). *The Timespace of Human Activity: On Performance, Society and History as Indeterminate Teleological Events.* Lanham, MD: Lexington Books.

Schatzki, T. Knorr Cetina, K. and von Savigny, E. (eds.) (2001) *The Practice Turn in Contemporary Theory.* London: Routledge.

Schouenborg, L. (2017). *Institutions in World History: Divorcing International Relations Theory from the State and Stage Models.* London: Routledge.

Smith, S. (2002). Historical Sociology and International Relations Theory. In: S. Hobden, and J. M. Hobson, eds., *Historical Sociology of International Relations*, Cambridge: Cambridge University Press, 223–243.

Spiegel, G. (2005). *Practicing History: New Directions in Historical Writing After the Linguistic Turn.* London: Routledge.

Wacquant, L. (2016). A concise genealogy and anatomy of habitus. *The Sociological Review*, 64 (1), 64–72.

Wallenius, T. (2019). The case for a history of global legal practices. *European Journal of International Relations*, 25 (1), 108–130.

50

QUANTITATIVE APPROACHES

Towards comparative and trans-regional approaches in Historical International Relations

Charles R. Butcher and Ryan D. Griffiths

How should research in Historical International Relations be carried out? Our task in this chapter is to discuss the advantages and disadvantages, as well as the opportunities, of taking a quantitative approach to Historical IR. Although we do not claim that the application of quantitative methods is the best way to conduct this research, we do argue that it can make substantive contributions. As the Editors have noted, there has been a recent increase in IR work with a historical dimension. Quantitative approaches are an important part of that turn.

It is useful to sort out two terms at the start. The first, 'Historical IR' has received a thorough treatment in this volume. For our part, we see it as IR's way of understanding history, an analysis of international relations of the past using concepts and approaches that are common to IR scholarship more generally. The second term is 'quantitative', and this is where our chapter offers a more specific discussion. While IR scholars often draw a distinction between qualitative and quantitative research, both approaches share an underlying logic of inference (King, Keohane, and Verba, 1994). The difference is more stylistic given that quantitative research utilizes numbers – at least more explicitly than qualitative work – and typically involves the use of statistical techniques and/or game theory. The boundaries between these two approaches are quite often blurred, and scholars frequently combine historiographical and interpretivist methods with quantitative data (Keene, 2014; de Carvalho, 2016), but scholars can usually see the difference.

Our goal in this chapter is to map out the quantitative approaches to Historical IR. We begin by discussing how the topic has been treated to date, and outlining the challenges inherent in the quantitative approach. We then develop what we see as a space wherein quantitative work can make an important contribution: namely, the move towards a more comparative and trans-regional focus in historical IR.

A brief history of quantitative Historical IR

The quantitative work in Historical IR, like IR research in general, can be divided roughly by whether the researchers are using statistics or game theory/formal theory. Both are methodological approaches that fall under the umbrella of quantitative research. Work using statistics is data-driven – in fact, it depends on the availability of useful data – and it looks for patterns among data. In contrast, formal game theoretic work can be done in the absence of comprehensive data. Instead, it utilizes mathematical models of reality, often quite abstract, to explain outcomes under specified conditions. Although statistical research tends to be more inductive while formal modelling is more deductive, in practice researchers typically employ both forms of reasoning. Indeed, some of the best work in IR combines both methods, often with other more qualitative approaches.

The work in Historical IR using statistics began in many ways with projects like the Correlates of War (COW). Started in 1963 by J. David Singer at the University of Michigan, COW has developed into a family of roughly a dozen datasets on issues pertaining to conflict, trade, and territorial exchange, among others. These datasets and the vast body of quantitative based on them are historical insofar as the datasets typically reach back to 1816 at the end of the Napoleonic Wars. Scholars using these data have 200 years of IR history to examine, leading to foundational work on, for example, interstate war (Geller and Singer, 1998; Sarkees and Wayman, 2010), the democratic peace (Russett and Oneal, 2001), and trade (Mansfield, 1995; Barbieri, 1996). Gradually, other data projects like Polity, Minorities at Risk (MAR), and the Uppsala Conflict Data Program (UCDP) were developed and helped expand the range of potential quantitative work (Gleditsch et al., 2002; Minorities at Risk Project, 2009). Similarly, the work in Historical IR using formal models and game theory is also noteworthy, although perhaps less common. It includes work on state formation (Alesina and Spolaore, 2003), institutions and economic development (Levi, 1989; Acemoglu and Robinson, 2005), and interstate war (Fearon, 1995; Butcher and Griffiths, 2018, 2020), among others.

Is it accurate to say that this work is Historical IR? After all, many of these scholars come from different fields like economics and might be surprised to find themselves placed in the Historical IR camp. Moreover, there is a sense in which Historical IR grew out of history studies, or is at least a close sibling, and quantitative methods like linear regression and game theory came to seem alien (see also de Carvalho, Costa Lopez, and Leira, 2021). Nevertheless, if one uses COW conflict data to study interstate war in the 1800s, then it is, by our terms, Historical IR. If one develops a formal model of premodern state formation, it can be classified as Historical IR. These are commonly studied topics in historical IR; it is the methods that differ.

Are quantitative methods less common in Historical IR than other areas of IR and political science? Although we have no hard data to back this up, we believe on a rather observational basis that the answer is yes. One reason for this difference has to do with data availability. For those using COW and competing data sets, it is difficult to study international relations prior to 1816, at least using statistical techniques. For obvious reasons related to historical record keeping, data projects struggle to collect accurate and comprehensive data in earlier periods, and the challenges generally increase the further back we look (see also Denemark, 2021). Time presents a kind of bulwark to data-driven Historical IR. Nevertheless, some of the most fascinating work in quantitative, data-driven Historical IR has looked back centuries to examine topics related to state formation (de Carvalho, 2016; Blaydes and Paik, 2016), economic development (Acemoglu and Robinson, 2005; Fenske, 2013; Blaydes and Chaney, 2013), and the legacy of historical conflict (Besley and Reynal-Querol, 2014; Wig, 2016; Paine, 2019).

A different challenge has to do with the use and generalizability of concepts over time (see also Kessler, 2021). For example, when we discuss interstate war in the post-1945 period, we can have a fair amount of confidence that we are talking about similar units – that is, sovereign states that are full members of the United Nations (UN). But if we are talking about interstate war in the Chinese Warring States Period, or Ancient India, or the European Middle Ages, then we have less confidence in the equivalence of our types. After all, what is a state, and how does it differ from other political forms like empires and city-states (Modelski, 1964; Tilly, 1992; Spruyt, 1994; Hui, 2005; Nexon, 2009)? This problem is even more salient once we begin to compare regions over time. Data collection requires not only records, but also clearly defined categories and types.

The complexity of sociopolitical life across history makes that difficult. Likewise, this presents a problem to formal modellers because they need clear concepts that can be applied across a given domain. Therefore, a formal model of state formation across time and space would need a concept of the state that extended across time and space.

It is important to note that these challenges also apply to qualitative work in Historical IR. A detailed analysis of interstate relations in 15th-century East Asia will depend on good records. Comparing units within that system will require robust concepts, and they will have to be more robust still if we want to compare that system with others in Southeast Asia, South Asia, West Africa, etc. We believe that this is one of the reasons that Historical IR has tended to focus on specific regions or specific political units and steer somewhat clear of the universalizing theory that is common in mainstream IR. Here, you can see the influence of the field of history and the practice of historiography on Historical IR. However, like the recent development of the subfield of global history, we see a current trend in Historical IR towards the comparison of systems and regions across space. As we discuss in the next section, this is one area where quantitative approaches can help.

Data, concepts, and Historical IR

This is an exciting time for Historical IR given the burgeoning scholarship on non-Western and pre-modern state systems and regional orders (Hui, 2005; Nexon, 2009; Kang, 2010; Phillips, 2011; Ringmar, 2012; Donnelly, 2012; Branch, 2014; Besley and Reynal, 2014; Møller, 2014; Suzuki, Zhang, and Quirk, 2014; Keene, 2014; Phillips and Sharman, 2015; Butcher and Griffiths, 2015; Buzan and Lawson, 2015; Kwan, 2016; Zarakol, 2017; Mackay, 2018; Nedal and Nexon, 2019, see also Quirk, 2021; Suzuki, 2021). This interest follows partly from a belief that past research has relied too heavily on the European experience of political development and neglected other areas of the world. In his call for a new agenda for international studies, Amitav Acharya argued that we need to examine non-European regional systems and orders and include societies that have hitherto been ignored (Acharya, 2014: 647–649). We contend that quantitative IR can make a valuable contribution to this turn by constructing comprehensive data using concepts that have historical reach.

At first glance, this is not so apparent, because quantitative IR is guilty of the same Eurocentrism that Acharya is critiquing. Take, for example, the COW family of data sets that are keyed to a core COW list of states in existence since 1816. Figure 50.1 shows the number of states according to that list for the pre-League of Nations period (1816–1919) and their approximate locations in relation to contemporary states. One would get the impression from this figure that the African continent was stateless, as was South Asia, Southeast Asia, and the Pacific. Yet, historical sources point to numerous state-like entities in these regions (Wilks, 1975; Tambiah, 1977; Herbst, 2000; Oliver and Atmore, 2001; Kang, 2010; Ringmar, 2012; Fenske, 2013; Besley and Reynal-Querol, 2014; Phillips and Sharman, 2015; Wig, 2016).

The regions appear empty because of the criteria used by COW to identify states in the pre-1920 era, before the League of the Nations. For an entity to qualify as a state in the COW registered during this period, it needed to satisfy both of the following conditions: (1) possess a population of at least 500,000 people and (2) receive diplomatic representation by France and Britain at the level of *charge d'affaires* or higher (Correlates of War Project, 2017). The purpose behind these criteria was to identify viable states that were internationally recognized – population size and diplomatic relations with the British and the French were used as proxies. Notably, the criteria for inclusion in the COW list changed from 1920 onwards, where states were now counted if they had membership in the League of Nations or the UN, or a population of 500,000

Figure 50.1 World map of states in the COW data, 1816–1919

or more and recognition by two or more major powers. As other scholars have noted, these criteria had two important consequences (Gleditsch and Ward, 1999; Bremer and Ghosn, 2003; Fazal, 2007; Griffiths and Butcher, 2013; Butcher and Griffiths, 2015, 2017). First, it generated a pre- and post-1920 inconsistency in population size given that small UN-member states like Tuvalu and Nauru with populations just over 10,000 make the COW list, and any state in the pre-1920 period with a population below 500,000 was excluded. Second, it tied international recognition to Britain and France because there were no globe-spanning associations of sovereign states like the League of Nations or the UN prior to 1920, and, as the originators of COW wrote, Britain and France were the two key legitimizers (Singer and Small, 1966: 246).

The downstream consequences of these criteria are fascinating. The architects of COW pinned international recognition in the pre-1920 era to Britain and France because those states maintained thorough records of diplomatic contact, and because they were arguably the core of the expanding European-based international system. But the international system of the 19th century was not fully connected and is better envisaged as a set of regional systems that were gradually drawing together (see also Leira, 2021). Neither Britain nor France had sufficient presence in all regions of the world to recognize states at the required level. For some states that operated independently in a sovereign fashion, France and Britain simply were not the relevant regional powers. For the Luba Kingdom in West Africa, the locally relevant states were Lunda and the Belgians, not Britain or France. In Bali, the relevant powers were the competing local kingdoms and the Dutch. At a basic level, Britain and France were simply more likely to recognize states that were geographically closer to them, which is perhaps one of the reasons for why China and Japan did not join the system, according to COW, until 1860. Importantly, diplomatic recognition is a strategic act (Teorell, 2017), and by conditioning statehood on the diplomatic practices of France and Britain, the biases and selection processes of French and British diplomats were encoded into the DNA of COW. As a thought experiment, consider that the COW list and the family of COW data sets keyed to it have formed the backbone of quantitative research in IR. Would that research have derived substantially different conclusions on a range of topics if the designers had pinned diplomatic relations not to Britain and France, but to China and the Ottoman Porte?

Although readers who are sceptical of quantitative methods may be rolling their eyes at this point, we see the contribution of COW as a kind of first cut at cataloguing states around the world since the early 1800s. There is a Eurocentric focus in the project, but, of course, the same bias exists in many other influential works in Historical IR (Gilpin, 1981; Tilly, 1992; Spruyt, 1994; Mearsheimer, 2001). Like the rest of Historical IR, the quantitative approaches have been taking up Acharya's challenge, even before he offered it (Acharya, 2014). For example, Gleditsch and Michael Ward (GW) were two of the first scholars to construct an historical state list using recognition criteria not pinned to European states (Gleditsch and Ward, 1999), and there have been more regionally focused efforts at identifying historical states (Besley and Reynal-Querol, 2014; Wig, 2016; Paine, 2019). In doing so, these authors were able to bring into the analysis of states that had previously been neglected.

We have joined this effort with the introduction of the International System(s) Dataset (ISD). Version 1 was published in 2013 (Griffiths and Butcher, 2013), and version 2 is the basis of a current book project. Our aim with these data was to move beyond the Eurocentric bias that sits at the heart of traditional quantitative IR scholarship, best signified by COW, and enable a more systematic investigation into precolonial, non-Western state systems that have largely been neglected. In doing so, we could provide a more accurate understanding of the development of the international system over the last two centuries and give scholars the tools to pursue a range of research topics such as the historical importance of state borders and boundaries, the practices surrounding recognition (Fabry, 2010; Visoka, 2022), and the frequency and intensity of conflict across regions.

To qualify as a state in the ISD, a political entity needs to have (1) a population of at least 10,000;[1] (2) autonomy over a specific territory; and (3) sovereignty that is either uncontested or acknowledged by the relevant international actors. These criteria reflect the conception of statehood at the heart of the ISD. Sovereignty has an internal and external dimension. Internally, states stand at the top of a hierarchy and are force-wielding organizations. In the ideal form, states possess a complete monopoly on the use of physical force within their borders (Weber, 1946). Externally, a sovereign state has recognized, formal control over its foreign relations. By using criteria that stresses the importance of internal and external control, we are following a well-charted path in Historical IR and IR more generally (Waltz, 1979; Spruyt, 1994; Ruggie, 1998; Krasner, 1999; Buzan and Little, 2000; Lake, 2009; Branch, 2014; see also de Carvalho, 2021).

Those who have created data sets know that the organizing criteria constitute a theoretical vision of a phenomenon. In our case, that phenomenon is the state. We have elaborated our criteria elsewhere (Griffiths and Butcher, 2013; Butcher and Griffiths, 2017), but let us draw attention to the third criterion: that sovereignty is either uncontested or acknowledged by the relevant international actors. Here, our purpose was to avoid the Eurocentric bias in COW and develop the concept of sufficient recognition. For a period until the late 1800s, Japan existed in a relatively hermetic condition with few diplomatic linkages, but its sovereign independence was uncontested. Others, like Nicaragua, engaged in diplomatic relations and were regarded by their neighbours as sovereign, but just not with both Britain and France. By taking a regionally sensitive approach, we can ascertain whether sufficient recognition was achieved by the polity in question. Accordingly, we define the relevant international actors as those states which, for all practical purposes, are the key legitimizers of the state in question. The general disconnectedness and gradual development of the international system prior to 1920 renders it problematic to make any one state the key legitimizer. While the key actors can vary depending on context, we argue (and have found) that they are always identifiable.

It is important to pause and recognize the challenge of applying concepts across diverse historical and geographical contexts. As Wittgenstein put it, 'every word has a different character in

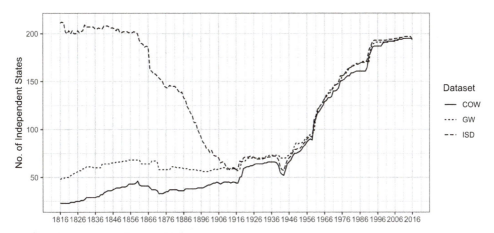

Figure 50.2   Independent states according to ISD, COW, and GW, 1816–2016

different contexts' (Wittgenstein, 2001: 181). Using words like 'state' or 'sovereignty' and claiming that they travel across contexts is a move that some will challenge. Although we offer a defence for our project elsewhere (Butcher and Griffiths, 2017), this is a critique that can be levelled at both quantitative and qualitative Historical IR in general. Nevertheless, scholars working in these areas tend to calibrate the depth of their concepts with their reach. Concepts that aim to capture a specific locale can afford to be highly contextualized; conversely, for concepts to travel, they cannot be rooted too deeply in a specific context.

Using our theoretical concepts and related data, we have been able to showcase a much more accurate portrait of the international system since 1816. As Figure 50.2 illustrates, the ISD Version 2 shows a very different picture of how the number of states around the world has changed over time, compared to the COW and GW lists. The three data sets are very similar from 1920 onwards and vary only slightly in relation to different rules around the inclusion of microstates and how periods of occupation are dealt with. However, the picture is altogether different in the pre-1920 era. Whereas COW identifies 23 states in 1816 and GW list 47, the ISD discovered 211. When taking the entire pre-1920 period as a whole, the ISD identifies 315 states, roughly 14 times the number of states in COW and 7 times the number in GW. Most of these states existed in the arc of territory stretching from Africa up through Central and South Asia and down to Southeast Asia. This is a vastly different picture of the international system, one that shows a concave trend to the number of states over time, rather than one in which the number has been gradually increasing. To some extent, the distance between the two trends in the early 1800s, particularly where COW is concerned, is a legacy of the Eurocentric bias in IR research.

We maintain that data sets like this are extremely useful for Historical IR. For example, our data permits a comparison of the densities of precolonial states systems around the world. Figure 50.3 shows the number of ISD-identified states that existed within what are now the boundaries of a contemporary sovereign state. Standouts include Nigeria, Indonesia, and, of course, India. These states were once the locations of regional systems.

Data sets of this type are essential for answering large global questions like whether war is declining. This is a contested topic, and one that is important for Historical IR. Recent works have recognized that understanding whether the probability of war has declined also requires accounting for the number of units with the potential to initiate or participate in conflict (Pinker, 2011; Fazal, 2014; Clauset, 2018; Braumoeller, 2019). Observing more wars in the past could be a consequence of a higher probability of war, but it also could be a function of incomplete data. In

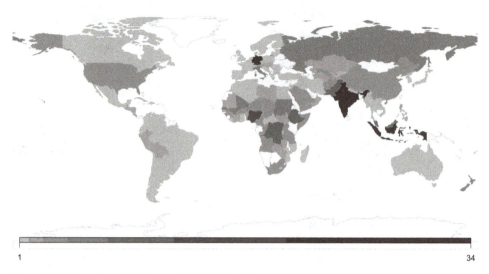

Figure 50.3 A number of ISD states, 1816–1920, within contemporary states

the same way that it is inaccurate to judge the likelihood of contracting a disease among two differently sized communities by looking only at the number of people who get the disease without adjusting for how many people there are in each community, it is also inaccurate to infer changes in the baseline probability of war by looking only at the number of wars.

Figure 50.4 illustrates the number of interstate conflicts per year depending on the state list used. Here, conflict data is taken from the Brecke conflict catalogue (Brecke, 1999). Using the COW data would lead us to conclude that the frequency of war (wars per state-year) has dropped sharply since the 19th century. Adjustments using the GW list suggest that armed conflicts were more common before World War II, after which the incidence fell. Adjusting for ISD states shows a more static picture in which the per-state war incidence was actually higher in the 1990s than it was in 1850. To be sure, we do not intend this to be the final word on whether war is declining. Rather, our point is simply that this debate can only be resolved with accurate, comprehensive data.

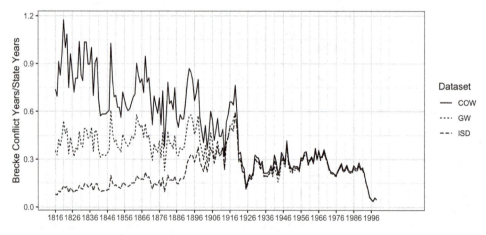

Figure 50.4 Armed conflicts per state-year, ISD, COW, and GW, 1816–1999

Conclusion

We do not claim that quantitative approaches will be applicable to all areas of Historical IR. Indeed, some scholars researching Historical IR will reject the positivist assumptions that underlie the approach, or the attempt to define, measure, and quantify sociopolitical phenomena across diverse settings. Some work in Historical IR will be more interpretivist or more historiographical and/or require deeper and more specific investigations into a given locale. Fair enough. For Historical IR to thrive, it should be inclusive and accommodate different approaches depending on the question at hand.

However, as we outline in a recent article (Butcher and Griffiths, 2017), one aspiration of the New Agenda is to engage in the comparative analysis of historical regions. For example, in their analysis of political order in the early modern Indian Ocean basin, Andrew Phillips and Jason Sharman showed how different institutional forms could co-exist (Phillips and Sharman, 2015). They naturally compared their findings to Hendrik Spruyt's earlier work that found institutional convergence, rather than enduring diversity, in early modern Europe (Spruyt, 1994). These sorts of comparisons, and the studies on which they are based, strike at deep themes in Historical IR regarding variation in political development over time. They are sure to advance the subfield. But they require theoretical frameworks for comparison and data to compare. This is one of the many areas in which quantitative approaches can contribute to Historical IR.

Suggestions for further reading

Acharya, A. (2014). Global international relations (IR) and regional worlds: a new agenda for international studies. *International Studies Quarterly*, 58 (4), 647–659.

Blaydes, L., and Paik, C. (2016). The impact of Holy Land Crusades on state formation: war mobilization, trade integration, and political development in medieval Europe. *International Organization*, 70 (3), 551–586.

Butcher, C., and Griffiths, R. (2017). Between Eurocentrism and Babel: a framework for the analysis of states, state systems, and international orders. *International Studies Quarterly*, 61 (2), 328–336.

Butcher, C., and Griffiths, R. (2020). States and their international relations since 1816: introducing version 2 of the International System(s) Dataset (ISD). *International Interactions*, 46 (2), 291–308.

Butcher, C., and Griffiths, R. (2020). War, interaction capacity, and the structures of state systems. *International Theory*, (forthcoming). Viewed on 20 October 2020, <https://doi.org/10.1017/S1752971920000019>.

de Carvalho, B. (2016). The making of the political subject: subjects and territory in the formation of states. *Theory and Society*, 45 (1), 57–88.

Keene, E. (2014). The standard of 'civilisation', the expansion thesis and the 19th-century international social space. *Millenium*, 42 (3), 651–673.

Paine, J. (2019). Ethnic violence in Africa: destructive legacies of pre-colonial states. *International Organization*, 73 (3), 645–684.

Note

1 In ISD Version 1, the population floor was 100,000.

References

Acemoglu, D., and Robinson, J. A. (2005). *Economic Origins of Dictatorship and Democracy*. Cambridge: Cambridge University Press.

Acharya, A. (2014). Global international relations (IR) and regional worlds: a new agenda for international studies. *International Studies Quarterly*, 58 (4), 647–659.

Alesina, A., and Spolaore, E. (2003). *The Size of Nations*. Cambridge, MA: MIT University Press.

Barbieri, K. (1996). Economic interdependence: a path to peace or a source of interstate conflict? *Journal of Peace Research*, 33 (1), 29–49.

Besley, T., and Reynal-Querol, M. (2014). The legacy of historical conflict: evidence from Africa. *American Political Science Review*, 108 (2), 319–336.

Blaydes, L, and Chaney, E. (2013). The feudal revolution and Europe's rise: political divergence of the Christian West and the Muslim World before 1500 CE. *American Political Science Review*, 107 (1), 16–34.

Blaydes, L., and Paik, C. (2016). The impact of Holy Land Crusades on state formation: war mobilization, trade integration, and political development in medieval Europe. *International Organization*, 70 (3), 551–586.

Branch, J. (2014). *The Cartographic State: Maps, Territory, and the Origins of Sovereignty*. Cambridge: Cambridge University Press.

Braumoeller, B. (2019). *Only the Dead: The Persistence of War in the Modern Age*. Oxford: Oxford University Press.

Brecke, P. (1999). Violent Conflicts 1400 AD to the Present in Different Regions of the World. In: 1999 Meeting of the Peace Science Society, Unpublished Manuscript.

Bremer, S., and Ghosn, F. (2003). Defining states: reconsiderations and recommendations. *Conflict Management and Peace Science*, 20 (1), 21–41.

Butcher, C., and Griffiths, R. (2015). Alternative international systems? System structure and violent conflict in 19th century West Africa, Southeast Asia, and South Asia. *Review of International Studies*, 41 (4), 715–737.

Butcher, C., and Griffiths, R. (2017). Between Eurocentrism and Babel: a framework for the analysis of states, state systems, and international orders. *International Studies Quarterly*, 61 (2), 328–336.

Butcher, C., and Griffiths, R. (2018). War and variation in the structure of historical international systems: a theoretical model. In: M. Hall, J. Bartelson, and J. Teorell, eds., *De-Centering State-Making: Historical and Geographical Perspectives*, Cheltenham: Edward Elgar.

Butcher, C., and Griffiths, R. (2020). War, interaction capacity, and the structures of state systems. *International Theory*, (forthcoming). Viewed on 20 October 2020, <https://doi.org/10.1017/S1752971920000019>.

Buzan, B., and Lawson, G. (2015). *The Global Transformation: History, Modernity and the Making of International Relations*. Cambridge: Cambridge University Press.

Buzan, B., and Little, R. (2000). *International Systems in World History: Remaking the Study of International Relations*. Oxford: Oxford University Press.

Clauset, A. (2018). Trends and fluctuations in the severity of interstate wars. *Science Advances*, 4 (2), eaao3580.

Correlates of War Project. (2017). State System Membership List, v2016. Online. Viewed on 20 October 2020, <http://correlatesofwar.org>.

de Carvalho, B. (2021). Sovereignty in historical international relations: trajectories, challenges and implications. In de Carvalho, B., Costa Lopez, J., & Leira, H., eds. *Routledge Handbook of Historical International Relations*. Abingdon: Routledge.

de Carvalho, B. (2016). The making of the political subject: subjects and territory in the formation of states. *Theory and Society*, 45 (1), 57–88.

de Carvalho, B., Costa Lopez, J., and Leira, H. (2021). Introduction: Historical International Relations. In de Carvalho, B., Costa Lopez, J., & Leira, H., eds. *Routledge Handbook of Historical International Relations*. Abingdon: Routledge.

Denemark, R. (2021). World-Systems Analysis: Past Trajectories and Future Prospects. In de Carvalho, B., Costa Lopez, J., & Leira, H., eds. *Routledge Handbook of Historical International Relations*. Abingdon: Routledge.

Donnelly, J. (2012). The elements of the structures of international systems. *International Organization*, 66 (4), 609–644.

Fabry, M. (2010). *Recognizing States: International Society and the Establishment of New States Since 1776*. Oxford: Oxford University Press.

Fazal, T. (2007). *State Death: The Politics and Geography of Conquest, Occupation, and Annexation*. Princeton, NJ: Princeton University Press.

Fazal, T. (2014). Dead wrong? Battle deaths, military medicine, and exaggerated reports of war's demise. *International Security*, 39 (1), 95–125.

Fearon, J. (1995). Rationalist explanations for war. *International Organization*, 49 (3), 379–414.

Fenske, J. (2013). Does land abundance explain African institutions? *The Economic Journal*, 123 (573), 1363–1390.

Geller, D. S., and Singer, J. D. (1998). *Nations at War: A Scientific Study of International Conflict*. Cambridge: Cambridge University Press.

Gilpin, R. (1981). *War and Change in World Politics*. Cambridge: Cambridge University Press.

Gleditsch, K., and Ward, M. (1999). A revised list of independent states since the congress of Vienna. *International Interactions*, 25 (4), 393–413.

Gleditsch, N. P., Wallensteen, P., Eriksson, M., Sollenberg, M., and Strand, H. (2002). Armed conflict 1946-2001: a new dataset. *Journal of Peace Research*, 39 (5), 615–637.

Griffiths, R., and Butcher, C. (2013). Introducing the International System(s) Dataset (ISD), 1816–2011. *International Interactions*, 39 (5), 748–768.

Herbst, J. (2000). *States and Power in Africa: Comparative Lessons in Authority and Control*. Princeton, NJ: Princeton University Press.

Hui, V. (2005). *War and State Formation in Ancient China and Early Modern Europe*. Cambridge: Cambridge University Press.

Kang, D. (2010). *East Asia Before the West: Five Centuries of Trade and Tribute*. New York, NY: Columbia University Press.

Keene, E. (2014). The standard of 'civilisation', the expansion thesis and the 19th-century international social space. *Millenium*, 42 (3), 651–673.

Kessler, O. (2021). Conceptual History in International Relations: From Ideology to Social Theory?. In de Carvalho, B., Costa Lopez, J., & Leira, H., eds. *Routledge Handbook of Historical International Relations*. Abingdon: Routledge.

King, G., Keohane, R., and Verba, S. (1994). *Designing Social Inquiry: Scientific Inference in Qualitative Research*. Princeton, NJ: Princeton University Press.

Krasner, S. (1999). *Sovereignty: Organized Hypocrisy*. Princeton, NJ: Princeton University Press.

Kwan, A. (2016). Hierarchy, status, and international society: China and the steppe nomads. *European Journal of International Relations*, 22 (2), 362–383.

Lake, D. (2009). *Hierarchy in International Relations*. Ithaca, NY: Cornell University Press.

Leira, H. (2021). Diplomacy: The World of States and Beyond. In de Carvalho, B., Costa Lopez, J., & Leira, H., eds. *Routledge Handbook of Historical International Relations*. Abingdon: Routledge.

Levi, M. (1989). *Of Rule and Revenue*. Berkeley, CA: University of California Press.

MacKay, J. (2018). Rethinking hierarchies in East Asian historical IR. *Journal of Global Security Studies*, 4 (4), 598–611.

Mansfield, E. (1995). *Power, Trade, and War*. Princeton, NJ: Princeton University Press.

Mearsheimer, J. (2001). *The Tragedy of Great Power Politics*. New York, NY: W.W. Norton and Company.

Minorities at Risk Project. (2009). *Minorities at Risk Dataset*. College Park, MD: Center for International Development and Conflict Management.

Modelski, G. (1964). Foreign policy and international system in the ancient Hindu world. *American Political Science Review*, 58 (3), 549–560.

Nedal, D., and Nexon, D. (2019). Anarchy and authority: international structure, the balance of power, and hierarchy. *Journal of Global Security Studies*, 4 (2), 169–189.

Nexon, D. (2009). *The Struggle for Power in Early Modern Europe: Religious Conflict, Dynastic Empires, and International Change*. Princeton, NJ: Princeton University Press.

Oliver, R., and Atmore, A. (2001). *Medieval Africa, 1250-1800*. Cambridge: Cambridge University Press.

Paine, J. (2019). Ethnic violence in Africa: destructive legacies of pre-colonial states. *International Organization*, 73 (3), 645–684.

Phillips, A. (2011). *War, Religion, and Empire: The Transformation of International Orders*. Cambridge: Cambridge University Press.

Phillips, A., and Sharman, J. (2015). *International Order in Diversity: War, Trade and Rule in the Indian Ocean*. Cambridge: Cambridge University Press.

Pinker, S. (2011). *The Better Angels of Our Nature: Why Violence Has Declined*. New York, NY: Penguin Books.

Quirk, J. (2021). Africa and international history. In de Carvalho, B., Costa Lopez, J., & Leira, H., eds. *Routledge Handbook of Historical International Relations*. Abingdon: Routledge.

Ringmar, E. (2012). Performing international systems: two East-Asian alternatives to the Westphalian order. *International Organization*, 66 (1), 1–26.

Ruggie, J. (1998). *Constructing the World Polity*. New York, NY: Taylor and Francis Group.

Russett, B., and Oneal, J. (2001). *Triangulating Peace: Democracy, Interdependence, and International Organizations*. New York, NY: W.W. Norton and Company.

Sarkees, M. R. and Wayman, F. W. (2010) *Resort to war : a data guide to inter-state, extra-state, intra-state, and non-state wars, 1816-2007*. Washington, D.C.: CQ Press

Singer, J., and Small, M. (1966). The composition and status ordering of the international system: 1815-1940. *World Politics*, 18 (2), 236–282.

Spruyt, H. (1994). *The Sovereign State and its Competitors.* Princeton, NJ: Princeton University Press.

Suzuki, S. (2021). International order in East Asia. In de Carvalho, B., Costa Lopez, J., & Leira, H., eds. *Routledge Handbook of Historical International Relations.* Abingdon: Routledge.

Suzuki, S., Zhang, Y., and Quirk, J., eds. (2014). *International Orders in the Early Modern World: Before the Rise of the West.* London: Routledge.

Tambiah, S. (1977). The galactic polity: the structures of traditional kingdoms in Southeast Asia. *Annals of the New York Academy of Sciences*, 293, 69–97.

Teorell, J. (2017). Rules of Recognition? Explaining Diplomatic Representation in the Long Nineteenth Century. Lund University, Department of Political Science, *STANCE Working Paper Series*, 3.

Tilly, C. (1992). *Coercion, Capital, and European States, AD 990-1992.* Hoboken, NJ: Wiley-Blackwell.

Visoka, G. (2022). *Statehood and Recognition: An Introduction.* London: Routledge.

Waltz, K. (1979). *Theory of International Politics.* Boston, MA: McGraw-Hill.

Weber, M. (1946). Politics as Vocation. In: H.H. Gerth, and W. Mills, eds., *Max Weber: Essays in Sociology*, New York, NY: Oxford University Press.

Wig, T. (2016). Peace from the past: pre-colonial political institutions and civil wars in Africa. *Journal of Peace Research*, 53 (4), 509–524.

Wilks, I. (1975). *Asante in the Nineteenth Century: The Structure and Evolution of a Political Order.* Cambridge: Cambridge University Press.

Wittgenstein, L. (2001 [1953]). *Philosophical Investigations.* New York, NY: Blackwell.

Zarakol, A., ed. (2017). *Hierarchies in World Politics.* Cambridge: Cambridge University Press.

51

CONCEPTUAL HISTORY IN INTERNATIONAL RELATIONS

From ideology to social theory?

Oliver Kessler

Introduction: concepts in IR

While the notion of 'concepts' has been used within International Relations (IR) for considerable time already (e.g. Baldwin, 1997; Buzan, 1984), it was for a long time taken as being unproblematic. The then prevailing positivism, which treated concepts as variables, meant that they were rendered invisible to the theorist's eye (King, Keohane, and Verba, 1994: 12). Meanwhile, the pendulum has changed direction and with the current reign of post-positivist social theories, the very term 'concepts' has started to raise eyebrows within International Theory (Berenskoetter, 2016, 2017; Ish-Shalom, 2021).

An early statement of this changed perception can be found in the advent of the securitisation literature which early on emphasised that security had to be understood as *a concept* and not merely as an empirical fact (Buzan, Waever, and de Wilde, 1998: 8). Something becomes and is turned into a security problem instead of just 'being' one. The very idea of securitisation highlighted that there is a certain *contingency* of whether or not something becomes a security problem. Whether or not the 'concept' of security is performed is not simply a function of some natural or material characteristic, but rather part of political processes themselves. It might be a case in point that the subsequent debate around securitisation did not focus predominantly on the notion of 'security as a concept' (but see Huysmans, 1998), but rather pursued different avenues like the identification of possible criteria for successful securitisation and desecuritisation (e.g. Balsacq, 2005: 171).

This link of concepts to contingency in the formation of objects, facts and meaning of events (Kessler, 2016) already highlights that concepts are irremediably linked to questions of ordering, (non-)knowledge and thus power. Concepts are not neutral devices, but carry inbuilt biases, hierarchies and performative consequences. It thus may come as no surprise that early contributions to the problematisation of concepts have come from scholars critical of positivist social science (see Bartelson, 1995, 2001: 21; Guzzini, 2005: 495; Hobson and Kurki, 2012; Jordheim and Neumann, 2011; Jordheim and Wigen, 2018; Wigen, 2014). For example, Nicholas Onuf (1991) and Friedrich Kratochwil (1995) have both early on inquired into the *conceptual history of sovereignty* to show how the concept came into being and subsequently became part of the 'constitutive' rules of today's language game, a line of thought that raised some debate within more historically minded scholars recently (Costa Lopez and de Carvalho, 2018; Leira, 2017).

It is at this juncture between historical IR and the contingency of and around the use of concepts where *conceptual history* becomes particularly interesting as possible future avenue for those interested in social theory and historical research. Conceptual history in IR is predominantly referred to as *Begriffsgeschichte*, a specific *approach* that gained prominence in Germany after 1945 and that in IR is associated with the work of Reinhart Koselleck.[1] As an introduction to conceptual history for those interested in historical IR, this chapter highlights how conceptual history frames the contingencies, ruptures, and discontinuities of the way our knowledge about the world is being formed. It shows how this approach highlights the discontinuities with the past with the implication that these discontinuities show on the conceptual level. Neither is it possible to project our contemporary concepts onto past events, nor can we take past concepts out of their historical context and simply 'apply' them to current events. Similar to current attempts to show the restricted use and translatability of concepts within the 'worlding beyond the West' literature, conceptual history may allow us to better understand the emergence of the modern mind through the emergence, change and configurations of specific conceptual fields.

At the same time, this chapter highlights that conceptual history becomes with its own particular history and context: *Begriffsgeschichte* emerged and was advanced within right-Hegelian if not even anti-modernist circles in Germany. The relation between their ideology and the key concepts of *Begriffsgeschichte* is still an open question, and thus, further debate is needed about how political projects and agendas align with particular conceptualisations of concepts. In order to pursue this question, this chapter argues that it is necessary to broaden conceptual history from an approach to *a set of questions* around the interdependence or co-evolution of semantic and social change.

In the following, this chapter moves in three steps. It opens with a reconstruction of the ideological origins of this approach in the midst of the German right Hegelian tradition closely linked with the thought of Martin Heidegger and Carl Schmitt. In a second step, this chapter introduces some key terms by Reinhart Koselleck with a focus on *temporalisation of concepts* and the idea of the mid-18th to mid-19th century as a *Sattelzeit*. The very term of Sattelzeit, however, seems to be bound by a certain politics that is prima facie insufficient for historical IR. As the third section then outlines, it is useful to rethink conceptual history as a set of questions which allows historical IR to broaden the perspective and see conceptual history as a problem of social theory that may come in many forms and guises.

Conceptual history before Reinhart Koselleck

Even though *Begriffsgeschichte* as an approach is predominantly associated with the work of Reinhart Koselleck (Koselleck, 1979e, 2000c), Koselleck neither invented the approach nor the term itself. Instead, Koselleck is part of an intellectual field that has a longer pedigree and that is worth looking into in order to better understand Koselleck's presuppositions and hence to better assess the potential promises and pitfalls for a historical IR. The first thing one has to note is that while it is the very philosopher of German *Romanticism* Georg Friedrich Hegel who first formulated the key ideas in his lectures on the history of philosophy (Hegel, 1989 (1836): 39), it is only in post-WWII *Adenauer* West-German Republic that this approach started to become highly influential in its own right (for general discussion: Joas and Vogt, 2011; Müller and Schmieder, 2016).

The *Adenauer* Republic is characterised by a gradual Westernisation of German politics and a general silence about the recent horrors conducted during the *Third Reich*. This ambiguity with its most recent past is also visible in the formation of this approach. For example, both, Martin Heidegger and Carl Schmitt continued to be highly influential in academic circles and were instrumental in advancing this approach. Heidegger's former assistant and regular visitor at *Tödtnauberg*, Hans-Georg Gadamer, in fact elevated *Begriffsgeschichte* to the level of philosophical hermeneutics. In his *Wahrheit und Methode*, his direct response to Heidegger's *Sein und Zeit*, Gadamer outlines that

> We have lost that naive innocence with which traditional concepts were made to serve one's own thinking. Since that time, the attitude of science towards these concepts has become strangely detached, whether it takes them up in a scholarly, not to say self-consciously archaizing way, or treats them as tools. Neither of these satisfies the hermeneutic experience. The conceptual world in which philosophizing develops has already captivated us in the same way that the language in which we live conditions
>
> (Gadamer, 1986 (1960): xxiii–xxiv).

As Gadamer highlights in these sentences, conceptual history as an approach is not simply about the reconstruction of changes in the use of concepts over time. *Conceptual history is not just about the history of concepts*. Instead, conceptual history as part of philosophical hermeneutics is linked to questions of being-in-the-world. It is linked to a very specific critique of modern sciences and instrumental rationality and thus to the limits of thought itself. A point Gadamer makes explicit in *Begriffsgeschichte als Philosophie* (Gadamer, 1970: 151) when he notes that *concepts are the true being*.

It is also Gadamer who, along with Erich Rothacker, took on a leading role in the *institutionalisation* of conceptual history in post-WWII Germany (see Müller and Schmieder, 2016, for a longer historical reconstruction). The German Research Foundation (Deutsche Forschungsgemeinschaft) for example created a special programme for which Gadamer not only took on the leading role but also assembled the group of scholars whose members still today are considered influential scholars in this approach. He also became a leading member of the *Mainzer Akademie der Wissenschaften und der Literatur* that published the leading outlet *Archiv für Begriffsgeschichte*.

Another major impact on conceptual history can be found in the *historical* writings of the 1920s and 1930s in Germany (on politics of history more broadly, see Subotic and Steele, 2021 in this volume). The grandeurs of what later would become *Begriffsgeschichte* like Otto Brunner, Erich Rothacker and Werner Conze were all highly active and influential during the Nazi Era (see Lehmann and Van Horn Melton, 1994; Van Horn Melton, 1996: 21ff). Brunner, for example, was in charge of the Austrian Institute for Historical Research (Österreichisches Institut für Geschichtsforschung) and a collaborator in a Research Institute for the Jewish Question (Forschungsabteilung Judenfrage). It is this context where a reconsideration of existing concepts and their history was of interest for both intellectual but foremost for political reasons.

The politics of historical research in the 1930s can be seen for example in Otto Brunner's *Land und Herrschaft* (Brunner, 1939, for a discussion see: Van Horn Melton, 1996). Following the incisive reconstruction of Van Horn Melton here, at first sight, this book can be read as a critique of how many of his contemporary colleagues were guided by modern (liberal) distinctions in their assessment of past practices. Their projection of contemporary concepts onto historical sources rendered them unable to actually understand medieval institutions and hence politics. For example, it is simply impossible to understand the importance of 'the feud' or 'the house' along modern distinctions of public and private. Neither of those terms existed in our sense. Brunner showed that these concepts operated quite differently in medieval politics where the 'house' was not simply linked to the private exchange (or extraction) of goods but encompassed also questions of government or the adequate 'distance' of relationships. It is only through an adequate reconstruction of the *historical use of concepts at that time* that one can aspire to understand the past.

In a slightly different reading, however, *Land und Herrschaft* is as much an historical inquiry into medieval politics as well as an inquiry into the contours of the 'true' German statehood, a statehood that certainly has nothing in common with democracies of the 1920s, and only finds its true, 'concrete' manifestation in the National Socialist Ideology. Conceptual history hence provided an avenue to 'cleanse' German vocabulary from any impact of Liberalism and the Enlightenment, which were seen as contrary to the 'true' German self. Brunner believed along with Carl Schmitt and many others that the 'new reality' of the Third Reich made it necessary to wipe out all liberal and bourgeois distinctions and concepts from our basic concepts (*Grundbegriffe*). As the Third Reich is the reincarnation of the 'true' Germany, the formation of all socio-political concepts had to align with this new reality in order to also allow Germans to re-become to their true selves.

It is only after the WWII that this folk-history (*Volksgeschichte*) was rewritten as European *social* history where references to *Volk* were simply replaced by *social*. While holding on to conceptual history, his pan-German ideology was written out and replaced by a pan-European one (see in particular van Horn Melton, 1996). Along those new lines and while holding on to the identified discontinuity with the past, the identified ruptures were now linked to the French and Industrial Revolutions which gave rise to 'industrial society' (See Van Horn Melton, 1996: 30), a term that was more in line with the post-WWII Germany and its integration into the West. This network of previously active scholars in the Nazi-Regime and their transformation from folk to social history after the Second World War provided the background in which conceptual history flourished. The key methodological insights around concepts, understanding and discontinuities prevailed while many grandeurs of conceptual history then had to adapt to the new – self-consciously – liberal reality.

Koselleck: the *Geschichtliche Grundbegriffe* and beyond

It is an open and certainly still-to-be-discussed question to what extent this political background is inscribed into the very basic concepts within the approach of conceptual history. While it is important to keep this political dimension in mind, it would be simply false to argue that everybody who is interested in *Begriffsgeschichte*, thereby instantly moves closer to Nazi ideology. At least, in the course of the last 50 years (see Steinmetz, 2007: 174ff), conceptual history has developed into a rich and quite diverse approach whose influence moved from historiography to social theory more broadly. The most prominent avenue was formulated by Reinhart Koselleck who,[2] along with Otto Brunner and Werner Conze, edited the globally appraised *Geschichtliche Grundbegriffe* (GG), a lexicon of eight densely written volumes that traces the discontinuities of our socio-political vocabulary from antiquity to the present. Each entry provides a nuanced presentation of different traditions, national trajectories and in particular the ruptures and discontinuities of their uses. Each article in GG is based on an almost infinite number of references that still today can serve as valuable entry points for historical inquiries. While of course the work of the editors has shifted in the course of the more than 20 years of its completion, it is useful to highlight some of Koselleck's key terms at this point in order to situate his approach within the context as outlined before and thus provide a better understanding of Koselleck's particular approach within it.

The concept of concept

A useful entrance point to the thought of Reinhart Koselleck is his epistemological triangle of word, concept and 'fact' that stands behind the construction of his key concepts.[3] In particular, this triangle helps Koselleck to separate a word from a concept. Words are used in specific contexts for specific purposes and are said to refer to facts.[4] In contrast, a concept 'encompasses' a plurality of experiences and incorporates a variety of theoretical and practical references (Koselleck, 1979d: XXIII). At best, concepts like democracy or capitalism trigger an entire history of arguments, images, and experiences from which they cannot be separated. As a consequence, concepts cannot be *true* in any positivist understanding. Since they encapsulate an entire array of different experiences and hence are 'valid' across situations, their meaning is not fully captured by a correct reference. To disentangle the meaning of concepts hence demands historical reflexivity and *interpretation* of their use in a particular period of time. Conceptual history thus had at the beginning for Koselleck a predominantly methodological function on how to use historical sources: sources have to be interpreted in terms of how language was used at that given period in time (Koselleck, 2000a (1971): 298).

Over the years, Koselleck moved to the position that conceptual history was more a social theory than merely a methodological yardstick, a social theory that was able to trace past political conflicts and constellations around conceptual battles. He developed this thought in his discussion on the Prussians Reform, where he showed that in particular *von Hardenberg* deliberately confused the established aristocracy by mixing names or by replacing *Stand*, a concept where entitlement is inherited and backward-looking, with *Klasse*, an administrative and economic concept inherently forward-looking. Conceptual history as a social theory thus is able to see these societal conflicts and transformations in predominantly temporal terms (see also Jordheim, 2014). The next section will develop this thought in some more detail.

Sattelzeit and temporalisation of concepts

While Koselleck's work can be approached from various angles, this *temporal* dimension provides a useful entry point to capture some of his themes (Koselleck, 1979d: 9; see also Hom, 2021; Guillaume, 2021; both in this volume). One of the key concepts that Koselleck always referred to was *Sattelzeit*. Sattelzeit indicates for Koselleck a time between 1750 and 1850, where a general *acceleration of society* led to a complete reorganisation of the sociopolitical vocabulary. This 'societal' temporality is characterised as a societal transformation from past to future orientation: today, for example, we frame science as the discovery of new knowledge rather than the 'search to the original foundations' which always referred back to the Bible and hence stabilised the celestial authority. We understand today 'revolution' as rapid transformation rather than 'move back' as the Latin word *revolvere* actually implies. According to Koselleck, we can trace a similar temporal shift in concepts like authority, power, hierarchy, sovereignty, the state, the public or any other sociopolitical concept (see Koselleck, 2006: 77ff). These concepts were all decoupled from their past-oriented meaning and are endowed with new meanings that are compatible with a future that is not anymore determined by the apocalypse, but a future that is now perceived to be *open* and unknown.

As intriguing as the assumption of a reconfiguration of the sociopolitical vocabulary is, it is noteworthy that Koselleck never *derived* the concept of *Sattelzeit* from within his own framework: there are explanations of how acceleration occurred (for instance the reduction of travel times), but there is no theoretical argument internal to his approach (instructive here is Koselleck, 1979b): *Sattelzeit* is introduced exogenously and serves more as a heuristic, a postulate that guides and highlights certain tendencies and dynamics, but that was never incorporated into his conceptual framework itself. To derive it internally would have required him to develop a theory of society or social theory which he never did. Without being critical, but being the historian that he was, his conceptual apparatus to describe *social and political* conflicts operates on a somewhat lower level than his discussions on historiography, theory, and 'ontology'.

Consequently, however, the very term of *Sattelzeit* also points to one of the potential limits of Koselleck's approach for IR: for a genuine conceptual history of the international or international relations, the concept of the social or the structural changes of society needs further scrutiny. To simply apply Koselleck's framework risks the danger to secretly presuppose a very European history based on the emergence of modern nation states, which presupposes the discovery of perspective in Renaissance Florence, the Reformation, and the European Revolutions of the 19th century. Within the approach of conceptual history, a genuine conceptual history of the international is missing, even though there are attempts to move in this direction such as the work of Jens Bartelson who has started to reconstruct the way in which unity and difference was articulated over time, for example through *Monarchia* and *Respublica Christiana* (Bartelson, 2009: 108).

Experience and existence

This temporalisation of concepts is a particular way for Koselleck to capture new ways of experiencing or a changed *mode of existence* (also Hoffmann and Lampert, 2010: 212 ff): for one, this temporalisation is linked to the emergence of *collective singulars*. Collective singulars like 'history' or 'progress' were invented in the 18th century and have become *objects* towards which human experience can be directed. While there were only histories in the plural, histories that incorporated certain lessons of lived life, history in the singular is different: it is an object whose regularities and dynamics can be studied in books. History as a singular becomes subject of scientific scrutiny from which is it endowed with rules and notions of progress or decay (Koselleck, 1979a: 40).

At the same time, the continuing acceleration of society produces a widening gap between the 'space of experience' and the 'horizon of expectations' (Koselleck, 1979c: 348ff). The space of experience (*Erfahrungsraum*) refers to the experiences gained through lived life. The 'horizon of expectations' highlights how human beings form and maintain expectations about future developments. Society, for Koselleck, is characterised by a widening gap between the past and the present, between experience and expectations. In particular, the advancement of scientific knowledge and technology constitute two examples where past experiences simply cannot translate into expectations anymore. In both instances, it was previously not even possible to name objects around which now expectations are to be formed. The more society is based on scientific knowledge and technology, the more concepts are not formed on the basis of past experiences, but they increasingly are oriented towards an unknown future. We may think here of our technological vocabulary from 'to google' to 'delete', from 'apps' to 'zooming': concepts that have not emerged or were shaped by past experience, but that have now already become part of daily life yet at the same time already carry their future decay within them; they will be replaced by other concepts that today are unknown but that technological advancement will bring into being.

Through the temporalisation of concepts history, *Begriffsgeschichte* always has one eye on questions of existence and thus in a sense on the pre-predicate, the prelinguistic forms of knowing and being. Past experience is never fully captured by text, but there is a prelinguistic form of experience that constitutes the conditions of possibility for historical inquiry and 'histories'. Contrary to what its very term may suggest, *Begriffsgeschichte* is not confined to the use of concepts through history that then analyses the continuities and discontinuities throughout the centuries, but there is an inbuilt diagnosis of modernity and of human existence (again see Hoffmann and Lampert, 2010): the more the gap widens, the less it is possible to bring the past and the future together for a meaningful present (ibid: 359; also Sebastián and Fuentes, 2006). The less the past is able to inform the present, the more emphasis is given on future developments where the keyword of progress as a collective singular operates (Koselleck, 1979c: 374). The temporalisation of concepts, for Koselleck, thus seems not only to serve the purpose of a diagnosis of the present. The temporalisation of concepts in relation to technology, science and progress seems to be a continuation of Heidegger's critique of modernity, technology and *man* of city life. To what extent conceptual history has an inbuilt reservation towards liberalism and the enlightenment can only be raised as a question here (see Koselleck, 2000b: 97ff). However, it is from here where many of his theoretical inquiries into historiography, hermeneutics and anthropological distinctions (asymmetrical counter-concepts) like before and after, life and death, friend and enemy take off. So the question is important for an assessment of conceptual history and indeed the *politics* of doing conceptual history which leads us now to the last section.

The politics of conceptual history?

For Koselleck, the acceleration of the 19th century leads to a cognitive discontinuity with the past which makes the past unintelligible for us. The very term 'Sattelzeit' is a continuation of the critique of Liberalism and Enlightenment as it was raised by others before him. Here, the impact of Carl Schmitt on his work on *Critique and Crisis* and *The Prussian Reforms* is already well documented. Koselleck shares his critique of the Enlightenment, its use of binaries and the construction of collective singulars. It is also this 'tradition' which leads Koselleck to focus more on philosophical anthropology rather than on social theory. He never developed an account of the social or showed particular interest in a sociological theory of society from where his interest in temporalisation of concepts could derive. There are of course references to the dissolution of *Stände or the rise of the bourgeoisie,* but these phenomena are never developed into a social theory which could point us towards *sociology of knowledge,* i.e. how knowledge formation is linked to questions of power and social inequality. In our pluriverse, this social theory is necessary to capture the coexistence of world views and hence problems of social contingency and reality formation (see Kessler, 2016). Conceptual history, thus, cannot be decoupled also from questions relevant to any International Political Sociology.

This implies that even though conceptual history is a fascinating and inspiring literature, we need to be cautious not to silently buy into a certain political project. Future contributions to conceptual history in IR eventually need to unpack how concept formation, politics and social formations are intertwined. This means that only through a future development of global 'sociology of knowledge' or 'global society' is it possible to free conceptual history from this particular politics and open it to other projects, ideas and in particular non-Western contexts. To advance this agenda, it is useful to reformulate conceptual history as a set of questions within social theory rather than simply a particular approach that carries within it Western (romantic) experiences. Conceptual history as a set of questions then operates in-between notions of politics, society, experience and (temporalisation of) concept formation. As *a problem of* or *set of questions within* social theory, conceptual history thus enters as soon as the problem of discontinuity and the co-dependence of social and semantic change are accepted.

With this redefinition, it is possible to broaden its confines and include other approaches with different political agendas. It is worth remembering, for example, that Michel Foucault similarly wanted to move away from any *history of ideas* (see Foucault, 1969: 177). A tradition of thought, for Foucault, with its resonating concepts of author, tradition, oeuvre and boundaries presupposes a (transcendental) subject whose authority then determines the meaning of texts. According to Foucault, the very idea of continuity and with it the idea of the sovereign subject are at the core of modern discourses from which he wanted to depart. *L'Archéologie du savoir* with its emphasis on discontinuity and plurality rejects the idea of the subject, the author and the assumption that meaning is to be derived from that position.

Foucault de-connects his observations from both the subject and the 'given' object and zooms into this space 'in-between' them, a space where history becomes not associated with the traces of ideas, but with ruptures, discontinuities and an entire reconfiguration of thought, a space where we find the rules and play of discourses. Through the play of the rules and groupings, statements establish discursive formations that allow for the manifestations of objects and sets of practices. It is here, where Foucault also in passing refers to questions of concept formation in the context of the logic of Port Royale (see also Hacking, 1975). The discourse as the ever-changing connectivity of statements hence is not simply a set of texts, but it is a set of practices.

It is also here, where we eventually are able to distil insights for conceptual history. In contrast to the focus on the temporalisation of concepts that we find in Koselleck, Foucault emphasises the changed way in which concepts are connected to 'series', how they are directed against new problems and constitute new practices and institutional arrangements that are discontinuous to previous 'arrangements'. *Conceptual history* along these lines is thus not the history of a concept that increasingly gets refined and purified like positivists and historians of ideas may have it, but its *operation* within different discursive fields, its productive power in practices: the strategies that concepts give rise to but also how concepts structure practices and stand at the boundary of the visible and the sayable, of inclusion and exclusion and hence of those to be heard and those whose who are silenced. A politics of conceptual history therefore cannot simply focus on the use of concepts, but on the implied oppositions, distinctions and separations that are then made operational and are continuously performed within institutions.

Michel Foucault and Reinhart Koselleck could be seen as opposite approaches to the problem of semantic and social change. Both share in a sense an emphasis on discontinuity, ruptures and reorganisations of entire vocabularies, modes of thought or discourses. At the same time, there are important differences in the way they understand history, how they deal with sources and how they organise their material: Koselleck focuses on concepts directly; he does not develop any theory of society or social theory from where key concepts like temporalisation or Sattelzeit could be derived. Foucault highlights the contours and the advent of modern society in the arrangement of the sayable and the visible yet does not particularly pay that much attention to any 'concept of the concept'. He cannot avoid talking about concepts, but it is quite telling that in the subsection with the title 'the Formation of Concepts' within the *Archaeology of Knowledge*, he actually does not talk about concepts themselves. For a historical IR interested in conceptual history, the tension that arises through a juxtaposition of their approaches helps to transform conceptual history from an approach to a set of questions and hence to adapt and explore further questions of concept formation with notions of society and discontinuities.

Conclusion

This chapter provided an introduction to conceptual history as *Begriffsgeschichte* with a particular focus on the contributions of Reinhart Koselleck. This chapter opened the discussion with its ideological origins that links it with the Third Reich and where further debate about discontinuities and continuities after WWII is needed (see Van Horn Merton, 1996, in particular). This is not to say that everyone interested in this approach buys into these early narratives and convictions, but it does want to open the conceptual apparatus of conceptual history for future scrutiny and critical reflection. His notion of *Sattelzeit* does indeed identify processes that had a longer pedigree and which could be read as diminishing the German guilt for the genocide(s) during and in the name of the Third Reich. Hence, to explore the possibility and limits of conceptual history for IR, the associated politics is of particular interest. This chapter showed that through a redefinition of *Begriffsgeschichte* as a set of questions, it is possible to open a debate on the co-dependence of discontinuities and the co-dependence of semantic and social change. As a set of questions, we may find of course inspirations in quite different sources than those outlined here. This chapter in particular pointed to Michel Foucault as a possible juxtaposition to Reinhart Koselleck in order to broaden the range of possible avenues. The point was not to say that Koselleck should have included Foucault's writing in his own, but to allow other approaches interested in the co-constitution of social and semantic change enter the scene. In particular, both could be seen as distinct avenues on how to organise the tensions and interdependencies of the social, history, language and thought in relation to questions of power, institutions and modes of inclusion and exclusion. It is thereby also possible not only to highlight the discontinuities with our pasts, but also to see how concepts operate, how the structure our way of knowing the world and how they are linked to power, knowledge and authority.

Suggestions for further reading

Ball, T., Farr, J., and Hanson, R. L., eds. (1989). *Political Innovation and Conceptual Change*. Cambridge: Cambridge University Press.

Bartelson, J. (2009). *Visions of World Community*. Cambridge: Cambridge University Press.

Koselleck, R. (2004). *Futures Past: On the Semantics of Historical Time*. Translated by K. Tribe. New York, NY: Columbia University Press.

Hacking, I. (1975). *The Emergence of Probability*. Cambridge: Cambridge University Press.

Richter, M. (1995). *On the History of Political and Social Concepts*. Oxford: Oxford University Press.

Notes

1 The so-called *Cambridge School* around Quentin Skinner, J.G.A. Pocock, James Tully, Peter Lasett and John Dunn could equally be seen as a distinct approach in conceptual history that identifies the 'speech acts' in the classics of political theory (Skinner, 2002).

2 Due to well-known page limitations, I cannot deal with further albeit important issues such as concepts as indicators vs. factors and the questions of basic concepts.

3 Koselleck uses the term *Sachverhalt* – for which I was unable to find an adequate translation.

4 As Koselleck notes, concepts and facts stand in a bilateral relationship: one can change independent of the other.

References

Baldwin, D. (1997). The concept of security. *Review of International Studies*, 23 (1), 5–26.

Bartelson, J. (1995). *Genealogy of Sovereignty*. Cambridge: Cambridge University Press.

Bartelson, J. (2001). *Critique of the State*. Cambridge: Cambridge University Press.

Bartelson, J. (2009). *Visions of World Community*. Cambridge: Cambridge University Press.

Berenskoetter, F. (2017). Approaches to Concept Analysis. *Millennium: Journal of International Studies*, 45 (2), 151–173.

Berenskoetter, F., ed. (2016). *Concepts in World Politics*. London: Routledge

Brunner, O. (1939). *Land und Herrschaft: Grundfragen der Territorialen Verfassungsgeschichte Südostdeutschlands im Mittelalter*. München, Wien: Rohrer.

Buzan, B. (1984). Peace, power and security: contending concepts in the study of international relations. *Journal of Peace Research*, 21 (2), 109–125.

Buzan, B., Waever, O., and de Wilde, J. (1998). *Security: A New Framework for Analysis*. London: Lynne Rienner.

Costa Lopez, J., and de Carvalho, B., (2018). The Emergence of Sovereignty: More than a Question of Time. In: Costa Lopez, J., De Carvalho, B., Latham A. A., Zarakol, A., Bartelson, J., and Holm, M. Forum: In the Beginning There was No Word (for it): Terms, Concepts, and Early Sovereignty. *International Studies Review*, 20 (3), 489–519.

Foucault, M. (1969). *L'Archéologie du savoir*. Paris: Gallimard.

Gadamer, H.-G. (1970). Begriffsgeschichte als Philosophie. *Archiv für Begriffsgeschichte*, 14, 137–151.

Gadamer, H.-G. (1986 (1960)). *Wahrheit und Methode*. Gesammelte Werke. Band 1. Tübingen: J.C.B. Mohr.

Guillaume, X. (2021). Historical Periods and the Act of Periodisation. In de Carvalho, B., Costa Lopez, J., & Leira, H., eds. *Routledge Handbook of Historical International Relations*. Abingdon: Routledge.

Guzzini, S. (2005). The concept of power: a constructivist analysis. *Millennium: Journal of International Studies*, 33 (3), 495–521.

Hacking, I. (1975). *The Emergence of Probability*. Cambridge: Cambridge University Press.

Hegel, G. F. (1989 (1836)). *Vorlesungen über die Philosophie der Geschichte. Einleitung. Werke*. Volume 18. Frankfurt/Main: Suhrkamp.

Hobson, C., and Kurki, M., eds. (2012). *The Conceptual Politics of Democracy Promotion*. London: Routledge.

Hoffmann, S.-L., and Lampert, T. (2010). Koselleck, Arendt and the anthropology of historical experience. *History and Theory*, 49 (2), 212–236.

Hom, A. R. (2021). Time and History in International Relations. In de Carvalho, B., Costa Lopez, J., & Leira, H., eds. *Routledge Handbook of Historical International Relations*. Abingdon: Routledge.

Huysmans, J. (1998) Security! What do you mean? From Concept to Thick Signifier. *European Journal of International Relations*, 4(2), 226–255..

Ish-Shalom, P., ed. (2021). *Concepts At Work: On the Linguistic Infrastructure of World Politics*. Ann Arbor, MI: Michigan University Press.

Joas, H., and Vogt, P., eds. (2011). *Begriffene Geschichte*. Frankfurt/Main: Suhrkamp.

Jordheim, H. (2014). Introduction. Multiple times and the work of synchronization. *History and Theory*, 53 (4), 498–518.

Jordheim, H., and Neumann, I. B. (2011). Empire, imperialism and conceptual history. *Journal of International Relations and Development*, 14 (2), 153–185.

Jordheim, H. and Wigen, E. (2018) Conceptual Synchronisation: From Progress to Crisis, *Millennium: Journal of International Studies*, 46(3), 421–439.

Kessler, O. (2016). The contingency of constructivism. *Millennium: Journal of International Studies*, 45 (1), 43–63.

King, G., Keohane, R. O., Verba, S. (1994). *Designing Social Inquiry: Scientific Inference in Qualitative Research*. Princeton, NJ: Princeton University Press.

Koselleck, R. (1979a). Historia Magistra Vitae. Über die Auflösung des Topos im Horizont neuzeitlich bewegter Geschichte. In: R. Koselleck, ed., *Vergangene Zukunft: zur Semantik geschichtlicher Zeiten*, Frankfurt/Main: Suhrkamp, 38–66.

Koselleck, R. (1979b). Begriffsgeschichte und Sozialgeschichte. In: R. Koselleck, ed., *Vergangene Zukunft*, Frankfurt/Main: Suhrkamp, 107–129.

Koselleck, R. (1979c). Erfahrungsraum< und >Erwartungshorizont< – zwei historische Kategorien. In: R. Koselleck, *Vergangene Zukunft: zur Semantik geschichtlicher Zeiten*, Frankfurt/Main: Suhrkamp, 349–375.

Koselleck, R. (1979d). *Vergangene Zukunft: zur Semantik geschichtlicher Zeiten*. Frankfurt/Main: Suhrkamp.

Koselleck, R. (2000a (1971)). Über die Theoriebedürftigkeit der Geschichtswissenschaft. In: R. Koselleck, *Zeitschichten. Studien zur Historik*, Frankfurt/Main: Suhrkamp, 298–316.

Koselleck, R. (2000b). Historik und Hermeneutik. In: R. Koselleck, *Zeitschichten. Studien zur Historik*, Frankfurt/Main: Suhrkamp, 97–118.

Koselleck, R. (2000c). *Zeitschichten*. Frankfurt/Main: Suhrkamp.

Koselleck, R. (2006). Die Verzeitlichung der Begriffe. In: R. Koselleck, *Begriffsgeschichten*, Frankfurt/Main: Suhrkamp, 77–85.

Kratochwil, F. (1995). Sovereignty as Dominium: Is there a Right of Humanitarian Intervention? In: G. M. Lyons, and M. Mastanduno, eds., *Beyond Westphalia? State sovereignty and international intervention*, Baltimore, MD: Johns Hopkins University, 21–42.

Lehmann, H., and Van Horn Melton, J., eds. (1994). *Paths of Continuity: Central European Historiography from the 1930s to the 1950s*. Cambridge: Cambridge University Press.

Leira, H. (2017). A Conceptual History of Diplomacy. In: Constantinou, C., Kerr, P., and Sharp, P., eds., *Sage Handbook on Diplomacy*, London: Sage, 28–38.

Müller, E., and Schmieder, F. (2016). *Begriffsgeschichte und historische Semantik: ein kritisches Kompendium*. Frankfurt/Main: Suhrkamp.

Onuf, N. (1991). Sovereignty: outline of a conceptual history. *Alternatives: Global, Local, Political*, 16 (4), 425–446.

Sebastián, J. F., and Fuentes J. F. (2006). Conceptual history, memory and identity: an interview with Reinhart Koselleck. *Contributions to the History of Concepts*, 2 (1), 99–127.

Skinner, Q. (2002). *Visions of Politics, Volume 1: Regarding Method*. Cambridge: Cambridge University Press.

Steinmetz, W. (2007). Vierzig Jahre Begriffsgeschichte- The State of the Art. In H. Kämper, L. M. Eichinger, eds., *Sprache – Kognition – Kultur. Sprache zwischen mentaler Struktur und kultureller Prägung*, Berlin: De Gruyter, 174–197.

Subotic, J. and Steele, B. J., (2021). History and Memory: Narratives, Micropolitics and Crises. In de Carvalho, B., Costa Lopez, J., & Leira, H., eds. *Routledge Handbook of Historical International Relations*. Abingdon: Routledge.

Van Horn Melton, J. (1996). Otto Brunner and the Ideological Origins of Begriffsgeschichte. In: H. Lehmann, and Richter, M., eds., *The Meaning of Historical Terms and Concepts. New Studies on Begriffsgeschichte*, Washington, DC: Deutsches Historisches Institut, 21–35.

Wigen, E. (2014). Two level language games: international relation as interlingual relations. *European Journal of International Relations*, 21 (2), 427–451.

52

HISTORICAL PERIODS AND THE ACT OF PERIODISATION

Xavier Guillaume

Historical periods are a central part of how the field of International Relations (IR) defines the subject of its analysis but also how it regards itself as a field of analysis.[1] On the one hand, historical periods represent the temporal unfolding of specific (spatial) logics of interactions – say, from the balance of power to Orientalism – among various and differentiated political units in a space that come to define what the international is. They are markers of dynamics researchers in the field of IR are set to uncover and study the evolution (see, for instance, the classical book by Ferguson and Mansbach, 1996, on polities). Moreover, historical periods are the markers of transition between temporally distinguished moments that are given a specific quality, often as chrononymous,[2] e.g. the 'long nineteenth century' (Hobsbawm, 1989 [1987]: 6, 8, 11) or the Cold War, and thus come to define a (largely European and western) space that de facto spills over and come to forcefully – physically, materially, symbolically or epistemically – include the rest of the world. In that sense, historical periods offer an implicit causal reading of the unfolding of history as per their design by a specific conceptual perspective.

On the other hand, historical periods are not simply a referential point the boundaries of which are set outside the writing of history (see de Certeau, 1975); they are not innocent descriptive tools. Quite the contrary, historical periods are constructed and as such offer a window into the practice of that writing in IR. An historical period thus is a *dynamic heuristic device*: what and how is defined a historical period may change. As a construct, a historical period inherently is simplifying and thus requires attention to 'the genesis of its constructions, the plurality of the processes [by which it is constructed], the diversity of the rhythms [that are taken into account to construct them], the complexity of the gazes [behind their construction]' (Gibert, 2014: 7). This is also at work for IR as a discipline or a field of study, since its own periodisation serves as a justification, from its origins to its unfolding, of its own legitimacy as a scholarly endeavour (see Schmidt, 2002; Ashworth, 2014, 2021). Unfortunately, a lack of attention to these dimensions largely is characteristic of Historical IR.

Historical periods are a particular place of contention in IR when 'international relations' takes on the form of homochronism (see Birth, 2008). Homochronism refers to the implicit or explicit conception in IR that only considers that one relevant historical time exists for every various and differentiated political units relevant to it. A first challenge then for IR is to consider whether the role of the field rather is to find ways to make sense of the multiple ways in which histories are written 'in their own terms and according to their own canonical veridicity'; thus seeking to study how they are juxtaposed, entangled, merged, destroyed, emerging, transformed, meeting or ignoring each other (see Bertrand, 2011: esp. 16–20, see also the contributions in Rüsen, 2001). The aim of this chapter is to set some of the parameters of this discussion by first defining what is a historical period as a necessary, but revealing, artifice when writing history. Importantly, historical periods, beyond their historical accuracies and robustness, should be seen as heuristic devices dependant on a scholar's working hypothesis. Working hypothesis are not something that need to be 'tested' in a 'positivist' sense, but rather a series of starting assumptions and premises – from the referent literature to someone's conceptual and critical apparatus – which are central in shaping a historical research's contours and how such research will be written within thus defined temporal boundaries.

I then move to reflect on why Historical IR tends to largely consider 'remarkable' periods – such as economic or systemic ruptures, the different times of the elites or the (Western European) state. Finally, I present some of the challenges and invitations that could be further explored by Historical IR, taking into account that while there are multiple ways in which we can construct historical periods, it is necessary to regard them as 'discontinuous continuities' (Revel, 2004: 2), precisely because we are, as researchers, those heuristically marking their boundaries and significance. History is often seen as a continuous unfolding through changes; this paradox should let us concentrate on how change is, implicitly or explicitly, thought through. Change, and more practically *what* change, is the interpretive key to identify the conceptual tools used to make sense of continuity. The ways by which we explain or understand change actually is key to how we construct a continuity that exists only through the identification of historical objects (events, thoughts, things, phenomena and so on) and their unfolding or evolution through time and how we periodise this.

What is a historical period? On the logic and politics of periodisation

To periodise, that is to say to determine a historical segment bounded by temporal markers of a 'before' and an 'after', is a necessary tool for historians. By cutting time into segments of a length that goes beyond the event, historians have a way to define, organise, hierarchise and select the latter, but also facts, moments, things, individuals or whichever historical objects, and to regroup and associate them in an intelligible order (Gibert, 2014: 7, 9). In the words of World War I historian Antoine Prost, to create a period is 'to substitute to time's elusive continuity, a meaningful structure' (Prost, 1996: 115). This 'meaningful structure' does not exist in isolation; as Stéphane Gibert (2014: 9) notes, its declination necessarily is plural. A historical period is as much defined by its set properties than it is by how it differs from or is in continuity with historical periods coming before and after it. As we will see in the next section, the type of continuities and ruptures Historical IR has focused on speak to how Historical IR has regarded what counts as 'international' history, largely naturalising historical periods (and its referent historical objects, such as the modern European state and its connoted concepts). This is largely the result of a lack of transparency and reflexivity as to the working hypothesis behind such periodisation.

Historical periods, or any concept which entail a specific deployment or evolution in time, while necessary to the work of any researcher, are not natural; they are/should be the source of scholarly justification, discussion, contestation and debate (see also Hom, 2021). One only needs, for instance, to think of specific historical objects (e.g. the state), historical periods themselves (e.g. the Cold War) or of intellectual and political movements (e.g. human rights) and the related debates about their periodisations to be convinced of this. For instance, the development of human rights as an intellectual and political movement is periodised differently by different authors. Hunt (2007) situates it in the 18th century, and even before, as an entrenched ideal that has forced its way as a civilisational process (in an Eliasian sense) in the world, while Moyn (2012) situates it in the 1970s in a time which, while certainly bearing the mark of past ideals, it took a prominence as a last utopia of justice, in a context when the ideals Hunt put forth were long dissipated outside of the revolutions they bore. Periodisation thus is a necessary tool, but it is not a neutral tool as it encapsulates the working hypothesis set to analyse a specific historical object; here namely 'human rights'. A historical period reveals the 'meaning and the value' historians hold about it (Le Goff, 2014: 12–13). If a historical period is a construct, then, the question becomes not why but rather *how* to periodise? As periods are artificial and an attempt at a heuristic rationalisation, they also risk however to be a 'simplification and a flattening of historical reality' (Le Goff, 2010 [2004]: 10–11). Beyond the attribution of a chronology, periods mirror 'an ideology and an imaginary' lying behind them (Le Goff, 2010 [2004]: 11).

Like Le Goff, Kathleen Davis highlights how behind the 'logic of periodisation' and the arbitrary of drawing a 'line through time' (Davis, 2008: 3, 18), there is a *political* logic, a 'political technique' (Davis, 2008: 5, 17), which is not only about defining but also about occluding and reifying (Davis, 2008: 4) the ways by which the present is set. In a thought provoking way, paralleling Paul Veyne's call to organise history not by temporal periods but through their conceptual delineations (Veyne, 1976: 49), Davis states that 'we cannot periodise the past'; in effect, to reflect on periodisation is not so much about asking 'when' was say the middle ages or modernity, but rather 'Where is the Now?' (Davis, 2008: 5). As a political technique, periodisation not only operationalises an occlusion of some histories, but also 'redistributes [the] terms' by which we are able to comprehend them as histories. In others words, a periodisation is reflective of, or rather performing (Davis, 2008: 19), a specific political order. That political order organises and hierarchises, sometimes at the cost of silencing or even denying, how certain actions, subjectivities, political entities or histories are legitimised, whereas other are not.[3] While an important heuristic tool for research, historical periods, as any methodological tool, need to be transparently established and discussed. An clear example of this situation is the elision of the 1791 Haitian revolution in any 'mainstream' reflections about Historical IR, or only paid a lip service, or any theoretical reflection about international relations (see, for instance, Buzan and Lawson, 2013), even though it may be strongly argued as it has been a central factor in the cementing of the western imposed international system in terms of a global colour line, questions of development and security (see Shilliam, 2008).

The next section provides a rapid and, by its limited nature, impressionistic and partial picture of Historical IR in terms of its approach to historical periods and the act of periodisation. Historical periods, because of their embeddedness and their necessary connected articulations, are a window as to how conceptions of continuity and ruptures are at work (Gibert, 2014: 9), at the level of which concepts or whichever historical objects, and thus what predominates as relevant in a specific (sub)field of study. As we will see, Historical IR has tended to privilege certain historical objects (e.g. the modern European state and the western international system) and correlated concepts (e.g. sovereignty, anarchy) as its focus of inquiry. This focus is reflective, I argue, of a lack of transparency in the act of periodisation which, while engaged in perfectly legitimate historical objects and their related working hypothesis, often lacks the historiographic reflexivity at the heart of crafting of historical work.

IR as grand (political) history: the myth of ruptures and exceptional time in Historical International Relations

Periodising necessitates marking off segments of time; such selection enables us to understand the hermeneutic logics behind the act of periodising (Davis, 2008; Gibert, 2014: 10; Le Goff, 2014). Doing so, we can see IR as dominated by the privileging of historical periods concentrating on three broad non-exclusive historical objects: modes of government (e.g. political regimes/ideas and the [anarchic] international system), modes of productions (e.g. capitalism) or modes of destruction (e.g. wars and conflicts). These acts of periodisation tend to privilege rupture as a modality (see Gibert, 2014: 11) in segmenting the past. Furthermore, IR generally takes Europe, or more generally the west, as its starting and ending point, as its conceptual matrix to design and define historical periods (see, for instance, Hobson, 2012). It may seem a paradox to make such claim for IR as one of its central traditions of thought, political realism, in its 'codeword' expression much dominant in IR, seems to privilege historical continuity and universality in so many ways (from its 'units', to its 'mechanics' and 'politics', and its cyclical 'dynamics'). Yet, two things can be said about this possible paradox (following Molloy, 2006). First, our current understanding, our 'codeword' understanding of political realism in its various IR forms is the result of the political technique of periodisation, notably from Kenneth Waltz on, giving us this impression of a compact and unified body of thought, rather than paying attention to its plurality and its nuances. Second, and in consequence, the assumed realist ideals of continuity and universality may less be understood as historical reality than a specific ethos of political action which may take a variety of forms depending on which realist thinker we concentrate on: ruptures and crisis are the reefs upon which such varied ethos are to be tested (see also Larson, 2021).

In Historical IR, this reliance on logics of ruptures and a western conceptual matrix is epitomised in IR by the concept of benchmark dates (Buzan and Lawson, 2012). One of the main issues with this concept is that it assumes a clear rupture between an epoch and another, when it is difficult *in actu* to establish such rupture because 'epochs' are enmeshed in one another (Le Goff, 2014). 'Ruptures are rare. The usual model is the more or less long, the more or less profound, mutation' (Le Goff, 2014: 137). Furthermore, the notion of historical period relies on 'an idea that during a certain period of time, a society, a civilisation, a state, an economy present a coherence, characteristics forming a structure, which, after a while, are undone and are replaced by others, according to a more or less long mutation or a sudden change' (Le Goff, 2010 [2004]: 10). One of the most iconic benchmark dates in IR, acting a rupture between 'periods', is 1648. 1648 and the 'Treaty of Westphalia' have become a mythical benchmark date to mark the entry point of the modern state system as an overarching system of intelligibility about what is the international. The chrononymous Westphalia has become iconic despite the fact that what is commonly assumed to be (re)presented in the two actual treaties – sovereignty, non-intervention or the famous principle of *cuius regio, eius religio* (whose realm, his religion) – is actually not present in it (see Osiander, 2001; de Carvalho et al., 2011). This historical inaccuracy, prevalent in our educational textbooks as well as in our scholarship, highlights the importance of unveiling the act of periodisation and what it theoretically, politically and empirically entails.

Buzan and Lawson's conceptual discussion about how and why benchmark dates are set aims at a less presentist understanding of the international, whence the latter is teleologically read in light of the present, as well as of a less western-centric conceptualisation of it (Buzan and Lawson, 2012: 438–439). Yet, it is striking that their act of periodisation nonetheless remains attached to a conception of history which still replicates a teleological framework as well as a western-centric conception of the international by which Historical IR is read as a macro-history of orthodox historical objects characteristic (for many) of the latter: the European expansion via its crystallisation in a specific political unit – the modern western state – its related ideology – liberal democracy – and economic system – capitalism. The clearest example of this is the privileging of the Russo-Japanese war of 1905 as a benchmark for the non-west to enter the world and modern stage rather than the Haitian revolution of 1791. Japan was already in IR western-logic a state with westernised institutions, westernised international dynamics (it was an empire) and was consciously doing so to compete with the west (see Guillaume, 2011). The principal issue behind this act of periodisation, legitimate in many other ways, is that it hides, behind an effort at conceptualising what benchmark dates are, its own premises by seeking to describe *what are in effect* the key historical international benchmarks, even if layered in stratified importance, rather than presenting them as working hypothesis based on the theoretical and political assumptions behind this conceptualisation.

This is rather predominant in IR which has largely been a history of the exceptional times of politics, concentrating on a type of grand History focusing on macro-historical objects (see Mabee, 2007) – modes of government, their relative modes of productions and modes of destruction – and what is usually read as diplomatic, security, intellectual or great power (systemic or otherwise) history. These objects are connected to their political importance as well as the exceptional times of political, military and economic elites, the intellectual history relative to the latter and/or to these different macro-historical objects.

A typical example of the difficulties of periodisation and its scholarly importance can be illustrated by the historiography of the Cold War, one of the most important chrononymous in IR. As Pierre Grosser (2014) has recently identified, the different interpretations behind what explains the Cold War – from great power rivalries to the clash of modernising politico-economic models – correlate with the different periodisations offered in the historiography of the Cold War. Yet, strikingly IR's take on the Cold War, even from a more 'constructivist' perspective, still privileges a classical, broadly understood, political History to determine what has led to the end of the Cold War or how to periodise it (see the contributions in Tannenwald and Wohlforth, 2005). At the same time, the historiography of the Cold War has moved to expand its horizon from the more traditional 'diplomacy, security and ideology' outlook, much fitting IR as it has usually approached it, to a 'bracing assortment of trans-national and domestic, cultural and social, human rights and media, economic and intellectual history approaches' (Romero, 2014: 686; see also Kwon, 2021). As this should make clear, the act of periodising should thus be read as a challenge but also an invitation to move beyond certain scholarly boundaries for Historical IR.

Challenges and invitations

The act of periodising, therefore, is as much a meaningful an act as is what is periodised itself. This act has faced many criticisms in the field of history and beyond (see Gibert, 2014: 15–21). Some of the most central for Historical IR are the questioning of the ideological frameworks (realism, liberalism, Marxism and other) behind the logics of periodising and how they naturalise rather than problematise (see above), the challenge to western and Eurocentric perspectives and their homochronism, and finally, the recognition of the ahistorical, I would argue anachronistic, qualities of historically driven scholarship (see Ashley on structural realism, but his argument can be extended beyond; Ashley, 1986 [1984]: 290–295). Beyond these challenges however, reflecting on the act of periodisation also offers at least two potential invitations, which I briefly delineate here: first, the most present one for our field, how can we research the 'discontinuous continuities' (Revel, 2004: 2) of multiple histories in light of contemporary connected and global histories; second, how could we shift away from our 'political' historical focus to a 'social' historical one, to historical rhythms rather than (temporal) segments.

One of the first challenges faced by Historical IR in terms of the act of periodisation is homochronism, that is to say to regroup any meaningful historical objects into 'a single all-encompassing set of temporal tropes' (Birth, 2008: 9), e.g. *the* international society. While homocronism does not need to be teleological, which would make it an anachronism (see below), it still tends 'to create a sense of coevalness [which] is consequently an imposition of one historical and culturally contingent, and presently powerful, temporality' (Birth, 2008: 15, 16).

These temporal tropes, in contemporary historical IR, can be such as the state, interstate wars, sovereignty, capitalism, democracy and so on. Homocronism also is related to the structuring of other 'historiographic rationalities' (see Bertrand, 2011: esp. 16–20) into a single temporal rationale through the fold of the (exploring, colonial, imperial, (post-)cold warring) west, the contact of which makes an Other take on meaning and existence (whether it is 1492 and the Americas or the colonial expansion in South East Asia, see Gruzinski, 2017). The issue and invitation here is to move away from a totalising discourse about the international, that it is a single spatio-temporal space that is simply more and more encompassing, even if it might be diverse. Historical IR scholars should strive to clearly unveil and problematise their situatedness, making apparent their historiographic rationality and their working hypothesis, without falling into such totalising discourse (see Douki and Minard, 2007: 21).

Another challenge facing the act of periodising in Historical IR stems from one of the forms homochronism can take: anachronism. Anachronism can be defined as using categories, concepts or chrononymous such as the Renaissance or Westphalia, that would be 'unintelligible to the figures being described' (Rorty et al., 1984: 2) through them. In this sense, anachronism has been and largely continues to constitute how IR conceptualises and treat history as either a stockpile of (past) facts that serve to explicate contemporary explanations or interpretations, based on contemporary concepts about the world, or as an ethical or practical exemplarity serving as an analogy to contemporary events (see, for instance, Walker, 1989: 171). Yet, anachronism, in any case a problematic historical practice, opens up another central challenge in thinking historically, or about history, in Historical IR: how to commensurate between events and facts of the past and our present? How do we hold a conversation with the past (see Rorty et al., 1984)? How do we connect differentiated polities into a historical narrative? How do we avoid anachronism while writing historical *IR* knowing it can take many forms? More broadly, how do/should we engage with the practice of periodisation in Historical IR (see, for instance, Green, 2019, on the 19th century)?

This challenge has been at the heart of a movement to rethink international history as more than a history of the west into the world but a connected or global history (on these conceptions see, for instance, Strayer, 1995; Subrahmanyam, 2007; Sachsenmaier, 2011; Çapan et al., 2021). Here lies a first invitation, in the form of a challenge, for historical IR, whether these global or connected forms of writing history are subsuming historical IR, and if not how to clearly situate the different orientations within the latter in a clear engagement regarding the former. Moreover, what does integrating the insight from connected and global histories mean for IR's own canonical periodisations (see, for instance, Abu-Lughod's challenge of European-centric reading of the international economic system, Abu-Lughod, 1991)?

A second less pressing invitation stems from a previous remark that Historical IR tends to be a *political* history of the international, and that this political reading tends to privilege the elites, states (or their functional and historical equivalents), diplomacy, security, ideology or the means of production and destruction. An invitation would be to design historical periods that are not attached to this political historical IR narrative but rather to a more social history of the international that may not be connected to elites but to the everyday (see Guillaume and Huysmans, 2019). By social history, I follow here Jürgen Kocka's definition which encompasses well the different historiographic traditions (French, German, British, United States and others) broadly related to this term: social history concentrates on 'social structures, processes, and actions in a specific sense (inequality, mobility, classes, strata, ethnicity, gender relations, urbanisation, work and life of different types of people, not just elites), in contrast to other sub-disciplines [of history] like economic history … or the history of ideas' (Kocka, 2003: 21); to which I would add a history of things and objects and thus of material culture (see Lubar and Kingery, 1993). So the question is what a social and/or material culture historical IR would look like and how would it effect the ways by which we can think in terms of historical periods about the international, and at which 'scale'?

Conclusion

Historical periods and the act of periodisation are a 'necessary evil' of our work as historians or historically driven scholars. As heuristic tools, we cannot do without them despite all the issues that are related to their designation, design and performance. As this chapter has highlighted, making use and designing historical periods should work hand in hand with a clear explicitness of the working hypothesis and the conceptual premises behind it. This a central feature to evaluate our craftsmanship (Bloch, 2007 [1949]) as historians or historically driven scholars. 'A period ... is the result of the know-how [*savoir-faire*] of the historian. They must guard from any selective history, only keeping data conforms to their interpretative model, thus creating a sense of ineluctability, hiding the potentialities, incapable to give back to the past the uncertainty of the future' (Gibert, 2014: 9). This is particularly true for Historical IR scholars as they are situated in a field that still largely is ahistorical in its relation to concepts – as we have seen in the prominence of homochronism and anachronism – and still takes what are standpoints from which working hypothesis could be formulated as unifying principles to do [H]istory, and not histories. Taking on the challenges of the act of periodisation and responding to some of its invitations could make Historical IR a much more prominent interlocutor in many social scientific and humanities fields.

Suggestions for further reading

Davis, K. (2008). *Periodisation and Sovereignty. How Ideas of Feudalism and Secularization Govern the Politics of Time*. Philadelphia, PA: University of Pennsylvania Press.
Le Goff, J. (2015 [2014]). *Must We Divide the History in Periods?* New York, NY: Columbia University Press.
Walker, R. B. J. (1989). History and structure in the theory of international relations. *Millennium: Journal of International Studies*, 18 (2), 163–183.

Notes

1 This chapter notably benefited from the comments of the participants of the 2018 EWIS workshop and an EISA panel dedicated to this Handbook. I would also like to thank Julia Costa López, Benjamin de Carvalho, Claire Vergerio and an anonymous reviewer for their comments. All translations, quirks and errors remaining are mine.

2 This qualifying practice can be termed chrononymy, the act of attributing specific characteristics to an historical period by naming it – as a chrononymous – after an individual, a place (Westphalia), a dynasty, an identifiable trait (the *Cold* War), or a temporal marker. Chrononymous usually confers, by its naming, and as does the act of periodising, a stabilising and conventional meaning to a specific artificial definition (see Bacot et al., 2008).

3 Periodisation is an act that opens up a window to analyse what is regarded as relevant, how and by whom: laying bare how and what the *histôr* is witnessing maybe at the cost of losing track of the act of being an 'arbiter' through inquiry, an act never detached to who 'signifies' (Hartog, 2000: 394–395).

References

Abu-Lughod, J. L. (1991). *Before European Hegemony. The World System A.D. 1250-1350*. Oxford: Oxford University Press.
Ashley, R. K. (1986 [1984]). The Poverty of Neorealism. In: R. O. Keohane, ed., *Neorealism and its Critics*, New York, NY: Columbia University Press, 255–300.

Ashworth, L. M. (2014). *A history of International Thought. From the Origins of the Modern State to Academic International Relations*. London: Routledge.

Ashworth, L. M. (2021). Disciplinary Traditions and Debates: The Subject Matters of International Thought. In de Carvalho, B., Costa Lopez, J., & Leira, H., eds. *Routledge Handbook of Historical International Relations*. Abingdon: Routledge.

Bacot, P., Douzou, L., and Honoré, J.-P. (2008). Chrononymes. La politisation du temps. *Mots. Les langages du politique*, 87, 5–12.

Bertrand, R. (2011). *L'histoire à parts égales. Récits d'une rencontre Orient-Occident (XVIᵉ-XVIIᵉ siècle)*. Paris: Seuil.

Birth, K. (2008). The creation of coevalness and the danger of homochronism. *Journal of the Royal Anthropological Institute*, 14 (1), 3–20.

Bloch, M. (2007 [1949]). *Apologie pour l'histoire. Ou Métier d'historien*. Paris: Armand Colin.

Buzan, B., and Lawson, G. (2012). Rethinking benchmark dates in international relations. *European Journal of International Relations*, 20 (2), 437–462.

Buzan, B., and Lawson, G. (2013). The global transformation: the nineteenth century and the making of modern international relations. *International Studies Quarterly*, 57 (3), 620–634.

Çapan, Z. G., dos Reis, F. and Grasten, M., (2021). Global Histories: Connections and Circulations in Historical International Relations. In de Carvalho, B., Costa Lopez, J., & Leira, H., eds. *Routledge Handbook of Historical International Relations*. Abingdon: Routledge.

Davis, K. (2008). *Periodisation and Sovereignty. How Ideas of Feudalism and Secularization Govern the Politics of Time*. Philadelphia, PA: University of Pennsylvania Press.

De Carvalho, B., Leira, H., and Hobson, J. M. (2011). The big bangs of IR: the myth that your teachers still tell you about 1648 and 1919. *Millennium: Journal of International Studies*, 39 (3): 735–758.

De Certeau, M. (1975). *L'écriture de l'histoire*. Paris: Gallimard/nrf.

Douki, C., and Minard, P. (2007). Histoire globale, histoires connectées: un changement d'échelle historiographique? Introduction. *Revue d'histoire moderne et contemporaine*, 54 (4bis), 7–21.

Ferguson, Y. H., and Mansbach, R. W. (1996). *Polities: Authority, identities, and change*. Columbia, SC: University of South Carolina Press.

Gibert, S. (2014). Les enjeux renouvelés d'un problème fondamental: la périodisation en histoire. *ATALA Cultures et sciences humaines*, 17, 7–31.

Green, D. M. (2019). Conclusions: The Value of Our New Historical Narrative. In: D. M. Green, ed., *The Two Worlds of Nineteenth Century International Relations*, London: Routledge.

Grosser, P. (2014). La guerre froide, une périodisation impossible? *ATALA Cultures et sciences humaines*, 17, 149–166.

Gruzinski, S. (2017). *La machine à remonter le temps. Quand l'Europe s'est mise à écrire l'histoire du monde*. Paris: Fayard.

Guillaume, X. (2011). *International Relations and Identity. A Dialogical Approach*. London: Routledge.

Guillaume, X., and Huysmans, J. (2019). The concept of 'the everyday': ephemeral politics and the abundance of life. *Cooperation and Conflict*, 54 (2), 278–296.

Hartog, F. (2000). The invention of history: the pre-history of a concept from Homer to Herodotus. *History and Theory*, 39 (3), 384–395.

Hobsbawm, E. J. (1989 [1987]). *The Age of Empire, 1875–1914*. New York, NY: Vintage Books.

Hobson, J. (2012). *The Eurocentric Conception of World Politics: Western International Theory, 1760–2010*. Cambridge: Cambridge University Press.

Hom, A. R. (2021). Time and History in International Relations. In de Carvalho, B., Costa Lopez, J., & Leira, H., eds. *Routledge Handbook of Historical International Relations*. Abingdon: Routledge.

Hunt, L. (2007). *Inventing Human Rights. A History*. New York, NY: W. W. Norton & Company.

Kocka, J. (2003). Losses, gains and opportunities: social history today. *Journal of Social History*, 37 (1), 21–28.

Larson, D (2021). Realism: Excavating a Historical Tradition. In de Carvalho, B., Costa Lopez, J., & Leira, H., eds. *Routledge Handbook of Historical International Relations*. Abingdon: Routledge.

Le Goff, J. (2010 [2004]). *Un long Moyen Âge*. Paris: Fayard/Pluriel.

Le Goff, J. (2014). *Faut-il vraiment découper l'histoire en tranches?* Paris: Seuil.

Lubar, S., and Kingery, W. D., eds. (1993). *History of Things. Essays on Material Culture*. Washington, DC: Smithsonian Institution Press.

Mabee, B. (2007). Levels and agents, states and people: micro-historical sociological analysis and international relations. *International Politics*, 44 (4), 431–449.

Molloy, S. (2006). *The Hidden History of Realism. A Genealogy of Power Politics*. Basingstoke: Palgrave Macmillan.

Moyn, S. (2012). *The Last Utopia. Human Rights in History*. Cambridge, MA: The Belknap Press of Harvard University Press.

Osiander, A. (2001). Sovereignty, international relations, and the Westphalian myth. *International Organization*, 55 (2), 251–287.

Prost, A. (1996). *Douze leçons sur l'histoire*. Paris: Seuil.

Revel, J. (2004). Michel Foucault: discontinuité de la pensée ou pensée du discontinu? *Le Portique. Revue de philosophie et de sciences humaines*, 13–14, 1–11.

Romero, F. (2014). Cold War historiography at the crossroads. *Cold War History*, 14 (4), 685–703.

Rorty, R., Schneewind, J. B., and Skinner, Q. (1984). Introduction. In: R. Rorty, J. B. Schneewind, and Q. Skinner, eds., *Philosophy in History. Essays in the Historiography of Philosophy*, Cambridge: Cambridge University Press, 1–14.

Rorty, R., Schneewind, J. B., and Skinner, Q., eds. (1984). *Philosophy in history. Essays in the historiography of philosophy*. Cambridge: Cambridge University Press.

Rüsen, J., ed. (2001). *Western Historical Thinking. An Intercultural Debate*. New York, NY: Berghahn Books.

Sachsenmaier, D. (2011). *Global Perspectives on Global History. Theories and Approaches in a Connected World*. Cambridge: Cambridge University Press.

Schmidt, B. C. (2002). On the History and Historiography of International Relations. In: W. Carlsnaes, T. Risse, and B. A. Simmons, eds., *Handbook of International Relations*, London, Sage, 3–22.

Shilliam, R. (2008). What the Haitian Revolution might tell us about development, security, and the politics of race. *Comparative Studies in Society and History*, 50 (3), 778–808.

Strayer, R. W., ed. (1995). *The Making of the Modern World: Connected Histories, Divergent Paths (1500 to the Present)*. 2nd edition. New York, NY: St. Martin's Press.

Subrahmanyam, S. (2007). Holding the world in balance: the connected histories of the Iberian overseas empires, 1500–1640. *American Historical Review*, 112 (5), 1359–1385.

Tannenwald, N., and Wohlforth, W. C. (2005). Introduction: the role of ideas and the end of the Cold War. *Journal of Cold War History*, 7 (2), 3–12.

Veyne, P. (1976). *L'inventaire des différences*. Paris: Seuil.

Walker, R. B. J. (1989). History and structure in the theory of international relations. *Millennium: Journal of International Studies*, 18 (2), 163–183.

PART VI

Afterword

53

AFTERWORD

Ahead to the past

Yale H. Ferguson and Richard W. Mansbach

It is both a privilege and a pleasure to write an Afterword to this pioneering Handbook of more than 50 chapters, produced by a wide range of scholars, all of whom—however, diverse their ages, genders, nationalities, disciplines, and analytical approaches—share a keen interest in and commitment to Historical International Relations (HIR). The Editors in their Introduction tell us that their aim has not been either to offer an overview of what they consider the most important subjects in HIR or of the history of IR. Rather, they have sought to give us a comprehensive look at the 'historical work undertaken by IR scholars over the past two-three decades.' A second intent has been, through the essays, to help set 'the agenda for where different conversations in Historical IR may want to go.' We believe, and are sure readers will agree, that the Editors have succeeded wonderfully well in meeting these ambitious goals.

The road to the 'historical turn'

Our reading and indeed personal experience of the evolution of the relationship between IR and History over the five-plus decades of our own professional careers neatly converges with the short survey of that progression in the Editors' Introduction. The Editors recall that when two of them five years ago edited a four-volume set of literature on HIR, 'it became clear to what extent Historical International Relations, unlike the fantasy of Cormac McCarthy, has, unfortunately largely been a country for (Western-based) old men' (de Carvalho, Costa Lopez, and Leira, 2021). Ferguson and Mansbach actually knew quite a few of those old men as teachers, mentors, friends, and/or university colleagues and many others as our teachers' teachers, fellow conference goers, and/or featured speakers. We are reminded of what passed for humour in our innocent youth: 'A few years ago I couldn't even spell "engineer," and now I *are* one.' Today we have to acknowledge that *we are* Western-based old men, although we must advise you, partner, to smile when you say that.

As the Editors observe, the Anglo-American/Commonwealth discipline of IR 'grew out of a number of academic traditions, including colonial administration, international law, history, and political science' (ibid.). In fact, at the outset, history was the primary inspiration and influence, even in the United States, where IR has always struggled to be recognized as a separate discipline. It was mainly housed in political science departments and taught under such course headings as 'international politics' or 'world politics' and 'US (or another country's) foreign policy.' In the early days, domestic and foreign were generally assumed to be two distinct and separate spheres. Tufts University called its IR school Fletcher School of Law and Diplomacy, and American University labelled theirs School of International Service, but most others settled for School of International Affairs. We shall return shortly to the still dicey 'International Relations' identity problem, as part of a much broader conceptual chaos situation plaguing all the constituent disciplines of IR-History.

The so-called behavioural revolution in US social sciences, not least political science, from the late 1950s well into the 1970s constituted a direct threat to fledgling IR's connection with History, except insofar as History could be mined as a data set. In fact, our own first book together with Donald Lampert, *The Web of World Politics* (Mansbach, Ferguson, and Lampert, 1976) was a quantitative events-data (plus some factor analysis) exploration of the *contemporary* role of non-state actors in world politics. The conclusion that non-state actors had been grossly underestimated seemed overwhelming supported by the data at the time and, of course, today is widely accepted. Although that was our only significant quantitative work, our position on the behavioural/quantitative approach was then and has remained the same: When any such project seems well-conceived, the concepts and theoretical frame are crystal clear, the quantitative method employed is convincing, and sufficient reliable data is available—why not, for those so inclined? Regrettably, those requirement boxes are far too often not ticked, with unfortunate results. Make no mistake: There has always been some excellent quantitative work in IR—for example Jack Levy's (1983) on war—that uses historical data in a responsible way to make important and convincing arguments. Also, to be sure, we who are not of that behavioural/quantitative methodological persuasion have our own glass houses to worry about.

In any event, our personal reading (see also Ferguson and Mansbach, 1988) is that the early 'scientific revolution' in IR—after much professional *Sturm und Drang*—eventually ran out of steam for two fundamental reasons. The first is that, with few exceptions, the prophets of the revolution failed to deliver on their promises; that is, their mountain moved to produce mostly mice. The second is that most British, Commonwealth, and European IR scholars were not converted to the 'scientific' gospel being preached in the United States. Here is where we need to spotlight the English School and not least Hedley Bull (1966) who, in his famous defence of 'the classical approach,' stood boldly on the transatlantic rampants and thundered 'they shall not pass.' In truth, thus far, they never have—not in any great numbers—although recently there has been a small beachhead landing at Oxford. More methodological diversity on the UK/European side of the pond is no doubt entirely healthy, but alas we in the United States are currently experiencing 'déjà vu all over again.' Entirely *un*healthy from our perspective is the fact that a second wave of very intolerant quantifiers has gradually managed to (re)colonize IR in many US political science departments, just when the dominant trend in IR elsewhere in the world has been in a much less 'strict-science' direction.

With the behavioural revolution in retreat, attention in IR theory shifted towards a reconsideration and reworking of traditional paradigms—and then in the late 1970s/early 1980s began an explosion of intellectual diversification and creativity that still shows no signs of abating. On the more traditional side of the activity were neorealism, neoliberalism/liberal institutionalism, and the expanding English School (soon to be simply ES). On the more 'reflective' side emerged constructivists (with very different orientations, e.g. compare Wendt, Kratochwil, Onuf—see also Leira and de Carvalho, 2016; Bruneau, 2021), world-systems analysis (see Denemark, 2021), self-styled 'critical' theorists (e.g. the Frankfurt School), marxists, historical sociologists, poststructuralists, feminist scholarship, postcolonial perspectives, and others. Although for us, 'critical' theory itself has a more specific connotation, the Editors are entirely correct that all of the foregoing were 'critical' in that they directly challenged the ideas and relatively narrow intellectual scope of traditional IR—and implicitly, the dominance of US scholarship. Not for nothing have we ourselves long felt more comfortable in the intellectual company with our United Kingdom, Commonwealth, European, and other colleagues than with many of our US counterparts. As we write, all worldwide surveys of IR theory (of which we are aware) suggest that constructivism has securely established itself as the leading approach in IR theory, although classical realism still seems to hold sway over national policymakers.

History too, of course, has been evolving as a discipline since long before the social sciences and IR found their homes in the academic enterprise. Diplomatic history and historical work on foreign policy and international law were thriving early on, but it is noteworthy how relatively little we have to mention in the global history category until well into the 20th century (Çapan, dos Reis, and Grasten et al., 2021). The reasons are that most specialist historians have been uncomfortable with general history, and most general historians have been Westerners principally concerned with Western history (Herborth and Nitzschner, 2021). The latter limitation has been somewhat mitigated by the facts that the Near East has often been included in accounts of the 'rise of the West' and some historians were also interested in the impact of European empires on their non-Western subjects, a concern that persists (from the recipient perspective) in post-colonial scholarship. A major exception to our observation about Western myopia is scholarship on 'civilizations,' notably Oswald Spengler, Arnold Toynbee, and Fernand Braudel. Toynbee, in turn, was one of the inspirations for global historian William H. McNeill, whose 20-plus books during his long and distinguished career included a biography of Toynbee. McNeill's initial focus was Western civilization but his work became more global over time.

Even as IR was breaking out of its traditional bounds in the late 1970s, 1980s, and beyond, History was also changing, but, in many universities, suffered a decline of enrolment relative to the social sciences and strictly career-oriented courses. Historians themselves reluctantly had to face the fact that History as a discipline was in some danger of no longer being a destination in itself, rather primarily a service industry for other fields of study, even as historical scholarship was actually burgeoning and at an impressive rate. Meanwhile, History departments were trending away from political, foreign policy, and diplomatic history, preferring to focus their new hires in such subfields as social history, cultural history, women, economic history, and also previously neglected countries or regions like Latin America, China, Africa, and the Middle East.

What was happening in History as a discipline was making it all the more attractive to IR scholars as a treasure house of information and data. IR itself had become so much more diverse in terms of constituent disciplines, theories, ethnicity, and gender, as well as more global in subject matter and academic membership. The International Studies (note: *not* Relations) Association (ISA), which started out as a fairly small group of North American IR scholars, skyrocketed in membership (now over 7000 from 110 countries) and established significant relations with an ever-expanding number of similar national and regional associations around the world. As the Editors put it: 'The growing diversity and globalization [of IR] led a number of scholars to look [to History] for theoretical precedents for current positions, and to question the existing meta-narratives' (de Carvalho, Costa Lopez, and Leira, 2021). An increasing number of scholars were 'self-consciously describing their work as historical, and engaging in ever more sophisticated theoretical and empirical historical analyses.' Thus, by the turn of the millennium, 'enough historically oriented scholarship was coming forward to comment on a possible "historical" or "historiographical" turn in [IR].'

There was plenty of significant IR-History scholarship in the decades leading up to the circa millennium 'historical turn,' but in the two decades since, what was once a steady flow of work and publications has become a veritable flood. The sheer abundance is not only extremely heartening but also almost overwhelming. As the Editors state, 'A mere decade ago, a handbook such as this one would have seemed unthinkable.' Five years ago, we noted earlier, two of the Editors (Leira and de Carvalho, 2015) put together a four-volume collection of Historical International Relations literature. Now we have the present Handbook—with over 50 new contributions from IR scholars seriously engaged with History—that its Editors rightly charac-terize as a major 'stock-taking exercise.' Another volume with different editors (Bukovsky, Keene, Spanu, and Reus-Smit) and including both historians and IR scholars, the *Oxford Handbook on History and International Relations*, is also forthcoming. These two handbooks are by no means competing, rather profoundly complementary, and together offer a powerful testimony as to how very far the relationship between IR and History has come to date, as well as intriguing specu-lation about where it might be heading in the years ahead.

There has also been important professional institutional affirmation of the IR-History rela-tionship. Most notably, in 2013, upon the initiative of Benjamin de Carvalho and Halvard Leira, the Historical International Relations Section (HIST) was established in the ISA and soon soared in membership to be one of the larger sections in the ISA. The European International Studies Association (EISA) also now devotes a series of panels to IR-History at its annual meetings. In addition, we should mention the British International Studies Association's (BISA) long-established History and International Relations Working Group, and—although IR is only a small part of its remit—the American Political Science Association's History and Politics Section (formed 1999).

The road beyond the historical turn: issues and opportunities

Unrequited love

The Editors comment in passing that 'this volume makes evident that the different disciplines and activities cannot easily be collapsed unto each other,' which (we are sure they would agree) is a diplomatic understatement. We occasionally think of the rather grand phrase spoken by officials at many university graduation ceremonies, conferring degree X 'with all the rights, responsibilities, privileges and immunities pertaining thereto.' Every discipline claims their own such, but as George Lawson reminded us in his 2010 article that is now a modern classic—'The Eternal Divide? History and International Relations'—few disciplinary relationships have been as fraught with hostility as these two, (in our view) coming mainly but certainly not exclusively from the History side.

A personal story here offers a partial illustration. In the 1990s, given our earlier interest in non-state actors and our long-standing concern about state-centric IR theory, we decided to turn to pre-Westphalian historical experience in search of enduring truths about political forms, their evolution and interaction, and association with human identities. The result was *Polities: Authority, Identities, and Change* (Ferguson and Mansbach, 1996). Our choices of pre-Westphalian systems were ancient Mesopotamia, Greece, China, Mesoamerica, Islam, and Italy after the Roman Empire. In due course, none other than famous macro-historian William McNeill (mentioned earlier), whose work we still admire and use, honoured our book with an extended review (McNeill, 1997: 269–274). Alas, he was not in the best of humour.

McNeill's critique 'seemed' to be a straightforward attack on the way IR political scientists (mis)use history. The authors, he declared, present their theoretical argument in the first two chapters and then devote almost all the rest of the book to illustrating how world politics 'has always involved a crazy quilt of polities–foci of authority of varying domain and influence; dis-tinctive in some respects and overlapping, layered, nested, and linked in others.' He continued, 'Given that they knew exactly what they were looking for, it is not surprising to find that they do indeed discover a "crazy quilt" of competing and "overlapping, layered, nested and linked" polities in each case.' He accuses us of being 'profoundly ahistorical': 'The authors seek general truths about polities and politics, and, sure enough, they find what they expect–a plurality of identities and loyalties in competition with each other everywhere and always.' 'Theory,' he says, 'allowed the authors to create a series of pigeon holes into which they have to fit an impressive variety of information gathered through energetic reading of the best available scholarly accounts dealing with each of the cases they analyze.' The authors 'radically discount chronology' and go so far as to compare different sorts of polities across cases and periods (empires with empires, for instance). McNeill's view was that 'collecting data about horizontal and then about vertical relations among rival polities, is like studying anatomy by describing organs torn from the bodies of different animals–comparing legs with legs, eyes with eyes, and so on–without ever trying to put the parts together into a single, living whole.'

Our first positive reaction to the review (after less charitable thoughts) was, well, at least McNeill couldn't fault us on our sources. Our subsequent thought was, hold on! hasn't McNeill himself regularly ransacked history for the things he expected to find, in order to support the sweeping generalizations he so convincingly advanced? Consider, for example, his books on *Plagues and People* (1976) and *Population and Politics Since 1750* (1990). Then, it dawned on us: perhaps, McNeill's *primary* disagreement with the book was one that he did not acknowledge; that is, our analysis he decried abandons key realist premises. Historian though he was, like all historians, McNeill was also himself a theorist—in this case, a realist—and he was offended to the point of outrage that the 'polities' approach puts a variety of polities and their need to generate multidimensional 'value satisfaction' at the centre of the analysis rather than the familiar realist categories of coercion, armed force, and states. He insisted that 'Ferguson and Mansbach are wrong to suppose that competition among all the diverse kinds of polity that they discovered will not continue to give pride of place to whatever authorities are able to organize and maintain superior armed force.' The Westphalian State is not under threat in the present era, because '[s]o far, no promising alternative to the territorial organization of armed force has even begun to emerge.' His book on *The Pursuit of Power: Technology, Armed Force, and Society Since A.D. 1000* (1982) came out five years later.

So, what is it about this discipline called History, the constituents of which so often seem to feel the need to mount such an aggressive defence. Admittedly, their practitioners have been around since Herodotus, but we, IR Political Science types, can claim Aristotle and Thucydides. Lawson (2010: 211) suggests, 'There is no shortage of ways to think about history: as definitive record, as science, as teacher, as art, as narrative, as happening, as chaos, even as nightmare.' He spotlights two common conceptions of the discipline, history as 'scripture' and as 'butterfly,' that is respectively, a straightforward narrative of 'what happened next' without theoretical speculation and (the butterfly part) 'the tracing of how one-thing-followed-another in the unfolding of events so contingent as to be unrepeatable.' In the latter understanding, 'tides of history have been turned on the minutest of details.'

Lawson (2010: 213) deplores 'disciplinary parlour games' and takes both historians and social scientists to the woodshed for playing 'their part in fostering a disciplinary partition based on apparently eternal distinctions about appropriate levels of abstraction, degrees of causal determinacy and "proper" methods.' He continues, 'Whether understood as scripture versus butterfly or as lumper versus splitter, the result of this failure to communicate is second-order noise masquerading as first order debate.' And he proceeds to discuss four 'ways in which history and social science are co-implicated': 'context, narrative, eventfulness and ideal-typifications.' His is a complex argument that we cannot detail here, but we urge anyone interested in the 'divide' to read it—and a number of closely related chapters in this Handbook.

We have also written elsewhere (Ferguson and Mansbach, 2008) about the divide and even have borrowed a little of that material for this Afterword. Suffice it to say that both of us have had a lifelong love affair with history, cannot imagine doing our own work without historical perspective, and, yes, some of our best friends and colleagues are historians. To those of them who decry 'theory,' we can only rejoin that all analysts are theorists and it is infinitely better to be aware of and honest about one's theoretical inclinations. Every choice an historian makes about which project to undertake speaks volumes about one's opinion (based on what?) that the topic pursued is 'important' or at least 'interesting.' Every generalization or insight that an historian produces is either overtly theoretical or has potential theoretical implications. Therefore, listen up historians, we need to talk, and perhaps we can help you discover your inner theory.

What *exactly* (deliberate choice of word) it is that historians can do for our IR endeavours is also, of course, debatable and indeed the contributors to this Handbook explore that question in a wide variety of intriguing ways. How eager we are to 'know' and long to 'learn' from the past that we are certain is actually 'there' for us to 'read'! As David H. Lowenthal (1985: 4) almost plaintively expresses it, '[We] feel quite sure that the past really happened; its traces and memories reflect undeniable scenes and acts. The airy and insubstantial future may never arrive; man or nature may destroy humanity; time as we know it may end. By contrast, the past is tangible and secure; people think of it as fixed, unalterable, indelibly recorded.' The eminent classicist Moses Finley (1986: 31), who wrote with such apparent authority about ancient Greece and Rome, nonetheless also wrote, 'One can really only know one's own time and that is sufficient anyway. The past can yield nothing more than paradigmatic support for the conclusions one has drawn from the present: the past, in other words, may still be treated in the timeless fashion of myth.'

There remain any number of reasons why historical truth is ever elusive. Every generation reinterprets the past in light of its own experience, the struggle over who controls the archives (literally or figuratively) has practical political and policy consequences, and every individual investigator has one's own personal capabilities and biases. However, as we view it, the fundamental problem has little to do with extreme-relativist postmodern premises about our inability to access 'reality' in any form. To the contrary, we insist there is an abundance of 'true' historical 'facts,' and empirical research is decidedly possible, definitely worth doing—and not least, fun. However, especially when we venture back through the fog of history, we are keenly aware of how difficult, if not impossible, it is to get ourselves attuned to the 'mindset' or 'world view' of the time. Moreover, even for the best-documented time frames, there are major information gaps and serious problems with sources. As for contemporary history, we frequently have to face the opposite challenge of sheer information overload.

At the end, there is the perennial and really killer central issue of interpretation, what our facts 'mean.' Here historian and IR-inclined social scientist both stand under the same wide sky and have numerous common concerns, whether commonly acknowledged or not. All we can do here is mention three examples.

Common concerns

Let us go first to what we term 'conceptual chaos,' and in that category, there is no better start than with the names of the two 'disciplines' involved in the historical turn. What is History? We have just discussed the fog of 'history,' which covers not only the 'past' (object of study) but also the 'Problems of History' that disciplinary practitioners offer courses about to their more advanced students. Sit in one of those classrooms and you will quickly become aware that not even the professionals are entirely clear about what 'misuse' of history actually is. McNeill in his early career took plenty of flak from his peers because he had the temerity to attempt macro-history. It is heartening that History as a discipline is now less-Eurocentric and charting the history of the rest of the world, including the influence 'the rest' had on European civilization (cf. Hobson, 2004 and 2021; Sharman, 2019; Bowden, 2021). Global History is booming, although it is not clear how literally 'global' it needs to be. Can we write the history of neglected regions and cultures without considering them in a broader context? Does it matter who is telling the story, where that person was educated, or where the scholarship is produced?

History as a discipline is much more clearly defined than IR. A literal reading would suggest that IR equals relations between and among nations—whatever 'nation' means. We ourselves tell our students that the only secure definition of nation is 'a people who think they are one.' Of course, the 'nation' in 'international' is shorthand for 'nation-state,' which only compounds the confusion. If we demand that a nation have some semblance of shared ethnicity, language, culture, or common history, then very few states could claim to be anything but multinational—and there are many nations that have substantial bits of themselves resident in more than one state. It is said that there are not enough letters in the alphabet to form enough acronyms to capture all of the factions among the Kurds, but for certain if they all got together in a new Kurdistan, it would be highly disruptive to Middle Eastern borders.

If nation is a fuzzy concept, we cannot solve our IR identity problem by substituting 'state' (e.g. Interstate Relations), but of course that is in effect what our putative discipline has traditionally done. Ferguson and Mansbach (2019) have always insisted that 'the state' has so many meanings that it is almost useless as an analytical concept, and if we limit ourselves to sovereign states, we are only on slightly firmer ground. Across the globe, there are some 200 states that range from superpowers to microstates. They are all 'sovereign' (see de Carvalho, 2021) and legally 'independent,' which normative status bolsters their claim to autonomy, but that still must be defended in practice. Every sovereign state is buffeted by external forces and many have to struggle mightily to keep some semblance of order domestically. Sovereignty itself is a concept that, arguably, has a finite Western lineage dating only back to the time of Bodin and Hobbes (or earlier, see Costa Lopez, 2021), but archaeologists and some historians muddy the water by referring to entities like the 'Athenian state,' the 'Aztec state,' and the 'ancient Egyptian state.' As for the present, even realist Stephen Krasner (1993) refers to sovereignty as 'organized hypocrisy' and Robert Jackson (1990) writes of 'negative sovereignty' associated with what he terms 'quasi-states.' Then, there are 'failed states.' Conceptual chaos indeed.

Next, the confusion between IR and IS. We have previously observed that IR, especially in the United States, has had difficulty establishing itself as a separate discipline and has mainly been housed in Political Science programs. Patrick Thaddeus Jackson's recent (2018) investigation of International Studies reaches a similar conclusion, that International Studies is not a separate discipline. Surveying 'consensus top-ranked' International Studies graduate programs, he finds that most of them offer Ph.D. degrees in Political Science, and most scholars who published in consensus top-ranked International Studies journals have degrees and appointments in Political Science. However, Jackson comments that other disciplines like Sociology, Economics, and History already have a 'presence' in International Studies, and IS thus has some potential for becoming a 'multidisciplinary meeting space.' He believes this ought to be encouraged and so do we. Many of the contributors to this Handbook are among the over 7000 members of the International Studies Association, which (although we have not seen a recent ISA membership profile) welcomes diversity in disciplines as well as membership and draws members and annual conference participants from around the world. The ISA's 28 sections also reflect a wide range of subject interests, many of which, like HIST, cross disciplinary lines.

A second challenge for both IR and History is to overcome traditional and still pervasive state-centricity. History decades ago implicitly started to break away by shifting emphasis from diplomatic and political history towards social and cultural history. IR theory has perennially debated such matters as the relative importance of international system structure vs. human agency, actors, types of structure(s) (e.g. Waltzian distribution of power, core-periphery, and more recently hierarchies), units of analysis, transnational processes, and so on. The ever-expanding schools and approaches to IR theory have had to sort out their own positions on these debates, what to privilege and what to downplay. Too often, in our opinion, the tendency has been to drift back into familiar realist currents and assumptions about the primacy of the state, national interest, and hard power. Even a path-breaking constructivist like Alexander Wendt (Wendt, 1992) could proclaim (rather like Hedley Bull) that 'anarchy is what states make of it.' At least Bull's (1977) speculation about a possible trend towards a 'new medievalism' acknowledged that there might be other actors than states in the mix. In fact, we have always insisted that there is hardly a major issue area in global politics where non-state actors are not actively involved. Each such actor has its own sources of legitimacy and capacity for influence and control within its respective domains and beyond. Moreover, globalising processes have been 'colonising' states and sometimes 'hollowing them out,' even as particular national constituencies have and have not strongly benefited from globalization. If we eventually have a postcolonial globalisation, where will we locate the metropole?

In their joint chapter in this Handbook, Julian Go, George Lawson, and Benjamin de Carvalho make similar observations about state-centricity in Historical Sociology. They write, '[The] point is that a dominant focus on the state has acted as an obstacle to effective analysis not only of other units, but also to how states interacted with these. What began as an analytical move became, over time, an ontological one: the state acted as a cage not just of social scientific enquiry, but of social relations *in toto*. In other words, analysts acted as if states really were containers of ideas and practices. Yet there are a myriad of actors, forms, and processes operating at different scales that states try to manage, regulate, or discipline but which they ultimately cannot' (2021: 50). Go, Lawson, and de Carvalho would like to see fulfilled 'the promise of a truly global historical sociology in IR, one that can make sense of units and interaction well beyond the confines of the state' (2021: 54).

A third and last issue is periodization. Xavier Guillaume (2021) maintains, 'Historical periods, or any concept which entails a specific deployment or evolution in time, while necessary to the work of any researcher, are not natural; they are/should be the source of scholarly justification, discussion, contestation and debate.' It is increasingly recognized that some traditional 'periods' like modern, medieval, early modern, pre-modern, classical, and ancient have probably reached their sell-buy date or at least need continual rethinking and qualification. Meanwhile, the race seems to be on to identify turning points, tipping points, benchmark dates, watersheds, transformations, and 'ruptures' (our favourite, perhaps because we keep thinking of spleens).

As for our own work, far from implying historical direction in our designation of historical periods, we argue that virtually every conceivable period exhibits something 'new' and much that is 'old' and also some that is 'reconstructed.' Of course, there are always genuinely new phenomena—science and technology are among the engines of change—and new ideas and concepts regularly arise. The European State was 'invented' by Europeans—likewise the much later European Union. Although both incorporated features from earlier polities, they were also different in some important ways from any of their predecessors. We ourselves commonly refer to the present of global politics as 'a living museum,' by which we mean that in looking at the contemporary world, we can find many polity types, variants of polity types, identities, and loyalties that have existed through much of history. Some of these are 'nested,' waiting to re-emerge, frequently at a highly inconvenient time. At a deeper level, many essential problems of politics are as old as history itself, even though they often appear in new guises and forms. There is change and continuity, and it is always important to try to specify how much of each we observe.

Our own inclination has been to emphasize continuities. For example, we trace the beginning of globalisation back to a hypothetical person or two in a dugout canoe who paddled out of a local river and made their way up a neighbouring coastline to trade with another village. Not surprisingly then, we admire Braudel's conception of the *'longue durée.'* We also applaud world-systems analysis (Denemark, 2021) for its sustained research tracing social and other processes across many centuries. Finally, we are impressed with new scholarship that explores different ways of thinking about (not just Western) time. The Editors write about the fact that temporal locations like the Middle Ages are linked to a space location, even as a place like Europe has its own time frame. In his appropriately titled article, 'The Times They Are a-Changin,' C. Lorenz (2017: 110) reviews debates about memory and the subsequent effects of 'trauma' and 'historical experience' upon peoples and countries. Also, 'discussions about the proposal to label the geological time block since the Industrial Revolutions as the "anthropocene"—because the human species has turned into a geological actor through man-made climate change.'

Conclusion

It is exciting to contemplate how far Historical International Relations has come in such a relatively short time. The issues that remain should be viewed as opportunities for further advance. This Handbook offers remarkable testimony to the scope and abundance of new scholarship and the growing number of active participants. Clearly, IR-History and associated disciplines have expanded the range of their subject matter, become more global in orientation, and are increasingly diverse in membership.

Looking to the future, we ourselves have three major items on our wish list. First, Historical International Relations should become even more *global* than it already is. HIR has only begun to explore lesser-known regions and cultures of the world and—recall the linkage between time and space—the same is true for the vast stretch of history prior to the Greeks. For instance, William Hamblin (2006: 1) reminds us that 'half of all recorded military history occurred before the battle of Marathon.' Second, our own field of IR theory has fragmented to such an extent that we now have 'islands of theory' that rarely converse with one another except in a 'critical' way. Frankly, we miss bold attempts at grand theory and hope that reports of its demise have been greatly exaggerated. Finally, Historical International Relations needs to recruit more historians. Finding ways of attracting them into an interdisciplinary adventure that well might expand their intellectual horizons and produce even more important scholarship should be an HIR mission priority.

References

Bowden, B. (2021). Eurocentrism and Civilization. In de Carvalho, B., Costa Lopez, J., & Leira, H., eds. *Routledge Handbook of Historical International Relations*. Abingdon: Routledge.

Bruneau, Q. P. (2021). Constructivism: History and Systemic Change. In de Carvalho, B., Costa Lopez, J., & Leira, H., eds. *Routledge Handbook of Historical International Relations*. Abingdon: Routledge.

Bukovansky, M., Keene, E., Spanu, M., and Reus-Smith, C. (forthcoming). *Oxford Handbook on History and International Relations*. Oxford: Oxford University Press.

Bull, H. (1966). International Theory: The Case for a Classical Approach. *World Politics*, 18 (3), 361–377.

Bull, H. (1977). *The Anarchical Society*. New York, NY: Columbia University Press.

Çapan, Z. G., dos Reis, F., and Grasten, M. (2021). Global Histories: Connections and Circulations in Historical International Relations. In de Carvalho, B., Costa Lopez, J., & Leira, H., eds. *Routledge Handbook of Historical International Relations*. Abingdon: Routledge.

Costa Lopez, J. (2021). International Relations in/and the Middle Ages. In de Carvalho, B., Costa Lopez, J., & Leira, H., eds. *Routledge Handbook of Historical International Relations*. Abingdon: Routledge.

de Carvalho, B. (2021). Sovereignty in Historical International Relations: Trajectories, Challenges and Implications. In de Carvalho, B., Costa Lopez, J., & Leira, H., eds. *Routledge Handbook of Historical International Relations*. Abingdon: Routledge.

de Carvalho, B., Costa Lopez, J., and Leira, H. (2021). Introduction: Historical International Relations. In de Carvalho, B., Costa Lopez, J., & Leira, H., eds. *Routledge Handbook of Historical International Relations*. Abingdon: Routledge.

Denemark, R. (2021). World-Systems Analysis: Past Trajectories and Future Prospects. In de Carvalho, B., Costa Lopez, J., & Leira, H., eds. *Routledge Handbook of Historical International Relations*. Abingdon: Routledge.

Ferguson, Y. H., and Mansbach, R. W. (1988). *The Elusive Quest: Theory and International Politics*. Columbia, SC: University of South Carolina Press.

Ferguson, Y. H., and Mansbach, R. W. (1998). *Polities: Authority, Identities, and Change*. Columbia, SC: University of South Carolina Press.

Ferguson, Y. H., and Mansbach, R. W. (2008). Historical Perspectives on Contemporary Global Politics. In: Y. H. Ferguson, and R. W. Mansbach, eds., *A World of Polities: Essays on Global Politics*, London: Routledge, 64–82.

Ferguson, Y. H., and Mansbach, R. W. (2019). The Sociology of the State: The State as a Conceptual Variable. In: N. Sandal, ed., *Oxford Research Encyclopedia of International Studies*, Oxford: Oxford University Press.

Finley, M. (1975). *The Use and Abuse of History*. London: The Hogarth Press.

Go, J., Lawson, G., and de Carvalho, B. Historical Sociology in International Relations: The Challenge of the Global. In de Carvalho, B., Costa Lopez, J., and Leira, H., eds. *Routledge Handbook of Historical International Relations. Abingdon: Routledge*.

Guillaume, X. (2021). Historical Periods and the Act of Periodisation. In de Carvalho, B., Costa Lopez, J., & Leira, H., eds. *Routledge Handbook of Historical International Relations*. Abingdon: Routledge.

Hamblin, W. J. (2006). *Warfare in the Ancient Near East to 1600 BC*. London: Routledge.

Herborth, B., and Nitzschner, P. (2021). Europe in Historical International Relations. In de Carvalho, B., Costa Lopez, J., & Leira, H., eds. *Routledge Handbook of Historical International Relations*. Abingdon: Routledge.

Hobson, J.M. (2021). Multicultural Origins of the Global Economy. Cambridge: Cambridge University Press.

Jackson, P. T. (2018). 'Does It Matter If It's A Discipline?' Bawled the Child. In: A. Gofas, I. Hamati-Ataya, and N. Onuf, eds., *SAGE Handbook of the History, Philosophy and Sociology of International Relations*, Newbury Park, CA: Sage Publications, 326–339.

Jackson, R. H. (1990). *Quasi-States: Sovereignty, International Relations and the Third World*. Cambridge: Cambridge University Press.

Krasner, S. D. (1993). *Sovereignty: Organized Hypocrisy*. Princeton, NJ: Princeton University Press.

Lawson, G. (2010). The eternal divide? History and international relations. *European Journal of International Relations*, 18 (2), 203–236.

Leira, H., and de Carvalho, B. (2015). *Historical International Relations*. Four volumes. Newbury Park, CA: Sage Publishing.

Leira, H., and de Carvalho, B. (2016). Construction time again: history in constructivist IR scholarship. *European Review of International Studies*, 3 (3), 99–111.

Levy, J. S. (1983). *War in the Modern Great Power System, 1495-1975*. Lexington, KY: University Press of Kentucky.

Lorenz, C. (2017). 'The Times They Are a Changin': On Time, Space and Periodization in History. In: M. Carretero, S. Berger, and M. Grever, eds., *Palgrave Handbook of Research in Historical Culture and Education*, London: Palgrave Macmillan, 109–131.

Lowenthal, D. (1985). *The Past Is a Foreign Country*. Cambridge: Cambridge University Press.

Mansbach, R. W., Ferguson, Y. H., and Lampert, D. E. (1976). *The Web of World Politics: Non-State Actors in the Global System*. Englewood Cliffs, NJ: Prentice-Hall.

McNeill, W. H. (1976). *Plagues and Peoples*. Garden City, NY: Anchor Books.

McNeill, W. H. (1982). *The Pursuit of Power: Technology, Armed Force, and Society Since A.D. 1000*. Chicago, IL: University of Chicago Press.

McNeill, W. H. (1990). *Population and Politics since 1750*. Charlottesville, VA: University Press of Virginia.

McNeill, W. H. (1997). Territorial states buried too soon. *Mershon International Studies Review*, 41 (Supplement 2), 269–274.

Sharman, J. C. (2019). *Empires of the Weak: The Real Story of European Expansion and the Creation of the New World Order*. Princeton, NJ: Princeton University Press.

Wendt, A. (1992). Anarchy is what states make of it: the social construction of power politics. *International Organization*, 46 (2), 391–425.

INDEX